9. Inform editors if you're submitting simultaneous or previously published poems. (Note: Some editors will not consider such submissions.)

10. Enclose a SASE or, for reply from outside your country, a SAE with IRCs (from the post office) with every query, submission and/or follow-up letter.

11. Weigh your manuscript before mailing to be sure you include sufficient postage and an appropriate size envelope for its return.

12. Mail submissions first class within your country; use airmail for submissions to other countries.

13. Always keep copies of your work as well as detailed records of where and when you submitted your poems.

For more information about submitting your poetry for publication, read:

1992 Poet's Market

1992
Poet's Market

Where & How to Publish
Your Poetry

Editor: Judson Jerome

Assistant Editor: Pat Beusterien
Editorial Assistants: Christine Martin
and Cathy Brookshire

Writer's
Digest
Books

Cincinnati, Ohio

If you are a poetry publisher and would like to be considered for a listing in the next edition of Poet's Market, *please request a questionnaire from* Poet's Market, *1507 Dana Ave., Cincinnati, Ohio 45207.*

Managing Editor, Market Books Department:
Constance J. Achabal
Assistant Managing Editor: Glenda Tennant Neff

International Standard Serial Number
0883-5470
International Standard Book Number
0-89879-475-7

Contents

The Markets

Resources

Indexes

From the Editor

In writing these pages and using this book daily for reference (for I can't possibly *remember* all the information it contains), I have come, since the first edition in 1986, to think of it increasingly as a kind of cultural barometer. All this information about poetic activities — not just the publication of magazines and books, but contests, awards, readings, publications about writing poetry, colonies, organizations — tells me a lot about what's really going on in the poetic world, a lot I never knew about in 30-odd years of active literary life before I began putting together the first **Poet's Market**.

Others, I find, are using the book that way, too. Its primary function was intended to be, of course, a guide to poets as to where to send — and, just as important, where *not* to send — their poetry. But from the beginning, the staff of Writer's Digest Books and I recognized that to some extent, too, it was also a book that fed fantasies, like a mail-order catalog, and reported on the literary scene. For that reason I have tried to make it *readable*, not simply a place to look up facts, such as addresses, rates of payment, submission requirements, and so on. It's a book to settle back and read. I've tried to get something beyond the facts: the *feel* of the various magazines and publishing activities it lists.

For example, I find that I am to appear on a panel with three other poets, people I've never heard of. Part of my preparation may be to look up in **Poet's Market** the magazines and book publishers that have taken their work and the awards they have won. It helps me understand whom I'm dealing with. Also, when foundations or government agencies get grant applications, when publishers are looking over the resumes of poets whose books they are considering, when committees at universities are deciding which poets to invite for readings, they may well use **Poet's Market** as a reference. So Henrietta Humpledinck has had six books published by Amorphous Press, has she? What's that? If there's no listing, or a very cryptic listing, in **Poet's Market**, one possibility is that Amorphous Press is Henrietta Humpledinck herself. Nothing wrong with that, but it helps to know.

There are some new features this year. For example, we asked editors of magazines to indicate whether they review books of poetry. And we have added information on readings — one of the means poets find most useful in reaching a public.

It also may help you understand **Poet's Market** to follow through the thinking behind one change from past years. I was always bothered by the **III** classification, which we said was for "prestigious" publishers, magazines and awards. Sez who? I wondered. Sometimes amateur publications that were no more than newsletters asked for a **III**, and, after one look at a sample copy, I decided to code them **I**, for beginners. Some magazines that I would be honored to have take my own poems asked for a **II** classification — the general market to which experienced poets should submit; others that might have been elegantly printed but seem to me to contain rather inferior work called themselves **III**, and I had no objective way of determining that they were not prestigious.

Finally it occurred to me why that troublesome **III** had been introduced in the first place. It was not intended as a mark of honor; it was a deliberate effort to discourage submissions. Many small magazines and presses are overwhelmed by the amount of material they receive, much of it inappropriate (no doubt sent to them by poets who hadn't studied their **Poet's Market**), material that a volunteer staff found burdensome to deal with. Some of them asked not to be listed at all, hoping to stem the tide of submissions. But a number of these were among the best-known and highly respected publishers in the country (which is why they had so many submissions in the first place), and to leave them out would be like leaving Cadillac out of a catalog of automobiles. Hence the **III** was born, intended to imply that you'd be lucky to make it into these pages, but, face it, there's next to no chance that will happen, so please send your poems elsewhere.

Prestige has little to do with it. I think it was one of our readers who first happened to call such markets "limited," and light bulbs flashed. True, the very names of some magazines and publishers attract more submissions than they can possibly handle, but obscure ones might be objectively classified as "limited" as well. Here's a fellow who has for some years regularly published a modest little magazine, mimeographed and stapled at the corner, using almost entirely poetry written by himself and his friends. Sometimes it uses a poem by a stranger. Fascinating publication, serving a genuine literary need, but certainly not prestigious. *Limited*! Yeah! Like *The Hudson Review*!

As **Poet's Market** has increasingly been used as a reference book, not just a market guide, the importance of the **V** category—no unsolicited manuscripts—has grown. An astonishing number of the publishers of the books that are reviewed, win prizes, get talked about, are publishers not open to submissions. Indeed, many of the most prestigious magazines publishing poetry use almost entirely solicited material. However, it would be misleading not to list these places at all, so when they ask for a **V** coding, I invite them to describe their activities simply because that information is needed by anyone trying to get an overview of poetry today.

As a poet looking for publishers to take my work, I am inclined to resent the policy of only using solicited material; yet, when I think about it, I understand it very well. If I were running a magazine or publishing house largely out of my own funds, I, too, would prefer to choose writers from those whose work I knew; I wouldn't be much interested in a lot of mail from strangers, though, of course, I might therefore fail to discover the Keats of the twenty-first century.

But the true wonderland of listings are those coded **IV**: specialized markets for poems about or by poets from a particular region; by poets of a particular religious or sexual persuasion or gender; or for poetry in a particular form or on a specific theme, be it mountaineering, Middle-Earth fantasy or world peace. Editors of the mainline literary magazines often find themselves at a loss for words when it comes to defining what they want to see, and many settle simply for the word *quality*. But those of the specialized publications may be less interested in quality, or how a poem is written, than what it is about. There's something refreshing to me about that approach. They are looking for material that they think their readers *want* to read. Too often, it seems to me, the editors of quality literary magazines are looking for what they think readers *ought* to want to read. That attitude seems moral, or medicinal, and not much fun.

If poets are going to reach large audiences, one thing they might aspire to in their work is not only quality, but fun. There are a whole lot of publishers and editors and organizations out there having fun, and I hope this book helps poets find them.

Judd Jerome

How to Use Poet's Market

Before studying the listings and making your marketing plans, read these suggestions for the most productive use of all the features in **Poet's Market**. Especially note the explanation of the information given in the sample listing.

● **Start with the indexes.** We have simplified this directory by grouping all imprints or publications located at one address into one listing. The General Index lists all titles in the book with cross references where necessary. For example, suppose you wanted to find *Nostoc Magazine*; you will find it under N in the General Index with a cross reference to "see **Arts End Books**" and you will be given the page number. There is also a Geographical Index that lists publications by state and foreign countries for those wanting to submit to a specific location. Listings coded **IV** are indexed by specialization in the Subject Index and if you're ready to have a chapbook of your work published, there is a Chapbook Publishers Index to consult.

● A double dagger symbol (**‡**) appears before the names of listings new to this edition.

● **Market categories:** Listing names are followed by one or more Roman numerals:

I. **Publishers very open to beginners' submissions.** For acceptance, some require fees, purchase of the publication or membership in an organization, but they are not, so far as I can determine, exploitative of writers, and they often encourage and advise new writers. They publish much of the material they receive and often respond with criticism and suggestions.

II. **The general market to which most poets familiar with literary journals and magazines should submit.** Typically they accept 10% or less of poems received and usually reject others without comment. They pay at least 1 copy. A poet developing a list of publication credits will find many of these to be respected names in the literary world.

III. **Limited markets,** typically overstocked. This code is used by many prestigious magazines and publishers to discourage widespread submissions from poets who have not published elsewhere — although many do on occasion publish relatively new and/or little-known poets.

IV. **Specialized publications** which encourage contributors from a geographical area, a specific age-group, specific sex or sexual orientation, specific ethnic background, or which accept poems in specific forms (such as haiku) or on specific themes. In most **IV** listings we also state the specialty (e.g. **IV-Religious**). Often a listing emphasizes a theme but is also open to other subjects; these listings are marked with two codes (e.g. **I, IV-Ethnic**).

V. **Listings which do not accept unsolicited manuscripts.** You cannot submit without specific permission to do so. If the press or magazine for some reason seems especially appropriate for you, you might query (write, with SASE). But, in general, they prefer to locate and solicit the poets whom they publish. I have included these listings because it is important to know not only where to send your poetry but also where NOT to submit it. Also, many are interesting publishers to know about, and this book is widely used as a reference by librarians, researchers, publishers, suppliers and others who need to have as complete a listing of publishers of poetry as possible.

● Always include a SASE (self-addressed, stamped envelope) or, for foreign publishers, a SAE with IRCs (self-addressed envelope with International Reply Coupons purchased at the post office) **for response when submitting, querying, or requesting other information.** Be sure you have enough return postage to cover the amount of material you want returned and that the return envelope is large enough to hold such material. This information is so important that we repeat it at the bottom of many pages throughout this book rather than include it in individual listings.

● **Consult the Glossary** in the back of this book for explanations of any unfamiliar terms you might encounter while reading the listings.

● **As a guide to the information in the listings,** match the numbered phrases in this sample listing with the corresponding numbers in the explanation that follows:

(1) THE BLACK SCHOLAR; THE BLACK SCHOLAR PRESS (2) (IV-Ethnic), P.O. Box 2869, Oakland, (3) CA 94609, (4), (5) founded 1969, (6) publisher Robert Chrisman, uses (7) **poetry "relating to/from/of the black American and other 'Third World' experience."** The (8) bimonthly magazine is basically scholarly and research-oriented. (9)They have recently published poetry by Ntozake Shange, Jayne Cortez, Andrew Salkey, and D. L. Smith. (10) As a sample the editor selected these lines from "Tata on the Death of Don Pablo" by Nancy Morejan:

> *your set mouth*
> *pausing like a great bird*
> *over the plain, speaks:*

I have not seen a copy, but the editor says it is (11) 64 pp., 7×10″, (12) with 10,000 subscribers of which 60% are libraries, 15% shelf sales. Single copy $5; subscription $30. (13) **Sample back issue: $6 prepaid. Send SASE for guidelines.** (14) **Pays 10 copies and subscription.** (15) **Enclose "cover letter & bio or curriculum vita, SASE, phone number, no originals."** (16) **Reports in 1 month.** (17) Reviews books of poetry. They also publish 1-2 books a year, average 100 pp., flat-spined. (18) **Send query letter.** For sample books, send 8½×11″ SASE for catalog, average cost $10.95 including postage and handling. (19) "We only publish one issue every year containing poetry. Please be advised—it is against our policy to discuss submissions via telephone. Also, we get a lot of MSS, but read *every single one,* thus patience is appreciated."

(1) **Names.** All imprints at the same address that publish poetry are listed in the heading—in this case the magazine, *The Black Scholar*, and the imprint under which they publish books of poetry, **The Black Scholar Press.** If the publisher offers a contest or award, that is also included in the heading. The publisher (usually) decides how its listing title(s) will appear and therefore determines alphabetization.

(2) **Market category.** The Roman numeral indicates the market category or categories. Some publishers have more than one code number. For example (II, IV-Humor) might be used if a magazine uses all kinds of poetry, but especially wants light or humorous verse. All publishers with **IV** listings are cross-indexed in the Subject Index. For example, you will find this publisher listed with all others that have an ethnic focus.

(3) **Postal codes.** Used for all U.S. states and areas (such as District of Columbia) and Canadian provinces. For a complete list of the codes, see page 19.

(4) **Phone number.** Sometimes included in this space (*The Black Scholar* chose not to) for business use of this directory. A poet should not, in general, telephone publishers about submissions; it is better to have such communication in writing.

(5) **Date of founding.** Most entries give this date. It helps you judge the stability of the publication or publisher. Recently founded publications may be more in need of material and thus more open to submissions—but they have not yet established continuity.

(6) **Contact person.** Names are provided by the publisher. If no name is given, I would address the submission to "Poetry Editor." Sometimes there are specific instructions, even a separate address, for the poetry editor. Note and follow such instructions carefully.

(7) **Boldface text.** Indicates important information to keep in mind when submitting—the preferred themes, for example, and the specifics of actual submission policies. Quotation marks indicate the description is in the words of the editor. I often quote to enable you to sense the editor's personality and attitude.

(8) **Frequency of publication.** Gives you some indication of how much poetry is needed and

how soon an acceptance is likely to appear.

(9) Poets published. The names of the poets are an indication of the caliber of poetry published. Also, reading the work of these poets can give you some insight into editorial preferences.

(10) Sample lines. These are brief excerpts representative of the quality of the poetry published, quoted whenever editors supply them or allow me to select them. If possible, the excerpts are somewhat self-contained in form and meaning. Samples are indented and italicized to make them easy to spot.

(11) Format. I ask all publishers to send me samples of their publications, but not all do so. When I have a copy I tell more about how it looks than is given here—whether it is flat-spined or saddle-stapled (see the Glossary for definitions of special terms), what kind of graphics and cover it has, and other details. I give as much information about the appearance of the publication as possible because poets, especially, like to imagine in what form their work will appear and the quality of the printing and binding.

(12) Circulation figures. Usually indicate the total of subscriptions (individual and library) plus off-the-shelf sales and free distribution.

(13) Sample copy, guidelines. Almost all editors advise you to read sample publications before submitting—and to obtain guidelines if they are available. If ordering a sample copy from England or other countries in the U.K., send a draft for sterling (from your bank) in payment, since U.K. banks charge a commission, sometimes in excess of the amount of a check, to exchange U.S. funds.

(14) Payment. Most small presses pay only in copies. If they pay cash, that information would be in the listing. A few (all in category I) do not even pay a copy; the poet has to buy the magazine (or book) to see the work in print.

(15) Submission requirements. Publishers state their individual requirements (see page 13 for a sample cover letter for magazine submission), and these may differ for a magazine and press within the same listing (see 18). Most magazines object to simultaneous submissions (poems sent to more than one publisher at the same time) and previously published poems. Unless the listing says otherwise, assume that simultaneous submissions and previously published poems are *not* acceptable.

(16) Reporting time. The length of time a publisher needs to respond to your submission is approximate and can fluctuate greatly. If you have had no response within the reporting time plus a week or so, it is appropriate to query politely (with SASE) whether the manuscript is still under consideration. If a second or third query, spaced a few weeks apart, gets no response, it is appropriate to notify the editor that you are submitting the manuscript elsewhere. Always, of course, keep copies of manuscripts submitted. Sometimes you will be unable to get them returned.

(17) Book reviews. Indicates that the magazine will accept material for possible review.

(18) Query letter. Publishers often require a query letter rather than a manuscript as a first contact. The query letter is written to a publisher to elicit interest in a manuscript (see page 17 for a sample cover letter for book or chapbook submission) or to determine whether the publisher is interested in receiving submissions.

(19) Editorial comments. I ask editors whether they would like to make any general comments about poetry, trends or their publishing plans, or offer advice for poets (especially beginners) and quote the editors—sometimes at length.

These special features of **Poet's Market** will help you select the best publishers for your poetry and submit it properly. Also read the introductions to the Publishers of Poetry and Contests and Awards sections for additional information on those markets.

Starting Where You Are

by Judson Jerome

I live in a village with fewer than 5,000 inhabitants, many of whom are poets. Some have published in national magazines; some have published books. But the best-known poet among us (until his death a few years ago) was a man in his 90s whose poetry had never been published except in our local weekly, *The Yellow Springs News*. If you were to accompany him on one of his brisk walks through the business district on a Thursday morning, you may well have heard people call from across the street to greet him. "Great poem, Deckard!" they would cry, referring to the little verse he had sent that week in a letter to the editor, published in the Wednesday paper. Often on those walks I envied Deckard. My poetry had been appearing in print for a half century, but Deckard had something I didn't have and sorely missed: an appreciative audience of at least hundreds who read every one of his poems with interest and delight.

You won't find *The Yellow Springs News* in **Poet's Market**, as you won't find the thousands of other small newspapers, organizational and church newsletters, inhouse publications of corporations and other media to which poetry is, just like all the other news, relevant to their readership. And these may well be the media publishing the poetry Americans most care about: poetry written by their friends and family, members of their congregations or clubs or hobby groups, fellow employees of some business, school children in their area, fellow advocates of a political or environmental cause, or people related to them by ethnic or national background, sexual preference, age or some other characteristic. These people read what you write because they want to know what you have to say or because they recognize you as a compatriot in one or another community of common interest.

I am delighted when, among the special interest markets we are able to list in **Poet's Market**, I find a magazine devoted to (and using poetry about) the Old West (*Ghost Town Quarterly*), "The Andy Griffith Show" (*The Mayberry Gazette*), rug hooking and fibre crafts (*The Rugging Room*), or mountains and mountaineering (*Climbing Art*). *Superintendent's Profile & Pocket Equipment Directory* has loyally, since **Poet's Market** began in 1986, described its interest in poetry pertaining to highway superintendents. They have more than 2,000 dedicated readers. And they pay $5 a poem, too, which is $5 more than most of the markets listed here. And if your work as a janitor inspires you to write poetry, you're missing a bet if you haven't shared it with others like you through the pages of *Cleaning Business Magazine*. The world is waiting.

Literary ambitions

These special interest markets, the most readily available avenues to publication of poetry, may seem beneath the aspirations of many readers. I advise poets not to get too haughty too quickly, however. There is no reason that the poetry in these publications should not be good poetry; and if it isn't, that is probably because the readers of the magazines haven't sent any, not because the editors wouldn't recognize literary quality if they saw it. I'm sure the editors of *Bird Watcher's Digest* (where I have seen some very fine poems) would have been delighted to have received a contribution from William Butler Yeats called "The Wild Swans at Coole," though they may have found themselves a bit squeamish had he submitted "Leda and the Swan." I think my own poetry has a lot more literary quality than did the poems of my friend Deckard, but mine have never been in *The*

Yellow Springs News. I didn't send them there. Maybe I'm a snob. I think the editor of our local paper would have been happy to have printed a few.

But even if you regard your ambitions as literary, if you want not only a gratified audience but also some critical recognition, it is still good advice to start where you are—in your own community or among like-minded people. These days poetry may be hard to distinguish from one or another variety of political activism or social commitment. The people who put out magazines focusing on such issues are very likely to have social as well as literary ties. Often they constitute a group of friends who are drawn together by their interests as surely as garden club members are drawn together by their interest in gardening. They support one another, and writing for them is likely to mean joining them in one way or another. Some poets resent the fact that the editors of literary magazines mostly publish work of their friends, but if you or I started such a magazine, that's probably what we would do, too. Logrolling is as important a skill in the literary life as it is in business or politics. Friendship counts. The emotional commitment that individuals make to one another provides the communal glue that holds the diverse groups in our society together. You may be grateful that literary magazines are not conducted by legal rules, such as those that attempt to assure fairness in state lotteries.

Indeed, the rules of literary advancement probably start with one you can't do much about: Rule 1 is be a genius—or, at least, develop a highly verbal, informed, engaged mind. Rule 2 might be, have influential friends. Rules 3 and beyond, having to do with such matters as learning how to write a good poem, will get you nowhere until you have met those first two requirements, though writing well may help you develop the kind of mind and find the kind of friends that help you. In practice, your capacities as a poet all develop together. Rule 2 in this scheme is rarely talked about, yet it is critical. The current name for making friends with those whose influence can benefit your career is *networking*.

Community resources

Poets network like mad. Sometimes I think they do more networking than writing. Almost every community has poetry readings from time to time, some of them open. At open readings the stage and microphone are made available to volunteers from the audience who want to participate. If you want to meet the other people in your area who write poetry, go to these functions and, when you get the opportunity, stand up and perform. (This year for the first time **Poet's Market** has given special attention to readings, both in the section Sponsors of Poetry Readings devoted to that topic and in the listings of publishers and organizations.) Some poets form writers' groups to meet regularly and discuss one another's work. You meet other poets at workshops, in classes, in a wide variety of literary and artistic gatherings. If, however, you prefer to be a hermit, as did Emily Dickinson, your publication record, if any, is likely to resemble hers: mostly posthumous.

Local contacts become especially important when poets begin thinking of collecting their work in chapbooks or books. Typically, their work has been in a dozen or so magazines, local or otherwise. They have made themselves known, to some degree, as poets in regional workshops or local readings and other gatherings. Now they would like to have a few of their poems published together—to give to friends and family, to sell at readings. Maybe they have a local bookstore that would be willing to stock their work (usually on a consignment basis: the poet gets paid only after the books are sold). There are literally hundreds of publishers listed in **Poet's Market** that are open to submission of manuscripts for chapbook or book publication—so many that the prospect of deciding where to send a manuscript is downright daunting. And the process of doing so, and continuing to circulate a manuscript until someone accepts it for publication, is often discouraging. It has taken me years to place some book manuscripts, and I know it takes at least that long for most poets to do so.

How do you begin your journey to publication? Well, start where you are. If I were picking up **Poet's Market** for the first time, I think I would turn first to the geographical index in the back. I would want to find out which magazines and presses were in my area. I would start submitting to those and, if possible, start getting acquainted with the individuals involved.

Go down to the local writers' center. What? There's none listed in your Yellow Pages? Maybe you should start one. One of the most eye-opening experiences of my life was a visit to the one in the Washington DC area (see listing for The Writer's Center under Organizations Useful to Poets). I had been invited there to give a reading and short workshop, and I learned that a poet would find such a place a one-stop community center for his or her interests. You could even rent their word processor, typeset your own book and print it on their facilities. As Allan Lefcowitz, its founder, showed me around, I began to understand why there were not more places like that around the country. The guy is a demon for getting grants, lining up sponsors and donors, and recruiting new members. Without an Allan Lefcowitz a community would have a lot of serious birth pangs before it brought forth a writers' center. But he and the center are living proof it can be done.

Sometimes there are beginnings of such centers at local Y's and public libraries, community centers or other institutions. Some publishers have devoted themselves to opening up community resources for writers in addition to their publishing activities. Often universities, especially those with creative writing programs, offer a wide range of activities open to the public. Look at the listing for *Footwork* (under Publishers of Poetry), the product of a seething forest of poetic activities sponsored by Passaic County Community College. Between those activities and the offerings of the Great Swamp Poetry Series (under Organizations), New Jersey seems in a fair way to becoming the hub of the American poetry universe. If you are lucky enough to live nearby, there is nothing to stop you from joining up. And if you don't, the example of such efforts may inspire you to initiate something in your own community.

Also, look at the section State and Provincial Arts Councils — and check to see whether you have a local arts council as well. Arts councils are one of the major sources of funding for individual artists (including poets), organizations and publications, and you should know what opportunities are available to you from these sources.

Pen pals

This morning I needed information on a listing for one of the largest poetry competitions, one sponsored by England's Arvon Foundation (see the listing in Contests and Awards). Often, because of the obstacles presented by international mail, publishers and organizations in other countries are slow to return the forms we send out every year to verify the information in their listings. I had received a brochure from the Arvon Foundation about the facility they run which offers short courses in writing, along with accommodations at a retreat much like American writers' colonies. But the addresses for the contest and their center at Totleigh Barton were different, and I had still a third address for the foundation headquarters. How to sort all that out? Fast, for we were in final stages of putting together this volume.

No problem. I popped out of my word processing program, popped into CompuServe (see their listing under Organizations) and explained the whole problem to a poet in England, Barry Fogden, whose Close-up I had recently written. In minutes my message was waiting for Barry to download the next time he went online, and within hours he had the answers I needed and sent them back to me through CompuServe — all at minimal cost and with great ease. Most days I tap into CompuServe's Litforum once or twice, and through it I have established a wide range of valuable contacts and literary friendships. Anyone can participate, and, I hear, similar literary discussion groups are conducted on the many electronic networks — most of them local — now functioning around the country. Litforum has a workshop section that anyone can join. You upload a manuscript for group critique and, when your turn comes, the other participants download it, read it, and comment on the bulletin board. But most of the chatter in the Poetry and Lyrics section is simply social and friendly. Other sections focus on fiction, nonfiction, humor, science fiction and other forms of writing, and in all of them the ongoing conversation is wide-ranging, informative and often of direct professional help.

I have always been an inveterate pen pal. Hundreds of people write me letters in response to my books and my column on poetry in *Writer's Digest*, and I always answer personally (with a printed information sheet, if nothing else), and in some cases these initial contacts have led to friendships lasting for years. A lot of my best friends are people I've never met! Correspondents have responded in detail to my poems and books through the mail, and I have similarly tried to help them with their work. That's networking.

Nothing stops you from writing letters to the writers whose work you find in the literary magazines or the library. You can address them in care of their editors and publishers, and many are listed with addresses and sometimes phone numbers in the various directories of writers published by such organizations as Poets & Writers (see their listing under Publications Useful to Poets). However, this is not an open invitation to be bothered. We are not public facilities, not institutions or agencies or corporations. When the phone in my house rings, I'm the guy who is most likely to pick it up. When a letter is addressed to me, I'm the guy who opens it—not a secretary. I am likely to react negatively to those who contact me (especially by telephone) when their motive seems merely to seek my attention or help, and they are oblivious to the fact that I am a person with a private life that I don't want heedlessly invaded. But it is also true that communication from strangers through the mail or CompuServe has immensely enriched my life—and helped my career.

Poet's Market is one small part of the iceberg that floats in the busy sea of literary life. Most of the important activity goes on outside of public view. If you're serious about wanting to be a poet, you'll have to explore below the surface and discover the interdependence of the members of the poetic community. You'll never find the channel that leads to recognition merely by sending out manuscripts and waiting to be noticed.

Reading list

Suppose you're someone just beginning to wonder what it means to become a poet. Here are some resources to help you think through that question.

First, ask yourself whether your interest is amateur or professional. To help you answer this, look at a current anthology such as **The Vintage Book of Contemporary American Poetry**, edited by J.D. McClatchy (Random House, 1990), $14.95 in paperback. If you don't identify with the kind of poetry you find there—and that doesn't mean you necessarily like it—your interest in poetry is probably amateur. That means you write it and read it for *love*, as the root of the word *amateur* implies.

Still uncertain? Try reading some of the most widely respected publications publishing poetry today, such as *Poetry, American Poetry Review, Sewanee Review, Kenyon Review, Negative Capability*. Most libraries have at least some of these in their periodicals sections. Is your goal to attain the level of accomplishment exhibited by the work you read in these magazines? If not, you'll be happiest using the listings in **Poet's Market** coded **(I)**, or those coded **(IV)** for a specialty that interests you.

But if your interests are professional, if you aspire to have your work appear in such journals as those mentioned above or anthologies such as the **Vintage**, you probably want a different range of resources. I try to address your concerns monthly in my poetry column in *Writer's Digest*, and I cover many of the basics in **The Poet's Handbook**, Writer's Digest Books, $11.95 paperback.

Other books you may find helpful are:

Creating Poetry, John Drury, Writer's Digest Books, $18.95 hardback.

Writing Poems, Robert Wallace, Scott, Foresman & Co., 3rd ed., $17 paperback.

Sound and Sense: An Introduction to Poetry, Laurence Perrine, 7th ed., Harcourt Brace Jovanovich, $14.50 paperback.

Princeton Encyclopedia of Poetry and Poetics, Princeton University Press, $24.95 paperback.

Webster's Compact Rhyming Dictionary, Merriam Webster, $4.95 hardback.

Words to Rhyme with, including A Primer of Prosody, Willard R. Espy, Facts on File, $40 hardback; Henry Holt & Co., $22.50 paperback.

Judson Jerome was professor of literature at Antioch College from 1953 to 1973 and poetry editor of Antioch Review. He has also had an active writing career with publication of his poetry, fiction, essays and plays in magazines and books. He began writing a monthly poetry column for Writer's Digest in 1960. Some of those columns and his other writing about poetry have been published by Writer's Digest Books in **The Poet and the Poem**, **The Poet's Handbook** *(1980) and* **On Being a Poet** *(1984). His most recent book of poetry is* **Jonah & Job** *(John Daniel & Co., 1991), and his most recent books of prose are* **The Youthful Look** *(The University of Arkansas Press, 1991) and* **Nude**, *a novel, (Applezaba Press, 1991). He became editor of the annual* **Poet's Market** *with the first edition (1986).*

"Jud" (as he prefers to be called) and Marty Jerome were married in 1948 and have four grown children. He and Marty live in Yellow Springs, Ohio, where he free-lances and edits **Poet's Market** *from his home.*

The Business of Poetry

by Judson Jerome

I think everyone who fantasizes about becoming a writer imagines sitting somewhere and writing—maybe lounging on a grassy slope, chewing a pen and scribbling into a notebook. Then all you have to do is turn over your precious manuscript to a typist, and, *voila*, some months later you are being interviewed on talk shows (letting your business manager take care of all those incoming checks). Right?

Wrong—especially if you are a poet. Not only are you likely to have to do your own typing or word processing, but you have to be your own agent, too, and that's not the end of it. But before we go too far, let's consider some of the basic steps in getting your poetry published.

Manuscript form

Many manuscripts submitted for publication today are written on word processors and printed with a *good* printer (that is, if it's dot matrix, it should be able to print near letter-quality). There's nothing wrong with submitting typewritten manuscripts, but they should be perfect in every detail. Type the poem exactly the way you want it to appear in print: punctuation, spelling, spacing. Use good white 8½×11" bond paper, with a good dark ribbon. Don't get fancy with typography by using italics, ALL CAPS or an offbeat font. Center the title (without quotation marks around it) above the poem. Put no more than one poem on a page. Unless a publisher advises otherwise, poems are usually single-spaced (unless they are *very* short) with double-spacing between stanzas, as that most nearly approximates their appearance on the printed page. Your name and address (ordinarily, though some contests require no names) should be at the top of the first page and your last name, at least, on subsequent pages (in case the pages get separated in the editorial process).

This little pig . . .

Preparing your manuscript is still the easy part—getting it accepted for publication is more difficult. And beware of any agent who offers to handle your poetry. Agents work for money, and none will do so for author's copies, which are likely to be all the pay poetry brings. If you write bestsellers, you need an agent—who works for a percentage of your income from your books. Otherwise, forget it. Most agents won't take you as a client, and those that will, ask you to pay a fee up front instead of—or in addition to—the percentage reputable agents collect from earnings. Few agents handle magazine submissions at all.

You are the one who goes to market. For the time being, forget about books. You will be ready to think about book publication only after you have racked up a substantial list of credits in magazines. (For the most part, forget about contests, too: see my introduction to Contests and Awards.) Throughout this book I try to help you decide to which magazines you should send your poems, but if you are new to the game, I especially hope you will read Starting Where You Are as an introduction to this process.

Some editors list specific submission procedures, but the following advice applies to most. Select a sampling of your poems (usually 3-5 with a total length of no more than about 10 pages) for each magazine to which you want to submit. When they are carefully proofread, put them into a business-size (#10, 4¼×9½") envelope. (Big envelopes, such as 9 × 12", for a few pages strike some editors as bothersome and/or pretentious.) Enclose a self-addressed, stamped envelope (SASE) large enough and with sufficient postage—or International Reply Coupons (IRCs) for foreign submissions—for return of your manuscript. The usual practice is to fold a business-size envelope into thirds for return.

Copyright

You *can* write the Copyright Office, Library of Congress, Washington DC 20559 and get the forms to copyright your poems, if you wish. Then you can mark each poem with © _____ (filling in the year and your name). But it's unnecessary, and I don't advise it. No one is going to steal your poem. (You should be so lucky!) Besides, in my opinion, a copyright notice on your manuscript looks amateurish. Most little magazines are copyrighted when printed, which covers your poem. You can use the poem elsewhere, as in a book, unless you gave the editor, in writing, more than first rights for his copyrighted magazine. If that's the case, you should write the editor for permission to use the poem or to have the copyright assigned to you, a request that will be granted automatically (and without cost) by almost all publishers. Book publishers ordinarily take out a copyright in the name of the author (if it is a collection of work by an individual; if it's an anthology, the same procedures apply as are used in copyrighted magazines). But if you have signed a book contract which authorizes only the publisher to reprint your work and you want to use the poetry elsewhere, you must request permission from the publisher, which is almost always granted as a courtesy.

Cover letters

Some editors discourage and others encourage cover letters, and some don't say. A letter usually isn't essential—especially if it has no more to say than, "The enclosed poems are submitted for your consideration." Most editors receiving a packet of poems can figure that out for themselves. But it doesn't hurt to enclose some information about yourself and recent publications, if any—but keep it short and, above all, don't try to tell editors in a letter what a good poet you are; your poems will speak for themselves. See the sample cover letter for magazine submissions. Note that it demonstrates a familiarity with the magazine. Most of us often submit to magazines we *haven't* seen, but you'll do a better job of marketing if you examine copies in a library or buy a sample before submitting. I've heard the editor of the *Antioch Review* speculate that he gets so many submissions because the name of the magazine starts with "A" and occurs early in market lists. You should have some more specific reason than that when selecting a magazine to which to submit.

Records

Never send the only copy of your work. (Good photocopies are usually acceptable for submissions.) And be sure to keep a running account of what you have submitted, where and when, and when you receive a response. This not only keeps your business records straight but also provides you with a guide for future submissions. Some magazines indicate in their listings an approximate length of time before you can expect a response, but that may indicate wishful thinking, especially when magazines are new and optimistic about how fast they'll work. If you get no reply within a couple of months of the published time of response, it is reasonable to query, with SASE. To avoid endless frustration with small presses that don't answer their mail, or are slow in doing so, I usually tell them that unless I hear from them by a given date (for example, in a couple of weeks), I will consider the submission withdrawn and submit it elsewhere.

And don't be surprised by sloppy office work on the other end. In my experience, sometimes even the mass-circulation magazines and large publishers lose manuscripts or fail to respond to queries with SASE. Don't get mad, get even. Send your manuscript

SAMPLE COVER LETTER
(for magazine submission)

321 Howard Drive
Benton AZ 12345
(602)111-3456

January 10, 1992

Linda Martin
Poetry Editor
Cloud Quarterly
123 Four St.
Capital ME 45678

Dear Ms. Martin: (use Dear Poetry Editor if no name is·
given in listing)

Enclosed are my poems "After the Storm," "Spring
Rain" and "Autumn Night" for your consideration. My
poetry has recently appeared in Nimbus, Seasons and
Equator Monthly.

I grew up in the Southwest and am now employed by the
U.S. Forestry Service. My poetry has been greatly influenced by my work in the outdoors and in the conservation of our natural resources.

In your most recent (Spring) issue I especially enjoyed
Rita Wilson's "Mountain Climber" and Robert Carson's
"Cyclone." It would be an honor to see my poetry in your
pages.

Sincerely,

Christopher Smith

Christopher Smith

elsewhere—after notifying the editor that you are doing so—and don't favor that publication with your submissions thereafter.

An editor receiving a manuscript for consideration assumes that it has not been published elsewhere (unless you advise otherwise), that it is your own work, and that it is not being simultaneously submitted to another magazine. That last assumption is controversial. If you had written a hot, well-documented article revealing the involvement of the CIA in a recent attempted assassination of the Pope, it is reasonable that a magazine might expect the right to exclusive consideration, and, because of the news value of your story, the magazine can reasonably be expected to respond within days. But I don't see that the same applies to poems submitted to little magazines that are sometimes months in responding. More and more poets are submitting simultaneously to several magazines. If you do that and get an acceptance from one of them, notify other editors who have the same poems to consider that the submission is withdrawn—and why. It is polite to notify editors when you are submitting elsewhere simultaneously. Some editors specify "no simultaneous submissions," and these are likely to be upset (or to reject your submission outright) if you engage in this practice. You have to use your judgment. But the process of circulating your work and garnering occasional acceptances is slow at best, and I think poets have some rights to be considered—as do editors. But there are no rules, only customs, and building a successful career as a poet is at least as tricky as succeeding in any other field.

Anthologies

Literary immortality requires getting into anthologies and textbooks, but, like any other immortality, that's not something you can do much about. It's a matter of "Don't call us; we'll call you." The editors of prestigious anthologies decide whose work they would like to include and, if the poet or writer is alive, solicit a contribution.

But in recent years there has emerged another variety of anthology to which you *can* submit work, and which, if you are smart, you will avoid. The vanity publishing industry began with such an anthology. Back in the 1920s an enterprising young man, later to head one of the largest vanity publishing houses in the country, got the bright idea of asking poets (whose work he found in literary magazines and whose addresses he got from phone books) to be represented in the anthology he was editing. Most, flattered by the invitation, quickly agreed. Then the entrepreneur explained to them that, because of the high cost of publication and the small market for poetry, contributors would be required to purchase at least one copy. When he had collected enough money from the poets to pay printing costs (and provide himself with a nice profit), he went to a printer and had the anthology published.

Today there are huge businesses profiting from the gullibility of poets. Every year I get a flood of letters from poets who tell me proudly that they have appeared in a half-dozen anthologies and reaped great honors (certificates, not cash) at poetry conventions, and are wondering why no magazines will accept their work. They do not stop to think that just about the only people who buy those anthologies are the poets who paid to have their work included, and those who go to such conventions are poets, like themselves, who paid to be there. Vanity is one of our most abundant natural resources, apparently. There seem to be, year after year, thousands of poets who accept without question the idea that their work has been chosen to appear in an anthology entitled **The Greatest Poems in the Western World**, or something of comparable pretention.

Some publishers listed in **Poet's Market** have "anthology" in their coding. Note that these are almost always in the **(I)** category, for beginners. Few experienced poets submit. Often the anthologies are annuals, or appear at regular intervals (such as quarterly), and are really no different from annual magazines. Not all require purchase of a copy for inclusion, but many do. Apparently these fill some public need of poets to be published even if they have to pay for the privilege, so I have included those that seemed to me to be harmless, though I have excluded others that, because of the high price of their antholog-ies or their methods of soliciting manuscripts, seem to be exploitative of poets. Some are regional publications that seem to be honest, though not profitable, ways of getting local poets into print.

But arm yourself with skepticism when dealing with anthologies and contests. There are really no good alternatives to building up a publication record the hard way—by patient submission to magazines and publishers that pay little or nothing to contributors, but refrain from flattery and advertisements to get them.

Book publication

It is important to understand the various methods of book publication. Here are some basic ways of distinguishing among these alternatives:

● *Commercial publishing:* Usually the publisher assumes all publication and promotion costs and pays the author 10 copies and a 10% royalty on the retail price of the book. In a few cases the 10% is on the wholesale price. You may buy additional copies of your book from the publisher, usually for the same discount (40%) that a bookstore pays.

Poets are generally not concerned with commercial publication at all. Many major pub-lishers publish books of poetry, but most are not open for submissions. They have estab-lished lists of a few poets whose work they publish regularly, and they may solicit work from others who come to their attention. But books of poetry generally sell poorly, so publishers' efforts in this regard are more for prestige. If you have a reputation as a poet sufficient to interest a commercial publisher, you probably aren't reading this book.

● *Self-publishing*, the other extreme: You pay all costs and get all copies and all proceeds. If the name of the publisher is not important to you, it is better to invent a name and self-publish. If you deal with a printer, rather than a company that calls itself "publisher," you own all the books you paid to have manufactured. If you do not expect your book to be a commercial success, you may want only a couple of hundred copies printed, or as many as you can gracefully dispose of.

Many eminent poets have self-published their work. Walt Whitman not only set the type for his books and brought them out at his own expense, but also, under pseudonyms, wrote many reviews of his own work. There is nothing dishonorable about self-publication (though reviewing oneself is a questionable practice).

● *Cooperative publishing:* Most of the better-known poets have published their work through various cooperative publishing arrangements. Most small presses, which publish the bulk of good poetry that appears in the United States, are, essentially, nonprofit and volunteer efforts. Considering that the cost of publishing a book may be thousands of dollars and sales are usually low, you can understand why that is. If a respected and established imprint (usually a small press) will bring your work critical attention and circu-lation, you may be interested in sharing both the risks and profits of publication. Most of these arrangements—though they vary in detail—require you to invest in the costs but usually provide you with a larger number of copies and/or larger royalties than in commer-cial publishing contracts.

● *Vanity presses:* (they usually refer to themselves as subsidy publishers) are the least desirable alternative. Such presses can hurt the sales of your book because many readers and reviewers assume that you must be, at best, an amateur if you resort to using subsidy services.

What, then, is a vanity press? There is no absolute definition, but here are some signals that warn you to be cautious:

Does the publisher advertise for manuscripts? (Trade publishers and cooperative pub-lishers never do.)

Does the publisher praise your work excessively? (Acceptance is praise enough from most non-vanity publishers.)

Is the amount the publisher asks far in excess of costs? (Get estimates from printers for the size, format and binding of the book you have in mind to make comparisons.)

Does the publisher promise an unrealistic publicity campaign? (Remember, you will be paying for all those review copies. A good publisher is extremely selective – to avoid sending out copies that will simply be trashed.)

If the publisher promises to advertise, look for samples of their advertising. (Vanity presses customarily, to fulfill contract obligations, take out ads that list all their books together indiscriminately. Ads – especially newspaper ads – rarely sell books anyway, and those that do are carefully targeted for specific audiences. Most commonly they are how-to books.)

How many copies of your book will you own? (Typically, vanity publishers print many copies, but bind only a few needed for the author and for review copies. As author, you get some as part of the contract, but if you want more, you have to buy them – at a discount, of course – and the publisher will then bind enough to fill your order. But you paid to have the whole run printed and bound.)

• *Competitions:* Getting your first book of poems published is hard enough, but subsequent volumes are likely to be even harder to place. For first books, look into the many competitions that are available, such as those held annually by some university presses. (There are fewer for subsequent books.) But I know many a poet who has spent a lot of time and money (reading fees are often required, and photocopying and postage costs mount up) seeking these awards, and, obviously, only a few are winners. The publicity attendant upon the awards sometimes sells a few books or elicits a few reviews. But the sad truth is that most books of poetry never earn for their publishers or authors the cost of publication, and most are never reviewed at all.

• *Chapbooks:* These are pamphlets of 30 pages or less. (See the Chapbook Publishers Index). Because pamphlets do not have readable spines, they are an anathema to a bookstore and they are reviewed only by some few lit mags. (This year, if the information is available, I have indicated in their listings which magazines review books of poetry.) Most chapbook distribution is done by the poet – at readings, when some in the audience may want to have an inexpensive sample of a poet's work to keep, or through the mail. Nonetheless, chapbooks are a popular and useful step between magazine and book publication.

For the reasons I've discussed here, cooperative publishing and self-publishing are the most common means of getting books of poetry into print. If you have some reputation already, you may find a respected small-press publisher interested in bringing out your work on some cooperative arrangement. (See sample cover letter for book or chapbook submissions.)

Self-publication

I often advise poets who are *not* widely recognized, especially if they are elderly, to self-publish. Recognition by the literary world is chancy at best, and often a rather hollow achievement. If what matters to you is to preserve your writing in some attractive and enduring way for your family and friends and posterity, your best course may be to take on the responsibility of publication yourself. So you don't go to Samoa this year or buy a new car or new computer. You have to decide what is important to you. If it's bringing out your own book, you may want to consult **The Complete Guide to Self-Publishing** by Tom and Marilyn Ross ($16.95 from Writer's Digest Books). The same authors also offer **Marketing Your Books** ($9.95 from their own self-publishing operation, Communication Creativity, 425 Cedar St., Buena Vista CO 81211) – with ideas about how to market all those books you paid to have printed. (Marketing poetry is often an exercise in futility, however; you may be better off recognizing ahead of time that you probably will be giving away most of your books.) **Complete Guide** has, along with a clear explanation of the whole printing and publication process (good for a writer to understand), a glossary of everything from "AA"

SAMPLE COVER LETTER
(for book or chapbook submission)

456 Campbell Drive
Bay Island NY 45678
(200)122-3345

January 15, 1992

Lawrence Marshall
Poetry Editor
Coastal Press
Merrymount CA 12345

Dear Mr. Marshall: (use Dear Poetry Editor if no name is given
in listing)

Enclosed is my manuscript End of the Forest, 32 pages, which
I hope you will consider for chapbook publication. Some of
these poems have appeared in Verdant Magazine, Lemon Tree
and Nature Quarterly. I have previously had one book collection, Trees and Sky, and one chapbook, Green Meadows, published by Moore Press.

I was attracted to Coastal Press by the fact that you have published books I admire, such as Penny Ander's Web of Doubt
and Arnold Parker's Winding Way, both of them handsome
examples of the art of printing as well as spellbinding in content. You seem to respect poets who are able to work within
the confines of form, and I believe I am such a poet.

I would be able to help you promote sales by supplying you
with a list of the subscribers to Nature Land Magazine, where
my articles and poetry have frequently appeared, and through
my freelance writing connections with local newspaper people
and arts groups. I would actively assist sales by soliciting reviews and poetry readings, and help in any other way I could
to make my book a financial success.

Sincerely,

Janice Cook

Janice Cook

(author's alterations) to "WF" (wrong font). Rather than try to keep the details of a rapidly changing industry in my head, I rely on handbooks such as these for reference.

Did you say business?

Poetry is, alas, a fairly expensive hobby—like photography or white-water canoeing—more than it is a business. Langston Hughes and Ogden Nash, I am told, made a living from their poetry, but few others have done so. Many poets do as I do—write poetry for love and prose for profit. (How many of you who bought this book—a respectable, even deductible professional expense—have bought a book of my poems?) We usually don't expect to make a profit on what we do for love. Yet, strangely, or not so strangely, the things we love, not those we do for money, are central to our lives.

Poetry has almost never in history been a paying proposition—and that makes some sense. It brings an intensely personal satisfaction, and there is no good reason that the public should pay for our personal satisfactions. Most poets have lived on patronage of one sort or another, sometimes the wealth of their own families. Shakespeare made a living in the hurly-burly of the theater—which was in his time, as it is now, a real business, with paying customers—but his poems were written for patrons. Tennyson (who didn't need the money) wrote bestsellers. Though it was relatively late in his life before an American publisher brought out his work, Robert Frost was a writer whose poetry earned a profit. But for the most part those who commit their lives, as I have committed mine, to writing poetry have not been able to *make* a living by writing it. Indeed, it costs most of us more than it earns in any given year.

If you find that discouraging, you're simply in the wrong line of endeavor. Poetry is a spiritual transaction between two individuals. Some of us dream of such transactions taking place with our poems, and anyone who has ever experienced a taste of that joy understands the power of its attraction. We may not succeed in what we're trying to do, but no one can stop us from trying. If you've read this far, you probably know what I mean.

Market conditions are constantly changing! If you're still using this book and it is 1993 or later, buy the newest edition of Poet's Market *at your favorite bookstore or order directly from* Writer's Digest Books.

U.S. and Canadian Postal Codes

United States

AL	Alabama	MI	Michigan	UT	Utah
AK	Alaska	MN	Minnesota	VT	Vermont
AZ	Arizona	MS	Mississippi	VI	Virgin Islands
AR	Arkansas	MO	Missouri	VA	Virginia
CA	California	MT	Montana	WA	Washington
CO	Colorado	NE	Nebraska	WV	West Virginia
CT	Connecticut	NV	Nevada	WI	Wisconsin
DE	Delaware	NH	New Hampshire	WY	Wyoming
DC	District of Columbia	NJ	New Jersey		
FL	Florida	NM	New Mexico		
GA	Georgia	NY	New York		

Canada

AB	Alberta
BC	British Columbia
LB	Labrador
MB	Manitoba
NB	New Brunswick
NF	Newfoundland
NT	Northwest Territories
NS	Nova Scotia
ON	Ontario
PEI	Prince Edward Island
PQ	Quebec
SK	Sasketchewan
YT	Yukon

More US:
GU Guam, HI Hawaii, ID Idaho, IL Illinois, IN Indiana, IA Iowa, KS Kansas, KY Kentucky, LA Louisiana, ME Maine, MD Maryland, MA Massachusetts, NC North Carolina, ND North Dakota, OH Ohio, OK Oklahoma, OR Oregon, PA Pennsylvania, PR Puerto Rico, RI Rhode Island, SC South Carolina, SD South Dakota, TN Tennessee, TX Texas

ALWAYS submit MSS or queries with a self-addressed, stamped envelope (SASE) within your country or a self-addressed envelope and International Reply Coupons (IRCs) purchased from the post office for other countries.

Key to Symbols and Abbreviations

‡ New listing
MS-manuscript; MSS-manuscripts
b/w-black-and-white (photo or illustration)
SASE-self-addressed, stamped envelope
SAE-self-addressed envelope
IRC-International Reply Coupon, for use on reply mail in foreign markets.

Important Market Listing Information

• Listings are based on questionnaires and verified copy. They are not advertisements *nor* are markets reported here necessarily endorsed by the editor of this book.

• Information in the listings comes directly from the publishers and is as accurate as possible, but publications and editors come and go, and poetry needs fluctuate between the publication date of this directory and the time you use it.

• **Poet's Market** *reserves the right to exclude any listing that does not meet its requirements.*

The Markets

Publishers of Poetry

Though you might get the impression that the publishers of books and magazines listed in this section are big corporations with secretaries and switchboards and fax machines, for the most part, what you will find are *people* – individuals. Perhaps a young mother who happens to love poetry may decide to devote her spare time to publishing a little magazine. When she gets an issue together, she goes to a local printer and pays to have a pile of messy manuscripts turned into something presentable for mailing. Or maybe it's a gang of college students who are disgusted that they couldn't find magazines to publish their work, so they start their own magazine. Or maybe it's a retired biologist who takes up publishing instead of stamp collecting as his hobby.

Such possibilities are important to keep in mind as you use this book. Recently a friend who writes very good poetry, but is only now, in her 50s, getting around to submitting her work for publication, came to me in a mixture of fury and tears. She was going to give up on poetry. She had sent some of her work to a magazine I had recommended and, along with her returned poems and a rejection slip, had received a printed notation in which the editor said that she commented on poetry that she regarded as promising. My friend had received no comment and so assumed that her poetry was not regarded as promising by someone who, I had told her, was a good judge and published good poetry.

I had to explain what I hope all users of this book will understand. For one thing, 90% of my own poems that I send out come back with rejection slips and no comment from the editors – and I've been publishing poetry for half a century. I happened to know that the particular editor my friend was dealing with has a fulltime job in addition to publishing the magazine. She keeps no backlog; when she has enough acceptances for the next issue, she returns any new manuscripts she receives so as not to hold poets up from submitting them elsewhere. She may not even be able to read all the manuscripts she receives. Having done some volunteer editing myself, I know, too, that one can get busy or distracted or for any number of other reasons pay less attention to submissions than they deserve.

I also know, as every poet should, that taste is ultimately personal and arbitrary. There's no predicting what will appeal to any particular editor (or contest judge). I told my friend that though her sensitivity might serve her well when she is *writing* poems, it could be a nuisance when she was marketing them. You have to develop a hide like a rhinoceros. Above all, don't take rejections personally. All a rejection slip means is that these particular poems didn't fit the needs or interests of some particular editor (or perhaps one of several friends who constitute an editorial board) at some particular time. Maybe the editor in question should take that promise out of her "manifesto." You can see why rejection slips and information from publishers tend to be vague and incommunicative; anything they say may kick off responses like that of my friend, who thought that a printed statement of policy meant something specific about her work and her talent.

Where to look

When I started **Poet's Market** I had been frustrated by other directories because separate listings of various contests, publishers' imprints, and activities conducted by the same people were scattered under a lot of individual listings, so it was hard to get an overview of any one publisher. How was I to know that the editor of the magazine *Nostoc* was the same fellow who edited Arts End Books? When I read about someone winning the Discovery Prize or the Lenore Marshall Prize, how was I to know the connection between those awards and *The Nation*? So I tried to combine all poetry activities of each publisher into one listing. It is important, therefore, to consult the General Index at the back of the book to find a particular magazine or publisher listing; then, when you read the listing, you will also get an overview of the publisher's related activities.

There are special sections in this book for Contests and Awards and other categories of activities such as poetry readings or organization membership pertaining to poetry. However, if a publisher also offers these activities, the information will be included in the publisher's listing in this section. For instance, The University of Arkansas Press publishes a lot of poetry, but the only avenue open to unsolicited manuscripts is their contest for poets who have not previously published books. So I might have put the listing under Contests and Awards; but it seemed to me much more informative to list them in this section, where I could indicate the range of their publishing activities pertinent to poetry.

Also, I was concerned about readability. I didn't want **Poet's Market** to be like a phone book. I know that as a poet I find it important to know as much as possible about *a lot* of publications and publishers although I may have no intention of submitting my work to all of them. Like government agencies, foundations, editors and many others, I need a reference book that will explain to me the meaning of a poet's credentials. I've tried to make **Poet's Market** just that kind of reference book.

If you are looking for a specific listing, start with the General Index. (Also check the Other Poetry Publishers list at the end of this section for the current status of publishers not included here.) If you are reading for general information, start anywhere in this section. I'll bet you will find yourself fascinated, as I am, even after editing **Poet's Market** for six years. I can't possibly *remember* all the information here so, as I hope you will, I use **Poet's Market** daily, both for casual but informative reading and to locate specific facts.

ABATTOIR EDITIONS (II), Annex 22, University of Nebraska, Omaha NE 68182, phone (402)554-2787, founded 1972, director/editor Bonnie P. O'Connell, is a "literary fine press—adjunct to a teaching laboratory (Collegiate Book Arts Press) called The Fine Arts Press, producing hand-printed, hand-bound, limited editions." They want **poetry other than song lyrics, epics, science fiction or religious poetry.** They have recently published poetry by Brenda Hillman and Sam Pereira, Ann Deagon, Bernard Copper, and, earlier, under editorship of Harry Duncan, James Merrill, Richard Wilbur, Ben Howard and Weldon Kees. As a sample they offer these lines from "Dreaming of Rio at Sixteen" by Lynn Emanuel:

> It was always Ramon's kisses, or sometimes, or never.
> Even grandmother's diamond earrings burned like Brazilian
> noons when you and she sheeted beds and found every
> beautiful mother an excuse to stop work and look out.

They publish 2-4 chapbooks (12-20 pp.) and flat-spined paperbacks and/or hardbacks (32-40 pp.) a year. **Query with 5-6 samples, bio and credits. Simultaneous submissions and photocopies OK. The editor accepts but dislikes dot-matrix. Poems should not have appeared in book form earlier. Reports on queries in 2-3 weeks, MSS in 1-2 months. Pays 10% royalties.**

ABBEY; ABBEY CHEAPOCHAPBOOKS (II), 5360 Fallriver Row Court, Columbia MD 21044, phone (301)730-4272, founded 1970, editor David Greisman. They want "**poetry that does for the mind what that first sip of Molson Ale does for the palate. No pornography & politics.**" They have recently published poetry by Richard Peabody, Vera Bergstrom, Margot Treitel, Harry Calhoun, Wayne Hogan and Tom Bilicke. *Abbey*, a quarterly, aims "to be a journal but to do it so informally that one wonders about my intent." It is magazine-sized, 20-26 pp., photocopied. They publish about 150 of 1,000 poems received per year. Press run is 200. Subscription: $2. **Sample: 50¢ postpaid. Guidelines available for SASE. Pays 1-2 copies. Reports in 1 month.** *Abbey Cheapochapbooks* come out 1-2 times a year averaging 10-15 pp. **For chapbook consideration query with 4-6 samples, bio, and list of publications. Reports in 2 months. Pays 25-50 copies.** The editor says he is "definitely seeing poetry from 2 schools—the nit'n'grit school and the textured/reflective school. I much prefer the latter."

‡ABIKO QUARTERLY LITTER-ARY RAG (I, IV-Translations), 8-1-8 Namiki, Abiko, Chiba Japan 270-11, phone 011-81-471-84-7904, founded 1988, poetry editor Vincent Broderick, is a quarterly "**heavily influenced by James Joyce,** Finnegan's Wake. **We publish all kinds, even religious poems, including original and translations**" They have recently published poetry by Kenji Mujazawa Saunders "scientist-scientific twist; a Canadian with a football/love twist; Suvin, a Canadian poet/professor with a Japanese/Chinese twist." It is a magazine-sized newsletter format, desktop publishing with laser printer. Press run 300 for 100 subscribers of which 10 are libraries. 50 shelf sales. **Sample postpaid: 1,500 yen. Pays 1 copy. Editors always comment on rejections.**

ABORIGINAL SF (IV-Science fiction), Box 2449, Woburn MA 01888-0849, founded 1986, editor Charles C. Ryan, is a full-color, slick magazine appearing every two months. "**Poetry should be 1-2 pp., double-spaced. Subject matter must be science fiction, science, or space-related. No long poems, no fantasy.**" The magazine is 68 pp., using coated stock, with 8-16 full-color illustrations. Circulation: 30,000, mostly subscriptions. Subscriptions for "special" writer's rate: $12/6 issues, $22/12 issues, $30/18 issues." **Sample: $3.50 postpaid. Pays $20 per poem and 2 copies. Reports in 2-8 weeks, has no backlog.** Poems should be double-spaced. No simultaneous submissions. Good photocopies, dot-matrix OK. Send SASE for guidelines.

ABRAXAS MAGAZINE; GHOST PONY PRESS (III), 2518 Gregory St., Madison WI 53711, phone (608)238-0175, *Abraxas* founded 1968, Ghost Pony Press in 1980, by editor/publisher Ingrid Swanberg, who says "Ghost Pony Press is a small press publisher of poetry books; *Abraxas* is a literary journal (irregular) publishing contemporary poetry, criticism, translations and reviews of small press books. *Do not confuse these separate presses!*" She wants to see "**contemporary lyric, some experimental.**" Does not want to see "political posing; academic regurgitations." They have recently published poetry by Andrei Condrescu, Ivan Argüelles, Denise Levertov, Cesar Vallejo and Charles Bukowski. As a sample I selected the opening stanza of "Gauguin" by T. L. Kryss:

> Baby kangaroos
> bounce like yellow lightning
> and under the volcano
> pear-breasted maidens
> hang colorforms of laundry

The magazine is 80 pp., flat-spined, 6 × 9″, litho offset, with original art on its matte card cover, using "unusual graphics in text, original art and collages, concrete poetry, exchange ads only, letters from contributors, essays." It appears "irregularly, 4-9 month intervals." They receive about 1,800 pp. of submissions per year, accept 2% of unsolicited material. Press run 600, 300 subscriptions of which 150 are libraries. **Sample: $3 postpaid. Send SASE for guidelines. Pays 1 copy plus 40% discount on additional copies.** "Suggest no more than 5 poems per submission." No simultaneous submissions or previously published poems. Reports in 3 weeks to 5 months, or longer. Up to a year between acceptance and publication. To submit to Ghost Pony Press, inquire with SASE plus 5-10 poems and cover letter. Photocopy, dot-matrix, previously published material OK for book publication by Ghost Pony Press, which reports on queries in 4 weeks to 3 months, MSS in 3 months. Payment varies per project. Send SASE for catalog to buy samples. Editor sometimes comments briefly on rejections. They have recently published **Zen Concrete & Etc.,** a selection of poetry by d.a. levy.

‡ACM (ANOTHER CHICAGO MAGAZINE) (II) LEFT FIELD PRESS (V), 3709 N. Kenmore, Chicago IL 60613, founded 1976, poetry editor Barry Silesky. *ACM* is a literary bi-annual, **emphasis on quality, experimental, politically aware** prose, fiction, poetry, reviews, cross-genre work, and essays. The editor wants "**no religious verse.**" They have recently published prose and poetry by Michael McClure, Jack Anderson, Jerome Sala, Nance VanWinkel, Nadja Tesich, Wanda Coleman, Thomas McGrath and Marilyn Krysl. As a sample, the editor selected these lines (poet unidentified):

> The black trunk of the ancient tree splits
> into two branches at eye level.
> Thus Lopo Gonclaveo crossed
> the equator. No boiling waters. No harm

Though I have not seen a copy, the editor says that *ACM* is digest-sized, 196 pp., offset, b/w art, and uses ads. Circulation 1,500, 500 subscriptions of which 100 are libraries. **Sample $5 postpaid.**

The double dagger before a listing indicates that the listing is new in this edition. New markets are often the most receptive to submissions.

Pays $5/page and 1 copy. Reports in 2-3 months, has 3-6 month backlog. Submit 3-8 pp. typed. Simultaneous submissions, clear photocopy OK. They do not accept freelance submissions for chapbook publication.

ACUMEN MAGAZINE; EMBER PRESS (I, II), 6, The Mount, Higher Furzeham, Brixham, S. Devon TQ5 8QY England, phone 08045/51098, press founded 1971. *Acumen* founded 1984, poetry editor Patricia Oxley, is a "small press publisher of a general literary magazine with emphasis on good poetry." They want **well-crafted, high quality, imaginative poems showing a sense of form. No experimental verse of an obscene type.** They have published poetry by Elizabeth Jennings, Roy Fuller, Boris Pasternak, D.S. Enright, Peter Porter and R.S. Thomas. As a sample Mrs. Oxley selected these lines from "Spring Night" by William Oxley:

> Spring night, night without suffering,
> Black mottled with stars.
> Peace's infinite clinging

Acumen appears in April and October of each year, digest-sized, 100 pp. flat-spined, professionally printed with illustrations and ads. Of about 2,000 poems received they accept about 80. Press run is 500 for 250 subscriptions (12 libraries). $10 per issue, $25 subscription. **Sample: $10 postpaid.** Pays "by negotiation" and one copy. Simultaneous submissions OK, no previously published poems. **Reports in one month.** Reviews books of poetry. Patricia Oxley advises, "Read as many literary and poetry magazines as possible, as well as books of poetry both past and present."

ADASTRA PRESS (II), 101 Strong St., Easthampton MA 01027, phone (413)527-3324, founded 1980 by Gary Metras, who says, "I publish poetry because I love poetry. I produce the books on antique equipment using antique methods because I own the equipment and because it's cheaper—I don't pay myself a salary—it's a hobby—it's **a love affair with poetry and printing of fine editions.** I literally sweat making these books and I want the manuscript to show me the author also sweated." All his books and chapbooks are **limited editions, handset, letterpress,** printed with handsewn signatures. "Chances of acceptance are slim. About 1 in 200 submissions is accepted, which means I only take 1 or 2 unsolicited mss a year." The chapbooks are in square-spine paper wrappers, cloth editions also handcrafted. He wants **"no rhyme, no religious. Poetry is communication first, although it is art. Long poems and thematic groups are nice for chapbooks. No subjects are tabu, but topics should be drawn from real life experiences. I include accurate dreams as real life."** Poets published include Judith Neeld, W.D. Ehrhart, Joseph Langland and David Chorlton. Here are some lines from the poem, "Mill Town," in the chapbook, **The Ballad of Harmonica George & Other Poems,** by David Raffeld:

> Every day a little more life beaten.
> Sons of creosote, daughters of wool and dye,
> children of the raw fiber,
> fathers of chain saw and pick up,
> grandfathers of marble, your names
> are dust to the lungs of this town.

1-4 such chapbooks are brought out each year. **Author is paid in copies, usually 10% of the print run. "I only read chapbook manuscripts in the month of February, picking one or two for the following year. Queries, with a sample of 3-5 poems from a chapbook manuscript, are read throughout the year and if I like what I see in the sample, I'll ask you to submit the MS in February. Do not submit or query about full-length collections. I will only be accepting chapbook manuscripts of 12-18 double-spaced pages. Any longer collections would be a special invitation to a poet.** If you want to see a typical handcrafted Adastra chapbook, send $5 and I'll mail a current title. If you'd like a fuller look at what, how and why I do what I do, send check for $11.50 ($10 plus $1.50 postage and handling) and I'll mail a copy of **The Adastra Reader: Being the Collected Chapbooks in Facsimile with Author Notes, Bibliography and Comments on Hand Bookmaking,** published in 1987. This is a 247-page anthology covering Adastra publishing from 1979-1986."

ADRIFT (II, IV-Ethnic), 4D, 239 East 5th St., New York NY 10003, founded 1980, editor Thomas McGonigle, who says, "The **orientation of magazine is Irish, Irish-American. I expect reader-writer knows and goes beyond Yeats, Kavanagh, Joyce, O'Brien."** The literary magazine is open to all kinds of submissions, but does not want to see "junk." Simultaneous submissions OK. Poets recently published include James Liddy, Thomas McCarthy, Francis Stuart and Gilbert Sorrentino. As a sample, the editor selected this poem, "Mussel" by Beatrice Smedley:

> eating with
> friend his other
> pleasure now
> more limpid

Adrift appears twice a year and has a circulation of 1,000 with 200 subscriptions, 50 of which go to libraries. Price per issue is $4, subscription $8. **Sample: $5 postpaid. Magazine pays, rate varies; contributors receive 1 copy.** Magazine-sized, 32 pp., offset on heavy stock, cover matte card, saddle-stapled. Reviews books of poetry.

THE ADROIT EXPRESSION (I), P.O. Box 73, Courtney PA 15029, phone (412)379-8019, founded 1986, editor/publisher Xavier F. Aguilar, appears 2 times a year, and is **"open to all types of poetry, including erotica that is well written."** They have recently published poetry by Patrick J. Cauchi and Lisa Rae Allen. As a sample the editor selected the poem "Empty Spaces" by Amy F. Bleser:

> *I want to swallow*
> *The entire*
> *Round world. Bite by*
> *Bite, tasting,*
> *Feeling every velvet*
> *Inch of the sky.*

I have not seen an issue, but the editor describes it as magazine-sized, 3-5 pp., circulation 75. **Sample postpaid: $3.** They sponsor an annual poetry competition "entry fee required; awards prizes (sometimes cash)." The editor says, "In publishing poetry—I try to exhibit the unique reality that we too often take for granted and acquaint as mediocre."

ADVOCACY PRESS (IV-Children), P.O. Box 236, Santa Barbara CA 93102, founded 1983, director of operations Penny Paine, publishes children's books using **"equity materials only, in 2 series: (1) an event in the life of a little-known woman of history that had significant impact** (see **Berta Benz and the Motorwagen** by Mindy Bingham); (2) self-esteem, self-sufficiency concept-story (see **Minou** by Bingham). **Must have rhythm and rhyme."** They have published **Father Gander** featuring nursery rhymes that are non-sexist and non-violent, such as in this sample:

> *Peter, Peter, pumpkin eater,*
> *Had a wife and wished to keep her.*
> *Treated her with fair respect,*
> *She stayed with him and hugged his neck.*

That book is available hardback for $16.45 postpaid. Their books average 32 pp. **Query with description of concept and sample. Simultaneous submissions and previously published poems OK. SASE required for reply. "Please do not submit manuscripts that do not meet our subject requirements."**

THE ADVOCATE (I), 301A Rolling Hills Park, Prattsville NY 12468, phone (518)299-3103, editor Remington Wright, founded 1987, is an advertiser-supported tabloid appearing bimonthly, 12,000 copies distributed free, **using original, previously unpublished works,** such as feature stories, essays, 'think' pieces, letters to the editor, profiles, humor, fiction, poetry, puzzles, cartoons, or line drawings. They want **"nearly any kind of poetry, any length, but not religious or pornographic. Poetry ought to speak to people and not be so oblique as to have meaning only to the poet. If I had to be there to understand the poem, don't send it."** As a sample here are the opening lines from "The Kerry Eileen" by Joyce A. Story:

> *It was June the thirteenth when the ship was first seen*
> *By the captain and crew of the* Kerry Eileen
> *She then seemed to dissolve in the darkening greys*
> *Of the sky and the sea and the leaden-like haze.*

Sample: $2 postpaid. Pays 3 copies. Reports in 6-8 weeks; publishes accepted material an average of 4-6 months after acceptance. No simultaneous submissions. Editor "occasionally" comments on rejections. Accepts about 25% of poems received. Reviews books of poetry. Offers occasional contests.

AEGINA PRESS, INC.; UNIVERSITY EDITIONS (I, II), 59 Oak Lane, Spring Valley, Huntington WV 25704, founded 1983, publisher Ira Herman, is **primarily subsidy for poetry,** strongly committed to publishing new or established poets. Publishes subsidy titles under the University Editions imprint. Aegina has published non-subsidized poetry as well. **Authors of books accepted on a non-subsidized**

ALWAYS submit MSS or queries with a self-addressed, stamped envelope (SASE) within your country or a self-addressed envelope and International Reply Coupons (IRCs) purchased from the post office for other countries.

basis receive a 15% royalty. "We try to provide a way for talented poets to have their collections published, which otherwise might go unpublished because of commercial, bottom-line considerations. Aegina Press will publish quality poetry that the large publishers will not handle because it is not commercially viable. We believe it is unfair that a poet has to have a 'name' or a following in order to have a book of poems accepted by a publisher. Poetry is the purest form of literary art, and it should be made available to those who appreciate it." Poets recently published include Barbara Everest. The editor selected these sample lines from Joanne Lowery's "Icarus":

> One foot firm on the seat of his bicycle,
> A boy on top of Everest on top of wheels
> Sails the street with arms outstretched
> To ruffle the flaming maples.

"Most poetry books we accept are subsidized by the author (or an institution). In return, the author receives all sales proceeds from the book, and any unsold copies left from the print run belong to the author. Minimum print run is 500 copies. We can do larger runs as well. Our marketing program includes submission to distributors, agents, other publishers, and bookstores and libraries." **Manuscripts should be typed and no shorter than 40 pages. There is no upper length limit. Simultaneous and photocopied submissions OK. Reporting time is 30 days for full manuscripts, 7-10 days for queries.** They publish perfect-bound (flat-spined) paperbacks with glossy covers. **Sample books are available for $5 each plus $1.50 postage and handling.**

AERIAL (II), Box 25642, Washington DC 20007, phone (202)333-1544, founded 1984, editor Rod Smith; editorial assistants Gretchen Johnson and Wayne Kline, a once- or twice-yearly publication. Issue #4 was a special issue on Douglas Messerli. They have published work by Carla Harryman, Eric Wirth, Charles Bernstein, Harrison Fisher, and Tina Darragh. The editor chose this sample from "My Ovaries Don't Have Enough Room" by Bruce Andrews:

> perform to be unlike meaning

The magazine is 6×9", offset, varies 60-180 pp. Circulation is 1,000. Single copy price is $6. **Sample available for $6 postpaid. Poets should submit 1-10 pages. Reporting time is 1 week-2 months and time to publication is 3-12 months.** Also looking for critical/political/philosophical writing.

AETHLON: THE JOURNAL OF SPORT LITERATURE (IV-Sports), East Tennessee State University, Johnson City TN 37614-0002, founded 1983, general editor Don Johnson, Professor of English, ETSU poetry editor Robert W. Hamblin, Professor of English, Southeast Missouri State University, Cape Girardeau MO 63701. (Submit poetry to this address.) *Aethlon* publishes a variety of sport-related literature, including scholarly articles, fiction, poetry, personal essays, and reviews; 6-10 poems per issue; two issues annually, fall and spring. **Subject matter must be sports-related; no restrictions regarding form, length, style or purpose. They do not want to see "doggerel, cliché-ridden, or oversentimental" poems.** Some poets recently published are Neal Bowers, Joseph Duemer, Robert Fink, Jan Mordenski, H.R. Stonebeck, Jim Thomas, Stephen Tudor and Don Welch. As a sample, the editor selected the following lines by Hillel Schwartz:

> Ground is all there
> is as you feel yourself grow old,
> and your small flights from it,
> a foot or two at the most,
> this jogging a consolation
> for the rest of the running,

The magazine is digest-sized, offset printed, flat-spined, with illustrations and some ads, 200 pp. per issue. Circulation is 1,000 of which 750 are subscriptions, 250 to libraries. Price per issue is $12.50; subscription is included with membership ($30) in the Sport Literature Association. **Sample $12.50 postpaid. Contributors receive 5 offprints and a copy of the issue in which their poem appears. Submissions are reported on in 6-8 weeks and the backlog time is 6-12 months; "only typed MSS with SASE considered." Will accept simultaneous submissions.**

AFRICA WORLD PRESS (IV-Ethnic), Box 1892, Trenton NJ 08607, founded 1979, editor Kassahun Checole, publishes poetry by Africans, African-Americans, Caribbean and Latin Americans. Two poetry publications by Africa World Press are: **Under A Soprano Sky,** by Sonia Sanchez and **From the Pyramid to the Projects** by Askia Muhammad Toure, winner of an American Book Award for 1989.

Market categories: (I) Beginning; (II) General; (III) Limited; (IV) Specialized; (V) Closed.

Authors receive 7½% royalty; number of copies negotiable. Considers simultaneous submissions. Send SASE for catalog.

AFRO-HISPANIC REVIEW (IV-Ethnic), Romance Languages, #143 Arts & Sciences, University of Missouri, Columbia MO 65211, founded 1982, editors Marvin A. Lewis and Edward J. Mullen, uses some **poetry related to Afro-Hispanic life and issues.** Appears 3 times a year. They have recently published poetry by Manuel Zapata Olivella, Melvin E. Lewis and Antar Al Basir. **Pays 5 copies. Sample copy $5. Reports in 6 weeks.** Reviews books of poetry.

‡**AFTER THE END; GA PRESS; THE IMPERFECT PITCH (I)**, 275 Woolwich St. Basement, Guelph, Ontario N1H 3V8 Canada, phone (519)767-1998, founded 1985, editor Greg Evason. *ATE* appears 1-2 times/year using poetry and visual art. GA Press, formerly Guardian Angel Press, publishes 1-2 chapbooks/year, leaflets, postcards and broadsides. *TIP* is newsletter format, "available for the asking, a collection of quotes from various sources." "I'll look at anything but do not like rhymes or traditional forms. Often 'experimental.' Not academic or stuffy. Also looking for visual poetry, collage & drawings. I appreciate some kind of brief cover letter but don't like to see lists of previous publications. I think the poems submitted should stand by themselves & not supported by previous accomplishments. Considers sexually explicit material. Short stories, too. Essays, etc." They have recently published poetry by F.A. Nettlebeck, bpNichol, John M. Bennett and Guy R. Beining. *ATE* is usually photocopied, photocopied from typescript, sometimes with card covers, press run 100 copies for 10 subscribers, including 1 library. Many distributed free. Price: $1-4, subscription: $10. **Sample: $3 postpaid. Pays copies. Accepts about 10% of submissions.** For chapbook submission: "Anybody can send any kind of MS as long as there's an SASE. No need for poems to be previously published. Reports within a month." **Pays 25% of run.**

AGENDA EDITIONS; AGENDA (II), 5 Cranbourne Ct., Albert Bridge Rd., London SW11 4PE England, founded 1959, poetry editors William Cookson and Peter Dale. *Agenda* is a 7×5″, 80 pp. (of which half are devoted to poetry), quarterly magazine (1 double, 2 single issues per year), circulation 1,500-3,000, 1,500 subscriptions of which 450 are libraries. They receive some 2,000 submissions per year, use 40, have a 5-month backlog. **Reports in 1 month. Pays £10 per page for poetry.** Subscription: Individuals U.S. $38, libraries and institutions U.S. $50. **Sample: £4 ($8) postpaid.** "We seek poetry of 'more than usual emotion, more than usual order' (Coleridge). We publish special issues on particular authors such as T. S. Eliot, Ezra Pound, David Jones, Stanley Burnshaw, Thomas Hardy, etc." Some of the poets who have appeared in *Agenda* are Peter Dale, Geoffrey Hill, Seamus Heaney, C. H. Sisson, Patricia McCarthy and W. S. Milne. The editors selected these sample lines (poet unidentified):
> How will you want the snowy impermanence of ash,
> your dust, like grass-seed, flighted over heathland,
> drifting in spinneys where the boughs clash,
> with matted needles laying waste beneath them.

To submit book MS, no query necessary, "as little as possible" in cover letter. SAE and IRC coupon for return. **Reports within a month. Payment in copies.** The editors say poets "should write only if there is an intense desire to express something. They should not worry about fashion."

AGNI (II), Boston University, 236 Bay State Rd., Boston MA 02215, phone (617)353-5389, founded 1972, editor Askold Melnyczuk, wants "wonderful poetry." They have recently published poetry by Seamus Heaney, Edwin Honig, Derek Walcott, Tony Harrison, Ai, William Harmon and Rita Dove. As a sample I selected the first of 16 stanzas of "In The Gap" by Glyn Maxwell:
> The road is dark and wet and red.
> I never went. I never was.
> It was an insult, what you said
> and you shall bleed for it, because
> I am the stranger up ahead.

Agni is 300+ pp, flat-spined, digest-sized, typeset, with glossy card cover with art, appearing twice a year. They take "1 out of 1,000" poems received. Their press run is 2,000 with 500 subscriptions. Subscription: $12. **Sample: $7 postpaid. Pays $10 per page, maximum $150, plus 2 copies and one-year subscription. Submit 3-5 poems. They will consider simultaneous submissions but not previously published poems. Reading period: Oct. 1 to June 1.** Mss received at other times will be returned unread. **Reports in 1-4 months.** Reviews books of poetry.

Use the General Index to find the page number of a specific publication or publisher.

‡AGOG (III), 340 22nd St., Brooklyn NY 11215, founded 1989, editor Scott Gray, is a quarterly. He wants **"something that'll jerk me out of my shoes."** They have recently published poetry by Miriam Sagan and Patrick Fusco. As a sample the editor selected these lines (by Patrick Fusco):

> *A shapeless bird*
> *beating its wings,*
> *tentative in the dark*
> *inside her ribcage.*
> *Looking out,*
> *probing the flat, white bars*
> *that bend around it.*

It is 35-50 pp., digest-sized, professionally printed, saddle-stapled. Press run 200, half given "to folks who express an interest." **Sample postpaid: $2. Pays 1 copy. "Response is swift and sure." Editor often comments on rejections.**

AG-PILOT INTERNATIONAL MAGAZINE (IV-Specialized), 405 Main St., Mt. Vernon WA 98273, phone (206)336-9737, editor Tom Wood, "is intended to be a fun-to-read, technical, as well as humorous and serious publication for the ag pilot and operator." It appears monthly, 48-64 pp., circulation 8,400. Interested in **agri-aviation (crop dusting) related poetry ONLY." Buys 1 per issue, pays $10-50.**

AHSAHTA PRESS; COLD DRILL; COLD-DRILL BOOKS; POETRY IN PUBLIC PLACES (IV-Regional), English Dept., Boise State University, Boise ID 83725, phone (208)385-1246. Ahsahta Press is a project to publish **contemporary poetry of the American West.** But, say editors Tom Trusky, Orv Burmaster and Dale Boyer, **"Spare us paens to the pommel, Jesus in the sagebrush, haiku about the Eiffel Tower, 'nice' or 'sweet' poems."** The work should **"draw on the cultures, history, ecologies of the American West."** They publish collections (60 pp.) of individual poets in handsome flat-spined paperbacks with plain matte covers, with an appreciative introduction, about 3 per year. Occasionally they bring out an anthology on cassette of their authors. And they have published an anthology (94 pp.) **Women Poets of the West,** with an introduction by Ann Stanford. Some of their poets are Susan Deal, Leo Romero, David Baker, Richard Speakes, Philip St. Clair, Judson Crews. Here are some lines from Marnie Walsh's "Dakota Winter," in the collection **A Taste of the Knife:**

> *it is where the long-fingered*
> *hand of winter*
> *clangs down a crystal lid*
> *to the sound of snow*

You may submit only during their January-March reading period each year—a sample of 15 of your poems with SASE. They will report in about 2 months. Multiple and simultaneous submissions, photocopy, dot-matrix OK. If they like the sample, they'll ask for a book MS. If it is accepted, you get 25 copies of the 1st and 2nd printings and a 25% royalty commencing with the 3rd. They seldom comment on the samples, frequently on the MSS. Send SASE for their catalog and order a few books, if you don't find them in your library. "Old advice but true: read what we publish before submitting. 75% of the submissions we receive should never have been sent to us. Save stamps, spirit, and sweat." *Cold Drill* publishes "primarily Boise State University students, faculty and staff, but will consider writings by Idahoans—or writing about Idaho by 'furriners.' " They do some of the most creative publishing in this country today, and it is worth buying a **sample of** *cold-drill* for $9 just to see what they're up to. This annual "has been selected as top undergraduate literary magazine in the US by such important acronyms as CSPA, CCLM and UCDA." It comes in a box stuffed with various pamphlets, postcards, posters, a newspaper, even 3-D comics with glasses to read them by. **No restrictions on types of poetry.** As yet they have published no poets of national note, but Tom Trusky offers these lines as a sample, from Patrick Flanagan, "Postcard From a Freshman":

> *The girls here are gorgeous, studying hard,*
> *many new friends, roommate*
> *never showers, tried to*
> *kill myself, doctor says*
> *i'm getting better*

Circulation is 400, including 100 subscribers, of which 20 are libraries. **"We read material throughout the year, notifying only those whose work we've accepted December 15-January 1st. Manuscripts should be photocopies with author's name and address on separate sheet, simultaneous submissions OK. Payment: 1 copy."** They also publish two 24 pp. chapbooks and one 75 pp. flat-spined paperback per year. **Query about book publication.** "We want to publish a literary magazine that is exciting to read. We want more readers than just our contributors and their mothers. Our format and our content have allowed us to achieve those goals, so far." I would advise discretion in regard to mothers. Poetry in Public Places is a series of 8 monthly posters per year "presenting the poets in Boise State University's creative students series and poets in

BSU's Ahsahta Press poetry series. These, like all publications emanating from BSU, are elegantly done, with striking art. The posters are on coated stock.

AILERON PRESS; AILERON: A LITERARY JOURNAL; VOWEL MOVEMENT (II), P.O. Box 891, Austin TX 78767-0891, founded 1980, editors Edwin Buffaloe and Cynthia Farar. *Aileron* is an annual periodical consisting of poetry and occasional short fiction, with some art. The editors are looking for "poetry that moves us, that makes us want to read it again and again. We are especially keen on innovative uses of language—the unexpected word and the unusual cadence. We would like to see more poetic craft displayed, and, though not inimical to rhymed work, feel that few contemporary poets handle rhyme well." The editor selected these lines by Elkion Tumbalé as an example of what he likes:

> Blue cup modal gorges
> Lurk frondly on
> Orchid Zontal
> Obsidian felines

Poets published there include Anselm Hollo, Simon Perchik, Hal J. Daniel III and Tomaz Salamun. It's a digest-sized format, saddle-stapled, typeset (in small type), b/w original line art up to 8 × 10″, stiff cover with art. Circulation is 350, with 25 subscriptions. **Sample $4 postpaid**, subscription $14 for 4 issues. Each issue contains 40-60 pages of poetry garnered from 400-600 submissions each year of which 60-100 are used, 6-month backlog. **All formats acceptable; must have name and address on each page; payment is 1 copy; no limitations on form, length or subject matter; guidelines available for SASE. Reporting time: 6 weeks.** *Vowel Movement*, "a 'pataphysical journal,' is published occasionally as a special issue of *Aileron*. It contains **avant-garde humor, satire, and work that is outrageous or experimental in nature.**"

AIM MAGAZINE (IV-Social issues, ethnic), 7308 S. Eberhart Ave., Chicago IL 60619, phone (312)874-6184, founded 1974, poetry editor Henry Blakely, is a magazine-sized quarterly, circulation 10,000, glossy cover, **"dedicated to racial harmony and peace."** They use 3-4 poems ("poetry with social significance mainly") in each issue, **paying $3/poem. They ask for 32 lines average length, but most poems in the sample issues I have seen were much shorter, and some were by children.** They have recently published poems by J. Douglas Studer, Wayne Dowdy and Maria DeGuzman. The editor selected the third stanza of "Afrique Unique" by Loretta A. Hawkins:

> In all of history, have yet I read
> where man's not been allowed to
> mourn his dead
> where truth has in a heavy blanket hid
> where God has seen yet not a word has said.

They have 3,000 subscriptions of which 15 are libraries. Subscription: $8; per issue: $2. **Sample: $3.50 postpaid. Pays $3/poem. You will not receive an acceptance slip: "We simply send payment and magazine copy." They publish only about 30 submissions per year of which they use half. Photocopy, simultaneous submissions OK, no dot-matrix. Reports in 3-6 weeks.** The editor's advice: "Read the work of published poets."

ALABAMA LITERARY REVIEW (II), English Dept., Troy State University, Troy AL 36082, phone (205)670-3000, ext. 3286, poetry editor Ed Hicks, a biannual, **wants poetry that is "imagistic—*but* in motion. Will look at anything."** They have published poetry by Larry McLeod, Coleman Barks, Leo Luke Marcello, George Ellenbogen, Roald Hoffman, Wayne Hogan, Elizabeth Dodd and James Ashbrook Perkins. I selected these sample lines, by Paul Grant from "Getaway":

> Mr. Piano man in the dark
> listening to his hands
> wanting words to hang in air

The beautifully printed 100 pp., 6 × 9″ magazine, matte cover with art, b/w art and some colored pages inside, receives 300 submissions per year, uses 30, has a 2-month backlog. **Will consider simultaneous submissions. Sample: $4 postpaid. Query not necessary. Reports in 1-2 months. Pays copies.** Sometimes comments on rejections.

ALASKA QUARTERLY REVIEW (II), Department of English, University of Alaska at Anchorage, 3221 Providence Dr., Anchorage AK 99508, phone (907)786-1750. Started in 1981, Ronald Spatz and J. Liszka, executive editors; Thomas Sexton, poetry editor. **"A journal devoted to contemporary literary art. We publish both traditional and experimental fiction, poetry, essays and criticism on contemporary writing, literature and philosophy of literature."** They publish two double-issues a year, **each using about 25 pp. of poetry.** They have a circulation of 1,000; 200 subscribers, of which 25 are libraries, $4 an issue, $8 per subscription, **$4 for a sample (postpaid).** They receive up to 2,000 submissions each year, of which they take about 50. **Pay depends on funding. They take up to 4 months to report, and**

there is usually no comment on MSS. No query. Manuscripts are not read during May, June, July and the first half of August.

THE ALCHEMIST (II), Box 123, Lasalle, Quebec H8R 3T7 Canada, founded 1974, poetry editor Marco Fraticelli, is a 100 pp., small digest-sized, flat-spined, handsomely printed and illustrated with b/w drawings, irregularly-issued literary journal, using mostly poetry. No restrictions on form, style or content, (though in the issue I examined, #8, there is a section of haiku and a useful catalog of haiku markets. Considers simultaneous submissions. They have a print-run of 500, 200 subscriptions, of which 30 are libraries, and they send out some 200 complimentary copies. Subscription $12 for 4 issues, $3 per issue. They have a 6 month backlog. Sample: $2 postpaid. Reports in 1 month. Payment: 2 copies. I selected these sample lines, the opening of "Dreams" by A. D. Winans:

> the dreams will not leave me alone
> they come and go through my skull
> opening the memory bank
> like an overfilled suitcase

ALCHEMY PRESS; FRAGMENTS (II, IV-Spiritual, political, ethnic, fantasy/horror), 1789 McDonald Ave., Brooklyn NY 11230, phone (718)339-0184, founded 1985, editor/publisher Fred Calero, who says, "I am interested in poetry that shakes conventional thought. A poetry that illuminates the soul and rattles the spirit. I am also interested in work that deals with the problems of good and evil. Also anything that is simple yet profound. I want honest poetry. There is so much poetry today that is contrived, and I just don't have the energy to read it all." They have published poetry by Richard Kostelanetz, Jim Feast and Eve Teitelbaum. As a sample the editor selected these lines from his own "Rage":

> There is a place where a dark flower blooms in the blackness of his mind
> Full of rage and savagery, he follows his destiny, a poetry too dark to comprehend.
> Like blue jays picking at the bones, in the dampness of her shallow grave.

Fragments is a quarterly. I have not seen an issue, but the editor describes it as digest-sized, saddle-stapled, photocopied. Press run: 1,000 for 400 subscriptions of which 20 are libraries. "I receive about 1,500 poems yearly and use about 15%." Subscription: $12. Sample, postpaid: $4. Send SASE for guidelines. Pays 25 copies. "Five poems at a time is fine. The poet's name and address should appear on each and every poem." Simultaneous submissions and previously published poems OK. "The backload is tremendous," but the editor usually responds in 2 months. For chapbook publication send 10 sample poems, cover letter, bio, and other publications. Pays 50 copies. Sample chapbook: $5. Editor comments on submissions "at times, if a poem seems to need a little more work, I may offer suggestions." He says, "Read, read, read. Be familiar with the great poets of various cultures. Look for work that has survived the test of time. Never limit yourself, like so many poets do, to just reading their contemporary writers. Never limit yourself to just poetry when reading. Be awake to the world around you and thrive."

‡ALDEBARAN (II), Roger Williams College, Old Ferry Rd., Bristol RI 02809, appears twice a year. "We accept poetry in nearly all forms, lengths, and subject-matters. We are interested in modern, as well as traditional styles." It is 50-100 pp., side-stapled, digest-sized. Press run 200. Sample postpaid: $3. Send SASE for guidelines. Pays 2 copies. Submit no more than 5 poems/time. Response in 6-12 weeks. Student-run publication. No comments on rejections.

ALGILMORE (I), 125 N. Main St., Galena IL 61036, phone (815)777-9688, founded 1968 as Studio Five, thought-merchant Jay Son, conducts new age sessions and publishes video tapes, cassettes and flyers, paying no less than $10 per use for "higher thoughts—New Age—no restriction on style, length, subject, good teaching thoughts. Longhand acceptable, spelling mistakes OK. Clarity important. No jokes, militant, smut. We are interested in the message. We would like a coverpage with bio of the poet and a snapshot if possible. SASE. We prefer to retain copies (due to the high cost of postage) and each poet has a personal file in our office. Allow 30 days for report. We are currently working with Larian, An-Dabney Faulkner, Lloyd A. Jackson, Jim Wheeler, Edward Ainsworth, Ruff Reiter and Lyn Hampel." As a sample the editor selected these lines:

> Do you know—your writing on the
> pages of my heart—.

"We will be having 8-12 contests a year and newsletters-open to all poets. Fee $2 per poem for contest poems only. All poets submitting poems are put on our contest list. Each month we create a subject to be written about. Reward with cash rewards. Winners are notified in monthly newsletter."

ALICEJAMESBOOKS; BEATRICE HAWLEY AWARD (IV-Regional, women, ethnic), 33 Richdale Ave., Cambridge MA 02140, phone (617)354-1408, founded 1973. "An author's collective, which publishes exclusively poetry, with an emphasis on poetry by women; authors are exclusively from the New

England Area. We strongly encourage submissions by poets of color." Offers Beatrice Hawley Award for poets who cannot meet the work commitment due to geographical or financial restraints. They publish flat-spined paperbacks of high quality, both in production and contents, no children's poetry, and their books have won numerous awards and been very respectably reviewed. "Each poet becomes a working member of the co-op with a two-year work commitment." That is, you have to live close enough to **attend meetings and participate in the editorial and publishing process.** The editor chose these lines from "Your Skin Is A Country" by Nora Mitchell:

> *In the background her village burns.*
> *I have always hoped*
> *that after he snapped his picture, the camerman*
> *threw down his camera, folded her in his arms,*
> *and listened to her cry.*

They publish about 4 books, 72 pp., each year in editions of 1,000, paperbacks—no hardbacks. **Query first, but no need for samples: simply ask for dates of reading periods, which are in early spring and early fall. Simultaneous submissions OK, but "we would like to know when a manuscript is being submitted elsewhere." Reports in 2-3 months. Send two copies of the MS. Payment: authors receive 100 paperback copies.**

ALIVE NOW!; POCKETS; WEAVINGS (IV-Religious, children); THE UPPER ROOM (V), 1908 Grand Ave., Box 189, Nashville TN 37202, phone (615)340-7200. This publishing company brings out about 20 books a year and four magazines: *The Upper Room, alive now!, Pockets* and *Weavings.* Of these, two use freelance poetry. *Pockets, Devotional Magazine for Children,* which comes out 11 times a year, circulation 68,000-70,000, is for children 6-12, "offers stories, activities, prayers, poems—all **geared to giving children a better understanding of themselves as children of God. Some of the material is not overtly religious but deals with situations, special seasons and holidays, ecological concerns from a Christian perspective.**" It uses 3-4 pp. of poetry per issue. **Sample: $1.70 plus 85¢ postage. Ordinarily 24-line limit on poetry. Pays $25-50. Send SASE for themes and guidelines.** The other magazine which uses poetry is *alive now!,* a bimonthly, circulation 75,000, for a general Christian audience interested in reflection and meditation. **Sample and guidelines free. They buy 30 poems a year, avant-garde and free verse. Submit 5 poems, 10-45 lines. Pays $10-25.** *The Upper Room* magazine does not accept poetry.

ALLARDYCE, BARNETT PUBLISHERS; POETICA (V), Allardyce Barnett Publishers, 14 Mount St., Lewes, East Sussex BN7 1HL, England, founded 1982, editorial director Anthony Barnett. Allardyce, Barnett publishes important substantial collections by current English language poets; "our financial situation does not currently allow for an extension of this programme into other areas. **We cannot at this time encourage unsolicited manuscripts.**" Some of the better-known poets they have published are J. H. Prynne, Andrew Crozier, Douglas Oliver and Veronica Forrest-Thomson. The press usually publishes simultaneous cloth and paper editions, currently less than 1 per year, with an average page count of 320, digest-sized. In the U.S., their books can be obtained through Small Press Distribution in Berkeley, CA. Also publishes the occasional review *Poetica,* founded 1989.

ALLEGHENY REVIEW (I, IV-Students), Box 32, Allegheny College, Meadville PA 16335, founded 1983, editors Vern A. Maczuzak and Richardson K. Prouty III. "Each year *Allegheny Review* compiles and publishes a review of the nation's best **undergraduate literature.** It is entirely composed of and by college undergraduates and is nationally distributed both as a review and as a classroom text, particularly suited to creative writing courses. We will print **poetry of appreciable literary merit on any topic, submitted by college undergraduates.** No limitations except excessive length (2-3 pp.) as we wish to represent as many authors as possible, although exceptions are made in areas of great quality and interest." They have published poetry by Eric Sanborn, Cheryl Connor, Rick Alley, and Kristi Coulter and selected these lines by Eric Schwerer (Allegheny College) as a sample:

> *I drop to the ground*
> *and make a melting slushy angel in the snow*
> *coming up heavy with water*
>
> *She rolls her eyes*
> *I remind her too much of potato soup*
> *and other clumsy memories*

The *Review* appears in a 6×9", flat-spined, professionally-printed format, b/w photo on glossy card cover. **Submissions should be accompanied by a letter "telling the college poet is attending, year of graduation, any background, goals and philosophies that the author feels are pertinent to the work submitted." Reports 1-2 months following deadline. Submit 3 to 5 poems, typed, photocopy, dot-matrix OK. Sample: $3.50 and 11 × 18" SASE. Poem judged best in the collection earns $50-75 honorarium.** "Ezra Pound gave the best advice: 'Make it new.' We're seeing far too much imitation; there's already been a Sylvia Plath, a Galway Kinnell. Don't be afraid to try new things. Be innovative. Also, traditional forms are coming 'back in style,' or so we hear. Experiment with them; write a villanelle, a sestina, or a sonnet. And when you submit, please take enough pride in your work to do so professionally. Handwritten or poorly-typed and proofed submissions definitely convey an impression, a negative one."

ALLY PRESS CENTER (V), 524 Orleans St., St. Paul MN 55107, founded 1973, owner Paul Feroe, publishes and distributes work by Robert Bly, Michael Meade, James Hillman and Robert Moore, including books, cassette tapes and video tapes. Two to three times a year a complete catalog is mailed out along with information about Bly's reading and workshop schedule. The press is not accepting unsolicited MSS at this time. Book catalog is free on request.

ALMS HOUSE PRESS (I), P.O. Box 668, Stony Point NY 10980, founded 1985, poetry editors Lorraine De Gennaro and Alana Sherman, holds an **annual poetry competition with $7 entry fee (contestants receive a copy of a chapbook). "We have no preferences with regard to style as long as the poetry is high caliber. We like to see previous publication in the small press, but we are open to new writers. We look for variety and excellence and are open to new and experimental forms as well as traditional forms. Any topics as long as the poems are not whiny or too depressing, pornographic or religious."** They have recently published chapbooks by Martin Anderson and Harry Waitzman. As a sample they selected these lines by Sandra Marshburn:

> *Beyond the house the woods are dark*
> *with vine and bramble. The things you threw*
> *from the back porch: can opener,*
> *nut pick, lock without key; their secret*
> *rusting lives still belong to you.*

Submit 16-24 pp. chapbook including all front matter, title page and table of contents, between March 1 and May 31. Name, address and phone number should apear on title page only. Winner receives 15 copies. Send SASE for current rules. Sample copy: $4 postpaid. They offer a critical and editorial service for $25.

ALOHA, THE MAGAZINE OF HAWAII AND THE PACIFIC (IV-Regional), Suite 309, 49 S. Hotel St., Honolulu HI 96813, editor Cheryl Chee Tsutsumi, is a bimonthly (every 2 months) "consumer magazine with Hawaii and Pacific focus," Circulation 65,000. **"Not interested in lengthy poetry. Poems should be limited to 100 words or less. Subject should be focused on Hawaii."** Poems are matched to color photos, so it is "difficult to say" how long it will be between acceptance and publication. As a sample the editor selected these lines from "Beautiful Hawaii," by Sheri Rice:

> *Someone washed the sky last night*
> *leaving a rainbow*
> *in the wispy suds*
> *of lonely clouds.*

Aloha is magazine-sized, 80 pp., flat-spined, elegantly printed on glossy stock with many full-color pages, glossy card cover in color. They publish 6 of more than 50 poems received per year. **Sample: $2.95 postpaid. Send SASE for guidelines. Pays $25 plus 1 copy (and up to 10 at discount). MS should be double-spaced, typed, name, address and phone number on all MSS. Reports within 60 days.**

ALPHA BEAT SOUP; ALPHA BEAT PRESS (I, IV-Form/Style), 68 Winter Ave., Scarborough, Ontario M1K 4M3 Canada, founded 1987, poetry editor David Christy, appears twice a year **emulating the Beat literary tradition.** *Alpha Beat Soup* is "an international poetry and arts journal featuring Beat, 'post-Beat independent' and modern writing." Christy says that **25% of each issue is devoted to little known or previously unpublished poets.** They have published works by Joy Walsh, Pradip Choudhuri, Joan Reid, Erling Friis-Baastad, Jack Micheline, Janine Pommy Vega and Diane Wakoski. As a sample the editor selected these lines by Peter Bakowski:

> *art goes wherever the "no entry" signs plead,*
> *plays happily in the universe of a vacant lot.*
> *art dances the arabesque with old steamships and streetcars*

ABS is 7×8½", 50-75 pp., photocopied from IBM laser printer, card cover offset, graphics included. They will use 50% of most poetry received. Press run is 600 for 400 paid subscriptions (11 of them libraries). Subscription: $5. Single copy: $3. **Sample: $5 (includes first-class postage). Pays 2 copies. Simultaneous submissions and previously published poems OK. Editor comments on rejections "only on request."** Reviews books of poetry. **Alpha Beat Press publishes chapbooks.**

ALTA NAPA PRESS; GONDWANA BOOKS (IV-Form), 1969 Mora Ave., Calistoga CA 94515, founded 1976, FAX 707-226-7708, publishes various kinds of books, but the imprint **Gondwana Books is for epic poetry only.** A number of the books in their catalog (available for 9×12" SASE and $1) are by

the editor, Carl T. Endemann. He **publishes other authors on a "co-operative basis," which means partial or full subsidy** but gives no details of how that works. Write directly for information, and when you do **send three poems, and your covering letter should include biographical background, personal or aesthetic philosophy, poetic goals and principles, and the hour, date and place of your birth.** He says "No, I am not a fortune teller!" but he is apparently interested in **astrology and reincarnation.** He says he wants poetry which is **"clear, clean, concise/rhythm, reason and 'rammar/rare rational rhymes" on any subject of universal appeal; spiritual OK, but effusions of personal frustrations no. No trite drivel. Sex yes, Porno no, no spectator sports.** Recently published Erme Burton Hand (2 books of poetry for children and juniors) and Carl Heinz Kurz (2 poetry translations from German). Here are some lines from the editor's poem "Dream Girl, Sweet Girl, Cream Girl":
> *Here comes my delightful spouse*
> *Singing dancing through the house*

He publishes 3-4 chapbooks (30-148 pp.) and 3-4 flat-spined paperbacks (50-240 pp.) per year. Advice: "Join a *good* creative writing class now for three years and read *Writer's Digest* in depth. Poetry is not a commercial endeavor, but it can eventually pay for itself—mainly give you the feeling of having done something *worthwhile* which *no* money can buy." He offers **criticism for $1.30 per page of MS.**

ALTERNATIVE PRESS MAGAZINE (I,II), Box 205, Hatboro PA 19040, founded 1989, editor Bob Lennon, co-editor Lynne Lennon Budnick, appears quarterly using **"experimental, philosophical poetry; open to many subjects or style as long as it's in good taste. Nothing pornographic, traditional, religious, no worn-out love poems."** They have recently published poetry by Dave Brock. As a sample the editor selected these lines from "The Iconoclast" by Glenn Bykowski:
> *The temples and mausoleums he desecrates at will*
> *Unscathed by objectors seething with hate*
> *He slams and he smashes their paraphernalia of gloom*
> *He laughs at their lovely naivete.*

"*Alternative Press* **will attempt to print many poems submitted unlike some magazines that print trash and reject most poems. Submit up to 5 poems—remember that we publish a digest-sized mag and longer pieces have a harder time finding a place." Responds on submissions within 2 weeks-2 months. Simultaneous submissions and previously published poems OK. Guidelines available for SASE.** It is photocopied from photoreduced typescript, digest-sized, 36 pp. with matte card cover, saddle-stapled. Press run 200. Subscription: $10 for 4 issues. **Sample postpaid: $3. Pays 1-3 copies and "occasionally small sums." Editor comments on submissions "sometimes."** He says, "We like to publish new poets, but they should read at least one copy to see what the magazine is about. Send poetry that comes from inside, not works that conform to outdated modes of writing. Response to this listing has been outstanding, but everyone who submits stands a fair chance at being published. This includes our friends in Europe and Canada too."

ALURA (II), P.O. Box 44, Novinger MO 63559, phone (816)488-5216, founded 1975, poetry editor Ruth Lamb, is a poetry quarterly whose "aim is to reach the general public with understandable poetry." Its format is 51 pp., saddle-stapled, with colored matte cover illustrated (as are many inside pages) with b/w amateur drawings. The magazine is typeset with small, dark type. They use **"well-written poetry in all styles but not 'typewriter gymnastics' nor uninterpretable symbolism. Poems must communicate. Prefer poems of not more than 48 lines and spaces. All subject-matter in good taste. Do not waste reader's time with obscure meanings."** They have published poetry by Martha Forstrom, Laura Sanders, Fontaine Falkoff, C. David Hay, Charles B. Dickson, Charles Roach and Gerald Burke. The editor selected an excerpt from "Harbinger" by Edward B. Kovar:
> *The breath of winter frosts the chastened sun*
> *And hones the hardened air to chiseled points;*
> *Lethargic insects crawl that once had run,*
> *An aging army with arthritic joints.*

They have a circulation of 325, with 93 subscriptions of which 5 are libraries, receive 1,500-2,000 submissions per year and use about 350. **Sample: $3. Subscription: $10. "Submissions should be folded and sent in a regular business envelope. We accept simultaneous submissions and previously published poems *if* poets have retained all rights. Poets published in *Alura* do retain all rights. Prefer no more than 5-6 poems at a time. Photocopies OK. Because of our filing system, we would appreciate receiving poems in a regular business envelope with poet's last name *first* in the upper left corner of envelope and *large enough* to be read in a file. Return address stickers are too small to read in a file drawer. Please use a dark ribbon!"** Poems should be typed single-spaced with the poet's name, address and phone number directly under each poem. They report **in 6 months, pay 2 copies. "We appreciate loose stamps (4) to help with postage."** The editor comments, "We accept both rhymed and unrhymed poetry as long as it is well-written and the meaning clear. We applaud the return of traditional poetry. We think poetry has decreased in popularity the last few decades because much of the poetry written has been unintelligible, shocking and far-out. We will accept no poetry with obscenities and expletives. Due to the diversity of religions, we accept no religious poetry."

THE AMARANTH REVIEW; WINDOW PUBLICATIONS (II), P.O. Box 56235, Phoenix AZ 85079, founded 1989, editor Dana L. Yost. "Window Publications is a small-press publisher of poetry, fiction and non-fiction. *The Amaranth Review* is a literary journal (twice a year) that exists as a forum for contemporary thought. All questions have answers, and we believe that literature provides a sound vehicle for the exploration of alternatives. **In poetry, quality, while subjective, is our main concern — no preferred form, length, subject-matter or style. We publish what we like and prefer to place few if any restrictions on those who contribute — I would rather wade through dozens of poems that I don't like rather than take the chance of discouraging someone and possibly missing that 'one' poem every editor is waiting for."** They have recently published poetry by Sunil Freeman, Larry O. Dean, David Lincoln Fisher and Marian Blue. As a sample the editor selected these lines from "Eating My Words" by Mali:

> *At the So Real Cafe, I come to the end of my mind.*
> *On this crimson edge I grow new eyes, tiny like*
> *those antenna eyes on deep sea fish, wide open*
> *without lids and slow, searching for other life*

Amaranth is magazine-sized, 60+ pp., offset professional printing in small type, 80# matte cover stock. "We average around 100 submissions per month; in our last issue we published 32 poems." Press run: 1,500 for 230 subscriptions of which 2 are libraries, 230 shelf sales. Subscription: $10. **Sample, postpaid: $5.50. Send SASE for guidelines. Pays 2 copies plus 40% discount on extras plus free subscription. Simultaneous submissions OK. Reports in 4 weeks. For books or chapbook publication query with 5-10 sample poems, bio, and publications. Pays 10-15% royalties.** Editor comments on submissions "usually only when requested to do so." **Sponsors Fall and Spring Edition contests offering cash prizes and publication. Send SASE for guidelines.** The editor says, "The advice I would give a beginning poet would be to write from the heart, to write honest poetry that means something to you — find out what you really care about and then tap into the power of those feelings. And never quit — I don't care how many times you are rejected or how many people laugh when you tell them you're a poet — if you are a poet you have no choice but to write, and quitting is never an option. There are hundreds of small magazines publishing poetry today, and with enough perseverance and some careful market analysis (treat your **Poet's Market** like a bible) you will see your work in print."

‡**AMBIT (III),** 17 Priory Gardens, Highgate, London N6 5QY, England, phone 340-3566, editor Martin Bax; poetry editors Edwin Brock, Carol Ann Duffy, Henry Graham; prose editor J. G. Ballard; and art editor Mike Foreman. A 96 pp. quarterly, **pay "variable plus 2 free copies," sample £5,** subscription £20. As a sample the editor selected these excerpts from "Two Poems For Two Suicides" by Henry Graham:

> *1*
>
> *All right then*
> *who would fardels bare?*
> *Or the world away out of earshot*
> *careless of your one foot in too many graves*
> *every waking hour.*
>
> *2*
> *It got to seem like a war,*
> *casualties*
> *I used to say,*
> *though no one was shooting at us.*
> *Or were they?*

AMELIA; CICADA; SPSM&H; THE AMELIA AWARDS (II, IV-Form), P.O. Box 2385, Bakersfield CA 93303, or 329 "E" St., Bakersfield CA 93304, phone (805)323-4064. *Amelia,* founded 1983, Frederick A. Raborg, Jr. poetry editor, is a quarterly magazine that publishes chapbooks as well. Central to its operations are a series of contests, most with entry fees, spaced evenly throughout the year, awarding more than $3,500 annually, but they publish many poets who have not entered the contests as well. Among poets published are Pattiann Rogers, Stuart Freibert, John Millett, David Ray, Larry Rubin, Charles Bukowski, Maxine Kumin, Charles Edward Eaton and Shuntaro Tanikawa. These sample lines are by Michael Lassell:

> *The hairs on my greying chest*

cast a lengthening shade,
pluck my father's name
from the hollow corridor where
my grandfather grows
into a legend, his
hair as steel as age.

They are "**receptive to all forms to 100 lines. We do not want to see the patently-religious or overtly-political. Erotica is fine; pornography, no.**" The digest-sized, flat-spined magazine is offset on high-quality paper and usually features an original four-color cover; its circulation is about 1,250, with 522 subscriptions, of which 28 are libraries. **Sample: $7.95 postpaid. Submit 3-5 poems, photocopies OK, dot-matrix acceptable but discouraged, no simultaneous submissions except for entries to the annual Amelia Chapbook Award. Reports in 2-12 weeks, the latter if under serious consideration. Pays $2-25 per poem plus 2 copies.** "Almost always I try to comment." The editor comments, "*Amelia* is not afraid of strong themes, but we do look for professional, polished work even in handwritten submissions. Poets should have something to say about matters other than the moon. We like to see strong **traditional pieces as well as the contemporary and experimental. And neatness *does* count.**" Subscriptions to *Amelia* are $25 per year. *Cicada*, is a quarterly magazine that publishes **haikus, senryu and other Japanese forms**, plus essays on the form — techniques and history — as well as fiction which in some way incorporates haiku or Japanese poetry in its plot, and reviews of books pertaining to Japan and its poetry or collections of haiku. Among poets published are Roger Ishii, H.F. Noyes, Knute Skinner, Katherine Machan Aal, Ryah Tumarkin Goodman and Ryokufu Ishizaki. These sample lines are by Irene K. Wilson:

Sipping the thin tea
made from young green leaves'
tranquility

They are receptive to experimental forms as well as the traditional. "Try to avoid still-life as haiku; strive for the *whole* of an emotion, whether minuscule or panoramic. Erotica is fine; the Japanese are great lovers of the erotic." The magazine is offset on high quality paper, with a circulation of 600, with 432 subscriptions of which 26 are libraries. Subscription: $14/year. **Sample: $4.50 postpaid. Submit 3-10 haiku or poems, photocopies OK, dot-matrix acceptable but discouraged, no simultaneous submissions. Reports in 2 weeks. No payment, except three "best of issue" poets each receive $10 on publication plus copy.** "I try to make some comment on returned poems always." *SPSM&H* is a quarterly magazine that publishes **only sonnets, sonnet sequences**, essays on the form — both technique and history — as well as romantic or Gothic fiction which, in some way, incorporates the form, and reviews of sonnet collections or collections containing a substantial number of sonnets. Among poets published are Margaret Ryan, Harold Witt, Sharon E. Martin, Rhina P. Espaillat and Robert Wolfkill. Fred Raborg selected these sample lines from my "On the Young Man's Perfection":

What if she, like a cranky child, knocks all
stacked blocks into a random distribution,
allows empires to rise so they may fall,
and cancels with an R our evolution?

They are "**receptive to experimental forms as well as the traditional, and appreciate wit when very good.** Perhaps it may help to know the editor's favorite Shakespearean sonnet is #29, and he feels John Updike clarified the limits of experimentation with the form in his "Love Sonnet" from **Midpoint**. The magazine is offset on high quality paper, with a circulation of 600, for 432 subscribers and 26 libraries. Subscription: $14/year. **Sample: $4 postpaid. Submit 3-5 poems, photocopies OK, dot-matrix acceptable but discouraged, no simultaneous submissions. Reports in 2 weeks. No payment, except two "best of issue" poets each receive $14 on publication plus copy.** "I always try to comment on returns." The following annual contests have various entry fees: The Amelia Awards (six prizes of $200, $100, $50 plus three honorable mentions of $10 each); The Anna B. Janzen Prize for Romantic Poetry ($100, annual deadline January 2); The Bernice Jennings Traditional Poetry Award ($100, annual deadline January 2); The Georgie Starbuck Galbraith Light/Humorous Verse Prizes (six awards of $100, $50, $25 plus three honorable mentions of $5 each, annual deadline March 1); The Charles William Duke Longpoem Award ($100, annual deadline April 1); The Lucille Sandberg Haiku Awards (six awards of $100, $50, $25 plus three honorable mentions of $5 each, annual deadline April 1); The Grace Hines Narrative Poetry Award ($100, annual deadline May 1); The Amelia Chapbook Award ($250, book publication, 50 copies and 7½% royalty, annual deadline July 1); The Johanna B. Bourgoyne Poetry Prizes (six awards of $100, $50, $25, plus three honorable mentions of $5 each), The Douglas Manning Smith Epic/Heroic Poetry Prize ($100, annual deadline August 1); The Hildegarde Janzen Prize for Oriental Forms of Poetry (six awards of $50, $30, $20 and three honorable mentions of $5 each, annual deadline September 1); The Eugene Smith Prize For Sonnets (six awards of $140, $50, $25 and three honorable mentions of $5 each); The A&C

Limerick Prizes (six awards of $50, $30, $20 and three honorable mentions of $5 each); The Montegue Wade Lyric Poetry Prize ($100, annual deadline November 1).

AMERICA; FOLEY POETRY CONTEST (II), 106 W. 56th St., New York NY 10019, phone (212)581-4640, founded 1909, poetry editor Patrick Samway, S. J., is a weekly journal of opinion published by the Jesuits of North America. They primarily publish articles on religious, social, political and cultural themes. **They are "looking for imaginative poetry of all kinds. We have no restrictions on form or subject-matter, though we prefer to receive poems of 35 lines or less."** They have recently published poetry by Howard Nemerov, Fred Chappell, William Heyen and Eve Shelnutt. *America* is magazine-sized, 24 pp., professionally printed on thin stock with thin paper cover, circulation 35,000. Subscription: $33. **Sample: $1 postpaid. Pays $1.40/line plus 2 copies. Send SASE for excellent guidelines. Reports in 2 weeks. Editor comments "if asked to do so."** The annual Foley Poetry Contest offers a prize of $500, usually in late winter. Send SASE for rules. The editor says, *"America* is committed to publishing quality poetry as it has done for the past 80 years. We would encourage beginning and established poets to submit their poems to us."

AMERICAN ASSOCIATION OF HAIKUISTS NEWSLETTER; RED PAGODA; WALPURGIS NIGHT (IV-Form, horror), 125 Taylor St., Jackson TN 38301, phone (901)427-7714. *RP* was founded in 1982, *AAH* and its newsletter in 1983, and *WN* in 1988, editor Lewis Sanders. *AAHN* and *RP* are both haiku publications. You may join the American Association of Haikuists for $10 and receive the newsletter, 10 or fewer pages on white paper of photocopied typescript stapled at the corner (1-2 a year). *Walpurgis Night* is a horror magazine. *RP* is a journal that will consider **"haiku, modern and traditional. Renga, tanka, heibun, senyru, linked poems,** articles and book reviews on books and subjects dealing with haiku." The editor says, "I try to publish 4 times a year, but sometimes run late." They have published haiku by Alexis Rotella, John J. Soldo and Elizabeth Lamb. As a sample the editor offers this haiku by Kiri:

> Fall out from Russia—
> may wind
> moans in the chimney

The Red Pagoda is digest-sized, 52 pp., saddle-stapled, photocopied from various typescripts on bond paper with red paper cover. Subscription (4 issues) is $16 in the U.S. mailed first class; $24 outside the U.S. mailed airmail. Libraries receive a 10% discount on subscriptions. Checks should be made out to Henry L. Sanders. **You must buy a copy to see your work in print (price is $4/copy), but poets do not have to subscribe or purchase a copy to be published. Editor sometimes comments on rejections.** *WN*, the newest of the publications, will appear intermittently using: **"gothic horror/modern horror/erotic vampire poetry not more than 2 pp. in length (1-page poems preferred). Nothing obscene or pornographic."** As a sample I chose this stanza of "The Hanging at Four" by R. Schmitz III:

> Seconds slowly sail away
> Down streams of muddied time.
> Will they bring me to the light of day,
> Or cast me in the Old One's way,
> and end this pantomime?

WN is newsletter format on colored paper. **Sample: $4 prepaid. Pays 1 copy. "Poets who are accepted do not have to purchase a copy to be published, but if they do I will give an extra copy. If this proves too costly, I will have to revert to simply charging per copy." Reports in 3 weeks. Editor comments on rejections "often."**

AMERICAN ATHEIST PRESS; GUSTAV BROUKAL PRESS; AMERICAN ATHEIST (IV-Theme), 7215 Cameron Rd., Austin TX 78752, phone (512)458-1244, founded 1958, editor R. Murray-O'Hair, publishes the monthly magazine with 30,000 circulation, *American Atheist* and, under various imprints some dozen books a year reflecting "concerns of Atheists, such as separation of state and church, civil liberties, and atheist news." **Poetry is used primarily in the poetry section of the magazine. It must have "a particular slant to atheism, dealing with subjects such as the atheist lifestyle. Anticlerical poems and puns are more than liable to be rejected. Any form or style is acceptable. Preferred length is under 40 lines."** Poets they have published include Julia Rhodes Pozonzycki, Allan Case and Thomas A. Easton. The editor chose these lines by Angeline Bennett from "Lowercasing the Fear Words":

> Old certitudes die hard . . .
> but die they have, and now
> inspiration is left clear and clean
> for those uncluttered minds who find
> that God is just another god.

Of their 17,000 subscriptions, 1,000 are libraries. The magazine-sized format is professionally printed, with art and photos, glossy, color cover; subscription, $25, single copy price $2.95,

sample: free. They receive over 20-30 poetry submissions per week, use about 36 a year. **Submit typed, double-spaced (photocopy, dot-matrix, simultaneous submissions OK). Time-dependent poems (such as winter) should be submitted 4 months in advance. Reports within 12-16 weeks. Pays "first-timers" 10 copies or 6-month subscription or $12 credit voucher for AAP products. Thereafter, $15/poem plus 10 copies. Guidelines available for SASE, but a label is preferred to an envelope.** They do not normally publish poetry in book form but will consider them. ("We no longer do subsidy books.") **Sometimes comments on rejected MSS.**

‡**AMERICAN COLLEGIATE POETS (I, IV-Students/alumni, foreign languages)**, P.O. Box 44044-L, Los Angeles CA 90044, founded 1975, editor and manager Dr. Val. M. Churillo, offers 2 contests/year for poems up to 14-16 lines by anyone who is or has ever been a college student (whether graduate or not) desiring to have their work anthologized. Winners and entrants are published in $15 perfect-bound anthologies. There is an entry fee of $3 for the first, and $1 for each additional poem; cash prizes of $100, $50, $30, and 2 of $20. You may purchase copies at $15 each (none are given free to contestants). Foreign language poems welcome. Send SASE for rules.

‡**THE AMERICAN COWBOY POET MAGAZINE (IV-Themes)**, P.O. Box 326, Eagle ID 83616, phone (208)888-9838, founded 1988 as *The American Cowboy Poet Newspaper,* magazine format in January 1991, publisher/editor Rudy Gonzales. *ACPM* is a quarterly "about real cowboys" using "**authentic cowboy poetry. Must be clean--entertaining.**" It publishes articles including "Featured Poet," stories of cowboy poetry gatherings and news of coming events. Subscription: $12/year. **Sample postpaid: $3. Send SASE for guidelines. Editor often comments on rejections.**

AMERICAN DANE (IV-Ethnic), 3717 Harney St., Omaha NE 68131-3844, phone (402)341-5049, founded 1916, editor Jennifer C. Denning, is the monthly magazine of the Danish Brotherhood in America, circulation 10,000, which uses **poetry with a Danish ethnic flavor. Sample: $1.50 postpaid. Send SASE for guidelines. Buys 1-3 poems a year. Pays $35 maximum plus 3 copies. Reports in 2 weeks, up to 12 month backlog. Simultaneous submission OK.** The magazine is 20-28 pp., magazine-sized. Subscription: $6.

AMERICAN KNIGHT (I); PAISLEY VOICES POETRY COMPETITION, Rt. 1, Box 274, South Haven MN 55382-9727, founded 1989, editor Nancy Morín, is a quarterly publishing **poetry by those who contribute poetry or subscribe. "Open-minded acceptance; we prefer poetry with reflective insight and that which encourages the reader to release the limitations of physical and emotional perception. Nothing trite, 'mushy-love' rhymes."** Poets recently published include An-Dabney Faulkner, Kent Clair Chamberlain and Ray Mizer. These sample lines are the editor's:

> *We are nothing but deep breaths*
> *In the world of life;*
> *Necessary, in the sense that the game continues,*
> *And yet, abusingly taken for granted.*

The editor says, "To make a living in America today is quite a rare thing. *AK* has been developed for poets and poetry. It is here to give those who love the excitement of seeing their work in print and knowing that their poetry is being read by others, a chance to reach and enhance a broader audience. **Never hold back for rhyming reasons. This can be a great blockade when trying to get a point across to readers. This is a nonprofit quarterly written by the writers who contribute poetry or prose. Cost per issue: $2 plus 85¢ loose stamps.** Donations are greatly appreciated however, and can be made to *American Knight.*" The editor describes it as 11 × 17″ folded at center, printed on 20# or heavier paper, typed, with art on cover, more than 8 pp. **Sample postpaid: $2.50. Send SASE for guidelines. Pays "at least 1" copy but requests 95¢ postage to receive "pay" copy. Deadlines February 20, May 23, August 23, November 20 (yearly). Send up to 5 poems. Do not staple. Reports in 3-4 weeks.** The Paisley Voices Poetry Competition, held annually, is open to all poets, all forms and themes. Cash awards of $75, $50, $25, $15, $10 and 5 awards of $5 plus 15 honorable mentions. $5 entry fee for up to 5 poems, original, unpublished, 60-line limit. Deadline Feb. 1 yearly, entries received after Feb. 1 will be entered in the following year's competition. Send SASE for guidelines.

AMERICAN LITERARY REVIEW, A National Journal of Poems and Stories, University of North Texas Press, P.O. Box 13615, Denton TX 76203. Declined listing.

THE AMERICAN LITERARY REVIEW, 45 Thurston Rd., Newton MA 02164. Declined listing.

AMERICAN POETRY REVIEW; WORLD POETRY, INC.; JEROME J. SHESTACK PRIZES (III), 1704 Walnut St., Philadelphia PA 19103, founded 1972, is probably the **most widely circulated (24,000 copies bimonthly) and best-known periodical devoted to poetry in the world.** Poetry editors are Stephen

Covers of The American Poetry Review feature "the poet who has the best or most interesting or most unusual work in a given issue," says editor David Bonanno. Pictured here is Donald Revell, associate professor of English at the University of Denver, editor of the Denver Quarterly and author of several books of poetry. Eight of Revell's poems are contained in this issue as well as his article "Without a Golden Age: Genre in Diaspora." The cover photo is by Annie Dawid.

Berg, David Bonanno and Arthur Vogelsang, and they have published most of the leading poets writing in English and many translations. The poets include Gerald Stern, Brenda Hillman, John Ashbery, Norman Dubie, Marvin Bell, Galway Kinnell, James Dickey, Lucille Clifton and Tess Gallagher. As a sample, I selected some lines of my own published there, from "Encounters Of Kind," a poem based on a journal entry by Anton van Leeuwenhoek of Delft:

> *The ladder down into the well appears*
> *to have infinite and ever-smaller rungs.*
> *Look up into the dark sky where it reaches*
> *and hear the wind stirred by those alien tongues.*

15,000 subscriptions, of which 1,000 are libraries, tabloid format. **Sample and price per issue: $2.75.** They receive about 4,000 submissions per year, use 200, **pay $1.25 per line, 12 weeks to report, 1-3 year backlog, no simultaneous submissions.** The magazine is also a major resource for opinion, reviews, theory, news and ads pertaining to poetry. The Jerome J. Shestack Prizes of $1,000, $500 and $250 are awarded by the editors each year for the best poems, in their judgment, published in *APR*.

THE AMERICAN SCHOLAR (III), 1811 Q St. NW, Washington DC 20009, phone (202)265-3808, founded 1932, associate editor Sandra Costich, is an academic quarterly which uses about 5 poems per issue, pays $50 each. Two-month response time. They have published poets such as Robert Pack, Alan Shapiro and Gregory Djanikian. "We would like to see poetry that develops an image, a thought or event, without the use of a single cliché or contrived archaism. The most hackneyed subject matter is self-conscious love; the most tired verse is iambic pentameter with rhyming endings. The usual length of our poems is 30 lines. From 1-4 poems may be submitted at one time; *no more* for a careful reading." Study before submitting (sample: $5.75, guidelines available for SASE).

AMERICAN SQUAREDANCE MAGAZINE (V), 216 William St., Huron OH 44839, phone (419)433-2188, founded 1945, co-editor Catherine Burdick, "deals with all phases of square dancing internationally. Currently not accepting poetry submissions. The monthly magazine is 100-112 pp., digest-sized, saddle-stapled with a colored card cover, and is 50-55% ads, circulation to 22,000 subscribers. Per issue: $1.25. Subscription $12 for 1 year, $22 for 2 years.

AMERICAN TOLKIEN SOCIETY; MINAS TIRITH EVENING STAR; W.W. PUBLICATIONS (IV-Themes), P.O. Box 373, Highland MI 48357-0373, phone (313)887-4703, founded 1967, editor Philip W. Helms. There are special poetry issues. Membership in the ATS is open to all, regardless of country or residence, and entitles one to receive the journal. Dues are $5 per annum to addresses in U.S. and $10 elsewhere. Their magazines and chapbooks use **poetry of fantasy about Middle-Earth and Tolkien.** They have published poetry by Thomas M. Egan, Anne Etkin, Nancy Pope and Martha Benedict. *Minas Tirith Evening Star* is magazine-sized, offset from typescript with cartoon-like b/w graphics. **Pays contributor's copies.** The editor selected a sample by Joe Christopher:

> *The hobbits have fallen in this fallen world,*
> *Who once in burrows lived with round doors burled,*
> *but now must make their livings as they can:*
> *with one a baker, and one an artisan*
> *and one a bagpipe player with notes that skirled . . .*

They have a press run of 400 for 350 subscribers of which 10% are libraries. Per issue: $3.50. Subscription: $5. **Sample: $1.50 postpaid. Send SASE for guidelines. Prefer photocopies. No simultaneous submissions; previously published poems "maybe." Reports in 2 weeks. Editor** sometimes comments on rejections. Under imprint of W.W. Publications they publish collections of poetry 50-100 pp. **For book or chapbook consideration, submit sample poems. Published 2 chapbooks per year.** They sometimes sponsor contests.

‡**AMERICAN WRITING: A MAGAZINE; NIERIKA EDITIONS (II)**, 4343 Manayunk Ave., Philadelphia PA 19128, phone (215)483-7051, founded 1990, editor Alexandra Grilikhes, appears twice a year using **"innovative work, strong imagery; interested in the voice of the loner. No cerebral, academic poetry."** They have recently published poetry by Ivan Argüelles, Nico Vassilakis, Charles Fishman, John M. Bennett and Portia Wright. As a sample the editor selected these lines from "The Snake" by Ruth L. Schwartz:

> *I want both of you*
> *to rub my skin to fire,*
> *the gray sparked into orange, stroked*
> *like magic back to blue,*
> *the bark as it sheds*
> *its burning strips, peels*
> *itself like fingers arms and legs*
> *hissing in every flaming limb*

AW is digest-sized, flat-spined, 70+ pp., professionally printed, with matte card cover. Press run 1,000 for 100 subscriptions in their first year. Subscription $8. **Sample postpaid: $5. Guidelines on subscription form. Reporting time varies. "If it's a 'possible,' we may keep it 3 months." Pays 2 copies per accepted submission group.** The editor says, "Many magazines print the work of the same authors [the big names] who often publish 'lesser' works that way. *AW* is interested in the work itself, its particular strength and energy, rather than in the long lists of credits. We like to know *something* about the authors, however."

AMERICAS REVIEW; AMERICAS REVIEW POETRY COMPETITION (II, IV-Political), Box 7681, Berkeley CA 94707, founded 1985, editor Gerald Gray, a "literary annual with **emphasis on political content of the poetry** and prose we publish. **Only limit is subject-matter; it is almost always political in some general sense (though a few items of poetry are not). We do print, for instance, the love poetry of political figures.** We deliberately publish little-known or obscure poets, but we have included works by Nicholis Guillen, Otto Rene Castillo, Julia Vinograd, Dorianne Laux, Sergio Ramirez, Claribel Algeria, and (probably) Gary Snyder." As a sample Gerald Gray selected these lines by Gioconda Belli:

> *That's why I sit down to brandish these poems;*
> *to build against wind and tide*
> *a small space of happiness*
> *having faith that all this will not end—*

I have not seen the annual, but the editors describe it as 6×9″, flat-spined, about 75 pp., offset, using b/w graphics. It has a press run of 1,000 for 50 subscriptions (10 of them libraries) and the rest are for shelf sales. Per issue: $4 ($6 to libraries). **Sample: $3 postpaid. "Submit Sept. 1-Dec. 31 for most timely consideration." Pays $10 per author, plus 1 copy.** Editor "sometimes" comments on rejections. Their annual contest has a reading fee of $4 for up to five poems. They award three prizes of $100 each for published, unpublished, or translated poetry. The contest runs September 1-November 30. They note, "Our poetry and fiction is usually, but not exclusively, political in nature. All poems submitted will be considered for publication. Poems other than the winners chosen for publication will be paid in cash at our usual rate. Winners and others accepted will appear in the annual issue."

THE AMICUS JOURNAL (V), 40 W. 20th St., New York NY 10011, phone (212)727-2700, poetry editor Francesca Lyman, is the **journal of the Natural Resources Defense Council, a quarterly with a circulation of about 60,000, which pays $25/poem.** The poetry is **"nature based, but** *not* **'nature po-etry.'** " **They will not be accepting submissions in 1992 "because our cup runneth over with poetry."** They have used poems by some of the best known poets in the country, including David Wagoner, Gary Snyder, David Ignatow, Marvin Bell and William Stafford. As a sample, I selected the opening stanza of Mary Oliver's "Starfish":

In the sea rocks,
in the stone pockets
under the tide's lip
in water dense as blindness

The Amicus Journal is finely-printed, saddle-stapled, on high quality paper with glossy cover, using much art, photography and cartoons. **Free sample for SASE.**

‡ANACONDA PRESS (I), Submit to the editor closest to you: editor-in-chief Angie Lowry, P.O. Box 146227, Chicago IL 60614; West Coast associate editor Bayla Winters, 2700 Scott Rd., Burbank CA 91504; Midwest associate editor Beij Beltrisi, P.O. Box 445, Richmond IN 47375-0445. They publish 2-6 poetry chapbooks and 2-4 paperback anthologies 2-4 times a year, using **"slice of life poetry—experimental, contemporary, political—nothing overly structured or academic, no humor or overly light-hearted poetry." Reports in 2-4 weeks. Submit maximum of 5 poems, with short bio. Pays 10-20 copies.** Write for most recent announcement of upcoming anthologies.

ANALECTA (IV-Students), Liberal Arts Council, FAC 19, University of Texas, Austin TX 78712, phone (512)471-6563, founded 1974, editor Lisa Barnett, is an annual of literary works and photography by **college/university students and graduate students chosen in an annual contest,** a 200 pp. magazine, glossy plates for interior artwork in b/w, 7×10″, flat-spined, soft cover. **No restrictions on type; limited to 7 poems/submission. Deadline is in mid-October; write for specifics.** Submissions cannot be returned. "Our purpose is to provide a forum for excellent student writing. **Works must be previously unpublished."** Of about 700 submissions received, they publish about 40. Press run 700 for 600 subscriptions, 100 shelf sales. **Sample postpaid: $7.50. Send SASE for guidelines. Prizes in each category. Pays 1 copy and monetary prizes vary. Entries must be typed; name should appear on cover sheet only.** As a sample, the editor selected this excerpt from "neglect" by Alvaro Rodriguez:

show me your caffree smile, babe.
france is so far away, unreachable as of yet.
terror plummets down on me like the coca-cola eagles in the
sunless sky.

THE AND REVIEW; MID-OHIO CHAPBOOK PRIZE (II), 10485 Iams Rd., Plain City OH 43064, founded 1987, publishes one double-issue a year. **They are "open to all forms and styles, but prefer shorter, imagistic poems. No self-indulgent first attempts."** They have recently published poetry by William Stafford, Diane Glancy and William Heyen. As a sample the editors selected these lines from "River's Mind" by Gordon Grigsby:

Beneath layers of silt, leaves turning to silt,
in bedrock limestone
the ghosts of brachipods
swim motionlessly forever

Their press run is 500 with 200 subscriptions of which 10 are libraries. The magazine consists of "all poetry with one or two reviews of new books of poetry. We also feature in each issue an author reviewing his/her own book." It is digest-sized, professionally printed with a matte card cover, using b/w photos and ink drawings. No ads. **They receive 4,000 poems annually and publish 50-55. Subscription: $5. Sample: $5 postpaid. Pays 1 copy. Reports in 1 month. Guidelines available for SASE.** The Mid-Ohio Chapbook Prize is awarded annually to the best 2 chapbooks of 15-20 pages received between April and June and between October and December. A $10 reading fee is required for entry and includes a 1-year subscription to *The And Review*. Winning manuscripts are published in a special supplement within the magazine. Each author receives 25 separately bound copies of the chapbook and 25 copies of the magazine. **Editor sometimes comments on rejections.** The editors pass on Marvin Bell's advice, "Making the simple compli-cated is commonplace; making the complicated simple, awesomely simple, that's creativity."

ANDROGYNE BOOKS; ANDROGYNE (IV-Themes), 930 Shields, San Francisco CA 94132, founded 1971, poetry editor, Ken Weichel. *Androgyne* is a literary journal (an issue about every 18 months) **on specific themes, such as alchemy, erotic fantasy, auto/biographical writing, Surrealism/Dada.** "The best guideline for submission is a sample copy." Graphics, especially collage, welcome. They have published poetry by Laura Beausoleil, Ivan Argüelles, Geoffrey Cook, Alice Polesky, Ronald Sauer,

Tonay D'Arpino and Toby Kaplan. As a sample, the editor selected these lines by Michael Koch:
> *We translate it 'sperm of a nightingale'*
> *then settle for 'candle drippings'*
> *Obsure slang for cliques of angels.*

Reviews books of poetry. Besides publishing the literary journal, Androgyne Books also publishes chapbooks. **Unsolicited book length mss are not encouraged. Please query first. Simultaneous submissions OK, reports in 1 month, payment 2 copies and a subscription. Sample copy and a catalogue: $4.**

ANIMA: THE JOURNAL OF HUMAN EXPERIENCE (II, IV-Women/Feminism), 1053 Wilson Ave., Chambersburg PA 17201, founded 1974, editor Barbara Rotz. *Anima* "celebrates the wholistic vision that emerges from thoughtful and imaginative encounters with the differences between woman and man, East and West, yin and yang—*anima* and *animus*. **Written largely by and about women** who are pondering new experiences of themselves and our world, this equinoctial journal welcomes contributions, verbal and visual, from the known and unknown. We publish very few poems, but they are carefully selected. **We are not interested in simply private experiences. Poetry must communicate. Advise all would-be poets to study the kinds of things we do publish. No restrictions on length, form, or such matters.**" As a sample I chose the first stanza of Kay Ryan's "Why Animals Dance":
> *Because of their clickety hoofs*
> *Because of their scritchety claws*
> *Because of their crackety beaks*
> *Because they don't have any boots*

There are 5-10 pages of poetry in each semiannual issue of the elegantly-printed and illustrated 8½" square, glossy-covered magazine, 1,000 subscriptions of which 150 are libraries. Price per issue: $5.95. **Sample: $3.95. Slow reporting—sometimes 3-6 months. Payment is offprints with covers.**

‡ANIMAL TALES; HOLIDAY WRITING CONTEST (I,IV-Themes), 2113 W. Bethany Home Rd., Phoenix AZ 85015, founded 1989, editor Berta I. Cellers, appears every other month, using **"light verse and traditional poems about animals and the people who love them."** It is 32 pp., saddle-stapled, magazine-sized. Press run 400 for 350 subscribers. Subscription: $19.95. **Sample postpaid: $4.95. Send SASE for guidelines. Pays $5-20 and 1 copy. Response in 6-8 weeks.** Holiday Writing Contests are offered occasionally for animal stories with Thanksgiving or Christmas themes, with a prize of $25, entry fee $5/poem.

ANJOU (V), P.O. Box 322, Station P, Toronto, Ontario M5S 2S8 Canada, founded 1980, edited by Richard Lush and Roger Greenwald, publishes broadsides of poetry. **"We do not wish to receive submissions because we publish only by solicitation."**

ANSUDA PUBLICATIONS; THE PUB (II), P.O. Box 158JA, Harris IA 51345, founded 1978, "is a small press operation, publishing independently of outside influences, such as grants, donations, awards, etc. Our operating capital comes from magazine and book sales only." Their magazine *The Pub* "uses some poetry, and we also publish separate chapbooks of individual poets. We **prefer poems with a social slant and originality**—we do *not* want love poems, personal poems that can only be understood by the poet, or anything from the haiku family of poem styles. No limits on length, though very short poems lack the depth we seek—no limits on form or style, but rhyme and meter must make sense. Too many poets write senseless rhymes using the first words to pop into their heads. As a result, we prefer blank and free verse." They have recently published Kelly Ann Averill, Sheryl L. Nelms, Paul M. Lamb, Rick Fruge and Carol Hamilton. They offer no sample because "most of our poems are at least 25-30 lines long and every line complements all other lines, so it is hard to pick out only four lines to illustrate." *The Pub*, which appears irregularly (1-3 times a year) is a low-budget publication, digest-sized, mimeographed on inexpensive paper, making it possible to print 80 or more pages and sell copies for $3 **(the price of a sample).** Its minimum print-run is 300 for 130 subscriptions, of which 7 are libraries. Each issue has 8-12 pages of poetry, but **"we would publish more if we had it; our readers would like more poetry."** Everything accepted goes into the next issue, so there is no backlog; **reports immediately to 1 month, payment 2 copies, guidelines available for SASE. They also publish 1-2 chapbooks (24-28 pp.) per year.** For these, query with 3-6 sample poems. "We need cover letters so we know it's for a book MS query, but you should only include information *relevant* to the book (education, experience, etc.). We are *not* interested in past credits, who you studied under, etc. Names mean nothing to us and we have found that small press is so large that big names in one circle are unknown in another circle. In fact, **we get better material from the unknowns who have nothing to brag about (usually)."** Replies to queries immediately, reports in 1-2 months on submissions, no dot-matrix, simultaneous submissions only if clearly indicated. Payment: royalties plus 5 copies. They will also subsidy publish if poet pays 100% of costs, picks own press name (Ansuda does not appear on subsidy publications) and handles distribution. Prices on request. Daniel Betz adds, "About all I have left to say is to tell the novice to keep sending his work out. It won't get published in a desk drawer. There are so many little mags out there that eventually you'll find homes for your poems. Yes, some poets get published on their first few tries, but I've made first acceptances to some who have been submitting for 5 to 10 years with no luck, until their poem and my mag just seemed to click. It just takes time and lots of patience."

‡ANT FARM (II,IV-Form), P.O. Box 15513, Santa Fe NM 87506-5513, founded 1990, editor Kate Bremer, appears twice a year using **poems of 4 lines or less, "immediate, impactful, available," not "ungrounded spiritual, philosophical stuff, poems about relationships that have ended, limericks, clever, cute."** They have recently published poetry by Joan Logghe, Diane Randolph and Miriam Sagan. As a sample the editor selected this complete poem, "Connections," by Mary McGinnis:
> the dead bird from your dream
> leaves feathers for our fence.
It is 4×5″ professionally printed with matte card cover, press run 300. **Sample: $3. Reports in up to 6 months. Editor comments "sometimes." Pays 1 copy.**

‡ANTAEUS; THE ECCO PRESS (II), 26 W. 17th St., New York NY 10011, phone (212)645-2214, editor-in-chief Daniel Halpern. *Antaeus* is a semiannual that has published poetry by many of our major poets, such as Czeslaw Milosz, Paul Bowles, Robert Hass, Louise Gluck, Robert Pinsky, Seamus Heaney, Joyce Carol Oates, W.S. Merwin, James Merrill, Carolyn Forché, Mark Strand and Charles Simic. It is 275 pp., 6×9″, offset, flat-spined, with 4-color cover. They have 7,000 subscribers. Subscription: $30. **Sample postpaid: $10. Send SASE for guidelines. Reports in 6-8 weeks. Pays $10/page.** The Ecco Press reports on MSS in 8-12 weeks.

ANTHOLOGY OF MAGAZINE VERSE & YEARBOOK OF AMERICAN POETRY (III, IV-Anthology), % Monitor Book Company, P.O. Box 9078, Palm Springs CA 92263, phone (619)323-2270, founded 1950, editor Alan F. Pater. The annual **Anthology** is a selection of the **best poems published in American magazines during the year and is also a basic reference work for poets.** Alan F. Pater says, "We want poetry that is 'readable' and in any poetic form; we also want translations. **All material must first have appeared in magazines.** Any subject matter will be considered; we also would like to see some rhyme and meter, preferably sonnets." They have recently published poetry by Margaret Atwood, Richard Eberhart, Stanley Kunitz, Stephen Spender, William Stafford, Robert Penn Warren, Richard Wilbur, Robert Bly, Maxine Kumin and John Updike. Indeed, the anthology is a good annual guide to the best poets actively publishing in any given year. For the most part selections are made by the editor from magazines, but some poets are solicited for their work which has been in magazines in a given year.

ANTIETAM REVIEW (IV-Regional), Washington County Arts Council, Bryan Center, 3rd Floor, 82 W. Washington St., Hagerstown MD 21740, an annual founded 1981, poetry editor Ann B. Knox, looks for **"well-crafted literary quality poems. We discourage inspirational verse, haiku, doggerel, uses poets only from the states of Maryland, Pennsylvania, Virginia, West Virginia, Delaware and District of Columbia. Needs 12 poems per issue, up to 30 lines each, pays $20/poem, depending on funding, plus 2 copies.** Poets they have published include Grace Cavalieri, David McKain and Eleanor Ross Taylor. The editor chose this sample by Theresa Elder called "Australian Pine Cones":
> I know a man who gathers and scatters
> He offers a miscellany of sleight of hand,
> propels old doves high into the air
> from his secret cages.
They have a press run of 1,000, 8½×11″ saddle-stapled, **sample: $2.50 back issue, $5 current postpaid. Do not submit MSS from April-September. "We read from October-March annually."**

THE ANTIGONISH REVIEW (II), St. Francis Xavier University, Antigonish, Nova Scotia B2G 1C0 Canada, phone (902)867-3962, FAX 902-867-5153, founded 1970, editor George Sanderson, poetry editor Peter Sanger. This high-quality quarterly "tries to produce the kind of literary and visual mosaic

Market conditions are constantly changing! If you're still using this book and it is 1993 or later, buy the newest edition of Poet's Market at your favorite bookstore or order directly from Writer's Digest Books.

that the modern sensibility requires or would respond to." They want poetry **not over "80 lines, i.e., 2 pp.; subject-matter can be anything, the style is traditional, modern or post-modern limited by typographic resources. Purpose is not an issue."** No **"erotica, scatalogical verse, excessive propaganda toward a certain subject."** They have recently published poetry by Milton Acorn, Andy Wainwright, Janice Kulyk-Keefer, M. Travis Lane, Douglas Lochhead, Lorna Crozier, Irving Layton, Peter Dale, Roger Finch, W.J. Keith and W.S. Milne. As a sample the editor selected these lines by Lloyd Abbey:

> *not jigs but threnodies:*
> *ancestral sounds,*
> *the thud of flame,*
> *collapsing bone,*
> *cold wind*
> *across chimneys*

TAR is flat-spined 6×9", 150 pp. with glossy card cover, offset printing, using **"in-house graphics and cover art, no ads."** They accept about 10% of some 2,500 submissions per year. Press run is 1,100 for 800 subscriptions. Subscription: $16. **Sample: $3 postpaid. Pays 2 copies. No simultaneous submissions or previously published poems. Editor "sometimes" comments on rejections.** The poetry editor advises, "The time for free verse form is exhausting itself as a technical possibility. **We are sympathetic to poets working with strong rhythmic patterns.** Poets will have to return to the traditional devices of rhythm, rhyme and manipulation of line length. Many more poets would and could be published if more of them were also readers of the full range of poetry in English, old and new. We are *not* responsible for return of submissions sent with improper postage. **Must include self-addressed stamped envelope (SASE) or International Reply Coupons (IRC) if outside Canada."**

THE ANTIOCH REVIEW (III), Box 148, Yellow Springs OH 45387, founded 1941, "is an independent quarterly of critical and creative thought . . . **For 45 years, now, creative authors, poets and thinkers have found a friendly reception . . . regardless of formal reputation."** Poetry editor: David St. John. "We get far more poetry than we can possibly accept, and the competition is keen. Here, where form and content are so inseparable and reaction is so personal, it is difficult to state requirements or limitations. Studying recent issues of *The Review* should be helpful. No 'light' or inspirational verse." Recently published poets: Molly Peacock, Joyce Carol Oates, Debra Nystrom, Karen Fish, Michael Collier and Andrew Hudgins. I selected these sample lines from Craig Raine's "Inca":

> *And the swans display*
> *their dripping beaks for us,*
> *but your lips are parted:*
> *to kiss, or to speak.*

Circulation is primarily to their 4,000 subscribers, of which half are libraries. They receive about 3,000 submissions per year, publish 20 pages of poetry in each issue, have about a 6-month backlog. Subscription: $20. **Sample: $5. Pays $15/published page plus 2 copies, general guidelines for contributors available for SASE, reports in 4-6 weeks.**

‡**ANYTHING THAT MOVES: BEYOND THE MYTHS OF BISEXUALITY (IV-Specialized, themes),** #24, 2404 California St., San Francisco CA 94115, phone (415)564-2226 (BABN), founded 1991, attention fiction/poetry editor, managing editor Karla Rossi. This quarterly uses **"material only considered from those who consider themselves bisexual, whether they identify as such or not. Pen names are permissible with written notification, however author's real name and address must accompany submission (not to be published). Submissions need not address bisexuality specifically, but may be on topics/ themes/subjects of interest to bisexuals. Special consideration given to people of color, those differently abled, those living with HIV disease or AIDS, and those whose work has been denied/censored/erased in mainstream literary communities and publications."** They have recently published poetry by Alta, Batya Weinbaum and Murcy Sheiner. As a sample, I selected these lines from "Pride" by M.S. Montgomery:

> *No longer coward, traitor to the cause,*
> *I walked Fifth Avenue with them today.*
> *Unpunished by the prejudicial laws,*
> *I wanted, still, to count as proud and gay.*

It is professionally printed, magazine-sized with glossy paper cover, 64 pp. saddle-stapled. Press run 5,000 for 1,000 subscribers of which 100 are libraries, 3,000 shelf sales. Subscription $25. **Sample postpaid: $10. Reports in 6-8 weeks. Pays 2 copies. No comments on rejections. "Accepted material cannot be returned. Do not send original copy. Shorter poems are more likely to be accepted. Notification of use will be in the form of 2-copy payment, although notification of acceptance will be given 6-8 weeks upon receipt of submission.** *ATM* is published by the Bay Area Bisexual Network (BABN), a nonprofit institution, and is distributed nationally, with a small international distribution."

APALACHEE QUARTERLY; APALACHEE PRESS (II, IV-Themes), P.O. Box 20106, Tallahassee FL 32316, founded 1971, editors Barbara Hamby, Pamela Ball, Claudia Johnson, Bruce Boehrer and Paul McCall, want **"no formal verse."** They have published poetry by David Kirby, Peter Meinke and Jim Hall. There are 55-95 pp. of poetry in each issue, circulation 500, with 250 subscriptions of which 50 are libraries, a 1-3 month backlog. "Every year we do an issue on a special topic. Past issues include a Dental, Revenge and Cocktail Party issues copies." Subscription: $15. **Sample: $5 postpaid. Submit clear copies of up to 5 poems, name and address on each, no dot-matrix; photocopied, simultaneous submissions OK. Payment 2 copies. Guidelines available for SASE. Sometimes comments on rejections. We don't read during the summer (June 1-August 31).**

APPALACHIAN HERITAGE (IV-Regional), Hutchins Library, Berea College, Berea KY 40404, phone (606)986-9341, ext. 5260, FAX 606-986-9494, founded 1973, editor Sidney Saylor Farr, a literary quarterly with Southern Appalachian emphasis. The journal publishes several poems in each issue, and the editor wants to see **"poems about people, places, the human condition, etc., with Southern Appalachian settings. No style restrictions but poems should have a maximum of 25 lines, prefer 10-15 lines."** She does not want "blood and gore, hell-fire and damnation, or biased poetry about race or religion." She has recently published poetry by Jim Wayne Miller, Louise McNeill and Bettie Sellers. As a sample, she selected the following lines by James Still:

> They have come down astride their bony nags
> In the gaunt hours when the lean young day
> Walks the grey ridge, and coal light flags
> Smooth-bodied poplars piercing a hollow sky.

The flat-spined magazine is 6¾×9", professionally printed on white stock with b/w line drawings and photos, glossy white card cover with four-color illustration. **Sample copy: $5. Contributors should type poems one to a page, simultaneous submissions are OK, and MSS are reported on in 2-4 weeks. Pay is 3 copies.** Reviews books of poetry.

APPLEZABA PRESS (II), P.O. Box 4134, Long Beach CA 90804, founded 1977, poetry editor D. H. Lloyd, is "dedicated to printing and distributing poetry to as wide an audience as we can." They publish both chapbooks and flat-spined collections of individual poets and occasional anthologies, about 3 titles per year. **"As a rule we like 'accessible' poetry, some experimental. We do not want to see traditional."** They have recently published poetry by Leo Mailman, Gerald Locklin, John Yamrus, Toby Lurie and Nichola Manning. These sample lines are from Lyn Lifshin's "Parachute Madonna":

> either quite manic or depressive
> either up and flying or down
> with a huge crash.

No query. Submit book MS with brief cover letter mentioning other publications and bio. Reports in 3 months. Simultaneous submissions, photocopy OK, dot-matrix accepted but not preferred. Pays 8-12% royalties and 10 author's copies. Send SASE for catalog to order samples. The samples I have seen are digest-sized, flat-spined paperbacks with glossy covers, sometimes with cartoon art, attractively printed.

APROPOS (I, IV-Subscribers), RD 4, Ashley Manor, Easton PA 18042, founded 1989, editor Ashley C. Anders, appears 6/year, and **publishes all poetry submitted by subscribers (subscription: $25/year) except that judged by the editor to be pornographic or in poor taste. Each issue awards prizes of $50, $25, and $10, as judged by readers (no entry fee). "Poems will not be returned; please retain copies. Maximum length 46 lines. One submission per publication." Sample: $3 postpaid. Simultaneous submissions and previously published poems OK.** It is digest-sized, 52 pp., plastic ring bound, with heavy stock cover, desk-top published. As a sample, I selected one stanza of a poem by the editor:

> No prize is worth the winning,
>   unless it is deserved.
> No dream is worth the dreaming,
>   unless it is preserved.

Special contests for subscribers are offered throughout the year at no additional fee. Prizes of $25, $10 and $5.

‡AQUARIUS (II), Flat 10, Room A, 116 Sutherland Ave., Maida-Vale, London, W9, England, poetry editor, Eddie Linden, is a literary biannual publishing quality poetry. **Payment is by arrangement. Sample: £2.50 or $10 US.** Subscription in US: $40.

ARARAT (IV-Ethnic), 585 Saddle River Rd., Saddle Brook NJ 07662, phone (201)797-7600. Editor-in-Chief: Leo Hamalian. 80% freelance written. **Emphasizes Armenian life and culture for Americans of Armenian descent and Armenian immigrants. They do not want to see traditional, sentimental love poetry.** "Most are well-educated; some are Old World." Quarterly magazine. Circ. 2,400. **Pays on**

publication. Publishes MS an average of 1 year after acceptance. Buys first North American serial rights and second (reprint) rights to material originally published elsewhere. Submit seasonal/holiday material at least 3 months in advance. Photocopied and previously published submissions OK. Computer printout submissions acceptable. Reports in 6 weeks. Sample copy $3 plus 4 first class stamps. Any verse that is Armenian in theme. Buys 6 per issue. Pays $10.

ARCHAE: A PALAEO-REVIEW OF THE ARTS (II); CLOUD MOUNTAIN PUBLISHING (III); RAPA NUI JOURNAL (V), 10 Troilus, Old Bridge NJ 08857-2724. Cloud Mountain founded 1971, publisher Alan Drake. *Archae* appears 2/year, uses "poems, chants, invocations, legends, myths, fiction, essays, any length. Does not use overly self-conscious poetry, with the private 'I' as its primary focus. If it's metered/rhymed we probably will not use it. Seeking reviews of poetry as well as in-depth interviews with thought-provoking poets. Proof sheets provided to all writers for approval before publication. Special effort taken to work with poets." They have published poetry or interviews with poets Michael Heller, Dan Masterson, Armand Schwerner, Mikhail Horowitz, Irving Weiss and Janine Pommy Vega among others. Accepts 13% of unsolicited submissions. *Archae* is $7 \times 8\frac{1}{2}$", 64-120 pp. Press run 505 for 342 subscribers of which 10 are libraries. Subscription $13 (2 issues), $17 foreign. Sample postpaid: $7 (US only). Reports in 1-4 weeks. Pays "in copies or by special arrangement." Send SASE for guidelines. Reviews books of poetry. Editors also produce the quarterly *Rapa Nui Journal*, an international journal of anthropological/archaeological studies and current events occurring on Easter Island and in the South Pacific, which rarely accepts poetry. Cloud Mountain publishes chapbooks, broadsides, etc., some by subsidy. Inquiries send SASE.

ARGONAUT (IV-Science Fiction/Fantasy), P.O. Box 4201, Austin TX 78765, founded 1972, editor/publisher Michael Ambrose, is an "annual magazine anthology of science fiction and weird fantasy, illustrated." They want "speculative, weird, fantastic poetry with vivid imagery or theme, up to 30 lines. Prefer traditional forms. Nothing ultramodernistic, non-fantastic." They have recently published poetry by Sardonyx, J.R. Ericson, Robert R. Medcalf, Jr. and Joey Froehlich. I have not seen an issue, but the editor describes it as 56 pp., digest-sized, typeset. They accept 5-8 of 100-200 poems received. Press run: 300 for 50 subscriptions of which 3 are libraries. Subscription: $5. **Sample, postpaid: $5. Send SASE for guidelines. Pays 2 copies. Submit no more than 5 poems at a time. Reports in 4-8 weeks. Editor comments on submissions "occasionally."** He says, "Too much of what I see is trite, limited in scope or language, and inappropriate for the themes of *Argonaut*. Poets should know what the particular market to which they submit is looking for and not simply shotgun their submissions."

ARJUNA LIBRARY PRESS; JOURNAL OF REGIONAL CRITICISM (I, II), 1025 Garner St., Space 18, Colorado Springs CO 80905, library founded 1963, press founded 1979, editor Joseph A. Uphoff, Jr. "The Arjuna Library Press is avant garde, designed to endure the transient quarters and marginal funding of the literary phenomenon (as a tradition) while presenting a context for the development of current mathematical ideas in regard to theories of art and literature; photocopy printing allows for very limited editions and irregular format. Quality is maintained as an artistic materialist practice." He wants to see "surrealist prose poetry, dreamlike, short and long works, not obscene, profane (will criticize but not publish), unpolished work." He is currently publishing work by B.Z. Niditch, Paul Carrington and Rich Murphy. As an example the editor has selected these lines from "Night Journey Of The Mathematician In Africa" by Mike Rawn:

> *Look;*
> *A thousand young boys casting*
> *Long bamboos . . .*
> *Silhouettes teeming round the flat moon,*
> *Fly-fishing for silvers . . .*
> *This frenzy . . .*
> *Of the quick-hearted species*
> *Teeming suicidal about a reflection of light.*

JRC is published on loose photocopied pages of collage, writing and criticism, appearing irregularly in an irregular format. Press run: 1 copy each. **Pays "notification." Previously published poems and simultaneous submissions OK.** "I like ingenuity, legibility, convenience, polish. I expect some sympathy for mathematical, logical and philosophical exposition and criticism. These arguments remain our central ambition." Arjuna Library Press publishes 6-12 chapbooks/year, averaging 50 pp. **To submit to the press, send complete MS, cover letter including bio, publications, "any information the author feels is of value." The press pays royalties "by agreement, if we ever make a profit" and copies. Send 50¢ for sample.** Reviews books of poetry "occasionally." The editor says, "The nature of irony is vicarious and self-defensive. There are elements of fantasy in the violence of fiction but, without any doubt, the experience of the author is the basis of the written conception. We should expect that such a nature has a potent implication in terms of real world values and possibilities; this cannot always be taken lightly. The attack that shocks the reader must, therefore, be a matter of responsibility belonging to the poet and those who refer to the poem. We want to discourage the practice of vigilante irony (or rhetorical attack). We think irony should bring about justice!"

THE ARK (V), 35 Highland Ave., Cambridge MA 02139, phone (617)547-0852, founded 1970 (as BLEB), poetry editor Geoffrey Gardner, publishes books of poetry. "We are unable to take on new projects at this time." They have published poetry by David Budbill, John Haines, Joseph Bruchac, Elsa Gidlow, W. S. Merwin, Eliot Weinberger, Kathy Acker, George Woodcock, Kathleen Raine, Marge Piercy and Linda Hogan. The editor selected these lines by Kenneth Rexroth (a translation from the Sanskrit) as a sample:
>You think this is a time of Shiva's waking
>You are wrong
>You are Shiva
>But you dream

THE UNIVERSITY OF ARKANSAS PRESS; ARKANSAS POETRY AWARD (III), Fayetteville AR 72701, founded 1980, acquisitions editor James Twiggs, publishes flat-spined paperbacks and hardback collections of individual poets. Miller Williams, director of the press, says, "We are not interested in poetry that says, 'Guess what I mean' or 'Look what I know.' " They have published poetry by Dan Masterson, Leon Stokesbury, George Garrett and John Ciardi. As a sample, I selected the opening stanza of "Navy Town Spring" by Debra Bruce:
>A big-bellied bouncer bangs
>the door open wide and leans
>on it and lights up the sun.
That's from her book Sudden Hunger, digest-sized, 66 pp., flat-spined, elegantly printed on eggshell stock with glossy 2-color card cover. Query with 5-10 sample poems. Replies to query in 2 weeks, to submissions in 2-4 weeks. No replies without SASE. MS should be double-spaced with 1½" margins. Clean photocopy OK. No dot-matrix unless letter quality. Discs compatible with IBM welcome. Pays: 10% royalty contract plus 10 author's copies. Send SASE for catalog to buy samples. The Arkansas Poetry Award competition is open to any original MS by a living American poet whose work has not been previously published or accepted for publication in book form. Chapbooks, self-published books, and books produced with the author's subsidy are not considered previously published books. No translations. Submit 50-80 pp., not more than one poem/page, counting title page in page count. An acknowledgments page listing poems previously published should accompany MS. Author's name should appear on the title page only. $10 reading fee. Postmark no later than May 1. Publication the following spring. A $500 cash advance is part of the award.

ARROWOOD BOOKS, INC. (II), P.O. Box 2100, Corvallis OR 97339, phone (503)753-9539, founded 1985, editor Lex Runciman, is a "small-press publisher of quality literary works." He publishes sewn paperbacks and hardcover books, always on acid-free papers, 1-2 per year, 60-80 pp. Poets recently published are Anne Pitkin, Lisa Steinman and Madeline DeFrees. Query first. Simultaneous submissions, photocopies, poems previously published in magazines all OK. Reports to queries in 3 weeks, on MSS in 2 months. Pays royalties and advance. I have not seen a sample. If you want one, he offers a 10% writer's discount (limit 1 copy). He advises, "Write well, and work hard to separate the act of writing from the fear of publishing (or not)."

ART TIMES: CULTURAL AND CREATIVE JOURNAL (II), Box 730, Mount Marion NY 12456-0730, phone (914)246-6944, editor Raymond J. Steiner, a monthly tabloid newspaper devoted to the arts that publishes some poetry and fiction. The editor wants to see "traditional and contemporary poetry with high literary quality." He does not want to see "poorly written, pointless prose in stanza format." The most well-known poet he has published recently is Helen Wolfert. As a sample, he selected the following lines by Anne Mins:
>Your finical ear, my friend
>Neat file of images, pile of esoteric words
>Compendium of rhymes, blend of assonance,
>Your pyrotechnic metric, Spare me, spare me.
Art Times focuses on cultural and creative articles and essays. The paper is 16-20 pp., on newsprint, with reproductions of art work, some photos, advertisement-supported. Frequency is monthly and circulation is 15,000, of which 5,000 are by request and subscriptions; most distribution is free through galleries, theatres, etc. They receive 700-1,000 poems per month, use only 40-50 a year. Subscription is $15/year. Sample: $1 postage cost. Guidelines available for SASE. They have a 2-year backlog. Pay is 6 free copies plus one year complimentary subscription.

Close-up

Miller Williams
Director
The University of Arkansas Press

People
When people are born
we lift them like little heroes
as if what they have done
is a thing to be proud of.

When people die
we cover their faces
as if dying were something
to be ashamed of.

Of shameful and varied heroic things we do
except for the starting and stopping
we are never convinced
of how we feel.
We say oh, and well.

Ah, but in the beginning
and in the end.

That wry poem, in which comedy and tragedy, like Estragon and Vladimir, seem to jostle one another in mute efforts to occupy stage center, is characteristic of Miller Williams's tolerant view of life. "What binds us together as human beings," he says, "is that we're all lonely and all frightened. Because we're lonely we reach out to one another, inventing love; because we're frightened we hurt one another when we do. And because our loneliness is greater than our fear and the need for love is greater than the pain, it's worth it."

He was born in the small hill town of Hoxie, Arkansas, in 1930. His father was a "free-thinking Methodist preacher who with my mother filled our home with good books, good music, good talk, love, discipline and populism." Miller's degrees are all in science, which he taught at the college level for nearly a dozen years before joining the English Department of Louisiana State University in 1962. He has wandered about as far as his numerous literary awards and honors and his two dozen books can take a man. He has lived and taught in Chile, Mexico and Italy. "I have," he says, "a fondness for languages and mythologies." But the earthiness and humor in his work keep telling us you can't take Arkansas out of the boy. "Though I've written all my literate life," he says, "my formal education is in the sciences. This may have something to do with my mistrust of mysticism, a fondness for the ordinary moment and a sense of the poet as reporter rather than prophet."

Since becoming director of The University of Arkansas Press in 1980, he has spearheaded an unusually ambitious and imaginative publishing program for a university press, making it one of our most important, especially in the publication of books of poetry and books by and about poets. "We are offered something over 400 poetry manuscripts a year," he says, "of which we publish two to four. This is apart from the Arkansas Poetry Award competition, which attracts about a thousand first-book manuscripts annually."

Miller says that some university presses see their mission as exclusively the publication of scholarly works. At The University of Arkansas Press, he says, "Our mission, more broadly stated, is to make available to the educated and interested generalist any worthy work that might be considered unattractive to a commercial house. Increasingly, that includes poetry. It's not for me to say that commercial houses ought to be publishing poetry, or more of it. Books of poetry don't sell in great numbers, but most university presses, for various reasons, can survive, break even and even make a small profit with print runs of 2,500 or 3,000 copies. Large commercial houses can't. Some do publish poetry, but it's esssentially a *pro bono* effort, and while the effort has to be appreciated, I have no right to demand that it be made. I do have an obligation, or so I believe, as director of a university press to take up what slack I can."

Should you try your book there? Well, if it is your first, the competition may offer you a chance of recognition, but that's for one out of a thousand. How will it be evaluated? Miller says, "We're looking for poetry in which line-breaks make sense, in which stanzas have some reason for existence and in which every word earns its way. We're pleased to find convincing poems in formal structures, for a number of reasons—one of which is simply that it's a joy to see a difficult thing done well—but we're dismayed by the frequency with which such poems fail to succeed for us. The prosodic structure of a formal poem is not a vessel into which a statement is poured; it's an integument that grows around an active language as the work comes into being. And we're not attracted to poems that seem to say, 'Guess what I mean.' We read in the conviction that the best and most abiding poems are written to reveal meaning and seduce the reader into a new and empirical experience."

I have often, in my column in *Writer's Digest*, recommended a book by Miller Williams: **Patterns of Poetry: An Encyclopedia of Forms**, available from Louisiana State University Press in paperback for $14.95. In that book he lucidly explains most of the forms of poetry from acrostics to villanelles and the terms of versification, providing a scintillating anthology of examples. My advice is that you read his book and *then* try to write poems that will capture the attention of editors at The University of Arkansas Press.

—Judson Jerome

Submissions are reported on in 6 months. There is a 20-line limit for poetry. Simultaneous submissions OK. Typed MSS should be submitted to the editor. Criticism of MSS is provided "at times but rarely."

‡ART-CORE (I), P.O. Box 49324, Austin TX 78765, founded 1988, editor Patty Morales, is a quarterly using poems of "one page or less, alternative, underground, off-beat, avant-garde, uncensored—any subject including erotic, typed or visual layout. No main stream or lengthy poems." I have not seen an issue, but the editor describes it as 24 pp., magazine-sized, offset. Press run 2,000 for 150 subscribers, 1,000 copies distributed free locally. They accept about 100 of 200 poems submitted/year. Subscription: $6. Sample postpaid: $2.50. Send SASE for guidelines. Pays 1 copy. Responds within 2 months.

ARTE PUBLICO PRESS; THE AMERICAS REVIEW (IV-Ethnic), University of Houston, Houston TX 77204-2090, founded 1972, poetry editor Julian Olivares, publisher Nicolas Kanellos. (Note: *The Americas Review* is also the name of another magazine with a political focus published in Berkeley CA.) The press publishes 20 books of fiction and 2 of poetry by U.S. Hispanic writers per year. They have published books by Gary Soto, Alberto Rios and Sandra Cisneros. *The Americas Review* is a triquarterly of fiction and poetry. I have not seen it, but the publisher says it is digest-sized, 120-200 pp., flat-spined, circulation 3,000; 2,100 subscribers (of which 40% are libraries). Pays a varying amount plus 5 copies. Reports in 4 months. No simultaneous submissions. For book publication, publish first in the magazine. They pay a $500 advance and 25 copies for book publication. There is an annual award for the best poetry published in the magazine.

ARTFUL DODGE (II, IV-Translations), Dept. of English, College of Wooster, Wooster OH 44691, founded 1979, poetry editor Daniel Bourne, is an annual literary magazine that "takes a strong interest in poets who are continually testing what they can get away with successfully in regard to subject, perspective, language, etc., but who also show mastery of current American poetic techniques—its varied textures and its achievement in the illumination of the particular. What all this boils down to is that we require high (and preferably innovative) craftsmanship as well as a vision that goes beyond *one's own* storm windows, grandmothers, or sexual fantasies—to paraphrase Hayden Carruth. **Poems can be on any subject, of any length, from any perspective, in any voice, but we don't want anything that does not connect with both the human and the aesthetic. Thus, we don't want cute, rococo surrealism, someone's warmed-up, left-over notion of an avant-garde that existed 10-100 years ago, or any last bastions of rhymed verse in the civilized world.** On the other hand, we are interested in poems that utilize stylistic persuasions both old and new to good effect. We are not afraid of poems which try to deal with large social, political, historical, and even philosophical questions—especially if the poem emerges from one's own life experience and is not the result of armchair pontificating. We often offer encouragement to writers whose work we find promising, but *Artful Dodge* **is more a journal for the already emerging writer than for the beginner looking for an easy place to publish. We also have a sustained commitment to translation, especially from Polish and other East European literatures,** and we feel the interchange between the American and foreign works on our pages is of great interest to our readers. We also feature interviews with such outstanding literary figures as Jorge Luis Borges, W. S. Merwin, James Laughlin, Czeslaw Milosz, Nathalie Sarauté, Stanislaw Baranczak, Omar Pound, Gwendolyn Brooks, John Giorno, Stuart Dybek, Edward Hirsch and William Matthews. Recent and forthcoming poets include Naomi Shihab Nye, Walter McDonald, Stuart Friebert, Nicholas Kolumban, William Stafford, Len Roberts, Karl Krolow (German), Tomasz Jastrun (Polish), Mahmud Darwish (Palestinian), Tibor Zalan (Hungarian) and Joseph Salemi's faithfully erotic versions of Martial. The editor selected these sample lines from "How to Eat in the House of Death" by Katharyn Machan Aal:

> *Absolutely, ignore the faces peering*
> *in through darkened windows. If—*
> *well, no need to warn you.*
> *They are hungry too.*

There are about 40 pp. of poetry in each issue, circulation 750 for 100 subscriptions of which 30 are libraries. They receive at least 2,000 poems per year, use 20-30, and the backlog is 1-12 months between acceptance and publication. **Sample: $5.75 for recent issues, $3 for others. "No simultaneous submissions but typed photocopies of any technological persuasion are OK. Please limit submissions to 6 poems. Long poems may be of any length, but send only one at a time. We encourage translations, but we ask as well for original text and statement from translator that he/she has copyright clearance and permission of author." Reports from immediately to four months. Pays 2 copies, plus, currently, at least $5 honorarium because of grants from Ohio Arts Council.** The digest-sized, perfect-bound format is professionally printed, glossy cover, with art, ads.

ARTS END BOOKS; NOSTOC MAGAZINE (II), P.O. Box 162, Newton MA 02168, founded 1978, poetry editor Marshall Brooks. "**We publish good contemporary writing. Our interests are broad and so are our tastes.** People considering sending work to us should examine a copy of our magazine and/or our catalog; check your library for the former, send us a SASE for the latter." Their publications are distinguished by excellent presswork and art in a variety of formats: postcard series, posters, pamphlets, flat-spined paperbacks and hardbacks. As a sample Brooks chose Rogue Dalton's "The Captain" (translated by Sesshu Foster):

> *The captain in his hammock the captain*
> *asleep under the chirping of the night*
> *the guitar hanging against the wall*
> *his pistol set aside his bottle*
> *awaiting like a rendezvous with love*
> *the captain the captain*
> *—he should know—*
> *under the same darkness as his prey.*

The magazine appears irregularly in printruns of 300-500, about 30 pp. of poetry in each, 100 subscriptions of which half are libraries. **Sample: $2.50 postpaid.** They receive a few hundred submissions per year, use 25-30; "**modest payment plus contributor's copies. A cover letter is a very good idea for any kind of submission;** we receive *very* few good, intelligent cover letters; what to include? That's up to the writer, whatever he/she feels important in terms of the work, in terms of establishing a meeting." **Tries to report within a few weeks, discourages simultaneous submissions, frequently comments on rejected MSS.** Reviews books of poetry. Brooks says, "We try to respond warmly to writers interested in making genuine contact with us and our audience."

‡ARTS INDIANA LITERARY SUPPLEMENT; POETRY ON THE BUSES (IV-Regional), Suite 701, 47 S. Pennsylvania St., Indianapolis IN 46204-3622. *Arts Indiana Literary Supplement* is an annual 33 pp. publication using poems and short stories by residents of Indiana. "Writers should send no more than

3 poems and/or one short story." Poems up to 40 lines. "New work will be given first consideration, but previously published work will be considered if the author has maintained copyright or can arrange written permission for re-publication." Simultaneous submissions OK if so noted. Payment $20 for each accepted poem (unpublished). One poem will receive a cash award of $500 in addition. Send SASE for guidelines. Deadline March. *Poetry on the Buses* selects 12 poems to be printed on placards 11 × 28″ each year to be displayed inside METRO buses, a new poem each month. Open to poets 18 or older living within Marion and contiguous counties. Submit 4 copies of no more than 3 poems no longer than 17 lines, 81 spaces/line. Deadline July 3. Send SASE for entry form.

ARUNDEL PRESS; MERCER & AITCHISON (III), 11349 Santa Monica Bl., Los Angeles CA 90025, phone (213)477-1640, founded 1984, managing editor Phillip Bevis, speaking for Arundel Press, "publishes only major texts (as we see them) in limited editions printed letterpress. We will consider only established authors. Most work is illustrated with original graphics. Mercer & Aitchison publishes definitive editions of major (as we see them) works of poetry, literature & literary criticism." They publish about 6 hardbacks/year. Phillip Bevis recommends to beginning poets the Mercer & Aitchison publication, Clayton Eshleman's **Novices: A Study of Poetic Apprenticeship** (paperback, $12.95). He says, "The only thing worth adding to what is said there is that there are only a handful of poets in America (at the most) making a living *as* poets. The majority of even the most prominent must teach or work in other fields to support their poetic endeavors. Poetry must be something you do because you want to—not for the money."

‡ASCENT (II), P.O. Box 967, Urbana IL 61801, founded 1975, editor Audrey Curley, appears 3 times/ year, using **poetry that is "eclectic, shorter rather than longer."** They have recently published poetry by Brendan Galvin, Ralph Mills and Nance Van Winckel. As a sample the editor selected these lines from "Sunday Falls" by E.G. Burrows:

> *Never the abbeys never*
> *sad stories of the death of kings*
> *but the water descending*
> *braid by braid a mute*
> *gaiety of the river out of cloudbreak*
> *and the sealed shafts in the hills*
> *miners their women and all*
> *holiday this grey jay*
> *these better ruins.*

I have not seen an issue, but the editor describes it as 6 × 9″, 64 pp, professionally printed with matte card cover. They accept about 5% of 750 poems received/year. Print run 900 copies for 250 subscribers of which 90 are libraries. Subscription $3/year. **Sample: $2. Pays 3 copies.** The editor says, "I am usually the sole reader. Poems are rejected or accepted from 2-8 weeks, usually closer to 2 weeks. Acceptances are usually published within the year."

‡THE ASCENT (I, IV-Students), Aldephi University U.C. 109, South Avenue Box 701, Garden City NY 11530, founded 1987, senior editor Kristina A. Uihlein, appears twice a year using **"poetry by students attending accredited colleges and universities or students, alumni or faculty of Aldephi University. Any form, preferably up to 5 pp. typewritten, mature, sophisticated work, nothing banal and trite."** As a sample the editor selected these lines from "Pain" by Angela Ward:

> *Chewing on glass*
> *the blood boils*
> *over*
> *my lips*

It is a handsomely produced magazine-sized journal with glossy card cover. "We accept about 80% of submissions from people affiliated with Adelphi University and 60% from outside sources." Press run 300. Shelf sales about 100. Price per issue: $1, subscription: $7. **Sample: $3.50 postpaid. Pays 1 copy. Submit by Apr. 1 for Spring, Nov. 1 for Fall. Previously published poems and simultaneous submissions OK. Editor seldom comments.** There is a vote on submissions but senior and junior editors have the final say. "We welcome correspondence with other college literary magazines."

THE ASHLAND POETRY PRESS (V, II, IV-Anthologies, themes), Ashland College, Ashland OH 44805, founded 1969, editor Robert McGovern, publishes anthologies on specific themes and occasional collections. He has recently published collections by Harold Witt, Alberta Turner and Richard Snyder. As a sample he selected lines from "Journey" by Hollis Summers:

> *Unless bored stands as another word*
> *For wise, they were not wise, only bored,*
> *And rich. Only the bored and rich wander.*

Wise men linger and produce at home.
That poem appears in Summers' book **After the Twelve Days**. **"Watch publications such as *Poets & Writers* for calls for MSS, but don't submit otherwise."** On collections, poet gets 10% royalty; anthologies, poets are paid stipulated price when sufficient copies are sold. Write for book and price list. **"We do not read unsolicited MSS; anthology readings take quite a bit of time."** Considers simultaneous submissions.

‡ASHOD (IV-Translations), P.O. Box 1147, New York NY 10159-1147, phone (212)475-0711, founded 1979, editor Jack Antreassian, publishes 2 paperbacks/year, **translations from Armenian plus limited original work.** They have recently published books of poetry by Michael Casey, Diana Der Hovanessian, Archie Minasian, Nahabed Kouchag, and editor Antreassian. **Pays 9% royalties, full royalty on 900 copies given on publication, plus 10 copies. Replies in 1 week to queries, 1 month to MSS.**

ASYLUM (II, IV-Form, translations), P.O. Box 6203, Santa Maria CA 93456, founded 1985, editor Greg Boyd, is "a literary semiannual journal with emphasis on short fiction, **the prose poem, and poetry. No restrictions on form, subject-matter, style or purpose, though we are especially receptive to prose poems.**" They have recently published poetry by Thomas Wiloch, Philip Dacey, Edouard Roditi and Tom Whalen. As a sample, I selected this poem, "Stain," by Pierre Jean Jouve, translated from the French by Eric Basso:

> *I saw a thick stain of green oil*
> *Drained from an engine and on*
> *The hot sidewalk in that sleazy district*
> *I thought long, long of my mother's blood.*

Asylum is digest-sized, 80-128 pp., professionally printed with matte card cover. They accept about 2% of submissions. Print run 700 for 160 subscriptions of which 10 are libraries. Subscription: $10. **Sample, postpaid: $3. Pays 3 copies. Put name and address on each page. Reports in 2 weeks-3 months.**

ATALANTIK (IV-Ethnic, foreign language), 7630 Deercreek Dr., Worthington OH 43085, phone (614)885-0550, founded 1979, editor Prabhat K. Dutta, is a "literary quarterly **mainly in Bengali** and containing short stories, poems, essays, sketches, book reviews, interviews, cultural information, science articles, cinema/theater news, children's pages, serialized novels, etc., **with occasional English writings (non-religious, non-political.)**" They have published "all major poets of West Bengal, India (Sunil Gangopadhyay, Manas Roychoudhury, Santosh Chakrabarty, Surajit Ghosh, Dibyendu Palit, Krishna Dhar, Ananda Bagchi, Debaroti Mitra, Kajal Chakrabarti, etc.)as well as of Bangladesh (Shamsur Rahaman, Begum Sufia Kamal, Abu Jafar Obeyadullah, Ashraf Siddique, Al Mahmood, etc.)" As a sample the editor selected four lines from "After the Vedas" by Diane Morgan:

> *The eye will enter the sun,*
> *The soul will enter the wind,*
> *The limbs will enter the earth,*
> *The place where they have sinned.*

"*Atalantik*, the first Bengali literary magazine in USA, was started to keep Bengali language alive to Bengalees in USA. Number of pages differ widely and average out to 60. Original printing by electric press in Calcutta, India; USA printing is by offset or photocopy and the number varies according to order; artwork both on the cover and inside the magazine." It is magazine-sized, flat-spined, with b/w matte card cover. The annual subscription is $20. Some copies are distributed free. **Sample: $6 postpaid. Send SASE for guidelines. Pays 1-2 copies. Simultaneous submissions and previously published poems OK. Reports in 1 month.** "We are actively and seriously considering publishing books under 'Atalantik Publications.' **For book consideration submit sample poems, cover letter with bio and publications. Simultaneous submissions, photocopies, dot-matrix OK. Pays "25 copies usually, may vary."** Editor sometimes comments on rejections. He adds, "Poetry is the unique vehicle of literature that transfers feelings in a subtle way." Reviews books of poetry. The operations of a smaller version of *Atalantik* are managed by Keshab Dutta, from 36B, Bakul Bagan Road, Calcutta-700025, India (phone 75-1620) for distribution in India.

THE ATLANTIC (III), 745 Boylston St., Boston MA 02116, phone (617)536-9500, founded 1857, poetry editor Peter Davison, publishes 1-5 poems monthly in the magazine. **Some of the most distinguished poetry in American literature** has been published by this magazine, including recent work by William Matthews, Mary Oliver, Stanley Kunitz, Rodney Jones, May Swenson, Galway Kinnell, Philip Levine, Red Hawk, Tess Gallagher, Donald Hall and W.S. Merwin. The magazine has a circulation of 500,000, of which 5,800 are libraries (**sample: $3 postpaid**). They receive some 75,000 poems per year, of which they use 35-40 and have a backlog of 6-12 months. **Submit 3-5 poems, no dot-matrix, no simultaneous submissions, payment about $3/line.** Peter Davison says he wants "to see poetry of the highest order;

we do *not* want to see workshop rejects. **Watch out for workshop uniformity. Beware of the present indicative. Be yourself."**

THE ATLANTIC MONTHLY PRESS, 19 Union Square W., New York NY 10003. Declined listing.

‡ATLANTIS: A WOMEN'S STUDIES JOURNAL (IV-Feminist), Mount Saint Vincent University, Halifax, Nova Scotia B3M 2J6 Canada, phone (902)443-4450, ext. 319, founded 1975, managing editor Maurice Michaud or literary editor Margaret Harry, appears twice a year using **poetry "certainly no longer than 5 MS pp; should have a feminist perspective, preferably academic. No cutsie greeting-card poems about marshmallow women or by men without a hint of feminist consciousness."** They have recently published poetry by Liliane Welch. I have not seen an issue, but the editor describes it as magazine-sized, 150 pp., flat-spined with card cover. They accept about 5-10% of submissions. Press run 1,000 with 600 subscribers of which 55% are libraries. Subscription: Canada $20; US $30 (Canadian). **Sample postpaid: $7.50 Canadian. Pays 1 copy. Reports in 6-12 weeks.**

ATTICUS REVIEW/PRESS (II, IV-Form), 720 Heber Ave., Calexico CA 92231, founded 1981, poetry editor H. Polkinhorn, is a "small-press publisher of cut-up and experimental and visual/verbal work," publishing the magazine, *Atticus Review*, chapbooks and flat-spined editions, wanting **"open form, open subject-matter, experimental." They do not want to see traditional forms.** As a sample I selected this stanza from "Serpent Rock" by Karl Kempton:

> *Atop any formation*
> *never again*
> *will I watch*
> *a young jackrabbit*
> *fifteen minutes*
> *chase*
> *a five foot rattler*

Atticus Review is magazine-sized, clipped on one side, glossy card cover, $4 a copy (plus $1 "transportation"). *AR* appears 2 times a year. They receive about 500 poems per year, 25-50 accepted. **Sample: $4 postpaid. Pays 2 copies. Simultaneous submissions, previously published OK. Reports in 4-6 weeks. They publish 1 chapbook a year. Submit samples. Chapbook publication pays 10% of run.**

AUGURIES (IV-Science fiction/fantasy), 48 Anglessy Rd., Alverstoke, Gosport, Hants, England, PO122EQ founded 1983, editor Nik Morton, uses **science fiction and fantasy poetry, "any length, any style, good imagery."** They have recently published poetry by Garry Legg, J.V. Stewart, Steve Sneyd, Dave W. Hughes and John Light. As a sample the editor selected these lines from "Chill Factor" by John Francis Haines:

> *Beneath our feet: the ice;*
> *Beneath the ice: the city,*
> *Its locked, distorted face*
> *Held static, without pity . . .*

The digest-sized periodical is lithographed from photoreduced typeset on bond paper, thin glossy card cover with b/w art, 52 or more pp., saddle-stapled. They take about 40% of 50 poems received per year. Press run 250 for 150 subscriptions, about 50 shelf sales. Price per issue: $5; subscription: $20. **Sample back issue $5 postpaid. Pays 1 copy. No simultaneous submissions. Previously published poems "not usually" used. Reports in 8 weeks. Editor comments on rejections "if possible."** Reviews books of poetry, "albeit briefly." He says, "My choice of poetry is very subjective, may even appear arbitrary: if it appeals to me, I will accept (perhaps offering advice where necessary before acceptance). Be patient, I have material for issues up to #18 and #13 is just out!"

AURA LITERARY/ARTS MAGAZINE (II), Box 76, University of Alabama at Birmingham, Birmingham AL 35294, phone (205)934-3216, founded 1974, editors David Good and Steven Smith, a semiannual magazine that publishes "fiction and art though majority of acceptances are poetry—90-100 per year. **Length—open, style open, subject matter open. We are looking for quality poetry. Both first-time and often published poets are published here.** *Aura* has published work by Lyn Lifshin, Adrian C. Louis and William Miller. As a sample the editors selected these lines by Robert Anderson:

> *I saw a movie once,*
> *They put a saint inside*
> *a bell and rang it.*
> *Poetry is like that.*

The 6×9″ magazine is 90-120 pp., perfect-bound, printed on white matte with b/w photos, lithography, and line art. Circulation is 500, of which 40-50 are subscriptions; other sales are to students and Birmingham residents. Price per issue is $2.50, subscription $6. **Sample available for $2.50 postpaid, guidelines for SASE. Pay is 2 copies. Writers should submit "3-5 poems, with SASE, no simultaneous submissions, will take photocopies or even neatly hand written."** Reporting time is 2-3 months. The editors say, "Quality is our quantity. If it's good we will find a place for it, if not this issue, the next."

AWEDE PRESS (II), Box 376, Windsor VT 05089, phone (802)484-5169, founded 1975, editor Brita Bergland. Awede is a small press that publishes letterpress books, sewn with drawn-on covers, graphically produced. The editor wants **"contemporary, 'language' poetry with a strong visual interest."** They have published poetry by Charles Bernstein, James Sherry, Rosemarie Waldrop and Hannah Weiner. The editor selected these sample lines by Charles Bunstein:

> *No priority other than the vanished*
> *Imagination of some other*
> *Time—inlets of dilapidated*
> *Incredulity harbored*
> *On the deleterious Bus to Air Landing*

Awede publishes two poetry chapbooks per year, 32 pp., 6 × 9″, flat-spined. **Freelance submissions are accepted, but author should query first. Queries are answered in 2 weeks, MSS reported on in 4-5 months, simultaneous submissions are acceptable, as are photocopied MSS. Pay is in author's copies, 10% of run.** No subsidy publishing, book catalog free on request, with SASE a must. Sample books available at list price of $4-8.

THE BABY CONNECTION NEWS JOURNAL (IV-Themes), Drawer 13320, San Antonio TX 78213-0320, phone Tues.-Sat. 12:30-5:30 CST (512)493-6278, founded 1986, Ms. Gina G. Morris, C.I.D.I./ editor, is "a monthly news journal **to support, educate, move and inspire new and expectant parents** in their role of rearing babies and pre-schoolers 0-5 years of age. Parenting is such a tough job—our publication strives to reward and motivate positive and nurturing parenting skills." They use **"poetry only on the subjects of mothering, fathering, birthing, pregnancy, child rearing, the power, the love, the passion and momentum, fertility. Humor a big plus. No Eastern mysticism, anything too far left or right. Ours is a straight and narrow journal, and I will not alienate my readers with weird poetry. Poets, be real; basic humanity is massively appealing. Be sure to include a very personable bio about who you are, not your publishing accomplishments. We don't care where or if you've been published. Your work makes the connection for us and for our readers. I need more, more, more poetry on pregnancy and birth."** They have recently published poetry by Alex Grayton, Barbara Kane, E.K. Alasky, Jim McConnell and Laura Rodley. As a sample the editor selected these lines from "Night Music" by Marc Swan:

> *The moon casts a mosaic of light and dark*
> *against her bedroom wall. I lean low to*
> *tuck her in & kiss her goodnight. Dad,*
> *she whispers, look at Peter Pan's shadow. I hug*
> *her tightly, close to my chest. If it gets lost*
> *you can sew it back on. Yes, she says,*
> > *I will.*

The tabloid-sized newsprint publication is 8 pp. **"We would like to receive and publish all poetry that specifically pertains to our publishing needs."** Press run: 30,000 for 1,700 subscriptions of which 10% are libraries. Subscription: $9/year. **Sample postpaid: $3 for 2 different issues. For $3 you get 2 issues and "writer's kit" giving guidelines, submission form and pre-routed return envelope. Pays 5 copies.** "We encourage a reduced rate subscription of $4.75 for 6 months so we can be assured the poet knows our context and cares enough to follow us for a term. However, there is no obligation. We encourage all caring persons." **Simultaneous submissions and previously published poems OK. Reports "immediately" if possible. Editor comments on submissions "if poet requests feedback."** Reviews books of poetry. They also publish 5-8 chapbooks and flat-spined paperbacks/year averaging 16-72 pp. **For book or chapbook publication, submit 3-4 samples, bio ("a very personable bio—about the real poet, not accomplishments"), publications. Pays 6 copies and honorarium averaging $25.** "We are preparing to publish a complete book of all poems submitted. Be a part of such a lovely collection. Payment is copy of book." They are open to subsidy arrangements for "small books of poetry specifically dealing with family, birthing and parenting, and we will advertise it free of charge in our newspaper and in our Baby's Mart catalog." Query for details of arrangements. The editor says, "Our Parent Center is very interested in collections of family and birthing poetry to inspire positive parenting. Be part of American-realized family values and give us basic, *almost* abrasive, blatant perspectives on womanhood, fathering, fertility and the joy of bringing a new life into this world."

‡**BABYFISH (LOST ITS MOMMA) (I, IV-Regional)**, P.O. Box 11589, Detroit MI 48211, founded 1988, editor/publisher Andy Sunfrog, appears "twice a year, or whenever we get it done." The editor says, **"We are a free form journal, but our emphasis leans toward experimental and anti-authoritarian writing; no boring poetry."** They have recently published poetry by Antler, Kim Hunter and Marie Mason. As a sample the editor selected these lines from "Blues Poem #1" by Willie Williams:

> *They say*
> *we*
> *Gave the Blues*
> *to America*
> *But*
> *i say*
> *she gave us*
> *The blues first*

I have not seen an issue, but the editor describes it as magazine-sized 70-100 pp., with card stock cover, "tons of art & graphics, wild layout, photocopy and offset." They accept 25-50% of poetry received. Press run 1,000 for 1 subscriber, ⅓ given away "to other publications for review, to poor people, prisoners, etc." **Sample postpaid: $3. Pays 1-5 or more copies.** "We love to get poetry from new, previously unheard of writers. Free Form to me means *anything goes* but my personal preference is **for Detroit area writers with a social/political edge.** We are poets who are visionaries, activists, witches, massage therapists and *much more* but *not* professional poets."

‡**BAD HAIRCUT (II, IV-Social issues)**, 3115 SW Roxbury, Seattle WA 98126, founded 1987, poetry editors Kimberlea and Ray Goforth, is a "small-press magazine with world-wide distribution, publication schedule varies. **Pro-peace themes, surrealistic, anything really. Free verse is preferred. Don't want to see anything by bad poets in** *love*." They have recently published poetry by Lyn Lifshin, Edward Mycue, Henry Mason, B. Z. Niditch and Ivan Argüelles. As a sample the editors selected these lines by Brian Burch:

> *There is a brown crow*
> *hovering over Guatemala*
> *pretending to be an eagle.*
>
> *Looking for outbreaks*
> *of still warm bodies*
> *it waits,*
> *beak open to pluck out eyes*
> *and tear off ears . . . .*

Their object is "to bring together thoughts of peace from around the world." *Bad Haircut* is digest-sized, using some art and ads. Of thousands of poems received each year, they say, they use 300. Press run is 1000 for 300 subscriptions (3 libraries), and it is carried by 4 stores. $4 per issue, $14 for a subscription. **Sample: $4 postpaid. Send SASE for guidelines. Pay is "a tearsheet, maybe one copy."** No simultaneous submissions. **Previously published poetry OK. Rejections in 1 day; acceptances can take up to 2 months. Editors comment on rejections "always – as poets ourselves, we learned to hate form rejections."** They also publish a line of poetry postcards.

THE BAD HENRY REVIEW; 44 Press (II), Box 150045, Van Brunt Station, Brooklyn NY 11215-0001, founded 1981, poetry editors Evelyn Horowitz, Michael Malinowitz and Mary du Passage. They have recently published poetry by John Ashbery, Gilbert Sorrentino, Stephen Sandy and William Mathews. Press run is 500-1,000 for 200 subscriptions of which 15 are for libraries; 200-300 for shelf sales. *The Bad Henry Review* is an annual publishing quality poetry, 64 pp., digest-sized. **Sample: $4.** Per issue $6; subscription $12/2 issues. **Pays 1 copy with half price discount for contributors. Submit no more than 5 poems, include SASE. No simultaneous submissions. No previously published poems unless advised. Rarely comments on rejected MSS.** The editor comments, "We've done one issue of long poems and we are doing an issue on translations in 1993." 44 Press publishes about 1 book of poetry per year.

‡**BANGTAIL (I)**, 3137 W. Paradise Ln., Phoenix AZ 85023, founded 1989, editor William Dudley, appears twice a year. **They want "contemporary poetry of any form and subject, quality in language & imagery, unique presentation & style – Experimental High Energy/Beat Culture/Avant-Garde Poetry."** As a sample the editor selected these lines by Patricia Gentner:

> *New York walkers*
> *move slyly,*
> *corner-eyed glances*
> *catch marauding*
> *yellow drones.*

I have not seen an issue, but the editor describes it as 30 pp., saddle-stapled, digest-sized, offset printed from large type. Press run 250. Subscription: $7. **Sample: $3.50. Pays 1 copy.**

THE BANK STREET PRESS; THE PORT AUTHORITY POETRY REVIEW (V), 24 Bank St., New York NY 10014, phone (212)255-0692, founded 1985, poetry editor Mary Bertschmann. A small group of poets meet at the Bank Street home of Mary Bertschmann and publish their poetry annually in a series of flat-spined paperbacks called *The Port Authority Poetry Review*. Review books of poetry. **Sample $7 including postage and handling.** Please make check payable to Mary Bertschmann. The Bank Street Press also publishes solo collections of poetry. The latest publication (November 1990) is a limited, signed, fine print edition, *Goslings on the Tundra* by Mary York Sampson ($20.00 including postage and handling). A sample poem from that work is "leech craft":

> the round autumn moon
> paving its way across the sky
> showers the woods with gauzy light
> conjures the trees to leak out inner secrets
> as black lacquer over milky ground

‡BANTAM DOUBLEDAY DELL PUBLISHING GROUP (V), 666 Fifth Ave., New York NY 10103, phone (212)765-6500, **accepts MSS only from agents.**

BAPTIST SUNDAY SCHOOL BOARD; LIVING WITH PRESCHOOLERS; LIVING WITH CHILDREN; LIVING WITH TEENAGERS; HOME LIFE (IV-Religious); MATURE LIVING (IV-Religious, senior citizen), 127 Ninth Ave. N., Nashville TN 37234, the publishing agency for Southern Baptists. "We publish magazines, monthlies, quarterlies, books, filmstrips, films, church supplies, etc., for Southern Baptist churches." **Query with samples.** For most of their publications they want "**inspirational and/ or religious poetry. No 'word pictures'. We want poetry with a message to inspire, uplift, motivate, amuse. No longer than 24 lines,**" typed, double-spaced, no simultaneous submissions. Reports within 60 days, rate of pay figured on number of lines submitted. The biggest of the monthlies is *Home Life*, which began in 1947. Circulation 750,000; 20,000 subscriptions—a magazine-sized 60+ pp., saddle-stapled slick magazine, illustrated (no ads). Its poetry editors, Charlie Warren and Mary Paschall Darby, say they want "**religious poetry; treating marriage, family life and life in general from a Christian perspective. We rarely publish anything of more than 25 lines.**" Sample: $1 to authors with SASE! Submit no more than 6 poems at a time. "**Prefer original, but photocopy and dot-matrix acceptable. Query unnecessary.**" Send SASE for guidelines. Reports in 6-8 weeks, pays $15-24. *Mature Living: A Christian Magazine for Senior Adults*, founded in 1977, is a monthly mass circulation (330,000) magazine providing "leisure reading for senior adults. All material used is compatible with a Christian lifestyle." The poetry they use is of Christian content, inspirational, about "nature/God," rhymed, 8-24 lines. Assistant editor Judy Pregel says, "We dislike free-verse or poems where a word is dragged in just to piece out a meter." Apparently you do not have to be a senior citizen to submit. The editor selected "Coloring Book" by Marion Schoeberlein:

> Spring is a new green meadow—
> A murmuring brook
> Spring is God filling in
> A coloring book!

Mature Living is magazine-sized, 52 pp., saddle-stapled, using large print on pulp stock, glossy paper cover, with color and b/w art. They "receive hundreds" of poems per year, use about 125-150. Most of their distribution is through churches who buy the magazine in bulk for their senior adult members. **For sample, send 9×12" self-addressed envelope and 85¢ postage. Pays $5-25. Reports in 6-8 weeks, but there might be a 3 year delay before publication.**

THE BASSETTOWN REVIEW (II), 72 Railroad St., Uniontown PA 15401, founded 1988, poetry editor George Swaney, is a literary annual. "No more silly listings for us. Suffice to say, **submit up to six poems, any subject, any style. Simultaneous submissions OK.**" They have published poetry by Peter Blair, Robert Cooperman, Arthur Winfield Knight and Michael Wurster. As a sample the editor has selected these lines from "A Silly Listing in **1991 Poet's Market**":

> No free translations of "Wooly Bully"
> —("Hadda whole Hannah")?—or
> anything beginning with a line
> by Pindar in boldface or italics, etc. . . .

It is tabloid format, 36 pp. with photos, professionally printed. *TBR* is distributed free to libraries and bookstores in Southwest Pennsylvania. **No samples ("We run out a week after it's printed") but send SASE for guidelines and 2 photoreduced pages from current issue. Pays 3 copies.**

Reviews books of poetry. The editor adds, "George Herbert said it best: 'Be as good as Donald Hall; take as long as you wish.' "

BAY AREA POETS COALITION (BAPC); POETALK (I), P.O. Box 11435, Berkeley CA 94701-2435, phone (415)236-7949, founded 1974, poetry editor Carter McKenzie. Coalition sends monthly poetry letter, *Poetalk*, to over 400 people. They publish annual anthology (12th–155 pp., out in 1991), giving one page to each member of BAPC who has had work published in *Poetalk* during the prior year. *Poetalk* publishes 50-60 poets in each issue. BAPC has 170 members, 80 subscribers, but *Poetalk* is open to all. **Predictable rhyme only if clever vocabulary. Each poem 3×4″ maximum. One poem from each new submitter will usually be printed. Typewritten, single-spaced OK. Simultaneous and previously published work OK. All subject matter should be in good taste. Poems appear on 3 legal-size pages. Send 4 poems every 6 months only. Response time 2 weeks-4 months. You'll get a copy of *Poetalk* in which your work appears. Write (with SASE) for 2 months' free copies.** Membership: $12 for 12 months' *Poetalk*, copy of anthology and other privileges if you live in the Bay Area. The editor chose these sample lines by Delbert Campbell:

> *By the sun-baked mall*
> *A wide sombrero slumbers*
> *On folded elbows.*

BAPC holds monthly readings, contests, etc.; has mailing list open to local members; a PA system members may use for a small fee. People from 27 states other than California and 8 countries have contributed to *Poetalk* or entered their 11th annual contest.

BAY WINDOWS (IV-Gay/lesbian), 1523 Washington St., Boston MA 02118, FAX 617-266-5973, founded 1983, poetry editors Rudy Kikel and Patricia A. Roth. *Bay Windows* is a weekly gay and lesbian newspaper published for the New England community, regularly using **"short poems of interest to lesbians and gay men. Poetry that is 'experiential' seems to have a good chance with us, but we don't want poetry that just 'tells it like it is.' Our readership doesn't read poetry all the time. A primary consideration is giving** *pleasure*. **We'll overlook the poem's (and the poet's) tendency not to be informed by the latest poetic theory, if it** *does* **this: pleases. Pleases, in particular, by articulating common gay or lesbian experience, and by doing that with some attention to form. I've found that a lot of our choices were made because of a strong image strand. Humor is** *always* **welcome—and hard to provide with craft. Obliquity, obscurity? Probably not for us. We won't presume on our audience."** They have recently published poetry by Randy Brieger, Robert Friend, Katherine Kotik, M.S. Montgomery, Sheila Harkens Rosencrans and Jill Spisak. As a sample Rudy Kikel picked these lines from "Icarus Flies Air France" by Lawrence Kinsman:

> *My hands tremble at the thought of you,*
> *eating miniature Coq au Vin, reading a book,*
> *chatting with a male model who will ask for your*
> *phone number, nothing beneath you but currents of*
> *treacherous air. Oh, my Icarus, why can't we sail to*
> *La Havre on the Mauretania as the Vanderbilts and the*
> *Carnegies did?*

"We try to run four poems (two by lesbians, two by gay men) each month," print run 13,000, 700 subscriptions of which 15 are libraries. Subscription: $35; per issue: 50¢. They receive about 1,000 submissions per year, use 1 in 20, have a 3 month backlog. **Sample: $1 postpaid. Submit 3-5 poems, "5-25 lines are ideal; include short biographical blurb." Poems by gay males should be sent care of Rudy Kikel,** *Bay Windows*, **at the address above; by lesbians, care of Patricia A. Roth % Schwartz, 11 Belmont Ave., Somerville MA 02143. Reports in 4 weeks, pays copies.** Editors "often" comment on rejections. Review books of poetry.

BEAR TRIBE PUBLISHING; WILDFIRE MAGAZINE (IV-Nature, themes, ethnic), P.O. Box 9167, Spokane WA 99209, phone (509)326-6561, founded 1965 (the magazine's former name, *Many Smokes Earth Awareness Magazine*), poetry editor Elisabeth Robinson. The magazine uses **short poetry on topics appropriate to the magazine, such as earth awareness, self-sufficiency, sacred places, native people, etc.** Press run is 10,000 for 6,000 subscriptions of which 5% are libraries, 3,500 shelf sales. Subscription $15. **Sample: $4 postpaid. Send SASE for guidelines.** They have published poetry by Gary Snyder, W. D. Ehrhart, P. J. Brown and Evelyn Eaton. The quarterly devotes 1-2 pp. to poetry each issue. They want a **"positive and constructive viewpoint, no hip or offensive language." Poets published receive 1 year subscription.** Reviews books of poetry. The press publishes books that incorporate Native American poems and songs, but no collections by individuals. They may comment on rejections, "especially on good poetry."

BELLFLOWER PRESS (III, IV-Humor, social issues, women/feminism), Box 87 Dept. WD, Chagrin Falls OH 44022-0087, founded 1974, poetry editor/owner Louise Wazbinski, **publishes poetry books 50% of the time on a subsidized basis.** She wants **"poetry that educates the feelings; poetry that**

crystallizes the attitudes held by our society; poetry that is laid out in rhythmical lines, i.e., *Good Poetry.*" They have recently published poetry by Judy Kronenfeld, from whose poem "Lente, Lente," in her collection **Shadow of Wings**, I selected these sample lines:

> Slowly my father wades into his ripe age.
> His great barrel chest, split and healed again,
> cleaves the pool . . .
> I remember when he took the cold air in,
> and threw his coat wide.

Reports in 2-4 weeks on queries, 6-8 weeks on MSS. "Contract depends upon subvention by author, usually 50%. Often the author will subsidize a small percentage and receive books as payment. In other cases, there is no subsidy and the author receives a royalty based on the specific arrangements made at the time of agreement."

"Since we are committed to publishing material that we feel demonstrates that life is meaningful and worth living, we look for illustrations that are well conceived and humanely executed," says Bellowing Ark editor Robert R. Ward. *"This particular drawing we felt emanated a sense of peace we found very appealing."* The illustrator is Carolyn A. Gardner of Newport News, Virginia, who began submitting her work to Bellowing Ark four years ago, when she was a high school student.

BELLOWING ARK PRESS; BELLOWING ARK (II), P.O. Box 45637, Seattle WA 98145, phone (206)545-8302, founded 1984, editor Robert R. Ward. *Bellowing Ark* is a bimonthly literary tabloid that **"publishes only poetry which demonstrates in some way the proposition that existence has meaning or, to put it another way, that life is worth living. We have no strictures as to length, form or style; only that the work we publish is to our judgment life-affirming."** They do not want **"academic poetry, in any of its manifold forms."** Poets recently published include Natalie Reciputi, John Elrod, Ray Mizer and Mark Allan Johnson. As a sample the editor selected "Contemplation on the 20th Anniversary of the Moonshot; July 20, 1989" by Bethany Reid:

> Above these dim, suburban lights
>
> The Universe unfolds, whole,
> Its precious molecular structures
> Recycling, recombining, invisible
> Wheels of science. And the spirit also,
>
> Rising unnoticed perhaps
> Like the moon over sleeping children

The paper is tabloid-sized, 24 pp. printed on electrobright stock with b/w photos and line drawings. Circulation is 1,000, of which 200+ are subscriptions and 600+ are sold on newsstands. Price is $2/issue, subscription is $12/year. **Sample: $2 postpaid. Pay is 2 copies.** The editors say, **"absolutely *no* simultaneous submissions, prefer not to see dot-matrix or photocopy."** They reply to submissions in 2-6 weeks and publish within the next 1 or 2 issues. Occasionally they will criticize a MS if it seems to "display potential to become the kind of work we want." Reviews books of poetry. Bellowing Ark Press publishes collections of poetry by invitation only.

BELL'S LETTERS POET (I), P.O. Box 2187, Gulfport MS 39505, founded 1956 as *Writer's Almanac*, 1958 as *Thunderhead for Writers*, 1966 as *Bell's Letters*, publisher and editor Jim Bell, is a quarterly which **you must buy ($3 per issue, $12 subscription) to be included.** The editor says "most fall in love with its family-like ties," and judging by the many letters from readers, I would judge that to be the case. **Though there is no payment for poetry accepted, many patrons send awards of $5-20 to the poets whose work they especially like. Subscription "guarantees them a byline each issue." Poems are "12-16 lines in good taste."** They have recently published poetry by David Collins, Vic Chapman, Carrie Quick and Patricia Johnson. As a sample of the spirit of *BL* poetry the editor chose these lines by Louis Bussolati:
> Wind murmurs through pine crowns
> clouds of insects hum in sunbeams
> and I stop like the fallen log before me
> devoid of old life, a host of the new

It is digest-sized, 72 pp., offset from typescript on plain bond paper (including cover). **Sample: $3 postpaid. Send SASE for guidelines. MS may be typed or even hand-written. No simultaneous submissions.** Previously published poems OK "if cleared with prior publisher." Reports in 10 days. Acceptance of poems by subscribers go immediately into the next issue. "Our publication dates fall quarterly on the spring and autumn equinox and winter and summer solstice. Deadline for poetry submissions is 30 days prior to publication." "50 BL Classics" is a competition in each issue. Readers are asked to vote on their favorite poems, and the winners are announced in the next issue, along with awards sent them by patrons.

THE BELOIT POETRY JOURNAL (II), Box 154, RFD 2, Ellsworth ME 04605, phone (207)667-5598, founded 1950, editor Marion K. Stocking, a well-known, long-standing quarterly of quality poetry and reviews. **"We publish the best poems we receive, without bias as to length, school, subject or form.** It is our hope to discover the growing tip of poetry and to introduce new poets alongside established writers. We publish occasional chapbooks on special themes to diversify our offerings." They want **"fresh, imaginative poetry, with a distinctive voice. We tend to prefer poems that make the reader share an experience rather than just read about it, and these we keep for up to 3 months,** circulating them among our readers, and continuing to winnow out the best. At the quarterly meetings of the Editorial Board we read aloud all the surviving poems and put together an issue of the best we have." They have recently published Bruce Cutler, Hillel Schwartz, Lola Haskins, Albert Goldbarth and Susan Tichy. The editor chose this sample from "Neuroanatomy" by Susan Kolodny:
> The fog over Grizzly Peak,
>   a thick cerebral cortex
> I enter its folds, its sulci and gyri;
>   the canyons beneath me,
> like ventricles; dusk
>   seeps from them like dark fluids.

It's an attractively printed digest-sized, 40 pp. format, with tasteful art on the card covers. **Sample copy: $2, includes guidelines, or SASE for guidelines alone.** They have a circulation of 1,200, 575 subscriptions, of which 325 are libraries. **Submit any time, without query, any legible form, *"No simultaneous submissions."*** (If you send photocopies or carbons, include a note saying the poems are not being submitted elsewhere.) **"Any length of MS, but most poets send what will go in a business envelope for one stamp. Don't send your life work." Payment: 3 copies.** No backlog: **"We clear the desk at each issue."**

‡**THE BENCH PRESS (V)**, 1355 Raintree Dr., Columbia SC 29212, phone (803)781-7232, founded 1985, editor and publisher Warren Slesinger, **considers no unsolicited MSS.**

BENNETT & KITCHEL (IV-Form), P.O. Box 4422, East Lansing MI 48826, phone (517)355-1707, founded 1989, editor William Whallon, publishes 3-4 hardbacks/year of **"poetry of form and meaning. Short pieces with perhaps one or two longer ones. Any subject. No free verse, sestinas or haiku; not much blank verse or slant rhyme."** As a sample of poetry he likes the editor selected these lines by Lord Alfred Douglas:
> And from the great gates of the East,
> With a clang and a brazen blare,
> Forth from the rosy wine and the feast
> Comes the god with the flame-flaked hair.

Bennett & Kitchel recently published a volume of verse for The Society for Creative Anachronism. **Sample postpaid: $6. Reports in 2 weeks. Terms "variable, negotiable." Simultaneous submissions and previously published poems OK if copyright is clear. Minimum volume for a book "might be 750 lines." If a book is accepted, publication within 9 months. Editor comments on submissions "seldom."** He advises, "Read 'Writing a Narrative in Poetry,' *Writer's Digest*, August, 1988."

BERKELEY POETRY REVIEW (II), 700 Eshleman Hall, University of California, Berkeley CA 94720, founded 1973, poetry editor Natacia Apostoles, editor-in-chief Jonathan Brennan, is an annual review "which publishes poems and translations of local as well as national and international interest. We are open to any form or length which knows how to express itself through that form." They have recently published poetry by Federico Garcia Lorca, Thom Gunn, August Kleinzahler, Robert Hass and John Tranter. I have not seen an issue, but the editors describe it as a flat-spined paperback, averaging 150 pp., circulation 500. Subscription: $10/year. **Simultaneous submissions, photocopies, dot-matrix, previously published poems (if not copyrighted) all OK, pays 1 copy.** They also publish books. For book publication **submit 5 sample poems with bio. Include SASE; allow 2-6 months for reply.**

BERKELEY POETS COOPERATIVE (WORKSHOP & PRESS) (II), Box 459, Berkeley CA 94701, founded 1969, poetry editor Charles Entrekin (plus rotating staff), is "a nonprofit organization which offers writers the opportunity to explore, develop and publish their works. Our primary goals are to maintain a free workshop open to writers and to publish outstanding collections of poetry and fiction by individual writers." The *New York Times* has called it **"the oldest and most successful poetry co-operative in the country."** Chapbooks recently published by Linda Watanabe McFerrin and Chitra Divakaruni. Charles Entrekin says he prefers **"modern imagist—open to all kinds, but we publish very little rhyme."** These sample lines are by Bruce Hawkins:
> *The sandtormented stingray lies*
> *up near the logline,*
> *a smouldering necktie,*
> *a suffering piece of geometry.*

They publish two 64 pp. chapbooks by individuals each year, for which the poets receive 50% of the profit and 20 copies. **You can order a sample book for $3.** Criticism sometimes provided on rejected MSS. Poets elsewhere might consider BPWP as a model for forming similar organizations.

‡BETWEEN THE LINES BOOK PUBLISHERS (IV-Political), Suite 203, 394 Euclid Ave., Toronto, Ontario M6G 2S9 Canada, founded 1977, managing editor Ian Rashid. **"We publish political non-fiction and none of our books are exclusively collections of poetry. We have published books that use poetry as an annex to a larger text.** Forthcoming titles that will include poetry are: **Notes from the Margin** by Marlene Nourbese Philip and **Living with AIDS** by Michael Lynch with Tom Hastings." As a sample the editor selected these lines from **Crumbs** by Claudia Lars:
> *I saw the masked men*
> *throwing truth into a well.*
> *When I began to weep for it*
> *I found it everywhere.*

"No strict rules about MSS, but we suggest that writers should not submit entire MSS. A sampling with a cover letter is preferable. A query is advised, but please remember that Canada is not yet an American state; US stamps mean nothing here. We will not respond without IRCs enclosed. If a project seems viable it is presented to our editorial collective which meets monthly. **Writers can expect a report within 2-4 months after we receive their submissions. We try and provide comments whenever possible."** They give no indication of payment policy. The editor says, "Between the Lines disseminates information around social change issues specific to Canada and/or the Third World. We value work that is analytical, accessible, sophisticated and, most importantly, political."

BEYOND (IV-Science fiction/fantasy), P.O. Box 136, New York NY 10024, phone (212)874-5914, founded 1985, editor Shirley Winston, a quarterly magazine of **science fiction and fantasy.** For poetry, the editor wants **"anything short of a major epic"** on those themes. She does not often use anything longer than 120 lines. *Beyond* does not print material in the horror genre. She has recently published poetry by Dan Crawford and Genevieve Stephens, from whose "Under a Lunar Canopy" she chose the following lines as a sample:
> *Under a lunar canopy*
> *One day*
> *Will there be*
> *A house?*

A yard?
A child at play?
The magazine-sized *Beyond* is 54 pp., saddle-stapled, offset from letter-quality word processor printout, with b/w drawings to illustrate the pieces and a b/w drawing on the cover. Circulation is 200. Price per issue is $5, subscription $17/year. **Sample available for $5 postpaid. Pay is 3¢/ line plus 1 copy. Submissions "must be legible (dot-matrix is OK if dark enough)." Reporting time is 3 months. The editor "always" provides criticism on rejected MSS.**

BILINGUAL REVIEW PRESS; BILINGUAL REVIEW/REVISTA BILINGÜE (IV-Ethnic, bilingual), Hispanic Research Center, Arizona State University, Tempe AZ 85287, phone (602)965-3867, journal founded 1974, press in 1976. Managing editor Karen Van Hooft says they are "a small-press publisher of U.S. Hispanic creative literature and of a journal containing poetry and short fiction in addition to scholarship." The journal contains some poetry in each issue; they also publish flat-spined paperback collections of poetry. **"We publish poetry by and/or about U.S. Hispanics and U.S. Hispanic themes. We do not publish translations in our journal or literature about the experiences of Anglo Americans in Latin America. We have published a couple of poetry volumes in bilingual format (Spanish/English) of important Mexican poets."** They have recently published poetry by Elías Miguel Muñoz, Marjorie Agosín, Martín Espada, Demetria Martínez and Pablo Medina. I have not seen the journal, which appears 3 times a year, but the editor says it is 7×10", 96 pp. flat-spined, offset, with 2-color cover. They use less than 10% of hundreds of submissions received each year. Press run is 1,000 for 850+ subscriptions. Subscriptions are $16 for individuals, $26 for institutions. **Sample: $6 individuals/$9 institutions postpaid. Pays 2 copies. Submit "2 copies, including ribbon original if possible, with loose stamps for return postage. For book submissions, send 4-5 sample poems, bio, publications." Pays $100 advance, 10% royalties and 10 copies.** Reviews books of U.S. Hispanic poetry only.

BIRD WATCHER'S DIGEST (IV-Nature), P.O. Box 110, Marietta OH 45750, founded 1978, editor Mary Beacom Bowers, is a specialized but promising market for **poems of "true literary merit" in which birds figure in some way, at least by allusion. 2-3 poems are used in each bimonthly issue and earn $10/poem.** Some poets who have appeared there recently include Susan Rea, Nancy G. Westerfield, Lois Barkett and William D. Barney. I liked these lines from David Hopes' "The Kingdom of the Birds," describing cranes:
pointed upward, flight a repose
between two agonies, striving and beating
as though together all might lift
the swamp up rung by rung into the sky.
"Preferred: no more than 20 lines, 40 spaces, no more than 3 poems at a time, no queries." Sample postpaid: $3.50. Reports in 2 months. They have up to a year's backlog and use 12-20 of the approximately 500 poems received each year.

BIRMINGHAM POETRY REVIEW (II, IV-Translations), English Department, University of Alabama at Birmingham, Birmingham AL 35294, phone (205)934-8573, founded 1988, editor Robert Collins, associate editor Randy Blythe. Appears twice a year using poetry of **"any style, form, length or subject. We are biased toward exploring the cutting edge of contemporary poetry. Style is secondary to the energy, the *fire* the poem possesses. We don't want poetry with cliché-bound, worn-out language."** Recently published poetry by Blumenthal, Carlson, Frost, Linda, Glaser, Harrod, Mueller, Horne and Jaeger. They describe their magazine as 50 pp., 6×9", offset, with b/w cover. Their press run is 600 for Fall Issue, 500 for Spring Issue, 275 subscriptions. Subscription: $3. **Sample: $2 postpaid. Guidelines available for SASE. Pays 2 copies and one-year subscription. Submit 3-5 poems, "no more. No cover letters. We are impressed by good writing; we are unimpressed by publication credits. It should go without saying, but we receive more and more manuscripts with insufficient return postage. If it costs you forty-five cents to mail your manuscript, it will cost us that much to return it if it is rejected. Hereafter, manuscripts with insufficient return postage will be discarded." No simultaneous submissions, and previously published poems only if they are translations. Reports in 1-3 months.** Editor sometimes comments on rejections. He says, "Advice to beginners: Read as much good contemporary poetry, national and international, as you can get your hands on. Then be persistent in finding your own voice."

BISHOP PUBLISHING CO. (IV-Themes), 2131 Trimble Way, Sacramento CA 95825, professor Roland Dickison, is a "small press publisher of **folklore in paperbacks, including contemporary** and out-of-print." They want to see **"American folk poetry, either current or historical. No modern free verse.** Folk poetry is usually anonymous."

BITS PRESS (III, IV-Humor), English Dept., Case Western Reserve University, Cleveland OH 44106, phone (216)795-2810, founded 1974, poetry editor Robert Wallace. **"Bits Press is devoted to poetry. We publish chapbooks (and sometimes limited editions) by young as well as well-known poets. Our**

main attention at present is given to light verse and funny poems." The chapbooks are distinguished by elegant but inexpensive format. They have published chapbooks by David R. Slavitt, George Starbuck and Margaret Lally. These sample lines are from Richard Wilbur's **Some Atrocities**:

> If a sheepdog ate a cantaloupe,
> Would it make him frisk like an antelope?
> Would he feel all pleased and jolly?
> Or would he be a Melon Collie?

The few chapbooks they publish are mostly solicited. Send $2 for a sample or two of the chapbooks; payment to poet in copies (10% + of run). Wallace sometimes offers criticism with rejections.

BLACK AMERICAN LITERATURE FORUM (IV-Ethnic), Dept. of English, Indiana State University, Terre Haute IN 47809, founded 1967 (as *Negro American Literature Forum*), poetry editors Sterling Plumpp, Thadious M. Davis and Pinkie Gordon Lane, is a "magazine primarily devoted to the analysis of Afro-American literature, although one issue per year focuses on poetry by black Americans." No specifications as to form, length, style, subject matter or purpose. They have recently published poems by Amiri Baraka, Gwendolyn Brooks, Leon Forrest, Jan Carew, Clarence Major, Dudley Randall and Owen Dodson. As a sample I selected the opening lines of "on the line (with 11 million unemployed 9/3/82)" by Mel Donalson:

> and still they wait
> no less in need than the generation before
> their names altered to percentage rates
> their faces mere decimal points along economic indicators

Forum is 6 × 9", 200 pp. with photo on the cover. Individual subscriptions: $20 USA, $25 foreign. They receive about 500 submissions per year, use 50. Sample: $8.50 postpaid. **Submit maximum of 6 poems to editor Joe Weixlmann. Pays in copies. Reports in 3-4 months. Send SASE for guidelines. The editors sometimes comment on rejections.**

‡**BLACK APPLE (II, IV-Regional, translations)**, % Lethbridge Community College, 3000 College Dr. South, Lethbridge, Alberta T1K 1L6 Canada, phone (403)320-3420, founded 1990, managing editor Richard Stevenson, appears twice a year using "all styles [modern or post-modern, formal metrical or free verse] provided the work is accessible, has something of value to say and displays a knowledge of craft and the tradition. We believe poets should extend, not abort, tradition and craft. No doggerel, sentimental greeting card verses or juvenile poetry, unless required by contest in the future. Also, no sexism, racism, gratuitous violence or (prurient) self-indulgence, no solopsistic navel-gazing Romanticism either; work should acknowledge socio-political realities of our time and look outward to the body politic as well as inward to self or soul." They have recently published poetry by Sid Marty, Susan Musgrave, Bert Almon and Claire Harris. As a sample the editor selected these lines from "Sacrifice" by Yvonne Trainer:

> We were talking about confusion
> The Doctor said "Brain"
> I said "Word"
> The Doctor said "Tumor"

It is magazine-sized, saddle-stapled, desktop-produced. "A teaching vehicle designed to showcase the best contemporary literature available. International in focus, but largely Canadian. Will take translations, but onus is on the translator to secure permissions." They accept less than 15% of 250-500 MSS received per year. Press run 500. Subscription: $10. **Sample: $5 postpaid. Send SASE for guidelines. Pays 2 copies. "Best to submit between September and April; we are quicker during the Jan.-April period when the magazine workshop is in session and there are more hands-on-deck." Reports in 3-8 weeks. Editor often comments on rejections, as time permits.** "We reject better than 85% of the material we receive, largely because prospective contributors send us descriptive, demotic prose arbitrarily shred and diced. Know what a line is and make full use of the resources of poetry (poetic devices, metaphor, mouth music). Poetry has to contain ideas as well as personal feelings. Think first of your audience: *other* intelligent readers of contemporary poetry."

 The double dagger before a listing indicates that the listing is new in this edition. New markets are often the most receptive to submissions.

BLACK BEAR PUBLICATIONS; BLACK BEAR REVIEW; POETS ELEVEN . . . AUDIBLE (II, IV-Political, social), 1916 Lincoln St., Croydon PA 19021-8026, phone (215)788-3543, founded 1984, poetry and art editor Ave Jeanne, review and audio editor Ron Zettlemoyer. *Black Bear Review* is a semiannual international literary and fine arts magazine that also publishes chapbooks and holds an annual poetry competition. Recent poets published in *BBR* include Walt Phillips, Gina Bergamino, Robert Nagler, Joe Salerno, Richard Wilmarth and Sean Thomas Dougherty. *Poets Eleven . . . Audible* has released poetry on tape by A. D. Winans, Tony Moffeit, Kevin Zepper and Mike Maggio. As a sample from *BBR*, the editor has selected the poem "Oatmeal Shirt" by Joy Oestreicher:

> You can wear your oatmeal
> Like you do a good shirt
> It's even good for your skin
> But if it dries that way
> Beauty masks in layers upon you
> They'll be more to
>   regaining your freedom
> Than just cracking you out.

Circulation of *BBR* is 500, of which 300 are subscriptions; 15 libraries. Price: $4/issue; subscription $8. Catalog is available for SASE. The magazine is perfect-bound, digest-sized, 64 pp., offset from typed copy on white stock, with line drawings, collages and woodcuts. The editors explain that *Poets Eleven . . . Audible* was started for accommodation of longer poems for the reader to take part in poetry as a listener; **the author may submit up to 10 minutes of original poetry. SASE for return of your tape; sample copies available for $4.50 postpaid. Contributor receives 25% royalties. "We like well crafted poetry that mirrors real life—void of camouflage, energetic poetry, avant-garde, free verse and haiku which relate to the world today. We seldom publish the beginner, but will assist when time allows. No traditional poetry is used. The underlying theme of *BBR* is social and political, but the review is interested also in environmental, war/ peace, ecological and minorities themes."** Submissions are reported on in 2 weeks, publication is in 6-12 months, any number of poems may be submitted, one to a page, photocopies are OK but they prefer not to read dot-matrix. They publish two chapbooks per year. **Chapbook series requires a reading fee of $5, samples and cover letter.** For book publication, they would prefer that *"BBR* has published the poet and is familiar with his/her work, but we will read anyone who thinks they have something to say." **Queries are answered in 2 weeks, MSS in 2; simultaneous submissions are not considered. "Submissions without SASE will be trashed." A sample of** *BBR*: **$4 postpaid; back copies when available are $3 postpaid. Guidelines available for SASE.** "We appreciate a friendly, brief cover letter. Tell us about the poet; omit degrees or any other pretentious dribble. All submissions are handled with objectivity and quite often rejected material is directed to another market. If you've not been published before—mention it. We are always interested in aiding those who support small press. We frequently suggest poets keep up with **Poet's Market** and read the listings and reviews in issues of *Black Bear*. Most recent issues of *BBR* include extensive reviews on small press markets—current releases of chapbooks and the latest literary magazines. We make an effort to keep our readers informed and on top of the small press scene. Camera-ready ads are printed free of charge as a support to small press publishers. We do suggest reading issues before submitting to absorb the flavor and save on wasted postage. Send your best! Our yearly poetry competition offers cash awards to poets." Annual deadline is November 1. Guidelines are available for a SASE.

‡BLACK BOOKS BULLETIN; THIRD WORLD PRESS (IV-Ethnic), 7524 S. Cottage Grove Ave., Chicago IL 60619, phone (312)651-0700. *BBB* is an annual about **"Black literature and current issues facing the African-American community using Afro-centric poetry, style open."** They have recently published poetry by Gwendolyn Brooks, Kalamu ya Salaam and Estella Conwill Majozo. Focus is on book reviews.

BLACK BUZZARD PRESS; BLACK BUZZARD REVIEW; VISIONS—INTERNATIONAL, THE WORLD JOURNAL; THE BLACK BUZZARD ILLUSTRATED POETRY CHAPBOOK SERIES (II, IV-Translations), 1110 Seaton Lane, Falls Church VA 22046, founded 1979, poetry editor Bradley R. Strahan, associate editor Shirley G. Sullivan. "We are an independent nonsubsidized press dedicated to publishing fine accessible poetry and translation (particularly from lesser known languages such as Armenian, Gaelic, Urdu, Vietnamese, etc.) accompanied by original illustrations of high quality in an attractive format. **We want to see work that is carefully crafted and exciting work that transfigures everyday experience or gives us a taste of something totally new; in all styles except concrete and typographical 'poems.' Nothing purely sentimental. No self-indulgent breast beating. No sadism, sexism or bigotry. No unemotional pap. No copies of Robert Service or the like. Usually under 100 lines but will consider longer."** They have published poetry by Ted Hughes, Marilyn Hacker, James Dickey, Allen Ginsberg and Marge Piercy; and though he protests that "no 4 lines can possibly do even minimal justice to our taste

or interest!" Bradley Strahan offers this 4 line poem, "Landscape," by Katherine Smith Manceron:
The wind coalesces. Suddenly, you have a name and a home.
This is your childhood.
Look closer. If you don't know, ask yourself
Who Loved this Light? This canvas filled with boats, rivers, refusals.
Visions, a digest-sized, saddle-stapled magazine finely printed on high-quality paper, appears 3 times a year, uses 56 pages of poetry in each issue. Circulation 750 with 300 subscriptions of which 50 are libraries, **sample: $3.50 postpaid. Current issue: $4.50.** They receive *well* over a thousand submissions each year and use 140, have a 3-18 month backlog. *Black Buzzard Review* is a "more or less annual informal journal, dedicated mostly to North American poets and entirely to original English-language poems. We are *letting it all hang out* here, unlike the approach of our prestigious international journal *Visions*, and taking a more wide-open stance on what we accept (including the slightly outrageous)." **Sample of *BBR:* $2.50 plus $1 postage. Current issue: $3.50 plus $1 postage.** It is magazine-sized, 36 pp., side-stapled, with matte card cover. **"Poems must be readable (not faded, light photocopy or smudged) and *not* handwritten. We resent having to pay postage due, so use adequate postage! No more than 8 pages, please." Reports in 3 days—3 weeks, pays in copies or $5-10** "if we get a grant. *Visions* is international in both scope and content, publishing poets from all over the world and having readers in 48+ US states, Canada and 24 other foreign countries." **To submit for the chapbook series, send samples (5-10 poems) and a *brief* cover letter "pertinent to artistic accomplishments." Reports in 3 days—3 weeks, pays in copies, usually provides criticism. Send $4 for sample chapbook.** Bradley Strahan adds that in *Visions* "We sometimes publish helpful advice about 'getting published' and the art and craft of poetry, and often discuss poets and the world of poetry on our editorial page."

BLACK FLY REVIEW (II), University of Maine, Fort Kent ME 04743, phone (207)834-3162, ext. 118, founded 1980, editors Roland Burns and Wendy Kindred. **"We want poetry with strong, sensory images that evoke a sense of experience, place, person; poetry that generates ideas; no overtly philosophical poetry, bad poetry."** They have recently published poetry by Walter McDonald, John Tagliabue, Terry Plunkett and Constance Hunting. As a sample the editors selected these lines (poet unidentified):
We listen to hail waste itself
on hardscrabble shale and cactus,
rain rushing in gullies to the creekbed.
Cramped in a cave
we share with snakes and scorpions
The annual is digest-sized, 56 pp., using woodcuts and prints by Wendy Kindred, professionally printed in small type on tinted, heavy stock with matte card cover with art. They accept 40-50 of 500-600 submissions per year. Press run of 700-1,000 for 50 subscriptions of which 30 are libraries, and 500 shelf sales. **Sample: $2 postpaid. Send SASE for guidelines. Pays 5 copies. No simultaneous submissions or previously published poems. Reports in 6 months.** Roland Burns advises, "The publishing situation for poets is good and getting better. There are more good poets writing in America than at any other time. The essence of poetry is the image that provides sensory focus and that generates a sense of experience, place, persons, emotions, ideas."

BLACK MOUNTAIN REVIEW; LORIEN HOUSE (IV-Themes), P.O. Box 1112, Black Mountain NC 28711-1112, phone (704)669-6211, founded 1969, editor David A. Wilson, is a small press publishing many books under the Lorien House imprint (poetry on a subsidy basis) and the annual *Black Mountain Review*. They want **poetry with "quality form/construction—a full thought, specifically fitting the theme, 16-80 lines. No blatant sex, violence, horror."** As a sample, the editor selected these lines from "Between Wakefulness and Sleep" by Susan Sheppard in *BMR #6* "on Edgar Allan Poe":
Wind comes knocking.
The room is cold. Tossed on the narrow cot
is the grey military coat smoothed into
the shape of a woman. Poe shuts his eyes
to wrestle with the festering arms of the dream.
BMR is digest-sized, saddle-stapled, 44 pp. with matte card cover, photocopied from typescript. The issue I saw was printed in blue ink. Press run "about 300" of which they sell about 200. They accept 1-5 poems of about 200 received per year. **Sample postpaid: $3.75. Send SASE for guidelines. Pays 2 copies plus $5 for poems. Previously published poetry OK. Reports in a few days.** Reviews books of poetry when an issue has room—usually 3-6 books. **Query regarding subsidized book publication. Editor comments on submissions "occasionally,"** and he offers **"full analysis and marketing help"** for $1/typed page of poetry. He says, "*Please* send for the current theme. Do *not* send general poetry. Research the theme and give me a well-constructed

work which reflects the theme—any style of poem. I demand quality . . . and want to see your best efforts."

BLACK RIVER REVIEW; STONE ROLLER PRESS (II, IV-Translations), 855 Mildred Ave., Lorain OH 44052-1213, phone (216)244-9654, founded 1985, poetry editor Michael Waldecki, editorial contact Kaye Coller, is a literary annual using **"contemporary poetry, any style, form and subject matter, 50 line maximum (usually), poetry with innovation, craftsmanship and a sense of excitement and/or depth of emotion. Do *not* want Helen Steiner Rice, greeting card verse, poetry that mistakes stilted, false or formulaic diction for intense expression of feeling."** They have recently published poetry by James Margorian, Adrian Louis, Christopher Franke, Catherine Hammond, Sylvia Foley and Leslie Leyland Fields. The editor selected these lines from "Drought" by Stephen R. Roberts:

> *The reptilian trunk of a pine crawls up*
> *to needles as loose as an old man's teeth.*
> *There is a fear of frictions.*
> *Poison ivy slumbers in green smiles,*
> *and the crow's harsh voice*
> *could spark the woodpile.*
> *Everything is burned and older.*
> *Children are telling children,*
> *four more weeks and we all die.*

The magazine-sized annual is photocopied from typescript on quality stock, saddle-stapled with matte card cover with art, about 60 pp., using ads, circulation 400 (sold in college bookstore). **Sample: $3 (backcopy); $3.50 (current issue); $6 (two copies of any issue) postpaid. Pays 1 copy. Submit between January and May 1, limit of 10, photocopy OK, no simultaneous submissions. Will consider previously published if acknowledged. Send SASE for guidelines. Editor may comment on submissions.** Reviews books of poetry. Kaye Coller comments, "We want strong poems that show a depth of vision beyond the commonplace. We don't care if a poet is well-known or not, but we don't publish amateurs. An amateur is not necessarily a new poet, but one who doesn't believe in revision, tends to be preachy, writes sentimental slush, tells the reader what to think and/or concludes the poem with an explanation in case the reader didn't get the point. If we think we can use one or more of a poet's poems, we keep them until the final choices are made in June; otherwise, we send them back as soon as possible. Follow the MS mechanics in **Poet's Market. We are also looking for poems written in Spanish. If selected, they will be published with English translation by either the poet or one of our staff."**

THE BLACK SCHOLAR; THE BLACK SCHOLAR PRESS (IV-Ethnic), P.O. Box 2869, Oakland CA 94609, founded 1969, publisher Robert Chrisman, uses **poetry "relating to/from/of the black American and other 'Third World' experience."** The bimonthly magazine is basically scholarly and research-oriented. They have published poetry by Ntozake Shange, Jayne Cortez, Andrew Salkey and D. L. Smith. As a sample the editor selected these lines from "Tata on the Death of Don Pablo" by Nancy Morejan:

> *your set mouth*
> *pausing like a great bird*
> *over the plain, speaks:*

I have not seen a copy, but the editor says it is 64 pp., 7×10", with 10,000 subscribers of which 60% are libraries, 15% shelf sales. Single copy $5; subscription $30. **Sample back issue: $6 prepaid. Send SASE for guidelines. Pays 10 copies and subscription. Enclose "letter & bio or curriculum vita, SASE, phone number, no originals."** Reviews books of poetry. They also publish 1-2 books a year, average 100 pp., flat-spined. **Send query letter.** For sample books, send 8½×11" SASE for catalog, average cost $10.95 including postage and handling. "We only publish one issue every year containing poetry. Please be advised—it is against our policy to discuss submissions via telephone. Also, we get a lot of MSS, but read *every single one*, thus patience is appreciated."

BLACK SPARROW PRESS (III), 24 Tenth St., Santa Rosa CA 95401, phone (707)579-4011, founded 1966, assistant to the publisher Julie Curtiss Voss, publishes poetry, fiction, literary criticism and bibliography in flat-spined paperbacks, hardcovers and deluxe/limited editions (hardback). "We do not publish chapbooks. Our books are 150 pp. or longer." They have recently published poetry by Tom Clark, Wanda Coleman, Robert Kelly, Diane Wakoski, John Weiners and Edward Dorn. As a sample the editor selected these lines by Charles Bukowski:

> *It's not the large things that send a man to the madhouse . . .*
> *No, It's the continuing of small tragedies*
> *that send a man to the madhouse . . .*
> *Not the death of his love*

but the shoelace that snaps
with no time left . . .
Reports in 60 days. Pays 10% minimum royalties plus author's copies.

‡BLACK TAPE PRESS (II), P.O. Box 14841, Long Beach CA 90803, founded 1989, editors Glenn Bach and Stephanie Bray, appears 2-3 times a year, using **"eclectic" poetry, "no high school or Hallmark."** They have recently published poetry by Michael C. Ford, Cheri D. Gibson and Gerald Locklin. As a sample the editor selected these lines from "The Mouth of Her Body" by Andrew Demcak:
He has convinced her,
she is not the space
her flesh fills.
He wrapped her up
in laws like chains.
BTP is 50-60 pp., digest-sized, photocopied from photoreduced typescript with matte card b/w cover, has a press run of 150. Subscription: $10. **Sample: $4 postpaid. Pays 1 copy. Reports within 1 month.** Editor Glenn Bach advises, "Write a lot, read at many open readings, write more, forget about the big shots and send your poems to small and beginning magazines. Wallpaper your house with acceptances not rejections."

BLACK TIE PRESS (III), P.O. Box 440004, Houston TX 77244-0004, phone (713)789-5119, founded 1986, publisher and editor Peter Gravis. "Black Tie Press is committed to publishing innovative, distinctive and engaging writing. We publish books; we are not a magazine or literary journal. We are not like the major Eastern presses, university presses or other small presses in poetic disposition. To get a feel for our publishing attitude, we urge you to buy one or more of our publications before submitting." **Sample postpaid: $7.** He is **"only interested in imaginative, provocative, at risk writing.** *No rhyme."* Recently published poets: Harry Burrus, Guy Beining, Sekou Karanja, Craig Cotter, Donald Rawley, Dieter Weslowski, Laura Ryder and Toni Ortner. He plans to publish 12 books in 1992. **"We have work we want to publish, hence, unsolicited material is not encouraged. However, we will read and consider material from committed, serious writers as time permits. Write, do not call about material. No reply without SASE. Reports in 2-6 weeks. Author receives 10% of press run.** Peter Gravis says, "Too many writers are only interested in getting published and not interested in reading or supporting good writing. Black Tie hesitates to endorse a writer who does not, in turn, promote and patronize (by actual purchases) small press publications. Once Black Tie publishes a writer, we intend to remain with that artist." Member COSMEP and Small Press Center.

THE BLACK WARRIOR REVIEW (II), P.O. Box 2936, Tuscaloosa AL 35486-2936, phone (205)348-4518, founded 1974. Poets whose work has recently appeared in the *Black Warrior Review* include Judith Berke, Jorie Graham, Mary Ruefle, Sherod Santos, Linda Gregg, Bill Knott and James Ulmer. **Address submissions to the Poetry Editor. Submit 3-6 poems, simultaneous (say so) and photocopied submissions OK, awards one $500 prize annually, payment $5-10/printed page plus two copies. Reports in 1-3 months.** It is a 6×9" semiannual of 144 pages, circulation 1,800. **Sample: $5 postpaid. Send SASE for guidelines.** The editor chose this sample from "Black Fish Blues" by Beckian Fritz Goldberg:
. . . I've got a view and a neighbor with a drainpipe
running off his roof. I've got a feel for the plumbing
broken in those shadows. I've got May light
coming in strong on all stations and branches

knocking their shadows flat on the blocks of the fence.
I've got a whole cluster of black fish bobbing
in the top block. Fish that touch you quick
constellations below the water . . .
"We solicit a nationally-known poet for the chapbook. For the remainder of the issue, we solicit a few poets, but the bulk of the material is chosen from unsolicited submissions. Many of our poets have substantial publication credits, but our decision is based simply on the quality of the work submitted." Reviews books of poetry.

‡BLAST MAGAZINE (I), P.O. Box 3514, Manuka, ACT 2603, Australia, phone (06)2480912, founded 1987, contact Ann Nugent, appears 4/year (I have not seen a copy). **Pays $20 for poetry; they indicate that they often provide comments or criticism on rejections.**

BLIND ALLEYS (II); SEVENTH SON PRESS (V), % Michael S. Weaver, Rutgers University, Box 29, Camden NJ 08102, founded 1981, *Blind Alleys* founded 1982 by Michael S. Weaver, editors Michael S. Weaver, Glenford H. Cummings, Charles Lynch and Aissatou Mijiza. *BA* appears twice a year, digest-sized, 78 pp., saddle-stapled, professionally printed on thin stock, matte card cover, circulation

500. Sample: $5 postpaid. All submissions must be addressed to Michael S. Weaver. Submit about 5 poems in a batch, none longer than 100 lines. Pays 2 copies. Reviews book of poetry. They have published poetry by Lucille Clifton, Arthur Winfield Knight, Kimiko Hahn, Peter Harris and Ethelbert Miller. As a sample I selected the first stanza of "Fells Point" by James Taylor:

> First step. Land fall. A site
> in near future of a colonial black painter,
> shipwrights and quick to please prostitutes.
> Some towns are born old and born hookers.

The press publishes broadsides but is not at present accepting unsolicited book MSS.

‡THE BLIZZARD RAMBLER (I), P.O. Box 54, Weiser ID 83672, founded 1983, editor Ron Blizzard, appears 2-3/year. "Open as to form, length, etc. No pornography, senseless violence." They have recently published poetry by John Grey and William P. Robertson. As a sample the editor selected these lines (poet unidentified):

> Now the drums beat ever louder
> to the tempo of too much,
> And the man-made this and that
> crowds ever closer to the touch;
> And the world, no longer satisfied
> to hum its axis 'round,
> Is a screaming, whirling dervish
> hurtling frenzily; hell-bound.

It is "about 80-120 pp. digest-sized, heavier paper cover." Press run 400. **Sample postpaid: $4. Send SASE for general guidelines for writers. Reports in 3-8 weeks. Pays ¼¢/word, $2 minimum, plus 1 copy.** The editor says, "*TBR* is not really a 'literary' magazine. We buy poetry based basically on whether I like it or not. I like **humorous, light-hearted poems; poems that tell stories; gloomy, moody poems; satirical poems.** I just don't know until I see them."

‡THE BLUE GUITAR (I), 3022 N. 5th St., Harrisburg PA 17110, founded 1989, editor Richard Kearns, is a quarterly using "**modern, lyric, experimental, political, social, haiku and almost any style if done well. Looking for anything compelling. No greeting card verse, nor most devotional poetry.**" They have recently published poetry by Gary Fincke, Arthur Winfield Knight, Kerry Shawn Keys and Jack Veasey. As a sample the editor selected these lines from "Paranoia Between Commercials (for Phillip K. Dick)" by Eugene Howard:

> I am a human
> My blood is as red
> as the blood of coyote
> My sperm is as white
> as the meat of a crab
> I am only doing my job:

It is handsomely printed (desktop publishing), 40-60 pp., digest-sized with matte card cover, b/w drawings, saddle-stapled. Press run is 260 for 15 subscribers. Subscription: $12. **Sample: $3 postpaid. Pays 2 copies.** "Usually takes 3-4 months to respond. I am the editorial board, publisher, typesetter, etc. and am funded by myself, friends and subscriptions. I find the current literary scene to be very depressing. There are many poets who have mastered some sort of style but are lacking in substance. I am tired of reading sterile, intellectual poetry written by fatuous poseurs. I need to be able to find a pulse in the work or some other sign of life."

‡BLUE LIGHT PRESS (V), P.O. Box 642, Fairfield IA 52556, phone (515)472-7882, founded 1988, partner Diane Frank, publishes 3 paperbacks, 3 chapbooks/year. "**We like poems that are emotionally honest and uplifting. Women, Blacks, Visionary Poets, Iowa Poets, San Francisco Poets. No rhymed poetry or dark poetry.**" They have recently published poetry by Diane Frank and Reginald Lockett. As a sample the editor selected these lines from **The Houses Are Covered in Sound** by Louise Nayer:

> There was something
> moving in a garbage can,
> a white light glowing in a spiral.
> I thought it was a child,
> no the wind, no the part
> of myself that glowed.

That book is flat-spined, digest-sized, professionally printed, 60 pp., with elegant matte card cover: $10. They have also published an anthology of 13 Iowa Poets. **Currently not accepting unsolicited MSS; reports on queries in 1-2 months. Pays 15-40% royalties.** They have an editorial board. They provide criticism for $20-30/hour. "We also work in person with local poets. We have an ongoing poetry workshop and give classes periodically."

BLUE LIGHT RED LIGHT (II), Suite F-42, 496A Hudson St., New York NY 10014, phone (201)432-3245, founded 1988, editors Alma Rodriquez and Joy Parker, appears 2-3 times a year using **"the finest works of new and established writers, fusing mainstream writing, magic realism and surrealism together with speculative fiction.** As an interdisciplinary periodical we seek not to isolate these genres but to discover the points of contact between them and mainstream writing itself. As contemporary life becomes fragmented, the search for meaning, for personal myths, becomes all the more intense. We want to participate in this search for meaning." They ask of submissions **"Does this piece have magic? Please, no cyberpunk or nihilist's declarations that there is no meaning."** They have recently published poetry by Susan Osberg, Juan Julian Caicedo, Steven Doloff, Janet Holbrook, Peter Beck, Joan Harvey and Z. As a sample the editor selected "Concerto for Astronauts" by Wahn Yoon. Here are the opening lines of this 7-page poem:

> *What could I give you,*
> *black panther sky,*
> *that you haven't already*
> *swallowed and transformed?*

It comes in a 6×9" flat-spined format with glossy cover, 176 pp. Press run: 2,000. Subscription: $15/3 issues. **Sample postpaid: $5.50. Pays small honorarium plus 5 copies. Submit only 3-4 poems at a time. Simultaneous submissions and previously published poems OK.**

‡**BLUE RYDER (II)**, P.O. Box 587, Olean NY 14760, founded 1989, editor Ken Wagner, is subtitled "excerpts from underground, small press and micropress publications, plus." It appears every other month. Submit **"2-5 poems that work together in terms of tone, content, intent and style. Beat generation and modernist best. No rhyme."** They have recently published poetry by Lyn Lifshin, Tom Krampf, John Bennett, Patrick McKinnon, Dan Sicoli and Cheryl Townsend. As a sample the editor selected these lines by Laura Albrecht:

> *You looked into the face of America and saw its stars and stripes teeth*
> *ripping children apart.*

BR reviews other magazines and reprints excerpts from them in addition to publishing original material. It is magazine-sized, 36 pp., saddle-stapled, with matte card cover. They use up to 18 poets per year. Press run 500 for 200 subscribers of which 2 are libraries, 80 shelf sales. Subscription: $15. **Sample postpaid: $3. Send SASE for guidelines. Pays 1 copy. Reports in 3 months.** "Because we publish reprints of poetry from other magazines, and because we publish the best underground poets, competition is fierce. Send very best stuff."

BLUE UNICORN, A TRIQUARTERLY OF POETRY; BLUE UNICORN POETRY CONTEST (II, IV-Translations), 22 Avon Rd., Kensington CA 94707, phone (415)526-8439, founded 1977, poetry editors Ruth G. Iodice, Harold Witt and Daniel J. Langton, wants **"well-crafted poetry of all kinds, in form or free verse, as well as expert translations on any subject matter. We shun the trite or inane, the soft-centered, the contrived poem. Shorter poems have more chance with us because of limited space."** Some poets they have published recently are James Applewhite, Kim Cushman, Charles Edward Eaton, Patrick Worth Gray, Joan LaBombard, James Schevill, John Tagliabue and Gail White. These sample lines are from "S Is for Sonnet" by Elizabeth Michel:

> *Sand whispers sibilants on soles, a storm shakes*
> *Them from sycamores, and the sea*
> *Shouts them out on shoals. And your mouth makes*
> *S's its own way: slurping soup noisily*
> *It sucks them in, from sky and star and space*
> *It spills a song of cosmos on the doily's lace.*

The magazine is **"distinguished by its fastidious editing, both with regard to contents and format."** It is 56 pp., narrow digest-sized, saddle-stapled, finely printed, with some art, **sample: $4 postpaid.** They receive over 35,000 submissions a year, use about 200, have a year's backlog. **Submit 3-5 poems on normal typing pages, original or clear photocopy or clear, readable dot-matrix, no simultaneous submissions or previously published poems. Reports in 1-3 months, payment one copy, guidelines available for SASE.** They sponsor an annual contest with small entry fee to help support the magazine, with prizes of $100, $75 and $50, distinguished poets as judges, publication of 3 top poems and 6 honorable mentions in the magazine. Entry fee: $3 for first poem, $2 for others to a maximum of 5. Write for current guidelines. **Criticism occasionally offered.** "We would advise beginning poets to read and study poetry—both poets of the past and of the present; concentrate on technique; and **discipline yourself by learning forms before trying to do without them.** When your poem is crafted and ready for publication, study your markets and then send whatever of your work seems to be compatible with the magazine you are submitting to."

BLUELINE (IV-Regional), English Dept., Potsdam College, Potsdam NY 13676, founded 1979, editor-in-chief Anthony Tyler, and an editorial board, "is an annual literary magazine dedicated to prose and **poetry about the Adirondacks and other regions similar in geography and spirit."** They want **"clear, concrete poetry pertinent to the countryside and its people. It must go beyond mere description,** however. We prefer a realistic to a romantic view. We do not want to see sentimental or extremely experimental poetry." Usually 44 lines or fewer, though "occasionally we publish longer poems" on "nature in general, Adirondack Mountains in particular. Form may vary, can be traditional or contemporary." They have recently published poetry by Phillip Booth, George Drew, Eric Ormsby, L. M. Rosenberg, John Unterecker, Lloyd Van Brunt, Laurence Josephs, Maurice Kenny and Nancy L. Nielsen. As a sample they offer these lines from "Eagle Lake" by Noelle Oxenhandler:

> Sometimes the lines fall this way,
> the canoe's narrowness
> filling my mind, and my arms
> sending their weight through the water.

It's a handsomely printed, 112 pp., 6×9″ magazine with 40-45 pp. of poetry in each issue, circulation 600. **Sample copies: $6 on request.** They have a 3-11 month backlog. **Submit September 1-December 1, no more than 5 poems with short bio. No simultaneous submissions. Photocopy, dot-matrix OK if neat and legible. Reports in 2-10 weeks. Pays copies. Guidelines available for SASE.** Occasionally comments on rejections. "We are interested in both beginning and established poets whose poems evoke universal themes in nature and show human interaction with the natural world. We look for **thoughtful craftsmanship rather than stylistic trickery."**

BOA EDITIONS, LTD. (III), 92 Park Ave., Brockport NY 14420, phone (716)637-3844, founded 1976, poetry editor A. Poulin, Jr., **generally does not accept unsolicited MSS.** They have published some of the major American poets, such as W. D. Snodgrass, John Logan, Isabella Gardner and Richard Wilbur, and they publish introductions by major poets of those less well-known. For example, Gerald Stern wrote the foreword for Li-Young Lee's **Rose.** The editor selected from that book "Eating Together" as a sample poem:

> In the steamer is the trout
> seasoned with slivers of ginger,
> two sprigs of green onion, and sesame oil.
> We shall eat it with rice for lunch,
> brothers, sisters, my mother who will
> taste the sweetest meat of the head,
> holding it between her fingers
> deftly, the way my father did
> weeks ago. Then he lay down
> to sleep like a snow-covered road
> winding through pines older than him,
> without any travelers, and lonely for no one.

Query with samples. Pays outright grants or royalties.

BOGG PUBLICATIONS; BOGG (II), 422 N. Cleveland St., Arlington VA 22201, founded 1968, poetry editors John Elsberg (USA), George Cairncross (UK: 31 Belle Vue St., Filey, N. Yorkshire YO 14 9HU, England) and Sheila Martindale (Canada: P.O. Box 23148, 380 Wellington St., London, Ontario NGA 5N9). ISSN: 0882-648X. "We publish *Bogg* magazine and occasional free-for-postage pamphlets. The magazine uses a great deal of poetry in each issue (with several featured poets)—**"poetry in all styles, with a healthy leavening of shorts (under 10 lines). Our emphasis on good work per se, and Anglo-American cross-fertilization."** This is one of the liveliest small press magazines published today. It started in England, and in 1975 began including a supplement of American work; it now is published in the US and mixes US, Canadian and UK work with reviews of small press publications on both sides of the Atlantic. It's thick (64 pp.), typeset, saddle-stitched, in a 6×9″ format that leaves enough white space to let each poem stand and breathe alone. They have published work by Ann Menebroker, Steve Richmond, Joyce Odam, Rochelle Ratner, Jon Silkin, Patrick McKinnon, Robert Peters, Harold Witt, Ron Androla, Charles Plymell, Steve Sneyd, Tina Fulker and Andy Darlington. They offer these lines from "Exorcism" by Winona Baker (Canada) as a sample:

> Get out of my room
> Get out of my bed
> Get out of my body
> Get out of my poems.

All styles, all subject matter. "Some have even found the magazine's sense of play offensive. Overt religious and political poems have to have strong poetical merits—statement alone is not sufficient. Prefer typewritten manuscripts, with author's name and address on each sheet. Photocopy OK. We will reprint previously published material, but with a credit line to a previous

publisher." **No simultaneous submissions. Prefers to see 6 poems.** About 40 pp. of poetry per issue, print run of 750, 400 subscriptions of which 20 are libraries, **sample $3 postpaid.** Subscription: $12, for 3 issues. They receive over 10,000 American poems per year and use 100-150. "We try to accept only for next 2 issues. SASE required or material discarded (no exceptions)." **Reports in 1 week, pays 2 copies, guidelines available for SASE.** Reviews books and chapbooks of poetry. Their occasional pamphlets and chapbooks are by invitation only, the author receiving 25% of the print run, and you can get **chapbook samples free for SASE.** Better make it at least 2 ounces worth of postage. John Elsberg advises, "Become familiar with a magazine before submitting to it. Always enclose SASE. Long lists of previous credits irritate me. Short notes about how the writer has heard about, or what he finds interesting or annoying in, *Bogg* I read with some interest."

BONE AND FLESH (V, II), P.O. Box 349, Concord NH 03302-0349, founded 1988, co-editors Lester Hirsh and Frederick Moe, *"Bone & Flesh* **is currently overstocked. In addition to this fact, we are changing our focus to concentrate on fewer writers and artists in order that the works of a select number may be featured in each issue. We will reopen to unsolicited material in September 1992."** *Bone & Flesh* appears twice yearly with the *Annual* and *Aside* issues. They want **"quality calibre work from seasoned writers with a literary slant. All forms: prose poems, short fiction, haiku, essays, artwork, are welcome. Themes may vary but should focus on the substance of our lives or the link with other lives and times. We do not want to see anything that is overtly religious, banal, trite or conventional. Submissions are accepted September-February only."** They have recently published works by Jean Battlo, Jack Veasey, Don Skiles, T. Kilgore Splake, Chelsea Adams, David Brooks and Bayla Winters. As a sample, the editors selected these lines by Bob Shannahan:

> *Our lives in both*
> *bone and flesh*
> *like a boy's footprint*
> *caught for centuries*
> *under the ash of Pompeii*
> *here and gone*

The *Annual* issue is magazine-sized, 75-100 pages. The *Aside* is digest-sized, 32 pp. Press run may vary from 200 to 300 or more, plus library distribution according to issue. **Payment is in contributor's copies. Reporting time and or correspondence averages 1-3 months.** "We sometimes hold work for final consideration." **Submit no more than 6 poems at a time. Editors** attempt to comment on rejections and provide suggestions when appropriate. **Guidelines available for SASE. Sample copies: $5 postpaid.** Occasionally reviews books of poetry.

BOREALIS PRESS; TECUMSEH PRESS LTD.; JOURNAL OF CANADIAN POETRY (V), 9 Ashburn Dr., Ottawa, Ontario K2E 6N4 Canada, founded 1972. Borealis and Tecumseh are imprints for books, including **collections of poetry, by Canadian writers only, and they are presently not considering unsolicited submissions.** Send SASE (or IRCs) for catalog to buy samples. Poets published recently include John Ferns and Russell Thornton. These sample lines are by Fred Cogswell:

> *Often in dreams, when powerless to wake*
> *Or move and thereby ease my pounding heart,*
> *I have felt like a mouse that cannot squeal*
> *When the sprung trap pins its broken spine or*
> *Like a rabbit mesmerized by a snake's*
> *Unchanging otherness of lidless eyes.*

The annual *Journal* publishes reviews and criticism, not poetry. **Sample: $6.95 postpaid.**

BOSTON LITERARY REVIEW (BLUR) (II), P.O. Box 357, W. Somerville MA 02144, phone (617)625-6087, founded 1984, editor Gloria Mindock-Duehr, appears twice a year using **"work with a strong voice and individual style; experimental work welcome. Submit 5-10 poems."** They have recently published poetry by Stuart Friebert, David Ray, Eric Pankey and Richard Kostelanetz. I have not seen an issue, but the editor describes it as "24 pp., 4×12", offset, no ads." They publish about 60 of 4,800 poems received per year. Press run: 500 for 55 subscriptions of which 5 are libraries. Subscription: $6/year. **Sample postpaid: $4. Pays 2 copies. Reports in 2-4 weeks. Editor comments on submissions** "sometimes."

BOSTON REVIEW (II), 33 Harrison Ave., Boston MA 02111, editor Margaret Roth, founded 1975, a bimonthly arts and culture magazine, uses about a **half-page of poetry per issue, or 10 poems a year,** for which they receive about 700 submissions. Circulation 10,000 nationally including subscriptions and newsstand sales. **Sample: $4 postpaid.** They have a 4-8 month backlog. **Submit any time, no more than 6 poems, photocopy OK, simultaneous submissions discouraged; reports in 2 months "if you include SASE,"** pay varies. Reviews books of poetry. The editor advises, "To save the time of all those involved, poets should be sure to send only *appropriate* poems to particular magazines. This means that a poet should not submit to a magazine that he/she has not read. Poets should also avoid lengthy cover letters and allow the poems to speak for themselves."

BOTTOMFISH (II), De Anza College, Creative Writing Program, 21250 Stevens Creek Blvd., Cupertino CA 95014, editor Robert Scott. This college-produced magazine appears annually. *Bottomfish Twelve* contains poems by Chitra Divakaruni, Janice Dabney and Charles Safford. Poetry sample is from "Blowout" by Walter Griffin:

> Suddenly you are there, out by the highway, arm
> wrestling the dark with the wheel in your hands
> gauging the distance between odometers and stars
> that shimmer like ghosts in the falling air
> as the wheel comes loose from the column and
> your brakeless car rolls toward the cliff

Bottomfish is 7 × 8¼", well-printed on heavy stock with tasteful b/w graphics, 60 pp. perfect-bound. Circulation is 500, free to libraries, schools, etc., but $4/copy to individual requests. "Before submitting, writers are strongly urged to purchase a sample copy; subject matter is at the writer's discretion, as long as the poem is skillfully and professionally crafted." Best submission times: September through February 1. Deadline: February 1 each year. Reporting time is 2-6 months, depending on backlog. Pay is 2 copies. The editor says, "Spare us the pat, generic greeting-card phrases. We want sharp, sensory images that carry a strong theme."

BOULEVARD (II), % editor Richard Burgin, 2400 Chestnut St. #2208, Philadelphia PA 19103, phone (215)561-1723, founded 1985, appears 3 times a year. "We've published everything from John Ashbery to Howard Moss to a wide variety of styles from new or lesser known poets. We're eclectic. Do not want to see poetry that is uninspired, formulaic, self-conscious, unoriginal, insipid." They have published poetry by Amy Clampitt, Kenneth Koch, Molly Peacock, Jorie Graham and Marvin Bell. As a sample editor Richard Burgin selected these lines from "Buying a Dress" by James Lasdun:

> Thirty a day and enough gin to float
> A goldfish, Guinness sluicing down her throat
> The barman's spaniel, one damp eye a-cock
> Wiggling his nose like a toe in a sock

Boulevard is 150 + pp., flat-spined, digest-sized, professionally printed, with glossy card cover. Their press run is 2,500 with 600 subscriptions of which 100 are libraries. Subscription: $10. Sample: $6 postpaid. Pays $25-250 per poem, depending on length, plus 2 copies. "Prefer name and number on each page with SASE. Encourage cover letters but don't require them. Will consider simultaneous submissions but not previously published poems." Editor sometimes comments on rejections. Richard Burgin says, "We believe the grants we have won from the National Endowment for the Arts etc., as well as the anthologies which continue to recognize us, have rewarded our commitment. My advice to poets: 'Write from your heart as well as your head.'"

BOX DOG PRESS; FEMINIST BASEBALL; AVANT-GARDE WORLD (I), P.O. Box 9609, Seattle WA 98109, founded 1983, editor Craig Joyce, publishes "chapbooks, flatsheets, fanzines" and wants **poetry, "experimental, innovative, good work in any genre/style"** but not **"metaphysical, racist, sexist, ultra-pretentious."** They have published poetry by Cholah Ciccone. I have not seen a copy of *Feminist Baseball,* but the editor describes its purpose as to "destroy art and literature, worship cool 10-year-old girls," and says it's 40 pp. magazine-sized, appearing 2-3 times a year, and that it uses ¾ of the 10 submissions it receives a year, press run 200 for 17 subscriptions. Per issue: $1. **Sample: $2 postpaid. Pays 1-2 copies. Simultaneous submissions, previously published poems OK. For chapbook consideration send sample poems. Charges $2 reading fee.** *Avant-Garde World* is a photocopied magazine of clippings and comments—no poetry.

BOX 749 MAGAZINE; THE PRINTABLE ARTS SOCIETY INC. (II), 411 W. 22nd St., New York NY 10011, phone (212)989-0519, founded 1972, editor-in-chief David Ferguson. *Box 749* is an annual using **"fiction and poetry of every length and any theme;** satire, belles-lettres, plays, music and any artwork reproducible by photo-offset. **We have no particular stylistic or ideological bias.** *Box 749* is directed to people of diverse backgrounds, education, income and age—an audience not necessarily above or underground. Such an audience is consistent with our belief that literature (plus art and music) is accessible to and even desired by a larger and more varied portion of our society than has generally been acknowledged." I have not seen it, but the editor describes it as 96 pp., magazine-sized. It has a circulation of 2,000 with 300 subscriptions of which 20 are libraries, other copies sold in the street by the editor. Per issue: $2.50. **Sample: $3.50 postpaid. Guidelines available for SASE. Pays 2-5 copies. Prefers letter-quality printing. Reports in up to 3 months or longer, depending on length. Publishes**

Close-up

Gloria G. Brame
Associate Editor, Boulevard
Advisory Editor, ELF

Beautiful is the flesh of 20
weaving its warmth into the sleeve
of 40, who would like to believe
undying in the spring of urgency
that youths possess and adults
wistfully recall and re-invent.
(first stanza of "Beautiful, Fleshly")

That cautionary poem may be the wisdom gleaned from the romantic life Gloria led before the age of 30, some of it as a financial analyst researching the chemical industry on Wall Street. It somewhat belies her present daily endeavors as a freelance writer; business consultant; teacher of English and creative writing at New College, Hofstra University and New York University; associate editor of *Boulevard*; advisory editor of *ELF*; and, most important, poet.

As a child Gloria Brame studied classical music and her family thought she would go on to become a virtuoso pianist, but her heart was in literature from the time she started reading at three. "My Euro-centric parents thrust the works of foreign novelists into my hands by age 10, and I began writing poems as soon as I learned to create complex sentences. I thought poetry was the only true language—or, at least, the only language worth speaking. I was always trying to get my arms around poetry; alas, my early attempts look to me now more like I was throttling it."

She graduated summa cum laude from York College (CUNY) in English (after taking a break to live in France for a couple of years and earn a diploma from the Alliance Francaise); she earned her master's at Columbia University, but then "took an office job out of financial desperation." She did well in business and, though she didn't know a thing about economics or what a stock was, soon found herself on Wall Street, where "female professionals were rare. I mostly worked *against*: sexism, bureaucracy, my own ignorance, salary inequities and a system that eased the way for some (mostly men) and shunted others (mostly women) into obscurity.

"One of my few consolations were the poems I tacked to bulletin boards. Roethke's 'Dolor' traveled with me from job to job because I thought I too knew 'the inexorable sadness of pencils,/ Neat in their boxes.' " She read poetry during coffee breaks and lunch hours "or when angst came knocking on my cubicle." But Wall Street *does* reward intelligence, no matter how unconventional, she found. She was doing well, but "by the time I attained a pretty decent salary and position, I looked around and realized I couldn't bear it anymore. I started waking up every day thinking I would die without ever having lived my real life." She gave notice, quit her job, launched herself into financial uncertainty and vowed that she would never put her heart into anything but writing.

"I remember feeling ashamed," she confesses, "the first time a poem actually appeared in print because the work had been pushed by a friend of mine who was herself fairly well known. I didn't think it really counted because I feared the poem might have been rejected without her enthusiastic recommendations. It took me a few years before I finally accepted that friends, contacts and the kind interventions of people who believe in what one's doing are an aspect of any business and something one ought to feel grateful for. I think the truth is that people will *not* help you if you don't have the talent yourself. It's foolish to *rely* on contacts. And I'm still happiest when an editor who's never heard of me responds warmly to a submission. This, to me, feels cleanest and most gratifying. But if someone wants to put in a good word for me somewhere, I no longer feel embarrassed by her gentle goodwill."

With a record of publishing credits that includes everything from erotic fiction to business reports, as well as poems in significant little magazines, she has now embarked on the task of looking for a publisher for her first book.

At *Boulevard* she and senior editor Phillis Levin read through the vast piles of submissions that reach their New York office. "I look for work that has an authoritative voice and a refined aesthetic. Intelligence, clarity and a mastery of language are key attributes of the work we select. While we tend to prefer formal verse, we stress craft and depth of thought above form, and many of the people whose work appears in *Boulevard* write non-traditional verse. Our huge backlog makes it impossible to respond personally to each submission, and turnaround can often be quite slow. However, we do read everything carefully, and most work is seen by at least two people before a decision is reached." She adds, "We do not return any manuscripts without a SASE, and we encourage those who are interested in submitting to first obtain a copy of *Boulevard* to get a sense of our editorial preferences."

When the new magazine *ELF* accepted one of Gloria's short stories, "they picked my brain for advice, based on my experience with *Boulevard*. I was impressed with their professionalism, sincerity and ambitious editorial goals." They subsequently asked her to serve as an advisory editor, in which capacity she gives them "advice on the nitty-gritties of publishing" and solicits work for them.

—Judson Jerome

MS an average of 1 year after acceptance. The editor says, "MSS are rejected because of lack of imagination for character, not well-written, or not about anything that is worth sharing with the general public."

BRADFORD POETRY (I), 9 Woodvale Way, Bradford, West Yorkshire BD7 2SJ England, phone 0274-575993, founded 1983, editor Clare Chapman, is a small-press quarterly using **poetry with "no restrictions at all. Prefer to print reasonably short poems, but happy to accept some longer work. Anything good is gratefully received." She doesn't want "the trite, the dull."** As a sample the editor selected these lines by Michael Levene:

>   *Above our heads, Queen Mary stared; stern, stony,*
>   *the hydrochloric gaze of an Indian chief*
>   *A rumour went. She won the war, you know,*
>   *she looked at Adolph Hitler and he died*

The quarterly is digest-sized, 8 pp. "Prontoprinted" from photoreduced typescript with Clare Chapman's own drawings as illustrations. She accepts about 10% of "hundreds" of submissions. She has about 30 subscriptions. **Sample: £1.70. Pays 1 copy. Simultaneous and previously published submissions OK. Editor sometimes comments on rejections.** She says, "I think this is a happy era for poets. There are many outlets for them. I receive many worthwhile MSS from poets in the US and Britain. Publishing poetry is not easy, but more people read it and see these 'little' magazines than the editors realize. The best advice I can give poets is to read the masters of the craft and find contemporary poetry that they can admire."

‡BRANCH REDD BOOKS; BRANCH REDD REVIEW; BRANCH REDD POETRY BROADSHEETS; BRANCH REDD POETRY CHAPBOOKS (III), 4805 B St., Philadelphia PA 19120, phone (215)324-1462, editor Bill Sherman, is a "small-press publisher of poetry" that **discourages unsolicited MSS.** They have recently published poetry by Allen Fisher, Pierre Joris, Asa Benveniste, Eric Mottram, Kate Ruse-Glason and Shreela Ray. As a sample the editor selected these lines (poet unidentified):

>   *Her hair, her blue nightslip, more*
>   *Frustration. Earlier*
>   *news of Bunting's death.*

The *Branch Redd Review* appears irregularly in varied formats with a press run of 500, pays at least 5 copies.

‡GEORGE BRAZILLER, INC. (II), 60 Madison Ave., New York NY 10010, phone (212)889-0909, founded 1955, editor Adrienne Baxter, is a major literary publisher. In 1980 they published **Classic Ballroom Dances** by Charles Simic, from which I selected this sample poem, "Bedtime Story":

> When a tree falls in a forest
> And there's no one around
> To hear the sound, the poor owls
> Have to do all the thinking.
>
> They think so hard they fall off
> Their perch and are eaten by ants,
> Who, as you already know, all look like
> Little Black Riding Hoods.

It is digest-sized, professionally printed, flat-spined, 64 pp. with glossy card cover, $3.95. **"We consider reprints of books of poetry as well as new poems. If submitting a book for reprint, *all* reviews of the book should be submitted as well. Submit sample of work, never *entire* original pp."** Response in 1 month or less. Payment varies in each case. The editor says, "We are a small publishing house that publishes few books (in general) each year. Still, we have published many well-known authors and are always open and receptive to new writers of every kind--and from all parts of the world."

BREAKTHROUGH!; AARDVARK ENTERPRISES (I, IV-Membership/subscription), 204 Millbank Dr. SW, Calgary, Alberta T2Y 2H9 Canada, phone (403)256-4639, founded 1982, poetry editor J. Alvin Speers. *Breakthrough!* is a general interest quarterly with 13 page "Poetry Corner." Aardvark publishes chapbooks on subsidy arrangements. *Breakthrough!*'s editor says, **"Prefer rhyme—no porn. Any length."** They have recently published poetry by Ellen Sandry, Edna Janes Kayser, Muriel Kovinow and W. Ray Lundy. As a sample the editor selected these lines from "Shared Legacy" by J. Alvin Speers:

> We miss them, but they are part of us,
> Though they crossed the great divide,
> Leaving us just the memories
> Of times with them by our side;
> To live a life that lets no one down
> Who trusts in our love and care
> Is the least we can do with the legacy
> That they passed this way to share.

The editor says *Breakthrough!* is "dedicated to life improvement, starting with primary re-source—the individual" and describes it as "52 pp., digest-sized, plus ad inserts periodically. Good quality photocopy, color heavy paper cover, using b/w illustrations." They receive about 100 poems a month, use approximately 20%. Press run is "over 200 and growing nicely." Price per issue is $4, subscription $15. **Sample: $4 postpaid. Send SASE for guidelines. Pays "small cash award to best 3 items per issue, chosen by readers' votes. Subscribers only submissions." Simultaneous submissions, previously published poems OK. Replies "prompt! Usually by return mail."** Reviews books of poetry for subscribers only. For subsidized chapbook publication query with 3-5 samples, bio, previous publications. "We publish for hire—quoting price with full particulars. We do not market these except by special arrangement. Prefer poet does that. We strongly recommend seeing our books first. Same goes for submitting to *Breakthrough!*; best to see magazine first." Send SASE for catalog to buy book samples. Periodic poetry contests close March 17th—small entry fee. Contest anthology published if sufficient interest. Details for SASE. Please note US stamps cannot be used in Canada. The editor advises, "Be professional and considerate. Our files bulge with abandoned manuscripts—we respond by return mail and never hear from authors again. Treat editors as you would like to be treated."

BREITENBUSH BOOKS, INC. (V), P.O. Box 82157, Portland OR 97282, founded 1977, managing editor Tom Booth, publishes 2-3 flat-spined paperbacks/cloth editions per year, 64-150 pp., 6×9". They have published books by Mary Barnard, Naomi Shihab Nye, Ingrid Wendt, William Greenway and Peter Sears. **"We have temporarily suspended the publication of new poetry volumes and won't be accepting submissions during 1992."**

THE BRIDGE: A JOURNAL OF FICTION AND POETRY (II), 14050 Vernon St., Oak Park MI 48237, founded 1990, editor Jack Zucker, appears twice a year using **"exciting, realistic, not trite, simplistic, poetry."** They have recently published poetry by James Reiss and Judith McCombs. It is digest-sized,

100 pp., flat-spined, press run 500. Subscription: $8. **Sample postpaid: $4. Pays 2 copies. Editor comments on submissions "occasionally."** An editorial board of 3 considers MSS; decision made by editor and 1 special editor. Reviews books of poetry and prose.

‡BRILLIANT STAR (IV-Children), % Hill, Baha'i National Center, Wilmette IL 60091, is a Bahai bimonthly for children, appearing in a magazine-sized format, using some poetry fostering Bahai's very general spiritual values. The editor selected these sample lines from "In Celebration of Black History" by Mary Lou McLaughlin:

> Then, a springtime arrived
> with colors, colors alive!
> Black is Beautiful, red and
> yellow blossomed above the
> richness of the brown earth.
> Hues by which to measure
> the standard,
>   and so it is
>   a challenging delight.

No pay. Considers simultaneous submissions. Sample: free with 9 × 12″ SASE (sufficient postage for 5 oz.); objectives are printed in the masthead.

‡BRISTOL HOUSE PUBLISHERS' POETRY REVIEW; BRISTOL HOUSE PUBLISHERS' POETRY NEWS-LETTER (I), Suite 105, 10343 Royal Palm Blvd., Coral Springs FL 33065, founded 1990, editor/publisher Richard David Behrens. The Review appears every other month; the Newsletter is monthly. **Both of these magazines have a $25 prize for the best poem appearing in each issue.** I have not seen either, but the editor describes the Review as "50-60 pp. digest-sized, saddle-stapled, photocopied from computer masters, heavy matte cover, press run 300" and the Newsletter as "magazine-sized, 10-15 pp., corner-stapled." **Sample: Review $5, Newsletter $3. Send SASE for guidelines.**

‡BROADSHEET MAGAZINE (IV-Feminist, regional) P.O. Box 56147, Aukland, New Zealand, phone 09-608535, founded 1972, has 11 issues/year. **"We publish only about 6 poems a year, all from NZ women poets from a feminist perspective."** They have recently published poetry by Margaret Berry and Sue Rifelelt. It is 48 pp. with glossy cover. Subscription: $50 NZ. **Sample postpaid: $9 NZ. No pay, not even copies.**

BROKEN STREETS (I, IV-Religious, children), 57 Morningside Dr. E., Bristol CT 06010, founded 1981, poetry editor Ron Grossman, is a **"Christian-centered outreach ministry to poets. Chapbooks are sent free to encourage poets."** The digest-sized magazine, photocopied typescript, 40-50 pp., card covers, appears 4-5 times a year—250 copies, **$3.50 for a sample.** The editor wants **"Christian-centered, city poetry, feelings, etc., usually 5-15 lines, haiku, no more than 5 poems at a time, not necessary to query, but helpful."** Reports in 1 week. **Uses about 150 of the 200 poems submitted per year—by children, old people, etc. No pay but copies.** Reviews books of poetry. He has recently published Bettye K. Wray and Naomi Rhoads. I selected this poem by Crystall Carman, age 10, as a sample:

> The sea runs against the shore
> while thunder roars beyond the distant sunset
> and God smiles at his creations
> while the thunder drifts away

BRUNSWICK PUBLISHING COMPANY (I), Rt. 1, Box 1A1, Lawrenceville VA 23868, founded 1978, poetry editor Walter J. Raymond, is a **partial subsidy publisher. Query with 3-5 samples. Response in 2 weeks with SASE. If invited, submit double-spaced, typed MS (photocopy, dot-matrix OK). Reports in 3-4 weeks, reading fee only if you request written evaluation. Poet pays 80% of cost, gets same percentage of profits for market-tester edition of 500,** advertised by leaflets mailed to reviewers, libraries, book buyers and bookstores. The samples I saw were flat-spined, matte-covered, 54 pp. paperbacks. **Send SASE for "Statement of Philosophy and Purpose," which explains terms, and catalog to order samples.** I quote from that Statement: "We publish books because that is what we like to do. Every new book published is like a new baby, an object of joy! We do not attempt to unduly influence the reading public as to the value of our publications, but we simply let the readers decide that themselves. We refrain from the artificial beefing up of values that are not there.... We are not competitors in the publishing world, but offer what we believe is a needed service. We strongly believe that in an open society every person who has something of value to say and wants to say it should have the chance and opportunity to do so."

BRUSSELS SPROUT (IV-Form), P.O. Box 1551, Mercer Island WA 98040, phone (206)232-3239, Francine Porad, art and poetry editor since 1988. This magazine of **haiku, senryu and art** appears each January, May and September. **They want "any format (1-4 lines); subject matter open; seeking work that captures the haiku moment in a fresh way."** It has recently published poetry by Elizabeth St. Jacques, Anne McKay, George Swede, Robert Spiess and Marlene Mountain. As a sample the editor selected these haiku by Wally Swist:

> brook's rush
> giving the stones
> a voice

and Anita Virgil:

> daybreak
> glittering
> thrush songs

The magazine is digest-sized, professionally printed, 44-48 pp. saddle-stapled with matte b/w card cover featuring an artist each issue. **Sample: $5 postpaid. Guidelines available for SASE. No payment, other than 3 $10 Editor's Choice Awards each issue. Submit only original work, 4-12 poems (can be on one sheet), name and address on each sheet. Do not submit MSS from May 25 to June 15. No simultaneous submissions or previously published poems. Reports in 3 weeks. Editor sometimes comments on rejections. Reviews books of haiku** "sometimes, but list those received with a brief comment or sample of work." *Brussels Sprout* sponsors Haiku Northwest, an informal group of writers meeting 5-6 times yearly to share work. The editor advises, "For the record, no editor enjoys saying 'no.' Keep writing, rewriting and sending out your manuscripts. If you value your work, you will find an editor who feels the same."

BUFFALO SPREE MAGAZINE (II), 4511 Harlem Rd., Buffalo NY 14226, founded 1967, poetry editor Janet Goldenberg, is the quarterly regional magazine of western New York. It has a controlled circulation (21,000) in the Buffalo area, mostly distributed free (with 3,000 subscriptions, of which 25 are libraries). Its glossy pages feature general interest articles about local culture, plus book reviews, fiction and poetry contributed nationally. It receives about 300 poetry submissions per year and uses about 25, which have ranged from work by Robert Hass and Carl Dennis to first publications by younger poets. As an example, the editor chose 5 lines of Martha Bosworth's "Alien in Spring":

> I am a tall pale animal in boots
> trampling forget-me-nots and scaring birds
> from the lemon tree: with my long-handled claw
> I pull down lemons — tear-shaped, dimpled, round,
> bouncing they vanish into vines and weeds.

They use 5-7 poems per issue, **paying $20 for each; these are selected 3-6 months prior to publication; sample copy: $3.75 postpaid. Considers simultaneous submissions, "but we must be advised that poems have been or are being submitted elsewhere."**

BYLINE MAGAZINE (IV-Themes), P.O. Box 130596, Edmond OK 73013, founded 1981, editor Marcia Preston, is a **magazine for the encouragement of writers and poets, using 9-12 poems per issue about writers or writing, paying $5-10 per poem.** They have about 3,000 subscriptions, receive 3,000 submissions per year, of which they use 144. These sample lines are from "On Receiving a Native Carving From Africa" by John D. Engle, Jr.:

> Thank you for the African poem,
> carved from ebony
> by ebony hands.
> Seeing and touching
> this tangible song
> of silent harmony
> awakens subtle senses
> too long aslumber.

Byline is professionally printed, magazine-sized, with illustrations, cartoons and ads. **Sample: $3 postpaid. No more than 4 poems per submission, photocopies OK, no reprints, reports within a month, rates $5-10, guidelines available for SASE.** Marcia Preston advises "We are happy to work with new writers, but please read a few samples to get an idea of our style."

CACANADADADA REVIEW (I, IV-Humor), P.O. Box 1283, Port Angeles WA 98362, founded 1989, editor Jack Estes, appears "every 4 months, or so we hope," using poetry, short fiction, cartoons, jokes, anecdotes, interviews, book and movie reviews, recipes, letters, "index items (as in *Harper's* index but goofier), personals, **all must be iconoclastic, satiric, parodic or just plain sophomoric. Don't want long long poems (3-4 pp.) Nothing sappy, religious, heavy. We have no use for rhyming ditties, 'once-upon-a-time' fable parodies, didactic/preachy, violent/aggressive/pornographic pieces, or cute pet stories."**

They have recently published poetry by J. Michael Yates, Susan Musgrave, Dick Bakken and David Ray. As a sample the editor selected these lines by William Slaughter:

> Laughing man, that's his name
> Never had another.
> His mother died having him.
> Never had another.

It is 48 pp., 5½×8½", saddle-stapled. They use about 10% of "tons of poetry" received. Press run 1,000 for 50 subscriptions of which 2 are libraries. Subscription: $6. **Sample postpaid: $3. Send SASE for guidelines. Reports in 1-8 weeks. Double-space everything, name on each page. Always include cover letter ("If you don't we won't know what to say about you when we publish you. Nothing returned without SASE.") Pays copies.** "Don't (oh please, oh please) put cardboard in your submission envelopes!" Reviews books of poetry. They also offer a Bad Poetry Contest. He says, "I like unusual cover letters listing credits. Let poem/story stand on its own. I want *clean* poems (without rusted paper clips from dozens of submissions)."

CADMUS EDITIONS (III), P.O. Box 687, Tiburon CA 94920, founded 1979, editor Jeffrey Miller, publishes hardback and paperback editions of poetry: **"only that which is distinguished."** They have recently published poetry by Federico García Lorca, Tom Clark, Bradford Morrow and Carol Tinker. These sample lines are by Ed Dorn:

> The common duty of the poet
> in this era of massive disfunction
> & generalized onslaught upon alertness
> is to maintain the plant
> to the end that the mumbling horde
> bestirs its pruned tongue.

Query first, no samples, with "an intelligent literate letter accompanied by a SASE." Answer to query in 30 days, to MS (if invited to submit) in 30-45 days. Contracts are for 5-10% royalties. Comments "occasionally but not often in that most unsolicited submissions do not warrant same."

‡CAGE (I, II), % Dr. Lynch, English Dept., 110 N. Grand Ave., Walnut CA 91789, founded 1986, appears "approximately quarterly. **Our preferences are extremely liberal. We want to hear whatever is on the artist's mind, however it may be expressed.** We accept illustrations and photographs suitable for photocopying, and prose pieces of 3 pp. or less. **No greeting card stuff, inspirational verse, racist, homophobic perspectives, propaganda."** They have recently published poetry by Lyn Lifshin, Dick Barnes and Annette Lynch. As a sample I selected the opening lines from "Einstein Was a Nerd" by Hugh Fox:

> Everyone's said the kid's
> impossible,
> short attention-span,
> crazy, wild, hyper,
> and he is,
> until he sits down in
> front of a video-game and
> plunges inside it

It is 35 pp., 8½×7", photocopied, saddle-stapled, with b/w paper cover. They accept about 20% of 500 poems from 50 poets received annually. Press run 100 for 25 subscribers. Subscription: $10. **Sample postpaid: $2. Send SASE for guidelines. Pays 1 copy "unless otherwise indicated.** *Cage* is very small but dedicated to publishing the underrated, underground artist."

‡CALAPOOYA COLLAGE; CAROLYN KIZER POETRY AWARDS (II), P.O. Box 309, Monmouth OR 97361, phone (503)838-6292, founded 1981, editor Thomas L. Ferte. *CC* is a literary annual using **"all kinds"** of poetry. They have recently published poetry by Robert Bly, Joseph Bruchac, Octavio Paz, Marge Piercy, William Stafford, Ursula K. LeGuin, Patricia Goedicke, David Wagoner and David Ray. It is tabloid-size, 48 pp. Press run 1,500 for 250 subscribers of which 16 are libraries. They accept about 6% of 6,000 poems received annually. **Sample postpaid: $4. Pays 2 copies. Reports in 4-8 weeks.** All poems accepted for publication are eligible for annual $700 Carolyn Kizer Poetry Awards.

JOHN CALDER (PUBLISHERS) LTD.; RIVERRUN PRESS INC (V), 9-15 Neal St., London WC2H 9TU England, phone (071)497-1741, editor John Calder, a literary book publisher. On their list are Samuel Beckett, Erich Fried, Paul Eluard, Michael Horovitz, Pier Paolo Passolini and Howard Barker. **"We do not read for the public,"** says John Calder, and he wants **no unsolicited MSS.**

‡THE CALIFORNIA QUARTERLY (II), 100 Sproul Hall, University of California, Davis CA 95616, founded 1971, poetry editor Jordan Jones, appears 2-4/year, using **poetry of "literary quality, no specs."** They have recently published poetry by Laura Jensen, Alan Williamson, Colette Inez and Sal Cetrano. As a sample I selected the concluding lines from "Waiting for the Bus" by Lee Bartlet:

Slowly thick snakes rouse themselves from under the vines.
Fear-Ball begins to sweat, holding his rifle tight to his chest. He wants his mamma
Do-da

It is digest-sized, flat-spined, 80+ pp., professionally printed, offset, with glossy card cover. They accept about 25 of 2,500 poems received per year. Press run 600. Subscription: $14/4 issues. **Sample postpaid: $4. Reports in 6-8 weeks. Pays $4/page plus 1 copy. Do not submit June-September.**

CALLALOO (IV-Ethnic), Johns Hopkins University Press, #275, 701 W. 40th St., Baltimore MD 21211, phone (301)338-6987, founded 1976, editor Charles H. Rowell. Devoted to **poetry dealing with North America, Europe, Africa, Latin and Central America, South America and the Caribbean.** They have recently published poetry by Rita Dove, Jay Wright, Alice Walker, Yusef Komunyakaa, Aimé Césaire, Nicolás Guillén and Michael Harper. These sample lines are by Clarence Major:

They've forced me to pose
in the picture with them.
I'm the unhappy one
standing next to the man
with sixty smiles
of summer in his smile

The magazine is a thick quarterly with a varying amount of poetry in its nearly 200 pp., circulation 1,400, with 1,400 subscriptions of which half are libraries. **"We have no specifications for submitting poetry except authors should include SASE." Reports in 6 months. Payment in copies.** The *Callaloo* Poetry Series is published by the University of Virginia Press.

CALYX, A JOURNAL OF ART & LITERATURE BY WOMEN (IV-Women, lesbian), P.O. Box B, Corvallis OR 97339, phone (503)753-9384, founded 1976, managing editor M. Donnelly, is a journal edited by a collective editorial board, **publishes poetry, prose, art, reviews and interviews by and about women.** They want **"excellently crafted poetry that also has excellent content."** Some poets they have published recently are Diane Glancy, Robin Morgan, Rebecca Seiferle, Lin Max and Carol Ann Russell. The editor selected these sample lines from "Watching My Mother Dress" by Cornelia Hoogland:

She, who loudhosannahed every chore,
cleaned and cared for us while she peeled potatoes,
in one deft spiral paring, who spun rooms
and bottles through her dusting cloth, lingered.

Each issue is 7×8", handsomely printed on heavy paper, flat-spined, glossy color cover, 125-200 pp., of which 50-60 are poetry. **Sample for the single copy price, $8 plus $1.50 postage.** *Calyx* is open to submissions twice annually: April 1-May 30 and Oct. 1-Nov. 30. MSS received when not open to reading will be returned unread. **Send up to 6 poems with SASE and short biographical statement. "We accept copies in good condition and clearly readable. We report in 2-6 months." Payment in copies. Guidelines available for SASE.** They say, "Read the publication and be familiar with what we have published."

CAMELLIA (I), P.O. Box 4092, Ithaca NY 14852, editor Tomer Inbar, "is a quarterly poetry magazine available for free in the San Francisco/Oakland Bay area, also Madison, Seattle, Ithaca and D.C., or by sending a 52¢ SASE. Subscription: $5/year. **"We publish poetry in the W.C. Williams tradition. The poetry of things, moment and sharpness. We encourage young writers and like to work with the writers who publish with us (i.e., publishing them again to widen the forum or exposure of their work). Our main goal is to get the poetry out. We do not want to see poetry where the poem is subordinate to the poet or poetry where the noise of the poetic overshadows the voice. We look for poetry that is honest and sharp and not burdened by noise."** As a sample the editor selected these lines from "This Time" by Miriam Sagan:

"It's just like Baden Baden," I said in the dream
"full of arsenic and mineral healing,"
But she stood still
Refusing to come down
Her breasts floating out over the water.

I have not seen an issue, but the editor describes it as digest-sized, 16-20 pp., desktop published using cartoons and drawings. "We receive approximately 200-250 poems per issue and publish 9-16." Press run 500-900. **Sample: 52¢ SASE. Pays 1 copy. Simultaneous submissions and pre-**

viously published poems OK. Reports "ASAP." Editor comments on submissions "if asked for or if I want to see more but am not satisfied with the poems sent." He says, "We want to get the poetry out to as many people as possible, put it out and it will be read. The idea is to do it and move forward. Poetry is only really about the poem and saying it and that is tied to the tradition of the poem and pushing beyond the previous – always forward."

CANADIAN AUTHOR & BOOKMAN; CANADIAN AUTHORS ASSOCIATION (III), Suite 104, 121 Avenue Rd., Toronto, Ontario M5R 2G3 Canada, poetry editor Sheila Martindale. *Canadian Author & Bookman*, a quarterly, is magazine-sized, 28 pp., professionally printed, with paper cover in 2 colors. It contains articles useful to writers at all levels of experience. **Sample: $4.50 postpaid. Buys 40 poems a year.** "The trend is toward thematic issues and profiles of featured poets, so query letters are recommended." Pays $15 plus one copy. Reviews books of poetry. (See also Canadian Authors Association Literary Awards in Contest and Awards section.)

CANADIAN DIMENSION: A SOCIALIST NEWS MAGAZINE (IV-Political), 707-228 Notre Dame Ave., Winnipeg, Manitoba R3B 1N7 Canada, phone (204)957-1519, founded 1964, editorial contact Tanya Lester, appears 8 times per year, using **"short poems on labour, women, native and other issues. Nothing more than one page."** They have recently published poetry by Tom Wayman and Milton Acorn. As a sample the editor selected these lines by Ishbel Solvason:

> *She must find a job quickly*
> *She has been told*
> *But the factory closed its doors*
> *Her English is poor*

It is 48-56 pp., magazine-sized, slick, professionally printed, with glossy paper cover. Press run: 4,500-5,000 for 3,000 subscriptions of which 800 are libraries, 1,000 shelf sales. Subscription: $30.50 US ($24.50 Canadian). **Sample, postpaid: $1.50. Pays 5 copies. Simultaneous submissions OK.** Reports in 1 month. Editor comments on submissions "rarely."

CANADIAN LITERATURE (IV-Regional), 2029 West Mall, University of British Columbia, Vancouver, British Columbia V6T 1W5 Canada, phone (604)228-2780, founded 1959, poetry editor L.R. Ricou, is a quarterly review which publishes **poetry by Canadian poets. "No limits on form. Less room for long poems."** They have recently published poems by Atwood, Ondaatje, Layton and Bringhurst. The following sample lines are from "Birds" by John Pass:

> *And a snowy owl*
>
> *is an exception. Once*
> *I stood by goalposts at the local school*
> *and watched one watch the hard white field*
> *from the crossbar, utterly unruffled, at home*
>
> *and extraordinary there, a genius*
> *of moonlight and the small hot shadows, of quickness*
> *subtleties, exquisite contrasts.*

Each issue is professionally printed, large digest-sized, flat-spined, with 190+ pp., of which about 10 are poetry. It has 2,000 circulation, two-thirds of which are libraries. **Sample for the cover price: $10 Canadian.** They receive 100-300 submissions per year, of which they use 10-12. **No photocopy, round-dot-matrix, simultaneous submissions or reprints. Reports within the month, pays $10/poem plus 1 copy.**

‡**CANADIAN WRITER'S JOURNAL (IV-Themes)**, Gordon M. Smart Publications, P.O. Box 6618, Depot 1, Victoria, British Columbia V8P 5N7 Canada, is a very **limited market for poetry using only** "short poems or portions thereof as part of 'how-to' articles relating to the writing of poetry and occasional short poems with tie-in to the writing theme." But it is a publication of interest to poets. "Every issue has a variety of how-to and motivational articles for writers, many by accomplished and well-published authors" and "several regular columns with interesting and useful information ranging from writing tips to the viewpoint from behind the editor's desk." It appears quarterly, subscription $15.

CANAL LINES (I, IV-Regional), 55 Main St. #2, Brockport NY 14420-1903, phone (716)637-0584, founded 1987, editor Joseph Hoffman, appears 3-4 times a year. **"Subject matter and style are open, although material connected to New England/Upstate New York is preferred. Length is limited to 100 lines."** They have published poetry by William Heyen, Steven Huff and David Michael Nixon. As a sample the editor selected these lines by William Blaine Durbin:

> *When lids of night dropped over harvest moons*

Close-up

Sheila Martindale
Editor, Canadian Author & Bookman
Canadian Poetry Editor, Bogg

Five O'Clock Flight
Late autumn
is almost overtaken by winter
as offices are exited
and we struggle home
through the sleet
our light shoes
no protection from icy puddles
and wet leaves flapping at our feet

Suddenly the wind
grasps an umbrella
snapping half its joints
in one vicious twist

the fabric collapses
onto its owner's head
she leaves it there
leans into the stinging rain

—a lopsided bird
flying on one wing

Photo by Clarke Leverette

"I have always written poetry," says Sheila Martindale, "so you could say it chose me rather than the other way around." And a wise choice it was, considering her six published books of poetry, the most recent, **No Greater Love** (Moonstone Press, Goderich, Ontario, 1989). Her poems have also appeared in anthologies and are published regularly in periodicals and literary magazines. In addition she writes magazine stories and feature-length pieces as well as reviews on the theater, art and books in all writing genres. She has received reading grants from The Canada Council and writing grants from the Ontario Arts Council.

Her involvement in the literary scene developed into a desire to "make things happen and to promote a better image of poets and poetry," so becoming an editor was a logical progression. In 1982 she became poetry editor of *Canadian Author & Bookman*, a quarterly trade journal for writers, published by the Canadian Authors Association, with articles on all aspects of the writing life, interviews with well-known writers and book reviews (mainly of writers' handbooks and books of poetry). Each issue also contains a poetry section.

Martindale enjoys being an editor because "it puts me in touch with a variety of interesting people and I get to read a lot of poetry." She credits Mattie Falworth of Vanier College in Montreal as her mentor—"the person probably most responsible for shaping my editorial career. And now I, in turn, have become something of a mentor for young poets. An awesome responsibility," she says, "but one with great possibilities."

In the approximately 100 poetry submissions received each month at *Canadian Author & Bookman*, she looks for "fresh imagery, a new perspective, the surprising twist, great lyricism. I work mostly with themes or features of particular poets," she adds, "so all poets would be wise to query for current requirements." Also, she urges, "Be professional, follow the rules." She wants crisp, clean copy that is not folded and a brief cover letter (they use capsule bios). And she reminds U.S. contributors to remember that American stamps cannot be used to mail from Canada; therefore, they should include International Reply Coupons, Canadian stamps (which can be ordered from any Canadian Post Office) or a U.S. dollar bill for return of manuscripts.

Martindale is also Canadian poetry editor for *Bogg*, a small press magazine published three times a year (see listing in this section). *Bogg* started in England and in 1975 began including a supplement of American work. It is now published in the U.S. and mixes British and North American work, using about 40 pages of poetry in each issue. "I handle the Canadian submissions," she explains, "but the selections are made by John Elsberg, *Bogg's* U.S. editor in Arlington, Virginia. He likes poetry which captures the personal experience but rises above it; which works on more than one level; which is composed with technical skill."

Following through on her desire to "make things happen" and to promote the poetic image, Martindale is active in the League of Canadian Poets, the Writers' Union of Canada and the Canadian Authors Association, all of which hold annual conferences. She also conducts workshops in poetry and creative writing. "Getting and giving feedback is important in the creative process," she says. "The stimulation of bouncing ideas around with people interested in the same things as you are is wonderful." She advises poets to start a workshop if there isn't one locally and believes that attending poetry readings is a good way for a novice poet to find out what is being written and published today. "Many new writers really need this," she says, "as some have no idea about contemporary writing. Giving a public reading is helpful, too, because it gives a poet a fair idea of what works and what doesn't."

As a published poet as well as editor, she comments on the merits of being published, "Seeing your work in print gives you a credibility, an authenticity as a poet. Submitting for publication and dealing with the inevitable rejections teaches you a lot about your work and also about yourself."

She considers networking in the pursuit of publication as "moderately" important. "But quality work," she says, "will surface whether or not a poet cultivates the right connections."

—Pat Beusterien

---

and the icy eye of winter took up watch
a hungry frost ate up their golden shoots
and planted in their fields a barrenness.
Canal Lines is digest-sized, 16 pp. saddle-stapled with matte card cover, photocopied from typescript, press run 100. They accept about 40-50% of 60-70 submissions per year. **Sample, postpaid: $1.25. Pays 2 copies. "A report on any submission takes 6-7 weeks or longer."** The editor says, "Patience and determination are a must. A well-written/thought-out poem may be rejected numerous times before finally finding a 'home.' A rejection slip is *not* a statement of failure, but an ongoing process to bring a poem into the proper light."

CANOE PRESS (II), 1587 Lake Dr., Traverse City MI 49684, phone (616)946-7680, founded 1988, publisher Brian Browning, poetry editor Joe Dionne. "We publish books of poetry, also chapbooks, broadsheets in quality letterpress on a hand-fed Chandler and Price. We do our own sewing and binding and in every way try to produce a *work of art*. **We publish modern poetry and have no restrictions as to form whatever. We are now open for submissions. Nothing from the Rod McKuen School, however."** They have recently published poetry by Lee Upton, Jack Driscoll, Al Drake, Barbara Drake and F. Richard Thomas. As a sample the editor selected these lines by Katy McConnell:
It's not caring that's important.
It's all the things that don't count.
It's all the days in the middle of a
storm no one sees. It's blue wind in the night;

They publish 3 chapbooks a year averaging 25 pp. **Reports in 1 month. Pays 15-20 copies. Accepts unsolicited MSS.**

THE CAPE ROCK (II), Department of English, Southeast Missouri State University, Cape Girardeau MO 63701, founded 1964, appears twice yearly and consists of **64 pp. of poetry and photography, with a $200 prize for the best poem in each issue and $100 for featured photography.** It's a handsomely printed, flat-spined, digest-sized magazine, **sample: $3, guidelines available for SASE. "No restrictions on subjects or forms. Our criterion for selection is the quality of the work. We prefer poems under 70 lines; no long poems or books, no sentimental, didactic, or cute poems."** They have published such poets as Stephen Dunning, Joyce Odam, Judith Phillips Neeld, Lyn Lifshin, Virginia Brady Young, Gary Pacernik and Laurel Speer. I selected these sample lines from Kevin Woster's "November Night":

> *The rough paved streets*
> *have crystalized with sudden beauty*
> *Even trash cans find*
> *an edgeless sort of grace*

Their circulation is about 500, with 200 subscribers, of whom half are libraries. They have a 2-8 month backlog and **report in 1-3 months. Do not read submissions in May, June or July. Pays 2 copies.**

THE CAPILANO REVIEW (III), 2055 Purcell Way, North Vancouver, British Columbia V7J 3H5 Canada, phone (604)984-1712, FAX (604)984-4985, founded 1972, editor Pierre Coupey. A "literary and visual media tri-annual; **avant-garde, experimental, previously unpublished work." They want poetry of sustained intelligence and imagination.** *TCR* comes in a handsome digest-sized format, 150 pp., flat-spined, finely printed, semi-glossy stock with a glossy full-color card cover. Circulation: 1,000. **Sample: $8 prepaid. Do not submit MSS during June and July. Pays an honorarium plus 2 copies. No simultaneous submissions. Reports in up to 6 months.**

CAPPER'S (I, IV-Nature, inspirational, humor), 616 Jefferson St., Topeka KS 66607, founded 1879, poetry editor Nancy Peavler, is a biweekly tabloid (newsprint) going to **370,000 mail subscribers,** mostly small-town and farm people. Uses 6-8 poems in each issue—payment $3-6 per poem. They want short poems **(4-10 lines preferred, lines of one-column width) "relating to everyday situations, nature, inspirational, humorous."** They have recently published Helen Harrington, Emma Walker, Sheryl Nelms, Alice Mackenzie Swaim, Ralph W. Seager, and Ida Fasel. The editor selected these lines from "Correction" by R.H. Grenville:

> *"Time heals," they say*
> *to those who bear*
> *the weight of grief.*
> *Oh, I've been there!*
> *And this I know:*
> *it isn't so.*
> *It's love that heals.*
> *Time doesn't care.*

"Most poems used in *Capper's* **are upbeat in tone and offer the reader a bit of humor, joy, enthusiasm or encouragement. Short poems of this type fit our format best." Submit 4-6 poems at a time with return postage, no photocopies or simultaneous submissions. Reports within 3-4 months. Send 85¢ for sample. Not available on newsstand.**

CARAVAN PRESS; EDGAR LEE MASTERS AWARD (III), Suite 279, 15445 Ventura Blvd., Sherman Oaks CA 91403, founded 1980, poetry editor Olivia Sinclair-Lewis, is "a small press presently publishing approximately 6-7 works per year including poetry, photojournals, calendars, novels, etc. We look for quality, freshness and that touch of genius." In poetry, **"we want to see verve, natural rhythms, discipline, impact,** etc. We are flexible but **verbosity, triteness and saccharine make us cringe."** As a sample of their publications, they sent **Litany** by Scott Sonders. It is a professionally printed, digest-sized, 100 pp., flat-spined book with 3-color glossy card cover ($9.95). The editor selected these lines from "Transformation" in that book as a sample:

> *A thin dog with one albino eye*
> *growls in sympathy for the dead*
> *or soon-to-be-dead, and sings,*
> *of metamorphosis, and slowly*
> *slowly, i feel us changing*
> *into implements of purest gold.*

In addition to Sonders they have published books by Bebe Oberon, Walter Calder, Exene Vida, Carlos Castenada, Claire Bloome and G. G. Henke. Their tastes are for poets such as Charles

Bukowski, Sylvia Plath, Erica Jong and Bob Dylan. **"We have strong liaisons with the entertainment industry and like to see material that is media-oriented and au courant." Sample, postpaid: $8. Query first, with 2-3 poems and résumé. If invited to submit, send double-spaced, typed MS (photocopy, dot-matrix OK). "No manuscripts will be read without SASE." Simultaneous submissions OK. They reply "ASAP." They offer 20% royalty contract, 10-50 copies, advance or honorarium depending on grants or award money. "Please study what we publish before submitting." Criticism offered on rejected MSS. (Note: Fee charged if criticism requested.)** "We sponsor the Edgar Lee Masters Awards, established in 1981, including a poetry award with a $2,500 grand prize annually plus each winner (and the five runners up in poetry) will be published in a clothbound edition and distributed to selected university and public libraries, news mediums, etc. There is a one-time only $10 administration and reading fee per entrant. Further application and details available with a #10 SASE."

THE CARIBBEAN WRITER (IV-Regional), Caribbean Research Institute, University of the Virgin Islands, RR 02, P.O. Box 10,000, Kingshill, St. Croix, USVI 00850, phone (809)778-0246, founded 1987, editor Dr. Erika Smilowitz, is an annual literary magazine **with a Caribbean focus. The Caribbean must be central to the literary work or the work must reflect a Caribbean heritage, experience or perspective. Blind submissions only: name, address and title of MS should appear on a separate sheet. Title only on MS. Payment is 1 copy.** They have recently published poetry by Audre Lorde, O.R. Dathorne, Opal Palmer Adisa and Julia Alvarez. As a sample I selected the opening lines of "Below Blue Mountain" by Joseph Bruchac:

> *The full moon touches the crest of the peak*
> *and all is quiet at Nannytown.*
> *The conch horns of the eastern Maroons,*
> *the hands of the old man on the drum*
> *are quiet, quiet, quiet.*

The magazine is handsomely printed on heavy pebbled stock, flat-spined, 110 pp., 6×9", with glossy card cover, using advertising and b/w art by Caribbean artists. Press run is 1,500. **Sample: $7 plus $1.50 postage. Send SASE for guidelines. (Note: postage to and from the Virgin Islands is the same as within the United States.) Simultaneous submissions OK. "Best to avoid submitting MSS in the summer." Deadline is Sept. 30 of each year.** The annual appears in the spring. Reviews books of poetry.

‡CARN; THE CELTIC LEAGUE, (IV-Ethnic), 33 Bōthar Bancroft, Tamhlacht, B.Â.C. 24, Ireland, founded 1973, editor Ms. P. Bridson, is a magazine-sized quarterly, circulation 2,000. "The aim of our quarterly is to contribute to a **fostering of cooperation between the Celtic peoples**, developing the consciousness of the special relationship which exists between them and making their achievements and their struggle for cultural and political freedom better known abroad. Contributions to *Carn* come **through invitation to people whom we know as qualified to write more or less in accordance with that aim. We would welcome poems** *in the Celtic languages* **if they are relating to that aim.** Reviews books of poetry if in the Celtic languages. If I had to put it briefly, we have a political commitment, or, in other words, *Carn* is not a literary magazine."

CAROLINA QUARTERLY (III), Greenlaw Hall CB# 3520, University of North Carolina, Chapel Hill NC 27599-3520, founded 1948, editor David Kellogg, is a small literary magazine that appears three times a year using poetry of "all kinds, **though we seek excellence always."** They have recently published poets such as David St. John, Richard Kenney, Charles Simic and Mary Kinzie. As a sample the editor selected these lines from a poem by Jim Daniels:

> *It's nice that he doesn't have to speak.*
> *Jeff gets letters about his loans. They burn like any paper.*
> *I rest my head on my hands and smell cleanser.*

It's a professionally printed, 6×9" flat-spined magazine, glossy cover, with 90 pp. of which about 30 are poetry, circulation 1,000, with 400 subscriptions, of which about half are libraries. They receive thousands of submissions per year, use 40-60. **Sample: $5 postpaid. Submit no more than 2-6 poems. Use of poems over 300 lines is impractical. No simultaneous submissions. Submissions read** *very slowly* **May—September; reporting time somewhat longer. Pays $15/author plus 2 copies. Guidelines available for SASE.** Sometimes comments on rejections. Reviews books of poetry.

CAROLINA WREN PRESS (IV-Women, ethnic, regional), P.O. Box 277, Carrboro NC 27510, founded 1976, editor-in-chief Elaine Goolsby, poetry editor Marilyn Bulman, publishes **"primarily North Carolina authors; primarily people whose work we have come to know through teaching, readings, consultation; focus on women and minorities, though men and majorities also welcome."** They have published poetry by Jaki Shelton-Green, Li Ch'ing-Chao (in translation), Amon Liner, T.J. Reddy and Mary Kratt. The editor chose this sample from **Traffic of the Heart** by Miranda Cambanis:

Poetry lives in perpetual insomnia
and not in damp houses with leaking roofs and hungry children
as has often been said between well paid intellectuals at cocktail parties,
wishing, in their drunkenness, to be poets with any other voice
except their own.

Send query letter. No more than 12 pages of poetry. Report time 6 months. Pays 10% of print run in copies. Publishes 4 books per year. Send SASE for catalog to purchase samples. Some free advice: "Become good and for feedback use friends and community resources." Founder of the press and former editor-in-chief Judy Hogan offers "consultation by mail" on poetry MSS. Send SASE for details.

CAROUSEL MAGAZINE (II), Rm. 217 University Center, University of Guelph, Guelph, Ontario N1G 2W1 Canada, founded 1983, editor Michael Carbert, is an annual using **"any type of well-written, typed poetry,** as well as short stories, graphics or short plays. **We do not usually publish rhyming poetry. MSS should be well-edited before they are sent. Original, minimalist, off-beat material is encouraged."** They have recently published poetry by John B. Lee, Anne Burke, James Harrison, Mary Melfi and W.P. Kinsella. It is flat-spined, 89 pp. Their press run is 500. They accept about 30-40 of 150 pieces received. **Sample: $4 postpaid. Send SASE for guidelines. Pays 1 copy. They will consider simultaneous submissions. Reports in 3-4 months. Type name and address on each page.**

CARPENTER PRESS (V), P.O. Box 14387, Columbus OH 43214, founded 1973, editor Bob Fox, publishes a **chapbook series and an occasional full-length collection, flat-spined. No unsolicited MSS. Query, no samples.** They have published poetry by Steve Kowit and David Shevin. **Pays 10% royalties, 10% of press run in copies. Send SASE for catalog to purchase samples.**

THE CARREFOUR PRESS (V), Box 2629, Cape Town, South Africa 8000, phone (021)477280, founded 1988, managing editor Douglas Reid Skinner, is a "small press specializing in poetry, criticism, philosophy," accepting **"manuscripts by invitation only."** They have recently published poetry by Basil Du Toit, Douglas Livingstone and Israel Ben Yosef. They publish about 6 paperbacks a year averaging 80 pp. Poets they publish **"should have an established reputation, primarily through magazines." Pays 7½-10% royalties and 20 copies.** About a third of their books are subsidized, and the poet "must assist in obtaining sponsorship."

‡**THE CARRIONFLOWER WRIT; NOSUKUMO (II)**, GPO Box 994-H, Melbourne Victoria, Australia 3001, Nosukumo founded 1982, *TCW* founded 1985, editor Javant Biarujia. *TCW* appears irregularly, about 2/year. Nosukumo publishes 1-2 chapbooks/year. **"Prefer language-oriented and experimental poetry, but not exclusively so. 1-200 lines. No street or performance poetry, realism, magic realism, dirty realism, doom and gloom political poems."** They have recently published poetry by Charles Bernstein, Kamala Das, Phillip Foss and B. Wongar. As a sample the editor selected these lines from "Eratosthenes at Swenet" by Ian C. Birks:

Taut to the stars
The random pitted sky
There to remind you
of something
That had long since slipped the mind
you

Their products are characterized by elegant printing on quality paper, sewn chapbooks. *TCW* is an 8 pp. quarto broadsheet (folding out to poster size). Press run 350 for 100 subscribers of which 10 are libraries, 100 shelf sales. **Sample postpaid: A$3. Money orders, postal orders etc. must be made out to Nosukumo. Reports in 6-8 weeks. Pays 10 copies. Chapbooks pay 5-10% royalties plus 30 copies.** Though they can publish very little of the poetry received, they do not wish to discourage submissions. The editor says he leans "toward experimental work, emphasis on interior writing, emotional honesty, effective wordplay. Interested in 'homotextuality,' for example."

CAT FANCY (IV-Themes, children), P.O. Box 6050, Mission Viejo CA 92690, phone (714)855-8822, founded 1965, editor K.E. Segnar. *Cat Fancy* is a magazine-sized monthly that uses **poems on the subject of cats. "No more than 30 short lines; open on style and form, but a conservative approach is recommended. In our children's department we occasionally use longer, rhyming verse that tells a story about cats. No eulogies for pets that have passed away."** They have published poetry by Lola Sneyd and Edythe G. Tornow. As a sample the editor selected these lines by Lynette Combs:

He trampolines
from chair to chair

> *and waits in ambush*
> *on the stair.*

It has a press run of 317,687 for 236,174 subscribers, 28,882 shelf sales. Subscription: $21.97. **Sample postpaid: $4. Pays $20/poem plus 2 copies. Name and address "in upper left-hand corner." Reports in 6 weeks. Editor sometimes comments on submissions, "especially if the MS is appealing but just misses the mark for our audience."** She says, "We have an audience that very much appreciates sensitive and touching work about cats. As for advice—get input from knowledgeable sources as to the marketability of your work, and be open to learning how your work might be improved. Then send it out, and hang on. Rejection may not mean your work is bad. We are able to accept very few submissions, and the competition is fierce. Timing and luck have a lot to do with acceptance, so keep trying!"

THE CATHARTIC (II), P.O. Box 1391, Ft. Lauderdale FL 33302, phone (305)474-7120, founded 1974, edited by Patrick M. Ellingham, "is a **small poetry magazine devoted to the unknown poet** with the understanding that most poets are unknown in America." He says, "While there is no specific type of poem I look for, **rhyme for the sake of rhyme is discouraged. Any subject matter except where material is racist or sexist in nature. Overly-long poems, over 80 lines, are not right for a small magazine normally.** I would like to see some poems that take chances with both form and language. I would like to see poems that get out of and forget about self ['I'] and look at the larger world and the people in it with an intensity that causes a reader to react or want to react to it. I am gravitating toward work that looks at the darker side of life, is intense and uses words sparingly." **Considers sexually explicit material.** Recently published poets include Joy Walsh, Harry E. Knickerbocker, Laurel Speer and Eileen Eliot. It's a modest, 28 pp. pamphlet offset printed from typescript, consisting mostly of poems, which appears twice a year. **Sample: $3 postpaid.** He receives over 1,000 submissions per year, of which he uses about 60. No backlog. **Photocopy, dot-matrix, simultaneous submissions OK, submit 5-10 poems. Reports in 1 month. Uses reviews of small press books as well as some artwork and photography. Guidelines available for SASE. Contributors receive 1 copy.** He advises, "The only way for poets to know whether their work will get published or not is to submit. It is also essential to read as much poetry as possible—both old and new. Spend time with the classics as well as the new poets. Support the presses that support you—the survival of both is essential to the life of poetry."

CATS MAGAZINE (IV-Themes), P.O. Box 290037, Port Orange FL 32029, editor Linda J. Walton, is a monthly magazine **about cats, including light verse about cats. Pays 50¢ a line. Free sample copy is available when accompanied by a 9 × 12″ envelope with $1.21 postage. All submissions or requests must have SASE. Payment on publication.**

‡WM CAXTON LTD. (I, II), Box 709—Smith Drive & Hwy 57, Sister Bay WI 54234, phone (414)854-2955, founded 1986, publisher K. Luchterhand. **"About 50% of our books involve an author's subvention of production costs with enhanced royalties and/or free copies in return."** They want **"any serious poetry, not children's, doggerel."** They have published poetry by David Koenig and by Caroline Sibr. Write or call to purchase sample copies.

CCR PUBLICATIONS (II), 2745 Monterey Hwy #76, San Jose CA 95111-3129, founded as Realities Library in 1975, as CCR Publications in 1987, editor and publisher Ric Soos. "I am going to take one book, and follow it through all stages with the author. I will not even consider a new book until the current project is finished. Please keep in mind when you contact me for projects, that I believe in Jesus Christ, and that anything I publish will be to help further the Gospel if it is for that purpose. In poetry, **I look for items that will not hinder the spread of the Gospel. In other words, the poet need not be Christian, does not need to mention Christ by name. But I will no longer be publishing for Shock Value."** He publishes those **"who support me in some respect . . . Support is not always financial."** Query with sample poems. He has published books of poetry by Ruth Daigon and Ella Blanche Salmi. As a sample I selected the complete poem, "To Carol" by Don MacQueen:

> *When gulls fly inland crying*
> *under a thin gauze sky*
> *it can mean storm, I told you.*

ALWAYS submit MSS or queries with a self-addressed, stamped envelope (SASE) within your country or a self-addressed envelope and International Reply Coupons (IRCs) purchased from the post office for other countries.

> *Now it is raining and*
> *you are not here to praise me.*

That poem is from **Far from the Garden,** a flat-spined digest-sized book, 64 pp., professionally printed on good stock with 2-color glossy card cover, $5.

‡CELERY/INKY BLUE (I), 5108 Elkmont Dr., Rancho Palos Verdes CA 90274, founded 1989, editors Cat Spydell and Andrew Demcak, appears quarterly. Both titles are bound into one cover. From one side it is *Celery* and from the other it is *Inky Blue.* The two titles have different requirements. *IB* wants **"thought-provoking, with a tendency to avoid the mundane."** For *Celery* they say **"Don't let it make sense. NO superficial overzealous religious poetry."** For both: **"No sexist poetry, red-neck-beer-bellied-middle-American-women-are-only-good-if-they-have-flat-heads poetry."** They have recently published poetry by Gerald Locklin, Ray Zepeda, Lyn Lifshin, Isa de Quesada, Elspeth Aubrey, Millicent Borges "and all well-known local, stunning celebrities." As samples the editors chose these lines by Cat Spydell from *Inky Blue*:

> *The small tortured soul whispering its will to live,*
> *she walked into the room sobbing*
> *as she climbed onto the metal table.*
> *The baby left this time like a dying red rose,*
> *unfolding its petals and yearning to fall.*

and by Baron Friedric Von Ubeldenken from *Celery*:

> *Stickly prickly yam weapon.*
> *Druid muffin decathalon.*
> *with a veneer soft cheese and vice grips.*

The double magazine ("from the sublime to the silly") is 48 pp. digest-sized with matte card cover, press run of 85-300 ("depending on funding"). They accept 75% or more of submissions ("usually at least one poem"). **Sample: $4. Pays 1 copy. Previously published poems and simultaneous submissions OK. "Please put name and address on each poem. 1-2 pp. with SASE OK."** The editors say that they began "to give deserving but struggling local Southern California poets a chance to see their work in print. We've grown since then, and now receive poetry from all over. We'll take a chance on raw poets. Everyone has to start somewhere! *Celery* is dedicated to the silly. Don't try this at home without first consulting your doctor! Like good wine, we're improving with age, SO WATCH OUT! You'll never get anywhere being a shrinking violet, just do it."

‡CELESTIAL ARTS (V), P.O. Box 7327, Berkeley CA 94707, founded 1970, publishes books of poetry but **accepts no unsolicited submissions.**

‡CENCRASTUS (IV-Ethnic), One Abbeymount Techbase, Edinburgh EH8 8EJ Scotland, phone (031)661-5687, founded 1979, editor Raymond Ross, is a quarterly magazine **to create the intellectual and imaginative conditions for a new Scottish nation"** which uses **"no light verse; long poem a specialty; all poetry to be relevant to Scotland or peripheral living."** They have published poetry by Edwin Morgan, Kenneth White, Sorley Maclean, Gael Turnbull, Douglas Dunn and international poets. There are 3-8 pages of poetry in each issue. Circulation to 1,000 subscriptions of which a fourth are libraries. **Sample: £1.85 postpaid from USA.** They receive over 400 submissions per year and use 30 with a 1-2 issue backlog. **Submit 4-8 poems, typed, no query, reports in 1-2 months. Pays £7.50 per poem or £30 per page.** Reviews books of poetry.

‡THE CENTENNIAL REVIEW (V), 312 Linton Hall, Michigan State University, East Lansing MI 48824-1044, phone (517)355-1905, founded 1955, is a well-established quality quarterly, **which is interested in that sort of poem which, however personal, bears implications for communal experience. They** currently have a backlog of submissions. They have published poetry by Joyce Carol Oates, David Ignatow and Susan Fromberg Schaeffer. It is an elegant 6×9″ format, flat-spined (160+ pp.), **sample** $5 postpaid, subscription $10 for 3 issues. Circulation: 1,200.

UNIVERSITY OF CENTRAL FLORIDA CONTEMPORARY POETRY SERIES (II), % Dr. Louis Trefonas, Dean of Graduate Studies, University of Central Florida, Orlando FL 32816, founded 1970, poetry editors Judith Hemschemeyer and Don Stap, publishes **two 50-80 pp. hardback or paperback collections each year.** They have recently published poetry by Rebecca McClanahan Devet, Don Stap, Roald Hoffmann and Edmund Skellings. Here is a sample from Don Stap's book, **Letter at the End of Winter.** These are the first nine lines of the poem "From a Photograph":

> *In your checkered dress you are smiling*
> *your blond hair diffused in the angelic light of a poor exposure.*
> *You are seven or eight,*
> *wearing white anklets and shoes with buckles*

standing with your hands behind your back.
But where is the farm on Territorial Road
and the fruit orchards of Coloma?
Where is the black bread and blood sausage
and where is Latvia, that dark stain on Russia's shoulder?

The only criterion is good poetry. **Reporting time: 8-12 weeks.**

‡**CENTRAL PARK (III)**, Neword Productions, Inc., P.O. Box 1446, New York NY 10023, phone (212)362-9151, founded 1979, poetry editor Eve Ensler, appears twice a year using **"either experimental or aggressively political poetry."** They have recently published poetry by Jackson Mac Low, Charles Bernstein and Ron Silliman. As a sample the editor selected these lines by Kathleen Fraser:

We gave them thirteen boxes. They left us with two
of our original four truths and news of flying horses.

It is 150 pp. offset. Press run 1,000. **Sample postpaid: $5. "We read submissions in October and February of each year. We prefer submissions from poets who have read or ordered the magazine."**

CHAKRA (I, IV-Erotica, spirituality, occult, science fiction/fantasy), P.O. Box 8551, Dept. P10, FDR Station, New York NY 10022, founded 1988, editor Liz Camps, appears 2-4 times per year using **poetry of "any length or style dealing with eroticism, mysticism, myth and magick. Prayers and ritual verse greatly encouraged."** They have recently published poetry by Stephen Gill, Kenneth Lumkin and Michael Hathaway. As a sample the editor selected these lines from "Letter to Sarah" by Ivan Argüelles:

that dark matter I mean your soul
wherever it is however capable it is
of extending itself through corporeal music
into the bathysphere or beyond its halos . . .

Chakra has a new format I have not seen: magazine-sized, photocopied. They accept about 10% of "hundreds of poems received a year." Press run: 200-1,000 ("varying"). Subscription: $3.50. **Sample postpaid: $2. Pays $1/poem plus contributor's copy. They want MSS "typed neatly on** *used* **paper (encourages amateur recycling)." Simultaneous submissions and previously published poems OK. Reports in "3 months maximum." Editor comments on submissions "seldom, but comments are extensive when offered."** They held their first contest in 1991. "Send SASE for details—with request on *used* paper."

CHALK TALK (IV-Children), 1550 Mills Rd., RR 2, Sidney, British Columbia V8L 3S1 Canada, phone (604)656-1858, founded 1987, editor Virginia Lee, is a "non-glossy magazine **written by children for** children (with parents' pages), stories, poems, drawings, published 10 months/year. **Any form or subject matter."** As a sample I selected this poem, "Trees," by Shalan Joudry, age 10, from Toronto:

Trees are tall and short
They make excellent tree houses and swings
They keep the ground and soil down flat
Children have joyful fun climbing and exploring the trees
I hope the trees grow forever

It is magazine-sized, 24 pp., newsprint. No July or August issues. Approximately 3 pp. per month are poems. Press run 3,000 for 1,500 subscribers of which 15% are libraries. Subscription: $14 (incl. GST) CDN, $17 US and foreign. **Sample postpaid: $2. Send SASE for guidelines. Pays "as many copies as requested."** Simultaneous submissions OK. Reviews books of poetry.

‡**CHAMINADE LITERARY REVIEW; THE UNTERECKER PRIZES (II, IV-Regional)**, 3140 Waialae Ave., Honolulu HI 96816, founded 1986, editor Loretta Petrie, appears twice yearly. **"No jingles, pop"** poetry. They have recently published poetry by John Unterecker, Cathy Song, Nel Altizer and Gene Frumkin. As a sample, I selected the first stanza of "Edward Hopper's Rooms by the Sea" by Joseph Stanton:

A house that opens wide its door
to an open expanse of sea is more
than a machine for living, and less.

The handsomely printed magazine averages 175 pp., flat-spined, 6×9″ with glossy card cover. They accept about 25% of 500 poems received/year. Press run 500 for 350 subscribers of which 6 are libraries. Subscription: $10/year, $18/2 years. **Sample postpaid: $4. Pays year's subscription. Previously published poems OK.** The Unterecker Prizes (cash awards) are awarded yearly to Hawaiian poets published in the magazine, and they give **special consideration to Hawaii's writers or Hawaii subject matter.**

‡CHANGING MEN: ISSUES IN GENDER, SEX AND POLITICS (IV-Feminist), 306 N. Brooks, Madison WI 53715, founded 1979, poetry editor Bob Vance, is described as **"a pro-feminist journal for men —** politics, poetry, graphics, news." He wants work which "expresses the emotional, intellectual and sensual complexity of living in America in an age enlightened by but not yet freed by feminism, gay liberation, socialism and ethnic beauty. A concern for form and invention is appreciated." They have published poetry by Sidney Miller, Louie Crew, T. Obatala, Sesshu Foster, Assotto Saint and Denis O'Donovan. Though the poetry is "so varied" the editor felt he could not select 4 representative lines, I chose the opening lines of James Broughton's "Afternoon in Ceylon" to illustrate the quality, if not variety, of poetry in the magazine:

> *Luncheon had made us hungry for one another*
> *After the curry and fried bananas*
> *we added our own heat to the hot afternoon*
> *simmering in sweat and coconut oil*

Uses about 6 pp. of poetry in each magazine-sized issue, circulation 2,000, 1,000 subscriptions of which few are libraries. They have a backlog for 2-4 issues. **Sample: $6 and 9 × 12″ SASE. Submit up to 5 poems, photocopy, simultaneous submissions OK. Reports in 2-6 months. Pays copies. Send SASE for guidelines. Editor sometimes comments on rejections.**

CHANNELS; CURRENTS (IV-Religious, membership), Rt. 2, Box 505, San Benito TX 78586-9414, phone (512)748-2138, founded 1974, editor Jean Hogan Dudley, a tri-annual magazine of the Christian Writer's League of America, **using the work of members.** Dues $12.50 per year. Uses about 100 poems a year, including some in *Currents*, CWLA news magazine, editor Lee Longenecker. **Pays in contributor copy, accepts photocopies, simultaneous and dot-matrix submissions, and previously published work. Sample: $4 postpaid; guidelines for SASE.** Reviews only books of poetry by members. Annual contest in February, open to all, $2 entrance fee. Write for details. "We are looking for quality poems in any form that speak both to mind and heart. Christian emphasis includes nature, home life, social problems and aspects of the Christian faith."

‡CHANTRY PRESS (III), P.O. Box 144, Midland Park NJ 07432, founded 1981, poetry editor D. Patrick, publishes **perfect-bound paperbacks of "high quality" poetry. No other specifications.** They have published work by Laura Boss, Anne Bailie, Ruth Lisa Schechter and Joanne Riley. These sample lines are from **Winter Light** by Maria Gillan:

> *Remember me, Ladies,*
> *the silent one?*
> *I have found my voice*
> *and my rage will blow*
> *your house down.*

That's from an 80 pp. book (usually books from this press are 72 pp.), flat-spined, glossy cover, good printing on heavy paper, author's photo on back, $5.95. **Send SASE for catalog to order sample. Don't send complete MS. Query first, with 5 sample poems, no cover letter necessary. Submission period October-April. Replies to query in 4 months, to submission in 4 months. Simultaneous submissions OK, photocopy OK. 15% royalties after costs met and 10 author's copies.** Very short comment sometimes on rejected MSS. The editor advises: "Do not be rude in inquiring about the status of your manuscript."

CHAPMAN (IV-Ethnic); CHAPMAN PRESS (V), 4 Broughton Place, Edinburgh EH1 3RX Scotland, phone (031)557-2207, founded 1970, editor Joy Hendry, "provides an outlet for new work by **established Scottish writers and for new, up-and-coming writers also,** for the discussion and criticism of this work and for reflection on current trends in Scottish life and literature. But *Chapman* is not content to follow old, well-worn paths; it throws open its pages to new writers, new ideas and new approaches. In the international tradition revived by MacDiarmid, *Chapman* also **features the work of foreign writers and broadens the range of Scottish cultural life."** They have recently published poetry and fiction by Alasdair Gray, Liz Lochhead, Sorley MacLean, T.S. Law, Tom Scott and Una Flett. As a sample the editor selected this poem by Naomi Mitchison, "The Rhodesian Woman":

> *It's Us or Them she said, dry-lipped, sun-faded, Us or Them,*
> *Why, I said, why? For she scared me, she, would-be destroyer*
> *Of the tenderness that I knew, the being together,*
> *The trust warm between equals, the more than trust,*
> *The joining of hands, of worlds, the gifts of both sides.*
> *Let me be far from you, woman of my colour, not of my heart.*
> *I go to my friends*

Chapman appears 4 times a year in a 6 × 9″ perfect-bound format, 104 pp., professionally printed in small type on matte stock with glossy card cover, art in 2 colors, circulation 2,000 for 900 subscriptions of which 200 are libraries. They receive "thousands" of freelance submissions of poetry per year, use about 200, **have an 8-12 month backlog. No simultaneous submissions. Sample: £2.50 (overseas). Pays £8 per page. Reports "as soon as possible."** Reviews books of poetry. **Chapman Press is not interested in unsolicited MSS.**

THE CHARITON REVIEW PRESS; THE CHARITON REVIEW (II), Northeast Missouri State University, Kirksville MO 63501, phone (816)785-4499, founded 1975, editor Jim Barnes. *The Chariton Review* began in 1975 as a twice yearly literary magazine and in 1978 added the activities of the Press, producing "limited editions (not chapbooks!) of **full-length collections ... for the purpose of introducing solid, contemporary poetry to readers.** The books go free to the regular subscribers of *The Chariton Review*; others are sold to help meet printing costs." The poetry published in both books and the magazine is, according to the editor, **"open and closed forms—traditional, experimental, mainstream. We do not consider verse, only poetry in its highest sense, whatever that may be. The sentimental and the inspirational are not poetry for us."** They have recently published poets such as Michael Spence, Neil Myers, Ruth Good, Judy Ray, Charles Edward Eaton, Wayne Dodd and Harold Witt. These lines offered as a sample are from "Deathbed Edition" by Elton Glaser:

> And though this throat, when young, was blessed
> By crossed candles, I want
> No gospel-volume bossed in gold, no Latin chatter
> And sweet smoke invoking
> Mansions for sale in the sunlit suburbs of heaven.

There are 40-50 pages of poetry in each issue of the *Review*, a 6 × 9″ flat-spined magazine of over a hundred pages, professionally printed, glossy cover with photographs, circulation about 600 with 400 subscribers of which 100 are libraries. **Sample: $2.50 postpaid. Do *not* write for guidelines.** They receive 7,000-8,000 submissions per year, of which they use 35-50, with never more than a 6-month backlog. **Submit 5-7 poems, typescript single-spaced, no carbons, dot-matrix or simultaneous submissions. Payment: $5/printed page. Contributors are expected to subscribe or buy copies. To be considered for book publication, query first—samples of magazine $2.50, of books $3 and $5. Payment for book publication: $500 with 20 or more copies. Usually no criticism is supplied.** The sample book I have seen, **The Tramp's Cup,** by David Ray, has an appearance much like the magazine and sells for $3. The prices of both the magazine and books seem remarkably low in view of the high quality of production. Jim Barnes advises poets "Submit only your *best* work."

CHARNEL HOUSE (IV-Form, anthology), P.O. Box 281, Station S, Toronto, Ontario M5M 4L7 Canada, phone (416)924-5670, founded 1979, editor Crad Kilodney, is **"only interested in very bad poetry."** They publish limited editions of fiction and poetry, mostly sold on the street. I have not seen one of their publications but the editor describes them as digest-sized, saddle-stapled paperbacks. *"Bad* **poetry only, for a series of anthologies of bad poetry. Intended as offbeat novelty items. Any style, from semi-illiterate to pretentious avant-garde. Any subject. Preferably less than 40 lines. Nothing that shows real talent."** They have recently published poetry by Richard Truhlar, Minnie Dalton, Jon Daunt and William McGonagall. As a sample the editor selected these lines (poet unidentified):

> Yes, this is a great nation,
> Lots of drugs but sex education.
> The streets are filled with perverts,
> And we get smog alerts.

They publish one chapbook a year, 64 pp. **Sample postpaid: $6. Submit to the anthology only. Previously published poems and simultaneous submissions OK. Reports in 1 week. Pays 1 copy "or by arrangement."** The editor explains, "Charnel House is mainly a fiction imprint, but we are doing a series of bad poetry anthologies because no one else is doing them."

CHASTITY & HOLINESS MAGAZINE; CHRISTIANIC POETIC MINISTRY; C.J.L. PRESS/ART CO.; THE POLYGLOT ARMY (IV-Religious), 22006 Thorncliffe P.O., Toronto, Ontario M4H 1N9 Canada, phone (416)423-6781, founded 1988, editor-in-chief Cecil Justin Lam, publishes "Christianic works, Christianic long poems and books by new inspirational writers. Old writers also accepted. Poetry should be **religious, Christianic, inspirational. All styles, all forms. No restriction as to poetic expressions. No limit to length. The longer is usually the more welcome; Christ and inspired poetry related, to spread the Gospel of love and truth. No Satanic or obscene poetry. No secular poetry with no fixed aim of life view. No garbage talker and poets who do not know what is happening and what they are doing with their words."** They have recently published poetry by Thomas Kretz, David Castleman and Hugh Alexander. As a sample the editor selected these lines by Joanna M. Weston:

> Explode into joy,
> oh my soul
> Explode into
> movement

into
dance
Swirl with
the cymbals
The magazine appears twice a year, 8½×7″, 28 pp., photocopied from typescript, paper cover. They accept about 30% of 100 poems received a year. Press run: 200 for 50 subscriptions of which all are libraries. Subscription: $10. **Sample postpaid: $5. Send SASE for guidelines. Pays "prayers and rewards plus 1 copy." Simultaneous submissions and previously published poems OK. Reports immediately. For book publication by C.J.L. Press submit 3 samples, bio, publications. Reports in 4 weeks. Pays 1 copy plus 20% royalties. "Awards will be granted on the basis of Christianic literary performance."** The editor says, "All living creatures, men or aliens may submit to us. The central goal of our publishing firm is to present the World and the Universe with the Holy Sacrifice and Resurrected life of Christ. Intensive Research must be carried out in ensuring all co-ordinative aspects of publishing and economics may match." He provides criticism for $100/100 pp. Reviews books of poetry. "Constructive comments will be used to encourage the on-going of writing ventures. The publication of any work may imply success at a premature timing; therefore considerable on-the-line efforts must be constantly attended."

THE CHATTAHOOCHEE REVIEW (II), DeKalb College, 2101 Womack Rd., Dunwoody GA 30338, phone (404)551-3166, founded 1980, editor-in-chief Lamar York, a quarterly of poetry, short fiction, essays, reviews and interviews, published by DeKalb College. **"We like to publish beginners alongside professional writers. We are open to poetry from traditional forms to avant-garde and any subject matter or length or style."** They have recently published poems by Fred Chappell, Rosemary Daniell, Ed Minus, Bettie Sellers and Jessie Hill Ford. *The Review* is 6×9″, professionally printed on white stock with b/w reproductions of artwork, 90 pp., flat-spined, with one-color card cover. Circulation is 1,000, of which 500 are complimentary copies sent to editors and "miscellaneous VIP's." Price per issue is $4, subscription $15/year. **Sample available for $4 postpaid, guidelines for SASE. Pay is 2 copies. Writers should send 1 copy of each poem and a cover letter with bio material. Reporting time is 6 months and time to publication is 3-4 months. Queries will be answered in 1-2 weeks. No simultaneous submissions. Photocopied or dot-matrix MSS are OK but disks are not.** Reviews books of poetry.

CHELSEA; CHELSEA AWARD COMPETITION (III, IV-Translations), P.O. Box 5880, Grand Central Station, New York NY 10163, founded 1958, editor Sonia Raiziss, associate editors Richard Foerster, Alfred de Palchi and Caila Rossi, is a long-established, high-quality literary annual aiming to promote intercultural communication. **"We look for intelligence and sophisticated technique in both experimental and traditional forms. Always interested in translations of contemporary poets. Length: 5-7 pp. per submission. Although our tastes are eclectic, we lean toward the cosmopolitan avant-garde. Do not want to see 'inspirational' verse, pornography or poems that rhyme merely for the sake of rhyme."** They have recently published poetry by Lucille Clifton, Rita Dove, Laura (Riding) Jackson, Len Roberts and William Van Wert. I have not seen a recent issue, but the editors describe it as "160-240 pp., flat-spined, 6×9″, offset, cover art varies, occasional use of photographs, ads." Circulation: 1,300, 600 subscriptions of which 200 are libraries. Subscription: $11. **Sample: $4 or more depending on issue. Send SASE for a brochure describing all past issues. Pays $5/page and 2 copies. Reports immediately to 3 months. 5-7 pp. of poetry are ideal; long poems should not exceed 10 pp.; must be typed; clean photocopy OK; include brief bio; no simultaneous submissions. "We try to comment favorably on above-average MSS; otherwise, we do not have time to provide critiques."** Guidelines for their annual Chelsea Award Competition, $500 for poetry, available for SASE to P.O. Box 1040, York Beach ME 03910. Richard Foerster, associate editor, comments: "Beginners should realize that a rejection often has more to do with the magazine's production schedule and special editorial plans than with the quality of the submission. They should also realize that editors of little magazines are always overworked (and almost invariably unpaid) and that it is necessary haste and not a lack of concern or compassion that makes rejections seem coldly impersonal."

CHICAGO REVIEW (III), 5801 S. Kenwood, Chicago IL 60637, founded 1946, poetry editor Anne Myles. **"A sure hand, showing originality and precision of language, form and tone—while avoiding the clichés of critical consensus—is the sole requirement for inclusion in *CR*,** overriding formal affiliation, regional bias or previous history of publication. We have recently published poets as diverse as Kathleen Spivack, J.B. Goodenough, Kathleen Norris, Turner Cassity, Michael Donaghy and Jim Powell; out of the 1,500 submissions we receive each year, we accept around 50." **New submissions read October through June. Payment in copies. Sample: $5.50 postpaid. Response time: 3-4 months, longer in some cases.** Circulation: 2,000. Does not presently review books of poetry, "but we will begin listing books received." Annual contest entries read October 15-December 15; $5 entry fee, $100 prize. Write for details.

‡CHICKADEE MAGAZINE; THE YOUNG NATURALIST FOUNDATION (IV-Children, nature), Suite 306, 56 the Esplanade, Toronto, Ontario M5E 1A7 Canada, founded 1979, editor Catherine Ripley, is a magazine **for children 3-9 about nature** appearing 10/year. They want **"evocative poetry; poems that play with words; humorous poetry; no longer than 50 lines. Nothing religious, anthropomorphic; no formal language; no poetry that is difficult to understand."** As a sample, I selected these lines from "The Nervous Mountain Climber" by Colin McKim:

> *To anyone who'll listen*
> *He mutters with a sigh*
> *"My big complaint with mountains*
> *Is they make them much too high."*

It is magazine-sized, professionally published, 32 pp. printed in full-color, with paper cover. They accept 1-2% of 500 poems received. Press run 40,000 for 21,000 subscribers of which 2,000 are libraries. Subscription: $14.95 US. **Sample postpaid: $3.75. Send SASE for writers' guidelines. Pays $10-75/poem plus 2 copies. Simultaneous submissions considered but not encouraged.** "*CM* is a 'hands-on' science and nature publication designed to entertain and educate 3-9 year olds. Each issue contains photos, illustrations, an easy-to-read animal story, a craft project, puzzles, a science experiment and a pullout poster."

CHICORY BLUE PRESS (V), 795 East St. N., Goshen CT 06756, founded 1988, publisher Sondra Zeidenstein, publishes poetry but **accepts no unsolicited MSS and "am not currently accepting queries."**

‡CHILDREN'S ALBUM (IV-Children), P.O. Box 6086, Concord CA 94524, phone (415)671-9852, founded 1984, editor Margo M. Lemas. *Children's Album* is a bimonthly literary magazine featuring **fiction and poetry written only by children 8-14.** Crafts, written by adults for children in that age group, are also included. Adult input is needed in the areas of crafts; science projects; covers; fillers; jokes; word puzzles; and cartoons. The magazine uses original artwork, graphics, no ads. Subscription: $15. **Sample: $3 postpaid. Guidelines available with SASE. Pays children 1 year free subscription. Reports in 2-8 weeks, backlog up to a year.**

CHILDREN'S BETTER HEALTH INSTITUTE; BENJAMIN FRANKLIN LITERARY AND MEDICAL SOCIETY, INC.; HUMPTY DUMPTY'S MAGAZINE; TURTLE MAGAZINE FOR PRESCHOOL KIDS; CHILDREN'S DIGEST; CHILDREN'S PLAYMATE; JACK AND JILL; CHILD LIFE (IV-Children), 1100 Waterway Blvd., Box 567, Indianapolis IN 46206. This publisher of magazines stressing health for children has a **variety of needs for mostly short, simple poems, for which they pay $15 minimum. Send SASE for guidelines.** For example, *Humpty Dumpty* is for ages 4-6; *Turtle* is for preschoolers, similar emphasis, uses many stories in rhyme—and action rhymes, etc.; *Children's Digest* is for preteens (10-13); *Jack and Jill* is for ages 7-10. *Child Life* is for ages 9-11. *Children's Playmate* is for ages 6-8. All appear 8 times a year in a 6½×9" 48 pp. format, slick paper with cartoon art, very colorful. The editors advise that writers who appear regularly in their publications **study current issues carefully. Samples: 75¢ each, postpaid.**

‡CHIMERA POETRY MAGAZINE FOR CHILDREN; CHIMERA SUMMER POETRY CONTEST (I, IV-Children), P.O. Box 1007, Merchantville NJ 08109, founded 1990, editor Michael Northen appears quarterly using **"poetry by children (ages 6-18), any form or subject; poetry by adults for children; and commentary by children on writing poetry. Prefer poems less than 30 lines, but will consider longer ones. No poetry by adults for adults, poetry with language which would offend children or poetry by adults for children that is 'cute,' condescending or saccharine."** The editor chose 2 sample poems, the first, "My Bear" by Jillian Gault, age 10:

> *He sits upon my shelf at night*
> *With fur so brown and eyes so bright*
> *He sits so still I know he will*
> *Watch me through the night.*

And the second by Amy Roselle, age 16:

> *Sprinkles of memories*
> *Drip down the windowsill*
> *Cloudy thoughts of*
> *Someone far away*
> *Bring a windy chill . . .*

The magazine is "to provide a publication where young writers can have poetry accepted and printed; to give writers for children a forum for writing." It is 40-52 pp., photocopied from typescript with printed card cover, digest-sized. Press run 200 copies for 100 subscribers. It is distributed free to teachers, schools and adult contributors. Subscription: $7/year. **Sample: $2. Pays adults 1 copy, nothing to children, not even copies. "The magazine is kept inexpensive so** that young writers, if they wish, can afford copies of issues with their poems in print. I work closely with schools and encourage class submissions by teachers. Schools with several students submitting receive a free copy. Since I encourage beginning poets I have no strict guidelines other than name, address and age. Name of school is appreciated. SASE is not necessary for young writers, but is appreciated also. I like comments from writers about their writing. Acceptance in about one month. I try to comment on serious poetry submitted by individuals. I encourage classroom submissions but cannot respond to each poem. Poems are printed uncorrected either in spelling or punctuation." Reviews books of poetry if written for children or by young writer (under 18). Summer poetry contest runs from June 1-July 20. Prizes awarded in 2 age groups (5-12, 13-18). No entry fee. Winners printed in summer issue of *Chimera*.

CHIRON REVIEW; CHIRON BOOKS; CHIRON REVIEW POETRY CONTEST (I, II), 1514 Stone, Great Bend KS 67530-4027, phone (316)792-5025, founded 1982 as *Kindred Spirit*, editor Michael Hathaway, assistant editor Jane Hathaway, contributing editor (poetry) Gerald Locklin, is a tabloid quarterly using photographs of featured writers. They have recently published poetry by Charles Bukowski, Federico Garcia Lorca, Edward Field and Elliot Fried. As a sample the editors selected these lines excerpted from "Youth And Car Stalled in Snowy Ravine," a poem from a series of poems by Robert Peters about Randy Kraft, notorious California serial killer:

Syllables of foam. My teeth are crumbling into
talc. Your body is mere skin and cartilage. You
are too young to be a fallen tree. Shall I
strangle you. Forgive me. I wallow in psychic
ditches of filth. Can I ever love you enough?

Their press run is about 2,000. Each issue is 24-32 pp. and "contains dozens of poems." **Sample: $2 postpaid ($4 overseas or institutions). Send SASE for guidelines. Send 5 poems "typed or printed legibly." They will consider simultaneous submissions but not previously published poems. Pays 1 copy. Reports in 2-4 weeks.** Reviews books of poetry. For book publication submit complete MS. They publish 1-3 books/year, flat-spined, professionally printed, **paying 25% of press run of 100-200 copies.** Their annual poetry contest offers awards of $100 plus 1-page feature in Winter issue, $50, and 5 free subscriptions and a Chiron Press book; entry fee $4 for up to 6 poems.

THE CHRISTIAN CENTURY (II, IV-Religious, social issues), 407 S. Dearborn St., Chicago IL 60605, founded 1884, named *The Christian Century* 1900, founded again 1908, joined by *New Christian* 1970, poetry editor Dean Peerman. This "ecumenical weekly" is a liberal, sophisticated journal of news, articles of opinion and reviews from a generally Christian point-of-view, **using approximately one poem per issue, not necessarily on religious themes but in keeping with the literate tone of the magazine. "No pietistic or sentimental doggerel, please."** They have recently published poems by Robert Beum, Joan Rohr Myers, Ida Fasel, Jill Baumgaertner, Louis Miles and J. Barrie Shepherd. As a sample the editor selected the short poem "Adam's Revenge" by James Worley:

Condemned to be cursed by memory,
he took four plants from paradise
to share his fate of wanting what had been:
the violet, made purpler by its loss;
forsythia, forever creeping back;
the willow drooping toward its roots;
the ivy clinging, even as it climbed,
to what it still remembered of un-time:
robbed of such beauty, paradise was left
with the same longing and the same regret.

The journal is magazine-sized, printed on quality newsprint, using b/w art, cartoons and ads, about 30 pp., saddle-stapled. **Payment: usually $20/poem. Sample: $1.50 postpaid. No simultaneous submissions. Submissions without SASE or IRCs will not be returned.** Reviews books of poetry "infrequently."

THE CHRISTIAN SCIENCE MONITOR (II), 1 Norway St., Boston MA 02115, phone (617)450-2000, founded 1908, a national daily newspaper with a weekly international edition. **Poetry used regularly in The Home Forum. Pays $25 and up.**

‡THE CHRISTIAN WAY (IV-Inspirational, subscription), 8131 Lemon Ave. #4, La Mesa CA 91941, founded 1984, editor/publisher Kae Carter Jaworski, is a monthly newsletter using **poems up to 24 lines** that are "inspirational, uplifting. Christian verse accepted, seasonal verse. Purpose is to uplift Christianity, build self-esteem and encourage new and professional poets: nature, inspirational, love, family, friends, people. No porno, meaningless verse, profanity-type." The newsletter has recently published poems by Liz Carter Richards, Henry W. Gurley, Betty B. Millar and Sister Mary Gemma Brunke. As a sample the editor selected these lines from "Those Who Truly Love," poet unidentified:

> Their eyes overlook much that would hurt,
> Their ears listen with empathy.
> Their tongues bring encouragement.
> Their hands are willing to be helpful,
> Their minds think with Christ.
> Their love is universal.

The newsletter is magazine-sized, 8-10 pp. The editor says she receives more than 300 pieces each month and "I accept 85-90% of it, keep some for future issues." Press run is 320 for 300 subscriptions. Subscription: $12. Sample: $2. Pays 1 copy. *Contributors must subscribe.* "I am touchy about misspelled words and sloppy work." Simultaneous submissions and previously published OK. Reports within two days. Editor sometimes comments on rejections. She says, "Subscribe to as many good magazines as you can, observing how well-known or widely published poets work. Join poetry clubs and write and rewrite your poems until they are as near perfect as you can make them. Do not get discouraged when you get rejection slips. Alway send SASE for reply. Do a professional job and you will be published. It is wise to order a sample copy before submitting poetry."

THE CHRISTOPHER PUBLISHING HOUSE (II), 24 Rockland St., Commerce Green, Hanover MA 02339, phone (617)826-7474, FAX (617)826-5556, managing editor Nancy Lucas, says "We will review all forms of poetry." Submit complete MS.

‡**THE CHRONICLE OF THE HORSE (IV-Themes)**, P.O. Box 46, Middleburg VA 22117, phone (703)687-6341, founded 1937, assistant editor Cynthia Foley, is a weekly magazine using short poetry related to horses "the shorter the better. No free verse." The magazine is devoted to English horse sports, such as horse shows and steeplechasing. It averages 68 pp., magazine-sized. Subscription: $42. Sample postpaid: $2. Pays $15/poem. "We review books submitted to us but do not accept reviews for publication." No simultaneous submissions. "We want first North American rights." Reports in 2-4 weeks. Summer "is not a good time" to submit. 2-3 editors read poems.

CIMARRON REVIEW (II), 205 Morrill Hall, Oklahoma State University, Stillwater OK 74078-0135, founded 1967, poetry editors Thomas Reiter, Randy Phillis and Sally Shigley, is a quarterly 96-pp. literary journal. "Reflecting humanity in contemporary society, we seek literary examples of Man Triumphant in a technological world. We emphasize quality and style. We like clear, evocative poetry (lyric or narrative) that uses images to enhance the human situation. No obscure poetry. No sing-song verse. No quaint prairie verse. No restrictions as to subject matter, although we tend to publish more structured poetry (attention to line and stanza). Also, we are conscious of our academic readership (mostly other writers) and attempt to accept poems that everyone will admire." Among poets they have published are Robert Cooperman, James McKean, David Citino and Lynn Domina. There are 10-12 pages of poetry in each issue, circulation of 500, mostly libraries. Submit to Deborah Bransford, managing editor, any time, 3-5 poems, name and address on each poem, typed, single- or double-spaced. Clear photocopies acceptable. No simultaneous submissions. Replies within 4-6 weeks. They pay when they have a grant to do so. Reviews books of poetry. Subscription rates: $3 per issue, $12 per year ($15, Canada), $30 for 3 years ($40, Canada), plus $2.50 for all international subscriptions.

CINCINNATI POETRY REVIEW (II, IV-Regional), Dept. of English (069), University of Cincinnati, Cincinnati OH 45221, founded 1975, editor Dallas Wiebe "attempts to set local poets in a national context. Each issue includes a quarter to a third of work by local poets (within about 100 miles of Cincinnati), but most are from all over." They use "all kinds" of poetry, have published such poets as James Baker Hall, Judith B. Goodenough, David Citino, Colleen McElroy, Harry Humes, Keith Wahle and Yusef Komunyakaa. The editor selected this sample from "The Big Picture" by Jeff Hillard:

> There were no changes in the forecast
> he was going, regardless,
> There's nothing the wind can't track down.

They try to get out two issues a year, but it's irregular—handsomely printed, flat-spined, 80 pp., digest-sized magazine, all poems, art on the glossy card cover. Circulation is about 1,000, with 92 subscriptions, 12 of which are libraries. They use about 120 of 2,000-3,000 submissions per year. Sample: $2. Subscription: $9 for 4 issues. Typed MSS with address on each poem, photocopies OK. Reports in 1-3 months. Payment is 2 copies. Each issue offers a poetry contest for poems of all types. The poems judged best and second in each issue receive cash awards of $150 and $50, and they hope to increase it.

THE CINCINNATI POETS' COLLECTIVE (II), 6910 W. Waters Ave. #1005, Tampa FL 33634, founded 1988, % Rebecca D. Sullivan, is an annual poetry magazine. "Prefer that the length of the poem be such that it lends itself to the poem's content; nothing hackneyed, didactic; no greeting-card subjects or rhyme." Poets recently published include Dr. Anthony Sean Koeninger, Beatrice G. Holt and Terry Watada. As a sample the editor selected the following lines from "No Harm Done" by Martha M. Vertreace:

> Yeast raises no warning about Turks outside Vienna.
> Holy Saturday: I shed my glasses,
> watch edges of your face grow soft, then fade,
> an owl scared awake as sun rises
> too fast in oaks. Going to the kitchen, the busboy
> swings a plastic pail of carrots

Send SASE for guidelines. Submit MSS Oct. 1-March 1 only. Pays 1 copy. Submit up to 5 poems at a time. Simultaneous submissions will be considered, but not previously published poems. Reports in 4-6 months.

CITY LIGHTS BOOKS (III), 261 Columbus Ave., San Francisco CA 94133, phone (415)362-1901, founded 1955, edited by Lawrence Ferlinghetti and Nancy J. Peters, achieved prominence with the publication of Allen Ginsberg's **Howl** and other **poetry of the "Beat" school**. They publish "**poetry and advance-guard writing in the libertarian tradition.**" Paper and cloth. Simultaneous submissions OK, payment varies, reporting time 4-6 weeks.

‡**CITY SCRIPTUM (I)**, City College of San Francisco, 50 Phelan Ave., San Francisco CA 94112, phone (415)239-3000, founded 1988, editor-in-chief Brown Miller, appears twice a year using "any form from closed (traditional) to open (so-called 'free verse') but must be inventive, resonant, memorable, worth reading, nothing trite, wordy, sentimental, or any kind that reveals lack of knowledge about 20th Century verse." They have recently published poetry by Lyn Lifshin, A.D. Winans and Seaborn Jones. As a sample the editor selected these lines from "Winter in Auschwitz" by Gayle Leyton:

> a small boy
> has lost his birthday
> his mother
> keeper of his secrets
> wanders under the earth
> calling his name

It is handsomely printed, magazine-sized, 58 pp. with matte card cover. Press run 1,000 for 10 subscribers of which 5 are libraries. 20 shelf sales. Subscription: $8. Sample postpaid: $4 (when available). Send SASE for guidelines. Reports in 2-6 months. Pays 2 copies. Do not submit July-August. The editor advises, "Read widely. Know the important poetry and poetic theories/criticism of this century. Then strive for a voice and vision of your own. Avoid too much of the discursive. Create surprise/magic that rings true."

THE CLASSICAL OUTLOOK (IV-Themes, translations), Classics Dept., Park Hall, University of Georgia, Athens GA 30602, founded 1924, poetry editors Prof. David Middleton (original English verse) and Prof. Jane Phillips (translations and original Latin verse), "is an internationally circulated quarterly journal (4,000 subscriptions, of which 250 are libraries) for high school and college Latin and Classics teachers, published by the American Classical League." **They invite submissions of "original poems in English on classical themes, verse translations from Greek and Roman authors, and original Latin poems. Submissions should, as a rule, be written in traditional poetic forms and should demonstrate skill in the use of meter, diction and rhyme if rhyme is employed. Original poems should be more than mere exercise pieces or the poetry of nostalgia. Translations should be accompanied by a photocopy of the original Greek or Latin text. Latin originals should be accompanied by a literal English rendering of the text. Submissions should not exceed 50 lines."** They have recently published work by Francis Fike. As a sample the editor selected the first two stanzas of Roy Fuller's "Somewhere in Socrates":

> Mysterious bodily changes in the night
> From powers far from understood; the force
> Of four o'clock, of just perceptible light!
>
> Socrates said: death is a dreamless sleep,
> Or the delightful prospect of questioning
> Old Homer. Though what answer from the deep-

There are 2-3 magazine-sized pages of poetry in each issue, and they use 55% of the approximately 150 submissions they receive each year. They have a 6-12 month backlog, 4 month lead time. **Submit 2 copies, double-spaced.** Receipt is acknowledged by letter. Poetry is refereed by poetry editors. Reports in 3-6 months. Pays in 5 complimentary copies. Sample copies available from the American Classical League, Miami University, Oxford OH 45056 for $7.50. Guidelines available for SASE. Reviews books of poetry "if the poetry is sufficiently classical in nature."

CLEANING BUSINESS MAGAZINE; WRITERS PUBLISHING SERVICE CO. (IV-Themes), 1512 Western Ave., P.O. Box 1273, Seattle WA 98111, phone (206)622-4241, founded 1976, poetry editor William R. Griffin. *CBM* (formerly Service Business Magazine) is "a quarterly magazine **for cleaning and maintenance professionals" and uses some poetry relating to their interests. "To be considered for publication in** *Cleaning Business,* **submit poetry that relates to our specific audience—cleaning and self-employment."** He has recently published poetry by Don Wilson, Phoebe Bosche, Trudie Mercer and Joe Keppler. I have not seen the magazine, but the editor says it is 8½ × 11", 100 pp., offset litho, using ads, art and graphics. Of 50 poems received, he uses about 10. Press run is 5,000 for 3,000 subscriptions (100 of them libraries), 500 shelf sales. Subscription: $20. Per issue $5. **Sample: $3** postpaid. Send SASE and $3 for guidelines. **Pays $5-10 plus 1 copy. Simultaneous submissions OK, no previously published poems.** Writers Publishing Service Co. is an imprint for subsidized publication of poetry (author's expense) and other services to writers. William Griffin suggests that "poets identify a specific market and work to build a readership that can be tapped again and again over a period of years with new books."

CLEVELAND STATE UNIVERSITY POETRY CENTER; CSU POETRY SERIES (II); CLEVELAND POETS SERIES (IV-Regional), Cleveland State University, Cleveland OH 44115, director Nuala Archer, editors Leonard Trawick and David Evett. The Poetry Center was founded in 1962, first publications in 1971. **The Poetry Center publishes the CSU Poetry Series for poets in general and the Cleveland Poets Series for Ohio poets.** "Open to many kinds of form, length, subject-matter, style and purpose. Should be well-crafted, clearly of professional quality, ultimately serious (even when humorous). No light verse, devotional verse, or verse in which rhyme and meter seem to be of major importance." They have published poetry by Martha Collins, Eric Trethewey, Naomi Clark and Stephen Tapscott. As a sample Leonard Trawick selected these lines from **Inland, Thinking of Waves** by Sarah Provost (CSU Poetry Center, 1991):

> It seems to be spring, sweetie,
> here in the heart of the green
> proprieties. The thirsty wind is a rascal,
> makes quick work of our splendid
> coifs . . . .

Books are chosen for publication from the entries to the CSU Poetry Center Prize contest. (Write for free catalog and sampler of some 65 Poetry Center books.) **Deadline March 1, entrance fee $10; which awards the winner $1,000 and publication;** they publish some other entrants in the Poetry Series: 50 copies (of press run of 1,000), 10% royalty contract. The Cleveland Poets Series (for Ohio poets) offers 100 copies of a press run of 600. To submit for all series, send MS between December 1 and March 1. Reports on all submissions for the year by the end of July. MSS should be for books of 50-100 pp., pages numbered, poet's name and address on cover sheet, clearly typed. Photocopies OK, and poems may have been previously published (listed on an acknowledgement page). Send SASE for guidelines. The Center also publishes other volumes of poetry, including chapbooks (20-30 pp.), with a **$5 reading fee for each submission (except for Ohio residents).**

THE CLIMBING ART (IV-Themes), P.O. Box 816, Alamosa CO 81101, phone (719)589-5579, founded 1986, editor David Mazel, is a quarterly magazine **"read mainly by mountain enthusiasts who appreciate good writing about mountains and mountaineering. We are open to all forms and lengths. The only requirement is that the work be fresh, well-written, and in some way of interest to those who love the mountains. If in doubt, submit it."** As a sample the editor selected these lines by Reg Saner:

> An hour or so . . . I'll have tracked the last snowfield
> and be far down this mountain, leaving
> bootprints that believed in themselves
> to brighten . . .

It is 32 pp., magazine-sized, professionally printed on heavy stock with glossy card cover. Press run: 1,050 for 800 subscriptions of which 5 are libraries, 350 shelf sales. They use 1-4 poems per issue of 100-200 submissions received/per year. Subscription: $10. **Sample postpaid: $2.75. Pays 3 copies and subscription. Simultaneous submissions and previously published poems OK. Reports in 2 months.** Reviews books of poetry only if they concern mountains.

CLOCKWATCH REVIEW (II, III), James Plath, Dept. of English, Illinois Wesleyan University, Bloomington IL 61702, phone (309)556-3352, founded 1983, James Plath is editor, and Lynn Devore, James McGowan and Pamela Muirhead are associate editors. "We publish a variety of styles, leaning toward poetry which goes beyond the experience of self in an attempt to SAY something, without sounding pedantic or strained. We like a **strong, natural voice**, and lively, unusual combinations in language. Something *fresh, and that includes subject matter as well. It has been our experience that extremely short/long poems are hard to pull off*. Though we'll publish exceptions, we prefer to see poems that can fit on one published page (digest-sized) which runs **about 32 lines or less**." They have recently published Peter Wild, Martha Vertreace, John Knoepfle, Rita Dove and Peter Meinke. Asked for a sample, the editors say "trying to pick only four lines seems like telling people what detail we'd like to see in a brick, when what we're more interested in is the design of the *house*." Nonetheless, they selected these sample lines from Philip Schultz's "The Horizon":

> *as a boy he climbed hills beyond Minsk*
> *to see the sky expanding like an accordion*
> *of stars drifting in fiery halos, light*
> *rooting a thousand million flowers*

The 80 pp., semiannual *CR* is printed on glossy paper with colored, glossy cover. They use 7-10 unsolicited poems in each issue, with 1 featured poet. Circulation is 1,400, with 120 subscribers, of which 25 are libraries. They send out 300 complimentary copies and "The balance is wholesale distribution and single-copy sales." Sample: $4 postpaid. They receive 18,000 submissions per year, use 20-30. No backlog. **Prefer batches of 5-6 poems. "We are not bowled over by large lists of previous publications, but brief letters of introduction or sparse mini-vitas are read out of curiosity. One poem per page, typed, single-spacing OK, photocopy OK if indicated that it is not a simultaneous submission (which we do NOT accept). Reports in 2 weeks; 2 months if under serious consideration. Payment is 3 copies, and, when possible, small cash awards — currently $10/poem."** They will comment "if asked, and if time permits."

CLOUD RIDGE PRESS (V), 2135 Stony Hill Rd., Boulder CO 80303, founded 1985, editor Elaine Kohler, a "literary small press for unique works in poetry and prose." They publish letterpress and offset books in both paperback and hardcover editions. In poetry, they want **"strong images of the numinous qualities in authentic experience grounded in a landscape and its people."** The first book, published in 1985, was **Ondina: A Narrative Poem**, by John Roberts. As a sample, the editor selected the following lines:

> *Some kill, and some get killed.*
> *But who's to say what's real or not,*
> *when dreams lay open spooky life,*
> *and life comes a-swirlin at you dreamin?*

The book is 6 × 9¼", handsomely printed on buff stock, cloth bound in black with silver decoration and spine lettering, 131 pages. Eight hundred copies were bound in Curtis Flannel and 200 copies (of which mine is one) bound in cloth over boards, numbered and signed by the poet and artist. This letterpress edition, priced at $18/cloth and $12/paper, is not available in bookstores but only by mail from the press. The trade edition was photo-offset from the original, in both cloth and paper bindings, and is sold in bookstores. The press plans to publish 1-2 books/year. **Since they are not accepting unsolicited MSS, writers should query first. Queries will be answered in 2 weeks and MSS reported on in 1 month. Simultaneous submissions are acceptable, as are photocopied or dot-matrix MSS. Royalties are 10% plus a negotiable number of author's copies.** A brochure is free on request; send #10 SASE.

CLUBHOUSE; YOUR STORY HOUR (I, IV-Children, teens), P.O. Box 15, Berrien Springs MI 49103, poetry editor Elaine Trumbo, **pays about $12 for poems under 24 lines plus 2 contributor's copies.** The publication is printed in conjunction with the **Your Story Hour** radio program, founded 1949, which is designed to teach the Bible and moral life to children. The magazine, *Clubhouse*, started with that title in 1982, but as *Good Deeder*, its original name, it has been published since 1951. Elaine Trumbo says, "We do like humor or mood pieces. Don't like mushy-sweet 'Christian' poetry. We don't have space for long poems. Best — 16 lines or under." They have recently published poetry by Lillian M. Fisher, Audrey Osofsky, Sharon K. Motzko, Bruce Bash and Craig Peters. As a sample the editor selected these lines from "A Magic Place" by C. Dell Turney:

> *In my room*
> *There's a magic place*
> *Where I can show*
> *Myself my face*
> *And every secret*
> *I won't tell*
> *My mirror keeps it*
> *Very well*

The magazine has a circulation of 10,000, with 10,000 subscriptions of which maybe 5 are libraries. Subscription: $5, 6 issues per year. **Sample: 3 oz. postage. Writer's guidelines are available** for SASE, submit MSS in April, simultaneous submissions OK. The "evaluation sheet" for returned MSS gives reasons for acceptance or rejection. The editor advises, "Give us poetry with freshness and imagination. We most often use mood pieces and humorous poems that appeal to children."

THE CLYDE PRESS (IV-Themes), 373 Lincoln Parkway, Buffalo NY 14216, phone (716)875-4713 or 834-1254, founded 1976, poetry editor Catherine Harris Ainsworth, specializes in folklore, oral literature, ethnic tales and legends, games, calendar customs, jump rope verses, superstitions and family tales—all edited and left in the words of the informants, and all taken from collections that cover about 30 years, 1952-82. They will consider submissions of **folk poetry and songs from bona fide folk collections, "i.e. recorded from the folk or written by the folk, really sung or recited."** Query with samples. Games and Lore of Young Americans, recipient in 1985 of an award from the National Endowment for the Arts.

COACH HOUSE PRESS (II, IV-Regional), 401 (Rear) Huron St., Toronto, Ontario M5S 2G5 Canada, phone (416)979-7374, FAX (416)979-7006, founded 1964, poetry editors Michael Ondaatje, Christopher Dewdney and Victor Coleman, publishes **"mostly living Canadian writers of 'post-modern' poetry and fiction, drama and literary criticism."** They have printed finely-printed flat-spined paperback collections by such poets as Phyllis Webb, Michael Ondaatje, Sharon Thesen, Betsy Warland and Roy Kiyooka. They want **"no religious, confessional stuff or traditional rhyme schemes. We lean toward experimental."** Query with 10 samples. Cover letter should include bio and other publications. **Double-spaced, photocopy or dot-matrix OK. Reports in 12-16 weeks. Contract is for 10% royalties, 5 copies.** Catalog sent on request, or "Beyond Baroque Foundation and Northwestern University receive everything we do. Also, samples are on display in the Small Press Centre in N.Y.C. **We expect poets to be familiar with the Coach House flavor and to have a few journal publication credits to their name.** You don't have to be famous, but you do have to be good. Make the effort to do a little research on us, and save yourself time and postage. No SASE, no reply . . . and Canada Post does not accept American postage."

COCHRAN'S CORNER (I, IV-Subscribers), P.O. Box 2036, Waldorf MD 20604, phone (301)843-0485, founded 1985, poetry editor Billye Keene, is a **"family type" quarterly open to beginners, preferring poems of 20 lines or less. You have to be a subscriber to submit. "Any subject or style (except porn)."** She has recently published poetry by J. Alvin Speers, Becky Knight and Francesco BiVone. As a sample she selected these lines from "Night of Unknown" (poet unidentified):

> *From under my door your breeze seeps confident and slow,*
> *Preparing a subtle path for your patchwork cold to creep.*

CC is 58 pp. saddle-stapled, desktop publishing, with matte card cover, press run of 500. **Subscription: $15. Send SASE for guidelines. Sample: $5 plus SASE. Pays 2 copies. Simultaneous submissions and previously published poems OK. Reports in average of 3 months.** Reviews books of poetry. Contests in March and July; $3 entry fee for 2 poems. "We provide criticism if requested at the rate of $1 per page. Write from the heart, but don't forget your readers. You must work to find the exact words that mirror your feelings, so the reader can share your feelings."

THE COE REVIEW (II), Coe College, 1220 1st Ave. NE, Cedar Rapids IA 52402, phone (319)399-8660, founded 1972, poetry editor James Nulick, is "an annual little literary magazine with **emphasis on the innovative and unselfconscious** poetry and fiction. We are **open to virtually any and all subject-matter."** They have recently published poetry by James Galvin and Jan Weissmiller. As a sample these lines were selected by the editor from "The Spider" by Steve Ketzer Jr.:

> *I saw him reeling web & building,*
> *And "Oh!" I thought, "It's life!"*
> *I looked up moments later,*
> *And he hung there, quite dead.*

The annual is 100-150 pp., flat-spined, digest-sized with matte card cover. "Each issue includes 4-8 reproductions of works of art, usually photographs, lithography and etched prints." Circulation is about 500. **Sample: $4 postpaid. Send SASE for guidelines. Pays 1 copy. Reports in 6-8 weeks. Accepted work appears in the next issue, published in Spring. No simultaneous submissions. Photocopy OK. Include "brief cover letter."** The editor says, "We are supportive in the endeavors of poets whose material is original and tasteful. We are eclectic in our publication choices in that variety of subject matter and style make the *Coe Review* exciting."

‡COFFEEHOUSE POETS' QUARTERLY (I), P.O. Box 15123, San Luis Obispo CA 93406, founded 1990, editor Ray Foreman, **pays nothing, not even copies. They want "free verse that is fresh and imaginative that lets the reader share the experience. Psychologically penetrating. Saccharine, pablum, religious, greeting cards, academic assignments are out."** They have recently published poetry by Will Inman,

Greg Boyd and James Cushing. As a sample the editor selected the first of 4 stanzas of "Cafe in a Small Town" by Alex Johnson:

> She sits alone at a table, but I lack the courage.
> The cold rain chills the static warm of this cafe
> with its papered walls of beaches and bikinied girls.
> Like my thoughts, they cover neglected hidden cracks.

It is 40-60 pp. Press run 300 for 47 subscribers, 130 shelf sales. They accept about 30% of 500 poems submitted/year. "We showcase actively writing poets and provide purpose for them to continue to write and take chances with their work. We don't look for safe poetry." Subscription: $8. **Sample postpaid: $2. Send SASE for guidelines. Reports in about 2 weeks. "Will critique poems lightly for subscribers as time permits."** The editor says, "Only your mother cares how smart you are. Poetry must communicate in accessible language. Private imagery, nightmares, gibberish and mental gymnastics belong in a journal. Poetry is language performance and needs clarity to be appreciated by an audience. If you don't hook your reader in the first few lines, you've had it. Now you do want an audience, don't you?"

COKEFISH (I), P.O. Box 683, Long Valley NJ 07853, phone (908)876-3824, founded 1990, editor Ana Pine, **is a monthly newsletter with an entry fee of $1/3 poems. "I want to see work that has passion behind it. From the traditional to the avant-garde, provocative to discreet, trivial to the significant. Am interested in social issues, alternative, avant-garde, erotica and humor for people with nothing to hide."** They have recently published poetry by Charles Bukowski, Lyn Lifshin, Joy Walsh and Tracy Lyn Rottkamp. As a sample the editor selected these lines from Tony Moffett's poem "Blue Highway":

> I cry apache I cry mojo
> I cry ghost dance
> I cry jazz oop boodelee skee bob adoo
> I cry blues woke up this mornin'
> dead walkin' in my shoes.

The format is 60 pp., side-stapled on heavy paper with a cover printed on both sides on colored photocopy paper. Press run 100 for 50 subscribers. Subscription: $15. **Sample postpaid: $4. Send SASE for guidelines. Pays 1 copy. Accepts 40% of MSS received. Note entry fee: $1/3 poems, additional $1 for additional poems. Simultaneous submissions and previously published poems OK. Reports in 1 week.** Reviews books of poetry. The editor advises, "Spread the word; don't let your poems sit and vegetate in a drawer. Send me stuff that will make may hair stand up on end."

CO-LABORER; WOMAN'S NATIONAL AUXILIARY CONVENTION (IV-Religious), P.O. Box 1088,

Nashville TN 37202, phone (615)361-1010, founded 1935, editor Lorene Miley, is "a bimonthly publication **to give women a missionary vision and challenge. We'll consider any length or style as long as the subject is missions."** They do not want to see poetry which is not religious or not related to missions. The editor selected this sample, "Mission," written by E.A. Dixon:

> A simple
> Clay conduit
> Lay nicked
> And scarred
> Amid the
> Arid expanse
> Of souls
> A sturdy grid
> Through which
> Living Water
> Must flow.

The 32 pp. magazine uses at least one poem per issue, circulation 18,000. **Sample postpaid: $1.**

COLLAGES & BRICOLAGES, THE JOURNAL OF INTERNATIONAL WRITING (I,II,IV-Translations, feminist, political, social issues, humor), Office of International Programs, 212 Founders Hall,

University of Pennsylvania, Clarion PA 16214, founded in 1986, editor Marie-José Fortis. *C&B* is a "small literary magazine with **a strong penchant for literary, feminist, avant-garde work.** Strongly encourages poets and fiction writers, as well as essayists, whether English-speaking or foreign. (Note: **Writers sending their work in a foreign language must have their MS accompanied with an English translation.)** We are presently looking for **poetry that is socially aware – politically engaged. No sexism, racism or glorification of war."** *C&B* recently published Cherokee Appalachian poet Marilou Awiakta, an anthologized writer and author of "Red Alert," a reflection of *Dances with Wolves* in the March-April 1991 issue of *Ms Magazine,* and *Selu: Spirit of Survival.* The editor selected these sample lines from Marilou Awiakta's "Women Die Like Trees":

> Women die like trees, limb by limb
> as strain for bearing shade and fruit
> drains sap from branch and stem
> and weight of ice with wrench of wind
> split the heart . . .

The annual is magazine-sized, 100+ pp., flat-spined, with glossy card cover. They accept 5% of 150 poetry submissions/year. Press run 400. **Sample postpaid: $5, or $2.50/back issue. Only submit MSS during the fall. Reporting time is 1-3 months. Pays 2 copies.** "It is recommended that potential contributors order a copy, so as to know what kind of work is desirable. **Enclose a personalized letter.** Be considerate to editors, as many of them work on a voluntary basis and sacrifice much time and energy to encourage writers." Marie-José Fortis says, "It is time to stop being too plastic and too polite and too careful. The Berlin Wall is down. The East will bring to us powerful, daring literary voices, with much to tell. The American writer should follow a similar path. With what was revealed as the temptation of war and the neglect of an effort for peace, too many things are left unsaid."

COLLEGE ENGLISH; NATIONAL COUNCIL OF TEACHERS OF ENGLISH (II), % James C. Raymond, Drawer AL, University of Alabama, Tuscaloosa AL 35487, phone (205)348-6488, editor Dara Wier, University of Massachusetts, Amherst, MA. This journal, which goes 8/year to members of the National Council of Teachers of English (membership: $30, includes subscription to *CE*), is a scholarly journal for the English discipline, but includes poetry by such poets as James Tate, Michael Pettit and Norman Stock. It is 100 pp., saddle-stapled, with matte card cover, 7½×9½", circulation 16,000. **Sample postpaid: $4.50. Pays 6 copies. Reports in 4 months maximum.**

COLORADO NORTH REVIEW (III), UC 208, University Center, University of Northern Colorado, Greeley CO 80639, founded 1963 as *Nova*, editor L. Christopher Baxter, appears twice a year (December and May). **"We consider all MSS without bias, regardless of style, form, genre, or so-called 'schools.'** I open all the mail myself and look primarily for poetic integrity, that is a synthesis between original vision and a unique and organic means of expressing it. Overly poetic language (i.e. artificial) and clichéd sentiments are frowned upon."** They have recently published poetry by Florence Elon, Anselm Hollo, Robert Long, Phyllis Koestenbaum and Eileen Myles. As a sample the editor selected these lines from "Les L'armes Sanglant ĎEnfer" by William Hathaway:

> Go ahead! Rename candy tears,
> red as bloody beads we pricked
> on fingertips for holy love
> as kids. The ones stinging spit-
> fire cinnamon we called "red hots."

It is 100-120 pp. flat-spined (with occasional double issues of up to 220 pp.), printed on 70 lb. vellum paper. They received over 900 MSS for a recent issue, accepted 74 poems from 39 poets (and 12 pieces of fiction). Press run is 2,500 for 65 subscriptions of which 40 are libraries. Subscription $8. **Sample postpaid: $4.50. Do not submit MSS during June or July. Send SASE for guidelines. Pays 2 copies plus CNR T-shirts when available. No simultaneous submissions please! Reports in 4-8 weeks. Editor comments "when time allows or in exceptional cases."** Reviews books of poetry.

COLORADO REVIEW (II, IV-Translations, themes), Dept. of English, 359 Eddy Bldg., Colorado State University, Ft. Collins CO 80523, phone (303)491-6428, founded 1955 as *Colorado State Review*, resurrected 1977 under "New Series" rubric, renamed *Colorado Review* 1985. General and poetry editor Bill Tremblay. *Colorado Review* is a journal of contemporary literature which appears twice annually; it combines short fiction, poetry, interviews with or articles about significant contemporary poets and writers, articles on literature, culture, and the arts, translations of poetry from around the world and reviews of recent works of the literary imagination. **"We're interested in poetry that explores experience in deeply felt new ways; merely descriptive or observational language doesn't move us. Poetry that enters into and focuses on the full range of experience, weaving sharp imagery, original figures and surprising though apt insight together in compressed precise language and compelling rhythm is what triggers an acceptance here."** They have recently published poetry by Bin Ramke, Frank Stewart, Jane Hirshfield and Marge Piercy. They have a circulation of 1,100, 200 subscriptions of which 75 are libraries. They use about 10% of the 500-1,000 submissions they receive per year. **Sample: $5 postpaid. Submit about 5 poems, typewritten or clear photocopy. Reports in 3 to 6 months. Pays $10/printed page. "When work is a near-miss, we will provide brief comment and encouragement,"** Bill Tremblay says. "Our attitude is that we will publish the best work that comes across the editorial desk. We see poetry as a vehicle for exploring states of feeling, but we aren't interested in sentimentality (especially metaphysical)."

COLUMBIA: A MAGAZINE OF POETRY & PROSE; EDITORS' AWARDS (II), 404 Dodge Hall, Columbia University, New York NY 10027, phone (212)280-4391, founded 1977, is a literary semiannual using "quality short stories, novel excerpts, translations, interviews, nonfiction and **poetry, usually no longer than 2 pp. Nothing juvenile, sentimental, simply descriptive.**" They have recently published poetry by Henri Cole, Theresa Svoboda, Eamon Grennan and Jimmy Santiago-Baca. It is digest-sized, approximately 180 pp., with coated cover stock. They publish about 12 poets each year from 400 submissions. Press run 1,250 for 1,000 subscriptions of which 100 are libraries, 150 shelf sales. $6/copy. **Sample postpaid: $6. Send SASE for guidelines. Pays up to 4 copies. Submit double spaced MSS. Reports in 1-2 months.** "Very brief comments at editor's discretion." They offer annual Editors' Awards of $350 and $150 for the best poems published annually. To be considered for these awards enclose fee of $6 (which covers the cost of an issue) and submit before April 1 for fall issue, and before December 1 for spring issue.

COLUMBUS SINGLE SCENE (IV-Themes, humor), P.O. Box 30856, Gahanna OH 43230, founded 1985, poetry editor Jeanne Marlowe, is a monthly magazine, circulation 5,000, for Ohio singles (18 and up), "**positive, upbeat approach to single living, but we're neither yuppies nor pollyannas. Humorous treatments get priority.**" Recently published poets include John Lange and Stephen Parker. The editor chose this sample from "The Pattern" by Paul Warad:

> *Once again you depart.*
> *But*
> *Standing in the darkness of my kitchen,*
> *Disposing your remains,*
> *I expect*
> *And anticipate*
> *Your return.*

Sample: $2 postpaid. Considers simultaneous submissions. Submit maximum 12 poems, dealing with single living or relationships, 1-50 lines. Reporting time is 4 weeks. Pays advertising trade or copy. Reviews books of poetry "only if very relevant to singles."

COMMONWEAL (III,IV-Religious), 15 Dutch St., New York NY 10038, phone (212)732-0800, poetry editor Rosemary Deen, appears every 2 weeks, circulation 20,000, is a general-interest magazine for college-educated readers **by Roman Catholics.** The editor selected this sample from "One is One," sonnets by Marie Ponsot:

> *Heart, you bully, you punk, I'm wrecked, I'm shocked*
> *stiff. You? you still try to rule the world—though*
> *I've got you: identified, starving, locked*
> *in a cage you will not leave alive . . .*

Sample: $3. Prefers serious, witty, well-written poems of up to 75 lines. Does not publish inspirational poems. Considers simultaneous submissions. Pays 50¢ a line.

COMMUNICATIONS PUBLISHING GROUP; COLLEGE PREVIEW, A GUIDE FOR COLLEGE-BOUND STUDENTS; DIRECTIONS, A GUIDE TO CAREER ALTERNATIVES; JOURNEY, A SUCCESS GUIDE FOR COLLEGE AND CAREER-BOUND STUDENTS; VISIONS, A SUCCESS GUIDE FOR NATIVE AMERICAN STUDENTS; FIRST OPPORTUNITY, A GUIDE FOR VOCATIONAL TECHNICAL STUDENTS (IV-Youth, themes, ethnic), 3100 Broadway, 225 PennTower, Kansas City MO 64111, phone (816)756-3039, editor Georgia Clark. These five publications are 40% freelance written. All are designed to inform and motivate their readers in regard to college preparation, career planning and life survival skills. All except *First Opportunity*, which is quarterly, appear in spring and fall. *College Preview* is for **Black and Hispanic young adults, ages 16-21.** Circ. 600,000. *Directions* is for **Black and Hispanic young adults, ages 18-25.** Circ. 500,000. *Journey* is for **Asian-American high school and college students, ages 16-25.** Circ. 200,000. *Visions* is for **Native American students, young adults, ages 16-25.** Circ. 100,000. *First Opportunity* is for **Black and Hispanic young adults, ages 16-21.** Circ. 500,000. All these magazines pay on acceptance. Submit seasonal/holiday material 6 months in advance. Simultaneous, photocopied and previously published submissions OK. Computer printout submissions OK; prefers letter-quality. "Include on manuscript your name, address, phone, Social Security number." Reports in 2 months. Sample copy of any for 9 × 12″ SAE with 4 first class stamps. Writer's guidelines for #10 SASE. They use free verse. Each magazine buys 5 poems per year. Submit up to 5 poems at one time. Length: 10-25 lines. Pays $10-50/poem.

COMMUNITIES: JOURNAL OF COOPERATION (IV-Social issues), 105 Sun St., Stelle IL 60919, phone (815)256-2252, founded 1972, managing editor Charles Betterton, is a "quarterly publication on **intentional communities, cooperatives, social and global transformation,**" using poetry relevant to those themes. **Pays 3 copies. Previously published poems and simultaneous submissions OK. No comment on rejections.** It is magazine-sized, professionally printed on newsprint stock with 2-color glossy paper cover, 56 pp., saddle-stapled. The sample issue sent me by the editor contained no poetry (most do not), so, as a sample, I selected these lines from my own "Middle Ages," published in *Communities* some years ago:

> *... now in our scattered communes in*
> *the crags we keep households where kids may grow*
> *outside the law. I cannot keep those brawling*
> *nations straight. There is only one weapon*
> *against the state: indifference ...*

‡**THE COMMUNITY ENDEAVOR (II)**, 240-B Commercial St., Nevada City CA 95959, phone (916)265-0824, founded 1986, poetry editor Debra Craig, is a monthly tabloid newspaper. **Address poetry submissions to Poetry Editors, Arts & Poetry, P.O. Box 1658, Grass Valley CA 95945. "Prefer 1 page or less in length; like to see the language of poetry expressed as directly as possible without losing the essential elements. This is the true challenge of poetry. No forced rhyme; disregard for effective use of language; lack of substance."** They have recently published poetry by David Plumb, Will Staple, Joy Phillips, Chris Olander and Brian Spittles. As a sample the editor selected these lines from "The Unweaving" by L. Ward:

> *Peeling away rocks and dead leaves,*
> *feeding them to the waiting shrubbery,*
> *she begins to dig rich river earth,*
> *asking forgiveness of the worms she cuts*
> *and reburying those she digs up whole.*

Press run is 8,000-10,000 for 400 subscribers of which 3 are libraries. They accept about 100 of 200-400 poems received/year. Most copies are distributed free to Northern Sierra Nevada Region and non-profit organizations. There are 2-3 pp. of poetry in the center of the tabloid. Subscription: $15/year. **Sample: $1 postpaid. Pays 1 copy. Previously published poems and simultaneous submissions OK. Reports in 1-2 months. Editor always comments "regarding our particular focus.** We sometimes work with themes. We match poems with drawings—and sometimes photos. We occasionally publish children's poetry and feature poets or artists in articles." She advises, "Read and write poetry. One must discover and experience what poetry *is, is not,* and *can be*; only then can we begin to find our voice within it. Be concerned with the writing—not the label. Be honest with yourself—and persevere."

A COMPANION IN ZEOR (IV-Science Fiction/fantasy), Rt. #5, Box #82, 17 Ashland Ave., Cardiff NJ 08232, phone (609)645-6938, founded 1978, editor Karen Litman, is a **"SF, fantasy fanzine involved with the writings of Jacqueline Lichtenberg" appearing irregularly (last published issue December 1990). "Prefer nothing obscene, usually related to the works of Jacqueline Lichtenberg. Homosexuality not acceptable unless very relevant to the piece. Prefer a 'clean' publication image."** As a sample, I selected these lines from "Almost Home" by Jill Stone:

> *To give life, not just fight for that which dies ...*
> *Everything is gathering, merging, intertwined.*
> *In the cold twilight, both growing blind,*
> *we have come at last to some familiar place.*
> *Beyond your shoulder is my brother's face,*
> *and I see the early snowfall in his eyes.*

It is magazine-sized, photocopied from typescript, press run 300. **Send SASE for guidelines. Pays copies. "Always willing to work with authors or poets to help in improving their work."** Reviews books of poetry.

CONCHO RIVER REVIEW; FORT CONCHO MUSEUM PRESS (IV-Regional), 213 E. Ave. D, San Angelo TX 76903, phone (915)657-4441, founded 1984, poetry editor Gerald M. Lacey. "The Fort Concho Museum Press is a small press having published 2 major books and is entering its fourth year of publishing *Concho River Review*, a literary journal published twice a year. **Work by Texas writers, writers with a Texas connection and writers living in the Southwest preferred. Prefer shorter poems, few long poems accepted; particularly looking for poems with distinctive imagery and imaginative forms and rhythms. The first test of a poem will be its imagery."** Short reviews of new volumes of poetry are also published. *CRR* is 120-138 pp. flat-spined, digest-sized, with matte card cover, professionally printed. They use 35-40 of 600-800 poems received per year. Press run: 300 for about 200 subscriptions of which 10 are libraries. Subscription: $12. **Sample postpaid: $4. Pays 1 copy. "Please submit 3-5 poems at a time. Use regular legal sized envelopes—no big brown envelopes. Please include full name and return address on outside of envelope. Type must be letter-perfect, sharp enough to be computer scanned." Reports in 1-6 weeks.** The editor says, "We're always looking for good work—from well-known poets and from those who have never been published before."

CONDITIONED RESPONSE PRESS; CONDITIONED RESPONSE; CONDITIONED RESPONSE ANNUAL CHAPBOOK SEARCH (V), P.O. Box 3816, Ventura CA 93006, founded 1982, poetry editor John McKinley, a small-press publisher of poetry only—magazine and occasional chapbooks. **They are not accepting unsolicited material at this time.** *Conditioned Response* appears biannually and has a circulation of 200; subscription: $4 for 2 issues. The digest-sized publication contains poetry only, no illustrations except a cover photograph. It is professionally printed on lightweight stock, 24 pp., matte card cover, saddle-stapled. Reviews books of poetry.

CONFLUENCE PRESS (II, IV-Regional), Lewis Clark State College, Lewiston ID 83501, phone (208)799-2336, founded 1975, poetry editor James R. Hepworth, is an "independent publisher of fiction, poetry, creative nonfiction and literary scholarship. **We are open to formal poetry as well as free verse.** No rhymed doggerel, 'light verse,' 'performance poetry,' 'streetpoetry,' etc. We prefer to publish work by poets who live and work in the northwestern United States." They have recently published poetry by John Daniel, Greg Keeler, Nancy Mairs and Robert Wrigley. As a sample the editor selected these lines from "For the Explainers" by Wendell Berry:

> Spell the spiel of cause and effect,
> Ride the long rail of fact after fact;
> What curled the plume in the drake's tail
> And put the white ring round his neck?

They print about 3 books and 2 chapbooks a year. **Query with 6 sample poems, bio, list of publications. No simultaneous submissions. Reports in 3 weeks to queries, 2 months to MSS. Pays $100 advance and 10% royalties plus copies.** Editor sometimes comments on rejections. Send SASE for catalog to order samples.

CONFRONTATION MAGAZINE (II), English Dept., C. W. Post of Long Island University, Greenvale NY 11548, founded 1968, editor-in-chief Martin Tucker, is "a semiannual literary journal with **interest in all forms.** Our only criterion is high literary merit. We think of our audience as an educated, lay group of intelligent readers. **We prefer lyric poems. Length generally should be kept to 2 pages. No sentimental verse.**" They have recently published poetry by Karl Shapiro, T. Alan Broughton, David Ignatow, Philip Appleman, Jane Mayhall and Joseph Brodsky. As a sample I selected the first stanza of David Galler's "Rotten Dreams":

> It's no disgrace
> To dream you look in a mirror
> And see your mother's face,
> Or the kitchen floor.

Basically a magazine, they do on occasion publish "book" issues or "anthologies." It's a digest-sized professionally-printed, flat-spined, 190+ pp. journal with a circulation of about 2,000. **Sample: $3 postpaid.** They receive about 1,200 submissions per year, publish 150, have a 6-12 month backlog. **Submit no more than 10 pp., clear copy (photocopy OK). Do not submit MSS July-August. "Prefer single submissions." Reports in 6-8 weeks. Pays: $5-50 and copy of magazine.** Reviews books of poetry.

‡CONJUNCTIONS (III), Bard College, Box 115, Annandale-on-Hudson NY 12504, founded 1981, managing editor Marlene Hennessy, is an elegant, fat journal appearing twice/year. **"Potential contributor should be familiar with the poetry published in the journal."** They have recently published poetry by John Ashbery, Robert Kelly, Charles Stein and Michael Palmer. As a sample, I selected these lines from "Paulownia" by Barbara Guest:

> ravenous the still dark a fishnet—
> robber walk near formidable plaits
> a glaze—the domino overcast—
> violet. shoulder.

Like *The Quarterly*, this publication is distributed by Random House. The issue I have seen is 400+ pp., 6×9", flat-spined, professionally printed. Press run 3,000 for 600 subscribers of which 200 are libraries. Subscription: $18. **Sample postpaid: $9.95. No pay.**

THE CONNECTICUT POETRY REVIEW (II), Box 3783, New Haven CT 06525, founded 1981, poetry editors J. Claire White and James William Chichetto, is a "small press that puts out an annual magazine. **We look for poetry of quality which is both genuine and original in content. No specifications except length: 10-40 lines.**" The magazine has won high praise from the literary world; they have recently published such poets as Gary Metras, Robert Peters, Mary Crow and Simon Perchik. Each issue seems to feature a poet. These sample lines are by Ann Douglas:

> The 11 o'clock light
> pulls the whole to a flatness
> like the flatness of water

> *on which the rest of the day turns*
> *and continues.*

The flat-spined, 60 pp. large digest-sized journal is "printed letterpress by hand on a Hacker Hand Press from Monotype Bembo." Most of the 60 pp. are poetry, but they also have reviews. Circulation is 400, with 80 subscriptions of which 35 are libraries. **Sample: $3.50 postpaid.** They receive over 900 submissions a year, use about 20, have a 3-month backlog, **report in 3 months, pay $5/poem plus 1 copy.** The editors advise, "Study traditional and modern styles. Study poets of the past. Attend poetry readings. And write. Practice on your own."

‡CONNECTICUT RIVER REVIEW; NATIONAL FALL POETRY CONTEST; BRODINE CONTEST; CON-NECTICUT POETRY SOCIETY (II), P.O. Box 2171, Bridgeport CT 06608, founded 1978, appears twice yearly. Editor Robert Isaacs. They want poetry that has **"depth of emotion, the truly seen (imaginary or actual), in which sound and sense are one. All forms are welcome, except haiku. We look for high quality, well-crafted poems."** They have recently published poetry by Joseph Bruchac, Donald Jenkins, Simon Perchik, Viola Shipley and Paul Zimmer. Each of the plain but attractively printed, digest-sized issues contains about 40 pp. of poetry, has a circulation of about 500, with 175 subscriptions of which 5% are libraries. They receive about 2,000 submissions per year, use about 70. Subscription: $10. **Sample: $5 postpaid. Deadlines: Feb. 15 and Aug. 15. Submit no more than 3-5 poems. No simultaneous submissions. Poems over 40 lines have little chance of acceptance, unless exceptional. Rejections within 2 weeks, acceptances could take 2 months. Pays 1 copy. Guidelines available with SASE.** The National Fall Poetry Contest, deadline August 1, has a $2 entry fee per poem and prizes of $100, $50, and $25. Send SASE for rules. The Brodine Contest, Box 112, Stratford, CT 06497, guidelines available in February; send SASE. Deadline is July 15, $2 fee per poem. Three cash awards plus publication in the *Connecticut River Review*.

‡CONTEXT SOUTH (II), P.O. Box 2244, State University AR 72467, founded 1988, editor/publisher David Breeden, appears twice a year using **"any form, length, subject matter. Looking for strong rhythms, clear vision. Nothing sentimental."** They have recently published poetry by Andrea Hollander Budy and William Greenway. As a sample the editor selected these lines by Wayne Dodd:

> *Not only thoughts*
> *and will we are rain*
>
> *falling through*
> *trees our hair*
>
> *wet about our faces our arms*
> *rising and falling*
>
> *the rhythm our*
> *life is*

It is 65 pp. digest-sized, saddle-stapled, using fiction, criticism and book reviews as well as poetry. They accept less than 1% of poems received. Press run 500 for 45 subscribers of which 3 are libraries. **Sample: $5. Pays 1 copy. Simultaneous submissions OK.** The editor advises, "read every poem you can find from the beginning of time. Every poem encapsulates the entire tradition."

CONVERGING PATHS (IV-Spiritual, themes), P.O. Box 63, Mt. Horeb WI 53572, founded 1986, editor Kyril Oakwind, is a quarterly **"Pagan/Wiccan magazine focusing on traditional Wicca, using a few poems: short, fits in one column or occasionally one page, inspirational, Pagan poetry. Suggested subjects: earth, mother, God of the hunt, death and rebirth, initiation, Celtic or British myths and gods. Our prime consideration is whether it is emotionally moving to our staff. If so, it doesn't *have* to be technically perfect or have traditional form. No long, long poems or those unrelated to the Pagan theme of our magazine or bad poetry."** I have not seen an issue, but the editor describes it as magazine-sized, 32 pp., stapled. Press run 200 for 100+ subscriptions of which 1 is a library, 20-30 shelf sales. Subscription: $14. **Sample postpaid: $4. Pays 1 copy. Reports in 1-2 months.** Reviews books of pagan poetry.

THE COOL TRAVELER (I, IV-Themes), P.O. Box 11975, Philadelphia PA 19145, phone (215)440-0592, founded 1988, editor Bob Moore, appears 4-6 times per year, using **"poetry that contains artistic references: painters, works, etc. and poetry about places, especially different countries, but I'll look at it all."** They have recently published poetry by Joe Farley, Addie Lee, Arthur Knight and Layle Silbert. As a sample the editor selected these lines by Nickie Arufo:

> *Gusting autumn winds*
> *sweep Washington Square,*

lift layers of fallen leaves—
tawny-hued magic carpets

Its format is long and slender, 10-25 pp., saddle-stapled, photocopied from typescript, with colored paper cover. His first year the editor received 60-70 pieces and accepted them all. Press run: 1,000 for 80-100 subscribers, ¾ of the copies go to cafes and galleries. Subscription: $10. **Sample postpaid: $1. Pays 1 copy (more if requested). Submitting poets should, in a cover letter, "say something about themselves—a short one or two lines to be printed with their work." Reports in 2 weeks, sometimes asks for rewrites. Editor comments on submissions "often."** Reviews books of poetry. He says, "There are many local papers and publications that want poetry."

COOP. ANTIGRUPPO SICILIANO; TRAPANI NUOVA (II, IV-Translations), Via Argenteria, Km 4, Trapani, Sicily, Italy, 91100, phone 0923-38681, founded 1968, poetry editor Nat Scammacca, is a group of over 100 poets involved in international activities pertaining to poetry including readings, sponsored visits, and publication in the weekly (except in August) cultural newspaper, *Trapani Nuova*, or in collections or anthologies. **Free samples.** Scammacca says, **"We translate and publish short poems almost every week in *Trapani Nuova* and, on occasion, in our anthologies.** We have published several thousand American poems and have included 20 American poets including Simpson, Stafford, Bly, Ferlinghetti, Corso, Ignatow, etc. We like **ironical poetry, committed poetry (anti-atomic), intelligent poetry; we do not want poetry that makes no sense, rhetorical stuff, sentimental, or poets who think each word or line is God-sent. The poem must *communicate*. We prefer short poems, but if the poem is exceptional, we want it. Short poems we can translate into Sicilian and Italian and use in our weekly in a week's time."** The editor selected a sample from his own "Lovingly":

Though this January morning's bitter cold the two roses I picked yesterday
Have spread their petals wide to bloom, lovingly—but not my wife
Who, with a dustpan and the broom in her hands muttered:
"Let's sweep up the trash," when I said:
"A poem is blooming in my head."

Send poems of 4-15 lines to Nat Scammacca. Considers simultaneous submissions. "The poet must send his best poetry. If it is difficult but makes sense he can explain why he wants us to publish the poem, why he wants us to suffer. We want, otherwise, enjoyable, witty, intelligent and if possible great poetry." Apparently one gets acquainted by submitting to the weekly. If you want **to send a book MS, query first, with cover letter giving biographical background, personal or aesthetic philosophy. Payment in copies of the published book.** "They are lucky when we publish them," says the editor. The nonprofit cooperative is supported by government funds; it organizes poetry tours, radio and TV appearances and readings for some of the authors they have published. "We want other poets to be sufficiently confident in themselves so as not to ask for our opinion concerning their poetry. We prefer having the poet himself explain why he writes, for whom and why he writes as he does. We do not want to substitute our methods for his methods." (See listing for Cross-Cultural Communications.)

COPPER BEECH PRESS (III), P.O. Box 1852, English Dept., Brown University, Providence RI 02912, phone (401)863-2393, founded 1973, poetry editor Randy Blasing, publishes **books of all kinds of poetry**, about three 48 pp., flat-spined paperbacks a year. Recently published Christopher Buckley, Gary Young, Charles O. Hartman and Robert Cording. I selected these lines by Kay Ryan as a sample:

Oh the brave and confident,
the habitual people of Egypt
who filled Heaven with Earth
by the cubit.

Free catalog. Query with 5 poems, biographical information and publications. Do not submit MSS from Memorial Day to Labor Day. Considers simultaneous submissions. Replies to queries in 1 month, to submissions in 3 months, payment: 10% of press run.

CORNERSTONE: THE VOICE OF THIS GENERATION (IV-Religious), Jesus People USA, 939 W. Wilson, Chicago IL 60640, phone (312)989-2080, editor Dawn Herrin, is a mass-circulation (50,000), low-cost ($2 per copy), bimonthly **directed at youth**, covering **"contemporary issues in the light of Evangelical Christianity."** They use avant-garde, free verse, haiku, light verse, traditional—"no limits except for epic poetry. (We've not got the room.)" **Buys 10-50 poems per year, uses 1-2 pp. per issue, has a 2-3 month backlog. Submit maximum of 5 poems. Pays $10 for poems having 1-15 lines, $25 for poems having 16 lines or more. Sample: $2. Send SASE for guidelines.**

CORNFIELD REVIEW (II), Ohio State University, 1465 Mt. Vernon Ave., Marion OH 43302-5695, phone (614)389-2361, FAX (614)389-6786, founded 1974, is an annual of poetry, artwork, short fiction and personal narrative. **"We are open to all forms of high quality poetry, and we are interested in new**

talent." The editor selected these lines by David Citino from "Sister Mary Appassionata Addresses the Marion County Writers' Guild" as typical of the quality they're looking for:

> . . . *There's no dark,*
> *writers, you can't see into,*
> *witnessing so ignites you, revisioning*
> *the world until you get it right.*

> *Everyone you care for lives forever.*

It is 6×9", flat-spined, printed on heavy slick stock with b/w graphics, glossy cover with art, approximately 40-48 pp. Their press run is about 500. **Sample: $4.50 postpaid. Pays 3 copies. Send no more than 5 poems with brief cover letter. No simultaneous submissions or previously published poems. Reports within 2-3 months.** "Submissions should be typed or letter-quality dot-matrix, copyright reverts to contributor."

CORONA (II), Dept. of History and Philosophy, Montana State University, Bozeman MT 59717, phone (406)994-5200, founded 1979, poetry editors Lynda and Michael Sexson, "is an interdisciplinary annual bringing together reflections from those who stand on the edges of their disciplines; those who sense that insight is located not in things but in relationships; those who have deep sense of playfulness; and those who believe that the imagination is involved in what we know." In regard to poetry they want "no sentimental greeting cards; no slap-dash." They have recently published poems by Richard Hugo, X. J. Kennedy, Donald Hall, Philip Dacey, Wendy Battin, William Irwin Thompson, Frederick Turner and James Dickey. Asked for a sample, they said, "See journal for examples. We are not interested in cloned poems or homogenized poets." Journal is perfect-bound, 125-140 pp., professionally printed, using about 20-25 pp. of poetry per issue, circulation 2,000. **Sample: $7 postpaid. Submit any number of pages, photocopy and dot-matrix OK, no simultaneous submissions. Reports in 1 week to 6 months.** Payment is "nominal" plus 2 contributor's copies. The editors advise, "Today's poet survives only by the generous spirits of small press publishers. Read and support the publishers of contemporary artists by subscribing to the journals and magazines you admire."

COSMIC TREND; PARA*phrase (I, IV-Themes, love/romance/erotica), P.O. Box 323, Clarkson Rd., Mississauga, Ontario L5J 3Y2 Canada, founded 1984, *Cosmic Trend* poetry editor George Le Grand, *PARA*phrase* editor Tedy Asponsen. *Cosmic Trend* publishes 3 chapbook anthologies a year of **"New Age mind-expanding material of any style, short or medium length; also: humorous, unusual, or zany entries (incl. graphics) with deeper meaning. We ignore epics, run-of-a-mill romantic and political material."** As a sample the editor selected these lines (poet unidentified):

> *Trinkets of sleepiness will shatter and blend*
> *into the solid state of the liquid crystal*
> *of the sun of love*
> *be it only half the frequency of creation*
> *time will carve*
> *into our b e i n g infinite!*

*PARA*phrase* — Newsletter of Cosmic Trend (irregular times: 2-3 times a year). Publishes "condensed life-stories and/or visions with insight, beyond the normal and related poetry." **They will consider simultaneous submissions and previously published poems "with accompanied disclosure and references." Pays 1 copy/published contribution. Send $1 for guidelines or $3 for sample publication and guidelines.** Brief guidelines: $1 for each two poems submitted, plus $1 for postage. Minimum fee $2 plus postage. ("No US postal stamps, please.") **Response time is usually less than 3 weeks. Editor "often" comments on rejections.** His advice is "don't give up in your gaining access to your source of being. The associated courage of expressing yourselves without compromises transcends us all in the end as one in our patterned love-learning beyond the immediate human involvements. *Cosmic Trend* wants to celebrate this courage in individuals who are ready to tune into their own creative sources and promote poetry as a high adventure of the spirit, rather than mere intellectual posing."

COSMOPOLITAN (IV-Women), 224 W. 57th St., New York NY 10019, founded 1886, is a monthly magazine "aimed at a female audience 18-34," part of the Hearst conglomerate, though it functions independently editorially. They want **freshly-written free verse, not more than 25 lines, either light or serious, which addresses the concerns of young women. Prefer shorter poems, use 1-4 poems each issue.** "We cannot return submissions without SASE." They have a circulation of 2,987,970. **Buy sample at newsstand. Reports in 3-5 weeks, pays $25.** "Please do not phone; query by letter if at all, though queries are unnecessary before submitting. Poems shouldn't be too abstract. The poem should convey an image, feeling or emotion that our reader could perhaps identify with. We do publish mostly free verse, although we're also open to well-crafted rhyme poems."

COTEAU BOOKS; THUNDER CREEK PUBLISHING CO-OP; WOOD MOUNTAIN SERIES (IV-Regional, children), 401-2206 Dewdney Ave., Regina, Saskatchewan S4R 1H3 Canada, phone (306)777-0170, founded 1975, managing editor Shelley Sopher, a "small literary press that publishes poetry, fiction, drama, anthologies, criticism, children's books—only by Canadian writers." Poetry should be "of general interest to Canadian or American audience." They have recently published poetry by Nancy Mattson, Kim Morrissey and Dennis Cooley and 2 anthologies of Saskatchewan poetry. Writers should submit 30-50 poems "and indication of whole MS," typed; simultaneous and American submissions not accepted. Letter should include publishing credits and bio and SAE with IRC if necessary. Queries will be answered in 2-3 weeks and MSS reported on in 2-4 months. Authors receive 10% royalty; 10 copies. Their attractive catalog is free for $9 \times 12"$ SASE or IRC and sample copies can be ordered from it. It says: "Membership has changed through the years in the Thunder Creek Publishing Co-op, but now stands at ten. Each member has a strong interest in Canadian writing and culture." As a sample, the editor selected these lines from "Crows" by Catherine Buckaway:

> *A black pillar of crows*
> *rises like dusty smoke*
> *from this land.*

The imprint Wood Mountain Series is for first collections, reflecting their commitment to publishing new writers.

COTTONWOOD; COTTONWOOD PRESS (II, IV-Regional), Box J, Kansas Union, University of Kansas, Lawrence KS 66045, founded 1965, poetry editor Philip Wedge. The Press "is auxiliary to *Cottonwood Magazine* and publishes material by authors in the region. Material is usually solicited. For the magazine they are looking for "strong narrative or sensory impact, non-derivative, not 'literary,' not 'academic.' Emphasis on Midwest, but publishes the best poetry received regardless of region. Poems should be 60 lines or less, on daily experience, *perception*. They have recently published poetry by Rita Dove, Allen Ginsberg, Walter McDonald, Patricia Traxler and Ron Schreiber. The editors selected these sample lines by Denise Low:

> *Last winter I slept long nights*
> *pressed against my husband,*
> *my thigh across his belly.*
> *Outdoors bulbs lay below ground,*
> *crisp white flesh cupped*
> *around and around flowerlets.*

The $6 \times 9"$, flat-spined (112+ pp.) magazine is published 3 times per year, printed from computer offset, with photos, using 20-30 pages of poetry in each issue. They have a circulation of 500-600, with 150 subscriptions of which 75 are libraries. They receive about 2,000 submissions per year, use about 30, have a maximum of 1 year backlog. Price per issue, $5, **sample: $3 postpaid.** **Submit up to 5 pp., dot-matrix, photocopy OK. No simultaneous submissions. Reports in 2-5 months.** They sometimes provide criticism on rejected MSS. **Payment: 1 copy.** The editors advise, "Read the little magazines and send to ones you like."

COUNCIL FOR INDIAN EDUCATION (V), 517 Rimrock Rd., Billings MT 59102, founded 1970, poetry editor Elnora Old Coyote, is a non-profit corporation publishing material (small paper-bound books) to use in schools with Indian students. **We have too much poetry on hand; we cannot accept any more until fall 1992."**

COUNTRY JOURNAL (II), P.O. Box 8200, Harrisburg PA 17105, phone (717)657-9555, poetry editor Donald Hall, editor Peter V. Fossel, is a bimonthly magazine featuring country living for people who live in rural areas or who are thinking about moving there. They use free verse, light verse and traditional. Circ. 200,000. Average issue includes 6-8 feature articles and 10 departments. They have recently published poems by Mary Oliver, Kate Barnes and Lorraine Ferra. As a sample, I selected these lines from Maxine Kumin's "The Confidantes":

> *Whoa, Ebony!—and I put my palms*
> *flat on the twitching satin skin*
> *that smells like old fruit, and memory begins.*

Of 450-500 poems received each year they accept 20-25. Subscription: $24. **Sample postpaid: $4.** Simultaneous submissions, previously published poems OK. Reports in 2-3 months. Editor comments on submissions "seldom." Pays $50/poem on acceptance. Submit seasonal material 1 year in advance. Photocopied and previously published submissions OK. Computer printout submissions acceptable, prefers letter-quality; "dot-matrix submissions are acceptable if double spaced." Reports in 2-3 months.

‡COUNTRY ROADS QUARTERLY (IV-Regional), P.O. Box 479, Oakland MD 21550, founded 1987, editor Carol Fox, uses **poetry related to the rural Appalachian region. They don't want "romance."** As a sample of what she especially wants to see, the editor referred to "The Ballad of West Virginia Rose" by Linda Beth Fristoe. Here is a sample stanza:

> Young lovers come from miles around
> in quest of pale rosebuds
> that began to grow out of coal
> the night Rose dreamed of love.

The quarterly is magazine-sized, professionally printed. Subscription: $12. **Sample: $2 postpaid. Pays $5-15/poem plus 2 copies. Reports in 3 months. Publishes 12 months after acceptance. "I'm very overloaded with poetry at this time, however."** She says, "I'm especially interested in encouraging new, unpublished people as well as established writers. Because poetry is so personally written and so personally received by the reader, it's a serious part of this new publishing venture. My advice to all writers is to write. To continue, even in the face of rejection. I like to see poetry the average person can relate to and appreciate. No spaced-out rambling. My readers appreciate nature, history, folklore, country way of life."

COUNTRY WOMAN; REIMAN PUBLICATIONS (IV-Women, humor), P.O. Box 643, Milwaukee WI 53201, founded 1970, managing editor Kathy Pohl. *Country Woman* "is a bimonthly magazine dedicated to the lives and interests of country women. Those who are both involved in farming and ranching and those who love country life. In some ways, it is very similar to many women's general interest magazines, and yet its subject matter is closely tied in with rural living and the very unique lives of country women. **We like short (4-5 stanzas, 16-20 lines) traditional rhyming poems that reflect on a season or comment humorously or seriously on a particular rural experience. Also limericks and humorous 4-8 line filler rhymes. No experimental poetry. Poetry will not be considered unless it rhymes. Always looking for poems that focus on the seasons. We don't want rural putdowns, poems that stereotype country women, etc. All poetry must be positive and upbeat. Our poems are fairly simple, yet elegant. They often accompany a high-quality photograph."** *CW* recently published poems by Hilda Sanderson, Edith E. Cutting and Ericka Northrop. As a sample the editor selected these lines from a poem by Betty Ekiss:

> There is a feeling in the air
> Born of sights and sounds,
> A subtle turning of the earth
> As nature makes her rounds . . .

CW, appearing 6 times a year, is magazine-sized, 68 pp., glossy paper with much color photography. Circulation to 700,000. Subscriptions, $14.98 per year, $2.50 per copy. They receive about 1,200 submissions of poetry per year, use 40-50 (unless they publish an anthology). Their backlog is 1 month to 3 years. "We're always welcoming submissions." **Sample: $2.50 postpaid. Submit maximum of 6 poems. Photocopy OK if stated not a simultaneous submission. Reports in 2-3 months. Pays $10-40 per poem plus copy.** They hold various contests for subscribers only. I examined one of their anthologies, *Cattails and Meadowlarks: Poems from the Country,* 90+ pp., saddle-stapled with high-quality color photography on the glossy card cover, poems in large, professional type with many b/w photo illustrations.

THE COUNTRYMAN (IV-Rural), Sheep St., Burford, Oxford OX8 4LH, England, phone Burford 2258, founded 1927, editor Christopher Hall, a bimonthly magazine "on rural matters." The editor wants **poetry on rural themes, "available to general readership but not jingles."** It is a handsome, flat-spined, digest-sized magazine, 200+ pp., using popular articles and ads. As a sample the editor selected this complete poem, "January omen," by Jane A. Mares:

> At the cold birth of the year
> I saw what was better unseen:
> The Raven or Grimcrag, the grief-bringer,
> With his tone of ill-tidings,
> A-top the tall stone,
> Wiping his bill clean.

They pay a maximum of £15/poem. Submissions should be short. Reporting time is "within a week usually," and time to publication is "3 months-3 years." The editor says, "Not all our poems are *about* birds or flowers or animals. Personal reactions to rural experience is valued if it comes in a form to which our readers (high-income, quiet not violently green British for the

Market categories: (I) Beginning; (II) General; (III) Limited; (IV) Specialized; (V) Closed.

most part) can relate. We get quite a few American submissions which I always read with much interest, not least because of my own love of the few American landscapes I know. Too often these submissions are too obviously American (because of tell-tale species or phrases) and I generally rule these out because 95% of my readers expect a British mag."

COYOTE CHRONICLES; NORTHLAND QUARTERLY PUBLICATIONS, INC. (I, II, IV-Themes), *(Coyote Chronicles* formerly *The Northland Quarterly*), #2161, 1522 E. Southern Ave., Tempe AZ 85282, founded 1987, editor Jody Namio Wallace, is a "small-press publisher of fiction, poetry, non-fiction and scholarly publications, publishing a quarterly literary journal. Limited subsidy publishing services offered to selected authors." She wants **"poetry with emphasis on progressive political themes and ideas, ecology etc. No religious, fantasy, or 'scenery' poetry."** They have published poetry by Norman German, John Grey, Mark Maire and Richard Davignon. As a sample she selected these lines (poet unidentified):

> *Last night I went to bed intoxicated again. You watched*
> *"Ghandi," repressing violence.*
> *Today, I am drinking too much coffee,*
> *smoking too many cigarettes.*
> *You say you'll be late . . .*

CC is digest-sized, 90-128 pp., professionally printed, flat-spined. They accept 10-15% of 1,000 poems received a year. Subscription: $18. **Sample: $4 postpaid. Guidelines available for SASE. Pays 3 copies. "Contributors encouraged to buy additional copies." Submit with cover letter and bio. They consider simultaneous submissions and previously published poems. Reports in 2-4 weeks. Editor sometimes comments on rejections, "more substantial critiques on request."** Publishes several chapbooks a year averaging 100 pp. For chapbook consideration either query or send MS with cover letter and bio. Reports in 12-14 weeks. **"Large backlog at this time, but we welcome all submissions." Payment "varies."** Send SASE for catalog to buy samples.

CRAB CREEK REVIEW (V), 4462 Whitman Ave. N., Seattle WA 98103, phone (206)633-1090, founded 1983, editor Linda J. Clifton, appears 3 times per year, 32 pp., attractively printed on newsprint. They publish **poetry which is "free or formal, with clear imagery, wit, voice that is interesting and energetic, accessible to the general reader rather than full of very private imagery and obscure literary allusion; also translations."** They have published poetry by Robert Bringhurst, Elizabeth Murawski, Laurel Speer, Maxine Kumin, William O'Daly translating Neruda, and William Stafford. They have about 20 pp. of poetry in each issue, circulation 350,200 subscriptions of which 20 are libraries, receive 400-500 submissions per year from which they choose 50-60 poems. **"We are currently backlogged through 1992; no unsolicited MSS until 1993."** Sample: $3 postpaid, subscription $8 per year. Listed in *Index of American Periodical Verse*.

CRAMPED AND WET (I), 1012 29th, Sioux City IA 51104, founded 1986, editor Kidd Smiley, is a quarterly. **"I like real stuff but I want to see fun too. There's room for hard tough stuff yet I like to end up with a real warm feeling. No real conceptual self-indulgent s***."** They have recently published poetry by John McKinley, Rob Treinen, Charles Luden, A.Q. Passmore and Jason Murphy. As a sample the editor selected these lines from "next exit 27 miles" by George DeChant:

> *i only say this so*
> *you know why i sometimes*
> *feel like a long stretch of asphalt*
> *heading towards a stuckey's*
> *standing next to you*

C and W's size varies. It is 20-30 pp., offset printed. They accept about 10-20% of 400-500 poems per year. Press run: 150. **Sample postpaid: $1.50. Pays 1 copy.** Editor comments on submissions "often. I usually write the poet within a couple of weeks either returning his submission or informing him of acceptance, etc.—that is if he includes a SASE." He advises, "Do what you want, feel good about yourself. The most radical attitude is the positive one. Practice self-parody like some practice self-discipline." **The magazine supports the right for anyone to say anything derogatory at anytime or anyplace.**

‡CRAZYHORSE (II), Dept. of English, University of Arkansas, Little Rock AR 72204, founded 1960, managing editor Zabelle Stodola, poetry editor Ralph Burns, is a highly respected literary magazine appearing twice a year. They have recently published poetry by Alberto Rios, Mark Jarman, Bill Matthews and Yusef Komunyakaa. As a sample, here are the closing lines from "For Victor Jara: Mutilated and Murdered, the Soccer Stadium, Santiago, Chile" by Miller Williams (see listing for University of Arkansas Press):

> *Would we have stayed to an end or would we have folded our faces?*
> *Awful and awful. Good friend. You have embarrassed our hearts.*

CRAZYHORSE

SPRING 1990

"We are pleased that the artist, Melinda B. Cameron, is an Arkansan since Crazyhorse is published through the University of Arkansas at Little Rock," managing editor Zabelle Stodola says of this illustration. *"We always try to use a horse motif on our cover, and we felt this bold, contemporary painting reflected some of the qualities we seek in fiction and poetry inside,"* she says. Ms. Cameron's painting is entitled "Zebra in Jewels II."

It is 145 pp., 6×9″ offset. Press run 900. Subscription: $10. Sample postpaid: $5. Pays $10/printed page plus 2 copies. Reports in 4-8 weeks. $500 award for best poem each year. No submissions June-August. Reviews books of poetry. To get a sense of the quality of the magazine, see the anthology, **The Best of Crazyhorse** (University of Arkansas Press, 1990).

CREAM CITY REVIEW (II), Box 413, Dept. of English, University of Wisconsin at Milwaukee, Milwaukee WI 53201, phone (414)229-4708, editor-in-chief Kit Pancoast, poetry editor Marilyn Taylor, is a nationally distributed literary magazine published twice a year by the Creative Writing Program. The editors will consider **any poem that is well-crafted and especially those poems that show an awareness of where poetry has come from and where it might be going;** but they have little patience with dogma, sentimentality, sexism or prose made to look like poetry. They have published poetry by Ted Kooser, David Ray, Amy Clampitt, George Garrett, Ann Lauterbach, Ronald Wallace, Lucien Stryk, William Stafford, Eve Shelnutt and Robert Pack. Magazine size is 5½×8½″, perfect-bound, on 70 lb. paper, circulation 1,000, 100+ subscriptions of which 15 are libraries. Sample: $5 postpaid. Send SASE for guidelines. Include SASE when submitting and please submit no more than 5 poems at a time. Payment varies with funding and includes 2 copies. Reports in 2 months. Simultaneous submissions OK. Editors sometimes comment on rejections. Always looking for new talent.

CREATIVE WITH WORDS PUBLICATIONS (C.W.W.); SPOOFING; WE ARE POETS AND AUTHORS, TOO (I, IV-Children, Seniors), Box 223226, Carmel CA 93922, phone (408)649-1682, founded 1975, poetry editor Brigitta Geltrich, **offers criticism for a fee.** It focuses "on furthering **folkloristic tall tales** and such; creative writing abilities in **children** (poetry, prose, language-art); creative writing in **senior citizens** (poetry and prose)." The editors organize and sponsor an **annual poetry contest, offer feedback on MSS submitted to this contest,** and publish on a wide range of themes relating to human studies and the environment that influence human behaviors. **$2 reading fee per poem, includes a critical analysis.** The publications are anthologies of children's poetry, prose and language art; anthologies of senior citizen poetry and prose; and *Spoofing: an Anthology of Folkloristic Yarns and Such,* which has an announced theme for each issue. "**Want to see:** folkloristic themes, poetry for and by children; poetry by senior citizens; topic (inquire). **Do not want to see:** too mushy; too religious; too didactic; expressing dislike for fellowmen; political; pornographic; death and murder poetry." Latest themes are "A CWW Christmas"; "It's a Matter of Love" and "A CWW Easter." Guidelines available for SASE, catalog for 25¢. The samples I have seen of *Spoofing!* and (*We are Poets and Authors, Too!*) an anthology of poems by children are low-budget publications, photocopied from typescript, saddle-stapled, card covers with cartoon-like art. **Submit 20-line, 40 spaces wide maximum, poems geared to specific audience and subject matter.** They have published poetry by Sarah Hammond, Mark Eaton and Hilary Hersom. The editor selected this sample by Angela Koehler:

> *Walking quietly*
> *Along the beach at sunrise*
> *I can feel the peace*
> *Of God's earth in the breeze and*
> *Hear it in the seagull's cry.*

"Query with sample poems, short personal biography, other publications, poetic goals, where you read about us, for what publication and/or event you are submitting." Their contests have prizes of $15, $10, $5, $1, but they hope to increase them. "No conditions for publication, but CWW is dependent on author/poet support by purchase of a copy or copies of publication." They offer a 20% reduction on any copy purchased. The editor advises, "Trend is proficiency. Poets should research topic; know audience for whom they write; check topic for appeal to specific audience; should not write for the sake of rhyme, rather for the sake of imagery and being creative with the language. Feeling should be expressed (but no mushiness). Topic and words should be chosen carefully; brevity should be employed."

‡CREATIVE WOMAN (IV-Women, feminist, themes), Governors State University, University Park IL 60466, phone (708)536-5000, ext. 2524, founded 1977, editor Helen E. Hughes, "is published three times a year. **We focus on a special topic in each issue, presented from a feminist perspective."** They want poetry **"recognizing, validating, celebrating women's experience, especially fresh and original style."** They have recently published poetry by Marge Piercy and Larissa Vasilyeva. As a sample Helen Hughes selected these lines from "The Fishwife's Declaration of Independence" by Olivia Diamond:

> *This fishwife cries to ply her cutter*
> *in deeper more crystal schools of marlin*
> *and never peddle her fry in any market;*
> *her coach is kinetic, her compass private,*
> *her steerage personal, her passage free,*
> *and no husband stands at the helm.*

The Creative Woman is magazine-sized, 48 pp., professionally printed on heavy coated stock with b/w graphics, ads. They use about 5% of several hundred unsolicited poems received per year. Press run of 2,000 for 600 subscriptions (65 libraries). Per issue: $5, subscriptions $12, institutions $20; **sample $5 postpaid. Pays 4 copies and opportunity to purchase more at half price. MSS should be double-spaced, name and address on each page. No simultaneous submissions or previously published poetry. Reports in "up to 1 year."** Helen Hughes comments, "It's wonderful that so many women are writing poetry, that so much of it is good and that poets are willing to submit for publication, knowing we cannot pay them."

CREEPING BENT (III), 1023 Main St., Bethlehem PA 18018, phone (215)866-5613, founded 1984, editor Joseph Lucia, a literary magazine that focuses on serious poetry, fiction, book reviews and essays, with very occasional chapbooks published under the same imprint. **"Please note that during much of 1992 we will be accepting very little (possibly no) unsolicited material. We publish only work that evidences a clear awareness of the current situation of poetry. We take a special interest in poems that articulate a vision of the continuities and discontinuities in the human relationship to the natural world."** The editor does not want "any attempt at verse that clearly indicates the writer hasn't taken a serious look at a recent collection of poetry during his or her adult life." He has recently published work by Turner Cassity, Charles Edward Eaton, Robert Gibb, Briget Kelly, Walter McDonald, Donald Revell, Harry Humes and Patricia Wilcox. As a sample, he chose these lines from Peter Yovu's "Once You Have a Name":

> *Once you have a name*
> *for things, things begin: trees,*
> *eucalyptus and mango like branching*
> *magnets draw green iron out of the air;*
> *bees drone; vines too young to strangle, spiral;*
> *violet stems flecked with aphids like sweated milk*
> *grow fur and here a hoopoe lifts its crest.*

Creeping Bent is digest-sized, nicely printed on heavy stock with some b/w artwork, 48-64 pp., saddle-stapled with glossy white card cover printed in black and one other color. It appears at least once a year, sometimes more often. Circulation is 250, of which 175 are subscriptions, 25 go to libraries, and 25 are sold on newsstands. Price per copy is $3, subscription $6/year. **Sample available for $3 postpaid, guidelines for SASE. Pay is 2 copies plus a 1-year subscription. "Absolutely no simultaneous submissions!"** Photocopied and dot-matrix MSS are OK. Reporting time is usually 2-3 weeks and time to publication is 6 months at most. The editor says, "Before submitting to any magazine published by anyone with a serious interest in contemporary writing, make certain you understand something about the kind of work the magazine publishes. Be familiar with current styles and approaches to poetry, even if you eschew them."

CRESCENT MOON (I), 18 Chaddesley Rd., Kidderminster, England DY10 3AD, founded 1988, editor Jeremy Robinson, publishes about 10 books and chapbooks/year **on arrangements subsidized by the poet.** He wants **"poetry that is passionate and authentic. Any form or length."** Not **"the trivial, insincere or derivative."** They have recently published studies of Robert Graves, D.H. Lawrence, Thomas Hardy, J.M.W. Turner, John Cowper Powys, Lawrence Durrell and Renaissance painting, including poetry by the editor. As a sample the editor selected the first of five stanzas from his "Aphrodite's Mirror":

> *Shaving one day in Aphrodite's mirror,*
> *Using her sea-foam as ointment and the shell*
> *For a basin, I caught sight of myself*
> *In that speckled glass and wondered if*
> *This love of ours was going to last beyond*
> *A mere Rising-From-The-Sea-Attended-By-Nymphs.*

The sample chapbook I have seen is the editor's **Black Angel**, 45 pp., flat-spined, photocopied from typescript, digest-sized, with matte card cover. **Sample, postpaid, in response to "written requests."** Inquiries welcome. **Reports on queries in 4 weeks, on MSS in 8.** "I am putting together some anthologies of new American poetry, and would like to hear from interested poets."

CRICKET, THE MAGAZINE FOR CHILDREN; LADYBUG, THE MAGAZINE FOR YOUNG CHILDREN (IV-Children), P.O. Box 300, Peru IL 61354, *Cricket* founded 1973, *Ladybug* founded 1990, publisher and editor-in-chief, Marianne Carus. *Cricket* is a monthly, circulation 120,000, **paying up to $3 per line for "serious, humorous, nonsense rhymes, limericks" for children. They sometimes use previously-published work.** The attractive 7×9″ magazine, 80 pp., saddle-stapled, color cover and b/w illustrations inside, receives over 1,000 submissions per month, uses 10-12, and has up to a 2 year backlog. **No query. Submit poems up to 25 lines, no restrictions on form. Sample: $2. Guidelines available for SASE. Reports in 3-4 months.** They hold poetry contests for children ages 5-9 and 10-14. Current contest themes and rules appear in each issue. *Ladybug*, also monthly, circulation 120,000, is similar in format (same price for sample copy) and requirements but is aimed at younger children (ages 2-7). **Payment for both is up to $3/line and 2 copies.**

‡CROOKED ROADS; POETS FOR PEACE & JUSTICE; E.P.A.F.A.P.N.V.R. (B.A.R.N) (II, IV-Themes); WHEEL OF FIRE PRESS (V), P.O. Box 32631, Kansas City MO 64111, founded 1988, poetry editor Sharon Eiker. *CR* is a literary magazine appearing 3/year, "each issue devoted (but not exclusively) to exploration of a theme, e.g., 'The Imp of the Perverse.' Brief capsule reviews of magazines only. **Looking for long narrative or meditative poems, socially-oriented poems, prose poems; no haiku, lavender fog, surrealism taking itself seriously, word salad, chopped prose, art as therapy."** They have recently published poetry by Linda Rodriguez and Phil Miller. As a sample the editor selected these lines from "Flat Graves" by Alfred Kisubi:

> *The earth is hunter's booty*
> *Which the quick must grab*
> *And grab quickly,*
> *Or lie low and die dismal*
> *Like those low dead do,*
> *To be disowned stories in history.*

It is 20-28 pp. magazine-sized, laser-printed and photocopied, saddle-stapled. They accept less than 10% of 750-800 poems received/year. Press run 500 for 200 subscribers of which 1 is a library, 50-75 shelf sales. Subscription: $5. **Sample postpaid: $1. Pays 1-3 copies. Reports in 4-6 weeks. Inquire about upcoming themes. Submissions accepted on 3½″ disks, MacWrite.** Poets for Peace & Justice is an organization whose newsletter, *E.P.A.F.A.P.N.V.R. (B.A.R.N)*, **"Elitist Proletarian Artists For A Preferably Non-Violent Revolution (But A Revolution Nevertheless),"** also uses poems on themes appropriate to its political purposes, and is available on request. Wheel of Fire Press publishes 1-3 paperbacks, 2-5 chapbooks per year, **almost half subsidized; no unsolicited MSS or queries. Send SASE for price list or $2 for sample chapbook.** "*Crooked Roads* takes its name and philosophy from a proverb of William Blake: 'Improvement makes strait roads, but the crooked roads without improvement are roads of Genius.' This proverb addresses originality and authenticity; Blake is not advising against revision. 'First thought, best thought,' but it takes some time and care to come to one's First thought."

‡CROSS TIMBERS REVIEW (II), Cisco Junior College, Cisco TX 76437, phone (817)442-2567, founded 1983, poetry editor Cleatus Rattan, appears twice a year. "No bias I admit to—no long (more than 50 lines) poems. Nothing obscene." It is 70 pp., 6×9" offset. Print run 250. Subscription: $6. Sample postpaid: $3. Pays 2 copies. Reports in 2 months. Do not submit in the summer.

CROSS-CULTURAL COMMUNICATIONS; CROSS-CULTURAL REVIEW OF WORLD LITERATURE AND ART IN SOUND, PRINT, AND MOTION; CROSS-CULTURAL MONTHLY; CROSS-CULTURAL REVIEW CHAPBOOK ANTHOLOGY; INTERNATIONAL WRITERS SERIES (II, IV-Translations, bilingual), 239 Wynsum Ave., Merrick NY 11566-4725, phone (516)868-5635, FAX 516-379-1901, founded 1971, Stanley H. and Bebe Barkan. Stanley Barkan began CCC as an educational venture, a program in 27 languages at Long Island University, but soon began publishing collections of poetry translated into English from various languages—some of them (such as Estonian) quite "neglected"—in bilingual editions. During the 70s he became aware of Antigruppo (a group against groups), a movement with similar international focus in Sicily, and the two joined forces. (See Coop. Antigruppo listing; CCC is the American representative of Coop. Antigruppo.) CCR began as a series of chapbooks (6-12 a year) of collections of poetry translated from various languages and continues as the Holocaust, Women Writers, Latin American Writers, Asian-American Writers, International Artists, Art & Poetry, Jewish, Israeli, Dutch, Turkish, Long Island and Brooklyn Chapbook Series—issued simultaneously in palm-sized and regular paperback and cloth-binding and boxed editions, as well as audiocassette and video-cassette. All submissions should be preceded by a query letter with SASE; the Holocaust series is for survivors. Send SASE for guidelines. Pays 10% of print run. In addition to publications in these series, CCC has published anthologies, translations and collections by dozens of poets from many countries. As a sample the editor selected the first stanza of "The Girl from Ipanema" by Vinícius de Moraes, as translated from the Portuguese by Gregory Rabassa:

> Look at her, see her, a beauty who passes, so full of grace.
> See her, a girl going past here, a soft swinging pace,
> A sweet side-to-side,
> On her way to the sea.

That's from the title poem of **Cross-Cultural Review Chapbook 34**, published in 1982, digest-sized, 32 pp., saddle-stapled, professionally printed with matte card cover, photo of the Brazilian poet on the back—$5. Sample: $7 postpaid. *Cross-Cultural Monthly* focuses on bilingual poetry and prose. Subscription: $36 postpaid. Sample: $3 postpaid. Pays 1 copy. CCC co-produces (with David Curzon, Vice-President of the UN Society of Writers) the Reading Series at the United Nations.

‡CRUCIBLE; SAM RAGAN PRIZE (II), Barton College, College Station, Wilson NC 27893, phone (919)237-3161, ext. 217, founded 1964, editor Terrence L. Grimes, is an annual using "poetry that demonstrates originality and integrity of craftsmanship as well as thought. Traditional metrical and rhyming poems are difficult to bring off in modern poetry. The best poetry is written out of deeply felt experience which has been crafted into pleasing form. No very long narratives." They have recently published poetry by Robert Grey, R.T. Smith and Sally Buckner. As a sample the editor selected these lines from "The Poet, the Lovers and the Nuns" by Anthony S. Abbott:

> It is cool for June. The sky, shockingly blue,
> aggravates the poet's dreams. Shaking the rust
> of solitude, he mounts the hill to the Cloisters

It is 100 pp., 6×9", professionally printed on high-quality paper with matte card cover. Press run 500 for 200 subscribers of which 50 are libraries, 100 shelf sales. Sample postpaid: $4. Send SASE for guidelines for contests (prizes of $150 and $100), and the Sam Ragan Prize ($150) in honor of the Poet Laureate of North Carolina. Submit between Christmas and mid-March. Reports in 3 months or less. "We require a short biography including a list of publications, in case we decide to publish the work." No comments on rejections.

CRYSTAL RAINBOW (V), 340 Granada Drive, Winter Park FL 32789, editor Louise M. Turmenne, is a quarterly inspirational newsletter using "seasonal, traditional rhyme or free verse, 24 lines maximum. Purpose to comfort, encourage, inspire our readers to improve themselves and reach out to others. No sexual situations. We are still over-stocked with acceptances for this year." Recently published poets include Angie Monnens, Flora Kosoff and Alice Cameron Bostrom. As a sample the editor selected these lines from "Love . . . It Is . . ." by Janet D. Dahlgren:

> Love, you know, is everywhere
> Everywhere the winds blow
> It is the tiny seed waiting
> Beneath the winter snow . . .

The newsletter is 28 pp., 7×8½", photocopy from typescript, with illustrations and classified ads—$3.50 per issue, $11.75 per year. Sample $3.50 plus SASE (75¢ postage). Send SASE for

guidelines. They sponsor quarterly contests with entry fees of $1-1.50 per poem, prizes from $4-8. Louise Turmenne says, "Touch the heart of the reader. Feel the joy and pain they feel. Embrace them with your words. Emphasize relationships. Keep it brief."

CUMBERLAND POETRY REVIEW (II, IV-Translations), P.O. Box 120128, Acklen Station, Nashville TN 37212, phone (615)373-8948, founded 1981, is a biannual with a 100+ pp., 6×9″ flat-spined format. *CPR* presents poets of diverse origins to a widespread audience. "Our aim is to support the poet's effort to keep up the language. We accept special responsibility for reminding American readers that not all excellent poems in English are being written by US citizens. We have published such poets as Laurence Lerner, Donald Davie, Emily Grosholz and Rachel Hadas." The editorial board selected these sample lines by Seamus Heaney:

> When Dante snapped a twig in the bleeding wood
> a voice sighed out of blood that bubbled up
> like sap at the end of green sticks on a fire.

Sample: $5 postpaid. Back issues: $5. Submit poetry, translations or poetry criticism with SASE or IRC. Reports in 3 months. Circulation: 500.

‡**CURLEY; BAY'S BROADSIDE (II, IV-Women, ethnic)**, P.O. Box 23521, Providence RI 02903, founded 1990, editor Sheila Smith. **"Especially interested in work by women and ethnic writers."** They give no indication of frequency of appearance of either *Curley* or *bay's broadside*, nor have I seen copies of either. **Sample: $3 postpaid. Pays 2 copies. Reports in 4 weeks.** Press run 200.

CUTBANK; THE RICHARD HUGO MEMORIAL POETRY AWARD (II), English Dept., University of Montana, Missoula MT 59812, phone (406)243-6730, founded 1973, coeditors Dennis Held and Peter Fong, an annual publishing "the best poetry, fiction, reviews, interviews and artwork available to us." Offers 2 annual awards for best poem and piece of fiction in each double issue, The Richard Hugo Memorial Poetry Award and The A. B. Guthrie Short Fiction Award. Winners announced in spring issue. Past contributors include James Crumley, William Pitt Root, Patricia Goedicke, Jim Hall, Richard Hugo, William Stafford, Harry Humes and Rita Dove. Sample lines by Hillel Schwartz:

> the miniatures are the essential us, . . .
> the last condensed edition.
> We have always wanted good
> uncluttered copy. Here we are,
> less than breviary, pruned
> to the absolute.

There are about 140 pp. of poetry in each issue, which has a circulation of about 400, 180+ subscriptions of which 10-20% are libraries. Price per issue: $12. **Sample: $4 postpaid. Submission guidelines for SASE. Submit 3-5 poems, single-spaced. Photocopies OK, dot-matrix discouraged, simultaneous submissions OK if informed. Reports in December** (i.e., "We may hold material until final choices are made in December"). **"Submit August 15-February 28. We don't read during the summer." Pays in copies.**

‡**CWM (II, IV-Themes)**, 112 S. Market St., Johnstown NY 12095, (or % David Kopaska-Merkel, 4801 Cypress St. #1004, Tuscaloosa AL 35405, phone (205)553-2284), founded 1990, co-geologians Ge(of Huth) and David Kopaska-Merkel. (These "geologians" also edit dbqp and *Dreams and Nightmares*, but *CWM* has no relation to their other imprints.) This magazine, published annually on **set themes**, is **"not tied down by ideas of proper style, form or substance, and presents work for the person of divergent tastes. The only considerations will be length and quality (as we see it). Extremely long poems will be at a disadvantage." Poems must be on the theme of the issue. Theme for the 1992 issue will be "What lies beneath the surface." "Unusual pieces of any kind are welcome, and should be** submitted in whatever form the author deems most suitable." Press run: 100. **Send SASE for guidelines. Pays "at least one copy."** Reviews books of poetry.

‡**D.C. (I)**, P.O. Box 624, Sherburne NY 13460, phone (315)691-9431, founded 1989, (*Der Gargling Cucumber*), editor Katrina Kelly, is a monthly 8-pp. publication (2 legal-sized sheets folded in the middle), using poetry "no more than one page, not in a foreign language." They have recently published poetry by Errol Miller, Paul Wienman and Ryan Reid. As a sample the editor selected these lines (poet unidentified):

> I see a buffalo
> Grazing on a Hill
> oh no, 'tis but a billboard

Sample postpaid: $1. Pays 1 copy. Press run 100+, 50 distributed free to "my established friends, trades." $20 gets you a lifetime subscription plus all back issues.

DAGGER OF THE MIND; K'YI-LIH PRODUCTIONS; BREACH ENTERPRISES (IV-Science Fiction/Fantasy/Horror), 1317 Hookridge Dr., El Paso TX 79925, phone (915)591-0541, founded 1989, executive editor Arthur William Lloyd Breach, wants "poetry that stirs the senses and emotions. Make the words dance and sing, bring out the fire in the human soul. Show flair and fashion. No four-letter words, nothing pornographic, vulgar, blasphemous, obscene and nothing generally in bad taste." They have recently published poetry by Jessica Amanda Salmonson. The quarterly *DOTM* is magazine-sized, saddle-stapled, with high glossy covers. They use about 50 of 100-150 poems received per year. Press run 4,000-5,000 with 100 subscribers. Subscription: $8/half year, $16/year. **Sample postpaid: $3.50. Pays $1-5/poem plus 1 copy.** "Send in batches of 10. I will consider simultaneous submissions only if told in advance that they are such. Length is open as is style. Be creative and try to reflect something about the human condition. Show me something that reflects what is going on in the world. Be sensitive but not mushy. Be intelligent not sophomoric. Don't try to carbon copy any famous poet. You lead the way—don't follow. I don't like the trend toward blood and gore and obscenity. Report back in 4 weeks tops. *DOTM* is devoted to *quality* horror. The key word is quality. *DOTM* is a publication under the division of K'yi-Lih Productions whose main heading is Breach Enterprises. All publications to appear in the market will come under K'yi-Lih Productions." The editor will evaluate work and review books of poetry for a fee, depending on length and quantity. He says, "I'm planning an anthology of Lovecraftian related material. The paperback will be predominantly Cthulhu Mythus fiction, but I do intend to publish some poetry."

THE DALHOUSIE REVIEW (II), Sir James Dunn Bldg., Suite 314, Halifax, Nova Scotia B3H 3J5 Canada, founded 1921, phone (902)494-2541, is a **prestige literary quarterly** with 165+ pp. per issue in a 6×9″ format, professionally printed on heavy stock with matte card cover. **Contributors receive $3 for a first poem. For each poem after (in the same issue) he or she will receive $2 per poem. They prefer poems of 40 lines or less.** Subscription: $17/year within Canada, $25/year outside Canada (both in Canadian dollars). Individual copies range in cost from $6-25. As a sample I selected these lines for "St. Cassian of Imola, Writing Teacher, Martyr" by U.S. poet David Citino:

> He ordered your writing students
> to stab you with their pens.
> A bad class, they were too happy
> to oblige, hating you
> for your stinging insistence
> on the spirit and law of each letter.

‡DANCE CONNECTION (IV-Themes), 604,815 1st St. SW, Calgary, Alberta T2P 1N3 Canada, phone (403)237-7327, founded 1983, editor Heather Elton, uses **poems about dance—"any length, format, subject except bad poetry talking about the extended graceful lines of ballet."** It is magazine-sized, 52 pp., desktop published, saddle-stapled. Press run 5,000 for 675 subscribers of which 35 are libraries. 4,000 distributed free to "serious dance readers." 400 shelf sales. Subscription: $16. **Sample postpaid: $4. Reports in 3 months. Pays 3 copies and "occasional honorarium."** Deadline for their literary issue is May 1. The editor says they "very occasionally publish poetry. When we get larger we will publish more, but now space is a precious commodity for review/calendars/news/columns and feature departments."

‡DANDELION (II), The Alexandra Centre, 922-9th Ave. SE, Calgary, Alberta T2G 0S4 Canada, phone (403)265-0524, founded 1975, poetry editors Nancy Holmes and Christopher Wiseman, managing editor John McDowell, appears twice a year. They want **"quality--We are open to any form, style, length. No greeting card verse."** They have recently published poetry by Claire Harris, Susan Ioannoce and Robert Hilles. As a sample the editor selected these lines by Roger Nash:

> On Sabbath evenings, a slow hand
> tuned the guitar. A fast hand
> moved the shifting stars. And, somewhere,
> while we were growing up, there was a street still
> made of gold of tin of slush

It is 6×9″, 102 pp., with full-color cover, professionally printed and bound. They accept about 10% of 600 MSS received. Press run 750. **Sample postpaid: $6.** Send SASE for a short statement of their needs. **Reports in 4-6 weeks. Pays $15/poem plus 1 copy.** Submit in Jan.-March and July-Sept. for issues in June and December.

JOHN DANIEL AND COMPANY, PUBLISHER; FITHIAN PRESS (II), P.O. Box 21922, Santa Barbara CA 93121, phone (805)962-1780, founded 1980, reestablished 1985. John Daniel, a general small-press publisher, specializes in literature, both prose and poetry. Fithian Press is a subsidy imprint open to all subjects. **"Book-length MSS of any form or subject matter will be considered, but we do not want**

to see pornographic, libelous, illegal or sloppily written poetry." He has recently published books by R.L. Barth, Charles Gullans and Judson Jerome. As a sample John Daniel selected these lines from "One Step Down from the Wilderness" by Julia Bates:

> Writing a poem should be
> simple as opening a window
> to breathe morning air,
> ordinary as turning pages of a book,
> concentrated, like the child with a spade
> who squats in the sand digging all the way to China,
> enriching as bread taken hot from the oven,
> placed on cooling racks, the aroma filling the kitchen

He publishes 10 flat-spined paperbacks, averaging 64 pp., per year. **For free catalog of either imprint, send 10 sample poems and bio. Reports on queries in 2 weeks, on MSS in 8 weeks. Simultaneous submissions, photocopy, dot-matrix OK, or disks compatible with Macintosh. Pays 10-50% of net receipts royalties. Fithian Press books (50% of his publishing) are subsidized, the author paying production costs and receiving royalties of 50% of net receipts. Books and rights are the property of the author, but publisher agrees to warehouse and distribute for one year if desired.** The samples I have seen (John Daniel imprint) are handsomely printed, digest-sized, with matte card covers. John Daniel advises, "Poetry does not make money, alas. It is a labor of love for both publisher and writer. But if the love is there, the rewards are great."

‡**DARK SIDE MAGAZINE; SHAMROCK PUBLICATIONS (IV-Horror/Fantasy)**, Rt. 3 Box 272-D, Ripley MS 38663, phone (601)837-3719, founded 1988 (formerly Southern Rose Productions, *Southern Rose Review, Tapestry*), editor and publisher Shannon Riley: "**I am seeking horror/dark fantasy/occult-related poems of high literary quality. No specific form or style. Length may be up to 40 lines. I have few taboos, if the work is of merit.**" They have recently published poetry by Janet P. Reedman and James A. Lee. As a sample the editor selected these lines from "Ask the Angels" by Wayne Edwards:

> we burn some stuff
> say some things
> it grows from our
> shit and sweat and sperm

Dark Side is a quarterly, digest-sized, photocopied from typescript, 80-100 pp. saddle-stapled with glossy card cover. "I receive approximately 50-60 poems each month of which I only have room for 3-4." Press run 250. Subscription: $15. **Sample: $4.50 postpaid. Send SASE for guidelines. Pays $5/poem plus 1 copy.**

‡**DAUGHTERS OF SARAH (IV-Feminist, religious, social issues, themes)**, 3801 N. Keeler, Box 411179, Chicago IL 60618, phone (312)736-3399, founded 1974, editor Reta Finger, a bimonthly magazine "integrating feminist philosophy with biblical-Christian theology and making connections with social issues." The magazine includes only "occasional" poetry. The editor says, "**Do not prefer rhyming poetry; must be short enough for one 8½×5½" page, but prefer less than 20 lines. Topics must relate to Christian feminist issues, but prefer specifics to abstract terminology.**" She does not want "greeting-card type verse or modern poetry so obscure one can't figure out what it means." As a sample she chose the following lines by Ann Bailey:

> Who would lay her head on stone,
> Would crush the dark to dust?
> What dreamstruck one will hurl herself toward holiness
> and fight for her own blessings?
> Who here would risk her life to wrestle with the Lord?

The magazine is digest-sized, 40 pp., with photos and graphics, web offset. Its circulation is 6,500, of which 6,400 are subscriptions, including about 250 libraries; bookstore sales are 70. Price per issue, $3.50; subscription $16/year. **Sample: $3.50 postpaid; guidelines are available for SASE.** *Daughters of Sarah* pays $15-30/poem plus 2-3 copies. **Poets should submit two copies of each poem (prefers shorter poems) to the editor, who reports in 1-2 months; time to publication is 3-18 months. Considers simultaneous submissions. "Write first for list of upcoming themes, since we mostly choose our poetry to fit with a particular theme.**" Reviews books of poetry.

THE DAYSPRING PRESS: THE NEW ANGLICAN REVIEW; THE NEW CATHOLIC REVIEW; POET'S FORUM (I, IV-Religious), 18600 W. 58 Ave., Golden CO 80403-1070, phone (303)279-2462, founded 1983, editor John C. Brainerd, who describes his operation as a "little-literary and religious forum. We publish almost everything received (or find its natural market)." They want "short lyrics, up to 5-page narrative poems, trading in the deeper human sensibilities. No prurient, scandalous or malicious material will be published." They have recently published poetry by Michael Davidson and Heland James. As a sample, I selected these lines from "Pan in Pain" by Aumbry Williams:

If I should contemplate the great god Pan,
He makes me sad, so little life and so much benumbed,
His beauty laid upon the mind and long his hope so dimly shine.

All magazines are in the same format: digest-sized (large print available), photocopied from Courier pica, elite and condensed, about 40 pp., with paper cover. All are monthly, with an annual "best of" edition. Press run: 1,000 for 200 subscriptions. Each sells for $2.57/issue. Subscription: $18 (12 issues). **Sample postpaid: $2.57. Send SASE and $2.57 for 20 pp. catalog (includes "writer's guidelines"). Pays 50% net over expenses (accounted). Reports in 1-4 weeks.** Reviews books of poetry. The editor says, "Discover—by intuition—where your heart is. Orbit (and write) very nearby."

DBQP; ALABAMA DOGSHOE MOUSTACHE; A VOICE WITHOUT SIDES; &; HIT BROADSIDES; THE SUBTLE JOURNAL OF RAW COINAGE; DBQPRESCARDS (IV-Form), 112 S. Market St., Johnstown NY 12095, founded 1987, poetry editor Ge(of Huth). "*dbqp* is the name of the overall press. *Alabama Dogshoe Moustache* publishes **language poetry (usually very short) & visual poetry.** *A Voice Without Sides* is an occasional magazine in very small runs (about 24 copies) and in strange formats (in jars, etc.); it uses the same type of poetry as *ADM.* *&* is a series of leaflets featuring 1 poem at a time. *Hit Broadsides* is a broadside series. *The Subtle Journal of Raw Coinage* is a monthly that publishes coined words but occasionally will publish an issue of *pwoermds* (one-word poems—that is, a word coined to be a poem, as Aram Saroyan's 'eyeye') or poems written *completely* with neologisms. *dbqprescards* is a postcard series publishing mostly poetry. These publications are generally handmade magazines, leaflets, broadsides and objects of very small size. **I am interested only in short language poetry and visual poetry. No traditional verse or mainstream poetry.**" They have recently published poetry by John M. Bennett, Karl Kempton and Bob Grumman. As a sample the editor selected this complete poem by David C. Kopaska-Merkel:

> *Yesterday's ice*
> */elbow grease/*
> *a brown pick*

Their major poetry "zine" is the quarterly *Alabama Dogshoe Moustache*, which appears in various formats up to 15 pp., magazine-sized, held together with thread, staples, fasteners, or packaged inside containers. Its press run is 50-100 with 10 subscriptions. Price per issue 75¢-$2. **Sample: $1 or $2 postpaid. Catalog available for SASE. Pays "at least 2 copies." Reports within 2 weeks. Editor "always" comments on rejections.** Occasionally reviews books of poetry. The editor says, "Most of the poetry I reject is from people who know little about the kind of poetry I publish. I don't mind reading these submissions, but it's usually a waste of time for the submitters. If you are familiar with the work of the poets I publish, you'll have a much better idea about whether or not I'll be interested in your work."

‡DEATHREALM (IV-Horror, fantasy), 3223-F Regents Park, Greensboro NC 27405, founded 1987, editor Mark Rainey, is a quarterly using "**mostly tales of horror/dark fantasy. Small amount of poetry in each issue. No poetry reviews. Use your imagination. I do not place restrictions on theme, style or length, though epic-scale pieces are not recommended. I like rhyming poetry (if it's not too elementary) as well as free-style. Small amount of poetry in each issue.**" They have recently published poetry by Fred Chappell, Jessica Amanda Salmonson and Mary Elizabeth Counselman. It is digest-sized, 56 pp., saddle-stapled. They accept 10-12 of 200-300 poems received/year. Press run 1,000 for 200 subscribers, 700-800 shelf sales. Subscription: $15. **Sample postpaid: $4. Send SASE for guidelines. Pays $2-5 plus 2 copies. Editor often comments on rejections. Reports in 2-6 weeks.**

DELAWARE VALLEY POETS, INC. (IV-Membership, anthology), P.O. Box 6203, Lawrenceville NJ 08648, phone (609)737-0222, publications director L.M. Harrod. "We publish contemporary anthologies and broadsides of **poetry by invitation to submit and books or chapbooks by members who are ready to publish.**" They have recently published poetry by Maxine Kumin, Alicia Ostreicher, Theodore Weiss, Geraldine Clinton Little, David Keller, Lois Marie Harrod and Jana Harris. As a sample, they selected these lines from "Mr. Kurtz, I Presume" by John Falk:

> *and a blue mantle of water unclasps,*
> *Slides down from the clouds and reclothes*
> *The worn and broken armature of stones.*

They publish 1-3 books per year averaging 90 pages. **Members submit 6 samples, bio, publications. Reports in 6 months.** "For anthologies, poets must have some connection with the basic organization. Anthologies are paid for by DPV, Inc., and all sales go to the organization. Individual authors pay printing costs; individual editorial services and distribution are provided by DVP. All sales go to the author." Patricia Groth advises, "Poets serious about their work need to read all the poetry they can find, write poetry, attend poetry readings and find someone to trade poetry and criticism with. If there is no workshop available, start one."

‡DELIRIUM (II), Rt. 1 Box 7X, Harrison ID 83833, founded 1989, editor Judith Shannon Paine, appears twice a year using **"vibrant poetry that is reader-friendly. Free verse is preferred, and poetry should not exceed 30 lines. Nothing obtuse."** They have recently published poetry by Richard Davignon, Elliot Richman and Claudette Bass. As a sample the editor selected these lines from "Demons Dance" by John Soldo:

> *Demons dance across the waves of my mind.*
> *Their waves insinuate*
> *like a car cutting in front of you—*

The editor says it has "a lively format." Press run 200 for 22 subscribers. Subscription: $16. **Sample postpaid: $4. Send SASE for guidelines. Pays 1 copy. Reports in 2 weeks.**

DENVER QUARTERLY (II), Dept. of English, University of Denver, Denver CO 80208, phone (303)871-2892, founded 1965, editor Donald Revell, a quarterly literary journal that publishes fiction, poems, book reviews and essays. **There are no restrictions on the type of poetry wanted.** They have recently published poetry by James Merrill, Linda Pastan and William Matthews. As a sample, the editors selected the following lines from "The Inns and Outs of Irony" by William Logan:

> *All Britain this hospital between the guts*
> *and what scavenges after, vulture blood fledged*
> *with lies, light; lab where the dusty wish*
> *of culture cultures the dawn in its dish*

Denver Quarterly is 6×9″, handsomely printed on buff stock, average 160 pp., flat-spined with two-color matte card cover. Circulation is 1,000, of which 600 are subscriptions (300 to libraries) and approximately 300 are sold on newsstands. Price per issue $5, subscription $15/year to individuals and $18 to institutions. **Samples of all issues after Spring 1985 are available for $5 postpaid, guidelines for SASE. Pay is 2 copies and a one-year subscription. No submissions read between May 15 and September 15 each year. Reporting time is 2-3 months.** Reviews books of poetry.

DEPOT PRESS (IV-Themes), P.O. Box 60072, Nashville TN 37206, founded 1981, publishes books, including poetry, relating to the **South, Old West and Civil War.** "Our 1981 booklet, *Jesse James and Bill Ryan at Nashville*, is about to enter its third printing. Our most recent title, however, is *Toreros*, the final collection of the late English lyric poet John Gawsworth (1912-1970)." **Query with letter only.**

DESCANT (III, IV-Regional), Box 314, Station P, Toronto, Ontario M5S 2S8 Canada, founded 1970, editor-in-chief Karen Mulhallen, is "a quarterly journal of the arts committed to being the finest in Canada. **While our focus is primarily on Canadian writing we have published writers from around the world."** Some of the poets they have recently published are Lorna Crozier, Tim Lilburn, Leona Gom and Libby Scheier. They selected this sample from "Journal" by Brian Henderson:

> *The dream light that folds*
> *through the page and washes over it*
> *like water is afternoon*
> *light and wells upward*

It is an elegantly printed and illustrated flat-spined publication with colored, glossy cover, over-sized digest format, 140+ pp., heavy paper, with a circulation of 1,000 (800 subscriptions, of which 20% are libraries). **Sample: $7.50 postpaid.** They receive 1,200 freelance submissions per year, of which they use less than 10, with a 2 year backlog. **Guidelines available for SASE. Submit typed MS, unpublished work not in submission elsewhere, photocopy OK, name and address on first page and last name on each subsequent page. SASE with Canadian stamps or coupons. Reports within 4 months.** They pay "approximately $100." Karen Mulhallen says, "Best advice is to know the magazine you are submitting to. Choose your markets carefully."

DESCANT: TEXAS CHRISTIAN UNIVERSITY LITERARY JOURNAL (II), English Dept., Texas Christian University, Fort Worth TX 76129, phone (817)921-7240, founded 1956, editor Betsy Colquitt, appears twice a year. They want **"well-crafted poems of interest. No restrictions as to subject-matter or forms. We usually accept poems 40 lines or fewer but sometimes longer poems."** They have recently published poems by Walter McDonald and Lyn Lifshin. As a sample I selected the first stanza of "Worth" by Alberta Turner:

> *She does so want to be right about the way*
> *smoke rises, about what a dish pan*
> *emptied into a stream will feed,*
> *about the worth of her oath.*

It is 6×9″, 92 pp. saddle-stapled, professionally printed, with matte card cover. Their press run is 500, going to 350 subscribers. "We publish 30-40 pp. of poetry per year. We receive probably 4,000-5,000 poems annually." Per issue: $4.50; subscription: $8. **Sample: $2.50 postpaid. Pays 2** copies. Simultaneous submissions OK. Reports in 6-8 weeks, usually no more than 8 months until publication.

DEVIANCE (II, IV-Feminist, political, spiritual, social issues), P.O. Box 1706, Pawtucket RI 02862-1706, founded 1985, editor Lin Collette. The magazine appears three times a year, "dedicated to publishing work by persons espousing views that may differ from the 'majority.' This includes **feminist, lesbian/gay, non-religious or religious (i.e.** discussions of religious issues that are not Judeo-Christian OR which may be an unorthodox view of Christianity or Judaism), political (non-Republican or Democratic, whether anarchist, socialist, etc.). We would like to see more work focusing on politics, our personal relationships with the world, etc. We prefer that people write poetry that answers specific questions they may have or poses a situation or tells a story of sorts. Length is wide-open (no book-length, though). Study the master poets, traditional, contemporary, etc., for style. If someone can write a good metered, rhymed poem, please send it! None of the usual nature meditations (green grass, falling rain) unless very well-done and unusual in thought; no homophobic, sexist, racist material; no gratuitous sex and violence. Please, none of the same old meditations on lovers, lost loves, etc. Unless well-done. We are getting too much of this." They have recently published work by Trish Lehman and Patricia Slattery. As a sample, the editor selected these lines by M.C. Alper:

> *Human nature entraps itself*
> *in its own web of*
> *Intellectual thread, skillfully spun*
> *by rhetorical tongues of ideological conviction.*

Deviance is magazine-sized, 37-50 pp., laser printed, with a taped spine, colored card cover, circulation 500 with 75 subscriptions, 275 shelf sales, $5 per issue, $13.50 for subscription of 3 issues. Sample: $5 postpaid, checks payable to Lin Collette. Pays 1 copy. Reports in 1 month. Submit maximum of 5 poems. SASE for guidelines or for replies to submissions; otherwise no reply will be sent. She comments on rejections "when appropriate; especially if it's something that might have worked for us." Reviews books of poetry. She says "Publishing poetry is probably one of the more difficult avocations anyone can have. However, it's a craft as much as a hobby and it deserves to be written well. Be familiar with current and past poetry styles, but develop your own in response to them. Pick up books on writing poetry, but the most important thing is to read poetry itself, not just handbooks. Avoid clichés, and tired situations and subjects. Most of the 'New Age' material we've been getting has been really awful—please be certain to write well on this subject, if you insist on doing so. Also, love poetry, if not done very well, can be really tiresome. Although *Deviance* is not specifically a women's publication and is for everyone, we'd like to see more feminist work than we've been getting."

THE DEVIL'S MILLHOPPER PRESS; THE DEVIL'S MILLHOPPER; KUDZU POETRY CONTEST (II), College of Humanities, University of South Carolina at Aiken, 171 University Parkway, Aiken SC 29801, founded 1976, editor Stephen Gardner, assistant editor Carol Jennings, publishes one magazine issue of *The Devil's Millhopper* each year and one chapbook, winner of an annual competition. They want to see any kind of poetry, except pornography or political propaganda, up to 100 lines. Some of the poets they have published recently are Susan Ludvigson, Ann Darr, Lynne H. de Courcy, Ricardo Pau-Llosa, Katherine Soniat, Walt McDonald, R.T. Smith and Dorothy Barresi. As a sample the editor chose these lines from "The Temporary Map" by David Graham:

> *All rain is acid, eating the landscape*
> *in memory. Any map's temporary,*
> *like a family tale altering itself,*
> *like a difficult friend improving with time.*

That is from the winner of their 1989 chapbook contest, **Doggedness**, handsomely printed 32 pp., saddle-stapled, on quality cream white stock with matte textured tan card cover. The print run of *Devil's Millhopper* is 500. The annual chapbook has a print run of 600, going to 375 subscribers of which 20 are libraries. The magazine is digest-sized, 28-40 pp., saddle-stapled, printed on good stock with card cover and using beautiful b/w original drawings inside and on the cover. Sample: $2.50 postpaid. Send regular, non-contest submissions September and October only. They want name and address on every page of submissions; simultaneous submissions acceptable. Photocopy and dot-matrix OK if it is dark, readable type. Pays copies. Reports usually in 2 months. Sometimes the editor comments on rejected MSS. Send SASE for their annual Kudzu Poetry Contest rules (prizes of $50, $100 and $150, $3/poem entry fee), chapbook competition rules and guidelines for magazine submissions. Send Kudzu contest submissions September 1-October 15; chapbook contest submissions January 1-February 1. Chapbook competition requires either $5 reading fee or $9 subscription for 2 years. Pays $50 plus 50 copies. The editor advises, "There is no substitute for reading a lot and writing a lot or for seeking out tough criticism from others who are doing the same."

JAMES DICKEY NEWSLETTER (II), DeKalb College, 2101 Womack Rd., Dunwoody GA 30338, founded 1984, editor Joyce M. Pair, a biannual newsletter devoted to study of James Dickey's works/ biography and bibliography. They **"publish a few poems of *high* quality."** The copy I have, which is 30+ pp. of ordinary paper, neatly offset (back and front), with a card back-cover in blue, stapled top left corner, contains 1 poem, "Haft Blossom," by R.T. Smith. Its opening lines are:

> Long-sleeping, I rose in the morning
> and opened the door to sunlight.
> Trough water woke me with sunlight,
> dark and the other stars having
> yielded their power . . .

The newsletter is published in the fall and spring. Single copy price is $3.50, subscription to individuals $5/year; $10 to institutions. **Sample available for $3.50 postage. Contributors should follow MLA style and standard MS form, sending 1 copy, double-spaced.** The editor's advice is: "Acquire more knowledge of literary history, metaphor, symbolism and grammar, and, to be safe, the poet should read a couple of our issues."

DICKINSON STUDIES; HIGGINSON JOURNAL (V); DICKINSON-HIGGINSON PRESS (I), 1330 Massachusetts Ave. NW, Apt. 503, Washington DC 20005-4150, phone (202)638-1671, founded 1968, poetry editor F. L. Morey. *Dickinson Studies* and *Higginson Journal* are publications of Dickinson-Higginson Press (membership $50 individuals, $100 for libraries for 3 years). **Both magazines are overstocked until 1993.** They are semiannuals, sometimes with bonus issues, all distributed free to about 250 subscribers of which 125 are libraries. *Dickinson Studies* **is principally for scholarship on Emily Dickinson, but uses poems about her.** *Higginson Journal* **has a special poetry issue about every two years and uses a few poems in each issue.** The journals are both digest-sized, about 30 pp., saddle-stapled, typeset with card covers and b/w art. **Sample: $4 postpaid.** The Dickinson-Higginson Press also has subsidy-published several collections of poems, the poet putting up all printing costs, plus 10% for editing and handling; 25 copies free to poet. "All payments in advance, before scheduling definitely."

‡DIE YOUNG (V), P.O. Box 11066, Milwaukee WI 53211, founded 1990, editors Jesse Glass, Jr. and Skip Fox, is a journal appearing irregularly, **accepting no unsolicited poetry**, that has published poetry by Robert Creeley, Karl Shapiro, Richard Eberhart, Kathleen Raine, Burton Raffel and Tom Clark. As a sample the editor selected these lines from "Provincetown" by Leo Connellan:

> Eons ago the sea came up out of the pit of itself
> to have a look at its roof the sky and
> vomited up a little spread of land to come
> and lie on its back and look at the ever
> changing heavens as we do...

Sample postpaid: $3. Those who wish to submit may query with SASE.

‡DIEHARD (III), 3 Spittal St., Edinburgh, Scotland EH3 9DY, phone (031)229-7252, founded 1990, editors Ian King and Sally Evans, publishes 6 hardbacks and 1-2 chapbooks/year. **They want "the heavyweight stuff, no fractured prose, politics and pious piffle."** As examples of poets published recently the editor lists Keats, Oscar Wilde and John Skelton. "A book is a book. Write me a book rather than ply me with a heap of scraps from magazines." **Reporting is "slow." They pay 5% royalties plus 6 copies. "No reply unless interested, do not send SAE. Use your own name, keep it accurate, keep it legible."** The editor says, "Anyone attempting subsidy will be booted out the door that fast and it might cause an international incident. We are actually quite a major antiquarian bookshop (Grindles of Edinburgh) with a bindery and letterpress printing facilities (for shop use only). As most of our staff are writers or former publishers of some description, we like to keep Diehard going as a sideline where quality of production really matters."

‡A DIFFERENT DRUMMER (II, IV-Translations); SONGS OF THE CITY ANNUAL POETRY CONTEST (II, IV-Themes), 84 Bay 28th St., Brooklyn NY 11214, founded 1989, editor/publisher Nicholas Stix. *ADD* appears 3 times a year. **"I am promiscuous in my likes (style and theme-wise) and don't want to discourage someone from submitting an excellent poem written in a generally undistinguished genre. I do not expect poetry to toe a political line. Spare me impostors, masquerading as poems: incoherent fragments, uninspiring prose set in short 'poetry-like' lines and literal statements of the writer's moral superiority or love of another person, place or thing. Also: no poems that explain themselves through a preface or epilogue, or poems on the difficulties of writing poetry, unless extremely witty."** They have recently published poetry by Bob Balo and Alysia Harpootian and translations by Clara Pierre. As a sample the editor selected these lines from "Napoleon's Donut" by John Misselwitz:

> The mailman left me
> Napoleon's head the other day
> And before I had time to catch him

The head had eaten my morning donut.
ADD is 8×11″ flat-spined, 83 pp., professionally printed, with glossy card cover. Press run 2,000 for about 300 subscriptions, about 900 shelf sales. Subscription: $9. Sample postpaid: $4. **Do not submit MSS in July, except those for contest, and August. Send SASE for guidelines. Pays a minimum of 2 copies. "Allow 3 months for a response. I read all submissions, screening out approximately 90%. Each remaining MS is read by one of my editors, who then discusses it with me. There are no requirements, but potential contributors are strongly urged to read** *ADD* **first, before going to the trouble and expense of submitting work."** They use translations with original works (author must secure rights of work not in public domain.) Their annual Songs of the City Contest (Prizes of $100, $75, $50, plus publication in *ADD* and copies; entry fee: $5/poem; deadline August 1) is for **poems on urban themes.** The editor says, "Don't be a slave to the muse, forcing all of your thoughts and feelings into a 'poetic' form. Work in as many forms of prose and poetry as possible. That way you are more likely to find the style appropriate to your expression. Be your own toughest critic. Proofread and analyze your work carefully. Never rush out a poem before its time. Avoid the company of poets. Above all, don't pay too much attention to the pious pronouncements of pompous publishers."

‡DIS-EASE (II), P.O. Box 4264, Westmount, Quebec H3Z 3B6 Canada, founded 1989 "from the ashes of the now (in)famous *Noovo Masheen*," editors Frank Manley, Claude Paradox and James Whittall, appears quarterly. **"Heavy emphasis on satire, irony and parody, and poems written so well they would fall apart if you pulled out one word. Favor shorter poems (less than 1 page). Form is still important to us dinosaurs."** It is magazine-sized, circulation 500. **Sample: $3 postpaid. Reports in 4 months, pays copies. "No US stamps please: IRCs or cash required."** Claude Paradox advises, "Don't do it unless you feel you have no choice."

‡DOC(K)S; EDITIONS NEPE; ZERROSCOPIZ; ANTHOLOGIES DE L'AN 2.000; LES ANARTISTES (II, IV-Bilingual/foreign language), Le Moulin de Ventabren, 13122 Ventabren, France 13122, uses "concrete, visual, sound poetry; performance; mail-art; metaphysical poetry," not "poesie à la queue-leu-leu" . . . whatever that means. Recently published work by J.F. Bory, Nani Balestrini, Bernard Heidsieck, James Koller, Franco Beltrametti, A. Arias-Missow, E. Miccini, E. Limonov, A. Spatola and Ma Desheng. The magazine *Doc(k)s* is published 4 times a year and has a circulation of 1,100, of which 150 are subscriptions. **Pay for poetry is 5 copies. There are no specifications for submissions.** *Doc(k)s* is an elegantly produced volume, 7×10″, over 300 pp., flat-spined, using heavy paper and glossy full-color card covers. Most of it is in French. I cannot quote a sample, because concrete poetry, a cross between poetry and graphic art, requires the visual image to be reproduced. Nepe Editions publishes collections of poetry, mostly in French.

DOLPHIN LOG (IV-Children, themes), 8440 Santa Monica Blvd., Los Angeles CA 90069, phone (213)656-4422, founded 1981, editor Pamela Stacey, is a bimonthly educational publication for children offered by The Cousteau Society. "Encompasses all areas of science, history and the arts as they relate to our global water system. Philosophy of magazine is to delight, instruct and instill an environmental ethic and understanding of the interconnectedness of living organisms, including people." They want to see **"poetry related to the marine environment, marine ecology or any water-related subject-matter to suit the readership of 7 to 15-year-olds and which will fit the concept of our magazine. Short, witty poems, thought-provoking poems encouraged. No dark or lengthy ones (more than 20 lines)."** The editor selected these sample lines from "I Found a Tiny Starfish" by Dayle Ann Dodds:

> *I found a tiny starfish*
> *In a tidepool by the sea.*
> *I hope whoever finds him next,*
> *Will leave him there like me!*
> *And the gift I've saved for you?*
> *The best that I can give:*
> *I found a tiny starfish,*
> *And for you, I let him live.*

It is magazine-sized, 20 pp., saddle-stapled, offset, using full-color photographs widely throughout, sometimes art, no advertising. It circulates to 100,000 members, approximately 860 library subscriptions. Membership: $28/year for a Cousteau Society family membership, $10/year for *Dolphin Log* only. **Sample: $2.50 postpaid. Pays $10-50 on publication and 3 copies. Reports within 2 months. Dot-matrix, photocopies OK. Double-spaced. First-time use preferred.** The editor advises, "Become familiar with our magazine by requesting a sample copy and our guidelines. We are committed to a particular style and concept to which we strictly adhere and review submissions consistently. We publish only a limited amount of poetry each year."

DOLPHIN-MOON PRESS; SIGNATURES (II, IV-Regional), P.O. Box 22262, Baltimore MD 21203, founded 1973, president James Taylor, managing editor Richard Byrne, is **"a limited edition (500-1,000 copies) press which emphasizes quality work (regardless of style), often published in unusual/ 'radical' format.** The writer is usually allowed a strong voice in the look/feel of the final piece. "We've published magazines, anthologies, chapbooks, pamphlets, perfect-bound paperbacks, records, audio cassettes and comic books. **All styles are read and considered, but the work should show a strong spirit and voice. Although we like the feel of 'well-crafted' work, craft for its own sake won't meet our standards either."** They have published poetry by Gian Lombardo, John Strausbaugh, John Logan, W. D. Snodgrass, Tom O'Grady and Nobel Laureate Jaroslav Seifert. As a sample, I selected these opening lines from James Taylor's "Fells Point," one of the poems in the Signature **Baltimore: A City in Four Poems:**

> First step. Land fall. A site
> in near future of a colonial black painter,
> shipwrights and quick to please prostitutes.
> Some towns are born old and born hookers.

The four poems in Signature collections are printed on one side of a folded 9×20″ card. On the other (title side) is a beautiful sepia photo cityscape of Baltimore. The other examples they sent are similarly elegant and unusual in design. I was sufficiently impressed that I sent them my own MS, *The Village: New and Selected Poems,* $8.95 paperback, $15.95 hardcover. **Send SASE for catalog and purchase samples or send $10 for their 'sampler' (which they guarantee to be up to $20 worth of their publications). To submit, first send sample of 6-10 pp. of poetry and a brief cover letter. Replies to query in 2-4 weeks, to submission of whole work (if invited) in 2-4 weeks. Payment in author's copies.** "Our future plans are to continue as we have since 1973, publishing the best work we can by local, up-and-coming and nationally recognized writers—in a quality package."

THE DOMINION REVIEW (II), Old Dominion University, Bal 200, English Dept., Norfolk VA 23529-0078, phone (804)683-3000, founded 1982, faculty advisor Wayne Ude, Creative Writing, who says, **"There are no specifications as to subject-matter or style, but we are dedicated to the free verse tradition and will continue to support it. No poetry which has no sense of discipline toward language or which does not give a new perspective on any subject provoked by *any* motivation."** They have published poetry by Bob Perlongo, Paul Genega and Grace P. Simpson. As a sample I selected these lines from "Pictures Looked at Once More" by Alberto Rios:

> August lightning opens the afternoon sky
> As one might open an egg.
> Opens, or breaks, the same way
> Those album photographs get ripped
> Then scotch taped back together.

TDR is flat-spined, 80 pp., digest-sized, professionally printed, and appears each spring. They have 300 subscriptions. **Submissions read from Sept. 1 to Dec. 7; allow to Feb. 15 for replies. Guidelines available for SASE. No more than 5 poems per submission. No pay. They will not consider previously published poems. "We would like a cover letter."**

DREAMS AND NIGHTMARES (IV-Science fiction/fantasy), 4801 Cypress Creek #1004, Tuscaloosa AL 35405, phone (205)553-2284, founded 1986, editor David C. Kopaska-Merkel, is published quarterly. The editor says, "I want to see intriguing poems in any form or style which are under about 60 lines (but will consider longer poems). All submissions must be either science fiction, fantasy or horror (I prefer supernatural horror to gory horror). Nothing trite or sappy, very long poems, poems without fantastic content, excessive violence or pointless erotica. Sex and/or violence is OK if there is a good reason." He has recently used poetry by Lisa Kucharsk, Robert Frazier, Donna Zelzer, John Grey, D.F. Lewis, Wendy Rathbone and Ann K. Schwader. As a sample he selected these lines from "A confusion of planets" by Alan Catlin:

> On the street she was a legend,
> creating something like a new world,
> eating cat food out of cans as she
> played, singing a song with no words
> no one who ever heard her could ever forget.

It has 20 pp., digest-sized, photocopied from typescript, saddle-stapled, with a colored card stock cover and b/w illustrations. They accept about 60 of 750-1,000 poems received. Press run is 200 for 70 subscriptions. **Samples: $1.25 in stamps.** Subscription: $5/4 issues. **Send SASE for guidelines. Pays $3/poem plus 2 copies. No simultaneous submissions. "Rarely" uses previously published poems. Reports in 1-4 months.** The editor says "Speculative poetry has gained much recognition of late; most professional speculative fiction magazines publish some poetry. My advice is to actively seek information about new markets, to write a lot of poems and to submit poems as often as necessary."

DRUID PRESS (II), 2724 Shades Crest Rd., Birmingham AL 35216, phone (205)967-6580, founded 1981, president Anne George. "We do individual chapbooks. **We want to see concrete images, free verse, any subject-matter. No June-moon rhymes.**" They have published poetry by R.T. Smith, Sue Walker, Sue Scalf, John Brugaletta and many others. As a sample the editor selected these lines (poet unidentified):

> *South of Montgomery along the interstate*
> *redtailed hawks perch on bare trees*
> *and watch the traffic pushing through*
> *the heaviness of late fall rain*

For chapbook or book consideration query with 5 samples, bio, publications. Simultaneous submissions, photocopies, dot-matrix OK, but no previously published material. Reports in 3 weeks. Pays "negotiable" number of author's copies. Sample books: $4 postpaid.

‡**DRY CRIK REVIEW (IV-Themes)**, P.O. Box 51, Lemon Cove CA 93244-0051, founded 1991, editor John C. Dofflemyer, is a quarterly of cowboy poetry. "Poetry must exhibit some *unique* perspective gained from or in terms of the cattle business. It must be authentic. No doggerel, please! Insightful. No more than 40 lines." They have recently published poetry by Wallace McRae, Paul Zarzyski and Vess Quinlan. As a sample the editor selected these lines from "For Woody" by Rod McQueary:

> *And now, I watch him strain to shuffle.*
> *I touch my rifle, 'neath my seat.*
> *A friend to suffering horses.*
> *At this range, I could not miss.*
> *He'd find green pastures in an instant.*
> *For my Dad, I do it neat,*
> *He'd never hear the whisper.*
> *Never feel the Nosler's kiss.*

It is digest-sized, 48 pp., photocopied from typescript on quality textured paper, matte card cover. Press run 500 for 200 subscribers of which 5 are libraries, 10% shelf sales. Subscription: $20. **Sample postpaid: $6. Send SASE for guidelines. Pays 2 copies. Reports within 90 days.**

‡**DUCKABUSH JOURNAL (II)**, P.O. Box 2228, Sequim WA 98382, founded 1988, editors Nancy Beres and Tom Snyder, appears twice a year. "**We consider all types of writing as long as it's correctly edited and spell-checked. No greeting card verse.**" They have recently published poetry by James Bertolino, Alice Derry and Tim McNulty. As a sample the editors selected these lines by Gloria Boyer:

> *Everything was a sensation she could never place:*
> *night dragging its thin fingers across the glass,*
> *a leaf bug clicking the beads of its abacus.*
> *Already winter was coming and her body curled*

It is digest-sized, flat-spined, 70+ pp., with matte card cover. Press run 350 for 25 subscribers of which 3 are libraries, 250 shelf sales. They accept about 10% of poetry received. Subscription: $10. **Sample postpaid: $3. Reports within 6 weeks. Pays 2 copies.** Nancy Beres says, "We read everything. The two editors have very different styles and ranges of taste. Anything is possible."

‡**DUST (FROM THE EGO TRIP); CAMEL PRESS (IV-Themes)**, HC 80, Box 160, Big Cove Tannery PA 17212, phone (717)573-4526, founded 1981, poetry consultant Katharyn Machan Aal, publisher James Hedges, who describes himself as "editor/printer of scholarly and scientific journals, does occasional poetry chapbooks for fun." *Dust (From the Ego Trip)* is "an intermittent journal of personal reminiscences." For it he wants "**autobiographical material (can address any subject, but written from the viewpoint of an active participant in the events described). MSS should average about 2,500 words and can be one long poem or a collection of related shorter poems. Any style OK, and any language using the roman alphabet. No religious (evangelizing) material or other material written primarily to advance a point of view. Any topic is OK, and coarse language is OK, but only if used artistically.**" As a sample James Hedges selected these lines by recent author Sheryl L. Nelms:

> *The gold lapel pin declares him Blessed.*
> *His yellow suit and tie announce it with day-glow intensity,*
> *and the money clip bulging with hundreds*
> *screams:*
> *Praise the Lord, brothers and sisters. I am blessed!*

He publishes 1-2 chapbooks a year under the Camel Press imprint, average 20 pp. **Query with "a few sample poems." No bio, publications needed because, "we judge on material only, status of poet is irrelevant. Simultaneous submissions, photocopies, previously published material OK,** but he prefers not to have dot-matrix. Reports in 10 days. **Pays 50 copies plus half of net after production costs are recovered.** He is open to subsidy publishing of poetry of "artistic merit," though he has never done any. To buy samples, request catalog. "I always write a cover letter, but I'm not a poetry critic, just a considerate publisher. I do a bit of poetry because I want to encourage the art and broaden my catalog. Everything I publish is handset in metal type and letterpress printed on fine paper. The authors are expected to do most of the promotion. Press run normally 500, and I give away about 400 copies to friends, plus 50 for the author. The author can order more copies in advance if he expects to sell a large number. Financial arrangements are negotiable."

DUSTY DOG; DUSTY DOG REVIEWS (II), P.O. Box 1103, Zuni NM 87327, phone (505)782-4958, founded 1990, editor/publisher John Pierce, appears three times a year using **"high caliber, well-crafted poetry, any style. No restrictions on form or length. No rhyming poetry, nothing** *overtly* **pornographic or religious. No light verse. No haiku."** They have recently published poetry by T.K. Splake, Belinda Subraman, Sue Saniel Elkind, Joanne Lowery, Hugh Fox, William Rodriguez, R. Nikolas Macioci, Janet McCann and Brian Walker. As a sample the editor selected these lines (poet unidentified):

> I work a ceremony: my shadow in front
> guarding the Earth from the sun. I draw
> this makeshift sled: a fence
> carrying off a season: a scraping
> as of the sun was afraid to come

It is 20-28 pp., 8½ × 7", sometimes 5½ × 8½", professionally printed on tinted paper with matte card cover. Saddle-stapled. Press run is 300 for 90 subscribers. Subscription: $7/3 issues. **Sample: $4 postpaid. Pays 1 copy. Send SASE for guidelines. Simultaneous submissions OK. Reports in 2-4 weeks.** *Dusty Dog Reviews* is a quarterly review magazine, reviewing small press poetry magazines and chapbooks, 20-40/issue. Subscription: $10. Sample: $4. The editor advises, "Become very familiar with **Poet's Market** and what Judson Jerome has to say at the beginning of the book. The small press magazines are often 1 person staff and work very hard for you, the poet. Be patient with them, and support the magazines you like. If poets don't subscribe to the magazines that publish them, it is very hard for the magazine to continue publishing."

EAGLE WING PRESS (IV-Ethnic), P.O. Box 579MO, Naugatuck CT 06770, phone (203)274-7738, founded 1981, poetry editor Ron Welburn, is an **American Indian newspaper** appearing every other month. **Poems must be on American Indian themes or written by American Indians. "Try to avoid 'typical' pieces that try to sound 'Indian'. We are looking for clear, concise, strong poetry."** They have recently published poetry by Joseph Bruchac and Ed Edmo. As a sample the editor selected lines from the poem "Just a Bundle of Twigs" by Mary Good Seeds Woman:

> just a bundle of twigs
> beautiful
> perfect
> tied together with a root
> to keep the dream alive

The newspaper is tabloid-sized, 28 pp., unstapled, with graphics and ads, circulation 4,700 with 300 subscriptions of which 120 are libraries, about 600 shelf sales. Subscriptions are $10 a year. **Sample: $2 postpaid. Pays 5 copies.** Reviews books of poetry by Native Americans.

EARTH'S DAUGHTERS: A FEMINIST ARTS PERIODICAL (IV-Women/Feminist, themes), Box 622, Station C, Buffalo NY 14209, phone (716)837-7778, founded 1971. The "literary periodical **with strong feminist emphasis**" appears 3 times a year, irregularly spaced. Its "format varies. Most issues are flat-spined, digest-sized issues of approximately 60 pp. We also publish chapbooks, magazine-sized and tabloid-sized issues. Past issues have included broadsheets, calendars, scrolls and one which could be assembled into a box." Those I have seen are elegantly printed and illustrated on glossy stock with glossy card covers. **Poetry can be "up to 40 lines (rare exceptions for exceptional work), free form, experimental—we like unusual work. All must be strong, supportive of women in all their diversity. We like work by new writers, but expect it to be well-crafted. We want to see work of technical skill and artistic intensity. We rarely publish work in classical form, and we never publish rhyme or greeting card verse."** They have published poetry by Christine Cassidy, Rose Romano, Lyn Lifshin, Helen Ruggieri, Joan Murray, Susan Fantl Spivack, "and many fine 'unknown' poets, writers and artists." They publish poetry by men if it is supportive of women. As a sample the editor selected *#36 Over the Transom* "A Shape Soft Enough to Wear" by Lynn Martin:

> . . . Two women can talk the night
> into a shape soft enough to wear
> one more time. It's almost as if

> *The same onion planted over & over,*
> *never decays, grows like a prayer . . .*

"Our purpose is to publish primarily work that otherwise might never be printed, either because it is unusual, or because the writer is not well known." Subscription: $14/3 issues for individuals; $22 for institutions. Sample: $4 postpaid. Send SASE for guidelines. Some issues have themes, which are available for SASE after April of each year. Pays 2 copies and reduced prices on further copies. Length of reporting time is atrociously long if MSS is being seriously considered for publication, otherwise within 3 weeks. Simultaneous submissions, photocopies, dot-matrix OK. "Per each issue, authors are limited to a total of 150 lines of poetry, prose or a combination of the two. Submissions in excess of these limits will be returned unread. Business-size envelope is preferred, and use sufficient postage—we do not accept mail with postage due." Editor comments "whenever we have time to do so—we want to encourage new writers." The collective says: "Once you have submitted work, please be patient. We only hold work we are seriously considering for publications, and it can be up to a year between acceptance and publication. If you must contact us (change of address, notification that a simultaneous submission has been accepted elsewhere), be sure to state the issue theme, the title(s) of your work and enclose SASE."

EASTERN CARIBBEAN INSTITUTE (I, IV-Regional), P.O. Box 1338, Frederiksted, U.S. Virgin Islands 00841, phone (809)772-1011, founded 1982, editor S.B. Jones-Hendrickson, editorial contact Sandra Thomas; is a "small-press publisher with plans to expand," **especially interested in poetry of the Caribbean and Eastern Caribbean "but open to all subjects, styles and forms."** As a sample the editor selected these lines from **On The Wings of Love and Time** (author/poet unidentified):

> *How often I wondered about your promises,*
> *And how long you'll be true. Now I know*
> *your promises were only to make me blue.*

Their books are softcover, averaging 60 pp. Sample copies available for purchase. **Submit 5 sample poems, cover letter with bio and previous publications. Simultaneous submissions and previously published poems OK. Reports in one month. Pays 50 copies.** The editor says, "In our part of the world, poetry is moving on a new level. People who are interested in regional poetry should keep an eye on the Caribbean region. There is a new focus in the Virgin Islands."

ECHOES (II), P.O. Box 365, Wappingers Falls NY 12590, founded 1985, editor Marcia W. Grant, "is a quarterly literary magazine that features quality prose and poetry from well-established as well as talented emerging writers. *Echoes* has no rigid specifications as to form, length, subject matter or style. Excellence is the determining factor. Usual length of accepted poems is 20-40 lines, longer if exceptional. Editors want to see poems whose ideas and imagery are clearly focused, well-crafted and unusual. No sing-song rhyme, erotica or effusive amateur efforts." They have recently published poetry by Robert Cooperman, Fr. Benedict Auer, Johy Grey, Ruth Daigon and Gayle Elen Harvey. As a sample the editor selected these lines from "Mother and Son Reunion" by Linda Back McKay:

> *Her finger traced the familiar shape*
> *of his nail, two hands that, but for dark*
> *leaps of time's hunger, should have known*
> *each other like gloves.*

Echoes is a 5½ × 8½", 44 pp., saddle-stapled, offset printed magazine, with matte cover. Press run 250 for about 100 subscriptions, of which 12 are libraries, some shelf sales. Subscription: $15 (libraries, $12.) **Sample postpaid: $4.50 current issue; $3 back issue. Send SASE for guidelines.** Reporting time generally 6-10 weeks. Pays 1 copy. "Five poems should be maximum submitted at one time. Contributor's notes requested." Previously published submissions OK if poet owns rights. Editor comments on submissions "rarely." The editor says poets must read good poetry to know good poetry. "Familiarize yourself with our magazine before you submit."

EDICIONES UNIVERSAL (IV-Ethnic, foreign language, regional), 3090 SW 8th St., Miami FL 33135, phone (305)642-3234, founded 1964, general manager Marta Salvat-Golik, is a small-press subsidy publisher of **Spanish language books. "We specialize in Cuban authors and themes."** They have recently published books of poetry by Olga Rosalo and Amelia del Castillo. **Poets "must be able to purchase in advance 75% of the copies, due to the fact that poetry does not sell well." Poets receive the copies they paid for. Submit sample, bio, publications. Reports in 4 weeks.**

‡EDINBURGH REVIEW (II, IV-Translations), 22 George Sq., Edinburgh, Scotland EH8, founded 1969, is a 160 pp. paperback literary quarterly, circulation 2,500, which uses **quality poetry. Especially interested in non-metropolitan work, translations, aphorisms, philosophy for the generalist and interviews with lesser known writers. Sample £4.95. Pays.** Reviews books of poetry.

Close-up

Imogene Bolls
Poet

Bird Bones
With time and direction
at ease in their sockets,
at home in the marrow,

they have borne up well,
these bones, scattered now,
encrusted with earth.

And since they have flown,
their falling at last
doesn't matter.

(from **Earthbound** in **Ohio Women: Poems**)

Photo by Nathan Bolls

For Imogene Bolls, a poem begins with an impulse "dancing about in the back of your brain." Everyone *has* the impulse, she says. But only some can grasp that thought, that unfinished dance, and exploit it enough to thrust it into the limelight, enabling that impulse to become its own form, its own feeling, and ultimately, its own poem.

Transferring that dancing impulse to a poetic phrase has become an art form for Bolls. She's published more than 400 poems in literary magazines and poetry journals; a collection, **Earthbound**, in **Ohio Women: Poems**; and a book, **Glass Walker**. She also has several travel grants and poetry awards to her credit.

"I've always wanted to be a poet . . . but not a poet with a capital 'p'," says Bolls. There is a difference, she explains: "I have a special love for the language and I'm a lover of poetry. I've always wanted to write poetry, but not necessarily be famous for it. I just want to play with words and make them come alive." In that mode, a 15-year-old Imogene Bolls set out to "express the inexpressible, to say the unsayable: to 'live-trap' with words a moment of psychic experience." And her poetry, mostly revolving around the topics of nature and the American Southwest, has certainly captured the experience and feeling of the outdoors.

Bolls believes that each poet, as each poem, has a distinct reason for existing and thriving. But at the same time, each successful poet must have a good base. And, although she admits that "rules and form in poetry are made to be broken," it's imperative to know those same rules in order to fully comprehend the poetic process. "I believe in form as a discipline for the contemporary poet. You must have the core, the base, before you can begin to express yourself poetically."

She sees young poets sometimes trying to surpass the learning stage (the base) before they're ready. To obtain the "base" she speaks of, one must *read*, stresses Bolls, and that means everything from the daily newspaper to the classics to the dictionary. "A poet must know history, as well as literature. Know the tradition of the literature you're writing about. If you're writing about a flower, know what kind of flower it is. Research it and know every little detail about it."

In the same sense it's good to study the trends in new poetry; not necessarily to copy or to follow, but to know them. "Don't follow the fads—the long, discursive poem; the lower case letters, the & signs—if they are not you. Learn from them, learn to love them, but write poems true to yourself."

Another problem of many young minstrels, she says, is that they sometimes attempt to take on topics too tough for the beginner to conquer. Emotions, for example, "are so abstract that they are hard to describe in poetry." She advises not to start with such topics because, as one's poetry develops and expands, it usually ends up at that point regardless. Start simply, she urges, with vivid descriptions of simple elements in your day-to-day life. Describe how your dog's ears stand up at mealtime, or the way a grounded leaf appears in autumn, and then move on to more complicated topics.

Sometimes the simplest ideas, sights and sounds will spur the most lively creative impulses, which may become good poems. Embarking upon a nature hike often creates a "shimmer" of an impulse for Bolls. She maintains that for other poets different methods to obtain an "askance concentration" (environment conducive to poetic creativity) are used, but her love for the outdoors seems to spark creativity.

Also, says the poet, getting away from her "natural" poetry style often helps her write better. "I don't consider myself a humorous poet at all, but writing in that style loosens me up; it encourages risk-taking, which can only improve my serious poetry."

Usually Bolls' humorous poetry (which makes up 10% of her work) stems from her "Odes to Words," poems about one single word. For example, one of her odes is about the word "balloon." In the poem, she actually tried to become the balloon—to squeeze into the balloon and express its short-lived existence, from the time it's blown up to the moment when all the air rushes out and propels it wildly through the air. In an even lighter moment, she wrote an ode to "belching."

Bolls can capture the dancing impulse and so eloquently lay it down for readers to enjoy that it seems she has deciphered the quirks associated with successful poetry writing. She assures that this assumption is far from true: "Writing does not get progressively easier as you go on . . . and your next poem is not necessarily better than the last one. Practice helps, but the most difficult 'dances' tax us again and again, every mental muscle. And we get stage fright every time."

—*Brian C. Rushing*

EGORAG; THE POET AND THE POEM; EGORAG PRESS (I, II, IV-Social), 4836 Ross St., Red Deer, Alberta T4N 5E8 Canada, founded 1989, editor Clarence Meinema, appears every other month using "5-25 lines of clear poetry that explores the struggles of mankind in the world today (social issues). No nature, religion." They have recently published poetry by Robert Stallsworthy, Melody Szabo, Macdonald Coleman and Brian Chan. As a sample I selected the opening lines from "Doubtless" by C.A. Kamenka:

> Entering the night doubtless
> our bodies follow an unseen choreographer
> under whose direction we dance the dance.

It is 30 pp., saddle-stapled, digest-sized, with matte card cover. Press run 150 for 85 subscribers. Subscription: $30. **Sample postpaid: $2.50. "Subscribers receive a small honorarium ($5); non-subscribers receive a submitter's copy." Submit MSS double-spaced.** *The Poet and the Poem* appears 4 times/year, publishes bio and 10-12 poems per poet, length 5-14 lines, 8 poets per issue. No information on payment. Egorag Press published 6 chapbooks in 1990. For chapbook consideration **submit 50 pp., $10 reading fee, brief bio, publications. Pays $35 plus 10 copies.** "Authors are expected to promote their own work by readings."

EIDOS MAGAZINE: EROTIC ENTERTAINMENT FOR WOMEN, MEN & COUPLES (IV-Erotica/ Women), P.O. Box 96, Boston MA 02137, founded 1982, poetry editor Brenda Loew Tatelbaum. "Our press publishes erotic literature, photography and artwork. Our purpose is to provide an alternative to women's images and male images and sexuality depicted in mainstream publications like *Playboy, Penthouse, Playgirl,* etc. We provide a forum for the discussion and examination of two highly personalized dimensions of **female sexuality: desire and satisfaction. We do not want to see angry poetry or poetry that is demeaning to either men or women. We like experimental, avant-garde material."** Poets they have recently published include Emilie Glen, Cynthia Lelos, Pamela Oberon Davis and Doug

Martin. *Eidos* is professionally printed, tabloid-format, with fine photography and art, **number of poems per issue varies**, print run 10,000, over 7,000 subscriptions. **Sample: $10 postpaid.** They receive hundreds of poems per year, use about 25. Backlog 6 months to a year. **1 page limit on length, format flexible, photocopy, dot-matrix, simultaneous submissions OK, reports in 4-8 weeks, payment: 1 copy, guidelines available for SASE. Only accepts sexually explicit material.** Comment or criticism provided as often as possible. Brenda Loew Tatelbaum advises, "There is so much poetry submitted for consideration that a rejection can sometimes mean a poet's timing was poor. We let poets know if the submission was appropriate for our publication and suggest they resubmit at a later date. Keep writing, keep submitting, keep a positive attitude."

THE EIGHTH MOUNTAIN PRESS; EIGHTH MOUNTAIN POETRY PRIZE (IV-Women, feminist), 624 SE 29th Ave., Portland OR 97214, founded 1985, editor Ruth Gundle, is a "small press publisher of **feminist literary works by women.**" They have published poetry by Karen Mitchell and Irena Klepfisz. They publish 1 book of poetry per year, averaging 115 pp. **"We now publish poetry only through the Eight Mountain Poetry Prize."** Pays 8-10% royalties. The Eighth Mountain Poetry Prize is an annual award of a $1,000 advance and publication for a book of 50-120 pp. written by a woman, no restrictions as to subject matter. Send SASE for rules. Submit during January and February. "The selection will be made anonymously. Therefore, the MS must have a cover sheet giving all pertinent information (title, name, address, phone number). No identifying information except the title should appear on any other MS page. The contest will be judged by a feminist poet each year, whose name will be announced after the winning MS has been chosen." The 1991 contest was judged by Judy Grahn.

EL BARRIO (IV-Ethnic, regional); CASA DE UNIDAD (V), 1920 Scotten, Detroit MI 48209, phone (313)843-9598, founded 1982, poetry editor Marta Lagos. They publish **poetry from Latino residents of the SW Detroit area concerning life, family, politics, repression, etc., but do not normally accept unsolicited material. Query first.** "Nothing obscene. We are family oriented." They have recently published poetry by Ana Cardona, Jose Garza, Victoria Gonzalez, Marta Lagos, Jacqueline Sanchez, Trinidad Sanches S.F., Abel Pineiro and Anibal Bourdon. As a sample the editor selected these lines from "from trinidad, the man" by Lolita Hernandez:

> now time and place
> has this same concept
> in one man
> with possibility
> to cross all those colors
> to show time
> that things like that
> can be done in another place

El Barrio is "to keep the Latino people of the SW Detroit area informed, to give them an opportunity to speak to the community." It appears 3-4 times a year, magazine-sized, about 28 pp., professionally printed with commissioned art on the matte card cover, using up to 3 poems per issue. Their press run is 5,000, $3 per issue, $12 for a subscription. **Sample: $3 postpaid. Send SASE for guidelines. Pays 1 copy upon request. They sometimes use previously published poems but no simultaneous submissions.** The press has published an anthology: **Detroit: La Onda Latina en Poesía** ($6). If you query about **book publication, send 3-5 copies and bio. You must be from the SW Detroit area.**

THE ELEVENTH MUSE; POETRY WEST; POETRY WEST CONTEST (II, IV-Regional), P.O. Box 2413, Colorado Springs CO 80901, editor Diane Robinson. Poetry West is a nonprofit organization seeking to foster poetry appreciation and skills in the Pikes Peak region and provide a national forum for local poets. They sponsor readings monthly September-November and January-May in local art galleries, colleges and universities. Membership is $15/year which includes a literary newsletter 2-3/year, and a literary magazine twice a year: *the eleventh Muse*, which **"welcomes quality submissions of contemporary poetry. No greeting card verse, *please*."** Submit from 3-5 poems; typewritten, single-spaced. Photocopy OK. "Neatness counts. No length restrictions; however, one-page poems have a better chance of publication." No simultaneous submissions/no previously published work. Pays 1 copy. Editor responds with personal comments, sometimes critique, within 6-8 weeks. "Books for review and essays relating to poetry are now welcome." **Sample copy: $3.85 postpaid.** Subscription (2 issues): $7/year. It is 42 pp. saddle-stapled, magazine-sized, photocopied from typescript, with matte card cover. Poets featured in a recent issue include Gayle Elen Harvey and Robert Cooperman. As an example of the quality of poetry preferred, Diane Robinson selected the following lines from "Sleeping Alone" by Constance Studer:

> Nothing lasts. Faces, sprawled pages
> of a fallen/book, the lost touch
> of palms, the fear of spring.

Copies of *the eleventh Muse* are available by subscription, at bookstores in the Colorado Springs area, at poetry readings and through Poetry West memberships. A Poetry West Contest is held annually with a May 1 deadline for poems up to 40 lines. Prizes of $100, $50 and $25 are offered, plus publication in *the eleventh Muse*. As the contest grows, so will the prize money. Entry fee is $3/poem for non-members. Members may enter 3 poems free. Submit poems in duplicate with name and address on one copy only. Previous judge was Jack Myers. Poets may apply to read by sending 10 poems and a brief bio. In addition to the reading, a guest poet leads a workshop on Saturday morning. Apply to Reading Committee.

‡**11TH ST. RUSE; BIG FISH (I)**, #23, 322 E. 11th St., New York NY 10003, phone (212)475-5312, founded 1987, editor R.L.S. Lucid. *11th St. Ruse* appears every 2 months, 4 pp. mimeo, wants poems **"short, preferably funny, written by someone who's read Browning, none with the word 'light' in it."** They have recently published poetry by Tom Savage and Ellen Carter. As a sample the editor selected these lines (poet unidentified):

> *Joyce Mandel,*
> *you are my love.*
> *I think of you when I*
> *buy drugs,*
> *when I sing*

Press run is 190. Price per issue: 25¢. **Sample postpaid: $1. Pays 2 copies. Reports in 1 day-3 months.** "I have another magazine, *Big Fish*, and I am urgently seeking material by poets without words—any picture, or lock of hair, etc. It may be signed."

‡**ELF: ECLECTIC LITERARY FORUM (Elf Magazine) (II)**, P.O. Box 392, Tonawanda NY 14150, founded 1990, editor C.K. Erbes, is a quarterly. **"Subject matter and form are open, but we are looking for well-crafted poetry. We prefer poems of 30 lines or less, but will consider longer poems. No trite, hackneyed, ill-crafted effluvia."** As a sample the editor selected these lines from "The Poet" by S.J. DiChristina:

> *The poet turns a perfect drop of water and*
> *rolls it round the yellow bowls of tulips*
> *—he combs the sable silks of Iowa corn as*
> *it tips and elbows in the flatland heat*
> *—he illusions in a speck of sand, and*
> *—nacres himself an orient pearl, . . .*

Elf is magazine-sized, 52-56 pp. with semi-gloss cover, professionally printed, saddle-stapled. They use approximately 140 poems/year. Press run 500-700. Subscription: $16. **Sample postpaid: $4. Send SASE for guidelines. Pays 2 copies. Editor comments when possible.** "Accepted writers are asked to submit a byline of 25 words or less." Poems are circulated to an editorial board; responses in 2-4 weeks.

‡**ELLIPSIS MAGAZINE (II)**, Westminster College of Salt Lake City, 1840 S. 1300 East, Salt Lake City UT 84105, founded 1967, appears twice a year using **"all kinds of good poetry. Limited on space."** They have recently published work by William Stafford, William Kloefkorn, Lyn Lifshin and Ron Carlson. I have not seen an issue, but the editor describes it as 80-112 pp., digest-sized, flat-spined. Subscription: $12/year. **Sample: $8 postpaid. Pays $10/page plus 1 copy. Responds within 3 months.**

EMBERS (II), P.O. Box 404, Guilford CT 06437, phone (203)453-2328, founded 1979, poetry editors Katrina Van Tassel, Charlotte Garrett and Mark Johnson, a "poetry journal of talented new and occasional well-known poets." The editors say, **"no specifications as to length, form or content. Interested in new poets with talent; not interested in lighter way-out verse, porn or poetry that is non-comprehensible."** They have published poetry by Brendan Galvin, Walker MacDonald, Marilyn Waniek and Sue Ellen Thompson. *Embers* is digest-sized, nicely printed on white stock with an occasional b/w photograph or drawing, 52 pp. flat-spined with one-color matte card cover handsomely printed in black; it appears twice a year—spring/summer and fall/winter. Price per issue is $6, subscription $11/year. **Sample available for $3 postpaid. Pay for acceptance is 2 copies. Submissions must be typed, previously unpublished, with name, address and brief bio of poet. Deadlines: basically March 15 and October 15, but we read continuously.** They sponsor a chapbook contest, deadline Dec. 15. Winner is

The double dagger before a listing indicates that the listing is new in this edition. New markets are often the most receptive to submissions.

reported by Feb. 15. Write for details. Editors' advice is "Send for sample copies of any publication you are interested in. Be patient. Most editors read as quickly as they can and report likewise. If a poet sends in work at the beginning of a reading time, or long before a deadline, he/she will have to wait longer for answers. *Embers* editors are interested in the poet's voice and would like to read up to five submissions showing variety of subject, form, etc."

‡EMERALD COAST REVIEW; WEST FLORIDA LITERARY FEDERATION; FRANCIS P. CASSIDY LITER-ARY CENTER; THE LEGEND; BACK DOOR POETS; WISE (WRITERS IN SERVICE TO EDUCATION) (IV-Regional), P.O. Box 1644, Pensacola FL 32597, located at WFLF/Cassidy Literary Center, Pensacola Cultural Center, 402 S. Jefferson St., Pensacola FL 32501. The WFLF was founded in 1987 and began the Cassidy Literary Center, a regional writers' resource and special collection library. One of their programs is WISE which provides over 50 area writers who volunteer their time to share their writing and writing experiences with local students. They sponsor a Student Writers Network for students in grades 9-12 and scholarships for area college student writers. They publish *The Legend*, a newsletter bringing literary arts news to 800-1,000 area writers and their supporters. Back Door Poets, one of their subgroups, conducts open microphone poetry readings the third Saturday of each month and sponsors "Poetry & Patriotism," a nonstop, 24-hour vigil reading of American poetry in Seville Square to commemorate American Independence Day. Membership in WFLF ranges from $5/year for students to $350 and up for lifetime memberships. The **Emerald Coast Review** is an annual **limited to Gulf Coast regional writers. Send SASE for guidelines. Submit with required form (included in guidelines) May 1-July 31. Pays copies. Sample: $12 postpaid.**

‡EMRYS JOURNAL (II), P.O. Box 8813, Greenville SC 29604, founded 1982, managing editor Linda Julian, an annual, wants **"all kinds of poetry, though we don't publish poems of more than 2-3 pp."** They have recently published poetry by Linda Pasten, Maxine Kumin, R.T. Smith, Neal Bowers, Jim Peterson and Carl Dennis. As a sample, I selected these lines from "Gargoyles" by Gail Regier:

> *Gray nights they vomit rain*
> *Out into the wind's skirl.*
> *They curse us*
> *And their curses come to pass.*

It is handsomely printed, 6×9″ flat-spined, up to 120 pp. "For our last issue we received about 650 poems from 40 states. We printed 10." Press run 350 for 250 subscribers of which 10 are libraries. **Sample: $7 postpaid. Pays 5 copies. Send SASE for guidelines. Editor never comments on rejections.** They say, "We try to report within 6 weeks of the end of our reading period," but don't indicate when the reading period is.

THE EMSHOCK LETTER (IV-Subscribers), P.O. Box 411, Troy ID 83871-0411, phone (208)835-4902, founded 1977, editor Steve Erickson, appears 3-12 times a year, occasionally with **poetry and other writings by subscribers. It is "a philosophical, metaphysical, sometimes poetic expression of ideas and events. It covers a wide range of subjects and represents a free-style form of expressive relation. It is a newsletter quite unlike any other."** I have not seen a copy, but the editor describes it as magazine-sized, 5-7 pp., photocopied from typescript on colored paper, subscription: $25. **Pays 2 copies following publication.** "Poets [who are subscribers] should submit poetry which contains some meaning, preferably centering on a philosophic theme and preferably 50 lines or less. Any good poetry (submitted by a subscriber) will be considered for inclusion and will receive a personal reply by the editor, whether or not submitted material is published in *The Emshock Letter*." Reviews books of poetry only if written by subscribers.

EN PASSANT POETRY (II), 4612 Sylvanus Dr., Wilmington DE 19803, founded 1975, poetry editor James A. Costello, a poetry review, irregular, **uses about 34 pp. of poetry per issue, pays 2 copies.** They have recently published poetry by Léon-Paul Fargue, Judith Goodenough, Robert King, Mark Nepo and Celia Strome. These sample lines are by Jim Costello:

> *Crickets grind the corn to dust.*
>
> *The couple sits fiddling*
> *the bones of their hands*
> *dreaming moonlight and loving*
> *slow as the owl's pulse.*

It is a flat-spined, digest-sized format with matte cover, tasteful b/w art, professional printing, circulation 300. **Sample copies $2.50.**

‡ENCODINGS; LIAUD: A WOMEN'S PRESS (IV-Women/Feminism), P.O. Box 6793, Houston TX 77265, founded 1989. *Encodings* appears "randomly, twice a year," using **"high quality poetry with a feminist perspective; especially interested in women's ways of knowing, women's invention and use of**

language." As a sample the editor selected these lines from "Puffer and Whale" by Jacquelyn Shawh:

> *With you, I'm a little fish,*
> *puffer used to being belly-up*
> *BB eyes bulging.*

> *You're a beached whale, with me,*
> *bleaching in our winter glare,*
> *fat sides going all dry.*

They aim "to give women who have little chance of being published elsewhere (because of radical content) a chance to be heard." It is 8½×7″ saddle-stapled, 40-60 pp., photocopied from typescript with glossy card cover. Press run 300 for 60 subscribers of which 1 is a library. Subscription: $9. Sample: $4.50 postpaid. Pays 2 copies. Send SASE for guidelines. Do not submit between October and December. Submit "3 copies of each poem with cover sheet listing name and address as well as a 50-word biographical sketch. Photocopies, dot-matrix OK. All submissions are peer reviewed by at least 2 reviewers, and it takes up to 6 months to report back to poets." Editor "occasionally" comments on rejections.

ENVOI; ENVOI POETS (II, IV-Anthology), Pen Ffordd, Newport Dyfed SA42 0QT U.K., *Envoi* founded 1957, *Envoi Poets* founded 1985, editor-in-chief Anne Lewis-Smith (plus panel of 28 editors), wants **"Just good poems, technically good, not too long unless superb! No religious, political, none full of swear words."** They have recently published poetry by Edward Storey, William Oxley, Marguerite Wood, Richard Vance and Anita Mathias. As a sample this poem titled "Bristol Docks" by Richard Bonfield:

> *Down at the docks you can still smell the slaves*
> *and the indigo*
> *and sense that spirit of place*
> > *umbered and silent*
> > > *ghosting down the riverway.*

Envoi is digest-sized, 44 pp. perfect-bound, professionally litho printed with plastic covered glossy card cover, few ads, using poetry and reviews. It appears 3 times a year, print run of 900, 800 subscriptions of which 20 + are libraries. Subscription: £6 or $11.50. Single copy: £2. **Sample: £1 or $2 in bills (no checks) postpaid. Pays 2 copies. "6 poems is an ideal number, with name and address on each page please. If they are really good we publish. We are looking for craftsmanship as well as that extra spark which makes a good poem. Subscribing to** *Envoi* **not necessary but welcomed." No simultaneous submissions. Photocopy and dot-matrix OK. Reports to queries in 1 week, to MSS in 2-8 weeks.** Reviews books of poetry; preference given to hardback. Each issue of the magazine has a poetry competition with prizes of £100, £50 and £25. She says, "An important factor of *Envoi* is that we welcome submissions at all times and do not solicit for poems. Out of the 2,000 plus poems we look at for each issue there are usually about 180-200 poems we want to print, but we only have space for 44. It is hard on editor and poet to return those. In the 34 years since *Envoi* was founded we have always had an editorial board of 29 poets/lecturers/teachers who write a short criticism on every poem returned. Sadly, due to the number sent in, this is only for subscribers, but we feel and know this free service is of great value. We are always looking for ways to further better understanding and relationships between poets and editors. We advise all those who write poetry not to send in work when the ink is hardly dry but to keep it a couple of months then look at it again. Often after this period of not seeing a poem the faults are very clear." *Envoi Poets* is an imprint under which about 12 subsidized individual collections, 20-50 pp., are published each year in a format much like the magazine except that the covers are matte card. The 80th individual collection of poetry has just been published. **For individual collections query with 6 samples, bio and credits.** *Envoi* published the first **Spring Anthology** in 1988, a hardback book containing work by over 90 modern poets. "This is a yearly feature and we welcome all enquiries accompanied by IRCs."

‡EOTU, MAGAZINE OF EXPERIMENTAL FICTION (II), 1810 W. State #115, Boise ID 83702, founded 1987, editor Larry D. Dennis, appears every other month using **"experimental, new voices, new styles, something unique. 3-4 pp. maximum length; no limitations on subject matter. Prose poems have the best chance with us. No traditional."** They have recently published poetry by Judson Crews, Bruce Boston, Joy Oestreicher and Edward Mycue. I have not seen an issue, but the editor describes it as 72 pp. digest-sized with color cover, saddle-stapled. Press run 500. Subscription: $18 (6 issues). **Sample: $4 postpaid. "We tend to be 'thematic'; send SASE for guidelines." Pays $5 plus 1 copy. Previously published poems OK, "just let us know when and where. Prefer a little bio info, in case we buy the poem, not necessarily a cover letter.** Usually poetry is used to fill odd pages between stories, so usually publication and acceptance are simultaneous (that's why 1 page poems have a better chance than long poems)." Editor "seldom" comments on rejections: "just depends." He advises, "Write what *you* want to write, not what you think I want to read."

EPOCH; BAXTER HATHAWAY PRIZE (III), 251 Goldwin Smith, Cornell, Ithaca NY 14853, founded 1947, has a distinguished and long record of publishing **exceptionally fine poetry** and fiction. They have published work by such poets as Ashbery, Ammons, Eshleman, Wanda Coleman, Molly Peacock, Robert Vander Molen and Alvin Aubert. The magazine appears 3 times a year in a professionally printed, 6×9″ flat-spined format with glossy b/w cover, 100+ pp., which goes to 900 subscribers. They use less than 1% of the many submissions they receive each year, have a 2-12 month backlog. **Sample: $4 postpaid. Reports in 2 months. "We *don't read* unsolicited MSS between May 15 and September 15." Pays $1/line. Occasionally provides criticism on MSS.** The annual Baxter Hathaway prize of $1,000 is awarded for a long poem or, in alternate years, a novella. Write for details. The editor advises, "I think it's extremely important for poets to read other poets. I think it's also very important for poets to read the magazines that they want to publish in. Directories are not enough."

‡EQUINOX PRESS; BRITISH HAIKU SOCIETY (IV-Form), Sinodun, Shalford, Braintree Essex CM7 5HN England, phone 0371-851097, founded 1990, c/o Mr. David Cobb. They publish a chapbook and a paperback per year. "No standard arrangements at the present time." **Haiku, senryu and tanka only.** As a sample the editor selected this haiku (poet unidentified):

> *a cloudless sky*
> *painters stretch ladders*
> *to their farthest rungs*

‡THE ESCAPIST (I, IV-Religious, fantasy, science fiction), 6861 Catlett Rd., St. Augustine FL 32095, founded 1987 as *Couch Potato Journal* and Thin Boundaries fanzines, editor T.M. Spell. *The Escapist* appears twice a year using "Christian fiction, nonfiction and **poetry in the tradition of C.S. Lewis. Looking for work rich with images that evoke what Lewis called 'joy' or the longing for it. 1-100 lines, traditional rhyming metered verse, prose poems, avant-garde, experimental.**" They have recently published poetry by Denise Dumars, Janet P. Reedman, John Grey and B.Z. Niditch. I have not seen an issue, but the editor describes it as digest-sized, saddle-stapled, 4-8 pp., desktop publishing. They accept 1-2 of 5-10 submissions/month. Press run 100. **Sample postpaid: $1.50. Reports in 2-8 weeks. Pays 2 copies. "Please enclose a cover letter saying where you heard about *TE*. If you would like a brief critique of your work, just ask."**

‡EUROPEAN JUDAISM (IV-Religious, ethnic), Kent House, Rutland Gardens, London, England SW7 1BX, phone (01)584-2754, founded 1966, poetry editor Edouard Roditi, is a "twice-yearly magazine with emphasis on European Jewish theology/philosophy/literature/history, with **some poetry in every issue. It should preferably be short, as it is often used as filler, and should have Jewish content or reference. We do not want hackneyed, overblown rubbish.**" They have recently published poetry by Alan Sillito, Erich Fried, Ruth Fainlight and Noris Farhi. I selected these sample lines from "Victims" by Bernard Kops:

> *their songs of praise will rise*
> *with the smoke of our bones*
> *and journalists will weep*
> *and history will shrug*

It is a glossy, elegant 7×10″ flat-spined magazine with no ads, rarely art or graphics, 48 pp. They have a print run of 950, about 50% of which goes to subscribers (few libraries). $9 per issue; subscription $18. **Sample can be obtained gratis from Pergamon Press, Headington Hill Hall, Oxford, England 0X3 0BW. Pays 1 copy.**

EVANGEL (IV-Religious), P.O. Box 535002, Indianapolis IN 46253-5002, weekly since 1897, poetry editor Vera Bethel, **publishes an 8-page paper for adults. Nature and devotional poetry, 8-16 lines, "free verse or with rhyme scheme."** The circulation is 35,000; it is sold in bulk to Sunday schools. **Sample for 6×9″ SASE. Pays: $5. Photocopy, simultaneous submissions OK. Reports in 1 month.** These sample lines are from "Spring Rain" by Dalene Workman Stull:

> *A punctured sky is leaking gentle rain*
> *Upon the rosery, the lawn, the hay.*
> *An iris wears a beading on its mane.*
> *And moisture films the mushroom's fawn beret.*

The editor advises, "Do not write abstractions. Use concrete words to picture concept for reader." SASE for reply or return.

EVENT (II, IV-Themes), Douglas College, Box 2503, New Westminster, British Columbia V3L 5B2 Canada, founded 1971, editor Dale Zieroth, is "a literary magazine publishing **high-quality contemporary poetry,** short stories and reviews. **Any good-quality work is considered.**" They have recently published Lorna Crozier, Tom Wayman, Heather Spears, Dieter Weslowski and Elizabeth Brewster. These sample lines are from "Poetry" by Don Domanski:

is it a side street or a cat's jaw?
cerecloth or the body's flesh?
I've named it the heart's pillow
wind in a mirror   cloud-rope
lighthouse on the edge of a wound
beadwork   the mote's halo   wolf-ladder

It appears three times a year as a 6×9″ flat-spined, 128+ pp., glossy-covered, finely printed paperback with a circulation of 1,000 for 700 subscriptions, of which 50 are libraries. **Sample: $5 postpaid. They have a 6 month backlog, report in 2-3 months, pay honorarium. Sometimes they have special thematic issues, such as: work, feminism, peace and war, coming of age. They comment on some rejections.** Review books of poetry.

‡THE EVERGREEN CHRONICLES (IV-Gay, lesbian), P.O. Box 8939, Minneapolis MN 55408, is "a biannual literary journal dedicated to presenting the best of lesbian and gay literary and visual artists. The artistry presented is not limited to 'gay' or 'lesbian' themes, but extends to life itself, in all its dimensions." I have not seen a copy. Subscription: $15. **Sample postpaid: $4. "Send 4 copies of your work, up to 10 pp. of poetry. Pays 1 copy. Deadlines: July 1 and January 1. Please include a short biographical paragraph describing yourself and your work."**

EXIT 13 (I), % Tom Plante, 22 Oakwood Ct., Fanwood NJ 07023, phone (908)889-5298, founded 1987, poetry editor Tom Plante, is a "contemporary poetry annual" using **poetry that is "short, to the point, with a sense of geography."** They have recently published poetry by Errol Miller, Alexis Rotella, Randy Fingland, Marijane Osborn and Simon Perchik. As a sample the editor selected the following lines by Claudette Bass:

Step after step after step I climbed
the exhausting wooden stairs
back to vacationers sitting
planted in rows like cabbages.

Their press run is 300. *Exit 13*, #3, was 48 pp. **Sample: $5 postpaid, payable to T. Plante. Guidelines available for SASE. Pays 1 copy. They accept simultaneous submissions and previously published poems. Reports in 2 months.** Reviews books of poetry and magazines. The editor advises, "Write about what you know. Study geography. *Exit 13* looks for adventure. Every state and region is welcome."

‡EXIT ZERO; STUDENT UNION FOR ETHNIC INCLUSION (SUEI); NAROPA INSTITUTE (IV-Ethnic, political), c/o Naropa Institute, 2130 Arapahoe Ave., Boulder CO 80302, phone (303)444-0202, founded 1990, co-editor Charles E. Pirtle, is an annual with **multicultural orientation**, magazine of the Student Union for Ethnic Inclusion (SUEI) at the Naropa Institute. **"We much prefer to publish solicited work; last year accepted 2 unsolicited poems. Prefer contributors to be familiar with the magazine and its orientation."** It is available at bookstores in Boulder, Denver, San Francisco Bay area, Seattle, Iowa City, Chicago and Ann Arbor. They have recently published poetry by Anne Waldman, Denise Levertov, Jack Hirschman and Jerome Washington. As a sample the editor selected these lines from "Yutang Kalaay" by Bataan Faigao:

I will not go home to smoky mountain
there how many people lie in state
dead & forgotten

their ghost cries
mingle with the smoke

rise incense to a terrible god

It is about 100 pp., flat-spined, magazine-sized, desktop publishing, with matte card cover. Appears approximately July 1. Press run 500. **Sample postpaid: $5. Pays "fame and glory" and 1 copy. Reports in one month. Submit anytime *but* March 15-July 31. Previously published poems OK with publication credits provided.** SUEI offers scholarships for poets of color for the summer writing programs at Naropa and sells *EZ* and sponsors poetry readings and other activities to support this program.

EXPEDITION PRESS (II, IV-Love, religious), Box A, 1312 Oakland Dr., Kalamazoo MI 49008, publisher Bruce W. White, who publishes chapbooks of **love poems and religious poems. "I dislike violence."** He likes to see **"fresh new approaches, interesting spatial relationships, as well as quality artwork. We dislike political diatribes."** Some poets he has published are J. Kline Hobbs, Jim DeWitt,

Martin Cohen and C. VanAllsburg. As a sample he chose this "Haiku" by himself:

> The sun low in the West.
> The warm clay courts. A
> moment of peace.

Submit MS of 20-30 pp. and brief bio. Photocopy, dot-matrix, simultaneous submissions OK. MS on cassette OK. Reports in 1 month. Pays 100 copies. Bruce White provides "much" criticism on rejected MSS.

‡EXPERIMENT IN WORDS; WRITER, POET AND ARTIST OF THE YEAR AWARDS (I), P.O. Box 470186, Ft. Worth TX 76147, founded 1990, editor/publisher Robert W. Howington. *EIW* appears annually. **The editor says, "I want stuff that is so far out there they don't even have a map to tell you where it is . . . create unique thoughts, images, dialogue and narrative . . . go outside the ordinary. Use a different structure, content, style or voice."** They have recently published poetry by Lyn Lifshin, Cheryl Townsend, Bob Z, B.Z. Niditch and Rogers Blanko. As a sample the editor selected these lines from "spark" by Charles Bukowski:

> *I always resented all the years, the hours, the*
> *minutes I gave them as a working stiff, it*
> *actually hurt my head, my insides, it made me*
> *dizzy and a bit crazy—I couldn't understand the*
> *murdering of my years*

EIW **is magazine-sized, stapled at the corners, photocopied from typescript on mimeo paper, 50-60 pp. Press run 500 for 250 subscribers. Subscription: $5. Sample: $5 check, cash or stamps. Make check payable to Robert W. Howington. Please send SASE for guidelines before submitting. Pays 1 copy. Reports in 1-3 months.** The editor comments, " 'It's Alive! It's Alive!' describes my magazine. I want the words to walk off of the page and jump onto my readers and show them something they've never seen before in the written word. Create new categories. Be bold. Be real. Be honest. No phonies allowed here!"

EXPLORATIONS (II), 11120 Glacier Highway, Juneau AK 99801, editors Professor Ron Silva and Professor Art Petersen, phone (907)789-4423, founded 1980. The annual literary magazine of the University of Alaska, Southeast. **"The editors look for meter in which form fits meaning but not meter that is insistent or thoroughly predictable. Standard form as well as innovation are encouraged, and such appropriate and fresh aspects of imagery as allusions, metaphors, similes and symbols draw editorial attention."** The editors selected this sample from "Fishing for Winter Kings" by T. M. Johnson:

> *Fishermen invited the night on deck,*
> *the uneasy fall of flakes*
> *like fireflies.*
> *Snow sting on warm skin*
> *is like the wrap of Jellyfish.*

It is digest-sized, nicely printed, with front and inside back cover illustration in one color, saddle-stapled. They offer a $100 prize for poetry and publish the best of the submissions received. **An entry/reading fee is required: $2 per poem (up to 10, 60 lines maximum); those paying reader/contest entry fees of $4 or more will receive a copy of the publication. Submit entries with 3- or 4-line biography December-March. Pay is 2 contributor copies. Submissions are reported on in May, publication is annual, out in May. MSS should be typed with name and address on the back, photocopies OK, simultaneous submissions OK.** "Replies for unselected manuscripts made only to SASE."

EXPLORER MAGAZINE; EXPLORER PUBLISHING CO. (I, IV-Inspirational, nature, love), P.O. Box 210, Notre Dame IN 46556, phone (219)277-3465, founded 1960, editor and publisher Raymond Flory, a semiannual magazine that contains **short inspirational, nature and love poetry** as well as prose. The editor wants **"Poetry of all styles and types; should have an inspirational slant but not necessary. Short poems preferred—up to 16 lines. Good 'family' type poetry always needed. No real long poetry or long lines; no sexually explicit poetry or porno."** He has recently published poems by Marion Schoeberlein, Edna James Kayser and Carrie Quick. As a sample, he chose the entire poem, "The Poet," by Jim Wyzard:

> *He puts his pen to paper,*
> *In hope that he might find,*
> *A spark of new conjecture,*
> *And a stairway to the mind.*

Explorer **is digest-sized, photocopied from typed copy (some of it not too clear) on thin paper, 31 pp., cover of the same paper with title superimposed on a water-color painting, folded and saddle-stapled. Circulation is 200, subscription price $6/year. Sample available for $3, guidelines** for SASE. Pay is 1 copy. Subscribers vote for the poems or stories they like best and prizes are awarded; four prizes each issue: $25, $20, $15 and $10. Writers should submit 3-4 poems, typed or photocopied; dot-matrix OK. Material must be previously unpublished; no simultaneous submissions. Reporting time is 1 week and time to publication 1-2 years. Explorer Publishing Company does not presently publish books except for an anthology about every 4 years; it is a paperback, digest-sized book with an average page count of 20. The editor says, "Over 90% of the poets submitting poetry to *Explorer* have not seen a copy of the magazine. Order a copy first — then submit. This will save poets stamps, frustration, etc. This should hold true for whatever market a writer is aiming for!"

EXQUISITE CORPSE (II), P.O. Box 25051, Baton Rouge LA 70894, founded 1983, editor Andrei Codrescu (whom you can often hear in commentary segments of "All Things Considered," The National Public Radio news program). This curious and delightful monthly ($15/year), when you unfold it, is 6" wide and 16" long, 20 pp., saddle-stapled, professionally printed in 2 columns on quality stock. The flavor of Codrescu's comments (and some clues about your prospects in submitting here) may be judged by this note in the January/February 1986 issue: "A while ago, alarmed by the number of poems aimed at the office — a number only the currency inflation and Big Macs can hold candles to — we issued an edict against them. Still they came, and some even came live. They came in the mail and under the door. We have no poetry insurance. If we are found one day smothered under Xerox paper, who will pay for the burial? The *Corpse* wants a jazz funeral. Rejections make poets happy. Having, in many cases, made their poems out of original, primal, momentary rejections, the rejection of these rejections affirms the beings forced to such deviousness." This issue has poems by Carol Bergé, Charles Plymell, Lawrence Ferlinghetti, a very long one by Alice Notley, and many others. As a sample I selected a complete poem, "Patterns" by Wanda Phipps:

> *there are patterns aren't there?*
> *designs for waves of confusion*
> *there are plans for internal battles:*
> *we will meet for massacre*
> *at exactly 6:00 a.m. on the dot*
> *careful of land mines as we march*
> *to the breakfast table*

Payment: "Zilch/Nada." You take your chances inserting work into this wit machine. As of 1990 this is their policy: ". . . we are abolishing the SASE-based privacy system . . . Your submissions will be answered directly in the pages of our publication. Look for your name and for our response to your work in the next *Corpse*. We will continue returning your submissions by SASE if you wish, but as to what we think of your *écriture*, please check 'Body Bag,' our new editorial column. Please rest assured that your work will receive the same malevolently passionate attention as before. Only now we are going to do it in public."

FABER AND FABER, INC. (V), 50 Cross St., Winchester MA 01890, phone (617)721-1427, editor Betsy Uhrig, has a distinguished list of poetry publications but is accepting **no unsolicited MS.**

‡FAITH . . . WORKS (IV-Religious), 122 N. Pearl, Buffalo NY 14202, founded 1990, editors Jack Shifflett and Ann Markle, a quarterly wanting **"free verse up to 24 lines, but will consider other forms and lengths; our only requirement is that poems must deal with some aspect of Christian faith and/ or Christian living, or must pertain in some way to those matters."** They have recently published poetry by Ann Goldsmith and Kenneth Feltges. As a sample the editor selected these lines from "The Mississippi Likened to Christ our Lord" by Diane Glancy:

> *Is it not that way with faith?*
> *We hear stories of Christ,*
> *then a factory with six smokestacks unloads its fog.*
> *But there is something left —*
> *somewhere in the skull faith twines like a worm,*
> *if a flock of birds fit the sky*
> *& a small trickle once passed over the hand.*

The magazine is digest-sized, 32-40 pp., desktop-formatted and laser-printed, high-quality paper, textured cover, saddle-stapled. Press run 500. Subscription: $10. **Sample: $3.50. Pays 4 copies. Send SASE for guidelines. Reports in 2 weeks if possible.** Editor seldom comments on rejections. The editor says, *"Faith . . . Works* aims to combine the quality of a literary journal with the specific content and concerns of a Christian magazine. We would like to suggest to contributors that sincerity is no substitute for poetry — we will not publish work of poor quality no matter how well-meant its "message.""

‡FAMILY EARTH (I, IV-Ecology), 135 Buford Ave., Gettysburg PA 17325, managing editor Denise Weldon-Siviy, founded 1990, is a family-oriented quarterly focussing on the environment, using poetry that **"must deal in some way with the environment. Shorter poems, 10-30 lines are preferred. Cannot consider material over 50 lines due to page layout. All forms and styles are acceptable. No overtly religious material or laments abusive to working mothers. I am currently receiving a high percentage of negative—world is awful will end any minute—poetry. Anything with a positive attitude has a good chance."** As a sample, I selected these lines from "Swan Song—USA" by Charlotte Partin:

> *Redwood, cypress, maples,*
> *cotton fields—celebrate me*
> *from freeway to Main Street.*

It is 24 pp., photocopied, digest-sized with colored paper cover. Press run is 200 for 100 subscriptions, 100 shelf sales. They accept about 25% of 100 submissions received/year. Subscription: $8/4 issues. **Sample: $2 postpaid. Pays $1-3/poem plus 1 copy. Send SASE for guidelines. Reports in 2 weeks. Editor always comments on rejections.** Reviews books of poetry if they deal with the environment, conservation, etc.

FARMER'S MARKET; MIDWEST FARMER'S MARKET, INC. (IV-Regional), P.O. Box 1272, Galesburg IL 61402, founded 1981, editors Jean C. Lee, John Hughes, Jim McCurry and Lisa Ress, is a biannual seeking **"to provide a forum for the best of regional poetry and fiction."** They want poems that are **"tightly structured, with concrete imagery, specific to Midwestern themes and values, reflective of the clarity, depth and strength of Midwestern life. Not interested in highly abstract or experimental work, or light verse."** They have recently published poetry by Kathleen Peirce, Mark Sanders, Gigi Marks, Judy Ray, Cory Brown and Simon Perchik. As a sample, they offer these lines by Alice George from "Remembering August in February":

> *It was the heat that made everyone give up*
>
> *the hoarded waters of winter and fear,*
> *sweat uniting them in a gleam and a musk;*
> *the head-back, throat-open repetition of lemonade,*
> *the lilting across of occasional speech*

FM is digest-sized, 100-140 pp., perfect bound with card cover, handsomely printed with graphics and photos. Circulation 500 for 150 subscriptions, of which 15 are libraries. **Sample: $4.50 plus $1 postage and handling.** They receive about 1,500 submissions per year, of which they use 50-60, have a 6-month backlog. **Submit up to 10 pages, typed or letter-quality printout, photocopies OK, would rather not have simultaneous submissions. Reports in 6-8 weeks (summer replies take longer). Pay: 1 copy.** They comment on rejections, **"only if we think the work is good."**

‡FAT TUESDAY (II), 8125 Jonestown Rd., Harrisburg PA 17112, founded 1981, poetry editors F. M. Cotolo, Kristen von Oehrke, B. Lyle Tabor and Lionel Stevroid, is an annual which calls itself **"a Mardi Gras of literary and visual treats featuring many voices, singing, shouting, sighing and shining, expressing the relevant to irreverent.** On Fat Tuesday (the Tuesday before Ash Wednesday, when Lent begins) the editors hold The Fat Tuesday Symposium. In ten years no one has shown up." They want **"prose poems, poems of irreverence, gems from the gut. Usually shorter, hit-the-mark, personal stuff inseparable from the voice of the artist. Form doesn't matter."** Poets they have published include Mark Cramer, Mary Lee Gowland, Chuck Taylor, Patrick Kelly and Randy Klutts. As a sample they offer these lines by John Quinnett:

> *It is enough to be alive,*
> *To be here drinking this cheap red wine*
> *While the chili simmers on the stove*
> *& the refrigerator hums deep into the night.*

The digest-sized magazine is typeset (large type, heavy paper), 36 pp., saddle-stapled, card covers, (sometimes magazine-sized, unbound) with cartoons, art and ads. Circulation 200 with 20-25 pp. of poetry in each issue. **Sample: $5 postpaid.** They receive hundreds of submissions each year, use 3-5%, have a 3-5 month backlog. **No previously published material. "Photocopy, dot-matrix, handwritten OK; we'll read anything." Reports in 1-2 weeks. Pay: 1 copy.** The editors say, "Our tip for authors is simply to be themselves. Poets should use their own voice to be heard. Publishing poetry is as lonely as writing it. We have no idea about current trends, and care less. We encourage all to buy a sample issue to see what they have which best fits our style and format, and also to help support the continuation of our publication. We rely on no other means but sales to subsidize our magazine, and writers should be sensitive to this hard fact which burdens many small presses."

FEELINGS; ANDERIE POETRY PRESS; QUARTERLY EDITOR'S CHOICE AWARDS (I, IV-Subscription), Box 2625, Lehigh Valley PA 18001, founded 1989, editor Carole Frew, a quarterly magazine, uses **"simple, understandable poems on any aspect of life, no more than 20 lines, no controversial,** abortion, pornography. Likes to see 'hearts and flowers' as well as hard-biting prose and poetry." As a sample, I selected these lines from "My Little Girl" by the editor:

> You've grown so very tall.
> The tiny hand that I once held in crossing streets
> Now holds mine in unfamiliar places.
> The voice that used to question, "Mommy, why?" a hundred times a day
> Gives me explanations of new and different things.

Feelings is magazine-sized, saddle-stapled with glossy paper cover, professionally printed on lightweight paper, using "photography appropriate to the season or subject." Subscription: $18. **Sample postpaid: $5.50. Send SASE for guidelines. Pays $10 for 3 Editor's Choice Awards in each issue. "Space and award priority to subscribers." Reports in 6 weeks. "We publish chapbooks, info/price list upon request with SASE."** MSS on "how-to" write, publish poetry welcome. Payment for articles varies.

FEH! A JOURNAL OF ODIOUS POETRY (IV-Themes, humor), P.O. Box 5806, Station B, Montreal, Quebec H3B 4T1 Canada, founded 1986, poetry editor Simeon Stylites, appears 3 times a year, using **"nasty stuff, but** *good* **nasty stuff; silliness and nonsense, but good silliness and nonsense; insanity; truth."** They have published poetry by John Grey and Renato Trujillo. As a sample the editor selected these lines by Francesca Bongiorno:

> so I shall wander happily
> ignoring everything I see
> and seeing things which aren't there
> and weaving hedgehogs in my hair

It is 20 pp., 7 × 8½" with photocopied paper cover. Their press run is 250 with about 40 subscriptions, and sales through bookstores. **Sample: $1 postpaid. Guidelines available for SASE. Pays 3 copies. Considers simultaneous submissions and previously published poems. Reports within 6 weeks. Editor sometimes comments on rejections, if asked.** The editor says, "We run the edge between the disgusting and the sublime. Some of the poems are funny and no more, but others of them are nasty little bits of truth, yapping at you and nipping at your ankles." Reviews books of poetry.

FELLOWSHIP IN PRAYER (IV-Religious), 291 Witherspoon St., Princeton NJ 08542, phone (609)924-6863, founded 1950, editor M. Ford-Grabowsky, is an interfaith bimonthly **"concerned with prayer, meditation, and spiritual life"** using poetry "pertaining to spirituality; brief." As a sample, I selected these lines from "Balm from the Twenty-third Psalm" by Tom Jurek:

> The Lord is My Time Giver
> I Shall Not Want
> In Short To-Do Lists and Prioritizing God Gives Me No Repose
> Beside Less Caffeine and Lower Blood Pressure God leads Me
> God Refreshes My Soul

It is digest-sized, professionally printed, 48 pp., saddle-stapled with glossy card cover. Press run: 20,000. They accept about 2% of submissions received. Subscription: $15. **Sample, postpaid: free. Pays 5 copies. Double-spaced submissions. Simultaneous submissions and "sometimes" previously published poems OK. Reports in 1 month.** Reviews books of poetry.

FEMINIST STUDIES (IV-Women), %Women's Studies Program, University of Maryland, College Park MD 20742, founded 1969, poetry editor Alicia Ostriker, **"welcomes a variety of work that focuses on women's experience, on gender as a category of analysis, and that furthers feminist theory and consciousness."** They have published poetry by Janice Mirikitani, Paula Gunn Allen, Cherrie Moraga, Audre Lorde, Judith Small, Milana Marsenich, Lynda Schraufnagel, Valerie Fox and Diane Glancy. The editor chose these lines by Nicole Brossard:

> She breaks the contract
> binding her to figuration.
> In the theatre of the past
> full of countless nostalgias,
> she alone, along with all women,
> creates the entire body
> of impressions

The elegantly-printed, flat-spined, 360 + pp., paperback appears 3 times a year in an edition of 7,000, goes to 6,000 subscribers, of which 1,500 are libraries. There are **4-10 pp. of poetry in each issue. Sample: $10 postpaid. Reports in 5 months. No pay.**

FENNEL STALK (II), 2448 W. Freeway Lane, Phoenix AZ 85021, phone (602)995-5338, FAX (602)864-9351, founded 1986, poetry editors Karen Bowden, Peter Bailey, Ron Dickson and August Shaefer. **"All forms, lengths, subject matter and styles except inspirational or sing-song rhyme or poems straining to be traditional. We select based on our response measured in spine tingles, shivers, skin temperature and neuro activity, as much as on how our lives are going when we read your work. Writers should not take rejection too seriously, although taking acceptance too seriously is probably deadlier."** They have recently published poetry by Rose Romano, Stacey Sollfrey and Jack Evans. As a sample they selected these lines by Lisa Helgesen from "The Wedding at Chief Joseph Battlefield":

> *Our stances our promises*
> *square as buttes as*
> *gulls are our witnesses*
> *their cries the rings*

Their magazine appears twice a year, digest-sized, typeset (desktop publisher) and printed on quality stock, saddle-stapled, with a b/w card cover using b/w art, photos, graphics. Their press run is 200-300 with 30 subscriptions (3 libraries). Subscription: $8. **Sample: $4 postpaid. Make checks payable to Ron Dickson. Please put name and address on each page. Reports in 2-4 months. Pays contributor's copy. Editors sometimes comment on rejections "if asked." Send SASE for information.** Reviews books of poetry "sometimes."

THE FIDDLEHEAD (II, IV-Regional, students), Campus House, University of New Brunswick, Box 4400, Fredericton, New Brunswick E3B 5A3 Canada, founded 1945, poetry editors Robert Gibbs, Robert Hawkes and Don MacKay. From its beginning in 1945 as a local little magazine **devoted mainly to student writers, the magazine retains an interest in poets of the Atlantic region and in young poets,** but in printing poetry from everywhere on the sole criterion of excellence, it is **open to good work of every kind, looking always for vitality, freshness and surprise.** Among the poets whose work they have published are M. Travis Lane, Robert Cooperman, Wm. Meyer, Mark Sanders and Tom Wayman. As a sample, the editor chose a stanza by Walt McDonald:

> *My father baked fresh loaves before he*
> *hit the road, hardscrabble dirt*
> *buckled over oil he believed he'd own.*
> *Yeast and sweet-rising honey oven-hot*
> *kept us begging him not to go,*
> *hot bread and butter dripping from our chins.*

The Fiddlehead is a handsomely printed, 6 × 9" flat-spined paperback (140+ pp.) with b/w graphics, colored cover, usually paintings by New Brunswick artists. Circulation is 1,000. Subscription price is $18/year (US). **Sample available for $6 (US). Pay is $10-12/printed page. They use less than 10% of submissions. Reporting time 6-10 weeks, backlog 6-12 months.** Reviews books of poetry by Canadian authors only.

FIELD; FIELD TRANSLATION SERIES (II, IV-Translations), Rice Hall, Oberlin College, Oberlin OH 44074, phone (216)775-8408, founded 1969, editors Stuart Friebert and David Young, is a literary journal appearing twice a year with "emphasis on poetry, translations and essays by poets." They want the **"best possible" poetry.** They have recently published poetry by Susan Cabot Black, Gerald Stern, Marin Sorescu, Sandra McPherson, W.S. Merwin, Linda Bierds and Seamus Heaney. A portion of "A Story" by Adrienne Rich was chosen as a sample:

> *Absence is homesick. Absence wants a home*
> *but Absence left without a glance at Home.*
> *Home tried to hold in Absence's despite*
> *Home caved, shuddered, yet held*
> *without Absence's consent. Home took a walk*
> *in several parks, Home shivered*
> *in outlying boroughs, slept on strange floors,*
> *cried many riffs of music, many words.*

The handsomely printed digest-sized journal is flat-spined, has 100 pp., rag stock with glossy card color cover, circulation 2,500, with 800 library subcriptions. Subscription: $12 a year, $20 for 2 years. **Sample: $6 postpaid. Pays $20-40 per page plus 2 copies. Reports in 2 weeks, has a 3-6 month backlog.** They also publish books of translations in the Field Translation Series, averaging 150 pp., flat-spined and hardcover editions. **Query regarding translations. Pays 10-15% royalties with $400 advance and 10 author's copies.** Write for catalog to buy samples.

‡FIGMENT: TALES FROM THE IMAGINATION; IMAGO: COMIX/ART DIGEST OF SF/F (IV-Science fiction/fantasy, form), P.O. Box 3566, Moscow ID 83843-0477, founded 1989, editors Barb and J.C. Hendee, *Figment* is a quarterly using **sci-fi and fantasy poems. Send SASE for guidelines.** They have recently published poetry by Thomas A. Easton and John Grey. As a sample, I selected these lines from "Advice from an Old Hand, to a Young Man Shipping Out" by Lori Ann White:

> Poor boy. I hear you weep for Mother Earth.
> Tell me, does your mother love you well?
> Does she cradle you on acid clouds? Swaddle you in muck?
> You should mourn a woman, not a heartless shell.
> Why praise a hunk of rock for giving birth?

Figment is digest-sized, 60 pp., saddle-stapled, printed in Times Roman 9.5, with glossy bond cover. Press run 500 for 150+ subscribers, 10-20 shelf sales. Subscription: $14.50. **Sample postpaid: $4.50. Pays $2-10 plus 1 copy. Reports in 8 weeks.** *Imago* considers poem/art combinations in the science fiction/fantasy genre.

THE FIGURES (V), 5 Castle Hill Ave., Great Barrington MA 01230-1552, phone (413)528-2552, founded 1975, is a small press publishing poetry and fiction. As a sample I selected these lines from Ron Padgett's **The Big Something:**

> in the slow
> rotation of the sphere
> you call a star,
> a flower, a mind.

They pay 10% of press run. They currently accept no unsolicited poetry.

FINE MADNESS (II), P.O. Box 31138, Seattle WA 98103-1138, founded 1980, president Louis Bergsagel. *Fine Madness* is a twice-yearly magazine. **They want "contemporary poetry of any form and subject. We look for highest quality of thought, language and imagery. We look for the mark of the individual: unique ideas and presentation; careful, humorous, sympathetic. No careless poetry, sexist poetry, greeting-card poetry, poetry that 10,000 other people could have written."** They have published poetry by Tony Esolen, Pattiann Rogers, Stuart Friebert, Andrei Codrescu, David Kirby, Naomi Shihab-Nye, William Stafford, Walter Pavlich, Beth Bentley and Barb Molloy-Olund. As a sample the editor selected these lines by Judith Skillman:

> She's left the fish's head on
> so it will bake slowly in foil, its milk eye
> turning on finally like a light the timer
> caused to open.

Fine Madness is digest-sized, 80 pp., perfect-bound, flat-spined, offset printing, 2-3 color card cover. Their press run is 800 for 100 subscriptions of which 10 are libraries. They accept about 40 of 1,000 poems received. Subscription: $9. **Sample: $4 postpaid. Guidelines available for SASE. Pays 1 copy plus subscription. Submit 3-10 poems, preferably originals, not photocopy, 1 poem per page. Reports in 2-3 months.** They give 2 annual awards to editors' choice of $50 each. Coeditor Sean Bentley says, "If you don't read poetry, don't send us any."

FIRST HAND (IV-Gay, subscribers), Box 1314, Teaneck NJ 07666, phone (201)836-9177, founded 1980, poetry editor Bob Harris, is a **"gay erotic publication written mostly by its readers."** The digest-sized monthly has a circulation of 70,000 with 3,000 subscribers of which 3 are libraries, and uses 1-2 pp. of poetry in each issue, for which they **pay $25 a poem.** They have published poems by Kelvin Beliele and Steven Finch. The editor selected these sample lines from "To a Model" by Karl Tierney:

> I assure you, I mean no
> disrespect when I discover,
> beyond sex and half asleep,
> you deflate to only half the monster
> and will be that much easier
> to battle out the door at dawn.

Submit poems no longer than 1 typed page. No queries. Reports in 6 weeks. Editor Bob Harris sometimes comments on rejected MSS. They have an 18-month backlog. The editor advises, "Make sure what you're writing about is obvious to future readers. **Poems need not be explicitly sexual, but must deal overtly with gay situations and subject matter."** Reviews books of poetry.

FISH DRUM (II, IV-Regional), 626 Kathryn Ave., Santa Fe NM 87501, founded 1988, editor Robert Winson, is a literary magazine appearing 2-4 times a year. **"I love West Coast poetry, the exuberant, talky, often elliptical and abstract 'continuous nerve movie' that follows the working of the mind and has a relationship to the world and the reader. Philip Whalen's work, for example, and much of** Calafia, The California Poetry, **edited by Ishmael Reed. Also magical-tribal-incantatory poems, exemplified by the future/primitive** Technicians of the Sacred, **ed. Rothenberg.** Fish Drum **has a soft spot for schmoozy, emotional, imagistic stuff. Literate, personal material that sings and surprises, OK?"** They have published poetry by Philip Whalen, Joy Harjo, Arthur Sze, Nathaniel Tarn, Alice Notley, John Brandi,

Steve Richmond, Jessica Hagedorn, Leo Romero and Leslie Scalapino. As a sample the editor selected these lines from "Advice to the Unborn Baby" by Miriam Sagan:

> *Angel, I felt you greedy at my neck*
> *Months before you were conceived*
> *You said I'm back, open the door*
> *I'm UPS with a package especially for you.*

FD is digest-sized, 40 pp., saddle-stapled, professionally printed, with glossy card cover. "Of 150 or so unsolicited submissions last year, accepted fewer than twenty." Press run 500 for 100 subscriptions of which 10 are libraries, 400 shelf sales. Subscription: $10 for 4 issues. **Sample, postpaid: $3. Pays 2 or more copies. Contributors may purchase advance copies at $1.50 each in addition to contributor's copies. Reports quickly. "We're looking for New Mexico authors,** also prose: fiction, essays, what-have-you, and artwork, scores, cartoons, etc.—just send it along. **We are also interested in music/poetry collaborations for our occasional cassette issues. We also publish chapbooks, but solicit these from our authors."** Reviews books of poetry.

FIVE FINGERS REVIEW; FIVE FINGERS PRESS (III, IV-Form, women, political, social issues, bilingual), P.O. Box 15426, San Francisco CA 94115, founded 1984, editors John High, Thoreau Lovell, Aleka Chase and Julia Ward, a literary biannual publishing "diverse, innovative writing by writers of various aesthetics who are **concerned with social issues.**" Some of the better-known poets they have published are Denise Levertov, Robert Bly, C.D. Wright, Kathleen Fraser, Philip Levine and Ron Silliman. An occasional poem is published in both English and Spanish. The editors chose a sample from "I've Forgotten Nothing" by Bella Akhmadulina, translated by John High and Katya Olmstead:

> *I've forgotten nothing-*
> *that I'm part of humanity*
> *saddens me.*

Five Fingers Review is 6×9", nicely printed on buff stock, 150 pp., flat-spined with one-color glossy card cover. Circulation is 1,000 copies, 25% of which go to libraries. Price per issue is $6, subscription $12/year. **Sample available for $7 postpaid. Pay is 2 copies. Reporting time is 3-6 months and time to publication is 4 months. Query for current deadlines. Simultaneous submissions OK.** Five Fingers Press also publishes a perfect-bound book series. The advice of the editors is: "Pick up a copy of the magazine. Be committed to craft and to looking at the world in fresh, surprising ways."

‡**FLEETING MONOLITH ENTERPRISES (II); VERTICAL IMAGES (IV-Regional),** 62 Langdon Park Rd., London N6 5QG England, phone (081)340-5807, founded 1986, editor Mike Diss. Fleeting Monolith publishes about 3 chapbooks/year. *Vertical Images* is an annual using primarily poets connected with the Vertical Images poetry group: "All those submitting work are given equal representation in the magazine, which grows largely out of consistent workshop practice every 2 weeks. We suggest moving to London, joining the group and taking it from there." For their chapbooks, Fleeting Monolith wants "**inspired/delirious/challenging/manic work—who cares about form! No dead/academic/po-faced/sensitive stuff.**" They have recently published poetry by Slaughter District, Chris Brown, Jondi Keane, and the editor, who chose the following complete poem (poet unidentified) as a sample:

> *not every inch a father do i go*

Their chapbooks are in a variety of formats and **payment depends "entirely on the format and scope of each work."** Sample postpaid: £2. The editor says, "*L'art, c'est un connerie.* Artaud said that, but we wish we had. Poetry can be a garden shed: Michaut said that (who cares about form! count this, count that!) and he wasn't English either—in fact, not many poets are, now that Keats and Lewis Carroll are dead. Buster Keaton was a poet and Jean Tinguely is a poet. At Fleeting Monolith, only a small part of the living process of poetry gets crystallized into books. Write us a letter, send us something, join the network of creative discontent."

‡**FLIPSIDE (II),** California University of Pennsylvania, Dixon Hall, California PA 15419, founded 1987, poetry editor L.A. Smith, is a literary tabloid appearing twice a year **using poetry. "Sentimentality is forbidden."** They have recently published poetry by Charles Bukowski and Arthur Winfield Knight. As a sample, I selected the opening lines of a full-page poem, "Midnight Lights up the Sky" by Jim Chaffee:

> *Midnight lights up the sky*
> *As I lie and listen to the hum of the neon business card*
> *buzzing outside my window*
> *about cheap rates and cheaper mates.*

The tabloid is 64 pp., professionally printed. Press run 5,000, distributed free to the public, libraries, writing schools, colleges, advertisers, poets, etc. They accept lesss than 5% of hundreds of poems submitted. **Sample postpaid: $2. Send SASE for guidelines. Reports in 1 month. Pays as many copies as you want.**

THE FLORIDA REVIEW (II), Dept. of English, University of Central Florida, Orlando FL 32816, phone (823)275-2038, founded 1972, poetry editor Russ Kesler, is a "literary biannual with emphasis on short fiction and poetry." They want **"poems filled with real things, real people and emotions, poems that might conceivably advance our knowledge of the human heart."** They have published poetry by Knute Skinner, Elton Glaser and Walter McDonald. As a sample, I selected these lines from "Needlepoint" by Lisa Rhoades:

> *The draw of the yarn*
> *through the canvas rasps*
> *uneven as the breath*
> *of an old man, the*
> *murmur of a cat.*

It is 128 pp., flat-spined, professionally printed, with glossy card cover. Press run 1,000 for 400 subscriptions of which 50 are libraries. Shelf sales: 50. **Sample postpaid: $4.50. Send SASE for guidelines. Pays 3 copies, small honorarium occasionally available. Submit no more than 6 poems. Simultaneous submissions OK. Reports in 1-3 months. Editor comments on submissions "occasionally."** Reviews books of poetry.

FLUME PRESS (II), 4 Casita, Chico CA 95926, phone (916)342-1583, founded 1984, poetry editors Casey Huff and Elizabeth Renfro, publishes poetry chapbooks. **"We have few biases about form, although we appreciate control and crafting, and we tend to favor a concise, understated style, with emphasis on metaphor rather than editorial commentary."** Considers simultaneous submissions. They have recently published chapbooks by Tina Barr, Randall Freisinger, Leonard Kress, Carol Gordon and Gayle Kaune. As a sample, the editor selected these lines from "Mother Pills" by David Graham:

> *I may also have drawn her long hair, eyes split*
> *behind bifocal lenses, but what remains*
> *is that sliver of light under my bedroom door,*
> *the voice my voice could waken, sure as rain.*

Chapbooks are chosen from an annual competition, deadline June 30. $6 entry fee. Submit 20-28 pp., including title, contents, and acknowledgments. Name and address on a separate sheet. "Flume Press editors read and respond to every entry. They choose the finalists and send them to the Final Judge, a nationally known poet, who selects the winner. Past judges include Frances Mayes, Madeline Defrees, David Wojahn, Sandra Cisneros and Linda Hogan." Winner receives $100 and 25 copies. **Sample: $5 plus $1 postage and handling.**

FOLIO: A LITERARY JOURNAL (II), Dept. of Literature, Gray Hall, American University, Washington DC 20016, phone (202)885-2973, founded 1984, editors change annually, a biannual. They have recently published poetry by Jean Valentine, Henry Taylor and Andrea Hollander Budy. The editors selected these sample lines from "The Longing" by Kathrine Jason:

> *I like it here*
> *in the realm of stone*
> *and unerring geometry*
> *where a word, spoken,*
> *flies back as an answer*
> *and a wind in decline*
> *is a gargoyle's breath.*

There are 55 pp. of poetry in each 74 p. issue, narrow digest-sized, thin flat spine, glossy cover, neatly printed from typeset. **Sample: $5 postpaid. Submit from August to November 1 or January to March 1, up to 6 pp., include a brief bio/contributor's note, photocopy, dot-matrix OK. Considers simultaneous submissions. Pays 2 copies. Comments on rejections "when possible."** They also sponsor a contest open to all contributors with a $75 prize for the best poem of the spring issue.

‡FOLLOW YOUR DREAMS; LONGRIFLE PUBLISHING (IV-Membership), 10500 15th St., Mojave CA 93051, founded 1990, editor Cyndi Lynne Turner. *FYD*, appearing 6/year, publishes **poetry by members. Membership: $15. The editor says she "would still like to see all."** Cyndi Lynne Turner is a counselor at The Alexander LongRifle Youth Reservation for battered and abused children and, finding that most of the children at the refuge wrote poetry, started a magazine for their poetry and others who would like to join. As a sample the editor chose these lines from "The Ordinary Female" by June Albrecht:

> *Without T.V. I'd never know*
> *Just what to use or wear*
> *My life would be just dull routine*
> *And no one else would care.*

There's just one thing though that bothers me
Before I joined the ranks
My life was simple and carefree
With money in the bank!

"Members can buy a full-page spread for $2; otherwise there will be 2-3 poems/page. The magazine will start out being 5-10 pp. and grow, with members' support." She wants "poetry that rhymes and can be understood — not too long — work they feel proud of, nothing that's prejudiced." Local members will participate in making editorial judgments. Samples $2.

FOOLSCAP (I, II), 78 Friars Road, East Ham, London E6 1LL England, phone 01-470-7680, founded 1987, editor Judi Benson, appears in January, April and September using poetry "that surprises and informs with attention paid to language and voice as well as to the world around us. We are looking for a confidence, a sense of humor and, of course, a vision. We are looking for a wide range of styles and opinions and most likely won't know what we want until we find it. We veer away from cliché, obvious rhyme, self-indulgence, overwriting, oversentimentalizing, lecturing, and general whittering on, not to mention that which is written in poetic line breaks but which is not poetry. We advise people to get a copy before submitting." They have recently published poetry by Carol Ann Duffy, Sean O'Brien and Frances Wilson. As a sample the editor selected these lines from "Blues In the Woodshed" by Libby Houston:

A knock at the door midnight and no one
there, the click of a dumb phonecall.
The night a brick smashed on the roughcast
out of the sallow empty
dark was worst. So
nights without speech.

I have not seen an issue, but the editor describes it as 52 pp., digest-sized, camera-ready photocopying, no reductions. Black and white illustrations and sometimes half-tones. Light card cover in design of child's exercise book. No ads. No frills. They accept about 120 of 1,200 poems received per year. Press run: 200 for 100-250 subscribers of which 10 are libraries, 50 shelf sales. Subscription: $15/£5. Sample postpaid: $5/£2.35. Pays 1 copy. Submit "not more than 6/time. Best if overseas not to have to return MSS. Include more than 1 International Postal Order as 1=24 pence and regular airmail is 34 pence, not to mention that which includes MS." Do not submit MSS in September (summer is better). No simultaneous submissions; previously published poems sometimes used. Editor comments on submissions "sometimes, if we feel a poem is close but not quite there and that there is a seriousness of intent. It may seem obvious, but I would advise beginning poets to share their work with others (this doesn't mean Mom and Dad) before even considering sending to magazines and that they study the market. *Foolscap* accepts a wide range of poetry from many different geographical locations, written by a variety of people, accepting both the unknown and the well-known. We are looking for poetry which represents today's thinking and feeling, however diverse. There is an urgency in much of the work we publish, and we want the word to get out."

FOOTWORK: THE PATERSON LITERARY REVIEW; HORIZONTES; THE PATERSON POETRY PRIZE; PCC POETRY CENTER POETRY CONTEST; PASSAIC COUNTY COMMUNITY COLLEGE POETRY CENTER LIBRARY (II, IV-Regional, bilingual/foreign language), Passaic County Community College, Cultural Affairs Dept., College Blvd., Paterson NJ 07509. A wide range of activities pertaining to poetry are conducted by the Passaic County Community College Poetry Center, including the annual literary magazine *Footwork*, founded 1979, editor and director Maria Mazziotti Gillan, using poetry of "high quality" under 100 lines. They have recently published poetry by David Ray, Diane Wakoski, William Stafford, Sonia Sanchez, Laura Boss and Marge Piercy. As a sample, the editor selected several lines from "Message From Your Toes" by Ruth Stone:

How now, if you should dig him up, the bones of his left foot
falling like dice, there would be one among them gnarled out of shape
a ridge of calcium extruding a pattern of unutterable anguish.
And your toes, passengers of the extreme
clustered on your dough white body,
say how they miss his feet, the thin elegance of his ankles.

Footwork: The Paterson Literary Review is magazine-sized, 144 pp., saddle-stapled, professionally printed with glossy card 2-color cover, using b/w art and photos, circulation 1,000 with 100 subscriptions of which 50 are libraries. Sample: $5 postpaid. Pays 1 copy. Reports in 3 months. Send no more than 5 poems per submission. *Horizontes*, founded in 1983, editor, José Villalongo, is an annual Spanish language literary magazine using poetry of high quality no longer than 20 lines. Will accept English translations, but Spanish version must be included. They have recently published poetry by Nelson Calderon, Jose Kozer and Julio Cesar Mosches. As a sample, the editor selected these lines by the editor of *Footwork*, Maria Gillan:

> Yo he aprendido de la litanía de mi vida,
> del patrón de ordenes repetidas
> y reclusiónes.
>
> Yo he aprendido más de lo que
> quisiera saber, sueño
> con retroceder a mi inocencia,
> la vida limpia de pesadumbre y el cielo
> sin obscurecerse

Horizontes is magazine-sized 120 pp., saddle-stapled, professionally printed with full color matte cover, using b/w graphics and photos, circulation 800 with 100 subscriptions of which 20 are libraries. **Sample issue: $4 postpaid. Pays 2 copies. Reports in 3-4 months. Accepts simultaneous submissions. "On occasion we do consider published works but prefer unpublished works."** The Poetry Center of the college conducts an annual poetry contest, no fees, prizes of $250, $125 and $100, deadline April 15. Send SASE for rules. They also publish a **New Jersey Poetry Resources** book, the **PCC Poetry Contest Anthology** and the **New Jersey Poetry Calendar**. The Paterson Poetry Prize of $1,000 is awarded each year (split between poet and publisher) to a book of poems published in the previous year. Publishers should write with SASE for application form to be submitted by Feb. 1. Winner in 1990, Denise Levertov; judge Diane Wakoski. Passaic County Community College Poetry Center Library has an extensive collection of contemporary poetry and seeks small press contributions to help keep it abreast. The Geraldine R. Dodge Poetry Festival, each September at Waterloo Village in Stanhope, New Jersey, features readings by many major poets, and the Distinguished Poetry Series also offers readings by poets of international, national and regional reputation. Poetryworks/USA is a series of programs produced for UA Columbia-Cablevision.

FOR POETS ONLY (I), P.O. Box 4855, Schenectady NY 12304, founded 1985, poetry editor L.M. Walsh, **requires a $3 entry fee for each poem submitted, which may win a $10 prize (at least five promised for each issue). Others accepted are paid for with one copy of the magazine.** The issue I have has 35 pp. of poems—some with more than one to a page. Of these, 16 were awarded prizes. They have published poems by J. Bernier, C. Weirich and Alice Mackenzie Swaim. As a sample I selected the first lines of one of the prize winners, "Poets Unite," by J. Mead:

> The Literary Poetry Queen
> of "For Poets Only" Magazine
> Has composed a wonderful, unique book,
> enjoy the works as you continue to look.

FPO is digest-sized, 36 pp., saddle-stapled, photocopied from typescript with glossy card cover. It appears quarterly. The editor rejects about 10% of poetry received. Press run is 200. Per copy: $3. **Sample: $3.50 postpaid. Any subject. No pornography. No comments on rejections.** The editor advises, "For beginning poets: a quote from Horst Bienek in his **The Cell**: 'We are distressed but *not in despair*, distressed but *not destroyed,* persecuted but *not forsaken,* cast down but *not destroyed.'* "

‡FOREST BOOKS (III, IV-Translations), 20 Forest View, Chingford, London E4 7AY U.K., phone 081-529-8470, founded 1984, director Brenda Walker, publishes 25-30 paperbacks/year. The sample I have seen, **Enchanting Beasts: An Anthology of Modern Women Poets in Finland**, is a handsomely printed flat-spined book of 126 pp. **Pays 10% royalties plus 20 copies.** Samples may be purchased through Dufour Editions, P.O. Box 449, Chester Springs PA 19425.

THE FORMALIST (II, IV-Form, translations), 525 S. Rotherwood, Evansville IN 47714, founded 1990, editor William Baer, appears twice a year, **"dedicated to *metrical* poetry written in the great tradition of English-language verse."** They have recently published poetry by May Swenson, Charles Causley, John Updike, X.J. Kennedy and Fred Chappell. As a sample the editor chose the opening stanza from "The Amateurs of Heaven" by Howard Nemerov:

> Two lovers to a midnight meadow came
> High in the hills, to lie there hand in hand
> Like effigies and look up at the stars,
> The never-setting ones set in the North
> To circle the Pole in idiot majesty,
> And wonder what was given them to wonder.

"We are interested in metrical poetry written in the **traditional forms, including ballads, sonnets, couplets, the Greek forms, the French forms, etc. We will also consider metrical translations of major formalist non-English poets—from the Ancient Greeks to the present. We are not,** however, interested in haiku (or syllabic verse of any kind) or sestinas. Although we do publish poetry which skillfully employs enjambment, we have a marked prejudice against excessive enjambment. Only rarely do we accept a poem over 2 pages, and we have no interest in any type of erotica, blasphemy, vulgarity or racism. Finally, like all editors, we suggest that those wishing to submit to *The Formalist* become thoroughly familiar with the journal beforehand." *The Formalist* considers submissions throughout the year, 3-5 poems at one time. We do *not* consider simultaneous submissions, previously published work, or disk submissions. A brief cover letter is recommended and a SASE is necessary for the return of the MSS. Subscription: $12. Sample postpaid: $6.50. Payment 2 copies. Reports within 8 weeks. See also the contest listing the World Order of Narrative and Formalist Poets. Contestants must subscribe to *The Formalist* to enter.

FOX CRY (I), University of Wisconsin Fox Valley, Midway Road, Menasha WI 54952, phone (414)832-2600, founded 1973, editor Professor Don Hrubesky, is a literary annual using poems up to 50 lines long, deadline February 1. They have recently published poetry by Shirley Anders, David Graham, Clifford Wood, Laurel Mills and Don Hrubesky. As a sample, the editor selected these lines (poet unidentified):

> She was out there with the leaves
> the old woman bent but broad of back
> In long even pulls, she collected
> the detritus of the sun's decline.

Their press run is 400. Sample: $5 postpaid. Send SASE for guidelines. Submit MSS from Sept. 1-Feb. 1. Submit maximum of 3 poems. They will consider simultaneous submissions. Pays 1 copy.

‡FOX VALLEY LIVING (IV-Regional), 707 Kautz Rd., St. Charles IL 60174, founded 1989, editor Francie Graham Smith, appears every other month using poems "on subjects of specific interest to region, 20 lines or less, or from poets *from* this region. Nothing not suitable for a general-interest family magazine. We receive far too much 'obscure' verse. Our readers want to be entertained and delighted. Humor and upbeat verse have a much better chance with us. We do not publish anything depressing, controversial or erotic, so there's no point in submitting such work." As a sample, I selected these lines from "Lament Upon Biting Into A Store Bought Tomato" by Krista Ravenscraft:

> Anemic imitation of a fruit
> You deserve to be called
> vegetable.
> You fall against my
> teeth with a thud
> Like a potato.

FVL is magazine-sized, on glossy paper with glossy paper cover, 96-128 pp., 4-color, saddle-stapled. Press run 35,000 for 15,000 subscribers of which 500 are libraries, 12,000 shelf sales. Subscription: $10.95/6 issues, $19.90/12. Sample post-paid: $3. Send SASE for guidelines. Pays $50-100/poem plus up to 5 copies (if requested). "Need *brief* bio. First of the year is the best time to submit; should request an editorial calendar so poems can be tied into subjects featured. Seasonal poems should be submitted at least 6 months in advance. Poems of possible interest to an upcoming issue are reviewed by editorial board that meets approximately every 2 months. All editorial material is subject to possible cut due to space limitations." Reviews books of poetry "if from Fox Valley region."

FRANK: AN INTERNATIONAL JOURNAL OF CONTEMPORARY WRITING AND ART (II, IV-Form, translations), B.P. 29, 94301 Vincennes Cedex France, founded 1983, editor David Applefield. *Frank* is a literary semiannual that "encourages work of seriousness and high quality which falls often between existing genres. Looks favorably at true internationalism and stands firm against ethnocentric values. Likes translations. Publishes foreign dossier in each issue. Very eclectic." There are no subject specifications, but the magazine "discourages sentimentalism and easy, false surrealism. Although we're in Paris, most Paris-poems are too thin for us. Length is open." They have published poetry by Rita Dove, Derek Walcott, Duo Duo, Raymond Carver, Tomas Tranströmer, James Laughlin, Breytenbach, Michaux, Gennadi Aigi, W.S. Merwin, Edmond Jabes, John Berger, and many lesser known poets. The journal is digest-sized, flat-spined 224 pp., offset in b/w with color cover and photos, drawings, and manuscript pages, 5 pages of ads. Circulation is 4,000, of which 2,000 are bookstore sales and subscriptions. Subscription $30 (individuals), $60 (institutional) for 4 issues. Sample: $18 postpaid airmail from Paris. Pay is $5/printed page and 2 copies. Guidelines available for SASE. Poems must be previously unpublished. Submissions are reported on in 8-10 weeks, publication is in 1-4 months. "Send only what you feel is fresh, original, and provocative in either theme or form. Work of craft that also has political and social impact is encouraged." The editor provides some criticism on rejected MSS. Editor organizes readings in US and Europe for *Frank* contributors. *Frank* also publishes *Paris-Anglophone*, a directory of English commercial and cultural activities in France, and *Paris Inside Out*, an insiders guide to Paris for students and discerning visitors, and sponsors a complete information service on cultural and commercial matters in France via fax called *Facts by Fax* (617)536-0068.

‡FREDRICKSON-KLOEPFEL PUBLISHING CO. (F-K BOOKS) (I, IV-Themes), 7748 17th SW, Seattle WA 98106, phone (206)767-4915, "established 1983 as an outlet for John (J. Fred) Blair's poetry and pamphlets, opened to the public 1990," editor John F. Blair, publishes **anthologies on specific themes.** They "try to publish at least one item by each contributor; 1,000 words max, like a strong viewpoint, backed by sound poetics, literal imagery, metaphor or strong story line, salty commentary, active verbs . . . It is a matter of provocative content." Send SASE for current theme. They have recently published poetry by Ralph La Charity, Joanne Seltzer, John Grey and Jeffrey Zable. As a sample the editor selected these lines from "Abel and Cain" by B.Z. Niditch:

> Teach me that a veil is fate
> Color only a brother murdered for meat
> Wishful yet unsatisfied with a beast's mark.

Send "cold turkey" 4-10 items that seem to fit the topic announced (e.g., in lit newsletters such as *Poetry Exchange*). Send SASE for current theme and available publications. Reports in 3-4 months. "After book is completed, contributors may purchase copies at print cost for promotion in their locales. They should make a small profit wholesaling them and get full mark-up on the ones they retail. Any profit I make will be shared across the board with contributors. I want to be known, not (necessarily) rich. It is not enough to write up your poetry and dump it into somebody else's lap to publish and peddle. There are 10 million competent poets in the U.S. who can't get off their high horses long enough to take a real look at what goes into marketing. F-K Books is recruiting a nationwide association of confrontational writers into a mutual promotion operation—as you promote them, they promote you. These anthologies thrive on mixed styles and opposing viewpoints that meld into a 'vox pop' dialogue (or polilogue polly-wolly doodlogue)."

FREE FOCUS; OSTENTATIOUS MIND (I, IV-Women/feminist), 224 82nd St., Brooklyn NY 11209, phone (718)680-3899, *Free Focus* founded 1985, *Ostentatious Mind* founded 1987, poetry editor Patricia D. Coscia. *Free Focus* "is a small-press magazine which **focuses on the educated women of today** and needs stories and poems. They want **all types except x-rated. The poems can be as long as 2 pp. or as short as 3 lines. The subject matter is of all types and the style, the same. The purpose of the magazine is to give women writers a place in literature, that women have a will to succeed and earn respect for their achievements.**" As a sample Patricia D. Coscia comments, "This 4-line poem by Gretchen Busch represents the basic doubts of a woman's successfulness in writing. Is it worth all the hard work?"

> I say I want to write, but don't
> Yet I could fill up a book with excuses
> It's fine just to say I'm awaiting a purpose
> But it's nothing my waiting produces.

Ostentatious Mind "is designed to encourage the intense writer—the cutting reality. The staff deals in the truth of life: political, social and psychological. Both magazines are photocopied on $8 \times 14''$ paper, folded in the middle and stapled to make a 10 pp. (including cover) format, with simple b/w drawings on the cover and inside. *Free Focus* appears in spring and fall. **Sample:** of either is $2 postpaid. Send SASE for guidelines. Pays 4 copies. Poems should be "single-spaced typed on single sheets of papers. Poem submission is 3." Simultaneous submissions and previously published poems OK. Reports "as soon as possible." Comments? "Yes, very much so. It is important to the writer." They plan to sponsor contests. Patricia D. Coscia says, "I think that the poet who is unknown will never be known unless she or he sends out their poems to a publisher or gets involved in a literary magazine such as this one."

FREE LUNCH (II), P.O. Box 7647, Laguna Niguel CA 92607-7647, founded 1988, editor Ron Offen, is a "poetry journal interested in publishing whole spectrum of what is currently being produced by American poets. Always try to comment on submissions. Especially interested in experimental work and work by unestablished poets. Hope to provide all serious American poets with free subscription. For details on free subscription send SASE. Prefer no more than 3 poems per submission. No restriction on form, length, subject matter, style, purpose. Don't want cutsie, syrupy, sentimental, preachy religious, or agressively 'uplifting' verse. No aversion to form, rhyme." Poets recently published include Neal Bowers, Billy Collins, Louis McKee, F.D. Reeve, Jim Reiss, Vern Rutsala, Bill Zavatsky and Leila Zeiger. As a sample the editor selected these lines from "My Father's Forecast" by Len Roberts:

> the chunk of oak snapped in the black stove
> as I sat with my father's face

> *in my hands, his*
> *nights of cigarettes rising with each breath . . .*

Published 3 times a year. The magazine is 32-40 pp., saddle-stapled, digest-sized, offset. Their press run is 850 with 75 subscriptions of which 10 are libraries. Subscription $10 ($13 foreign). **Sample: $4 ($5 foreign) postpaid. Pays 1 copy plus subscription. Send SASE for guidelines. Will consider simultaneous submissions. Editor usually comments on rejections and tries to return submissions in 8 weeks.** He quotes Archibal MacLeish, " 'A poem should not mean/ But be.' Poetry is concerned primarily with language, rhythm and sound; fashions and trends are transitory and to be eschewed; perfecting one's work is often more important than publishing it."

‡**FRENCH BROAD PRESS (III)**, The Asheville School, Asheville NC 28806, phone (704)255-7909, founded 1989, publishers Jessica Bayer and J.W. Bonner, publishes 20-40 pp. chapbooks. **"Any style or form welcome. Considers sexually explicit material."** They have recently published poetry by Thomas Meyer, Jeffrey Beam and Jonathan Williams. **"We're slow. May take 6 months to respond to a MS, and up to 2 years before publication. Many of our poets have paid 'in kind': typesetting MSS and covers on disks or pasting up the book for printing." Pays 10% of press run.** Write to buy samples or order from The Captain's Bookshelf, 26½ Battery Park Ave., Asheville NC 28801.

FRIENDS JOURNAL (II, IV-Themes), 1501 Cherry St., Philadelphia PA 19102, phone (215)241-7277, founded 1827 as *The Friend*, 1844 as *Friends Intelligencer* and 1955 as *Friends Journal*, appears monthly, magazine-sized, circulation 9,000+. **"The *Journal* seeks poetry that resonates with Quakerism and Quaker concerns, such as peace and nonviolence, spiritual seeking, the sanctuary movement, the nuclear freeze."** These sample lines are from "For a Friends' Wedding" by Pulitzer Prize poet Henry S. Taylor:

> *We have been schooled in silence in this place;*
> *whatever words I frame to wish you well*
> *dwindle toward the spirit in this air . . .*

No multiple or simultaneous submissions. Pays 2 copies per poem. Subscription: $18 per year.

FROG GONE REVIEW (I, IV-Subscription), Box 46308, Mt. Clemens MI 48046, phone (313)263-3399, founded 1988-89, editor Greg Schindler, is an annual poetry magazine. **Submit 5 poems (120-line maximum). Poetry accepted September 1 through January 15. Reports February and early March.** Very seldom uses poems over 40 lines. **"Economy of words and good fresh imagery wanted. No porno."** They have recently published poetry by Marcia Kester, Edwin Pilmer, Ruth Forman, Heather Renouf and John Grey. As a sample the editor selected "Sweater Weather" by Darlene Roether:

> *Wind wraps itself, spiraling*
> *undulating about the island*
> *is a young child caught*
> *in an unruly sweater.*

"Submitting poets must order a copy of the magazine for $4. The five best poems are designated and awarded $10 each." Send SASE. The format is unusual. The green card cover and pages turn up like pages from a calendar. Cursive type, black ink on cream yellow-colored paper, saddle-stapled, several illustrations.

FROGMORE PAPERS; FROGMORE POETRY PRIZE (II), 42 Morehall Ave., Folkestone, Kent, England, founded 1983, poetry editor Jeremy Page, is a literary quarterly with emphasis on new poetry and short stories. **"Quality is generally the only criterion, although pressure of space means very long work (over 100 lines) is unlikely to be published."** They have recently published poetry by B.C. Leale, Geoffrey Holloway, Myra Schneider, Frances Wilson, Linda France, Merryn Williams and Ivor C. Treby. As a sample the editor selected these lines by Elizabeth Garrett:

> *I rock on my heels and test*
> *My breath's spillage on the air.*
> *I shall fold it with the weather*
> *For safe keeping, in a camphor chest.*

The magazine is 22 pp. saddle-stapled with matte card cover, photocopied in photoreduced typescript. Their press run is 250 with 70 subscriptions. They accept a tenth of poetry received. Subscription: £7 ($12). **Sample: £2.50 ($4) postpaid. Pays 1 copy. Reports in 3-6 months. Considers simultaneous submissions. Editor sometimes comments on rejections.** Write for information about the annual Frogmore Poetry Prize. The editor says, "My advice to people starting to write poetry would be: read as many recognized modern poets as you can and don't be afraid to experiment."

FROGPOND: QUARTERLY HAIKU JOURNAL; HAIKU SOCIETY OF AMERICA; HAIKU SOCIETY OF AMERICA AWARDS/CONTESTS (IV-Form, translation), % Japan Society, 333 E. 47th St., New York NY 10017, has been publishing *Frogpond* since 1978, now edited by Sylvia Forges-Ryan, and submissions should go directly to her at 87 Bayard Ave., North Haven CT 06473. *Frogpond* is a stapled spine quarterly of 48 pp., 5½×8½", of haiku, senryu, haiku sequences, renga, more rarely tanka, and translations of haiku. It also contains book reviews, some news of the Society, contests, awards, publications and other editorial matter—a dignified, handsome little magazine. Poets should be familiar with modern developments in English-language haiku as well as the tradition. **Haiku should be brief, fresh, using clear images and non-poetic language. Focus should be on a moment keenly perceived. Ms. Forges-Ryan hopes contributors will be familiar with contemporary haiku and senryu as presented in** *The Haiku Handbook* **(Wm. J. Higginson) and** *The Haiku Anthology* **(Cor van den Heuvel, Ed.).** Recent contributors include Charles Dickson, Sandra Fuhringer, Carol Montgomery, Patricia Neubauer, H.F. Noyes, Francine Porad, Tom Tico, Michael Dylan Welch and Ruth Yarrow. Considerable variety is possible, as these two examples from the magazine illustrate:

> *lost to a field*
> *of Queen Anne's lace*
> *the woman in white*
> —Elizabeth St. Jacques

> *The firefly*
> *folding, unfolding*
> *its moonlight*
> —Vincent Tripi

Each issue has between 25 and 35 pages of poetry. The magazine goes to more than 600 subscribers, of which 15 are libraries, as well as to over a dozen foreign countries. **Sample postpaid: $5.** Make check payable to Haiku Society of America. They receive about 8,000 submissions per year and use about 400-450. **Accepted poems usually published within 6-12 months, reporting within 6 weeks. They are flexible on submission format: haiku on 3×5" cards or several to a page or one to a page or half-page. Ms. Forges-Ryan prefers 5-20 at one submission, no photocopy or dot-matrix. No simultaneous submissions. They hope contributors will become HSA members, but it is not necessary, and all contributors receive a copy of the magazine in payment. Send SASE for Information Sheet on the HSA and submission guidelines.** The Society also sponsors the Harold G. Henderson Haiku Award Contest, The Gerald Brady Senryu Award Contest, The Haiku Society of America Renku Contest, The Nicholas A. Virgilio Memorial Haiku Competition for High School Students and gives Merit Book Awards for books in the haiku field. Two "best-of-issue" prizes are given "through a gift from the Museum of Haiku Literature, Tokyo."

FROM HERE PRESS; XTRAS; OLD PLATE PRESS (II), Box 219, Fanwood NJ 07023, phone (201)889-7886, founded 1975, editors William J. Higginson and Penny Harter, a small-press publisher of a chapbook series called *Xtras* and flat-spined paperback anthologies and solo collections. The editors want **"contemporary work; we have a particular interest in haiku, but also have done everything from haibun and renga to long poems." They do not want "5-7-5 nature poems, poorly crafted traditional verse."** The *Xtras* series of books is published on a co-op basis; the author pays half the cost of production and receives half the press run. Other book contracts are individually negotiated. They have recently published poetry by Ruth Stone, Dee Evetts and themselves. I have seen two sample volumes—a chapbook of haiku, **Casting Into a Cloud**, by Elizabeth Searle Lamb, and a flat-spined paperback, **Lovepoems**, by Penny Harter. As a sample, I chose the beginning lines from Harter's "Our Hair Is Happy":

> *Our hair is happy.*

> *You pull the brush through my hair.*
> *It crackles, lifts, curls on your wrist.*
> *My head streams into your hands.*

Lovepoems is handsomely printed on heavy beige stock with b/w drawings by Gilbert Riou, 70 pp. **"Please query with 10 pp. first." MSS should be "clear, typed double-spaced, no simultaneous submissions." Queries will be answered in 1 month. Pay is usually ½ of the press run in author's copies.** The press publishes 2-4 books each year, mostly digest-sized, with an average page count of 40. A catalog is free for #10 SASE; average price of books is $3. The editors say, "If you do not read 10-12 books of poetry by living authors each year, please do not consider submitting work to us."

FRONTIERS: A JOURNAL OF WOMEN STUDIES (IV-Feminist), University of New Mexico, Mesa Vista Rm 2142, Albuquerque NM 87131-1586, founded 1975, is published 3 times a year, circulation 1,000, magazine-sized format, flat spined, 80-92 pp. **Sample: $8. Uses poetry on feminist themes.** Recently published Audré Lorde, Janice Mirikitani, Carol Wolfe Kenek and Opal Palmer Adiga. **Pays 2 copies. Reports in 3 to 5 months. No simultaneous submissions.**

‡FURRY CHICLETS: A LAWPOETS CREATION (I), 914 5th St., Santa Monica CA 90403, founded 1990, editors Charles Carreon and Tom Brill, an annual, wants **"impact poetry, stories and anything else that fits, to dislodge tired, useless concepts and replace them with free energy; test your freedom here. Poems: 1 page."** As a sample the editor selected these lines from "Pocket Essay Re: *Ramones,*" (poet unidentified):

> *What you can do with it:*
> *Cut LA in half with one clean stroke*
> *Raze Century City with a backhand swipe,*
> *Vaporize the Hollywood sign with a glance, and*
> *Blow away all eight lanes of the*
> *Freeway with a single puff of breath*

It consists of photocopied pages stapled at the top to a blue matte backing, 30-40 pp. Press run of first issue was 100, but they hoped to increase the number. **"We hope to be able to pay in 1 copy." Sample: $4 postpaid. Editors often comment on rejections. They try to respond in 6 weeks.** The editor advises, "Poetry is inspirational writing. Poetry is a mirror fallen in the gutter, randomly reflecting changing scenes. Time passes. Do not imitate, unless to embellish. Creeping through cracks of dense legal prose like vines breaking concrete, post-punk lawyers send forth shoots of verse that blossom in publication, revealing bouquets of Furry Chiclets, brightly colored, cryptic, inedible; we solicit others to do likewise, whether legal-minded or just imprisoned in the thicket of world law."

FUTURIFIC MAGAZINE (IV-Themes), Foundation for Optimism, 280 Madison Ave., New York NY 10016, phone (212)684-4913, founded 1976, publisher Balint Szent-Miklosy, is a monthly newsmagazine dealing with **current affairs and their probable outcomes. "We pride ourselves on the accuracy of our forecasting. No other limits than that the poet try to be accurate in predicting the future." They want to see "positive upbeat poetry glorifying humanity and human achievements."** *Futurific* is magazine-sized, 32 pp., saddle-stapled, on glossy stock, with b/w photos, art and ads, circulation 10,000. Subscription: $48. **Sample: $5 postpaid. Pays 5 copies.** The editor says, "*Futurific* is made up of the words Future-Terrific. Poets should seek out and enjoy the future if they want to see their work in *Futurific.*"

G.W. REVIEW (II, IV-Translations), Marvin Center Box 20, George Washington University, Washington DC 20052, phone (202)994-7288, founded 1980, editor Adam H. Freedman, appears 2 times a year. "The magazine is published for distribution to the University community, the Washington, D.C. metropolitan area, and an increasing number of national subscribers." They have recently published poetry by William Stafford, Robin Becker, Gary Fincke and Julia Alvarez. It is 64 pp., perfect-bound with cover photograph. They receive about 3,300 poems a year and accept 50-60. Their annual press run averages 4,000 copies. Subscriptions: $5/year, $8/2 years. **Sample postpaid: $3. Pays 5 copies. They consider simultaneous submissions but not previously published poems. Reports in 1-3 months. The staff does not read manuscripts from May 15-August 15. Editor sometimes comments on rejections when the staff likes the work but thinks it needs to be revised.**

GAIRM; GAIRM PUBLICATIONS (IV-Ethnic, foreign language), 29 Waterloo St., Glasgow, G2 6BZ Scotland, editor Derick Thomson, founded 1952. *Gairm* is a quarterly, circulation 2,000, which uses **poetry in Scottish Gaelic only.** It has published the work of all significant Scottish Gaelic poets, and much poetry translated from European languages. An anthology of such translations, *European Poetry in Gaelic,* appeared in August 1990 (price £7.50 or $15). **All of the publications of the press are in Scottish Gaelic. Sample of *Gairm*: $3.** Reviews books of poetry.

‡GALAXY PRESS (III), 71 Recreation St., Tweed Heads, N.S.W. 2485 Australia, phone 075-361997, founded 1979, editor Lance Banbury, is a small-press publisher of short modernist to semi-traditional poems in chapbooks. He wants **"post-modernist short to medium-length verse, or didactic blank verse. No poetry of an anecdotal type."** As a sample he chose these lines from "Dressing for dinner" by Harry Burrus:

> *His opponents then are thriving now.*
> *A long line of young and old customers,*
> *propelled by sunrise worship at Sunday*
> *drive-in services, whose Good Book*
> *crushes with roots and sepulcher-like thought*
> *swallow primrose verse and walk*
> *the garden path, guarded and malignant.*

Query with 5 samples. Reports in 4 weeks. Pays 2 copies. Lance Banbury says, "Market pressures have severely pruned all my plans for publications in the last few years. However, this press needs to join in a thematic synchronicity, with other author/s, and concurrence of statement is more important than style or form."

THE GALLEY SAIL REVIEW (II), Suite 42, 1630 University Ave., Berkeley CA 94703, phone (415)486-0187, editor Stanley McNail. *The Galley Sail Review* was originally founded in 1958 and published until 1971 in San Francisco; second series is now based in Berkeley. Publication appears three times a year: spring, summer, and fall-winter. The editor says, *"GSR* is like many other 'littles' in that it **compensates its contributors in copies.** Since its inception it has survived without recourse to governmental or foundation grants, but is supported out of the editor's pocket and produced as a 'one-man' magazine entirely. We (editorial 'We') do not conduct contests or offer prizes, but **we endeavor to find and publish the best, most insightful and imaginative contemporary poetry extant. We do not promote any literary 'school' or ideological clique. We use both poetry and reviews."** Some recent contributors include Errol Miller, Thomas Krepz, Marjorie Power, Alan Atkinson and Barbara McCauley. The editor chose these lines from "The Last Walk" by Scott E. Thomas:
> *Spring is here and this is our last walk*
> *on this familiar path, this ribbon of worn-out earth,*
> *a stream bed in the rainy weeks.*

The Galley Sail Review is digest-sized, offset on fairly thin paper, 44 pp., saddle-stapled, with cover of the same paper. Single copy price is $3, subscription $8/3 issues; "a 6-issue minimum subscription at $15 required from institutions. Outside US and Canada add $4 for postage."

THE GAMUT (II), English Dept., Cleveland State University, 1218 Fenn Tower, Cleveland OH 44115, editors Leonard Trawick and Louis T. Milic, first published in 1980. *The Gamut, a Journal of Ideas and Information*, is "a general interest magazine with literary and art emphasis." **Send SASE for guidelines.** Leonard Trawick says they want **"poems that are more or less accessible to the educated reader, but not too simple, no trivial, greeting card, 'inspirational' poetry."** They have recently published poetry by David Citino, Roy Bently, Lynn Luria-Sukenick and Jeff Gundy. The magazine has a press run of 1,500 going to 900+ subscribers of which 50 are libraries. Price per issue: $6. Subscription: $15. **Pays an average of $15 per page plus 2 copies. Reports within 2 months. On rejection, editor comments "on the good ones."** As a sample Prof. Trawick selected these lines from "Visit to the Polygamists" by Marilee Richards (*The Gamut #32* Spring 1991):
> *"Hardworking sons of bitches" was all*
> *my grandfather said. The played-out land*
> *absorbed the silence of the endless afternoon.*
> *On every steep incline the Studebaker stalled.*

Professor Trawick says, "In selecting a poem perhaps the first thing we require is that the language be right. It may be complex and challenging, or it may be ostensibly simple, but if the poem doesn't work on the level of diction and syntax, it doesn't work at all for us."

GÁVEA-BROWN PUBLICATIONS; GÁVEA-BROWN: A BI-LINGUAL JOURNAL OF PORTUGUESE-AMERICAN LETTERS AND STUDIES (IV-Ethnic, bilingual), Box O, Brown University, Providence RI 02912, phone (402)863-3042, founded 1980, editors Onésimo T. Almeida and George Monteiro, is a small-press publisher of books and a journal **relating to the Portuguese-American experience.** They publish flat-spined collections of poetry in their journal. They have published poetry by Jorge de Sena, João Teixeira de Medeiros and Thomas Braga. As a sample I chose the first stanza of "At the Portuguese Feast" by Nelson H. Vieira:
> *Pushing my way through the jostling crowds*
> *Where Lusitanian ancestry strikes me in every face,*
> *I celebrate my annual sensation of pride and discomfort*
> *Knowing I shall never resolve the tug-of-war that is my fate.*

Gávea-Brown is handsomely printed, 100+ pp., digest-sized, flat-spined, with a glossy colored card cover. Its "purpose is to provide a vehicle for the **creative expression of the Portuguese immigrant experience."** It has a circulation of 450. $15 for a subscription (double issue). **Sample: $15 postpaid for a double issue, $7.50 for a pre-1982 single issue. Pays 3 copies. Reports in 3 months. Has a 1-year backlog.** Reviews books of poetry "related to the area covered by our journal." **Submit sample poems and query regarding book publication. Photocopy, dot-matrix OK. Pays copies.** The books I have seen much resemble the journal in format.

THE GAY MEN'S PRESS; GAY VERSE (IV-Gay), P.O. Box 247, London N17 9QR, England, phone (081)365-1545, founded 1979, poetry editor Aubrey Walter. "We are the major British publishers of books of gay interest, aiming to reflect and record the extent and variety of our gay culture." **Gay Verse** is a series of poetry publications by various writers. They publish flat-spined paperbacks and want **"poetry that has something to say about the experiences of being gay in the context of wider society. No form, style, length restrictions. No egocentric coming out reflections or self-indulgent**

pornography." They have published poetry by John Gambril Nicholson, Martin Humphries and Steve Cranfield. As a sample the editor selected these lines (poet unidentified):

> I'm into pain, I must be or I guess
> I'd stop handcuffing us in poetry
> Making us M's to serve love's mighty S.
> That's tough on you, true, tougher still on me.

"**Prefer introductory letter in advance.**" Send 4-8 sample poems, bio, and statement of aesthetic or poetic aims. "**We actively seek new and unpublished poets with something of pertinence to say.**" Pays advance ("varies").

GAZELLE PUBLICATIONS (V), 5580 Stanley Dr., Auburn CA 95603, founded 1976, editor Ted Wade, is a publisher for home schools and compatible markets including **books of verse for children. He is not currently considering unsolicited manuscripts. Currently inactive in area of poetry.**

‡GENERATION MAGAZINE (IV-Regional, specialized), Box G, SUNY at Buffalo, Buffalo NY 14214, contact literary editor, is a weekly magazine (during the academic year) using work by **local writers and students, faculty and alumni of SUNY Buffalo. Nothing "overly lengthy."** It is 32 pp., glossy cover. They accept 25% of poetry received. Press run 10,000, distributed to campus community. **Sample for price of postage. Send SASE for guidelines.**

GENERATOR (IV-Form/style); GENERATOR PRESS (V), 8139 Midland Rd., Mentor OH 44060, founded 1987, poetry editor John Byrum, is a yearly magazine "devoted to the presentation of **language poetry and 'concrete' or visual poetic modes." If you don't know what these terms mean, I advise you not to submit without having seen a sample copy.** They have recently published poetry by Susan Bee, Charles Bernstein, Bruce Andrews, Sheila E. Murphy, Stephen Ratcliffe and Ron Silliman. As a sample the editor selected these lines by Tom Beckett:

> Sex and thought are identical — only reversed
> Insulated between witness and wetness
> one never knows what one needs
> Things get done in a major miniseries
> The world is all that takes the place
> of allegorical invasions

Generator is magazine-sized, side-stapled, using b/w graphics, photocopied, with matte card cover. John Byrum says he receives work from 300 poets a year, of whom 10% are accepted. Press run is 200 copies for 20 subscriptions of which 5 are libraries. **Sample: $5 postpaid. Do not submit MSS in May, June, July or August. Send SASE for guidelines. Pays 1 copy. "Visual works should be adaptable to 7 × 8½" page size. Poems should be no longer than 5 pages."** Simultaneous submissions OK, previously published poems used "occasionally." Reports "usually 2-4 weeks." Does not review books of poetry but "will print reviews by others: reviews on visual/concrete and language poetry, and mail art." Generator Press also publishes the **Generator Press chapbook series. Approximately 4 new titles per year. "We do not accept unsolicited manuscripts."** The editor adds, "Worthwhile writers do not need advice and should not heed any but their own."

GEORGIA JOURNAL (IV-Regional), P.O. Box 27, Athens GA 30603-0027, phone (404)354-0463, poetry editor Janice Moore. The *Georgia Journal* is a quarterly magazine, circulation 5,000, covering the state of Georgia. Send SASE for guidelines. Sample: $3. **They use poetry "mostly from Southern writers but not entirely. It should be suitable for the general reader."** Publishes 20-30 poems per year. **Submit maximum of 3-4 poems, maximum length 30 lines. Pays in copies. Reports in 2-3 months.**

UNIVERSITY OF GEORGIA PRESS; CONTEMPORARY POETRY SERIES (II), Terrell Hall, University of Georgia, Athens GA 30602, phone (404)542-2830, press founded 1938, series founded 1980. Series editor Bin Ramke, publishes four collections of poetry per year, two of which are by poets who have **not had a book published,** in simultaneous hardcover and paperback edition. "Writers should query first for guidelines and submission periods. Please enclose SASE." There are no restrictions on the

Market conditions are constantly changing! If you're still using this book and it is 1993 or later, buy the newest edition of Poet's Market at your favorite bookstore or order directly from Writer's Digest Books.

Close-up

Michael Heffernan
Poet

Photo by David Sanders

Look to the blue above the neighborhood
and nothing there gives any help at all.
We have seen the fuschia, and it doesn't work.
Time flows away. The mystery it fills
with our undoing moves aside awhile
and brings a new reality into play
apparently—and here is the main idea:
the wind of time appears to blow through here,
the periwinkle and the may-apple
trembling in wind that is of their own kind,
a gorgeous color of a clarity
that fills our eyes with brightness to see through,
for all the good it does us, and to tell
the morning glory from the glory of God.

Aside from the excellence of his poems, like "Merciless Beauty," printed above, Michael Heffernan is a typical example of that untypical American career, Working Poet. "My current living situation involves a lot of administrative work directing a graduate writing program at the University of Arkansas, which I enjoy a great deal. I also have a very active home life, raising three boys with my beautiful wife of 16 years." Heffernan previously taught at Pittsburg State University in Pittsburg, Kansas, and at Oakland University in his native Michigan at the beginning of his career in the late '60s.

He has three books published by distinguished university presses: **The Cry of Oliver Hardy** and **To the Wreakers of Havoc** (University of Georgia Press, 1978 and 1984) and **The Man at Home** (University of Arkansas Press, 1988). He has also won two NEA Fellowships. But he says, "I sometimes think it's strange not only that I wanted to be a poet in the first place but that I actually became one and have been able to find a living as a poet all these years. It is not a normal line of work. Most of the guys I went to school with are bankers and lawyers and corporate executives. The Jesuits gave me my Vergil, and I thought they meant him as an inspiration to would-be poets. How was I to know they intended the Latin as a discipline for the CEO?"

The Jesuits also gave him an insistent, questioning religious sensibility that informs many of his poems (he describes himself as a good bad-Catholic in his entry in **Contemporary Authors**). Many of his poems are meditative and inquire toward the meaning in seemingly mundane experiences in the house, the yard or the neighborhood. Other poems deal with his ancestral Ireland. He has also been marked by the regions of America where he was born and has worked, though he is no uncomplicated regionalist. "I was born in Detroit in a multi-ethnic, inner-city neighborhood," he says, "where I lived until I left in 1964" for graduate study in Massachusetts. "I left Michigan for good in 1969 and lived for 17 years in rural Kansas, where I taught at a small regional university, followed by my most recent move (and I hope my last) in 1986 to Fayetteville, Arkansas. So I am an urban northerner with very strong ties to the middle and mid-southern part of the country, though my dreams often send me back to the old neighborhood, with its hand-lettered storefront churches, rancid bars and alleys of ailanthus trees, while in the backdrop to many of my poems I find a blue sky broken by catalpas full of blackbirds, in Kansas, or somewhere past the gray-blue mountains where I live now.

"It's a mixed condition for the growth of a poet's mind. Kansas probably never was the way I thought I found it. Other writers there (natives) . . . seemed to breathe a jingoism about combines and windmills that made me hate the regional as a conscious element in poetry, while the old neighborhood in Detroit has fallen into total murderous chaos as a result of crack cocaine. In Arkansas, I've come to feel more and more like a lucky exile, whose home is in his head."

Heffernan wrote his doctoral dissertation on the poet in whose work many find the paradigm of American speech: William Carlos Williams. He says now, "I later grew to dislike him intensely, because of his incoherence, his sloppiness, his passionately misinformed opinions. His hatred of T.S. Eliot—which prompted him to write a poem, in 1941, calling on the Nazis to bomb London and kill Eliot—is utterly appalling. I am glad, though, that I studied Williams closely enough to discover what is deeply mistaken about one of the great models of contemporary poetry. For all of his proclamations about the spoken idiom, his poems haven't the quality of speech at all. They are not to be read aloud. The poems of Yeats and Frost speak to you off the page.

"I wanted to get that duality into my own work. So my work tends to be formal, but I hope not formalist." He denies being a "New Formalist," saying, "There have been important poems written in form throughout the twentieth century, despite the ascendancy of free verse. And the new formalists have a program, an ideology. My only ideology is what works on the page."

Part of his job as a working poet/teacher is helping students find out what works on the page. He says, "I would tell young writers to take good notes, read widely, travel as much as possible, avoid politics [though some of his own poems like "Presidents" and "Fishing Cow Creek During the Grenada Invasion" deal wonderfully with political themes], eat well and get good sleep. Leave drugs and alcohol alone. You don't need them for inspiration, and you write better without them. I suppose I have old-fashioned, probably substandard habits for a writer in the age of the word processor. I write longhand on legal pads or clipboards. I keep extensive notebooks in which poems get germinated. I have several wonderful old manual typewriters—one of which seems to have a facility for composing blank verse, so I often compose longer iambic poems on it."

At the time of this interview, Heffernan was preparing a new volume of poems for publication. "I'm not particularly bothered," he says, "by the small readership for poetry. In a way, I embrace it. The readership for poetry is highly intelligent and well read. I have the opportunity to earn my living while practicing my art and teaching it to students who continue to enroll in poetry classes along with their other coursework in accounting or zoology. In the general culture, poets have seldom gained great fame or remuneration for their work. And that I think is the reality that we need to recognize, and live with, while we continue to do our work. Poetry is not finally about fame or monetary gain. It is about love and joy, about the soul, and what it means to have one."

—Jim Henley

Use the General Index to find the page number of a specific publication or publisher.

type of poetry submitted, but "familiarity with our previously published books in the series may be helpful." **$10 submission fee.**

THE GEORGIA REVIEW (III), The University of Georgia, Athens GA 30602, phone (404)542-3481, founded 1947, editor Stanley W. Lindberg, associate editor Stephen Corey. This is a distinguished, professionally printed, flat-spined quarterly, 200+ pp., 7×10″, glossy card cover. They use 60-70 poems a year, less than one-half percent of those received. Subscription: $12 a year. Circulation: 5,300. **Sample: $4 postpaid. No submissions accepted during June, July and August. Rarely uses translations. Submit 3-5 poems. Pays $2 per line. Reports in about 8 weeks. No simultaneous submissions.** They have recently published poetry by Galway Kinnell, Gerald Stern, Lisel Mueller, Seamus Heaney, Linda Pastan, Albert Goldbarth, Rita Dove and Charles Simic. As a sample, Stephen Corey selected these lines from "Not the Occult" by Stephen Dunn:

> . . . *I love the local and crude*
> *somehow made beautiful, all the traces*
> *of how it got that way erased.*
> *And I love the corporeal body itself,*
> *designed to fail,*
> *and the mind, the helpless mind,*
> *regularly impelled to think about it.*

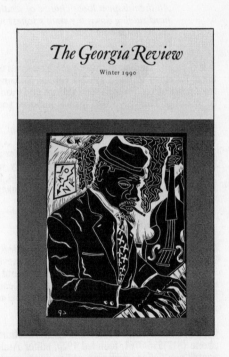

"Each issue of The Georgia Review since 1978 has featured the work of a contemporary artist," says editor Stanley W. Lindberg. This issue carries a portfolio of George Davidson's linocuts from which one of Thelonious Sphere Monk, entitled "t sphere," was selected for the cover "because it combines significant and immediate visual appeal with an inviting complexity of subject matter," Lindberg says. "Although some of our quarterly issues carry an announced thematic focus, this particular issue was one of our more customary eclectic gatherings of some of the best in American art and thought."

THE GETTYSBURG REVIEW (II), Gettysburg College, Gettysburg PA 17325, phone (717)337-6770, founded 1988, editor Peter Stitt, is a multidisciplinary literary quarterly using **any poetry except that which is "badly written."** I have not seen a copy. They accept 2-3% of submissions received. Press run 3,000 for 1,500 subscriptions. **Sample postpaid: $6. Pays $2/line.**

GHOST TOWN QUARTERLY (IV-Themes), P.O. Box 714, Philipsburg MT 59858, phone (406)859-3365, founded 1988, editor Donna B. McLean, is a "quarterly magazine devoted to preserving the **history surrounding ghost towns and abandoned sites** and presenting it in a manner both interesting and informative, using **poetry to provide variety and act as 'fillers.'** Any form; length open, up to approximately 350 words. Pertaining to heritage, history or the 'old West.' Can also support a photograph or historical document by the poem and have a definite value in what it says by historical content. Nothing vulgar or obscene, no modern-day crusaders or poetry having no relation to our themes." They have recently published poetry by Harold K. Armstrong. As a sample I selected the poem, "Wild Roses," published with a photo by the author, Garnet Stephenson:

> *'Tis summer and roses are blooming*
> *Throughout Montana and.*
> *The lovely flowers are cherished*
> *For beauty and fragrance grand.*
>
> *The old, log building does shelter,*
> *And so these beauties grow tall,*
> *Here in the golden sunshine,*
> *Against the old, log wall.*

It is magazine-sized with glossy pages, side-stapled, front and back covers in color. They use 20-30 poems/year, receive about 4 times that many. Press run: 6,000 for 650 subscriptions of which 11 are libraries, 3,800 shelf sales. Subscription: $11.50. **Sample postpaid: $3.50. Send SASE for guidelines. Pays 5¢/word plus 1 copy. Simultaneous submissions OK, first (one-time) rights preferred.**

‡GIANTS PLAY WELL IN THE DRIZZLE (I), 326-A 4th St., Brooklyn NY 11215, founded 1983, editor Martha King, is a poetry newsletter appearing 2-6/year. The editor wants **"energy in breath, sound, intellect, passion in wit, in irreverence, in high seriousness, and oh those dirty dogs."** They have recently published poetry by Robert Creeley, Sheila Murphy, Laurie Price and Tom Clark. As a sample the editor selected these lines from "Found in a Finch Egg" by Brent MacKay:

> *All the misspent loose change of youth*
> *hard raining down the skull's softest rut*
> *seems but a blue folded fin*
> *tucked in a pocket*
> *lost in the wash.*

It is 6-10 pp., stapled at the corner. Press run 600 for 550 on a free mailing list. **Sample postpaid for a 1st class stamp. Pays 3-5 copies. Editor "sometimes" comments on rejections.** "This is a free publication. Friends send stamps and money to keep it going. Please ask for a sample before submitting! The very small format imposes some limits as to length."

‡GINGER HILL (I, II), c/o English Dept., Room 314, Spotts World Cultures Building, Slippery Rock University, Slippery Rock PA 16057, phone (412)738-2043, founded 1963, is an annual literary magazine using **"academic poetry, with preference for excellent free verse, but all forms considered. 27 line limit. No greeting card verse, no sentimentality, no self-serving or didactic verse."** They have recently published poetry by Gay Brewer, William Boggs, Elizabeth R. Curry, Ralph Hills and Frank Treccase. As a sample, I selected these lines from "Monkeys" by Jimmy Ross:

> *Monkeys watch the moonlight*
> *in primeval states of mind.*
> *One drops from the trees*
> *And makes a social climb.*

It is digest-sized, printed in italic type on tinted blue paper with gold-embossed matte card cover, 70 pp. Press run 2,000 distributed free, mostly to the State System of Higher Education in Pennsylvania. **Sample: $1.50 for mailing. Send SASE for guidelines. Pays 2 copies. Submissions must be postmarked on or before Dec. 1 of each year.** The editor says, "The staff now seeks to broaden the base of *GH* and reach a national audience for both established poets and excellent amateurs."

DAVID R. GODINE, PUBLISHER (V), Horticultural Hall, 300 Massachusetts Ave., Boston MA 02115, phone (617)536-0761, founded 1970, editor Audrey Bryant, is a "small publisher of quality fiction, poetry, non-fiction, gardening, calligraphy/typography, art and architecture, children's books and photography. Godine has a wide scope of publishing, and is known for the quality of its production." They publish poetry in simultaneous hardcover/softcover editions. They have recently published books of poetry by Robert Pack, Roger Weingarten and Gail Mazur. As a sample the editor selected these lines by Ben Belitt, from his book **Possessions:**

> *The orange is ceremonious. Its sleep*
> *is Egyptian. Its golden umbilicus*
> *waits in pyramidal light, swath over swath, outwitting*
> *the Caesars. It cannot be ravaged by knives,*

They print 4 books per year, averaging 96 pp. The editor advises, **"We are committed into 1992 and therefore cannot consider new submissions for some time to come."**

‡GOING DOWN SWINGING (I, II), Box 64, Coburg, Melbourne Victoria 3058 Australia, founded 1980, editors Kevin Brophy and Myron Lysenko, is an annual using **"poetry that's tackling contemporary literary, social, political issues. Poetry that's alive now. No racist or sexist poetry."** They have recently published poetry by Grant Caldwell, Bev Roberts, Ania Walwicz, Steven Herrick and Warwick Anderson. As a sample the editor selected these lines from "6 PM" by Gillian Mears:

> *I dial your eight digit number slowly*
> *from a country town call box where*
> *someone has left their keys. I jangle these*
> *and grind my teeth like that old goat we laughed at,*
> *tethered under red frangipani, the day we swam to Susan Island*

It is flat-spined, digest-sized. Press run 800 for 150 subscribers of which 15 are libraries, 500 shelf sales. **Sample postpaid: $6 (A). Reports in 2-4 months. Pays 1 copy and a "small fee." Editors often comment on rejections.** "We are primarily an Australian magazine, but we are open to new and outstanding writing from overseas. Our aim is to publish the work of new, young and generally unknown writers whose work excites and interests us. We review small press books."

‡GOING GAGA (IV-Form), 2630 Robert Walker Pl., Arlington VA 22207, phone (703)527-6032, founded 1988, editor Gareth Branwyn, is a quarterly "free-form exploration of experimental art, writing, culture and fringe ideas. We do review books, chapbooks and magazines." He wants **"experimental, concrete, verbo-visual, free form" poetry.** They have recently published poetry by Geof Huth, Ron Buck and Philip Hughes. As a sample the editor selected these lines from "Yesterday" by Paul Weinman:

> *I said to myself—Don't walk into*
> *that Super M wearing nothing*
> *but boots.*
>   *But, I did.*

I have not seen an issue, but the editor describes it as "half-legal, 38 pp., offset, saddle-stapled, original graphics and collage." Press run 350 for 175 subscribers of which 6 are libraries, 60 shelf sales. Subscription: $12/3 issues. **Sample postpaid: $4. Send SASE for guidelines. Pays 1 copy. "I only respond if I'm going to use immediately, otherwise I send a copy of the issue on publication."**

GOLDEN ISIS MAGAZINE; GOLDEN ISIS PRESS; POEM OF THE YEAR CONTEST (IV-Mystical/ Occult), 23233 Saticoy St., Bldg. 105, Box 137, West Hills CA 91304, founded 1980, editor Gerina Dunwich. "**Golden Isis** is a mystical literary magazine of poetry, magick, pagan/Egyptian artwork, Wiccan news, occult fiction, letters, book reviews and classified ads. **Poetry: Occult, Egyptian, cosmic, euphonic and Goddess-inspired poems, mystical haiku and magickal chants are published. "We are also interested in New Age spiritual poetry, astrological verses and poems dealing with peace, love and ecology. All styles considered; under 60 lines preferred. We do not want to see religious, pornographic, Satanic, sexist or racist material."** Recently published poets include Lady Jenny, Fletcher DeWolf, Vashti, and Jane Wallace Weigel. As a sample the editor chose "Ode to the Crone" by Gina Landers:

> *Queen of darkness, death and birth,*
> *Olden One with power of night,*
> *Casting magick to the Earth*
> *In shadows on a secret flight.*

The magazine is digest-sized, 25-30 pp., desktop publishing, saddle-stapled with paper cover. International circulation is 5,000. Single copy $3.95 postpaid, subscription $15/year. **Payment: $10 and 1 free contributor's copy. Reports within 2-3 weeks. Occasionally comments on rejected material. Submit 1 poem/page, typed single-spaced, name and address on upper left corner and the number of lines on upper right corner; photocopied, previously published and simultaneous submissions OK. All rights revert back to author upon publication.** Golden Isis Press **is now accepting MSS for chapbook publication. Terms and payment negotiable. $5 reading fee for chapbook submissions required. Please make checks payable to Golden Isis.** The magazine sponsors an annual "Poem of the Year" contest that offers cash prizes. Entry fee: $5/poem, deadline December 1, no limit on number of poems entered. Poems should be up to 60 lines, any form, with author's name and address on upper left corner of each page. Free guidelines and contest rules for SASE.

‡GOLDEN QUILL PRESS (I), RFD #1, Avery Rd., Francestown NH 03043, publishes a great deal of poetry on a subsidy basis "depending on past sales record." **Pays maximum 10% royalties. Submit complete MS. Photocopy, dot-matrix OK. Reports in 2 weeks on queries, 1 month on submissions.**

GOOD HOUSEKEEPING (II, IV-Humor, women), Hearst Corp., 959 8th Ave., New York NY 10019, poetry editor Andrea Krantz, circulation 5,000,000, **women's magazine, uses up to 3 poems per issue for which they pay $10 per line. Light verse and traditional. Submit up to 10 poems; maximum length: 25 lines."** They no longer return or critique manuscripts. "We look for poems of emotional interest to American women. Must be wholesome, clever, upbeat or poignant. Poets whose work interests us will hear from us within 4-5 weeks of receipt of a manuscript. We ask that poets send inexpensive copies of their work, and do *not* enclose SASE's or postage. We do accept multiple submissions." Send seasonal material 6-12 months before publication date. Submit short humorous verses, anecdotes and 'daffinition' to "Light Housekeeping" editor, Rosemary Leonard. Enclose SASE because they do return these MSS. Pays $25 for 2-4 lines; $50, 5-8 lines. Usually overstocked.

GOOSE LANE EDITIONS (III, IV-Regional), 248 Brunswick St., Fredericton, New Brunswick E3B 1G9 Canada, phone (506)450-4251, FAX (506)459-4991, managing editor S. Alexander, founded 1956, a small press publishing Canadian fiction, poetry and literary history. **Writers should be advised that Goose Lane considers manuscripts by Canadian poets only.** They receive approximately 400 MSS per year, 10-15 books published yearly, 3-4 of these being poetry collections. Writers recently published include Dorothy Roberts, Douglas Lochhead and Claire Harris. The following poem, "The purpose of cats", is from **Night Flying** (1990) by Roger Nash:

> When the sun isn't house-trained,
> it leaves a yellow puddle
> in each room. Cats
> sit in them, and accept the blame.

"Unsolicited Canadian MSS considered if individual poems have been previously published in literary journals. SASE essential (IRCs or Canadian postage stamps only). Reports in 10-12 weeks. Authors receive royalty of 10% of retail sale price on all copies sold. Copies available to author at 40% discount."

‡**THE GOPHERWOOD REVIEW (II)**, Box 58784, Houston TX 77258, founded 1990, editors Sandra Reiff and Sharron Crowson, appears twice a year. **They solicit most material, but "accept** *some* **unsolicited poetry. Experimental, surreal and imagistic, only very high quality; it must leave us speechless, breathless, and/or changed. Nothing cliched, sentimental, bland, overwritten, underdone, or voiceless."** They have recently published poetry by B.Z. Niditch, Arthur Winfield Knight, Philip Dacey and Janet McCann. As a sample the editor selected these lines from "Eleventh Hour" by Jeff Vetock:

> At long last the quartz
> has given way to winter.
> Thin fisssure in the ice
> where the hand has struck.

It is magazine-sized, 44 pp., desktop and laser printed, with matte card cover. Press run 200 for 100 subscribers. Subscription: $9. Sample: **$3.50 postpaid. Pays 1 copy. Send SASE for guidelines.** "We like interesting cover letters and bio, try to respond within 3 weeks, have 6-month backlog, often comment on rejections." Reviews books of poetry. The editors advise, "Good poetry does not come easily; revise and rewrite. Compare your work with those you admire. If it lacks something—power, impact, a voice—don't submit it until it's your best effort. There is a great deal of lukewarm poetry out there. Don't settle for that. Make it catch fire." They are planning an annual contest. Send SASE for rules.

GOSPEL PUBLISHING HOUSE; PENTECOSTAL EVANGEL; LIVE; HI-CALL; JUNIOR TRAILS (IV-Religious, children/teens), The General Council of the Assemblies of God, 1445 Boonville, Springfield MO 65802, phone (417)862-2781, FAX (417)862-8558, editor Richard G. Champion. *Pentecostal Evangel* is a weekly magazine containing **inspirational articles and news of the Assemblies of God for members of the Assemblies and other Pentecostal and charismatic Christians,** circulation 280,000. **Religious and inspirational poetry.** "All poems submitted to us should be related to religious life. We are Protestant, evangelical, Pentecostal, and any doctrines or practices portrayed should be in harmony with the official position of our denomination (Assemblies of God)." **Free sample copy and writer's guidelines. Submit maximum 3 poems. Submit seasonal/holiday material 6 months in advance.** Computer printout submissions acceptable, prefers letter-quality. Reports in 3 months. **Pays 50-75¢/line on acceptance.** *Live*, is a weekly for adults in Assemblies of God Sunday schools, circulation 200,000. **Traditional free and blank verse, 12-20 lines.** "Please do not send large numbers of poems at one time." Submit seasonal material 1 year in advance; do not mention Santa Claus, Halloween or Easter bunnies. Computer printout submissions acceptable. Free sample copy and writer's guidelines for 7 × 10 SASE and 40¢ postage. Letters without SASE will not be answered. **Pays 25¢/line on acceptance.** *Hi-Call* is a weekly magazine of **Christian fiction and articles for teenagers,** 12-17, circulation 78,000. **Free verse, light verse and traditional, 10-40 lines. Buys 50 poems per year.** Submit seasonal/holiday material 18 months in advance. **Simultaneous, photocopied and previously published submissions OK** if typed, double-spaced, on 8 × 11 paper. Computer printout submissions acceptable; prefers letter-quality. Reports in 6 weeks. Sample copy for 8 × 11 SAE and 2 first class stamps; writer's guidelines for SAE. **Pays 25¢/line first rights, 15¢/line second rights. Minimum of $2.50 and $5 on acceptance.** *Junior Trails* is a weekly tabloid covering **religious fiction and biographical, historical and scientific articles with a spiritual emphasis for boys and girls ages 10-11,** circulation 75,000. **Free verse and light**

verse. Buys 6-8 poems per year. Submit seasonal/holiday material 15 months in advance. **Simultaneous and previously published submissions OK. Computer printout submissions acceptable, prefers letter-quality. Reports in 3-6 weeks. Sample copy and writer's guidelines for 9 × 12 SAE and 2 first class stamps. Pays 20¢/line on acceptance.** "We like poems showing contemporary children positively facing today's world."

GOTTA WRITE NETWORK LITMAG; MAREN PUBLICATIONS (I, IV-Science fiction/Fantasy, subscription), 612 Cobblestone Circle, Glenview IL 60025, founded 1988, editor/publisher Denise Fleischer, is a desktop published quarterly saddle-stapled, 60-page magazine featuring "general poetry, articles, short stories and market listings. *GWN* now spans 39 states, Canada and England. Half of the magazine is devoted to science fiction and fantasy in a section called 'Sci-Fi Fan Galleria.' **"I'm open to well-crafted, clear poetry that doesn't have to be dissected to understand its message. Poetry that leaves the reader with a special feeling. Can be of any genre. No sexually graphic material, obscenities, or lengthy poetry."** She has published poetry by H.R. Felgenhauer, John Grey, C.R. Riehle, Anne Simon and C. David Hay. As a sample, the editor selected these lines from "i saw isolde once" by Charles Rampp:

> *hidden more fully than warblers*
> *in forest's morning woods, quiet*
> *as mushroom fairy dance ring*
> *in the churchyard, this love of ours.*

"*Gotta Write Network* subscribers receive more than a quarterly magazine. In subscribing, they become part of a support group of both beginners and established poets. I offer critiques at request, will even retype a poem to point out spelling errors and suggest other appropriate markets. Members are from all walks of life: housewives, religious persons, seniors, nursing home residents. Five reside in prisons." Press run: 200 for 70 subscribers. "I'm striving to give beginners a positive starting point and to encourage them to venture beyond rejection slips and writer's block. Publication can be a reality if you have determination and talent. There are over a thousand U.S. litmags waiting for submissions. So what are you waiting for?" Subscription: $15. **Sample, postpaid: $3.75.** The editor says, **"I encourage poets to purchase a sample copy before subscribing. This way they can see just how varied the information is." Pays 1 copy. Reports in a few days to a few weeks. Include a cover letter and SASE. If there's an entry fee, pay it up front."** Reviews books of poetry; "prefer that a b&w photo of book accompany the submission." Maren Publications has published 1 chapbook, **Poetry Cafe.** She adds, "Write the way you feel the words. Don't let others mold you into an established poet's style. Poetry is about personal imagery. Write clearly or ask your family for a typewriter for Christmas. Most of all, love what you do."

GRAHAM HOUSE REVIEW (II, IV-Translations), Box 5000, Colgate University, Hamilton NY 13346, phone (315)824-1000, ext. 262, founded 1976, poetry editors Peter Balakian and Bruce Smith, appears yearly. "We publish contemporary poetry, poetry in translation, essays and interviews. **No preferences for styles or schools, just good poetry.**" They have published poems by Seamus Heaney, Marilyn Hacker, Maxine Kumin, Michael Harper and Carolyn Forché. The editor selected this sample from Derek Walcott's "Winter Lamps":

> *Are they earlier, these*
> *winter dark afternoons,*
> *whose lamps, like croziers*
> *ask the same questions*

GHR is digest-sized, flat-spined, 120 pp., professionally printed on heavy stock, matte color card cover with logo, using 100 pp. of poetry in each issue, circulation 500, with 300 subscriptions of which 50 are libraries. They receive about 2,000 freelance submissions of poetry per year, use 20-50. **Sample: $7.50 postpaid. No photocopies. Reports in 2 months or less, pays 2 copies.**

GRAIN; SHORT GRAIN CONTEST (II), Box 1154, Regina, Saskatchewan S4P 3B4 Canada, phone (306)757-6310, is a literary quarterly. "*Grain* strives for artistic excellence, seeks material that is accessible as well as challenging to our readers. Ideally, a *Grain* **poem should be well-crafted, imaginatively stimulating, distinctly original.**" They have recently published poems by Su Croll and Anne Marriott. It is a digest-sized format, professionally printed with chrome-coated cover, 112 pp., circulation 1,000+, with 650 subscriptions of which 90 are libraries. Subscription: $15 (Canadian). They receive about 400 freelance submissions of poetry per year, use 60-100 poems per year. The editor selected as a sample the opening of "The Children" by Patrick Lane:

> *The children are singing.*
> *Hear them as they rise out of the deep hollows,*
> *the tangles of wildwood and wandering vines.*
> *They are lifting from the shadows*

> *where the black creek water flows*
> *over mud and stones. They have left behind*
> *the green whip of a snake*
> *thrown like a thin necklace into the trees ...*

Sample: $5 plus IRC (or 80¢ Canadian postage). They want "no poetry that has no substance." Submit maximum of 6 poems. Photocopies OK. Prefers letter-quality to dot-matrix. Pays $30+ per poem. Send SASE for guidelines. Reports in 3-4 months. The editor comments, "Only work of the highest literary quality is accepted. Read several back issues." *Grain* holds an annual Short Grain Contest. Entries are either prose poems (a lyric poem written as a prose paragraph or paragraphs in 500 words or less) or post-card stories (also 500 words or less). Prizes in each category, $250 first, $150 second, $100 third and honorable mentions. All winners and honorable mentions receive regular payment for publication in *Grain*. Entry fee of $15 (Canadian) includes a one-year subscription. Additional entries are $5 each. Entries are normally accepted between January 1 and April 30.

‡GRAND UNION; WHITE LION PRESS; NY CENTER FOR ART AND AWARENESS (II, IV-Regional), 225 E. 5th St., #4D, New York NY 10003, assistant editor Neil Hackman. *GU* appears 3/year. White Lion Press publishes 1 paperback/year. The New York Center for Art and Awareness "is a non-profit organization that seeks to promote art which heals, uplifts, inspires, transforms, or informs. It sponsors a poetry reading series and allocates funds on a small scale to worthy artistic endeavors." **They do not want "greeting card poetry, untyped, confessional or 'dark' (self-pitying) poetry. We like poetry that celebrates, sings, opens our eyes, hearts, and minds. We like to publish New York writers because there are so many good writers here that it is hard for many of them to get any kind of recognition whatsoever, but we also publish writers from anywhere."** They have recently published poetry by Anne Waldman, Maureen Owen and D.S. Sulaitis. As a sample the editor selected these lines by Ravi Singh:

> *I am listening to rivers*
> *of opalescent earth.*
> *Some are winding*
> *Through the snow night*
> *Into arms of*
> *Burning helicopters*
> *Of dawn.*
> *I have given myself over*
> *To white rapids;*
> *Ambidexterous epiphany*
> *Of the sands.*

GU is digest-sized, 55 pp., saddle-stapled, professionally printed with glossy card cover with b/w illustration. **Sample postpaid: $4. Pays copies ("usually, within reason, as many as they want").**

GRASSLANDS REVIEW (I, II), NT Box 13706, Denton TX 76203, phone (817)565-2050, founded 1989, editor Laura B. Kennelly, is a magazine **"to encourage beginning writers and to give creative writing class experience in editing essays, fiction, poetry, using any type; shorter poems stand best chance."** Poets published: LaDelia Leech-Tomlinson, James Hoggard, José García, Carol Schneck, Peter Brett, Adriana Craciun, Gary Glazner, Tony D'Arpino, Laurie Suzanne Lessen, Linda McFerrin and Edward Mycue. As a sample the editor selected these lines by Darrel g.h. Schramm:

> *Under the olive boughs*
> *cattle egrets, bored*
> *   with their white-as-snow,*
> *stand beside their Holstein cows*
> *and wait for their own*
> *   black to grow.*

The copy I have seen is 94 pp., professionally printed, digest-sized, photocopied, saddle-stapled with soft cover. **They accept 10-15 of 200 submissions received. Press run 200. Subscription: $4/ year (2 issues). Sample postpaid: $1. Pays 2 copies. Submit only during October and March. Reports in 8-10 weeks. Editor comments on submissions "sometimes."**

GRAYWOLF PRESS (V), Suite 203, 2402 University Ave., Saint Paul MN 55114, phone (612)641-0077, founded 1975, poetry editor Scott Walker, **does not read unsolicited MSS.** They have published poetry by Tess Gallagher, Linda Gregg, Jack Gilbert, Chris Gilbert and William Stafford. **Pays 7½-10% royalties, 10 author's copies, advance negotiated.**

GREAT ELM PRESS; UPRIVER CHAPBOOK SERIES (V), 1205 Co. Rt. 60, Rexville NY 14877, phone (607)225-4592, founded 1984, editor/publisher Walt Franklin. Great Elm is a small press dedicated to the writing of rural affairs, to bio-regionalism, to the universal qualities found in local life. The press produces chapbooks and anthologies in limited editions. **"We are currently not accepting unsolicited submissions in order to complete other necessary projects."** They have recently published poetry by Jared Carter, William Vernon and Patricia Shirley. As a sample the editor selected these lines from "The Red Efts" by K.W. Jaynes:

> *They floated there, euphorically outstretched.*
> *And I was with them till an alder leaf*
> *disturbed the stream and bent me back to life.*

GREAT LAKES POETRY PRESS; POETICS (I, IV-Anthology), Box 56703, Harwood Heights IL 60656, phone (312)631-3697, founded 1987, poetry editor Chuck Kramer, publishes the annual **American Anthology of Contemporary Poetry.** "This book provides new poets with the opportunity to publish their work and is **open to poetry that deals with almost any topic. We do not, however, publish poems that are obscene, violent or racist."** The anthology is published each December and **submissions may be sent during May and June.** The anthology sells for $19.99 plus $3 postage and handling. It is digest-sized, professionally printed, two poems to a page, 100+ pp., flat-spined with varnished card cover. **"You do not have to purchase a copy to be included."** Sample anthology: $4. Great Lakes also publishes books that are organized around specific themes or topics. For instance, in 1991 they published a book on drug and alcohol addiction. **"Manuscripts for these books are solicited through our newsletter,** *Poetics*, **advertising and personal contact. To learn the topic of our current project, send us a SASE and request that information. To receive free copies of future issues of** *Poetics*, **send your name and address."** They also publish **single author collections** of poetry on both a **commercial and subsidy basis. "For more information, let us know what you have in mind (include a SASE) and we'll get back to you."** As a sample the editor selected these lines from "Ecuador" by Mary Hiles:

> *Andean songs, Andean songs*
> *whispered words, knife kisses*
> *bare heels pounding, pounding*
> *muted sounds on red, dusty earth*
> *swift fingers on Spanish guitar and Indian pipe*
> *sing of lithe feet on vine-slung bridges, green caverns*
> *and high airless places.*

‡GREAT PLAINS CANAL AND AVALON DISPATCH (I, IV-Nature/Rural/Ecology), 212 W. First St., San Angelo TX 76903, phone (915)655-3792, founded 1963 as *Cyclotron*; name change to *Cyclo*Flame* in 1966; to Annual in 1970; hiatus from 1976-1986. *Avalon Dispatch* was a newsletter from 1967; added *Great Plains Canal* in 1985. Editor Vernon Payne describes the publication as a "literary newsletter, emphasis on conservation of resources by poetry and letters; nonfiction." He wants **poetry of "timely significance . . . does not want light verse, trite or trivial preachments, work lacking in an elementary knowledge of poetry."** He has published poetry by Lilith Lorraine, Archibald Henderson, Walter Kidd, Alice Makenzie Swaim, Ed Falkowski, Sandra Fowler, Goldie L. Morales, Jack Murphy and Stella Tremble. As a sample he selected these lines from sonnet-series "To Be a Poet" by Lucia Clark Markham:

> *We freed the pinions of poetic powers,*
> *A rich and rhythmic cataract of words*
> *And rose-hued thoughts in effervescent hordes*
> *Came lilting through the evening's perfume showers*

The editor advocates a canal to carry excess water from the Yukon to the Rio Grande, or Antarctic icebergs drawn to Australia for its Outback, or great bladders of water drawn from the Amazon River to Mediterranean coasts. "Armies of the world now engaged in destructive warfare could use their efforts infinitely better to, with one accord, cease from destruction and bring a navigable canal from Siberia, with the melt of its icecaps, to the deserts of USSR, Turkey, Iraq, Iran, Saudi Arabia, Jordan, and the lands of North Africa." The newsletter is magazine-sized, photocopied from typescript on bond paper, 10 pp. side-stapled. Press run is 500. Subscription is $10 a year. **Sample: $1 postpaid. Pays $1 "token plus 2 (or more) copies. Reports in "matter of weeks."** Published poems OK if credit line included. "Cuss or dirty words should be abandoned for more accurate and factual adjectives, etc." Reviews books of poetry.

GREAT RIVER REVIEW (II), 211 W. 7th, Winona MN 55987, founded 1977, poetry editor Orval Lund, is published "three times every two years." They want **"high quality contemporary poetry that uses image as the basis for expression." Suggested submission: 4-6 poems."** They have published poetry by Jack Myers, Thom Tammaro, Margaret Hasse, Michael Dennis Browne, Pam Harrison and Tom Hennen. *GRR* is elaborately printed, $6 \times 8''$, with a featured poet per issue. They use about 50 poems per issue, receive about 500, use 5-10%. Press run of 750 goes to 300-400 subscriptions of which 30-50 are libraries, and have 200-300 newsstand or bookstore sales. Single copy: $4.50, subscription $9 for two issues. **Sample: $4.50 postpaid. Pays 2 copies. Reports on submissions in 4-10 weeks, 4-12 months between acceptance and publication. Simultaneous submissions discouraged. Editor "sometimes" comments on rejections.** Reviews books of poetry.

GREEN FUSE (II, IV-Political, ecology), 3365 Holland Dr., Santa Rosa CA 95404, phone (707)544-8303, founded 1984, editor Brian Boldt, is published in April and October. **"We are looking for work that celebrates earth's beauty, the harmony in diversity and poetic sanity in an age of prosaic madness. Simultaneous submissions are OK, but we much prefer unpublished work, unless it is the perfect** *Green Fuse* **poem. We seek contemporary free verse; sentimental and religious work, poems submitted without an SASE and work stinking of nicotine will be folded into origami."** They have recently published poetry by Antler, Elliot Richman, Maureen Hurley and Bryan Dietrich. As a sample the editor selected the following lines by Paul Willis:

> *Is there something about*
> *a rainwashed Padre's shooting star*
> *hung new and purple above the earth*
> *about yucca spears and the*
> *aching flourish of crimson paintbrush*
> *that suggests to our inmost minds*
> *the truth?*

Green Fuse is 6×9″, 48 pp., offset, perfect-bound, with black and white illustrations on the cover and throughout. Press run is 400 for subscriptions, shelf and reading sales. Subscriptions: $9 for two issues, $13 for three. **Sample postpaid: $4.50. Do not submit MSS February-March and August-September. Send SASE for guidelines. Pays 1 copy, more to featured poets. Editor "sometimes" comments on rejections and reports within 12 weeks.** Of 1300 poems received a year, he accepts about 80.

‡GREEN ZERO (I), P.O. Box 3104, Shiremanstown PA 17011, founded 1990, editor Jeff Vetock, a quarterly magazine. **"I am looking for poetry with roots in objectivism — prefer relatively short, imagistic or surreal poems which engage the mind on many levels. I generally dislike strictly narrative poetry. Innovation encouraged! Please, no sentimental, needlessly obscure, or 'tragically hip' Romantic poetry!"** They have recently published poetry by Joseph Farley and Pam Rehm. As a sample the editor selected these lines from "William Carlos Williams" by Ed Webster:

> *All that time attending*
> *a remarkable suchness,*
> *singing: This is it.*
> *This is the sound of my vigor.*

It is 8-12 pp. photocopied from typescript and side-stapled. "At this point I'm accepting about 20% of the submissions I receive." Press run 130 copies ("available to anyone who supplies postage.") **Sample: 55¢ stamp. Pays 2 copies. Send SASE for guidelines. Reply within 2-4 weeks. Editor usually comments on work.** "Please remember to send error-free copy whenever you submit material! Careless MSS hurt much more than they help!"

THE GREENFIELD REVIEW PRESS (V); THE GREENFIELD REVIEW LITERARY CENTER; ITHACA HOUSE (V), P.O. Box 308, Greenfield Center NY 12833, phone (518)584-1728, founded 1971, poetry editor Joseph Bruchac III, all from a nest of literary activity, The Greenfield Review Literary Center, which publishes a regular newsletter, has a poetry library and offers workshops and lectures in a former gas station. **Send large SASE with 2 oz. postage for a handout on "marketing tips" and sample copy of the newsletter.** Joe Bruchac advises, "Buy books of poetry and literary magazines. The community you support is your own. Don't be in too much of a hurry to be published." Ithaca House, an imprint acquired in 1986, has been one of the longest-going and highly respected small press publishers in the country since 1970, and will continue under Greenfield Review Press. **Neither is accepting unsolicited MSS until at least 1993 because of their involvement in several large projects.**

GREENHOUSE REVIEW PRESS (V), 3965 Bonny Doon Rd., Santa Cruz CA 95060, founded 1975, publishes a series of poetry chapbooks and broadsides."**No unsolicited MSS will be accepted until 1993 due to backlog of titles in production.**" Send SASE for catalog to buy samples. Pays copies.

GREEN'S MAGAZINE (I, II); CLOVER PRESS (V), P.O. Box 3236, Regina, Saskatchewan S4P 3H1 Canada, founded 1972, editor David Green. *Green's Magazine* is a literary quarterly with a balanced diet of short fiction and poetry; Clover Press publishes chapbooks. They publish **"free/blank verse examining emotions or situations." They do not want greeting card jingles or pale imitations of the masters.** Some poets published are Sheila Murphy, Mary Balazs, Robert L. Tener, David Chorlton, Helene Scheffler-Mason and Fritz Hamilton. As a sample the following lines are from "Signals" by Winifred Scheffler:

The counsellor talks in clipped and rapid tones,
voice rising, and then abruptly still,
And there you are, disconcerted, the space to
respond thrust suddenly under your nose.

The magazine is digest-sized, 100 pp., with line drawings. A sample chapbook is also digest-sized, 60 pp., typeset on buff stock with line drawings, matte card cover, saddle-stapled. Circulation is 400, subscriptions $12. **Sample: $4 postpaid. Guidelines available for SASE. (International Reply Coupons for U.S. queries and/or MSS). Payment is 2 free copies. Submissions are reported on in 8 weeks, publication is usually in 3 months. The editor prefers typescript, complete originals.** Occasionally reviews books of poetry. **Freelance submissions are accepted for the magazine but not for books; query first on latter. Comments are usually provided on rejected MSS.** "Would-be contributors are urged to study the magazine first."

THE GREENSBORO REVIEW; GREENSBORO REVIEW LITERARY AWARD; AMON LINER POETRY AWARD (II), English Dept., University of North Carolina, Greensboro NC 27412, phone (919)334-5459, founded 1966, editor Jim Clark. *TGR* appears twice yearly and has published poetry by Mary Kratt, Starkey S. Flythe, Jr., Kelly Cherry and Bobby Caudle Rogers. As a sample the editor selected these lines from "Cats Mating" by Susan O'Dell Underwood:

Yawn of scalping sound
arches brawling, vaults caterwauling,
opening wide the mouth of dark,
stretches bristling hisses of rash skirmish
into the belly-hide of night.

The digest-sized, 120+ pp., flat-spined magazine, colored matte cover, professional printing, uses about 25 pp. of poetry in each issue. Circulation 500 for 300 subscriptions of which 100 are libraries. Uses about 3% of the 1,200 submissions received each year. **Sample postpaid: $4. Submissions accepted August 15-February 15 (deadlines for the 2 issues: September 15 and February 15). No simultaneous submissions, reports in 2-4 months, pays 3 copies.** They offer the Amon Liner Poetry Award and a $250 Greensboro Review Literary Award in poetry and in fiction each year.

GROVE WEIDENFELD, Div. of Grove Press Inc., 841 Broadway, 4th Flr., New York NY 10003-4793. Declined listing.

GRUE MAGAZINE (IV-Horror), Box 370, New York NY 10108, founded 1985, editor Peggy Nadramia, a horror fiction magazine "with emphasis on the experimental, offbeat, rude." The editor wants **"Poems of any length including prose-poems, with macabre imagery and themes. Not interested in Poe rip-offs, (although we'll look at rhyming poems if subject is weird enough), 'straight' vampire, ghost or werewolf poems."** She has recently published poems by t. Winter-Damon, W. Gregory Stewart, Steve Sneyd, Robert Frazier, G. Sutton Breiding and Bruce Boston. As a sample she selected these lines from "Angels of Anarchy" by Andrew Darlington:

in the red light from the dashboard
my mistress hands me the knife,
she wears a carnelian in her fly,
her needle extracts the moth from my tongue,
where its eggs are laid beneath my skin.
The moon sheds blood over the Headrow
where I dissolve in double shadows.

The magazine is digest-sized, 96 pp., offset, with a glossy b/w cover, "sharp" graphics, and "a centerfold that is unique." It appears 3 times a year and has a circulation of 3,000, of which 500 are subscriptions and 1,000 are newsstand sales. Price per issue is $4.50, subscription $13/year. **Sample: $4.50 postpaid; guidelines are available for SASE. Poets receive 2 copies plus $5 per poem upon publication to a maximum of $5 per issue. They should submit up to 5 poems at a time, photocopied or dot-matrix MSS are OK. Submissions are reported on in 3 to 6 months and time to publication is 12 to 18 months.** The editor usually provides criticism of rejected MSS. Her advice is: "We like poems that go for the throat, with strong, visceral controlling images. We're also interested in poems that comment upon, or challenge the conventions of, the horror genre itself."

GUERNICA EDITIONS INC.; ESSENTIAL POET SERIES, PROSE SERIES, DRAMA SERIES; INTERNATIONAL WRITERS (IV-Regional, translations), Box 633 Station NDG, Montreal, Quebec H4A 3R1 Canada, founded 1978, poetry editor Antonio D'Alfonso. "We wish to bring together the **different and often divergent voices that exist in Canada. We are interested in translations. We are mostly interested right now in prose poetry and essays.**" They have recently published poetry by Paol Keineg

(France, USA), Roland Morisseau (Haiti), Bert Schierbeek (Holland), Nadine Ltaif (Lebanon), Dacia Maraini (Italy), Dorothy Livesay (Canada) and Claude Péloquin (Quebec). **Query with 1-2 pp. of samples. Send SASE or IRC (Canadian stamps only) for catalog to buy samples.** The editor comments, "We enjoy reading what other people are doing, to go beyond our country and study and learn to love what you originally thought little of."

‡GUILD PRESS; FULL CIRCLE SERIES (I, IV-Ethnic), P.O. Box 22583, Robbinsdale MN 55422, founded 1978, senior editor Leon Knight: **"The Leading Publisher of Minority Authors in Minnesota." wants poems to 40 line max., nothing sexually graphic.** They have recently published poetry by Gary Smith, Bernard U. Finney, Jr. and Nancy Ellen Williams (Big Mama). As a sample the editor selected these lines (poet unidentified):

> *I thought poetry*
> *made a difference*
> *. . .*
> *But photography*
> *doesn't alter sunsets:*
> *poetry does not*
> *restrain the wind*

The Full Circle Series are **annual anthologies of 35-50 poets. Individual collections are published "by invitation only" to poets who have appeared in the "open-invitation" anthologies. Send SASE for guidelines. Pays copies.**

GULF STREAM MAGAZINE (II), English Dept., Florida International University North Miami Campus, N. Miami FL 33181, phone (305)940-5599, founded 1989, editor Lynne Barrett, associate editors Pam Gross and Virginia Oesterle, is the biannual literary magazine associated with the creative writing program at FIU. They want **"poetry of any style and subject matter as long as it is of high literary quality."** They have recently published poetry by Gerald Costanzo, Judith Berke and Mike Carson. As a sample, Pam Gross selected these lines from "Those People Once" by Alan Peterson:

> *They stand looking at each other from three feet away.*
> *A whole galaxy could fit now in that space,*
> *though there is nothing there but maddening black minutes*
> *folding over each other so loud they can both hear*
> *a shuffling like cards, all clubs and spades.*

The handsome magazine is digest-sized, flat-spined, 90+ pp. on quality stock with glossy card cover. They accept less than 10% of poetry received. Press run: 750. Subscription: $7.50. **Sample postpaid: $4. Send SASE for guidelines. Pays 2 free subscriptions. Submit no more than 5 poems. Do not submit MSS during summer. Reports in 6-8 weeks. No simultaneous submissions. Editor comments on submissions "if we feel we can be helpful."**

‡GUYASUTA PUBLISHER (I), (formerly Tiffany and Shore Publishers); Suite 200, 1687 Washington Rd., Pittsburgh PA 15228, phone (412)831-1731, founded 1988, owner Cynthia Sterling. **"Guyasuta offers both straight and co-op publishing. We prefer to publish chapbooks and collections of poetry; however, we are considering self-help, how-to, and quality short fiction. Our publishing needs in the children's category have been filled through 1992. We supply original artwork for each collection of poetry by such artists as Helen Kita, Sally Stormon and Sue Zak. We are expanding our line of poetry to 100 titles a year." They accept MSS throughout the year.** They have a 67-acre farm that is being developed to offer housing, workshops and seminars for poets, writers and artists. As a sample, Cynthia Sterling selected these lines from Diana Rubin's poem "Let Them Eat Cake" from her book **Spirits In Exile:**

> *Yet, the homeless woman interjected and still persisted.*
> *"Cake, please, cake."*
> *As an unending saga unfolded before*
> *my eyes in gruesome repetition:*
> *Those who haven't bread are often forced to eat cake.*

They will consider simultaneous submissions and unsolicited manuscripts of 25-60 poems. For further information send SASE for catalog and guidelines. Sample: $5.95 (includes shipping).

GYPSY (II); VERGIN' PRESS (V), % Belinda Subraman and S. Ramnath, 10708 Gay Brewer, El Paso TX 79935, founded 1984 (in Germany), general editor Belinda Subraman, publishes poetry, fiction, interviews, articles, artwork and reviews. She wants **poetry that is "striking, moving, but not sentimental, any style, any subject-matter."** They have published poetry by Peter Wild, Robert Cooperman, Albert Huffstickler, Jennifer Olds and Charles Webb. As a sample, she selected these lines by Peter Bakowski:

Blood still runs in my veins
and I can look out the window
seeking ants and nightingales
not pain.

Gypsy appears twice a year, with subscribers and contributors from the U.S., Canada, England, Europe, and other foreign countries. It is magazine-sized, offset, usually a hard spine, around 56-90 pages. Circulation is 1,000 to 300 subscriptions of which 40 are libraries, about 20 shelf sales. Subscription: $12 a year; per issue: $7. **Sample: $6 postpaid. Pays 1 copy. Reports in 1-3 months.** Reviews books of poetry. She publishes **2-3 chapbooks per year under the Vergin' Press imprint but at present is not accepting unsolicited submissions for these.** New writers establish themselves with her by acceptance in *Gypsy*. **She sometimes comments on rejections.** "I'm looking for material for an anthology tentatively titled *Of Global Concern*. Would like to see anthing related to the Middle Eastern Crisis/War and saving the environment." Belinda Subraman says, "This is not a place for beginners. I'm looking for the best in all genres. Although I don't have anything against work of total self-absorption (guess I write some of that myself), I am just about fed up with it. I'd like to see work with a more universal appeal, a searching to connect, an understanding or a trying to understand other peoples in the universe."

HAIGHT ASHBURY LITERARY JOURNAL (II, IV-Social issues), 558 Joost Ave., San Francisco CA 94127, phone (415)221-2017, founded 1979-1980, editors Lena Diethelm, Joanne Hotchkiss, Alice Rogoff and Will Walker, is a newsprint tabloid that appears 1-3 times a year. They use **"all forms and lengths, subject-matter sometimes political, but open to all subjects. Poems of background—prison, minority experience—often published, as well as poems of protest and of Central America. Few rhymes."** Themes of recent issues include erotic poetry and Latin American poets. They have recently published poetry by Leslie Simon, Jack Micheline, Gary David, Bill Shields and Eugene Ruggles. As a sample, the editors selected these lines from "Deep in the Evening" by Quill:

Deep in the evening
when others are cold, limp creatures
on damp beds, you hold the sun
like a lucky stone to remind me
that daybreak is only a nightmare away

The tabloid has photos of featured poets on the cover, uses graphics, ads, 16 pp., circulation 2,000. $25 for lifetime subscription, includes all back issues. **Sample: $2.50 postpaid. Make checks payable to Alice Rogoff. Send SASE for guidelines. Pays 3 copies, reports in 2 months. Submit up to 6 poems or 8 pp. Photocopy OK, simultaneous OK "if we are informed. Each issue changes its theme and emphasis.** Don't be discouraged if rejected, and please submit again."

‡HAIKU ALIVE: MONTHLY ISSUE OF ONE-LINE HAIKU (IV-Form), 6914 Compass Court, Orlando FL 32810, founded 1991, editor/publisher Dennis Kalkbrenner, uses **one-line haiku only.** As a sample the editor selected these haiku (author unidentified):

The roaring ocean moon
Dancing red dragon   Kiss of the reptile
Traffic noise   Urban music

The publication is 2-4 pp. on quality paper, 25-50 haiku per issue, suitable for folder and/or hole punching for ringed notebook, desktop publishing. They accept 10-20% of submissions. **Both beginners and experienced are encouraged to submit, 10 haiku per single page at a time, name and address in upper left-hand corner, date of submission in upper right-hand corner, no simultaneous or previously published submissions. Pays 1 copy, or an extra copy for subscribers.** Subscription: $24/year. **Sample: $2 with SASE, sample serves as guidelines.** "No contests, prizes or gimmicks. We want to see one-line haiku only. Haiku: transient moments of poetic impact that are concise, intense, engaging images of sincere experience expressed in word(s) and/or phrase(s). **Innovative and experimental encouraged. No line should be longer than 17 syllables. We do not want to see: mawkish haiku images lacking vitality." Responds in 2 weeks. Editor frequently comments.** He adds, "Study classical haiku of Bashō, Buson, Issa and Shiki—and then using your senses and feelings move beyond them."

HAIKU CANADA (IV-Forms, membership), 67 Court St., Aylmer, Quebec J9H 4M1 Canada, founded 1977, is a society of haiku poets and enthusiasts from Canada, the U.S., Japan and elsewhere. Its members share information on haiku (and related forms), haiku events, societies, markets and publications. *Haiku Canada Sheets* are "an excellent way to share **haiku**," each containing about 20 haiku by one poet, a bio-bibliographical notice on the poet and a photograph. **You must be a member to submit. Pays 10 copies.** Review some books on haiku. They have a large haiku library, sponsor readings, and a Haiku Canada Weekend. They publish *Haiku Canada Newsletter*, "a fact-oriented exchange of information on events, projects and publications. In addition to haiku, senryu, renga and haiku selections, it provides an annual listing of haiku magazines, as well as information on haiku markets, contests, and other societies." **Sample $5. Membership: $20 per year.** Membership secretary Marco Fraticelli, Box 123, Lasalle, Quebec H8R 3T7 Canada.

HAIKU HEADLINES: A MONTHLY NEWSLETTER OF HAIKU AND SENRYU (IV-Form), 1347 W. 71st, Los Angeles CA 90044, founded 1988, editor/publisher David Priebe, uses **haiku and senryu** only. They have recently published haiku by Matthew Louviere, Dorothy McLaughlin, Mark Arvid White and Catherine Buckaway. As a sample the editor selected these haiku by Rengé:

> Elusive moments   A puppy crying
> of communion with nature   at the door of the schoolhouse
> the Tao of haiku   summer is over

The newsletter is 6-8 pp. on a double magazine-sized folded sheet punched for a three-ring notebook, desktop publishing. They accept about 10% of submissions. Their press run is 250 with 150 subscriptions of which 3 are libraries. Subscription: $18. **Sample: $1.50 postpaid. Pays 1 copy with SASE, or free extra copy to subscribers. Haiku may be submitted with up to 10 per single page. Submissions are "answered with proof sheets of acceptances, suggested revisions sheets, with occasional notes on originals — within 4-6 weeks."** Monthly contest Readers' Choice Awards: 1st place $5, 2 runners-up $2.50.

HAIKU JOURNAL; GEPPO HAIKU JOURNAL; HAIKU JOURNAL MEMBERS' ANTHOLOGY (I, IV-Form, membership), P.O. Box 1250, Gualala CA 95445, phone (707)882-2226, *HJ* founded 1977 and first published by the Yuki Teipei Haiku Society, editor Jane Reichhold. *HJ* is devoted to haiku and haiku criticism; contest winners and **"members' haiku only are published here.** *Geppo* is a mimeographed newsletter for members using **haiku, especially traditional haiku: 17 syllables with a KIGO."** I have not seen an issue, but the editor describes these as "around 60 pp., 6×9", nicely printed on heavy paper, card stock cover." Press run 300 for 100 subscriptions of which 10 are libraries. **Sample postpaid: $4.50. Send SASE for guidelines. Simultaneous submissions and previously published poems OK. Editor comments on submissions "especially if response is requested."** They have an annual contest in the spring. Send SASE for rules.

HAIKU QUARTERLY (II, IV-Form), 542 E. Ingram, Mesa AZ 85203, founded 1989, editor Linda S. Valentine. *Haiku Quarterly* **welcomes unpublished haiku, senryu and haiku sequences from new and established writers.** They have published haiku by Alexis Rotella, Gary Hotham, Adele Kenny, Geraldine C. Little, Elliot Richman, Francine Porad, vincent tripi, Anthony J. Pupello, Paul O. Williams and Matthew Louvière. As a sample the editor selected this haiku by Charles B. Dickson:

> into the silence
> after the church bells
> a thrush's song

Haiku Quarterly contains 36 pp., is professionally printed, saddle-stapled, 70 lb., with glossy 80 lb. cover, press run 250. Subscription: $16. **Sample: $4.50 postpaid. Send SASE for guidelines. No pay, but awards $5 to 4 outstanding poets in each issue. Reports in 4 weeks.** They hold periodic contests; send SASE for rules. "Capture the essense of the moment in clear, concise language."

HALF TONES TO JUBILEE (II), English Department, Pensacola Junior College, 1000 College Blvd., Pensacola FL 32504, phone (904)484-1400, founded 1986, faculty editors Walter Spara and Allan Peterson. *HTTJ* is an annual literary journal featuring poetry, short fiction, art. They have published poetry by R.T. Smith, Sue Walker, Larry Rubin and Simon Perchik. As a sample the editors selected these lines by Peter Wild from "Smokejumper's Pants," the winner of the 1989 *HTTJ* poetry contest:

> There may be lions in the trees, thistles that
> when the sun hits them just right
> make the amateur photographer famous
> even verbena, diminutive ice cream
> that they shout at underfoot . . .

HTTJ is digest-sized, 100+ pages, perfect-bound with matte card cover, professionally printed. Their press run is 500. They receive 1,000 submissions per year, use 50-60. **Reports 2-3 months, faster when possible. Pays 1 copy.** Subscriptions $4. Sample: $4. **No previously published work, no simultaneous submissions, SASE mandatory.** *HTTJ* sponsors an annual poetry competition, $300 first prize, $200 second, two $50 third prizes, entry $2/poem or 3 poems for $5. Send SASE for rules, deadlines.

HAMMERS; DOUBLESTAR PRESS (II), 1718 Sherman #205, Evanston IL 60201, founded 1989, editor Nat David. *Hammers* appears irregularly. Most of the poets whom they have published are from the Chicago area. Poets recently published include Luis Rodriguez, Michael Warr, Victor di Suvero, David

Whyre and Effie Mihopoulos. He says he wants **"honest poetry from the depths of the poet's universe and experience, which is cognizant of our interconnectedness."** As a sample he selected these lines from "Einstein's Daughter" by Barbara Pamp:

> We are all daughters of Einstein
> our inertia grows greater
> the closer we get
> our reflections disappear
> from the mirror
> and our fathers all
> move away from us
> traveling at the speed of light.

Price per issue: $3. **Reports ASAP. Sample copy postpaid: $4. Editor comments on submissions "seldom." Pays 1 copy.**

‡THE HAMPDEN-SYDNEY POETRY REVIEW (III, IV-Translations), P.O. Box 126, Hampden-Sydney VA 23943, poetry editor Tom O'Grady, has published such poets as A. R. Ammons, Dick Allen, James Dickey, X. J. Kennedy, William Stafford and James Schevill. **"We also publish translations."** The handsomely printed quarterly is in a flat-spined, glossy-covered 6 × 9" format. As a sample I chose the first stanza of Michael Egan's "The Hex":

> There are hexes here in our country.
> The farmers touch-up hexsigns; the Brethren
> sidestep crones, arointing
> the evil eye.

Sample: $5 postpaid. 1975-90 Anthology, 140 poets, 330 pp., $12.95 postpaid.

‡HANDSHAKE EDITIONS (V); CASSETTE GAZETTE (II), Atelier A2, 83 Rue de la Tombe-Issoire, Paris, France 75014, phone 4327-1767, founded 1979. *Cassette Gazette* is an audio cassette issued "from time to time." Poets published include Ted Joans, Yianna Katsoulos, Judith Malina, Elaine Cohen, Amanda Hoover and Jayne Cortez. **Payment in copies. Handshake Editions does not accept unsolicited MSS** for book publication. Jim Haynes, publisher, says, "I prefer to deal face to face."

HANGING LOOSE PRESS (V); HANGING LOOSE (I, II, IV-Teens/students), 231 Wyckoff St., Brooklyn NY 11217, founded 1966, poetry editors Robert Hershon, Dick Lourie, Mark Pawlak and Ron Schreiber. The Press accepts no unsolicited book MSS, but welcomes work for the magazine. The magazine has published poets such as Paul Violi, Donna Brook, Kimiko Hahn, Ron Overton, Jack Anderson and Frances Phillips. As a sample I selected the opening lines of "Bald" by Bill Zavatsky:

> In the mirror it's plain to see:
> Soon I'll be bald, like the two faceless men
> Staring at each other in the word "soon."

Hanging Loose is flat-spined, 96 pp., offset, now in its 25th year, on heavy stock with a 2-color glossy card cover. One section contains **poems by high-school-age poets. The editor says it "concentrates on the work of new writers."** It comes out 3 times a year. **Sample: $6.50 postpaid.** Submit 4-6 **"excellent, energetic"** poems, no simultaneous submissions. **"Would-be contributors should read the magazine first." Reports in 1-12 weeks. Pays.**

HANGMAN BOOKS (II), 32 May Rd., Rochester, Kent ME1 2HY England, founded 1982, editor Jack Ketch, publishes selected books of poetry on a cooperative basis. Jack Ketch says, "We receive no grant, **therefore we expect the writers to put their money where their mouth is. We don't advertise this fact as we are not a vanity press, we only approach writers with this proposal if we are sufficiently impressed with their work and want to help them** (this is very rare)." They want **"personal" poetry, "none rhyming, none political, bla bla bla."** 60% of press run belongs to poet. They have recently published poetry by B. Lewis, Criss Broderick and N. Sparkes. As a sample the editor selected these lines from **The Deathly Flight of Angels** by B. Childish:

> money: the langwidge
> of all
> the assholes
> of
> the world

That is from a handsomely printed flat-spined book, 70+ pp., with matte card cover in color.

HANSON'S: A MAGAZINE OF LITERARY AND SOCIAL INTEREST (II), 113 Merryman Court, Annapolis MD 21401, phone (410)626-0744, founded 1988, poetry editor Shannon Rogowski, is a semi-annual using **"all forms, styles, subjects and points of view reflective of intelligence and a sense of beauty."** As a sample the editor selected these lines from "Voices" by Robert Johnson:

> *Will the Spirits of the Age forgive a man,*
> *If he speaks of small concerns?*
> *Or the Spirits of All Time,*
> *If he speaks of himself?*
> *Poetry is lost upon those who question it,*
> *And dead to those who take up pen*
> *To write a perfect line.*

It is magazine-sized, 75-100 pp., saddle-stapled with matte card cover in full color. Press run 3,000 for 1,500 subscriptions including 2 library systems. "We receive 400-500 poems per year, publish about 30-40 per year." Subscription: $8. Sample postpaid: $4. Send SASE for guidelines with 2 first-class stamps. Pays $20-40 plus 1 copy. **"Previous publication is not a prerequisite. We'd rather see honest, careful art, than a resume." Reports in 2-3 weeks. Editor comments on submissions "seldom."**

‡**HAPPY LAMB (I, IV-Subscription)**, 8019 N.E. 132nd St., Kirkland WA 98034, founded 1990, publisher David Bissell, is a monthly newsletter **"open to beginners and previously published poets."** The editor describes it as "4-8 pp., typeset on typewriter—clean style, very readable." Subscription ($10/ 1 year) required with all submissions; "does not guarantee acceptance of poetry submitted." Sample postpaid: $2. Pays 1 copy. Reports in 1-3 weeks. Cover letter preferred ("should tell me who they are, or where they have published; be friendly and avoid egotism!") The editor says, "Poets, be yourself. I try to respond with friendly encouragement. Keep it short, and keep it simple, and most of all, don't give up."

‡**HARBOUR PUBLISHING (V)**, P.O. Box 219, Madeira Park BC V0N 2H0 Canada, publishes 12-15 books/year, 2-4 of them poetry by **Canadian authors.** They have recently published Glen Sorestad, Tom Wayman, Maureen McCarthy, Ken Mitchell and Peter Trower. **"We're not looking for more."**

HARCOURT BRACE JOVANOVICH, PUBLISHERS; HBJ CHILDREN'S BOOKS; GULLIVER BOOKS (IV-Children), 1250 Sixth Ave., San Diego CA 92101, phone (619)699-6810, HBJ Children's Books and Gulliver Books publish hardback and trade paperback books for children. They have recently published books of children's poetry by Jane Yolen, Arnold Adoff, James Dickey, e.e. cummings, Lee Bennett Hopkins and Carl Sandburg. **Submit complete MS. No dot-matrix. Pays favorable advance, royalty contract and copies.** Send SASE for guidelines and book catalog.

HARD ROW TO HOE; MISTY HILL PRESS (I, IV-Rural), P.O. Box 541-I, Healdsburg CA 95448, phone (707)433-9786. *Hard Row to Hoe*, taken over from Seven Buffaloes Press in 1987, editor Joe E. Armstrong, is a "book review newsletter of literature from rural America with a section reserved for short stories (about 2,000 words) and **poetry featuring unpublished authors. The subject matter must apply to rural America including nature and environmental subjects. Poems of 30 lines or less given preference, but no arbitrary limit. No style limits. Do not want any subject matter not related to rural subjects."** As a sample the editor selected this poem by Terri McGill:

> *We thought it were a fence post,*
> *looked like it, with the sun goin down*
> *b'hind it like that. It weren't.*
> *It were Old Man Dew leanin gainst his hoe*
> *Like he's ponderin . . .*
> *could he finish the choppin*
> *or was the day dyin out*
> *too fast.*

HRTH is magazine-sized, 12 pp. side-stapled, appearing 3 times a year, 3 pp. reserved for short stories and poetry. Press run 300, subscription $7/year. Sample $2 postpaid. **Send SASE for guidelines. Pays 3 copies. Editor comments on rejections "if I think the quality warrants."** Reviews books of poetry.

‡**HARDWARE: THE MAGAZINE OF TECHNOPHILIA (IV-Themes)**, 710 Adeline St., Trenton NJ 08611, founded 1989, editor Jimm Gall, appears 3/year using **"any style or length, as long as the poem espouses the abnormal/obsessive relationship between Man and Technology—especially machines. No aliens!"** They have recently published poetry by Lee Ballentine, Bruce Boston, Robert Frazier and John Grey. As a sample the editor selected these lines from "Wired In" by Ann K. Schwader:

> *Disembodied*
> *in our own born forms we drift*
> *flesh circuits in a bloodless current*
> *soul of the machine.*

It is magazine-sized, 40 pp., offset, saddle-stapled, with 2-color glossy card covers. They accept about 10% of 200 poems received/year. Press run: 2,500 for 400 subscribers. Subscription: $11. **Sample postpaid: $4. Send SASE for guidelines. Pays $2-10/poem plus 3 copies. Reports in 3-5** months. "Essentially a 1-man operation—I read and decide everything. Publication can be up to a year after acceptance."

HARPER COLLINS (V), (formerly, Harper and Row), 10 East 53rd St., New York NY 10022, founded 1817. HarperCollins, as you can tell from the date of founding, is an old-line, highly respected publishing house. Among the 300 titles Harper's publishes each year only 1-2 are books of poetry. **They accept no unsolicited MSS, but the questionnaire they returned does say that poets can submit 6 sample poems.** The poets they publish are, obviously, likely to be fairly well-known before Harper's publishes them; on my shelves I have, for example, volumes published by Harper and Row by William Stafford, Hayden Carruth (in the Colophon imprint), Yehuda Amichai and Gwendolyn Brooks. All are handsomely produced. As a sample I chose the beginning lines from Gwendolyn Brooks's "Jessie Mitchell's Mother":

> *Into her mother's bedroom to wash the ballooning body.*
> *"My mother is jelly-hearted and she has a brain of*
>   *jelly:*
> *Sweet, quiver-soft, irrelevant. Not essential.*
> *Only a habit would cry if she should die."*

If your poetry is good enough to be published by HarperCollins, you probably don't need this directory.

‡HARP-STRINGS; EDNA ST. VINCENT MILLAY HARP-WEAVER CONTEST (I), 310 S. Adams St., Beverly Hills FL 32665, founded 1989, editor Madelyn Eastlund, appears 3/year. **They want poems of "14-70 lines, narratives, lyrics, ballads, sestinas, rondeau, redouble, blank verse. Nothing 'dashed off,' trite, broken prose masquerading as poetry."** They have recently published poetry by Anne Marx, James Proctor, Betsy Kennedy and Grace Haynes Smith. As a sample the editor selected the last stanza of "Magnet" by Charles Dickson:

> *Today he rows slowly upstream from the new*
> *power dam. He often wonders what magnet*
> *still pulls him here on Sunday afternoons,*
> *with his fields, his fences, his terraces,*
> *his locked, empty house fifty feet below*
> *the shimmering sunset surface of the lake.*

It is 36 pp. digest-sized, saddle-stapled, professionally printed in colored ink on quality colored matte stock with matte card cover. She accepts 5-10% of poems received **in February, June and October only.** Press run 100 for 75 subscribers. Subscription: $20. **Sample postpaid: $5.50 for previous year, $6.50 for current year. Pays 1 copy.** "I am interested in seeing poems that have won awards but have not been published. The annual Millay contest has cash awards of $10-40 and publication in December issue—$2/poem, $5/3 poems entry fee. "Stanley Kunitz once said, 'Poetry today has become easier to write but harder to remember.' *Harp-Strings* wants poetry to remember, poetry that haunts, poetry the reader wants to read again and again."

THE HARTLAND POETRY QUARTERLY; HARTLAND PRESS (I, II, IV-Children, themes), 168 Fremont, Romeo MI 48065, phone (313)752-5507. Founded 1989, contact David Bock, **"prefer 24 lines or less; no style restrictions; no pornography—none—nada—nill! Looking for serious poems by Viet Nam veterans and I mean serious—don't send the one-and-only angry poem—I got that stuff coming out of my ears. Very, very open to good children's poems written only by children under 15 for a special 'coming out' part of the magazine."** They have recently published poetry by Loriann Zimmer, T. Kilgore Splake and Laurence W. Thomas. As a sample the editor selected these lines (poet unidentified):

> *And*
> *you see*
> *as I see,*
> *a rainstorm of children*
> *with tumbling hair*
> *picking buttercups in a yellow field.*

Their quarterly is digest-sized, spine-stapled, 25-30 pp. They accept about 15% of 300-500 poems received/year. Press run 500, with 70 subscribers of which 15 are libraries, 300 shelf sales. Subscription: $8. **Sample postpaid: $1. Pays 2 copies. Reports in 2-4 weeks. Include bio with submission.** Reviews books of poetry. They publish 2 chapbooks/year of poets already published in the quarterly. Pays 20 copies. The editor says, "Write about what you have lived. Read, read, write, write—repeat cycle 'till death. Support as many small publications as you can afford."

HATBOX (II), P.O. Box 336, Miller N.S.W. Australia 2168, founded 1989, editor David Zarate, is a quarterly using **"any contemporary poetry. No specifications as to form, length, subject-matter, style, etc., only that it be quality work. Nothing overly 'Romantic,' wordy."** They have recently published poetry by Dorothy Porter. As a sample the editor selected these lines from "On the Railway Near the Sea" by Chris Mansell:

> *phrases become stranded*
> *in the doppler effect*
> *sirens sing islands dance*

It is A5 sized, 96 pp., cover using b/w art. Press run 300 for 70 subscribers. Subscription: $9/2 issues (add $6 for overseas, $20 for institutions). **Sample: $5. Pays 1 copy plus subscription. Reports in 2 months. Submission reading times are December/January and May/June. Editor comments on submissions "often."** Reviews books of poetry. He says, "New poets (especially young poets) should definitely read as much poetry as they can; both from their own country and others. Also from outside their language if quality translations are available. Gives perspective."

‡THE HAUNTED SUN (IV-Horror), 22000 Mauer, St. Clair Shores MI 48080, founded 1990, managing editor John Habermas, is a tabloid appearing 4/year, using **"poetry of any style involving dark or fantastic themes and macabre tones. Length open, though we prefer shorter works. No taboos. Originality stressed and innovation encouraged."** As a sample the editor selected these lines from "Family" by John Grey:

> *through halls of terror*
> *in rooms drunken with screams*
> *on walls that mirror cruel death*
> *their legends survive*
> *for evil self-perpetuates*
> *and blood stains*
> *last longer than blood*

It is tabloid size, webb-offset printing, folded, b/w with ads and strong attention to art. Press run 3,000-5,000. **Sample: $2.50 postpaid. Send SASE for guidelines. Pays $2-5 plus 1 copy. Previously published poems and simultaneous submissions OK. Reports in 1-3 weeks. Unacceptable poetry returned immediately.** The editor advises, "Use original themes, and never let form interfere with content."

HAUNTS (IV-Science Fiction, fantasy, horror), Nightshade Publications, P.O. Box 3342, Providence RI 02906, phone (401)781-9438, is a "literary quarterly geared to those fans of the 'pulp' magazines of the 30s, 40s and 50s, with tales of **horror, the supernatural and the bizarre. We are trying to reach those in the 18-35 age group."** Circulation: 1,000. **Sample: $3.95 plus $1 postage. Send SASE for guidelines. Photocopies OK. Uses free verse, light verse and traditional, about 12-16 poems a year. Send a maximum of 3 poems. Pays copies.**

HAWAIÍ REVIEW (I, II), % Department of English, 1733 Donaghho Rd., University of Hawaii, Honolulu HI 96822, phone (808)956-8548, poetry editor Lani Kwon. "We are interested in **all sorts of poetry, from free verse to formal lyricism, rhyme and meter; heroic narrative, haiku, light verse, satire and experimentation; we're also interested in poems translated from other languages; and while** *Hawaii Review* **has published poets with established reputations like lifshin, Bly and Merwin, the absolute beginner is very welcome here as well."** They have recently published poetry by lyn lifshin, Michael J. Bugeja, Joseph Stanton and Tony Quagliano among others, and translations by Carolyn Tipton and Alexis Levitin. As a sample the editor selected the poem "Alice and Max" by Kathleen Postma:

> *He deals designer*
> *Shoes out of*
> *a backroom in Barcelona*
> *That's where they meet.*
>
> *She's nineteen.*
> *He's fifty-four*
> *It's sordid.*
>
> *When he can't sleep,*
> *he can count off*
> *the years in between*
>
> *them.*

HR appears 3 times yearly, 160 pp., flat-spined, 6½ × 9½", professionally printed on heavy stock with b/w or color cover, 150 subscriptions of which 40 are libraries. Up to 500 are used by University of Hawaii students. Subscription: $12/one year; $20/two years; $5/single issue. **Sample: $4. Do not submit MSS from May 31-August 15. Send SASE for guidelines. "Artwork to accompany poetry is welcomed." Pays $10-60 plus 2 copies.** Editor sometimes comments on rejections. Reporting time: 1-3 months. Does not normally review books, but "authors can query." The editor says, "Good poetry shows more than psuedo-literary erudition – a good poem *speaks* to people, not just intellectually but at the gut level."

HAYDEN'S FERRY REVIEW (II), Matthews Center, Arizona State University, Tempe AZ 85287-1502, phone (602)965-1243, founded 1986, managing editor Salima Keegan, is a handsome literary magazine appearing twice a year. **"No specifications other than limit in number (6) and no simultaneous submissions. We would like a brief bio for contributor's note included." Reports in 8-10 weeks of deadlines. Deadlines: Feb. 28 for Spring/Summer issue; Sept. 30 for Fall/Winter. Submissions circulated to two poetry editors.** Contributors receive galley proofs. Editor comments on submissions "often." They have recently published poetry by Dennis Schmitz, Maura Stanton, Ai, and David St. John. As a sample the editor selected these lines from "Cherish" by Ray Carver:

> From the window I see her bend to the roses
> holding close to the bloom so as not to
> prick her fingers. With the other hand she clips, pauses and

HFR is 6 × 9", 120 + pp. flat-spined with glossy card cover. Press run 1,000 for 100 subscribers of which 30 are libraries. 500 shelf sales. They accept about 3% of 800 submissions annually. Subscription: $10. **Sample postpaid: $6.20. Send SASE for guidelines. Pays 2 copies.**

‡**THE HEADWATERS REVIEW (II)**, P.O. Box 13682 Dinkytown Station, Minneapolis MN 55414, founded 1990, editor-in-chief Frank J. Laurich, appears twice a year **"to publish poetry of the very finest quality."** They published poetry by Robert Bly in their first issue. It is 65 pp., digest-sized, flat-spined. **Sample postpaid: $6.50. Reports in 1-4 months. Send SASE for guidelines. Pays 1 copy. No critiques.**

HEART (I), Box 3097, Durango CO 81302, phone (303)247-4107, founded 1989, editor Marcia Mulloy, is a literary tabloid appearing twice a year. They want **poetry of "any style, length, subject-matter. Preference is for clean, muscular writing, writing that has substance regardless of style. If you can make a sonnet sing the ginhouse blues and be believable, I'll probably print it. No song lyrics."** The editor says it is approximately 30 pp., newsprint with cover art in color, b/w art inside, ads relating to literature/art. Subscription: $18/4 issues. Per issue: $5. **Sample: $2.50 postpaid. Send SASE for guidelines. Pays 2 copies. Reports in 6-8 weeks. "Do not send only copy of MS."** Editor comments on rejections "often."

HEAVEN BONE PRESS; HEAVEN BONE MAGAZINE (II, IV-Spiritual, nature, ecology), P.O. Box 486, Chester NY 10918, phone (914)469-9018, founded 1986, poetry editor Steve Hirsch, publishes poetry, fiction, essays and reviews with **"an emphasis on spiritual, metaphysical, esoteric and ecological concerns."** Issue #8 includes poetry and fiction by Joe Richey, Kirpal Gordon, Miriam Sagan, Fielding Dawson, Mikhail Horowitz, Bob Arnold and Jack Collom. As a sample the editor chose these lines from "Physics One" by Marie Harris:

> Each cord of woods that warms this house:
> > ragged hickory, chalky birch, maple
> > oak rounds that hold a fire overnight
> > arthritic apple, biscuit wood,
> has been carried –
> > hauled, cradled, thrown,
> > turned, stacked, handled
> – from standing timber to ashes
> for the outhouse
> eleven times.
> Figured this way, the cord
> weighs forty-four thousand pounds.

Heaven Bone is magazine-sized, saddle stapled, 56 pp., using b/w art, photos and ads, on recycled bond stock with glossy recycled card cover. They have a press run of 800. Of 250-350 poems received they accept 18-30. Subscription: $14.95. **Sample: $5 postpaid. Pays 2 copies. Submit 3-10 poems. Simultaneous submissions and previously published poems OK "if notified." Reports in 2 weeks to 6 months, up to 6 months until publication.** Reviews books of poetry. Editor advises, "Please be familiar with the magazine before sending MSS. Break free of common 'poetic' limitations and speak freely with no contrivances. No forced end-line rhyming please."

Featuring: The Woodcuts of Latin American Artist Alejandro Mario Yllanes

For editor Steven Hirsch, this cover represents Heaven Bone's theme through its "excellence, subtlety, warmth and spiritual ascension." It appears as "the entrance into an inner realm of discovery," he says. The cover features a woodcut by Alejandro Mario Yllanes, a Latin American artist whose work is also included inside the issue. "His work is considered a re-discovered treasure of modern Latin (Bolivian) art and we are proud and privileged to be part of its renaissance," Hirsch says. The Foundation for Latin-American Fine Art, Harriman, New York, is restoring Yllanes' work.

Channel the muse and music without being an obstacle to the poem." Annual chapbook contest; send SASE for guidelines.

‡HELICON NINE, INC.; HELICON NINE EDITIONS; MARIANNE MOORE POETRY PRIZE (III), P.O. Box 22412, Kansas City MO 64113, phone (913)722-2999, founded 1977, editor Gloria Vando Hickok. Helicon Nine, formerly a literary magazine, now is a publisher of books of poetry. **"Our one requirement is excellence; nothing pedestrian."** They have published poetry by Joyce Carol Oates, Grace Paley, Ellen Gilchrist and James Dickey. As a sample the editor selected these lines from "At Emily's in Amherst" by David Ray (from their first book, **The Helicon Nine Reader**):

> *Sipping wine from the dandelions of her yard, I ask her*
> *about the lover, if there was one. And I feel certain*
> *I am that lover, all she could look forward to.*
>
> *Yet I am not such a bad choice. I sit devoted for hours,*
> *loving her well, sharing the wine, the growing darkness,*
> *and I promise to come back, to think of her always.*

They are not encouraging submissions at this time. Please query. "Payment varies, but we're in the publishing business to *help* poets and authors, not to hinder them or take advantage. We publish *beautiful* books and try to get them into the hands of readers. We have national distributors making sure our books are made available throughout the States. We also aggressively pursue new markets and book reviews and advertise in many trade publications as well as exhibit at the ABA, etc." The Marianne Moore Poetry Prize is given annually, $1,500 for an unpublished poetry MS of at least 50 pp. The award includes a $500 honorarium and publication by Helicon Nine Editions. Deadline Jan. 1.

HELLAS: A JOURNAL OF POETRY AND THE HUMANITIES (II, IV-Form), 304 S. Tyson Ave., Glenside PA 19038, phone (215)884-1086, founded 1988, editor Gerald Harnett. *Hellas* is a semiannual that wants poetry of **"any kind but especially poems in meter. We prize elegance and formality in verse, but specifically encourage poetry of the utmost boldness and innovation, so long as it is not willfully obscurantist; no ignorant, illiterate, meaningless free verse or political poems."** They have recently accepted poetry by Marcus, Moore, Butler, Kessler and many others. It is 172 pp, 6×9″ flat-spined, offset, using b/w art. Their press run is 750. Subscription: $12. Sample: $7.50 postpaid. Send SASE for guidelines. Pays 1 copy. They will consider simultaneous submissions and previously published poems **"if they let us know, but please don't bother unless it's specifically suited to *Hellas*." Reports in 2** months. Editor comments on rejections "happily if requested. If I don't understand it, I don't print it. On the other hand, we don't want obvious, easy, clichéd or sentimental verse." Their flyer says, "*Hellas* is a lively and provocative assault on a century of modernist barbarism in the arts. A unique, Miltonic wedding of *paideia* and *poesis*, engaging scholarship and original poetry, *Hellas* has become the forum of a remarkable new generation of poets, critics and theorists committed to the renovation of the art of our time . . . Meter is especially welcome, as well as rhymed and stanzaic verse. We judge a poem by its verbal artifice and the formal harmonies of its internal order. Lines should not end arbitrarily, diction should be precise: we suggest that such principles can appear 'limiting' only to an impoverished imagination. To the contrary: we encourage any conceivable boldness and innovation, so long as it is executed with discipline and is not a masquerade for self-indulgent obscurantism. . . . We do not print poems about Nicaragua, whales or an author's body parts. We do specifically welcome submissions from newer authors."

HELTER SKELTER; SCREAMSHEETS; SCREAM PRESS (I), 26524 Fisher Dr., Carmel CA 93923, founded 1987, editor Anthony Boyd. Boyd, who says his press promotes "new and established literary thinkers." Both the annual magazine, *Helter Skelter*, and broadsheets "include a short bio and photo with each poet's work to give them more exposure." **Nothing over 50 lines can be printed.** Poets recently published include Jim DeWitt, Mary Ann Henn and Walt Phillips. As a sample the editor selected these lines by Sara Boyd:

> Somewhere in the distance water flows
> So serenely that it calms my heart
> It reminds me of days long ago
> When kindness came as easily as breath

Helter Skelter is magazine-sized, 12-20 pp., saddle-stapled. Circulation is 500. Subscription: $10. **Sample postpaid: $2. Pays 2 copies. Reports within a month.** "Cover letters are appreciated. I look for poetry of laughter and eloquence. Rhyme isn't important to me, rhythm is. I love groups like U2, King's X and Undercover. If you like their style, write me. We'll talk."

HEMISPHERES; PAISANO PRESS (I), Rt. 1, Box 28, Eden WI 53019, phone (414)477-6861, founded 1989, editor Gary Scheinoha, appears twice a year using "**poems up to 40 lines, open as to form, subject-matter, and style; no pornography, occult.** Writers published in this magazine are pretty well open to explore their own personal hemispheres." They have recently published poetry by Betty Pyle, Ken Stone and Evelyn Scheinoha. As a sample the editor selected these lines from "The Meals Now" by John Grey:

> We don't come to
> this restaurant to eat
> but to spar like weary boxers,
> each jabbing away
> at the sound of the
> other's voice.

Hemispheres is a digest-sized, 20-24 pp., photocopied from photoreduced typescript, with colored paper cover. Press run 50 copies for 13 subscriptions. Subscription: $4. **Sample postpaid: $2. Send SASE for guidelines. Pays "varying number of copies." Submit MSS in January for March issue, June for Sept. issue. Simultaneous submissions and previously published poems OK. Reports in 1 month.** Reviews books of poetry. **Authors of books "usually appear in the magazine first. This is not a requirement."** The editor says, "Hang tough. Poetry is a game for survivors. Those who keep submitting despite rejections and discouragement are the ones who will make it. Never forget it requires endless revision. If you are willing to work hard at your writing, I'm sure you'll find there is a special place for it; someone willing to publish it."

HEN'S TEETH (V), P.O. Box 689, Brookings SD 57006, founded 1988, editor Janice H. Mikesell. As a sample of poetry she liked, she picked these lines from her poem, "My Mother's Back Yard":

> . . . there are other memories as well, so fragile that
> I dare not dust them off
> for fear that I will break

That poem appears in **Women Houses & Homes: an anthology of prose, poetry and photography,** $6 (plus $1 postage), a 52-page saddle-stapled book cut with a roof-line top, professionally printed with a cover photograph of a "painted lady" Victorian house. She expects to publish a book every 2 years but **will not be open for submissions.** Most recent publication is **A Survivor's Manual: a book of poems,** $6 (plus $1 postage), a 52-page perfect-bound quality paperback with an arresting cover photo. Sample lines from "Closing Thoughts" are:

> . . . the fire's in the belly now
> the final tyrant, time.

HERBOOKS (IV-Lesbian), P.O. Box 7467, Santa Cruz CA 95061, founded 1984, owner Irene Reti, is a small-press publisher of lesbian-feminist writing and photography, essays, poetry, short story collections and anthologies. **"We wish to achieve better balance of poetry and prose within HerBooks titles."** They want **"lesbian-feminist poetry with a strong personal voice; free verse or traditional form, 1-10 pp., written out of conviction, non-rhetorical, specific, written out of a strong sense of lesbian culture and identity."** They do not want **"anything racist, or pro s/m, anything vague and mushy."** They have published poetry by Lesléa Newman, Ellen Bass and Judith Barrington. As a sample Irene Reti chose these lines from "Household Deities" by Penelope J. Engelbrecht:

> *Everyone wants to get inside*
> *out of the cold*
> *but the plea of a tiny cat*
> *carries more weight than a thousand*
> *sapphic lyrics*
> *upon a tender breast.*

The poem appears in **Cats (and their Dykes)**, an anthology edited by Irene Reti and Shoney Sien, 160 pp., perfect-bound, $10.

HERESIES (IV-Women, themes), P.O. Box 1306, Canal St. Station, New York NY 10013, founded 1977, editorial collective, is a "feminist publication on art and politics." **Poetry "must be by women and fit into the specific issue theme."** They have recently published poetry by Adrienne Rich, Alice Walker and Margaret Randall. As a sample I chose the opening lines of "Dance Instruction for a Young Girl" by Kimiko Hahn:

> *Stand knees slightly*
> *bent, toes in posed*
> *you watch the hawk over the river*
> *curve, until his voice, shoulders back*
> *gently overcome by Seiji's mouth*
> *against you, the white breath, and elbows*
> *close to your side . . .*

Heresies, one of the oldest and best-known feminist publications, appears 2 times a year in a 96 pp. flat-spined, magazine-sized format, offset with half-tones, 2-color glossy card cover, using non-profit, book related exchange ads. They accept about 10 out of 100 submissions. Press runs 5,000 for 3,000 subscriptions of which a fourth are libraries, 50% shelf sales. Per issue: $6.75; subscription: $23/4 issues. **Sample, back issues: $6 postpaid. Send SASE for guidelines. Pays small honorarium plus 3 copies. Simultaneous submissions OK. Reports in 6-12 months.**

THE HEYECK PRESS (V), 25 Patrol Ct., Woodside CA 94062, phone (415)851-7491, founded 1976, poetry editor Robin Heyeck, is "essentially a private press, publishing very fine poetry in letterpress editions. We are able to produce only 2-3 books per year and not all of these are going to be poetry in the future. We sometimes do dual editions of paperback and fine volumes on handmade paper with special leather and marbled paper bindings." They want to see **"well crafted, well organized poetry which makes sense — poetry which shows particular sensitivity to the precise meanings of words and to their sounds."** They have published poetry by Frances Mayes, Sandra Gilbert, William Dickey, Charlotte Muse, Edward Kleinschmidt and Bernard Gershenson. Robin Heyeck selected these sample lines from Adrienne Rich's book **Sources**:

> *I refuse to become a seeker for cures.*
> *Everything that has ever*
> *helped me has come through what already*
> *lay stored in me. Old things, diffuse, unnamed, lie strong*

The sample books I have seen are, indeed, elegantly printed on heavy stock, lavish with b/w drawings. **The Summer Kitchen**, poems by Sandra Gilbert, drawings by Barbara Hazard, is a series of poems on vegetables, titles on the cover and on individual poems in red ink; and **Herbal**, poems by Honor Johnson, drawings by Wayne and Honor Johnson, is a series on herbs. **No unsolicited mss; query with 5-6 samples and cover letter stating other publications, awards and a "brief" biography. Replies to query in 3 weeks. Photocopy, dot-matrix OK. Contract is for royalties 10% of net sales.**

HIGH PLAINS LITERARY REVIEW (III), Suite 250, 180 Adams St., Denver CO 80208, phone (303)320-6828, founded 1986, editor Robert O. Greer, associate poetry editor Ray Gonzalez, appears 3/year using "high quality poetry, fiction, essays, book reviews and interviews." The format is 135 pp., 70 lb paper, heavy cover stock. Subscription: $20. **Sample postpaid: $7. Pays $10/published page for poetry.**

HIGH PLAINS PRESS (IV-Regional), P.O. Box 123, Glendo WY 82213, phone (307)735-4370, founded 1985, poetry editor Nancy Curtis, considers **poetry "specifically relating to Wyoming and the West, particularly those poems based on historical people/events. We're mainly a publisher of historical**

nonfiction, but do publish a book of poetry about every other year." They have recently published poetry by Peggy Simson Curry, Robert Roripaugh and Mary Alice Gunderson. As a sample she quoted these lines from the book *No Roof But Sky* by Jane Candia Coleman. The poem is "Geronimo photographed at Ft. Sill (1905)"

> *Bring me the elusive images*
> *of my life, and I will smile for you—*
> *over and over—an exchange of illusions*
> *like the dying change into light.*

Reports in 2 months, publication in 18-24 months. Pays 10% of sales. Catalog available on request; sample chapbooks $5.

HIGH/COO PRESS; MAYFLY (IV-Subscriber, form), 4634 Hale Dr., Decatur IL 62526, phone (217)877-2966, founded 1976, editor Randy Brooks. High/Coo is a small press publishing nothing but **haiku in English.** "We publish haiku poemcards, minichapbooks, and a bibliography of haiku publications in addition to flat-spined paperbacks and hardbound cloth editions, and the magazine *Mayfly,* evoking emotions from contemporary experience. We are not interested in orientalism nor Japanese imitations." They publish no poetry except haiku. They have recently published haiku by Elizabeth S. Lamb, Virgil Hutton and Lee Gurga. As a sample the editor selected this haiku by Ruth Yarrow:

> *Warm rain before dawn:*
> *my milk flows into her*
> *unseen*

Mayfly is a 16 pp. saddle-stapled magazine, 3×5″, professionally printed on high-quality stock, one haiku/page. It appears in February, May and September. They publish "about 50" of an estimated 3,000 submissions. Subscription: $10. Sample: $3.50 postpaid. A Macintosh computer disk of samples and haiku-related stacks is available for $1 postage and handling. Guidelines available for SASE. Pays $5/poem and no copies. "Contributors are required to be subscribers." Submit no more than 5 haiku per issue. No simultaneous submissions or previously published poems. High/Coo Press considers MSS "by invitation only." Randy Brooks says, "Publishing poetry is a joyous work of love. We publish to share those moments of insight contained in evocative haiku. We aren't in it for fame, gain or name. We publish to serve an enthusiastic readership of haiku writers."

HIGHLIGHTS FOR CHILDREN (IV-Children), 803 Church St., Honesdale PA 18431, phone (717)253-1080, founded 1946, associate editor Greg Linder, appears every month except July-August is a combined issue. Using **poetry for children aged 2-12.** "Meaningful and/or fun poems accessible to children of all ages. Rarely publish a poem longer than 16 lines, most are shorter. No poetry that is unintelligible to children, poems containing sex, violence or unmitigated pessimism." They have recently published poetry by Nikki Giovanni, Aileen Fisher, John Ciardi, A.A. Milne, Myra Cohn Livingston, Langston Hughes and William Jay Smith. It is generally 44 pp., magazine sized, full-color throughout. They purchase 6-10 of 300 submissions per year. Press run 3.3 million for approximately 3 million subscribers. Subscription: $19.95 (one year; reduced rates for multiple years). **Sample postpaid: free. Payment** "money varies plus 2 copies. MS typed with very brief cover letter. Please indicate if a simultaneous submission." Reports "generally within 30 days." Editor comments on submissions "occasionally, if MS has merit or author seems to have potential for our market." He says, "We are always open to submissions of poetry not previously published. However, we purchase a very limited amount of such material. We may use the verse as 'filler,' or illustrate the verse with a full-page piece of art. Please note that we do not buy material from anyone under 16 years old."

‡HILLTOP PRESS (V), 4 Nowell Place, Almondbury, Huddersfield, West Yorkshire England HD5 8PB, founded 1966, editor Steve Sneyd, publishes books of **"mainly SF poetry nowadays,"** but currently accepts no unsolicited MSS. They have recently published poetry by Andrew Darlington, John Brunner and Dave Calder. As a sample the editor selected these lines from **Voyager** by John Francis Haines:

> *Blast off:*
> *Rattled our teeth and hooped pig-iron onto our chests*
> *Freefall:*
> *Made us feel sick and left us grasping for our possessions*

The double dagger before a listing indicates that the listing is new in this edition. New markets are often the most receptive to submissions.

Landfall:
Restored us the gift of gravity and buckled our knees
They offer **"FREE FOR SAE—'Workshopping' leaflet on some unusual poetry forms (while stocks last)."** They publish 2-3 chapbooks/year, pay "ample" author's copies. "I have limited quantities of a number of earlier chapbooks. These can be had as samples, 5 all different, for £1.50 UK or $3 US, postage paid. (Checks payable to S. Sneyd. U.S. orders, will also accept $ bills or small denomination, unused US stamps). My advice for beginning poets is (a) persist—don't let any one editor discourage you. 'In poetry's house are many mansions,' what one publication hates another may love; (b) be prepared for the possibility of long delays between acceptance and appearance of work—the press is mostly self-financed and part time, so don't expect it to be more efficient than commercial publishers; (c) *always* keep a copy of everything you send out, and put your name and address on *everything* you send."

HIPPO (II), 28834 Boniface Dr., Malibu CA 90265, phone (213)457-7871, founded 1988, publisher/editor Karl Heiss, appears twice a year. *"Hippo* has two feet sunk in surreality . . . the rest firmly dedicated to standing ground in the (sometimes all-too-depressing, awakening, sobering) real world. The main emphasis is fiction—also poetry, art and essays. *Hippo* loves the unpretentious and lives for subtle revelations. Nothing stuffy. Words that reform language, create new understandings or meaning, and image flashes, or very very short stories. *Hippo* also likes to try and understand people and the narrator is important sometimes to that end." They have published poetry by Lyn Lifshin, Paul Weinman, Belinda Subraman, Thomas Wiloch and Dan Raphael. As a sample the editor selected these lines from "Multiples" by M. Kettner:

Cloning myself
to be nearer you

I am everywhere
like lost pennies,
they are my eyes

while you are away . . .
It is photocopied from photoreduced typescript, 48 pp. digest-sized, saddle-stapled, with 2-color paper cover. The editor accepts about 1 of 10 poems submitted. Press run: 150 for 70 subscriptions of which 2 are libraries. Subscription: $6. **Sample postpaid: $2.50. Pays 1 copy.** *"Hippo* spends many hours in a lonely river and likes cover letters written by real people."** Previously published poems may be used. Reports in up to 5 months.

HIPPOPOTAMUS PRESS; OUTPOSTS POETRY QUARTERLY; OUTPOSTS ANNUAL POETRY COMPETITION (II, IV-Form), 22 Whitewell Rd., Frome, Somerset, BA11 4EL, England, *Outposts* founded 1943, Hippopotamus Press founded 1974, poetry editor Roland John, who explains, *"Outposts* is a general poetry magazine that welcomes all work either from the recognized or the unknown poet. The Hippopotamus Press is specialized, with an affinity with Modernism. No Typewriter, Concrete, Surrealism. The Press publishes 6 full collections per year." They have recently published in *OPQ* poetry by John Heath-Stubbs, Peter Dale and Elizabeth Jennings. As a sample (though it is by no means typical, it amused me) I chose the opening quatrain of "A Reply to Keats' 'To One Who Has Been Long in City Pent' " by Shaun McCarthy:

To one who has been long enclosed by fields,
deterred by gates wired shut and seeded land,
these streets excite dulled senses—each has scanned
and, dazed by choice, knows banishment repealed.

That is from a 1984 60 pp. collection, **The Banned Man**, published in a flat-spined paperback, elegantly printed, digest-sized, with a matte card cover and pasted on matte paper flaps, selling for £3.90. *Outposts* is digest-sized, 70-100 pp. flat-spined, litho, in professionally set small type, using ads. Of 120,000 poems received he uses about 300. Press run is 3,000 for 2,800 subscriptions of which 10% are libraries, 2% of circulation through shelf sales. Subscription: $24. **Sample: $8 postpaid. Pays $8 per poem plus 1 copy. Simultaneous submissions, previously published poems OK. Reports in 2 weeks plus post time.** Hippopotamus Press publishes 6 books a year, averaging 80 pages. **For book publication query with sample poems. Simultaneous, previously published, dot-matrix, photocopies all OK. Reports in 6 weeks. Pays 10% minimum royalties plus 20 paper copies, 6 cloth.** Send for book catalog to buy samples (available in U.S. from their distributor, State Mutual Services, 521 Fifth Ave., New York NY 10175). The magazine holds an annual poetry competition.

HIRAM POETRY REVIEW (II), P.O. Box 162, Hiram OH 44234, founded 1967, poetry editors Hale Chatfield and Carol Donley, is a semiannual with occasional special supplements. **"We favor new talent — and except for one issue in two years, read** *only* **unsolicited MSS." They are interested in "all kinds of high quality poetry"** and have published poetry by Grace Butcher, Hale Chatfield, David Citino, Michael Finley, Jim Daniels, Peter Klappert and Harold Witt. They offer these sample lines from "Fat People at the Amusement Park" by Rawdon Tomlinson:

> . . .*chattering as though they'd entered*
> *the kingdom, they step into the cars*
> *of the tilt-a-whirl, tilting, and take off*
> *into a scream of weightlessness.*

There are 30+ pp. of poetry in the professionally printed digest-sized saddle-stapled magazine (glossy cover with b/w photo). It has a circulation of 400, 250 subscriptions of which 150 are libraries. $4 per subscription, $2 per copy. They receive about 7,500 submissions per year, use 50, have up to a 6 month backlog. **Sample: free! No carbons, photocopies or simultaneous submissions. "Send 4-5 fresh, neat copies of your best poems." Reports in 2-4 months. Pays 2 copies plus year's subscription.**

HOB-NOB (V), 994 Nissley Rd., Lancaster PA 17601, phone (717)898-7807, founded 1969, poetry editor Mildred K. Henderson, is a small literary semiannual with certain 'family' emphasis. About ⅓ poetry, ⅔ prose. They are **"filled up with poetry from first-time submitters for 1992. They use "poetry up to 16-line limit, light or humorous verse, serious poetry on vital current themes, people, nature, animals, etc. Religious poetry is also acceptable. No erotica, horror, suicide, excess violence, murder, overly depressing themes, especially utter hopelessness."** They have recently published poems by Gayle Elen Harvey, Andrew J. Grossman and Ronald Smits. As a sample Mildred Henderson chose these lines by Sigmund Weiss:

> *Armies of daffodils rise massed for war,*
> *their spears silvered by rays of sun.*
> *Above and around horsemen ride*
> *on wings light as air.*

Hob-Nob is 64 pp. magazine-sized, saddle-stapled, offset, on 20 lb. bond and heavier cover, printed from photoreduced typescript. It offers free ads to subscribers and exchange publications. About 20 new poets are featured in each issue. Print run is 350. Subscription: $6. **Sample: $3.50 postpaid. Send SASE for guidelines. Pays 1 copy for first appearance only. After that you have to subscribe to be accepted. She accepts submissions only in January and February of each year, 2-year wait for first-time contributors. Material received at other times will be returned unread. She prefers not to have simultaneous submissions or previously published poems. Publication is copyrighted; buys first rights only. Reports in 2 months. The editor comments on rejections "especially if I can think of a way a rejected item can be salvaged or made suitable to submit elsewhere."** The Readers Choice contest, every issue, pays $10 for first prize, lesser amount for other place (unless special prizes are offered by readers). Awards are on the basis of votes sent in by readers. The editor advises, "Poets and would-be poets should read contemporary poetry to see what others are doing. Most of what I receive does not seem to be rhymed and metered anymore, and unless a poet is extremely skilled with rhyme and meter (few are), he will find free verse much easier to deal with. I told one poet recently that the content is vital. Say something new, or if it's not new, say it in a new way. Nobody wants to see the same old 'June-moon-spoon' stuff. Patterns can be interesting, even without formal rhyme and meter. Take an unusual viewpoint."

HOBO JUNGLE: A QUARTERLY JOURNAL OF NEW WRITING (I), Rucum Rd., Roxbury CT 06783, phone (203)354-4359, founded 1987, publishers Ruth Boerger and Marc Erdrich, is a literary quarterly of new writing using poetry **"well written with no restrictions as to length or content."** They have recently published poetry by Lyn Lifshin, Davyne Verstandig and Alvin Laster. As a sample the editor selected these lines by Deborah Lattizori:

> *Come out of your skin*
> *Hang it on the windowless wall that widows watch*
> *as they*
> *quietly spin their web*

It is professionally printed on newsprint, 64-102 pp., with textured, heavy paper cover. They accept about 25-30% of 600-800 submissions received annually. Press run: 11,000, **distributed free throughout Connecticut and parts of New York City.** ("but small contribution helps—for postage; currently offering subscriptions for $12 for anyone who would like to have the magazine mailed.") **"All submissions should be cleanly typed or photocopied, or may be submitted electronically via modem: phone (203)355-8295. Pays $10 upon publication. Reports in 10-12 weeks." Editor comments on submissions "always."** Marc Erdrich says, "In issue No. 6 we published more than 80 writers. As a free publication, we can easily reach a large audience. New writers, especially poets, need to hear their work read aloud."

HOLIDAY HOUSE, INC. (IV-Children), 425 Madison Ave., New York NY 10017, phone (212)688-0085, founded 1936, editor-in-chief Margery Cuyler, is a trade children's book house. They have published hardcover books for children by Myra Cohn Livingston. They publish 3 books a year averaging 32 pages but are interested in publishing more poetry books for ages 8-12. **Submit 5 sample poems. No simultaneous submissions or previously published poems. Photocopy and dot-matrix OK. They offer an advance and royalties. Editor rarely comments on rejections.**

THE HOLLINS CRITIC (II), P.O. Box 9538, Hollins College VA 24020, phone (703)362-6317, founded 1964, editor John Rees Moore, publishes critical essays, poetry and book reviews, appears 5 times yearly in a 20 pp. magazine-sized format, circulation 550, **uses a few short poems in each issue, interesting in form, content or both.** They have recently published poetry by Sandra G. Teichmann, Knute Skinner and Claudia Andrews. As a sample, here are a few lines from "Shifting Night" by Mattie F. Quesenberry:

> I slip out of my bone-bordered enclave,
> wave my hands in the air.
>
> The night shifts, shorn from the sky.
> The stars fall away from their center.
> This tilting, timed for now,
> lifts my feet from the ground.
> I fix my eyes to the network of lights
> tacked to night's blanket of curved space.

Sample: $1.50. Submit up to 5 poems, none over 35 lines. No photocopies. Reports in 6 weeks (slower in the summer). Pays $25/poem plus 5 copies.

HOLMGANGERS PRESS; KESTREL CHAPBOOK SERIES (V), 95 Carson Ct., Shelter Cove, Whitethorn CA 95489, phone (707)986-7700, founded 1974, poetry editor Gary Elder, was "founded primarily to bring out **young or unjustly ignored 'older' poets.** We have since published as well collections of fiction, novels, history, graphic art and experimental works." **Holmgangers Press and the Kestrel Series will be inactive through 1992.**

HENRY HOLT & COMPANY (V), 115 W 18th St., New York NY 10011, **accepts no unsolicited poetry.**

‡HOME PLANET NEWS (II), P.O. Box 415, Stuyvesant Station, New York NY 10009, phone (718)769-2854, founded 1979, editors Enid Dame and Donald Lev, is a 3-4 times a year tabloid (newsprint) journal presenting a "lively, eclectic and comprehensive view of contemporary literature." They want **"honest, well-crafted poems, open or closed form, on any subject, but we will not publish any work which seems to us to be racist, sexist, ageist, anti-semitic, or has undue emphasis on violence. Poems under 30 lines stand a better chance. We lean somewhat toward poetry with urban sensibility but are not rigid about this."** They have published poetry by Hayden Carruth, Cornelius Eady, Norman Rosten, Daniel Berrigan, Will Inman, Toi Derricotte, Fritz Hamilton, Leo Connellan, Lyn Lifshin, Antler, William Packard, and Denise Duhamel. The editors selected these sample lines from "Clotheslines" by Robbie Casey:

> Clothes on a rope
> gallop in the wind
> freer than the bodies they cover
> will ever be

They use approximately 13 full 11 × 16″ pp. of poetry in each 24 pp. issue, circulation 1,000 with 400 subscriptions of which 8 are libraries. Of 1,200 submissions per year, they use about 50-60. Publication could take one year from acceptance. **Sample: $2 postpaid. Subscription: $8 per year. Submit 3-6 poems typed double-spaced, with SASE. Reports within 3 months. Payment: 4 copies and year's subscription.** Reviews books of poetry. "We co-sponsor 'Day of the Poet,' a poetry festival and contest which takes place each October in Ulster County, New York."

HONEST ULSTERMAN (II, IV-Regional), 102 Elm Park Mansions, Park Walk, London, U.K. SW10 0AP, founded 1968, editors Robert Johnstone and Ruth Hooley, is a literary magazine appearing 3-4 times a year using **"technically competent poetry and prose, book reviews. Special reference to Northern Irish and Irish literature. Lively, humorous, adventurous, outspoken."** They have published poetry by Seamus Heaney, Paul Muldoon, Gavin Ewart, Craig Raine, Fleur Adcock, and Medbh McGuckian. I have not seen an issue, but the editor describes it as "75-100 pp., A-5 (digest-sized), photolithographic, phototypeset, photographs and line drawings. Occasionally color covers." Press run: 1,000 for

300+ subscriptions. Subscription: $28. **Sample postpaid: $7. Pays "a nominal fee" plus 2 copies. Editor comments on submissions "occasionally."**

HONEYBROOK PRESS (V), P.O. Box 883, Rexburg ID 83440, phone (208)356-1456, founded 1984, proprietor Donnell Hunter, specializes in fine printing, letterpress, handset type, of chapbooks of poetry. Donnell Hunter says, "this is more of a hobby press, so I ask some 'name' poets for MSS; but I have done some subsidized work for friends." He has published books by himself, William Stafford, Marvin Bell and Leslie Norris.

‡HOPSCOTCH: THE MAGAZINE FOR GIRLS (IV-Children), Box 12923, Saratoga Springs NY 12866, phone (518)587-2268, founded 1989, editor Donald P. Evans, is a bimonthly magazine for **girls 6-12. "No length restrictions. Nothing abstract, experimental."** They have recently published poetry by Bette Killion, Sue Carloni and Cathy Drinkwater Better. I have not seen an issue, but the editor describes it as "full-color cover, 48 pp. of 2-color inside, 7×9", saddle-stapled." They use about 30-35 of some 2,000 poems received/year. Press run 7,500 for 7,000 subscribers of which 5,500 are libraries, 200 to inquiring schools and libraries. Subscription: $15. **Sample postpaid: $3. Reports in 2 weeks. Pays $10-40. Submit no more than 6 poems/submission.**

HOUGHTON MIFFLIN CO. (V), 2 Park St., Boston MA 02108, founded 1850, poetry editor Peter Davison. Houghton Mifflin is a high-prestige trade publisher that puts out both hardcover and paper-back books, but **poetry submission is by invitation only.** They have recently issued poetry books by Donald Hall, May Swenson, Ai, William Matthews, Margaret Atwood, Andrew Hudgins and Rodney Jones. **Authors are paid 10% royalties; advance is $1,000 and up.**

‡HOUSE OF MOONLIGHT (I), 15 Oakwood Rd., Bracknell, Berkshire RG12 2SP U.K., founded 1981, editor John Howard, publishes 4 pp. leaflets of poems by individual poets at irregular intervals. **"Poems on love, death and the universe — common themes expressed in an uncommon way. Long poems up to 100 lines preferred."** They have recently published poetry by Steve Sneyd and John Francis Haines. **Pays 5 copies. Reports in a month.**

HOUSEWIFE-WRITER'S FORUM (IV-Children, humor), P.O. Box 780, Lyman WY 82937, phone (307)786-4513, founded 1988, editor/publisher Diane Wolverton, is a magazine of "prose, poetry, information and open forum communication for and by housewives or any woman who writes while juggling a busy schedule. **We have no specifications as to form, length, subject, style or purpose. We publish both serious poetry and humorous. Nothing pornographic, but erudite expression is fine."** As a sample she selected these lines from "Female Justice" by Carole Brost:

> . . . *this is nine months*
> *of lopsided respite,*
> *a holiday from monthly worries*
> *of blood in my shoe.*

Diane Wolverton describes the magazine as "a small market for women who aspire to write for larger women's markets; or support each other in the quest for finding time and energy to write." It is 40 pp., desktop published, using some art, graphics and ads, appearing bimonthly. Press run is 1,200. **Sample: $4 postpaid. Send SASE for guidelines. Pays 1 copy plus 1¢ and up per word. "Simultaneous submissions are fine." Reports in 2 months.** She holds contests in several catego-ries, humorous and serious, with $2 per poem fee, April 15 deadline."

HOWLING DOG (II), 8419 Rhode, Utica MI 48317, founded 1985, editor Mark Donovan, a quarterly literary journal of "letters, words, and lines." The editor likes **"found poetry, graphically interesting pieces, humorous work, avant-garde, experimental, fun and crazy. All forms. All subjects, but we tend to have a light satirical attitude towards sex and politics."** He has recently published poems by Arthur Winfield Knight, Keith Wilson, John Sinclair, Alan Catlin and M. L. Liebler. As a sample the editor selected these lines by Richard Myers:

> *I ran into Idi Amin*
> *at the Safeway in Jeddah*
> *He was stocking up*
> *on Sara Lee pound cake*

Howling Dog appears 2 times a year in a 64 pp. digest-sized, flat-spined format, offset, press run 500 for 80 subscriptions of which 1 is a library. They receive some 4,000 submissions per year, use maybe 150. Subscription: $20/4 issues. **Sample: $4 postpaid. Send SASE for guidelines. Pays with copies and discount. Submit 3-5 poems with name and address on each page. "We don't use much rhyme or poems under 10 lines." Simultaneous submissions OK. Previously published poems OK "but let us know." Reporting time 2-3 months, longer if we like it.** Reviews books of poetry. **They are not presently considering book MSS.** Mark Donovan says, "We desire to produce an effect similar to the howl of a dog with its foot caught in the fence. Something that may not be pleasant or permanent, yet still heard by everyone in the neighborhood until the time comes to unleash the poor beast to whatever other endeavors it may become involved in. Send your wildest pieces."

‡THE HOWLING MANTRA; THE HOWLING MANTRA PRESS (II, IV-form), P.O. Box 1821, LaCrosse WI 54602, founded 1988, is an annual using "short poems. I would like minimal and experimental poems under 20 lines (including haiku). Poems that bring out erotic or natural metaphor. No suicide poems or verbal diarrhea. No long-winded bs." They have recently published poetry by Charles Bukowski, Allen Ginsberg, Judson Crews, Antler, Ellen Bryant Voight and Robert Schuler. As a sample the editor selected these lines from "ecology of love, in the forest" by Walter Hamady:

> we let ourselves love,
> that is the setting of
> ourselves on fire.
> in the ashes there,
> new things grow
> that cannot burn again.

It is 4¼″ × 5½″, professionally printed in small type, 40-60 pp., "stitched no binding, handmade paper cover, b/w art, small pocket mag good to take to the woods and read." Press run is 150 for 20 subscribers of which 2 are libararies, 40 shelf sales. Subscription: $5. **Sample: $5 postpaid. Do not submit mss from March through May. Pays 1 copy. "I read all submissions immediately and respond within 2 weeks."** Editor seldom comments on rejections. He says, "There is an overall abundance of small press markets for poets. Find the one which means something to you, and support it. As far as poetry, be brief and honest. Send, send, send it out! Proclaim it from the highest small press. Read Keats and Han Shan, and drink a lot of Black Label in the park hours of August." Howling Mantra Press will "design and publish a book with the help of the author. Cost and distribution is a shared problem between the two of us."

HRAFNHOH; LANGUAGE INFORMATION CENTRE (IV-Religious, political, spirituality, ethnic, themes), 32 Stryd Ebeneser, Pontypridd, Wales via GB, phone 0443 492243, founded 1987, editor Joseph Biddulph, is a "small press publishing linguistic and literary works, with historical, heraldic and genealogical subjects added, in the irregular magazine *Hrafnhoh.*" They use "**Poetry in traditional verse forms with a spiritual, Christian inspiration and purpose, with an active concern for technique and conveying a serious message in an evocative and entertaining style. No expressive free verse with iconoclastic or cynical attitude, self-indulgent, blasphemy, or indecency or verse that doesn't say anything.**" They have recently published poetry by John Waddington-Feather. As a sample the editor selected these lines (poet unidentified):

> Charles Spurgeon didn't fit a fashion's frame
> (Although he hangs brown-tinted on this wall) —
> He unexpected raised the neglected name,
> To which all dominations kneel and fall . . .

I have not seen an issue, but the editor describes it as digest-sized, 12-24 pp., photocopied from typescript, illustrated with sketches and old prints. He accepts about 2 of 6-10 poems received. Press run: 100-500. **Sample postpaid: £3 outside Europe. Pays "as many copies as required." Simultaneous submissions and previously published poems OK. Reports as soon as possible. Editor comments on submissions "not at any length and only if specifically requested." He offers criticism for £2 for up to 4 poems of 1-2 pp. each.** Reviews only a selection of books of poetry. He says, "Almost all unsolicited submissions are in one form—free verse—and without substance, i.e., without a definite purpose, message or conclusion. I am anxious to obtain verse with a strong technique and understanding of meter, with some real and substantial message."

THE HUDSON REVIEW; THE BENNETT AWARD (III), 684 Park Ave., New York NY 10021, assistant editor Kate Swisher, *The Hudson Review* is a high-quality flat-spined quarterly, which **pays 50¢ a line for poetry. Reports in 6-8 weeks. Poetry is read from April 1 through September 30.** They also sponsor the Bennett Award, established in memory of Joseph Bennett, a founding editor of *HR.* Every other year $15,000 is given to honor a writer "of significant achievement, in any literary genre or genres, whose work has not received the full recognition it deserves, or who is at a critical stage in his or her career—a stage at which a substantial grant might be particularly beneficial in furthering creative development. There are no restrictions as to language or nationality. **The Bennett Award is not open to nominations, and *The Hudson Review* will not accept nominations or applications in any form.**"

THE HUMAN QUEST (IV-Political), 1074 23rd Ave. N., St. Petersburg FL 33704, editor Edna Ruth Johnson, is a "humanistic monthly dealing with society's problems, especially peace. We use practically no poetry." It is magazine-sized, appears 9 times a year, circulation 10,000, of which 1,000 go for library subscriptions. **Send for free sample. Pays copies.**

‡HUMOR (IV-Humor), P.O. Box 41070, Philadelphia PA 19127, founded 1985, editor Edward Savaria Jr. is a quarterly magazine using **short humorous poems**. As a sample the editor selected "Driver's License?" by Danny Lee:

> *I studied all the rules of the road.*
> *The test was a pain in the neck.*
> *But, I had to get my license.*
> *How else could I cash a check?*

They accept 1 out of 10 pieces submitted. It is professionally printed, magazine-sized, 24 pp. with color glossy card cover. Press run 10,000 for 5,000 subscriptions, 5,000 shelf sales. Subscription: 16. **Sample: $5 postpaid, first class. Send SASE for guidelines. Pays $5-100 plus 1 copy. Previously published poems and simultaneous submissions OK. Reports in 30+ days.** The editor says, "If you get a response of 'that's cute' to your poem—don't send it."

HURRICANE ALICE (IV-Feminist), 207 Lind Hall, 207 Church St. SE, Minneapolis MN 55455, founded 1983, acquisitions editor Toni McNaron, a quarterly feminist review that publishes a maximum of 1-2 poems per issue; "we are not willing to read a great deal of poetry." Poems should be **infused by a feminist sensibility (whether the poet is female or male) and "should have what we think of as a certain analytic snap to them."** They have published poems by Alice Walker, Ellen Bass, Meridel LeSueur, Patricia Hampl, and Nellie Wong. The magazine is a "12-page folio, table of contests on cover, plenty of graphics." Circulation is 500-1,000, of which 350 are subscriptions and about 50 go to libraries. Price per issue is $1.95, subscription is $10 (or $8 low-income). **Sample available for $2.50 postpaid. Pay is 5-10 copies. Reporting time on submissions is 3-4 months and time to publication 3-6 months. Considers simultaneous submissions, "If we know."** Reviews books of poetry. The editor says, "Poets—read what one another are doing. If someone has already written your poem(s), listen to the message. Read what good poets have already written. Spare the trees—."

HUTTON PUBLICATIONS; RHYME TIME; MYSTERY TIME; WRITERS' INFO (I, IV-Themes), P.O. Box 1870, Hayden ID 83835, poetry editor Linda Hutton. *Rhyme Time*, founded 1981, and published bimonthly beginning in 1987, consists of 3-5 sheets of typing paper, stapled at the corner, offset both sides from typescript, "**featuring rhymed poetry with some free verse and blank verse. We sponsor several contests each year, both with and without entry fees. 16 lines maximum, no avant-garde, haiku or sugary work.**" As a sample the editor selected these lines from "Night Whispers" by Helen V. Johnson:

> *Hum to me, wind;*
> *Whisper, spring rain;*
> *Rustle, green leaf—*
> *Dim aching pain,*
> *Solace my grief.*

Sample and guidelines free for SASE (two stamps), price regularly $1.25, subscription $7.50, circulation 200, 75 subscriptions (2 libraries). She uses about half of the 300 submissions received annually, **pays one free copy.** *Mystery Time*, founded 1983, is an annual 44-52 pp. digest-sized chapbook, stapled-spine, containing 1-2 pages in each issue of **humorous poems about mysteries and mystery writers.** The editor selected these lines from "Who Done It?" by R.C. McIntyre:

> *Halfway through the plot,*
> *When the plot's not so hot,*
> *Wouldn't it be better than not*
> *If somehow the writer was shot?*

Circulation: 100, sample $3.50, uses 4-6 of the 12-15 submissions received. **Guidelines available. Pays 25¢ per line.** *Writers' Info*, founded 1984, is a monthly consisting of 3 sheets of typing paper, stapled at the corner, offset both sides from typescript. Tipsheet for the beginning freelancer. The editor selected this sample from "Nothing to read" by C.D. Russell:

> *I bought a new poetry book today.*
> *The reason for it I can't say;*
> *But black and white are never gray.*
> *The poet lost me somewhere on his way.*

Writers' Info "**needs short poems about freelancing (fewer than 16 lines) and pays up to $10 for first rights. Payment in copies for reprint rights. A sample copy of this monthly newsletter is free for a #10 SASE with two ounces postage.**

‡ICON; HART CRANE AWARD (II), English Dept., Kent State University, Trumbull Campus, 4314 Mahoning Ave. NW, Warren OH 44483, phone (216)847-0571, founded 1966, faculty advisor Dr. Robert Brown, appears twice a year. "**We prefer experimental poetry, poetry that takes risks in terms of form and subject matter, but will consider anything well-written. No religious, sentimental, formulaic or prosaic poetry.**" They have recently published poetry by Gay Brewer and William Greenway.

As a sample the editor selected these lines from "To Bartleby..." by Margaret Pinkerton:

> Bartleby, you bother me.
> I find the words that brought you fame
> more distinctive than your name....

It is digest-sized, 40-80 pp., saddle-stapled, with matte card cover, printed in colored type. They accept 20% of 200 poems submitted. Press run 1,000 for 50 subscribers of which 10 are libraries. Distributed free to students and faculty. Subscription: $4. **Sample postpaid: $2. Pays 2 copies. No submissions April-July. Reports in 1-3 months.** The Hart Crane Award of $100 for poetry and a Kenneth Patchen Award of $100 for prose are given annually.

‡IHCUT (I), P.O. Box 612, Napavine WA 98565, founded 1989, contact Larry L. Randall, is an inexpensively produced newsletter appearing every other month. **"I am open to anything so long as it is exciting and original. Length does not matter, and the purpose should be to writhe, cry or explode. I would rather not see rhyming poetry."** As a sample the editor selected these lines from "Corridors" by Njuzu:

> down
> the dark
> secret
> passages
> of my mind

It is 15-20 pp. photocopied, side-stapled on ordinary paper. Press run 20. **Sample postpaid: $2. Send SASE for guidelines. Pays 1 copy. Reports in 1 week. Previously published poems and simultaneous submissions OK.**

UNIVERSITY OF ILLINOIS PRESS (III), 54 E. Gregory Dr., Champaign IL 61820, phone (217)333-0950, founded 1918, poetry editor Laurence Lieberman, publishes **collections of individual poets, 65-105 pp.** Some poets they have published are Roland Flint, Brendan Galvin, S.J. Marks, Laura Mullen and Robert Wrigley. **Open for poetry submissions one month a year—usually February. There is a $10 handling fee. Query with "brief resume of publications, awards, etc." Samples optional. Typescript preferred. Royalty contract and 10 copies. Editor comments on many submissions.** Laurence Lieberman comments: "Poets would do well to acquaint themselves with at least a few books from our list before deciding whether to submit their work to Illinois." Send SASE for poetry list.

‡IMAGINATION MAGAZINE (I), P.O. Box 781, Dolton IL 60419, founded 1990, editor Lisa Hake, is a monthly using **poems up to 24 lines. "I prefer poetry that is rhymed and follows traditional forms although I'm open to new styles and forms. I like to see good imagery. The poems should move me. They've got to have bang!"** They have recently published poetry by Jocelyne Kamerer, Michael Colin Murphy and S.R. Sheppard. As a sample the editor selected these lines from "You Can Go Home Again" by H. Ray Nail:

> The soul of night comes out to wear
> Moonbeams of gold within her hair,
> And I in rapture wander there.
> My harried friends seem quite aware
> I've surely been away somewhere.
> I tell them with a gentle grace
> I've just been to the Old Home Place.

It is 32 pp., photocopied on 8½×11" sheets, folded in half, saddle-stapled, with stock cover, desk-top publishing. Press run 100 for 35 subscribers of which 4 are libraries. Subscription: $21/year. **Sample: $3 postpaid. Send SASE for guidelines. Pays 1 copy. Editor sometimes comments. Reports in one month.** Reviews books of poetry. Send books to the attention of Book Reviewer. "We also began publishing chapbooks in March 1991. No requirements, no membership fee, no reading fee, nothing. Just send me your stuff."

‡IMAGO LITERARY MAGAZINE; CITY OF BRISBANE POETRY AWARD (II, IV-Regional), School of Communication and Organisational Studies, GPO Box 2434, Brisbane 4001 Queensland, Australia, phone (07)223-2976, founded 1988, appears twice a year, publishing "the best **Australian writing, placing particular emphasis on Queensland writing and culture, but also welcomes submissions from overseas. Poems preferably short—up to about 50 lines, most from 12-25 lines. Our main criterion is good writing."** They have recently published poetry by Tom Shapcott, Bruce Dawe, Roger McGough and Nancy Cato. It is digest-sized, 90 pp., with glossy card cover. They accept about 10% of 500 poems from about 150 writers. Press run 800 for 350 subscribers of which 36 are libraries. Subscription: $A12.50 in Australia. **Sample postpaid: $A7.50. Reports in 1-6 months. Pays $A30-40 plus 1 copy.** Comments "sometimes, if requested." They publish the winning poems of the City of Brisbane Poetry Award (annual).

IMPLOSION PRESS; IMPETUS (I, II, IV-Erotica, women), 4975 Comanche Trail, Stow OH 44224, phone (216)688-5210, founded 1984, poetry editor Cheryl Townsend, publishes *Impetus*, a quarterly literary magazine, chapbooks, special issues. The editor would like to see "strong social protest with raw emotion exuded. No topic is taboo. Material should be straight from the gut, uncensored and real. Absolutely no nature poetry or rhyme for the sake of rhyme, oriental, or 'Kissy, kissy I love you' poems. Any length as long as it works. All subjects okay, providing it isn't too rank. *Impetus* is now publishing an annual erotica and all female issue. Material should reflect that theme." They have published poetry by Charles Bukowski, Ron Androla, Todd Moore, Gerald Locklin and Lyn Lifshin. As a sample the editor selected these lines from "And He Closes 91.43% of His Sales" by Joan McMenomey:

> never go to bed with a man
> whose sheets look like graph paper
> when he comes inside you
> it will feel like a transaction
> he will have timed the strokes
> learned foreplay from a Zig Ziglar book
> mirror-rehearsed his pitch
> calculated your measurements
> into the price of the wine

The 7½×9″ magazine is photocopied from typescript, saddle-stapled. Circulation about 1,000, with 300 subscriptions. Generally a 3 month backlog. **Sample: $3 postpaid; make check payable to Cheryl Townsend. The editor says, "All I ask is that they send me what best represents them, but I prefer shorter, to-the-point work."** Previously published work OK if it is noted when and where. Usually reports the same day. Pays 1 copy. Send SASE for guidelines. In her comments on rejection, the editor usually refers poets to other magazines she feels would appreciate the work more. Reviews books of poetry. She says, "Bear with the small press. We're working as best as we can and usually harder. We can only do so much at a time. Support the small presses!"

INDIANA REVIEW (II), 316 N. Jordan Ave., Indiana University, Bloomington IN 47405, founded 1982, editor Allison Joseph, is a triquarterly of new fiction and poetry. "In general the *Review* looks for fresh, original poems of insight, poems that are challenging without being obtuse. We'll consider all types of poems — free verse, traditional, experimental. Reading a sample issue is the best way to determine if *IR* is a potential home for your work. Any subject matter is acceptable if it is written well. No poetry that is cliché, amateurish or fake. Recently published David Mura, Silivia Curbelo, Naomi Shihab Nye, Pattiann Rogers and Stephen Dobyns. The magazine uses about 30-40 pp. of poetry in each issue (6×9″, flat-spined, 128 pages, color matte cover, professional printing). The magazine has 600 subscriptions of which 120 are libraries. They receive about 8,000 submissions per year of which they use about 60. Sample: $5 postpaid. Submit no more than 4-5 pp. of poetry. Photocopy, dot-matrix OK if readable. Please indicate stanza breaks on poems over 1 page. "Simultaneous submissions very strongly discouraged." Pays $5 per page when available ($10 minimum per poem), plus 2 copies and remainder of year's subscription. "We try to respond to manuscripts in two to three months. Reading time is often slower during summer months."

‡INDIGO MAGAZINE: THE SPANISH-CANADIAN PRESENCE IN THE ARTS (IV-Foreign Languages, Translations, Themes), Rm 252, Atkinson College, York University, North York, Ontario M3T 1P3 Canada, phone (416)736-2100 Ext. 6632, founded 1989, editor-in-chief Prof. Margarita Feliciano, appears twice a year using "poetry to be thematically of Hispanic contents if written in French or English (not the case if written in Spanish)." They have recently published poetry by Rafael Barreto-Rivera and Rosemary Sullivan. As a sample the editor selected these lines (poet unidentified):

> I was born on this lip of stone
> Jutting out over the jungle
> I've never wanted to go down.
> As a child I would run to the edge to catch the birds
> or follow the lizards with my hand along the ledges.

It is professionally printed, flat-spined, 150+ pp., with glossy card cover. "I accept 50% of submissions (about 40). Press run 300 for 50 subscribers. Subscription: $25. **Price of sample, payment, reporting time not given. The editor says she always comments on rejections.**

INFINITY LIMITED: A JOURNAL FOR THE SOMEWHAT ECCENTRIC (II), P.O. Box 2713, Castro Valley CA 94546, phone (415)581-8172, founded 1988, Editor-in-Chief Genie Lester, is a "literary quarterly dedicated to presenting emerging talent attractively illustrated. Staff artists illustrate most work, but we encourage writer-artists to submit their own illustrations." They want poetry that is **"clever, amusing, interesting, thoughtful, original, moving."** They have recently published poetry by Thomas Kretz, Errol Miller and Thomas Chase. It is magazine-sized, "printed on 60 pound bond with parchment cover (2-3 color)" and says it appears "more or less quarterly, 4 times a year. We receive about 25 submissions per week, use about 25 poems per issue." Press run 1,000 for 150+ subscriptions. Subscription: $10. **Sample postpaid: $3.95. Send SASE for guidelines. Pays 2 copies. Simultaneous submissions and occasionally previously published poems OK. Reports within 3 months. Editor comments on submissions "if writing or art shows promise."** The editor says, "We are small but growing rapidly, probably because we are willing to work with our writers and artists. We make an effort to present material attractively. The poetry we publish usually deals in an original way with concerns common to all of us."

INKSHED—POETRY AND FICTION (II); INKSHED PRESS (V), 387 Beverley Rd., Hull, N. Humberside HU5 ILS England, founded 1985, editorial director Anthony Smith, poetry editor Lesli Markham, is a quarterly using **"any good quality poetry, traditional or contemporary, not sexist or racist."** They have recently published poetry by Gerald Locklin, George Gott and Shelia Murphy. As a sample the editors selected these sample lines by Sam J. Bruno:

> *Aunt Clara says she has made the news.*
> *Enclosed are the paper clippings*
> *Of her dressed as Santa Claus,*
> *Outside the Salvation Army.*
> *One clipping shows the Catholic in her*
> *Blessing the drunk with holy water.*
> *Another shows the poverty in her*
> *Lighting a match*
> *To a Sears Roebuck catalogue.*

Inkshed is digest-sized, saddle-stapled, 44 pp., printed on gloss paper from typeset. Their press run is 400 with 100 subscriptions. Subscription: $10 for 3 issues. **Sample: $3 postpaid. "Please send cash only & U.S. dollars or Sterling—dollar cheques are too expensive to exchange." Pays 1 copy. They consider simultaneous submissions and previously published poems. Reports in 1 month.** Reviews books of poetry. **Inkshed Press publishes 1 chapbook a year averaging 30 pp., but only by invitation.** Anthony Smith advises, "Please study what is being written today—note trends but don't copy—be an individual, that's what poetry is about."

INKSTONE: A MAGAZINE OF HAIKU (IV-Form), P.O. Box 67, Station H, Toronto, Ontario M4C 5H7 Canada, founded 1982, poetry editors Keith Southward, Marshall Hryciuk and J. Louise Fletcher, "is a publication dedicated to the development of a distinctive English language haiku and to the craft of writing as it relates to haiku. Submissions reflecting these concerns are welcomed. We publish haiku and related forms, plus reviews, articles related to haiku. **Poems must be haiku or related but we use a very liberal definition of haiku."** They have published haiku by Carol Montgomery, Alexis Rotella, Akira Kowano, Guy Beining and this sample by Le Roy Gorman:

> *dusk*
> *cicada*
> *husk*

There are roughly 20 pp. of poetry and reviews/articles in the digest-sized format, 40 pp., offset from typescript, matte card cover, circulation 100, accepting "perhaps 10%" of the poems submitted each year, poems appear as space permits, usually in the next issue after acceptance. **Sample: $5.50 postpaid. Submit any number of poems, preferably 1 per 5½ × 8½" sheet, typewritten. Reports within 6 weeks. Pays 1 copy. Editor "occasionally" comments on rejections.**

INLET (II), Virginia Wesleyan College, Norfolk VA 23502, phone (804)455-3238, founded 1971, editor Joseph Harkey, is an annual **"publishing the best poems and stories we can get, by established or unknown writers. Well-written, serious poetry—even if humorous; no sentimental stuff, no doggerel, and nothing that is indistinguishable from prose. Short (8-16 lines) in great demand; poems of 36-46 lines had better be *very* good; anything longer had better be immortal."** They have published poetry by Sister Mary Ann Henn, Carol Reposa, Ruth Moon Kempher, Robert Cooperman, and James Sutherland-Smith. 20-30 pp. of poetry are used in each 37 pp. issue, 7 × 8", pebbled matte cover with art, circulation 700, distributed free. **Sample: $1 in stamps. MSS accepted from September 1st through March 1st; publishes in spring or summer (it varies). Photocopy OK, with name of the poet and number of lines on the first page of each poem; 7 poems or fewer, prefer 8-30 lines but will consider longer ones. Reports within 3 months,** "*usually*." **Payment in copies.** The editor advises, "Write as well as you can and present neatly typed, readable manuscripts worthy of a professional. Don't wait for one batch to come back before trying *other* magazines with new poems. No dual submissions."

‡INNISFREE (II), P.O. Box 277, Manhattan Beach CA 90266, phone (213)545-2407, founded 1981, editor Rex Winn, appears every other month using short stories, one or two essays and **poetry. "We are not interested in sentimental verse. A frequent mistake we find in submitted poetry is a lack of attention to syntax or other clues to the intended meaning."** They have recently published poetry by

Norman Silverman, Lyn Lifshin and Ana Pine. As a sample the editor selected these lines by William Doreski:

> *I don't know how to inscribe so vague a fear,*
> *like a tatoo*
> *glimpsed on the arm of a stranger*
> *in a coffee shop.*

It is magazine-sized, 56 pp., professionally printed with matte card cover. They accept about 50% of poetry received. Press run 200-300 for 125 subscribers of which 3 are libraries. Subscription: $18. **Sample: $3 postpaid. Send SASE for guidelines. Pays "splattered awards" but no copies. "If a person asks, I will comment. Sometimes I can't resist anyway!" Previously published poems and simultaneous submissions OK.** Reviews books of poetry.

INSIGHT PRESS (V), P.O. Box 25, Drawer 249, Ocotillo, CA 92259, founded 1983, publishers John and Merry Harris. The Harrises publish short poetry chapbook anthologies containing the work of **"pre-selected writers (no submissions without invitation, please.)" The work published must be "short, non-academic poetry for the layman — clarity and lucidity a must. Prefer humorous, inspirational poetry."** They have recently published poems by L.C. Dancer, Elizabeth Lee, Jack Adler, Falling Blossom (Cherokee) and Merry Harris, who selected as a sample the following "4-liner" from "Road-runner" by Ma-Lee Ridge:

> *To Mona Lisa*
> *I've seen that smile*
> *On other faces,*
> *I know your secret:*
> *You're wearing braces.*

The chapbooks are paperback, flat-spined, 40-50 pp. "We sell our chapbooks at cost and send out at least 50 of first run for promotion of our poets, who are then widely reprinted." **Sample: $3 for "Laughter: a Revelry."** Merry Harris advises, "1) one tip for beginners: Join an amateur press association, as I did 40 years ago, to learn basics while being published. Amateur does NOT mean 'Amateurish.' AMAT = LOVE! 2) Join a local writers' co-op. 3) *Avoid those who exploit writers.* 4) As for technique, keep it simple, avoid erudite phrasing and pseudo-intellectualism." We do not publish other people's books. We publish *Merry-Go-Round*, *Contest Carousel* and *Roadrunner*, literary newsletters containing essays or writing by Merry. **Not open to submission.**

INTERNATIONAL BLACK WRITERS; BLACK WRITER MAGAZINE (I, IV-Ethnic), P.O. Box 1030, Chicago IL 60690, founded 1970, contact Mable Terrell executive director. *BWM* is a "literary magazine to showcase new writers and poets; educational information for writers. **Open to all types of poetry."** The editors selected these lines as a sample:

> *When, in life, a pebble*
> *becomes a boulder,*
> *Then you'll know*
> *that you're barefooted!*

I have not seen the quarterly, but the editor describes it as magazine-sized, 30 pp., offset printing, with a glossy cover, circulation 1,000, 200 subscriptions. Subscription $19 per year. **Sample: $1.50 postpaid. Pays 10 copies. Reports in 10 days, has 1 quarter backlog. For chapbook publication (40 pp.) submit 2 sample poems and cover letter with short bio. Simultaneous submissions OK. Pays copies. For sample chapbook send SASE with bookrate postage.** They offer awards of $100, $50 and $25 for the best poems published in the magazine, and presented to winners at annual awards banquet. *IBW* is open to all writers.

‡**INTERNATIONAL POETS ACADEMY; INTERNATIONAL POETS (I, IV-Membership)**, 5, Mohamed Hussain Khan Lane, Royapettah, Madras 600-014, India, founded 1981, poetry editor Prof. Syed Ameeruddin. The Academy publishes books by members (for a price). *International Poets* is a quarterly publishing poetry by members. **Membership is $30 a year. Life membership is $100.** They have recently published poetry by Ellis Ovesen (U.S.A.), William S. Kim (U.S.A.), Nadine C. Carey (U.S.A.) and Joy B. Cripps (Australia). The editor describes the quarterly as magazine-sized, (9½ × 5½"); printed in Madras. Reviews books of poetry. They publish 3 chapbooks per year subsidized by the poets. For details contact the academy.

INTERNATIONAL POETS OF THE HEART; THE LAY POET (IV-Membership), P.O. Box 463, Midvale UT 84047-0463, founded 1988, poetry editor Bob Curtis. International Poets of the Heart is an organization (membership $10 year/$12 year outside U.S.) "for the mutual interaction of the ideas and ideals as concepts from the heart. Our purpose is the meaningful communication of these concepts, 'heart to heart.'" They publish a newsletter, *The Lay Poet* of "how-to and general commentary on poetry submissions on a quarterly basis. **We solicit poetry for the newsletter, and ask comments from the**

membership. We recognize that 'feelings' are not only 'mushy love songs,' but emotions that may range from anger to euphoria. However, for the purposes of this organization, we seek those feelings from the positive side of life's experience." As a sample the editor selected these lines by Bob Curtis:

> But each of us are searching deep
> For memories that are lasting;
> A friendship or acquaintance rare,
> Maybe, a touch in passing.

The editor says, "We want to have **poetry submissions by members, and then we will print what we can and ask comments on those pieces." Submissions accepted only from members. No payment.** "We hope to collect the best and publish a book entitled 'The Best of The Best' in the future." Contest for members only (no fee), 3 categories: romantic, humorous and serious. Entry deadline: July 1, 1992. SASE for guidelines. "Let the words flow from the heart, organized by the mind. Don't 'force' feeling, let feeling 'force' you to write."

INTERSTATE RELIGIOUS WRITERS ASSOCIATION (IRWA) NEWSLETTER AND WORKSHOPS (IV-Membership, religious), 300 Cherry Hill Rd. NW, Cedar Rapids IA 52405, phone (319)396-2732, founded 1981, co-editors Marvin Ceynar and Barbara Ceynar, publishes a newsletter that "gives information mostly about religious writing but also information about secular publication that religious people feel comfortable publishing in." It uses **poetry by members suitable for an ecumenical Christian readership.** As a sample Barbara Ceynar selected these lines by Delma Yost:

> Keeping the bend intact
> Smooth and rub and shine
> Until the inner value lies
> exposed to witness to the spark
> That is needed to motivate another person;
> So observers can see the beauty of the wood
> And yearn to communicate that beauty.

IRWA Newsletter appears 6 times a year, magazine-sized 11 pp., 200 subscribers. They receive about 24 poems a year and "accept many of them." Subscription: $12. **Sample: $2.15 postpaid. Pays 2-5 copies.** Simultaneous submissions and previously published poems OK. **Reports immediately.** Editor sometimes comments on rejections.

INTERTEXT (III, IV-Translations), 2633 East 17th Ave., Anchorage AK 99508-3207, founded 1982, poetry editor Sharon Ann Jaeger, is "devoted to producing lasting works in every sense. We specialize in poetry, translations and short works in the fine arts and literary criticism. **We are looking for work that is truly excellent—no restrictions on form, length or style. Cannot use religious verse.** Like both surrealist and realist poetry, poetry with intensity, striking insight, vivid imagery, fresh metaphor, musical use of language in both word sounds and rhythm. Must make the world—in all its dimensions—come alive." To give a sense of her taste she says, "I admire the work of Louise Glück, William Stafford, Jim Wayne Miller, Eleanor Wilner, Antonio Ramos Rosa and Rainer Maria Rilke." The editor chose these sample lines from Louis Hammer's *The Mirror Dances*:

> Because the human body is always beautiful,
> because there are paths through the thighs
> to the bones of lightning,
>
> because a single kiss
> rolls up the blood
> like a shade before the light

The sample of their publishing I have seen, **17 Toutle River Haiku** by James Hanlen, is beautifully printed and illustrated with "oil and mixed media" and calligraphy: sells for $12. **Query first with 3 samples only, from May to August.** "Cover letter optional—the sample poems are always read first—but no form letters, please. If sample poems are promising, then the complete MS will be requested." Photocopy OK. Simultaneous queries OK. **Payment: 10% royalty after costs of production, promotion and distribution have been recovered. Send 6×9″ SASE for catalog to purchase sample.** No longer comments on rejected poems. No longer publishes chapbooks but only "full-length collections by poets of demonstrated achievement."

INTRO (IV-Students), AWP, Old Dominion University, Norfolk VA 23529-0079, phone (804)683-3839, founded 1970, publications manager D.W. Fenza. See Associated Writing Programs under Organizations Useful to Poets. **Students in college writing programs belonging to that organization may submit to this consortium of magazines publishing student poetry, fiction and plays.** They are open as to the type of poetry submitted except they do not want "non-literary, haiku, etc." As to poets they have published, they say, "In our history, we've introduced Dara Wier, Carolyn Forché, Greg Pope,

Norman Dubie and others." Circulation 9,500. **Programs nominate *Intro* works in the fall. Ask the director of your writing program for more information.**

INVERTED-A, INC.; INVERTED-A HORN (I), 401 Forrest Hill, Grand Prairie TX 75051, phone (214)264-0066, founded 1977, editors Amnon Katz and Aya Katz, a very small press that evolved from publishing technical manuals for other products. "Our interests center on justice, freedom, individual rights and free enterprise." *Inverted-A Horn* is a periodical, magazine-sized, offset, usually 6 pages, which appears irregularly; circulation is 300. **Freelance submissions of poetry for *Horn* and chapbooks are accepted. They publish 1 chapbook per year. The editors do not want to see anything "modern, formless, existentialist."** As a sample, they quote the following lines by John Grey:

> *In wrinkled eyes the color gleams tenfold*
> *As they extract the beauty from the blur . . .*
> *The husks may shrivel in December's cold*
> *But, oh, what golden fields of wheat they were.*

Pay is one free copy and a 40% discount on further copies. **Queries are reported on in 2 weeks, MSS in 2 months, simultaneous submissions are OK, as are photocopied or dot-matrix MSS.** Samples: "A recent issue of the *Horn* can be had by merely sending a SASE (subject to availability)." The editor says "I strongly recommend that would-be contributors avail themselves of this opportunity to explore what we are looking for. Most of the submissions we receive do not come close."

IO; NORTH ATLANTIC BOOKS (V), 2800 Woolsey St., Berkeley CA 94705, phone (415)652-5309, founded 1964, editors Richard Grossinger and Lindy Hough. *Io* appears irregularly, circulation 2,000. The editors say that **in general they do "not consider unsolicited MSS. We will consider those MSS** that come with clear cover letters indicating that the author has read books published by our press and is submitting with an accurate sense of what our guidelines are," and they **do not consider unsolicited poetry.**

IOTA (II), 67 Hady Crescent, Chesterfield, Derbyshire S41 0EB, Great Britain, phone +44246-276532 (UK: 0246-276532), founded 1988, poetry editor David Holliday, is a quarterly wanting **"any style and subject; no specific limitations as to length, though, obviously, the shorter a poem is, the easier it is to get it in, which means that poems over 40 lines can still get in if they seem good enough.** No concrete poetry (no facilities), or self-indulgent logorrhea." They have recently published poetry by Stanley Cook, steve sneyd, Betty Parvin, Joan Downar, Alun Rees, James Deahl and Thomas Land. As a sample the editor selected these lines by M. Munro Gibson:

> *Mellow stone bridge curves*
> *across the looking glass mere*
> *a perfect oval*

Iota is duplicated from typescript, saddle-stapled 32 pp., with colored paper cover. Their press run is 350 with 200 subscriptions of which 6 libraries. They publish about 160 of 2,500 poems received. Subscription: $5 (£3). **Sample: $1.25 (75p) postpaid "but sometimes sent free." Pays 2 copies. The editor prefers name and address on each poem, typed, "but provided it's legible, am happy to accept anything."** He considers simultaneous submissions, **but previously published poems "only if outstanding." Reports in 1-3 weeks. Editor usually comments on rejections, "but detailed comment only when time allows and the poem warrants it."** Reviews books of poetry. He says, "I am after crafted verse that says something; self-indulgent word-spinning is out. I hope, in the future, to start a series of chapbooks in the same style and format as the magazine. All editors have their blind spots; the only advice I can offer a beginning poet is to find a sympathetic editor (and you will only do that by seeing their magazines) and not to be discouraged by initial lack of success. Keep plugging!"

UNIVERSITY OF IOWA PRESS; EDWIN FORD PIPER POETRY AWARDS (III), Iowa City IA 52242. The University of Iowa Press offers annually the Edwin Ford Piper Poetry Awards **for book-length (50-120 pp.) MSS by poets who have already published at least one full-length book in edition of at least 750 copies. Two awards are given each year of $1,000 plus publication with standard royalty contract. (This competition is the only way in which this press accepts poetry). Manuscripts are received annually in February and March only.** Judges are nationally prominent poets. **All writers of English are eligible, whether citizens of the United States or not. Poems from previously published books may be included only in manuscripts of selected or collected poems, submissions of which are encouraged. Simultaneous submissions OK if press is immediately notified if the book is accepted by another publisher.** No reading fee is charged, but stamped, self-addressed packaging is required or

MSS will not be returned. "These awards have been initiated to encourage poets who are beyond the first-book stage to submit their very best work."

IOWA REVIEW (II), 308 EPB, University of Iowa, Iowa City IA 52242, phone (319)335-0462, founded 1970, editor David Hamilton (first readers for poetry and occasional guest editors vary), appears 3 times a year in flat-spined, 170-200 pp., professionally printed format. The editor says, "We simply look for poems that at the time we read and choose, we admire. **No specifications as to form, length, style, subject-matter, or purpose.** There are around 30-40 pp. of poetry in each issue and currently we like to give several pages to a single poet." Circulation 1,200-1,300 with 1,000 subscriptions of which about half are libraries. They receive about 5,000 submissions per year, use about 100. **Sample: $5 postpaid. Their backlog is "around a year. Sometimes people hit at the right time and come out in a few months." They report in 1-4 months, pay $1 a line, 2-3 copies, and a year's subscription. Occasional comments on rejections or suggestions on accepted poems.** The editor advises, "That old advice of putting poems in a drawer for 9 years was rather nice; I'd at least like to believe the poems had endured with their author for 9 months."

IOWA WOMAN (IV-Women), P.O. Box 680, Iowa City IA 52244, phone (319)338-9858, founded 1976, poetry editor Sandra Witt. "We are a literary quarterly with interest in women's issues. It is a literary magazine that has received national recognition for editorial excellence. We are publishing work **by women, about women, and for women. Prefer contemporary poetry that is clear and concise. Prefer narrative and lyric. No greeting-card verse.**" They have recently published poetry by Peggy Shumaker, Lyn Lifshin, Patricia Clark, Ann Struthers and Theresa Pappas. As a sample the editor selected these lines by Laurie Blauner:

> *the same way our dreams pass us by each year.*
> *Her only pleasure is left lying in pools*
> *of colorless light, shaped like shadows*
> *that spread over the world by the next morning.*

Iowa Woman is elegantly printed, 48 pp., magazine-sized, 4-color cover with "original cover art and illustrations." Of 2,000 poems received "I accept about 30." Press run is 4,000 for 2,000 subscriptions. **Sample: $3 postpaid. Guidelines available for SASE. Pays subscription and extra copies. No simultaneous submissions.** They hold an annual poetry contest with first place prize of $150. $6 entry fee, 3 poems, for non-subscribers. All entrants receive a copy of the issue with the winners. Deadline December 15.

IRON PRESS; IRON (II), 5 Marden Terrace, Cullercoats, North Shields, Tyne & Wear, NE30 4PD England, phone (091)2531901, founded 1973, poetry editors Peter Mortimer and David Stephenson, "publishes contemporary writing both in magazine form (*Iron*) and in individual books. Magazine concentrates on poetry, the books on prose and drama." They are "**open to many influences, but no 19th century derivatives please, or work from people who seem unaware anything has happened poetically since Wordsworth.**" Peter Mortimer says, "Writing is accepted and published because when I read it I feel the world should see it—if I don't feel that, it's no good. What's the point of poetry nobody understands except the poet?" The poets they have recently published include James Kirkup, John Latham and Carol Rumens. As a sample the editor selected this haiku by David Cobb:

> *the gnat confides*
> *a large secret in my ear—*
> *one it told last year*

Iron is 8¼ × 7¾", flat-spined, professionally printed in small type, 1-3 columns, using b/w photos and graphics, three-color glossy card cover, about 50 pp. of poetry in each issue, circulation 800, 500 subscriptions of which 30 are libraries. **Sample: $8 (bills only, no checks) postpaid, or £2.50p. Submit a maximum of *five* poems. "Just the poems—no need for long-winded backgrounds. The poems must stand by themselves." He reports in "2 weeks maximum," pays £10 per page. He always comments on rejections "provided poets keep to our maximum of 5 poems per submission."** They do not invite poetry submissions for books, which they commission themselves. The editor advises, "don't start submitting work too soon. It will only waste your own and editors' time. Many writers turn out a few dozen poems, then rush them off before they've learnt much of the craft, never mind the art." And about his occupation as editor, this journalist, poet, playwright and humorist says, "Small presses are crazy, often stupid, muddle-headed, anarchic, disorganized, totally illogical. I love them."

ISRAEL HORIZONS (IV-Ethnic), Suite 902, 27 West 20th St., New York, NY 10011, founded 1952, editor Ralph Seliger; poetry consultants Jon Shevin and Rochelle Ratner. A quarterly Socialist-Zionist periodical, circulation 5,000, 8½ × 11", 32 pp., **uses poetry reflecting Israeli and Jewish culture and concerns.** *Israel Horizons* deals with the Israeli left and the peace camp in Israel, including but not exclusively *Mapam* and the Kibbutz Artzi Federation; Israeli culture and life and current challenges

Close-up
Akua Lezli Hope
Poet

Survival Is Its Own Revenge

and when air you breathe like manna
whole, serene, second-stride thresholds
of splintered light, mumbled hues through
tears. quiet hymns sung until trains
stop. arrivals aren't your glory
this road soon thin before third gear.
you've invented greater figures than those
fourscore foundling dreams so toehold.
arthritic, contrite, once wagging fingers
dumbfounded, mute, once snakecoiled tongues
crazy crazy you   like many dreamlashed
daughters, sons   so even minute
confirmations, just a trembling clockstroke
not even revolution, just life's side
smiled wink, is a proof. is enough
to sing. to Shout. to work well.

That is one of the poems that won Akua Lezli Hope a Creative Writing Fellowship from the National Endowment for the Arts in 1990. She has also received an Artists Fellowship from the New York Foundation for the Arts (1987). She has had many publications in magazines and anthologies, such as ***Black American Literature Forum, Hambone, Contact II, Obsidian, IKON Magazine, Isaac Asimov's Science Fiction Magazine*, Confirmation**, an anthology of African-American women writers, and **Extended Outlooks**, an Iowa Review anthology of contemporary American women writers, and has given many readings to audiences in colleges, prisons, parks, museums and bars. She is now looking for a publisher for her first book.

She describes herself as "third generation New Yorker/amurkin" with "three ivy degrees" in psychology, journalism and business at Williams and Columbia, "arrived in Manhattan, grew in the Bronx, fled Queens, breathed in Brooklyn, survives in the Glass Valley," where she earns a living as a corporate marketing communications employee in a Fortune 200 company. "I don't like to talk about it," she says of her job. "I am annoyed by the assumptions of both the business and the literary communities about the meaning of my endeavors. For me, it's just fulfilling the psycho-social imperative of my West Indian upbringing; you always have at least *two* existences/jobs/endeavors, if not four."

Her parents, she says "were sophisticated purveyors of culture; I grew up with novels, poetry, three sets of encyclopedias, African-American and European music. Countee Cullen, a well-beloved African-American poet, was one of my father's teachers. I was read to and encouraged to read and write. I began *writing* before I could write. My mother was my scribe and would record and read my creations to me. My father was a great storyteller and mentor. He made science and math as exciting as the timestep. I learned calculus, but I've yet to master the timestep."

Because she spent so much of her "youthful training time" reading science, psychology and then business texts, she has compensated by reading, she says, "a lot more than my peers." She found journalism school "the most memorable, enjoyable and practical academic experience. They taught me how to write. This science has been immeasurably useful in all aspects of my life. It enabled me to improve my poetry."

She advises young writers to "write daily and read daily. I find the time, daily, though it's seldom as much as I want; it's the only way the work gets done." But literature is inseparable from life for Akua. "I have a social duty. Kujichagulia—one of the seven principles of the Nguzo Saba—says 'we must define ourselves, name ourselves and speak for ourselves, instead of being defined or spoken for by others.' That's the crux of my endeavor. There are others like me, there are others like pieces of me, there are my ancestors whose sacrifice and daring informs me. I must fuse different kinds of knowing and speak.

"I write to record the urban, Black, emigré, technopeasant mythos; to conduct a mythopoeic exploration of ethnicity and interculturality, neo-African-American psycho-graphics and semiology, the reinvestment of indigenous jazz and funk with motive force and votive power, identity and acculturation, struggle and joy, transcendence and passion. I work to improve my craft, to lengthen my reach, to better block, strike, pluck or embrace—to create world-class literature, to be a force for good in the world (this relentless call to sing!) and to make peace irresistible."

Her intensity and dedication seem to me to burn on her pages.

—Judson Jerome

---

to Israeli Society; the world Jewish community and its achievements and current problems, from a Socialist-Zionist world view; and general examinations of questions confronting socialism in our day. It also contains editorial comments, regular columns on various topics, and book and film reviews. "We also print letters to the editor on occasion." They have an international readership with readers in the U.S., Israel, Canada and 22 other countries. **Sample: $3 and SASE; subscription: $10/year.**

ISSUE ONE, (II, IV-Humor); EON PUBLICATIONS (V), 2 Tewkesbury Dr., Grimsby, South Humberside, England DN34 4TL, founded 1983, poetry editor Ian Brocklebank, is an attractive quarterly pamphlet, professionally printed on colored card stock folded accordian-style into 5-8 letter-sized panels. A typical issue contains 8-10 short poems. The editor says he "aims to publish not only a broad mix of styles of poetry by new and established poets the world over but also strives to a consistently high standard with regard to the actual presentation of this work. **I prefer short pieces with modern themes, concise but comprehensive images. Metre etc. unimportant. Poems with a point to make. My own criterion for selection is based firmly on whether images within the poem stir something, anything else in my imagination than what seems to be the subject. No epics required. Usually nothing above 14 lines overall. Bad taste, racism, sexism are not encouraged. Humour is welcome but no limericks please!** *Issue One* will intermittently use guest editors." He has recently used poetry by KV Skene, Arnold Lipkin, Sheila E. Murphy and Brian Daldorph. As a sample, the editor selected these lines from "Breathe" by Lisa Kucharski:

> when I walk
> air trails by
> it forms a breeze
> and that is how
> you will recognize me
> if we spend our lives
> walking past each other

Issue One has a circulation of about 200 for 50+ subscriptions of which 8 are libraries. He receives 300-500 submissions per edition of which he uses a maximum of 15. No backlog: "I do not hold over work but will allow re-submission." **Sample free for envelope and postage. Submit no more than 5 typed or photocopied pages "with a covering note and SASE/IRC if they require a response. Simultaneous submissions OK. General queries will be welcome with a SASE/IRC." Reports in a maximum of 2 months. Pays in single contributor's copies. Send SASE for guidelines. Prefers not to comment but "will provide observations if specifically requested." Book publication by Eon Press is by invitation only.** Ian Brocklebank says, "For someone starting out writing poetry I would advise trying out as much of your poetry on as many different magazines as you can afford. Do not become discouraged by rejection of your work. Try to keep variety in your subject matter."

ISSUES (IV-Religious), P.O. Box 11250, San Francisco, CA 94101, founded 1973, is an 8-12 pp. newsletter of Messianic Judaism distributed free, circulation 50,000, which uses some **poetry relevant to that cause. Considers simultaneous submissions. Send SASE for free sample. Pays.**

‡ITALIAN AMERICANA (IV-Ethnic), URI/CCE, 199 Promenade S., Providence RI 02908, founded 1974, editor Carol Bonomo Ahearn, appears twice a year using **2-4 poems "on Italian American subjects, no more than 3 pp. No trite nostalgia or food poems; no poems about grandparents."** As a sample the editor selected these lines from "Inside the Inside of the Moon" by Brian McCormick:
> *Armstrong's hop from module videos*
> *To earth: Mom Vecchio lays down a heart.*
> *She asks, "When is he going to go in?"*
> *This puts a stop to the conversation.*

It is 150-200 pp., 6×9″ professionally printed, flat-spined. Press run is 2,000 for 1,000 subscribers of which 100 are libraries. 1,000 go free to students. Subscription: $25. **Sample postpaid: $12.50. Reports in 4-6 weeks. Pays year's subscription. Do not submit in December or January. Name on first page only. Editor occasionally comments on rejections.** They have 2 readers, anonymous peer review of MSS.

ITALICA PRESS (IV-Translations), 595 Main St., #605, New York NY 10044, phone (212)935-4230, founded 1985, publishers Eileen Gardiner and Ronald G. Musto, is a small press publisher of **English translations of Italian works** in Smyth-sewn paperbacks, averaging 175 pp. **Query with 10 sample translations of important 20th Century or medieval and Renaissance Italian poets with bio, list of your publications. Simultaneous submissions, photocopies, dot-matrix OK, but material should not be "totally" previously published. Reports on queries in 3 weeks, on MSS in 3 months. Pays 7-15% royalties plus 10 author's copies. Editor sometimes comments on rejections.** 1991 Publication: Poems by Guido Cavalcanti (in dual-language Italian-English edition), translated by Marc Cirigliano.

‡IT'S A MAD MAD MAD MAD MAD WORLD; FLYBREEDER PUBLICATIONS (I), 8830 Nesbit Ave. N., Seattle WA 98103, founded 1989, editor Steve Anger, is a quarterly using **"weird, sick, psychotic, painful, violent distorted drug induced and especially weird—not more than a page. Nothing sweet, sentimental, trite, suburban, Robert-Frost-type s*."** As a sample the editor selected these lines from "Wishing Well" by Steve Sibra:
> *My naked body is like a perverse citrus*
> *tree; I am covered with bulbous cancers. Mutely I remove one,*
> *offer it to myself, replace it. Then another.*

It is 40 pp. magazine-sized, photocopied, folded. They accept about 90% of 20 poems received/year. Press run 300. Subscription: $1 for postage. **Sample postpaid: $1 or "equal in U.S. Postage." Reports in 2 months. Pays 1-2 copies. No comments on rejections.** The editor says, "Just be cool and don't bog me down with a buncha copyright legalese bulls*. We are an underground 'zine that publishes stuff that is too deranged for more normal format. There is no censorship and no ©rap. We are very small time and want to keep it that way."

JACARANDA REVIEW (II, IV-Translations), Dept. of English, University of California at Los Angeles, Los Angeles CA 90024-1530, phone (213)825-4173, founded 1984, poetry editor Katherine Swiggart, is a literary journal appearing twice a year. **"We publish all kinds, from poems by poets who publish in the *New Yorker* to L.A. Beat poets, to translations from the Japanese. Subject matter and style are open. As to length, we'd be interested in a good long poem, but they seem hard to come by. No inspirational verse, etc."** They have recently published poetry by Carolyn Forché, Barry Spacks, Alfred Corn and Phyllis Janowitz. I have not seen the magazine, but the editor describes it as digest-sized, 100-124 pp., with 2- or 4- color covers, no art inside the magazine, 4-6 ads per issue. They accept 40-50 of 750-1,000 poems received a year. Press run is 1,000 for 100 subscriptions (25 of them libraries), about 400 shelf sales. Subscription: $8. **Sample: $4 postpaid. Pays 3 copies plus 20% discount on additional copies. Simultaneous submissions OK. Reports in 4-6 weeks. Editor often comments on promising rejections.** The editor says, "We'd like to see more emotionally adventurous poetry, poetry which could but chooses not to hide behind its technical proficiency. We want poetry that matters, that changes the way people think and feel by the necessity of their vision. That's a lot to ask, but good poets deserve demanding readers."

‡JACKSON'S ARM (V,II), % Sunk Island Publishing, Box 74, Lincoln LN1 1QG, England, founded 1985, editor Michael Blackburn, a small-press publisher of poetry chapbooks and translations. **"No specifications as to subject or style. The poetry I want to publish should be vigorous and imaginative,**

with a firm grasp of everyday realities. Nothing bland, safe or pretentious." The press publishes up to 3 chapbooks per year with an average count of 18 saddle-stitched pages. However, the editor says he does not usually accept freelance submissions. Writers should query, sending 6 sample poems, credits and bio. Queries will be answered immediately. Payment is in copies: 10% of print run. Mr. Blackburn advises, "Read everything you can, in particular *contemporary* poets and writers. Get hold of all the 'small' poetry magazines you can, as well as the more commercial and prestigious."

JAPANOPHILE (IV-Ethnic), P.O. Box 223, Okemos MI 48864, phone (517)349-1795, founded 1974, poetry editor Earl R. Snodgrass, is a literary quarterly about Japanese culture (not just in Japan). Issues include articles, art, a short story and **poetry (haiku or other Japanese forms or any form if it deals with Japanese culture).** Note: karate and ikebana in the US are examples of Japanese culture. They have published poetry by Mary Jane Sanadi, F. A. Raborg, Jr., Geraldine Daesch, Anne Marx, Egean Roggio, Mimi Hinman and reprints of Basho. As an example the editors selected this haiku by Michael Elsey:

> The glass sings crystal
> a moist finger gently
> dancing on the rim.

There are 10-15 pp. of poetry in each issue (digest-sized, about 50 pp., saddle-stapled). They have a circulation of 400 with 100 subscriptions of which 30 are libraries. They receive about 500 submissions a year, use 70, have a 1 month backlog. **Sample: $4 postpaid. Summer is the best time to submit. Photocopy OK. Reports in 6 months. Pays $1 for haiku to $15 for longer poems. Send SASE for guidelines.** They also publish books under the Japanophile imprint, but so far none have been of poetry. Query with samples and cover letter (about 2 pp.) giving publishing credits, bio.

‡JEOPARDY (II), College Hall 132, Western Washington University, Bellingham WA 98225, phone (206)676-3118, founded 1964, is an annual. **"We are willing to look at anything, but space limitations make publishing overlong stories, poems, essays difficult."** They have recently published poetry by William Stafford, James Bertolino, Daniel Halpern and Jonathan Holden. I have not seen an issue, but the editor describes it as 108 pp., size varies, offset. They occasionally review poetry. They use about 50 of 500 submissions received. Press run 4,000. **Sample postpaid: $2. Send SASE for guidelines. Accepts submissions Sept. through January, reports in February. Pays 2 copies.** When funds are available they offer competition for cash prizes. **"Prefer poetry of no more than 3 single-spaced, legal paper in length."** Their editorial staff usually consists of 3-5 people.

JEWISH CURRENTS (V), Suite 601, 22 E. 17th St., New York NY 10003, phone (212)924-5740, founded 1946, editor Morris U. Schappes, is a magazine appearing 11 times a year that publishes **poetry on Jewish themes.** "We have been forced to declare a temporary moratorium on all poetry acceptances owing to the size of our backlog of material already accepted and awaiting publication in this category." Reviews books of poetry.

JEWISH SPECTATOR (IV-Religious), 4391 Park Milano, Calabasas CA 91302, phone (818)883-5141, founded 1935, poetry editor Robert Bleiweiss. A 64 pp., Judaic scholarly quarterly that uses **Judaically oriented poetry.** Subscribers: 1,200. **Pays "nothing." Simultaneous submissions and previously published poems are not OK.**

JOE SOAP'S CANOE (II), 30 Quilter Rd., Felixstowe, Suffolk, IP11 7JJ England, phone 0394-275569, founded 1978, poetry editor Martin Stannard, is engaged in "magazine and occasional booklet/chapbook publication; for a new poetry of optimism and despair, **caters especially to poets who are awake. I really only ever want to see good poetry, but life isn't like that. I'll promise to read whatever I'm sent. No limits, as long as it's in English."** He has recently published poetry by John Ashbery, Tom Raworth, Peter Sansom, Ian McMillan and Lydia Tomkiw. The editor selected these lines from "Yellow" by Mandy Payne:

> Another interesting train ran over my aunt's mauve carrier bag, and
> she didn't wince like wild fowl would

> Twenty-seven million stitches per half second have indeed left me with
> a daunting task to follow exactly

joe soap's canoe appears annually, 100 pp. perfect-bound format—"it's really a paperback book." The editor describes the magazine as "quite brilliant—in fact, of all the poetry magazines published in the U.K. it's one of the 2 or 3 always worth reading. It's certainly never boring. Some people hate it. I can relate to that . . ." Circulation 400-500, 200 subscriptions of which 32 are libraries. Subscription: £3 or $10 overseas; per copy: £1. He receives "thousands" of submissions each year, uses 60-70. **Sample $2 or £1.25. Reports within a month. Pays in copies. Photocopy,** dot-matrix OK. **No simultaneous submissions.** Send 9×5" envelope with return postage for catalog to buy samples. **The editor comments on rejections "only when I'm provoked."** Any advice for poets? "No—the world is too large and poetry too various. I'm no advice agency and no tipster. Beginners should simply begin. And know when to stop."

THE JOHNS HOPKINS UNIVERSITY PRESS (V), Suite 725, 701 W. 40th St., Baltimore MD 21211, founded 1878, Eric Halpern, Editor-in-Chief. "One of the largest American university presses, Johns Hopkins is a publisher mainly of scholarly books and journals. We do, however, publish short fiction and poetry in the series Johns Hopkins: Poetry and Fiction, edited by John Irwin on 10% royalty contracts. **Unsolicited submissions are not considered."**

THE JOURNAL (II), Ohio State University, Department of English, 164 W. 17th Ave., Columbus OH 43210, founded 1972, co-editors Kathy Fagan and Michelle Herman, appears twice yearly with reviews, essays, quality fiction and poetry. **"We're open to all forms; we tend to favor work that gives evidence of a mature and sophisticated sense of the language."** They have published poetry by David Baker, T.R. Hummer, Maura Stanton, Heather McHugh, Edward Kleinschmidt, Lawrence Raab, Cynthia Ozick and Carol Frost. The following sample is from the poem "The Helmet of Mambrino" by Linda Bierds:

> *I would know that tumble often, that*
> *explorer's slide, belief to belief, conviction*
> *to its memory, to conviction. Once I placed*
> *my marker-coin on Mt. Whitney's double, lost in a mist,*
> *convinced I had climbed to the highest land. Once*
> *I charted a lake from opal air.*

The Journal is 6×9" professionally printed on heavy stock, 80-100 pp., of which about 40 in each issue are devoted to poetry, circulation 1,500. Subscription: $8; per copy: $5. They receive about 4,000 submissions per year, use 200, and have a 3-6 month backlog. **Sample: $5. Photocopy, dot-matrix OK. Pays copies and an honorarium of $25-50 when funds are available. On occasion editor comments on rejections.** Reviews books of poetry. Contributing editor David Citino advises, "However else poets train or educate themselves, they must do what they can to know our language. Too much of the writing that we see indicates that poets do not in many cases develop a feel for the possibilities of language, and do not pay attention to craft. Poets should not be in a rush to publish—until they are ready." (Also see Ohio State University Press/*The Journal* Award in Poetry.)

JOURNAL OF NEW JERSEY POETS (IV-Regional), English Dept., County College of Morris, Randolph NJ 07869, phone (201)328-5471, founded 1976, editor Sander Zulauf. This biannual periodical uses poetry from **current or former residents of New Jersey. They want "serious work that is regional in origin but universal in scope." They do not want "sentimental, greeting-card verse."** Poets recently published include Kenneth Burke, Joe Salerno and Lois Marie Harrod. As a sample, the editor selected the following poem by Joe Malone:

> *clothing your body lay*
> *flowers of june,*
> *myrtle from may.*
> *Kissing your body, say*
> *when*
> *my God*

Published January (spring) and June (autumn), digest-sized, offset, with an average of 64 pp. Circulation is 500, price per issue and **for sample, $4.** Subscription: $7/year. **Pay is 2 copies per published poem. There are "no limitations" on submissions; SASE required, reporting time is 3-6 months and time to publication within 1 year.** "We plan to offer brief reviews or listings of books by New Jersey poets."

‡JOURNAL OF PAN AFRICAN STUDIES (IV-Ethnic), P.O. Box 13063, Fresno CA 93794, phone (209)266-2550, founded 1987, editor Prof. Itibari M. Zulu, is an annual using **"short Afrocentric poetry via social, economic, political development of African people."** They don't want poetry from "those who lack wisdom/knowledge of Afrocentric culture." I have not seen an issue, but the editor describes it as magazine-sized, 22 pp., with a cover photo. Press run is 1,000 copies for 700 subscribers of which 10 are libraries, 30 shelf sales. **Sample postpaid: $4. Reports in a month. No pay, not even copies. Editor often comments on rejections.** "Unpublished (new) poets welcomed who focus on African world community (Pan African) ideas."

JOURNAL OF THE AMERICAN MEDICAL ASSOCIATION (JAMA) (II, IV-Themes), 515 N. State, Chicago IL 60610, phone (312)464-2417, founded 1883, associate editor Charlene Breedlove, has a "Poetry and Medicine" column and publishes poetry **"in some way related to a medical experience,**

whether from the point-of-view of a health care worker or patient or simply an observer. No unskilled poetry." They have recently published poetry by Diane Ackerman and Daisy Aldan. As a sample the editor selected these lines from "Surgical Haiku" by Barbara Seaman:

> *they wear foliage green;*
> *I am the blue horizon*
> *sutured to the earth*

> *two willows bending;*
> *a sovereign silver birch*
> *with serrated leaves*

JAMA, magazine-sized, flat-spined, with glossy paper cover, has 360,000 subscribers of which 369 are libraries. They accept about 5% of 300 poems received per year. Subscription: $66. **Sample postpaid: free. Pays up to 3 copies.**

‡JOURNEYS (I), Suite 201, 1512 11th St., Santa Monica CA 90401, founded 1990, editor George Kalmar, appears 3/year. **"We are looking for poetry that gives thought to nature, man's role in nature and the current human condition in general. However, we are not interested in 'nature poetry' or poetry which is a simple description of nature; rather we are looking for work that treats the subject of one's relationship to nature. We will consider any poetry from writers who have been writing for some time. We will reject racist and hate poetry."** Each issue will include a poem from Theodore Roethke to whose memory this magazine is dedicated, and the editor quoted one of these to indicate his taste:

> *I would with the fish, the blackening salmon,*
> *   and the mad lemmings,*
> *The children dancing, the flowers widening.*
> *Who sighs from far away?*
> *I would unlearn the lingo of exasperation,*
> *   all the distortions of malice and hatred;*

I have not seen an issue, but the editor describes it as being digest-sized, 30-40 pp., saddle-stapled. Press run 1,000. Subscription: $12. **Sample: $4 postpaid. Pays 2 copies. Previously published poems and simultaneous submissions OK, if you indicate where they have been published or are being sent. Reports in 2 weeks. Poems circulated to an editorial board.** "We strongly suggest that those submitting their work should be familiar with Roethke's work and the work of his contemporaries. As editor, I am interested in poetry in the voice of the modern post-war American poets (Williams, Stevens, etc.). We will review all submissions in English from any part of the world."

JAMES JOYCE BROADSHEET (IV-Themes), School of English, University of Leeds, Leeds LS2 9JT, England, founded 1980, editors Pieter Bekker, Richard Brown and Alistair Stead, a "small-press specialist literary review, mainly book reviews connected with James Joyce; we include relevant poems in the magazine." **Poems must be short, of good quality and connected with James Joyce. They do not want anything "long, self-indulgent."** The issue I have contains two poems, "The Ballad of Erse O. Really?" by Gavin Ewart and "Keeping Awake Over Finnegan" by Alamgir Hashmi. As a sample, the editor chose the following lines by Seamus Heaney:

> *Then I knew him in a flash*
> *out there on the tarmac among the cars*
> *wintered hard and sharp as a blackthorn bush.*

The magazine is "literally a broadsheet (i.e. A2) folded into A5 [digest] sized." It is professionally printed on good paper and includes b/w line drawings and other artwork. When unfolded, it is 4 pages, 11½ × 16¼". It appears in February, June and October and has a circulation of 700, of which 70 go to libraries; complimentary copies go to "eminent Joyceans." Subscription price is £5 (UK or Europe) or $12 (US), sent by air. **Sample available for £2 or $4. Pay is 3 copies. Writers should send 2 copies of their work. Reporting time is 1 month and time to publication 4 months. Simultaneous submissions, photocopied or dot-matrix MSS are OK.**

JUDI-ISMS; K'TUVIM: WRITINGS—A JEWISH JOURNAL OF CREATIVITY (IV-Ethnic, themes, anthology), 27 W. Penn St., Long Beach NY 11561, phone (516)889-7163, founded 1986, poetry editor Judith Shulamith Langer Caplan. Judi-isms is the overall name of the press. Judi-isms published its first chapbook in 1990, **Long Beach 11561**, featuring the poems of Shulamith Surnamer from which these lines are taken:

> *Oh, you stiff-necked people*
> *who still seek*
> *the answer*
> *from the rabbi within you.*

> *You will yet cast all your sins*
> *into the depths of this sea.*

The Long Beach 11561 chapbook was digest-sized, 16 pages, saddle-stapled; sample copy $3.50. Judi-isms expects to publish a chapbook within the next year and is currently interested in submissions dealing with the following themes for future chapbooks: a) From Adam to Zipporah, poems about Jewish personalities, past, present and future, such as The Daughters of Zelophe-had, Rashi, Maimonides, Bruria, Anne Frank, Ben Gurion; b) It's All Relative, poems about grandparents, aunts and uncles; c) Containers of Judaism, poems and drawings about Jewish ceremonial objects and ceremonies such as a mezuzah; and d) Inspired by Shakespeare, works that tie in with Shakespeare and his work. "I am open to all styles of poetry, including free verse, but I also enjoy seeing formal verse such as sestinas, pantoums, villanelles and alphabet poems." Pays copies. Reports within 3-6 months. Typed, photocopy, dot-matrix, simultaneous submissions, reprints, all acceptable. Name and address should be on each page. Editor sometimes comments on rejections.

JUGGLER'S WORLD (IV-Themes), % Ken Letko, Department of English, BGSU, Bowling Green OH 43403, phone (419)352-5722, founded 1982, literary editor Ken Letko, is a quarterly magazine, press run 3,500, using poems about juggling. **"Only restriction is that all content is focused on juggling."** They have recently published poems by Robert Hill Long, Barbara Goldberg and Margo Wilding. As a sample I selected these lines from "For Benjamin Linder" by Shirley Powers:

> *in a remote village in Nicaragua*
> *A young man watches all night*
> *from a nearby hillside,*
> *his first hydroelectric plant*
> *complete. At dawn he juggles for village*
> *children*
> *in celebration.*

JW is magazine-sized, about 40 pp., saddle-stapled, professionally printed on glossy stock with 2-color glossy paper cover. It is circulated to more than 3,000 jugglers in more than 20 countries. They receive 50-100 poetry submissions per year, use 4-8 poems per year. Subscription: $18. **Sample: "$2 or $3 depending on issue." Pays 1 copy. They will consider previously published poems. Reports in 1-4 months. Editor sometimes comments on rejections, suggesting some revision.** He advises, "Provide insights."

‡**JULIAN ASSOCIATES; NIGHT OWL'S NEWSLETTER; OUR WRITE MIND (I, IV-Themes)**, 6831 Spencer Hwy. #203, Pasadena TX 77505, editor Debbie Jordan, associate editor of *NON* R.S. Cooper, associate editor of *OWM* Robin Kendle Parker. Julian Associates publishes NON, a newsletter, and OWM, a magazine, both of which use poetry relevant to their themes only: living by night or writing. **"Anything with a clear message. Humor is a plus! Poems that are all image and no clear meaning waste our time."** They have recently published poetry by Lynn Bradley. **Previously published poems and simultaneous submissions OK, but tell the editor about them.** *OWM* appears irregularly, *NON* is quarterly. The latter is magazine-sized, corner-stapled, press run 100-200. **Sample postpaid: $3.50. Send SASE for guidelines. Reports in one month. Both publications pay at least $1 plus at least one copy.**

JUNIPER PRESS; NORTHEAST; JUNIPER BOOKS; THE WILLIAM N. JUDSON SERIES OF CONTEMPORARY AMERICAN POETRY; HAIKU-SHORT POEM SERIES; INLAND SERIES; GIFTS OF THE PRESS (III, IV-Form), 1310 Shorewood Dr., La Crosse WI 54601, founded 1962, poetry editors John Judson and Joanne Judson, is one of the oldest and most respected programs of publishing poetry in the country. *Northeast* is a semiannual little magazine, digest-sized, saddle-stapled. **Most poets published in book form have first appeared in *Northeast*. Authors wishing to submit book MS *must* first send query letter and samples of work *plus* SASE. Any MS sent without query will be returned without being read. Reports in 2-4 months.** A subscription to *Northeast*/Juniper Press is $33/year ($38 for institutions), which brings you 2 issues of the magazine and the Juniper books, haiku-short poem booklets, WNJ Books and some gifts of the press, a total of about 5-8 items. (Or send SASE for catalog to order individual items. **Sample: $2.50 postpaid.**) The Juniper Books are perfect-bound books of poetry by several poets; the WNJ Books are poetry books by one author; the haiku booklets are 12-40 pp. each, handsewn in wrappers; Inland Sea Series is for larger works; Gifts of the Press are usually letterpress books and cards given only to subscribers or friends of the press. **Payment to authors is 10% of the press run of 300-1,000.** "Please read us before sending MSS. It will aid in your selection of materials to send. If you don't like what we do, please don't submit."

K (I), 351 Dalhousie St., Brantford, Ontario N3S 3V9 Canada, phone (579)753-8737, founded 1985, editor G.J. McFarlane, is **"a free form exercise in terms of the turbulent technocratic social environment and the human condition thereof, appearing sporadically as funds and material allow."** I have not seen an issue, but the editor says he has a press run of 75 for 30 subscriptions. **Sample postpaid: $4.50. Pays 1 copy.** He says, "Poetry/literature provides a balance to technological progression in a primitive, human fashion. There has been a vast relinquishment of humanity in the latter twentieth century. Poetry allows the human voice in the mire of technocratic human diminishment."

‡**KAIMANA: LITERARY ARTS HAWAII; HAWAII LITERARY ARTS COUNCIL (IV-Regional),** P.O. Box 11213, Honolulu HI 96828, founded 1974, editor Tony Friedson. *Kaimana*, a quarterly, is the magazine of the Hawaii Literary Arts Council. **Poems with "some Pacific reference are preferred--Asia, Polynesia, Hawaii--but not exclusively."** They have recently published poetry by Howard Nemerov, Lyn Lifshin, John Yau, Reuben Tam and Joe Stanton. As a sample the editor selected these lines from "The Ride to Ho'omaluhia" by Tony Quagliano:

> as the tide rises and the rain-
> waters ride the red cliffs
> to fill the low land
> and the bay of Kane'ohe swells
> to take back the town . . .

It is 64-76 pp., 7½×10″, stapled, with high-quality printing. Press run 1,000 for 600 subscribers of which 200 are libraries. Subscription: $10. **Sample postpaid: $4. Pays $20 plus 2 copies. Reports with "reasonable dispatch." No comments on rejections.**

KALDRON: AN INTERNATIONAL JOURNAL OF VISUAL POETRY AND LANGUAGE ART (IV-Form), P.O. Box 7164, Halcyon CA 93421-7164, phone (805)489-2770, editor and publisher Karl Kempton. *Kaldron* is a "journal of visual poetry and language art interested only in works which are a true wedding of language/poetry/literature and the other arts. This is a journal which publishes works from around the world." Mr. Kempton says, **"A visual poem is a poem which takes the patterns and densities of language and molds them with other art forms, mainly the visual arts in such a way that without either element the work falls apart, that is to say the entire image is what is on the page."** It is handsomely printed in an oversized magazine format. The "poems" are graphic, using little verbal text, and can be reproduced only photographically. It is impossible to quote works from the magazine without photographing them; contributors include Doris Cross, Scott Helmes, Alan Satie, Hassan Moussady, Paula Hocks, Shoji Yoshizawa and Giovanni Fontana. *Kaldron* appears "irregularly" and has a circulation of 800; single copy price $10 (issue 20/21). **Sample $5 postpaid. Contributors receive 2 to 10 copies. The only instruction for contributors is: "no image should be larger than 10¼×16″." Submissions will be reported on in "one day to a month," and time to publication "varies, but contributor kept informed of any delays." Criticism will be given "if submissions are accompanied with a cover letter."** Mr. Kempton says, "Visual poetry and language art published in *Kaldron* may be considered examples of an ongoing development of an international meta-language/poetic/artistic gesturing which attempts to express what language is unable to express. Such concerns have created a strong international dialogue. The roots of this expression are ancient; the modern roots are found in movements like futurism and dadaism in the early part of this century and the more contemporary roots are found in the concrete poetry movement of the 50's and 60's, a poetry held by many to be the first true international poetic expression. Around 100 serious visual poets and language artists are at work in this country and hundreds more at work around the globe."

KALEIDOSCOPE PRESS; KALEIDOSCOPE: INTERNATIONAL MAGAZINE OF LITERATURE, FINE ARTS, AND DISABILITY (IV-Themes), 326 Locust St., Akron OH 44302, phone (216)762-9755, founded 1979, editor Dr. Darshan C. Perusek; consulting poetry editor Christopher Hewitt. *Kaleidoscope* is based at United Cerebral Palsy and Services for the Handicapped, a nonprofit agency, and has the mission "to provide a viable national and international vehicle **for literary and artistic works dealing with the experience of disability;** stimulate ongoing literary and art programming among organizations which serve persons with disabilities; and to serve as a forum for the issues inherent to the experience of disability that popular culture and most serious art forms neglect." **Must deal with being disabled but not limited to that when artist is disabled. Photocopies with SASE. Reports in 6 months, pays up to $50 for a body of work, $100 for feature length articles. Considers simultaneous submissions. All submissions must be accompanied by an autobiographical sketch.** Sketch should include general background information, any writing experiences, artistic achievements, a listing of previous publica-

ALWAYS submit MSS or queries with a self-addressed, stamped envelope (SASE) within your country or a self-addressed envelope and International Reply Coupons (IRCs) purchased from the post office for other countries.

tions (if applicable) and nature of disability. The editor says: "Poetry can be based on personal experience, though it must reach beyond the particular and must communicate vividly." They have recently published poetry by Fritz Hamilton, Patricia Ranzoni and Sandra Lindow. As a sample, they offer these lines by Meridel Le Seur:

> *I am luminous with age*
> *In my lap I hold the valley.*
> *I see on the horizon what has been taken*
> *What is gone lies prone, fleshless.*

Circulation 1,500, including libraries, social service agencies, health professionals, disabled student services, literature departments and individual subscribers. A subscription is $9 individual, $12 agency, $4.50 single. **Sample $2.** Reviews books of poetry. "*Kaleidoscope* presents work that challenges stereotypical perceptions of people with disabilities by offering balanced, realistic images. Writers with disabilities need not restrict themselves to writing about disability."

KALLIOPE, a journal of women's art (IV-Women, translations, themes), 3939 Roosevelt Blvd., Jacksonville FL 32205, phone (904)387-8211, founded 1978, editor Mary Sue Koeppel, a literary/visual arts journal published by Florida Community College at Jacksonville; the emphasis is on women writers and artists. The editors say, **"We like the idea of poetry as a sort of artesian well—there's one meaning that's clear on the surface and another deeper meaning that comes welling up from underneath. We'd like to see more poetry from Black, Hispanic, Native American women, and more translations. Nothing sexist, racist, conventionally sentimental. We will have one special theme issue each year. Write for specific guidelines."** Poets recently published include Beatrice Hawley, Marge Piercy, Kathryn Machan Aal, Judith Sornberger and Sue Saniel Elkind. As a sample, the editor selected the following lines by Laurie Duesing:

> *Now I am rapt and looking for the still point*
> *between earth and air. I am willing*
> *to wait while the world turns red,*
> *to watch while everything comes at me.*

Kalliope calls itself "a journal of women's art," and it publishes fiction, interviews, drama and visual art in addition to poetry. The magazine, which appears 3 times a year, is 7¼ × 8¼", handsomely printed on white stock with b/w photographs of works of art and, in the sample copy I have, a photographic (no words) essay. Average number of pages is 80. On my copy, the glossy card cover features a b/w illustration of a piece of sculpture; the magazine is flat-spined. The circulation is 1,250, of which 400-500 are subscriptions, including 50 library subscriptions, and 500 copies are sold on newsstands and in bookstores. Price is $7/issue, subscription $10.50/year or $20/2 years. **Sample: $7 and guidelines can be obtained for SASE. Contributors receive 3 copies. Poems should be submitted in batches of 3-10 with bio note, phone number and address. Because all submissions are read by several members of the editing staff, response time is usually 3-4 months. Publication will be within 6 months. Criticism is provided "when time permits and the author has requested it."** Reviews books of poetry, "but we prefer groups of books in one review." The editor says, "Don't be discouraged by rejection slips—keep trying. We have to send back a lot of good poetry because we simply can't publish it all. Send for a sample copy, to see what appeals to us, or better yet, subscribe!"

‡KANGAROOS AND BEANS (I, II), P.O. Box 52304, Livonia MI 48152-9998, phone (313)537-9425, founded 1989, editor Gregg Nannini, appears twice a year using **"most types of poetry as long as it appears there had been some thought behind it. Poems of nature. Poems that are spiritual, not necessarily religious. Nothing pornographic or violent."** They have recently published poetry by Glen Armstrong and Nancy Rice. As a sample the editor selected these lines from "Random Thoughts on a Lazy Sunday" by Christine Donovan:

> *I can't find myself tonight*
> *Where did I leave me behind?*
> *I usually carry myself with me . . .*

It is digest-sized, 20 pp., photocopied from typescript with matte b/w card cover. Press run 500. Subscription: $3.50. **Sample: $1 postpaid. Pays 2 copies. Simultaneous submissions OK. Reports in 3 months.**

KANSAS QUARTERLY; KANSAS ART COMMISSION AWARDS; SEATON AWARDS (II, IV-Regional, themes), Denison Hall 122, Kansas State University, Manhattan KS 66506, phone (913)532-6716, founded 1968 as an outgrowth of *Kansas Magazine*, poetry editors Jonathan Holden and Ben Nyberg, is "a magazine devoted to the culture, history, art and writing of mid-Americans, but not restricted to this area." It publishes poetry in all issues. They say, **"We are interested in all kinds of modern poetry except humorous verse, limericks, extremely light verse or book-length MSS."** They have published poetry by David Ray, Tom Hansen, Eugene Hollahan, Elizabeth Rees, Kathleen Spivack, David Citino, Lyn Lifshin, Robert McNamara, Roger Finch, Ronald Wallace, Mark Nepo, Peter Cooley, Denise Low and David Kirby. As a sample the editors offer these lines from "Margaret Love" by Andrew Klavan:

> She died by fire. Lying on the couch
> and posing questions to herself,
> she slipped into a doze;
> her right arm drifted down her side;
> her fingers settled on the floor,
> the cigarette in them dropping;
> and the flames went flashing through the house
> like inspiration through the brain.

There are an average of 80 pp. of poetry in each creative issue, circulation 1,150-1,350 with 721 subscriptions of which 50% are libraries. They receive 10,000 submissions per year, use 300-400. There is at least a 12- to 18-month backlog unless a poem fits into a special number—then it may go in rapidly. **Sample: $6 postpaid ($8 for double number). Submit "enough poems to show variety (or a single poem if author wishes), but no books. Typed, double-spaced, photocopy OK, but no dot-matrix. No queries. We consider, reluctantly, simultaneous submissions." Reports in 1-3 months. Pays 2 copies and yearly awards of up to $200 per poet for 6-10 poets.** The *Kansas Quarterly*/Kansas Art Commission Awards are $200 (1st prize), $150 (2nd), $100 (3rd), $75 (4th), and up to 5 honorable mentions ($50). There are also similar prizes in the Seaton Awards (to native-born or resident Kansas poets). The editors **often comment on rejections, even at times suggesting revision and return.** Editors say, "Our only advice is for the poet to *know* the magazine he is sending to: consult in library or send for sample copy. Magazines need the support and their published copies should provide the best example of what the editors are looking for. We believe that we annually publish as much generally good poetry as nearly any other U.S. literary magazine—between 250 and 400 poems a year. Others will have to say how good it really is."

KAPOK POETRY PRESS; KAPOK POETRY CHAPBOOK AWARD (I), P.O. Box 111102, Memphis TN 38111, founded 1991, editor LaNita Moses offers a semiannual award of publication of a chapbook. **$10 entry fee. Pays 20 copies plus 30% discount on additional copies. No haiku. Send 35-50 pp. with name, address, phone number, publication credits and index on separate sheet. Send SASE for rules. Deadlines end of June and December.**

KARAMU (II), Dept. of English, Eastern Illinois University, Charleston IL 61920, phone (217)581-5614, founded 1966, editor Peggy Brayfield, is an annual whose "goal is to provide a forum for the best contemporary poetry and fiction that comes our way. We especially like to print the works of new writers. **We like to see poetry that shows a good sense of what's being done with poetry currently. We like poetry that builds around real experiences, real images and real characters and that avoids abstraction, overt philosophizing and fuzzy pontifications. In terms of form, we prefer well-structured free verse, poetry with an inner, sub-surface structure as opposed to, let's say, the surface structure of rhymed quatrains. We have definite preferences in terms of style and form, but no such preferences in terms of length or subject matter. Purpose, however, is another thing. We don't have much interest in the openly didactic poem. If the poet wants to preach against or for some political or religious viewpoint, the preaching shouldn't be so strident that it overwhelms the poem. The poem should first be a poem."** They have recently published poetry by Rosmarie Waldrop, Allen Ginsberg, Marianne Andrea and Rich Haydon. The editor chose these sample lines from "African Violet" by Janet McCann:

> Soft green tongues utter
> from the center, they say
> moist, they say warm. A circle
> of green voices rising, tropical
> chant here in the house of sleep.

The format is 60 pp., 5×8", matte cover, handsomely printed (narrow margins), attractive b/w art. The most recent issue carries 42 pages of poetry. They have a circulation of 350 with 300 subscriptions of which 15 are libraries. They receive submissions from about 300 poets each year, use 20-40 poems. Never more than a year—usually 6-7 months—between acceptance and publication. **Payment is one contributor's copy. Sample: $3; 2 recent issues: $4. "Poems—in batches of no more than 5-6—may be submitted to Peggy Brayfield at any time of the year. Photocopied work OK, although we don't much care for simultaneous submissions. Poets should not bother to query. We critique a few of the better poems. We want the poet to consider our comments and then submit new work.** Follow the standard advice: know your market. Read contemporary poetry and the magazines you want to be published in. Be patient."

KATUAH: BIOREGIONAL JOURNAL OF THE SOUTHERN APPALACHIANS (IV-Regional), P.O. Box 638, Leicester NC 28748, founded 1983, editor Marnie Muller. *Katuah* is a quarterly tabloid journal "concerned with developing a sustainable human culture in the Southern Appalachian Mountains." The editor wants to see "**only regional poems or poems dealing with Appalachia and/or ecological feelings.**" They have recently published poems by Jim Wayne Miller, Kay Byers, Bennie Lee Sinclair, Michael Hockaday, Scott Bird, Oliver Loveday and Patricia Shirley. The issue I have contains two poems by Stephen Knauth. As a sample, I selected the beginning lines of his "1836. In the Cherokee Overhills":

> In a pasture of the Milky Way
> where the Little Pigeon glides down over the dark
> rocks
> of Tennessee,
> a man has landed on his belly,
> drinking water from a cup made of hands,

The tabloid has 32 pp., offset on newsprint, nicely laid out with attractive b/w drawings and other illustrations, folded for mailing, not stapled. Price per copy is $1.50, subscription $10/year. Circulation is 3,500, of which 300 are subscriptions; 80% of circulation is newsstand sales. **Sample available for $2 postpaid. Pay is 10 copies. Reporting time and time to publication are both 6 months.**

THE KAU KAU KITCHEN NEWSLETTER; HAKU MELE (I, IV-Regional, themes, children), 372 Haili St., Hilo HI 96720, phone (808)961-3984, founded 1988, editor Leilehua Yuen, comes out 6 times per year, **dealing with food, nutrition, homemaking, family health specific to Hawai'i, and using poetry related to those themes as well as poetry by children on a children's page. No erotic poetry.** They have recently published poetry by Fumie Uratani. As a sample the editor selected these lines from "Okazu" by Lehua Pelekapu:

> In a thin electric dawn
> the men line up.
>
> "Like one makizushi.
> No cut 'em too t'in!
> E-Koji!
> Where you was,
>   yesterday?"
>
>   Koji grins

The newsletter is digest-sized, saddle-stapled, typeset and photocopied, using line drawings, 40+ pp. Their press run is 200 with 40 subscriptions. Subscription: $10. **Sample: $2 postpaid.** Guidelines available for SASE. Buys one-time rights. Pays "copies or cash or subscription or ad space." Poem should be "typed exactly as it should appear. I won't edit poetry. If there are errors it will be tossed, unless they look like part of the poem, then I'll run it with errors." She considers simultaneous submissions and previously published poems. "We are also interested in recipes written in poem form for publication in the newsletter and a possible cookbook/anthology. *Please* limit submissions to those in our subject area. No 'glorious God' poems, unless He's in the kitchen. No poems about Cape Cod with a palm tree. We are most likely to publish poems about food or with food/eating in them. 'Kau Kau' means 'food' or 'to eat' in Hawai'i pidgin." Will consider reviewing books of poetry. *Haku Mele* is a "sporatically published poetry magazine with variable format. We publish when we get enough material." It is a **specialized publication limited to the Pacific and surrounding area** and interested in **bilingual/foreign language, ethnic/nationality, nature/ecology and women/feminism poetry, including translations.**

‡KAWABATA PRESS; SEPIA POETRY MAGAZINE (II, IV-Anthology), Knill Cross House, Millbrook, Torpoint, Cornwall, U.K., founded 1977, poetry editor Colin David Webb, publishes "**nontraditional poetry, prose and artwork (line only), open to all original and well thought-out work. I hate rhymes, traditional poems and dislike 'genre' stories. I want original and thought-provoking material.**" They have recently published poetry by Jacques de Lumiére and Steve Walker. *Sepia* is published 3 times a year, an inexpensively produced, digest-sized, 32 pp. saddle-stapled format, photoreduced from typescript, with narrow margins, bizarre drawings, press run 150, 75 subscriptions of which 5-6 are libraries. It sells for 50 p, or £1 ($3) per year. They receive 250 submissions per year, use 50-60. **Sample: 50p ($1). Submit 6-10 pp., typed**—photocopy, dot-matrix, simultaneous submissions OK. Reports in 10 days. Payment free copy. Reviews books of poetry. Under the imprint of Kawabata Press, Colin Webb also publishes **anthologies and collections. Query with 6-10 poems and "maybe a brief outline of intent." Poet gets 50% of profits after cost of printing is covered and 4 copies.** A book catalog of Kawabata Press publications is on the back of *Sepia*, for ordering copies. The editor **always comments**

on **rejections** and advises, "Strike out everything that sounds like a cliché. Don't try any tricks. Work at it, have a feeling for what you write, don't send 'exercise' pieces. Believe in what you send."

KENNEBEC: A PORTFOLIO OF MAINE WRITING (IV-Regional), University of Maine, Augusta ME 04330, phone (207)622-7131, founded 1975, editors Carol Kontos and Terry Plunkett, is an annual tabloid of creative writing by Maine writers (whether or not currently residents) supported by the University of Maine at Augusta. 5,000 copies are distributed free as a service to the community in an effort to bring Maine writers to the attention of a wide public. **Qualified writers may submit (with a statement of their relationship to Maine) between September 15 and December 1 each year. Sample free for SASE. Pays copies.** I selected these sample lines from "North Into Love" by David Adams:

> *A little on we inspect the ponds for frogs,*
> *guess at the names of shrubs,*
> *transversing a green geometry, like*
> *a dream through a dream.*

‡**KENNESAW REVIEW (II)**, English Dept., Kennesaw State College, P.O. Box 444, Marietta GA 30061, phone (404)423-6297, founded 1987, poetry editor Don Russ, editor Robert W. Hill, appears twice a year. **"Open to any form, style or subject; we are looking for high-quality, finely crafted contemporary poetry of all kinds."** They have recently published poetry by David Bottoms, Malcolm Glass, Larry Rubin, Eve Shelnutt, R.T. Smith and Lewis Turco. As a sample the editor selected these lines from "Raising the Dead" by Ron Rash:

> *The quick left weeks ago, most voluntarily.*
> *Those who remain are brought up, row by row,*
> *into the fading light*
> *of this November afternoon.*

It is 100 + pp., flat-spined, professionally printed, 6 × 9″, with embossed matte card cover. They accept about 20 of 2,000 poems received. Press run 1,000. Subscription: $5. **Sample postpaid: $1. Submit no more than 5 poems. Reports within 3 months. Pays 5 copies.**

"*Because Key West is an island city in the Florida Keys, we felt that a sailboat might represent the area, although* Key West Review *publishes the work of writers from all over the United States," says editor William J. Schlicht, Jr. This cover also lists the names of several well-known fiction writers and poets featured inside, illustrating the review's taste. The cover was prepared by associate editor Marion H. Smith, who is also* Key West Review's *poetry editor.*

THE KENYON REVIEW (III), Kenyon College, Gambier OH 43022, phone (614)427-3339, founded 1939, editor Marilyn Hacker, associate editor David Lynn, assistant editor for poetry David Baker, is a quarterly review containing poetry, fiction, criticism, reviews and memoirs. Long recognized as **one of the most distinguished of our literary journals**, it is constantly extending its tradition to affirm and represent the fruitful diversity of contemporary writing. Upcoming issues contain work by such poets as Cyrus Cassells, Judith Ortiz Cofer, Joy Harjo, Richard Howard, Josephine Jacobsen, Alicia Ostriker, Sherod Santos and Quincy Troupe. *De Colores*, the Fall 1991 special issue, focuses on the work of North American writers of color. The elegantly printed, flat-spined, 7×10″, 180+ pp. format has a circulation of 3,800 with 3,000 subscriptions of which 1,100 are libraries. They receive about 3,000-4,000 freelance submissions a year, use 50-60 (about 50 pp. of poetry in each issue), have a 1 year backlog. **Sample: $7 postpaid.** Unsolicited submissions are read from September through March *only*. Reports in 3 months, pays $15/page for poetry, $10/page for prose.

KEY WEST REVIEW (III), 9 Ave. G., Key West FL 33040, phone (305)296-1365, founded 1987, associate editor for poetry (Ms.) Marion H. Smith, appears twice a year. **"No restrictions on form or content of poetry. Nothing sentimental, amateurish or pornographic."** They have recently published poetry by Richard Wilbur, Marge Piercy, Eleanor Ross Taylor, Richard Eberhart, James Merrill and George Starbuck. As a sample the editor selected these lines from a poem by Judith Kazantzis called "Dusk and a Portuguese Man o' War":

> We are in the tropics. I'm sorry to say
> what slews round the corner
> is no fun: winningly, slidingly
> under its indigo puff sleeve
> under its beacon blue eye, its arms
> outspread to me.

MSS are not read during the summer. Editor comments on submissions "seldom." *KWR* is 100+ pp., digest-sized, flat-spined, professionally printed, with matte card cover. Press run: 1,000 for 250 subscribers of which 25 are libraries. 100 copies go free "to well-known authors from whom we are soliciting contributions." Subscription: $17. **Sample postpaid: $5. Pays "token only" and 2 copies, "sometimes more."**

‡KEYSTROKES; COMPUWRITE ANNUAL POETRY CONTEST; WRITERS ALLIANCE (IV-Themes), P.O. Box 2014, Setauket NY 11733, founded 1981, executive director of Writers Alliance, Kiel Stuart. Writers Alliance sponsors, in addition to its quarterly newsletter *Keystrokes*, workshops and other activities devoted to building a "dedicated arts community." Membership: $15. You needn't be a member to enter its annual poetry contest (poems about writing or computing, prize of $25, subscription to and publication in the newsletter, Jan. 1 deadline) or to submit poetry to the newsletter **"up to 10 lines on the subject of writing or using a computer or word processing system. 4-6 lines works best. We don't want anything that strays from the subject matter of writers, writing and using computers for that task."** They have recently published poetry by Karen Elizabeth Rigley and Carole Stein Holien. As a sample the editor selected this poem, "Dilemma," by Beatrice G. Davis:

> Free-lancer—hyphenated
> Freelancer—compounded
> Free lancer—separated
>
> Which am I?
> That's a typesetter's decision
> It would seem.

Keystrokes is 12 pp. desktop publishing (folded sheets of 8½×11″ paper). "Receive about a dozen poems a year; room for 8-10 but less than 50% accepted." Subscription: $15 (with membership). **Sample: $3.50 postpaid. Send SASE for guidelines. Pays 2 copies. "All checks are payable to Kiel Stuart. This is essential."** Previously published poems OK if they did not appear in a competing magazine or more recently than 6 months. **Reply in 6-8 weeks. Editor seldom comments.** Reviews books of poetry. The editor advises, "Treat your craft with respect. Learn the business aspects of being a poet and adhere to those rules. Sloppiness or failure to stick to standard MS format or (worst of all) failure to enclose SASE with ANY communication does NOT indicate an artistic soul."

‡KINGS REVIEW MAGAZINE; KINGS REVIEW PRESS (I, II), P.O. Box 1933, S. San Francisco CA 94083-1933, founded 1987, editor Larry Sparks. The press publishes flat-spined chapbooks of poetry. The frequency of the magazine was not given. They want **"avant-garde, educated and metrical, even rhymed poetry. We use translations."** They have recently published poetry by Errol Miller, Geoffrey Cook, Whitman McGowan and Martin Matz. As a sample the editor selected these lines from his own "For Our Recent American West":

> These are lines of great distress
> concerning events in our late American West
> of those days of not so long ago when
> the cattle of this great nation outnumbered men.

The editor says it is "fifty pages. Size may vary. Original cover art. Binding is very original."

Press run is not indicated. **Sample postpaid: $3.50. Pays 1 copy. "We might charge criticism fees." Payment for chapbooks varies. For chapbook publication, "query first with sample poems etc. It is not necessary to have published the poems previously."**

KITCHEN TABLE: WOMEN OF COLOR PRESS (IV-Women, ethnic), P.O. Box 908, Latham NY 12110, phone (518)434-2057, founded 1981, is "the only publisher in North America committed to producing and distributing the **work of Third World women of all racial/cultural heritages, sexualities and classes.**" They publish flat-spined paperback collections and anthologies. **"We want high quality poetry by women of color which encompasses a degree of consciousness of the particular issues of identity and struggle which women of color face."** The editors selected these lines from **Healing Heart, Poems 1973-1988** by Gloria T. Hull:

> we love in circles
>   touching round—
> faces in a ritual ring
>   echoing blood and color
> nappy girlheads in a summer porch swing
> belligerent decisions to live
>   and be ourselves.

That book is a digest-sized, flat-spined paperback, glossy card cover, 140 pp., $8.95, with critical praise on the cover by Gwendolyn Brooks, Ntozake Shange and Stephen E. Henderson. They publish an average of one book of poetry every other year and have published three anthologies, two of which contain poetry. All books are published simultaneously in hardback for library sales. **Submit a sample of 10 pages of poems with background information about your writing and publishing career and "a general description of the poetry collection as a whole." They reply to queries in 8 weeks, to full MS submissions (if invited) in 6 months. Simultaneous submissions OK if they are informed. MS should be typed, double-spaced. Clear photocopies OK. No dot-matrix. Payment is 7% royalties for first 10,000 copies, 8% thereafter, and 10 copies. Write for catalog to purchase samples. General comments usually given upon rejection.** The editors say, "We are particularly interested in publishing work by women of color which would generally be overlooked by other publishers, especially work by American Indian, Latina, Asian American and African American women who may be working class, lesbian, disabled or older writers."

ALFRED A. KNOPF (V), 201 E. 50th St., New York NY 10022, poetry editor Harry Ford. Over the years Knopf has been one of the most important and distinguished publishers of poetry in the United States. **"The list is closed to new submissions at this time."**

KOLA; AFO ENTERPRISES REG'D (IV-Ethnic), C.P. 1602 Place Bonaventure, Montréal, Quebec H5A 1H6 Canada, AFO Enterprises Reg'd founded 1983, Kola founded 1987, editor Dr. Horace I. Goddard. **"Poetry must reflect the black experience worldwide."** They have recently published poetry by Chezia Thompson-Cager (U.S.A.) and Ezenwa-Ohaeto (Nigeria). As a sample I selected these lines from "I Can't Go Home Again" by Shirley Small:

> I long to reach out
> and touch the earth of the mother-land
> land that will not reach out to me:
> earth of my fathers washed with bloody tears.

Kola is digest-sized, 40 pp. printed (lithographed) from typescript with matte card cover. It appears in spring, summer and fall each year and they accept 95% of the manuscripts received. Their press run is 300 with 150 subscriptions of which 4 are libraries. **Sample: $4 US, $3 Canada, postpaid. Pays 2 copies. Reports in 6-8 weeks. Editor sometimes comments on rejections.** Reviews books of poetry. AFO Enterprises Reg'd publishes paperbacks and does accept unsolicited MSS. Dr. Goddard says, "Poetry is not a saleable commodity. To be known a poet must try to read to many audiences. Try new forms and be bold with new techniques."

KRAX; RUMP BOOKLETS (II, IV-Humor), 63 Dixon Lane, Leeds, Yorkshire LS12 4RR England, founded 1971, poetry editors Andy Robson et al. *Krax* appears twice yearly, and they want poetry which is **"light-hearted and witty; original ideas. Undesired: anything containing the words 'nuclear' or 'Jesus.'"** 2,000 words maximum. All forms and styles considered. The editor chose these lines from "Night Yacht in Harbour" by Cynthia Kitchen:

> On the water
> something lisps,
> sick visitor
> in a stained white gown . . .

Krax is 6 × 8", 48 pp. of which 30 are poetry, saddle-stapled, offset with b/w cartoons and graphics. Price per issue: £1.50 ($3), per subscription: £6 ($12). They receive up to 1,000 submissions per year of which they use 6%, have a 2-3 year backlog. **Sample: $1 (75p). "Submit maximum of 6 pieces. Writer's name on same sheet as poem. SASE or IRC encouraged but not vital." Reports within 10 weeks. Pays 1 copy.** Reviews books of poetry. *Rump Booklets* are miniature format 3 × 4″ 16 pp. collections. **Query with "detailed notes of projected work." Send SASE for catalog.** The editor says, "Don't send money to publishers, etc., without written proof of their existence. Keep copies of your work—all things may be lost in transit, so query if no reply. Name poets tend to shun us in favor of glossy paperbacks and hard cash, but diamonds don't come in garish packages and no one can start at the top."

‡KUMQUAT MERINGUE; PENUMBRA PRESS (I, II), P.O. Box 5144, Rockford IL 61125, phone (815) 968-0713, founded 1990, editor Christian Nelson, appears 3/year using **"short poetry about the small details of life. Poetry about love, but especially the quirky side of love found or lost. Don't like long poems over 20 lines. Usually don't like rhyming. No preaching."** They have recently published poetry by Keith Abbott, Dwight E. Humphries, Gina Bergamino and Larry O. Dean. As a sample the editor selected these lines from "The Blues" by Terry J. Fox:

> *If your soul*
> *was the notes*
> *of a song*
> *only black guys*
> *would know how*
> *to sing you*

It is digest-sized, "professionally designed with professional typography but low resolution printing (copy machine)." Press run 100 for 35 subscribers. Subscription: $5. **Sample postpaid: $2.50. Send SASE for guidelines. Reports in 60 days. Pays 1 copy. "We like cover letters but not necessary. Previously published and simultaneous submissions sometimes OK, but please let us know."** The magazine is "dedicated to the memory of Richard Brautigan." The editor advises, "Read a lot of poetry, as much as you can stand, before you start sending yours out. Don't copy Brautigan. And don't copy those people who have copied him. We just want the same feeling. When you get discouraged, write some more. Don't give up. Send your stuff everywhere until it finds a home."

KWIBIDI PUBLISHER; KID'S PLAYYARD; THE JOURNAL OF THE NATIONAL SOCIETY OF MINORITY WRITERS AND ARTISTS; THE WRITERS' AND ARTISTS' AID (IV-Ethnic, membership, children), P.O. Box 3424, Greensboro NC 27402-3424. Kwibidi founded 1979, *JNSMWA* 1981, *KP* 1986. Editor Dr. Doris B. Kwasikpui. Kwibidi Publisher **"needs poems, one-act plays, short stories, articles, art, jokes, book reports, research papers and how-to-do and make, for books,** *Kid's Playyard* (a magazine for kids of all ages) and *JNSMWA*.**" Publication limited to minorities. Pay in copies. Upon acceptance, require membership in the National Society of Minority Writers and Artists ($15/year). Publishes much of the material received and often responds with suggestions. Send SASE for guidelines. Reports in about 3 weeks.** *KP* appears twice a year. As a sample of the poetry they publish I selected this poem (poet unidentified):

> *When snow comes down very fast*
> *And piles upon the ground*
> *We'll make a big snow man*
> *A tall one and very round . . .*

LA BELLA FIGURA (I, IV-Ethnic), P.O. Box 411223, San Francisco CA 94141-1223, founded 1988, editor Rose Romano, is a quarterly **using poetry "any form, any length, about Italian-American culture and heritage or anything of special significance to Italian-Americans. Nothing insulting to I-As: no negative stereotypes, no complaining about I-A ways without affection, no spelling accents (such as tacking an *a* to the end of every other word) and no apologies for being I-A."** They have recently published poetry by Rina Ferrarelli, Rachel DeVries, Dan Sicoli and Gigi Marino. As a sample the editor selected these lines from "Public School No. 18: Paterson, New Jersey" by Maria Gillan:

> *Remember me, ladies,*
> *the silent one?*
> *I have found my voice*
> *and my rage will blow*
> *your house down.*

La Bella Figura is 10 pp., magazine-sized, quality offset. Their press run is 200 with 100 subscriptions of which 2 are libraries. Subscription: $8. **Sample: $2 postpaid. Send SASE for guidelines. Pays 2 copies. "All potential contributors are asked to fill out a very short form to describe their Italian background and experience as an Italian-American. Part of the reason for** *LBF* **is to create family. Therefore, I welcome friendly, informative cover letters. I will gladly consider** previously published poems. **No simultaneous submissions.**" The editor adds, "Few people understand our culture and, therefore, cannot appreciate poetry based on its symbols and secrets. Many I-As are simply 'writing American' or not being published. Write what you are—not what you saw in a movie by an American. I'd like to include work by all I-As—lesbians, gays, heterosexuals and those who are half-Italian but who feel Italian very strongly, first through fourth or fifth generations."

LA NUEZ (II, IV-Foreign language), P.O. Box 1655, New York NY 10276, phone (212)260-3130, founded 1988, poetry editor Rafael Bordao, associate editor Celeste Ewers, is a quarterly international magazine of literature and art, **published entirely in Spanish.** The focus is primarily on poetry, but essays, criticism, interviews, short fiction and reviews of poetry books are also of interest, as well as original artwork and photography. They have published work by Frank Dauster, Reinaldo Arenas, Justo Jorge Padrón, Clara Janés and José Kozer. As a sample the editor selected these lines by Amparo Amorós:

> *Si la noche se acerca y vienes de muy lejos*
> *porque sientes la vida pesando sobre el alma*
> *es hora de sentarse sereno y en penumbra*
> *a contemplar, absorto, como queman el tiempo*
> *los leños del invierno.*

La Nuez is magazine-sized, 32 pp. saddle-stapled and professionally printed, with glossy paper cover. Their press run is 1,000. Subscription: $12. **Sample: $3.50. No simultaneous submissions. Only unpublished work with brief biographical info and SASE. Reporting time 6-8 weeks. Payment 2 copies.**

LACTUCA (II), P.O. Box 621, Suffern NY 10901, founded 1986, editor/publisher Mike Selender, appears 3 times a year. **"Our bias is toward work with a strong sense of place, a strong sense of experience, a quiet dignity and an honest emotional depth. Dark and disturbing writings are preferred over safer material. No haiku, poems about writing poems, poems using the poem as an image, light poems or self-indulgent poems. First English language translations are welcome provided that the translator has obtained the approval of the author."** They have recently published poetry by Charles Bukowski, James Purdy, Juliette Graff, Gail Schilke, Julia Nunnally Duncan, Judson Crews and Michael Pingarron. As a sample he selected these lines from "Brook" by Joe Cardillo:

> *Out in the fields,*
> *chainsaws elbow-greasing it*
> *all day*
> *tire and click off one at a time*
> *as if to say in relief*
> *this day is finally over*

Lactuca is digest-sized, 72 pp. saddle-stapled, laser printed or offset on 24 lb. bond with matte card cover, no ads. They receive "a few thousand poems a year of which less than 5% are accepted." Circulation 500 for 150 subscriptions. Subscription: $10/year. **Sample: $4 postpaid. Send SASE for guidelines. "We do not print previously published material." Pays 2-5 copies "depending on length." Reports within 3 months, "usually within one. We comment on rejections when we can. However the volume of mail we receive limits this."** Reviews books of poetry. He says, "The purpose of *Lactuca* is to be a small literary magazine publishing high-quality poetry, fiction and b/w drawings. Most of our circulation goes to contributors' copies and exchange copies with other literary magazines. *Lactuca* is not for poets expecting large circulation. Poets appearing here will find themselves in good company, appearing with that of other good writers. We've found that our acceptance rate is less than 5% for those responding to announcements in *Poets & Writers,* but significantly higher for poets who find out about *Lactuca* from other magazines."

LADIES' HOME JOURNAL (IV-Humor), 100 Park Ave., New York NY 10017, phone (212)351-3500, founded 1883, a slick monthly, circulation 5½ million, no longer accepts serious poetry. But they do consider **light verse (1-3 stanzas) for the "Last Laughs" page. Put "Last Laughs" on the outside of the envelope. No SASE necessary because they neither return nor acknowledge submissions. If your poem is accepted you'll know when you get the check for $100.** For a sample the editor chose the poem "How Did It Happen?" by Sara Gadeken:

> *They're always needing money,*
> *My two delightful teens.*
> *He takes his dates to restaurants.*
> *She wears designer jeans.*
>
> *He's going on a ski trip.*

She's going to the prom.
There's a Springsteen concert Friday
("You're only young once, Mom!").

I don't know how it happened.
It wasn't my design.
But my children's standard of living
Is considerably higher than mine!

LAKE EFFECT (I, II, IV-Humor, regional), Box 59, Oswego NY 13126, phone (315)342-3579, founded 1985, poetry editors Joan Loveridge-Sanbonmatsu and Carol Sue Muth, is a quarterly literary tabloid using art (graphics and b/w photographs), short fiction, non-fiction, poetry, book reviews, humor (poems and cartoons), essays and guest editorials. **"We look for imaginative, evocative, well-crafted poetry with fresh insights and images. Any style or theme, under 50 lines if possible."** As a sample, the editors selected these lines from "The Shooting of Cannons Over Rivers" by Patricia M. Smith:
> *So much in life we bring things up:*
> *the digging of potatoes, the resting of crocus bulbs.*
> *Then there are some arousals:*
> *anger and cream*
>
> *We are the resurrectors:*
> *coal and carrots and old hatreds.*

Their purpose is to "provide upstate New York readers poetry and prose of regional interest; we also include quality work by artists from other parts of the country." The tabloid quarterly runs 24-28 pp., professionally typeset and laid-out, circulation 9,000 with 198 subscriptions of which 9 are libraries. Subscription: $6. Sample: $2. **Send SASE for guidelines. Pays $5 per poem. Reports in 8 weeks, no backlog at present (seasonal material is held). Double-space MS. Photocopy, dot-matrix OK if legible. 2-5 poems per submission, no simultaneous submissions.** "A short bio with submission is nice but not necessary." **Put name, address, phone number in upper right corner.**

LAKE SHORE PUBLISHING; SOUNDINGS (I, IV-Anthology), 373 Ramsay Rd., Deerfield IL 60015, phone (708)945-4324, founded 1983, poetry editor Carol Spelius, is an effort "to put out decent, economical volumes of poetry." **Reading fee: $1/page. They want poetry which is "understandable and *moving*, imaginative with a unique view, in any form. Make me laugh or cry or think. I'm not so keen on gutter language or political dogma—but I try to keep an open mind. No limitations in length."** They have recently published poetry by Richard Calisch, Margo LaGattuta and Gertrude Rubin. The editor selected these sample lines from "Butch Bond's Funeral" by Kay Meier:
> *. . . His widow smug with survival and her secret*
> *that Butch had not fathered their youngest*
> *was deciding whether to keep*
> *the electric fence. Before Butch,*
> *only small animals had been stunned.*

The 253 pp. anthology included over 100 poets in 1985, is a paperback, at $7.95 (add $1 mailing cost), was published in an edition of 2,000. Soundings II is scheduled for late 1991. It is flat-spined, photocopied from typescript, with glossy, colored card cover with art. **Pays 1 copy and half-price for additional copies. Submit any number of poems, with $1/page reading fee, and a cover letter telling about your other publications, biographical background, personal or aesthetic philosophy, poetic goals and principles. Simultaneous submissions, photocopy, dot-matrix, all OK. Any form or length. Reports within 4 months. The editor will read chapbooks, or full length collections, with the possibility of sharing costs if** Lake Shore Publishing likes the book ($1/page reading fee). "I split the cost if I like the book." She advises, "Keep reading classics and writing modern. Try all forms. Pray a lot." **Sample copy of anthology or random choice of full-length collections to interested poets: $5.**

‡LANCASTER INDEPENDENT PRESS (IV-Feminist, political), P.O. Box 275, Lancaster PA 17603, founded 1969, editor Frank J. Pitz, a tabloid monthly, **uses "poetry included in newspaper on occasion. Feminist, political, free-form. Try to keep under 30-40 lines. Nothing religious."** As a sample the editor selected these lines (poet unidentified):
> *descending darkness clouds the vision*
> *A glut of sounds assault;*
> *the denizens of the street*
> *dance across the stygian scenery.*

They accept about 20 of 40 poems received. Press run 1,000. Subscription: $10. **Sample: $1.50 postpaid. No pay. Previously published poems and simultaneous submissions OK.**

LANDFALL; CAXTON PRESS (IV-Regional), Box 25-088, Christchurch, New Zealand, founded 1947, poetry editor Michele Leggott. *Landfall* is a literary quarterly of **New Zealand poetry**, prose, criticism, reviews, correspondence and interviews. Caxton Press publishes a poetry series of books. **They do not want to see poetry except by New Zealanders.** They have recently published poetry by Allen Curnow, Jenny Bornholdt and Fiona Kidman. As a sample the editor chose the first of two stanzas of "My Lost Youth" by Bill Manhire:

> *'My lost youth*
> *as in a dream,'*
> *begins this poem*
>
> *beginning with a line*
> *in what I think is Polish*

The handsome quarterly is digest-sized, 124 + pp., flat-spined, with full-color glossy card cover, circulation 1,800, 1,600 subscriptions of which 200 are libraries. Subscription: $44 (New Zealand dollars). Sample: $11 (New Zealand dollars) plus postage. **Pays about $40 plus 1 copy for 3-4 poems. Can be delay of up to 3 months for replies.** ("Editors have full time occupations—*Landfall* work in their spare time. Submit 10-12 poems, "a range." **Editor always comments on rejections.** Her advice: "Read poetry."

PETER LANG PUBLISHING, INC. (IV-Translations), 62 W. 45th St., New York NY 10036, phone (212)302-6740, FAX 212-302-7574, publishes primarily scholarly monographs in the humanities and social sciences. List includes **critical editions of great poets of the past. Complete MSS preferred, 200 pages minimum, with descriptive cover letter and *curriculum vitae*.**

LANGUAGE BRIDGES QUARTERLY (I, IV-Ethnic, foreign language), P.O. Box 850792, Richardson TX 75085, founded in 1988, editor Eva Ziem, "is a **Polish-English bilingual forum for Polish matters. One of its purposes is to introduce the English-speaking reader to Polish culture. The subject is Poland and the Polish spirit:** a picture of life in Poland, mainly after World War II, with emphasis on the new and ponderous Polish emigration problems." As a sample the editors selected these lines from "Wrak" (or Zombie—I will quote only the English) by TB (3 June 1987), translated by Karon Campbell and Eva Ziem:

> *I am a zombie.*
> *My soul*
> *is a void, hopelessly*
> *ruined, eternally pained*
> *by injustice.*

For more information send SASE.

LAUREL REVIEW (II); GREENTOWER PRESS (V), Dept. of English, Northwest Missouri State University, Maryville MO 64468, phone (816)562-1265, founded 1960, co-editors Craid Goad, David Slater and William Trowbridge. *LR* is a literary journal appearing twice a year; **Greentower Press accepts no unsolicited MSS.** *LR* wants "**poetry of highest literary quality, nothing sentimental, greeting card, workshop, spit and whistle.**" They have recently published poetry by George Starbuck, Marcia Southwick, Albert Goldbarth, David Citino and Pattiann Rogers. It is 128 pp., 6×9". Press run: 750 for 400 subscriptions of which 53 are libraries, 10 shelf sales. Subscription: $8/year. **Sample postpaid: $5. Pays 2 copies plus 1 year subscription. Submit 4-6 poems/batch.** "Closed to submissions May-Sept." Reports in 1 week-4 months. Editor "does not usually" comment on submissions.

THE LEADING EDGE (IV-Science fiction/fantasy), 3163 JKHB, Provo UT 84602, phone (801)378-2456, managing editor Scott R. Parkin. *The Leading Edge* is a magazine, appears 3 times a year. They want "**high quality poetry related to science fiction and fantasy, not to exceed 3-4 typewritten, double-spaced pages. No graphic sex, violence or profanity.**" They have recently published poetry by Michael Collings and Thomas Easton. As a sample the editors picked these lines from "An Astronaut Discusses a Black Hole Binary System" by Russell W. Asplund:

> *It looks like a sink*
> *A cosmic drainhole slightly clogged in*
> *Some cosmic downpour*
> *The star a carelessly dropped*
> *Bar of soap slowly dissolving*
> *In God's shower*

I have not seen the magazine, but the editors describe it as 6×9", 140 pp., using art. They accept about 15 out of 150 poems received per year. Press run is 500, going to 100 subscriptions (10 of them libraries) and 300 shelf sales. $2.50 per issue, $7.50 for a subscription. **Sample: $2 for back issue, $2.50 for current issue postpaid. Send SASE for guidelines. Pays $5 per typeset page plus 2 copies. Submit with no name on the poem, but with a cover sheet with name, address, phone number, length of poem, title and type of poem. Simultaneous submissions OK, but no previously published poems. Reports in 3-4 months.** They say, "We accept traditional science fiction and fantasy poetry, but we like innovative stuff. If a poet has a good idea, go with it."

THE LEDGE POETRY AND PROSE MAGAZINE (II), 64-65 Cooper Ave., Glendale NY 11385, phone (718)366-5169, founded 1988, editor Timothy Monaghan, appears 2/year and is looking for **quality poetry. "We are a free-verse publication and open to most slants, except that which is explicitly offensive or pornographic. We also do not want material which is preachy or religious-oriented. Looking for hard and strong stuff that moves me enough to grab hold of the author's vision. We consider poetry up to a maximum of 3 pages double-spaced."** Recent contributors are Les Bridges, Simon Perchik, Elizabeth Hansen and Kathy Scaccia. As a sample, the editor selected "Queen of Hell" by Jackie Maslowski:

> *Flower-like you leaned toward me;*
> *Hunger exploded; your distance I severed*
> *Into morsels and felt the fever of your*
> *Tenderness, at last, slipping down my throat.*

The Ledge is 5 × 7", usually 72-80 pp. with glossy cover. They accept 5% of some 700 submissions per year. Press run is 400 with 70+ subscribers, 275+ shelf sales. Subscription: $13.50 for 1 volume (6 issues) or $7.75 for one-half volume (3 issues). **Samples of current issue postpaid: $3.75. Previously published poems and simultaneous submissions OK. Reports in 4-8 weeks, longer if under serious consideration. Pays 1 copy.** The editor says, "We are constantly on the lookout for young and little-known talent. My best advice for submitters is to know the magazine they are submitting to. Pick up a sample issue and read through it. Nothing is more perplexing than receiving material that is totally outside the guidelines of the publication. It winds up being a waste of time for both the writer and editor."

‡LEFT CURVE (II), P.O. Box 472, Oakland CA 94604, phone (415)763-7193, founded 1974, editor Csaba Polony, appears "irregularly, about every 10 months." They want poetry "**critical culture, social, political, 'post-modern,' not purely formal, too self-centered, poetry that doesn't address in sufficient depth today's problems.**" They have recently published poetry by Jack Hirschman, Suzh Menefee and Etel Adam. As a sample the editor selected these lines by HM:

> *my unfriend the machine awakens me*
> *to a world one step removed*
> *from the dark, from the grave*

The editor describes it as "about 100 pp., offset, flat-spined, Durosheen cover." Press run 1,200 for 150 subscribers of which 50 are libraries, 800 shelf sales. Subscription: $18/3 issues (individuals). **Sample postpaid: $6. Reports in 3-6 months. Pays 3 copies.**

‡LEFT-FOOTED WOMBAT; VISHNU-ALA DAV PRESS (I), M31 Jardine Terrace, Manhattan KS 66502, founded 1988, editors David and Laura McGhee. Vishnu-Ala Dav Press publishes *LFW*, which appears twice a year using "**something with an unusual twist, either in form or subject matter. No specific length.**" As a sample, I selected these lines from "A Monument to Wonder" by Rochelle Hope Mehr:

> *I think that's when this menstrual mess all began.*
> *Lot's wife looked back from behind him*
> *"And she became a pillar of salt."*

It is 16-24 pp. photocopied from typescript on plain paper, digest-sized with paper cover, saddle-stapled. Press run 75. **Sample postpaid: $1. Pays 2 copies. Do not submit MSS in February, March, August and September. Send SASE for guidelines. Previously published poems and simultaneous submissions OK.** Editor "always" comments on rejections.

LEGEND (I, IV-Fantasy), 1036 Hampshire Rd., Victoria, British Columbia V8S 4S9 Canada, phone (604)598-2197, founded 1989, editor Janet P. Reedman, appears approximately once a year. She wants "**fantasy poetry dealing with/based on episodes of the British TV series 'Robin of Sherwood.'** " **Length is open. No porn or dull poetry about mundane matters.** She has recently published poetry by Cathy Bubaruz, J.P. Reedman, Owen Neill, J.M. Rattray, David Cavangh, D. Linn and Denysé Bridger. The editor selected these sample lines from "Sacrifice" (poet unidentified):

> *Red blood and dark earth a communion form,*
> *earth is England and the blood is mine,*
> *I am loth to leave when my love's lying warm,*
> *but I am sworn to be the King Divine.*

Magazine is 170+ pages, spiral-bound, photocopied from typescript, uses much b/w art. Press run: 120+. Accepts 80-90% material from 2 dozen or so. **"Will help with rewrites; prefer to outright rejection."** Sample: $17 US, $17.50 Canadian. Payment: a substantial discount. Typed or handwritten MSS acceptable. No previously published poems. Reports in 1-10 weeks, usually sooner. For US submissions/inquiries: rather than IRCs please send 2 loose US stamps. Nearly always comments on rejections.

L'EPERVIER PRESS (V), 1326 NE 62nd, Seattle WA 98115, founded 1977, editor Robert McNamara, a "small press publisher of contemporary American poetry in perfect-bound and casebound books." **Currently not accepting submissions.** He has recently published books by Bruce Renner, Linda Bierds, Frederic Will and Paul Hoover. As a sample, he chose the following lines from "The Hopper Light" by David Rigsby:

> *A slow burn. And then, even the cells*
> *whisper goodbye in a slow, vegetal loneliness.*
> *Today the stem goes to a stump, a seam*
> *along which the leaf is cloven and rains*
> *down in this vain. If the separation*
> *defines the kiss, I have seen so many*
> *falling out of love today*

The press publishes 2 poetry books each year, 6 × 9″ with an average page count of 64, some flat-spined paperbacks and some hardcovers. The book they sent me, **Second Sun** by Bill Tremblay, is handsomely printed on heavy buff stock, 81 pp., with glossy card cover in grey, yellow and white; there is a b/w landscape photo on the front cover and a photo of the author on the back; the book is priced at $6.95.

LIBIDO: THE JOURNAL OF SEX AND SEXUALITY (I, IV-Erotica, humor), P.O. Box 146721, Chicago IL 60614, founded 1988, editors Marianna Beck and Jack Hafferkamp, is a quarterly. **"Form, length and style are open. We want poetry of any and all styles as long as it is erotic and/or erotically humorous. We make a distinction between erotica and pornography. We want wit not dirty words."** They have recently published poetry by Ovid, Pietro Aretino and Arno Karlen. As a sample the editor selected these lines by Eliot Richman:

> *On our lips,*
> *liquid concupiscence*
> *like the sea*
> *where we came from, sailing with life*
> *eons like us, fins and scales*
> *wet with sex . . .*

It is digest-sized, 72 pp., professionally printed, flat-spined, with 2-color matte card cover. Press run: 7,000 for 3,000 subscriptions, shelf sales of 3,000 ("it's growing quickly"). They accept about 5% of poetry received. Subscription: $20 in US, $30 outside. **Sample postpaid: $6. Pays $0-25 plus 2 copies. Reports in 4-6 months.**

LIBRA PUBLISHERS, INC. (I), Suite 383, 3089C Clairemont Dr., San Diego CA 92117, phone (619)581-9449, poetry editor William Kroll, publishes two professional journals, *Adolescence* and *Family Therapy*, plus books, primarily in the behaviorial sciences but also some general nonfiction, fiction and poetry. "At first we published books of poetry on a standard royalty basis, paying 10% of the retail price to the authors. Although at times we were successful in selling enough copies to at least break even, we found that we could no longer afford to publish poetry on this basis. Now, unless we fall madly in love with a particular collection, **we require a subsidy.** They have published books of poetry by Martin Rosner, William Blackwell, John Travers Moore and C. Margaret Hall, the author of these sample lines selected by the editor:

> *Writing poetry means*
> *That I can take up the brush at any minute,*
> *That I can put down the thought*
> *That was flying high.*

Prefer complete MS but accept query with 6 sample poems, publishing credits and bio. Replies to query in 2 days, to submissions (if invited) in 2-3 weeks. MS should be double-spaced. Photocopy, dot-matrix OK. Send 9 × 12″ SASE for catalog. Sample books may be purchased on a returnable basis.

LIFTOUTS MAGAZINE; PRELUDIUM PUBLISHERS (V), 1503 Washington Ave. S., Minneapolis MN 55454, phone (612)333-0031, founded 1971, poetry editor Barry Casselman, a "publisher of **experimental literary work and work of new writers in translation from other languages."** Currently accepting no unsolicited material. *Liftouts* appears irregularly. New format: 5½×8" on offset, 50-150 pp., press run 1,000. Reviews books of poetry.

LIGHTHOUSE (I, IV-Children), P.O. Box 1377, Auburn WA 98071-1377, founded 1986, associate editor Lorraine Clinton, is a magazine "with a delightful variety of fiction and poetry that maintain time-honored values," appearing every other month. It has a children's section. **Uses poems up to 50 lines, "G-rated, ranging from light-hearted to inspirational."** They have recently published poetry by Dawn Zapletal, Joyce Parchman and Louise Hannah Kohr. As a sample the editor selected these lines from "Eventide" by Muriel Larsen:

> *Magenta splashed across the sky*
> *Has fallen on the tide,*
> *And mixed among the gold and blue*
> *Through twilight hour doth ride.*

I have not seen it, but the editor describes it as 56 pp., digest-sized, "professionally printed, some simple illustrations in Children's Section." Circulation is 300 for 100 subscriptions. Subscription: $7.95. Sample: $3 **(includes guidelines, postage and handling). Send SASE with first class stamp for guidelines. Pays up to $5 per poem.** "Prefer typed, double-spaced, each poem on a separate sheet for evaluating purposes." Reports in 2-8 weeks, publication within a year.

‡**LIGHTWORKS (IV-Form),** P.O. Box 1202, Birmingham MI 48012, phone (313)626-8026, "shimmering, flickering, shining and projecting new and creative art and art forms." Published irregularly, 21 issues to date, the magazine is highly visual with coverage of intermedia and fringe arts. "No straight lit but some **visual poetry, 'poeMvelopes', and plenty of mail art."** See *Kaldron* listing for a definition of "visual poetry." **SASE always. Payment with copies. Brochure available.** $1-5 for back issues.

Lilith *is a quarterly independent magazine with a Jewish feminist perspective, says publisher Paula Gantz. It seeks articles and poetry by Jewish women about the Jewish woman's experience. Poems, preferably short ones, should be addressed to poetry editor Alicia Ostriker. Pictured here is Anna Rael Delay, subject of the story "New Mexico's Secret Jews: Now is it Safe to Tell?" by Maria Stieglitz. The cover photo is by Doug Handel.*

LILITH MAGAZINE (IV-Women, ethnic), Suite 2432, 250 W. 57th St., New York NY 10107, phone (212)757-0818, founded in 1975, publisher Paula Gantz, poetry editor Alicia Ostriker, "is an independent magazine with a Jewish feminist perspective" which uses **poetry by Jewish women "about the Jewish woman's experience. Generally we use short rather than long poems. Do not want to see poetry on other subjects."** They have published poetry by Irena Klepfisz, Lyn Lifshin, Yael Messinai, Sharon Neemani, Marcia Falk and Adrienne Rich. It is glossy, magazine-sized. "We use colors. Page count varies. Covers are very attractive and professional-looking (one has won an award). Generous amount of art. It appears 4 times a year, circulation about 10,000, about 5,000 subscriptions." Subscription: $14 for 4 issues. **Sample: $4.50 postpaid. Send SASE for guidelines. Reports in 6-8 weeks.** "Please send no more than 6 poems at a time; advise if it is a simultaneous." Editor "sometimes" comments on rejections. She advises: "(1) Read a copy of the publication before you submit your work. (2) Be realistic if you are a beginner. The competition is *severe*, so don't start to send out your work until you've written for a few years. (3) Short cover letters only. Copy should be neatly typed and proofread for typos and spelling errors."

LILLIPUT REVIEW (II, IV-Form), 207 S. Millvale Ave. #3, Pittsburgh PA 15224, founded 1989, editor Don Wentworth, is a tiny (4½×3.6″) 12 pp. magazine, appearing irregularly and **using poems in any style or form no longer than 10 lines.** They have recently published poetry by Lyn Lifshin, Louis McKee, David Chorlton, Sheila Murphy and Tony Moffeit. As a sample the editor selected "Fourth of July Poem" by Steven Doering:

> *countless*
> *inconspicuous*
> *hordes of illegal*
> *aliens can't be*
> *wrong*

Press run 150. *LR* is offset printed from typescript on colored paper, side-stapled. **Sample: $1 or SASE. Currently, every other issue is a broadside featuring the work of one particular poet. Send SASE for guidelines. Pays 2 copies per poem. Submit no more than 3. Reports usually within 60 days. Editor comments on submissions "occasionally — always at least try to establish human contact."**

LIMBERLOST PRESS; THE LIMBERLOST REVIEW (II), HC 33, Box 1113, Boise ID 83706, phone (208)344-2120, founded 1976, editor Richard Ardinger. Limberlost Press publishes poetry, fiction and memoirs in letterpressed chapbooks, flat-spined paperbacks and other formats. *Limberlost Review* appears "fairly regularly." **"We want the best work by serious writers. No restrictions on style or form."** They have recently published poetry by William Stafford, Lawrence Ferlinghetti, Charles Bukowski, Allen Ginsberg and John Clellon Holmes. I have not seen their publications, but the editor describes *LR* as digest-sized ("varies. One issue recently has been devoted to a series of 20 letterpressed poem postcards.") It has a press run of 500-1,000. **Sample: $10 postpaid. Pays 2 copies ("varies"). No simultaneous submissions. For chapbook submission (2-3 a year), submit samples, bio and prior publications. Reports on queries in 1 week, on submissions in 1-2 months. Pays a varied number of author's copies. Editor sometimes comments on rejections. "Issues often are devoted to chapbooks by poets in lieu of anthologies."**

LIMESTONE: A LITERARY JOURNAL (II), Dept. of English, 1215 Patterson Office Tower, Lexington KY 40506-0027, founded as *Fabbro* in 1979, as *Limestone* in 1986, editor Matthew J. Bond, is an annual seeking **"poetry that matters, poetry that shows attention to content and form. We're interested in all poetics, but we do watch for quality of thought and a use of language that will wake up the reader and resonate in his/her mind."** They have recently published poetry by Wendell Berry, Guy Davenport, Michael Cadnum, Noel M. Valis and James Baker Hall. It is 6×9″, perfect-bound, offset. They accept 5-10 of 100-150 poems submitted annually. Press run is 500 for 30 subscriptions (20 of them libraries). **Sample: $3 postpaid. Pays 3 copies. Submit 1-10 pages. Simultaneous submissions and previously published poems OK. Reports in 3-6 months.** "If you're considering publication," the editor advises, "read as much poetry as possible. Listen carefully. Work over your poems till you're sick of them. The lack of such care shows up in many of the MSS we receive."

LIMITED EDITIONS PRESS (V); ART: MAG (II), P.O. Box 70896, Las Vegas NV 89170, phone (702)597-0943, founded 1982, editor Peter Magliocco, an "ultra-small purveyor of 'art/mort fantasies' and sometimes gross fictions." He describes *Art: Mag* as "unusual, off-beat, even 'avant-garde' mag." He also publishes chapbooks ("art: maggies") and original limited editions of poetry. He wants to see poetry that is **"well-crafted, hopefully meaningful work of no definite formal restrictions." He does not want to see "erotic fixations bordering on the pornographic or bland academic stuff going nowhere."** He has recently published poetry by John Grey, Paul Dilsaver, James Purdy, charlie mehrhoff, Mark Weber, and Steven Jacobsen. As a sample the editor selected "Straddling The Brink" by Belinda Subraman:

> *The mirror is a foreign object*
> *these days. We don't know*
> *what we're seeing.*
> *We are victims of our own making,*
> *paralyzed children,*
> *mental quadriplegics*
> *with no pity for them*
> *or else too much.*

The unusual magazine is sometimes oversized, hand crafted, many poems in handwriting, photo-copied on many different kinds of paper, including a great variety of graphics (including an original oil painting in one issue I have seen), side-stapled (or bound with a plastic clasp). It appears 1-2 times a year, about 100 copies given to "friends and patron believers." **Sample: $2.50 postpaid. Send SASE for guidelines (if you're not squeamish). Pays 1 copy. Reports within 3 months.** He usually publishes 1-3 chapbooks per year (photocopied, stapled, 15 pp.), but **"not planning any for '92."** Peter Magliocco, who calls himself "mag man," advises, "Poets can't editorially dictate or expect to run the show. Brilliant small press poetry is struggling against becoming an endangered species, with little exploration of the meaningful 'Word,' the guiding everyday ethic of an artist's Life. Pursue your own vision as an artist, even if it puts you at odds with others."

‡**LINCOLN BULLETIN (I, IV-Gay)**, P.O. Box 94629, Lincoln NE 68509, founded 1986, editor Darla Brown, publishes occasional one-page photocopied flyers of various sizes with line drawings or clip art using **"poems, rants, commentary from queers, criminals, women, drunks, children, Christians and other weirdos. We like plants, sex, drinking, politics, religion, literary criticism, translations and the blurring of genre distinctions. Nothing that JUST SAYS NO."** They have recently published poetry by Kirstin Nelson and Ed Chaberek (and Francis of Assisi in translation). As a sample the editor selected these lines by "Ken":

> *His damn mother brought him here, before he was born.*
> *But she didn't tell him why. That's his excuse.*
> *(Went to Northeast J-S High)*
> *Everytime I sit down they wheel out the damn vacuum cleaner.*

They claim not to have rejected anything yet. **"Submit anything, in any form. If previously published tell us where and when. Long rambling cover letters preferred. I read them right in the post office. Then they go in a box under Don's desk [Don Smith is co-editor] until they strike a nerve in one of us. Then we put them out. This takes one week or two years. Tell us if you're impatient."** Press run is 10-60 for 5 subscribers. **"5-55 copies left in libraries, or student unions, or laundromats, stapled to bulletin boards, telephone poles in Lincoln." Sample: "send stamps." Pays 1-2 copies.** Reviews books of poetry. The editor says, "The rant is *the* literary form of the 20th century. The most powerful, moving and dangerous. Ezra Pound ranted. So did Valerie Solanas. Ranting combines poetry, fiction, history, theater, music, film, ritual, and martial arts. Hitler and Mussolini are obvious examples. But also Allen Ginsberg, the rap group Public Enemy, Alfred Jarry, the Apocalypse Society, the films 'Faces of Death,' the extemporaneous speeches of George Bush and other political figures ... Actually, I should say the rant is the *male* literary form of the 20th century—used mostly for patriarchal ends." Go figger, sez Jud.

‡**LINES N' RHYMES (I)**, 5604 Harmeson Dr., Anderson IN 46013, phone (317)642-1239, founded 1989, editor Pearl Clark, appears every other month using **"some poetry to 40 lines—use some 4 lines, most between 12-20 lines. I like poems concerning life, belief in God's guidance. Nothing pornographic or occult."** They have recently published poetry by Ainsley Jo Phillips, Ruth E. Cunliffe and Rosina Clifford. As a sample the editor selected these lines from "Ben Franklin's Bird" by Dr. Harry Snider:

> *For had the Congress stood with Ben,*
> *The turkey would be national;*
> *Protected in its coop or pen*
> *By federal law, irrational.*
> *And then upon Thanksgiving Day,*
> *With turkey kills illegal;*
> *Around our tables folks would pray,*
> *"Lord, help us eat this eagle."*

It is photocopied on 4 legal-sized colored sheets, sometimes 5. Press run is 50. 20 are distributed free to "my church group." 3-5 shelf sales. Subscription $5/6 issues. "I receive 170 poems/year—accept 70%. **I pay nothing for poetry used. I award 'Editor's Choice' to 2 poets/issue at $1. I give preference to subscribers. However, I use poetry from non-subscribers." Previously published poems OK.** Reviews books of poetry and comments in current issue. She holds a limerick contest each September with 3 cash prizes of $5/each, open only to subscribers. **For a sample copy send $1 to *Lines N' Rhymes*.**

‡**LINES REVIEW (II, IV-Translations); LINES REVIEW EDITIONS (V)**, Edgefield Rd., Loanhead, Edin-burgh Scotland EH20 9SY, phone (031)440-0246, founded 1952 ("the oldest continuing Scottish liter-ary magazine"), editor Tessa Ransford. *LR* is a quarterly. **"I like to accept from 4-6 poems in traditional page format, though with energy and intelligence in use of language, form and content. No unusual typography, concrete, sensation-seeking, nostalgic, dully descriptive or fanatically political poetry."** They have recently published poetry by Norman MacCaig, Gozo Yoshimasu, George Szistes and Amy

Clampitt. They review books of poetry. Press run 750 for 500 subscribers of which 100 are libraries, 100 shelf sales. **Sample postpaid: £1.75. Reports in 2-3 weeks. Pays £10/page plus 1 copy. "Double spacing helps, and clear indication whether a page break is or is not also a stanza break, and careful attention to punctuation—that it is as it will be printed."** Tessa Ransford is also director of Scottish Poetry Library (see listing under Organizations) and offers a School of Poets and Critical Service through the library. *LR* often has special issues devoted, for example, to poetry from Glasgow, Japan, America, Canada. They publish translations. Their spring, 1992, issue will celebrate the magazine's 40th anniversary. Lines Review Editions publishes 2 paperbacks/year, "a dozen or so published poets whose work has regularly appeared in the magazine. **We are not accepting any unsolicited MSS."**

LINTEL (II), P.O. Box 8609, Roanoke VA 24014, phone (703)982-2265 or 345-2886, founded 1977, poetry editor Walter James Miller, who says, **"We publish poetry and innovative fiction of types ignored by commercial presses. We consider any poetry except conventional, traditional, cliché, greeting card types, i.e., we consider any artistic poetry."** They have recently published poetry by Sue Saniel Elkind, Samuel Exler, Adrienne Wolfert and Edmund Pennant. As a sample the editor selected these lines by Nathan Teitel:

> *loneliness*
> *is a Mexican earring*
> *and fear*
> *a crushed cigarette*

The book from which this was taken, **In Time of Tide**, is 64 pp. flat-spined, digest-sized, professionally printed in bold type, hard cover stamped in gold, jacket with art and author's photo on back. Walter James Miller asks that you **query with 5 sample poems. He replies to the query within a month, to the MS (if invited) in 2 months.** "We consider simultaneous submissions if so marked and if the writer agrees to notify us of acceptance elsewhere." **MS should be typed, photocopy OK. Pays royalties after all costs are met and 100 copies. To see samples, send SASE for catalog and ask for "trial rate" (50%).** "We like our poets to have a good publishing record, in the literary magazines, before they begin to think of a book."

‡LINWOOD PUBLISHERS (II), Suite 16, 481 Hambrick Rd., Stone Mountain GA 30083, phone (404)296-3950, founded 1982, poetry editor Bernard Chase, was "organized as an independent small press, primarily to publish the poetry of known, unknown and little known poets." They publish in both paper and hardback editions. The editor says he is interested in **"quality poetry of any form."** They have recently published poetry by Simon Perchik, Carl Lindner, Barbara Unger, T.S. Wallace and George Gott. The editor selected these sample lines by Isabella Matsikidze from "The Zimbabwean Collectibles":

> *I am a writing*
> *beginner. One with*
> *a world of words*
> *to tell a message*
> *to a world of people.*

They will consider freelance submissions of book MSS. **It is your option whether to query first or send samples. Your cover letter should give publication history and bio. They try to reply to queries within 30 days, to MSS within 30-60 days. Preferably typed MS: photocopies, dot-matrix, simultaneous submissions OK; contracts are for 5-10% royalties and author's copies (negotiated). Send SASE with 7 × 10″ envelope, 3 oz. postage, for catalog.** "Sample copies of our publications can be purchased directly from the publisher." Bernard Chase advises, "Feel no intimidation by the breadth, the depth of this craft of which you have chosen to become a part. Although we are very open to beginners, we do not as a rule respond with comments, suggestions or criticisms."

‡LITERARY CREATIONS (I), P.O. Box 1339, Albany OR 97321, phone (503)928-7093, founded 1990, publisher Margaret L. Ingram, is a monthly 4-pp. tabloid using **"all types, except pornography, up to 24 lines."** They have recently published poetry by Tim Monaghan and Alexandre Amprimoz. As a sample, I selected this stanza (the first of 5) from "The Dustbunny Creation" by George A. Hancock:

> *They gather at night*
> *Consolidating their might*
> *Despite their fiendish gleams*
> *I sleep in dreams.*

Press run 300 for 15 subscribers. Subscription: $10. **Sample: $2 postpaid. Send SASE for guidelines. Pays up to 5 copies. "Accepts simultaneous submissions. Cover letter is preferred, giving information about the submission and requesting a sample copy or guidelines. Submissions are accepted as space is available. Contributors will receive a 'thank you' within 2 weeks."** They accept 90% of submissions, publish 15-30 poems/issue. Reviews books of poetry for a minimum fee of $15. The editor advises, "Write about things, places or people that you know or have experienced. Read, write and rewrite. Poetry is alive and doing well."

‡LITERARY FOCUS POETRY PUBLICATIONS; ANTHOLOGY OF CONTEMPORARY POETRY; INTER-NATIONAL POETRY CONTESTS: FALL CONCOURS, SPRING CONCOURS, SUMMER CONCOURS (I), P.O. Box 36242, Houston TX 77236-0242, phone (713)779-2804, founded 1988, editor-in-chief Adrian A. Davieson. **Purchase of anthology may be required of poets accepted for publication.** Literary Focus publishes anthologies compiled in contests, 3/year, with prizes of $500, $300 and $100, plus "Distinguished Mention" and "Honorable Mention." **"Contemporary poetry with no restriction on themes. 20 line limit. Maximum submission 15 poems, minimum 3 poems. No abusive, anti-social poetry."** As a sample the editor selected these lines from "Delayed Journey" by himself:

> *I saw the footsteps retracing to*
> *A lost moment, then there was a*
> *Whisper of ancient sorrows long*
> *Left in the trail of endless*
> *Struggles.*

The digest-sized anthologies are either flat-spined or saddle-stapled, 70 pp., typeset. **Previously published poems and simultaneous submissions OK. "Poems are evaluated on an individual basis by a panel of five editors chaired by editor-in-chief. Poets are notified of acceptance two weeks after deadlines."** Send SASE for guidelines. Reviews books of poetry.

THE LITERARY REVIEW: An International Journal of Contemporary Writing (II), Fairleigh Dickinson University, Madison NJ 07940, phone (201)593-8564, founded 1957, editor-in-chief Walter Cummins, a quarterly, seeks **"work by new and established poets which reflects a sensitivity to literary standards and the poetic form." No specifications as to form, length, style, subject matter or purpose.** They have published poetry by Robert Cooperman, Gary Fincke, José Bergamin, Tomasz Jastrun and R.S. Thomas. The editors selected these sample lines by Robert M. Chute:

> *Their savage, ragged screams*
> *are music here between*
> *jagged lines of hemlock, water maple,*
> *pine. The sun's nimbus*
> *is around them. Set wings,*
> *fantails, dried-blood brown*
> *translucent feathers shine*

The magazine is 6×9", flat-spined, 128+ pp., professionally printed with glossy color cover, using 20-50 pp. of poetry in each issue, circulation 1,800, 900 subscriptions of which one-third are overseas. They receive about 1,200 submissions per year, use 100-150, have 6-12 months backlog. **Sample: $5 postpaid, request a "general issue." Submit no more than 5 poems at a time, clear typing or dot-matrix, simultaneous submissions OK, no queries. Reports in 2-3 months. Pays copies. At times the editor comments on rejections.**

LITERATURE AND BELIEF (II, IV-Religious), 3134 Jesse Knight Humanities Building, Brigham Young University, Provo UT 84602, phone (801)378-2304, founded 1981, editor Jay Fox, is the "annual journal of the Center for the Study of Christian Values in Literature." **It uses poetry "with Christian-based themes"** in a handsomely published flat-spined format. Price per issue: $5 US, $7 outside US. They conduct an annual contest with $100 first prize for poetry. They have recently published poetry by Ted Hughes, Donnel Hunter, Leslie Norris and William Stafford. As a sample the editor selected these lines from "Obsidian" by Dixie L. Partridge:

> *Cold, this blind glass*
> *carries more heat than topaz*
> *and ruby, more strokes*
> *from the mother-earth,*
> *and more sorrow.*

‡THE LITHIC REVIEW (II); NOMAD (IV-Themes); THE PREHISTORIC PRESS, P.O. Box 40624, Bellevue WA 98004, phone (206)453-9211, founded 1990, editor Denise Buckner. *The Lithic Review* is a literary quarterly. **"Want to see insight and imagination. Any style. Enjoy poems dealing with nature or the environment, but any subject is OK. (Bonus points for poems that have anything to do with ancient cultures or anthropology.) I enjoy Beat poetry, poetry with a sense of humor, poetry that takes risks, breaks new ground. Be an original. Don't want to see bad rhyme or gushy poetry."** They have recently published poetry by A.D. Winans, Arthur Winfield Knight, Joy Walsh, B.Z. Niditch and Douglas Powell. As a sample the editor selected these lines from "Telegram" by Sherry Brandon:

> *The future race is coming in,*
> *signal please:*

> breaker to breaker,
> dream to dream,
> are you there?

It is digest-sized, 32 pp., saddle-stapled, with card cover. Press run 250-300. Subscription: $5 for 2 issues, $10 for 4 issues, $30 lifetime subscription. Please make checks payable to Denise Buckner. **Sample: $2.50 postpaid. Pays 1-3 copies. "I appreciate cover letters which convey the personality or outlook of the poet, but a cover letter isn't required. It would be nice to hear how the poet heard of** *The Lithic Review. Please* **include name and address on every page and be sure to include a SASE. Usually respond to submissions within a few weeks. Seldom provide comments or criticism on rejections."** Reviews books of poetry. *Nomad* is an occasional poetry publication on announced themes. "It will be published on five papers in various formats at irregular intervals." **For a list of upcoming themes send SASE. Pays copies.** She advises, "Read lots of current poetry. Cultivate your own style—be authentic. Write a lot. Don't be discouraged by rejections. Enjoy yourself!"

‡**THE LITTLE MAGAZINE (II)**, SUNY-Albany, 1400 Washington Ave., Albany NY 12222, founded in mid-60s, poetry editor Sharon Stenson, is an annual. **"No specifications as to form, length or style, or purpose or subject-matter. Open to experimental or language-oriented poetry, well-crafted. No clichés, sentimental pap, or junk!"** They have recently published poetry by Simon Perchick, Diane Glancey, Lori Anderson, Jim Daniels and Sharon Stenson. As a sample the poetry editor selected "A Cambodian Woman's Lament" by Suzette Bishop:

> See, our written language is sinuous as my arms
> > in coral bracelets,
> As the waters I have crossed.
> I hear Cambodian music, the dry bamboo leaves.
> Your pastels are unknown to me. I know of reds
> > taking into
> themselves such deeply shaded greens.

It is digest-sized, 300+ pp., flat-spined, professionally printed, with glossy full-color card cover. Press run 1,500 for 500 subscribers of which 200 are libraries, 500 shelf sales. **Sample postpaid: $6. Reports in 4-8 weeks. Pays 2 copies. Submit between Sept. 15 and Dec. 15. No comments on rejections.** The editor advises, "Poetry must have strong images--must communicate."

LITTLE RIVER PRESS (V), 10 Lowell Ave., Westfield MA 01085, phone (413)568-5598, founded 1976, editor Ronald Edwards, publishes **"limited editions of poetry collections, chapbooks and postcards of New England Poets."** They have recently published poetry by Steven Sossaman, Wanda Cook and Frank Mello. As a sample the editor selected these lines from "The First of May" by Anne Porter:

> All over the marshes,
> and in the wet meadows,
> wherever there is water,
> the companies of peepers
> who cannot count their members,
> gather with sweet shouting.

I have not seen any of their publications. **No unsolicited poetry. Pays 60% of run.**

LIVING STREAMS (IV-Christian, membership), P.O. Box 1321, Vincennes IN 47591, phone (812)882-4289, founded 1988, editor/founder Kevin Hrebik, a national, quarterly, "subscriber written," 80-page journal. Subscription: $15/year. They **"prefer non-controversial Christian material, especially good poetry, prose and fiction, also all special forms."** They use 150-200 poems per year, 3-25 lines and 25-30 prose pieces, average length 1,000 words. Pays in contributor's copies, tearsheets and free subscriptions. Photocopied, simultaneous, previously published submissions are acceptable (no dot-matrix). Reporting time is 2-4 weeks. Sample available for $3.75 postpaid, guidelines free. Uses original art and photography; will consider submissions (nature scenes with water) for cover (pay is $50). The editor says, "Send 4-6 good poems and 1 prose piece at a time. Don't write Christian 'baby' material. Assume reader is intelligent, literate and a mature Christian. Write clearly, make specific points, yet try to be original and artistic. Show off your skill."

‡**LMNO PRESS (I)**, P.O. Box 862, Westminster MD 21157, founded 1991, editor Laurie Precht. LMNO Press publishes yearly in July. It accepts **concrete, narrative poetry under 100 lines and short stories.** *"Whatever gets published must make sense!* **And please, no poetry about cats, death, religion or about writing poetry. Also, no chapbooks."** As a sample she selected these lines from "Manzanar" by Laurie Watanabe:

> The first sound
> in town

I remember
was sweep. It made songs
in my crib. If you think sweep
is not a song
you should hear my mama
play her broom.

LMNO Press is digest-sized, 40 pp., press run 200. It is distributed through subscription and at poetry readings and literary fairs. Subscription or **sample copy: $3 postpaid. "Don't send cash; please send check or money order made out to Laurie Precht." Pays 1 copy. MSS should be typed with name on everything. Submit 3-6 poems, simultaneous submissions OK, no previously published work. Reports in 3-6 months. Editor comments if the poem needs work before it is published.** She advises, "Let the words speak for you and let your ideas invoke the imaginations of your audience. Poetry is *the* most powerful communication avenue — don't get lost on Main Street. Try going down Parsons Way or Loch Raven Boulevard or any of a thousand avenues where you'll find something different."

LODESTAR BOOKS (IV-Children/teen, anthology), 375 Hudson St., New York NY 10014, phone (212)366-2627, affiliate of Dutton's Children's Books, a division of Penguin USA, founded 1980, editorial director Virginia Buckley, is a trade publisher of **juvenile and young-adult nonfiction, fiction and picture books. "A good anthology would be OK, or poetry for the very young child. No adult poetry. Although we have not published any poetry or anthologies, we are open to submissions; writers should be familiar with the juvenile market. Best place to start is in the library rather than bookstore."**

LOLLIPOPS, THE MAGAZINE FOR EARLY CHILDHOOD EDUCATORS (IV-Themes), Good Apple, Inc., 1204 Buchanan, Box 299, Carthage IL 62321, phone (212)357-3981, editor Jerry Aten, is a magazine published 5 times a year providing easy-to-use, hands-on practical **teaching ideas and suggestions for early childhood education. Uses light verse on themes appropriate to the focus of the magazine.** Circulation 18,000. Subscription $16.95. Sample postpaid: $4.50. **Writer's guidelines for #10 SAE with 2 oz. postage. Submit seasonal/holiday material 6 months in advance. Computer printout submissions acceptable; prefers letter-quality. Pays "variable" rates on publication.**

LONDON MAGAZINE (II), 30 Thurloe Place, London SW7 England, founded 1954, poetry editor Alan Ross, is a literary and art monthly using **poetry "the best of its kind."** They accept about 150 of 2,000 poems received a year. Press run is 5,000 for 2,000 subscriptions. Subscription: £28.50 or $67. **Sample: £3 postpaid. Pays £20 per page. Reports "very soon."** Alan Ross says, "Quality is our only criterion."

‡**LONG ISLAND QUARTERLY (IV-Regional)**, 14 Center St., Northport NY 11768, founded 1990, editor-publisher George Wallace, is a quarterly using **poetry by people on or from Long Island. "Surprise us with fresh language. No conventional imagery, self-indulgent confessionalism, compulsive article-droppers."** They have recently published poetry by David Ignatow and William Heyen. As a sample, I selected these lines from "Watermill" by Claire Nicholas White:

> *This pioneer's house, lonely as a shroud*
> *once housed the trapped soul of a sad wife.*
> *I knew her there chained to her loom*
> *in a land not her own, bending her head*
> *to peer through small panes over land eastward*
> *from where she came*

It is digest-sized, 28 pp., professionally printed on quality stock with matte card cover. Press run 250 for 130 subscribers of which 15 are libraries, 50-75 shelf sales. Subscription: $10. **Sample: $3 postpaid. Pays 1 copy. Responds in 3 months. Submissions without SASE not returned.** The editor advises "(1) Go beyond yourself; (2) Don't be afraid to fictionalize; (3) Don't write your autobiography — if you are worth it, maybe someone else will."

LONG ISLANDER; WALT'S CORNER (II), 313 Main St., Huntington NY 11743, phone (516)427-7000, FAX (516)427-5820, founded 1838 by Walt Whitman, poetry editor George Wallace, is a weekly newspaper, 25,000 circulation, using **unrhymed poetry up to 40 lines "grounded in personal/social matrix, no haiku, inspirational."** They have used poetry by David Ignatow, David Axelrod and R.B. Weber. As a sample I selected the first 3 stanzas of "Love Poem-12" by Sandra Kohler:

> *A woman wakes to a midnight perfume.*
> *It is her own, transformed by sleep*
> *into something rich and strange*
> *as the words we speak dreaming,*
> *a geography of need.*

It is "48 pp. newsprint." They use 52 of about 1,000 poems submitted each year. Subscription: $12 on Long Island, $17 off Long Island. **Sample: $2.50 postpaid. Simultaneous submissions OK. Pays 1 copy. Editor "normally" comments on rejections.**

LONG SHOT (II), P.O. Box 6231, Hoboken NJ 07030, founded 1982, published by Danny Shot, edited by Jack Wiler, Jessica Chosid and Tom Polhamus, is, they say, a "good magazine." They have published poetry by Charles Bukowski, Sean Penn, Allen Ginsberg, Marianne Faithfull, Amiri Baraka and June Jordan. It is 120+ pp., flat-spined, professionally printed with glossy card cover using b/w photos, drawings and cartoons. It comes out twice a year, press run 1,500. They say they accept about 35 of 1,000 submissions received. Subscription $18−2 years (4 issues). **Sample: $5. Pays 2 copies. Simultaneous submissions OK. Reports in 8 weeks.**

‡LONGHOUSE (II); SCOUT (V); ORIGIN PRESS (V), Green River R.F.D., Brattleboro VT 05301, founded 1973, editor Bob Arnold. *Longhouse* is a literary annual using **poems "from the serious working poet" from any region in any style.** They have recently published poetry by Hayden Carruth, Keith Wilson, Barbara Moraff, James Koller, Cid Corman, Janine Pommy-Vega, Bobby Byrd and Sharon Doubiago. Its format is unusual: a thick packet of looseleaf 8½×14″ sheets, photocopied from typescript, in a handsomely printed matte cover. Press run 200. **Sample postpaid: $8. Pays 2 copies.** Reviews books of poetry. **They publish chapbooks and books (manuscripts solicited only) under the imprints of Longhouse and Scout.** "We are also a bookshop and mail-order business for modern 1st editions and modern poetry and small presses. We encourage poets and readers looking for collectible modern 1st editions and scarce−and not so scarce−books of poetry and small press magazines to write for our free catalog." Bob Arnold says, "Origin Press is best known as Cid Corman's press. One of the quiet giants in American poetry/plus the wide scope of international work. Established in the early 1950s in Boston, it has moved around as Cid went with his life: France, Italy, for many years now in Kyoto, Japan. Cid has merged with Longhouse in that we now edit and publish a few items together. He continues to edit, translate and publish from Kyoto. His own books are heavily based in our bookshop and mail order catalog."

THE LOOKOUT (IV-Themes), Seamen's Church Institute of New York and New Jersey, 241 Water St., New York NY 10038, phone (212)349-9090, founded 1834, poetry editor Carlyle Windley, is the "external house publication of the Institute and has been published continuously since 1909, 3 times a year, circulation 5,700. Basic purpose of the publication is to engender and sustain interest in the work of the Institute and to encourage monetary gifts in support of its philanthropic work among merchant seamen. Emphasis is on the *merchant marine*; NOT Navy, power boats, commercial or pleasure fishing, passenger vessels." It is magazine-sized, normally 20-24 pp., printed offset in two color inks. Subscription is via a minimum contribution of $5 a year to the Institute. It **"buys small amount of short verse (sea-faring related but *not* about the sea per se and the clichés about spume, spray, sparkle, etc.), paying $10."** They have published poetry by Wendy Thorne, June Owens, Irene Abel and Kay Wissinger. The editors selected this sample poem by John E. Hall:

> In the winter
> When I can . . .
> And the norther's high . . .
> I trudge to the headland
> and stand . . .
> Just to feel her shiver. . . .

Sample free for 9 × 12″ SASE. Submit any number of poems. No photocopies. Typed originals. Reports within 2 weeks. Send SASE for guidelines.

LOOM PRESS; LOOM; BEAT SCENE (II), P.O. Box 1394, Lowell MA 01853, founded 1978, editor Paul Marion, a small-press publisher of poetry chapbooks and broadsides. The broadside series, which appears irregularly, is called *Loom* and publishes **"good contemporary poems in any form, style."** Poets recently published include Susan April, Dana White, Juan Delgado and Eric Linder. As a sample, the editor selected the following lines from "Dreaming of Sugar Cane" by George Chigas:

> Your father sat engoldened upon the lotus
> amused by the cricket's gossip
> while you learned English in the camp

The broadsides range from magazine-sized to 11 × 17″. They have a circulation of 100-500. Price per issue varies, but a **sample is available for $2. Pay is 10 copies. "Clear copies" are OK for submissions which will be reported on in 1 month; time to publication is 3-6 months. Writers should query first for chapbook publication, sending credits, 5 sample poems and bio. Queries will be answered in 1 month, MSS reported on in 6 weeks. Simultaneous submissions will be considered, and photocopied or dot-matrix MSS are OK. Royalties of 10% are paid on chapbooks, plus 5% of print run. Sample chapbooks are available at $5 each. The editor comments** on MSS **"when time allows."** The chapbooks are saddle-stitched, 6×9", with an average page count of 20. The editor advises, "The publishers of poetry need your support as well as your poems." The editor of Loom Press is also a contributing editor for *Beat Scene*, an English magazine specializing in American literature and culture. Loom Press accepts U.S. poetry submissions for *Beat Scene*.

‡LOS HOMBRES PRESS (IV-Form), P.O. Box 632729, San Diego CA 92163-2729, phone (619)234-6710 or 688-1023, founded 1989, publisher Jim Kitchen, publishes **haiku only.** As a sample, I selected this haiku by Marlene Mountain:

> *my art my life hidden from mother.*

That appears in an anthology, **the rise and fall of sparrows**, edited by Alexis Rotella, a digest-sized, flat-spined professionally printed paperback (glossy card cover), $9.95. "We publish only one book per year." **Pays 10% royalties plus 10 copies.**

‡LOST MAGAZINE; LUPUS ENTERPRISES (I, IV-Horror), 67 Seyler St., New Hamburg, Ontario N0B 2G0 Canada, phone (519)662-2725, founded 1990, editor Adam Thornton. *Lost* appears every other month using **"any horrific or eerie poetry, any length, preferably not rhyming. No sci-fi or fantasy or poems with predictable themes or rhyme schemes."** They have recently published poetry by John Grey, james siple and Lynda Walter. As a sample the editor selected these lines from "Dorothy's Minion" by David Hunter Sutherland:

> *in this land of milk & honey,*
> *saints of plywood, 2' by 4',*
> *nail sweet Dorothy to its entrance,*
> *then pray mankind will heed her call.*

It is 40 pp. digest-sized, saddle-stapled, photocopied from typescript on ordinary paper. They accept about 25% of 60 poems received/year. Press run 100, 6 shelf sales. Subscription: $2. **Sample postpaid: $2. Send SASE for guidelines. Reports immediately. Pays 1 copy.** "Cover letters are a *must*, preferably ones that are creative and interesting, containing biographical info. Anyone can submit. We encourage amateurs and anyone unsure of their work—very friendly and personal." Editor always comments on rejections.

LOTHROP, LEE & SHEPARD BOOKS (V), 105 Madison Ave., New York NY 10016, founded 1859, editor-in-chief Susan Pearson. **"We do not accept unsolicited MSS."**

LOTUS PRESS INC. (V), P.O. Box 21607, Detroit MI 48221, phone (313)861-1280, FAX (313)342-9174, founded 1972, poetry editor Naomi Long Madgett. "With one exception of a textbook, we publish books of **poetry by individual authors,** although we have two anthologies and two sets of broadsides, one with a teachers' guide for use in secondary schools. We occasionally sponsor readings. **Most, but not all, of our authors are black."** Currently, they are not accepting unsolicited MSS. Poets recently published include May Miller, Monifa Atungaye, Selene de Medeiros and Naomi F. Faust. The following lines are by Oliver LaGrone:

> *Dawn is eternally somewhere.*
> *The eagle's nest,*
> *Crag in the windborne mists*
> *Has noisy witness: cry the foragers'*
> *Return in hours of bending light . . .*

Payment is made in copies. Poets are not expected to contribute to the cost of publication. Response is usually within 6 weeks. "Copies may be ordered from our catalog, which is free upon request. We do not give samples."

‡LOUDER THAN BOMBS; SEMINAL LIFE PRESS (II), 2313 Santa Anita Ave., S. El Monte CA 91733, phone (818)575-1887, founded 1990, editor Bryan Ha. *LTB* is a quarterly. Seminal Life Press publishes books of poetry. They want **"fresh images, strong language. Any form, length or style is fine. Nothing dull, sentimental, banal, ordinary."** They have recently published poetry by Steve Abee, Antler, Laurel Speer, S.A. Griffin, Joel Ensana, Sigmund Weiss, Michael C. Ford, Gerald Locklin, Lyn Lifshin and James Snydal. As a sample the editor selected these lines from "psalm 122" by Andrew Demcak:

> *that huge blue face of the sky*
> *sat yawning*
> *like some bloated cannibal.*
>
> *it had worn the sun and moon*
> *like Siamese twins*
> *twisted into the shape of earrings.*

LTB is magazine-sized, photocopied, spiral bound. Press run 200 for 9 subscribers, 140 shelf sales. Subscription: $10. **Sample postpaid: $3. Pays 1 copy. Reports in 2 weeks.** Reviews books of poetry. *A Piece of Paper,* a weekly broadside, is distributed free to cafés and bookstores throughout Los Angeles. **Terms for book publication are worked out personally with each poet.** The editor advises, "Write whatever you feel like. Use the style best for your own expression. Just because your poem is rejected doesn't necessarily mean that it's not good. Try to buy a sample copy if you can. **Cover letters are always appreciated."**

LOUISIANA LITERATURE; LOUISIANA LITERATURE PRIZE FOR POETRY (II, IV-Regional), P.O. Box 792, Southeastern Louisiana University, Hammond LA 70402, editor Tim Gautreaux, appears twice a year. They say they **"receive MSS year round. We consider creative work from anyone though we strive to showcase our state's talent. We like poetry with original language use and strong images which go beyond themselves."** They have published poems by Sue Owen, Catharine Savage Brosman, Katharyn Machan Aal, David Tillinghast, Elton Glaser, Jo McDougall and Glenn Swetmann. The editor chose these sample lines by Kathy Andre-Eames:

> *You mumbled to the shed,*
> *shaved a desk, wrote impatiently*
> *slow music for a violin and bow,*
> *wasps droning low in the gutterpipes.*

The magazine is a large (6¾ × 9¾") format, 100 pp., flat-spined, handsomely printed on heavy matte stock with matte card cover (using pen drawing). Subscription: $10 for individuals; $12.50 for institutions. The Louisiana Literature Prize for Poetry offers a $300 award. **Guidelines for SASE.**

LOUISIANA STATE UNIVERSITY PRESS (II), Baton Rouge LA 70893, phone (504)388-6294, founded 1935, poetry editor L.E. Phillabaum, is a highly respected publisher of collections by poets such as Lisel Mueller, Julia Randall, Fred Chappell and Henry Taylor. The editor selected a sample from "In The Market" by Margaret Gibson:

> *I thought of lillies—how they pull water*
> > *clear through*
> *their green channels.*
> *In them was presence,*
> > *and ease of future.*

Query with 6-8 sample poems, publication credits. Replies to query in 1 month, to submission (if invited) in 3-4 months. Simultaneous submissions, photocopies OK. Royalty contract plus 10 author's copies.

THE LOUISVILLE REVIEW (II, IV-Children/Teen), 315 Bingham Humanities, University of Louisville, Louisville KY 40292, phone (502)588-6801, founded 1976, faculty editor Sena Jeter Naslund, appears twice a year. **They use any kind of poetry except translations, and they have a section of children's poetry (grades K-12). "Poetry must include permission of parent to publish if accepted. In all of our poetry we look for the striking metaphor, unusual imagery and fresh language. We do not read in summer. Poems are read by 3 readers; report time is 1-2 months and time to publication is 2-3 months."** They have recently published poetry by Richard Jackson, Jeffrey Skinner, Maura Stanton, Richard Cecil, Roger Weingarten and Greg Pape. *TLR* is 200 pp., flat-spined, 8¼ × 6". They accept about 10% of some 700 pieces received a year. **Sample: $4 postpaid. Pays 1 copy.**

‡**LOW-TECH PRESS (V),** 30-73 47th St., Long Island City NY 11103, founded 1981, editor Ron Kolm, has published work by Hal Sirowitz, John Yau and Jennifer Nostrand. As a sample the editor selected these lines (poet unidentified):

> *They firebombed*
> *the dinner table*
> *taking us completely*
> *by surprise.*

"I am only interested in short poems with clear images. Since almost nobody gets paid for their work, I believe in multiple submissions and multiple publishings. Even though we publish only solicited MS, I respond right away to any mail the press receives."

LUCIDITY; BEAR HOUSE PRESS (I), Route 2, Box 94, Eureka Springs AR 72632-9505, founded 1985, editor Ted O. Badger. *Lucidity* is a quarterly of poetry. **Submission fee required—$1 per poem for "juried" selection by a panel of judges or $2 per poem to compete for cash awards of $20, $10 and $5.** Other winners paid $1 cash and in copies. In addition, the editor invites a few contributors to submit to each issue. Contributors are encouraged to subscribe or buy a copy of the magazine. The magazine is photocopied from typescript, digest-sized, saddle-stapled, 56 pp. with matte card cover, press run 250, 140 subscribers. Subscription: $8. **Sample: $2 postpaid. Send SASE for guidelines.** The magazine is called *Lucidity* because, the editor says, "I have felt that too many publications of verse lean to the abstract in content and to the obscure in style." Ted Badger says the magazine is **"open as to form. 40 line limit due to format.** No restriction on subject matter except that something definitive be given to the reader." Purpose: "to give a platform to poets who can impart their ideas with clarity." He does not want "religious, nature or vulgar poems." Recently published poets include Betty Benoit, Sue Austin, Michael Estabrook and Mary Stickney Strand. As a sample of the type of verse sought, the editor offers these lines:

> I shall not dread snow
> nor bone-chilling winds of time;
> your love gives me warmth.

Reports in 2-3 months, a 3-month delay before publication. Simultaneous submissions, previously published poems OK. Bear House Press is a subsidy arrangement by which poets can pay to have booklets published in the same format as *Lucidity,* prices beginning at 50 copies of 32 pp. for $140. Publishes 8 chapbooks per year. The editor says, "Poets become known by being published in national journals."

‡THE LULLWATER REVIEW (II), Box 22036 Emory University, Atlanta GA 30322, phone (404)727-6182, founded 1989, editor Robert T. Webb, appears twice a year. They want **"original, imaginative treatment of emotional and intellectual topics. No mere wordplay. Ideas and concepts should be emphasized. Nothing overtly sentimental or with little craftsmanship."** They have recently published poetry by Howard Nemerov, Eve Shelnutt, Harold Witt and John Stone. As a sample the editor selected these lines from "Lucky Pierre" by Turner Cassity:

> Working with radium gave Dr. Curie cancer;
> Being struck by horses in the street, however,
> Killed him. So much for the natural as answer.

It is a handsome 6×9" flat-spine magazine, 96-112 pp. with glossy card cover. Press run 2,000. 500 copies go to Emory students. Subscription: $10. **Sample: $5 postpaid. Pays 3 copies. Send SASE for guidelines. Will consider simultaneous submissions. Reports in 3-6 weeks "unless heavy load arrives."** Editor comments "whenever possible." An editorial board of poets, Emory faculty and students discuss and determine which poems will be published. The editor says, "There are good poets today. There are fewer great ones. *LR* seeks to publish both. We recommend our potential submitters be well read, aware of current trends in poetry and take their craft seriously. If you are unaware of the meaning of new formalism or postmodernism, try Hallmark, not the *LR*."

LUNA BISONTE PRODS; LOST AND FOUND TIMES (IV-Style), 137 Leland Ave., Columbus OH 43214, founded 1967, poetry editor John M. Bennett, may be the zaniest phenomenon in central Ohio. John Bennett is a publisher (and practicioner) of **experimental and avant-garde writing,** sometimes sexually explicit, and art in a bewildering array of formats including the magazine, *Lost and Found Times,* post card series, posters, chapbooks, pamphlets, labels and audio cassette tapes. You can get a sampling of Luna Bisonte Prods for $3 plus $1 postage and handling. Numerous reviewers have commented on the bizarre *Lost and Found Times,* "reminiscent of several West Coast dada magazines"; "This exciting magazine is recommended only for the most daring souls"; "truly demented"; "Insults . . . the past 3,000 years of literature," etc. Bennett wants to see **"unusual poetry, naive poetry, surrealism, experimental, visual poetry, collaborations—*no* poetry workshop or academic pablum."** He has published poetry by I. Argüelles, G. Beining, B. Heman, R. Olson, J. Lipman, B. Porter, C. H. Ford, P. Weinman, E. N. Brookings, F. A. Nettelbeck, D. Raphael, R. Crozier, S. Sollfrey, S. Murphy, M. Andre, N. Vassilakis, and himself. The editor selected these lines from the poem "Ab:Prophetics #10" by Jake Berry:

> I am a pearly ecumenical. Severely cornered in
> a retort. Effeminate with octopus. And they
> shall creosote the price of parading. It's
> that ovum. Leaping stink in a habit of tires.

The digest-sized 40 pp. magazine, photoreduced typescript and wild graphics, matte card cover with graphics, has a circulation of 350 with 60 subscriptions of which 25 are libraries. **Sample: $4 postpaid. Submit any time—preferably camera-ready (but this is not required). Reports in 1-2 days, pays copies.** Luna Bisonte also will consider book submissions: query with samples and cover letter (but "keep it brief"). Chapbook publishing usually depends on grants or other subsidies and is usually by solicitation. Photocopy, dot-matrix OK. He will also consider subsidy arrangements on negotiable terms.

‡THE LUNDIAN (I), The English International Association of Lund, P.O. Box 722, 220 07 Lund, Sweden , phone 046-184550-Info., founded 1976, copy editor March Laumer, is an 8 pp. newsletter using **short poems, no more than 20 lines, nothing romantic.** They publish 5 of 15 poems received.

Press run 3,000 for 400 subscribers of which 12 are libraries. Subscription: $10.

THE LUTHERAN JOURNAL (IV-Religious), 7317 Cahill Rd., Edina MN 55439, phone (612)941-6830, editor The Rev. Armin U. Deye, is a family quarterly, 32 pp., circulation 136,000, for Lutheran Church members, middle age and older. They use **poetry "related to subject matter," traditional, free verse, blank verse. Pays. Sample free for SASE. Simultaneous and photocopied submissions OK.**

LYNX, A QUARTERLY JOURNAL OF RENGA (IV-Form, subscribers), P.O. Box 169, Toutle WA 98649, phone (206)274-6661, formerly APA-Renga founded 1986, editor Terri Lee Grell, one of the first APA-Renga contributors, "changed the name to *Lynx* to link an endangered species of poetry with an endangered animal and to inspire the traditional wit of renga. The magazine, published quarterly, is **based on the ancient craft of renga, linked verse with origins in Zen and Japanese culture, publishes renga, mostly by subscribers.** A renga is a non-narrative series of linked images as a group effort." The editor selected this sample renga (excerpt) by Tundra Wind, Eric Folsom, Jane Reichhold and Terri Lee Grell:

> Redwood shadows at river's edge
> Approaching auto's distant headlights
> Two white fangs of a bobcat
> The whimper of illuminated lovers

Lynx also publishes essays, book reviews, articles, interviews, experimental linked forms, linked prose, art, commentaries and "whatever encourages poets to link ideas." Published poets include Hiroaki Sato, Marlene Mountain and Miriam Sagan. *Lynx* **encourages submissions by those experienced and experimenting with collaborative forms. Subscribers participate in ongoing rengas, start trends and otherwise determine the content. Reports in 4 weeks. Editor responds to all who submit.** Currently 100 subscribers. *Lynx* is a newsprint publication, 5½ × 4", 24 pp., unstapled. **Sample copy: $2 postpaid, includes guidelines. Pays copies.**

THE LYRIC; LYRIC ANNUAL COLLEGE POETRY CONTEST (II, IV-Form, students), 307 Dunton Dr. SW, Blacksburg VA 24060, founded 1921 ("the oldest magazine in North America in continuous publication devoted to the publication of **traditional poetry**"), poetry editor Leslie Mellichamp, uses about 50 poems each quarterly issue. **"We use rhymed verse in traditional forms, for the most part, with an occasional piece of blank or free verse. 35 lines or so is usually our limit. Our themes are varied, ranging from religious ecstasy to humor to raw grief, but we feel no compulsion to shock, embitter or confound our readers. We also avoid poems about contemporary political or social problems — grief but not grievances, as Frost put it. Frost is helpful in other ways: if yours is more than a lover's quarrel with life, we're not your best market. And most of our poems are accessible on first or second reading. Frost again: don't hide too far away. Poems must be original, unpublished and not under consideration elsewhere."** Pays 1 copy, and all contributors are eligible for quarterly and annual prizes totaling over $900. They have recently published poetry by Anne Barlow, John J. Brugaletta, R.H. Morrison, Rhina P. Espaillat, Barbara Loots, Amy Jo Schoonover, Paul Ramsey, Alfred Dorn, Charles Dickson, Gail White and Tom Riley. The editor selected these sample lines by Tom Merrill:

> Unwithered by all casting out,
> My demon drives me yet
> Down the dark path that always ends
> In sorrow and regret

It is digest-sized, 32 pp. format, professionally printed with varied typography, matte card cover, has a circulation of 850 with 800 subscriptions of which 290 are libraries. They receive about 5,000 submissions per year, use 200, have an average 3 month backlog. **Sample: $3 postpaid. Subscription $10 US, $12 Canada and other foreign countries. Submit up to 5 poems. Photocopy, dot-matrix OK. Reports in 1 month (average). Send SASE for guidelines.** *The Lyric* also offers a poetry contest in traditional forms for fulltime undergraduate students enrolled in any American or Canadian college or university, prizes totaling $500. Send SASE for rules. Leslie Mellichamp comments, "Our *raison d'être* has been the encouragement of form, music, rhyme and accessibility in poetry. We detect a growing dissatisfaction with the modernist movement that ignores these things and a growing interest in the traditional wellsprings of the craft. Naturally, we are proud to have provided an alternative for over 70 years that helped keep the true roots of poetry alive."

M.A.F. PRESS; THIRTEEN POETRY MAGAZINE (V, I, IV-Form), Box 392, Portlandville NY 13834-0392, phone (607)286-7500, founded 1982, poetry editor Ken Stone. *Thirteen Poetry Magazine* **"publishes only 13-line poetry; any theme or subject as long as in 'good' taste. We seek to publish work that touches the beauty of this life." Do not submit mss until July, 1992; "currently overstocked." The M.A.F. Press publishes a chapbook series, however, not reading through end of 1991 — no reading fee. Chapbooks must be a total of 32 pages.** They have published poetry recently by Pamela Pontwood,

Ida Fasel, Will Inman, Stan Proper, Janet Carncross Chandler and Marion Cohen. As a sample the editor selected "Leaving" by John Craig:

> *And still the memory*
> *of you standing, waving good-bye.*
> *I should have turned around then*
> *for the sadness of your eye.*

Thirteen appears quarterly in a magazine-sized 40 pp., saddle-stapled format, photocopied from typescript, matte card cover with b/w cartoon, circulation 350 for 130 subscriptions of which 20 are libraries. Ken Stone accepts about 100 of the 300 submissions he receives each year. **Sample: $2.50 postpaid. Submit 4-6 poems. Photocopies are acceptable, no reprint material. "We have even taken hand-written poems. As to queries, only if 13 lines gives the poet problems." Reports "immediately to 2 weeks." Pays 1 copy. Send SASE for guidelines. Comments on rejections "especially if requested."** Reviews books of poetry. The editor advises, "Send more poetry, less letters and self-promotion. Read the 'want lists' and description listings of magazines for guidelines. When in doubt request information. Read other poets in the magazines and journals to see what trends are. Also, this is a good way to find out what various publications like in the way of submissions."

MACFADDEN WOMEN'S GROUP; TRUE CONFESSIONS; TRUE ROMANCES; TRUE LOVE; TRUE STORY; SECRETS; MODERN ROMANCES (I), 233 Park Ave. S., New York NY 10003, phone (212)979-4800. **Address each magazine individually; do not submit to Macfadden Women's Group.** Each of these romance magazines uses poetry—usually no more than one poem per issue. **Their requirements vary, and I suggest that readers study them individually and write for guidelines.** These mass-circulation magazines (available on newsstands) are obviously a very limited market, yet a possible one for beginners—especially those who like the prose contents and are tuned in to their editorial tastes.

THE MACGUFFIN (II), Schoolcraft College, 18600 Haggerty Rd., Livonia MI 48152, phone (313)462-4400, ext. 5292, founded 1983, editor Arthur Lindenberg, who says, "*The MacGuffin* is a literary magazine which appears three times each year, in April, June and November. We publish the best poetry, fiction, non-fiction and artwork we find. We have no thematic or stylistic biases. **We look for well-crafted poetry. Long poems should not exceed 300 lines. Avoid pornography, trite and sloppy poetry.**" *The MacGuffin* has recently published poetry by Danny Rendleman, Jim Daniels and Wendy Bishop. As a sample, the editor selected the following lines from "An Evening Walk in Snowfall" by Janet Krauss:

> *... within that hollow turn into a trap unleashing*
> *fear, I return home to stand and watch*
> *the ice stars melt down on the black woolen hat*
> *while I remember them as gentle whisks on*
> *my eyes and face along a cumulous*
> *place where I could not stumble.*

The MacGuffin is digest-sized, professionally printed on heavy buff stock, 128 pp. with matte card cover, flat-spined, with b/w illustrations and photos. Circulation is 500, of which 75 are subscriptions and the rest are local newsstand sales, contributor copies, and distribution to college offices. Price per issue is $3.75, subscription $10. **Sample: $3 postpaid. Pay: two copies,** "occasional money or prizes. **The editorial staff is grateful to consider unsolicited manuscripts and graphics.**" MSS are reported on in 8-10 weeks and the publication backlog is 6+ months. Writers should submit no more than 6 poems of no more than 300 lines; they should be typewritten, and photocopied or dot-matrix MS are OK. "We will always comment on 'near misses.' Writing is a search, and it is a journey. Don't become sidetracked. Don't become discouraged. Keep looking. Keep traveling. Keep writing." The magazine recently sponsored a contest with a $100 first prize for Michigan poets only; they hope to be able to sponsor a national competition soon.

MACMILLAN OF CANADA (V), 29 Birch Ave., Toronto, Ontario M4V 1E2 Canada, phone (416)963-8830, editorial assistant Joanne Ashdown, is a "leading publisher of Canadian fiction, non-fiction, biography, and children's books. Exclusive agent for William Morrow Company, Hearst Books, Andrews & McNeel and Harraps. **They publish no unsolicited poetry or fiction MSS.**

MACMILLAN PUBLISHING CO.; CHARLES SCRIBNER'S SONS; ATHENEUM; COLLIER, 866 Third Ave., New York NY 10022. Declined listing.

MCPHERSON & COMPANY PUBLISHERS; TREACLE PRESS (V), Box 1126, Kingston NY 12401-0126, founded 1974, publisher Bruce McPherson, **publishes little poetry and has "no real plans for poetry."** The only example of poetry I find in his catalog is Novalis, "Hymns to the Night," translated by Dick

Higgins. He says **"Even when I'm listed for 'no unsolicited submissions' it seems I receive stuff in the mail; it might be appropriate to caution the overzealous not to waste time with wishful thinking."** But this young publisher has developed an outstanding reputation for his finely made books of experimental literature, and if you write the "brave and often brazen" kind of material he likes ("I've always been attracted to outrageous comic invention," for instance) you should send a SASE for his catalog and see whether you might fit into his publishing plans.

‡MAD RIVER PRESS (V), State Road, Richmond MA 01254, phone (413)698-3184, founded 1986, editor Barry Sternlieb, publishes 1 or 2 chapbooks/year, **all types of poetry, no bias," but none unsolicited.** They have recently published poetry by Gary Snyder, John Haines, Paul Metcalf and Janine Pommy Vega. Write for information.

THE MAGE (IV-Science fiction/Fantasy), Colgate University Student Association, Hamilton NY 13346, founded 1984, poetry editor Sonja Gulati, a student-run journal of science and fantasy fiction, essays, poetry, and art. It publishes 4-7 poems in each issue. The editor says, **"We will consider poems of science fiction and/or fantasy themes or subjects. We do not have any categorical specifications as to form or length. We do not print erotic poetry or limericks."** They have published poems by Tom Rentz, Deborah A. Dessaso, Dawn Zapletal, Kathleen Jurgens and Terry McGarry. In order to suggest quality, the editor selected these lines from "Skyship I, On the Seas" by J. L. Chambers:

> *In the Skyship we ride the cloud-swell,*
> *dark, bulging hull swinging low*
> *and snow white sails stacked up high*
> *camouflaged on the round cumulus waves.*

The Mage is 8½ × 11", professionally printed with occasional pen-and-ink illustrations, 64 pp. saddle-stapled with white textured card cover illustrated by a b/w drawing. The magazine appears each semester (twice a year) and has a press run of 800, with subscriptions and book catalog sales plus individual sales by the staff. Price per issue is $3.50, $6/year postpaid. **Sample available for $3 postpaid. Pay is 2 copies. Submissions "only have to be readable. Desired punctuation and spacing should be clear so that we don't have to write for clarification during typesetting."** Reporting time is 4-8 weeks, and accepted work is generally published in the next issue. **"We usually endeavor to make some constructive criticism on all MSS."** The editor offers three pieces of advice: **"1) Our needs are very specific: if your poetry does not have an element of fantasy, science fiction, or horror, it will not fit the tone of our publication. 2) Avoid the cliches which are all too common in these genres. 3) An unusual and interesting first line is much better than an unusual format (with apologies to e. e. cummings)."**

MAGIC CHANGES (IV-Themes), P.O. Box 658, Warrenville IL 60555-0658, phone (708)416-3111, founded 1978, poetry editor John Sennett, is now published every 18 months, still in an unusual format. Photocopied from typescript on many different weights and colors of paper, magazine-sized, stapled along the long side (you read it sideways), taped flat spine, full of fantasy drawings, pages packed with poems of all varieties, fiction, photos, drawings, odds and ends—including reviews of little magazines and other small-press publications, it is **intended to make poetry (and literature) fun—and unpredictable.** Each issue is on an announced theme. *"Magic Changes* **is divided into sections such as 'The Order of the Celestial Otter, 'State of the Arts,' 'Time,' 'Music' and 'Skyscraper Rats.' A magical musical theme pervades."** There are about 100 pp. of poetry per issue, circulation 500, 28 subscriptions of which 10 are libraries. They have published poetry by Roberta Gould, A. D. Winans, Lyn Lifshin and Dan Campion. As a sample of their poetry I selected the closing stanzas from "Time" by Sri Chinmoy:

> *O lover,*
> *You are the fulfiller of Time.*

> *O God,*
> *You are the Player of Time.*

Sample: $5 postpaid. Reports in 8 weeks. Submit 3-5 poems anytime. Photocopy OK. He says **"no query,"** but I would think poets would need to know about upcoming themes. The editor sometimes comments on rejections and offers criticism for $5 per page of poetry. Pays 1 or 2 copies.

Market categories: (I) Beginning; (II) General; (III) Limited; (IV) Specialized; (V) Closed.

‡MAGIC REALISM; PYX PRESS (II,IV-Fantasy), Box 620, Orem UT 84059-0620, founded 1990, editor C. Darren Butler. *Magic Realism* appears 2-3/year using poetry that is **"well-written, carefully imagined. I hope to publish work that will sustain subsequent readings."** It is photocopied, typeset, digest-sized, 60 pp. with card cover using b/w art. They use 5-6 poems/issue. **Sample postpaid: $4.95. "Please order a sample copy before submitting." Pays 1 copy. Reports in 4-6 months. Editor often comments.** He says, "I am looking for literary work based in exaggerated realism. Fantasy should permeate the reality, give it luster. My needs are somewhat flexible. For example, I occasionally publish genre work, or glib fantasy of the sort found in folktales and fables."

‡MAINICHI DAILY NEWS, HAIKU IN ENGLISH (IV-Form), 1-1-1 Hitotsubashi, Chiyoda-ku, Tokyo, Japan 100, phone 212-0321. The "Haiku in English" column was established in January, 1982, poetry editor Kazuo Sato. "The *Mainichi Daily News (MDN)* publishes **selected haiku submitted in English from poets around the world** in a weekly (Sunday) column entitled "Haiku in English." **Entries are selected on basis of quality; some seasonal reference preferred.** *MDN* **does not copyright selections but does publish the name and country of their authors. Authors selected for publication living outside of Japan are sent complimentary copies (1 each) of the column in which their haiku appear. Authors are not paid for their entries. However, an annual haiku contest is held every January with prizes."** They have published haiku by James Kirkup, Edith Shiffert and Virginia Brady Young. As samples, I chose the first prize winners of a past contest in "Free Style" and "Syllabic Style":

> *after the foghorn*
> *silence*
> *drifts towards shore*
> "Free Style" haiku by Carol Wainright

> *Wards Island in snow*
> *the cold harbour holds the call*
> *of a single goose.*
> "Syllabic Style" haiku by James Deahl.

The first prizes were 20,000 yen along with a Brother electronic typewriter, the second prizes were 10,000 yen. **All haiku published in the column throughout the year are automatically considered as entries.** I will quote some of the editor's comments on these haiku to give you a sense of his taste. On the "Free Style" example: "A good haiku or any good poem surprises the reader pleasantly . . . Silence moves and drifts. Through this expression the lonely and intermittent sounds of a foghorn reach the heart of the reader. The desolate scene of the foggy seashore emerges from this short poem." On the "Syllabic Style" example: "In traditional Japanese literature poets have written tanka and haiku about *kari* (wild goose) and *kamo* (wild duck). Both *kari* and *kamo* are season words for winter in Japanese haiku . . . The verb 'holds' is superb. This haiku reminds me of Basho's masterpiece, 'The sea darkens;/The voices of the wild ducks/Are faintly white' (tr. by R. H. Blyth)."

THE MALAHAT REVIEW (II); LONG POEM PRIZES (II, IV-Form), Box 3045, University of Victoria, Victoria, British Columbia V8W 3P4 Canada, phone (604)721-8524, founded 1967, editor Constance Rooke, is "a high quality, visually appealing literary quarterly which has earned the praise of notable literary figures throughout North America. Its purpose is to publish and promote poetry and fiction of a very high standard, both Canadian and international. **We are interested in various styles, lengths and themes. The criterion is excellence."** They have recently published poems by Angela Ball, Stephan Torre and Carolann Russell. The editor selected these sample lines from "Sleep Movements of Leaves" by Toni Sammons:

> *imagination is like being slightly deaf*
> *— what you almost hear*
> *keeps you balanced on precipices of air*
> *your head woven from cobwebs*
> *like a white-eye's nest*

They use 50 pp. of poetry in each issue, have 1,800 subscriptions of which 300 are libraries. Subscription: $15. They use about 100 of 2,000 submissions received per year, have no backlog. **Sample: $7 postpaid. Submit 5-10 poems, addressed to Editor Constance Rooke. Reports within 3 months, pays $20 per poem/page plus 2 copies and reduced rates on others. Send SASE for guidelines. The editors comment if they "feel the MS warrants some attention even though it is not accepted."** Reviews books of poetry. The Long Poem Prizes of $300, plus publication and payment at their usual rates, entry fee $15 (which includes a year's subscription), is for a long poem or cycle 5-20 pp., (flexible minimum and maximum), deadline March 1.

‡MALCONTENT (I), P.O. Box 703, Navesink NJ 07752, founded 1984, editor Laura Poll, appears "approximately every 2 months" using **"whatever—will consider most anything." The editor says they publish about 98% of work received.** It is magazine-sized, 100 pp. photocopied with side-clip binding and "customized by-hand covers." Press run is 100-150, most distributed free "as trades and contributors' copies and offers of appreciation." **Sample: $3 postpaid.** "A personalized note must be included with contributions or else you become a member of the 'Rubber Band Club'—I put your poems in your SASE, rubberband you with the rest who also neglect a note, and toss the lot into the bottom of my 'to-do' box, to be ignored until I feel like acknowledging your rudeness. I take the time to read the stuff, I expect the courtesy of taking the time to say 'hi' to me." Editor always comments on submissions. Previously published poems and simultaneous submissions OK. Pays 1 copy. "Communicate! Don't just let your work 'speak for you.' What a cop-out! The current literary scene is a silent, impersonal wasteland of bloated egos."

THE MANDEVILLE PRESS (V), 2 Taylor's Hill, Hitchin, Hertfordshire, SG4 9AD England, founded 1974, poetry editors Peter Scupham and John Mole, publishes hand-set pamphlets of the work of individual poets, but **will not be considering new submissions through 1991.** Send SASE for catalog to buy samples.

MANHATTAN POETRY REVIEW (II), Box 8207, New York NY 10150, phone (212)355-6634, founded 1981, editor Elaine Reiman-Fenton, **"publishes about half prestige market and half new and/or little-known poets who deserve an audience, wanting carefully crafted poems in any form or style; interesting subject-matter.** There are no restrictions as to length of poems although it has become the custom to avoid very long poems (more than 3 pp.); MSS should be typed, double-spaced, 5-6 pp. of poetry plus cover letter giving previous publication credits, honors, awards, teachers, etc. and SASE. New poets and unsolicited MSS are welcomed. Nothing obscene, ungrammatical, or handwritten. MSS must be ready for the typesetter in case they are accepted." They have published poetry by Marge Piercy, David Ignatow, Diane Wakoski, Marilyn Hacker, Judith Farr, and Robert Phillips. *MPR* appears twice a year, 52-60 pp., digest-sized, saddle-stapled, offset print, paper cover, using only poetry—no art, graphics, ads, prose or reviews. They receive about 1,500 MSS per year, accept 1-2 poems from about 10% of those submitting. Press run is 750. Subscription: $12. **Sample: $7 postpaid. Pays 1 copy. No simultaneous submissions or previously published poems. Reports in 3-4 months. Editor seldom comments on rejections.** She says, "I believe that this is an exciting period in the history of American poetry. The diversity of 'little' magazines reflects the vitality of contemporary poetry and suggests that there is a forum for virtually every type of poem. But recently many little magazines have failed for financial reasons. We need to develop a large dedicated readership, and poets must lead the way! Everyone should subscribe to and read a selection of literary magazines—especially poets."

THE MANHATTAN REVIEW (II, IV-Translations), 440 Riverside Dr. Apt. 45, New York NY 10027, phone (212)932-1854, founded 1980, poetry editor Philip Fried, tries **"to publish American and foreign writers, and we choose foreign writers with something valuable to offer the American scene. We like to think of poetry as a powerful discipline engaged with many other fields. We want to see ambitious work. Interested in both lyric and narrative. Not interested in mawkish, sentimental poetry.** We select high-quality work from a number of different countries, including the U.S." They have published poetry by A. R. Ammons, Ana Blandiana, Bronislaw Maj, Christopher Bursk, Colleen J. McElroy, D. Nurkse, Judson Jerome and Penelope Shuttle. The editor selected these sample lines by Peter Redgrove:

> *The waters shall be healed the spinet declares,*
> *And like gardens of flowers be full of fish*
> *As the flow-er plays; and the moths*

> *Shall carry all leprosies away on their backs,*
> *On their scaly backs, with formal magnitude*

The *MR* is "once again a semiannual." The magazine has 60+ pp., digest-sized, professionally printed with glossy card cover, photos and graphics, circulation 500, with 85 subscriptions of which 35 are libraries. They receive about 300 submissions per year, use few ("but I do read everything submitted carefully and with an open mind"). "I return submissions very promptly." Subscription: $10; per issue: $5. **Sample: $6.25 with 6×9" envelope. Submit 3-5 pp., no photocopy, no simultaneous submissions, with short bio. Reports in 10-12 weeks. Pays copies. Sometimes comments "but don't count on it."** Reviews books of poetry. Philip Fried advises, "Don't be swayed by fads. Search for your own voice. Support other poets whose work you respect and enjoy. Be persistent. Keep aware of poetry being written in other countries."

MANIC D PRESS (I, II), P.O. Box 410804, San Francisco CA 94141, founded 1984. **manic d is interested in books/broadsides/etc.** of **poetry by talented unknowns who are looking for an alternative to establishment presses. Considers simultaneous submissions. Reports in 3 months. Pays copies. Send SASE for catalog to buy samples (or $5 for one of their books of their choice).**

MANKATO POETRY REVIEW; GOOD THUNDER READING SERIES (II), Box 53, English Dept., Mankato State, Mankato MN 56001, phone (507)389-5511, founded 1984, editor Roger Sheffer, a semiannual magazine that is **"open to all forms of poetry. We will look at poems up to 60 lines, any subject matter."** They have recently published poems by Edward Micus, Judith Skillman and Walter Griffin. As a sample, the editor chose the following lines from a poem by Richard Robbins:

> Sage connects to lava rock mile by mile.
> West of Atomic City, blue flowers
>   in the craters of the moon.

The magazine is $5 \times 8''$, typeset on 60 lb. paper, 30 pp. saddle-stapled with buff matte card cover printed in one color. It appears usually in May and December and has a circulation of 200. Price per issue is $2.50, subscription $5/year. **Sample available for $2.50 postpaid, guidelines for SASE. Pay is 2 copies. Do not submit MSS in summer (May through August). "Readable dot-matrix OK. Please indicate if simultaneous submission, and notify." Reporting time is about 2 months;** "We accept only what we can publish in next issue." The editor says, "We're interested in looking at longer poems—up to 60 lines, with great depth of detail relating to place (landscape, townscape)." They sponsor the annual Good Thunder Reading Series in which a number of poets give readings each academic year. Pay varies. Apply to Richard Robbins, director of the series, in their English Department.

‡MANNA (I, II), 2966 W. Westcove Dr., West Valley City UT 84119, founded 1978 by Nina A. Wicker, poetry editors Roger A. Ball, Robert Raleigh, Nina A. Wicker and Rebecca Bradley, is **"a small magazine for the middle-of-the-road poet. We like humor, short poems with feeling, farm poems, inspirational poetry; we mostly use free verse, some rhyme. We do not want long poems. Prefer short quality poems with feelings. Images, tone and thoughtful use of language important."** The digest-sized, 45 pp. magazine, photocopied from laser printed type, matte card cover with simple art, comes out twice a year, using nothing but poetry, circulation 200+, with 100 subscriptions. They receive 500 submissions per year, use about 200, and have less than a year's backlog. **Sample postpaid: $3. Submit 3-5 poems any time (please do not submit a lone poem), reports in 3 weeks or less. No pay, but they give 3 small prizes ($7, $5, and $3) for the best in each issue. "No simultaneous submissions please."** The magazine has recently changed hands and address, with little change in policy or format planned. The new editor advises, "Trust instinct and *write*. Submit poems that give your audience a unique vision; use language and images worthy of that vision. Don't send sentimental love poetry."

‡MANOA: A PACIFIC JOURNAL OF INTERNATIONAL WRITING (II), 1733 Donaghho Rd., Honolulu HI 96822, founded 1989, associate editor Frank Stewart, appears twice a year., **"We are a general interest literary magazine, open to all forms and styles. We are not for the beginning writer, no matter what style. We are not interested in Pacific exotica."** They have recently published poetry by John Updike, Norman Dubie, Alberto Rios and Eugene Ruggles. They review current books and chapbooks of poetry. It is 200+ pp., $7 \times 10''$, offset, flat-spined using art and graphics. They accept about 2% of 3,000 submissions received/year. Press run 1,800 for 700+ subscribers of which 30+ are libraries, 300+ shelf sales. Subscription: $12/year. **Sample postpaid: $7. Send SASE for guidelines. Reports in 6 weeks. Pay "competitive" plus 2 copies. Seldom comments on rejections.** The editor says, "We welcome the opportunity to read poetry submissions from throughout the country. We are not a regional journal, but we do feature work from the Pacific Rim, national and international, especially in our reviews and essays. We are not interested in genre or formalist writing for its own sake, or picturesque impressions of the region."

MANROOT BOOKS (V), Box 762, Boyes Hot Springs CA 95416, founded 1969, publisher Paul Mariah, is "America's oldest gay press." **Currently not accepting submissions.**

‡THE WILTON MARKS STUDIO (IV-Children, romance), P.O. Box 30153, Baltimore MD 21270, founded 1988, programming director Timothy Parker. **This company produces audio and video cassettes from original material. "We purchase all rights and all fees are negotiable. All types and lengths are acceptable. We particularly prefer romance, children's [for use in audio programming]."** All the poets they have used have been beginners. Send SASE for more information.

MAROVERLAG (II, IV-Foreign language), Riedingerstr. 24, 8900 Augsburg, West Germany, phone 0821/416033, founded 1970, editor Lothar Reiserer. **Maroverlag publishes paperbacks and some hardcover books of poetry, one a year, averaging 80 pages.** The books are in German, but they have published a number of English and American poets (for example, Charles Bukowski). **Submit sample of 8-10 poems and bio. Pays 5-10% royalties.**

‡**MARYLAND POETRY REVIEW; MARYLAND POETRY AND LITERARY SOCIETY: (II)**, Drawer H, Catonsville MD 21228, founded 1985, edited by Rosemary Klein, "is interested in promoting the literary arts in Maryland as well as nationally and internationally. **We are interested in strong, thoughtful poetry. All submissions are read carefully.** *MPR* **is open to good poets who have not published extensively as well as to those who have.**" Recent contributors include William Stafford, Josephine Jacobsen, Seamus Heaney and Lucille Clifton. As a sample I selected the first stanza of "The Poetry of Earth" by James McKusick:

> *The earth is given to silence, the gray silence*
> *of dawn on the lakeshore as mist rises*
> *twisting its form above the dark waters.*

The issue I have seen is professionally printed in small type on quality egg-shell stock, 7×11″, 75 pp., saddle-stapled with a glossy b/w card cover. It appears twice a year in double issues (Spring/Summer and Fall/Winter). In the past they have done special issues on confessional, Irish, Hispanic and Australian poetry. Query about possible future special issues. **Submit brief bio with submission. No simultaneous submissions. Sample copy: $5 plus $2 for postage and handling. Pays 1 copy. Reports in 8-12 weeks.** Subscription and Maryland Poetry and Literary Society membership is $17 ($12 for students; $20 for member and spouse; $12 for senior citizens). Book reviews are generally solicited.

THE MASSACHUSETTS REVIEW (II), Memorial Hall, University of Massachusetts, Amherst MA 01003, founded 1959, editors Paul Jenkins and Anne Halley. They have published poems by Andrew Salkey, Dara Weir, Paul Muldoon and Eavan Boland. The editor chose this poem "Love In the Ether" by Adélia Prado:

> *There's a landscape inside me*
> *between noon and two p.m.*
> *Long-legged birds, their beaks slicing the water*
> *enter and don't enter this memory-place,*
> *a shallow lagoon with slender reeds along the shore. . . .*

I have not seen it, but the editors describe this quarterly as "off-set (some color used in art sections) 6×9″. Of 2,500 poems received they accept about 50. Press run is 2,000 for 1,200-1,300 subscriptions (1,500 of them libraries), the rest for shelf sales. Subscription is $14 (U.S.), $20 outside U.S., $17 for libraries. **Sample: $5.25 postpaid. Send SASE for guidelines. Don't read submissions June 1 to October 1. Pays minimum of $10, or 35¢ per line plus 2 copies. No simultaneous submissions or previously published poems. Reports in 6 weeks. No submissions returned without SASE.** "Read the magazine."

MATRIX (IV-Regional), Box 100, Ste. Anne de Bellevue, Quebec H9X 3L4 Canada, founded 1975, is a literary appearing 3 times a year which publishes **quality poetry by Canadians without restriction as to form, length, style, subject matter or purpose.** They have published poems by George Elliott Clarke, Joy Kogawa, David McFadden, Carolyn Smart and Douglas Barbour. There are 5-8 pp. of poetry in each issue. The magazine is 8½×11″, 80 pp., stapled, professionally printed, glossy cover with full-color art and graphics, circulation 2,000. Subscription: $15 Canadian, $20 international. They receive about 500 submissions per year, use 20-30, have a 6-month backlog. **Sample: $10 postpaid (Canadian funds). Submit 6-10 poems. No simultaneous submissions. Reports in 12 weeks. Pays $10-40 per poem.** Editor sometimes comments on rejections. Reviews books of poetry.

‡**MATTOID (II)**, School of Humanities, Deakin University, Geelong, Victoria, Australia 3217, founded 1977, Dr. Brian Edwards, appears 3/year. **"No special requirements but interesting complexity, quality, experimentation. No naive rhyming verse."** They have recently published poetry by Lauris Edmond, Kevin Hart and Judith Rodrigues. It is 200 pp., flat-spined with 2-color cover. They publish about 10-15% of 800 poems received/year. Press run 600 for 400 subscribers of which 10 are libraries, 30-50 shelf sales. **Sample postpaid: $10 overseas. Reports in 2-3 months. Pays 2 copies.**

MATURE YEARS (IV-Senior citizen), P.O. Box 801, 201 8th Ave. South, Nashville TN 37202, phone (615)749-6292, founded 1954, editor Marvin W. Cropsey, is a quarterly, circulation 80,000. They use poetry of no more than 16 lines: **"fun poetry and poetry especially suited to persons in retirement or over 55 years of age."** They do not want to see **"anything that pokes fun at older adults or which is too sentimental or saccharine."** It is magazine-sized, 100+ pp., saddle-stapled, with full-color glossy paper cover. Guidelines are available for writers. They pay 50¢-$1 per line, report in 2 months, a year's delay before publication.

MAYAPPLE PRESS (V, IV-Regional, women), 5520 Briarcliff Dr., Edinboro PA 16412, phone (814)734-3488, founded 1978, publisher/editor Judith Kerman, publishes **"women's poetry, Great Lakes regional poetry"** in chapbooks. They want **"quality contemporary poetry rooted in real experience and strongly crafted. No greeting card verse, sentimental or conventional poetry."** They have recently published chapbooks by Judith Minty and Toni Ortner-Zimmerman. They **"rarely"** accept freelance submissions. **Query with 5-6 samples. Check** *Poets & Writers* **for open times.** "We are not likely to publish unless poet accepts a *primary* role in distribution. Reality is only poets themselves can sell unknown work." **Pays 10% of run. Publishes on "cooperative" basis.** "Generally poet agrees to purchase most of the run at 50% of cover price." Editor **"usually comments (very briefly)"** on rejections. She says, "Poets must create the audience for their work. No small press 'white knight' can make an unknown famous (or even sell more than a few books!)."

THE MAYBERRY GAZETTE (IV-Themes, humor), Wake Forest University, 8955 Renolda Station, Winston-Salem NC 27109, phone (919)998-2860, founded 1986, editor John Meroney, is a newsletter appearing 6 times a year using poetry **about the fictional town of Mayberry, North Carolina, as presented through television's "Andy Griffith Show" (CBS, 1960-1968), "which has become a permanent fixture in Americana. The publication maintains the original mood and theme expressed in the series. Writers should look to the program and issues of the publication for direction. Writer's guidelines available for large SASE."** As a sample the editor selected this piece by Danny Hutchins:

> *Mayberry beats everything, we all know that.*
> *Mayberry's where all the good things are at.*
> *Fair or foul weather, we all stick together.*
> *We are Mayberrians forever and ever.*

The newsletter is 4 pp., folded, professionally printed. Their press run is 7,000 with 5,000 subscriptions. Subscription: $17 one year, $29 two years. **Sample: $3 postpaid. No simultaneous submissions. "Include details as to how you were influenced by the series, why you feel it was/is popular, etc." Reports in 4-6 weeks. "Please include a large SASE with all material."** Editor comments on rejections **"often."** Reviews books of poetry. They occasionally have contests announced through the newsletter.

THE EDWIN MELLEN PRESS (II), 240 Portage Rd., Lewiston NY 14092, phone (716)754-2795, founded 1974, poetry editor Mrs. Patricia Schultz, is a scholarly press. **"We do not have access to large chain bookstores for distribution, but depend on direct sales and independent bookstores."** They pay 2 copies, no royalties. **"We require no author subsidies. However, we encourage our authors to seek grants from Councils for the Arts and other foundations because these add to the reputation of the volume."** They want **"original integrated work—living unity of poems, preferably unpublished poetry, encompassable in one reading."** They have recently published poetry by Toby Lurie and Robert Carter. As a sample the editor selected these lines by John W. Crawford:

> *The lotus blossom calls again.*
> *Away to blue enchanted isles*
> *Where doves descend in quiet drift*
> *And sleepy men lie all about.*

Their books average 64 pp. The sample I have seen, Eleanor Snouck Hurgronje's **Quietly My Captain Waits**, is a handsome hardbound, digest-sized, flat-spined, unpaginated, on good stock. **Submit 40+ sample poems, bio, publications. "We do not print until we receive at least 75 prepaid orders. Successful marketing of poetry books depends on the author's active involvement. Authors provide us with an extensive list of names and addresses of potential readers of their book.** We send out up to 12 free review copies to journals or newspapers, the names of which may be suggested by the author. Authors may purchase more copies of their book (above the 2 free copies provided) at the same 40% discount (for quantities of 10 or more) which we allow to bookstores. An author may (but is not required to) purchase books to make up the needed 75 prepublication sales. Soft covers are also available.

‡MEMES (II), 38 Molesworth Rd., Plympton Plymouth, Devon PL7 4NT U.K., founded 1989, editor Norman Jope, appears twice a year, **"is particularly responsive to work that exhibits awareness of the *wider* dimensions of human experience and which is conscious both of contemporary realities and their possible denouements.** The title of the magazine refers to the linguistic equivalent of genes (legacies passed on from present to futurity) and the aim of the magazine is to drop as many potent memes as possible into the human timestream. Preference for more 'modernist' material (especially with 'occult' or generally 'speculative' themes). Work from authors seeing themselves as 'surrealists' is also liable to please." They have recently published poetry by Dan Raphael, Thomas Wiloch, Shela E. Murphy and Belinda Subraman. As a sample I selected the opening lines of "Dream (Undated)" by Hilary Hayes:

> *Fast fading it flies—this memory on night-dark wings*

This memory of dreams I dreamed last night.
A tent of night-dark hair, the sudden shock
Of recognition bent over me.

It is 36-44 pp. digest-sized, saddle-stapled, desk-top published in small type on light paper with light card cover. They review books, including poetry. Press run 200+ ("rising"), for 25 subscriptions by libraries, about 25 shelf sales. Subscription and samples for **cash only:** $10/3 issues, $4 copy. **Reports in 4 weeks. Pays 1 copy.**

MEMORY PLUS ENTERPRISES PRESS; LIFT THE COVER (I); WRITERS' NEWSLETTER, Box 225, Oakwood IL 61858, founded 1985, chairman Karl Witsman, publishes two books of poetry per year in their Lift the Cover series. They **publish "poetry with some sort of lyrical or rhythmical structure; can be free-verse; does not have to rhyme. Nothing racist. Do not like poems with lines of only one word (except the title line). Poems must make sense and have a point."** The series began with **Erindonia** by Donna Carlene ($3.50 postpaid). As a sample the editor selected these lines from "My One Love" in that collection:

Deep brown eyes I lose myself in,
Turn this way and look at me.
Let me sun myself in your dark light.
Sparkle and shine,
Laugh and cry, my brown eyes,
Let me comfort you.

Pays in copies. "Due to the number of poets responding, those wishing comments or critiques should either buy sample copy or send $2 reading fee per 5 poems. Would encourage participation in our Writers' Group if poet lives in central Illinois or Indiana. Not required. We are still new in poetry and are very flexible."

MENNONITE PUBLISHING HOUSE; PURPOSE; STORY FRIENDS; ON THE LINE; WITH (IV-Religious, children), 616 Walnut Ave., Scottdale PA 15683-1999, phone (412)887-8500. **Send submissions or queries directly to the editor of the specific magazine at address indicated.** The official publisher for the Mennonite Church in North America seeks also to serve a broad Christian audience. **Each of the magazines listed has different specifications, and the editor of each should be queried for more exact information.** *Purpose*, editor James E. Horsch, a "monthly in weekly parts," circulation 18,250, is **for adults of all ages,** its focus: "action oriented, discipleship living." It is 5⅜ × 8⅜", with two-color printing throughout. **They buy appropriate poetry up to 12 lines.** *Purpose* uses 3-4 poems per week, receives about 2,000 per year of which they use 150, has a 10-12 week backlog. MSS should be typewritten, double-spaced, one side of sheet only. **Simultaneous submissions OK. Reports in 6-8 weeks. Pays $5-15 per poem plus 2 copies. Sample copy: free. Send SASE for guidelines.** *On the Line*, edited by Mary C. Meyer, another "monthly in weekly parts," is **for children 10-14,** a "story paper that reinforces Christian values," circulation 10,000. It is 7x10", saddle-stapled, with 2-color printing on the cover and inside, using art and photos. **Sample: free. Pays $5-15 per poem plus 2 copies. Poems 3-24 lines. Submit "as many as desired, but each should be typed on a separate 8 × 11½" sheet." Simultaneous submissions, previously published poems OK. Reports in 1 month, backlog "varies."** *Story Friends*, edited by Marjorie Waybill, is **for children 4-9,** a "story paper that reinforces Christian values, also a "monthly in weekly issues, circulation 10,500, uses poems **3-12 lines, pays $5-10. Send SASE for guidelines/sample copy.** *With*, Editorial Team, Box 347, Newton, KS 67114, telephone (316)238-5100, is for **"senior highs, ages 15-18,"** focusing on helping "high school youth make a commitment to Christ in the context of the church amidst the complex and conflicting values they encounter in their world," circulation 5,300, uses **poetry "dealing with youth in relation to their world." Poems should be short (15-25 lines). No information on payment given.**

MERLYN'S PEN: THE NATIONAL MAGAZINE OF STUDENT WRITING, GRADES 7-10 (IV-Students, young adults), Dept. PM, Box 1058, East Greenwich RI 02818, phone (800)247-2027, founded 1985, editor R. Jim Stahl, is a quarterly using young adult writing as indicated by its title. It is magazine-sized, professionally printed, 36 pp. with glossy paper color cover. Press run: 22,000 for 20,000 subscriptions of which 5,000 are libraries. Subscription: $16.95. **Sample, postpaid: $3. Send SASE for guidelines. Pays 3 copies. Reports in 2 months.** As a sample the editor selected the opening lines of "Shakespeare" by tenth grader Joanna Hearne:

Shakespeare, did you live in the sea?
The beauty of the salty, unsmooth waves is yours,
beating roaring rhythms on the shore,
where tides have come and gone.

METHUEN, INC., Routledge, Chapman & Hall, 29 W. 35th St., New York NY 10001. Declined listing.

METRO SINGLES LIFESTYLES (I), Box 28203, Kansas City MO 64118, phone (816)436-8424, founded 1984, editor Robert L. Huffstutter. *MSL* is a tabloid publication for women and men of all ages: single, divorced, widowed or never-married. Not a lonely hearts type of publication, but positive and upbeat. Published 6 to 9 times per year and has a circulation of 25,000 (approximately 5,000 subscribers in Kansas City and throughout the USA), newsstand, bookstore sales and limited complimentary copies to clubs, organizations and singles groups. Interested in seeing **"free verse, lite verse, philosophical, romantic, sentimental and Frost-type poetry. All subjects considered.** They have recently published poetry by Patricia Castle, Milton Kerr and Mary Ann McDonnell. As a sample, the editor selected these lines from "The Women of Cairo" by Phillip Slattery:

> *Eyes made of the Egyptian night*
> *Sparkling like an oasis pool*
> *Skin the color of the endless sand*
> *Beauty of forgotten goddesses lives on.*

Each issue features at least 12 poems by poets living throughout the USA. "Poets are invited to send a photo and a brief paragraph about their goals, single status and lifestyle. This is optional and does not influence selection of poetry, but does add interest to the publication when space for this extra feature permits." **Reports in 6-8 weeks; pays from $5/poem or in subscriptions plus complimentary copies. Sample copy of current issue is $2 and mailed postpaid immediately.** Each issue about 36 pp. and printed on Webb Offset press. **MS should be typewritten, double-spaced or written in easy-to-read format. Prefer to look at original poetry. No simultaneous or previously published work.** The editor says, "We do not limit or restrict subject of poems, but insist they convey an emotion, experience, or exercise the reader's imagination."

MICHIGAN QUARTERLY REVIEW (III), 3032 Rackham Bldg., University of Michigan, Ann Arbor MI 48109, phone (313)764-9265, founded 1962, editor-in-chief Laurence Goldstein, is "an interdisciplinary, general interest academic journal that publishes mainly essays and reviews on subjects of cultural and literary interest." They use **all kinds of poetry except light verse. No specifications as to form, length, style, subject matter or purpose.** Poets they have recently published include Amy Clampitt, Stuart Dybek, Tess Gallagher, Robert Creeley, Marge Piercy and Jorie Graham. As a sample, the editor chose these lines by Robert R. Anderson:

> *How bored the stars must be*
> *by their own heavenly floorshows*
> *dragging eternities through*
> *predictable moves, dazzling*
> *the darkness, because they have to.*

The *Review* is 6×9", 160+ pp., flat-spined, professionally printed with glossy card cover, b/w photos and art, has a circulation of 2,000, with 1,500 subscriptions of which half are libraries. Subscription: $13; per copy: $3.50. They receive 1,500 submissions per year, use 30, have a 1-year backlog. **Sample: $2 postpaid. They prefer typed MSS, photocopies OK. Reports in 4-6 weeks. Pays $8-12 per page.** Reviews books of poetry. Laurence Goldstein advises, "There is no substitute for omnivorous reading and careful study of poets past and present, as well as reading in new and old areas of knowledge. Attention to technique, especially to rhythm and patterns of imagery, is vital."

MID COASTER (II), 2750 N. 45th St., Milwaukee WI 53210-2429, founded 1987, editor Peter Blewett, is an annual. **"I would like good, tough poetry. No restrictions on form, length or subject matter. Experimental, nonsensical OK. Nothing sentimental."** They have published poetry by Edward Field and F.D. Reeve. As a sample the editor selected these lines from "I Hear the Wife of the Governor of Wisconsin Singing" by James Liddy:

> *Over the bluff your rock-like song*
> *   passes,*
> *over soft shade me who*
> *forgets or dislikes most literature.*

Mid Coaster is magazine-sized, 36 pp. saddle-stapled, professionally printed in small type with glossy heavy paper cover. Press run: 1,000 for 50 subscribers. **Sample postpaid: $4. Send SASE for guidelines. Pays 2 copies.** Reviews books of poetry. The editor quotes Owen Felltham: "Poetry should be like a coranto, short and nimble-lofty, rather than a dull lesson of a day long . . . . He is something the less unwise that is unwise but in prose."

MID-AMERICAN REVIEW; JAMES WRIGHT PRIZE FOR POETRY (II, IV-Translations), Dept. of English, Bowling Green State University, Bowling Green OH 43403, phone (419)372-2725, founded 1980, editor-in-chief Ken Letko, poetry editor John Bradley, appears twice a year. **"Poetry should emanate from strong, evocative images, use fresh, interesting language, and have a consistent sense of voice. Each line must carry the poem, and an individual vision should be evident. We encourage new as well**

as established writers. There is no length limit." As a sample I selected the first stanza of Walter MacDonald's "The Truth Trees Know":

> *Mice die because their world is level.*
> *They never dream wings wait in trees*
> *above them. Whatever they fear*
> *springs on four feet over dirt,*

The review appears twice a year, 200 pp., flat-spined, offset, professional printing, using line drawings, glossy card cover. They receive a thousand MSS a year, use 60-80 poems. Press run is 1,000. Subscription: $8. Per issue: $5. **Sample postpaid: $4. Send SASE for guidelines. Pays $7 per printed page plus 2 copies. They do not consider MSS June-August. Publishes chapbooks in translation.**

MIDDLE EAST REPORT (IV-Regional, ethnic, themes), Suite 119, 1500 Massachusetts Ave. NW, Washington DC 20005, phone (202)223-3677, founded 1971, editor Joe Stork, is "a magazine on contemporary political, economic, cultural and social developments in the Middle East and North Africa and U.S. policy toward the region. We occasionally publish **poetry that addresses political or social issues of Middle Eastern peoples."** They have recently published poetry by Dan Almagor (Israeli). The sample lines are from "It was Beirut, all over again" by Etel Adnan (Lebanese):

> *And it is Beirut all over again*
> *with water on the horizon*
> *cemeteries outcrowding hotels*
> *airplaines bringing the worst*
> *of news*
> *and infinite processions*
> *of sorrow*

It is magazine-sized, 48 pp. saddle-stapled, professionally printed on glossy stock with glossy paper cover, 6 issues per year. Press run: 7,500. "We published 9 poems last year, all solicited." Subscription: $25. **Sample postpaid: $6 domestic; $8 air mail overseas. Pays 3-6 copies. Simultaneous submissions and previously published poems OK. Reports in 6-8 weeks. "We key poetry to the theme of a particular issue. Could be as long as 6 months between acceptance and publication." Editor sometimes comments on submissions.**

MIDDLE EASTERN DANCER (IV-Themes, ethnic), P.O. Box 181572, Casselberry FL 32718-1572, phone (407)831-3402, founded 1979, editor/publisher Karen Kuzsel, is a "monthly international magazine for Middle Eastern dancers and culture enthusiasts. **No specs for poetry other than sticking to the subject matter. Do not want to see anything not related to Middle Eastern dancing."** As a sample the editor selected these lines from "The Dance of Life" by Shariah:

> *The eternal drummer*
> *pounds out the timeless rhythm*
> *which is the heartbeat of the universe—*
> *and the dance of life goes on . . .*

The monthly is magazine-sized, usually 36 pp., printed in 2-color on heavy stock with glossy paper cover, using b/w photos and graphics. They receive about 20 poems per year, accept 6-10 ("depends on room"). The press run is 2,500+. Subscription: $24/year; per issue: $3 plus $1 postage and handling. **Sample: SASE ($1 stamps). Pays 2 copies. Poems can be in "any form that's legible." Simultaneous submissions (if not to other Middle Eastern dance publications), previously published poems OK. Reports within 2 weeks. Editor occasionally comments on rejections.**

MIDLAND REVIEW (II), English Dept., Morrill Hall, Oklahoma State University, Stillwater OK 74078, phone (405)744-9474, founded 1985, a literary annual that publishes "poetry, fiction, essays, ethnic, experimental, women's work, contemporary feminist, linguistic criticism, drama, comparative literature, interviews." The editors say, **"style and form are open." They do not want long or religious poetry."** Poets published include Amy Clampitt, William Stafford, Medbh McGuckian and Richard Kostelanetz. As a sample, the editors chose the following lines by James Doyle:

> *The pressured houses squat*
> *beneath a black sky. Smoke*
> *passes back and forth between*
> *them down the street. Gilled*
> *animals swim the thin odors*
> *home, calling themselves planets . . .*

Midland Review is digest-sized, 100-120 pp., with photography, artwork and ads. Circulation is 500, of which 470 are subscriptions. Price per issue is $6. **Sample available for $5 postpaid. Pay is 1 copy. Writers should submit 3-5 poems, typed MS in any form. "We no longer read during the** summer (May 1-Aug. 31)." **Reporting time is 3-6 months and time to publication 6-12 months.**

‡MIDMARCH ARTS PRESS; WOMEN ARTISTS NEWS (IV-Women), 300 Riverside Dr., New York NY 10025, founded 1979, editor Sylvia Moore. They have recently published poetry by Muriel Rukeyser, Eve Merriam and Jane Cooper. *WAN* is a 40 pp. magazine focusing **on women in the arts,** using some poetry. **Sample postpaid: $3.75. Send SASE for guidelines. Reports in 6 weeks. Pays 5 copies.** Midmarch Arts Press publishes 6 paperbacks/year.

‡MIDNIGHT ZOO; EXPERIENCES UNLIMITED WRITER'S AND ARTIST'S ORGANIZATION NEWS-LETTER (I, IV-Horror/science fiction/fantasy), 544 Ygnacio Valley Rd. #A273, Walnut Creek CA 94596, phone (415)942-5116, founded 1990, editor/publisher Jon L. Herron. *MZ* appears every other month using **poems of 4-100 lines, "horror, sci-fi, fantasy. No haiku, no mainstream. Submit up to 20 poems. Light verse, traditional OK."** They have recently published poetry by Ray Faraday Nelson, J.C. Hendee and Jacie Ragan. I have not seen an issue, but the editor describes it as magazine-sized, 100+ pp, flat-spined with glossy cover. They review other magazines. They accept 60-100 of 200-300 poems received. Press run 3,800 for 1,214 subscribers of which 37 are libraries, 1,800 shelf sales. Subscription: $29.95. **Sample postpaid: $6. Send SASE for guidelines. Pays $3-10/poem plus 1 copy. Reports within 8 weeks. Editor often comments on rejections. "Want a short cover letter with a bio."** *EUWAON*, new in September 1991, publishes reviews. The editor says it is magazine-sized, 32 pp., saddle-stapled, with glossy cover. **Sample postpaid: $2.50. Send SASE for guidelines. Pays $2-8/poem plus 1 copy.**

MIDSTREAM: A MONTHLY JEWISH REVIEW (IV-Ethnic), 110 E. 59th St., New York NY 10022, phone (212)752-0600, editor Joel Carmichael, is a magazine-sized, 64 pp., flat-spined national journal, circulation 10,000, appearing monthly except June/July and August/September, when it is bimonthly. It uses **short poems with Jewish themes or atmosphere.** They have published poetry by Yehuda Amichai, James Reiss, Abraham Sutzkever and Liz Rosenberg. The editor selected these lines from "Yahrzeit" by Rodger Kamenetz as a sample:

> *She lights a candle in a jar. I put*
> *it on the mantle. The candle burns because*
> *it's the custom and our grief doesn't know*
> *where to put itself . . .*

> *. . . We don't believe. Despair*
> *would tell us nothing, but that's no good.*
> *We do what we can. We did what we could.*

Subscription: $21; per issue: $3. They receive about 300 submissions per year, use 5-10%. **Sample: free. No query. Reports in 1 month. Pays $25 per poem.**

MIDWEST POETRY REVIEW (IV-Subscribers); RIVER CITY PUBLICATIONS (V), P.O. Box 4776, Rock Island IL 61201, founded 1980, poetry editors Tom Tilford, Grace Keller and Jilian Roth, is a "subscriber-only" quarterly, with no other support than subscriptions—that is, **only subscribers ($20/year; $25 Canadian, $30 foreign, both in US funds) may submit poetry and/or enter their contests. Subscribers may also get help and criticism on one poem per month.** "We are attempting to encourage the cause of poetry and raise the level thereof by giving aid to new poets, to poets who have lapsed in their writing, and to poets who desire a wider market, by purchasing the best of modern poetry and giving it exposure through our quarterly magazine. We want **poetry from poets who feel they have a contribution to make to the reader relating to the human condition, nature, and the environment. Serious writers only are sought. No jingly verses or limericks. No restrictions as to form, length or style. Any subject is considered, if handled with skill and taste."** They have recently published poetry by Jacie Ragan, William Appel, Eva Harding, Fritz Wolf, Hugo Thomas, Nancy Graham, Barb Abendschein, Dorothy Heller, B R Culbertson and Raymond Farr. The editors selected these sample lines from "Endangered Species" by John Robert McFarland:

> *At final dusk, the rhino came,*
> *the last one, mateless,*
> *thus by definition, last,*
> *and last by nature's way;*

The digest-sized, 52 pp., saddle-stapled magazine is professionally printed in various type styles, matte card cover, some b/w art. They have quarterly and annual contests plus varied contests in each issue, with prizes ranging from $25-500 (the latter for the annual contest), with "unbiased, non-staff judges for all competitions. Paid-up subscribers enter the contests with fees. **Sample: $5 postpaid. Subscription fee of $20 ($25 Canadian, $30 foreign, both in US funds) must accompany first submission. No photocopies. Reports in 2 weeks. Pays $5-500 per poem. Send SASE and $1 for guidelines.** River City Publications is not currently publishing books. The editor advises, "We are interested in serious poets, whether new or published. We will help those who wish to consider serious criticism and attempt to improve themselves. We want to see the poet improve, expand and achieve fulfillment."

THE MIDWEST QUARTERLY (II), Pittsburg State University, Pittsburg KS 66762, phone (316)235-4689, founded 1959, poetry editor Stephen Meats, "publishes articles on any subject of contemporary interest, particularly literary criticism, political science, philosophy, education, biography, sociology, and each issue contains a **section of poetry from 10-30 pages in length. I am interested in well-crafted, though not necessarily traditional poems that see nature and the self in bold, surrealistic images of a writer's imaginative, mystical experience of the world. 60 lines or less (occasionally longer if exceptional)."** They have recently published poetry by Amy Clampitt, Marguerite Bouvard, Jared Carter, Chris Howell, Walter McDonald and Greg Kuzma. These are sample lines from "Yellow Woman" by Denise Low:

> The river is a woman of yellow sand.
> I lie down in her, leaving a print
> of hips and breasts. Soft water touches inside me.

The digest-sized, 130 pp., flat-spined, matte cover, magazine is professionally printed, has a circulation of 650, with 600 subscriptions of which 500 are libraries. They receive approximately 2,500 poems annually; publish 80. Subscription: $10; per issue: $3. "My plan is to publish all acceptances within 1 year." **Sample: $3. MSS should be typed with poet's name on each page, 10 poems or fewer. Photocopies, legible dot-matrix, OK; simultaneous submissions accepted, but first publication in** *MQ* **must be guaranteed. Reports in 8 weeks, usually sooner. Pays 3 copies. Editor comments on rejections "if the poem or poems seem particularly promising."** He says, "Keep writing; read as much contemporary poetry as you can lay your hands on; don't let the discouragement of rejection keep you from sending your work out to editors."

MILIM (I, IV-Religious), (formerly Mosaic: A Torah Magazine of the Arts), 324 Ave. F, Brooklyn NY 11218, founded 1990, editor Y. David Shulman, appears 3/year, using **"poems by those engaged in Torah lifestyle."** They have recently published poetry by Roberta Chester. As a sample the editor selected these lines by Yedidich Shalom:

> A letter which swept through the nile-blue sky
> And splashed into my hand;
> A parchment in my reverent hand,
> A silver fish, alive in my wondering hand,
> A comet showering the paths of my hand,
> A cinder spinning fire in my hand,

It is 40 pp. 8 × 7", offset, saddle-stapled, with matte card cover. Press run 500. Subscription: $8. **Sample: $3 postpaid. Pays 3 copies. Reports in 2 weeks. Editor comments "upon request."**

MILKWEED EDITIONS (II), Box 3226, Minneapolis MN 55403, phone (612)332-3192, founded 1979, poetry editor Emilie Buchwald. Three collections published annually. Recent books of poetry include: **The Color of Mesaki Bones**, by John Caddy; **Forgiveness**, by Dennis Sampson; and **Paul Bunyon's Bearskin**, by Patricia Goedicke. **Unsolicited MS accepted in June and January; please include return postage. Poetry titles are set through 1992.** Catalog available on request, with 74¢ in postage.

MIND IN MOTION: A MAGAZINE OF POETRY AND SHORT PROSE (I, II), P.O. Box 1118, Apple Valley CA 92307, phone (619)248-6512, founded 1985, a quarterly, editor Céleste Goyer wants **poetry "15-60 lines. Explosive, provocative. Images not cliched but directly conveyant of the point of the poem. Use of free association particularly desired. We encourage free verse, keeping in mind the essential elements of rhythm and rhyme. Traditional forms are acceptable if within length restrictions. Meaning should be implicit, as in the styles of Blake, Poe, Coleridge, Stephen Crane, Emily Dickinson, Leonard Cohen. Submit in batches of 5-6. Not interested in sentimentality, emotionalism, simplistic nature worship, explicit references."** She has recently published poetry by Robert E. Brimhall, Charlie Mehrhoff, Paul Forster and Michael Alter. As a sample she selected these lines (poet unidentified):

> If Promise had intended mankind ill,
> Exalted but sadly privileged still,
> Then must we with perverted will
> Genially immerse ourselves in swill.
>
> But wisdom must eventually decide
> What reality can and cannot hide,
> A toppled wall against the tide
> Of freshly soiled, laundered lies.

MIM is 54 pp., digest-sized, saddle-stapled, photocopied from photoreduced typescript with a heavy matte cover with b/w drawing. Of approximately 2,400 poems per year she accepts about 200. Press run is 350 for 250 subscriptions. Subscription: $14. **Sample: $3.50 postpaid (overseas: $4.50, $18 per year). Send SASE for guidelines. Pays 1 copy "when financially possible." Reports in 1-6 weeks. Unpublished works only. Simultaneous submissions okay if notified. Magazine is copyrighted; all rights revert to author. Editor usually comments on rejected MSS.**

MIND MATTERS REVIEW (I), 2040 Polk St. #234, San Francisco CA 94109, founded 1988, editor Carrie Drake, is a **"literary quarterly with emphasis on use of science as a tool for responsible organization of information;** analysis of the role of language in conscious knowledge intelligence; social criticism particularly of metaphysics. Book reviews, poetry, short stories, art, satire." They want **"short poems for fillers; will publish collections of poems by a single author if suitable to theme of a particular issue of *MMR*. Would like to see inspirational poetry; but open to satire and contemporary subjects that reflect the struggle between the 'inner voice' and external pressures. Rhythm important, but rhyme isn't."** They have recently published poetry by Benny Williams from whose "Conflict" the editor selected these lines:

> *The guns are silent; no sound of cannons roar;*
> *Somber eyes with gazes fixed somewhere in space.*
> *Another pause to dwell*
> *And taste the blood of hell*
> *And feel the sorrow of the human race.*

MMR is magazine-sized, desktop published, includes graphics, sketches, b/w photos. Subscription: $15 U.S., $20 foreign. **Sample, postpaid: $3.50. Send SASE for guidelines. Pays 1 copy. Poets are encouraged to buy a copy before submitting. Simultaneous submissions and previously published poems OK.** The editor says, "Poetry should reflect the deeper layers of consciousness, its perceptions, observations, joys and sorrows; should reflect the independence of the individual spirit. Should not be 'trendy' or 'poetic' in a forced way."

THE MINNESOTA REVIEW (II), English Dept., SUNY, Stony Brook NY 11794-5350, phone (516)632-7400, founded 1960, co-editor Michael Sprinker, poetry editor Helen Cooper, appears twice a year, a literary magazine, wanting **"poetry which explores some aspect of social or political issues and/or the nature of relationships." No nature poems, and no lyric poetry without the above focus."** As a sample Michael Sprinker selected these lines from "Hotel Kitchen" by Jonathan Holden:

> *Downstairs in those steel kitchens, in the loud*
> *bucket-brigade of orders, pots and shuttling*
> *of dishes hand-to-hand, you couldn't hear*
> *the murmurous conversation of the rich . . .*

TMR is digest-sized, flat-spined, 160 pp., with b/w glossy card cover and art. Circulation: 1,000 for 500 subscriptions. Subscription: $8 to individuals, $16 to institutions. **Sample: $4.50 postpaid. Pays 2 copies. Reports in 2-4 months.** Reviews books of poetry.

‡MINORITY LITERARY EXPO (IV-Membership, Ethnic, Regional), Fondren Enterprises 2000, P.O. Box 370171, Birmingham AL 35237, phone (205)798-8916, founded 1989, editor Kervin Fondren, is an annual poetry anthology of an **"organization membership open to all minority poets. I want poems from minority poets, less than 24 lines each, no vulgar or profane poetry accepted, any style, any form, any subject matter. Poetry that can be interpreted as therapeutic is very acceptable and holistic poetry. No vulgar, sexual lewd, hate-poems, slang or poems without any social or literary value. I am soliciting** at least 20 out-of-town/state of Alabama 'Special Guest Contributing Minority Poets' to be included in *Minority Literary Expo*. No fee is charged for inclusion, but only selected poets will be featured. No organization membership fee will be charged to 'Guest Poets.' " As a sample the editor selected these lines from "It's Lonely at the Top," (poet unidentified):

> *No Man Can Reach the Top of the Mountain*
> *With Hate, Greed and Despair;*
> *Because in Reaching the Top, He Soon Will Find Out,*
> *That he is the Only One There.*

MINOTAUR PRESS; MINOTAUR (II), Box 4039, Felton CA 95018, founded 1974, editor Jim Gove. *Minotaur* is a "small press literary quarterly **with emphasis on contemporary and experimental styles. Must be relevant. No rhymed and/or traditional verse."** They have recently published poetry by Judson Crews, Ed Mycue, Julia Vinograd and e.m. As a sample the editor selected these lines from "For Jack Spicer" by William Talcott:

> *No one listens to poetry*
> *Jack Spicer.*
> *Salt & Pepper*

Are just another passida laugh
in the mashed potatoes

I have not seen an issue, but the editor describes it as digest-sized, photocopied, "stock cover—cover graphics—sometimes use interior graphics, but rarely." They publish about 12 of 100 poems received. Press run: 400 for 300 subscriptions of which 50 are libraries. Subscription: $14. **Sample, postpaid: $3.50 Send SASE for guidelines. Pays 1 copy. Submit 4-8 poems. "Best of issue from subscribing contributors receives 1-year subscription. You do not need to subscribe to be published." Editor comments on submissions "if requested only."** Reviews books of poetry. Minotaur Press publishes a "Back to Back" chapbook with each issue. **"We ask for MSS from regular magazine contributors." Pays 20 copies of chapbooks.** They "rarely" subsidy publish "if quality merits and poet comes to us. Author pays; we distribute to our readership as a bonus book." The editor says, "Subscribe to the magazines that publish your work. Few poetry magazines run in the black."

MIORITA: A JOURNAL OF ROMANIAN STUDIES (IV-Ethnic), Department of Foreign Languages Literatures and Linguistics, University of Rochester, Rochester NY 14627, is a scholarly annual, digest-sized, 100 pp., circulation 200, focusing on **Romanian culture and using some poetry by Romanians or on Romanian themes. Sample: $5. Pays copies.** Reviews books of poetry "occasionally; must be Romanian-connected."

THE MIRACULOUS MEDAL (IV-Religious), 475 E. Chelten Ave., Philadelphia PA 19144-5785, phone (215)848-1010, founded 1928, editor Rev. Robert P. Cawley, C.M. is a religious quarterly. **"Poetry should reflect solid Catholic doctrine and experience. Any subject matter is acceptable, provided it does not contradict the teachings of the Roman Catholic Church. Poetry must have a religious theme, preferably about the Blessed Virgin Mary."** They have recently published poetry by Gladys McKee. As a sample the editor selected these lines (poet unidentified):

God-Man Jesus! Is it true that You did the things I do?
Did You count the stars at night,
See a firefly's glowing light,
Watch the wild geese winging by,

I have not seen a copy, but the editor describes it as digest-sized, 32 pp., saddle-stapled, 2-color inside and cover, no ads. *The Miraculous Medal* magazine is no longer circulated on a subscription basis. It is used as a promotional piece and is sent to all clients of the Association. The circulation figure is now 340,000. **Sample and guidelines free for postage. Pays 50¢ and up per line payable on acceptance. Reports in 6 months-3 years, backlog is 6 months to 3 years. Poems should be a maximum of 20 lines, double-spaced. No simultaneous submissions or previously published poems. Buys first North American rights. Photocopy, dot-matrix OK.**

MIRIAM PRESS; UP AGAINST THE WALL, MOTHER (I, IV-Women, theme), 9114 Wood Spice Lane, Lorton VA 22079, phone (703)690-2246, founded 1980, poetry editor Lee-lee Schlegel. The quarterly is **"concerned with poetry as therapy first, literary excellence second.** Our philosophy is that there are many good literary markets but few who 'help' those in trouble. They want **anything on women in crisis (we deal with the darker side here—death, rape, abuse, the frustrations of mothering/wives, etc.).** *Mother* has published poetry by Jill DiMaggio, Serena Fusek, Joan Payne Kincaid, John Fiore and John Grey. Lee-lee Schlegel selected this untitled poem by Jadene Felina Stevens:

"but he loves me," she says
to herself through torn lips
as her blood reddens the snow,
smears her cheek, her chin—
drops like visual screams
to shock the whitened ground.

Each issue of the digest-sized magazine has 39-52 pp. of poetry. It has a circulation of about 500 with 400 subscriptions of which 25 are university libraries. It is inexpensively produced, laser, card covers with simple art. They receive about 6,000 submissions per year, use 800. Subscription: $12. **Sample: $3.50. Submit 4-6 poems. Simultaneous submissions, photocopies, dot-matrix OK. Usually reports the same or next week. No pay, not even a copy. Send SASE for guidelines.** "We are a friendly press open to all. We are also very poor and appreciate support. Our immediate goals include being able to pay poets in copies, eventually money. Advice: 1) study your market, 2) always send SASE, 3) please don't tell me how good your poetry is!"

‡MISNOMER (I, II), P.O. Box 1395, Prestonsburg KY 41653, founded 1990, editors Eric W. Cash and Jeff Weddle, appears twice a year. **"We like to see poetry that is vibrant and honest, poetry that communicates the human experience by dancing on the matchhead of reality, yet conveys true human compassion. We want real images, real situations. If your head is in the clouds, leave it there. Send**

us those poems that you would be afraid to show your mother, poems that scream to the reader. If it's good, we'll publish it. No religious, light verse, rhymed, overly sentimental pieces about your grandmother, your dog, or your grandmother's dog. We occasionally review books, chapbooks, and other magazines. Send them to us and we may review them." They have recently published poetry by George Eklund, Paula Fountain, George Barnette and Karl Vermillion. As a sample the editors selected these lines from "moon chakra" by Jeff Weddle:

> *three stars*
> *wind like a gone electrolux*
> *tuned out on acid*
> *the clouds an X-ray:*
> *I see a rib cage*
> *over your moon chakra*

I have not seen an issue, but the editor describes it as 40-60 pp., digest-sized, saddle-stapled, photocopied from typescript. They use about 10% of work submitted. Press run 300. Subscription: $6. Sample postpaid: $3. Send SASE for guidelines. Pays 1 copy. "Need short bio to be included with cover letter: tell us who you are (no bearing on acceptance)." Simultaneous submissions OK.

The cover of the Mississippi Review is "temporal" says editor Frederick Barthelme. It is "what seems interesting to us at the time we're putting together the issue," he says. However, recent special issues of the review not only have a title, such as this "Workshops" issue, but they also promote the issue to follow. Mississippi Review's special "Poetry" issue contains poems and commentary by A.R. Ammons, Marvin Bell, Amy Clampitt, Norman Dubie and Denise Levertov, among others.

MISSISSIPPI REVIEW (II), University of Southern Mississippi, Southern Station, Box 5144, Hattiesburg MS 39406-5144, phone (601)266-4321. Editor: Frederick Barthelme. Managing Editor: Rie Fortenberry. Literary publication for those interested in contemporary literature. **Does not read manuscripts in summer. Sample: $5.50. Payment in copies.**

MISSISSIPPI VALLEY REVIEW (II), English Dept., Western Illinois University, Macomb IL 61455, phone (309)298-1514, founded 1973, editors John Mann and Tama Baldwin, is a literary magazine published twice a year which uses **poems of high quality, no specifications as to form, length, style, subject matter or purpose.** They have published poetry by Denise Levertov, David Citino, A.E. Stringer, Dave Etter, Daniel J. Langton, Walter McDonald, Vince Gotera, Tony Curtis and Catherine Sutton. The editors selected these sample lines by Daniel Bourne:

> *Her voice*
> *each syllable, tangled in the roots of my hair.*
> *She said you are a tree, leafed for summer,*
> *deaf to all the world but the rain.*

MVR uses a handsomely printed, digest-sized, flat-spined, 60+ pp. format, glossy, color cover, circulation 400. Subscription: $10; per copy $5. They have about 25 pp. of poetry in each issue, receive 1,000-2,500 submissions per year, use about 30, and have a 6-12 month backlog. **Considers simultaneous submission. Sample: $5 postpaid. Submit 5 pp. or less. Reports in 4 months. Pays 2 copies and a year's subscription. Editor comments on rejections "occasionally, particularly if we are interested in the MS. Send us poems of high quality which speak authentically from human experience."** Occasionally reviews books of poetry.

‡**UNIVERSITY OF MISSOURI PRESS; DEVINS AWARD (II)**, 2910 LeMone Blvd., Columbia MO 65201, phone (314)882-7641, founded 1958, editor Clair Willcox. The Devins Award will be given for the **best poetry manuscript, not necessarily a first book, already accepted for publication by the University of Missouri Press during the year. The Press now accepts poetry MSS from both published and unpublished authors throughout the year. Write or call for more information.**

MISSOURI REVIEW (II), University of Missouri, 1507 Hillcrest Hall, Columbia MO 65211, phone (314)882-4474, founded 1978, poetry editor Greg Michalson, is a quality literary journal, 6×9″, 250 pp., which appears 3 times a year, **publishing poetry features only—6-10 pages for each of 3 to 5 poets per issue. No simultaneous submissions. Photocopies, dot-matrix OK. Reports in 8-10 weeks. Pays $15-20/printed page. Sample: $5.** Reviews books of poetry occasionally.

MR. COGITO PRESS; MR. COGITO (II), U.C. Box 627, Pacific University, Forest Grove OR 97116 or 3314 S.E. Brooklyn, Portland OR 97202, founded 1973, poetry editors John M. Gogol and Robert A. Davies. *Mr. Cogito*, published 2-3 times per year, is a tall, skinny (4½×11″) magazine, 24-26 pp. of poetry. The copy I examined was printed in a variety of type styles. The editors want **"no prose put in lines. Yes: wit, heightened language, craft. Open to all schools and subjects and groups of poets."** They have published poetry by Dian Million, Elizabeth Woody, Mark Osaki, Kevin Irie and Tomacz Jastrum. As a sample the editors selected these lines from "The Three Kings" by Stanislaw Baranczak:

> . . . *as bewildered as a new-born babe,*
> *you'll open the door. There will flash*
> *the star of authority.*
> *Three men. In one of them you'll recognize . . .*

They use poems in both English and translation, **"preferably representing each poet with several poems."** The magazine has a circulation of 400, sells for $3 a copy. Subscription for 3 issues: $9. **Sample: $3. Submit 4-5 poems. Simultaneous submissions and photocopies OK. Pays copies. Reports in 2 weeks-2 months.** Mr. Cogito Press publishes collections by poets they invite from among those who have appeared in the magazine. Send SASE for catalog to buy samples. They also conduct special theme and translation contests with prizes of $50 or $100. The editors advise, "Subscribe to a magazine that seems good. Read ours before you submit. Write, write, write."

MOBIUS (I), Orion Art Center, P.O. Box 674, Lake Orion MI 48361, phone (313)693-4986, founded 1982 by the Orion Art Center, current editor Jean H. Herman. "We welcome beginners as well as previously published poets. We are looking for your best work even though we are not a college-based forum. **No restrictions on type of poetry (please, no pornography or obscenity). Poets may submit up to five poems, up to 80-85 lines."** Published poets include John Williams, Claudette Bass, Gina Bergamino, Stephen Gill, Ana Pine, Linda Principi, Rod Farmer and E. Matthew Lewis. As a sample the editor selected these lines from "Consider the Cat" by A.M. Peoples:

> *She's nobody's subject and not a doormat,*
> *Has her own dignity, will, and a brain.*
> *No Tabby's enticement, no Tom's caveat*
> *Pries a pale from her fence, puts a bend in her lane.*
> *She's fond of her friends but wears her own hat.*
> *Not all need to love her, but must, she makes plain,*
> *Consider the Cat.*

"*Mobius* has been published twice a year with a press run of 500, but will be expanding due to public response." It is magazine-sized, 60+ pp., professionally printed, saddle-stapled with matte card cover. **Sample: $5 postpaid. Subscription: $10 year. Guidelines available for SASE. "Printed authors receive one copy free. Editor will try to comment on all rejections."**

MODERN BRIDE (IV-Love/romance), 475 Park Avenue South, New York NY 10016, phone (212)779-1999, managing editor Mary Ann Cavlin, a slick bimonthly, occasionally buys **poetry pertaining to love and marriage. Pays $25-35 for average short poem.**

MODERN HAIKU; KAY TITUS MORMINO MEMORIAL SCHOLARSHIP (IV-Form, students), P.O. Box 1752, Madison WI 53701, founded 1969, poetry editor Robert Spiess, "is the foremost international journal of English language haiku and criticism. We are devoted to publishing only the very best haiku being written and also publish articles on haiku and have the most complete review section of haiku books. Issues average over 100 pages. They use **haiku only. No tanka or other forms.** The Kay Titus Mormino Memorial Scholarship of $500 is for the best haiku by a high school senior, deadline early March. Send SASE for rules. **"We publish all 'schools' of haiku, but want the haiku to elicit intuition, insight, felt-depth."** They have published haiku by Geraldine Little, Paul O. Williams, Wally Swist and Cor van den Heuvel. The editor selected this sample by Peter Fennessy:

> *soft spring rain*
> *the priest with AIDS*
> *sits by the window*

The digest-sized magazine appears 3 times a year, printed on heavy quality stock with cover illustrations especially painted for each issue by the staff artist. There are over 260 poems in each issue, circulation 650. Subscription: $12.50; per copy: $4.50. They receive 16,000-18,000 freelance submissions per year, use 800. **Sample: $4.50 postpaid. Submit on "any size sheets, any number of haiku on a sheet; but name and address on each sheet." Reports in 2 weeks. Pays $1 per haiku (but no contributor's copy). Send SASE for guidelines. The editor "frequently" comments on rejected MSS. No simultaneous submissions.** Robert Spiess says, "In regard to haiku, Daisetz T. Szuki said it succinctly well: 'A haiku does not express ideas but puts forward images reflecting intuitions.' "

‡MOKSHA JOURNAL; VAJRA PRESS OF YOGA ANAND ASHRAM (IV-Spiritual), 49 Forrest Pl., Amityville NY 11701, phone (516)691-8475, founded 1984, assistant Director Yogi Ananda Viraj, is a "small press publisher of **spiritual and/or philosophical literature, poetry, non-fiction and limited fiction/poetry** pertaining to the concept of 'Moksha,' defined by Monier-Williams as a 'liberation, release' (A Sanskrit-English Dictionary, 1899). Perspectives include, but are not limited to: Yoga, various schools of Buddhism, Sufism, Mystical Christianity, etc." *Moksha Journal* appears twice a year, 40-55 pp., 7¼×9½", offset, litho. Press run 400-500 for that many subscribers. Subscription: $8. **Sample: $4. Pays 1 copy. Simultaneous submissions OK. Reports in 4-6 weeks.** The press publishes flat-spined paperbacks.

MONOCACY VALLEY REVIEW (II), William Heath, Department of English, Mount Saint Mary's College, Emmitsburg MD 21727, founded 1985, poetry editor Mary Noel, editor William Heath, is an annual literary review. **Submissions should be received by January 15th.** "In general, we cannot publish longer poems; we also publish short stories, nonfiction prose, book reviews and artwork. We pride ourselves in being a review that is always local but never provincial. If we have a bias, it is in favor of clarity of vision and eloquence of language. We dislike poems that 'hurt the ear and unfit one to continue.' " A sample short poem, "A Song for Bernadette" by Bradley Strahan:

> *Trees climb a ridge.*
> *The train speeds*
> *through a painting*
> *of pink and lavender.*
> *A great grey church*
> *mounts the morning light.*
> *Transfixed I pass Lourdes,*
> *kneeling at the edge*
> *of the Pyrenees.*

MVR is magazine-sized, 60 pp. saddle-stapled, high quality paper. "We reject over 95% of submissions, publish 15-20 poems an issue." Press run 500 with 200 subscriptions of which 10 are libraries. Subscription: $8. **Sample: $5 postpaid. Include a 50-word or less biographical statement with all submissions. Pays $10-25/poem plus 2 copies. All submissions are judged anonymously; no backlog. If MSS sent in December and early January, response time is 6-8 weeks.**

WILLIAM MORROW AND CO. (V), 1350 Avenue of the Americas, New York NY 10019, phone (212)889-3050, publishes poetry on standard royalty contracts, **but accepts no unsolicited MSS. Queries with samples should be submitted through an agent.**

MOSAIC PRESS (V), 358 Oliver Rd., Cincinnati OH 45215, phone (513)761-5977, poetry editor Miriam Irwin. The press publishes fine hardbound small books (under 3" tall); they want **"interesting topics beautifully written in very few words — a small collection of short poems on one subject."** The editor **does not want to see haiku.** She has recently published collections by Marilyn Francis; the following lines, selected by her, are from "The Tin Snips" by Robert Hoeft:

> *A metal woodpecker*
> *jaws like sharpened sin*
> *harmless to lumber*
> *nemesis to tin.*

Close-up

James A. Autry
Poet/Businessman

The Meaning of Rich
When we said someone was rich,
we meant only one thing:
He never had to work another day in his life.
We did not know how much money it would take,
but as we entered the sweepstakes
and jingle contests
and shouted our quiz-show answers at the radio,
we figured sixty-four-thousand dollars would do just
    fine,
fifty dollars a week forever
and never work another day in our lives.

Money comes and goes,
and so does the meaning of rich,
but most of us retired before we learned
that nothing pays off
like having work to do.

That poem is from James Autry's book **Love and Profit** (William Morrow and Company, Inc., 1991), a unique combination of essays and poetry on the art of "caring leadership" — a book about management skills and the "sacred trust in which the well-being of other people is put in your care during most of their waking hours."

As president of Meredith Corporation's magazine group (which includes *Better Homes and Gardens*, of which he was once editor-in-chief, *Ladies' Home Journal* and a dozen other magazines), Autry brings to this book his 28 years of direct management experience. As an accomplished poet with two bestselling volumes of poetry, he adds his keen observations and poetic sensitivity. "The essays speak to the philosophy and techniques of business," he says, "the poetry to the feelings and emotions of it."

Despite his impressive publishing credits, Autry is a relative newcomer to poetry. "I came to poetry rather late," he says. "As a student at the University of Mississippi, living in the shadow of William Faulkner, I figured that I was probably going to be a novelist or a short story writer, and I tried to write some fiction over the years, but it was not really until I was 46 years old that I came to poetry.

"I had gone through quite a few emotional times in my life and it was quite an unsettled sort of period for me. I needed something, some way to express what I was feeling. I also needed some form, some voice beyond what I was doing every day in life." He found what he was looking for when he attended a poetry reading by James Dickey. "I was just *stunned* by the efficiency of the language and yet the evocative power of it," he says. Though he hadn't really studied poetry very much and hadn't tried to write it, he began to write poetry that very same night, "and I've been writing ever since, although the early poems were not really very good."

He also began to read a lot of contemporary poetry and to study on his own. "And I had a wonderful teacher, mentor and friend, Dr. Betty Sue Flowers, a published poet, mythologist, teacher of English and associate dean of the graduate school at the University of Texas, whom I met at a seminar she was moderating at The Aspen Institute. She helped me a great deal in writing poetry and knowing what to read," he says.

In the early '80s, a few years after he started writing poetry, Autry was doing a seminar on magazines with Willie Morris at the University of Mississippi and read him some of his poetry. He also shared some of it with Lawrence Wells, who with his wife, Dean Faulkner (the niece of William Faulkner), owns the Yoknapatawpha Press in Oxford, Mississippi. "Larry Wells said, 'I love this. If you can do a book manuscript of it, I'll publish it.' So," explains Autry, "my first book, **Nights Under A Tin Roof**, was published in 1983." It was also the collection he read from in Bill Moyers' PBS series "The Power of the Word."

"I truly *never* expected to publish my poetry—that was something I hadn't even thought of," explains Autry. "I was writing it very much for myself. I had never even sent it out to anybody." Reflecting on his good fortune, he adds, "I've thought many times of all the poets out there, and good ones, who are struggling to get published. I sort of fell into it by having my poetry seen by some of the right people at the right time at the right place."

His second book of poetry, **Life After Mississippi**, was published by Yoknapatawpha Press in 1989, and his poems have also been published in many literary and general magazines including frequent publication in *Kentucky Poetry Review*, which featured Autry in their Fall 1991 issue.

Autry grew up in the hill country of northern Mississippi, and his poetry reflects the religion, friendships and family ties of the region. His poetry is "about home and yet about never leaving home. It's about family, it's about love and community, it's about ritual." He adds, "I think that's true of my 'business poetry' as well." He sees work as "a community we come into. The workplace is filled with all the passions of life."

Why is it important for a poet to be published? Autry says, "From the very beginning I was sharing my poems with friends and family and other people who were important to me, because it was extremely important, and always has been, to me as a writer to 'close the loop'—to have someone at the receiving end to react and, I hope, get some pleasure from what I have written. So, while I hadn't sought being published at the beginning, I must say I didn't know what I was missing, because being published and getting reaction from people has just been one of the highlights of my life."

To assure that real communication is going on, he tries to make his poetry as accessible as possible. "I think the reason I'm not very taken with minimalist, sort of obscure poetry is not that I don't understand it, and it's not that I think it's bad poetry or that it isn't valid, because I'm not qualified to say that, it's that I would prefer to have real understanding going both ways.

"I know that some of my poems operate on different levels. I've read poetry in elementary schools—poems about fishing and snakes and things—and the kids get it at some level, and yet those same poems are enjoyed by adults who get it at another level.

"I'll tell you another thing that makes me happy," he says. "I'll be down South reading my poetry and have a *man* come up to me and say something like, 'Mr. Autry, I never read no poetry, but I sure do like yours.' I feel like that helps create a new audience for poetry."

And something poets should keep in mind, says Autry, "When you make it, when you are being published and doing readings, you have to be open to helping other people."

—*Pat Beusterien*

Market categories: (I) Beginning; (II) General; (III) Limited; (IV) Specialized; (V) Closed.

The sample miniature book the editor sent is **Water and Windfalls,** by Marilyn Francis, illustrated by Mada Leach. It is ¾×⅞", flat-spined (⅛" thick), an elegantly printed and bound hardback, with colored endpapers and gold lettering on spine and front cover. The press publishes 1 book per year, average page count 64. She is "booked up—going to finish existing projects before starting new ones." But writers can query, sending 3 or more sample poems and "whatever you want to tell me." She says, "We don't use pseudonyms." Simultaneous submissions are OK, as are photocopied and dot-matrix MSS, although she doesn't like the latter. Payment is in author's copies (5 for a whole collection or book) plus a $50 honorarium. She pays $2.50 plus 1 copy for single poems. Criticism will be provided only if requested and "then only if we have constructive comments. If work is accepted, be prepared to wait patiently; some of our books take 4 years to complete." The press publishes private editions but does not call it subsidy publishing. Catalog and writers manual free for large SASE with 52¢ postage. The editor advises, "Type neatly, answer letters, return phone calls, include SASE."

‡(m)ÖTHÊR TOÑGUÉS (II, IV-Translations), RR#2 Alders C-14, Ganges, British Columbia V0S 1E0 Canada, founded 1990, editor and publisher Mona Fertig, appears twice a year. She wants "**unpublished, new, volatile, political, well-written poetry, no clichés or unstimulating poetry," includes translations from many languages. Include "Writers Notes."** They have recently published poetry by Thich Tue Sy, Erin Mouré, Dorin Tudoran and Ann Diamond. *MT* is magazine-sized, 70 pp., photocopied. Press run 500. Subscription: $12 Canadian, $14 USA, $18 international. **Sample postpaid: $7. Reports in 3 months. Pays 1-year subscription.**

‡MOVING OUT: A FEMINIST LITERARY AND ARTS JOURNAL (IV-Women/feminist), Box 21249, Detroit MI 48221, founded 1970, co-editor Margaret Kaminski, is a magazine appearing 1 time a year with poetry, fiction, nonfiction and artwork **by and about women. Submit "at least 6 poems, no special length. We especially like thematic groupings by poets. We also like work which develops a feminist/ women's aesthetic, or that of a particular minority or ethnic group. Nothing that is sexist or pornographic."** They have published poetry by Marge Piercy, Margaret Atwood, Susan Fromberg Schaeffer and Ursula K. LeGuin. As a sample the editor selected the poem "Questions for Karen Silkwood" by Nancy Weber:

> *Was it long enough*
> *to see him rifle through your purse*
> *and grab your notebook?*
> *Did you have time to ask him*
> *why the cancer wasn't enough?*

I have not seen a copy of *Moving Out,* but Margaret Kaminski describes it as magazine-sized, 50-100 pp., offset, glossy cover, with b/w high-contrast photos and graphics, using commercial and exchange ads, with a circulation of 500-1,000, with 300 subscriptions of which 250 are libraries, selling for $9. **Sample: $6 plus 75¢ postage. Pays 1 copy. Reports in 6-12 months, a 6-12 month delay before publication. No simultaneous submissions or previously published work.** Sponsors contest for poetry and prose. $100 award. Submit 1-5 poems, $1 fee per poem. SASE for guidelines. "Sometimes we suggest minor changes to improve a poem, especially if we are interested in publishing it."

‡MSS/NEW MYTHS; JOHN GARDNER POETRY AWARD (II), Box 6000, SUNY Binghamton NY 13902-6000, phone (607)777-2168, founded 1961, editor Robert Mooney, appears twice a year. **They want "only excellence for whatever it is. It must be beautiful, carefully crafted, and in some way, moving. Nothing commercial. Please send bewtween 3-8 poems at a time."** They have recently published poetry by John Montague, Jack Myers, Joyce Carol Oates, Maxine Kumin and William Stafford. As a sample the editor selected these lines from "Summary" by David Ignatow:

> *In life we solve no problems*
> *just bend them like crowbars.*
> *A person takes one up*
> *where we laid it aside*
> *and advances upon us.*

It is 220 pp. 6×9". Press run 1,000 for 450 subscribers of which 125 are libraries, 125 shelf sales. Subscription: $8.50 for individuals. **Sample postpaid: $5. Reports in 2-8 weeks. Submit only Sept. 1-May 1. Payment "depends on funds available" plus 2 copies.** Editor often comments on rejections. "**We** *strongly* **recommend you read a copy of the magazine before submitting work!**" The John Gardner Poetry Award is "only by announcement, not annual."

MUDFISH; BOX TURTLE PRESS (I, II), 184 Franklin St., New York NY 10013, phone (212)219-9278, founded 1983, poetry editor Jill Hoffman, art editor Vladimir Urban. *Mudfish,* published by Box Turtle Press, is a journal of poetry and art that appears once a year and is looking for **energy, intensity, and** originality of voice, mastery of style, the presence of passion." They have recently published poetry by Charles Simic, Harvey Shapiro, Nicholas Kolumban, Denise Duhamel and John Ashbery. As a sample the editor selected these lines by Eric Gregory:

> *The bed shudders beneath the weight of dreams*
> *as the abandoned buildings surround the night.*
>
> *The aching bed splinters and settles.*
> *Nothing escapes the ascension of buildings.*

The next issue will have a press run of 1,500. **Mudfish 5 and 4 are $8; Mudfish 3, $6; and Mudfish 2, $7; plus $1.50 shipping and handling. These issues are available as sample copies. Pays 2 copies. They will not consider simultaneous submissions or previously published poems. Reports from "immediately to 6 months."**

‡**MULBERRY PRESS (II)**, P.O. Box 782288, Wichita KS 67278, founded 1991, publisher G.M. Frey. This is an arrangement for publishing chapbooks only. mulberry press (they prefer lower-case) will consider **chapbooks (any length) for a $5 reading fee, for which you get a critique and 2 sample chapbooks if your MS is rejected, 50 copies if it is accepted (more copies at cost). Press run 150-200 copies. Poems may be previously published in magazines. Make checks payable to G.M. Frey.** They are also open to co-op publishing: poet pays "a modest fee to cover cost" and receives 80% of press run. They have published chapbooks by Gina Bergamino and Michael Hathaway, from whose **god poems** I quote the complete poem "seven":

> *God drips luv*
> *He forgives people sinning*
> *people writing poems about His colors*
> *God's lucky luv drips all around us*
> *get on your knees*
> *lick it up*

The editor advises, "Take your art seriously, make it a priority in your life. Be persistent and patient and eventually you will endure and prevail. If you keep on writing, you can only get better."

MY LEGACY (I); OMNIFIC (I); FELICITY (I, IV-Themes); THE BOTTOM LINE, Star Route, Box 21AA, Artemas PA 17211, phone (814)458-3102, editor/publisher Kay Weems. *My Legacy* is a quarterly of poetry and short stories using **36-line, sometimes longer, poems, "anything in good taste" with an Editor's Choice small cash award for each issue. No contributor copies. Subscription: $12/year; $3.50/copy.** *Omnific,* a "family-type" quarterly publishes poetry only, **36 lines, sometimes longer; readers vote on favorites, small cash award or copy to favorites. Send SASE for guidelines. No contributor copies. Subscription: $12/year; $3.50/copy.** *Felicity,* founded 1988, is a monthly newsletter for contests only, 30-40 pp. They offer 10 contests per month including a monthly theme contest, 36 lines, $3/poem entry fee; other contests may be for theme, form, chapbook, etc. Entry fees vary. Send SASE for guidelines and upcoming themes. Payment for contest winners is small cash award and/or publication. No work is returned. They consider simultaneous submissions and previously published poems. All winning entries including honorable mentions are printed in the newsletter which also publishes market and other contest listings. Subscription: $15/year; $2.50/copy. *The Bottom Line,* founded 1988, is a monthly newsletter listing over 100 publications and contests for writers, reproducing guidelines of still others. Information is presented in chronological order by deadline date, and then in alphabetical order. Circulation 50-100. Subscription: $25/year; $3/copy.

NADA PRESS; BIG SCREAM (II, IV-Themes, bilingual), 2782 Dixie SW, Grandville MI 49418, phone (616)531-1442, founded 1974, poetry editor David Cope. *Big Scream* is **"a brief anthology of mostly 'unknown' poets, 1 time per year. We are promoting a continuation of objectivist tradition begun by Williams and Reznikoff. We want objectivist-based short works; some surrealism; basically short, tight work that shows clarity of perception and care in its making. Also poems in Spanish—not** translations." They have published poetry by Antler, James Ruggia, Richard Kostelanetz, Andy Clausen, Allen Ginsberg, John Steinbeck, Jr., Bob Rixon and Janet Cannon. As a sample David Cope selected some lines of his own:

> *an old blind black vet blows*
> *Camptown Races on his harp,*
> *stomping his one foot in time;*
> *another, legless, claps his hands*

Big Scream is 35 pp., magazine-sized, xerograph on 60 lb. paper, side-stapled, "sent gratis to a select group of poets and editors; **sample copies $3; subscriptions to institutions $6 per year."** He has a print run of 100. He receives "several hundred (not sure)" freelance submissions per year, uses "very few." **Submit after July. Send 10 pp. Simultaneous submissions OK. Reports** in 1-14 days. Pays copies. No cover letter. "If poetry interests me, I will ask the proper questions of the poet." No dot-matrix. Pays as many copies as requested within reason. Order sample chapbooks $3 each. Comments on rejections "if requested and MS warrants it." David Cope advises: "Read Pound's essay, "A Retrospect," then Reznikoff and Williams; follow through the Beats and NY School, especially Denby & Berrigan, and you have our approach to writing well in hand. I expect to be publishing *BS* regularly 10 years from now, same basic format."

‡NAHANT BAY (II), 45 Puritan Rd., Swampscott MA 01907, founded 1990, editors Kalu Clarke and Kim A. Pederson, appears twice a year. **"Open submissions; submit a maximum of 6 poems."** They have recently published poetry by Lyn Lifshin, Stuart Peterfreund and Robert Bixby. As a sample the editor selected these lines from "The Woman Next Door" by Ron E. McFarland:

> She does not ask much, but life
> eludes her. She would be satisfied
> with so little, just a man
> stumbling by half drunk in the last sun
> or even a boy driving a baseball hard
> against the door of her neighbor's new Ford.

The handsome magazine is digest-sized, 60-100 pp., saddle-stapled, professionally printed, with matte card cover. Subscription: $8. **Sample postpaid: $4. Reports in 2-4 months. Pays 1 copy.**

NANCY'S MAGAZINE (IV-Theme), P.O. Box 02108, Columbus OH 43202, founded 1983, editor Nancy Bonnell-Kangas, who describes her publication as a "variety magazine." **She wants to see "experimental, everyday life" poetry, but not "sentimental." Sophisticated humor and cynicism are always appreciated.** She has published work by Camille Blanchette and William Talcott. As a sample she selected this complete poem, "Rhyme: Love: Shadow" by George Myers Jr.:

> It went wherever
> I went, or would
> if only I could go

The magazine is **"often thematic,** leaning towards literary (without ever getting there)." It appears twice a year, 7×8½", 36 pp., saddle-stapled, offset from various sizes of photoreduced copy (some of it sideways, at angles, or upside down), using cartoons, b/w photos, ads, decorations, with light matte card cover, circulation 1,000, of which 200-250 are shelf sales. **Sample: $2 postpaid. Send SASE for guidelines. Pays 2 copies. Reports in 1 month.** Nancy Bonnell-Kangas advises, "Send work that helps explain why we are where we are."

THE NATION; LEONORE MARSHALL/NATION PRIZE FOR POETRY; DISCOVERY/THE NATION (III), 72 Fifth Ave., New York NY 10011, founded 1865, poetry editor Grace Schulman. *The Nation's* only requirement for poetry is "excellence," which can be inferred from the list of poets they have published: Marianne Moore, Robert Lowell, W.S. Merwin, Maxine Kumin, Donald Justice, James Merrill, Richard Howard, May Swenson, Garrett Hongo and Amy Clampitt. **Pay for poetry is $1 per line, not to exceed 35 lines, plus 1 copy.** The magazine co-sponsors the Leonore Marshall/Nation Prize for Poetry which is an annual award of $7,500 for the outstanding book of poems published in the U.S. in each year; and the "Discovery/The Nation" ($200 each plus a reading at The Poetry Center, 1395 Lexington Ave., New York, NY 10128. Submit up to 500 lines by mid-February. Send SASE for application). The editor chose this as a sample from a poem in the *Nation*, 1939, by W.B. Yeats:

> Like a long-legged fly upon the stream
> His mind moves upon silence.

NATIONAL ENQUIRER (II, IV-Humor), Lantana FL 33464, assistant editor Michele Cooke, is a weekly tabloid, circulation 4,550,000, which uses **short poems, most of them humorous and traditional rhyming verse.** "We want poetry with a message or reflection on the human condition or everyday life. Avoid sending obscure or 'arty' poetry or poetry for art's sake. Also looking for philosophical and inspirational material. Occasionally uses longer poetry (up to 12 or 16 lines) of either a serious or a humorous nature. Submit seasonal/holiday material at least 3 months in advance." Send SASE with all submissions. **Pays $25 after publication; original material only.**

‡NATIONAL FORUM (III), 129 Quad Center, Mell St., Auburn University, AL 36849-5306, phone (205)826-5200, founded 1915, editor Stephen W. White, is the quarterly of Phi Kappa Phi using **quality poetry, no "profanity, brutality, love poems."** They have recently published poetry by William Stafford, Bin Ramke, Mary Oliver, and Marge Piercy. As a sample the editor selected these lines from "The Bird Carver" by R. T. Smith:

> In the hearth, flame's bright plumage
> rises, a thicket of frail reeds,
> a nest. My eyes linger there, privileged.

> *Out the window, then, I watch the thin*
> *gray woodgrain of sky, the late sun*
> *a knot from which all sap unfurls. Alone, ...*

NF is magazine-sized, professionally printed, 48 pp. saddle-stapled, with full-color paper cover. They publish about 20 poems of 300 received a year. Their press run is 118,000 with 115,000 subscriptions of which 600 are libraries. Subscription: $10. **Sample: $1.65 postpaid. Pays "small honorarium" and 10 copies. Reports in 4-6 weeks, published within 9-12 months. Submit 3-5 poems.** The editor advises, "Do not send out work that has not been proofread by a couple of helpfully critical friends. Enclose a biographical sketch with recent publications. We do not include comments on rejected work."

‡NAUGHTY NAKED DREAMGIRLS; NAUGHTY LINGERIE (I, IV-Erotic, science fiction, humor), Andrew Roller, P.O. Box 221295, Sacramento CA 95822, phone (916)429-8522, founded 1986, editor Andrew L. Roller. These newsletters appear "approximately monthly." They want **erotic poetry.** Also willing to look at **"weird, occult or sci-fi, or humorous poetry (political or comics related)."** They have recently published poetry by Cheryl Townsend, P.D. Wilson, William Dockery and Norma Lee Edwards. As a sample the editor selected these lines from his own "Permanent Perigee," which he describes as "a poem converted to prose":

> *Anton was hungry. He peered through the gloom at the bulkhead. A winding flight*
> *of stairs clung to the upright partition. A clutter of splintered crates and heavy*
> *appliances lay at the bottom of the stairway. A tangle of corpses sprawled amidst*
> *the makeshift barrier. Anton wondered whether there were any dead Controllers*
> *left in the heap.*

The newsletters are corner stapled, 18 pp. Press run 105 for 20 subscribers of which 2 are libraries. **Sample postpaid: $2 US, $3 Canada, $4 foreign. Pays 1 copy ("2 for regulars"). Reports "at once." Editor always comments on rejections. "Don't send me more than a few pages of poems."**

NAZARENE INTERNATIONAL HEADQUARTERS; STANDARD; WONDER TIME; LISTEN; BREAD; TEENS TODAY; HERALD OF HOLINESS (IV-Religious, children), 6401 The Paseo, Kansas City MO 64131, phone (816)333-7000. Each of the magazines published by the Nazarenes has a separate editor, focus, and audience. *Standard*, circulation 177,000, is a weekly **inspirational "story paper" with Christian leisure reading for adults. Send SASE for free sample and guidelines. Uses a poem each week. Submit maximum of 5, maximum of 50 lines each. Pays 25¢ a line.** *Wonder Time*, poetry editors Evelyn Beals and Robyn Ginter, a publication of the Children's Ministries Department, Church of the Nazarene, **"is committed to reinforcement of the Biblical concepts taught in the Sunday School curriculum, using poems 4-8 lines, simple, with a message, easy to read, for 1st and 2nd graders. It should not deal with much symbolism."** The editors selected this sample poem by Sharon Briggs-Fanny:

> *You're with me, Lord, when I am weak;*
> *I only have to pray.*
> *And when the evil seems so strong,*
> *You show me the right way.*

Wonder Time is a weekly 4 pp. leaflet, magazine-sized, newsprint, circulation 37,000. **Sample free for SASE. Reports in 8-12 weeks. Pays minimum of $3—25¢/line, and 4 contributor's copies. Send SASE for guidelines. For** *Listen, Bread, Teens Today* and *Herald of Holiness*, write individually for guidelines and samples.

‡NCASA NEWS (NEWSLETTER OF THE NATIONAL COALITION AGAINST SEXUAL ASSAULT) (IV-Themes/Women/Feminism), 123 S. Seventh, Suite 500, Springfield IL 62701, founded 1986, editor Becky Bradway. Appears 3/year using **"well-written poetry by survivors of sexual assault and incest. Poems may deal with aspects of the sexual assault experience or recovery from sexual assault. Poems may also concern other topics relevant to women with a feminist perspective."** It is 36 pp., magazine-sized, professionally printed, with matte card cover, saddle-stapled. Press run 700 for 600 subscribers. Subscription: $20. **Sample: $4 postpaid. Pays 3 copies. Previously published poems and simultaneous submissions OK.** The editor says, *"NCASA News* is a nationally circulated magazine. Its 'Voices of Survivors' section includes poetry and fiction by survivors of sexual assault. While not a requirement, contributors are encouraged to subscribe or join NCASA ($25/year)."

Use the General Index to find the page number of a specific publication or publisher.

NEBO: A LITERARY JOURNAL (II), English Dept., Arkansas Tech University, Russellville AR 72801-2222, founded 1982, poetry editor Michael Ritchie, appears in May and December. Regarding poetry they say, **"We accept all kinds, all styles, all subject matters and will publish a longer poem if it is outstanding. We are especially interested in formal poetry."** They have published poetry by Jack Butler, Turner Cassity, Wyatt Prunty, Charles Martin, Julia Randall and Brenda Hillman. As a sample they selected the first 4 lines of "Sage Counsel" by Timothy Steele:

> *If, stung to rage, you'd quell your boiling blood,*
> *Regard the one who happens to annoy,*
> *And think, The man is mortal. The thought should*
> *Convert your heart to pity—or to joy.*

Nebo is digest-sized, 50-70 pp., professionally printed on quality matte stock with matte card cover. The press run "varies." Per issue: $5. Subscription: $5. Sample: $5 postpaid. Pays 1 copy. **"Please no onion skin or offbeat colors."** Do not submit mss between May 1 and August 15 of each year. Simultaneous submissions OK. Reports in 1 week-3 months, except for May 1 to August 15. Editor comments on rejections **"if the work has merit but requires revision and resubmission. We do all we can to help."** Reviews books of poetry.

THE NEBRASKA REVIEW; TNR AWARDS (II), ASH 212, University of Nebraska, Omaha NE 68182-0324, phone (402)554-2771, founded 1973, co-editor Art Homer, a semi-annual literary magazine publishing fiction and poetry with occasional essays. The editor wants **"Lyric poetry from 10-200 lines, preference being for under 100 lines. Subject matter is unimportant, as long as it has some. Poets should have mastered form, meaning poems should have form, not simply 'demonstrate' it."** He doesn't want to see **"concrete, inspirational, *poesa vivsa*, didactic, merely political."** He has published poetry by Laurie Blauner, David Hopes, Leslie Adrienne Miller, Richard Robbins, and Vern Rutsala. As a sample, he selected the following lines from "Matisse's Antoinette" by Peggy Shumaker:

> *In the bath, she stretches full-length—*
> *two bruised red peonies surface.*
> *Because she did not love him, she allowed*
> *one young man to stroke the sleek slope*
> *of her hip, wondering what he would find*
> *to possess, what she had*
> *to parcel, what one*
> *needs must conserve always. How little*
> *it has to do with the body.*

The magazine is 6×9", nicely printed, 60 pp. flat-spined (but the glue doesn't hold), glossy card cover with b/w illustration on green. It is a publication of the Writer's Workshop at the University of Nebraska and it was formerly called *Smackwarm*; it retains the volume and issue number of that publication. Circulation is 400, of which 260 are subscriptions and 80 go to libraries. Price per issue is $3.50, subscription $6/year. **Sample available for $2 postpaid. Pay is 2 copies and 1-year subscription. "Clean typed copy strongly preferred. Dot-matrix strongly discouraged."** Reporting time is 3-4 months and time to publication 3-6 months. The editor says, "Your first allegiance is to the poem. Publishing will come in time, but it will always be less than you feel you deserve. Therefore, don't look to publication as a reward for writing well; it has no relationship." The TNR Awards of $300 each in poetry and fiction are published in the spring issue. Entry fee: $6 subscription. You can enter as many times as desired. Deadline November 30th.

NEGATIVE CAPABILITY; NEGATIVE CAPABILITY PRESS; EVE OF ST. AGNES COMPETITION (II), 62 Ridgelawn Rd. E, Mobile AL 36608-2465, founded 1981, poetry editor Sue Walker. *Negative Capability* is a tri-quarterly of verse, fiction, commentary, music and art. The press publishes broadsides, chapbooks, perfect-bound paperbacks and hardbacks. They want **both contemporary and traditional poetry. "Quality has its own specifications—length and form."** They have recently published Diane Wakoski, W.D. Snodgrass, Rosaly Roffman, Roald Hoffman, Laurel Speer and John Brugaletta. Sue Walker selected these lines from Elizabeth Claman's "Love Song—for my mother":

> *Mother*
> *of the jazz scat and the scraped uterus,*
> *the dull pencil and words*
> *that can never come out, especially in anger,*
> *this*
> *I tell you, sweet mother of mine,*
>
> *is a love song.*

The editor says, "Reaching irritably after a few facts will not describe *Negative Capability*. Read it to know what quality goes to form creative achievement. Shakespeare had negative capability;

do you?" In its short history this journal has indeed achieved a major prominence on our literary scene. It is a flat-spined, elegantly printed, digest-sized, 130+ pp. format, glossy card color cover with art, circulation 1,000. About 60 pp. of each issue are devoted to poetry. Subscription: $12; per copy: $5. They receive about 1,200 freelance submissions per year, use 350. **Sample: $4 postpaid. Do not submit mss during the summer (June, July and August). Reports in 6-8 weeks. Pays 2 copies. Send SASE for guidelines. For book publication, query with 10-12 samples and "brief letter with major publications, significant contributions, awards. We like to know a person as well as their poem."** Replies to queries in 3-4 weeks, to submissions (if invited) in 6-8 weeks. Photocopy, dot-matrix OK. Payment arranged with authors. Editor sometimes comments on rejections. Reviews books of poetry. They offer an Annual Eve of St. Agnes Competition with major poets as judges.

‡**NEW CHICANO WRITING (IV-Ethnic)**, Dept. of Spanish & Portuguese, Mod. Lang. Bldg. 545, Univ. of AZ, Tucson AZ 85721, founded 1991, phone (602)621-7347, editor Chuck Tatum, is an annual anthology, uses **"poetry in Spanish or English or a combination of the two languages. Send an original and a photocopy of MS and return postage."** It is 6×9″, flat-spined, hardback and paperback professionally designed. Press run 1,000. **Sample: $20-25. Pays contributor's copies and a small fee. Editorial board reports in 3-5 months. Editors seldom comment on rejections. Cover letter required.**

NEW CICADA (IV-Form), 40-11 Kubo, Hobara, Fukushima, 960-06 Japan, phone 0245-75-4226, founded 1984, editor Tadao Okazaki. *New Cicada* is "the first and only magazine introducing the universal definition of haiku that is applicable to all languages. Of all existing Japanese haiku magazines in English, has the longest history of publication." As a sample, he chose the following by an unidentified poet:

> *White birch tree*
> *brushing another tint*
> *on a spring cloud*

The purpose of the magazine, which appears twice yearly in March and September, is "to raise the quality of haiku in English, and to introduce the universal definition of traditional haiku." Volumes 1 through 5 of *Cicada* were published in Toronto, Canada, by Eric W. Amann, founding editor, and later by the Haiku Society of Canada. The digest-sized publication is offset from dot-matrix copy with a b/w frontispiece; one-color matte card cover, saddle-stapled. Price is $4/issue, $6 for a 1-year subscription. **Sample: $4 postpaid by US personal check or 7 international reply coupons. The editor requests a self-addressed postcard and an IRC for reports. No MSS returned. It will take up to approximately 6 months to get a report. No payment in any form is offered for published poems.** The editor who says he "introduced the universal definition of haiku for the first time" maintains that "(1) the haiku form in any language is a triplet verse of 3-4-3 beats; (2) the 3-4-3 syllable verse is the shortest, and trimeter-tetrameter-trimeter triplet in general is the longest classical haiku form in English; and (3) the Japanese haiku is recited in iambic trimeter—tetrameter—trimeter form, and is fundamentally a ballad." The editor says, "The traditional haiku is an unrhymed triplet ballad; the old definition of haiku as a form of syllabic verse is wrong. Free verse haiku must be no longer than 3 lines, preferably with subject matter of nature or man and nature."

THE NEW CRITERION (II), The Foundation for Cultural Review, Inc., 850 7th Ave., New York NY 10019, poetry editor Robert Richman, is a monthly (except July and August) review of ideas and the arts, 7×10″, flat-spined, 90+ pp., which uses poetry of high literary quality. They have recently published poems by James Ulmer, Alan Shapiro, Elizabeth Spires and Herbert Morris. I selected these sample lines from "A question" by Luke Zilles:

> *The picket fence in front*
> *is a crotchety row of sticks.*
> *On the rotted sill of the window*
> *snow scrolls against the glass.*

Sample: $4 plus postage.

NEW DELTA REVIEW; THE EYSTER PRIZE (II), English Dept., Louisiana State University, Baton Rouge LA 70803, editor Janet Wondra, who says, "We call ourselves a 'breakthrough magazine'; we publish work of merit by **writers who for one reason or another are still slightly outside the mainstream. Most of them are younger writers who have not yet built a reputation. We are wide open: poets who are brave enough to take chances and skilled enough not to get spattered. No minimalist, compromised workshop voice. Stay young and write poems."** They have recently published poetry by Michael J. Rosen, Eve Shelnutt, Alice G. Brand and Gary Duehr. *NDR* appears twice a year, 6×9″ flat-spined, 90-120 pp., typeset and printed on quality stock with glossy card cover with art. Its press run is 300, with 100 subscriptions of which 10 are libraries, the rest for shelf sales. Subscription: $7. **Sample:**

$4 postpaid. Pays 2 copies (and 50% off for others)." Photocopy OK, no dot matrix, simultaneous submissions, or previously published poems. Reports in 1-3 months. MSS read in summer. Poetry editor "sometimes" comments on rejections. "Often I will return a piece and ask for revision." Reviews books of poetry. The Eyster Prize of $50 is awarded to the best story and best poem in each issue. Kathleen Fitzpatrick says, "The question we get asked most often is 'what sort of poetry are you looking for?' What can I say? The *good* sort. Sparks should fly from your typewriter keys. Read the magazine for specific examples, but mostly, keep writing."

NEW DIRECTIONS PUBLISHING CORPORATION (III, IV-Translations), 80 Eighth Ave., New York NY 10011, founded 1936, address "Poetry Editor." New Directions is "a small publisher of 20th-Century literature with an emphasis on the experimental," publishing about 36 paperback and hard-back titles each year. **"We are looking for highly unusual, literary, experimental poetry. We can't use traditional poetry, no matter how accomplished. Ninety-five percent of the time we publish poets who have built up a reputation in the literary magazines and journals. It is generally not financially feasible for us to take on unknown poets."** They have published poetry by William Carlos Williams, Ezra Pound, Denise Levertov, Jerome Rothenberg, Robert Creeley, Michael McClure, Kenneth Rexroth, H.D., Robert Duncan, Stevie Smith, David Antin, Hayden Carruth, George Oppen, Dylan Thomas, Lawrence Ferlinghetti, Jimmy Santiago Baca, Rosmarie Waldrop and Gary Snyder. As a sample I selected these lines from Thomas Merton's verse play, "The Tower of Babel, a Morality" in his collection, **The Strange Islands**:

> *Words have always been our best soldiers.*
> *They have defeated meaning in every engagement*
> *And have almost made an end of reality.*

Reports on submissions in 4 months; may be 2 years until publication. "Please send a sampling of about 10 typed, photocopied poems, preferably not a simultaneous submission." They look at all submissions but "chances are slight." Terms for book publication "all depend." To see samples, try the library or purchase from their catalog (available), local bookstores or their distributor, W. W. Norton. New Directions advises, "Getting published is not easy, but the best thing to do is to work on being published in the magazines and journals, thus building up an audience. Once the poet has an audience, the publisher will be able to sell the poet's books. Avoid vanity publishers and read a lot of poetry."

‡**NEW EARTH PUBLICATIONS; CO-OP PRESS (IV-Spiritual, political, translations)**, P.O. Box 4790, Berkeley CA 94704, phone (415)549-0575, founded 1990, editor Clifton Ross, publishes **"book length collections (up to 96 pp.) dealing with struggle for peace and justice, well crafted work and translations. 50% publications are author subsidized paying 10% of press run."** They publish 1-2 paperbacks, 2-3 chapbooks/year. Reports on queries in 2 weeks, on MSS in 6 weeks. Pays 10% royalties.

NEW ENGLAND REVIEW (III), (formerly NER/BLQ), Middlebury College, Middlebury VT 05753, phone (802)388-3711, ext 5075, founded 1978, editor T.R. Hummer, associate editor Devon Jerslid, *New England Review* is a prestige literary quarterly, 6×9", 160+ pp., flat-spined, elegant make-up and printing on heavy stock, glossy cover with art. Pays. Reports in 6-8 weeks. Poets published recently include Toi Derricotte, Albert Goldbarth, Norman Dubie, Philip Booth and Carol Frost. As a sample the editors selected these lines from Chase Twichell's "The Cut":

> *I had a sorrow that misled me.*
> *Because we were childless,*
> *I had, out of some sovereign,*
> *stupid longing in my body,*
> *invented a ghost-child,*
> *a third person. . . .*

New England Review also sponsors an annual narrative poetry competition, first prize $500, publication of the poem and a lifetime subscription, entry fee $2 per poem. Deadline June 1. Length: up to 400 lines. Subscription: $18. Sample: $4 postpaid. **"Poems for the competition or for regular publication in the magazine must demonstrate craft, inventiveness and visceral appeal."**

NEW HOPE INTERNATIONAL (II), 20 Werneth Ave., Gee Cross, Cheshire U.K. SK14 5NL, founded 1969, editor Gerald England, is a **"magazine of poetry, fiction, translations, literary essays, news and reviews."** They also publish chapbooks. **"Most types of poetry are acceptable, no limit on length. Content without form and form without content are equally unacceptable. Poems must be well-written within the form chosen but also have something to communicate in the widest sense. Don't send any depressive self-abusive poems."** They have recently published poetry by John Brander, Jennifer Footman, Ann Keith, Russell Smith, Steve Sneyd and Randy Wilson. The following lines are from "Haiku" by Kotude Iwal-a:

Ringing the small bell
Attached to my scissors
I sew the autumn.
The digest-sized magazine, 36 pp., is lightly photocopied from computer typesetting, mimeograph paper, saddle-stapled, color paper cover, using b/w artwork. Circulation 500 for 275 subscriptions of which 20 are libraries. $4 per issue, $20 for 6 issues including chapbooks and the *New Hope International Review* (A4 size, 40 pp. cost separately $4). **Sample: $4 postpaid. "Those who subscribe can expect much more in the way of feedback. Manuscripts read at anytime." Reports in "maximum 6 months" (usually no more than 5 weeks). Pays 1 copy. Put name and address on each sheet; not more than 6 at a time; simultaneous submissions *not* encouraged. Photocopy OK, dot-matrix OK, "NLQ please!"** Translations should include copy of original. For book publication, query first with 50 samples and bio. "Poets must fully participate in book marketing—buy copies at 50% discount for resale." Reviews books of poetry. The editor advises, "New poets should read widely and keep their minds open to work of different styles. 'Progress is a going forward from—not towards.' "

NEW LETTERS; NEW LETTERS POETRY PRIZE (II), University of Missouri-Kansas City, Kansas City MO 64110, phone (816)235-1168, founded 1934 as *University Review*; became *New Letters* in 1971, managing editor Bob Stewart, editor James McKinley, "is dedicated to publishing the best short fiction, best contemporary poetry, literary articles, photography and art work by both established writers and new talents." They want **"contemporary writing of all types—free verse poetry preferred, short works are more likely to be accepted than very long ones."** They have recently published poetry by Joyce Carol Oates, Hayden Carruth, John Frederick Nims, Louise Glück, Louis Simpson, Vassar Miller and John Tagliabue. As a sample I selected the first 2 of 9 stanzas of "Unrequited Love" by Marilyn Chin:
Because you stared into the black lakes of her eyes
you shall drown in them.
Because you tasted the persimmon on her lips
you shall dig your moist grave.
The flat-spined, professionally printed quarterly, glossy 2-color cover with art, 6×9", uses about 65 (of 120+) pp. of poetry in each issue, circulation 1,845 with 1,520 subscriptions of which about 40% are libraries. Subscription: $17; per copy: $5. They receive about 7,000 submissions per year, use less than 1%, have a 6 month backlog. **Sample: $5 postpaid. Send no more than 6 poems at once, no simultaneous submissions. "We strongly prefer original typescripts rather than photocopy or dot-matrix. We don't read between May 15 and October 15. No query needed." They report in 4-10 weeks, pay a small fee plus 2 copies.** Occasionally James McKinley comments on rejections. The New Letters Poetry Prize of $750 is given annually for a group of 3-6 poems, entry fee $10 (check payable to New Letters Literary Awards). Deadline May 15. They also publish occasional anthologies, selected and edited by McKinley.

‡NEW MADRID (II), Dept. of English, Murray State Univ., Murray KY 40071, poetry editor Claudia Keenlan, is a literary annual using poetry with **"no restrictions on form or content."** Their first issue, early 1991, will have poetry by Christopher Davis, Bill Knott and Laura Mullen. I have not seen an issue, but the editor describes it as 140-220 pp. with glossy cover. **Pays 2 copies.**

NEW METHODS: THE JOURNAL OF ANIMAL HEALTH TECHNOLOGY (IV-Specialized/animals), P.O. Box 22605, San Francisco CA 94122-0605, phone (415)664-3469, founded as *Methods* in 1976, poetry editor Ronald S. Lippert, AHT, is a "monthly networking service in the animal field, open forum, active in seeking new avenues of knowledge for our readers, combining animal professionals under one roof." They want poetry which is "animal related but not cutesy" They get few submissions, but if they received more of quality, they would publish more poetry. They publish a maximum of one poem in each monthly issue, circulation 5,600 to subscribers, of which over 73 are libraries. Price per issue, $1.50; subscription $18. **Sample: $2. Include SASE. A listing of all back issues and the topics covered is available for $5. Reports in 1-2 months. Double space with one-inch margins, include dated cover letter. Everything typed. Guidelines are available for SASE. Pays complimentary copies. Comment on rejected MSS?** "Always!" Ronald Lippert advises, "Keep up with current events."

NEW MEXICO HUMANITIES REVIEW (II, IV-Regional), Humanities Dept., New Mexico Tech, Socorro NM 87801, phone (505)835-5200, founded 1978, editors Jerry Bradley, John Rothfork and Lou Thompson, *NMHR* is published twice a year, invites MSS **"designed for a general academic readership and those that pursue Southwestern themes or those using interdisciplinary methods."** There are no restrictions as to type of poetry; *"NMHR* publishes first class, literary poetry," but does not want "sentimental verse, shallow, pointlessly rhymed ideas." Poets published include George Garrett,

Ralph Mills, Jr., Fred Chappell, Peter Wild and Walter McDonald. As a sample the editor selected the following lines by M. L. Hester:

> Stainless steel is the percentage sink.
> It will not chip, rust scratch or peel.
> And it shines. The beauty of light
> bouncing in the AM kills all germs democratically;

The review is digest-sized, 150 pp., printed by offset on white stock, with an embossed, one-color matte card cover, flat-spined; there are graphics and ads. Circulation is 650, of which 350 are subscriptions; other copies are sold at poetry readings, writers' workshops, etc. Price per issue is $6, subscription $11/year. *NMHR* **pays one year's subscription. Reports in 6 weeks, 6 months between acceptance and publication. No simultaneous submissions.** Reviews books of poetry. Also has a poetry contest supported by Witter Bynner Foundation for Poetry. Best three poems from two issues. Current issues being judged by Poet Laureate Mark Strand. Awards: 1st prize $500, 2nd $300, 3rd $200.

NEW ORLEANS POETRY JOURNAL PRESS (II), 2131 General Pershing St., New Orleans LA 70115, phone (504)891-3458, founded 1956, publisher/editor Maxine Cassin. **"We prefer to publish relatively new and/or little-known poets of unusual promise or those inexplicably neglected—'the real thing.'" She does not want to see "cliché or doggerel, anything incomprehensible or too derivative, or workshop exercises." Query first. She does not accept freelance submissions** for her chapbooks, which are flat-spined paperbacks. She has recently published books by Charles de Gravelles, Vassar Miller, Everett Maddox, Charles Black and Martha McFerren. As a sample, the editor selected these lines from "Millenary" by Raeburn Miller:

> The sun is an old terror.
> we know it is wrong
>
> to deduce from the eyeless denizens
> of caves acquired characteristics—

Their most recent book is **Illuminated Manuscript** by Malaika Favorite. **The editor reports on queries in 2-3 months, MSS in the same time period, if solicited. Simultaneous submissions will possibly be accepted,** and she has no objection to photocopied MSS. **Pay is in author's copies,** usually 50 to 100. Ms. Cassin does not subsidy publish at present and does not offer grants or awards. For aspiring poets, she quotes the advice Borges received from his father: "1) Read as much as possible! 2) Write only when you *must*, and 3) Don't rush into print!" As a small press editor and publisher, she urges poets to read instructions in **Poet's Market** listings with utmost care!

NEW ORLEANS REVIEW (II), Box 195, Loyola University, New Orleans LA 70118, phone (504)865-2294, founded 1968, poetry editor John Biguenet. It is 104+ pp., flat-spined, elegantly printed with glossy card cover using a full-color painting. Circulation is 1,500. **Sample: $9 postpaid.** As a sample I selected these lines from "End of the Party" by James Nolan:

> We spend life asking: "how much?"
> and we catch "how much?" in our parent's eyes,
> in their voices, hands, how much for this,
> for that, how much land, how much bread, . . .

Pays for published poems. Reports in 3 months.

THE NEW POETS SERIES, INC.; CHESTNUT HILLS PRESS (II), 541 Piccadilly, Baltimore MD 21204, phone (301)830-2863 or 828-0724, founded 1970, editors/directors Clarinda Harriss Raymond and Michael Raymond. The New Poets Series, Inc. brings out **first books by promising new poets. They want "excellent, fresh, nontrendy, literate, intelligent poems. Any form (including traditional), any style. No poetry riding any one particular political, social, sexual or religious hobbyhorse."** Provides 20 copies to the author, the sales proceeds going back into the corporation to finance the next volume (usual press run: 1,000). "It has been successful in its effort to provide these new writers with a national distribution; in fact, The New Poets Series was recently named an Outstanding Small Press by the prestigious Pushcart Awards Committee, which judges some 5,000 small press publications annually." Chestnut Hills Press publishes author-subsidized books—"High quality work only, however. CHP is itself achieving a reputation for prestigious books, printing only the top 10% of MSS CHP and NPS receive." The New Poets Series also publishes an occasional anthology drawn from public reading series. They have recently published books by Medbh McGuckian and Nuala Archer, Richard Fein, Shelley Scott, Carole Glasser Langille, Peter Wessel, Charles Stuart Roberts and Steven Sills. Books by Gail Wronsky and Beryl Schlossman are forthcoming. Clarinda Harriss Raymond selected "Calling Canada," a complete poem by Irish writer Medbh McGuckian, as a sample:

> I talk to the darkness as if to a daughter

Or something that once pressed from inside
Like a street of youth. My striped notebook
Is just a dress over my body, so I will waken
At a touch, or for no reason at all. In it
I learn how to cut into other people's dreams,
How to telephone them Paris-style and how
Like sunshine, a tenderness roughened
Because there was so little time for snow-months
To paint my woman's walls into sea.

Query with 10 samples, cover letter giving publication credits and bio. Reports in 6 weeks-6 months. Simultaneous submissions, photocopies OK. No dot-matrix. Editor sometimes comments briefly on rejections. MSS "are circulated to an editorial board of professional, publishing poets. NPS is very, very backlogged, but the best 10% of the MSS it receives are automatically eligible for Chestnut Hills Press consideration," a subsidy arrangement. **Send $4 for a sample volume.**

‡**THE NEW PRESS; THE NEW PRESS POETRY CONTEST (I, II)**, 87-40 Francis Lewis Blvd. #A44, Queens Village NY 11427, founded 1984, poetry editor Harry Ellison, is a quarterly magazine using poems **"less than 200 lines, accessible; imaginative. No doggerel, sentimentality."** They have recently published poetry by Les Bridges, Bruce Isaacson, Barbara Weekes and Robert Parody. As a sample the editor selected these lines by Lisa Campbell:

The wrong moon waxed strongly
but it was still the wrong moon.
The real one moved when Joshua
tampered with the sun.

It is magazine-sized, 28 pp., desktop published, with glossy cover, saddle-stapled. They accept about 10% of 700 poems received per year. Press run 1,000 for 200 subscribers of which 1 is a library, 800 shelf sales. Subscription: $12. **Sample postpaid: $3. Pays 3 copies. Reports in 2 months.** The New Press Poetry Contest, annually, deadline July 1, entry fee of $3 for up to 3 poems or 200 lines, has prizes of $120, $60, and ten 2-year subscriptions.

THE NEW QUARTERLY (II, IV-Regional), ELPP University of Waterloo, Waterloo, Ontario N2L 3G1 Canada, phone (519)885-1211, ext. 2837, founded 1981, managing editor Mary Merikle, is a "literary quarterly—new directions in Canadian writing." For the poetry they want, the editors have **"no preconceived conception—usually Canadian work, poetry capable of being computer typeset—4½″ line length typeset lines. No greeting card verse."** I have not seen *TNQ*, but the editor describes it as 120 pp., flat-spined, 6 × 8½″, with a photograph on the cover, no graphics or art, some ads. Of 2,000 poems received per year they use 100. Press run is 600 for 300 subscriptions (10 of them libraries) and additional shelf sales. Subscription: $15 (add $2 for US or overseas subscriptions). **Sample: $4 Canadian, $4 US postpaid. Send SASE for guidelines. Pays $20 per poem plus 3 copies. Submit no more than 5. Reports in 3-6 months. No comments on rejections of poetry.**

THE NEW RENAISSANCE (II, IV-Translations, bilingual), 9 Heath Rd., Arlington MA 02174, founded 1968, poetry editor James E.A. Woodbury. *the new renaissance* is "intended for the 'renaissance' person, the generalist rather than the specialist. Seeks to publish the best new writing, to offer a forum for articles of public concern, and to highlight interest in neglected writers and artists in its essay/review section. They have recently published Paul Snock (C.J. Stevens translation), Leslie Tompkins and Dori Appel. As a sample, the editor selected these lines from "Chiaroscuco" by A.S. Cohen and William Laufer:

That last flush of amber
just before dusk,
the sudden hesitancy
of warm before cool,
color backing into shadow
and once hidden,
its reluctance to be named.

tnr is flat-spined, professionally printed on heavy stock, glossy, color cover, 144-192 pp., using 16-34 pp. of poetry in each issue; usual print run 1,600, for 680 subscriptions of which approximately 132 are libraries. Subscriptions: $12.50/3 issues. **"We're an unsponsored, independent small litmag."** Contributors are expected to buy copies—$4.80 for an '82 issue or $6.45 for an '87 or '88 issue; current issue $7.50. They receive about **600 poetry submissions per year, use about 22, have about a 30-month backlog. "Will be reading manuscripts from January 2 through June 30, 1992." Pays $13-20, more for (occasional) longer poems, plus 1 copy. Reports in 3-6 months.** "We believe that poets should not only be readers but lovers of poetry. We're looking for 'literalists of the imagination—imaginary gardens with real toads in them.' **Our range is from traditionalist poetry to post-modern and experimental (the latter only occasionally, though). We also like the occasional 'light' poem and, of course, translations. We're especially interested in the individual voice. We aren't interested in greeting card verse or prose set in poetic forms."**

THE NEW REPUBLIC (II), 1220 19th St. NW, Washington DC 20036, phone (202)331-7494, founded 1914, poetry editor Richard Howard. *The New Republic* is a weekly journal of opinion. I chose the following sample poetry lines from "Our Days," by Gary Soto:

> *We get up to our feet, stretch, and throw practice kicks*
> *At the air, and bowing to one another,*
>
> *Begin to make bruises where the heart won't go,*
> *A hurt won't stay. I like that, the trust of bone,*
>
> *And how if I'm hit I'll step in, almost crazed,*
> *And sweep, back fist, and maybe bring him down.*

The New Republic is magazine-sized, printed on slick paper, 42 pp. saddle-stapled with 4-color cover. Subscription rate $69.97/year, back issues available for $3.50 postpaid. **I have no submission or payment information.**

NEW RIVERS PRESS; MINNESOTA VOICES PROJECT, INC. (II, IV-Regional, translation), Suite 910, 420 N. 5th St., Minneapolis MN 55401, founded 1968, publishes collections of poetry, translations of contemporary literature, collections of short fiction, and is also involved in publishing **Minnesota regional literary material. Write for free catalog, or send SASE for guidelines/inquiries. New and emerging authors living in Iowa, Minnesota, North and South Dakota and Wisconsin are eligible for the Minnesota Voices Project. Book-length manuscripts of poetry, short fiction, novellas, or familiar essays are all accepted. Send SASE for entry form. Winning authors receive a stipend of $500 plus publication by New Rivers. Second and subsequent printings of works will allow 15% royalties for author.**

‡NEW SPOKES (II), (formerly Spokes), The Orchard House, 45 Clophill Rd., Upper Gravenhurst, Bedford MK45 4JH, England, founded 1985, editor Donald Atkinson, a biannual journal of **new poetry,** reviews and b&w and monochrome art work. *New Spokes* is 64 pp., perfect-bound, with still gloss cover and pictures. Its circulation is in the UK, Europe, North America and Australia. Price per issue £3.75. Subscription £7.50/year (UK), £9/year (overseas). **Sample: £3.75. No particular specifications. Reporting time 6-8 weeks and time to publication approximately 4-6 months.** Reviews books of poetry.

NEW WELSH REVIEW (II, IV-Ethnic), St. David's University College, Lampeter, Dyfed, UK, phone 0570-423523, founded 1988, editor Belinda Humfrey. *NWR* is a quarterly publishing articles, short stories and poems. They have recently published poetry by Joseph Clancy, Gillian Clarke, Lawrence Ferlinghetti, John Heath-Stubbs, Les A. Murray, Peter Porter and Anne Stevenson. I have not seen it, but the editor describes it as 88 pp., glossy paper in three colors, laminated cover, using photographs, graphics and ads. Their press run is 1,500. Subscription: £12. **Sample: £3.50 postpaid. Submit double-spaced. No simultaneous submissions or previously published poems. Reports in 6 weeks. Publication within 1-7 months.** Editor sometimes comments on rejections. Reviews books of poetry.

NEW YORK QUARTERLY (II), P.O. Box 693, Old Chelsea Station, New York NY 10113, founded 1969, poetry editor William Packard, appears 3 times a year. They seek to publish "a cross-section of the best of contemporary American poetry" and, indeed, **have a record of publishing many of the best and most diverse of** poets, including W. D. Snodgrass, Gregory Corso, James Dickey, Charles Bukowski, Leo Connellan, Helen Adam, Macdonald Carey, Pat Farewell, and Judson Jerome. It appears in a 6×9″ flat-spined format, thick, elegantly printed, color glossy cover. Subscription: $15 to 305 Neville Hall, University of Maine, Orono, ME 04469. **Submit 3-5 poems. Reports within 2 weeks. Pays copies.** This magazine is sponsored by the National Poetry Foundation, listed under Organizations Useful to Poets.

THE NEW YORKER (III, IV-Translations, humor), 25 W. 43rd St., New York, NY 10036, founded 1925, poetry editor Alice Quinn, circulation 640,000, uses **poetry of the highest quality (including translations) and pays top rates. Replies in 6-8 weeks. MSS not read during the summer. Must include SASE for a reply.** Price: $1.75 (available on newsstands).

NEWSLETTER INAGO (I), Box 26244, Tucson AZ 85726-6244, phone (602)294-7031, founded 1979, poetry editor Del Reitz, is a 4-5 pp. corner-stapled, monthly newsletter. **"Free verse preferred although other forms will be read. Rhymed poetry must be truly exceptional (nonforced) for consideration. Due**

to format, 'epic' and monothematic poetry will not be considered. Cause specific, political, or religious poetry stands little chance of consideration. A wide range of short poetry, showing the poet's preferably eclectic perspective is best for *NI*. No haiku, please." They have recently published poetry by John Brander, Cal Rollins, Jori Ranhand, Sam Silva, Mark J. Isham, Barbara Elovic, Ana Pine, Gail White, Tom O. Jones and Salvatore Galioto. The editor says, "since editorial taste in poetry especially is such a subjective and narrow thing," a short selection cannot be chosen "with any fairness to either that taste or the poet whose material might be quoted." Below are lines from Harriet B. Shatraw's "A Late Fall Day in the Woods.":

> Light footsteps shuffle
> the cornflake leaves
> and a grey doe statues herself
> in stillness

Their press run is approximately 200 for that many subscriptions. **No price is given for the newsletter, but the editor suggests a donation of $2 an issue or $16 annually (overseas: $3 and $18). Guidelines available for SASE. Pays 4 copies. They consider simultaneous submissions and previously published poems. Reports ASAP (usually within 2 weeks). Editor sometimes comments on rejections.**

NEXT EXIT (II, IV-Regional), 92 Helen St., Kingston, Ontario K7L 4P3 Canada, founded 1980, editor Eric Folsom, a twice-yearly magazine that features poetry and reviews and focuses on Ontario and Eastern North American writers. The editor wants to see poetry that is **"lyric, narrative, meditative, concrete, explorative; any form done well,"** but nothing **"misogynist."** He has recently published work by John Barlow and Sheila E. Murphy. As a sample, he chose the following lines from "Well Woman" by Terri Lee Grell:

> The sleek, shining body
> of the new woman slips
> away, breathless.

The magazine is 5 × 8½" photocopied typed copy on 32 pp., saddle-stapled and folded with black lettering and illustration on cover. Circulation is 150, of which 75 are subscriptions and 10 go to libraries. Price per issue is $3, subscription $6/year. **Sample available for $3 postpaid. Pay is 1 copy plus 1-year subscription, more if requested. Submissions will be reported on in 90 days and time to publication is 6 months.** Reviews books of poetry.

NEXUS (II), 006 University Center, Wright State University, Dayton OH 45435, phone (513)873-2031, founded 1967, editor Chris Rue. *"Nexus* is a student operated magazine of avant-garde and street poetry; also essays on environmental and political issues. We're looking for truthful, direct poetry. Open to poets anywhere. We look for contemporary, imagistic work as well as traditional rhyme and meter."** Recent issues have featured themes on Japan and American West. *Nexus* appears 3 times a year—fall, winter and spring, using about 20 pp. of poetry (of 36-40) in each issue, circulation 2,000. They receive 1,000 submissions per year, use 30-50. **Send a 10 × 15" SASE with 5 first class stamps and $2 for first copy, $1 for each additional issue. Submit up to 6 pp. of poetry, September to May. Photocopy and simultaneous submissions OK. Send bio with submissions. Reports in 10-12 weeks except summer months. Pays 2 copies. Send SASE for guidelines. Editor sometimes comments on rejections.** Reviews books of poetry.

‡NEXUS (I), English Dept., Simon Fraser University, Burnaby, British Columbia V5A 1S6 Canada, founded "198-something," editor G.P. Lainsbury, appears 3/year, using **poetry. "No specifications other than quality; nothing sentimental, derivative."** They have recently published poetry by Christopher Wiseman, Jennifer Footman and Stan Rogal. As a sample, I selected these sample lines from "Jimmy S, out of his confused period, briefly" by John Barlow:

> Brother Jimmy of Baton Rouge, Louisiana
> warm sliding reminiscent of warm
> verily dolphin-like on the
> pancreatic piano
> claiming victory now and ever over
> New York devils and erzats Christians alike

It is digest-sized, 30 pp., with matte card cover. They accept about 30% of poetry received. Press run 200 for 150 shelf sales. **Sample postpaid: $2.50. Pays 2 copies. Reports in 2 months. "Please include short bio sketch."**

‡NIGHT MOUNTAINS (IV-Horror/Fantasy), Suite 188, 8605 Allisonville Rd., P.O. Box 50462, Indianapolis IN 46250-0462 (must use *complete* address), founded 1989, editor Lorrie Beaver, appears 2-3/year using **"poems no longer than 20 lines. Horror and/or fantasy with an almost surreal feeling to it. May be rhymed or unrhymed. No sex, no excessive gore, no profanity."** Have recently published poetry by John Grey, Steve Sneyd, Dory Hulburt and Jacie Ragan. As a sample the editor selected these lines by William P. Robertson:

> Out on the celestial outback
> heathens still worship the stars.
> At dusk they light mountains of fires
> that are seen from wherever you are . . .

I have not seen an issue, but the editor describes it as "around 30 pp., magazine-sized, corner stapled or bound at side. Definitely 'no frills' philosophy." They use 3-4 poems/issue, about 10-20% of that submitted. Press run 30 copies. **Sample: cost varies. Pays 1 copy. "May submit work anytime — accepted work may not be published until 3-6 months later due to publishing schedule. I don't deal with IRC's. Response time is 3-10 days. Submissions without SASEs are tossed. Often comment on rejections.** Don't send me smeared, soiled submissions with spelling errors. I have limited time as editor since I work full-time. Therefore, I can advise you to *take some pride in your work* by sending clean, crisp copy free of errors. Send for guidelines (with a SASE) first! Follow your own poetry voice — don't imitate others. Be original. *NM* is a humble venture. I refuse to get in over my head. . . . My goal is to break even on production costs."

NIGHT ROSES; MOONSTONE BLUE (I, IV-Anthology, teen/young adult, student), P.O. Box 393, Prospect Heights IL 60070, phone (708)392-2435, founded 1986, poetry editor Allen T. Billy, appears 2-4 times a year. "I plan to do special poetry anthologies from time to time. We publish *Moonstone Blue*, which is a science fiction/fantasy, psychic/occult anthology, but we have no set dates of publication on this series. We look for women/feminism themes for *Bikini* series, and love/romance/nature for special *Roses* series." For *Night Roses* they want **"poems about dance, bells, clocks, nature, ghost images of past or future, some haiku, romance poems, poems about flowers, roses, wildflowers, violets, etc. Do not want poems with raw language."** They have recently published poems by John DiMauro, James L. Wilson, Edna Janes Kayser, Michael Fraley, Linda Bornstein and Ida Fasel. As a sample the editor chose these lines by Rev. Benedict Auer:

> A moon
> in full mask
> frosts night,
> one last glare
> before ice
> slick woods.

Night Roses is 44 pp., saddle-stapled, photocopied from typescript on offset paper with tinted matte card cover, press run 200-300. Subscription: $8 for 3 issues, $3/copy. **Sample: $2.50 postpaid. Pays 1 copy. "Desire author's name and address on all sheets of MSS. If previously published — an acknowledgement must be provided by author with it."** No simultaneous submissions; some previously published poems used. **"I prefer submissions between April and September." Reports in 4-10 weeks. "Material accepted for current issue and 2 in progress. If I like a poem — I may ask a poet if I can put it in the 'hold file' to close out a future issue."**

NIGHTSUN (II), Dept. of English, Frostburg State University, Frostburg MD 21532, founded 1981, poetry editors Douglas DeMars and Barbara Wilson, is a 64 pp., digest-sized literary annual. They **want "highest quality poetry. Subject matter open. Prefers poems not much longer than 40 lines. Not interested in the "extremes of sentimental, obvious poetry on the one hand and the subjectless 'great gossamer-winged gnat' school of poetry on the other."** They have recently published poetry by William Stafford, Linda Pastan, Marge Piercy, Diane Wakoski and Dennis Brutus. They accept about 1% of poetry received. **Do not submit MSS during summer months. Sample: $6.95 postpaid. Pays 2 copies.** "Contributors encouraged to subscribe." Reports in 3 months. *Nightsun* is affiliated with the annual Western Maryland Writers' Workshop.

NIMROD INTERNATIONAL JOURNAL OF CONTEMPORARY POETRY AND FICTION; RUTH G. HARDMAN AWARD: PABLO NERUDA PRIZE FOR POETRY (II), 2210 S. Main St., Tulsa OK 74114, phone (918)584-3333, founded 1956, poetry editor Fran Ringold, "is an active 'little magazine,' part of the movement in American letters which has been essential to the development of modern literature. *Nimrod* publishes 2 issues per year: an Awards Issue in the fall featuring the prize winners of our national competition and a thematic issue each spring which in 1991 was "Clap Hands and Sing: Writers of Age." They want **vigorous writing that is neither wholly of the academy nor the streets, typed MSS."** They have published poetry by Pattiann Rogers, Denise Levertov, Willis Barnstone, Alvin Greenberg, Francois Camoin, Tess Gallagher, McKeel McBride, Bronislava Volek, Josephine Jacobson, William Stafford and Ishmael Reed. As a sample he chose these lines from "Hum-Drum Days" by Lisa Steinman:

> It's late, and daylight ends early.
> Outside, everything smells of winter;

the forsythia has abandoned its leaves, leans
against the window, pointing in.
The empty clothesline's taut.
We are clearly waiting for something.

The 6 × 9″ flat-spined, 160 + pp., journal, full-color glossy cover, professionally printed on coated stock with b/w photos and art, uses 50-90 pp. of poetry in each issue, circulation 3,500, 700 subscriptions of which 100 are public and university libraries. Subscription: $10/year plus $1.50 inside USA; $3 outside. Per copy: $6.90. They use about 1% of the 2,000 submissions they receive each year, have a 3 month backlog. **Sample: $6.90 for a recent issue, $5 for an issue more than 2 years old postpaid. Reports in 3 weeks-4 months, pays in copies. "Poets should be aware that during the months that the Ruth Hardman Awards Competition is being conducted, reporting time on non-contest manuscripts will be longer."** Send business-sized SASE for guidelines and rules for the Ruth G. Hardman Award: Pablo Neruda Prize for Poetry ($1,000 and $500 prizes). Entries accepted January 1-April 1 each year $10 entry fee for which you get one copy of *Nimrod*.

‡**1992 QUARTERLY (II)**, #3, 52 Berkeley Place, Brooklyn NY 11217, founded 1990, editor Steve Mason, "is a quarterly chronicle of the decade in poetry, prose, essay, and artwork—**fresh and meaningful work is encouraged and, indeed, any work that respects the powers and purposes of language is desired. Experimentalism, in the form of refuting contemporary publishing pressures, is also sought, as we wish to represent (and forecast) change.**" They have recently published poetry by Rika Lesser, Goran Sonnevi and Theo Dorgan. As a sample the editor selected these lines from "Pacificus" by Lucy Logsdon:

Your hand fills mine, from all angles
translucent blue and emeralds dart,
bubbles in their wake. Pools of light
beam beyond our fingertips, our noses
ledged against the plexiglass.

It is digest-sized, professionally printed with card cover.

9TH ST. LABORATORIES; ABSCOND; EXPERIMENTAL AUDIO DIRECTIONS; MODOM; ANOMALY (Audio Magazine) (IV-Form), P.O. Box 3112, Florence AL 35630, phone (205)760-0415, founded 1986, "front man" Jake Berry. "*9th St. Laboratories* is the overall name for anything we publish: poetry, fiction, collages, graphics—all experimental, in a variety of formats, from postcards and magazines to broadsheets. Print falls under *Abscond*. *Experimental Audio Directions* is the tape label for spoken/sound poetry and other audio explorations. *MODOM* is an ongoing series of broadsheets, objects, booklets, etc. **The key words are *experiment* and *explore*. Poetry that breaks new ground for the poet personally, that comes from the commitment to a vision. Also graphic poetry. Poetry using devices other than straight linear narrative, that makes use of things otherwise considered nonsensical or absurd. No sentimental pablum please, no puritanical or purely superficial religious versifying, no weepy, confessional poetry.**" They have recently published poetry by Jack Foley, Chris Winkler, Malok, Richard Kostelanetz, Ivan Argüelles and John M. Bennett. As a sample the editor selected these lines by Mike Miskowski:

blendering on reverb dice, my feet. corner inta that plasterer or,
couch the sprinkling mechanism greenwise a sunsetter. circuit
clippings. thermostat though ink in.

MODOM and *Anomaly* appear irregularly: "something appears 2 to 4 times a year." They use about 10 of 150 submissions received a year. Press run is 100-200. **Sample $4 postpaid. "All checks or money orders should be made out to Jake Berry, not the name of the mag and not to *9th St. Laboratories*." They pay 1 copy. "Of course poems submitted for the tape mag should be on tape and include an SASE for its return." No simultaneous submissions. They use some previously published work. They publish chapbooks by invitation only, pay 15-20 copies. Editor sometimes comments on rejections.** He says, "We publish as much as we can as often as we can, attempting to expand the area of poetic, visionary concentration. Going to the mailbox to find it full of work that ignores conventional limitations and is highly involved with creating new things, bringing new insights, is what makes us happy. It makes no difference if the material is marketable or not. If you're trying to get rich or famous or both don't send it to us. Overambition creates thin, superficial art."

NOMOS PRESS INC.; NOMOS: STUDIES IN SPONTANEOUS ORDER (IV-Political), 9421 S. Longwood, Chicago IL 60620, phone (708)858-7184, poetry editor John Enright, editorial contact person Carol B. Low. *Nomos* is a quarterly magazine "**dedicated to individual freedom and responsibility.**" **One page of each issue is devoted to poetry up to 24 lines, "although longer pieces are considered. Poetry must promote individual freedom and responsibility, skepticism toward government solutions for economic and social ills and/or celebrate the human condition. No contrived rhymes, pedestrian**

prose or cryptic charades. Clarity of meaning and direct emotional appeal are paramount; form should contribute to, not detract or distract from these." They have recently published poetry by John Harllee. As a sample, the editor selected these lines by Christopher Brockman:

> *I've thought at some length and it seems to me*
> *The problem has its roots in the fact that we*
> *Have allowed ourselves to become only means*
> *To the end of someone else's bandwagon dreams.*

"*Nomos'* purpose is to call attention to the erosion of civil and economic rights, much of which erosion has government as its catalyst." I have not seen an issue, but the editor describes it as magazine-sized, generally 40 pp. in length, offset, matte cover occasionally printed 2-color. Ad copy, line art for cover and article illustrations are solicited. It has a circulation of 1,000 with 450 subscriptions of which 10 are libraries, 300 sent out to potential subscribers. Subscription: $18. **Sample: $4.50 postpaid. Send SASE for guidelines. Pays 3 copies. "Reviewing sample copies strongly encouraged." Reporting time varies, up to 12 months to publication. Photocopies, dot-matrix OK, name and address on each page. "SASE a must."**

THE NORTH; THE POETRY BUSINESS; SMITH/DOORSTOP PUBLISHING (II), 51 Byram Arcade, West-gate, Huddersfield HD1 1ND England, phone 0484-434-840, founded 1986, editors Peter Sansom and Janet Fisher, is a small press and magazine publisher of contemporary poetry. **"No particular restrictions on form, length, etc. But work must be contemporary, and must speak with the writer's own authentic voice. No copies of traditional poems, echoes of old voices, poems about the death of poet's grandfather, poems which describe how miserable the poet is feeling right now."** They have recently published poetry by Susan Bright, "the only U.S. poet we publish at the moment." As a sample, the editor selected these lines from "Swimming the English Channel" by Ms. Bright:

> *I did not intend to be a theater.*
> *I do not like the man in the basement who controls me.*
> *I do not want to be a house, a hotel, a car.*
> *I do not like being exposed!*

The North is "²⁄₃ A4 format 48-52 pp. offset litho, graphics, ads, colored card cover, staple-bound." It appears 3 times/year, press run 400 for 200 subscriptions. Subscription: £8 (£10 U.S. rate). **Sample postpaid: £25 (U.S. rate). Pays 2 copies.** Smith/Doorstop publishes 6 perfect-bound paperbacks/year. **For book consideration, submit 6 sample poems, cover letter, bio, previous publications. Responds to queries in 2 weeks, to MSS in 3 months. Pays 20 copies.** They hold an annual book (perfect-bound, laminated) competition for 16 pp. MSS; prize—joint publication with the other winner. They also publish an anthology of the runners-up. They also have a Reading Service which provides poets with detailed criticism of their work. Send 12 pages of poems plus SAE. Fee $75. The editors say, "Read plenty of poetry, contemporary and traditional. Attend workshops, etc., and meet other writers. Keep submitting poems, even if you fail. Build up a track record in magazines before trying to get a book published."

NORTH AMERICAN REVIEW (III), University of Northern Iowa, Cedar Falls IA 50614, phone (319)273-6455, founded 1815, poetry editor Peter Cooley, is a slick magazine-sized quarterly of general interest, 72 pp. average, saddle-stapled, professionally printed with glossy full-color paper cover. In their 171st anniversary issue they had poetry by Richard Terrill, Jeannine Savard and Katherine Soniat, from whose "That Far from Home" I selected the opening stanza (of 15) as a sample:

> *If it only depended on the young*
> *circus elephant, swaying by the river*
> *eating kudzu, or*
> *the reeling paddlewheeler*

The editor says they receive 15,000 poems a year, publish 20-30. Press run 5,200 to 2,200 subscriptions of which 1,100 are libraries, some 2,000 newsstand or bookstore sales. Single copy: $4; subscription: $14. **Sample: $4 postpaid. Send SASE for guidelines. Pays 50¢ per line and 2 copies. No simultaneous submissions or previously published poems. Reports in 1-2 months, as much as a year between acceptance and publication.**

THE NORTH CAROLINA HAIKU SOCIETY PRESS (V), NCHSI CONTEST (IV-Form), P.O. Box 14247, Raleigh NC 27620, phone (919)231-4531, founded 1984, editor/publisher Rebecca Rust. The North Carolina Haiku Society International Contest has a $1 entry fee for each haiku. Eleven awards. Deadline in hand is Dec. 31. Send a SASE for copy of rules. **The press, temporarily on hold and not accepting submissions in 1992,** was established "solely as a vehicle for publishing books by those authors who have received a grant from the North Carolina Haiku Society." They publish flat-spined paperbacks of, or about, haiku only. The sample book I have seen is attractively printed on white stock with line drawings, shiny card cover with b/w art work, priced at $6.95 plus $1.50 postage and handling.

NORTH DAKOTA QUARTERLY (II), Box 8237, University of North Dakota, Grand Forks ND 58202, phone (701)777-3323, FAX 701-777-3650, founded 1910, poetry editor Jay Meek, a literary quarterly published by the University of North Dakota Press that includes material in the arts and humanities — essays, fiction, interviews, poems, and visual art. "We want to see poetry that reflects an understanding **not only of the difficulties of the craft, but of the vitality and tact that each poem calls into play.**" Poets recently published include Stephen Dunn, Elton Glaser and Alane Rollings. As a sample, the editor selected lines from "Analgesic Balm" by William Kloefkorn:

> *Or was it atomic balm?*
> *Applied too liberally, as the trainer did*
> *after the hit I incurred against Kiowa,*
> *it explodes the skin, fires its way*
> *all the way to the bone . . . .*

The issue I have of *North Dakota Quarterly* is 6 × 9″, 261 pp. flat-spined, professionally designed and printed with b/w artwork on the white matte card cover and b/w photographs inside. Circulation of the journal is 700, of which 500 are subscriptions and 200 go to libraries, 100 are newsstand sales. Price per issue is $5, subscription $15/year. **Sample available for $5 postpaid. Pay is 2 copies and a year's subscription. No simultaneous submissions. Reporting time is 4-6 weeks and** time to publication varies. The press does not usually publish chapbooks, but "we will consider."

UNIVERSITY OF NORTH TEXAS PRESS; TEXAS POET SERIES (IV-Regional), P.O. Box 13856, Denton TX 76203, phone (817)565-2142, series editor Richard Sale, has recently published work by these Texas poets: Naomi Nye, William Davis, R. S. Gwynn, and Jan Seale. As a sample the editor selected these lines by Walt McDonald:

> *Fishing in hardscrabble, a man keeps his tackle*
> *handy, ready to rise up and walk on water.*
> *Rattlesnakes there are bad,*
> *sneaking up behind and shaking like gourds*
> *of holy rollers in tent meetings, half the congregation*
> *   speaking in tongues and quaking, some picking up snakes*
> *and writing, on fire in the spirit, ignoring*
> *us boys outside and laughing.*

Books in the series average 120-128 pp. **Query with sample poems, bio, and list of publications. Simultaneous submissions OK. Reports on queries or MSS in 8-10 weeks. Pays 10% of net sales in royalties plus 5 copies.** To buy samples, request the Texas A&M University Press catalogue, Drawer C, College Station, TX 77843.

‡NORTHEAST ARTS MAGAZINE; BOSTON ARTS ORGANIZATION, INC. (II), P.O. Box 6061 J.F.K. Station, Boston MA 02114, founded 1990, editor/president Mr. Leigh Donaldson, is a quarterly using **poetry that is "honest, clear, with a love of expression through simple language, under 30 lines. No airy, pompous dribble."** They have recently published poetry by Sandy Macebuh, Martina Umbach, K. Carlson and Joseph Bathanti. As a sample the editor selected these lines from "Ray Seabeck Shows Slides of Haiti in New Hampshire" by Robert J. Begiebing (from their first issue, which featured New Hampshire poets):

> *On the concrete floor*
> *a slab of cardboard stained*
> *by someone's dying.*
> *Street drain a clotted*
> *mucous of paper and sewage.*

It is digest-sized, 32 or more pp. professionally printed with matte 1-color card cover. They accept 20-25% of submissions. Press run 500-750 for 150 subscribers of which half are libraries, 50 to arts organizations. Subscription $8. **Sample postpaid: $3.50. Send SASE for guidelines. Pays 2 copies. Reports in 1-2 months.** "A short bio is helpful."

NORTHEAST JOURNAL (II, IV-Regional), P.O. Box 2321, Providence RI 02906, phone (401)785-0553, founded 1969, editors Dennis Holt and Dawne Anderson, is a literary annual published by The Poetry Mission, a nonprofit literary arts organization. The journal is **"open to conventional-experimental poetry."** They have recently published poetry by John Grey and Janet Gray. As a sample the editors selected these lines from "The Surface and Depths of Southern Friendship" by Janet McCann:

> *I wait, Alice poised*
> *   on the giant chair, an obedient child.*
> *Men in brown suits discuss the Kuwait War*
> *   and problems with their software. I don't*
> *snicker.*

The purpose of *NJ* is "to encourage local (state and area) writers while remaining open to

Close-up

Leigh Donaldson
Editor/Publisher
NorthEastARTS

Fire-House
The silent group sits in front of a building
made of brick and mortar
that houses red, childlike trucks.

They smoke half-lit cigarettes as they wait
for the shriek of catastrophe
That springs them into sudden life.

We all sit numbly outside the structures of our lives
waiting for a pillar to fall
because, we believe, only then,
will we know
why we sat and waited.

The clarity and directness of that poem seem to me to grow out of the life of a man who refuses to be baffled by words or the paradoxes of experience. His parents were "both educators in schools and colleges," and the books in Leigh Donaldson's home were mostly textbooks, so he spent a good deal of his youth reading novels and comic books in libraries. "I leaned toward English classes in grammar school. In high school I became editor of the school newspaper. I believe that is where the seed was first planted to become a publisher."

He majored in journalism and political science at the University of Michigan, wrote for the college newspaper and began writing poetry "because so much around me seemed so odd. By *odd*, I mean divided and peculiar. For example, I couldn't, or perhaps refused to, understand why there was so much conflict between white and black students. I was trapped in the middle most of the time because I had friends of every nationality and race, so when I was challenged to take sides for one over the other, I was left speechless. Poetry was my out."

After graduation he attended Georgetown University Law School for a year, but he quit in 1979. He felt the administration was trying to force him to write in the manner of their in-house publications. "Legal terms," he says, "must be used a certain way, usually to cloud truth, and my inner spirit couldn't tolerate that." He moved to New York City and began working at any job that provided some writing experience, "including direct mail, advertising copy, radio jingles; you name it." He took graduate courses in English and comparative literature at Columbia. "That's when poetry took over my head. I studied every poet from W.B. Yeats to Sylvia Plath; Allen Ginsberg to Langston Hughes."

Weary of New York congestion he moved to Los Angeles in 1984, where he found a job in the sun, if no particular peace. A couple of years later he moved to Boston thinking of resuming law school, but instead "landed a job as permissions editor at Houghton Mifflin"—which strikes me as a neat way to use law to get into literature. "That was an eye-opening experience from a publishing standpoint, and when I left, I had all the determination I needed to start a publication."

On a grant from the National Press Foundation he began working on a book about the history of the Afro-American press. "When I wasn't in the libraries, I was walking up and down the Boston streets to arts organizations and corporations, hustling grant funding" for a magazine. With the advice of a friendly attorney, and after studying the records of arts organizations on microfiche, he was able to write his own application for incorporation, and, five years later, obtain nonprofit status for his Boston Arts Organization (another use of his legal study) on "thirty bucks and a prayer."

After years of work he and friends have been able to get their quarterly magazine, *NorthEastARTS*, underway. "Some might ask why an Afro-American poet would start a publication open to everyone. My response is: 'Why ask?' I believe in creative expression, from whomever's voice it springs." He considers the magazine "adventuresome. We don't *care* about money or literary prestige. How could we, when our goal is to find artists from every corner of the world? I believe there is an 'artist in us all.' Contributors should send well-crafted work to us, and it will always have a chance of publication."

Meanwhile, Leigh's own poetry and prose have appeared in publications such as *Poetry South, Obsidian II, Colorlines Magazine* and *Manhattan Poetry Review*. He has completed several collections of poems as well as theater and screen plays.

—*Judson Jerome*

---

national submissions." It is a digest-sized, flat-spined, 100 pp. format, typeset, with glossy card cover, circulation 500, with 200 subscriptions of which 100 are libraries. **Sample: $5 postpaid. Pays 1 copy. Reports in 3-6 months.** Reviews books of poetry.

NORTHEASTERN UNIVERSITY PRESS; SAMUEL FRENCH MORSE POETRY PRIZE (III), Northeastern University, 360 Huntington Ave., Boston MA 02115. The Samuel French Morse Poetry Prize, % Prof. Guy Rotella, Editor, Morse Poetry Prize, English Dept., 406 Holmes, Northeastern University, Boston, MA 02115, for book publication (MS 50-70 pp.) by Northeastern University Press and an **award of $500,** entry fee $10. Deadline of August 1 for inquiries, September 15 for single copy of MS. MS will not be returned. Open to U.S. poets who have published no more than 1 book of poetry.

‡**NORTHERN PERSPECTIVE (II),** Northern Territory University, P.O. Box 40146, Casuarina NT Australia 0811, founded 1977, managing editor Dr. Lyn Riddett, appears twice a year. This liberal arts journal is magazine-sized, 115-125 pp., using a full-color cover, professionally printed. Press run 750 for 250 subscribers of which 20 are libraries, 300 shelf sales. **Sample postpaid: $7.50 AUD. Pays minimum of $20 AUD/poem. Reports** "hopefully within 10 weeks." **Submit in March and September. Editor often comments on rejections.**

THE NORTHERN REVIEW (II, IV-Themes), Academic Achievement Center, University of Wisconsin, Stevens Point WI 54481, phone (715)346-3568, founded 1987, managing editor Richard Behm, wants **"quality literary poetry"** that appeals to an intelligent, general readership. They have recently published poetry by Donald Murray, William Kluefkorn, Laurel Mills and Colette Inez. As a sample, the editor selected these lines from "Northern Cardinal, December" by Rhoda Carroll:

> . . . *He cocks*
> *his head right, left,*
> *right, left, then dares*
> *a black seed. Against*
> *a snowscape of relentless*
> *white and black branches*
> *scraping shapes out of monochrome*
> *his red body is a heart,*
> *defiant.*

TNR, appearing spring and fall, is 8½ × 11", 48-64 pp., saddle-stapled, professionally printed on glossy stock, using b/w graphics and ads, circulation 1,000. **Sample: $4 postpaid. Send SASE for guidelines. Pays 2 copies. Reports in 4-6 weeks. No simultaneous submissions. Photocopy, dot-matrix OK. Editor sometimes comments on rejections.** He says, "We often have theme issues, and it would benefit poets interested to subscribe to our journal or to write to inquire about specific editorial needs."

NORTHWEST REVIEW (II), 369 PLC, University of Oregon, Eugene OR 97403, phone (503)686-3957, founded 1957, poetry editor John Witte, is "seeking excellence in whatever form we can find it" and uses **"all types" of poetry.** They have recently published poetry by Alan Dugan, Olga Broumas, William Stafford and Richard Eberhart. The 6 × 9″ flat-spined magazine appears 3 times a year, uses 25-40 pp. of poetry in each issue, circulation 1,300, with 1,200 subscriptions of which half are libraries. They receive 3,500 submissions per year, use 4%, have a 0-4 month backlog. **Sample: $3 postpaid. Submit 6-8 poems clearly reproduced. No simultaneous submissions. Reports in 8-10 weeks, pays 3 copies. Send SASE for guidelines.** The editor comments **"whenever possible"** on rejections.

NORTHWOODS PRESS; DAN RIVER PRESS; CONSERVATORY OF AMERICAN LETTERS NEWSLETTER (C.A.L.) (II), P.O. Box 88, Thomaston ME 04861, phone (207)354-6550, founded 1972, C.A.L. (Conservatory of American Letters) founded 1986. "Northwoods Press is designed for the excellent *working poet* who has a following which is likely to create sales of $2,000 or more. Without at least that much of a following and at least that level of sales, no book can be published. Request 15-point poetry program. **Northwoods Press will pay a minimum of $250 advance on contracting a book."** C.A.L. is a nonprofit tax exempt literary/educational foundation; Harley Fetzer edits their newsletter. Four anthologies of poetry and prose are published each year. **There is a $1 reading fee for each submission to their anthologies, which goes to readers, not to the publisher. Poets are paid $5/page on acceptance, shorter poems pro-rata page rate. Payment is advance against 10% royalties on all sales we can attribute to the influence of the author."** Robert Olmsted regards his efforts as an attempt to face reality and provide a sensible royalty-contract means of publishing many books. He says, **"If you are at the stage of considering book publications, have a large number of poems in print in respected magazines, perhaps previous book publication, and are confident that you have a sufficient following to insure very modest sales, send 8½ × 11″ SASE (3 oz. postage) for 'descriptions of the Northwoods Poetry Program and C.A.L."** His advice is **"Poetry must be non-trite, non-didactic. It must never bounce. Rhyme, if used at all, should be subtle. One phrase should tune the ear in preparation for the next. They should flow and create an emotional response."** Query with cover letter dealing with publication credits and marketing ideas. Submit **"entire MS as desired for final book form."** No simultaneous submissions, generally no previously published poems. Pays 10% royalties. Bob Olmsted **"rarely"** comments on rejections, but he offers commentary for a fee. Query. Membership in C.A.L. is $24 a year, **however, membership is not required.** Members receive a quarterly newsletter plus 10% discount on all books and have many services available to them. C.A.L. sponsors an annual writers' conference with no tuition, only a $10 registration fee. Dan River Press, which publishes books of prose, also publishes an annual **Dan River Anthology,** using short fiction and **poetry. Pays $5/page on acceptance.**

W. W. NORTON & COMPANY, INC. (III), 500 Fifth Ave., New York NY 10110, phone (212)354-5500, founded 1925, poetry editor Jill Bialosky. W. W. Norton is a well known commercial trade publishing house that publishes only original work in both hardcover and paperback. They want **"quality literary poetry"** but no **"light or inspirational verse."** They have recently published books by Ellen Bryant Voigt, Rosanna Warren, Melissa Green, Michael Burkard, James Lasdun, Charlie Smith, Rita Dove, Norman Dubie and Eavan Bolann. W. W. Norton publishes two books of poetry each year with an average page count of 64. The samples I have are flat-spined paperbacks, attractively printed (one has b/w illustrations), with two-color glossy card covers; they are priced at $9.95. **Freelance submissions are accepted, but authors should query first, sending credits and 15 sample poems plus bio.** Norton will consider only poets whose work has been published in quality literary magazines. They report on queries in 2-3 weeks and MSS in 16 weeks. Simultaneous submissions will be considered if the editor is notified, and photocopied MSS are OK. Royalties are 10%, but there are no advances. Catalog is free on request. Criticism of rejected MSS is sometimes given.

NOSTALGIA: A SENTIMENTAL STATE OF MIND (I), Box 2224, Orangeburg, SC 29116, founded 1986, poetry editor Connie Lakey Martin, appears spring and fall using **"nostalgic poetry, style open, prefer *non* rhyme, but occasional rhyme OK, relatively short poems, never longer than one page, no profanity, no ballads."** As a sample the editor selected these lines of her own:

> *Locked away, but unrestrained*
> *and limitless — little fuzzy, fragile flashbacks,*
> *figured forgotten.*
> *Forming without warning*
> *whether I am still*
> *or stirring —*

Nostalgia is digest-sized, 20 pp. saddle-stapled, offset typescript, with matte card cover. Its press run is 1,000. Subscription: $5. **Sample: $2.50 postpaid. "Most poems selected from Contest." Guidelines available for SASE.** There are contests in each issue with award of $100 and publication for outstanding poem, publication and 1-year subscription for Honorable Mentions. Entry fee $2.50 reserves future edition, covers 3 entries. Deadlines: June 30 and December 31 each year. **No simultaneous submissions or previously published poems.** Connie Martin says, "I offer criticism to most rejected poems and feature a poet each edition as 'Poet of the Season.' " Reviews books of poetry.

NOTEBOOK/CUADERNO: A LITERARY JOURNAL; ESOTERICA PRESS (I, IV-Ethnic, bilingual, subscription), P.O. Box 170, Barstow CA 92312-0170, press established 1983, magazine 1985, editor Ms. Yoly Zentella. Esoterica is a small-press literary publisher. *Notebook* is an annual journal. "*Notebook* reflects the ethno-cultural diversity of the Americas. **Particularly interested in Latino-American, Native American, Black, Asian and Muslim Arab American writing. Will accept Spanish. Themes based on culture, history and literature welcome. No frivolities, explicit sex, obscenities.**" Recently published poets include Aisha-Eshe, Antonia Pigno, Koryne Ortega and Arthur W. Knight. As a sample, the editor chose these lines by Real Faucher:

> The festival is over.
> Disorderly conduct
> on the subway,
> the slapping of a conga drum
> too loud,
> an illegal guanguanco

Notebook is digest-sized, 100 pp. perfect-bound, offset from typeset copy, with b/w illustrations inside and one-color matte card cover. Circulation is 150, subscription $12/year. **Guidelines available for SASE, pays 1 copy, subscriptions are required upon acceptance of work. Sample can be obtained from editor. The editor wants MSS "typewritten and proofread with name and current address on top of the page. No limit in number of poems or length. Solicits unpublished work. Will not consider simultaneous submissions but will consider previously published with name of previous publisher for credit. Address all submissions with bio and SASE of appropriate size to editor."** She reports on submissions in 8-16 weeks. Reviews books of poetry. Esoterica Press has published several chapbooks and now publishes paperback books as well. **She will accept MSS for chapbooks and book publication. Queries will be answered in 6 weeks and MSS accepted or rejected in 8-16 weeks; no simultaneous submissions. Original copy or photocopy OK. Pay for chapbooks is 1 copy;** for book publication expenses paid first, profits shared 60%-40% (author, publisher). The editor says, "We are very interested in publishing and promoting poets that represent the present state of the Americas."

‡NOVA SF (IV-Science fiction), 3 Ashfield Close, Bishops Cleeve, Cheltenham, Gloucester, England GL52 4LG, founded 1990, editor/publisher Adrian Hodges, is a quarterly using **"science fiction and fantasy in its widest sense, any length. No cliched stereotyped space opera and swords and sorcery."** They have recently published poetry by Andy Darlington. As a sample the editor selected these lines from "Extra Vehicular Activity" by John Francis Haines:

> Tonight the vandals have been out again,
> Risking their lives to daub their tribal signs
> Across the airlock doors; scooting around . . .

It is digest-sized, 40+ pp., saddle-stapled, professionally printed with glossy paper cover. Press run 300 for 63 subscribers. Subscription: £4/ 4 issues. **Sample postpaid: £1.25 ($4 US). Send SASE for guidelines. Reports immediately. Pays 1 copy. Submit at least 4 poems for "Featured Poet" section.**

NOW AND THEN (IV-Regional, themes), Box 19180A, ETSU, Johnson City TN 37614-0002, phone (615)929-5348, founded 1984, poetry editor Jo Carson, a regional magazine that deals with Appalachian issues and culture. **The editor does not want any poetry not related to the region. Issues have themes**—previous issues have focused on Appalachian veterans, working Cherokees, blacks, children and rural life. Themes for issues coming up: media, new Appalachian writing, Scottish-Appalachian connection, sports and recreation. **"No haiku or sentimental, nostalgic, romantic, religious poems."** They have published poems by Jim Wayne Miller and George Ella Lyon. As a sample the editor selected these lines from "The Real Volunteers" by Colleen Andersen:

> "You're part of the problem,
> and if that's the case, you might as well see
> the ones who are solving this mess we have
> made."
> Saying goodbye at the Saginaw airport,
> my parents in Sunday polyester:
> "We love you, you'll never finish school."
> And a boy from New York City and I,
> and a married couple and two tall girls

were sent to West Virginia two weeks later
to join the real volunteers.

Now and Then appears three times a year, 40 pp., magazine-sized, saddle-stapled, professionally printed, with matte card cover. Its press run is 1,600-2,000 for 600 subscriptions of which 200 are libraries. Of 200 poems received they accept 6-10 an issue. Subscription: $9. **Sample: $3.50 postpaid. Guidelines available for SASE. Pays 2 copies plus subscription. Submit up to 5 poems, "include 'contributors notes.' " Reports in 3-4 months. They will consider simultaneous submissions but "not usually"** previously published poems. Reviews books of poetry.

NRG; SKYDOG PRESS (V), 6735 SE 78th, Portland OR 97206, founded 1975, poetry editor Dan Raphael. **"NRG is going dormant. Not reading any manuscripts until 1993." In order to have a book published by Skydog Press you have to be invited."**

NUTSHELL (I, II), 8 George Marston Rd., Binley, Coventry CV3 2HH U.K., founded 1988, editor Tom Roberts, is a quarterly using poetry **"all subjects considered, any length. Nothing hateful, pornographic, badly assembled."** They have recently published poetry by Amryl Johnson, Ian MacDonald, Avril Redman, Kenneth Pobo and Carol Lee Saffiotti. As a sample the editor selected these lines from "Nutshell (for Roger & Jeff)" by Gillian Ewing:

> ... *There's not a walnut tree in half a mile*
> *But sheer determination brought it here;*
> *Grey and effacing two soft paws picked it out*
> *From all the tendered harvest one small hoard,*
> *Piled it in triumph on the whitened leaves,*
> *Crowned the achievement with this offering.*

I have not seen an issue, but the editor describes it as "A5 size, stapled, card cover, 64 pp." They accept about 10% of some 500 poems submitted per year. Press run 200 for 130 subscribers. **Sample, postpaid: £2.50. Pays £1.50, extra copy, or reduced rate subscription. Editor comments on submissions when requested.**

THE OAK (I); THE ACORN (I, IV-Children), 1530 7th St., Rock Island IL 61201, phone (309)788-3980, poetry editor Betty Mowery. *The Oak*, (formerly *Writer's Newsletter*) founded 1991, is a "newsletter for writers with short articles, poetry, fiction (no more than 500 words), and writers conferences." They want poetry **"no more than 32 lines. No restrictions as to types and style but no pornography."** Only one page is devoted to poems. *The Oak* appears 6 times a year. They take more than half of about a hundred poems received each year. Press run is 100, with 10 going to libraries. Subscription: $6. **Sample: $1. Pays 1 copy. Simultaneous submissions and previously published poems OK. Reports in 1 week.** *The Acorn* is a "newsletter for young authors and teachers or anyone else interested in our young authors. **Takes only MSS from kids K-12th grades.** Takes also articles and fiction, no more than 500 words." It appears 6/year and **"we take well over half of submitted MSS."** Press run 100, with 6 going to libraries. Subscription: $6. **Sample postpaid: $1. Pays 1 copy. Young authors, submitting to** *The Acorn*, **should either put age or grade on manuscripts. Simultaneous submissions and previously published poems OK. Reports in 1 week.** Editor Betty Mowery advises, "Beginning poets should submit again as quickly as possible if rejected. Study the market: don't submit blind. Always include a SASE or rejected manuscripts will not be returned."

OASIS BOOKS; OASIS SERIES; OASIS MAGAZINE, 12 Stevenage Rd., London, England SW6 6ES. Declined listing.

OBLATES (IV-Religious, spirituality/inspirational), Missionary Association of Mary Immaculate, 15 S. 59th St., Belleville IL 62223-4694, phone (618)233-2238, editor Jacqueline Lowery Corn, is a magazine circulating free to 750,000 benefactors, **"We use well-written, perceptive traditional verse, average-16 lines. Avoid heavy allusions. Good rhyme and/or rhythm a must. We prefer a reverent, inspirational tone, but not overly 'sectarian and scriptural' in content."** They have recently published poetry by Helen Kitchell Evans, Hilda Sanderson, Claire Puneky, and Susan Showers. As a sample the editor selected these lines by Connie Brown:

> *Dainty, diamond droplets*
> *Held fast by limb and lawn;*
> *Liquid gems He scatters*
> *Beneath the brimming dawn.*

Oblates is digest-sized, 20 pp., saddle-stapled, using color inside and on the cover. **Sample and guidelines for SASE and 55¢ postage. Six back issues — $1.25. Pays $25 plus 3 copies. Reports within 4-6 weeks. Time to publication "is usually within 1 to 2 years." Editor comments "occasionally, but always when MS 'just missed or when a writer shows promise.' " Considers simultaneous submissions.** She says, "We are a small publication very open to MSS from authors—

beginners and professionals. We do, however, demand professional quality work. Poets need to study our publication, **and to send no more than one or two poems at a time. Content must be relevant to our older audience to inspire and motivate in a positive manner."**

O-BLEK (OBLIQUE) (III), Box 1242, Stockbridge MA 01262, founded 1987, poetry editors Peter Gizzi and Connell McGrath, appears each April and November, a "journal of language arts" publishing a range of contemporary writing with an emphasis on poetry. **"We do not limit ourselves to any particular poetic; our foremost criterion is excellence. We are particularly interested in new alternative forms and styles. Poems may be of any length."** They have recently published poetry by Edmond Jabès, Barbara Guest, Michael Palmer, Charles Simic, Leslie Scalapino, Keith Waldrop, Rosmarie Waldrop, Fanny Gowe and Clark Coolidge. As a sample the editors selected these lines from "The Risingdale" by Michael Gizzi:

> *Men in the minds of their women*
> *Slickrock in a slot canyon. Even a morgue's got rules*
> *Cremated fore we sold 'em on the sound*
> *Musician diaphanous*

The issue of **o-blek** I have seen is digest-sized, 160-200 pp., flat-spined, professionally printed, with glossy, full-color cover. They have 250 subscriptions of which 30 are libraries. Subscription: $10. **Sample: $6 postpaid. Guidelines available for SASE. They do not consider simultaneous submissions or previously published poems. Reports in 4 months. "The editors strongly recommend that writers interested in submitting work to this journal read a copy *before* sending work. An average of one unsolicited manuscript is accepted per issue."**

OBSIDIAN II: BLACK LITERATURE IN REVIEW (IV-Ethnic), Box 8105, North Carolina State Univ., Raleigh NC 27695-8105, phone (919)737-3870, founded 1975, editor Gerald Barrax, appears three times a year "for the study and cultivation of creative works in English **by Black writers worldwide,** with scholarly critical studies by all writers on Black literature." They are **open as to subject-matter but want poetry (as well as fiction and drama) from Black writers only.** I have not seen an issue, but the editor describes it as 126 pp., 6×9″, press run of 700 for 500 subscriptions of which an eighth are libraries. Subscription: $12; single issue: $5. **Sample: $11 postpaid. Send SASE for guidelines. Pays 2 copies. Submit double-spaced MS on 8½×11″ paper. Reports in 3-4 months.**

‡OCCIDENT MAGAZINE; OCCIDENT PRESS; OCCIDENT POETRY COMPETITION; BERKELEY PO-ETRY PRIZE BOOK CONTEST (II), 700 Eshelman Hall, U. of CA, Berkeley CA 94720, founded 1868, editor P. Michael Campbell, a small press publisher of books (poetry, stories, prose) and an annual magazine, *Occident*. They want **"good poetry of any sort."** They have recently published poetry by Robert Pinsky, Thom Gunn, Michael Palmer, Charles Bernstein, August Kleinzahler, Charles Simic, Brenda Hillman, Susan Howe, Leslie Scalapino and Lyn Hejinign. As a sample, I selected these sample lines from "Rattling the Food Chain" by Leonard Nathan:

> *And someday, yes, the lion shall eat straw*
> *like the ox, but shall also catch in the wolf's eye*
> *and certain red glitter even here*
> *among the lambs, among God's plenty*

The magazine is 300 pp., 6×10″, flat-spined, professionally printed with glossy card cover. Press run 750-1,000. **Sample: $3.50 postpaid. Pays 1 copy. They prefer no simultaneous submissions. Previously poems accepted, but "depends on where they were published." Reports in 3-12 mo.** They publish 2 poetry chapbooks/year. Their annual contest has prizes of $75, $50, $25, and publication in the magazine. Deadline in April. Fee: $2/poem. Send SASE for information about the Berkeley Poetry Prize Book Contest.

THE OHIO REVIEW (II); OHIO REVIEW BOOKS (V,II), Ellis Hall, Ohio University, Athens OH 45701-2979, phone (614)593-1900, founded 1959, editor Wayne Dodd, attempts "to publish the best in contemporary poetry, fiction and reviews" in the *Review* and in chapbooks, flat-spined paperbacks and hardback books. They use **"all types"** of poetry and have recently published poems by William Stafford, Hayden Carruth, Deborah Boe, Joan Campbell, Gayle Roby, Campbell McGrath and Bin Ramke, from whose work the editor selected these sample lines:

> *Not even abstraction can save us,*
> *but the abstract endures, like her body*
> *slick across the page, the woman*
> *glistening photographically*
> *like any given convert, any born-again*
> *to sex or salvation, the more furious*
> *forms of knowledge.*

The *Review* appears 3 times a year in a professionally printed, flat-spined, 140+ pp. format, matte cover with color and art, circulation 2,000, featuring about 18 poets per issue. Subscription: $12; per copy: $4.25. They receive about 3,000 freelance submissions per year, use 1% of them, and have a 6-12 month backlog. **Sample: $4.25 postpaid. Reports in 1 month. Pays $1/line for poems and $5/page for prose plus copies. Editor sometimes comments on rejections. Send SASE for guidelines. Do not submit poetry MSS during June, July or August.** Reviews books of poetry. **They are not at present accepting freelance submissions of book MSS. Query with publication credits, bio.**

OHIO STATE UNIVERSITY PRESS/JOURNAL AWARD IN POETRY (II), 180 Pressey Hall, 1070 Carmack Rd., Columbus OH 43210-1002, poetry editor David Citino. Each year *The Journal* (see that listing) selects for publication by Ohio State University Press for the Ohio State University Press/Journal Award **one full-length (at least 48 pp.) book MS submitted during September, typed, double-spaced, $12.50 handling fee (payable to OSU). Clear photocopies OK.** Send SASE for return of MS; self-addressed, stamped postcard for notification of MS receipt. **Some or all of the poems in the collection may have appeared in periodicals, chapbooks or anthologies, but must be identified. Along with publication** *The Journal* **Award in Poetry pays a $1,000 cash prize from the Helen Hoover Santmyer Fund "in addition to the usual royalties." Each entrant receives a subscription (2 issues) to** *The Journal.*

OLD HICKORY REVIEW (I), Box 1178, Jackson TN 38302, phone (901)422-5832, founded 1969, president Jeff Woods, is a "literary semi-annual, 2 short stories and approximately 75-80 poems each issue. **No more than 24-30 lines, any form, any subject, no obscenities, no pornographic.** We publish poets from Maine to California. We are adding lyrics and hope to publish three publications during the 1991-1992 year." It is digest-sized, 120+ pp., professionally printed with matte card cover, about 300 press run for that many subscribers of which 15 are libraries. Subscription: $8/year for two; if three, $12. **Sample: $3.50 postpaid. Guidelines available for SASE. Pays 1 copy/poem.**

THE OLD RED KIMONO (I, II), P.O. Box 1864, Rome GA 30163, phone (404)295-6312, founded 1972, poetry editors Ken Anderson and Jon Hershey, a publication of the Humanities Division of Floyd College, has the "sole purpose of putting out a magazine of original, high-quality poetry and fiction. *ORK* **is looking for submissions of 3-5 short poems. "Poems should be very concise and imagistic. Nothing sentimental or didactic."** They have published poetry by Walter McDonald, Peter Huggins, Kim Thomas, Dev Hathaway, John C. Morrison and Mark R. McCulloh. The magazine is an annual, circulation 1,200, 7½ × 10½", 64 pp., professionally printed on heavy stock with b/w graphics, colored matte cover with art, using approximately 40 pp. of poetry (usually several poems to the page). They receive 1,000 submissions per year, use 60-70. **Sample $2 with 9 × 12" SASE. Reading period Sept. 1-March 1. Reports in 3 months. Pays copies.**

‡**THE OLIVE PRESS PUBLICATIONS (V)**, Box 99, Los Olivos CA 93441, phone (805)688-2445, founded 1979, editor Lynne Norris, is a general small press publisher for whom "poetry is incidental effort at this time. We specialize in local and family history."

‡**ONE & ONLY (IV-Themes)**, P.O. Box 35351, Station E, Vancouver, British Columbia V6M 4G2 Canada, founded 1989, publisher Pamela A. Miller, is a newsletter appearing 6/year using **poems about parenting. "Prefer upbeat, light-hearted or reflective. 160 words or 20 lines maximum."** It is 4-6 pp., press run 500 for 250 subscribers of which 3 are libraries. Subscription: $17.50/year. **Sample postpaid: $1.50. Reports in 1 month. Previously published poems and simultaneous submissions OK. Pays $10/poem plus up to 10 copies.** They use fewer than 6 poems/year.

ONIONHEAD; ARTS ON THE PARK, INC. (THE LAKELAND CENTER FOR CREATIVE ARTS); WORD-ART, THE FLORIDA POETS COMPETITION; ESMÉ BRADBERRY PRIZE (II), 115 N. Kentucky Ave., Lakeland FL 33801, phone (813)680-2787. Arts on the Park founded 1979; *Onionhead* founded 1988. *Onionhead* is a literary quarterly. **"Our focus is on provocative political, social and cultural observations and hypotheses. Controversial material is encouraged. International submissions are welcome. We have no taboos, but provocation is secondary to literary excellence. No light verse please."** They have recently published poetry by Jessica Freeman, Arthur Knight, Lyn Lifshin, B.Z. Niditch and A.D. Winans. As a sample I selected the last of four stanzas of "Apart" by June Goodwin:

> I mull and rock, a by-and-by evasion
> and possession of a yearning that satisfies and
> pains, ripping off the leaves, leaving
> boney limbs to claw across the space.
> Here where your absence makes love more imagined
> I drape myself like wings to try, as if
> distance, like apartheid, were only attitude.

The magazine is digest-sized, 40-50 pp., photocopied from typescript with glossy card cover.

Their press run is 250. Complimentary distribution to universities, reviews and libraries world-wide. They use 100 of 2,500 submissions received per year. Subscription: $8 U.S., $16 other. **Sample: $3 postpaid. Pays 1 copy. Poet's name and title of poems should appear on the upper right-hand corner of each page. Poem "should be submitted exactly as you intend it to appear if selected for publication." Editor comments on rejections "rarely."** Poems are reviewed by an Editorial Board and **submissions are reported on within two months. If accepted, poems will normally appear within one year.** WORDART, The Florida Poets Competition, established 1983, is now open to all American authors. Cash awards, "including the prestigious Esmé Bradberry Prize, are announced at a reading and reception during the first part of March." $8 reading fee. For guidelines and specific dates send SASE to the sponsoring organization, Arts on the Park, Inc., at the above address.

‡ONTARIO REVIEW (III); ONTARIO REVIEW PRESS (V), 9 Honey Brook Dr., Princeton NJ 08540, founded 1974. The *Ontario Review* appears twice a year. They have recently published poetry by William Heyen, Alice Ostriker, Albert Goldbarth and Jana Harris. *OR* 112 pp., 6×9″ offset, flat-spined. Press run 1,200 for 650 subscribers of which 450 are libraries. 150 shelf sales. Subscription $10. **Sample postpaid: $4.95. Reports in 4 weeks. Pays $10/printed page + 3 copies. Ontario Review Press is not considering new poetry MSS now. They publish 1-2 hardbacks and that many paperbacks/year, paying 10% royalties plus 10 copies.**

ONTHEBUS; BOMBSHELTER PRESS (II), 6421 ½ Orange St., Los Angeles CA 90048, founded 1975. *Onthebus* editor Jack Grapes. Bombshelter Press poetry editors Jack Grapes and Michael Andrews. *Onthebus* uses "contemporary mainstream poetry—no more than 6 poems (10 pp. total) at a time. No rhymed, 19th Century traditional 'verse.'" They have published poetry by Charles Bukowski, Lyn Lifshin, Ai, Norman Dubie, Kate Braverman, Stephen Dobyns, Allen Ginsberg, David Mura, Richard Jones, and Ernesto Cardenal. As a sample I selected these lines that conclude "The Point of Departure" by Doraine:

> *How terrifying to have no where to go.*
> *To have only this present*
> *to unwrap.*

Simultaneous submissions and previously published poems OK, "if I am informed where poem has previously appeared and/or where poem is also being submitted. I prefer cover letters with list of poems included plus poet's bio." Onthebus is a magazine appearing 2/year, 200 pp. offset, flat-spined, with color card cover. Press run 2,500 for 400 subscribers of which 20 are libraries, 700 shelf sales ("300 sold directly at readings"). Subscription: $24 for 3 issues; Issue #6/7, special double issue: $15. **Sample: $9 postpaid. Send SASE for guidelines. Do not submit MSS between Nov. 1 and Jan. 1 or June 1 and Aug. 1. Submissions sent during those times will be returned unread. Pays 1 copy. No comments on rejections. Reports in "up to 16 weeks."** Bombshelter Press publishes 4-6 flat-spined paperbacks and 5 chapbooks per year. **Query first. Primarily Los Angeles poets. "We publish very few unsolicited MSS." Reports in 3 months. Pays 50 copies.** As a sample the editors selected these lines by editor Jack Grapes from his book **Trees, Coffee and the Eyes of the Deer:**

> *VOWS:*
> *We're going to get married*
> *and have kids*
> *and live together*
> *and be bloody*

Jack Grapes advises, "Read the publication you are submitting to *first*. Send poems *neatly* typed. Sloppiness and cramped and excessively folded pages are not cute, signs of eccentric genius, but unprofessional and make my job of reading poems harder. Buy or subscribe to publications you care about or they will die."

OPEN HAND PUBLISHING INC. (V), Box 22048, Seattle WA 98122, phone (206)323-3868, founded 1981, publisher P. Anna Johnson, is a "literary/political book publisher" bringing out flat-spined paperbacks. They have recently published **Puerto Rican Writers at Home in the USA,** "an anthology of seventeen of the most well known Puerto Rican writers." **They do not consider unsolicited MSS.**

‡ORACLE POETRY; ASSOCIATION OF AFRICAN WRITERS; RISING STAR PUBLISHERS (I, IV-Ethnic/ Membership), P.O. Box 3883, Langley Park, Hayattsville MD 20783, phone (301)422-2665, founded 1989, editorial director Obi Harrison Ekwonna. *Oracle Poetry* and *Oracle Story* appear quarterly using work **"mainly of African orientation; must be probing, and must have meaning—any style or form. Writers must have the language of discourse and good punctuation. No gay, lesbian or erotic poetry."** As a sample, "Nostalgia" by Harrison Obi Ekwonna:

> *I feel you my mother.*
> *Though the distance is far, but*
> *I can still feel your inspiring breath.*
> *No matter the distance, the nature and*
> *Nurture that bind us are strong and*
> > *inseparable.*
> *In life and death, our bound must*
> *be one and strong.*

Membership in the Association of African Writers is $20/year. I have not seen an issue (unpublished at time of listing), but the editor describes it as magazine-sized, saddle-stapled, print run 500. Subscription, $12/year. **Pays copies. Reports in 4-6 weeks.** Reviews books of poetry. The editor says, "Read widely, write well and punctuate right."

ORBIS: AN INTERNATIONAL QUARTERLY OF POETRY AND PROSE(II), 199 The Long Shoot, Nuneaton, Warwickshire CV11 6JQ, England, founded 1968, editor Mike Shields, considers **"all poetry so long as it's genuine in feeling and well executed of its type."** They have published poetry by Sir John Betjeman, Ray Bradbury, George Mackay Brown, Christopher Fry, Seamus Heaney, Thomas Kinsella, James Kirkup, Norman MacCaig, Naomi Mitchison, President Jose Sarney of Brazil and R.S. Thomas, "but are just as likely to publish absolute unknowns." As a sample the editor selected the closing lines of "Stop at the Bridge" by Georgia Tiffany (Spokane, USA):

> *Frost crawls along the hoods of cars.*
> *The clock tower climbs out of the fog.*
> *Threaded across the once intimate blaze*
> *a web of ice.*
> *the enviable rage of spiders.*

The quarterly is 6 × 8½", flat-spined, 64 pp. professionally printed with glossy card cover, circulation 1,000 with 600 subscriptions of which 50 are libraries. Subscription: £14 ($30); per copy: £3.50 ($7.50). They receive "thousands" of submissions per year, use "about 5%." **Sample: $2 (or £1) postpaid. Submit typed or photocopied, 1 side only, one poem per sheet. No bio, no query. Enclose IRCs for reply, not U.S. postage. Reports in 1-2 months. Pays $10 per acceptance plus 1 free copy automatically. Each issue carries £50 in prizes paid on basis of reader votes. Editor comments on rejections "occasionally—if we think we can help.** *Orbis* is completely independent and receives no grant-aid from anywhere."

ORE (II, IV-Themes), 7 The Towers, Stevenage, Hertfordshire, SG1 1HE England, founded 1955, editor E.H. Ratcliffe, a magazine that appears 2-3 times per year. They want **"folk, legend, Celtic, Arthurian, fairy, spiritual, religious. No nasty dirty words. Too much materialism. No pop poetry."** They have recently published poetry by Jan Ramsay and Manumet Toms. As a sample the editor selected these lines (poet unidentified):

> *Ashurnasipal worships the sun-god Shamash*
> *in front of the Sacred Tree*
> *priest of Ashur*
> *beloved of Anu and Dagan*
> *son of Tukulti-Ninurta.*

They receive about 1,000 poems/year, accept 5%. **Sample: £1.60 or 6 IRCs. Pays 1 copy, others at half price. Simultaneous submissions OK. Editor "always" comments—"no curt rejection slips."** He advises: "1. Realize what your type of interest is and your educational and expression limits. 2. Read lots of poetry consistent with 1. Dwell internally on imagery, etc. 3. Write poetry when something comes in the head—don't intend to write first. 4. Put it away for a week and rewrite it."

‡ORIEL BOOKSHOP (IV-Regional), The Friary, Cardiff, Wales, UK, CF2 SAT, phone 0222-395548, founded 1974, head of bookshop Peter Finch, publishes **Anglo-Welsh poetry, nothing else.** They have recently published poetry by Dylan Thomas, T. Harri Jones and R.S. Thomas. As a sample the editor selected these lines from Dannie Abse's "Return to Cardiff":

> *No sooner than I'd arrived the other Cardiff had gone,*
> *smoke in the memory, these but tinned resemblances,*
> *where the boy I was not and the man I am not*

met, hesitated, left double footsteps, then walked on.
That poem is printed on a handsomely printed, large color poster.

ORPHIC LUTE (II, IV-Form), 526 Paul Pl., Los Alamos NM 87544, founded 1950, editor Patricia Doherty Hinnebusch, is 5½×8½", 40 pp. quarterly (photocopied from typescript, saddle-stapled, matte card cover) which used **"only short poems during 1991. Focus on sequences of haiku, senryu, lanternes, and cinquains. Light verse forms welcome also, and free verse 11 lines and under. No pornography."** They have recently published haiku by H.F. Noyes, Matthew Louviere, Jane Andrew and Marian Olson. The editor selected these sample lines by Matthew Louviére:
> Moonlit beach
> a single wave
> pleats the wind

The magazine has a circulation of 250, 200 subscriptions of which 6 are libraries. Subscription: $10; per copy: $2.50. They receive about 4,000 submissions per year, use 300, have a 2-3 month backlog. "I publish seasonal poetry in season; other poems ASAP. I work on 2 issues at a time." **Sample: $2.50 postpaid; subscription is $10/year. Submit 6-10 poems; no simultaneous submissions, no query; no unclear type or light photocopies. Reports in 8-12 weeks. Payment is one copy. Send SASE for guidelines. "Whenever asked, we critique submissions. We frequently make minor revisions a condition of acceptance."** The editor advises, "Every poem is a working poem. The poet can make improvements in successive revisions over many years. If it is worth saying, it is worth saying well."

ORTALDA & ASSOCIATES (V), 1208 Delaware St., Berkeley CA 94702, phone (415)524-2040, FAX (415)527-3411, founded 1985, poetry editor Floyd Salas, director/editor Claire Ortalda, publishes quality flat-spined paperbacks of poetry but **is not accepting submissions at this time.** They have published poetry by Czeslaw Milosz, Robert Hass, Ishamel Reed, Gary Soto, Jack Micheline, and Carolyn Kizer. As a sample Claire Ortalda selected these lines from "He Will Bleed Me Down to Serum for his Veins" by their poetry editor Floyd Salas:
> There is no honor among theives
> He will bleed me down to serum for his veins
> and pop me into his arm
> He will sell me to the fence . . .

The editors offer criticisms at $25 an hour. They advise: "It is your own integrity that matters. Honesty is transforming."

OSIRIS, AN INTERNATIONAL POETRY JOURNAL/UNE REVUE INTERNATIONALE (II, IV-Translations, bilingual), P.O. Box 297, Deerfield MA 01342, founded 1972, poetry editor Andrea Moorhead, a 6×9", saddle-stapled, 40 pp. semiannual **publishes contemporary poetry in English, French and Spanish without translations and in other languages with translation, including Polish, Danish and Italian.** They also publish graphics and photographs. They want poetry which is **"lyrical, non-narrative, multi-temporal, well crafted."** They have recently published poetry by Loss Glazier, Simon Perchik, Helene Dorion (Quebec), Robert Marteau (France), Gyula Illyes (Hungary), and Owen Davis (England). The editors selected these sample lines (poet unidentified):
> Aachen and Sinsheim, under the shadow of a thin tall steeple
> when the noon sun is low and warm
> and we have walked along the banks of a river in Aachen
> copper in light and full of grace

There are 10-14 pp. of poetry in English in each issue. They have a print run of 500, send 40 subscription copies to college and university libraries, including foreign libraries. Subscription: $8; per copy: $4. They receive 50-75 freelance submissions per year, use 12. **Sample: $1 postpaid. Include short bio with submission. Reports in 4 weeks. Pays 5 copies.** The editor advises, "It is always best to look at a sample copy of a journal before submitting work, and when you do submit work, do it often and do not get discouraged. Try to read poetry and support other writers."

THE OTHER SIDE MAGAZINE (II, IV-Political, religious, social issues), 1225 Dandridge St., Fredericksburg VA 22402, phone (703)371-7416, founded 1965, poetry editor Rod Jellema, is a "magazine (published 6 times a year) concerned with **social justice issues from a Christian perspective. The magazine publishes 1-2 poems per issue. We will consider no more than 4 poems at one time from the same author. Submissions should be of high quality and must speak to and/or reflect the concerns and life experiences of the magazine's readers. We look for fresh insights and creative imagery in a tight, cohesive whole. Be warned that only 0.5% of the poems reviewed are accepted. Seldom does any published poem exceed 40-50 lines. Do not want to see pious religiosity, sentimental schlock, haiku."** They have recently published poetry by Eric Ormsby, Elisabeth Murawski, Nola Garrett, and Gail

White; the editors selected these lines as a sample (poet unidentified):

> On our knees we see under
> the dark side of things,
> playgrounds everywhere
> wait to grind skin
> and we must rise bleeding,
> healing ourselves again.

The Other Side is magazine-sized, professionally printed on quality pulp stock, 64 pp., saddle-stapled, with full-color paper cover, circulation 13,000 to that many subscriptions. Subscription: $29.50. **Sample: $4.50 postpaid. Send SASE for guidelines (material pertaining to poetry is quoted above). Pays $15 plus 4 copies and free subscription. No simultaneous submissions.** Previously published poems rarely used. Editor "sometimes" comments on rejections.

‡OTTER (IV-Regional), Parford Cottage, Chagford, Devon U.K. TL13 8JR, founded 1988, editor Christopher Southgate, appears 3/year **using poetry by contributors associated with the County of Devon, "poems concerned with local community and with issues—social, political, religious. Like: poems in strict forms."** They have recently published poetry by Lawrence Sail, Ron Tamplin, Harry Guest and Jane Beeson. As a sample, I selected these lines from "The Yellow and Green Daughter" by Sandra McBain:

> She dances like a daffodil
> or wind driven forsythia
> like a petal whirled in water

It is digest-sized, 48 pp. flat-spined, with glossy card cover, professionally printed. They accept about 25% of 400-500 poems/year. Press run 300 for 70 subscribers of which 5 are libraries. Subscription: £5. **Sample postpaid: £2 (or $5 US; dollar checks OK). Reports within 3 months. Pays £2/poem plus 1 copy. "Those not resident in Devon should indicate their connection with the county."** Editor always comments on rejections.

OUR FAMILY (IV-Religious), Box 249, Battleford, Saskatchewan, S0M 0E0, Canada, phone (306)937-7771, FAX (306)937-7644, founded 1949, editor, Nestor Gregoire, o.m.i., is a monthly religious magazine **for Roman Catholic families. "Any form is acceptable. In content we look for simplicity and vividness of imagery. The subject matter should center on the human struggle to live out one's relationship with the God of the Bible in the context of our modern world. We do not want to see science fiction poetry, metaphysical speculation poetry, or anything that demeans or belittles the spirit of human beings or degrades the image of God in him/her as it is described in the Bible."** They have published poetry by Nadene Murphy and Arthur Stilwell. The editor selected these sample lines from "I Asked" by Jean Woodward Larson:

> I asked to be more open
> to receiving love;
> I was made more open
> in giving it.

Our Family is magazine-sized, 40 pp., glossy color paper cover, using drawings, cartoons, two-color ink, circulation 13,500 of which 48 are libraries. $1.95 per issue, subscription $15.98 Canada/$21.98 US. **Sample: $2.50 postpaid. Send SASE with IRC or personal check (American postage cannot be used in Canada) for writer's guidelines. Will consider poems of 4-30 lines. Pays 75¢-$1 per line. Reports within 30 days after receipt. Simultaneous submissions OK, prefers letter-quality to dot-matrix.** The editor advises, "The essence of poetry is imagery. The form is less important. Really good poets use both effectively."

OUT LOUD: THE MONTHLY OF LOS ANGELES AREA POETRY EVENTS (IV-Regional), 1350 Third St. Promenade, Santa Monica CA 90401, founded 1989, editor Carrie Etter, "is distributed at poetry venues throughout the Los Angeles area: performance spaces, theaters, bookstores, etc." and **accepts poetry from poets living in Los Angeles or Orange County, up to 40 lines. No "sentimental work or work that demonstrates that the writer is not an avid reader of modern poetry."** Previously published poetry OK if cover letter indicates when and where it was published. "Otherwise cover letters are not necessary." Subscription: $6/year. Format is an 11×17" sheet, printed and folded in half, "high quality." Circulation 2,000, all copies distributed free except subscriber copies. **Sample postpaid: 75¢. Pays 2 copies "unless poet requests more. Responses are made within a month."**

OUT MAGAZINE (I, IV-Gay), #5-359 Davenport Rd., Toronto, Ontario M5R 1K5 Canada, phone (416)921-1496, founded 1986, editor Shawn Venasse, poetry editor Brian Day, is a literary magazine appearing 6 times/year, celebrating all that it means and all that it can mean to be gay and male through interviews, essays, short stories, poetry, drawings, photographs and more." They use **"strong, imagistic, passionate, free verse, intelligent, challenging, aware" poetry, not that which is "inane,** rhyming, sophomoric." *Out* is tabloid size, press run "6,000+ and growing. In a slow year we receive 100 pieces and use about 20." It is distributed free. Subscription: $15. **Sample: $1 postpaid (or just postage). Deadlines are the 15th of: December, February, April, June, August and October. Reports in 3-6 weeks. Pays 5-10 copies "depending on size."** They prefer covering letter and bio with submissions. Reviews books of poetry. The editor says, "Poems are chosen by an intuitive gut response upon first reading—if they don't leap off the page we don't publish them. Be original and daring—avoid clichés at all cost and know your market."

OUTERBRIDGE (II), English A323, The College of Staten Island, 715 Ocean Terrace, Staten Island NY 10301, phone (718)390-7654, founded 1975, editor Charlotte Alexander, publishes "the most crafted, professional poetry and short fiction we can find (unsolicited except special features—to date rural, urban and Southern, promoted in standard newsletters such as *Poets & Writers, AWP, Small Press Review*), interested in newer voices. **Anti loose, amateurish, uncrafted poems showing little awareness of the long-established fundamentals of verse; also anti blatant PRO-movement writing when it sacrifices craft for protest and message. Poems usually 1-4 pp. in length."** They have recently published poetry by P. B. Newman, Cathryn Hankla, Marilyn Throne, and Candida Lawrence. The editors selected these sample lines from "Discovering Musicians" by Sharyn November:

> *They understand operations better than surgeons,*
> *how the sharpness of hair against cat-gut*
> *cuts more cleanly than a scalpel.*
> *Pasteboard and velvet cases cushion their unstrung*
> *cellos, basses, instruments whose scroll-work*
> *coils into a bass clef.*

The digest-sized flat-spined, 100+ pp. annual is about half poetry, circulation 500-600, 150 subscriptions of which 28 are libraries. They receive 500-700 submissions per year, use about 60. **Sample: $4 postpaid. Submit 3-5 poems anytime except June-July. "We dislike simultaneous submissions and if a poem accepted by us proves to have already been accepted elsewhere, a poet will be blacklisted as there are many good poets waiting in line." Reports in 2 months, pays 2 copies (and offers additional copies at half price).** The editor says, "As a poet/editor I feel magazines like *Outerbridge* provide an invaluable publication outlet for individual poets (particularly since publishing a book of poetry, respectably, is extremely difficult these days). As in all of the arts, poetry—its traditions, conventions and variations, experiments—should be studied. One current 'trend' I detect is a lot of mutual backscratching which can result in very loose, amateurish writing. Discipline!"

‡OUTREACH FOR ELDERLY HOUSEBOUND AND DISABLED (IV-Senior citizens, specialized: disabled, religious), Grayson Close, Stocksbridge, Sheffield S30 5BJ, South Yorks, England, editor J. Kirby, founded 1980, is a monthly newsletter using **"short religious, semi-religious poetry. This is a magazine for elderly housebound and disabled who need cheering up not made more depressed or bored!"** It is photocopied from typescript on ordinary paper, folded and saddle-stapled. As a sample, I selected these lines from "Stairs to God" by Helen S. Rice:

> *Prayers are the stairs*
> *We must climb every day,*
> *If we would reach God*
> *There is no other way.*

‡OUTRIDER PRESS (I, IV-Women), Suite C-3, 1004 E. Steger Rd., Crete IL 60417, founded 1988, president Phyllis Nelson, publishes 1-2 chapbooks/year. They want **"poetry dealing with the terrain of the human heart and plotting inner journeys; growth and grace under pressure. No bag ladies, loves-that-never-were, please."** As a sample the editor selected these lines from "Elegy" in **Listen to the Moon** by Whitney Scott:

> *He slipped*
> *Away,*
> *Gently as the rustle of silk*
> *He so favored in his shirts.*

That chapbook is digest-sized, 16 pp., photocopied from typescript with matte card cover, $4. **Responds to queries in 3 months, to submissions in 6 months. Pay negotiable.**

THE OVERLOOK PRESS; TUSK BOOKS (V), 149 Wooster St., New York NY 10012, phone (212)477-7162, founded 1972, are trade publishers with about 8 poetry titles. They have published books of poetry by David Shapiro and Paul Auster. The editors selected these sample lines from "Mannequins" by Daniel Mark Epstein:

> *This indecent procession of the undead invades*
> *the Avenue windows, dressed to kill, sporting*

tomorrow's clothes and yesterday's faces.
Tusk/Overlook Books are distributed by Viking/Penguin. **They publish on standard royalty contracts with author's copies. Query before submitting.**

‡OWENS PUBLICATIONS; THE WRITER'S HAVEN; KID'S KORNER!; OPEN DIARY POETRY FORUM; EMOTIONS POETRY NEWSLETTER (I, IV-Themes, romance, children), (formerly Writer's Haven), P.O. Box 413, Joaquin TX 75954, founded 1990, editor Marcella Owens. *TWH* is bimonthly with articles on writing, poetry and market listings, using **"poetry 20-25 lines max. No certain style or subject-matter."** Owens Publications also publishes *ODPF*, also bimonthly, using **poetry up to 16 lines about the writing life;** *Kid's Korner*, a monthly 3-4 pp. newsletter **"for kids, by kids,"** 10 **lines max.;** and *Emotions*, a bimonthly **newsletter using "romantic-type poetry"** 16-20 lines, no erotica. **Sample postpaid: $2/each for *WH, OD, Emotions;* $1 for *KK*.** *KK* has monthly contests with cash prizes. Reviews books of poetry.

‡OXALIS; STONE RIDGE POETRY SOCIETY ANNUAL POETRY CONTEST; DAY OF THE POET (II), Box 3993, Kingston NY 12401, founded contest 1983, *Oxalis* 1988, a literary quarterly. **"We are generally open as to form and subject matter. Usually would not take over 50 lines per poem. No gratuitous sex, violence, ugh types."** They have recently published poetry by Robert Cooperman and Emilie Glen. As a sample I selected the complete poem, "Mortuary" by Mildred Barker:

> *Outside the mortuary*
> *a hearse parked at the curb, engine running*
> *spreads carbon monoxide on the living*
> *while inside a metal coffin*
> *the corpse lies protected from fumes.*

Oxalis is magazine-sized, 40+ pp., saddle-stapled, desktop publishing with matte card cover using some b/w art. Their press run is 300 with 70 subscriptions of which 15 are libraries. They receive about 700 poems a year, use 120. Subscription: $18 for 4 issues, $14 for members of Stone Ridge Poetry Society. Single copies $5. **Sample: $4 postpaid. Send SASE for guidelines and contest rules. Pays 2 copies. Submit double-spaced with cover letter. "We return unread anything that comes without adequate postage. Please send SASE for our reply even if you don't want your poems returned."** Reviews books of poetry. Stone Ridge Poetry Society sponsors weekly poetry readings March-September. They seldom pay readers. They co-sponsor, with *Home Planet News* (a literary tabloid based in Brooklyn), an annual Day of the Poet in early October, at Ulster County Community College, which features a poetry reading contest, open readings, a book fair, music and refreshments. They have a paid featured poet for that event, and the $5 entry fees for poets participating in the contest are used for winners' prizes (as well as benefit for *Oxalis* and *Home Planet News*). SRPS also sponsors an annual poetry contest.

‡OXFORD MAGAZINE (II), 276 Bachelor Hall, Miami University, Oxford OH 45056, phone (513)529-7357, founded 1984, appears twice a year. **"We are open in terms of form, content, length and subject-matter."** They have published poetry by David Ignatow and Diane Wakoski. As a sample I selected these lines from "Burning the Fields" by C.L. Rawlins:

> *Between the grass and rolling flame, a pact;*
> *the farmers with their torches: custom, wisdom, lore.*
> *The fierce green rises blind above the black.*
> *Dry orchard prunings blaze in bony stacks*
> *at equinox, the land bare of snow and poor.*
> *Between the grass and rolling flame, a pact.*

It is a 6×9", 80-100 pp., flat-spined, professionally printed with matte card cover, press run 500. **Sample: $5 postpaid. "We accept submissions from September 1 until May 1 only."** No **simultaneous submissions or previously published poems. Reports in 8-10 weeks. Pays 1 copy and small honorarium.**

OXFORD UNIVERSITY PRESS (V), 200 Madison Ave., New York NY 10016, phone (212)679-7300, founded 1478, poetry editor Jacqueline Simms (U.K.), is a large university press publishing academic, trade and college books in a wide variety of fields. **Not accepting any poetry MSS.** "Our list includes Conrad Aiken, Richard Eberhart, Robert Graves, Geoffrey Hill, Peter Porter, M.L. Rosenthal, Stephen Spender, Anne Stevenson and Charles Tomlinson. These indicate our direction."

OYEZ REVIEW (II), 430 S. Michigan Ave., Chicago IL 60605, phone (312)341-2017, founded 1965, editor Angela Lewis. An annual literary magazine published by Roosevelt University. They have published poetry by Lisel Mueller, John Jacob, and Barry Silesky. "*Oyez Review* is in its 26th year of publication and is an award-winning publication which has maintained its high level of excellence by encouraging submissions from serious writers and artists." The digest-sized review is flat-spined, about

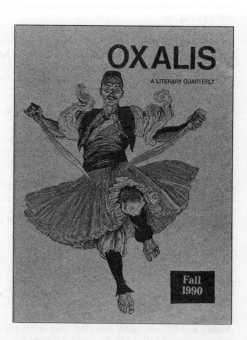

OXALIS
A LITERARY QUARTERLY

Fall
1990

"Many of our covers come from the public domain and are chosen to go with featured poems," says Oxalis editor Shirley Powell. "The dancing figure on this cover was chosen to go with B.D. Love's poem 'Kingdom Come' because it has the same spirit," she says. Assistant editor Mildred Barker, a 75-year-old writer, finds the cover illustrations and also makes collages to go with some of the work inside. This illustration is from the book Men: A Pictorial Archive from Nineteenth-Century Sources (Dover).

100 pp., using b/w photography and line drawings, poetry and fiction, has glossy, color card cover. Circulation 500. It is sold at Roosevelt University events and bookstores in Chicago and throughout the nation. Sample copies are $4. Guidelines available for SASE. **Pays 3 copies. Reports in 10-12 weeks. Deadline in October or November. Published in spring.**

PABLO LENNIS (IV-Science fiction, fantasy), 30 N. 19th St., Lafayette IN 47904, founded 1976, editor John Thiel, appears irregularly, is a **"science-fiction and fantasy fanzine preferring poems of an expressive cosmic consciousness or full magical approach. I want poetry that rimes and scans and I like a good rhythmic structure appropriate to the subject. Shorter poems are much preferred. I want them to exalt the mind, imagination, or perception into a consciousness of the subject. Optimism is usually preferred, and English language perfection eminently preferable. Nothing that is not science fiction or fantasy, or which contains morbid sentiments, or is perverse, or does not rime, or contains slang."** They have recently published poetry by Lorraine A. Donfor, Christian Amsler, Gary Baker and Alana Lucci. As a sample the editor selected these lines from "Wargames Players" by Gerald Zenger:

> Meeseemeth that his mâge is féy
> Who standeth in the tower;
> I see by his fell countenance
> He cannot hold an hour—
> The curmudgeons are put to rout
> For they have not the power.
> And last, who reads these words of wit
> Shall succumb in a grand mâl fit.

It is magazine-sized, 30 pp. side-stapled, photocopied from typescript, with matte card cover, using fantastic ink drawings and hand-lettering. "I get maybe fifty poems a year and have been using most of them." Press run "up to 100 copies." Subscription: $10/year. **Sample, postpaid: $1. Pays 1 copy, 2 if requested. Reports "at once. I generally say something about why it was not used, if it was not. If someone else might like it, I mention an address."** Reviews books of poetry if they are science fiction or fantasy. The editor says, "Poetry if well-written can elate the reader, and it adds magic to existence. I hope poets will remember good poetic form and keep in mind the qualities poetry can have when writing poems; they have a definite positive effect upon the culture."

PAINTBRUSH: A JOURNAL OF POETRY, TRANSLATIONS, AND LETTERS (III), Dept. of Language & Literature, Northeast Missouri S.U., Kirksville MO 63501, founded 1974, editor Ben Bennani. *Paintbrush* is a 6×9", 64+ pp. literary biannual, circulation 500, which uses **quality poetry. Sample: $5. Send SASE with inquiries and request for samples. No submissions June, July and August.** Reviews books of poetry.

PAINTED BRIDE QUARTERLY (II), 230 Vine St., Philadelphia PA 19106, phone (215)925-9914, editors Lee W. Potts and Teresa Leo, founded 1973, **"We have no specifications or restrictions. We'll look at anything."** They have recently published poetry by Robert Bly, Charles Bukowski, S.J. Marks and James Hazen. The editors selected these sample lines from a poem by Etheridge Knight:

> *Grand leaps and the girl-giggles. We*
> *are touch-tender in our fears.*
> *You break my eyes with your beauty.*
> *Oouu-ou-baby . . .I love you.*

"PBQ aims to be a leader among little magazines published by and for independent poets and writers nationally." The 80 pp. perfect-bound, digest-sized magazine uses 40+ pages of poetry per issue, receiving over a thousand submissions per year and using under 150. Neatly printed, it has a circulation of 1,000; 850 subscriptions, of which 40 are libraries. $5 per copy, $16 for subscription, **sample: $5** postpaid. *Quarterly* deadlines: ongoing. **Submit no more than 6 poems, any length, typed, photocopies OK, only original, unpublished work. Payment 1-year subscription and half-priced contributor's copies.** "Submissions should include a *short* bio." Editors seldom comment on rejections. They have a 6-9 month backlog. Reviews books of poetry.

‡PAINTED HILLS REVIEW (II,IV-Regional), P.O. Box 494, Davis CA 95617-0494, phone (916)756-5987, founded 1990, editors Michael Ishii and Kara Kosmatka, is a quarterly using **"well-crafted poetry. Poems must sustain themselves. Rather than abstractly generalizing, make a poem detailed and real — full of 'real' people and 'real' situations. Nothing abstract, general, sloppy and unsustained, trite, 'greeting-card' verse, no philosophy or religion (i.e., dogmatism and didactic). Special interest in poetry of West Coast."** Recent contributors include William Stafford, Ingrid Wendt, Walter Pavlich, Lisa M. Steinman, Robert R. Ward and James Sallis. *PHR* is 48 pp., digest-sized, professionally printed and typeset, saddle-stapled, with matte card cover, all on recycled paper. Press run 250-300. Subscription: $10. **Sample: $3 postpaid. Pays 1-2 copies. $15 for best-of-issue. Send no more than 8 poems at a time, no more than 100 lines/poem. Reports in 4-6 weeks.** Reviews books of poetry. Sponsors "Paintbrush Award in Poetry," yearly contest. Deadline is May 20. Send SASE for info. Winners win cash prize and are published in *PHR*. The editors advise, "Read other poets; revise and revise again; keep trying."

‡PAISLEY MOON (I, II), Box 2373, Santa Cruz CA 95063, founded 1990, publisher and editor Michael Spring. *PM* is a quarterly magazine. **"Prefers poems around 35 lines or less, but will consider longer poems if exceptional. Open to all forms/style, even haiku! Editor prefers strong imagery, rich language, and explorative verse, original twists in vision and metaphor. No didactic, greeting-cardish, cliche-ridden verse."** They have recently published poetry by Joyce Odam, Antler, Wm. Everson, Martha F. Bosworth, Helen B. Glass, Donald McLeod and Jane Blue. As a sample the editor selected these lines from "The Triggering" by Dianna Henning:

> *Opening the door, there in the dark, eyes, all the eyes*
> *of the dead peered out. "But really mom," my daughter said,*
> *"it's just knots in the wood." Yes, it's just knots;*
> *all that stuff that collects, rounds out, grows hard.*

PM is digest-sized, 32-40 pp., photocopied from typescript on ordinary paper with matte card cover (with art). Press run 300. They accept about 15% of 1,000 poems received. Subscription: $9. **Sample: $2.50 postpaid. Pays 1 copy. Will consider previously published poems and simultaneous submissions. Reports in 1-4 months.** They sponsor an annual contest. All poems in contest are considered for publication. Winners are featured in winter issue. Prizes of $50, $25, $15, 5 honorable mentions; fee $1/poem, limit 35 lines. Deadline October 31. The editor advises, "Read past and present masters (critically); read everything you can on poetry; read enough to know what is and isn't a cliche. Write and rewrite often. Be patient and persistent with your craft and vision."

PALANQUIN; PALANQUIN POETRY SERIES (II), 9 Kerry Place, Flanders NJ 07836, phone (201)927-5751, founded 1989, editor Phebe Davidson. The Palanquin Poetry Series has **an issue every 2 months consisting of 3 columns of poetry showcasing a single poet, professionally printed on a folded card.** Press run: 100 for 50 subscribers. Subscription: $12.50. **Sample, postpaid: $2. Pays one-half press run.** She wants **no "sentimental, religious, clotted academic" poetry.** They have recently published poetry by Jean Hollander, Joe Weil and Patricia Celley Groth. As a sample the editor selected these lines from "Harp" by Lois Harrod:

> This gentle plucking of all my strings now,
> these ferns like green fingers when
> I walk the road, these vines like wild serpents
> tongues like threads, this thrush nagging me

"I read January-March for the following year." No previously published poems. Reports in 2 months. Annual fall chapbook contest for spring publication.

PANCAKE PRESS (V), 163 Galewood Circle, San Francisco CA 94131, phone (415)665-9215, founded 1974, publisher Patrick Smith, a small-press publisher of hand-bound paperbacks with sewn signatures. "Current projects are selected. At present we can consider only solicited mss for publication. Unsolicited mss will be returned with brief comment and thanks." The editor publishes "poetry aware of its own language conventions, tuned to both the ear and eye, attentive to syntax, honest about its desires, clear about something, spoken or written as a member of the species." He has recently published books by John Logan, David Ray, and Stephen Dunning. As a sample, he selected the following lines by an unidentified poet:

> words hard as stone that can fall down
> a mountain and not change but we are not
>
> made for such a plunge spirits such as
> we who breathe air and drink water thrive
>
> on what takes shape every moment i cant
> say this except in words dont keep them

The two thin chapbooks I have seen are handsomely printed on fine paper; one has b/w illustrations. Covers are either matte or glossy cards, and one is illustrated with a drawing of the author. Pancake Press publishes 2-3 chapbooks each year, with an average page count of 36, flat-spined.

PANDORA; PANDORA'S ALL YOUTH ISSUE (I, IV-Science fiction/fantasy, children/teen), 2844 Grayson, Ferndale MI 48220. Send poetry to Ruth Berman, 2809 Drew Ave. S., Minneapolis, MN 55416, founded 1978, editor Meg Mac Donald, poetry editor Ruth Berman, appears 2 times yearly (hoping to return to quarterly in 1992), using 12-15 poems in each issue of "science fiction, fantasy, offbeat, any form. No horror! Long poems must be of extremely high quality. Most of what we purchase is under 30 lines. No poems unrelated to the themes of our magazine." They have recently published poetry by Sandra Lindow, Melanie A. Rawls, W. Gregory Stewart, and D.A. Bach. As a sample these lines are from "three steps" by Roger E. Moore:

> will i lay down in the
> wet long grass of heaven, to
> breathe the loam and sleep
> under the blue forever?

It is digest-sized, 72 pp., offset, on white stock with glossy card stock cover in b/w and 1 additional color, perfect bound, using b/w graphics and ads, circulation 1,000, including some libraries, newsstand and bookstore sales. Subscription: $10 for 2 issues (U.S.); $15 for 2 issues (Canada); $20 for 2 issues. Sample: $5 postpaid (U.S.); $7 (Canada); $10 overseas. All payments must be made in U.S. funds. Send SASE for guidelines. Payment per poem averages $5 and 1 copy. "Please submit no more than 6 poems at once. Simultaneous submissions OK, but discouraged. Previously published poems used "rarely." Specify previous publisher. Reports in 8 weeks. Delay to publication 6-12 months. Editor comments on rejections. *Pandora's* All Youth issue accepts poetry by those in grades K-12 of the current year. Send SASE for guidelines, 1990-91 issue $4 postpaid. "Researching your market is probably the most valuable time you will spend as a poet. You've already spent precious time in the creation process; don't waste time and postage on blind submissions. Send for guidelines. Better yet, acquire a few issues of the magazine you are interested in submitting to. Spend some serious time scrutinizing the contents. Watch for trends, for changes in editorial tastes. Be careful not to send work that only repeats what you've seen recently. Trying to win the editor over with what you already know 'isn't quite right' is risky. When an editor can't use your work, take any comments to heart. Above all, don't be discouraged and never take rejection personally. Poetry is a very personal thing for many editors—it may not be the technical form that makes or breaks it, it may just be a gut reaction to that particular poem on that day. Take whatever clues you're given to improve your chances—or your poetry—in the future."

PANTHEON BOOKS INC., 201 E. 50th St., New York NY 10022. Declined listing.

THE PAPER BAG (I, II), Box 268805, Chicago IL 60626-8805, phone (312)285-7972 (an answering service), founded 1988, editor M. Brownstein, is a quarterly using poetry **"any kind, any style. We look for strong and original imagery."** As a sample, I selected this haiku by Mikael Larsson:

> Though snow is black
> With tossed-out seed, no birds come:
>   nightfalling

The Paper Bag is photocopied from typescript, 24 pp. digest-sized, saddle-stapled, with matte card cover. "Our circulation varies from 20-300+ and we sell out every issue." Subscription: $10/4-5 issues plus "anything else we publish." They publish about 30 of 200 poems received per issue. **Sample, postpaid: $2.50. Pays copies. Editor comments on submissions "always." They want a brief bio with each submission, typed MSS only, address and phone on each submission.** All checks or money orders should be made out to M. Brownstein. Reviews books of poetry in their broadside series. The editor says, "Be persistent. Because we reject one group of submissions does not mean we will reject another batch. Keep trying."

PAPER RADIO (IV-Form/style), P.O. Box 85302, Seattle WA 98145-1302, founded 1986, poetry editor N.S. Kvern, is a literary journal appearing 2 times a year. **"Actually what we want doesn't have a descriptive moniker because it is at the vanguard but not yet a movement. Suffice it to say, we are more in the line of descent from Wallace Stevens and the French dadaist and surrealists than from, say, W. C. Williams. Length: up to 100 lines. Style: from** *ambient* **to** *grand mal.* **Do not want to see mainstream theocratic bathos."** They have recently published poetry by Sheila E. Murphy, Bradley Goldman, Judson Crews and Stacey Sollfrey. As a sample the editor chose these lines (poet unidentified):

> credo a face with my hands like crabbark, a face framed
> in terraglia permanence an Art and my knabenhaftigkeit in
> the new words to tinct it out like old gaunt beckettfarces
> like astolfo-moons like symposia weeped off my feet

I have not seen a copy of *Paper Radio*, but the editor describes it as intended for "pointedly experimental poetry, fiction, graphics and criticism." It is digest-sized, "mixed printing (computer-generated, offset 8 or photocopy), generally ½ words and ½ graphics." They receive about 3,000 poems per year, accept 25-50. The circulation is 500+, 150+ subscriptions of which 10 are libraries. Subscription: $10. **Sample: $4 postpaid. Pays 1 copy.** "No specifications (we're anarchists) but more than 5-6 poems seems pointless or downright unstrategic (makes us feel Sisyphean)." **Best to submit mss in January and July. Simultaneous submissions OK. Reports in 1-2 months, 1-8 months delay till publication.** On rejections, **"we try to give some indication that a human read the work, but it depends on its quality and our workload.** Always remember Borges' comment: 'I write for myself and my friends, and to ease the passing of time.' Greed and mundane equivocation would seem, fortunately, to have no place in poetry—it's the useless utterance that is our greatest fulfillment." Reviews books of poetry "sometimes."

‡THE PAPER SALAd POETRY JOURNAL (II), 627 E. 100 S. #A, Salt Lake City UT 84102, founded 1990, editor Eldon Holt, is an annual using **"new and daring poetry, any poetry by a poet who takes his/her work seriously. Not poetry written just for writing a poem's sake rather than actually trying to say something. Sing-song and terribly obvious rhyme is also not appreciated."** As a sample the editor selected these lines by Richard Cronshey from "She Abandons Her Hands":

> Your body remembers the emptiness at the horizon of touches,
> the moment touch becomes nothing and you feel your own absence
> suddenly everywhere.
> And you are a city of rivers falling through the sky.
> And your fingers have the precise brightness of stars.

I have not seen an issue, but the editor describes it as 80 pp. flat-spined, digest-sized. Press run 200. **Sample: $5 postpaid. Pays 1 copy. Replies in 1 month, often comments on rejections.** The editor says, "I think it's absolutely important for poets to be experimental because anything else is only mimicking, therefore dead."

PAPIER-MACHÉ PRESS (IV-Themes, anthologies), 795 Via Manzana, Watsonville CA 95076, phone (408)726-2933, FAX (408)726-1255, founded 1984, editor Sandra Martz, is a small-press publisher of anthologies, poetry and short fiction in flat-spined paperbacks and case-bound books. They typically **"work on specialized projects, that explore a particular aspect of women's experience, e.g. sports, aging, parental relationships, work, etc. Any length acceptable; primarily interested in well-written, accessible material."** They have recently published poetry by Jenny Joseph, Sue Saniel Elkind, Shirley Vogler Meister, Michael Andrews, Ursula Hegi, Maude Meehan and Elisavietta Ritchie. As a sample the editor selected these lines from "To Fish, to Remember" by Enid Shomer:

> Daddy is with me here on the pier

at Cedar Key. The fish strung by their gills,
the shower of water from the bait bucket
bring him back. Night fishing
from Biscayne Bridge. I'm six,
chewed by mosquitoes, sticky with cocoa butter.
They publish 1-2 anthologies and 1-2 poetry collections each year. Each anthology contains 30-40 poems; collections contain 60-80 poems. Query before submission to obtain current themes and guidelines. They report on queries in 4 weeks, on MS in 3 months. Legible photocopies and dot matrix OK. Simultaneous submissions must be identified as such. Pays 2 copies on work accepted for anthologies. Royalties and modest advances are negotiated on individual collections. Send SASE for booklist to buy samples, typically $4 to $10. *"Papier Mache*'s primary objective is to publish anthologies, poetry and short story collections by, for and about midlife and older women. Material from socially aware men is welcome. Our strategy is to select subjects of particular importance to women, find well-written, accessible material on those themes, develop attractive, high quality book formats and market them to an audience that might not otherwise buy books of poetry. We take particular pride in our reputation for dealing with our contributors in a caring, professional manner."

PARADISE EDUCATIONAL PARTNERSHIP; LOVING MORE (I, IV-Themes, erotica), (formerly Polyfidelitous Education Productions, Inc.), P.O. Box 6306, Captain Cook HI 96704-6306, founded 1984, editor Ryam Nearing. *Loving More* "publishes articles, letters, poems, drawings, reviews, related to polyfidelity, group marriage and multiple *intimacy*." They use "relatively short poems, though a quality piece of length would be considered, but topic relevance is essential. Please no swinger or porno pieces." Magazine-sized, 14 pp., few ads. Quarterly. Circulation 500. Subscription $25 a year. **Sample:** $2 to poets. Pays 1 copy. Responds "ASAP," delay to publication 2-6 months. MS should be "readable." Considers simultaneous submissions. Editor comments on rejections "sometimes—if requested."

‡PARAGON HOUSE PUBLISHERS (III), 90 5th Ave., New York NY 10011, phone (212)620-2820, founded 1983, editor-in-chief Ken Stuart, has published books of poetry by Louis Simpson and Leo Connellan.

‡PARANOIA PRESS; BACKDROP (II, IV-Regional), 35 Percy St., Middlesbrough, Cleveland TS1 4DD United Kingdom, founded 1984, poetry editor Richard Briddon, publishes 4-5 paperbacks per year. "We are inclined towards winners of the Cleveland Writearound festival for first collections of local writers. Contemporary mainstream poetry, but quality is the main thing." As a sample the editor selected these lines from Brian Burr's "Document," a poem in his collection **Fear of Language:**
I knew a man who would not name himself;
whose skull was clothed in thin cartography,
a document of flesh. A library
of bright tattoos, dreamt sentences, sprouted
from his skin—a coat of consonant and vowel.
Pays 7-10% royalties, honorarium of £50, and 6 copies. Their poets "will usually have published in a quality press previously—e.g. *Stand, London Magazine, Iron*, etc."

THE PARIS REVIEW; BERNARD F. CONNORS PRIZE; JOHN TRAIN HUMOR PRIZE (III, IV-Humor), 45-39 171st Pl., Flushing NY 11358, founded 1952, poetry editor Patricia Storace. (**Submissions should go to her at 541 E. 72nd St., New York, NY 10021**). This distinguished quarterly (circulation 10,000, digest-sized, 200 pp.) has published many of the major poets writing in English. Sample: $6.90. Study publication before submitting. Pays $35 to 24 lines, $50 to 59 lines; $75 to 99 lines; $150 thereafter. The Bernard F. Connors prize of $1,000 is awarded annually for the best previously unpublished long poem (over 200 lines), submitted between April 1 and May 1. The John Train Humor Prize of $1,500 is awarded annually for the best previously unpublished work of humorous fiction, nonfiction or poetry submitted before March 31. All submissions must be sent to the 541 E. 72nd St., New York, NY 10021 address.

PARNASSUS: POETRY IN REVIEW; POETRY IN REVIEW FOUNDATION (V), Rm 804, 41 Union Square W., New York NY 10003, phone (212)463-0889, founded 1972, poetry editor Herbert Leibowitz, provides "comprehensive and in-depth coverage of new books of poetry, including translations from foreign poetry." They have published special issues on Words & Music and Women & Poetry, and a special issue on the long poem in 1992. "We publish poems and translations on occasion, but we solicit all poetry. Poets invited to submit are given all the space they wish; the only stipulation is that the style be non-academic." Writers recently published include Alice Fulton, Eavan Boland, Ross Feld, Debora Greger, William Logan, Tess Gallagher, Seamus Heaney and Rodney Jones. They do consider unsolicited essays, but strongly recommend that writers study the magazine before submitting.

They report on essay submissions within 4-10 weeks (response takes longer during the summer), dislike multiple submissions and dot-matrix printing, and pay $25-250 plus 2 gift subscriptions—the contributors can also take one themselves. **Editor comments on rejections—from one paragraph to 2 pages.** Reviews books of poetry. Subscriptions are $18/year, $36/year for libraries; they have 1,100 subscribers, of which 550 are libraries. The editor comments, "Contributors should be urged to subscribe to at least one literary magazine. There is a pervasive ignorance of the cost of putting out a magazine and no sense of responsibility for supporting a magazine."

PARNASSUS LITERARY JOURNAL (I, IV-Humor), P.O. Box 1384, Forest Park GA 30051, founded 1975, edited by Denver Stull: "Our sole purpose is to promote poetry and to offer an outlet where poets may be heard." **One copy in payment.** This is an amiable, open magazine **emphasizing uplift.** It is photocopied from typescript, uses an occasional photo or drawing, 84 pp., saddle-stapled. Poets recently published include Eugene Botelho, Louis Daniel Brodsky, Rod Farmer, Ruth Wildes Schuler, Alice MacKenzie Swaim and Bernard Hewitt. As a sample the editor selected these lines from "Kokro" by George Gott:

> *The grass seldom complains*
> *of the mountain heights*
> *that keep the narrow village*
> *in its gorge,*
> *or of cherry blossoms scattered*
> *by the ineluctable wind:*
> *and tonight is no exception*

Denver Stull says, **"We are open to all poets and all forms of poetry, including Oriental. Prefer 24 lines and under but will take longer poetry if it is good. Do not see enough humor."** The magazine comes out three times a year with a print run of 300 copies. Subscribers presently number 200 (5 libraries). They receive about 1,500 submissions per year, of which they use 350. Circulation includes: Japan, England, Greece, India, Korea, Germany, and Nederlands. **Reports within one week. Sample: $3.50. (regularly $4.25 per copy, $12 per subscription). Make checks or money order payable to Denver Stull.** "Editor's Choice" award is given for one poem and one haiku each issue. Readers vote of best of the issue each issue. Also conducts a contest periodically. **"Definitely" comments on rejected MSS.** Reviews books of poetry by subscribers only. The editor advises: "Write about what you know. Study what you have written. Does it make sense? A poem should not leave the reader wondering what you are trying to say. Improve your writings by studying the work of others. Be professional."

PARTING GIFTS; MARCH STREET PRESS (I), 3006 Stonecutter Terrace, Greensboro NC 27405, founded 1987, poetry editor Robert Bixby. **"I want to see everything.** I'm a big fan of Jim Harrison, C. K. Williams, Amy Hempel and Janet Kauffman. If you write like them, you'll almost certainly be published. But that's pretty useless advice unless you're one of those people." He has recently published poetry by Eric Torgersen, Lyn Lifshin, Elizabeth Kerlikowske, Stuart Dybek and Russell Thorburn. As a sample I selected these lines from "Bed" by Katharyn Machan Aal:

> *A week ago I said goodbye*
> *and we pressed close in final*
> *coupling, mouth and mind and all*
> *our bodies knew to give.*

PG is digest-sized, 36 pp., photocopied, with colored matte card cover, press run 200, appearing twice a year, **send SASE for guidelines.** Subscription: $6. **Sample: $3 postpaid. Pays 2 copies.** "Best time to submit MSS is early in the year." Reports in 1-2 weeks. **Submit in "groups of 3-10 with SASE and cover letter." No previously published poems, but simultaneous submissions OK. March Street Press publishes chapbooks; $10 reading fee.**

PARTISAN REVIEW (III, IV-Translations, themes), 236 Bay State Rd., Boston MA 02215, phone (617)353-4260, founded 1934, editor William Phillips, is a distinguished quarterly literary journal (6×9", 160 pp., flat-spined, circulation 8,200 for 6,000 subscriptions and shelf sales), using **poetry of high quality.** They have recently published poetry by Joseph Brodsky, Eavan Boland, W.S. Merwin and C.H. Sisson. As a sample the editor chose these lines from "Daybreak" by Adam Zagajewski:

> *At daybreak, from the train window I see cities*
> *which sleep left deserted,*
> *open and defenseless like huge animals*
> *lying on their backs.*
> *Through the vast squares, only my thoughts*
> *and a cold wind are wandering . . . .*

Submit maximum of 6. Sample $5 plus $1 postage. Pays $50 and 50% discount on copies. No simultaneous submissions. Reports in 2 months. Editor "occasionally" comments on rejections.

"Our poetry section is very small and highly selective. We are open to fresh, quality translations but submissions must include poem in original language as well as translation. We occasionally have special poetry sections on specified themes."

PASQUE PETALS; SOUTH DAKOTA STATE POETRY SOCIETY, INC. (I, IV-Regional, subscribers), 909 E. 34th St., Sioux Falls SD 57105, phone (605)338-9156, founded 1926, editor Barbara Stevens. This is the official poetry magazine for the South Dakota State Poetry Society, Inc., but it is open to non-members. **Those not residents of SD are required to subscribe when (or before) submitting. They use "all forms. 44 line limit, 50 character lines. Count titles and spaces. Lean toward SD and Midwest themes. No rough language or porno—magazine goes into SD schools and libraries."** As a sample the editor chose "Kleptomaniac" by Emma Dimit:

> *Lady-like,/ my silver Gruen/ picks up time/ as if life/*
> *is not already/ stealing away/ too fast./ Cogs rackets/*
> *click tick/ fast faster/ shop lift/ sun lit moments/*
> *of my life.*

PP appears 10 times a year (no August or November issues), digest-sized, 16-20 pp., using small b/w sketches. Circulation is 250 to member/subscribers (16 to libraries). Subscription: $15/year. **Sample: $1.50 postpaid. Send SASE for guidelines. Pays non-members only 1 copy. Reports in 3 months. 2-3 month backlog. Submit 3 poems at a time, 1 poem (or 2 haiku) per page. Editor "always" comments on rejections.** $5 prize for the best poem in every issue. They sponsor one yearly contest—and sometimes smaller ones are offered by members.

PASSAGER: A JOURNAL OF REMEMBRANCE AND DISCOVERY (II, IV-Senior citizen), University of Baltimore, 1420 N. Charles St., Baltimore MD 21201-5779, phone (301)625-3041, founded 1989, editors Kendra Kopelke and Sally Darnowsky. *Passager* is published quarterly and publishes fiction, poetry, essays and interviews that give voice to human experience. **"We seek powerful images of remembrance and discovery from writers of all ages. One of our missions is to provide exposure for new older writers; another is to function as a literary community for writers across the country who are not connected to academic institutions or other organized groups."** The journal is 8×8″, 32 pp., printed on white linen, saddle-stitched. Includes photos of writers. **Poetry, 30 line maximum; fiction and essays, 3,000 words maximum. Pays one year's subscription. Reports in 8 weeks. Simultaneous submissions acceptable if notified. No reprints.**

‡PASSAGES NORTH (II), Kalamazoo College, 1200 Academy, Kalamazoo MI 49007, founded 1979, poetry editor Mark Cox, is a **semiannual tabloid** (i.e., white uncoated paper, folded, unstapled), though the quality of paper and printing are higher than that term implies. "The magazine not only publishes established writers, but also encourages students in writing programs. It fosters interchange between the Upper Midwest and other parts of the nation." They have recently published poetry by Jack Driscoll, Diane Wakoski, Tess Gallagher, Stuart Dybek and Grace Butcher. As a sample the editor selected these lines from "Sail Baby Sail" by Dan Gerber:

> *Now I sing to my mother, the lullabies she sang*
> *to me as a child. Her hand trembles to her mouth,*
> *as if to find the lips that once formed words, as*
> *if to move them again with her fingers into speech.*

PN is 24 pp., tabloid size, offset on quality white paper, using graphic arts and photography, limited ads, with a circulation of 2,500 for 1,000 subscriptions of which 12 are libraries; 1,000 copies distributed free as promo at conferences and colleges. Subscription: $5/year; $8/2 years. **Sample postpaid: $3. "Best time to submit: August-September; January-March." Send SASE for guidelines. Pays $10-20 per poem when grants permit plus 3 copies. Reports in 3 weeks to 3 months, delay to publication 6 months. Prefers groups of four, typed single-spaced, or clear copy. Simultaneous submissions only if informed at once of acceptance elsewhere.**

PASSAIC REVIEW (II), % Forstmann Library, 195 Gregory Ave., Passaic, NJ 07055, founded 1979, Richard Quatrone, poetry editor, has published **a number of our most notable poets, such as Allen Ginsberg and David Ignatow.** Here are some lines from "June 17, 1983" by Richard Quatrone:

> *These could be the lines of a dying man.*
> *Dying here in Passaic, in the fumes and poisons*
> *of modern greed and hatred, dying in the flesh*
> *of cynicism, caught within its grip with nowhere*
> *to go, with no one to listen, with only one hope*

It comes out twice a year in an offset, typescript, saddle-stapled, 48 pp. digest-sized format, with occasional artwork. The editor says he wants **"direct, intelligent, courageous, imaginative, free writing."** They print a thousand copies, have 75 subscriptions (20 libraries). Each issue is $3.75, subscription $6, **sample back-issue $2.75**, have a 4-6 month backlog and **report in 4-6 months. Pays 1 copy. Rarely comments.**

PATH PRESS, INC. (IV-Ethnic), 53 W. Jackson Blvd., Suite 724, Chicago IL 60604, phone (312)663-0167, FAX: (312)663-5318. founded 1969, president Bennett J. Johnson, executive vice president and poetry editor Herman C. Gilbert, a small publisher of books and poetry primarily **"by, for, and about African American and Third World people."** The press is open to all types of poetic forms except **"poor quality."** Submissions should be typewritten in manuscript format. Writers should send sample poems, credits, and bio. The books are "hardback and quality paperbacks."

‡PAUPER'S PRESS/PHAERWIND REVIEW; PIERROT POETRY COMPETITION (I,II, IV-Children), RR #1, Chesterville ON K0C 1H0 Canada, phone (613)448-2972, founded 1990, editor Heather O'Neil, uses **"any kind"** of poetry **"from traditional, haiku, free-verse to experimental. Nothing obscene, violent, abusive, horror."** They have recently published poetry by Emily Madsen and David Skyrie. As a sample the editor selected these lines from "Mobius" by G. Baillargeon:

> *The soft mist flows, with moon beam glows*
> *and dew drops on the sand.*
> *A whispered thread of voices led*
> *by some forgotten hand.*

Pauper's Press/Phaerwind Review appears every two months. **They have a "Junior Edition for kids under 16," the 7th edition, appearing each June.** It has a minimum of 30 pp. but Christmas and Kids' issues run to 40-50 pp. They describe it as "a literary magazine the whole family can enjoy!" It is magazine-sized, photocopied, side-stapled with b/w card cover, illustrations throughout. Press run 150 for 5 subscribers of which 2 are libraries; 75 shelf sales. Subscription: $25 Canadian, $30 foreign. **Sample postpaid: $4. Send SASE for guidelines. Pays 1-2 copies.** The Pierrot Poetry Competition, held in March of each year, is for poems up to 40 lines, $2/poem entry fee, prizes of $50, $25 and $15. Query regarding chapbook publication. The editor says, "Never stop submitting your work. Eventually you will find that one editor who thinks you're terrific. Don't stop short of your goal. Keep on truckin'."

PEACE AND FREEDOM; PEACE AND FREEDOM TAPE MAGAZINE (I), 17 Farrow Rd., Whaplode Drove, Spalding, Lincs. PE12 OTS England, phone 0406-330242, editor Paul Rance, founded 1985, is a "small-press publisher of poetry, music, art, short stories and general features, tapes," and also is a distributor. *Peace and Freedom* is a magazine appearing 2 times a year. **"We are looking for poetry particularly from U.S. poets who are new to writing, and women. The poetry we publish is anti-war, of environmental slant, poems reflecting pop culture, science fiction, love poetry; erotic, but not obscene, poetry, spiritual, humanitarian poetry. With or without rhyme/metre.** Recently published poetry by Janette Clutton, Hayley Tagg, Sara Burlace, Andy Savage and Andy Bruce. These sample lines are by Susan C. Thomson:

> *These lines, painfully personal,*
> *I may as well*
> *strip naked*
> *before you.*

Peace and Freedom has a card cover, normally 28 pages. "Pen pal ads included, and a correspondence section for poets is planned. 50% of submissions accepted. Poetry is judged on merit, but non-subscribers may have to wait longer for their work to appear than subscribers." **Sample:** U.S. $2; 75 p and SAE UK. "Sample copies can only be purchased from the above address, and various mail-order distributors too numerous to mention. Advisable to buy a sample copy first. Banks charge the equivalent of $5 to cash foreign cheques in the U.K., so advisable to send bills, preferably by registered post. We're not too impressed by poems sent without an accompanying note or letter. We like the personal touch." Subscription U.S. $7, U.K. £3 for 4 issues. **Payment 1 copy. Simultaneous submissions and previously published poems OK.** "Replies to submissions normally under a month, without IRC/SAE. Reviews books of poetry. *Peace and Freedom Tape Magazine* is a quarterly tape version of *Peace and Freedom*. Poems are read out by either the editor or a guest reader. Music, plays, stories, reviews also featured. Sample copy £2.50/$6. Poets are requested to send in bios. Guidelines same as magazine. No reply likely. 'New' poets are often too introverted about showing their work, which is why we try and feature/encourage 'new' poets. A burgeoning talent can often be nipped in the bud by an insensitive editor. Have belief is my advice to any writer."

‡THE PEACE NEWSLETTER (IV-Social issues, political), Syracuse Peace Council, 924 Burnet Ave., Syracuse NY 13203, founded 1936, is a magazine-sized 24 pp. publication circulating 12 times a year to 5,000 people mostly in upstate and central NY with news about the peace movement and using **some**

poetry relating to that movement. Subscription: $12/year. **Unable to pay for submissions. Considers simultaneous submissions. Sample free for SASE.**

PEARL; PEARL CHAPBOOK CONTEST (II), 3030 E. Second St., Long Beach CA 90803, phone (213)434-4523, founded 1974, folded after 3 issues, resurrected in 1987, poetry editors Joan Jobe Smith, Marilyn Johnson, and Barbara Hauk, is a literary magazine appearing twice a year. "**We are interested in accessible, humanistic poetry that communicates and is related to real life. Humor and wit are welcome, along with the ironic and serious. No taboos stylistically or subject-wise. Prefer poems up to 35 lines, with lines no longer than 10 words. We don't want to see sentimental, obscure, predictable, abstract, or cliché-ridden poetry. Our purpose is to provide a forum for lively, readable poetry that reflects a wide variety of contemporary voices, viewpoints, and experiences—that speaks to *real* people about *real* life in direct, living language, profane or sublime.**" They have recently published poetry by Billy Collins, Ann Menebroker, Michael C. Ford, Linda King, Robert Peters, Laurel Ann Bogen, Bill Shields and Denise Dumars. As a sample they selected these lines from "Lovesick" by Fred Voss:

> At the cliffs he gambols and scrambles down the point
> to fall and bounce and roll off of rocks
> and land head up on the wet sand,
> his finger through the handle of the jug,
> the waves rushing toward his bare feet,
> as he stares out at the sea
> and calls it his woman
> and weeps.

Pearl is digest-sized, 72 pp., saddle-stapled, professionally printed (offset from camera-ready copy). Their press run is 500 with 70 subscriptions of which 7 are libraries. Subscription: $10 per year. **Sample: $5 postpaid. Guidelines available for SASE. Pays 2 copies. "Handwritten submissions and unreadable dot-matrix print-outs are not acceptable. Cover letters appreciated." Reports in 6-8 weeks. No simultaneous submissions or previously published poems.** Each issue contains the work of 25-30 different poets and a special 10-15 page section that showcases the work of a single poet. "We now sponsor an annual chapbook contest, judged by one of our more well-known contributors. Winner receives publication, $100, and 50 copies, with an introduction by the final judge. (To date, judges have been Gerald Locklin, Laurel Speer and Robert Peters). Entries accepted during the months of May and June. There is a $10 entry fee, which includes a copy of the winning chapbook." Send SASE for complete rules and guidelines. "Advice for beginning poets? Just write from your own experience, using images that are as concrete and sensory as possible. Keep these images fresh and objective, and always listen to the music. . . ."

PEBBLE; BEST CELLAR PRESS, Dept. of English, University of Nebraska-Lincoln, Lincoln NE 68588. Declined listing.

‡PECKERWOOD (I), 1503-1465 Lawrence W., Toronto, Ontario M6L 1B2 Canada, phone (416)248-2675, founded 1987, editors Ernie Ourique and Ibi Kaslik, appears 3 or 4 times/year. **It could be any style you wish, any length. Haiku—yes. Rhymes—yes. Beauty—yes. Ugliness—yes. No clones of good poets, creative writing class crap, or poems written by television housewives.**" They have recently published poetry by Chris Wood, Stan Rogal, John Bennett and Hank Stace. As a sample the editor selected these lines from "Lost Cow" by editor Ibi Kaslik:

> it's dry skin stretched over
> its week, weaks
> needing some kind of moisture
> like the kind
> your eyes
> give me.

It is 30-40 pp., saddle-stapled, photocopied from typescript with matte card cover. They accept about 30% of poems received. Press run 150, 60 shelf sales. **Sample postpaid: $1. Pays 5 copies. "We're very quick." Editors always provide comments on rejections.** Ernie Ourique says, "No one can teach you how to write poetry. Don't accept the 'masters' of poetry (Pound, Eliot, Yeats) as the greatest. Explore poetry from all over the world. This means reading more than writing. Also get a job that doesn't involve brains: construction, washing toilets. You'll meet the greatest and worst human beings in the working class. Never insult people."

PEGASUS (I), 525 Ave. B., Boulder City NV 89005, founded 1986, editor M. E. Hildebrand, is a poetry quarterly for serious poets who have something to say and know how to say it using sensory imagery. Publishes 10-15% of the work received. **Submit 3-5 poems, 3-40 lines. Avoid "religious, political,**

pornographic themes." They have recently published poetry by Carla Davis, Gayle Elen Harvey, Robert K. Johnson and Elizabeth Perry who provides the opening lines of "The Meeting Hour" as a sample:

> *Before Dawn drops*
> *her luminous petals*
> *I wake and listen*
> *for your muted voice*
> *to break the silence*
> *of our worlds*
> *like rustlings*
> *in the deep woods.*

Pegasus has 32 pp., digest-sized, saddle-stapled, offset from typescript, colored paper cover, subscription $12.50, circulation 200. **Sample or single copy: $4.50, includes postage. Send SASE for guidelines. Reports in 2 weeks. Previously published poems OK, but no simultaneous submissions. Publication is payment.**

THE PEGASUS REVIEW (I, II, IV-Themes), P.O. Box 134, Flanders NJ 07836, founded 1980, is a 14-page (counting cover) pamphlet entirely in calligraphy, illustrated on high-quality paper, some color overlays. Poetry editor Art Bounds says, "This magazine is a bimonthly, **based on specific themes:** January/February—Courage; March/April—Dreams; May/June—Friends; July-August—America; September/October—Autumn; November/December—Christmas. Poetry not more than 24 lines, the shorter the better; (short short, about 3 pages would be ideal); essays and cartoons. Approach themes in a unique manner. Looking for brevity as well as clarity." Poets recently published: Joan Payne Kincaid, Arlene L. Mandell and Leslie D. Foster. The editor has selected these lines as a sample from "Armchair Traveler" by Tilitha Waicekauskas:

> *I travel near, I travel far,*
> *And never leave my nook.*
> *How bored and lonely people are*
> *Who never read a book.*

Sample: $2. Subscription: $7. Query if there are any questions or additional information needed. 158 copies are printed for 150 subscriptions, of which 3 are libraries. **Reports within a month, often with a personal response. Payment: 2 copies.** Occasional book awards throughout the year. The editor advises, "Discipline yourself to write rather than talk about what you're planning to write. Try to work on a daily basis, even if its an hour or two. Zealously guard this precious time for your work only. Continue to read what is vital today because that will be your market."

PEMBROKE MAGAZINE (II), Box 60, Pembroke State University, Pembroke NC 28372, founded 1969 by Norman Macleod, edited by Shelby Stephenson, a heavy (252+pp., 6×9"), flat-spined, quality literary annual, has published Fred Chappell, Stephen Sandy, Charles Edward Eaton, M.H. Abrams and Betty Adcock. Here is one of A.R. Ammons' poems "Cold Rheum":

> *You can't*
> *tell what's*
>
> *snot from*
> *what's not*

Print run: 500, subscriptions: 125, of which 100 are libraries. **Sample: $5 postpaid,** the single copy price, **reports within 3 months, payment in copies, sometimes comments on rejections.** Stephenson advises, "Publication will come if you write. Writing is all."

PENNINE PLATFORM (II), Ingmanthorpe Hall Farm Cottage, Wetherby, W. Yorkshire, England LS22 5EQ, phone 0937-64674, founded 1973, poetry editor Brian Merrikin Hill, appears 3 times a year. The editor wants any kind of poetry but concrete ("lack of facilities for reproduction"). No specifications of length, but poems of less than 40 lines have a better chance. "All styles—effort is to find things good of their kind. Preference for religious or socio-political awareness of an acute, not conventional kind." They have recently published poetry by Elizabeth Bartlett, Anna Adams, John Ward, Stanley Cook, Judith Kazantzis, John Latham and John Sewell. The editor selected these sample lines by Martyn Lowery, from a poem on his father's death:

> *While all I ever seem to say*
> *and not in any grand or gesticulating way*
> *concerns the peacetime pity of it all. So much is missed*
> *behind these barricades where we build*
> *a myth and fly a flag as best we may;*
> *where we live and where word by word are killed.*

The 6×8", 48 pp. journal is photocopied from typescript, saddle-stapled, with matte card cover with graphics, circulation 400, 300 subscriptions of which 16 are libraries. Subscription £5.40 for 3 issues (£9 abroad; £20 if not in sterling); per copy: £1.50. They receive about 300 submissions per year, use about 30, have about a 6-month backlog. **Sample: £1 postpaid. Submit 1-6 poems, typed or photocopied. Reports in about a month. No pay.** Editor occasionally comments on rejections. Reviews books of poetry. Brian Hill comments, "It is time to avoid the paradigm-magazine-poem and reject establishments—ancient, modern or allegedly contemporary. Small magazines and presses often publish superior material to the commercial hyped publishers."

PENNSYLVANIA ENGLISH (II), Penn State-Erie, Erie PA 16563, founded 1988 (first issue in March, 1989), contact poetry editor, is "a journal sponsored by the Pennsylvania College English Association." They want poetry of **"any length, any style."** It is magazine-sized, saddle-stapled, and appears twice a year, press run 300. Subscription: $15, which includes membership in PCEA. **Pays 2 copies. Submit 4-5 typed poems. Do not submit MSS in the summer. They consider simultaneous submissions but not previously published poems. Reports in 1 month.**

THE PENNSYLVANIA REVIEW (II), English Dept., 526 CL, University of Pittsburgh, Pittsburgh PA 15260, phone (412)624-0026, founded 1985, editor Lori Jakiela. This ambitious new journal was described by *Choice* as "a fine small literary magazine." **There are no restrictions on subject matter, style or length, although they do not want to see "light verse or greeting card verse."** Some poets recently published are Nance Van Winckel, Eric Pankey, Maggie Anderson, Sharon Doubiago, Harry Humes, Debra Bruce, Leslie Adrienne Miller, and translations of Karl Krolow by Stuart Friebert. As a sample the editor selected lines from "A Few Arguments With The Conspicuous," by Jeff Worley:

> *What if all the substantial*
>
> *evidence is nothing but a trick*
> *light plays, every sharp*
>
> *penetrating image*
> *really a marvelous blur?*

The Pennsylvania Review announces that it publishes "the best contemporary prose and poetry twice yearly." It is a handsome magazine, 7 × 10″, 80 pp. flat-spined, professionally printed on heavy stock with graphics, art and ads, glossy card cover with b/w illustration on grey. Circulation is approximately 1,000 with 300 subscriptions, price per issue $5, subscription $10. **Sample: $5 postpaid. Pay is 2 copies. Submission deadlines are November 30 for Spring issue, April 1 for Fall issue. Submissions are not accepted between June 1 and September 1. Submissions are reported on in 8-12 weeks. Writers should submit 3-6 poems, typewritten only, clear photocopies OK but no dot-matrix.** Reviews books of poetry.

‡**PENNYWHISTLE PRESS (IV-Children)**, 1000 Wilson Blvd., Arlington VA 22229-0002, is a weekly tabloid newspaper supplement with stories and features for children 7-14 years old, circulation 2,000,000 which uses "traditional poetry for children." **Buys 5-10 poems per year. Submit maximum of 1 poem. Pays variable rate. Send SASE for guidelines, 75¢ and 9 × 12″ SASE with 2 stamps for sample.**

‡**PENSIVE POEMS (I)**, 270 Baker St., Batesville AR 72501, founded 1990, editor Lewis Blue Price, is an annual, the first issue to appear about February, 1992. They want **poetry including elegies "solacing the disconsolate with charming, apt, honest verse—rhymed, metered, capitals, punctuation, 1-40 lines. No obscenity, zealotry, raw optimism. We value melancholy, cynicism, pesssimism, philosophy, didactics."** As a sample the editor selected these lines (poet unidentified):

> *My prayers at speed of light*
> *may take ten million years*
> *to reach the throne of One*
> *Who'd wipe away my tears.*

They plan for it to be 5 pp, magazine-sized, photocopied. Press run 30. **Pays 1 copy. Send SASE for guidelines. Editor often comments on rejections. Reports in 1 month or less.** The editor says, "For centuries millions liked blues and straight talk. Pathos, nostalgia, biting truth, 'gloomy magnificence' are out there and we want some. Plus epigrams and nature poems."

PENTAGRAM PRESS (V), 212 N. Second St., Minneapolis MN 55401, phone (612)340-9821, founded 1974, poetry editor Michael Tarachow, who is also printer and publisher. **Not reading new manuscripts.** Pentagram publishes broadsides, postcards and pamphlets in addition to books. They have recently published poetry by Philip Gallo, Theodore Enslin, and Robie Liscomb; a book by Clifford Burke is forthcoming. "Pentagram uses handset metal type to publish letterpress books of contemporary poetry. *Time* is the invisible factor: even a small project can take 300-500 hours. What would *you* sell that portion of your life for?"

PEOPLENET (IV-Specialized, romance), P.O. Box 897, Levittown NY 11756, phone (516)579-4043, founded 1987, editor/publisher Robert Mauro, is a newsletter **for disabled people focusing on dating, love and relationships.** The editor wants **"any poetry on relationships, love and romance in any form. But the length should remain 10-20 lines. 3 or 4 poems at a time. We publish beginners, new poets."** As a sample the editor chose the first stanza of his poem "How Many Times Have I Counted on Your Fingers":

> How many times have I
>   counted on your fingers
> the ways of love
>   one finger at a time
> touching this one first
> and that one in this place

Peoplenet appears 3 times a year, 12-15 pp., magazine-sized, offset, using graphics and ads, press run about 200, with that many subscriptions. Subscription $17. **Pays tearsheets only.** (Copies of the newsletter, which contains personal ads, go to subscribers only. Free brochure available.) **Poems should be double-spaced, with name and address on each page. No simultaneous submissions. Reports "immediately." Editor comments on rejected MSS.** He says, **"We want to publish poems that express the importance of love, acceptance, inner beauty, the need for love and relationship."**

PEQUOD: A JOURNAL OF CONTEMPORARY LITERATURE AND LITERARY CRITICISM (II, IV-Translations), Dept. of English, Room 200, New York University, 19 University Place, New York NY 10003, contact poetry editor, is a semiannual literary review publishing **quality poetry, fiction, essays, and translations.** They have published poetry by Deborah Digges, Donald Revell, and Theodore Weiss. As a sample I selected the concluding lines of "At the Atlantic City Bus Station" by Stephen Dunn:
> ...A man
> with dredlocks
> is selling crack in the men's room.
>
> The tattooed man is making a muscle
>   and oh, the little heart
> on his bicep has started to dance.

Subscription: $10 annually. **Sample: $5 postpaid.** It is a professionally-printed digest-sized, 130+ pp., flat-spined magazine with glossy card cover. This magazine is sponsored by the National Poetry Foundation, listed under Organizations Useful to Poets.

PERCEPTIONS (IV-Women), 1945 S. 4th W., Missoula MT 59801, founded 1982, poetry editor Temi Rose, is a "small prize-winning **women's poetry magazine for the promotion and development of women's consciousness of peace and hope and freedom to be ourselves.**" They have recently published poetry by Doreen Cristo. As a sample the editor selected this haiku by Kitty Cutting:

> As silver birds soar
>   so my heart and whole being
> ache to be with them.

Perceptions is digest-sized, 30 pp., photocopied from typescript, colored paper cover, and comes out three times a year. They publish about 250 of 1,000 poems received per year; their press run is 100 with 30 subscriptions of which 3 are libraries. Subscriptions: $10. **Sample: $3 postpaid. Guidelines available for SASE. Pays 1 copy. They consider simultaneous submissions and previously published poems and report in 1-3 months.**

PEREGRINE: THE JOURNAL OF AMHERST WRITERS & ARTISTS (II); AWA CHAPBOOK SERIES (V), Box 1076, Amherst MA 01004, *Peregrine* founded 1983, Amherst Writers & Artists Press, Inc., 1987. **Open to all styles, forms, subjects but greeting-card verse.** They have recently published poetry by William Packard, Doug Anderson and Barbara Van Noord. As a sample the editors selected these lines by Anna Kirwan Vogel:

> Nothing winged at the hummingbird feeder
> But us girls, taking the sun, and notes.
> We lean, like young broccoli, slightly forward
> Under green whirligig hats, ready
> To catch words, and if possible, whole sentences
> As they dart up from the ground.
> Shrubbery tells only the truth,

For this we are grateful . . .
"We try to publish twice a year, but sometimes cannot because of finances. **We may hold poems for several months, and so we encourage simultaneous submissions.**" *Peregrine* is digest-sized, 70 plus pp., flat-spined, professionally printed, with matte card cover. Their press run is 500. **Payment in contributors' copies. Sample: $4.50 postpaid.** The AWA Chapbook Series publishes handsome collections on a cooperative basis. **No unsolicited chapbook manuscripts, please. Query only.**

PERIVALE PRESS; PERIVALE POETRY CHAPBOOKS; PERIVALE TRANSLATION SERIES (II, IV-Translations, anthology), 13830 Erwin St., Van Nuys CA 91401-2914, founded 1968, editor Lawrence P. Spingarn, publishes **Perivale Poetry Chapbooks, Perivale Translation Series,** anthologies. The collections by individuals are usually translations, but here are some lines from R. L. Barth from "Da Nang Nights: Liberty Song" in **Forced-Marching to the Styx:**
> *In sudden light we choose*
> *Lust by lust our bar:*
> *And whatever else we lose,*
> *We also lose the war.*

They publish an average of one 20 pp. saddle-stapled chapbook, one perfect-bound (20-70 pp.) collection, one anthology per year, all quality print jobs. Send SASE for catalog. Perivale publishes both on **straight royalty basis (10%, 10 author's copies) usually grant supported, and by subsidy, the author paying 100%, being repaid from profits, if any. "Payment for chapbooks accepted is 50 free copies of press run.** Authors should agree to promote books via readings, talk shows, orders and signings with local bookshops. **Contributors are encouraged to buy samples of chapbooks, etc., for clues to editor's tastes." Samples of previous poetry chapbooks: $5 postpaid.** (Barth title out of print.) Latest title: **Going Home** (chapbook) by Sheryl St. Germain. **To submit, query first, with sample of 6-10 poems, bio, previous books. Do not submit MSS from June 15 to September 1.** Spingarn, a well-known, widely published poet, offers criticism for a fee, the amount dependent on length of book.

PERMAFROST (II, IV-Regional), English Dept., University of Alaska, Fairbanks AK 99775-0640, phone (907)474-5237, founded 1977. "Editors change annually." *Permafrost* is a biannual journal of poems, short stories, essays, reviews, b/w drawings and photographs. "We survive on both new and established writers, and hope and expect to see your best work (we are not the Siberia of mediocre poetry). **We publish any style of poetry provided it is conceived, written, revised with care; favor poems with strong, unusual images or poems with abstraction backed up by imagery; both must have universal applications. We discourage 'tourist poetry' which rarely works because of its hackneyed imagery and lack of universal theme; encourage poems about Alaska and by Alaskans, but they are works and writers at ease with their setting. We also encourage poems about anywhere and from anywhere. We are not a regional publication, but in order to support contemporary Alaskan literature, publish reviews only of work by Alaskan authors or publishers."** They have published poetry by Wendy Bishop, Jerah Chadwick, Leslie Leyland Fields, Linda Gregg, Patricia Monaghan, John Morgan, Peggy Shumaker and Kim Stafford. The editors selected these sample lines from "Ancient Forests of the Near East" by Jerry Cable:
> *This year, no scavenging hip-deep*
> *in dead-white snow for twigs*
> *and scraps of lumber crusted*
> *with icy leaves.*

The digest-sized 100+ pp. journal is flat-spined, professionally printed, two-color paper cover with b/w graphics and photos, has a circulation of 500 with 100 subscriptions of which 20 are libraries. Subscription: $7; per copy: $4. **Deadlines are December 1 and April 1. Return time is 1-3 months; "longer if work was submitted well before deadline and is under serious consideration." Do not accept submissions between April 1 and August 1. Sample: $4 postpaid. Submit no more than 5 poems, neatly typed or photocopied; considers simultaneous submissions but "expects to be told." Guidelines available for SASE, ("although most are listed here"). Pays 2 copies, reduced contributor rates on others.** Editors comment only on manuscripts that have made the final round and then are rejected. Depth of comments vary.

‡**PERSEA BOOKS (III),** 60 Madison Ave., New York NY 10017, editor Michael Braziller, publishes books of **"serious"** poetry. They have recently published poetry by Thylias Moss, Paul Blackburn and Les Murray. They publish 4-6 paperbacks and the same number of hardbacks/year. **Reports in 4-6 weeks. Payment "negotiable."**

THE PET GAZETTE (IV-Themes), 1309 N. Halifax, Daytona Beach FL 32118, phone (904)255-6935, founded 1984, editor Faith A. Senior, a quarterly journal that wants **"poems about animals, nature and/or ecology. Simple and easily understood, in behalf of animals overall, short poems preferred."**

She does not want "haiku, and ultra-contrived and/or highly intellectual." Poets frequently in *The Pet Gazette* are Vincent Hathaway, John Coulbourn, Rhoda Rainbow, Johnathan Russell, C. David Hay and S. Mary Ann Henn. As a sample, she selected the following stanza from "The Crow" by Nellie S. Richardson:

> I asked a crow the other day
> "Why not sing soft and low?"
> He said, "I do the best I can,
> It's the only way I know,
>   CAW! CAW!

Pet Gazette is magazine-sized, offset on 60 lb opaque paper, in many type styles with b/w photos and drawings, folded and saddle-stapled with b/w photos on cover, inserts from various pro-animal organizations. Circulation is 300, subscription $12.50 yearly. **Sample copy available for $2 postpaid. Payment is in copies. Reporting time is "upon receipt," and time to publication is "sometimes a year, though usually much sooner."**

PETERLOO POETS; POETRY MATTERS (II), 2 Kelly Gardens, Calstock, Cornwall PL18 9SA Great Britain, founded 1977, poetry editor Harry Chambers. *Poetry Matters* is an annual house journal to which you may not submit, but they publish collections of poetry under the Peterloo Poets imprint: flat-spined paperbacks, hardbacks and poetry cassettes. **Query with 10+ sample poems, bio and list of publications. Considers simultaneous submissions and previously published poems if they have not been in book form. Pays 10% royalties, $100 advance (for first volume, $200 for subsequent volumes) and 12 copies. Editor "normally, briefly" comments on rejections.**

‡PETRONIUM PRESS (V), 1255 Nuuanu Ave., 1813, Honolulu HI 96817, founded 1975, editor Frank Stewart. Petronium is a small-press publisher of poetry, fiction, essays and art—"**primarily interested in writers in and from Hawaii, but will publish others under special circumstances.** Interested in fine printing, fine typography and design in limited editions." They publish chapbooks, trade books, limited editions, broadsides and "other ephemera," but they "**are not accepting unsolicited material at this time.**" They publish 3-6 poetry chapbooks per year, with an average page count of 32, flat-spined paperbacks. The editor says, "**Query letters are welcome, with SASE.**" He replies to queries within 3 weeks and reports on MSS in the same amount of time. He has "no special requirements," but will not accept photocopied or dot-matrix MSS or discs. "**Payment of authors is negotiated differently for each book.**" The editor does not comment on rejections "**unless the material is exceptionally good.**" He says, "We are not really for beginners nor, in general, for people outside the Pacific region. We are not strict regionalists, but believe in nurturing first the writers around us. Beginning writers might do well to look for publishers with this same philosophy in their own cities and states rather than flinging their work to the wind, to unknown editors or to large publishing houses. All writers should consider supporting quality publishing in their own region first." Some of Petronium's books are distributed by the University of Hawaii Press (2840 Kolowalu St., Honolulu HI 96822) and may be obtained from them; "send for their literature catalog or ask for our titles specifically."

PHASE AND CYCLE; PHASE AND CYCLE PRESS (II), 3537 E. Prospect, Fort Collins, CO 80525, phone (303)482-7573, founded 1988, poetry editor Loy Banks. *Phase and Cycle* is a poetry magazine published semiannually. "**We look for short-to-moderate-length poems of all kinds, especially those that set out 'the long perspectives open at each instance of our lives' (Larkin). We are looking for poetry that will pass technical inspection in the academic community.**" They have recently published poetry by Richard Mishler, Lawrence Minet, B.Z. Niditch, R.T. Smith and Karen Kowalski Singer. The magazine is digest-sized, 48 pp., saddle-stapled. **Sample: $2.50 postpaid. Guidelines available for SASE. Pays 2 copies. "A brief bio note may accompany poems." No simultaneous submissions or previously published poems. Reports in 5-10 weeks. Submissions are accepted throughout the year. Editor sometimes comments on rejections.** Phase and Cycle Press has just published two poetry chapbooks, **Breathing In The World**, by Bruce Holland Rogers and Holly Arrow and **Out of Darkness**, by Mary Balazs.

PHILOMEL; PHILOMATHEAN SOCIETY (II), Box H, College Hall, University of Pennsylvania, Philadelphia PA 19104, phone (215)898-8907, founded in 1813. *Philomel* is a literary annual using "**any kind of poetry, no more than 300 words or 3 pp. per poem.**" They also use stories, essays and "witty recipes." As a sample, they selected these lines from "Page B6, B7, or B8" by William Keckler:

> It will happen; something violent
> Fusing images onto glass—
> An atomic flowerbust
> That flashes you translucent
> As an orange illuminated
> By a flashlight in a child's hand.

Philomel comes out each spring. It is flat-spined, 64 pp., 6×9", with matte card cover. Poems are selected by a committee of the Philomathean Society. Press run: 1,500 for 20 subscribers of which 3 are libraries, 1,400 distributed free to the university community. Price per issue: $4. **Sample postpaid: $2. Deadline for submissions: February 1, annually.**

PHOEBE, THE GEORGE MASON REVIEW (II), 4400 University Dr., Fairfax, VA 22032, phone (703)323-3730, founded 1970, poetry editors Greg Grummer and Evan Oakley, is a literary quarterly which uses **"any contemporary poetry of superior quality."** They have recently published poetry by C. K. Williams, Peter Klappert and William Matthews. Circulation 3,500, with 30-35 pp. of poetry in each issue. Subscription: $13/year; $3.25/single issue, $6.50/double issue. *Phoebe* receives 2,500 submissions per year. **Submit up to 5 poems; submission should be accompanied by SASE and a short bio. No simultaneous submissions, no dot-matrix. Reports in 6-8 weeks. Pays in copies.**

PHOENIX BROADSHEETS; NEW BROOM PRIVATE PRESS (II), 78 Cambridge St., Leicester, England LE 3 0JP, founded 1968, poetry editor Toni Savage, publishes chapbooks, pamphlets and broadsheets on a small Adana Horizontal Hand Press. The editor wants poetry which is **"descriptive—not too modern, not erotica or concrete, up to 12 lines (for the sheets).** Also some personal background of the poet." He has recently published poems by Spike Milligan, Elizabeth Bewick, Gina Bergamino, Sue Townsend, Jane Bradbury Lord, Chris Challis, Roger McGough and Arthur Caddick. Toni Savage selected these sample lines from "Muse" by Sue Mackrell:

> *Soft sadness in what might have been*
> *soothed and shared*
> *by touch of hand.*

The broadsheets are letterpress printed on tinted paper (about $5 \times 8"$) with graphics. **Submit no more than 3 poems with cover letter giving "personal backgrounds and feelings." No pay. Poet receives 20-30 copies.** "My *Broadsheets* are *given* away in the streets. Edition is usually 200-300. They are given away to Folk Club, Jazz Club and theater audiences. The broadsheets started as a joke. Now much sought after and collected. This is my hobby and is strictly part-time. Each small booklet takes 1-3 months, so it is impossible to ascertain quantities of publications." *Phoenix Broadsheets* may be obtained by sending adequate postage, approximately $1-50.

‡PIE (POETRY IMAGERY AND EXPRESSION) (V), P.O. Box 739, Parramatta, New South Wales Australia 2124, founded 1984, co-compiler Bill Tibben, is a publication of the poets who attend and participate in **readings sponsored by the group. "The publications are a record of the readings. We will return all unsolicited work without comment.** Our reason for requesting an entry in **Poet's Market** is that we think what we do is a good idea and one worth promoting. The people who come to the readings and who see themselves in print on the night (plus getting copies for their friends, etc.) get a good buzz! This is poetry as she is happening in the here and now and the day-to-day world!" They publish the poetry in an attractive oversize format, photocopied from typescript, side-stapled with card cover.

PIEDMONT LITERARY REVIEW; PIEDMONT LITERARY SOCIETY (I, II, IV-Form), Rt. 1, Box 512, Forest VA 24551, founded 1976; poetry editor Gail White, 1017 Spanish Moss Lane, Breaux Bridge LA 70517 (and **poetry submissions should go to her address).** If you join the Piedmont Literary Society, $12 a year, you get the quarterly *Review* and a quarterly newsletter containing much market and contest information. Gail White says, **"I prefer all types of poems up to 32 lines. Each issue has a special section for oriental forms with an emphasis on haiku." Each also includes short fiction. She does *not* want: "smut, overly romantic, greeting-card verse."** She has recently taken poetry by Harold Witt, Michael Brugeja, John Brugaletta, Enid Shomer and Charles B. Dickson. As a sample, these lines from a sestina by Ann Menebroker:

> *There is no need to deal with memory.*
> *She feels like a dirty picture, a woman*
> *denying poetry, feeling, like the blind, slowly*
> *across this tense reality. She sees sorrow*
> *as a platter of bland noodles, a non-color*
> *that doesn't shadow her world or dreams.*

The quarterly is digest-sized, saddle-stapled, offset from typescript, matte card cover, using b/w graphics, with 40-50 pp. of poetry in each issue, circulation 300 with 200 subscriptions of which 10 are libraries. **Sample: $3 postpaid. Welcomes all submissions. Send SASE for guidelines. Pays copies. Reports within 6 months.** She "usually" comments on rejections. Reviews "a few" books of poetry in accompanying newsletter. They sponsor occasional contests; write to Forest, VA address for rules and dates. Gail White advises, "Be introspective while showing empathy for mankind. Show some structure. No poems disguised as broken lines of prose."

PIG IRON (II, IV-Themes), P.O. Box 237, Youngstown OH 44501, phone (216)783-1269, founded 1975, poetry editors Jim Villani and Nate Leslie, is a literary annual devoted to special themes. They want **poetry "up to 300 lines; free verse and experimental; write for current themes."** Forthcoming themes: Epistolary Fiction and the Letter as Artifact, The Environment: Essence and Issue. They do *not* **want to see "traditional" poetry.** They have recently published poetry by Eve Shelnutt, Reg Saner, Grace Butcher, Antler, and Laurel Speer. As a sample the editor selected these lines from Mildred J. Nash:

> *Some arbitrary point will mark the end*
> *of what I'm saying and about to cast*
> *off into envelope and mailbox, destined*
> *for someone who will never spend as much*
> *time on these choice capricious words as I.*
> *It hardly matters. so long as I can touch*
> *the reader in myself and clarify*
> *some fleeting vision otherwise too dim*
> *among the words that spill out, whim by whim.*

Pig Iron is magazine-sized, flat-spined, 128 pp., typeset on good stock with glossy card cover using b/w graphics and art, no ads, circulation 1,000. They have 200 subscriptions of which 50 are libraries. Price per issue: $8.95. Subscription: $8/1 year, $15/2 years. **Sample: $3 postpaid. Send SASE for guidelines. Pays $5/poem plus 2 copies. Reports in 3 months, 12-18 months delay to publication. No simultaneous submissions. Dot-matrix, photocopies OK.**

THE PIKESTAFF FORUM; PIKESTAFF PUBLICATIONS, INC.; THE PIKESTAFF PRESS; PIKESTAFF POETRY CHAPBOOKS (II, IV-Children, teens), P.O. Box 127, Normal IL 61761, phone (309)452-4831, founded 1977, poetry editors Robert D. Sutherland, James R. Scrimgeour and James McGowan, is "a not-for-profit literary press. Publishes a magazine of national distribution, *The Pikestaff Forum*; and a poetry chapbooks series." They want **"substantial, well-crafted poems; vivid, memorable, based in lived experience**—*Not*: self-indulgent early drafts, 'private' poems, five finger exercises, warmed over workshop pieces, vague abstractions, philosophical woolgathering, 'journal entries,' inspirational uplift. **The shorter the better, though long poems are no problem; we are eclectic; welcome traditional or experimental work. We won't publish pornography or racist/sexist material."** They have recently published poetry by Gayl Teller, J.W. Rivers, Lucia Cordell Getsi, Frannie Lindsay and Fritz Hamilton. The editor selected these sample lines from Jeff Gundy's "C.W. Ponders the Pomes Even Now Winging Their Way Back to Him":

> *So, they come home. It's not their fault.*
> *They crook their heads and try to look*
> *on the bright side: they're back safe, still young.*
> *Maybe they'll grow.*

The Pikestaff Forum is an annual newsprint tabloid, 40 pp., "handsome, open layout. Trying to set a standard in tabloid design. Special features: poetry, fiction, commentary, reviews, young writers (7-17 in a special section), editors' profiles (other magazines), The Forum (space for anyone to speak out on matters of literary/publishing concern)." Circulation 1,200 with 200 subscriptions of which 5 are libraries. Price per copy: $2. Subscription: $10/6 issues. They receive 2,000-3,000 submissions per year, use 3%, have a year's backlog. **Sample: $2 postpaid. "Each poem should be on a separate sheet, with author's name and address. We prefer no simultaneous submissions—but if it is, we expect to be informed of it."** No more than 6 poems per submission. **Reports within 3 months. Pays 3 copies. Send SASE for guidelines. Query with samples and brief bio for chapbook submission. Replies to queries in 2 weeks, to submission (if invited) in 3 months. Photocopy OK, but "reluctantly" accepts dot-matrix. Pays 20% of press run for chapbooks. The editors "always" comment on rejections.** Reviews books of poetry if published by small presses or self-published. They advise, "For beginners: don't be in a hurry to publish; work toward becoming your own best editor and critic; when submitting, send only what you think is your very best work; avoid indulging yourself at the expense of your readers; have something to say that's worth your readers' life-time to read; before submitting, ask yourself, 'Why should *any* reader be asked to read this?'; regard publishing as conferring a responsibility."

PIKEVILLE REVIEW (II), Humanities Dept., Pikeville College, Pikeville KY 41501, founded 1987, editor James Alan Riley, who says **"There's no editorial bias though we recognize and appreciate style and control in each piece. No emotional gushing."** *PR* appears once yearly, accepting about 10% of poetry received. Press run is 500. **Sample $3 including postage. Send SASE for guidelines. Pays in 5 copies. No simultaneous submissions or previously published poetry. Editor sometimes comments on rejections.** They also sponsor contests.

PINCHGUT PRESS (V), 6 Oaks Ave., Cremorne, Sydney, NSW 2090, Australia, founded 1948, publishes **Australian poetry. Not currently accepting poetry submissions. Send SASE for catalog to order samples.**

‡**THE PINEHURST JOURNAL; PINEHURST PRESS (I)**, P.O. Box 360747, Milpitas CA 95036, founded 1990, editor Michael K. McNamara, is a quarterly. **"Generaly open, 24-line limit. Some sort of rhyme, meter or alliteration is a plus as well as good haiku. No religious, porno or dire despair. Work should be original, no reprints."** They have recently published poetry by Dan Green. As a sample, I selected the whole poem "Sneaking Out" by Anita M. Barnard:

> *The evening wind*
> *that chills us,*
> *Night things we fear*
> *that blow us, bear us, befriend us,*
> *that shake our leaves*
> * are really*
> *Demons in the trees*
> *that stir a young boy's blood.*

It is magazine-sized, 36 pp., offset from typescript, saddle-stapled. Of 400 poems/year received they use 55-60. Press run 150 for 70 subscribers of which 2 are libraries, 20 shelf sales. **Subscription: $16. Sample postpaid: $4.50. Send SASE for guidelines. Pays 1 copy. Reports in 6-8 weeks. Submit no more than 6 poems at a time.**

THE PIPE SMOKER'S EPHEMERIS (IV-Themes), 20-37 120th St., College Point, NY 11356, editor/publisher Tom Dunn, who says, "The *Ephemeris* is a limited edition, irregular quarterly **for pipe smokers and anyone else who is interested in its varied contents.** Publication costs are absorbed by the editor/publisher, assisted by any contributions—financial or otherwise—that readers might wish to make." There are 66 pages, offset from photoreduced typed copy, colored paper covers, with illustrations, stapled at the top left corner. The following lines are from "Coterie Fellowship" by R.W.:

> *There is no comparable moment*
> *When I light up my briar,*
> *To tamp that bowl of contentment,*
> *And to mix that gold with fire.*

PITT POETRY SERIES; UNIVERSITY OF PITTSBURGH PRESS; AGNES LYNCH STARRETT POETRY PRIZE (II), 127 N. Bellefield Ave., Pittsburgh PA 15260, founded 1968, poetry editor Ed Ochester, publishes **"poetry of the highest quality; otherwise, no restrictions—book MSS minimum of 48 pages."** Simultaneous submissions OK. They have published books of poetry by Etheridge Knight, Alicia Ostriker, Maggie Anderson, David Wojahn, Robley Wilson Jr., Liz Rosenberg, Larry Levis, Jane Flanders and Leslie Ullman. **"Poets who have not previously published a book should send SASE for rules of the Starrett competition ($10 handling fee),** the *only* **vehicle through which we publish first books of poetry."** The Starrett Prize consists of cash award of $2,000 and book publication. Poets who have previously published books should query.

‡**THE PITTSBURGH QUARTERLY (II)**, 36 Haberman Ave., Pittsburgh PA 15211-2144, phone (412)431-8885, founded 1990, editor Frank Correnti, who says, **"our first criterion is good writing with the variety of content that is common to a broad community interest. Generally, writing with narrative and real-life elements. We don't want doggerel or most rhyme."** They have recently published poetry by Michael Wurster, Jane Candia Coleman, Dennis Brutus and Susan Jacobson. As a sample the editor selected these lines from "The Poem as Labrador" by d steven conkle:

> *the poem as labrador*
> *rises rock-faced from a swirling sea*
> *brushes man aside*
> *as easily as*
> *a moose snapping at a black fly.*

It is digest-sized, 76 pp., professionally printed, saddle-stapled with matte card cover. Press run 500 for 150 subscribers of which 5 are libraries, 200 shelf sales. Subscription: $12 ($14 Canadian). **Sample postpaid: $4. Reports in 2-3 months. Pays 1 copy. "We will reply by letter to queries." Editor often comments on submissions.** Published books are reviewed as space is available, 1-2/issue. "We are responding in part to the network of writers whose crafted creativity made the magazine possible, but also we are attempting to provide a readership that will connect more strongly to the community of poets and writers through this quarterly."

PIVOT (II), 250 Riverside Dr. #23, New York NY 10025, phone (212)222-1408, founded 1951, editor Martin Mitchell, is a poetry annual that has published poetry by Philip Appleman, William Matthews, Eugene McCarthy, Craig Raine, W.D. Snodgrass and Robert Wrigley. As a sample I selected "Prescription" by David Ignatow:

> *What does he want of himself?*
> *How to write without reservation,*
> *yet without repugnance*
> *so that to value it,*
> *teeth, tongue and terror,*
> *he will accept the terror.*

It is a handsome 6 × 9″ flat-spined, professionally printed magazine with glossy card cover, press run 1,200. Price per issue: $5. **Pays 2 copies. Reports in 2-4 weeks. They read MSS between January 1 and June 1 only.**

Editor Jane Greer says she chose this cover illustration because "Plains Poetry Journal *is out of North Dakota, and I wanted to make that clear." However, she says, the journal "does not limit its acceptances to North Dakota or prairie poetry. Plains Poetry Journal's content is catholic and eclectic and its subscribers/contributors live all over the world." This illustration of the North Dakota landscape was created by Trygve Olson of Christine, North Dakota, who also does editorial cartoons and illustrations for the Fargo Forum.*

PLAINS POETRY JOURNAL; STRONGHOLD PRESS (II, IV-Form), P.O. Box 2337, Bismarck ND 58502, founded 1982, editor Jane Greer, publishes "meticulously crafted, language-rich poetry which is demanding but not inaccessible. We love rhyme and meter and poetic conventions used in vigorous and interesting ways. I strive to publish unpublished poets as well as old pros. I do *not* want broken-prose 'free verse' or greeting card-type traditional verse. I want finely-crafted poetry which uses the best poetic conventions from the past in a way that doesn't sound as if it were *written* in the past. No specifications. I'm especially interested in compelling long poems and essays on poetry. Our credo is, 'no subject matter is taboo; treatment is everything.'" They have recently published poetry by Gail White, Rhina P. Espaillat, Richard Moore, Judson Jerome, Paul Ramsey, R. L. Barth, Jack Flavin and Edmund Conti. As a sample Jane Greer chose "Yielding" by Neill Megaw:

> *Softer than silk or swansdown, than newborn baby's skin,*
> *Softer than tones still heard after the music's death,*
> *Than the remembered touch of a long-ago lover's breath—*
> *The first, faintest sense of sweetly approaching sin.*

Plains Poetry Journal is a quarterly, digest-sized, 44 pp. (of which about 40 are poetry), saddle-stapled, professionally printed on tinted paper with matte card cover, graphics, circulation 500, 400 subscriptions of which 50 are libraries. Subscription: $18. They receive 1,500-2,000 submissions per year, use about 200, seldom have more than 3 month backlog. **Sample: $4.50 postpaid. Submit "not less than 3 poems, not more than 10 at a time. Photocopy, hand-written, dot-matrix, simultaneous submissions, all OK." Reports in 1-3 weeks. Pays copies. Send SASE for guidelines.**

Has ceased book publishing. "Considering the rude and totally unnecessary slowness of most publishers, an author is *crazy* not to submit simultaneously." Jane Greer says **she comments on rejections "occasionally, especially if the MS is especially promising or if I think the poet is a child or teen** (it happens)." She comments, "Do enclose an SASE, and *don't* enclose an explanation of the poems. Above all understand that a poet never 'gets good,' he or she just keeps *working* at it. If you're willing to do this, I am, too."

PLAINSONG (II), Box 8245, Western Kentucky University, Bowling Green KY 42101, phone (502)745-5708, founded 1979, poetry editors Frank Steele, Elizabeth Oakes and Peggy Steele, is an occasional poetry journal. "Our purpose is to print the best work we can get, from known and unknown writers. This means, of course, that we print what we like: poems about places, objects, people, moods, politics, experiences. **We like straightforward, conversational language, short poems in which the marriage of thinking and feeling doesn't break up because of spouse-abuse (the poem in which ideas wrestle feeling into the ground or in which feeling sings alone — and boringly — at the edge of a desert). Prefer poems under 20 lines in free verse. No limits on subject matter, though we like to think of ourselves as humane, interested in the environment, in peace (we're anti-nuclear), in the possibility that the human race may have a future."** They have recently published poetry by William Matthews, Ted Kooser, William Stafford, Del Marie Rogers, Betty Adcock, Julia Ardery and Abby Niebauer. The editors selected these sample lines from "Dream of an Afternoon with a Woman I Did Not Know" by Robert Bly:

> *Frost has made clouds out of the night weeds.*
> *In my dream we stopped for coffee, we sat alone*
> *Near a fireplace, near delicate cups.*
> *I loved that afternoon, and the rest of my life.*

The magazine is 48-56 pp., 6×9", professionally printed, flat-spined, matte color card cover with photos and graphics, print run 600 with 250 subscriptions of which 65 are libraries. They use about 100 of the 2,000 submissions received each year. Subscription: $7; per copy: $3.50. **Sample: $3.50 postpaid. "We prefer poems typed, double-spaced. Simultaneous submissions can, of course, get people into trouble, at times."** Reports "within a month, usually." Payment in copies. **Send SASE for guidelines.**

PLAINSONGS (II), Dept. of English, Hastings College, Hastings NE 68902, founded 1980, editor Dwight C. Marsh, a poetry magazine that **"accepts manuscripts from anyone, considering poems on any subject in any style."** Some recurrent contributors printed in the last year include Mellanee Kvasnicki, Lyn Lifshin, Edward C. Lynskey, Nikolas Macioci, Nancy Peters, Ron Rash, Ionna-Veronika Warwick and Nancy G. Westerfield. In the January, 1991 issue, which included 39 poets, Katie Kingston's poem "Airlines" begins:

> *I fold these words into pages*
> *as the wheels leave the ground*
> *tucking themselves into this huge,*
> *metal belly. We are floating now.*

Plainsongs is digest-sized, 40 pp., saddle-stapled, set on laser, printed on thin paper with b/w illustrations, one-color matte card cover with black logo. The magazine is financed by subscriptions, which cost $9 for three issues per year. **Sample copies are $3. Pay is two copies and a year's subscription, with three award poems in each issue receiving small monetary recognition. MS deadlines are August 15 for fall issue; November 15 for winter; March 15 for spring. Notification is mailed about three weeks after deadlines.**

PLAINSWOMAN (IV-Women, regional), P.O. Box 8027, Grand Forks, ND 58202, founded 1977, is a 16 pp. magazine-sized literary journal appearing 10 times a year, circulation 500, using some **poetry by and about women in the Great Plains. Guidelines available, include SASE. Pays two copies of issue in which poem appears. Sample: $2.**

PLANTAGENET PRODUCTIONS (V), Westridge, Highclere, Nr. Newbury, Royal Berkshire RG15 9PJ, England, founded 1964, director of productions Miss Dorothy Rose Gribble. Plantagenet issues cassette recordings of poetry, philosophy and narrative (although they have issued nothing new since 1980). Miss Gribble says, "Our public likes classical work ... We **have published a few living poets, but this is not very popular with our listeners, and we shall issue no more."** They have issued cassettes by Oscar Wilde, Chaucer, Pope, as well as Charles Graves, Elizabeth Jennings, Leonard Clark and Alice V. Stuart. The recordings are issued privately and are obtainable only direct from Plantagenet Productions; write for list. Miss Gribble's advice to poets is: "If intended for a listening public, let the meaning be clear. If possible, let the music of the works sing."

THE PLASTIC TOWER (I, II), P.O. Box 702, Bowie MD 20718, founded 1989, editors Carol Brown and Roger Kyle-Keith, is a quarterly using **"everything from iambic pentameter to silly limericks, modern free verse, haiku, rhymed couplets—we like it all! Only restriction is length—under 40 lines preferred."** They have published poetry by John Bennett, Johy Grey, Jonathan Levant, Lyn Lifshin, Richard Peabody, Walt Phillips, Cheryl Townsend, A.D. Winans and Bob Z, "as well as a bunch of folks nobody's heard of yet . . . but hopefully will soon." As a sample, I selected the prose poem "1939" by Jennie VerSteeg:

> You pass your thumb so lightly over my mouth, as though I am a fading charcoal sketch
>   of a woman who could have loved you once—in France, in a daguerreotype, with
>   absinthe, belly hair wet and curling in a bow.

It is digest-sized, 38-54 pp., saddle-stapled; "variety of typefaces and b/w graphics on cheap photocopy paper." Press run: 200. Subscription: $8/year. Copy of current issue: $2.50. **We'll send a back issue free for a *large* (at least 6×9″) SASE with 75¢ postage attached." Send SASE for guidelines. Pays 1-3 copies. Simultaneous submissions OK. Reports in 4-8 weeks. Editor comments on submissions "often."** Roger Kyle-Keith says, "*The Plastic Tower* is genuinely eclectic—we've published the entire spectrum of modern poetry, from bathroom wall limericks to minutely crafted academic verse. We never quite know what we're going to like until we see it! But we especially look of poetry that's exciting, fresh and elicits a strong reaction from the reader—good or bad. *The Plastic Tower* is user friendly, and we encourage poets to laugh off the crummy little form rejections and *have some fun*, 'cause this whole business of submitting for puiblication can be a real ego-buster if it's taken too seriously. Yeah, we practice what we preach; though we publish quite a bit of serious (and downright downbeat) poetry, we always try to maintain a good *fun* quotient."

‡PLEIADES MAGAZINE (I, IV-Form), Box 357, Lakewood CO 80214, phone (303)237-3398, founded 1983, editor-in-chief John L. Moravec, poetry editor Hadrian K. Zve, appears twice a year using **"rhyming poetry, any length, on modern subjects."** It is magazine-sized, 75 pp. Press run 1,200. Subscription: $9. **Sample postpaid: $3. Responds in 2 weeks. Pays copies and cash awards.**

PLOUGHSHARES (III), Emerson College, 100 Beacon St., Boston MA 02116, phone (617)926-9875, founded 1971, **The magazine is "a journal of new writing edited on a revolving basis by professional poets and writers to reflect different and contrasting points of view."** Recent editors have included Gerald Stern, Rita Dove, James Alan MacPherson, and M.L. Rosenthal. They have recently published poetry by Donald Hall, Li-Young Lee, Robert Pinsky, Brenda Hillman and Thylias Moss. The quarterly is 5½×8½″, 200 pp., circulation 3,800. Subscription: $15 domestic; $19 foreign. They receive approximately 3,000 poetry submissions per year. **Sample: $5 postpaid. "Due to revolving editorship, issue emphasis and submission dates will vary. We suggest you read a few issues and check editorial announcements in current issue." Do not submit MSS from May 1 to September 1. Reports in 3-5 months, pays $10 minimum per poem, $5/printed page per poem over 2 printed pages, up to $50 maximum per poet, plus contributor copies. Simultaneous submissions acceptable.** Reviews books of poetry.

‡THE PLUM REVIEW (II), P.O. Box 3557, Washington DC 20007, founded 1990, editors M. Hammer and Christina Daub, appears twice a year. **"We are open to original, high quality poetry of all forms, lengths, styles and subject-matters. No cliché-ridden or overly sentimental work."** They have recently published poetry by Mark Strand, William Stafford, Jean Valentine, Linda Hogan, Jane Hirschfield, Henri Cole and Michael Collier. As a sample the editor selected these lines by James McCorkle:

> The danger is that you and I remain unscathed—
> We continue to dream heavily on this raft, watching
> Frigate birds sweep along the inner folds of thermal drafts.
> Tomorrow we will disembark among the small craft in a harbor
> Whose first name was lost, leaving only the dry sorrows of palms.

It is 100 pp., flat-spined, professionally printed, 6×9″. Press run 1,000. **Sample postpaid: $5. Send SASE for guidelines. Reports in 2 months. Pays 1 copy. "Absolutely no simultaneous submissions. Include a brief bio indicating previous publications and/or awards. Submit a few strong poems, not your life's work." Seldom comments on rejections.** They welcome reviews of recently published books of poetry. They sponsor a reading series. They are planning creative writing workshops for the handicapped.

‡POCAHONTAS PRESS, INC.; MANUSCRIPT MEMORIES (V), 2805 Wellesley Ct., Blacksburg VA 24060, phone (703)951-0467, founded 1984, president Mary C. Holliman, publishes hardback and chapbook collections of poetry, but is temporarily not considering new MSS "because I am trying to finish those already accepted." Inquire before submitting. **"Most of the poetry books I have published have been subsidized to some extent by the author. So far one of those authors' books has sold enough**

copies that the author has received a significant reimbursement for his investment. We continue to market all of our books as aggressively as possible. The idea is to make a profit for both of us (though we have yet to do so)." She offers editorial critiques for $20/hour. Reviews books of poetry "sometimes." She has published books by Leslie Mellenchamp, Lynn Kozma, Mildred Nash, Hubert J. Davis, Clyde Kessler and David R. Wones; forthcoming: Preston Newman and Elaine Emans. As a sample the editor selected these lines by Cecil J. Mulline:

> In the East, time has been divorced
> From things. No clocks hem the hours
> In, and time, not being firmly forced,
> Slops around.

Pays 10% royalties on all sales receipts, 10 free copies of book, and any number of copies at 50% for resale or "whatever use author wishes. If author helps with printing costs, then an additional percentage of receipts will be paid."

POCKET INSPIRATIONS (I, IV-Inspirational), P.O. Box 796, Weaverville CA 96093, founded 1989, editor Janey Mitchell, a "newsletter to uplift the heart and nourish the spirit. It has something for everyone, appearing quarterly, using **soul-stirring, all types of spiritual/inspirational poetry.**" Open to reprints. **They prefer short poems. "If you are not a subscriber or have not been previously published in *Pocket Inspirations*, there is a $1/poem reading fee."** The editor says the magazine is approximately 28 pp., photocopied and stapled, and that "since each publication has a unique flavor of its own," she suggests you read an issue of the newsletter before submitting to them. Subscription: $12/year. **Sample: $3. Pays copies. Reports in 2-6 weeks.**

POEM; HUNTSVILLE LITERARY ASSOCIATION (II), English Dept., University of Alabama at Huntsville, Huntsville AL 35899, founded 1967, poetry editor Nancy Frey Dillard, appears twice a year, a flat-spined 4½ × 7¾", 70 pp. journal, circulation 400 (all subscriptions, of which 90 are libraries), matte card cover, tinted paper, consisting entirely of poetry. "We are open to traditional as well as non-traditional forms, but we favor work with the expected compression and intensity of good lyric poetry and a high degree of verbal and dramatic tension. We welcome equally submissions from established poets as well as from less known and beginning poets. We do not accept translations or previously published works. We prefer to see a sample of 3-5 poems at a submission, with SASE. We generally respond within a month. We are a nonprofit organization and can pay only in copy to contributors. Sample copies are available at $5." They have recently published poetry by R. T. Smith, Simon Perchik and Charles Edward Eaton. The editor selected as a sample the following poem by Jonathan Stark, "Eve of All Saints":

> One night, at least, we remember
> that Adam, for all his faults,
> was a good Christian, that nature abhors
> a cultivated cabbage, that the world
> does not end at the garden wall. Beyond,
> among weed and shrub and sucking parasite swell
> berries bright with secret dying;
> there shadows couple,
> spawn; there squats
> the jeweled toad, unblinking, lifting
> doleful orisons to the virgin moon.

They receive about 2,000 submissions per year, use 210.

‡POEMS FOR A LIVABLE PLANET (I, IV-Nature/ecology, translations), #12, 1295 Federal Ave., Los Angeles CA 90025, founded 1990, editor Jeffrey Dellin, appears "once or twice a year" using **"poems dealing with the beauty/peril of the Earth & Her creatures. Prefer a political slant. Any form, language given equal consideration; length limit 50 lines. Non-English should include translation." Sample postpaid: $3.75. Reports in 4-6 weeks. Pays 1 copy.** No previously published material "I am a novice editor. I rely on my passion. I don't know names or reputations. Everyone has an equal chance of getting in."

‡POET; COOPER HOUSE PUBLISHING INC.; JOHN DAVID JOHNSON POETRY COMPETITION; IVA MARY WILLIAMS INSPIRATIONAL POETRY COMPETITION; ANNUAL CHAPBOOK COMPETITION; AMERICAN COLLEGE & UNIVERSITY POETRY COMPETITION–STUDENT AND TEACHER DIVISIONS (I, II);, Box 1334, El Reno OK 73036, founded 1985, managing editor Peggy Cooper. *Poet*, a quarterly, is **"open to beginners' submissions. The poets we publish don't have to buy anything or join anything or subscribe; however, they may if they wish subscribe or buy single copies. They may request free copies of the pages on which their work appears. Some of our competitions have entry fees. These fees are used to help publish *Poet* Magazine."** They have recently published poetry by Lyn Lifshin,

Karen Douglas and Lewis Turner. As a sample the editor selected these lines from "Woman at the Fruit Stand" by Marcia Gale Kester:

> *Mattie, on the corner of Eighth and Ash*
> *brown dough stomach bulging in damp*
> *polyester print. A bucket of mangos*
> *at fifty cents apiece*
> *her fingers are sticky sweet with juice.*
> *She smiles wide, teeth like piano keys*
> *laughter thick in molasses and ginger.*

It is magazine-sized, professionally printed, 48-56 pp. with glossy cover, saddle-stitched. Of 2-5 thousand submissions they use about 10%. Subscription: $20/year. **Sample: $5.50 postpaid. Send SASE for guidelines. Pays 1 copy. Previously published poems and simultaneous submissions OK. Reports within 3 months. Editor sometimes comments on rejections.** Reviews books of poetry. They sponsor an annual chapbook competition (up to 24 pp., $20 entry fee, prize-publication in book form); John David Johnson Poetry Memorial Competiton (Prizes of $200, $100, $50, and honorable mentions, award certificates and publication, $5/poem entry fee, Dec. 25 deadline); Iva Mary Williams Inspirational Poetry Competition (prizes of $100, $50, $25 and honorable mentions; $3/poem fee; July 1 deadline); American College & University Poetry Competition with divisions for students and for teachers (prizes of $200, $100, $50, ten $10 honorable mentions, 20 special merit certificates, no entry fee, deadlines and official entry forms for both the student division and the teacher division are published in *Poet* magazine).

POET AND CRITIC (II), 203 Ross Hall, Iowa State University, Ames IA 50011, phone (515)294-2180, founded 1961, editor Neal Bowers, appears 3 times a year, 6x9", 48 pp. staple bound, professionally printed, matte card cover with color, circulation 400, 300 subscriptions of which 100 are libraries. Subscription: $16; per copy: $6. **Sample: $6 postpaid. Submit 3-5 poems. "We do not read MSS between the end of May and mid-August." Reports in 2 weeks (often sooner). Pays 1 copy. Send SASE for guidelines.** The sample copy I examined focused on humorous poetry—10 poets, some represented by more than 1 poem. I selected as a sample the opening of "Kong Settles Down" by William Trowbridge:

> *They've locked me in with this goddam lady gorilla,*
> *Russian bred, bulged up on steroids*
> *till she's damn near big as me. Shot-putter,*
> *they say. Couldn't pass the hormone test.*

Reviews books of poetry. Neal Bowers advises beginning poets, "Read *Poet and Critic.*" I found I couldn't put this sample copy down!

‡**POET GALLERY PRESS (IV-Specialized)**, Box 1206, New York NY 09221, founded 1970, editor E.J. Paulos, publishes **work by American poets living outside the U.S. He wants "serious, learned, quality"** not **"greeting card level."** They have recently published poetry by S. Hakim, I. Roverso and Gamela. As a sample the editor selected these lines from Pavia:

> *Bramante had been there,*
> *and Da Vinci contributed to the plan*
> *the third largest dome in Italy*
> *before there had been Charlemagne,*
> *. . . the tower—and the iron crown, marks of a medieval heritage*
> *symbols of the once royal town.*

Reports on queries in 1 month, on MSS in 2 months. Payment "depends upon sales, etc." but includes copies.

POET LORE (II), The Writers Center, 7815 Old Georgetown Rd., Bethesda MD 20814-2415, founded 1889, managing editor Sunil Freeman, editors Philip Jason and Barbara Goldberg, is dedicated "to the best in American and world poetry and objective and timely reviews and commentary. We look for **fresh uses of traditional form and devices, but any kind of excellence is welcome. The editors encourage narrative poetry and original translations of works by contemporary world poets.**" They have recently published poetry by Sharon Olds, John Balaban, William Heyen, Walter McDonald, Reginald Gibbons and Howard Nemerov. As a sample (though it is not representative) I chose the first stanza of "Hieroglyphics" by Amy Rothholz:

> *September is lying on its side*
> *So blackberry brandy and professions of love*
> *Can swim down my throat.*
> *Put another quarter in the jukebox.*
> *Let the pretty lies fly.*

The 6×9", 64 pp. saddle-stapled, professionally printed quarterly, matte card cover, has a circulation to 600 subscriptions of which 200 are libraries. Subscription: $12; per copy: $4.50. They receive about 3,000 poems in freelance submissions per year, use about 100. **Sample: $4 postpaid. Submit typed author's name and address on each page. Photocopies OK. Reports in 3 months. Pays 2 copies.** Reviews books of poetry.

POETIC JUSTICE (II), 8220 Rayford Dr., Los Angeles CA 90045, founded 1982, poetry editor Alan C. Engebretsen, publishes "contemporary American poetry. **Quality poetry is what I want—no-nos are raw language and blue material.**" Poems about relationships and positive features of life are welcome. They have recently published Tony Moffeit, Arthur Winfield Knight, Pearl Bloch Segall, Sheila Golburgh Johnson, Charles B. Dickson and Michael Fraley. The editor selected these sample lines from "Nursery Rhyme" by Ida Fasel:

> *When I was too young for the words*
> *music on the way to sleep*
> *gave me the deep rest of warm dark.*

The magazine is digest-sized, 44 pp., professionally printed, tinted matte card cover, published irregularly, circulation 200 with 55 subscriptions of which 2 are libraries, **43 pp. of poetry per issue.** Subscription: $10, 4 issues; per copy: $3. They receive about 1,500 poems per year, use 160. No current backlog. **Sample: $3 postpaid. Prefer submissions of 4 poems at a time, typewritten. No query. Reports in 1-2 weeks. Pays contributor's copy. Send SASE for guidelines. No oversize envelopes. Use #10 legal size envelopes only. Editor comments on rejections "when I have something to say."**

‡THE POETIC KNIGHT: A FANTASY ROMANCE MAGAZINE (IV-Fantasy, romance), 805 Applegrove St. NW Apt #1002, North Canton OH 44720-8618, founded 1990, editor Michael While, appears 3-4 times/year. **"looking for fantasy oriented poetry that exemplifies the classical romantic in all of us. Poetry can be of any length, but prefer under 30 lines. No profanity or explicit sex. Like to see work that is more uplifting than depressing."** They have recently published poetry by John Grey, J.C. Hendee and P.R.S. Schwartz. As a sample the editor selected these lines from "Crystal Queen" (poet unidentified):

> *She says she will love him forever*
> *Her soul is one with his.*
> *She'll flee her icy kingdom*
> *if with her he will stay.*

It is 40-52 pp., digest-sized, laser set with heavy bond cover, saddle-stapled. They accept "about 3 to 1 ratio and we get 3-4 submissions a week." Press run 300 for 100 subscribers of which 3 are libraries, 150 shelf sales. Subscription: $11/4 issues. **Sample postpaid: $3. Send SASE for guidelines. Pays 1 copy. Editor "always" comments on rejections.**

POETIC PAGE (I), P.O. Box 71192, Madison Heights MI 48071-0192, phone (313)548-0865, founded 1989, editor Denise Martinson, appears bimonthly. **Each issue has a contest, $1/poem fee, prizes of $25, $15 and $10. All poetry published is that of contest winners. "All forms are used except explicit sex, violence, and crude. 20-24 lines."** They have published poetry by Dan Gallik, Kay Weems, Alice McKenzie Swaim, Marian Ford Park, Denise Martinson and Pearl Bloch Segall. As a sample the editor selected these concluding lines from "At the Post Office" by Charles Corry:

> *Big Chief chaws*
> *flavor awesome tales,*
> *dripping like quivering shaped notes*
> *past tobacco-curled grins*
> *as wrinkled WW-I vets*
> *enhance old glories.*

Poetic Page is 24-32 pp., magazine-sized, photocopied from typescript on 20 lb. paper, press run 250-350, 10 to libraries. Subscription: $10. **Sample, postpaid: $2. Simultaneous submissions and previously published poems OK. Nonsubscribers receive 1 copy.** "We only accept one-third of the poetry we receive." The editor adds, "We want poets to say, 'now that's an excellent poem.' If I read a poem, submitted or read elsewhere, I'll climb the highest mountain, swim the deepest sea to obtain it for our readers. We illustrate the pages because we feel that poems are work and that work should be shown in the best possible way. We publish a quality publication. We like to print the beginner's poem alongside the seasoned pro's. In other words, we love poetry." They review books of poetry and pay $5 for articles about poetry.

POETIC SPACE: POETRY & FICTION (I, IV-Social issues, political), P.O. Box 11157, Eugene OR 97440, founded 1983, editor Don Hildenbrand, is a literary magazine with emphasis on contemporary poetry, fiction, reviews, interviews and market news. Accepts poetry and fiction that is **"well-crafted and takes risks. We like poetry with guts. Would like to see some poetry on social and political issues. Erotic and experimental OK. No traditional, rhymed (unless of high-quality), sentimental, romantic."**

They have published John M. Bennett, Barbara Henning, Albert Huffstickler, Arthur Winfield Knight, Crawdad Nelson, Tyrone Williams and Lawson Fusao Inada. The editor selected these sample lines from "Critic" by Sesshu Foster:

> Just for the sake of peace and quiet I'd say
> go ahead and shoot all the poets
> but then the few would lie silenced
> bleeding with actual compassion like anyone
> else, while from the wounds of the rest
> would pour words words words words

The magazine is 8½×11", saddle-stapled, 16 pp., offset from typescript and sometimes photoreduced. It is published twice a year. They use about 25% of the 200-300 poems received per year. Press run: 800-1,000 with 50 subscriptions of which 12 are libraries. Price per issue: $3. Subscription: $15. **Sample: $2. Guidelines for SASE. Pays 1 copy, but more can be ordered by sending SASE and postage. MS should be typed, double-spaced, clean, name/address on each page. Reports in 2-4 months. No simultaneous submissions or previously published poems. Editor provides some critical comments.** Reviews books of poetry. Don Hildenbrand says, "We like poetry that takes chances, from the heart and guts. Originality, not mediocrity, is what we wish to see. Reputations are not considered."

POETICAL HISTORIES (IV-Regional), 27 Sturton St., Cambridge, CB1 2QG, U.K., founded 1985, editor Peter Riley, is a "small press publishing **poetry only.**" **They publish poetry that is "British, modernist,"** not "concrete, experimental, translated, homely." They have recently published poetry by J.H. Prynne, John James and Nicholas Moore. **They publish 3-4 hand-printed chapbooks averaging 8 pp. each per year.**

POETPOURRI; COMSTOCK WRITERS' GROUP INC.; SUMMER SIZZLER CONTEST (II), P.O. Box 3737, Taft Rd., Syracuse NY 13220, founded 1987, phone (315)451-1406, published by the Comstock Writers' Group, Inc., biannually, Jennifer B. MacPherson and Kathleen Bryce Niles, co-editors. **They use "work that is clear and understandable to a general readership, that deals with issues, ideas, feelings and beliefs common to us all—well-written free and traditional verse. No obscene, obscure, patently religious or greeting card verse."** They have recently published poems by Katharine Howd Machan, Robert Cooperman, Simon Perchik, Joseph Bruchac, Patrick Lawler and R. Nikolas Macioci. The group selected the closing lines from "Unfastened" by Michael Morgan:

> One-eyed buttons,
> Parading illusion,
> Can't see far;
> They just hold on
> As best they can.

Poems may be submitted anytime for possible publication, 3-6 at a time, unpublished poems only. Return time: about 6 weeks. Editors usually comment on returned submissions. They offer a yearly Summer Sizzler contest with over $400 in prizes, $2 per poem, 30 line limit. *Poetpourri* is 100 pp., digest-sized, professionally printed, perfect-bound, raised cover. Circulation 500. Subscription $8. **Sample: $4 postpaid. Pays copies.** The Comstock Writers' Group also publishes a newsletter periodically, which reviews books of poetry.

POETRY; THE MODERN POETRY ASSOCIATION; BESS HOKIN PRIZE; LEVINSON PRIZE; OSCAR BLUMENTHAL PRIZE; EUNICE TIETJENS MEMORIAL PRIZE; FREDERICK BOCK PRIZE; GEORGE KENT PRIZE; RUTH LILLY POETRY PRIZE, (III), 60 W. Walton St., Chicago IL 60610, founded 1912, editor Joseph Parisi, "is the oldest and most distinguished magazine devoted entirely to verse," according to their literature, though *Poet Lore* is considerably older, as is *North American Review*, which publishes both prose and poetry. Nonetheless the historical role of *Poetry* in modern literature is incontrovertible: "Founded in Chicago in 1912, it immediately became the international showcase that it has remained ever since, publishing in its earliest years—and often for the first time—such giants as Ezra Pound, Robert Frost, T. S. Eliot, Marianne Moore and Wallace Stevens. *Poetry* has continued to print the major voices of our time and to discover new talent, establishing an unprecedented record. There is virtually no important contemporary poet in our language who has not at a crucial stage in his career depended on *Poetry* to find a public for him: John Ashbery, Dylan Thomas, Edna St. Vincent Millay, James Merrill, Anne Sexton, Sylvia Plath, James Dickey, Thom Gunn, David Wagoner—only a partial list to suggest how *Poetry* has represented, without affiliation with any movements or schools, what Stephen Spender has described as 'the best, and simply the best' poetry being written." Although its offices have always been in Chicago, *Poetry*'s influence and scope extend far beyond, throughout the U.S. and in over 45 countries around the world. Asked to select 4 lines of poetry "which represent the taste and quality you want in your publication" Joseph Parisi selected the opening lines of "The Love Song of J. Alfred Prufrock" by T. S. Eliot, which first appeared in *Poetry* in 1915:

Let us go then, you and I,
When the evening is spread out against the sky
Like a patient etherized upon a table;
Let us go, through certain half-deserted streets . . .

The elegantly printed flat-spined 5½×9″ magazine appears monthly, circulation 7,000, 6,000 subscriptions of which 65% are libraries. Subscription: $25; $27 for institutions; per copy: $2.50. They receive over 70,000 submissions per year, use 300-350, have a 9 month backlog. **Sample: $3.50 postpaid. Submit no more than 6 poems. "Photocopy OK; no dot-matrix; letter-quality OK." Reports in 8-10 weeks. Longer for MSS submitted during the summer. Pays $2 a line. Send SASE for guidelines.** Six prizes (named in heading) ranging from $100 to $1,000 are awarded annually to poets whose work has appeared in the magazine that year. Only verse already published in *Poetry* is eligible for consideration and no formal application is necessary. *Poetry* also sponsors the Ruth Lilly Poetry Prize, an annual award of $25,000. Reviews books of poetry.

‡POETRY & AUDIENCE; PELICANS POETRY MAGAZINE; POETRY & AUDIENCE ANNUAL POETRY COMPETITION; GREAT NORTHERN UNION (I, II), School of English, University of Leeds, Leeds, West Yorkshire LJ2 9JT England, founded 1953, editor Michael Paraskos. *P&A* and *PPM* each appear 3-4/year. Both are "general poetry journals accepting work from new and established poets," both with press runs of 300-500 for 100 subscribers of which 20 are libraries. *P&A* is somewhat larger and more elegant. **"We do not discriminate against any form of poetry although there is a general move towards a more lyrical style. This said, we have and will continue to publish even the most obscure poetic forms."** They have recently published poetry by Carol Ann Duffy, Iaian Duhig and John Goodby. As a sample the editor selected these lines from "As She Left Us" by Peter Redgrove:

As she left us, the tension
From the thundercloud grazing
The land lessened. We lifted
Our glasses to her absence and took
A sip. . . .

"Poetry must be sent either to *P&A* or *PPM*, not both. Indicate on envelope which. Please double or a least use 1.5 spacing for all lines with triple-line spacing of stanzas. Please give birth date and place in any correspondence as well as previous publications, if applicable. No comments on rejections." The editor of *P&A* has a small consultative council. *Pelicans* is a more personal magazine with a rotating or sometimes joint editorship. Replies for either: 2 months. Subscription for either: £10 (overseas). **Sample: £1.50. Pays 1 copy.** *P&A* holds an annual contest with "minor cash awards and publications of winners." They founded Great Northern Union, "which brings together the university poets of Northern England."

POETRY BREAK; BEING; ANNUAL POETRY CONTEST (I, IV-Spirituality/occult/horror), P.O. Box 417, Oceanside CA 92049-0417, founded 1988, (*Poetry Break* formerly *The Creative Urge*, founded 1984), editor and publisher Marjorie Talarico. *Poetry Break* is a bimonthly magazine that publishes poetry and sometimes articles and short stories. **All subjects and styles of poetry are welcomed. There is a Youth Poetry Page for ages 5-12 and a Young Adult Poetry Page for ages 13-18.** *Being* is a bimonthly "New Age, Metaphysical, magickal, wholisstic health and healing journal." For *PB* the editor wants **rhyming, traditional, haiku, experimental poetry. No restriction in length.** For *Being*, **"poems, prose, haiku, experimental poetry, up to 100 lines. "Poems can be erotic, no porno, however." Guidelines for both magazines are available for SASE.** They have recently published poetry by Chester Ray Mattox, Marguerite Bell, Michael R. Roth, Sister Mary Ann Hern and Terry Lee. As a sample the editor selected these lines from "Fire" by Paul Truttman:

From the pit of despair comes a rekindled fire,
dressed for battle in regimental attire.
With order and precision, going again to meet,
the forces once contributing to its defeat.

Poetry Break is digest-sized, 32-36 pp., sometimes illustrated with pen and ink drawings; it uses 80 to 100 poems bimonthly. Circulation is about 375. **Pays in copies only. "We accept photocopy, dot-matrix printed, handwritten (legible, please)." Reporting time is 6-12 weeks and time to publication is 2-6 months.** Subscription for *Poetry Break* is $10/year, $2 per issue. **Sample: $2 plus 7½×10½ SASE with 75¢ postage.** Subscription for *Being* is $12/year, $3 per single issue. **Sample: $3 plus 7½×10½ SASE with 75¢ postage. Please make checks/money orders for samples/subscriptions payable to Marjorie Talarico.** They are planning to publish a horror anthology in 1992 and are considering contributions.

THE POETRY CONNEXION (II, IV-Specialized), Wanda Coleman and Austin Straus, co-hosts, P.O. Box 29154, Los Angeles CA 90029-0154, founded 1981, contact person Austin Straus. **"The Poetry Connexion" is a radio program, usually live; poets coming to the LA area make contact several months**

in advance and send work with SASE just as though the program were a press. "We are especially interested in poets who are planning to do readings in the Los Angeles area. Please notify us at least three months in advance for consideration as a guest on our program. Always include at least 6 poems and a vita in any submission." The program is heard on the first, third, and fifth Saturdays of each month from 6:00 to 7:00 p.m. Its purpose is "to broaden the audience, reading and listening, for poetry in the Southern California area which is now experiencing a cultural 'boom' of sorts. We are volunteer Pacifica Radio broadcasters and do not pay." The co-hosts say, "We have a preference for the 'serious' poet who has published in recognized magazines. The poet may not necessarily have a book but must be on the verge of publishing, participating in workshops, readings, residencies, etc." Submissions are open, but they "prefer the accessible. We are also always most interested in poets whose lives are as committed and intense as their work."

POETRY DURHAM (II), English Dept., University of Durham, New Elvet, Durham, England DH1 3JT, edited by David Hartnett, Michael O'Neill and Gareth Reeves, founded 1982, appears 3 times a year, 44 pp., digest-sized, professionally printed on good stock with glossy card cover, circulation 300, using **quality poetry and essays on modern poetry. Pays £12 per poem.** Reviews books of poetry. **All overseas subscriptions by international money order.** Subscription: £4.50 for 3 issues). As a sample I selected the complete poem "Deadly Nightshade" by Sally Carr:

> *Strange on the tongue*
> *those names that proffer ill—*
> *monkshood, hemlock and deadly nightshade.*
>
> *Offering the very sensation of death,*
> *the moment of coming sleep*
> *in a room suffused with dark—*
>
> *they dare you to pick them.*

POETRY EAST (II), Dept. of English, 802 West Belden Ave., De Paul University, Chicago IL 60614, phone (312)341-8330, founded 1980, editor Richard Jones, "is a biannual international magazine publishing poetry, fiction, translations, and reviews. We suggest that authors look through back issues of the magazine before making submissions. **No constraints or specifications, although we prefer open form.**" They have published poetry by Tom Crawford, Thomas McGrath, Denise Levertov, Calway Kinnell, Sharon Olds, and Amiri Baraka. As a sample the editor chose "Cobalt" by David Ray:

> *Cobalt wouldn't*
> *leap out to join*
> *the bomb, not*
> *the cobalt of*
> *this blue ming*
> *vase, not the cobalt*
> *of a bluejay's wing,*
> *not the cobalt of*
> *your eyes, my love.*

The digest-sized flat-spined, 100+ pp., journal is professionally printed, glossy color card cover, circulation 1,200, 250 subscriptions of which 80 are libraries. They use 60-80 pp. of poetry in each issue. Subscription: $10; per copy: $7. They receive approximately 4,000 freelance submissions per year, use 10%, have a 16-week backlog. **Sample: $4.50 postpaid. Reports in 4 months. Pays copies. Editors sometimes comment on rejections.**

THE POETRY EXPLOSION NEWSLETTER (THE PEN) (I), Box 2648, Newport News VA 23609-0648, phone (804)874-2428, founded 1984, editor Arthur C. Ford, Sr., is a "quarterly newsletter dedicated to the preservation of poetry." Arthur Ford wants **"poetry—40 lines maximum, no minimum. All forms and subject-matter with the use of good imagery, symbolism, and honesty. Rhyme and non-rhyme. No vulgarity."** He has recently published poetry by Ursula T. Gibson, Veona Thomas and Rose Robaldo. As a sample he chose his own poem, "Racism":

> *Whether white as light*
> *Black, or still another,*
> *Only painters have the right*
> *To be, biased toward color.*

The Pen is a newsletter containing 4 sheets (saddle-stitched) mimeographed on both sides of each sheet. He accepts about 80 of 300 poems received, press run 350, with 165 subscriptions of which 5 are libraries. Subscription: $12. **Send $3 for sample copy and more information. Pays 1 copy. Submit maximum of 5 poems. Include $1 for reading time. Simultaneous submissions and previously published poems OK. Editor comments on rejections "sometimes, but not obligated."** He holds poetry contests twice a year. He will criticize poetry for 15¢ a word. He comments:

"Even though free verse is more popular today, we try to stay versatile."

POETRY FORUM (I); THE JOURNAL (IV-Subscription), 5713 Larchmont Dr., Erie PA 16509, phone (814)866-2543, poetry editor Gunvor Skogsholm, appears 3 times a year. **"We are open to any style and form. We believe new forms ought to develop from intuition. Length up to 50 lines accepted. Would like to encourage long themes. No porn or blasphemy, but open to all religious persuasions."** As a sample the editor selected these lines (poet unidentified):

> Is it anger I see in your eyes
> when they look at mine
> Because I see no smile or happiness
> there—merely a blank stare.

The magazine is 7 × 8½", 38 pp., saddle-stapled with card cover, photocopied from photoreduced typescript. **Sample: $3 postpaid. Send SASE for guidelines. They will consider simultaneous submissions and previously published poems. They give awards of $50, $25, and $10 and 3 honorable mentions for the best poems in each issue.** *The Journal* appears twice a year, accepts **experimental poetry of any length from subscribers only. Sample $2.** Reviews books of poetry. They offer a poetry and short story chapbook contest, grand prize $100, send SASE for information. **Editor comments on poems "if asked, but respects the poetic freedom of the artist."** He says, "I believe today's poets should experiment more and not feel stuck in the forms that were in vogue 300 years ago."

POETRY HALIFAX DARTMOUTH; BS POETRY SOCIETY; NOVA SCOTIA POETRY AWARDS (I, II), BS Poetry Society, 7074 North, Halifax, Nova Scotia B3K 5J4 Canada, founded 1986, poetry editor Mark Hamilton, publishes the bimonthly literary magazine, *Poetry Halifax Dartmouth* with a calendar of literary activities, markets and announcements and the work of 5-12 writers in each issue, and articles relevant to writing. **"We're interested in quality writing with a broad span of interest. We are not specifically a regional magazine. Our contributors and readers are both national and international in range. We also publish short fiction, Canadian book reviews and b&w art. Encourage new writers. Rhymes rarely used. Will not accept material which is racist, sexist, homophobic or classist."** They have recently published poems by Joanne Light, Rick Armstrong and John Doull, Jr. *PHD* is 24-36 pp., 7 × 8½", saddle-stapled, with matte card cover and b&w art and photos. They accept about 75 poets a year or ¼-⅓ of authors who submit. Press run is 250 for 75 subscriptions of which 12 are libraries. Subscription: $15. **Sample: $2 postpaid. Pays in 2 contributor's copies plus $5. Submit up to 6 poems with short bio. Reports in 2 months.** Reviews books of poetry. Send SASE for information on the annual Nova Scotia Poetry Awards, open to national and international entries. Entry fee.

POETRY IRELAND REVIEW (II, IV-Regional), 44 Upper Mount St., Dublin 2, Ireland, founded 1981, "provides an outlet for **Irish poets; submissions from abroad also considered. No specific style or subject matter is prescribed."** Occasionally publishes special issues—recently Latin American Poetry. The 6 × 8" quarterly uses 60 pp. of poetry in each issue, circulation 1,000, with 450 subscriptions of which 50 are libraries. Subscription: $30; per copy: $8 (U.S.). They receive about 2,500 submissions per year, use 250, have a 3 month backlog. **Sample: $7 postpaid. Submit photocopies, no simultaneous submissions, no query. Reports in 3 months. Pays in copies.** Reviews books of poetry. The editors advise, "Keep submitting: good work will get through."

‡POETRY KANTO (V, II, IV-Translation), Kanto Gakuin University, Mutsuura, Kanazawa-Ku, Yokohama, Japan 236, founded 1984, editor William I. Elliott. *Poetry Kanto* is a literary annual published by the Kanto Poetry Center, which sponsors an annual poetry conference. It publishes well-crafted original poems in English and in Japanese (the Summer 1988 issue was devoted to translations). The magazine is **"open to anything except pornography, English haiku and tanka, and tends to publish poems under 30 lines."** They are not currently accepting submissions because the 1990 issue will specialize in contemporary French poetry with Japanese translations thereof. They have recently published work by Seamus Heaney, Desmond Egan, Shuntaro Tanikawa and Les Murray. As a sample, I selected the final stanza from "A Suite . . ." by Serge Gavronsky:

> Is it perverse to be inspired
> by poems when outside
> a pine tree
> waits
> for my pen to move
> in a respectful manner?

The magazine is digest-sized, nicely printed (the English poems occupy the first half of the issue, the Japenese poems the second), 60 pp. saddle-stapled, matte card cover. Circulation is 700, of which 400 are complimentary copies sent to schools, poets, and presses; it is also distributed at poetry seminars. The magazine is unpriced. **Guidelines are on the editorial page. "Because** special numbers are planned, do not submit poems before querying." Pay is 3-5 copies. Submissions should be typed, double-spaced. September-January is the best time to submit MSS. Reporting time is usually 2 weeks and there is no backlog except in special cases. The editor advises, "Read a lot. Get feedback from poets and/or workshops. Be neat, clean, legible, and polite in submissions. *SAE with international reply coupons absolutely necessary when submitting poems or requesting sample copy.*"

POETRY MAGIC PUBLICATIONS (I, IV-Love/Romance, anthology), 1630 Lake Dr., Haslett MI 48840, founded 1987, editor Lisa R. Church. Publishes an anthology and newsletter for writers, looking for **"no specific style. Open to all types, including haiku. Length should be no longer than one 8½×11"** page but will consider longer poems. We want work from the writer/poet's heart and soul — not something that is 'forced.' No pornographic. Sexual themes are okay but will be left to the editor's decision." They have published poetry by Maria Bakkum. As a sample she selected these lines from "Gauntlets of Threadbare Silk" by Scott Sonders:

> *i begin again*
> *when mind and soul are through*
> *to start the walk long down the hall*
> *to lie alone and think of you*

The anthology is digest-sized, 170 pages, flat-spined, 1-3 poems per page, with a matte cover with color art. $16.95 list price. **No payment. Discount to authors.** Newsletter features articles, contest information, market listings and **poem relating to the art of writing.** Subscription: $13.50 for newsletter. **Sample postpaid: $4. Pays 1 copy to $100 for newsletter. Send SASE for guidelines. MS should be typed on one side of paper. "Will accept hand-written material only if it is legible —otherwise, it ends up in file 'trash.' "** Submit MSS for newsletter anytime; anthology deadline: March of each year. Simultaneous submissions, previously published poems OK if stated as such. Reports in 4-6 weeks. Editor comments **"if time permits us to."** Reviews books of poetry "sometimes." She says, "I have found those individuals who persistently work at their craft will receive the deserved recognition. I suggest that beginners circulate their poems and their name to many editors, which will allow the editors to become familiar with the name and the work. It is strongly suggested that at all times beginners present themselves in a professional manner. If SASE not enclosed, work will be discarded."

‡THE POETRY MISCELLANY (II), English Dept., University of Tennessee at Chattanooga, Chattanooga TN 37403, founded 1971 (in North Adams, MA), poetry editor Richard Jackson. "We publish new and established writers—poems, interviews, essays, translations. We are truly a miscellany: **we look at all schools, types, etc..**" They have recently published poetry by Robert Penn Warran, Charles Simic, Mark Strand, William Matthews, John Ashbery, Richard Wilbur, Maxine Kumin, Donald Justice and David Ignatow. As a sample I selected the opening lines of "In No Particular Season" by Linda Pastan:

> *On a day like this of tatterned leaves*
> *in no particular season,*
> *I seem to have outgrown my life*
> *like last year's winter coat—unravelling . . .*

The 6×8½", 75 pp. biannual, professionally printed, blue ink on tinted blue, grey, or white paper, matte card cover, stapled spine, has a circulation of 650, 450 subscriptions of which 150 are libraries. Subscription: $4; per copy: $2. They receive about 8,000 submissions per year, use 30, have a 6-12 month backlog. **"We will also start doing chapbooks of 6-8 poems in 1989, probably 3 a year. Sample: $2.50 postpaid. Send 3-4 clear copies per submission. Reports in 3-3½ months. Pays 1 copy. Send SASE for guidelines.** They sometimes hold contests **"when grants allow."** Editor **"rarely"** comments on rejections.

POETRY MOTEL; SUBURBAN WILDERNESS PRESS, BROADSIDES AND CHAPBOOKS; (I, II), 1619 Jefferson, Duluth MN 55812, founded 1984, editors Pat McKinnon, Bud Backen and Jennifer Willis-Long aim **"to keep the rooms clean and available for these poor ragged poems to crash in once they are thru driving or committing adultery."** No specifications. They have recently published poetry by Jesse Glass, Robert Peters, Paul Fericano, Ligi and Janet Gray. *Poetry Motel* appears 1-2 times a year, 8½×7", digest, various covers, including wallpaper (issue 16) and chrome plated mylar (issue #10), circulation 500 (to 450 subscriptions), 50-60 pp. of poetry, prose, essays and reviews. Sample: $4.95. They receive about 1,000 submissions per year, take 150, have 6-8 month backlog. **Submit 3-5 pp., informal cover letter, name and address on each page. Photocopy OK. Simultaneous submissions OK. Reports in 1-3 weeks. Pays in copies.** Editors are **"always glad to comment, on request."** Reviews books of poetry. They advise, "Poets should read as much poetry as they can lay their hands on. And they should realize that although poetry is no fraternal club, poets are responsible for its survival, both financially and emotionally. Join us out here—this is where the edge meets the vision. We are very open to work from 'beginners.' "

POETRY NEW YORK: A JOURNAL OF POETRY AND TRANSLATION (II, IV-Translations, themes), PhD Program in English, CUNY, 33 W. 42nd St., New York NY 10036, phone (212)642-2206, founded 1985, editors Burt Kimmelman and Cheryl Fish, is an annual. The have recently published poetry by John Ashbery, Jerome Rothenberg, Enid Dame, Weatherly, Armand Schwerner, Ann Lauterbach, and translations of Mallarme, Hesiod and Makoto Ooka. I have not seen an issue, but the editor describes it as 4¼×5½″ saddle-stapled, 80 pp., with glossy card cover. They accept about 20% of "blind submissions." Press run: 500 for 300 shelf sales. **Pays 2 copies. Reports in 3-4 months. Editor comments on submissions "at times." Some issues are on themes. "Query to see what we're up to."** They sometimes sponsor readings.

POETRY NIPPON PRESS; THE POETRY SOCIETY OF JAPAN; POETRY NIPPON; POETRY NIPPON NEWSLETTER (II, IV-Form, translations), 5-11-2, Nagaike-cho, Showa-ku, Nagoya, Japan 466, phone (052)833-5724, founded 1967, poetry editors Atsuo Nakagawa and Yorifumi Yaguchi (and guest editors). *Poetry Nippon,* a quarterly, uses **translations of Japanese poems into English, poems by Western and Japanese poets, tanka, haiku, one-line poems, essays on poetry and poets, poetry book reviews, poetry news, home and abroad. They want tanka, haiku, one-line poems and poems on contemporary themes and on Japan.** They have published poetry by Yorifumi Yaguchi and Toshimi Horiuchi and Naoshi Koriyama. The editor selected these sample lines by James Kirkup:

> There is no other place
> like the room we were born in,
> The moment no one remembers
> is enshrined in it for ever.

Poetry Nippon has a circulation of 500 with 200 subscriptions of which 30 are libraries. Subscription: $29; per copy: $8. They use 25% of the 400 submissions they receive each year, have a 6-12 month backlog. **Sample free for 4 IRCs. Submit 2 poems, 5 tanka or 6 haiku, unpublished and not submitted elsewhere. "Deadline March 31 for nonmembers." Reports in 6 months for members. Payment is made in copies. Send SAE with 2 IRC's for guidelines.** Apparently you can join the Poetry Society of Japan, receive the *Newsletter* and *Poetry Nippon* and have other benefits. For example, **the editors provide criticism "on members' MSS only."** They sponsor contests for tanka and haiku and publish collections by individuals and anthologies.

POETRY NORTHWEST (II), 4045 Brooklyn NE, Seattle WA 98105, phone (206)543-2992, founded 1959, poetry editor David Wagoner, is a quarterly which uses 48 pp. of poetry in each issue, circulation 2,000. Subscription: $10; per issue: $3. They receive 30,000 poems in freelance submissions per year, use 160, have a 6 month backlog. **Sample: $3 postpaid. Reports in 1 month maximum, pays 2 copies. They award prizes of $100, $50 and $50 yearly, judged by the editors. Occasionally editor comments on rejections.**

POETRY NOTTINGHAM; LAKE ASKE MEMORIAL OPEN POETRY COMPETITION (II); NOTTING-HAM POETRY SOCIETY (IV-Regional); QUEENIE LEE COMPETITION (IV-Membership/subscription), Summer Cottage West St., Shelford, Notts. NG12 1EJ Nottingham England, phone 0602 334540, founded 1941, poetry editor Claire Piggott. Nottingham Poetry Society meets monthly for readings, talks, etc., and publishes quarterly its magazine, *Poetry Nottingham: The International Magazine of Today's Poetry,* which is open to submissions from all comers. **"We wish to see poetry that is intelligible to and enjoyable by the intelligent reader. We do not want any party politics or religious freaks. Poems not more than 40 lines in length."** They have recently published poetry by Bert Almon, William Davey and Ken Pobo from the USA. The editor selected these sample lines by Maurice Rutherford from "Half-Term":

> And if you've ever wondered what goes on
> inside the heads of men who sit on seats
> and ogle passers-by, come, sit with me,
> it's marvelous . . . fantastic's more the word!
> I chose at will, make this one rich, that poor . . .

There are 36 pp. of poetry in each issue of the 6×8″, magazine, professional printing with occasional b/w graphics, color matte card cover, circulation 325, for 200 subscriptions of which 20 are libraries. Subscriptions: £7 ($50 for 2 years USA); per copy: £1.50 ($6 USA). They receive about 1,500 submissions per year, use 120, usually have a 1-4 month backlog. **Sample: $6 or £1.50 postpaid. Submit at any time 3-5 poems, not more than 40 lines each, not handwritten, and previously unpublished. Send SAE and 2 IRC's for stamps. No need to query. Reports "within 3 months plus mailing time." Pays one copy.** Nottingham Poetry Society publishes collections by individual poets who were born, live or work in the East Midlands of England. Reviews books of poetry, but space allows only listings or brief review. The Lake Aske Memorial Open Poetry Competition offers cash prizes, annual subscriptions and publication in *Poetry Nottingham*. Open to all. The Queenie Lee Competition is for members and subscribers only, offers a cash prize and publication. **Editor accepts "when I feel the poet learned the craft and says something objectively worth hearing."** Her advice, especially for beginners, is "read the magazine before submitting anything; write the kind of poetry you believe in, which, if it is any good, will find a magazine to publish it." As a footnote, to help US poets understand some of the problems of editors in other countries, I'd like to quote Claire Piggott at length: "May I suggest that a general note about how to pay for small magazines from England that sell only a few copies in the USA, with a recommendation to send a draft for sterling, would be helpful to your readers. The price of our magazine is low (£7 annual subscription in the U.K.). If, however, I wish to exchange a draft from the USA, the bank charges me £3 commission (their commission being the same whether I am exchanging $10 or $10,000). Therefore, we are now asking that overseas subscribers who cannot arrange a draft for sterling should take out a two-year subscription for $50 to include all postage at increased rates. The advice about sterling drafts applies equally to sample copies; please allow £2.50 to include airmail post."

POETRY OF THE PEOPLE (I,IV-Anthology, humor, political, love/romance/erotica, nature, fantasy, themes), Box 13077, Gainesville FL 32604, founded 1986, poetry editor Paul Cohen. *Poetry of the People* appears once a month. **"We take all forms of poetry but we like humorous poetry, love poetry, nature poetry and fantasy. No racist or highly ethnocentric poetry will be accepted."** As an example the editor selected lines from a poem by Jenny L. Kelly:

> *And then we two walk naked into the town*
> *Hand in hand among hordes of people*
> *Who stop and stare in utter disbelief*
> *Not at our nakedness*
> *But rather at our radiance*

Poetry of the People has a circulation between 300 and 2,300. Copies are distributed to Gainesville residents for 25¢ each. **"I feel autobiographical information is important in understanding the poetry." Poems returned within three months. Editor comments on rejections "often."** In depth Critique: $3. He advises, "be creative: there is a lot of competition out there." **A dozen leaflets (8-16 pp., 4½×5¼", sometimes stapled on colored paper)** of poetry are published each year, usually theme anthologies. **Pays 5 copies. Subscription: $8 per year. Sample $1.50. Make checks payable to Paul Cohen.**

POETRY ONLY; FORESTLAND PUBLICATIONS (I), P.O. Box 213, Canterbury CT 06331-0213, founded 1988, editor Geraldine Hempstead. *Poetry Only* is a magazine. **"No restrictions on form, length or subject-matter. If it's a long poem, it better be exciting enough to keep me awake. No porn."** They have published poetry by Ray Mizer, Gary Scheinoha, Winnie Fitzpatrick, R. Allen Dodson and Ken Stone. As a sample the editor quoted these lines by John Rautio:

> *The world is nothing more you see*
> *than a Reflection of you and me*
> *the Rich are the ones in Poverty*
> *when they don't understand Life's simple poetry*

Press run 100, with 15 subscribers, 75 distributed free. Subscription: $8.50. **Sample: $2 postpaid. All orders must be made payable to Geraldine Hilliard not *Poetry Only*. Pays 1 copy. Send SASE for guidelines. They will consider simultaneous submissions and previously published poems.**

THE POETRY PEDDLER; SNOWBOUND PRESS (I, II), P.O. Box 250, West Monroe NY 13167, founded 1988, poetry editors J. J. Snow and A. M. Ryant. Snowbound Press publishes chapbooks by special arrangement. *PP* is a literary magazine of poetry and essays on poetry appearing six times a year, using **"poems of clarity and intensity of feeling. We will consider rhymed poetry of a serious nature providing the rhyme doesn't overwhelm the message. Seldom does a rhymed poem meet this standard. Rhyme used to augment humor is welcome. No bigotry, pro-war, graphic violence, obscure poems."** Poetry recently published by Susan Manchester, Walt Phillips, Jack Karpan, Asha Eshe and Helene Shrier. As a sample J. J. Snow chose the last lines from "Sidewalk Sale" by Kathleen Lee Mendel:

> *She trashes her cigarette*
> *sways catlike*
> *and advances*
> *toward her next paycheck.*

PP is 20 pp., magazine-sized, desktop publishing, with card covers, using some comptuer-generated graphics. **Send SASE for guidelines. Subscription: $10. Sample: $2. They will consider previously published poems** (send complete publications information and statement that you now control rights) but no simultaneous submissions. "Handwritten OK if legible." Editor always comments on rejections. Pays 1 copy.

POETRY PLUS MAGAZINE; GERMAN PUBLICATIONS (I, IV-Subscribers), Route 1, Box 52, Pulaski IL 62976, founded 1987, publisher/editor Helen D. German. *PPM* is a quarterly with articles about poetry, stories and poems. "We accept all styles. Length should be no more than 24 lines. Poets can write on any subject that offers a meaningful message. We want our poets to write poems that will make the reader really think about what has been said. Reader should not have to guess at what was said. We do *not* want any holiday poems, obscene poems or sexual poems. Poems should not be indecent." As a sample the editor selected this complete poem by Terry Lee Armstrong:

A Poet:
One who reads, writes, and thinks
While dwelling in the silence
of the light of thought.

PPM is magazine-sized, 25-35 pp., photocopied from typescript, bound with tape, paper cover. Subscription: $12. **Sample: $3 postpaid. Send SASE for guidelines. Subscribers are paid up to $5 for outstanding poems; no payment to non-subscribers.** The editor says, *"Poetry Plus* is a fresh magazine that offers poets and writers the opportunity to see their poems in print. We want poems that are written to stimulate the deeper side of the reader. Rhymed or unrhymed, poems should offer a message that is meaningful. They should leave a memorable impression. Always send a large SASE with sufficient postage to return your unused poems. We publish both the work of our subscribers and nonsubscribers. Of course due to limited space in each issue, subscribers get their poems published first. If you haven't been published yet or if you have, order a sample copy today and see what you've been missing in literary refreshment."

POETRY REVIEW; NATIONAL POETRY SOCIETY: NATIONAL POETRY COMPETITION: EUROPEAN POETRY TRANSLATION PRIZE: NATIONAL POETRY CENTRE: WH SMITH POETS IN SCHOOLS SCHEME: PUFFIN PROJECT: POEMS ON THE UNDERGROUND (II, IV-Children), 21 Earls Court Sq., London, SW5 9DE England, founded 1909, The National Poetry Society is Britain's largest and most influential poetry organization. In addition to their quarterly journal, *Poetry Review*, they maintain the directory of the National Poetry Society (including lists of poets' publications and fees), and conduct educational programs for school children and others, and other activities (including Poems on the Underground, for publishing poems in subways). Membership in the Society is available for poets throughout the world, with group rates. The only instructions as to the type of poetry wanted in *PR* (editor Peter Forbes) are, **"Intending contributors should study the magazine first."** They publish "all the leading UK poets, many American and European poets." Recent poets featured include Joseph Brodsky, Anthony Hecht, Derek Walcott, Tony Harrison, Howard Nemerov, Primo Levi, and Vikram Seth. As a sample, the editor chose four lines from David Sutton's "Geomancies":

Like a careful Chinese geomancer
I play the game: where shall I build my house?
As if my days and money left more choice
Than standard boxes, twenty to the acre.

Poetry Review is 6¾ × 9¾", 76 pp., offset on rough paper, with b/w graphics and photos. Stiff card cover, printed in two colors plus black on white, flat-spined. Circulation is 5,000, price per issue £3.95, subscription £19 ($40). All subscriptions, payable to *Poetry Review*, to: Central Books, 99 Wallis Rd., London E95LN, England. **Sample available for £5 ($9) postpaid, guidelines for SASE. Pay is £10-15 poem, plus 1 copy. Reporting time is 10 weeks and time to publication** varies. Reviews books of poetry. The National Poetry Competition offers prizes of £2,000, £1,000, £500 and 15 smaller prizes, for 40 lines or less on any subject, open worldwide. The winning poems are published as an anthology. Write for information regarding the European Poetry Translation Prize, membership, or their other activities.

POETRY TODAY (I), Suite 60, 4950 Richard St., Jacksonville FL 32207, founded 1989, editor Diane Chehab, appears monthly with poetry of **"any length or style, no restrictions. Looking for first-rate poetry, carefully-crafted and original. Very open to beginning poets. Use good taste, judgment. No smut."** As a sample the editor selected these lines from her own "Angel of Death":

Empty halls
Shadows
Eclipse my tears
Clutching at her shawl
In the corner
Full of fear
A mourner—
I stand near.

I have not seen an issue, but the editor describes it as digest-sized, 20-30 pp., saddle-stapled, color cover with b/w drawing. Subscription: $24. **Sample postpaid: $3. Checks should be made out to D. Chehab. Pays 2 copies. "Refrain from using dot matrix please."** They hope to have contests with monetary prizes in the future and to pay for poetry. They also encourage submissions of drawings for their covers. The editor says, "One must endeavor to read as much as possible, especially other poets. Study people for their reactions. Be the fly on the wall. Write as much as possible and save everything; don't throw anything away. You can use it later to gauge your progress and rewrite what you once thought belonged in the wastebasket."

POETRY: USA QUARTERLY: POEMS FOR PLANETARY SURVIVAL; (I, II, IV-Themes, children, membership), Ft. Mason Cultural Center, San Francisco CA 94123, founded 1985, editor Herman Berlandt, who describes *Poetry: USA Quarterly* as "a quarterly for **bold and compassionate poetry.** Every issue has a thematic focus: for example, love and experience, four dozen ways of looking at the moon, in praise of other muses, etc. Send SASE for upcoming themes. The editor does not want "trite and phoney, 'elevated' stuff using contrived rhymes."** He has published poetry by Amy Gerstler, Mary Mackey, Diane di Prima, Neeli Chekovski and Robert Bly. As a sample he selected these lines (poet unidentified):

> When I called your name
> it was a question
> glimmering in the high air
> so beautiful
> it had no answer

It is a typeset unstapled tabloid, 16 pp., with photos, graphics and ads, circulation 10,000, distributed free "to reach 40,000 literati in the Bay Area" and available to others by subscription at $7.50/year. **Sample: $1.50 postpaid. "Big backlog, active file for a year. Suggest poems under 32 lines. No SASEs. Just send photocopies — if published, contributor will get copies." No other pay "as yet. Suggest that contributors subscribe to maintain good contact." One section of the tabloid is devoted to poetry by young poets.** They hold four annual contests, on the theme of each issue. Contributors are encouraged to subscribe. Send SASE for guidelines. Previously published poems OK (if the editor knows).

‡POETRY VOICE (I, II), 32 Ridgemere Rd., Pensby Wirral Merseyside, U.K. L61 8RL phone (051)648-5683, founded 1988, editor George Robinson, appears 1-2/year using **"poetry of good quality (modern), good imagery and musical to the ear. Humour possible. Vivid and arresting is what I like. Concrete poems. No traditional end-stopped rhyming stuff or archaic imitations."** They have recently published poetry by Matt Simpson, Gladys May Coles, Carole Satyamuski and David Scott. As a sample the editor selected these lines by George Spirtes:

> A voice in another room calls out a name
> you do not recognize but know is yours
> So many ways with so few syllables that you must claim
> along with clothes as dead men's metaphors.

I have not seen an issue, but the editor describes it as "A5 glossy card cover, astroluxe cartoons." Press run 500 for 90 subscriptions of which 20 are libraries. They use about 10% of poetry received. Subscription: $4.50. **Sample: $1.25 postpaid. Send SASE for guidelines. Pays 1-2 copies. Editor comments "sometimes if asked."** He operates a criticism service at $10/100 lines.

POETRY WALES PRESS; POETRY WALES (II, IV-Ethnic), Andmar House, Trewsfield Ind. Estate, Tondu Rd., Bridgend, Mid-Glamorgan, CF31 4LJ Wales, founded 1965. *Poetry Wales,* a 72 pp. 253×185mm. quarterly, circulation 1,000, has a primary interest in **Welsh and Anglo-Welsh poets but also considers submissions internationally. Sample: £1.95. Pays.** Reviews books of poetry. The press publishes books of **primarily Welsh and Anglo Welsh poetry,** also biography, critical works and some fiction, distributed by Dufour Editions, Inc., Box 449, Chester Springs, PA 19425. I selected the first of 6 stanzas of "The Dark" by Richard Poole as a sample:

> And now, it seems, you are fearful
> of the dark. You people black vacancies
> with monsters of your own imagining.

 The double dagger before a listing indicates that the listing is new in this edition. New markets are often the most receptive to submissions.

POETRY/LA, PEGGOR PRESS (IV-Regional), P.O. Box 84271, Los Angeles CA 90073, phone (213)472-6171, founded 1980, editor Helen Friedland, assistant editor Barbara Strauss, "is a semi-annual anthology of **high quality poems by established and new poets living, working or attending school in the Los Angeles area. Otherwise, high literary quality is our only constraint.**" They have published poetry recently by Peter Levitt, Charles Bukowski, Carol Lem, Gerald Locklin, Amy Uyematsu and Lee Chul Bum. As to selecting a sample, the editor says, "Since our orientation is eclectic, quoting one poem would draw too many submissions with that poem's traits." With that warning, I selected the opening lines of "Errant" by Ron Koertge, hoping his style is inimitable but does represent the quality of the magazine:

> You wanted me to take care
> of that dragon who was bothering
> you, and I was glad to. He wasn't
> much bigger than a pig and had breath
> like a kitchen match.

The flat-spined, digest-sized biannual, professionally printed, color matte card cover, circulation 500, 200 subscriptions of which 20 are libraries, uses about 120 pp. of poetry in each issue. Subscription: $8; per copy: $4.25. They receive 2,750 submissions per year, use 200. Almost all poems are published within 2-6 months from date of acceptance. **Sample: $3.50 postpaid. "We prefer about 4-6 pp., but will review all poems received. Clean photocopy is fine, simultaneous submissions are not. And, *please*, name and address on each poem (anonymous entries drive us crazy)."** They report in 1-6 months, pay copies only (one per printed page of the poet's work). Send SASE for guidelines. Editor comments "in general, only if we believe the poem merits publication if certain difficulties can be resolved."

‡POETS OF NOW (I, IV-Anthology, membership), 6100 Longmeadow Blvd. S., Saginaw MI 48603, phone (517)793-9036, founded 1987, editor Rosemary J. Schmidt. They publish a quarterly magazine, 2 annual anthologies, and chapbooks. **You have to be a member ($10/year) to submit to the magazine. All poets may submit to the anthology, 40 line limit (you have to buy a copy to get one). Chapbook publication is on a subsidy basis. No line limit for chapbooks. "No vulgarity."** They have recently published poetry by Irene Warsaw, Alice Mackinzie Swaim, Ann Gasser and Grant E. Henson. As a sample the editor selected these lines from "Closing Time" by James. A. Edgerton:

> So love must take
> a hastened gait
> and hurry
> through time's closing gate
> where we at last
> in leisure mate.

The magazine is digest-sized, 32 pp., saddle-stapled, with paper cover. Free book ads to members. They accept 125-150 poems of 4,000 submitted/year. Press run 1,100+ for 960 subscribers. Subscription: $10 (membership). **Sample for two 29¢ stamps, guidelines included. Do not submit MSS June/July. Reports in maximum of 6 mo. Editor often comments on rejections.** Will consider reviewing books of poetry if requested. They have 2 contests/year with prizes of $100, $50, $25, 3 of $10 and 3 of $5. Both contests are for anthology publication only—100 to 120 poems are selected per anthology. ($1/poem fee, at least 50 magazines from each issue are sent free to libraries).

POETS ON: (IV-Themes), 29 Loring Ave., Mill Valley CA 94941, phone (415)283-2824, founded 1976, poetry editor Ruth Daigon, is a 48 pp. poetry semiannual, **each issue on an announced theme. "We want well-crafted, humanistic, accessible poetry. We don't want to see sentimental rhymed verse. Length preferably 40 lines or less, or at the very most 80 lines (2 page poems)."** They have published poetry by Marge Piercy, Charles Edward Eaton, Joseph Bruchac, Sharon Olds and Lyn Lifshin. As a sample the editor chose these lines from "Today" by William Stafford:

> And it is already begun, the chord
> that will shiver glass, the song full of time
> bending above us. Outside, a sign:
> a bird intervenes; its wings tell the air,
> "Be warm." No one is out there, but a giant
> has passed through the town, widening streets touching
> the ground, shouldering away the stars.

The digest-sized, professionally printed magazine, matte card cover with b/w graphics, has a circulation of 450, 350 subscriptions of which 125 are libraries. Subscription: $8; per copy: $4. They use about 5% of the 800 submissions they receive each year, have a 2-3 month backlog. **Sample: $4 postpaid. Query with SASE to find out the current theme. Submit 1-4 poems (40 lines or shorter). "We generally do not publish rhymed or overly-sentimental poems although** we are open to experimentation. Again it's a good idea to read the magazine before submitting poetry." Submit only between September 1-December 1 or February 1-May 1. Photocopy, dot-matrix OK. No handwritten MSS. Include short bio. Reports in 2-3 months. Pays 1 copy. Editor sometimes comments on rejections. Ruth Daigon advises, "The poet should make him/herself open to whatever is being done in the world of poetry, whether they like it or not, whether they agree with it or not, whether they understand it or not."

POETS. PAINTERS. COMPOSERS; COLIN'S MAGAZINE (II), 10254 35th Ave. SW, Seattle WA 98146, phone (206)937-8155, founded 1984, editor Joseph Keppler, who says *"Poets. Painters. Composers.* is an avant-garde arts journal which publishes poetry, drawings, scores, criticism, essays, reviews, photographs and original art. **If poetry, music or art is submitted, the work should be exciting, knowledgeable and ingenious."** The journal, which appears once or twice a year, has published such artists as Carla Bertola, Fernando Aguia, Ana Hatherly and Sarenco and such poets as Carol Barrett, Carletta Wilson, D. Bauer and Gregory Jerozal. "We also publish *Colin's Magazine, A Special Review from Poets. Painters. Composers.* with a focus on the interface of literature and computer technology." As a sample the editor selected these lines from "Carpenter Mondrian" by Gregory Jerozal:

> . . . *Forget*
> *Green fields; they are*
> *The summer places of*
> *Regret, forgetfulness,*
> *The past we watch with others*
> *Reassembled on the screen.*

The very handsome, expensively printed fifth issue of the journal is magazine-sized, 86 pp. Each cover has an original painting on it. Mr. Keppler says, "each odd-numbered issue appears in an 8½×11″ format; each even-numbered issue changes format: No. 2, for example, is published as posters; No. 4 appears on cassettes." No 6 will be an exhibition of sculpture with a catalog and a collection of multiples. Circulation is 300, no subscriptions. Each issue of the magazine carries an individual price tag, A copy of **Poets. Painters. Composers. No. 5 is $50. Sample of No. 2 available for $10.50 postpaid. Sample of *Colin's Magazine* is available for $7. Contributors receive 1 copy. "Contributors' poetry receives great care. All material is returned right away unless (a) it's being painstakingly examined for acceptance or (b) it's being considered as right for some other way of publishing it or (c) we died."** He expects to publish 3 chapbooks of poetry a year and will accept freelance submissions. **For chapbook publication poets should query first "if poet prefers," sending credits, 7 sample poems, bio, philosophy and poetic aims. Pay for chapbooks will be in author's copies, number negotiable ("We're generous"); honorariums are given whenever possible.** Format of the chapbooks is expected to be "small, avant-garde, distinguished, exciting, experimental." Joseph Keppler says, "Poets' work is important work, and poetry is a most difficult art today. We maintain absolutely high standards, yet offer a hopeful critique . . . We want to develop the avant-garde here and everywhere. We expect to last well into the 21st Century and to change the way this culture understands literature. We intend to transform the role of poets in society. Advice for beginning poets? We're all beginning poets today."

POET'S REVIEW (IV-Subscribers), 806 Kings Row, Cohutta GA 30710, phone (404)694-8441, founded 1988, publisher Bob Riemke, is a monthly booklet, digest-sized, 20 pp., photocopied from typescript with paper cover, using poetry by subscribers and making cash awards monthly and annually on basis of votes by subscribers. **"Prefer rhyme. 44 lines or less. Any subject. No porn! No foreign languages."** They have recently published poetry by Helen Webb. As a sample the editor selected this stanza from "The Captain and the Queen," a $500 winner in a 1988 issue, by Ashley C. Anders:

> *They had grown up together,*
> *the Captain and his Queen;*
> *She was a strong majestic ship . . .*
> *He, a lad tall and lean.*

Subscription: $36. Sample: $4 postpaid. **"Subscribers are sent a ballot along with their monthly booklet to vote for the poems they believe to be the best." Monthly prizes are $75, $50 and $25, plus 7 honorable mentions. "All $75 winners are presented to the subscribers again at the end of the year and compete for a $500, $250 and $100 prize."** 20-30 poems are printed each month along with the names of winners for the previous month. Reviews books of poetry.

POETS' ROUNDTABLE; POETS' STUDY CLUB OF TERRE HAUTE; POETS' STUDY CLUB INTERNA-TIONAL CONTEST (I, IV-Membership), 826 S. Center St., Terre Haute IN 47807, phone (812)234-0819, founded in 1939, president/editor Esther Alman. Poets' Study Club is one of the oldest associations of amateur poets. It publishes every other month, *Poets' Roundtable*, a newsletter of market and contest information and news of the publications and activities of its members in a mimeographed, 10 pp. bulletin (magazine-sized, stapled at the corner, on colored paper), circulation 2,000. They have also published an occasional chapbook-anthology of poetry by members "but do not often do so." **Dues: $6 a year, sample free for SASE. Uses short poems by members only. Simultaneous submissions and previously published poems OK.** They offer an annual Poets' Study Club International Contest, open to all, with no fees and cash prizes—a $25 and $15 award in 3 categories: traditional haiku, serious poetry, light verse, deadline February 1. Also contests for members only each two months. "We have scheduled criticism programs for members only."

POGMENT PRESS (V,IV-Regional), 11939 Escalante Ct., Reston VA 22091, phone (703)758-0258, founded 1985, editor Jefferson D. Bates, an elderly man who writes, "I still have enough energy and enthusiasm to publish 3-4 chapbooks/year, but how long this will continue I have no idea. I publish area poets with whose work I am familiar. **I am not seeking MSS from outside my immediate area of Washington DC, Maryland and Northern Virginia.** As long-time member of the Board of Director of the Writer's Center (now a member emeritus) I have an opportunity to meet (and hear readings by) many excellent poets. **I'm more concerned with the traditional forms and the niceties of rime and meter than are most publishers today. I love light, well-crafted verse** in the vein of Dorothy Parker, Ogden Nash, Samuel Hoffenstein and others that I've admired from my youth. I love the 'Grooks' of Piet Hein." He has published books by Dean Blehert, Werner Low and Marlene S. Veach, **10% royalties plus 10 copies. Sample: $2, for postage and handling.** "I do have a co-op arrangement somewhat similar to that of Northwoods Press. The author agrees to purchase a minimum of 200 copies at 50% off the list price." **He sometimes comments on rejections.**

‡THE POINTED CIRCLE (II), 705 N. Killingsworth, Portland OR 97217, phone (503)244-6111, ext. 5405, founded 1980, advisor Mary McNeill, is an annual using **"under 60 lines, mostly shorter. 1-page poems on any topic of any form. Nothing trite."** They have recently published poetry by Judith Barrington, William Stafford, Dianne Averill and Barbara Drake. As a sample, I selected these sample lines from "Greenwood" by D.M. Wallace:

> lain out naked and long
> iI mocked all my surfaces,
> all that remains green and
> mirrored in a Catskill pool

It is handsomely printed, 7×8", flat-spined, 80 pp, with b/w glossy card cover, professionally printed. Press run 400. **Sample: $3.50 postpaid. Submit MSS from December 1-March 1 only.** Send SASE for guidelines. Pays 1 copy. "Place name, address, etc. on cover sheet only, listing titles of submissions. Limit 5 poems/poet. All submissions are read anonymously by student editorial staff; notification about June 1 for submissions received by March 1.

‡POKED WITH STICKS; POKED PRESS; RED STAR PRODUCTIONS (II), 648 Winthrop #B, Toledo OH 43620, founded 1987, editor Stephen E. Toth, co-editor Star Bowers. *PWS* appears once or twice/year. Poked Press Publications publishes a chapbook/year. They want poetry "any style from traditional to experimental. No gender bashing, no contrived rhyme or 'praise be to god' rhetoric. 'Sweet little kitty' verse should be sent to greeting card manufacturers, not here." They have recently published poetry by Joel Lipman, William Merricle, Todd Moore and Lynne Walker. As a sample the editor selected these lines from "Bury the Moon" by Ronald Edward Kittell:

> poems essays lovenotes novels
> words buzz the page like flies
> on feces & more often than not
> the moon sticks out like a
> festering boil

I have not seen an issue, but the editor describes it as 40 pp. photocopied. Press run 300. They accept about 10% of 600 poems received/year. Subscription: $10/4 issues. **Sample postpaid: $2.** Pays 1 copy. "Because *PWS* is a collection of poetry, writing and mail art, I accept pieces in the exact form in which they are sent. Line length and spacing remains as the creator intended. All submitted copies must be dark enough for photoduplication and very rarely is anything retyped." Reports in 1-3 months. To be considered for chapbook publication, a poem must have been published in *PWS* previously.

POLYPHONIES (III, IV-Translations), BP189, Paris 75665 CEDEX 14 France, founded 1985, editors Pascal Culerrier. Editorial committee: Laurence Breysse, Jean-Yves Masson, Alexis Pelletier, Patrick Piguet. Appears twice a year. **"Every case is a special one. We want to discover the new important voices of the world to open French literature to the major international productions. For example, we published Brodsky in French when he was not known in our country and had not yet the Nobel Prize. No vocal poetry, no typographic effects."** They have recently published poetry by Marie Luzi (Italy), Jeremy Reed (Great Britain), Octavio Paz (Mexico) and Claude Michel Cluny (France). I have not seen an issue, but the editor describes it as "16/24 cm." Press run: 1,000 for 300+ subscriptions. **Pays 2 copies. They use translations of previously published poems.** The editor says, "Our review is still at the beginning. We are in touch with many French editors. Our purpose is to publish together, side-by-side, poets of today and of yesterday."

PORTABLE WALL; (I, IV-Humor), 215 Burlington, Billings, MT 59101, phone (406)256-3588, founded 1977, publisher Daniel Struckman. He wants **"humor, political, poetry as wisdom-friendship mind."** He has recently published poetry by Peter Koch, Michael Fiedler, and Anne Harris. As a sample he selected these lines by Wilbur Wood:

> One step: snap twig.
> Next step: crunch pinecone.
> Magpie, high in tree,
> Tilting head, eying me:

PW is published twice a year and open to beginners, 40 pp., saddle-stapled, on heavy tinted stock with 2-color matte card cover, press run 200. **Sample: $5 postpaid. Pays 3 copies. Reports in 6 weeks, 6 months between acceptance and publication.** Price per issue is $5, subscription $15 for 2 years.

PORTLAND REVIEW (II), Box 751, Portland OR 97207, phone (503)725-4533, founded 1954, contact editor, is a literary annual published by the Portland State University 3 times a year. **"Experimental poetry welcomed. No poems over 3 pages. No rhyming poetry."** The annual, which I have not seen, is magazine-sized, about 128 pp. They accept about 30 of 300 poems received each year. Press run is 500 for 100 subscriptions of which 10 are libraries. **Sample: $5. Send SASE for guidelines. Pays 1 copy. Simultaneous submissions OK.**

‡PORTRAITS POETRY MAGAZINE (II), 8312 123rd St. E., Puyallup WA 98373, phone (206)848-5827, founded 1989, editor Jay L. Chambers, appears 3/year. They want **"poems that create snapshot word pictures communicating visual, yet lasting impressions, poems that speak to our deeper selves and poems that appreciate an obvious style. We have yet to publish a rhyming poem due to their general lack of sophistication. We do not like experimental poetry or rambling prose."** They have recently published poetry by Frank Sibley, Ivan Kershner and Joanne McCarthy. As a sample the editor selected these lines from "Alberto's" by Don Larsen:

> Even the wall-paper reeks of garlic
> and stale smoke
> in that cramped upstairs room
> where piles of pasta and oily lettuce
> are delivered by the brown-faced, braless woman
> who speaks best with her body.

I have not seen an issue, but the editor describes it as 28 pp. magazine-sized, saddle-stapled. Press run 150 for 25 subscribers, 50 shelf sales. Subscription: $9. **Sample: $3 postpaid. Pays 1 copy/poem accepted. Reports in 1-4 months.** Editor comments **"if promising. We prefer to have no other publisher considering submissions sent to us but will read simultaneous submissions and occasionally make an exception. We do want to be** *told.*" Reviews books of poetry "if solicited. Query first." They have a contest ($1/poem fee) for each issue awarding free subscription plus small cash awards and copies. **"We accept both contest and non-contest submissions."**

POTATO EYES; NIGHTSHADE PRESS (II, IV-Regional), P.O. Box 76, Troy ME 04987, phone (207)948-3427, founded 1988, editors Roy Zarucchi and Carolyn Page, is a semiannual literary arts journal **"with a focus on writers who live along the Appalachian chain from southern Quebec to Alabama, though all U.S. and Canadian writers are welcome."** They have published poetry by Fred Chappell, R.T. Smith, Robert Morgan, Pat Anthony, Shelby Stephenson, Karen Blomain and Barbara Crooker. As a sample the editors selected these lines from Michael Chitwood's **Martyrdom of the Onions**, the title poem from a 1991 chapbook:

> In a garden, they are knots along a rope of dirt.
> Pulled out and hung in a bundle on the back porch,
> they chime in deep tones against the wood frame.
> I have seen my father rub a half on the lintel
> of a rabbit trap, to erase the smell of his hands.
> Lines of longitude describe their globe; . . .

Circulation is 800. *PE* is 5½×8½", 100+ pp. flat-spined, professionally printed, with block cut matte card cover. Subscription: $11 (Canadian $14). **Sample: $6 postpaid (back issue $5), or $7 Canadian. Reports in 4-8 weeks,** and **"those who submit receive a handwritten rejection/acceptance. We are open to any form other than rhymed, in batches of 3-5, but we tend to favor poetry with concrete visual imagery, solid intensity, and compression. We respect word courage and**

Close-up

Barry Fogden
Poet

Skinny-Dipping in Wiltshire:
1. The Bourne at West Gomeldon

Climbing the melting hill turned my legs to rhubarb:
freewheeling down, knees smell the fear of hot gravel.
I sweat noise into the normal sounds,
intrude barbed breath into wavy air,
wade agitation into the placid pool.

A trout hears me blink, kicks away from the shallows
and strokes without strain, its dorsal fin
drawing the water's veneer like a needle
pulling a single thread through shot silk.

I follow it and come up in a garden,
eye to gimlet-eye with a worming yaffle
that laughs without mirth, splattering a parasol
as it yoyos into the elder trees.

I'm a stranger here myself,
and not yet in my element.

Barry Fogden knows pools so quiet a trout can hear one blink, so still the trout's fin skims away as smoothly as a needle draws a thread through irridescent silk. Born in Lavant, near Chichester, West Sussex, he comes from a family that worked the land in rural southern England for centuries. "My childhood," he says, "was something resembling the rural idyll beloved of 19th century poets. I attended the old village school, where the headmaster was far keener on taking us on instructive nature walks into the countryside than on drumming the three Rs into us. To morning assembly, supposed to be a session of prayer and hymn-singing, he tended to bring dead things—badgers, hares and all manner of wild birds—for inspection and explication. I never had any difficulty understanding what Wordsworthian Pantheism was all about!"

His grandfather was a shepherd, of the sort that Hardy depicted. "I was privileged, as I was born late to his youngest daughter, to know something of a way of life that has almost died. Whatever else, I have learned to overlay the country ways of thinking that guided me as a child," Barry says. "I still feel that magical place calling me back to refresh me, to sharpen my values and put my deepest concerns, global and personal, into a sane perspective."

Jump ahead a few years and you'll find him playing lead guitar in a professional rock band, or later, "having got rid of a lot of hair," in a suit as a respectable "legal draftsman," drafting deeds and other documents. "The legal work taught me that it was possible, indeed necessary, to say almost anything with accuracy and economy, and to respect the structures of grammar and syntax, even sometimes while bending them!"

The first person in his family to attend college, he found the transition from a rural working-class boy to urban middle-class education at times bumpy. Nonetheless, after "too many years and too many degrees," he began experiments in writing in several forms before coming "almost reluctantly to the conclusion that I should write poetry. I chose it, rather perversely, because I'd become aware of a kind of magnificent impossibility about the poetic undertaking—quite simply, I'd found something so difficult that it would stretch me to the limit, always, and every time I thought I'd made an advance, I'd see baffling complexities, and even more baffling simplicities, staring me in the face."

He began getting work steadily accepted by magazines and began winning prizes, but also discovered the frustrations all poets encounter with long lapses of time between writing and acceptance and then, after what seems interminable delay, finally seeing his work in print. He has had a "friendly and welcoming" reception from editors in North America, in addition to those in the British Isles, and he's now at the point of seeking a publisher for his first book.

The first work of his to appear in a hardback book was in Norwegian, which he couldn't read. "Living on an island," he says, "I am acutely conscious of how *insular* we all tend to be, and I have made a special effort to acquaint myself with the poetry of other nations, other languages. I believe we need continual cross-fertilization with other poetries if our own work isn't to become inward-looking and sterile."

Should American poets be seeking publication in Britain? "It seems to me that American poets are welcomed in Great Britain. British editors tend to guard their independence fiercely and don't like being bullied by detailed bio notes and lists of publications with submissions, but in my experience they give everything a fair reading and often take the trouble to write a personal letter rather than a form rejection, if rejection it must be. The answer's still no, but you feel better about it." What do British editors like? "I think the standard thing is just a brief, friendly letter, with short details of your track record, if any, and no old bull about your artistic *raison d'etre*, dominant aesthetic and so on. Don't overdo it. I have a friend whose covering letters are a damn sight more entertaining than his actual work."

Unfortunately, as Barry notes, editors tend to hate International Reply Coupons, or IRCs, and these are fairly essential to poets who want to submit overseas. He suggests a "pairing" arrangement, such as he has with an American poet, in which each of two poets in different countries sends the other checks to buy postage to use on return envelopes.

Teaching literature, writing and philosophy at the University of Sussex, Barry finds that one of the hardest lessons for his students to accept is that "it wouldn't *matter* if we weren't fully recognized until 50 years after our deaths. That gives us tremendous freedom, of course: We are at liberty to write about anything we like, in any way we like. And if our work isn't utterly personal to us, in touch with our deepest selves, as well as, hopefully, having something to say about experience in general, it fails."

—Judson Jerome

---

risk-taking, along with thoughtful lineation. We prefer rebellious to complacent poetry. We prefer a cover letter with brief bio along with SASE. Nightshade Press is the imprint under which they publish about 12 chapbooks/year, each 24-48 pp. "usually with hand-blocked open/ink covers, endsheets, and recycled 24 lb text, 65 lb. cover text. Nightshade Press chapbooks are published on a somewhat cooperative arrangement based on poets' promotion with royalties paid to us. We only publish poets with futures, poets whose work shows promise." For chapbook consideration query with bio and list of publications. "We prefer that poets appear first in our magazine. We like to feel that they are supportive enough to subscribe." Send SASE for catalog or $5 for sample chapbook. They advise, "Beginning poets should devour as much good poetry as possible in order to delineate their own style and voice. Look for a match between substance and sound."

POTES & POETS PRESS, INC.; ABACUS (II), 181 Edgemont Ave., Elmwood CT 06110, phone (203)233-2023, press founded in 1981, magazine in 1984, editor Peter Ganick. The press publishes avant-garde poetry in magazine form under the *Abacus* imprint, one writer per 16-page issue. The P+Pinc books are perfect-bound and range from 80-120 pages in trade editions." **In addition to avant-garde, they want experimental or language-oriented poetry, not too much concrete poetry. No** *"New Yorker* **magazine,** *Ploughshares* **magazine, mainstream poetry."** They have published poems by Ron Silliman, Jackson Mac Low, Charles Bernstein, Cid Corman, and Theodore Enslin. The editors did not quote lines, and I have not seen samples. *Abacus* is magazine-sized, photocopied, no graphics, 12-18 pp.; it appears every 6 weeks. Circulation is 150, of which 40 are subscriptions and 10 go to libraries. Price per issue is $2.50, subscription $17/year. **Sample available for $2.50 postpaid. Pay is 12 copies. Simultaneous submissions are OK, as are photocopied or dot-matrix MSS. Reporting time is within 8 weeks and time to publication is 1 year. Freelance submissions are accepted for book publication. Writers should "just send the manuscript."** The press plans to publish 3 books of poetry per year with an average page count of 100, flat-spined paperbacks.

‡POTPOURRI (II), P.O. Box 8278, Prairie Village KS 66208, founded 1989, poetry editor Pat Anthony, is a monthly tabloid "to publish works of writers, **including new and unpublished writers. No religious, confessional, racial, political, erotic, abusive, or sexual preference materials unless fictional and necessary to plot or characterization. No concrete/visual poetry (because of format)."** They have recently published poetry by David Ray and Lloyd Van Brunt. As a sample the editor selected these lines from "An Artist's Lines" for "Grandma Elizabeth Layton" by Judy Ray:

> You say you don't have visions.
> Yet your drawings fill with unsprung
> coils of our lives, harmony
> and chaos, dancing and screams

It is 20-24 pp., press run 6,000-10,000 for 550 subscribers of which 20 are libraries, 5,000 distributed free to libraries, bookstores, universities, hospitals, community centers and others. Subscription: $12. **Sample postpaid: $1. Send SASE for guidelines. Pays 1-20 copies (poet's request). Submit no more than 3 poems, no more than 1/page, length to 75 lines (approximately 30 preferred). Submit seasonal themes 6 mo. in advance. Reports in 6-8 weeks at most.** The editor advises, "Keep your new poems around long enough to become friends with them before parting. Let them ripen, and above all, learn to be your own best editor. To borrow from William Carlos Williams, strive to let your particular 'specific' idea or poem be window to universality for your reader. Let them *in* to your work and write *for* an audience in terms of professionalism and clarity. Unrequited love, favorite pets, and description that seems to be written for its own sake find little chance."

‡THE POTTERSFIELD PORTFOLIO (IV-Regional), P.O. Box 1135, Station A, Fredericton, New Brunswick E3B 5C2 Canada, phone (506)454-5127, founded 1979. "Wild East's *The Pottersfield Portfolio* is a semiannual magazine of new English and French fiction, poetry, drama, articles and essays **from and by Atlantic Canadians.** Both new and more established writers are featured." They are **open to poetry by writers from or living in Atlantic Canada. They do not accept "sexist, racist, homophobic or classist material and no erotica or greeting card sentimentalism."** They have recently published poetry by Phyllis Rowan and Robert Gibbs. As a sample the editors selected these lines by Shari Andrews:

> He cradles them against his rib cage
> like a flap of skin to muffle his heart
> which hangs like a door on a broken hinge.
> Each beat; the snap of bones breaking in his head:
> bent thoughts that don't line up.
> His mind in traction.

The semiannual is handsomely printed in a 2-column format, 2-color glossy cover, using b/w art, ads, press run 1000, roughly 400 subscriptions. subscriptions (individual) $10/year or $12 in U.S.). **Sample: $5 postpaid. No simultaneous submissions or previously published poems. Buys first Canadian Serial Rights. Include MSS-sized self-addressed envelope with Canadian postage or IRC. Reports in 8-12 weeks. Editors sometimes comment on rejections. Pays $10/poem and 2 copies.** The editors say, "Read, read, read. Look inside yourself for the emotional intensity that will give your writing impact."

‡POWER ANIMAL (I), Joe Skyfoot Word and Music Creations, Suite 303, 245 Lakeshore Dr., Etobicoke Ontario M8V 2A8 Canada, phone (416)582-7414, editor Phillip Boucher, is a biannual magazine-sized newsletter, 10-20 pp., of **"poetry, humour, and the New Age. Needs all types of poetry: religious, horror, lesbian, children's, fantasy, and anything else you could think of. Nonsense verse or unintelligible poetry gets sent back. I love poems that make sense on the first reading."** As a sample, I selected these lines from "Dragon in my Tea Cup" by Linda Robitaille:

> Swirling, storming,
> Shapes are forming,

Trying to escape
This porcelain confinement
It hopes to overtake.

It is photocopied from typescript, corner stapled. Subscription: $10/year. **Sample postpaid: $5. Pays 1 copy. Send 1-3 poems. Reports in 4-6 weeks.**

THE PRAIRIE JOURNAL (II); PRAIRIE JOURNAL PRESS (IV-Regional, themes), P.O. Box 997, Station G, Calgary, Alberta T3A 3G2 Canada, founded 1983, editor A. Burke, who wants to see **poetry of "any length, free verse, contemporary themes (feminist, nature, urban, non-political), aesthetic value, a poet's poetry."** Does not want to see **"most rhymed verse, sentimentality, egotistical ravings. No cowboys or sage brush."** They have published poetry by Mick Burrs, Lorna Crozier, Mary Melfi, Art Cuelho and John Hicks. As a sample I selected the opening lines of "In His Presence" by Ronald Kurt:

My father lifts
me in his presence
I am lowered in prayer
in awe of bullet wounds
and a will to live

That is from a chapbook collection, **A Vision of Birds,** published by Prairie Journal Press, $7 \times 8\frac{1}{2}$" saddle-stapled, 36 pp., professionally printed on thin stock with Cadillac cover stock. Kurt is an Edmonton, Alberta, poet, his poetry having been published mostly in Canadian journals and by Canadian presses. *Prairie Journal,* is $7\frac{1}{2} \times 8\frac{1}{2}$", 40-60 pp., offset with card cover, with b/w drawings, ads, appearing twice a year. They accept about 10% of the 200 or so poems they receive a year. Press run 500 per issue, 150 subscriptions of which 60% are libraries. Subscription: $6 for individuals, $12 for libraries. **Sample: $3 postpaid. Guidelines available for postage (but "no US stamps, please" — get IRCs from the Post Office). Pays 1 copy. Reports in 2 weeks. No simultaneous submission or previously published poems. For chapbook publication Canadian poets only (preferably from the region) should query with 5 samples, bio, publications. Responds to queries in 2 weeks, to MSS in 2 weeks. Pays $100.** "We also publish anthologies on themes when material is available. We receive very little poetry we can use." They are offering a contest for poems, short fiction and nonfiction on the theme "Does literature have a role to play in armed conflict?" Personal perspectives OK. Entry fee $1. Work of winner will be published and receive a small cash prize and/or quality book(s). Closing date is end of 1992 but may be extended if response warrants. Write for further details. Reviews books of poetry. A. Burke advises, "Read recent poets! Experiment with line length, images, metaphors. Innovate."

THE PRAIRIE PUBLISHING COMPANY (III, IV-Regional), Box 2997, Winnipeg, Manitoba R3C 4B5 Canada, phone (204)885-6496, founded 1963, publisher Ralph E. Watkins, is a "small-press catering to regional market, local history, fantasy, poetry and non-fiction," with flat-spined paperbacks. They want **"basically well-crafted poems of reasonable length"** and do not want to see **"the work of rank amateurs and tentative and time-consuming effort."** They have published collections of poetry by Brian Richardson and Brian MacKinnon. As a sample Nancy Watkins selected these lines by Brian Richardson:

Tame grass grows in city parks
Tarmac grows round windowless schools
we're growing fast, we're getting big
to make more room for bigger fools.

Their books I have seen are handsomely produced, 6×9", using b/w photos and art along with the poems, glossy card covers. They publish about 1 a year, 68 pp. **Query with samples. Do not submit MSS during summer. Responds to queries in 6 weeks. Simultaneous submissions OK. Samples available at a 20% discount—send SASE or IRC for catalog.** Nancy Watkins notes, "Robert E. Pletta's point that most poets need to do more reading is well taken. We would endorse this suggestion."

PRAIRIE SCHOONER; STROUSSE—PRAIRIE SCHOONER PRIZE; SLOTE PRIZE; FAULKNER AWARD (II), 201 Andrews, University of Nebraska, Lincoln NE 68588, phone (402)472-3191, founded 1927, editor Hilda Raz; "one of the oldest literary quarterlies in continuous publication; publishes poetry, fiction, personal essays, interviews and reviews." They want **"poems that fulfill the expectations they set up." No specifications as to form, length, style, subject-matter or purpose. No simultaneous submissions.** They have recently published poetry by Cathy Song, Anneliese Wagner, Eric Pankey, Pat Mora, Reynolds Price, Marianne Boruch, Dabney Stuart, Nancy Esposito and Michael Waters. The editors selected these sample lines from "How Can She Rise, Earth-Born" by Claudia Van Gerven:

with her pithos, her great jar full
Pandora, Anesidora, gifted-girl, girl spilling

> *blessings, how can she matronly*
> *and involved in incessant car pools come*
> *in snow, in violets, or wild*
> *slender moon, quiver full of arrows*

The magazine is 6×9″, flat-spined, 144 pp., circulation 2,000, and uses 70-80 pp. of poetry in each issue. Subscription: $15/year; $4/copy. They receive about 4,000 MSS (of all types) per year from which they choose 300 pp. of poetry. **Sample: $2 postpaid. "Clear copy appreciated." Reports in 2-3 months; "sooner if possible." Pays copies.** Reviews books of poetry. The $500 Strousse-Prairie Schooner Prize is awarded to the best poetry published in the magazine each year, the Slote Prize for beginning writers ($500) and six other *PS* prizes will also be awarded, and the Faulkner Award for Excellence in Writing is also offered ($1,000). Editors serve as judges. Hilda Raz comments, *"Prairie Schooner receives a large number of poetry submissions; I expect we're not unusual. Our staff time doesn't allow criticial comments on MSS, but the magazine's reputation is evidence of our careful reading. We've been dedicated to the publication of good poems for a very long time and have published work early in the career of many poets."*

PRAKALPANA LITERATURE; KOBISENA (I, IV-Form), P-40 Nandana Park, Calcutta 700034, West Bengal, India, *Kobisena* founded 1972, *Prakalpana Literature* press founded 1974, magazine 1977, editor Vattacharja Chandan, who says, "We are small magazines which publish only *Prakalpana* (a mixed form of prose and poetry), Sarbangin (whole) poetry, essays on Prakalpana movement and Sarbangin poetry movement, letters, literary news and very few books on Prakalpana and Sarbangin literature. **Purpose and form: for advancement of poetry in the super-space age, the poetry must be really experimental and avant-garde using mathematical signs and symbols and visualizing the pictures inherent in the alphabet (within typography) with sonorous effect. That is Sarbangin poetry. Length: within 30 lines (up to 4 poems). Subject matter: society, nature, cosmos, humanity, love, peace, etc. Style: own. We do not want to see traditional, conventional, academic, religious and poetry of prevailing norms and forms."** They have published poetry by Dilip Gupta, Irving Weiss, John Byrum and Geof Huth. As a sample the editor chose these lines from "The God of Energy" by Richard Frankfother:

> *Anti − Electron + Electron = Energy.*
> *Anti − Universe + Universe = Engergy.*
> *Existence = Energy.*
> *Continued Energy.*
> *Therfore All Is Energy.*

Prakalpana Literature, an annual, is 70 pp., digest-sized, saddle-stapled, printed on thin stock with matte card cover. *Kobisena*, which appears at least twice a year, is 16 pp., digest-sized, a newsletter format with no cover. Both are hand composed and printed by letterpress. Both use both English and Bengali. They use about 10% of some 400 poems received per year. The press run is 1,000 for each, and each has about 450 subscriptions of which 50 are libraries. **Samples: 6 rupees for *Prakalpana*, 2 rupees for *Kobisena*. Overseas: 4 IRCs and 2 IRCs respectively or exchange of avant-garde magazines. Send SAE with IRC for guidelines. Pays 1 copy. Simultaneous submissions OK. Previously published poetry OK. Reports in 6 months, publication within a year.** After being published in the magazines, poets may be included in future anthologies with translations into Bengali/English if and when necessary. **"Joining with us is welcome but not a pre-condition." Editor comments on rejection "if wanted."** Reviews books of poetry, "but preferably experimental books." He says, "We believe that only through poetry, the deepest feelings of humanity as well as nature and the cosmos can be best expressed and conveyed to the peoples of the ages to come. And only poetry can fill up the gap in the peaceless hearts of dispirited peoples, resulted from the retreat of god and religion with the advancement of hi-tech. So, in an attempt, since the inception of Prakalpana Movement in 1969, to reach that goal in the avant-garde and experimental way we stand for Sarbangin poetry. And to poets and all concerned with poetry we wave the white handkerchief saying (in the words of Vattacharja Chandan) 'We want them who want us.'

THE PRESBYTERIAN RECORD (IV-Inspirational, religious), 50 Wynford Dr., Don, Mills, Ontario M3C 1J7 Canada, phone (416)441-1111, founded 1876, is "the national magazine that serves the membership of The Presbyterian Church in Canada (and many who are not Canadian Presbyterians). We seek to: stimulate, inform, inspire, to provide an 'apologetic' and a critique of our church and the world (not necessarily in that order!)." They want **poetry which is "inspirational, Christian, thoughtful, even satiric but *not* maudlin. No 'sympathy card' type verse a la Edgar Guest or Francis Gay. It would take a *very* exceptional poem of epic length for us to use it. Shorter poems 10-30 lines preferred. Blank verse OK (if it's not just rearranged prose). 'Found' poems. Subject matter should have some Christian import (however subtle)."** They have published poetry by Jean Larsen, Jeanne Davis, Joan Stortz, Marlow C. Dickson, Len Selle and J.R. Dickey. The magazine comes out 11 times a year, circulation 67,000. Subscription: $11. **Submit seasonal work 6 weeks before month of publication. Double-spaced, photocopy OK. "Dot-matrix semi-OK." Simultaneous submissions OK. Reports usually within a month. Pays $20-50 per poem.**

PRESCOTT STREET PRESS (IV-Regional), Box 40312, Portland OR 97240-0312, founded 1974, poetry editor Vi Gale: "**Poetry and fine print from the Northwest.**" Vi Gale says, "Our books and cards are the product of many hands from poet, artist, printer, designer, typesetter to bookstore and distributor. Somewhere along the line the editor/publisher [herself] arranges to pay one and all in the same way. Sometimes we have had grant help from the NEA and also from State and Metropolitan arts organizations. But most of our help has come from readers, friends and the poets and artists themselves. Everyone has worked very hard. And we are immodestly pleased with our labors! **We pay all of our poets. A modest sum, perhaps, but we pay everyone something. We are not a strictly regional press, although the poets I take on are connected with the Northwest in some way when we bring out the books.**" Vi Gale publishes a series of postcards, notecards, paperback and hardback books of poetry in various artistic formats with illustrations by nationally known artists. Send SASE for catalog to order copies. I selected these sample lines by Rolf Aggestam from a postcard:

> *muttering. cold*
> > *hands split fresh kindling*
> > > *damn*
> *what a life. you are far away.*
> > *in the darkness we used to call*
> > *each other forth*
> > > *with fingers and a few small words.*
> *we created a little border*
> > *between darkness and darkness.*

Considers simultaneous submissions. "No UPS submissions, please."

THE PRESS OF MACDONALD & REINECKE (II); PADRE PRODUCTIONS (I), P.O. Box 840, Arroyo Grande CA 93421-0840, phone (805)473-1947, founded 1974, poetry editor Lachlan P. MacDonald. Padre Productions prints books on a fee basis, as a book packager. MacDonald & Reinecke requires **the poet to "purchase 200 copies of an edition (at liberal discounts)" but they do not consider themselves subsidy publishers. They publish under the M&R imprint only work they consider of merit and in which they, like the poet, must invest.** "The press is a division of Padre Productions bringing together under one imprint drama, fiction, literary, nonfiction, and poetry. We publish poetry in broadsides, flat-spined paperbacks, chapbooks and hardcover. We are looking for **poetry of literary merit and also poetry suitable for travel and nature photo books. We are averse to tightly rhymed conventional poetry unless designed to appeal to the general humor market.**" They recently published Terre Ouenhand's **Voices from the Well** and Steven Schmidt's **Avigation and Other Poems. Query with 5-6 samples,** publication credits, bio. The editor also wants to know "do they give readings or have marketing opportunities? Some authors distribute flyers to build up pre-publication orders sufficient to justify the print order." **Replies to queries in 2-4 weeks, to submissions (if invited) in 2-6 months. Simultaneous submissions, photocopy, dot-matrix OK. MS should be double-spaced. Pays minimum of 4% royalties, 6 copies. The editor "frequently makes brief comments"** on rejections. Send 6×9″ SASE for catalog. The editor advises, "Poets who have not published 10 or 20 poems in literary magazines are unlikely to have developed the craft we require. We also prefer books with a unifying theme rather than a sampling reflecting the author's virtuosity."

‡THE PRESS OF THE THIRD MIND; BILE MAGAZINE (IV-Form), 65 E. Scott St. #6P, Chicago IL 60610, phone (312)337-3122, magazine began in 1978, press founded 1985, poetry editor Dada Ram Das, is a "literary/art monthly with avant-garde emphasis of small-press publisher of artist books, poetry and fiction' in magazines, paperbacks, broadsides, T-shirts and Tarot cards. "**We are especially intereted in the cut-up/fold-in technique, concrete poetry, translations, collaborative** (*Exquisite Corpse*) **poetry, found poems, dada, surrealism, etc. Nothing in braille, please!**" They have recently published poetry by "Pessoa, Spiro, Cesariny, Mansour and Lamantia." As a sample the editor selected these lines from the poem, "Clarksdale" by Bradley Lastname:

> *We've come to the township of hog maws and grits*
> *To sample the rich delta soil.*
> *As I ponder the natives object and throw fits,*
> *My hambone goes into a boil.*

Asked to describe the purpose and contents of *Bile Magazine,* which I have not seen, the editor said, "In a world of weeds, we are an opium poppy in a vase of ether." He described it as "from 8½×7″ to 11×17″ depending on the issue, usually offset, art-to-verbiage ratio is 10/1." It appears 12 times a year. Asked how much poetry they typically received per year and how much they accept, he said "We get about 6 metric tons and accept it all for fireplace logs." They have a press run of 200 with 100 subscriptions of which 38 are libraries. Subscription: $8. **Sample: $2 postpaid. Pay?** *"Surely you jest!"* **But contributors can have all the copies they can photocopy.** *"No dot matrix!!!"* **Simultaneous submissions OK. They have sometimes used previously published poetry and have simultaneously published with** *Exquisite Corpse.* Press of the Third Mind publishes 2 flat-spined paperbacks, 56 pp., per year. They recently published **Concave Buddha and Other Public Disservice Announcements** (paperback). **For book publication submit 20 sample poems, bio and credits. Responds to queries in 1 week, MSS in 3 weeks. "Just ask for free samples and include a substantial 'love offering.'"** Editor provides criticism on rejections. Reviews books of poetry. "We sponsor a contest for the poem with the longest line. Last winner wrote a line with 507 words." His advice: "Don't give up your day job at Walgreen's."

‡**PRIMAL VOICES; VISIONS AND REVISIONS; LAMBERT/MCINTOSH ENTERPRISES (I, IV–Children, Senior Citizens),** P.O. Box 3179, Poughkeepsie NY 12603, founded 1989, editors Carol Lambert and Susan McIntosh. Lambert/McIntosh publishes 3 periodicals. *Hamlet News* is for local news for and about New Hamburg "for local commuters and visitors." Both *PV* and *VAR* are quarterlies using **poetry other than pornographic. Both use poetry by and for children and senior citizens.** *Primal Voices* describes its focus as: "children, war veterans, senior citizens, the homeless, the environment, the handicapped, retarded persons, the incarcerated, the endangered animal—anyone with a need to be heard!" and *Visions and Revisions* is "for children of all ages!". Both are professionally printed, magazine-sized, saddle-wired on heavy stock with glossy b/w card covers. Press run 200. **Subscription (to either): $20. Sample postpaid: $5. Send SASE for guidelines. Pays 1 copy. Reports in 4-6 weeks. Previously published poems and simultaneous submissions OK.**

PRINCETON UNIVERSITY PRESS; LOCKERT LIBRARY OF POETRY IN TRANSLATION (IV-Translations, bilingual); PRINCETON SERIES OF CONTEMPORARY POETS (V), 41 William St., Princeton NJ 08540, phone (609)452-4900, literature editor Robert E. Brown. The Princeton Series of Contemporary Poets **is by invitation only.** "In the Lockert Library series, we publish simultaneous cloth and paperback (flat-spine) editions for each poet. Clothbound editions are on acid-free paper, and binding materials are chosen for strength and durability. Each book is given individual design treatment rather than stamped into a series mold. We have published a wide range of poets from other cultures, including well-known writers such as Hölderlin and Cavafy, and those who have not yet had their due in English translation, such as Ingeborg Bachmann and Faiz Ahmed Faiz. Manuscripts are judged with several criteria in mind: the ability of the translation to stand on its own as poetry in English; fidelity to the tone and spirit of the original, rather than literal accuracy; and the importance of the translated poet to the literature of his or her time and country. Originals are printed facing the translations." The editor says, "All our books in this series are heavily subsidized to break even. We have internal funds to cover deficits of publishing costs. We do not, however, publish books chosen and subsidized by other agencies, such as AWP. **Our series is an open competition, for which the 'award' is publication. We comment on semifinalists only." Send SASE for guidelines to submit. Send MSS only during respective reading periods stated in guidelines. Reports in 2-3 months. Simultaneous submissions OK if you tell them; photocopy, dot-matrix OK. Pays royalties (5% or more) on paperback and 12 author's copies.**

‡**PRINTED MATTER (II),** Hikari Biru 303, 3-7-10 Takadanobaba, Shinjuku-ku, Tokyo 169 Japan, phone (03)3362-7589, founded 1977, editor Stephen Forster, is a quarterly literary journal, featuring poetry, fiction, reviews, photos and graphics. It has recently published poetry by Cid Corman, Shuntaro Tanikawa, Xavier Villaurrutia and Ira Cohen. As a sample, the editor selected these lines by Joe Cozzo:

> *All that seems open*
> *in this missile weather*
> *are mouths of cannons*
> *and eyes too widened with fright*
> *to admit any darkness.*

Printed Matter is 54 pp. in professionally printed A5 format. Press run is 600. The magazine appears four times a year plus one special issue. Subscription: 3,000 yen (US $25), **Sample: 600 yen (US $5)**—both prices include postage. Unless otherwise arranged, submissions to *Printed Matter* **are accepted on condition that they have not previously been published and that the material is not under consideration elsewhere. Submissions should be accompanied by the usual materials. Reports in 1-2 months.** *Printed Matter* runs an annual poetry contest with prizes of 20,000 and 10,000 yen. The do not use rejection slips: **editor comments on rejections.**

PRISONERS OF THE NIGHT; AMARANTH; MKASHEF ENTERPRISES (IV-Psychic, erotica), P.O. Box 368, Poway CA 92074-0368, poetry editor Alayne Gelfand. *Prisoners of the Night,* founded 1987, **focusing on vampire erotica, uses poetry that is "erotic, unique, non-horror, non-pornographic, original visions of the vampire."** *Amaranth,* founded 1989, first issue early 1991, "erotic or not, visionary supernatural themes. *No* vampires, 'sword & sorcery', or devil worship." Poets who have appeared recently in *POTN* include Charles Jacob, Alex Grayton and Ann K. Schwader. As a sample the editor selected the poem "The Flock" by Wendy Rathbone:

> When laughter echoes in the basalt sky
> and wind sounds like the unfurling of
> a thousand wings
> look to the tender moon
> for final reassurance
> as caped forms descend
> and cavort
> to the rhythm of
> your manic heart

The intent of *POTN* is "to show the erotic, rather than the horrific aspects of the vampire." It is 150-200 pp., magazine-sized, perfect bound, with color cover, produced by high-speed photo-copying with "full color cover art. All poems are illustrated." It appears annually, usually in May. Of over 500 poems received per year they use between 10 and 30. It has an initial print run of 3,000, but each issue is kept in print. **Sample (the per-issue price): $15 postpaid. Reading schedule for *POTN*: September-March annually. Send SASE for guidelines. Pays $2/poem plus 1 copy. No more than 6 poems per submission. No simultaneous submissions or previously published poems. Reports "within 4 months."** Editor sometimes comments on rejections. *POTN* wants unusual visions of the vampire as well as unusual poetic styles. "We prefer non-rhyme and find humor too subjective to appeal to our readers. We really enjoy the unusual image, the brilliant juxtaposition of words." Same general guidelines for *Amaranth*, SASE for specifics, same payment. Reading schedule: April-August annually. Poets who appear in the first issue of *Amaranth* include Janet Reedman, Ann K. Schwader, Eugene Gryniewicz, Wendy Rathbone and Ree Young.

PROOF ROCK PRESS; PROOF ROCK (I, II, IV-Humor), Box 607, Halifax, VA 24558, founded 1982, poetry editors Serena Fusek and Don R. Conner. "We try to wake up a passive readership. We challenge our writers to search for something new under the sun; and improve on the old." The poetry they want is: "adventure, contemporary, humor/satire, fantasy, experimental. Avoid overt sentimentality. Poems up to 32 lines. All subjects considered if well done." As a sample I chose the opening lines of "The Hidden Reader" by Kurt J. Fickert:

> They have forbidden me to read.
> Go bowling, they say; watch TV.
> Share a pizza with a friend.
> But I cheat: I plummet into a book,

The digest-sized magazine appears 2-3 times per year, is offset from typescript copy, colored matte card cover, with 30-40 pp. in each issue, circulation 300, 100 subscriptions of which 8-10 are libraries. They receive 800-1,000 submissions per year, use 120-150, have a 3-6 month backlog. Subscription: $4; per copy: $2.50. **Sample: $2.50 postpaid. Submit no more than 6 pieces, year round. No query needed, though some issues are on announced themes. Photocopy, dot-matrix, simultaneous submissions OK. Reports "usually within 30 days." Pays 1 copy. Send SASE for guidelines.** Proof Rock Press publishes an occasional anthology and collections by individuals. Query with 8-10 samples, bio and publishing credits. Reply to queries in 30 days, to submissions (if invited) in 1-3 months. Simultaneous submissions, photocopies, dot-matrix OK. Pays copies. Send $2.50 for a sample chapbook. Editor sometimes comments on rejections. His advice is, "Be introspective. Accept the challenge of looking within and write from experience."

PROPHETIC VOICES (II); HERITAGE TRAILS PRESS (V), 94 Santa Maria Dr., Novato CA 94947, founded 1982, poetry editors Ruth Wildes Schuler, Goldie L. Morales and Jeanne Leigh Schuler. "Our goal is to share thoughts on an international level. We see the poet's role as that of prophet, who points the way to a higher realm of existence." They publish *Prophetic Voices* twice a year and chapbooks. They want "poetry of social commentary that deals with the important issues of our time. Poetry with beauty that has an international appeal. Do not want religious poetry or that with a limited scope. Open to any kind of excellent poetry, but publish mostly free verse. Limited number of long poems accepted due to lack of space." They have published Jack Brooks, Hazel F. Goddard, A. Manoussos, B. Z. Niditch, H. F. Noyes, Gloria H. Procsal, and Bo Yang. As a sample the editors selected these lines from "Illegitimate" by Mogg Williams:

> My manuscripts were maladjusted words
> Which became a pregnancy in my head,
> An illegitimate thing with no abode. Hesitant, I cut
> the umbilical cord and gave the thing a home, and name.

Its home was the asylum of my heart
And its name was poetry.

Prophetic Voices is digest-sized, 144 pp., perfect-bound, offset from typescript with matte card cover, colored stock with graphics. They have 100 pp. of poetry in each issue, circulation to 400 subscribers of which 10 are libraries. Subscription: $12; $14 to libraries; per copy: $6. They receive 4,000 submissions per year, use 800, have a 2 year backlog. **Sample: $5 postpaid. Photocopy OK. Submit 4 poems or less. Reports in 1-8 weeks. Pays 1 copy. Heritage Trails does not consider unsolicited MSS.** The editors advise, "Be aware of what is going on in the world around you. Even the personal poem should have universal appeal if it is to survive the test of time."

‡**THE PROSE POEM (II, IV-Form)**, 1004 Sycamore, San Marcos TX 78666, phone (512)353-4988, founded 1990, editor Steve Wilson, is an annual using **prose poems only. "I hope and pray the author knows what prose poetry is before submitting to me. For me 'prose poems' run from margin to margin, with no line breaks, and use intense, compact language."** I have not seen an issue, but the editor describes it as 40 pp., professionally printed with card stock cover, saddle-stapled. The first issue was scheduled for summer, 1991. Press run 200. **Sample postpaid: $3. Pays 1 copy. Submit only between Jan. 1-Mar. 31. Reports in 1 month after deadline.** "*TPP* is a journal focussing on one particular genre, and publishing only the best work done in that genre. This does not mean an author cannot experiment. I encourage it. It also does not mean I don't want to see work from new writers. Please send, but only your best. I publish this magazine with my own money, so sales are very important. I won't take grants. I like my freedom. If you think prose poetry matters and like the idea of a journal dedicated to it, please help me keep it going by sending great work and subscribing."

PROSETRY: NEWSLETTER FOR, BY AND ABOUT WRITERS (IV-Subscription, themes), The Write Place, P.O. Box 117727, Burlingame CA 94011, phone (415)347-7613, editor P.D. Steele, founded 1985. *Prosetry* is a monthly newsletter featuring "new and newly published poets and prose writers with a 'guest writer' column each month. Includes original poetry, new markets, contests, seminars, workshops and **general poetry potpourri gleaned from our subscribers." 50% freelance. Guidelines available for SASE. Sample for $2. Invites new writers. Send up to 3 poems, no more than 20 lines, English only. No profanity. Reports in less than 4 weeks. Payment is one year subscription.** Reviews books of poetry. "For 'guest writer' column we would prefer information relevant to the beginning or newly published writer/poet." They sponsor a yearly Horsepoem Competition with equine theme for traditional poetry or haiku between Sept. 1 and Dec. 1. Send for guidelines.

‡**THE PROSPECT REVIEW; ¡ESTO BUENO! (II)**, 557 10th St., Brooklyn NY 11215, founded 1990, editor Peter A. Koufos, appears once a year. "**We actively seek vital work that is often overlooked. We want compelling, innovative work that crosses a line and speaks of humanity. Submit 3-5 poems; all subjects and styles considered. Nothing sexist, racist nor separatist.**" They have recently published poetry by E. Ethelbert Miller, Jana Harris and Michael Petit. As a sample the editor selected these lines by K. Lardas:

and the fiery words
as once they breathed,

no longer in the dust
or in Egyptian tombs,
but breathing now, —
and breathless to be known.

It is 6×9", professionally printed, flat-spined, 85-90 pp., with glossy card cover. Press run 500+. **Sample postpaid: $6. Send SASE for guidelines. Always query first. Reports prior to issue release. No MSS June through August.** "It is essential that writers receive our guidelines and letter. It is a pleasure and part of our job to offer comments when they are requested." ¡Esto Bueno! Press, inaugurated in 1992, is an imprint for chapbooks. **Pays 1 copy. "All MSS should ideally follow a guidelines request. If not: all MSS should be double spaced. Cover letter is a good idea."** Editor comments "as time permits." The editor says, "If poets are truly legislators on this planet then the time is here for these artists to cast aside confessional affectations in their work and, in light of social problems now existing, create poetry for a new society in great need of heightened imagination and bonding. Concerned with building our experimental powers, and our craft, into no uncertain splendor. To do this we need to keep our work on our desks longer."

PROTEA POETRY JOURNAL (II), P.O. Box 876, Sutter Creek CA 95685, phone (209)267-0332, founded 1987, poetry editor Carol Lynn Gunther, biannual. **They prefer "imagism that is hard-edged and veering towards objectivist work. Surrealism can be nice, too, especially if it opens a dialogue with the reader. Didactic and/or sentimental poems are not welcome."** The editor chose these lines from John Owens' poem "Troubled Moon" as a sample:

The grass is agreeable.
Birds tread the meadow.
The mirror, breathless, blooms.

Protea is "produced on an off-set press, Ventura Desktop Publishing. Top-notch within small budget." **Send SASE for guidelines; $5 for sample copy. Pays 2 copies. No previously published poems, simultaneous submissions. Reports in 2-3 weeks. Comments on rejections.**

‡PROVINCETOWN ARTS; PROVINCETOWN ARTS PRESS (II), 650 Commercial St., Provincetown MA 02657, phone (508)487-3167, founded 1985, editor Christopher Busa, is an elegant 170+ pp. flat-spined annual with full-color glossy cover, using quality poetry. They have recently published poetry by Alan Dugan, Carolyn Forché, Susan Mitchell and Olga Broumas. As a sample, I selected the first of five stanzas of "Twilight Polka Dots" by Barbara Guest:

The lake was filled with distinguished fish purchased
at much expense in their prime. It was a curious lake, halfsalt,
wishing to set a tone of solitude edged with poetry.
This was a conscious body aware of shelves and wandering
rootlings, duty suggested it provide a scenic atmosphere
of content, a solicitude for the brooding emotions.

Press run 8,000 for 300 subscribers of which 20 are libraries, 5,000 shelf sales. **Sample postpaid: $7.50. Pays $25-100/poem. Reports in 2-3 months.** The Provincetown Arts Press and a poetry award are being developed.

PSYCH IT (I, IV-Themes, subscribers), 6507 Bimini Ct., Apollo Beach FL 33572, founded 1986, editor Charlotte L. Babicky, is a quarterly newsletter using **"any style, any psychologically-themed poetry. Any length. The purpose is to leave the reader with a message; one which will be remembered through images presented by the writer of the poetry. Well-thought-out, well-written poems."** Poets recently published include Cecil T. Tresslar, Marian F. Park, Tracy L. Rottkamp and Pam T. Owens. As a sample the editor selected these lines from "The Heiress" by Kenneth G. Geisert:

Once the jewels of her father's eye,
she has been reduced
to a millstone,
in a sea of insanity.

It is a 10 pp. side-stapled, magazine-sized newsletter photocopied from typescript, with heavy natural parchment paper. Press run under 100. **Subscription: $8. Sample, postpaid: $2.50. Pays $1/poem. Guarantees to publish at least one of 3-5 poems submitted by subscribers. Non-subscribers may enter contests but not submit. Send SASE for guidelines. Contest prizes vary, entry fee $1 for each poem.**

PSYCHOPOETICA (II, IV-Themes), Dept. of Psychology, University of Hull, Hull HU6 7RX England, founded 1979, editor Dr. Geoff Lowe uses **"psychologically based poetry."** Judging by the examples I have read, that is not a very narrow category, though many of the poems in *Psychopoetica* are explicitly about psychology or psychological treatment. But most good poetry is in some sense "psychologically based," as the editor seems to recognize in these comments (from his guidelines): **"I prefer short, experimental, rhymed and unrhymed, light verse, haiku, etc., (and visual poems) I will read and consider any style, any length, providing it's within the arena of 'psychologically-based' poetry. I'm not too keen on self-indulgent therapeutic poetry (unless it's good and original), nor 'Patience Strong' type stuff. I like poetry that has some (or all!) of the following: humour, vivid imaginary, powerful feelings, guts and substance, originality, creative style, punch or twist, word-play, good craftsmanship, etc."** Recently published poets include Sheila E. Murphy, Wes Magee, Andrew Gettler, and Ruth Wildes Schuler. As a sample the editor selected this stanza from "The And Language" by Linda McFerrin:

Waking up from a dream
I fell back,
into the arms of language.
Nursery rhymes ricocheted off the walls.

The magazine appears 2-3 times a year, circulating to "several hundred and increasing." It is magazine-sized, loose-bound (pages held together by a plastic clasp), photocopied from typescript. **Sample: £1 ($2). Send SASE for guidelines. Pays 1 copy. Reports within 1 month. Considers simultaneous submissions. Editor "always" provides comments on rejections.** Occasionally reviews books of poetry. He says, "Careful presentation of work is most important. But I continue to be impressed by the rich variety of submissions, especially work that shifts boundaries."

PTOLEMY/BROWNS MILLS REVIEW, Box 908, Browns Mills NJ 08015. Declined listing.

THE PUCKERBRUSH PRESS; THE PUCKERBRUSH REVIEW (IV-Regional), 76 Main St., Orono ME 04473, phone (207)581-3832, press founded 1971, *Review* founded 1978, poetry editor Constance Hunting, is a "small-press publisher of a literary, twice-a-year magazine focused on Maine and of flat-spined paperbacks of literary quality." The editor **does not want to see "confessional, dull, feminist, incompetent, derivative" poetry.** They have recently published poetry by Amy Clampitt, and the editor selected these sample lines from "Not a Navigable River" by Muska Nagel:

> *flow seaward, seaward*
> *my river, filled to the brink—*
> *(but no king's horses, no more*
> *will ever come to drink).*

Submit with SASE. For book publication, query with 10 samples. Prefers no simultaneous submissions. Pays 10% royalties plus 10 copies. Editor comments on rejections. She offers criticism for a fee: $100 is usual.

PUDDING HOUSE PUBLICATIONS; PUDDING MAGAZINE: THE INTERNATIONAL JOURNAL OF APPLIED POETRY; PUDDING WRITING COMPETITIONS; PUDDING HOUSE BED & BREAKFAST FOR WRITERS; OHIO POETRY THERAPY CENTER & LIBRARY (II, IV-Social issues), 60 N. Main St., Johnstown OH 43031, phone (614)967-6060 (after 5 p.m.), founded 1979, poetry editor Jennifer Welch Bosveld, attempts to provide "a sociological looking glass through poems that provide 'felt experience' and share intense human situations. To collect good poems that speak for the difficulties and the solutions. To provide a forum for poems and articles by people who take poetry arts into the schools and the human services." They publish *Pudding* every several months, also chapbooks, anthologies, broadsides. They **"want experimental and contemporary poetry—what hasn't been said before. Speak the unspeakable. Don't want preachments or sentimentality. Don't want obvious traditional forms without fresh approach. Long poems are happily considered too, as long as they aren't windy."** They have recently published poetry by James Belcher, Lowell Jaeger, Rick Clewett, Alan Catlin and Alfred Bruey. The editor selected these sample lines from "The Stroke" by Douglas M. Swisher:

> *The blister of his wristwatch burst:*
> *Time, a puddle to be sopped up.*

Pudding is a literary journal with an emphasis on poetry arts in human service. They use about 80 pp. of poetry in each issue—digest-sized, 80 pp., offset composed on IBM 1st Publisher, circulation 2,000, 1,800 subscriptions of which 50 are libraries. Subscription (3 issues): $12.75. Per copy: usually $4.75. Sample: $4.75 postpaid. Submit 5-10 poems. No simultaneous submissions. Photocopies and previously published submissions OK but include credits. Send SASE for guidelines. Reports on same day (unless traveling). Pays 1 copy—to featured poet $10 and 4 copies. For chapbook publication, no query. $5 reading fee. Send complete MS with cover letter with publication credits and bio. Editor often comments, will critique on request for $3 per page of poetry or $25 an hour in person. Reviews books of poetry. Jennifer Welch Bosveld shares, "Editors have pet peeves. Mine include: Postcards instead of SASE's (I won't respond); individually-folded rather than group-folded poems; cover letters that state the obvious." The Pudding Writing Competitions are for single poems (deadline September 30, fee $1/poem) and for chapbook publication ($9 entry fee). Pudding House Bed & Breakfast for Writers offers "luxurious rooms with desk, electric typewriter and all the paper you can use." Free breakfast, large comfortable home ½ block from post office. Location of the Ohio Poetry Therapy Center and Library. $40 single/night. Reservations recommended 3 months in advance. Send SASE for details.

‡**PUEBLO POETRY PROJECT (IV-Regional)**, 1501 E. 7th St., Pueblo CO 81003, Tony Moffeit, Director, founded 1979, **publishes poets from the Pueblo area only. If you qualify, inquire.**

PUERTO DEL SOL (II, IV-Translations, regional), New Mexico State University, Box 3E, Las Cruces NM 88003, phone (505)646-3931, founded 1972 (in present format), poetry editors Joseph Somoza and Kathleene West (on alternate years). "We publish a literary magazine twice per year. Interested in poems, fiction, essays, photos, translations from the Spanish. Also (generally solicited) reviews and dialogues between writers. We want **top quality poetry, any style, from anywhere. We are sympathetic to Southwestern work, but not stereotype (cactus and adobe). Anything that is interesting and/or moving. Poetry, of course, not verse (light or otherwise).**" They have recently published poetry by Bill Evans, Naton Leslie, Anselm Hollo, Philip Garrison, Cecelia Hagen, J.B. Goodenough and Marilyn Hacker. The 6×9″ flat-spined, professionally printed magazine, matte card cover with art, has a circulation of 650, 300 subscriptions of which 25-30 are libraries. 40-50 pp. are devoted to poetry in each 150 pp. issue, which also includes quite a lot of prose. Subscription $7.75; per copy: $5. They use about 60 of the 700 submissions (about 3,500 poems) received each year to fill up the 90 pp. of poetry two issues encompass. "Generally no backlog." Sample: $3 postpaid. Submit 5-6 pp., 1 poem to a page. Simultaneous submissions not encouraged. Reports within 10 weeks. Pays copies. Editor comments "on every MS." They advise: "Be true to yourself rather than worrying about current fashions—but *do* read as much of the best of contemporary poetry as you can find."

‡PURDUE UNIVERSITY PRESS; VERNA EMERY POETRY COMPETITION (II), So. Campus Courts-D, West Lafayette IN 47907-1131, phone (317)494-6259, founded 1960, managing editor Margaret Hunt. They select 1 book/year to publish through the Verna Emery Poetry Competition, reading fee $15, pays $500 plus 10 copies. **Send SASE for guidelines. Reading period Jan. 15-Feb. 15. It is 65 pp. double-spaced. "No particular style, but poetry accessible to general audience is favored. No devotional, patriotic, overly ideological poetry."** They have recently published poetry by Jim Barnes, editor of *Chariton Review* and Fleda Jackson, whose book won GLCA New Writers Award.

PURPLE PATCH; PROMOTION; THE FIRING SQUAD (I), 8 Beaconview House, Charlemont Farm, West Bromwich, England, founded 1975, editor Geoff Stevens, an "approximately quarterly" poetry and short prose magazine with reviews, comment, and illustrations. The editor says, **"prefer maximum of one page length (40 lines), but all good examples of poetry considered."** He does not want **"poor scanning verse, concrete poetry, non-contributing swear words and/or obscenities, hackneyed themes."** They have recently published poetry by Taylor Reese, T.L. Rottkamp, Sheila Jacob, Brian Daldorph and Ken Price. As a sample the editor selected "Dreams of Home" by Derek Korblandt:

> *A Fisherman's terrace, a spit from the sea,*
> *Huddled in comradeship against the world;*
> *A scuttled walk to the pub on the corner*
> *Where authors can sit and impersonate greatness.*

Purple Patch is magazine-sized, 14-20 pp. offset on plain paper, cover on the same stock with b/w drawing, side-stapled. Circulation "varies." Price is 3 issues for £2.50 in Great Britain; U.S. price is $5 per issue (submit dollars). **Contributors have to buy a copy to see their work in print.** "All legible formats" are accepted. **Reporting time is 1 month to Great Britain, longer to USA; time to publication is a maximum of 4 months.** *Promotion* "published as demand requires, is a new idea to provide a platform of introduction of poets to editors, publishers, arts bodies, etc. **Five or six poets are included in each issue, with photograph, brief biography, a summary of their future aims, poems, and extracts of poems.** Copies are sent free of charge to publishers, editors, and others. **Included poets pay for inclusion."** It is magazine-sized. 14-26 pp. offset on plain paper, cover of same stock with b&w drawing or photo. Circulation 50, not to general public but targeted recipients. *The Firing Squad* is a broadsheet of short poetry of a protest or complaint nature. **Send SASE or SAE and IRCs for guidelines.**

PYGMY FOREST PRESS (II), Box 36, Caspar CA 95420, founded 1987, editor/publisher Leonard Cirino, publishes flat-spined paperbacks. **"Forms of any kind/length to 64 pp., subject matter open; especially ecology, prison, asylum, Third World, anarchist to far right. Prefer Stevens to Williams. I like Berry-man, Roethke, Jorie-Graham; dislike most 'Beats.' Open to anything I consider 'good.' Open to traditional rhyme, meter, but must be modern in subject-matter."** He has published **The Sixth Day** by James Doyle; **Fresh Water** by Crawdad Nelson; **For You/on stones** by L. Cirino; **The Elk Poems** by Kate Dougherty; **Low-Tech In the Great Northwest** by Gordon Black; **Obeli** by Sheila Murphy; **Windows** by Philip Corwin. **Submit 10-15 poems with bio, publications. Simultaneous submissions, previously published material, photocopies OK (no dot-matrix). Reports on queries in 1-3 weeks, submissions in 2-4 weeks. Pays 10% of run**—about 30-50 copies. He comments on "almost every" MS. They also publish (on a subsidized basis) poetry on 30-60 minute audio tapes: $200-250 fee for production costs, for which author gets 60 copies of the tape. Leonard Cirino says, "I am basically an anarchist. Belong to no 'school.' I fund myself. Receive no grants or private funding. Generally politically left, but no mainline Stalinist or Marxist. Plan to publish 3 books yearly."

QUARRY MAGAZINE; QUARRY PRESS; POETRY CANADA (II, IV-Regional, teens), Box 1061, Kingston, Ontario K7L 4Y5 Canada. Quarry Press founded 1952, *Poetry Canada* founded 1979, managing editor Melanie Dugan, reviews editor Barry Dempster. "Quarry Press is designed to extend the range of material, poetry and prose, generally handled by *Quarry Magazine*—that is, to represent, as accurately as may be, the range of contemporary writing. We publish chapbooks, soft-bound books of stories and poetry—collections ranging from 60-150 pp., in addition to the quarterly *Quarry Magazine*. **We are interested in seeing any and all forms of contemporary verse.** *Quarry Magazine* **maintains a practical limit on length of submissions—that we cannot consider any single piece or series by one author that would print at more than 10 pages. Quarry Press considers MSS on an individual basis."** They have published poetry by Roo Borson, Kim Maltman, Roger Nash, Jane Munro, Fred Cogswell, and Don Bailey. The editor selected these sample lines from "I Met a Poem" by Dennis Cooley:

> *they say earth*
> *shifts & glides*
> *like a figure*

skater double-axeling her way
across the screen

Quarry is a digest-sized, 130+ pp., flat-spined publication with an unusually attractive cover—textured matte ivory card with striking b/w drawing trimmed so the front is a half-inch short—professionally printed on egg-shell stock. There are 40-50 pp. of poetry in each issue, circulation 1,000, 600 subscriptions of which 140 are libraries. Subscription: $18 ($4 surcharge outside Canada); per copy: $5. They use about 70 of over a thousand submissions of freelance poetry received each year. "We are prompt. Very small backlog if any. 3-6 month lead time." **Sample: $5 postpaid. No limit on number or time of submissions; prefer typed (or WP) double-spaced; clear photocopies acceptable; query not necessary, though it will be answered. Reports in 6-8 weeks. Pays $10 per poem plus 1 year subscription. Send SASE for guidelines. For book consideration, query with 6-10 samples, publication credits, brief bio and current projects. "We give priority to Canadians because of our Arts Council funding and our own interest in promoting Canadian writing." Replies to queries in 30 days, to submissions (if invited) in 6-8 weeks. Photocopy, dot-matrix OK. Contract is for 10% royalties, 10 author's copies. Send 5 × 7″ SASE for catalog to order samples. Editor "frequently" comments on rejections.** They conduct a High School Writers' Contest every second year. *Poetry Canada* is a quarterly magazine featuring interviews, essays, international criticism, and comprehensive reviews of every Canadian poetry book published. Each issue features a major Canadian poet on the cover and center spread (recent issues feature Marlene Nourbese Philip, Bronwen Wallace, and George Bowering). Circulation: 1,800 with 600 subscribers, 600 newsstand. Subscription: $15/year ($30/year institutions). **Sample: $4 postpaid. Submit average 10 poems with SAE, IRC. Reports within 4-8 weeks. Pays $20/poem.**

THE QUARTERLY (III), 201 E. 50th St., New York NY 10022, phone (212)572-2128 or 872-8231, founded 1987, editor Gordon Lish, is a literary quarterly publishing poetry, fiction, essays and humor. They want **poetry of the "highest standards."** They have published poetry by Sharon Olds, Bruce Beasley, Jack Gilbert and Thomas Lynch. It is 256 pp, digest-sized, flat-spined, with glossy card cover. Circulation: 15,000. Subscription: $40. **Sample postpaid: $9.95. Pay: "rates vary but are modest" plus 2 copies. "Do not submit a batch of poems folded separately!"**

QUARTERLY REVIEW OF LITERATURE; QRL AWARDS (III, IV-Subscription, translation), 26 Haslet Ave., Princeton NJ 08540, founded 1943, poetry editors T. Weiss and R. Weiss. After more than 35 years as one of the most distinguished literary journals in the country, *QRL* now appears as the *QRL Poetry Series*, in which 4-5 book length collections are combined in one annual volume, each of the 4-5 poets receiving a $1,000 Quarterly Review of Literature Award as a prize. The resulting 300-400 pp. volumes are printed in editions of 3,000-5,000, selling in paperback for $10, in hardback for $20. Subscription—2 paperback volumes containing 10 books: $20. **Manuscripts may be sent for reading during the months of November and May. The collection need not be a first book. It should be between 50-80 pp. if it is a group of connected poems, a selection of miscellaneous poems, a poetic play, a work of poetry translation, or it can be a single long poem of 30 pp. or more. Some of the poems may have had previous magazine publication. Also considers simultaneous submissions. SASE must be included for returned manuscripts. Manuscripts in English or translated into English are also invited from outside the U.S. Only one MS may be submitted per reading period and must include an SASE.** "Since poetry as a thriving art must depend partly upon the enthusiasm and willingness of those directly involved to join in its support, the editors require that **each MS be accompanied by a subscription to the series.**"

‡QUARTOS MAGAZINE (IV-Subscribers), BCM-Writer, London WC1N 3XX U.K., founded 1987, editor Suzanne Riley, appears every other month. This is a "creative writers publication which includes reviews usually submitted by subscribers. **Poems included are usually those previously accepted by other editors or competition judges to help other readers establish a clear idea of editorial requirements. Submissions accepted are the work of our readers."** The newsletter is magazine-sized, 24 pp. folded. Press run is 1,000 for that many subscribers, of which 20 are libraries. Subscription: £18. **Sample postpaid: £2. Pays 1 copy.** "The Writers Handbook lists us as the 'best single source of UK poetry competitions anywhere.' We would accept articles of 800 words on poetry writing from any source." Pays £10.

QUEEN OF ALL HEARTS (IV-Religious), 26 S. Saxon Ave., Bay Shore NY 11706, phone (516)665-0726, founded 1950, poetry editor Joseph Tusiani, a magazine-sized bimonthly, uses **poetry "dealing with Mary, the Mother of Jesus—inspirational poetry. Not too long."** They have published poetry by Fernando Sembiante and Alberta Schumacher. The editor selected these sample lines (poet unidentified):

The toddler falters, Mary, catch him up
(Gethsemane reveals the sombre cup.)

Now the Passover Lamb dwells in the land
(Amid wood shavings stands he fresh and tanned.

The 48 pp. professionally printed magazine, heavy stock, various colors of ink and paper, liberal use of graphics and photos, has approximately 5,000 subscriptions at $12 per year. Per copy: $2.50. They receive 40-50 submissions of poetry per year, use 2 per issue. **Sample: $3 postpaid. Submit double-spaced MSS. Reports within 3-4 weeks. Pays 6 copies (sometimes more) and complimentary subscription. Sometimes editor comments on rejections.** His advice: "Try and try again! Inspiration is not automatic!"

QUEEN'S QUARTERLY: A CANADIAN REVIEW (II,IV-Regional), Queen's University, Kingston, Ontario K7L 3N6 Canada, phone (613)545-2667, founded 1893, editors Martha J. Bailey and Boris Castel is "a general interest intellectual review featuring articles on science, politics, humanities, arts and letters, extensive book reviews, some poetry and fiction. **We are especially interested in poetry by Canadian writers. Shorter poems preferred.**" They have recently published poetry by Katie Campbell, Sue Nevill and Raymond Souster. There are about 12 pp. of poetry in each issue, 6×9″, 224 pp., circulation 1,500. Subscription: $20 Canadian; U.S. and foreign, $22 U.S. funds; per copy: $6.50 U.S. They receive about 400 submissions of poetry per year, use 40. **Sample: $5 U.S. postpaid. Submit no more than 6 poems at once. Photocopies OK but no simultaneous submissions. Reports in 12-16 weeks. Pays usually $25 (Canadian) per poem, plus 2 copies.**

RADCLIFFE QUARTERLY (IV-Specialized), 10 Garden St., Cambridge MA 02138, phone (617)495-8608, editor Ruth Whitman, is an alumnae quarterly that **publishes alumnae and college-related poets.** They have published poetry by Patricia Filipowska and Rhea Kovar Sossen. As a sample the editor selected these lines (poet unidentified):
Except to say it was brown, black
or in between, you can't describe it
nor any terror, guilt, fantasy . . .
Full-color cover, magazine-sized, with glossy paper cover. They accept 3 poems per issue, 12 per year, receive about 30 per year. Press run: 30,500 for 30,000 subscribers. **No pay. Samples free to alumnae.** The Dean's office sponsors a contest for poets, winners printed in the quarterly. Must be a Radcliffe student to enter.

‡RADDLE MOON (II, IV-Form), 9060 Ardmore Dr., Sidney, British Columbia V8L 3S1 Canada, phone (604)656-4045, founded 1985, editor Susan Clark, appears twice a year using **"language-centered and 'new lyric' poetry."** They have recently published poetry by Claude Royet-Journoud, Lyn Hejinian, Rosmarie Waldrop and Leslie Scalapino. The editor describes it as 6×9″ flat-spined, 100+ pp. Press run 700. **Sample postpaid: $5. Reports in 2-3 months. Pays subscription.**

RADIANCE: THE MAGAZINE FOR LARGE WOMEN (I, IV-Women), Box 31703, Oakland CA 94604, phone (415)482-0680, founded 1984, publisher/editor Alice Ansfield, who **"wants to include poetry for women all sizes of large. Need to have poetry reach women all over the country; hence not too political in language. It should be personal, empowering."** As a sample she quotes these lines from "I Have Known So Fine A Time" by Charlene Mary-Cath Smith:
When sweat pants
treadmills seven-cal dinners
were nonexistent
When beauty was all
voluptuous breasts
ample hips luxuriant
thighs were lovingly
stroked on canvas
painstakingly duplicated
in immortal marble
The quarterly is magazine-sized, professionally printed on glossy stock with full-color paper cover, 60 pp., saddle-stapled, using b/w graphics, photos and ads, circulation 20,000 to 4,000 subscriptions, 6,000 selling on newsstands or in bookstores, 2,000 sent as complimentary copies to media, clothing stores for large women, therapists, etc. Subscription: $15/year. **Sample: $3.50 postpaid. Send SASE for guidelines. Pays $10-40. Double-spaced, typed MS. Editor comments on rejections.**

RAG MAG; BLACK HAT PRESS (I), P.O. Box 12, Goodhue MN 55027, phone (612)923-4590, founded 1982, poetry editor Beverly Voldseth accepts **poetry of "any length or style. No pornographic SM violent crap."** They have recently published poetry by Myra L. Sullivan, Robert Edwards and Harry Brody. As a sample the editor selected these lines from "All Slipped Away" by John M. Solensten:

All slipped away on a wink of the dial.
Then all we could hear
was the crackling of tired static—
little dry electric whispers
trying to say goodbye, goodbye,
while the house sat on the narrow shelf of darkness
dimming, dimming—cooling down, down
like a big, shut-off wooden radio.

Rag Mag, appearing twice a year, is 80 pp., perfect-bound, digest-sized, professionally printed in dark type with tipped-in colored ads for books, with matte colored card cover. The editor says she accepts about 10% of poetry received. Press run is 200 for 50 subscriptions of which 4 are libraries. Subscription: $10. **Sample: $6 postpaid. "Send 6-8 of your best. Something that tells a story, creates images, speaks to the heart. Always send SASE." Pays 1 copy.** Reviews books of poetry. **They may publish chapbook or paperback collections of poetry under the imprint of Black Hat Press. Query first. $25 reading fee for book or chapbook MS. Detailed comments provided. Submit 6-8 poems, bio, publications. Simultaneous submissions, previously printed material, photocopies OK. No dot-matrix. Reports in 6 weeks. Financial arrangements for book publication vary.** Recently published Riki Kölbl Nelson's English/German poems about living in 2 worlds/2 languages. Title: *Borders/Grenzen.* 128 pages plus the author's artwork.

RAINBOW CITY EXPRESS (I, IV-Spiritual, nature, women), P.O. Box 8447, Berkeley CA 94707-8447, founded 1988, editor Helen B. Harvey, is a quarterly using **"excellent evocative material pertaining to individual spiritual insights and experiences, God-in-nature, women's issues. 30 lines maximum. No rhyming poems! No infantile beginners.** Please obtain and study at least one issue of *RCE* prior to submitting any manuscript." They have recently published poetry by James Dillet Freeman. As a sample the editor offered these lines from one of her poems:

The sparkle on the spider's web,
a dust mote on the air,
the purple and white of columbines
unseen, in dark, thick woods—
Cloaked in this Seamless Garment,
I am them All.

They offer "sporadic contests with cash prizes and publication of winners." I have not seen an issue, but the editor describes it as 60-80 pp. magazine-sized, side-stapled, with "exquisite art and graphics, uplifting essays and poems, and ads." They accept about 25-45 poems per year. Press run 500-1,000 for 400-500 subscriptions, including several libraries. Subscription: $24. **Sample, postpaid: $6. Pays 1 copy.**

RAMBUNCTIOUS PRESS; RAMBUNCTIOUS REVIEW (II, IV-Regional), 1221 W. Pratt, Chicago IL 60626, phone (312)338-2439, founded 1982, poetry editors Mary Dellutri, Richard Goldman, Beth Hausler, and Nancy Lennon. The *Review* appears once yearly in a handsomely printed, saddle-stapled, 7 × 10″ format, 48 pages. They want **"spirited, quality poetry, fiction, short drama, photos, and graphics. Some focus on local work, but all work is considered."** Recently they have published Richard Calisch and Sean Lawrence and offer these lines by Demetrice Worley as a sample:

every Thursday
I am two-dimensional,
thin enough
to walk down her hall
cluttered tables
containing small, still
figurines.

They have a circulation of about 500 with 200 subscriptions, single copy $3.50 (**sample: $4 postpaid**). They receive 500-600 submissions a year and use 50-60, **reporting in 6-9 months. No special requirements for submission, will consider simultaneous submissions. No submissions accepted June 1 through August 31. No queries. Payment 2 copies. Occasional comments on MSS.** They run annual contests in poetry, fiction, and short drama.

‡THE RAMPANT GUINEA PIG (IV-Fantasy, form), 20500 Enadia Way, Canoga Park CA 91306, founded 1979, editor Mary Ann Hodge, appears twice a year using **"traditional verse forms, fantasy subjects, humorous or serious. No words scattered unevenly across the page, pretending to be lines of poetry. I don't want to hear about your love life, real or imagined."** They have recently published poetry by Donald K. Grundy as part of a parody of scholarship: **"The Cat in the Hat: An Accurate Rendering of the [Ps.-] Vergilian Fragments."** Here is how Dr. Seuss's poetry might have been written by Dryden:

> *Failed the sullen Sun, nor might we to Game,*
> *As chill time's wanton Children Time are wont to lame;*
> *We sat within, together twinned, throughout the day—*
> *A day, but Cold, Frigid, Chill, & Watery with rain.*
> *With sibling Sally sitting, I let slip a sigh:*
> *"O sister, would that there were What to Do, Whereby,...*

It is 30-40 pp., magazine-sized, desktop publishing, side-stapled, with matte card cover. "I accept very little poetry." Press run 100. **Sample postpaid: $3. Reports in 6 weeks. Send SASE for guidelines. Pays 1 copy.**

RANGER INTERNATIONAL PRODUCTIONS; LION PUBLISHING; ROAR RECORDING (V), P.O. Box 71231, Milwaukee WI 53211-7331, phone (414)332-7474 (formerly Albatross Press, then Lion Publishing), founded 1969, editor Martin Jack Rosenblum, publishes **"objectivist/projectivist poetry, primarily with action subjects by adventurers—such as the Harley poetry—** in flat-spined paper and hardcover chapbooks." They have recently published poetry by Karl Young, Howard McCord, Toby Olson, and Carl Rakosi. As a sample the editor selected his own poem "Late Fall on a Harley-Davidson" (in the book **The Holy Ranger**):

> *the leaves scatter into heaps still wet*
> *from night rain & the fog lifts valleys*
> *onto shaded helmet visor visions coming*
> *— — — —upon a road kill*
> *— — — —as though a ranger*
> *— —having followed the trail*
> *—that led to frigid air*
> *impossible to breath quick*
> *so head down right over the stench*

That book is 84 pp. flat-spined, digest-sized, with matte card cover, $14.95. They publish about 3 books a year. **Query regarding submissions. Payment "negotiable." Editor comments on submissions "always."** Reviews books of poetry. He says, "Poetry has been swept into an academic corner and dusted off of daily living spaces and this is what Ranger International Productions works against: we went to bring poetry out of academics and back into life's daily platform. Write hard, accept no public money and achieve honesty and integrity personally while studying the master poets in school or out. Control of the forms is essential. Control of the life is absolutely required."

‡RARACH PRESS (V), 1005 Oakland Dr., Kalamazoo MI 49008, phone (616)388-5631, founded 1981, owner Ladislav Hanka, is a "small bibliophilic press specializing in hand-printing, hand-binding with original artwork. The material is either in Czech or, if English, dealing with environmentalist subject matter." He has printed books of poetry by James Armstrong, Richard Neugebauer, Bennet Mitchell, and Rainer Maria Rilke. "Authors tend to be friends, acquaintances, or dead. They are given a portion of the books or a portion of sales after the fact. **I do not care to receive unsolicited MSS.** I pity the lot of you. I fully expect most of my books to eventually be taken apart and sold for the artwork when they pass from the present collector of bibliophili to some philistine. This means the poetry will be lost . . . I really sell my books for the price of the binding and artwork."

‡RARITAN QUARTERLY (III), 31 Mine St., New Brunswick NJ 08903, phone (908)932-7887, founded 1982, editor Richard Poirier. **"We publish very little poetry. We publish** *almost* **no unsolicited poetry, so it would be misleading to encourage submissions."** They have recently published poetry by J.D. McClatchy, James Merrill, Richard Howard and Robert Pinsky. They review recent poetry books and chapbooks. It is 6 × 9" flat-spined, 150+ pp., with matte card cover, professionally printed. Press run 4,000 for 3,500 subscriptions of which 800 are libraries. Subscription: $16. **Sample postpaid: $5. Pays $100/submission if accepted.**

RASHI (IV-Ethnic), Box 1198, Hamilton, New Zealand, founded 1985, editor Norman Simms, uses poetry on **"Jewish topics in English or any Jewish language such as Hebrew, Yiddish, Ladino, etc."** They do not want poetry that is "pompous, self-indulgent nonsense." They have recently published poems by Anne Ranasinghe and Simon Lichman. *Rashi*, now the literary supplement of the monthly *New Zealand Chronicle*. They accept about 25 of 40 poems received per year. Circulation is over 2,000. Subscription: $15. **Sample $2 postpaid. Pays 1 copy. Subscription "recommended, but not necessary." Reports in 1 month. Editor comments on rejections for $5 per page.** He says, "This is a special part of our overall projects. We would like to see multi-lingualism develop, reinterpretation of ancient and medieval traditions."

‡RAW DOG PRESS; POST POEMS (IV-Humor), 128 Harvey Ave., Doylestown PA 18901, phone (215)345-6838, founded 1977, poetry editor R. Gerry Fabian, "publishes Post Poems annual—a postcard series. We do chapbooks from time to time and there is always a special project that crops up. **We want short poetry (3-7 lines) on any subject. The positive poem or the poem of understated humor always has an inside track. No taboos, however. All styles considered. Anything with rhyme had better be immortal.**" They have recently published poetry by ave jeanne, Lyn Lifshin, Philip Miller, Conger Beasley, Jr., and the editor, who selected his sample poem, "The Nothing on Television Spring":

> It was terrible—
> Raw, damp and gray
> with weeks and weeks
> of Lawrence Welk rain.

Query with 7-10 samples for chapbook publication. "We are small and any poet is expected to share half the responsibility and often that includes cost—not always, however. No photocopies or dot-matrix. Pays copies. Send SASE for catalog to buy samples. The editor "always" comments on rejections. Sometimes reviews books of poetry. He says he will offer criticism for a fee; "if someone is desperate to publish and is willing to pay we will use our vast knowledge to help steer the MS in the right direction. We will advise against it, but as P. T. Barnum said . . . . Raw Dog Press welcomes new poets and detests second-rate poems from 'name' poets. We exist because we are dumb like a fox but even a fox takes care of its own."

REAL (RE ARTS & LETTERS) (II, IV-Bilingual, translations, humor), (formerly RE:AL, RE: Artes Liberales), Box 13007, Stephen F. Austin State University, Nacogdoches TX 75962, phone (409)568-2101, founded 1968, editor Lee Schultz, is a "Liberal Arts Forum" using short fiction, drama, reviews and interviews; contains editorial notes, personalized "Contributors' Notes," reviews. Printed in the spring and fall, they "hope to use from 15 to 35 pages of poetry per issue, one poem per page (typeset in editor's office). Last two issues had submissions from thirty-eight states, Great Britain, Italy and Israel." **They receive between 10-35 poems/week. "We presently do not receive enough formal or witty/ ironic pieces. We need a better balance between open and generic forms. We're also interested in critical writings on poems or writing poetry and translations with a bilingual format (permissions from original author).** The editor selected this sample from "Within the Womb of This Mountain" by Jenna Fedock:

> We will not see him again,
> "Lord have mercy,"
> but only in the black box wedged in an aisle,
> heavy lid crushing our heads. We chant
> "Vichnaya pamyat, Vichnaya pamyat, Vichnaya pamyat,"
> trying to cast it off—but cannot.

It is handsomely printed, "reserved format," perfect-binding with line drawings and photos. Circulation approx. 400, "more than half of which are major college libraries." Subscriptions also in Great Britain, Ireland, Italy, Holland, Puerto Rico, Brazil and Canada. **Submit original and copy. "Editors prefer a statement that MSS is not being simultaneously submitted; however, this fact is taken for granted when we receive a MS." Sample postpaid: $4.50. Writer's guidelines for SASE. Pays in copies.** They acknowledge receipt of submissions and strive for a 1-month decision. Submissions during summer semesters may take longer. **"We will return poems rather than tie them up for more than a one-issue backlog (6-9 months)."**

‡REALITY STUDIOS (V), 4 Howard Court, Peckham Rye, London SE15 3PH U.K., founded 1978, editor Ken Edwards, has published books of poetry by Allen Fisher, Tom Raworth and Charles Bernstein, but **accepts no unsolicited MSS.** They publish 2 paperbacks/year. Their U.S. distributor is Small Press Distribution, 1814 San Pablo Ave., Berkeley CA 94302.

‡RECORDING & PUBLISHING NEWS; ANTERIOR BITEWING LTD. (I), 7735 Brand Ave., St. Louis MO 63135, founded 1988, editor Thomas Bergeron, appears 6 times a year using **poetry, not necessarily related to the themes of the magazine.** It is a "newsletter full of fact, figures, guidelines, and practical information. It's about services, markets, copyrights, technology, and techniques,—**but there's room for a few really good poems in every issue."** They have recently published poetry by C. David Hay, J.

Alvin Speers, Joyce Carbone and Vivian Bogardus. As a sample the editor selected these lines from "Lonely Poet" by James K. Halsey:

> *I admit that I am a lonely poet;*
> *But I do not dwell on the thought.*
> *I just open up my arms, and my heart—*
> *Then do or say what I have been taught.*

It is desktop published, magazine-sized, 20 pp. Press run 200-300 for 110 subscribers. Subscription: $15.99. **Sample: $3 postpaid. Please make checks payable to Anterior Bitewing Ltd. Pays $5/poem. Send SASE for guidelines. "We like cover letters."** Anterior Bitewing Ltd. is an imprint for job printing of newsletters and "magazettes." Send SASE for rate sheet. The editor says, "Always re-submit. There's some editor out there somewhere who will love your work. Take advice, make changes accordingly, and keep on re-submitting."

RECOVERING POET'S REGISTRY AND EXCHANGE; BLACKBERRY PRESS (IV-Specialized), 2902 N. 21st Ave., Phoenix AZ 85015, phone (602)340-0906, editor Susan Smith, is a small-press operation publishing chapbooks twice a year **"with work of poets recovering from chemical, behavioral, and emotional addictions. Include bio with address and phone number for communication and poetry exchange with other recovering poets."** They want **"powerful recovery poetry, well-thought-out, edited. Any style. All subjects (life is a process of recovery). Limit poems to 1 page whenever possible. The purpose is to encourage and unite recovering poets who write poetry as therapy and healing. Nothing hyper-religious, preachy, self-righteous, promotion of any organized religion."** As a sample the editor selected these lines from a poem by Roy R. Gosnell, "Hello . . . I Love You":

> *I found inside my heart one day,*
> *a child who'd somehow lost his way.*
> *He never grew as I had done,*
> *he never got to see the sun.*

Submit 2 or 3 samples and bio. Send poetry and letters, but not queries alone. Simultaneous submissions and previously published poems OK. You pay a one-time fee of $15 "includes one chapbook (with poetry and bio). An additional $10 for each publication thereafter with or without poet's contribution." Sample copies of publication available for $5 at above address. Reviews books of poetry "sometimes." The editor advises, "Ignore snobbish remarks about what makes 'good poetry.' Be totally honest and committed to communication. Write, edit, live with your creations and edit more whenever needed. Poetry can be therapeutic, but it doesn't have to be serious. It can be funny, cynical, sarcastic, morbid and bitter—as well as all the other poetic possibilities. Be yourself and capture moods, experiences, and feelings."

‡RECURSIVE ANGEL (IV-Science Fiction/Spirituality), 210 Wilbur Blvd., Poughkeepsie NY 12603, or 1412 N.E. 35th St., Ocala FL 32670, phone (914)485-3866, founded 1990, managing editor David H. Sutherland, appears twice a year, **"looking for hard-hitting tightly composed sci-fi with a spiritual and metaphysical slant. Open to all forms."** The have recently published poetry by G. Sutton Breiding and Robert Frazier. As a sample the editor selected these lines from "Future Texts" by Bruce Boston:

> *Without beginning or end,*
> *without rector or verso*
> *or colored cover to judge,*
>
> *unreeling like a worded carpet*
> *directly into our brains,*
> *the software melange with*
>
> *envelopes our days and nights . . .*

It is magazine-sized, 30-40 pp. "high quality typeset, hardbound and softbound distribution." Press run is 250 copies. Subscription: $14.95. **Sample postpaid: $7.95. Pays $10-40/poem/prose/ short story. "Send only 3-5 poems/prose. Cover letter A.O.K." Reports 6-8 weeks. Editor occasionally comments on rejections. 5″ disk, IBM ASCII submissions OK. Or you can upload 2 text submissions between 9-11 AM EST Sundays to (914)485-3866-1200, N, 8, 1.** The editor advises, "Buy **Poet's Market** and study it in the same vein as if you were taking an exam. Finally, Read! Read! Read!"

RED ALDER BOOKS; PAN-EROTIC REVIEW (II, IV-Erotica, feminist), P.O. Box 2992, Santa Cruz CA 95063, phone (408)426-7082, founded 1971, poetry editor David Steinberg. **"We specialize in publication of books on re-examination of traditional male roles, and creative, provocative erotica that is imaginative, top-quality, non-exploitative, especially if unconventional or explicitly sexual. It is our desire to demonstrate that erotica material can be evocative, sexy, powerful and energizing, without being cliché, exploitive of men's and women's frustrations, or male-dominant. Our work demands**

respect for the best of our erotic natures, for life, for love, and for our wonderful bodies." They have published poetry by Lyn Lifshin, James Broughton, Leslie Simon, Arthur Knight and Cheryl Townsend. **Query with 5-10 sample poems. Replies to queries and/or submissions in 1-2 months. Simultaneous submissions, photocopies OK. Pays copies, occasional royalties. Sample book available for $9, postpaid.** The editor advises, "Tell the truth; avoid playing the poet; pursue humility; be useful to someone beyond yourself; say something new, something unnoticed, about the life-force."

‡RED DANCEFLOOR (I, II); RED DANCEFLOOR PRESS (V), P.O. Box 3051, Canoga Park CA 91306, phone (818)785-7650, founded 1990, editor David Goldschlag, is a poetry quarterly: **"no restrictions on form, length or subject matter. We want poetry that is well thought out—not a first draft. If you send us rhyme it should have a specific purpose and work; would consider a good villanelle."** They have recently published poetry by Michael C. Ford, David Lake, Glenn Bach, Mario Rene Padilla and Mary Armstrong. As a sample the editor selected these lines from "Blind Women of Laos" by Elizabeth Ziemba:

> *in sepia stone courtyards*
> *they drift*
> *like pieces of confetti*
> *incased in silk.*

The magazine is digest-sized, 80-100 pp., flat-spined, laser printed, with glossy card cover. Press run 400. **Sample postpaid: $3.50. Send SASE for guidelines. Pays 1 copy and % off additional copies. Previously published poems and simultaneous submissions OK, "but please note." Reports in 2-6 weeks. "We will try to comment on all rejections, definitely if asked. A short cover letter is fine, but get to the point. Submit 5-7 poems."** Reviews books of poetry. The editor advises, "Do not avoid criticism: ask for it, accept it and use it to improve your work. Make rewriting as important as inspiration and don't be afraid to trust your instincts."

‡RED HERRING POETS; MATRIX; RED HERRING PRESS; RED HERRING CHAPBOOK SERIES; CHANNING-MURRAY FOUNDATION (IV-Membership), 1209 W. Oregon St., Urbana IL 61801, phone (217)344-1176, founded 1975, director of Red Herring Poets Ruth S. Walker. The Red Herring Poets is a workshop that publishes its members' work after they have attended at least 5 meetings, in their annual magazine, *Matrix*, and, for those who have been members for at least 2 years and given 2 public readings, one chapbook/year.

RED RAMPAN' PRESS (V); RED RAMPAN' REVIEW (V); RED RAMPAN' BROADSIDE SERIES (IV-Form), 4707 Fielder St., Midland TX 79707-2817, phone (915)697-7689, founded 1981, poetry editor Larry D. Griffin. **"For 1992 we will consider long poems for Red Rampan' Broadside Series."** *RRR* is an "eclectic review quarterly." I have not seen a copy, but the editor says it is 6×9", 48-60 pp., with a press run of 300, **"presently not accepting poetry."** The Press plans to publish flat-spined paperback collections.

THE REDNECK REVIEW OF LITERATURE (IV-Regional), P.O. Box 730, Twin Falls ID 83301, phone (208)734-6653, editor Penelope Reedy, semiannual magazine publishing poetry, fiction and essays dealing with the contemporary West. The editor wants to see **"any form, length or style." She does not want "ethereal ditties about nothing; obscure."** She has published poetry by Tom Trusky, Thomas McClanahan, Gail-Marie Pahmeir, Bill Studebaker, Gerald Locklin, Rane Arroyo and Mack Rozema. The magazine, which appears in the spring and fall each year, is magazine-sized, offset, perfect bound, some advertising. Circulation is 500, of which 200 are subscriptions and 100-150 are newsstand sales. Price per issue is $7 postpaid. **Sample: $7 postpaid. Pay is 1 copy. Rejected MSS are reported on immediately, and no accepted MSS are held beyond 3 issues. Writers should submit "2-3 poems at a time, letter quality—don't like simultaneous submissions. Please send SASE with *enough* postage to return MSS."** Criticism is sometimes given. Reviews books of poetry. The editor says, "Take time—have something to say. Learn how to pull images out of your head, to cover an idea completely. Read nursery rhymes to your kids, listen and observe."

REFLECT (IV-Themes), 3306 Argonne Ave., Norfolk VA 23509, founded 1979, poetry editor W. S. Kennedy. They use **"spiral poetry: featuring an inner-directed concern with sound (euphony), mystical references or overtones, and objectivity—rather than personal and emotional poems. No love poems, pornography, far left propaganda; nothing overly sentimental. (Don't write yourself into the poem.)"** They have recently published poetry by Marikay Brown, B.Z. Niditch, Pearl Bloch Segall, and Stan Proper. As a sample the editor selected these lines by Ruth Wildes Schuler:

> *An oyster white Southern gypsy, you burst in a psychotic passion*
> *upon a sterile rigid world—Faulkner shades followed in*
> *mocking vermillion, haunting your tan golden footsteps and*
> *dropping seeds of corrupting decay from the Ritz Bar to the*

Riviera. They sought to lock you in the gilded cage of
conformity, but you escaped them all, Zelda, by dancing a pale
orchid waltz to madness.
The quarterly is digest-sized, 48 pp., saddle-stapled, typescript. Subscription: $8. **Sample: $2**
postpaid. Guidelines available for SASE. All submissions should be single-spaced and should
fit on one typed page. Reports within a month. No backlog. Pays 1 copy. Editor sometimes
comments on rejections. Occasionally reviews books of poetry.

REFLECTIONS (IV-Children/teens), P.O. Box 368, Duncan Falls OH 43734, phone (614)674-5209,
founded 1980, is **"a poetry magazine by students from nursery school to high school"** – a project of
the 7th and 8th grade journalism students from Franklin Local Schools, Duncan Falls Junior High
School. Editor Dean Harper says it **"is an avenue for publishing young writers to encourage their**
writing and to help motivate students to write and to become involved when their teachers teach
writing." *Reflections* also features excellent writing programs across the United States. They consider
all forms and lengths of poetry. These are sample lines selected by the editor from "A Tear" by Beth
Decoteau, age 18:

> *A tear slices my cheek*
> *as it glides down my face*
> *smoothly*
> *like the blade*
> *of an ice skater's skate*
> *then falls*
> *disappointedly to the ground.*

Reflections comes out twice a year in an elegant magazine-sized format with a glossy, color
photograph by a student on the front. Its 32 large pages are filled with poems (in rather small
type), often with a b/w photograph of the student, and a few ads. It has a circulation of 1,000,
with 700 subscriptions, of which 15 are libraries. **Sample $2,** subscription $5. **Reports within 10**
days, 6 month backlog. Send SASE for guidelines. Pays in contributor's copy. This is one of the
few good places publishing poetry by children. They receive about 3,000 submissions a year, use
about 200. **Considers simultaneous submissions.**

RENDITIONS: A CHINESE-ENGLISH TRANSLATION MAGAZINE (IV-Translations), Research Center for Translation, CUHK, Shatin, NT, Hong Kong, editor Dr. Eva Hung, appears twice a year.
"Contents exclusively translations from Chinese, ancient and modern." They also publish a paperback
series of Chinese literature in English translation. They have recently published translations of the
poetry of Gu Cheng, Shu Ting, Mang Ke, and Bei Dao. As a sample the editor selected a poem by
Bing Xin, translated by John Cayley:

> *The waves constantly press the cliff.*
> *The rocks are always silent, never answer,*
> *Yet this silence,*
> *has been pondered down the ages.*

Renditions is magazine-sized, 180 pp., flat-spined, elegantly printed, often with side-by-side Chinese and English texts, using some b/w and color drawings and photos, with glossy card cover.
Sample: $9 postpaid. Pays "honorarium" plus 2 copies. Reports in two months. Use British
spelling. They "will consider" book MSS, for which they would like a query with sample poems.
Books pay 10% royalties plus 10 copies. MSS usually not returned. Editor sometimes comments
on rejections.

RENEGADE (II), Box 314, Bloomfield Hills MI 48303, phone (313)972-5580, founded 1988, editors
Miriam Jones and Michael Nowicki, appears twice a year using stories, essays and poems. **"We are an**
eclectic publication. There is no preference for form or style; we simply wish to see polished work of
good quality. Poems are generally of a length no more than 200 lines, no less than 10 lines. We try to
avoid anything that is anarchistic, antifeminist, or of a derogatory nature to any group of persons or
individuals." They have recently published poetry by John Sinclair, M.L. Liebler, Linda Nemec Foster,
and Laurence Pike. As a sample, I selected the first 2 of 5 stanzas of "Night Chain" by Murray Jackson:

> *Extended hands with purple plums*
> *shine in the half light of night and*
> *reflect the glare of patent leather.*
>
> *The long sleeves of night reach*
> *to find nightmares to pour –*
> *we all stand in a circle and wait our turn.*

Renegade is 32 pp. digest-sized, laser-printed, with matte card cover, b/w drawings and graphics.
Ads welcome. They accept about 5% of 300 MSS of 5 poems or less. Press run: 200 for 20

subscriptions, free to libraries and editors of other literary journals. 50 shelf sales. Subscription: $5.90. **Sample, postpaid: $2. Pays 1 copy, 2 on request. Reports in 3-6 months. Editor comments on submissions "often."** Reviews books of poetry.

‡RESIN (I), P.O. Box 2453, Athens GA 30612, founded 1989, edited by Gregory Mann and Charlotte Eubanks, is a quarterly. **"We want good poetry with concise images. No pornography; no sentiment."** They have recently published poetry by Charlotte Eubanks, Tatiana Prowell and Megan E. Ray. As a sample the editors selected these lines by Charlotte Eubanks:

> *Old man, bent and carving*
> *Slow steps from webs of roots,*
> *Splayed like spilled lightning bolts,*
> *Stilled by hob-nailed boots.*

It is magazine-sized, saddle-stapled with a glossy paper cover, printed in a variety of large type styles. They publish "less than a quarter" of poems received. Press run 65-75. **Sample: $2 postpaid. Pays 1 copy. Reports within a month.** Submissions are read by a staff of 3. When asked, they comment on rejections.

RESPONSE (IV-Ethnic, students), 27 W. 20th St., 9th Floor, New York NY 10011, phone (212)675-1168, FAX (212)-929-3459, founded 1966, poetry editor Bennett Graff, is a "contemporary Jewish review publishing poetry, fiction and essays **by students and young adult authors." The only specification for poetry is that it be on a Jewish theme and have some significant Jewish content.** They have recently published poetry by Esty Schachter, Mark Zuss, Robert Paul Silverman, and Barbara Foster. As a sample the editor chose these lines by Estelle Gershgoren Novak:

> *Memory, like a stranger,*
> *speaks a foreign language*
> *understood only by those*
> *who have studied*
> *the strange grammar of the dead.*

They look for "creative, challenging and chutzapadik writing" from young writers. The quarterly is "between 96 and 120 pp.," flat-spined, 6×9", professionally printed on heavy stock, with a glossy "varnished" cover with art work. Circulation 2,000 with 1,000 subscribers of which 30% are libraries. 1,000 distributed through bookstores and newsstands. Subscription: $16 ($8 for students); $20 for institutions. **Sample: $2 postpaid. Pays 5 copies. Reports in about 8 weeks. 6 months between acceptance and publication.** Occasionally reviews books of poetry.

‡RESURGENS (II), P.O. Box 725006, Atlanta GA 30339-9006, founded 1989, editors David Blanchard and Paul Beard, appears twice a year. **"We're looking for moments in people's lives—epiphanies—told with a poetic grasp of language. Short poems 20-30 lines preferred. We mostly publish free verse. No overtly political poems or poems with 'agendas.' Also, no simplistic rhymed meters or love poems."** They have recently published poetry by Michael Bailey, Reja-e Busailah, Tom Benediktsson and Tonja Harrison. As a sample the editor selected these lines from "Babel" by Michael Maschinot:

> *Feed my dust to the archeologists,*
> *Let them riddle my withered limbs, and let*
> *their manifestos all agree; here rests*
> *a city ached to death, crushed by the weight*
> *of towering dreams . . .*

It is digest-sized, 32-64 pp., professionally printed, saddle-stapled, with matte card cover. They use 5-10% of about 250 submissions/year. Subscription: $12/4 issues. **Sample postpaid: $4. Send SASE for guidelines. Reports in 2-3 months. Pays 2 copies. "Please include brief bio. We want to know who our contributors are!" Editors often comment on rejections.** "We're looking for writers with a love of language and who are committed to their craft."

‡REVIEW LA BOOCHE; A.B. HATTON AWARD (I, II), 110 S. 9th St., Columbia MO 65201, phone (314)874-8772, founded 1976, editors Gerald Dethrow and Michel Jabbour, appears each summer. They want **all forms, any subject, not "self-indulgent."** They have recently published poetry by John Ciardi, Leslie Mueller, X.J. Kennedy, Tom McAfee, R.P. Dickey, Lerry Levis, E.S. Miller, Warren Thomas and William Stafford. As a sample the editor selected these lines (poet unidentified):

> *Walk with me now, I'll have the setting right:*
> *a pond, idyllic pasture, woods, an orange sun—*
> *down, breeze, quiet*
>   *Now tell me what is love.*

It is handsomely printed, flat-spined, 100 pp., digest-sized. They accept about 3% of MSS received. Press run 500-1,000. **Sample: $6 postpaid. Send SASE for guidelines. A.B. Hatton Award of $100 for best poem and story per issue. Pays 4 copies. "Generally like 3-6 poems from author.**

if we like what we read will request more ourselves." The editor advises, "stay away from all schools of poetry that have proven to drown out your personal voice and also perpetuate easy formula poems that seem hollow and unmeaningful."

RFD: A COUNTRY JOURNAL FOR GAY MEN EVERYWHERE (I, IV-Gay), Box 68, Liberty TN 37095, founded 1974, poetry editor Steven Riel. *RFD* "is a quarterly for gay men with emphasis on lifestyles outside of the gay mainstream—poetry, politics, profiles, letters." They want **poetry with "personal, creative use of language and image, relevant to journal themes, political themes. We try to publish as many poets as we can so tend to publish shorter poems and avoid epics."** They have recently published poetry by Antler, James Broughton, Gregory Woods and Winthrop Smith. The issue I examined had 4 magazine-sized pp. of poetry, some dozen poems photoreduced from typescript arranged at various angles on the page, with b/w photos and drawings interspersed. As a sample the editor selected the opening lines of "Shadow" by L.E. Wilson:

> *I am a shadow among shadows*
> *a name whispered in a hurricane*
> *not immortal and nothing of the magic*
> *(but I remember magic) . . .*

RFD has a circulation of 2,600 for 1,300 subscriptions—per year: $25 first class, $18 second class; per copy: $5.50. **Sample: $5 postpaid. Submit up to 5 poems at a time. Photocopies, simultaneous submissions OK. Reports in 6-9 months. Pays copies. Send SASE for guidelines. Editor sometimes comments on rejections.** "*RFD* looks for interesting thoughts, succinct use of language and imagery evocative of nature and gay men and love in natural settings."

‡**RHINO (II)**, 8403 W. Normal, Niles IL 60648, founded 1976, editors: Kay Meier and Martha Vertreace, "is an annually published poetry journal. We seek well-crafted work with fresh insights and authentic emotion by known or new writers, **poems which show careful attention to form and contain surprise. Poems no longer than 3 pp. double-spaced.**" They have recently published poetry by Elaine Mott, Lyn Lifshin, Christopher Merrill, and Mark Pawlak. The editors chose as a sample the opening lines of "A Poem After the Wedding" by Nicole Niemi:

> *Our house is dark now.*
> *You and I slide into each other's arms like*
> *rain spinning onto a roof.*
> *I would like to say*
> *for the matter of poetry,*
> *that our love shimmers like a July hot rainbow.*
> *But this is not true.*

The digest-sized 96 pp. journal, perfect-bound, matte card cover with art, is offset from typescript on high-quality paper, circulation 500, 100 subscriptions of which 10 are libraries. They use 50-60 of 1,000+ submissions received. **Sample: $5 plus 90¢ postage. Submit 3-5 double-spaced poems; photocopies, dot-matrix OK. Reports in 2 months, pays one copy.** Annual *Rhino* Poetry Contest with $100 prize and publication in *Rhino*. Regular reading period January 1-May 31. Contest reading period ($2 per poem submitted) March 1-May 31.

‡**RHODODENDRON (I)**, 879 Bell St., E. Palo Alto CA 94303, founded 1984, poetry editor Steven Jacobsen. Regarding the poetry he is looking for, the editor says: **"Unconcerned about form, length and so on. Do not print anonymously-voiced, well-polished bits of faceless craft. Particularly interested in longer work, especially when narrative in nature. A mild prejudice against first-person material. If you write confessional poetry, confess elsewhere."** He has recently used poetry by Turquoise Q. Appendix, Robert Greenfield, Greg Boyd, Don Raphael, Joe Pjerrou, Steve Richmond, Douglas Goodwin, and Wanda Coleman. As a sample he selected these lines (poet unidentified):

> *A Heart   A knife*
> *the rough come by sucking the head of a gun*
> *a red bath with open arms*
> *eating the world through the mouth*

The digest-sized quarterly is typeset (large, dark type), photocopied, with matte card cover. Uses graphics, ads. Press run is 200+ for 77 subscriptions (2 of them libraries), the rest for shelf sales. Of 500+ poems received per year he uses about 50. Subscription: $15. **Single copy: $3 (limited supply of back issues—$2.50 each). Pays 3 copies. "Don't use red ink on lavender paper." Simultaneous submissions OK. Previously published poems—"maybe." Reports in 1-3 months.** Steven Jacobsen says, "I try to offer useful comments and suggestions to all MSS." Publishes 1 chapbook per year. Payment is ½ of press run. "Be faithful to your vision, whatever that vision might be. There is an alarming trend for writers to compose for the audience; literature as a marketable commodity. Screw that. Don't attempt to manipulate; be truthful. Write for yourself.

In addition to paying contributors copies, we mail copies of each issue to 50 different magazines as a means of introducing new talent to other editors."

THE RIALTO (II), 32 Grosvenor Rd., Norwich, Norfolk NR2 2PZ England, founded 1984, poetry editors John Wakeman and Michael Mackmin, wants **"poetry of intelligence, wit, compassion, skill, excellence, written by humans. Potential contributors are strongly advised to read *The Rialto* before submitting."** They have recently published poetry by Peter Porter, Tadeusz Rózewicz and Carol Ann Duffy. As a sample the editors chose the last half of "Finnish Tango," an elegy by Hans Magnus Enzensberger for Felix Pollak, translated by Reinhold Grimm:

> All is so bright   It was half dark
> The little boat will not always return
> It is the same and yet isn't
> No one's around   The rock is a rock
> The rock ceases being a rock
> The rock turns into a rock again
> It's always like that   Nothing
> dissolves and nothing remains   What existed
> is and isn't and is   No one
> can grasp that   That which existed last night
> That's easy to say   How bright
> the summer here is and how brief

The Rialto, which appears 3 times a year, is magazine-sized, 48 pp. saddle-stapled, beautifully printed on glossy stock with glossy b/w card cover, using b/w drawings. They accept subscriptions at $24. **Sample: $8.50 postpaid. Pays £5 per poem. No simultaneous submissions or previously printed poetry. Reports within 3 months. Editor "only rarely" comments on rejections.**

RIDGE REVIEW MAGAZINE; RIDGE TIMES PRESS (IV-Regional), Box 90, Mendocino CA 95460, phone (707)964-8465, founded 1981, poetry editors Jim Tarbell and Judy Tarbell, is a "bio-regional quarterly looking at economic, political and social phenomena of the area" which uses **only poets from Northern California.** They have recently published poetry by Michael Sykes and Judith Tannenbaum. As a sample the editors chose these lines from "New Broom" by Kay Ryan:

> New broom sweeps stiff,
> graceless thatch rakes,
> leaves tracks, but change
> comes unseen makes bristles
> sway that or this way
> turns tasks
> segue

The 7×10″ magazine, saddle-stapled, 50+ pp., linen card cover with art, photos and ads with text, circulation 3,500, 1,000 subscriptions, uses about 1 page of poetry per issue. Subscription: $10; per copy: $3. They use about 1 out of 20 poems submitted each year. **Considers simultaneous submissions. Sample: $3.85 postpaid. Photocopy, dot-matrix OK. Reports in about a week. Usually pays $10 per poem.**

RIO GRANDE PRESS; SE LA VIE WRITER'S JOURNAL (I, IV-Themes); EDITOR'S DIGEST (IV-Subscribers), P.O. Box 371371, El Paso TX 79937, founded 1987, editor Rosalie Avara. *Se La Vie Writer's Journal* is a quarterly journal, digest-sized, with articles, cartoons and humorous fillers about poetry and writing; and contests in poetry, essays and short stories. Prizes are $5-125 for poems, entry fee $5 for 2 poems. Publishes 70% of MSS received per quarter, **"dedicated to encouraging novice writers, poets and artists; we are interested in original, unpublished MSS that reflect the 'life' theme (La Vie). Poems are judged on originality, clarity of thought and ability to evoke emotional response."** They have recently published poetry by Marian Ford Park, Alice Mackenzie Swaim and Marianne McNeil. As a sample the editor selected some lines from a prize-winning poem, "The Flinders Ranges" by Keevil Brown:

> The desert reduced
> to a heat wave of colours
> with tooth-proof rocks reflecting images
> as were mirrors reflecting
> each others' dreaming
> down infinite aisles of memories,
> and sand dunes crystallized
> from the thought waves of a god.

SLVWJ is 80 pp., photocopied from typescript, with blue cover, saddle-stapled. **Sample: $4 postpaid. Deadlines: end of March, June, September and December. Send SASE for guidelines. Pays**

1 copy. *Editor's Digest* is "for editors and by editors," quarterly, digest-sized, 50 pp., **dealing with issues concerning small press editors: "an opportunity for editors to express their side of writing and exchange views, with peers."** Free advertising for subscribers. **Send SASE for details or $4 for sample. Uses some poetry from subscribers only.** Annual Publications Contest for subscribers only; cash prizes.

RIVER CITY; HOHENBERG AWARD (II), English Dept., Memphis State University, Memphis TN 38152, phone (901)363-4438, founded 1980, editor Sharon Bryan. *River City* publishes fiction, poetry, interviews and essays. Contributors have included John Updike, Marvin Bell, Philip Levine, Maxine Kumin, Robert Penn Warren, W. D. Snodgrass, Mary Oliver, Fred Busch, Beth Bentley, Mona Van Duyn and Peter Porter. The biannual is 6×9", perfect-bound, 100 pp., 40-50 pp. of poetry in each issue, professionally printed, two-color matte cover, circulation 1,000, subscription: $6. **Sample: $4 postpaid. Submit no more than 5 poems, none June-August. Photocopy OK. Reports in 2-12 weeks. Pays 2 copies (and cash when grant funds available).** $100 Hohenberg Award is given annually to best fiction or poetry selected by the staff.

RIVER RAT REVIEW (III), Box 24198, Lexington KY 40524, founded 1987, editor Daryl Rogers, is published once a year, **"designed for mainly non-academic readership, though open to anything that is clear, concise and striking. There are no real restrictions but it's advisable to sample an issue before submitting. If you can't afford it, write me and we'll work something out."** Poets last published include Charles Bukowski, Douglas Goodwin, Steve Richmond and Serena Fusek. As a sample I give you the following lines by Marcus Cafagna:

> *Jamming Sheet metal in a*
> *punch press. In the same motion*
> > *beating hissing jaws by seconds*
> *and lifting it out. Their faces dripping*
> *soap and oil.*

The review is digest sized, 48 pp., printed by offset on white stock, with a one color cover, saddle-stapled; there is some b&w artwork. Circulation is 200. Price per issue is $4, subscription $4/year. **Submit MSS between Oct. 1 and Nov. 1 *only*. No simultaneous submissions. Pays one copy. Reports in 1-2 months. Publishes "short mention of chaps, etc. I think deserve it."**

RIVER STYX MAGAZINE; BIG RIVER ASSOCIATION (II), 14 S. Euclid, St. Louis MO 63108, phone (314)361-0043, poetry editor Ms. Lee Schreiner, founded 1975, is "an international, multicultural journal publishing both award-winning and relatively undiscovered writers. We feature fine art, photography, poetry and short prose." They want "excellent poetry—thoughtful." They have published work by Adrienne Rich, Amy Clampitt, Toni Morrison, Amiri Baraka, Simon Ortiz, Milosz, and Margaret Atwood. As a sample the editors chose these lines by Derek Walcott:

> *What's missing from the Charles is the smell of salt*
> *though the thawed river, muscling toward its estuary,*
> *swims seaward with the Spring, then with strong shoulders*
> *heaves up the ice. The floes crack like rifle fire.*

River Styx appears 3 times a year. I have not seen it, but the editors describe it as 90 pp., digest-sized with b/w cover. They accept less than 10% of 500 MSS received a year. **Sample: $7 postpaid. Reading period Sept. 1-Oct. 31. Guidelines available for SASE. Pays $8 a page plus 2 copies. Submit "legible copies with name, address on each page. Submissions read in September and October only." Reports in 1 week to 2 months, publication within a year.** Editor sometimes comments on rejections.

RIVERRUN (I, II), Glen Oaks Community College, Centreville MI 49032-9719, phone (616)467-9945, ext. 277, founded 1977, poetry editor Harvey Gordon, is a literary biannual, using **30-40 magazine-sized pp. of poetry in each issue**—"no prejudices. We would like to receive more formal verse." As a sample, the editor chose the complete poem "Dining in Winter" by Philip Miller:

> *Almost forgotten,*
> *a red sun swims at dusk,*
> *catching the edge of his eye*
> *before he turns back to their meal*
> *and to the silence hung*
> *above the cool ring of silver.*

They have a print run of 600. **Sample: $3 postpaid.** They receive 500-600 poems per year, use "as much as possible," have a 6-12 month backlog. **Reports immediately, except from June 15-Sept. 15. Pays 2 copies.**

RIVERRUN

Fall 1990

All of Riverrun's illustrations are chosen "for the purpose of embellishing the publication with high quality artwork," says editor Harvey Gordon, adding that "No thematic representation is intended." All of the artists are art students at Glen Oaks Community College, Centreville, Michigan, where Riverrun, a poetry biannual, is published. This particular cover was done in ink by Jory Meisterheim.

RIVERWIND (II), General Studies, Hocking College, Nelsonville OH 45764, phone (614)753-3591 ext. 2375, founded 1982, poetry editor C.A. Dubielak, is a literary annual wanting **"work from serious writers. We are most open to work with serious content, though humor may be the vehicle. Do not want to see poetry from those who view it as a 'hobby.' We have not published limericks."** They have published poetry by Naton Leslie, Gloria Ruth, Charles Semones, Walter McDonald, John Haines, John Aber, James Riley and Greg Anderson. As a sample the editor selected these lines (poet unidentified):

> *Sometimes I wake on the sofa, sleep on*
> *the sofa, or wake walking in the middle*
> *of a talk out of sense. Only while no one*
> *tears me out does it have sense for me.*

Riverwind is 6×9″ flat-spined, 80 pp., typeset, offset, with 2-color semiglossy card cover. Of 80-100 poems received they accept approximately 40. Press run is 500. Per issue: $2.50. **Sample back issue: $1 postpaid. Pays 2 copies. Submit batches of 3-5, no previously published poems, no simultaneous submissions. Reports in 2-8 weeks. Response slow during summer months. Editor comments "particularly if we would like to see more of that person's work."** Reviews books of poetry. They hope to begin publishing chapbook collections.

‡ROADS (I), 49 Meynell Heights, Leeds Yorkshire U.K. L511 9P5, founded 1988, editors Gordon Smith and David Mitchell, appears twice a year. They want **any poetry except "excessively long."** They have recently published poetry by Joy Walsh, Peter Bakowski, Tina Fulker and Peter Thabit-Jones. As a sample the editor selected these lines by L.E. Scott:

> *After making love*
> *lying in my mind*
> *watching the clouds, making skeletons*
> *the earth is full of mirrors*

It is a small oblong magazine of 36 pp. offset, "litho on recycled paper" with b/w card cover. They accept about 20% of 300 poems received a year. Press run 250. Subscription: £3. **Sample: £1.50. Pays 1 copy. Poets are encouraged to buy copies. Reports in 1 month.** The editor advises, "Be persistent, be patient and do your best to support small presses."

ROANOKE REVIEW (II), Roanoke College, Salem VA 24153, phone (703)389-2351, ext. 367, founded 1968, poetry editor Robert R. Walter, is a semiannual literary review which uses **poetry that is "conventional; we have not used much experimental or highly abstract poetry."** They have published poetry by Peter Thomas, Norman Russell, Alan Seaburg, Mary Balazs and Irene Dayton. I selected as a sample the second of two stanzas of "Of Shoes and Ships" by Ernest Kroll:

> *The shoes in snow divide a waveless sea*
> *Whose wake congeals as if it thought a trough*
> *Redress enough for snow's discourtesy,*
> *Redress enough—by fresh snow leveled off.*

RR is 6×9″, 52 pp., professionally printed with matte card cover with decorative typography, using 25-30 pp. of poetry in each issue, circulation 250-300, 150 subscriptions of which 50 are libraries. Subscription: $5.50; per copy: $3. They receive 400-500 freelance submissions of poetry per year, use 40-60, have a 3-6 month backlog. **Sample: $3 postpaid. Submit original typed MSS, no photocopies. Reports in 8-10 weeks. No pay.** The editor advises, "There is a lot of careless or sloppy writing going on. We suggest careful proofreading and study of punctuation rules."

THE ROCKFORD REVIEW; TRIBUTARY (II, IV-Membership, regional), P.O. Box 858, Rockford IL 61105, *The Rockford Review*, founded 1971, editor David Ross, is a quarterly publication of the Rockford Writers Guild, **publishing their poetry and prose, that of other writers in the Illinois-Wisconsin region and contributors from elsewhere. "We look for the magical power of the words themselves, a playfulness with language in the creation of images and fresh insights on old themes, whether it be poetry, satire, or fiction."** They have recently published Todd Moore, Dwight E. Humphries and Olivia Diamond. The editor selected these sample lines by Christine Swanberg:

> *My legs are where? I feel nothing*
> *must be ohohdead but amnot amnot!*
> *Get out! No pain must be dead*
> *should hurt but this can't be*
> *heaven: WLS is playing*
> *Cracklin Neil Diamond's*
> *I'm a rose upside in glass*
> *I smell the earth. Siren?*

It is digest-sized, 92 pp., flat-spined, glossy cover with b/w photos. Circulation 750. Price per issue $6; subscription $8 (2/year). **Reports in 2-4 weeks. Considers simultaneous submissions. Pays 1 copy.** Editor's Choice Prize of $25-50 (one each issue). They also desktop publish triquarterly *Tributary*, 20 pages of poetry featuring a reader poll to select the best poem which wins a $25 prize each edition. **Poetry not accepted for *Rockford Review* is automatically considered for *Tributary*, or poets may submit separately.**

ROCKY MOUNTAIN REVIEW OF LANGUAGE AND LITERATURE (IV-Membership, translations), Boise State University English Dept., Boise ID 83725, phone (208)385-1246, founded 1947, poetry editor, **Marcia Southwick, to whom poetry submissions should be sent, English Department, 202 Andrews Hall, University of Nebraska, Lincoln NE 68588-0333. Contributors to the literary quarterly must be members of Rocky Mountain Modern Language Association. Poetry should be "generally relatively short," but otherwise they will consider anything but "bad poetry."** The review has recently published poetry by Scott P. Sanders and translations of Antonio Cisneros and David Huerta. As a sample, the editor selected the following three lines (opening stanza) of "The Bathers" by Jerry Bradley:

> *In Cezanne's canvas the bathers are angels,*
> *Clean and without men, their clothes banked*
> *where earthwarm river, sky, and green field*
> *blend.*

The 6×9″, 276 pp. flat-spined quarterly publishes work of interest to college and university teachers of literature and language; **poetry may be in English or other modern languages. Contributors are not paid and do not receive extra copies; subscription is part of RMMLA membership. Poets should submit two copies, *without author's name*. They report on submissions in 4-8 weeks and publish usually within 6 months but no more than 12 months after acceptance.** Circulation of the review is 1,100-1,200, all membership subscriptions. They accept a few ads from other journals and publishers.

ROHWEDDER: INTERNATIONAL JOURNAL OF LITERATURE & ART (II, IV-Translations), P.O. Box 29490, Los Angeles CA 90029, founded 1986, editors Robert Dassanowsky-Harris, Nancy Antell, and Hans-Jurgen Schacht, who say their "international journal seeks the highest quality poetry and prose. It is **open to all styles and subject matter—foreign language with translation, multi-cultural also, experimental, open text and language-oriented poetry and prose.** We have published poetry from Lithuania, East and West Germany, Central America, Argentina, Portugal, Denmark, Poland, Canada and the U.S." Writers recently published include Jean Chapdelaine-Gagnon, Luis Alfaro, Susana

Close-up

Robert Dassanowsky-Harris
Editor
Rohwedder

Photo by Patrick Bristow

Knowing the Time is Nothing
A God has been stained into
our eyes since birth

The baroque domes collapse
and others say there is no music
the Queen of the Night flounders
with no friends

It is just a sky:
breath adds to the desert
and the spine is a final
tether to the earth

which is ours, worked to death
and then we try to escape.

That poem will be in Robert Dassanowsky-Harris's first book of selected poems, **Telegrams from the Metropole**. He started out as an actor, then became a playwright, and, he says, "my poetry grew simultaneously with writing for the theater, as a way to present the visions that wouldn't stand expansion, generating their strength from brevity and symbols."

But theater is not the influence that most distinguishes his work as poet and editor of *Rohwedder*. Rather, it is his commitment to poetry as an international cultural endeavor. He was born in the United States, but his family is Austrian, and he was raised in a bilingual environment "where Central European culture was very accessible and nurturing." He currently teaches German language and literature at UCLA, is completing his doctorate in that field, and co-edits *New German Review*. "Although my aesthetic sensibilities are rooted in my cultural background (I write in English and German language), the poet developed quite independently from the academic. I have been particularly influenced by German, Austrian and French art movements in style and subject matter and this blends — often competes — with the overriding American and specifically West Coast elements."

During the last decade his poetry has appeared internationally, the first publications being Canadian, European and Australian before reaching a readership in the U.S. He also writes widely published literary and film criticism and continues to write for theater and, recently, television. "But poetry remains the creative core."

It was impatience with what they regarded as the "cliquishness" and isolation of the Los Angeles literary scene — and the complaint that L.A. poetry is often not well-known outside that city — that moved Hans-Jürgen Schacht and Nancy Antell, soon joined by Robert, to begin Rough Weather Press and *Rohwedder* in 1986. "I felt this polyglot, multi-cultural city did not have an independent publication that introduced new or established foreign writers and ethnic American voices and visions." Now the magazine is no longer local. It has grown to reach an audience across the U.S. and abroad.

"I encourage poets to become familiar with all types and periods of literature, art, philosophy and history. I find that in many poetry programs too much emphasis is placed on being 'gritty and natural' in style, and too little is placed on content or even going beyond imitation. Exploring self is important, but knowing what has come before, what is happening around you, beyond self, is a powerful challenge that may activate a stronger, more unique 'voice'. Read the work of English language and translated (original language if you can) contemporaries, and don't neglect the past. Postmodernism, for all its myriad definitions, has made revision of older styles, forms and directions a vital tool for new writing. Collect ideas, images, entire worlds. Do not fear elegance, as you must not fear being political, sensual or experimental. Poetry remains an activist's genre and is reclaiming wide social importance as we approach our own *fin de siècle.*"

If the editorial staff of *Rohwedder* cannot deal with the language of the poetry submitted, they call in experts who can. Poets who publish there are likely to feel the need to participate in a movement and art that is not bound by any particular language or ethnic viewpoint. "I believe that my experience," Robert says, "as a bilingual poet—publishing in the U.S. and finding foreign venues (a difficult situation given the limited poetry publications in most countries)—might be encouraging to others who shy from using all their talents."

—*Judson Jerome*

Thénon and Robert Peters. As a sample the editors selected lines from "Confessions Noir" by Wanda Coleman:

> *i prefer commercials over programming*
> *black & white over color*
> *informed silence over ignorant applause*
>
> *i pray only on airplanes*
> *occasionally one of my dreams*
> *comes true*
> *once in a while I pass myself going*
> *in the other direction.*

Rohwedder (Rough Weather) is 8½×11", 50 pp., saddle-stapled, offset from typesetter with b/w art inside and on the glossy card cover. About half the issue is poetry. Press run: 1,000; subscription: $12. **Sample: $5, $4/back issue. "We often do theme issues; poets should check." Submit five poems. Pays in contributors' copies. No simultaneous submissions or previously published poems. Photocopy, dot-matrix OK. Cover letter with bio and credits. Reports in approximately 2 months. Editor sometimes comments on rejections.** Nancy Antell includes this quote for writers: "On the one hand, the correct political line is demanded of the poet; on the other, it is justifiable to expect his/her work to have quality." Walter Benjamin, "The Author as Producer" *Reflections* (1978).

ROLLING COULTER (II, IV-Religious), Messiah College, Grantham PA 17027, phone (717)766-2511 (ext 7026), founded 1988, editor William Jolliff, appears twice a year. **"I look for poetry that is not necessarily religious but which shows some evidence of being informed by a religious world-view. I'm open to most forms, but work in traditional forms must be especially good to be printable. I don't want to see greeting card, calendar, or bulletin cover stuff."** They have recently published poetry by Jeff Gundy, David Radavich and Joanne Lowery. As a sample the editor selected these lines from "Mourning the Dead" by Gene Doty:

> *mourning the dead in old grey photos*
> *crammed helter skelter in a widow's trunk*
> *a dead god stinking behind their gloss*
> *mourning the wheedling dead*
> *made of cardboard and gas*

The Rolling Coulter is digest-sized, 40-60 pp., laser printed with 2-color cover. Their press run is 400 with 104 subscriptions. "We distribute to libraries at religious colleges, with or without charge." Subscription: $6/2 issues. **Sample: $2.50 postpaid. Pays 1 copy. Reports in 6-12 weeks. "We respond slowly in summer." Editor occasionally comments on rejections on request.** "There's really no substitute for becoming familiar with a magazine before submitting work. We get in lots of work that we can enjoy reading, but far less that we can use. Tremendous variety exists in the little magazine scene, and poets should celebrate that fact by doing more reading of what is being written and published right now, *in addition to* what has been anthologized for their college courses."

‡ROMANCING THE PAST (IV-Themes), 17239 S. Oak Park Ave #207, Tinley Park IL 60477, founded 1989, editor Michelle Regan, appears every other month using **"poetry of historical or nostalgic theme only."** They have recently published poetry by Martha Vertreace and Robert Klein. As a sample, I selected these lines from "Toy Soldier" by C. David Hay, a poem originally published by *Tucumcari Review,* apparently derived from Eugene Fields' "Little Boy Blue":

> *Now the cannon sits tarnished with age,*
> *The soldiers stand frozen in stare,*
> *Awaiting the touch of tiny hands*
> *That loved and placed them there.*

It is digest-sized, 64 pp., saddle-stapled, photocopied from typescript with matte card cover. Press run 350 for 57 subscriptions of which 4 are libraries (45 distributed free to doctor's offices; 160 shelf sales). Subscription: $12. **Sample postpaid: $2.75. Send SASE for guidelines. Pays 1 copy. Replies within 45 days. Editor always comments on rejections.** The editors advise, "Poets should not worry so much about keeping within a certain form or rhyming. Rhymes should come naturally if the poet prefers to write structured verse, not be forced. The poetry should evoke a feeling and should have something to say."

‡THE ROMANTICIST; ATLANTEAN PRESS (II, IV-Themes, translations), 354 Tramway, Milpitas CA 95035, founded 1990, publisher Patricia LeChevalier. Atlantean Press was founded to publish Romantic fiction, drama, and poetry, beginning with republication of work by Victor Hugo that is out-of-print. *The Romanticist* is a quarterly seeking **"intelligibility, thoughtfulness, poetry that is interesting. Choice of subject is most important. I would prefer to see poems whose subjects involve human actions, emotions, choices, aspirations, values and virtues — though poems need not be explicitly about people."** The magazine is 64 pp., $7 \times 7''$, saddle-stapled, with 2-color cover. Subscription: $20. **Sample postpaid: $5. Pays up to $2/line. Send SASE for guidelines. Reports in 2 weeks. Editor often comments on rejections.** "We'd be very interested in competent translations of Victor Hugo's poetry."

THE ROMANTIST (IV-Fantasy, Horror, Science Fiction), Saracinesca House, 3610 Meadowbrook Ave., Nashville TN 37205, phone (615)226-1890, poetry editor Steve Eng, founded 1977, is a "literary magazine of non-fiction articles on fantasy, horror, and romantic literature, using **lyrical poetry — prefer fantasy and horror content. No homespun, gushy, trite verse with forced rhyme."** They have published poetry by Donald Sidney-Fryer, Joey Froehlich, Stephanie Stearns and Richard L. Tierney. As a sample the editor selected these lines by John Gawsworth:

> *The worthy are not always just*
> *Nor are the noble always brave,*
> *And yet all mingle in the dust*
> *Of the one grave.*

The annual is magazine-sized, press run 300 numbered copies for 150 subscriptions of which 50 are libraries. **Sample: $10 postpaid. Contributors may purchase a copy for 50% of its price. They receive tear sheets. Submit no more than 3 poems at a time, double-spaced. Reports in 4 weeks. Editor sometimes comments on rejections.** He says, "Too much contemporary poetry is easy to write and hard to read. We resist the depressed, carefully jaded tone so often fashionable. We prefer lyric verse that reflects some knowledge of traditions of poetry, though we do not require the slavish adherence to any school."

‡ROOM OF ONE'S OWN (IV-Women), P.O. Box 46160 Sta. G, Vancouver, British Columbia V6R 4G5 Canada, phone (604)327-1432, founded 1975, is a quarterly using **"poetry by and about women, written from a feminist perspective. Nothing simplistic, clichéd."** It is 80 pp., digest-sized. Press run 1,250 for 500 subscribers of which 50-100 are libararies, 350 shelf sales. Subscription $15 ($20 US or foreign). **Sample: $5 plus postage or IRC. Send SASE for guidelines. Reports in 6 months. Pays "honorarium plus 2 copies."** The MSS are circulated to a collective, which "takes time."

‡ROPE BURNS (IV-Themes), Working Cowboy, P.O. Box 35, Gene Autry OK 73436, founded 1987, editor Bobby Newton, is a monthly tabloid of rodeo events using cowboy poetry. "I like to publish poems and stories about the average old cowboy, some good some bad, but they must have thought it was good if they took time to send it." As a sample, I selected the opening of a full-page poem, "The Old Cowboy's Christmas," by Howard Norskog, in the December, 1990 issue of *Rope Burns*:

> *The cowboy woke up at the first light of day*
> *And anyone there would of heard the man say*
> *It's Christmas and time that all should relax*
> *And enjoy good tidings, now this is a fact*

Sample postpaid: 2 stamps. Pays copies.

THE ROUND TABLE: A JOURNAL OF POETRY AND FICTION (II), 375 Oakdale Dr., Rochester NY 14618, founded 1984, poetry editors Alan Lupack and Barbara Lupack. "We publish a journal of poetry and fiction. Currently, 1 issue a year. **Few restrictions on poetry—except high quality. We like forms if finely crafted. Very long poems must be exceptional.**" They have recently published poetry by Kathleene West, John Tagliabue, Wendy Mnookin and Paul Scott. As a sample I chose the opening lines of "Homestead in Union" by David Memmot:

> We live in a house we did not build
> and cannot revise overnight
> generations of unfinished dreams.
> These walls recall many weavers . . .

The Round Table is digest-sized, 64 pp., perfect-bound, professionally printed (offset) with matte card cover. Circulation 125, for 75 subscriptions of which 3 are libraries. Subscription: $7.50. Sample: $5 postpaid. "**We like to see about 5 poems (but we read whatever is submitted but only from October 1-June 30).**" Cover letter. Simultaneous submissions OK. "**But we expect to be notified if a poem submitted to us is accepted elsewhere. Quality of poetry, not format, is most important thing. We try to report in 2 months, but—especially for poems under serious consideration—it may take longer.**" Pays copies. They will alternate Arthurian and general issues.

‡RUBBER PUPPY (I), P.O. Box 50454, Austin TX 78763-0454, founded 1988, corresponding editor Eddy Jersey, is a quarterly "**especially interested in the stuff of personal experience. Any format other than standard left-justified should be** *camera ready*! **No S&M, Satanism, elves, nature poems.**" They have recently published poetry by Leo Obrst, Wayne Henderson, Lawrence Oberc and Paul Weinman. As a sample the editor selected these lines by -A-Lynx-in-the-Mist:

> Days come, as they will
> when I feel like a candy wrapper, crumpled,
> on the sidewalk of my memories.
> Visions of the bad times come
> Without invitation
> to tread on my face.

It is digest-sized, 32 pp. with light card cover, photocopied from typescript. They use about half of over 100 submissions/year. Press run 300 for 200 subscribers. Subscription: $10. **Sample postpaid: $2.50 (back issues $1.50). Send SASE for guidelines. Pays 2 copies. Reports in 1-3 months. Previously published poems and simultaneous submissions OK.** The editor says, "We are looking for good poetry (among other things) from people outside the mainstream. Basically we're looking for well-written stuff that because of content/politics/whatever just wouldn't fly in the *Atlantic Monthly* or *Ladies' Home Journal*. We have no particular bias as to content but reserve the right to arbitrarily distinguish erotica from pornography. The name "Rubber Puppy" was derived as a symbol of bouncing around in a world frightened by my ideas/humor."

THE RUGGING ROOM; RUGGING ROOM BULLETIN (IV-Themes), 10 Sawmill Dr., Westford MA 01886, founded as a press in 1983, periodical in 1987, poetry editor Jeanne H. Fallier, publisher of "how-to books **related to traditional rug hooking and related subjects of interest to people in fibre crafts.**" Verses of a philosophical theme or concerning nature are acceptable if they **refer to hand works, wool or fibers, the therapeutic value of hand-made fiber crafts, etc.** She accepts "**very short poems related to fibre arts (especially hooking) crafts—not more than ½ page.**" The *Rugging Room Bulletin* is a newsletter, 8-16 pp., 8½×11" appearing 4 times a year printed on white stock, with b/w illustrations, ads and graphics. Circulation 300 but wide-spread, coast to coast. Subscription: $9. **Sample: $2.50 postpaid. Pays 3 copies plus 1 year subscription. Contributors are expected to buy 1 copy. Simultaneous submissions OK. Reports within about 2 weeks.**

RURAL HERITAGE (I, IV-Theme), Box 516, Albia IA 52531, phone (515)932-5084, founded 1975, editor Florence Holle and publisher D.H. Holle, **uses poetry related to rural living, Americana, is open as to length and form.** As a sample the editor selected these lines from "To Green Lea Trojan" by Brooks H. Rohde:

> Green Lea Trojan, you're for sale
> With ribbons in your mane and tail.
> Are you nervous thus not knowing
> Just to whom or where you're going?

RH is magazine-sized, quarterly, using b/w photos, graphics and ads, circulation 3,000. Subscription: $14. Per issue: $4. **Sample: $4.50 postpaid. Guidelines available for SASE. Pays on publication 3-15¢ a word and 1 copy. Reports ASAP, 4-6 months between acceptance and publication.** Florence Holle says "**submission must in some way be connected to celebrating our rich American rural heritage.**"

SACHEM PRESS (II, IV-Translations, bilingual), P.O. Box 9, Old Chatham NY 12136, phone (518)794-8327, founded 1980, editor Louis Hammer, a small-press publisher of poetry and fiction, both hardcover and flat-spined paperbacks. **No new submissions, only statements of projects, until January 1992. Submit MSS January-March.** The editor wants to see "**strong, compelling, even visionary work, English-language or translations.**" He has recently published poetry by Cesar Vallejo, Yannis Ritsos, 24 leading poets of Spain, Miltos Sahtouris and himself. As a sample, he selected the following lines from a poem by Felix Grande in the anthology, **Recent Poets of Spain**, translated by Louis Hammer and Sara Schyfter:

> *I offend the way the cypresses offend. I'm*
> *the depressor. I'm the one who contaminates*
> *with his kisses a vomit of dark silences,*
> *a bleeding of shadows. I offend, love, I offend.*

I have 5 sample publications by Sachem Press, all handsome flat-spined paperbacks with glossy two- or four-color covers; all are translations (from Greek or Spanish) except one by Louis Hammer. The small paperbacks average 120 pp. and the anthology of Spanish poetry contains 340 pp. Each poem is printed in both Spanish and English, and there are biographical notes about the authors. The small books cost $6.95 and the anthology $11.95. **Royalties are 10% maximum, after expenses are recovered, plus 50 author's copies.** Book catalog is free "when available," and poets can purchase books from Sachem "by writing to us, 33⅓% discount." Rainer Maria Rilke's *Duino Elegies*, translated by Louis Hammer and Sharon Ann Jaeger, forthcoming.

‡SACKBUT PRESS (II), 2513 E. Webster Pl., Milwaukee WI 53211, founded 1978, poetry editor Angela Peckenpaugh. "I publish mainly **poem notecards. I take short, neatly-typed poems that lend themselves to illustration by line drawing or b/w photo.** I get the illustrations through **Artist's Market. These are not greeting cards! I like anything that leaves me with refreshment or delight.**" She has recently published poetry by Ron Ellis, Fae Korsmo, Ron Schreiber and Antler. She selected this sample by Kathleen Dale:

> *Here is a coin newly struck*
> *ready to shine like sun*
> *polished by fog:*
> *a newborn tongued clean.*

They publish about 1 new card line per year. **Cards are 50¢ each or 5 for $3 postpaid. Maximum 10 lines. Submit no more than 3 poems for notecard series. Considers simultaneous submissions. Reports in 1 month. Payment is 25 cards.**

‡SA-DE PUBLICATIONS (I), P.O. Box 42607, Portland OR 97242, founded 1986, owner Sam L. Vulgaris, publishes annual anthologies. **Those included are required to buy a copy for $14.95.** They are flat-spined, digest-sized 200+ pp. books photocopied from typescript. **Submit "4 pieces with name/address in upper righthand corner of each sheet, each piece on separate page—all kinds, any length." Reports in 1-2 months.** As a sample, I selected these sample lines from "Fall" by Storm B. Barrett:

> *As the leaves turn brown and gold*
> *Mother nature takes a hold*
> *Of the season while it turns*
> *To fall and summer slowly burns*

ST. ANDREW PRESS (IV-Religious), Box 329, Big Island VA 24526, phone (804)299-5956, founded 1986, poetry editor Jean Horne, is a "small-press publisher of religious material (worship materials, lyrics and music, etc.), **specializing in meditations, lifestyle, church renewal, spirituality, hunger, peace and justice issues.**" Any form or style up to 64 lines on subjects listed. "**No profanity for shock value only; no sickeningly sweet idealism.**" As a sample the editor selected these lines from "Mary's Song" by Katherine Meyer which appeared in their newsletter:

> *I follow*
> *the seam of light*
> *stitched*
> *by my mothers,*
> *Eve's grief*
> *flows unbroken*
> *into Elizabeth's joy.*

They say they will publish 3 chapbooks and flat-spined paperbacks, averaging 64 pp., per year. **Submit 6 samples, bio, other publications. Simultaneous submissions, photocopies, dot-matrix, previously published poems OK. Reports in 2-4 weeks. Payment usually $10 minimum, averages more.** They will consider subsidy publishing. The editor says, "We are looking forward to doing more with poetry in the next couple of years. The amount we do will be largely determined by quality of submissions we receive."

ST. ANTHONY MESSENGER (IV-Religious), 1615 Republic St., Cincinnati OH 45210, is a monthly 56 pp. magazine, circulation 380,000, for Catholic families, mostly with children in grade school, high school or college. In some issues, they have a **poetry page which uses poems appropriate for their readership. Their poetry needs are very limited but poetry submissions are always welcomed.** In the issue I examined there were 2 poems of 11 and 30 lines each. As a sample I selected "Necessity" by Catherine Curtin Fenzel:

> *I gave my gift*
> *To children of the poor —*
> *Full well aware*
> *They had the need of bread —*
> *And watched them as*
> *They hurried from the door*
> *To buy a magic*
> *Red balloon instead.*

"Submit seasonal poetry (Christmas/Easter/nature poems) several months in advance. Submit a few poems at a time; do not send us your entire collection of poetry. We seek to publish accessible poetry of high quality." Pays $2 a line on acceptance. Send SASE for guidelines and free sample.

ST. JOSEPH MESSENGER AND ADVOCATE OF THE BLIND (I, IV-Religious), 541 Pavonia Ave., P.O. Box 288, Jersey City NJ 07303, phone (201)798-4141, founded 1898, poetry editor Sister Ursula Maphet, C.S.J.P, is a 30 pp. quarterly (16 pp., 8×11"), circulation 27,000, which wants **"brief but thought-filled poetry; do not want lengthy and issue-filled."** Most of the poets they have used are previously unpublished. The editor selected a sample by Priscilla Snell:

> *While lo from heaven's all healing*
> *hands,*
> *gentle and soft and slow,*
> *falls cool upon earth's fevered brow*
> *God's sacrament of snow.*

There are about 2 pp. of poetry in each issue. Subscription: $5. They receive 400-500 submissions per year, use 50. **Send SASE for guidelines and free sample. Reports within 2 weeks. Pays $5-20/poem. Editor sometimes comments on rejections.**

ST. MARTIN'S PRESS, 175 5th Ave., New York NY 10010. Declined listing.

SALMAGUNDI (III), Skidmore College, Saratoga Springs NY 12866, founded 1965, edited by Peggy Boyers and Robert Boyers, has long been **one of the most distinguished quarterlies** of the sciences and humanities, publishing poets such as Robert Penn Warren, Louise Gluck, John Peck, Howard Nemerov and W. D. Snodgrass. These lines, for instance, are from "During Holy Week" by Seamus Heaney:

> *Dippings. Towellings. The water breathed on.*
> *The water mixed with chrism and with oil.*
> *Cruet tinkle. Formal incensation*
> *And the psalmist's outcry taken up with pride:*
> *Day and night my tears have been my bread.*

Each issue is handsomely printed, a thick, flat-spined book, priced at $5-10 (**sample: $4 postpaid.**). Subscriptions are $12 a year, $18 for two years. The magazine has a paid circulation of 5,400 with 3,800 subscriptions of which about 900 are libraries. **They use about 10-50 pages of poetry in each issue, receive 1,200 submissions per year and use about 20, have a year to 30 month backlog, and report in 3 months. Payment in copies only, no need to query, photocopies OK, with permission for sets of more than 5.**

SALMON PUBLISHING; THE SALMON INTERNATIONAL LITERARY MAGAZINE (II, IV-Translations), Bridge Mills, Galway, Ireland, phone 62587, magazine founded 1981, Salmon Publishing in 1985, director/editor Jessie Lendennie, who says, **"It is hard to describe what good poetry is. I am open-minded as to style, subject matter, length, but prefer innovative work and poetry of some social relevance. Translations from all languages welcome, and I am interested in seeing more contributions from women." She doesn't like "overtly sentimental or doggerel verse, sloppily put-together work, obscure work."** She has recently published poetry by Mary O'Malley, R.T. Smith, Clarinda Harriss Lott, Michael D. Higgins, Mary O'Donnell, John Unrau, Octavio Paz and Clairr O'Connor. As a sample she selected these lines from "Manchild" by Michael Heffernan:

> *. . . Whatever they said*
> *was there I took for granted, what was not*
> *was not, and what a man could do I did*
> *about the things I had some say about.*
> *Anything much else was in the mind of God,*
> *even the daybreak, what there was of it.*

The Salmon appears 3 times a year (autumn, spring, summer), 96 pp., flat-spined, 6 × 8½", professionally printed on quality stock with two-color glossy card cover with b/w art. Its aim is "to present a quality journal with an international voice which also speaks intimately of Ireland." Jessie Lendennie says she accepts about 200 of 5,000 poems received. Press run is 1,000 for 300 subscriptions of which 50 are libraries, the rest of the copies going to shelf sales. Subscription: £5 (or $22 air mail, $18 surface for the US, including postage). **Sample: £3 (or $5) postpaid. Pays 1 copy. (Payment to contributors depends on Arts Council funding.) Submit no more than 5 at a time. No simultaneous submissions or poems previously published in Ireland. Reports in 6-12 weeks. Backlog.** Salmon Publishing publishes 12-15 flat-spined collections of poetry per year. **For book publication, query with 20 sample poems, bio and publishing credits. Reports on queries in 6 weeks. Pays 10% royalties. Editor sometimes comments on rejections.** She says, "Beginners must be open to the whole world of poetry, not just their little corner of it. That is, read contemporary poetry, think about what you're writing, be open to change."

SALT LICK; SALT LICK PRESS; SALT LICK SAMPLERS; LUCKY HEART BOOKS (II), 1909 Sunny Brook Dr., Austin TX 78723-3449, founded 1969, poetry editor James Haining, publishes "new literature and graphic arts in their various forms." They have published poetry by Robert Creeley, Martha King, Susan Firer, Paul Shuttleworth, Wm. Hart, Robert Slater, Gerald Burns and Sheila Murphy. As a sample I selected this poem, "Stride Time" by the editor, James Haining:

> *her walking into the*
> *room from the rain*
> *what you would*
> *in the length say*
> *I hear so time*
> *for time*

The magazine-sized journal, 48 pp., saddle-stapled, matte cover, experimental graphics throughout, appears irregularly, print run of 1,500. They receive 400-600 poems per year, use 1-2%. **Sample: $5 postpaid. Reports in 1-6 weeks. Pays copies. To submit for book publication under the Lucky Heart Books imprint, send 20 samples, cover letter "open." Simultaneous submissions, photocopies, dot-matrix OK. Pays copies.**

SAMISDAT (II), 436 Monroe Turnpike, Monroe CT 06468, founded 1978, editor Merritt Clifton, is an annual magazine, but subscribers ($15/year) get both the magazine and all chapbooks published in a given year (about 250 pp. total). The editor wants **"socially, politically and environmentally aware material for an extremely well-informed, committed activist audience. No preaching to the choir. No personal fulminations, lamentations, doggerel, rewrites of the daily news, mere cant of any kind or any other form of masturbation on paper."** They have recently published poetry by Miriam Sagan, Gary Metras, Robert Peters and W.D. Ehrhart. As a sample the editor selected these lines by Walt Peterson:

> *Fists rising; looking for that death's head*
> *right, the locomotive coming out of the fog,*
> *all white light, all crimson trimmed in gold;*
> *remember the snap slap of jump rope on the gym floor,*
> *remember the legs, the legs die first,*
> *never the heart.*

All **Samisdat** magazines and chapbooks are in an inexpensive, desktop published format, digest-sized, saddle-stapled, with matte card covers. Press run 300 for 200 subscribers of which 20 are libraries. Subscription: $15 (for about 250 pp.). **Sample postpaid: $3. "I'll throw in a chapbook or two for another buck." Pays 2 copies. Reports in 2 weeks maximum. Previously published poems OK if they last appeared at least 3 years ago and the original publisher is clearly identified.** "June, Sept. and Nov. are always especially hectic months for me." Often comments on rejections — sometimes in language that may offend some readers. "Chapbooks are published under a cooperative arrangement whereby authors furnish the cost of paper and printing supplies, we provide basic production services, and press runs are proportionally divided, usually half-and-half." Send SASE for description of this plan. Editor Clifton's "literary philosophy" is available in a recently updated The Pillory Poetics, $2. I suggest you read some material published by Samisdat (a word which refers to clandestine publishing in the Soviet Union) before submitting. Inappropriate submissions are likely to be treated rudely.

SAN DIEGO POETS PRESS; LA JOLLA POETS PRESS; AMERICAN BOOK SERIES (II), P.O. Box 8638, La Jolla CA 92038. San Diego Poets Press is a nonprofit press founded 1981 by present editor/publisher Kathleen Iddings. She has published poetry magazines, anthologies and individual poets. As a sample of the type of poetry she's published, Kathleen Iddings selected these lines from "At Eighteen" in Joan LaBombard's **The Counting of Grain:**

> *The grass is his; he is lord of greenness,*
> *Especially of meadows lush and overgrown.*
> *He is a prince of stones.*
> *See how they skim the water, how they skip*
> *Obedient to his wish . . .*

Kathleen Iddings originated La Jolla Poets Press as another imprint in 1985. **For either press send cover letter, 6 poems, bio, SASE. Simultaneous submissions OK.** The 1992 "American Book Series" winner ($500 and publication) will be selected from work submitted to her presses throughout the year. Winners since 1984 have included Joan LaBombard, Regina McBride and Charles Atkinson. Samples of winning book: $12.

SAN FERNANDO POETRY JOURNAL; KENT PUBLICATIONS. INC.; CERULEAN PRESS (MINI AN-THOLOGY SERIES), (I, IV-Social issues, anthologies), 18301 Halsted St., Northridge CA 91325, founded 1978, poetry editors Richard Cloke, Shirley Rodecker and Lori Smith (and, for the Mini Anthology Series, Blair H. Allen, 9651 Estacia Court, Cucamonga, CA 91730). The *San Fernando Poetry Journal* uses poetry of social protest. According to Richard Cloke, "Poetry, for us, should be *didactic* in the Brechtian sense. It must say something, must inform, in the tenor of our time. We follow Hart Crane's definition of poetry as architectural in essence, building upon the past but incorpo-rating the newest of this age also, including science, machinery, sub-atomic and cosmic physical phe-nomena as well as the social convulsions wrenching the very roots of our present world." **Send SASE for guidelines which explain this more fully.** For example, I quote this passage from one of them for its general usefulness for poets: "In some, the end-line rhyming is too insistent, seeming *forced;* in others the words are not vibrant enough to give the content an arresting framework. Others do not have any beat (cadence) at all and some are simply not well thought out—often like first drafts, or seem like prose statements. Please try reworking again to get some energy in your statement. If your poetry is to succeed in impelling the reader to act, it must electrify, or at least command interest and attention." **They welcome new and unpublished poets.** As a sample the editor chose these lines by Jack Bernier:

> *We buy stock on the installment*
> *plan in a company rated high*
> *on stock market exchanges.*
> *This company files bankruptcy.*
> *No dividends. No profit. No checks.*
> *There is something in signs on cars;*
> *Money talks. Mine only knows*
> *how to say goodby.*

The flat-spined quarterly, photocopied from typescript, uses 100 pages of poetry in each issue, circulation 400, 350 subscriptions of which 45 are libraries. They use about 300 of the 1,000 submissions (the editor rightly prefers to call them "contributions") each year. **Sample: $2.50 postpaid. No specifications for MS form. Simultaneous submissions OK. Reports in 1 week, pays in copies.** The press, under its various imprints, also publishes a few collections by individu-als. **Query with 5-6 pp. of samples. For the Mini Anthology Series, query Blair Allen at the address above.**

SAN JOSE STUDIES; CASEY MEMORIAL AWARD (II), San Jose State University, San Jose CA 95192, phone (408)924-4476, founded 1975, poetry editor O. C. Williams. This "journal of general and schol-arly interest, featuring critical, creative and informative writing in the arts, business, humanities, science and social sciences" uses poetry of **"excellent quality—no kinds excluded. Tend to like poems with something to say, however indirectly it may be communicated. Usually publish 7-12 pp. of verse in each issue. We like to publish several poems by one poet—better exposure for the poet, more interest for the reader."** They have recently published poetry by Leonard Nathan, lyn lifshin and James Sutherland-Smith. As a sample the editor chose these lines from "Mountain Woman" by Virginia de Araújo:

> *. . . But place in her is deep root:*
> *hand, brain, nerve, tooth. Planted, she will*
> *spill upward in fern fronds, tight buds and fists.*
> *Overhead, winter and summer secretly will move,*
> *and she remain planted in true place.*

SJS appears thrice yearly in a 6 × 9″ flat-spined, 100+ pp. format, professionally printed, matte card cover, using b/w photos, circulation of 400-450 of which 70-75 are libraries. Subscription: $12; per copy: $5. They receive about 120 submissions per year, use 8-10 authors, have a 2 year backlog. **Sample: $4 postpaid. No simultaneous submissions. Reports in 4-6 weeks. Pays 2 copies. Annual award of a year's subscription for best poetry printed that year and a Casey Memorial Award of $100 for the best contribution in prose or poetry.** O. C. Williams comments, "Poetry is both an art and a craft; we are not interested in submissions unless the writer has mastered the craft and is actually practicing the art."

‡**SANGRÉ SANGRÉ (I, II, IV-Themes, Regional, women),** P.O. Box 3774, St. Augustine FL 32085-3774, founded 1985, editor Joel Bradford Cooper, is a monthly 4 pp. photocopied paper **"designed to reveal Hollywood and LA to the general reader. Only poetry with a Hollywood flavor, or written about LA, will be printed. Female poetry strongly encouraged. I want to see Truth. Stomp-bite and cold stare. Hollywood as it really is. Los Angeles as it stands. Thrash-angst. Poetry baptized in water and fire. Prophetic. Torque. Insanity.** *Above all: whispered hope.* **Give me blood and underbelly. No pornography or misplaced expletives. Well-placed expletives and erotica are fine. Women have a beautiful perspective of life that men can't see. I want youthfulness, no matter the age."** They have recently published poetry by John R. Williamson, Sean Asunder, Bandhaven Scorn, Idy Oliver, Layne Schroeder and Angel Nuevo-Hijo. As a sample the editor selected these lines from his own "Something Worse Than Blood-Loss":

> *Rage, rage on this page. Read and weep and wail.*
> *Direct Anger for this land on precipice of hell.*
> *Thrash all night in dream-filled sweat.*
> *Rash, and right, for what you meant*
> *was good and forthright; honored true*
> *by all those there watching you.*

Press run 200. Subscription: $10. **Sample: $1 postpaid. Send SASE for guidelines. Pays 2 copies. "I would like queries requesting guidelines, but if my poet spent all night dealing in angst and blood, and cries out to me today without, and not wanting to heed, temporal law, choosing spirit-guidance instead, I will receive them, bloody and torn, with open, loving, unconditional arms. All submissions are read, thought about, filed either accepted or rejected. No comments. Published author will know when they receive paper in the mail. Could be as long as three months. Send SASE for returned MS. A short bio must be included: 1) I want to know if they live in LA; or 2) if they don't and simply wrote** *of* **the area. They need not live anywhere near California, need not mention Hollywood or LA. Terms and places and phrases and things used and seen in the Southland are definite plusses. Español poetry submissions are encouraged, but** *must* **be accompanied by a reliable, non-literate 'feel of the emotion' translation in American. For example, Sangré Sangré does not translate 'blood blood.' It translates 'blood' or 'flowing blood,' 'blood rhythmic,' et cetera."** *Sangré Sangré* is a member of Orthodox Christian Poet Solidarity.

SANTA MONICA REVIEW (V), 1900 Pico Blvd., Santa Monica CA 90405, founded 1988, poetry editor Jim Krusoe, appears twice a year. **They are temporarily overstocked.**

SANTA SUSANA PRESS (V), CSU Libraries, 18111 Nordhoff St., Northridge CA 91330, phone (818)885-2271, founded 1973, editor Norman Tanis, a small-press publisher of limited edition fine print books, history, literature and art, some poetry, all hardcover editions. **They do not accept freelance submissions of poetry. Poets should query first, and queries will be answered in 2 weeks. Honorariums paid depend on grant money.** The press has recently published books by George Elliott, Ward Ritchie and Ray Bradbury, from whose "The Last Good Kiss" the editor selected the following lines as a sample:

> *What's past is past*
> *And the memory of mouths*
> *In a dry season, soon or late,*
> *Makes salivate the mind*

Book catalog is free on request; prices are high. For instance, **Reaching: Poems by George P. Elliott,** illustrated, is published in an edition of 350 numbered copies at $35 and 26 lettered copies at $60.

‡**SARGASSO (IV-Regional/bilingual),** P.O. Box 22831 UPR Station, San Juan PR 00931-2831, founded 1984, editor Lowell Fiet, appears "irregular, but at least once/year" **using poetry of the Caribbean or related in English or Spanish (with English translations). "Unsolicited poems should be short, roughly 20-30 lines, in batches of no more than 5 or so; narrative poems but as image-laden and visually voiced as possible; Caribbean experience as lived and, at times, as observed."** They have recently published poetry by Edward Kamu Braithwaite, Lorna Goodison, Rosario Ferré and Ian McDonald. As a sample, I selected these lines from "The Gas Mask" by James Collins:

> *Digging for his roots*
> *Beneath the cellar stairway*
> *His garden spade turned up*
> *The faceplate of an ancient warrior.*

It is magazine-sized, flat-spined, photocopied from typescript, 100+ pp. with matte card cover. Press run 300 for 200 subscribers of which 30 are libraries. **Sample: $5 postpaid. Pays 1 copy.** "Sometimes we are slow. Poems are read blind by each member of the editorial committee. But we try to get answers back as soon as possible." **Editors often comment on rejections.**

SATURDAY EVENING POST (IV-Humor), 1100 Waterway Blvd., Indianapolis IN 46202, phone (317)636-8881, founded 1728 as the *Pennsylvania Gazette*, since 1821 as *The Saturday Evening Post*, Post Scripts editor Steve Pettinga. *SEP* is a general interest, mass circulation monthly with emphasis on preventive medicine, using "**humorous light verse only. No more than 300 words per poem. Stay away from four-letter words and sexually graphic subject matter. No experimental verse (haikus, etc.) Morally, the *Post* is an anachronism of the early 50s; most of its readers are elderly. Other than that, anything goes, as long as it's in good taste.**" As a sample the editor selected these lines (poet unidentified):

> *I find the witness box*
> *Is far too demanding.*
> *I can't stand lying.*
> *And I can't lie standing.*

Payment is $15/all rights. "Work for hire."

SATURDAY PRESS, INC.; EILEEN W. BARNES AWARD SERIES; INVITED POETS SERIES (II, IV-Women), Box 884, Upper Montclair NJ 07043, phone (201)256-5053, founded 1975, poetry editor Charlotte Mandel with guest editors for contest which have included Maxine Kumin, Colette Inez, Sandra M. Gilbert, Maxine Silverman and Rachel Hadas. "Saturday Press, Inc., is a nonprofit literary organization. The Press has a **special—though not exclusive—commitment to women's poetry, and by sponsoring the Eileen W. Barnes Award Competition for first books by women over 40 seeks to offer opportunity for new poets who have delayed their writing careers. The MS is selected by means of open competition or, in alternate years, by editorial board decision. Query for current information.** Not an annual event, the contest is widely posted when announced. The Invited Poets Series offers publication to established or less-known poets. We want **authoritative craft, strong, fresh imagery, sense of imagination and a good ear for syntax, sounds and rhythms. Language should lead the reader to experience a sense of discovery. Any form, content or style, but do not want polemic, jingles or conventional inspiration.**" They have published books of poetry by Colette Inez, Janice Thaddeus, Jean Hollander, Anne Carpenter, Anneliese Wagner, Charlotte Mandel and Geraldine C. Little. As a sample the editor chose these lines from Geraldine C. Little's "Looking at a Pompiian Lady in an Exhibit":

> *Everywhere, the spill*
> *of summer, air cracked*
> *by only birdbells, sails*
> *moving like old dances.*

Do not send book MS without query. Enclose 1-3 samples and minimum summary of publications. Replies to queries in 2 weeks. If invited, book MS may be photocopied; simultaneous submission OK. No dot-matrix. "Prefer no binder, simple folder or paper clip." Pays 25-50 copies and possible honorarium ("depends on grants"). Send SASE for catalog to buy samples.

SCARP (II), School of Creative Arts, University of Wollongong, Box 1144, Wollongong, New South Wales, Australia 2500, phone (042)270985, founded 1982, editor Ron Pretty "is a small press publisher of poetry, prose fiction and new art. *Scarp* also contains articles and reviews. Both new and established writers are encouraged to contribute." It appears twice a year. "**Not restricted by genre or form or subject-matter or style or purpose, however we would prefer not to publish anything of an epic length.**" They have published poetry by Marvin Bell, Bruce Beaver, John Millet, Manfred Jurgenson and Debbie Westbury. As a sample the editor selected these lines by Steven Herrick:

> *St. Mark's Bookstore, New York*
> *Hemingway's in the corner*
> *drinking his way through France*
> *& shooting up the bad guys in Spain*

Scarp is 64-80 pp., A4 landscape format, perfect-bound, card cover, b/w graphics, some (mainly local) ads. "*Scarp 17* received about 600 poems from 100+ contributors. We published 14 poems from these." Press run: 1,000 for approximately 300 subscriptions of which 30 are libraries. Some shelf sales. Subscription: $24/4 issues. **Sample, postpaid: $5. Send SASE for guidelines. Pays $20 (Aust.) plus 2 copies and 2-year subscription. Subscription encouraged but not required. No** more than 5 poems per submission. Poems previously unpublished in Australia OK. Submit during March and August. Editor comments on submissions. He says, "We're looking for poetry and prose that leaps off the page at you, and that usually means there's a lot of life in the language." Reviews books of poetry.

‡SCAT! (I, II), Innis College, 2 Sussex Ave., Toronto, Ontario M5S 1S5 Canada, founded 1982, editor Yukie Koglin Hood, is an annual, with **"dedication to new, wordy, smart poetry, any length, sure of speed and delivery, get to the point! Believe that 'It's all in the delivery.' Disdain for Blakean tragedies being writtten in the 1990s. Poet must be aware of the time and thought s/he's writing in."** They have recently published poetry by Brian Burke, Robbie Newton Drummond and Debbie Ferst. As a sample the editor selected these lines from "The Altar" by Jonathan Hyman:

> *It is night, wind*
> *and we storm together.*
> *There is nothing that binds*
> *like fury, nothing as quiet as air,*
> *The other corners*
> *are sunlit,*
> *holy.*

They sent no sample and give no indication of its price or format or terms of publication, but the editor says she comments "occasionally."

SCAVENGER'S NEWSLETTER; KILLER FROG CONTEST (IV-Science fiction/fantasy/horror), 519

Ellinwood, Osage City KS 66523-1329, may seem an odd place to publish poems, but its editor, Janet Fox, uses 3-4 every month. The *Newsletter* is a **32-page booklet packed with news about science fiction and horror publications,** (printed at an instaprint shop). **Janet prefers sf/fantasy/horror poetry, and will read anything that is off-beat or bizarre. Writing-oriented poetry is occasionally accepted but avoid "Oh poor pitiful me" themes. Poetry is used as filler so it must be 10 lines or under.** Recently published poets include: M.B. Simon, Paul Weinman, Ken Stone and Joey Froehlich. As a sample she selected "Kindling" by Herb Kauderer:

> *In the interface of mind & computer*
> *neurons strike electrons*
> *& ignite whole new realities.*

Janet Fox says, "I wouldn't call *SCAV* a typical inspirational writers' magazine. The rat on the cover says it all. I prefer lean, mean poetry with bite. Maybe my latest pet peeve is a poem made up of disparate words that the reader is somehow to make something of. I don't mind if the connections are obscure, but for me they have to be there." She has around 760 subscribers. Subscription: $11.50/year; $5.75/6 months. Sample copy plus guidelines for $1.50, guidelines alone for SASE. Response: 1 month or less. **"I like poems with sharp images and careful craftsmanship."** At last report was "accepting about 1 out of 10 poems submitted." You can use photocopy, dot-matrix, multiple submissions, simultaneous submissions (if informed) — **even reprints if credit is given. No need to query. Payment: $2 on acceptance plus one copy.** "I hold an annual 'Killer Frog Contest' for horror so bad or outrageous it becomes funny. There is a category for horror poetry. Has been opening April 1, closing July 1 of each year. Prizes $25 each in four categories: poetry, art, short stories and short short stories, plus the 'coveted' Froggie statuette." The '91 contest had no entry fee but entrants wanting the anthology pay $2.50 postpaid. Winners list for a SASE.

SCIENCE FICTION POETRY ASSOCIATION; STAR*LINE; THE RHYSLING ANTHOLOGY (IV-Science

fiction, anthology), 2012 Pyle Rd., Schenectady NY 12303, for membership information. For poetry submissions: Richard Rowand, 5545 Homeward Dr., Virginia Beach VA 23464. Founded 1978. The Association puts out two publications which use poetry: *Star*Line*, a bimonthly magazine, editor Robert Frazier, and an annual, *The Rhysling Anthology*. The magazine is the newsletter of the Association; the anthology is a yearly collection of final nominations from the membership "for the best SF/Fantasy long and short poetry of the preceding year." The Association also publishes a cassette tape anthology and a Science Fiction Poetry Handbook. The magazine has published poetry by Bruce Boston, Thomas Easton, Andrew Joron, Steve Rasnic Tem, Nancy Springer, Joe Haldeman and Diane Ackermann. Here are some sample lines from "Dactyl" by W. Gregory Stewart:

> *a wreck of pterodactyl*
> *lay across the yard this morning*
>
> *(I didn't know about it*
> *until Fred Mulvaney*
> *from across the street*
> *called up complaining.)*

Close-up

Robert Frazier
Editor
*Star*Line*

Photo by Timalyne Lindquist-Frazier

I can't really say I knew the heavens better.
But who can, considering how long
their pale light journeyed to join us.
Considering that though father and daughter,
sharing the binoculars like prospectors
with their last canteen,
we are sometimes as far apart
as neighboring galaxies.
Each barely visible to the other,
even on cold clear nights.

Robert Frazier's poem, "Relative Distances," contains no spaceships. No one travels physically to the future or the past. Its subject matter, a father watching Halley's Comet with his daughter, could be that of a poem in almost any literary magazine. Indeed, he says, "Science fiction poetry is a misleading term. Most poets hear in it connotations of bodice-ripping pulp magazines." In fact, "The term has come to mean everything from the surreal to Poe's macabre to poetry informed by the most up-to-date science."

Robert Frazier can speak of SF poetry with great authority. He has published five collections of verse, including **Co-Orbital Moons** (Ocean View Books, 1988), **A Measure of Calm** (Ocean View, 1985 in collaboration with poet Andrew Joron) and **Chronicles of the Mutant Rain Forest** (Mark V. Ziesing Books, 1991; coauthor Bruce Boston). His poems have appeared in the major SF newsstand magazines such as *Omni* and *Isaac Asimov's Science Fiction Magazine*, as well as small press periodicals devoted to SF poetry such as *Ice River* and *The Magazine of Speculative Poetry*. He won the Rhysling Award from the Science Fiction Poetry Association for his short poem "Salinity" in 1989, and he edits the SFPA newsletter, *Star*Line*, which publishes poetry, essays, reviews and news of the field.

"The SFPA is meant to be a forum for poets and poetry readers," says Frazier, "and they tend to come from all walks of life, but with at least a portion of their reading and writing in the fantastic vein. The organization has two volunteer secretaries, and a printing/production person for the newsletter. The newsletter itself is both a networking device for our members and a much needed outlet" that has published about 1,000 poems since 1978. *Star*Line* is not precisely a literary magazine, nor entirely a club newsletter. Frazier publishes several poems in each issue as well as market listings, award news and a workshop section that explains various poetic forms (recently Frazier covered the pantoum) and invites reader experiments with them, some of which he publishes.

Two Rhysling Awards are given each year, one each in the categories short poem and long poem. The Rhysling is named for a character who was a poet in a Robert Heinlein science fiction novel, but the connection between the SF prose and SF poetry genre, or the reading and writing communities, is not necessarily that close. Most readers of SF novels are like most readers of non-SF novels: they don't read much poetry. So SF poets don't enjoy the same followings that science fiction novelists do. A few popular SF novelists, such as Joe Haldeman, Ursula K. LeGuin and Gregory Benford, have extensively published their poetry, but most SF poets are not published SF novelists. Frazier doesn't feel that a deep familiarity with science fiction prose is important to anyone interested in writing SF poetry: "Read lots of poetry; forget the science fiction." His favorite poets include Gary Snyder, Charles Olson and Margaret Atwood. He also recommends nonfiction by popular science writers such as David Quammen and Oliver Sacks.

For *Star*Line* Frazier likes to see "nothing vague, that's for sure. General evocations of the stars, dragons, dread darkness, man's urge to spaceflight, etc. all leave me cold, as would general bits of poetry on anything. Who needs a greeting card when you can have a cross section of the actual tissue, the substance of life. I want specifics—about you, about the world, about the future. I want to see, feel, taste the poem. It has to buzz in the gut. For beginning poets who wander into the twilight zone of the surreal or the scientific, the macabre or the science fictional, I advise them to work past the trappings. Find the heart of what they want to say, what they feel. And don't be afraid to try new things." If you feel uncertain about whether or not what you've written can be considered a "science fiction poem," the standard advice to the working poet applies, study the magazine *before* you submit.

Frazier feels, "Science fiction poetry, with its visionary language, is not just a matter of visible trappings, or its obvious examples—warp drives, aliens, death stars. It has the potential to apprehend the present, the implications of the present, by dealing with its extensions." Frazier's present unfolds on Nantucket Island, off Cape Cod. As an amateur naturalist, he loves "salt marshes, bird migrations, marine biology," but not the isolation. "I want access to bookstores with the latest science books. I want museums. Poetry readings." He traces his aesthetics and love of language to his parents: His mother painted landscapes and his father taught cryptology to Army Security. Frazier started college as a geology major but eventually took undergraduate writing courses from the Iowa University Writer's Workshop.

"I muse about life and death, about the people I know, about science, about history, about heartfelt things, yet a goodly portion of what I write can be called science fiction poetry. It's my impetus. I live in hardwired times, the Information Age, where old-fashioned, industrial age progress no longer exists. Information now moves by the nanosecond, and technological innovation seems mutable, unable to be wholly grasped, because it changes as we speak. That can be scary. Unlike our parents or grandparents, you and I will die in a future radically different from our youths.

"To understand this force that transforms our times, to use its imagery and explore its implications, this feels natural to me. We are what we eat is true of knowledge as well as calories."

—Jim Henley

They have 200 subscribers (1 library) paying $10 for the 6 issues per year (**sample: $1.50 postpaid**). **Submissions to *Star*Line* only.** They receive two or three hundred submissions per year and use about 80—mostly short (**under 50 lines**). They are **"open to all forms—free verse, traditional forms, light verse—so long as your poetry shows skilled use of the language and makes a good use of science fiction, science, fantasy, or speculative motifs."** Reports in a month, likes 2-3 poems per submission, typed, photocopy OK, dot-matrix "difficult but not refused," no simultaneous submissions, no queries, pays $1 for first 10 lines, 5¢/line thereafter. The digest-sized magazines and anthologies are saddle-stapled, inexpensively printed, with numerous illustrations and decorations. (You can order the anthology for $2.50.)

SCORE MAGAZINE; SCORE CHAPBOOKS AND BOOKLETS (IV-Form), 491 Mandana Blvd., #3, Oakland CA 94610, poetry editors Crag Hill, Laurie Schneider and Bill DiMichele, is a "small-press publisher of **visual poetry** in the magazine *Score*, booklets, postcards and broadsides. They want **"Poetry which melds language and the visual arts such as concrete poetry; experimental use of language, words and letters—forms. The appearance of the poem should have as much to say as the text. Poems on any subject; conceptual poetry; poems which use experimental, non-traditional methods to**

communicate their meanings." They don't want "traditional verse of any kind—be it free verse or rhymed." They have published poetry by Stephen-Paul Martin, Bruce Andrews, Karl Kempton, Larry Eigner and Bern Porter. They say that it is impossible to quote a sample because "some of our poems consist of only a single word — or in some cases no recognizable words." **I strongly advise looking at a sample copy before submitting if you don't know what visual poetry is.** *Score* is 18-40 pp., magazine-sized, offset, saddle-stapled, using b/w graphics, 2-color matte card cover, appearing 1 time a year in a press run of 200 for 25 subscriptions (6 of them libraries) and about 40 shelf sales. **Sample: $6 postpaid. Send SASE for guidelines. Pays 2 copies. Photocopies OK "as long as strong black." No simultaneous submissions. Previously published poems OK "if noted." For chapbook consideration send entire MS. No simultaneous submissions. Pay 8-16 copies of the chapbook. Almost always comments on rejections.** They subsidy publish "if author requests it."

‡SCREAM MAGAZINE; ALTERNATING CRIMES PUBLISHING (II, IV-Fantasy), P.O. Box 10363, Raleigh NC 27605, phone (919)834-7542, founded 1985, editor Katherine Boone. *Scream* appears twice a year using **"fiction and poetry in a fantastic vein."** Alternating Crimes publishes poetry chapbooks, short story collections, and illustrated fiction. **"Open in form, length and style. *Scream* focuses on darker themes and on poetry which emphasizes images of experience. Shorter poetry preferred. Nothing religious."** They have recently published poetry by Charles Bukowski and M. Kettner. As a sample the editor selected these lines from "Death Dream Two: A Friend Story" by Kate Meads:

> *Walking alongside, your lover of late ponders his dones*
> *and might-have-dones, his failure to win the heart encased*
> *in glass. Dead and still reading his thoughts, you face*
> *west, laughing: the symbolism redundant.*

I have not seen an issue, but the editor describes it as magazine-sized, 64 pp., with 4-color cover, using illustrations with most poems, laser printed. They accept about 10% of poetry received. Press run 1,500 for 100 subscribers of which 5 are libraries, 800 shelf sales. Subscription: $10. **Sample: $5 postpaid. Send SASE for guidelines. Pays 3 copies. Reports in 1-4 months. Editor "frequently" comments on rejections.** Alternating Crimes Publishing brings out 1 chapbook/year, 32 pp. **For chapbook consideration, submit 1-4 samples and a statement of why you chose A-C Publishing. Pays 20-50% of profit after printing cost plus varied number of copies.** The editor says, "Submit it. Everyone (every editor) can spot what they consider unpublishable poetry, but there is that large gray area where the editor's personal taste and judgment makes the decision between acceptance and rejection, not the quality of the poetry."

‡SCREAM OF THE BUDDHA; BUDDHA ROSE PUBLICATIONS; CRYPTIC WHITE PRESS (I), P.O. Box 902, Hermosa Beach CA 90254, phone (213)543-3809, founded 1988, publisher Dr. Scott Shaw, editor Elliot Sebastian: **"We want to see poetry that screams; be it: erotic, mystical, street wise, or religious. Any form, length, or subject matter. We don't want to read rhyming boring love junk; unless there is a stake through the heart at the end."** They have recently published poetry by Charles Bukowski, Scott Shaw (their publisher), James F. Spezze III and Hae Won Shin. As a sample the editor selected these lines (poet unidentified):

> *I drink a glass of suicide*
> *redemption in a cup*
> *a lady she lays next to me*
> *I do not know her name*

I have not seen an issue, but the editor describes it as digest-sized, 10-20 pp, saddle-stapled. They accept about 30% of 200 poems received/year. Press run 400 for 45 subscribers of which 2 are libraries. Subscription: $25. **Sample: $2. Pays up to 5 copies. "Simultaneous submissions, AOK; who knows, anyway. Poetry written on napkins is fine. The freer the better. If it screams, it is in. We here do not judge what it screams about. Report on submissions one day to one month." Editor often comments on rejections.** Reviews books of poetry. Buddha Rose Publications and Cryptic White Press are imprints for publication of flat-spined paperbacks, chapbooks and hardbacks. **For book consideration, "It is not important to us if poets were previously published. For then, how does one begin. It is better to send us at least some of the MS. Queries tell one little." Pays 15-25% royalties plus varied number of copies.** The editor says, "Buddha Rose Publications accepts no subsidized work. It is involved in the publication of mystical, poetic, philosophic, modern novels, and cultural studies type of work. It is the parent organization of *Scream of the Buddha* and Cryptic White Press." Submissions to Buddha Rose must be "meaning-

Market categories: (I) Beginning; (II) General; (III) Limited; (IV) Specialized; (V) Closed.

ful. Cryptic White Press, on the other hand, is far more open, as it does not have to hold the entire financial responsibility of any publishable work."

‡**SCREAMING TREES (I, IV-Ecology/themes)**, P.O. 1563, San Bruno CA 94006, founded 1990-91, editor Caren Beicker, is a quarterly using **"environmental/urban poetry, free form or rhyming, prefer not longer than 1 page. Nothing sentimental, dogmatic, didactic, propaganda."** The magazine was new at the time of the listing, but the editor said it would use "recycled paper with cover art" and she planned to accept about 50% of poetry received. **Pays 1-3 copies. Response in 4-8 weeks. Editor never comments on rejections.**

‡**SCRIPSI (II)**, Ormond College, University of Melbourne, Parkville, Victoria, Australia 3052, phone (03)3476-360, founded 1981, poetry editors Peter Craven and Andrew Rutherford, is an "international literary quarterly publishing poetry, fiction, essays, reviews and interviews." Recent issues feature verse by Les Murray, John Ashbery, David Shapiro and James Laughlin. As a sample the editors selected Laurie Duggan's translation of Martial II, vii:

> You'll tackle anything
> O products of writing schools:
> you read well, you're socially conscious,
> you compose sestinas, sonnets,
> villanelles, epics, epigrams,
> you've set work to music,
> written several librettos . . .
> So what's wrong with you?
> It's your competence.

I have not seen a copy, but the editors describe it as 200+ pp. "150mm × 210mm" (6 × 8") offset printing, "graphics published in each issue." They have a press run of 2,500 for 1,000 subscriptions of which 100 are libraries. Subscription: $40. **Send subscriptions to Oxford University Press Australia, GPO Box 2784Y, Melbourne, Victoria 3001, Australia. Pay is "variable." No simultaneous submissions or previously published poetry. Reports in 8 weeks. Editor "occasionally" comments on rejections.** Reviews books of poetry.

‡**SCRIPTOR (I)**, P.O. Box 1032, Hackensack NJ 07602, founded 1990, editors/owners D.S. Mandrake and Diane S. Mandrake, is a new periodical hoping to become a quarterly. **"We like poetry that emphasizes the fluidity of language, that 'flows' from word to word and sound to sound. Any style or subject except obscenity, pornographic, or poetry calculated to advance a political or social 'cause.' "** As a sample the editor selected these lines (poet unidentified):

> Tumbling freefall from an autumn moon,
> Crystal elements in swift procession multiply
> And press with ardent passion their select evangel
> songs of velvet and of scarlet and of perfumed vessels
> Slipping swiftly into windflight to become immortal . . .

I have not seen an issue, but the editor describes it as 64 pp. digest-sized, saddle-stapled. **Send SASE for guidelines. Pays 1 copy. "We're not impressed by who has published you before; a work stands or falls solely on its own merit. Previously published work OK. We don't need to own your work forever. Just use it once; rights revert to the author upon publication. Replies ASAP, not more than 30 days. We comment when appropriate and when possible."**

SCRIVENER (II), 853 Sherbrooke St. W., Montreal, Quebec H3A 2T6 Canada, founded 1980, is an annual review of contemporary literature and art published by students at McGill University. With a circulation of 2,000 throughout North America, *Scrivener* publishes the best of new Canadian and American poetry, short fiction, criticism, essays, reviews and interviews. *"Scrivener* **will consider and respond to all submissions; however, it especially encourages writing that challenges generic conventions of literature and thought."** Recent contributors include David Solway, Mary di Michele, Corey Brown, Louis Dudek and Leonard Cohen. As a sample the editors have selected these lines from "Ear of the Bat" by Travis Lane:

> The bat's ear, so honed it hears
> The changes ring among the leaves,
> dew swelling, or the bones
> that creak in a blue mouse wrist
> hears only sound.

Scrivener uses about 50 of 1,000 submissions received each year. It is a book-sized review, 120 pp., printed on natural recycled paper and bound with a flat spine and one color matte card cover; all graphics and ads are black and white. Cover price is $5; subscriptions $4/year. **Sample postpaid $4. Feb. 1 deadline for submissions for May 1st publication; contributors encouraged** to submit in early fall. Send 5-15 poems, one poem per page; be sure that each poem be identified separately, with titles, numbers, etc. .... Editors comment individually on each submission. Reports in 8-12 weeks. Pays 2 copies or 2 year subscription.

SEATTLE REVIEW (II), Padelford Hall, GN-30, University of Washington, Seattle WA 98195, phone (206)543-9865, founded 1978, poetry editor Colleen McElroy, appears in the fall and spring using "contemporary and traditional" poetry. They have published poetry by William Stafford, Tess Gallagher, Marvin Bell and Walter McDonald. As a sample the editor selected these lines from "Car Mechanic Blues" by Jan Wallace:

> He lords his wrench over me like
> a magic wand. His ease with grease, the way
> he calms the speeding idle should convince
> me, this man's got the power. He wants
> to show me how the sparks fire. I say,
> No thanks, I'll get the book.

It is professionally printed, flat spined, 110+ pp., with glossy card cover. Press run 800 for 250 subscribers of which 50 are libraries, 400 shelf sales. Subscription: $8; per issue $4.50. **Sample postpaid: $3. Send SASE for guidelines. Reports in 1-3 months (up to 5 months for summer submissions). Pay "varies, but we do pay" plus 2 copies.** The editors offer these "practical suggestions. Cover letters with submissions do help. A cover letter provides something about the author and tells where and for what s/he is submitting. And don't let those rejection letters be cause for discouragement. Rejections can often be a matter of timing. The journal in question may be publishing a special issue with a certain theme (we've done a number of themes—"all-fiction," "all-poetry," "Asian-American," "Northwest," "science fiction," etc.) Also, editorial boards do change, and new editors bring their individual opinions and tastes in writing. Good poetry will eventually be published if it is circulated."

SECOND AEON PUBLICATIONS (V), 19 Southminster Road, Roath, Cardiff, Wales, phone 0222-493093, founded 1966, poetry editor Peter Finch, is a "small press concerned in the main with **experimental literary works.**" He has recently published poetry by Bob Cobbing and himself. **Pays copies. Accepts no unsolicited MSS.** Editor reviews poetry as a freelancer for a broad range of publications.

‡SECRET GOLDFISH (I, IV-Horror, science fiction, fantasy), 311 Rosemary Lane, Danville VA 24541, founded 1990-91, editor publisher R. Monk Habjan, appears twice a year. "**I want to see primarily horror, sf, fantasy, and experimental. I lean toward darker themes, dark humor and occasional unusual approaches to F/SF. Not afraid to take a chance on an unusual idea when it catches my eye. I also like new, fresh approaches to religion and infinity. No run-of-the mill F/SF, gore, and sex. Not interested in pornography. Blood and sex are often unneeded, should be used to enhance.**" As a sample the editor selected these lines from "Dreaming of Icarus" by Donald McLeod:

> "My waxed wings
> are floating in the sea
> and my father's mourning
> has turned to murder,"
> I cried.

Print run minimum is 100. It is about 50 pp., 5 × 8" photocopied from typescript, with card cover, staple-bound. **Send SASE for guidelines. Pays 1 copy.**

‡SECRETS FROM THE ORANGE COUCH (I, II), Box 688, Killam, Alberta T0B 2L0 Canada, founded 1988, appears twice a year. "**We appreciate an eclectic range of styles: magic realism, traditional, experimental, deconstruction, cross-over writing etc. Above all, we insist on good quality writing.**" They have recently published poetry by Cecilia Frey, Chad Norman, Fred Wah and Birk Sproxton. As a sample the editor selected these lines from "Simile" by Brian Burke:

> "Dad"—my daughter calling—
> "I got a cramp crawling like a smile
> across my stomach."
> —& yes I am hit by the perfect simile
> for smiling at loss

It is 48 pp. magazine-sized, saddle-stapled, professionally printed (desktop) with matte card cover. Press run 300 for 150 subscribers of which 3 are libraries, 100-150 shelf sales. Subscription: $10 plus $2.50 postage (Canadian). **Sample postpaid: $6. Reports within 4 months. Pays $12.50 (Canadian)/published page. "A brief bio would be appreciated."**

SEEMS (II), Box 359, Lakeland College, Sheboygan WI 53082-0359, founded 1971, published irregulary (27 issues in 20 years). This is a handsomely printed, nearly square (7 × 8¼") magazine, saddle-stapled, generous with white space on heavy paper. Two of the issues are considered chapbooks, and the editor, Karl Elder, suggests that a way **to get acquainted would be to order** *Seems #14, What Is The Future Of Poetry?* **for $5,** consisting of essays by 22 contemporary poets, and "If you don't like it, return it, and we'll return your $5." There are usually about 20 pages of poetry per issue. Karl Elder says, **"For a clear idea of what I'm after by way of submissions, see my essay 'The Possibilites of Poetry'** in #19-20 ($6), a special double issue of poetry." He has recently used poetry by Dori Appel, Philip Asaph, Frank Miele, Scott Owens and Sapphire. He said it was "impossible" to select four illustrative lines. The magazine has a print run of 350 for 200 subscriptions (20 libraries) and sells for $4 an issue (or $16 for a subscription—four issues). There is a **1-2 year backlog, reports in 1-3 months, pays copies.**

SEGUE FOUNDATION; ROOF BOOKS; SEGUE BOOKS (V); 303 E. 8th St., New York NY 10009, phone (212)674-0199, president James Sherry, is a small-press publisher of poetry, literary criticism, and film and performance texts. Most of their books are flat-spined paperback, some hard cover. They have published books by Jackson MacLow, Charles Bernstein, Ron Silliman and Diane Ward, but they **do not consider unsolicited MSS. Query first. Pays 10% of run.** The Foundation is also a distributor of a number of prestigious small-press magazines and books. Write for their catalog to buy samples.

SENECA REVIEW (II, IV-Translations), Hobart and William Smith Colleges, Geneva NY 14456, phone (315)781-3349, founded 1970, editor Deborah Tall. They want **"serious poetry of any form, including translations. No light verse. Also essays on contemporary poetry."** Recently they have published poetry by Seamus Heaney, Rita Dove, Denise Levertov, Stephen Dunn and Hayden Carruth. *Seneca Review* is 100 pp., $6 \times 9''$ flat-spined, professionally printed on quality stock with matte card cover, appearing twice a year. Of 3,000-4,000 poems received they accept approximately 100. Press run is 600 for 250 subscriptions of which half are libraries. About 50 shelf sales. Subscription: $8/year, $15/2 years. **Sample: $5 postpaid. Pays 2 copies. They read Sept. 1-May 1; do not read in summer. Submit 3-5 poems. No simultaneous submissions or previously published poems. Reports in 3-10 weeks.**

SENIOR EDITION USA/COLORADO OLD TIMES (IV-Seniors, regional, themes), SEI Publishing Corporation, Suite 218, 1385 S. Colorado Blvd., Denver CO 80222-3312, phone (303)758-4040, managing editor Rose Beetem, is a monthly tabloid "Colorado newspaper **for seniors (with national distribution)** emphasizing legislation, opinion and advice columns, local and national news, features and local calendar aimed at over-55 community." They want **"usually no haiku, religious/inspirational. Subject matter often to match** *Colorado Old Times.*" **Circ.** 25,000. **Pays on publication. Publishes MS an average of 1-6 months after acceptance. Submit seasonal/holiday material 3 months in advance. Sample copy $1; writer's guidelines for SASE.** Senior Overlook column features **opinions of seniors about anything they feel strongly about: finances, grandkids, love, life, social problems, etc. (May be editorial, essay, prose or poetry). Buys 2-6 MSS per year. Send complete MS. Length: 250-900 words. Pays $20, maximum.** Rose Beetem says, "Although we are not refusing manuscripts, the time to hear back from us has lengthened."

SENSATIONS MAGAZINE (I,IV-Membership), 2 Radio Ave., A5, Secaucus NJ 07094, founded 1987, founder David Messineo. **Subscription required before submission of material.** "*Sensations* is a literary magazine which **accepts poetry and short stories, themes varied and controversial, yet aimed for an intelligent, open-minded audience. We'd love material dealing with contemporary issues and current or historical events. No abstract material that only the writer can understand, no minimalist stories, and if it's a love poem, it should be remarkable and something others can appreciate."** As a sample, the founder selected these lines from "Friends and Other Strangers" by Angela Consolo Mankiewicz:

> *Instead of plaster, massive plates of glass*
> *pretend to be a wall; they pass me by*
> *like funhouse mirrors mocking window panes,*
> *grinning through a summer sun that snatches*
> *at my eyes and steals unanchored images.*
> *It isn't right, a hospital you see through;*
> *a hospital you see through has no shame.*
> *I need my wall. I want my yesterday,*

Sensations is magazine-sized, 70 pp., printed on LaserWriter, color front and back covers. **"To join and receive writers' guidelines and samples of previously published poetry, send a $3 check payable to David Messineo along with 52¢ SASE or send $7 for a sample issue. Do not send any poetry until after you've received our writers' guidelines." Simultaneous submissions OK if so indicated. New unpublished material preferred. Legible dot matrix accepted. Reports 4-6 weeks after deadline. No complimentary copies.** The founder says, "All amounts raised go directly toward costs of publishing, marketing and mailing. Advice? A good writer can work as easily with meter or rhyme as with free verse. Beginning writers are advised to first work within the limitations of meter and rhyme, to help them improve their ability to choose the best words to say what they want to say in the best possible way. Read *any* magazine before sending material; throwing material into an envelope without reading the publication or samples of published material is a sure-fire way to waste your time and money." Final reminder: "Poetry submitted by non-members will neither be read nor criticized—we get an abundance of fine material from active magazine patrons and focus our efforts on those who financially support our magazine."

SEQUOIA (II), Storke Publications Building, Stanford CA 94305, founded 1892, poetry editor Carlos Rodriguez, appears twice a year. "We are eclectic but would especially like to see **new kinds of beautiful language. Formal/metrical work is welcome. Rhythm is important to us.**" They have recently published poetry by Susan Howe, Seamus Heaney, Adrienne Rich, Rita Dove, James Merrill. As a sample the editor selected these lines by Ken Kesey:

> She promised light to a secret land
> Took you gentle by the hand
> Picked your locks just like she planned
> and let the stranger in . . .

Sequoia is 80-100 pp., 6 × 9", professionally printed, flat-spined, with a glossy card cover with art. Their press run is 800 with 400 subscriptions, of which half are libraries. They publish a small percentage of hundreds of unsolicited submissions. Subscription: $10. **Sample: $4 postpaid. Pays 2 copies. Reports in "2 months or more." They consider simultaneous submissions but not previously published poems.** The editor says, "*Sequoia* has a long tradition of encouraging 'formal' poetry. Nowadays it seems especially appropriate to remind poets that there is nothing inherently embarrassing about the craft of verse."

SEVEN BUFFALOES PRESS; AZOREAN EXPRESS; BLACK JACK; VALLEY GRAPEVINE; HILL AND HOLLER ANTHOLOGY SERIES (IV-Rural, regional, anthologies), Box 249, Big Timber MT 59011, founded 1973, editor Art Cuelho, who writes, "I've always thought that Rural and Working Class writers, poets and artists deserve the same tribute given to country singers." These publications all express that interest. For all of these publications Art Cuelho wants **poetry oriented toward rural and working people, "a poem that tells a story, preferably free verse, not longer than 50-60 lines, poems with strong lyric and metaphor, not gay, romantical, poetry of the head and not the heart, not poems written like grocery lists, or the first thing that comes from a poet's mind, no experimental or ivory tower, no women's lib (but half my contributors are women)."** He has published poetry by R.T. Smith, James Goode, Leo Connellan and Wendell Berry. As a sample he selected these lines by Jim Wayne Miller:

> and black as a shrew in a snowy field of foxtracks,
> and move toward a setting winter sun
> red on the snow, musky—a sun
> that snaps small bones in a mouth of night.

The Azorean Express, 5½ × 8½", 35 pp., side-stapled, appears twice a year, circulation 200. **Sample: $2.50 postpaid. Pays 1 copy. Reports in 1-2 weeks. Submit 4-8 poems. No simultaneous submissions.** *Black Jack* is an anthology series on Rural America that uses rural material from anywhere, especially the American West; *Valley Grapevine* is an anthology on central California, circulation 750 that uses rural material from central California. Sample: $4. Hill and Holler, Southern Appalachian Mountain series takes in rural mountain lifestyle and folkways. Sample copy: $4. Seven Buffaloes Press does not accept unsolicited MSS but publishes books solicited from writers who have appeared in the above magazines. Art Cuelho advises, "Don't tell the editor how great you are. This one happens to be a poet and novelist who has been writing for 25 years. Your writing should not only be fused with what you know from the head, but also from what you know within your heart. Most of what we call life may be some kind of gift of an unknown river within us. The secret to be learned is to live with ease the darkness. Because there are too many things of the night in this world, but the important clue to remember is that there are many worlds within us."

SEVENTEEN (IV-Teens), 850 3rd Ave., New York NY 10022, phone (212)759-8100, founded 1944, poetry editor Liza DiPrima, is a slick monthly, circulation 1,750,000, for teenage girls which is open to "**all styles of poetry up to 40 lines by writers 21 and under. We are looking for quality poetry by new young poets.**" Purchase sample ($1.75) at newsstands. Reports in 6-8 weeks. Pays $15. Send SASE for guidelines. They receive about 3,000 submissions per year, use 24-30, have a 12-18 month backlog.

SEWANEE REVIEW; AIKEN TAYLOR AWARD FOR MODERN POETRY (III), University of the South, Sewanee TN 37375, founded 1892, thus being our nation's oldest continuously published literary quarterly, and one of the most awesome in reputation. George Core is editor. Each of the 4 issues per year is a hefty paperback of nearly 200 pages, conservatively bound in matte paper, always of the same

THE SIGNAL (II, IV-Translation), P.O. Box #67, Emmett ID 83617, phone (208)365-5812, poetry editors Joan Silva and David Chorlton, "art, opinion, review, interview, exploratory short fiction, articles, essays. **Encourage scientific lit. speculation. Translations. Approach can be a little wild—but not tacky. As to poetry, no restrictions! We want an attitude that reveals caring what goes on in our world, planet caring, people caring, clear-minded, informed opinion, sharp, questioning outlook. Do not want to see poetry that is muddled, wishy-washy, impressed with image as opposed to substance, style as opposed to passion or personal conviction.**" Recently published poets include Robert Peters, Wanda Coleman, Philip K. Jason, Maurice Kenny and Hans Raimund. As a sample Joan Silva selected these lines by Sharon Kubusak:

> —*three marzipan candles, blue flames,*
> *the singed black pearls of tears. This is the card*
> *of leeches. Palm it until it hurts, cuts*
> *in its crown, until your fortune tingles*
> *and squirms and tentacles feeling for wheels*
> *are all you know. The chance card. Listen, the*
> *train. Listen, the world is just beginning.*

The Signal is magazine-sized, 64 pp., saddle-stapled, beautifully printed on heavy ruled stock with matte card cover, using b/w photography and art. It appears twice yearly. Subscriptions are $10 a year domestically, negotiable for foreign subscriptions. **Sample: $6, $3 (back issues) postpaid. Do not submit MSS during June, July or August. Reporting time: 6-12 weeks. Pays in contributors' copies.** Occasionally reviews books of poetry, "but don't count on it." The editors announce a "Cup Award" in each issue for a "currently underappreciated" poet and feature work by that poet in the following issue. "*The Signal* has *no* grant, corporate, or academic funding. We depend 100% on reader support. Help keep us independent."

THE SIGNPOST PRESS; THE BELLINGHAM REVIEW; 49TH PARALLEL POETRY CONTEST (II), 1007 Queen St., Bellingham WA 98226, phone (206)734-9781. Founded 1975, magazine editor Susan Hilton; book editor Knute Skinner. Publishes *The Bellingham Review* twice a year, runs an annual poetry competition, and publishes other books and chapbooks of poetry occasionally. "**We want well-crafted poetry but are open to all styles**," no specifications as to form. Poets they have published recently include Sean Bentley, Fabian Worsham, Marty Ennes, Joseph Green and James Bertolino. As a sample, Knute Skinner selected these lines by John Doorty:

> *Out of the cold reserve*
> *came the warmth of a kiss;*
> *Out of that mumbling marrow*
> *where no kisses came from,*
> *Came a kiss for the road*
> *on the lips of the recently dead.*

Each issue of the *Review* has about 38 pp. of poetry. They have a circulation of 700 with 500 subscriptions. It's digest-sized, saddle-stapled, typeset, with art and glossy cover. **Sample: $2 postpaid. Submit up to 6 pp. Photocopy, simultaneous submissions OK. Reports in 1-3 months, pays 1 copy plus a year's subscription.** Reviews books of poetry. Send SASE for rules for the next 49th Parallel Poetry Contest and query regarding book publication.

SILVER APPLES PRESS (V), Box 292, Hainesport NJ 08036, phone (609)267-2758, founded 1982, poetry editor Geraldine Little. "We're a very small press with very limited funds. Published our first chapbook in 1988; open contest for same. We plan to publish randomly, as things turn us on and as funds permit—pamphlets, chapbooks, a set of postcards. **We are over-committed at present. Not currently accepting poetry submissions.**" They have published **Contrasts in Keening: Ireland** by Geraldine C. Little, **Abandoned House** by Susan Fawcett, **The Verb to Love** by Barbara Horton and **Keeping Him Alive** by Charlotte Mandell.

SILVER WINGS (IV-Religious, spirituality, inspirational), Box 1000, Pearblossom CA 93553-1000, phone (805)264-3726, founded 1983, and now published by Poetry on Wings, Inc., poetry editor Jackson Wilcox. "As a committed Christian service we produce and publish a quarterly poetry magazine. We want **poems with a Christian perspective, reflecting a vital personal faith and a love for God and man. Will consider poems from 3-20 lines. Quite open in regard to meter and rhyme.**" They have recently published poems by William T. Burke, Andrew Peterson, C. David Hay and Harriett Hunt. The editor chose these sample lines from "Night to Night" by Joyce G. Bradshaw:

> *The sky is crystalline.*
> *No clouds*
> *obscure the view.*
> *Stars, like laser points,*
> *punctuate*

> *the ebony expanse.*
> *A chorus of mute voices*
> *proclaims aloud*
> *God's creatorship.*

The 32-36 pp. magazine is digest-sized, offset from typescript with hand-lettered titles on tinted paper with cartoon-like art, circulation 450 with 225 subscriptions. They receive 1,000 submissions per year, use 200. Another 300-400 come in as entries in contests sponsored by Silver Wings—send SASE for details. Subscription: $7. **Sample: $2 postpaid. Typed MSS, double-spaced. Reports in 3 weeks, providing SASE is supplied. Pays $9 in subscription and copy value. Rarely comments on rejections.** Reviews books of poetry in a separate newsletter (announced) going out free 6 times a year. "We also now have a new form which we publish: Chaplets. A Chaplet is a 10 page booklet measuring 4¼×5¼" with 8 poems of 20 short lines or less and a prayer of acceptance, commitment, confession, petition or thanksgiving on the inside of the back cover. We will mail one anywhere for $1. The price for two or any larger quantity will be 75¢ each postpaid. We want to do more of these in cooperative modest financial partnership with poets. If you have an interest, write to **Silver Wings** for details." The editor says, "If a poet has had a faith experience, share it freely from the heart, using whatever words are warm and expressive. Thus the shared message becomes a powerful communication to bless others. We are glad to look at poetry that has an uplift to it. We are Christian by design and openly ecumenical in spirit."

SILVERFISH REVIEW; SILVERFISH REVIEW PRESS (II, IV-Translations), P.O. Box 3541, Eugene OR 97403, phone (503)344-5060, founded 1979, poetry editor Rodger Moody, is an irregularly appearing digest-sized 48 pp. literary magazine, circulation 750. "The only criteria for selection is **quality. In future issues** *Silverfish Review* **wants to showcase translations of poetry from Europe and Latin America** as well as continue to print poetry and fiction of quality written in English." They have published poetry by Walter McDonald, Jon Davis, Dick Allen, Ivan Arguelles, D. M. Wallace, Walter Pavlich, Ralph Salisbury, Bob Austin, Christine Zawadiwsky and Kathleen Spivack. As a sample the editor selected these lines by Floyd Skloot:

> *The thick-lipped bowl*
> *spun slowly, its rim*
> *stroked by her blade*
> *scraping down the liver.*

There are 36-48 pp. of poetry in each issue. The magazine is professionally printed in dark type on quality, stock, matte card cover with art. Subscription: for institution: $12; for individuals: $9; per issue: $3. They receive about 1,000 submissions of poetry per year, use 20, have a 6-12 month backlog. **Sample: $3, single copy orders should include $1 for postage and handling. Submit at least 5 poems to editor. Photocopies OK. No simultaneous submissions. Reports in 6 weeks. Pays 5 copies plus small honorarium when grant support permits.** Silverfish Review Press will **consider MSS for chapbook publication and conducts an annual chapbook competition with an award of $100 and 25 copies (with a press run of 750). Send SASE for rules.** Reviews books of poetry.

SING HEAVENLY MUSE! (IV-Feminist), Box 13299, Minneapolis MN 55414, founded 1977, editor Sue Ann Martinson, fosters "the work of women poets, fiction writers, and artists. The magazine is **feminist in an open, generous sense: we encourage women to range freely, honestly, and imaginatively over all subjects, philosophies, and styles. We do not wish to confine women to women's subjects,** whether these are defined traditionally, in terms of femininity and domesticity, or modernly, from a sometimes narrow polemical perspective. We look for explorations, questions that do not come with ready-made answers, emotionally or intellectually. **We seek out new writers, many before unpublished.** The editors try to reduce to a minimum the common bureaucratic distance between a magazine and its readers and contributors. Although our staff is small, we encourage writers by discussing their work, and we solicit comments from our readers. This relationship makes *Sing Heavenly Muse!* a community where women with widely varying interests and ideas may meet and learn from one another." For poetry they have "**no limitations except women's writing.**" They have published poetry by Alexis Rotella, Jill Breckenridge and Amirh Bahati. The editor selected these sample lines from "Sons of Soweto" by June Jordan:

> *Words live in the spirit of her face*
> *and that sound will no longer yield . . .*
> *she will stand under the sun!*
> *She will stay!*

The magazine appears two times a year in a 6×9" flat-spined, 125 pp. format, offset from typescript on heavy stock, b/w art, glossy card color cover, circulation 1,000, 275 subscriptions of which 50 are libraries. Subscription: $14 (2 issues); per copy: $7. They receive 1,500+ submissions per year, use 50-60. **Sample: $4 postpaid. Submit 3-10 pp., name and address on each page. Photocopy OK. No simultaneous submissions. Reports in 4-5 months at reading periods. Reads only spring and fall. Pays "usually $25 plus 2 copies." Generally accepts manuscripts for consideration in April and September. Inquire about special issues, contests. Send SASE for guidelines. Editors sometimes comment on rejections.**

SINGLE TODAY (I, IV-Romance/love), 2500 Mt. Moriah #185, Memphis TN 38115, phone (901)365-3988, founded 1986, president/owner P.M. Pederson, appears every other month, a small-press magazine for **singles, widowed, divorced, using "short free verse on love and romance, appealing to singles. Nothing vulgar, tasteless, rhyming."** As a sample the editor selected these lines by Kathleen S. McGown:

> *But most of all*
> *You taught me*
> *How to love openly*
> *To search for the ends of the rainbow*
> *And to believe in the magic of one's dreams.*

I have not seen an issue, but the editor describes it as magazine-sized. Press run 15,000 for 2,026 subscriptions. Subscription: $25. **Sample, postpaid: $4. Send SASE for guidelines. Pays 1 copy. Simultaneous submissions and previously published poems OK. Reports "same week." Editor sometimes comments on submissions.** Reviews books of poetry.

SINGULAR SPEECH PRESS (II, IV-Translations), 10 Hilltop Dr., Canton CT 06019, phone (203)693-6059, founded 1976, editor Don D. Wilson. "Although initially a means of publishing the editor's verse translations, Singular Speech Press nonprofitably lives that we may present to *some* public a few, fine examples of the thousands of real poets now at work, playing — probably our most unsupported artists. To this end, **we plan to publish at least 3-4 MSS per annum, 24-64 pages. We have hardly any biases, are delighted by formal and informal verse, are made glad by unknown and well-known poets, and eschew only the egregiously confessional, so boring, and the patently prosy, lined out as though poetic."** They have published Wiliam Burns, David Cloutier, Charles Fishman, Deborah Ford, Susan Whitmore and Stephen Smith. Soon to publish Kenneth Pobo, Rose Rosberg and Ron McFarland. "Impossible to find four representative and self-contained lines, but here are 4 from K. Pobo's "Yes: Irises":

> *My friends have moved. Only butterflies*
> *widening in the grass are the same.*
> *Let dusk come, falling pink straw.*
> *I do not live here any more, but yes: irises.*

Query with 5-10 typed samples and bio. Simultaneous submission, photocopies OK. Payment is half of printed copies. Editor usually comments on rejections. Reports within 1-2 weeks.

SINISTER WISDOM (IV-Lesbian, feminist), P.O. Box 3252, Berkeley CA 94703, founded 1976, editor and publisher Elana Dykewomon, a lesbian feminist journal. The editor says, **"We want poetry that reflects the diversity of lesbian experience — lesbians of color, Third World, Jewish, old, young, working class, poor, disabled, fat, etc. — from a lesbian and/or feminist perspective. No heterosexual themes. We will not print anything that is oppressive or demeaning to women, or which perpetuates negative stereotypes."** The journal has recently published work by Gloria Anzaldúa, Sapphire and Betsy Warland. The editor chose the following lines from Minnie Bruce Pratt's poem "#67 To Be Posted on 21st Street, Between Eye and Pennsylvania":

> *Like a movie, sudden threat*
> *Predictable. I get so tired of this disbelief.*
> *My tongue, faithful in my mouth, said: Yes, we are.*
> *the shout: Lesbians. Lesbians. Trying to curse*
> *us with our name. Me louder: That's what we are.*

The quarterly magazine is digest-sized, 128-144 pp. flat-spined, with photos and b/w graphics; I have not seen it. Circulation is 3,500 of which 1,000 are subscriptions and 100 go to libraries; newsstand sales and bookstores are 1,500. Price per issue is $5, subscription $17 US, $22 foreign. **Sample available for $6.50 postpaid. Pay is 2 copies. No simultaneous submissions. Reporting time is up to 9 months and time to publication 6 months-1 year.** Reviews books of poetry.

SISTERS TODAY (II, IV-Religious), The Liturgical Press, Collegeville MN 56321, phone (612)363-2213, poetry editor Sister Audrey Synnott, 1437 Blossom Rd., Rochester NY 14610, editor Sister Mary Anthony Wagner, has been published for about 60 years. Though it is a Roman Catholic magazine, **not all of the poetry it uses is on religious themes, and the editors do not want poetry that is "overly religious." They want "short (not over 25 lines) poems on any topic, using clean, fresh images and appeal to the reader's feelings and thoughts in a compelling way." They do not want poetry that depends "heavily on rhyme and on 'tricks' such as excessive Capitalization, manipulation of spacing,**

etc." They have recently published poetry by Evelyn Mattern, Eileen Curteis and Pat McKinnon. As a sample, poetry editor Sister Audrey Synnott chose these lines from "Father's Lesson" by Frank Accuardi:

> *In that frozen moment I see his face*
> *Through the cloudy cold. Neck veins*
> *taut as tree limbs hold the heavy chin.*
> *Dark creases branch around knotted eyes.*

ST, appearing 6 times a year beginning with January 1990, is 6×9″ 64 pp., saddle-stapled, professionally printed with matte card cover, press run 9,000 for 8,500 subscribers. They receive about 100 poems per month, accept about 3. Subscription: $15 USA; $17 foreign. **Sample: $2 postpaid. Send SASE to poetry editor at Rochester, NY address (above) for guidelines. Pays $10/poem and 2 copies. They like you to put your "complete legal name, address and social security number typed in the upper right corner." No simultaneous submissions. Previously published poems OK with publisher's release, but original poems much preferred. Reports within 1 month, 6-12 months until publication. Poetry editor comments when a poem has come close to being accepted.**

‡**SISYPHUS (I)**, 8 Asticou Rd., Boston MA 02130, founded 1990, editor Christopher Corbett-Fiacco, appears every other month using **"meaningful poetry and prose of substance and style that speaks of and to humanity, human emotion, and life (whatever it may be). The editor likes to see up to 5-7 poems at a time. No length limit for poetry; prose to 5,000 words. Also uses artwork, including cover art (up to 7½×9″). No self-conscious, beatniks obsessed with body functions and numbers and types of sex partners. Nothing too radical."** As a sample I selected these lines from "Promises of Roses" by their "Featured Artist" in their first issue, Mary Duffye Forte:

> *and you pull me to your side,*
> *holding me against myself*
> *you stab at me*
> *your hardness*
> *strangling me of love*
> *I drank in fully once*
> *before I tasted bitterness on your tongue.*

It is magazine-sized, 20 pp. photocopied from typescript, with card cover, stapled along one side. They accept 10-20% of work received. Subscription: $12 US; $18 international. Current issue $2.50. **Sample: $1.75. Send SASE for guidelines and contest flyers. Pays 1 copy.** Bimonthly contest theme "exercises" with modest prizes.

‡**SKOOB QUARTERLY REVIEW; SKOOB BOOKS PUBLISHING LTD. (III, IV-Translations)**, 43 Old Bethnal Green Rd., London E9 6PR U.K., founded 1987, editor Lucien Jenkins. *SR* appears quarterly, 48 pp. with colored cover, with a circulation of 2,000. **"As a publishing house we are interested in translations, particularly from Modern European poetry."** As a sample the editor selected these lines from Michal Hamburger's translation of "Inventory" by Gunter Eich:

> *This pencil lead*
> *is what I love most:*
> *by day it writes verses*
> *I thought up in the night*

The magazine pays 1 copy. Reports ASAP. Books pay 7% royalties plus 6 copies. "We run a major international poetry competition in partnership with Index on Censorship." Lucien Jenkins gives this advice to people who write: "It takes time, it takes work, it takes courage *and* it takes talent. Do not be buttered up by friends who reassure you otherwise. Expect no money, no fame, no gratitude, no respect, no success, no pleasure, no comfort. Do it *only* because not doing it is not a possibility."

SKYLARK (I, II, IV-Themes), Purdue University Calumet, 2233 171st St., Hammond IN 46323, phone (219)989-2262, founded 1972, editor Pamela Hunter, is "a fine arts annual, including **special theme.**" They are looking for **poems up to 30 lines. No horror, nothing extremely religious, no pornography.** They have recently published poetry by Robert Cooke, Michael Kulycky, Ray Mizer and Charles Tinkham. As a sample the editor selected these lines from "He Said Ease Was Just Picking Up, Hearing My Voice" by lyn lifshin:

> *crocus slithering*
> *up to the morning*
> *Frost   planted in*
> *the fall   an act*
> *of faith in a*
> *grey November*
> *sleet in the air*

Skylark is magazine-sized, saddle-stapled, 100+ pp., professionally printed, with matte card cover. Press run is 500-1,000 for 60 subscriptions of which 10 are libraries. Price: $6. **Sample: $3.50 postpaid. Pays 1 copy. "Typed or computer printout manuscripts OK. Will accept simultaneous submissions. Inquire as to annual theme for special section." Do not submit MSS between June 1st and September 30th. Reports in 4 months (longer in summer). Editor may encourage rejected but promising writers.**

SKYLARK (I), 2110 Charleroi, #8, Beauport, PQ G1E 3S1 Canada, founded 1989, editor Suzanne Fortin, appears every other month. **"The editor reads everything but generally accepts poetry that is traditional. Rhyme and free verse considered. Any subject matter. No Dadaist."** As a sample the editor selected these lines from "Praying for the Rapturous Bombs to Fall" by Brian Burke:

> You pray for the rapturous bombs to fall
> your ears tuned to the apocalyptic blast
> convinced some nimble god
> will save those fevered few of you

I have not seen an issue, but the editor describes it as digest-sized, 20-24 pp., photocopied with card cover. They accept 40% of submissions. Circulation: 50. Subscription: $12. **Sample, postpaid: $2; *all checks* must be paid to Suzanne Fortin. Pays 1 copy. "Poems' titles to be listed on cover, name & address on each page. 100 lines per poem, maximum; 10 poems, maximum." Previously published poems OK. Reports in 1 week-2 months. Editor comments on submissions "infrequently."** Reviews books of poetry. She says to beginning poets, "Don't be trendy to be trendy. Don't give in to people who say 'this type of poetry is fashionable, not *your* kind' or to groups or individuals who say there isn't an audience for your poetry."

SLANT: A JOURNAL OF POETRY (II), Box 5063, University of Central Arkansas, Conway AR 72032, founded 1986, is an annual using *only* poetry. They use **"traditional and 'modern' poetry, even experimental, moderate length, any subject on approval of Board of Readers; purpose is to publish a journal of fine poetry from all regions of the United States. No haiku, no translations."** They have recently used poetry by Marge Piercy, Andrea Budy and Gary Whitby. As a sample the editor selected this excerpt from "Sheltering the Enemy" by Suzanne Harvey:

> I should evict you from this house
> You're no fit tenant for a landlord turned fifty
> You and this feeling that I'm twenty
> And ripe to launch my skiff on an uncertain sea
> Where the tide will never ebb or the wind subside
> Where the moon will wax out of season . . .

Slant is professionally printed on quality stock, 145 pp. flat-spined, with matte card cover. They publish about 80-90 poems of the 2,500 received each year. Press run is 350 for 70-100 subscriptions. **Sample: $10 postpaid. Pays 1 copy. "Put name and address top of each page." Submit no more than 5 poems of moderate length. Allow 3-4 months from November 15 deadline for response. No multiple submissions or previously published poems. Editor comments on rejections "on occasion."**

SLATE & STYLE (IV-Specialized), 2704 Beach Dr., Merrick NY 11566, phone (516)868-8718, editor Loraine Stayer, is a **quarterly for blind writers available on cassette, large print, and Braille, "including** articles of interest to blind writers, resources for blind writers. Membership/subscription $5 per year, $10 for Braille only (specify format). Division of the National Federation of the Blind." **Poems may be "5-30 lines. Prefer contributors to be blind writers, or at least writers by profession or inclination. No obscenities. Will consider all forms of poetry."** They have recently published poetry by Mary McGinnis, Milton Kerr and Sonja Kershaw. As a sample the editor selected "Lost Hills" by Carol Ann Lindsay:

> Hundreds of pumping oil wells
> Secure upon a hill,
> Far from man, mountain, and sea
> Owned by one giant company;
> Taking a resource
> Natural to earth,
> Not giving it back
> But leaving steel fists
> To rot in the sand.

The print version is magazine-sized, 28-32 pp., stapled, circulation 200 with 150 subscribers of which 4-5 are libraries. Subscription: $5 a year, Braille $10. Per issue: $1.25 except Braille. **Sample $2.50 postpaid. Do not submit MSS in July. Send SASE for guidelines. Pays 1 copy. Reports in "2 weeks if I like it." No simultaneous submissions. Interested in new talent. Editor** comments on rejections "if requested." Reviews books of poetry. They offer annual contests, added a fiction and poetry section to the magazine. Loraine Stayer says, "Poetry is one of the toughest ways to express oneself, yet ought to be the easiest to read. Anything that looks simple is the result of much work."

SLIPSTREAM; SLIPSTREAM AUDIO CASSETTES (II, IV-Themes), Box 2071, New Market Station, Niagara Falls NY 14301, phone (716)282-2616 (after 5pm, EST), founded 1980, poetry editors Dan Sicoli, Robert Borgatti and Livio Farallo. *Slipstream* is a "small-press literary mag, uses about 70% poetry and 30% prose, also artwork. The editors like **new work with contemporary urban flavor. Writing must have a cutting edge to get our attention. Occasionally do theme issues. We like to keep an open forum, any length, subject, style. Best to see a sample to get a feel. Like city stuff as opposed to country. Like poetry that springs from the gut, screams from dark alleys, inspired by experience.''** No "pastoral, religious, traditional, rhyming" poetry. They have recently published poetry by Mary Ann Lynch, Lisa Harris, Gerald Locklin, M. Kettner, Charles Bukowski, Robert Underwood, Michael Basinski, Belinda Subraman, Kurt Nimmo and Andrew Gettler. The editors selected these sample lines from "No One Will Report You" by Susan Holahan:

> *Define the world for your child:*
> *if you beat him, he thinks beatings*
> *are life,*
> *ordinary as orange juice or the lingering taste*
> *of castor oil on silver years ago.*

Slipstream appears 1-2 times a year, $7 \times 8\frac{1}{2}$" format professionally printed, saddle-stapled, using b/w graphics, circulation 300, with 200 subscriptions of which 10 are libraries. About 60 of the 80+ pp. are devoted to poetry. They receive over 1,000 freelance submissions of poetry per year, use less than 10%. Subscription: $7.50/2 issues. Sample: $4.95 postpaid. Reports in 2-8 weeks. Editor sometimes comments on rejections. Pays copies. Send SASE for guidelines. **Some issues are on announced themes — e.g., a "working stiff" theme issue is planned for 1992 but is already full. Also producing an audio cassette series. "Spoken word, songs, audio experiments, etc. are all welcome. Query for current needs."** Annual chapbook contest has December 1 deadline. Reading fee: $5. Submit up to 40 pp. of poetry, any style, previously published work OK with acknowledgments. Winner receives 50 copies. All entrants receive copy of winning chapbook. Past winners have included Gerald Locklin, Serena Fusek, Robert Cooperman and Richard Amidon. Dan Sicoli advises, "Most poetry mags publish for a specific audience, usually writers. Support the ones you like best. Funding is difficult and many mags live a very short life."

SLOW DANCER; SLOW DANCER PRESS (II), Box 3010, RFD 1, Lubec ME 04652, founded 1977, American editor Alan Brooks. *Slow Dancer* is a semi-annual magazine of British and American writing published by John Harvey in Nottingham, England (address: 58 Rutland Rd., West Bridgford, Nottingham NG2 5DG); Slow Dancer Press publishes (very) occasional chapbooks of poetry and prose. The editor says, **"All types, lengths, subjects [of poetry] considered. We prefer to print multiple selections from contributors. We look for freshness of image and language, clarity and individuality, whatever the subject. We encourage submissions from previously unpublished poets and always judge the poem, not the 'name.'** Prospective contributors should buy a sample copy if they want to learn our preferences. **We will reject all poems which display knee-jerk alienation, cutesy formalism, or New Yorker-ese, as well as those which come with a cover letter explaining what they really mean."** He has recently published poems by Martin Stannard, Lyn Lifshin, Erika Brady, Brian Patten and Roger McGough. As a sample, he selected the following lines from "Riding The Wish of A Horse" by Grace Cavalieri:

> *From the place of no nurture*
> *I climb into a bed of birdsong*
> *moving further and further away*
> *from what matters*

Most issues of *Slow Dancer* "feature a mix of British and North American writers, with a smattering of writers (in English) from all over." The magazine is digest-sized, offset from typed copy, on white stock, some line drawings and b/w photographs, short fiction, 48 pp., saddle-stitched with b/w glossy photo cover. Circulation is about 500, of which approximately 300 are subscriptions. Price per copy is $5. Sample back issue $4. Subscriptions: $20/4 issues, $36/8 issues (**all prices postpaid**). Poems, previously unpublished, should be submitted one to a page, photocopy or dot-matrix OK if clear, simultaneous submissions OK. **"The reading period is November 1-April 30: poems submitted outside this period will be returned unread."** Reporting time is 2 months. Slow Dancer Press publishes 1 or 2 chapbooks of poetry per year, 12-48 pp., format like that of the magazine, but **freelance submissions for chapbooks are not accepted. "We publish manuscripts by poets who have regular appearances in the magazine."** Pay is in author's copies. The editor says, "We are returning to an old *Slow Dancer* tradition: publishing fewer poets but more work by each contributor. If you like what you see in a sample issue, send a reasonable selection of your work. And please, do check your spelling."

SMALL POND MAGAZINE OF LITERATURE (II), Box 664, Stratford CT 06497, phone (203)378-4066, founded 1964, poetry editor Napoleon St. Cyr, a literary tri-quarterly that features poetry ... "and anything else the editor feels is original, important." Poetry can be **"any style, form, topic, so long as it is deemed good, except haiku, but limit of about 100 lines."** Napoleon St. Cyr wants **"nothing about cats, pets, flowers, butterflies, etc. Generally nothing under 8 lines."** Although he calls it name-dropping, he "reluctantly" provided the names of Heather Tosteson, Deborah Boe, Richard Kostelanetz, Fritz Hamilton, and Emilie Glen as poets recently published. He preferred not to supply sample lines, but I have, from a recent issue, selected the opening stanza of "Mother" by Vicky L. Bennett:

> *sits in splendid silence*
> *her dead fox collar*
> *wrapped high around her throat*

The magazine is digest-sized, offset from typescript on off-white paper, 40 pp. with matte card cover, saddle-stapled, art work both on cover and inside. Circulation is 300-325, of which about half go to libraries. Price per issue is $2.75; subscription $7.50 (for 3 issues). **Sample: $2.50 postpaid for a random selection, $3 current. Guidelines are available in each issue. Pay is two copies.** The editor says he doesn't want 60 pages of anything; "dozen pages of poems max." He reports on submissions in 10-45 days (longer in summer), and publication is within 3-18 months. Reviews books of poetry.

SMALL PRESS WRITERS & ARTISTS ORGANIZATION (SPWAO); SPWAO SHOWCASE; SPWAO NEWSLETTER (IV-Membership, Sci-fi/horror/fantasy), 1210 Greer Ave., Holbrook AZ 86025; president Mike Olson; newsletter editor Valerie Massie. The organization publishes a newsletter, with an emphasis on aiding members, advice columns, short poetry, art, reviews, short fiction and providing a poetry commentary service. **You must be a member to submit. They don't want to see "mainstream, religious, highly sentimental, pornography, racial or political poetry."** They have recently published poems by Marge Simon, John Grey, D.M. Vosk, Cathy Buburuz, Joey Froehlich and Mark Fewell. Doni A. Lazenby, Director of SPWAO Promotion Committee, says: "Learn to paint a poem the way an artist paints a picture. Understand not only what words mean, but how they sound, how they relate to each other and how they emphasize a poem's theme. Don't just throw words on paper hoping for some sort of rhyme or cadence. Instead, weave the elements of meaning, sound and pattern into a poetic tapestry that catches and keeps the reader's attention."

‡**THE SMALL TIMES (I, IV-Subscription)**, 62 Queen St., Lalor, Victoria, Australia 3075, founded 1988, editor Trixie Perren, appears every other month, using poetry—"prefer not too long; any subject or style." They have recently published poetry by Peter Bakowski, John Montgomery, Myron Lysenko, Joy Walsh and Amelia Angove. As a sample, I selected these lines from "The Race of Life" by editor "Trixi":

> *Burn brightly, stark reality*
> *(Is this a game? I thought I had it won!)*
> *Clinging to the dreams*
> *Yet let go the fantasy.*

It is digest-sized, 28 pp., saddle-stapled, photoreduced type-script on yellow paper with cover of the same paper. The editor says she accepts **"at least one poem from each contributor."** Press run 150 for 80 subscribers of which 10 are libraries. Subscription $A22, $A35 overseas. **Sample free for postage. Reports within 3 months. Pays non-subscribers 1 copy, subscribers get 2. "Cover letters give me an idea about the poet. I love them."** They review books of poetry and publish notes on literary events in Melbourne. "Contents are 75% by subscribers."

‡**THE SMITH; THE GENERALIST PAPERS (II)**, 69 Joralemon St., Brooklyn NY 11201, founded 1964, editor Harry Smith, publishes 2 hardbacks and 4 paperbacks/year and is considering a chapbook series. They have recently published poetry by Menke Katz, Lloyd Van Brunt, Richard Nason and Karen Swenson. As a sample the editor selected these lines from "Hawk Forever in Mid-Dive" by Lance Lee's **Wrestling with the Angel:**

> *Her feet on the patio are leaves blown*
> *over flagstones. Aimed at her head,*
> *beak thrust out wings angled severely*
> *a hawk hangs frozen in mid-air,*
> *fanned to permanent fire in her sky.*

"Send 3-6 poem sampling with query. No jingles, no standard academic verse." Pays 15% royalties, $500 advance, 10 copies. "The decision process is relatively slow—about three months—as many MSS are offered. Readers' reports are often passed along and the editor often comments.

Write for catalog (free) or send $2 for a 'slightly irregular' book (with bumped corners or a little dust)." Harry Smith advises, "Revert to earlier models. *Avoid* university wordshops where there are standard recent models leading to standard mod verse. A close reading of **The Pearl Poet** will be more nourishing than all the asparagus of John Ashbery or Robert Bly." *The Generalist Papers*, appearing 6/year, consists of lively critical commentaries on contemporary poetry—more candor than you will find in most reviews. Subscription: $12. **Sample: $2 postpaid.**

GIBBS SMITH, PUBLISHER; PEREGRINE SMITH POETRY COMPETITION (II), P.O. Box 667, Layton UT 84041, phone (801)544-9800, founded 1971; poetry series established 1988, contact Steve Chapman, publicist. **They want "serious, contemporary poetry of merit. No specs except book is only 64 pp."** They have recently published books of poetry by David Huddle and Carol Frost. Books are selected for publication through competition for the Peregrine Smith Poetry Prize of $500 plus publication. Entries are received in April only and require a $10 reading fee. All titles are printed in a uniform 5×9″, 64 pp. paperback format on acid-free archival stock with covers featuring a facsimile design of early Victorian marbleized paper. A die-cut widow in the covers will reveal an original watercolor commissioned for each title. The first 1,500 copies of each edition will be personally signed by the author. The judge for the series and editor is Christopher Merrill, director of the Santa Fe Writers' Conference.

‡SMOKE; WINDOWS PROJECT (II), 22 Roseheath Dr., Halewood, Liverpool L26 9UH England, founded 1974, poetry editor Dave Ward, appears 2 times per year, digest-sized, 20 pp., b/w graphics, paper cover, circulation 1,500 with 800 subscriptions of which 10 are libraries. They have recently published poetry by Douglas Dunn, Lorena Cassady, Matt Simpson and Frances Horovitz. Subscriptions: £2 for 3 issues (plus postage for foreign mailing); per issue 50p plus postage. They use about 50 of 1,000 submissions received annually. **Sample: 50p postpaid. Submit up to 6 poems. Photocopy OK. Name and address on each poem. Reports "as soon as possible."** Editor comments on rejections "only if asked to and if I've something helpful to say."

SMOKE SIGNALS (II), Meander Box 232, Flushing NY 11385-0232, founded 1989, editor Joshua Meander, is a quarterly. **"No curse words in poems, little or no name-dropping, no naming of consumer products, no two-page poems, no humor, no bias writing, no poems untitled. 9-30 lines, poems with hope. Simple words, careful phrasing. Free verse, rhymed poems, sonnets, half page parables, myths and legends, song lyrics. Subjects wanted: love poems, protest poems, mystical poems, nature poems, poems of humanity, poems with solutions to world problems and inner conflict."** They have published poetry by Brenda Charles, Joseph Gourdji, Dorothy Wheeler and Jeff Swan. As a sample the editor selected these lines from "Loves Giant Piano" by Connie Goodman:

> Walk a giant piano . . .
> Destination, the stars
> Along love's entrancing melody;
> The night, it is ours.

I have not seen an issue, but the editor describes it as 5 pp., 2-3 poems per page, typeset. They receive 150 poems per year, use about 50. Press run 400, all distributed free. **Subscription $5; per copy $1.25. Make check payable to Joshua Meander. Pays one copy. Reports in 6-8 weeks.** The editor says, "Stick to your guns; however, keep in mind that an editor may be able to correct a minor flaw in your poem. Accept only minor adjustments. Go to many open poetry readings. Respect the masters. Read and listen to other poets on the current scene. Make pen pals. Start your own poetry journal. Do it all out of pure love."

SNAKE NATION REVIEW; SNAKE NATION PRESS (II), 2920 N. Oak, Valdosta GA 31602, phone (912)242-1503, founded 1989, editor Roberta George, appears twice a year. **"Any form, length of 60 lines or less."** They have recently published poetry by Irene Willis and William Fuller. As a sample the editor selected these lines by David Kirby:

> It need only sound,
> not be right,
> for all unhappy families
> are not unhappy
> in different ways.

The handsome 6×9″ flat-spined, 100 pp. magazine, matte card cover, has a press run of 1,000 for 200 subscriptions of which 11 are libraries. Subscription: $6. **Sample postpaid: $5. Send SASE for guidelines. Pays 2 copies or prizes. Reports in 3 months. Editor comments on submissions sometimes.** Beginning in 1991, Snake Nation Press publishes books of poetry. **Submit 50 pp. MS, $10 reading fee. Pays $500 on publication.**

SNAKE RIVER REFLECTIONS (I, IV-Themes), 1863 Bitterroot Drive, Twin Falls ID 83301, phone (208)734-0746, appearing 10 times a year using **short (up to 20 lines) poems, "especially related to writing topics." Pays 2 copies. Guidelines available for SASE. Sample: 25¢ postpaid.** Subscription: $5.50. It is 4 pp., stapled at the corner, press run 100-200. Reviews books of poetry.

SOCIAL ANARCHISM (IV-Political, social issues), 2743 Maryland Ave., Baltimore MD 21218, phone (301)243-6987, founded (Vacant Lots Press) 1980, poetry editor Howard J. Ehrlich, is a digest-sized 96 pp. biannual, print run 1,200, using about 10 pp. of poetry in each issue which **"represents a political or social commentary that is congruent with a nonviolent anarchist and feminist perspective."** They have recently published poetry by Jacqueline Elizabeth Letalien, L.M. Harrod, Mark Colasurdo, Bridget Balthrop Morton and Bert Hubinger. As a sample I selected the first stanza of "The Saga of Dick and Jane" by Bruce E. Hopkins:

> My recollection is
> That it was a college town
>   a university town
> Where people had degrees
> And ate their chicken with knives and forks

Sample: $3 postpaid; $3.50 outside U.S. Submit up to 5 poems, "not in crayon." Considers simultaneous submissions. Reports in 4-6 weeks. Pays 5 copies.

SOCIAL JUSTICE: A JOURNAL OF CRIME, CONFLICT, WORLD ORDER (IV-Political, social issues), P.O. Box 40601, San Francisco CA 94140, phone (415)550-1703, founded 1974, editor Gregory Shank, is a "quarterly journal addressing violations of international law, human rights and civil liberties; the 'law and order' crime policies of the New Right, including the death penalty; crime and social justice under capitalism and socialism; community approaches to crime control and justice, using a **few poems, not in every issue."** They want **"political poetry, reflecting personal experiences or expressing the aspirations of broader movements for social justice. Do not want anything unrelated to criminal justice themes or social movements."** They have published poetry by Adrienne Rich, Jeremy Cronin and Luis Talamantes. As a sample I selected the closing lines from "A First Night in El Sing Sing" by Piri Thomas:

> Hey—you're not a numba
> You got a name—
> They only got your body
>   not your brain—

I have not seen it, but the editor describes it as 6×9″, laser printed, then photo offset, no graphics, 180-200 pp., flat-spined. They use 3-4 of 10-15 poems received. Press run is 2,000 for 1,700 subscriptions of which 700 are libraries, others distributed through bookstore sales. Subscription: $30; per issue: $10. **Sample: $12 postpaid. Pays 1 copy. No simultaneous submissions, previously published poems—"maybe." MS should be double-spaced, one inch margins, pica or elite, Courier if possible or on IBM compatible 5¼″ floppy. Reports in 6 weeks, time to publication 90 days or more. Editor sometimes comments on rejections.**

THE SOCIETY OF AMERICAN POETS (SOAP); IN HIS STEPS PUBLISHING COMPANY; IN HIS STEPS RECORDS (I, IV-Religious, membership), 102 Demetree Rd., Warner Robins GA 31093, phone (912)923-6687, founded 1984, editor Rev. Charles E. Cravey. *SOAP* is a literary quarterly of poetry and short stories. In His Steps publishes religious and other books and publishes music for the commercial record market. **"Open to all styles of poetry and prose—both religious and secular. No gross or 'X-rated' poetry without taste or character."** They have recently published poetry by Henry Gurley, Pat Stephenson, Carrie Hereford, Elizabeth Horne and the editor. As a sample the editor selected these lines by Edward Bernstein:

> Battered fortresses, hewn in time by men of warfare—
> Death, destruction, both weave their way through the myriads of time—
> Like a cancer growing deep within the soul.

SOAP, the quarterly newspaper, uses **poetry by member/subscribers only.** (Membership: $15/year.) **For book publication query. No pay. Editor "most certainly" comments on rejections.** The newspaper has poetry competitions in several categories with prize of $25-100. The editor says, "My future plan is to publish a nice 'slick' magazine for poets, religious articles, and short stories. Poets should be more careful in metering each line and in finding 'new' words to describe 'old' emotions, events, etc. Poetry should never 'bore' the reader, but serve to 'spark' the imagination and lead us on to higher realms of thought."

SOJOURNERS (IV-Religious, political), Box 29272, Washington DC 20017, phone (202)636-3637, founded 1975, appears 10 times per year, "with approximately 46,000 subscribers. **We focus on faith, politics and culture from a radical Christian perspective. We use shorter poetry (not over 30 lines),** which must be original. We are very open to various themes and seasonal poetry. We look for poetry related to the political and cultural issues covered by our magazine, but also publish poems which simply celebrate life. Poetry using noninclusive language (any racist, sexist, homophobic poetry) will not be accepted." As a sample the editor selected these lines (poet unindentified):

> old ogala woman,
> i taste your hot salt tears
> burning slowly
> through a thousand wrinkles
> down a thousand years.

I have not seen an issue, but the editor describes it as 52 pp., offset printing. It appears monthly except that there is one issue for August/September and February/March. Of 400 poems received per year they publish 8-10. Press run: 50,000 for 46,000 subscriptions of which 500 are libraries; 2,000 shelf sales. Subscription: $27. Sample, postpaid: $2.75. Send SASE for guidelines. Pays $25/poem plus 5 copies. Submit no more than 3 at a time. Occasionally they use a previously published poem with reprint permission. Reports in 4-6 weeks. Editor comments on submissions "sometimes."

SOLEIL PRESS (IV-Ethnic), Box 452, RFD 1, Lisbon Falls ME 04252, phone (207)353-5454, founded 1988, contact Denis Ledoux, publishes and distributes **writing by and about Franco-Americans** in chapbooks and paperbacks. **Not interested in the continental French experience. Pays copies.**

SOLO FLYER; SPARE CHANGE POETRY PRESS (I), 2115 Clearview NE, Massillon OH 44646, Spare Change Poetry Press founded 1979, editor David B. McCoy. "Three 4-page flyers are published a year; each by an individual author. All styles of poetry using punctuation and capitalization will be considered, but send only from May through Labor day." Send up to 10 poems at a time. Payment: 20-25 copies. Free samples on request with SASE. Reports in 1-3 months. No submissions returned without SASE. As a sample I selected the closing lines of "The Tornado's Eye" by Margaret Alder Eaves:

> In the black windows of our house,
> my eyes are as empty as the one-armed doll's,
> washed as clear as the rain-swept streets
> in wake of the storm.

"We chose this cover for its humor and its nostalgia, and because the image suggests a situation or a narrative and in this way seemed literary," says Sonora Review's chief editor Joan Marcus. The cover "represents an individual artist's vision, just as each individual piece in our journal represents a unique aesthetic, rather than being one small part of a uniform aesthetic," she says. The artist, Sally Geier, is a Rhode Island School of Design graduate now living and working in San Francisco.

SONORA REVIEW (II), Dept. of English, University of Arizona, Tucson AZ 85721, phone (602)626-8383, founded 1980, poetry editors Andrea Werblin and Jennifer Rocco, a semiannual literary journal that publishes "non-genre" fiction and poetry. **The editors want "quality poetry, literary concerns."** They have published poems by Olga Broumas, Jon Anderson, Jane Miller and Charlie Smith. Some poems are published both in English and Spanish. As a sample, the editors chose the following lines by Linda Gregg:

> *I love the places on your body where*
> *the patina is worn through to the bright metal*
> *by touching and kissing. Toe or knee.*
> *Nose or cheek or nipple. Your belly*
> *as you recline. Pity is where you are.*

Sonora Review is a handsome magazine, 6×9″, professionally printed on heavy off-white stock, 130 pp. flat-spined, with 2-color glossy card cover. Circulation is 650, of which 250 are subscriptions and 300 go to libraries. Price per copy is $5, subscription $8/year, $15/2 years. **Back issue available for $4 postpaid. Pay is 2 copies. Poets should submit typed copy; dot-matrix, simultaneous submissions OK. Reporting time is 8 weeks and time to publication 6 months.** The magazine sponsors annual poetry awards with prizes of $150 and $50.

‡**SOUNDINGS: A NEWSLETTER FOR SURVIVORS OF CHILDHOOD SEXUAL ABUSE; ECHOES NETWORK, INC. (IV-Themes)**, Suite 541, 700 NE Multnomah, Portland OR 97232, founded 1983, executive director Wendy Ann Wood, M.A. Echoes Network is an organization devoted to therapy of victims of childhood sexual abuse. Their quarterly newsletter, *Soundings* uses **poetry on the theme of survival of childhood sexual abuse.** As a sample, I selected this complete poem, "Little One," by Lynn:

> *It hurt to be so small*
> *And have her for the mom*
> *And need a little help*
> *To tie my shoe*
> *To print my name*
> *Or learn a prayer for school.*
> *She was never nice to me.*
> *No one was.*

It is 8 pp. laser printed, stapled at top left. They use 30% of poems received. Press run 1,000-1,500 for 1,000 subscriptions. Subscription: $8. **Sample: $2 plus SASE. Pays 1 copy. Editor often comments on rejections. Reports in 6-8 weeks.** Reviews books of poetry. The editor advises, "Focus on what you have *personally* done to heal from the trauma of childhood sexual abuse. Stay present rather than reliving your life story. If your material is past-oriented then include a progress report explaining where you are now in recovery. Read **Triumph Over Darkness** by W. Wood and L. Hatton [published by Beyond Words Publishing and Echoes Network in 1988] for specific examples."

SOUNDINGS EAST (II), Salem State College, Salem MA 01970, phone (508)741-6270, founded 1973, advisory editor Rod Kessler. "*SE* is published by Salem State College and is staffed by students. We accept short fiction (15 pp. max) and **contemporary poetry (5 pp. max).** Purpose is to promote poetry and fiction in the college and beyond its environs. We **do not want graphic profanity.**" They have recently published poetry by Martha Ramsey, Walter McDonald and Linda Portnay. The editor selected these sample lines from "Muscatine" by Debra Allbery:

> *That night she dreams about California.*
> *The sun there is different—leisurely, decorative,*
> *shining like something you could never afford.*
> *Not like in the Midwest, where the sun is just*
> *one more day—laborer with a job to do. Traveling*
> *its rheumy eye over the fields in winter,*
> *burning too hard on summer weekends, desperate*
> *as anyone to have a good time. In her dream*
> *California is as seasonless as heaven.*

SE appears twice a year, 64-68 pp. digest-sized, flat-spined, b/w drawings and photos, glossy card cover with b/w photo, circulation 2,000, 120 subscriptions of which 35 are libraries. They receive about 500 submissions per year, use 40-60. **Sample: $3 postpaid. Fall deadline November 15; Spring March 15. No manuscripts read over the summer. Photocopies, dot-matrix, simultaneous submissions OK. Reports within 1-4 months. Pays 2 copies.**

‡**SOUNDINGS: JOURNAL OF THE LIVING ARTS; EDGE CITY (II)**, P.O. Box 7075, St. Joseph MO 64507, phone (816)279-6037, founded 1989, is a quarterly. **"We are open-minded. We are an open forum which likes to see traditional forms, but we also prefer insightful, incisive free verse. We do not**

wish to see greeting card verse, predictable rhyme or cutesy poems." They have recently published poetry by William Stafford. As a sample, I selected these lines from "Robert Lowell" by John Gilgun:

> *They said you were a Boston blue blood,*
> *But I knew better. I'd seen mad eyes like yours*
> *In the mirrors of taxis driven by*
> *Lunatic Ukrainian immigrants on Thorazine.*

It is digest-sized, 60 pp., saddle-stapled, professionally printed with matte card cover, using line drawings and photos. They use 10-15% of about 800 submissions/year. Press run 400. Subscription: $8. **Sample postpaid: $3. Pays 1 copy. Previously published poems and simultaneous submissions OK. "We request cover letters from each submission . . . We want to know who you are, not where you've been published before."** Reports in 3 months by handwritten note. Query **regarding chapbook publication under the imprint Edge City.** They review chapbooks and other magazines. "We'd like to see more people read the small presses. No press is an island."

SOUTH CAROLINA REVIEW (II), English Dept., Clemson U., Clemson SC 29634-1503, phone (803)656-3229, founded 1968, editor Richard J. Calhoun, is a biannual literary magazine "recognized by the *New York Quarterly* as one of the top 20 of this type." They will consider **"any kind of poetry as long as it's good. Format should be according to new MLA Stylesheet."** They have recently published poems by Jay A. Blumethal, J. W. Rivers and Claire Bateman. The editor selected these sample lines by John Lane:

> *Who is to say if bodies wrapped in a slow roll*
> *are mounted rock in a spreading floor,*
> *or if he did see a child grind off a bench*
> *like a loose glacier? I loved him with all his faults.*

It is a 6×9", 200+ pp., flat-spined, professionally printed magazine which uses about 8-10 pp. of poetry in each issue, has a circulation of 600, 400 subscriptions of which 250 are libraries. Subscription: $7. They receive about 1,000 freelance submissions of poetry per year of which they use 10, have a 2-year backlog. **Do not submit during June, July, August or November. Sample: $5 postpaid. Reports in 6-9 months, pays in copies.** Reviews books of poetry.

SOUTH COAST POETRY JOURNAL (II), English Dept., California State University, Fullerton CA 92634, founded 1986, editor John J. Brugaletta. The twice-yearly (January and June) magazine publishes poetry only. **"We'd like to see poems with strong imagery and a sense that the poem has found its best form, whether that form is traditional or innovative. We prefer poems under 40 lines, but we'll look at others. Any subject-matter or style.** We have recently published Denise Levertov, Mark Strand, X.J. Kennedy and Robert Mezey." As a sample, the editor selected these lines from "All That Jazz" by Sue Walker:

> *This year my brother's on probation*
> *with the law, but I've got a Sugar*
> *Daddy who comes down with hard cash.*
> *He says we'll do the Quarter,*
> *listen to Al Hirt's horn sing*
> *"Way Down Yonder In New Orleans."*
> *I tell him I want to ride*
> *the streetcar "Desire," breakfast*
> *at Brennans — all that jazz.*

The journal is digest-sized, 60 pp., perfect-bound, offset, heavy paper cover, some line art. Print run is 500, 150 subscribers, 25 of which are libraries, 50 shelf sales. Subscription: $9, $5/issue. **Sample: $3.50 postpaid. Guidelines are available for SASE. Pay is 2 copies. Do not submit in June, July or August. No simultaneous submissions. Every submission is read by at least three editors. Submissions will be reported on in 6-8 weeks.** They conduct an annual poetry contest judged by eminent poets — most recently: Philip Levine. Entry fee is $3/poem.

SOUTH DAKOTA REVIEW (II,IV-Regional, themes), University of South Dakota, Vermillion SD 57069, phone (605)677-5220 or 677-5229, founded 1963, editor John R. Milton, is a "literary quarterly publishing poetry, fiction, criticism, essays. **When material warrants, an emphasis on the American West; writers from the West; Western places or subjects; frequent issues with no geographical emphasis; periodic special issues on one theme, or one place or one writer. Looking for originality, some kind of sophistication, significance, craft—i.e., professional work. Nothing confessional, purely descriptive, too filled with self-importance.** They use 6-10 poems/issue, "receive tons, it seems." Print run 650-900 for 450 subscriptions of which half are libraries. Subscription: $15/year, $25/2 years. **Sample, postpaid: $4. Pays 1 copy per page. Reports in 1-12 weeks. Editor comments on submissions "rarely."** He says, "Find universal meaning in the regional. Avoid constant 'I' personal experiences that are not of interest to anyone else. Learn to be less self-centered and more objective."

THE SOUTH FLORIDA POETRY REVIEW (II), 7190 N.W. 21 St., Ft. Lauderdale FL 33313, *Review* founded 1983, poetry editor S.A. Stirnemann, uses "previously unpublished free verse or traditional poetry, none that is religious without ingenuity. We try to attract a variety of poetic styles with a common denominator of quality. We take pride in finding 'new' talent, and admit to delight in publishing Florida poets who deserve the recognition, but we also publish nationally recognized poets." They have published poetry by Marvin Bell, Mark Jarman, Philip Levine, Lisel Mueller, William Stafford and Diane Wakoski. The editors selected these sample lines from "At the Edge of the Hollow" by Edward Byrne:

> *A crane raises large rocks*
> *and spins slowly at the edge of the hollow.*
> *I watch it circle and admire the driver's skill,*
> *the way he seems to have a soft touch, able*
> *to balance the load fished from the bottom silt*

They have a new poetry review section and are looking for essay reviews of recently published books of poetry (published in the previous year) as well as interviews with established poets and essays on contemporary American poetry. The *Review* is perfect-bound, a magazine-sized triquarterly, 68 pp. (including tinted paper cover), circulation 500 with 400 subscriptions of which 20 are libraries. They receive about 2,000 submissions per year, use 130. **Sample: $3.50 postpaid; subscription: $7.50. "We read all year but less in the summer. Submit up to 6 poems, previously unpublished, with SASE and brief bio sketch." Reports within 3 months. Considers simultaneous submissions. Pays 2 copies.** "If we are attracted to a good MS we sometimes reject with suggestions. Submissions that are illegible or hand-corrected make a bad impression. We tend to like subtly strong images; poems, which have something new to say, with originality, even if the subject matter is old."

THE SOUTHERN CALIFORNIA ANTHOLOGY; ANN STANFORD POETRY PRIZES (III), c/o Master of Professional Writing Program, WPH 404, University of Southern California, Los Angeles CA 90089-4034, phone (213)743-8255, founded 1983, is an "annual literary review of serious contemporary poetry and fiction. **Very open to all subject matters except pornography. Any form, style OK.**" They have recently published poetry by Robery Bly, John Updike, Denise Levertov, Peter Viereck, Donald Hall, James Merrill and Yevgeny Yevtushenko. As a sample the editor selected these lines from "The Tent People of Beverly Hills" by James Ragan:

> *Faceless on the Boulevard of Mirrors,*
> *North along the flats of Rodeo's stripped*
> *baldhead mannequins*
> *they come treading on*

The anthology is digest-sized, 144 pp., paperback, with a semi-glossy color cover featuring one art piece. Circulation is 1,500, 50% going to subscribers of which 50% are libraries. 30% are for shelf sales. **Sample: $5.95 postpaid. Send SASE for guidelines. Pays 3 copies. Reports in 4 months. Submit 3-5 poems between September 1 and January 1. All decisions made by mid-February. Legible photocopied submissions OK, computer printout submissions acceptable, no dot-matrix, no simultaneous submissions, no previously published poems.** The Ann Stanford Poetry Prizes ($750, $250 and $100) has a March 1 deadline, $10 fee (5 poem limit), for unpublished poems. Include cover sheet with name, address and titles and SASE for contest results. All entries are considered for publication.

SOUTHERN HUMANITIES REVIEW (II, IV-Translations), 9088 Haley Center, Auburn University AL 36849, poetry editor R. T. Smith, co-editors T. L. Wright and D. R. Latimer, founded 1967, is a 100+ pp. 6×9″ literary quarterly, circulation 800. **Interested in poems of any length, subject, genre. Space is limited, and brief poems are more likely to be accepted. "Several poems at a time recommended. Avoid sending faint computer printout. Pays 1 copy and $50 for the best poem published during the year. Translations welcome."** They have recently published poetry by Lars Gustaffson, Donald Hall, Reynolds Price, Mary Ruefle, James Seay, Robert Morgan and John Engels. **Sample copy, $4,** subscription $12/year. **Responds in 30-60 days, possibly longer in summer.** Reviews books of poetry. The editors advise, "For beginners we'd recommend study and wide reading in English and classical literature, and, of course, American literature – the old works, not just the new. We also recommend study of or exposure to a foreign language and a foreign culture. Poets need the reactions of others to their work: criticism, suggestions, discussion. A good creative writing teacher would be desirable here, and perhaps some course work too. And then submission of work, attendance at workshops. And again, the reading: history, biography, verse, essays – all of it. We want to see poems that have gone beyond the language of slippage and easy attitudes."

SOUTHERN POETRY REVIEW; GUY OWEN POETRY PRIZE (II), English Dept., University of North Carolina, Charlotte NC 28223, phone (704)547-4225, editor Robert Grey, founded 1958, a semiannual literary magazine "with emphasis on effective poetry. **Not a regional magazine, but a natural outlet for new Southern talent."** There are no restrictions on form, style or content of poetry; **length subject to limitations of space. They do not want to see anything "cute, sweet, sentimental, arrogant or preachy."** They have recently published work by Linda Pastan, Judith Ortiz Cofer, David Ray, Stephen Sandy, Betty Adcock and Walter McDonald. As a sample, I chose the first stanza from "Museum Piece" by Barbara Fritchie:

> Past survival, he killed for
> trophies. His wife said dead things
> have no decorative value.
> She never understood
> the importance of a good mount.

Southern Poetry Review is 6×9", handsomely printed on buff stock, 78 pp. flat-spined with textured, one-color matte card cover. Circulation is 1,000+, price per copy $3.50, subscription $6/year. **Sample available for $2 postpaid; no guidelines, but will answer queries with SASE. Pays 1 copy. Writers should submit no more than 3-5 poems. Reporting time is 4-6 weeks, and poems should be printed within a year of acceptance.** There is a yearly contest, the Guy Owen Poetry Prize of $500, to which the entry fee is a subscription; deadline is normally about May 1.

‡SOUTHERN REVIEW (II), University of Adelaide, Adelaide South Australia 5001, founded in the 1960s, poetry editor Anne Brewster, Curtain University of Technology, appears 3 times a year **using poetry that is not sexist, racist.** They have recently published poetry by Andrew Lansdown. As a sample the editor selected these lines from "On the Ask" by Geoff Goodfellow:

> Outside a city bluestone squat
> he struggles for balance
> TRY ME screams off his tee-shirt
> in six inch block
> eases from eyes bottle brown—
> port red

It is digest-sized, 100 pp., flat-spined. Press run 500 for 375 subscribers. **Sample postpaid: A$12. Reports in 3 months. Pays 1 copy.**

THE SOUTHERN REVIEW (II), 43 Allen Hall, Louisiana State University, Baton Rouge LA 70803, phone (504)388-5108, founded 1935 (original series); 1965 (new series), poetry editors James Olney and Dave Smith, "is a literary quarterly which publishes fiction, poetry, critical essays, book reviews, with emphasis on contemporary literature in the US and abroad, and with special interest in Southern culture and history. Selections are made with careful attention to craftsmanship and technique and to the seriousness of the subject matter." By general agreement this is one of the most distinguished of literary journals. Joyce Carol Oates, for instance, says, "Over the years I have continued to be impressed with the consistent high quality of *SR*'s publications and its general 'aura,' which bespeaks careful editing, adventuresome tastes, and a sense of thematic unity. *SR* is characterized by a refreshing openness to new work, placed side by side with that of older, more established, and in many cases highly distinguished writers." The editors say they want "**No particular kinds of poetry. We are interested in any formal varieties, traditional or modern, that are well crafted, though we cannot normally accommodate excessively long poems (say 10 pp. and over).**" They have recently published poetry by A.R. Ammons, Yvonne Sapia, Nancy Schoenberger and Miller Williams. The editors selected these sample lines by Mary Oliver:

> The story about Jesus in the cave
> is a good one,
> > but when is it ever like that
>
> as sharp as lightning,
> > or even the way the green sea does everything—
> > quickly,
> > and with such grace?

The beautifully printed quarterly is massive: 6¾×10", 240+ pp., flat-spined, matte card cover, print-run 3,100 with 2,100 subscriptions of which 70% are libraries. Subscription: $15. They receive about 2,000 freelance submissions of poetry, use 10%. **Sample: $5 postpaid. Prefer 1-4**

Use the General Index to find the page number of a specific publication or publisher.

pp. submissions. Reports in 2 months. Pays $20/printed page plus 2 copies. Send SASE for guidelines.

SOUTHWEST REVIEW; ELIZABETH MATCHETT STOVER MEMORIAL AWARD (II), 6410 Airline Rd., Southern Methodist University, Dallas TX 75275, phone (214)373-7440, founded 1915, editor Willard Spiegelman. *Southwest Review* is a literary quarterly that publishes fiction, essays, poetry and interviews. "It is hard to describe our preference for poetry in a few words. We always suggest that potential contributors read several issues of the magazine to see for themselves what we like. But some things may be said: We demand **very high quality in our poems; we accept both traditional and experimental writing, but avoid unnecessary obscurity and private symbolism; we place no arbitrary limits on length but find shorter poems easier to fit into our format than longer ones. We have no specific limitations as to theme."** No simultaneous submissions, no previously published work. Photocopies OK. They have recently published poetry by George Bradley, Debora Greger, Rachel Itadas, Marie Ponsot and Howard Nemerov. As a sample I selected "The Fifteenth Summer" by James Merrill:

> Why were we here?
> To flow. To bear. To be.
> Over the view his tree
> In slow, slow motion
> Held sway, the pointer of a scale so vast,
>
> Alive and variable, so inlaid
> As well with sticky, pungent gold,
> That many a year
> Would pass before it told
> Those mornings what they weighed.

The 6 × 9″ 144 pp. perfect-bound journal is professionally printed, matte text stock cover, circulation 1,500 with 1,000 subscriptions of which 600 are libraries. Subscription: $20. They receive about 700 freelance submissions of poetry per year, use 24. **Sample: $5 postpaid. Reports within a month. Pays cash plus copies. Send SASE for guidelines.** $150 annual Elizabeth Matchett Stover Memorial Prize for best poem, chosen by editors, published in preceding year.

SOU'WESTER (II), Box 1438, Southern Illinois University, Edwardsville IL 62026, phone (618)692-3190, founded 1960, editor Fred W. Robbins, appears 3 times a year. **"We like poetry with imagery and figurative language that has strong associations and don't care for abstract poetry. We have no particular preference for form or length."** They have recently published poetry by J.D. Smith, Walter Griffin and Douglas Leonard. The editor selected the first stanza of "Casting the Friendship Circle" by Susan Swartwout:

> In this singular season, words
> rise like sap, darkness
> lifts, green buds appear
> along branches in
> roughest bark. Secure
> with unleaving, we ripen,
> turn, drift down to the river's
> surface filmy with our dreams.
> We are free.

There are 25-30 pp. in each 6 × 9″ 80 pp. issue. The magazine is professionally printed, flat-spined, with textured matte card cover, circulation 300, 110 subscriptions of which 50 are libraries. Subscription: $10 (3 issues). They receive some 2,000 poems (from 600 poets) each year, use 36-40, have a 2 month backlog. **Sample: $5 postpaid. Simultaneous submission, photocopy and dot-matrix OK. Rejections usually within four weeks. Pays 2 copies. Editor comments on rejections "usually, in the case of those that we almost accept. Read poetry past and present. Have something to say and say it in your own voice. Poetry is a very personal thing for many editors. When all else fails, we may rely on gut reactions, so take whatever hints you're given to improve your poetry, and keep submitting."**

THE SOW'S EAR (II, IV-Regional, children), 245 McDowell St., Bristol TN 37620, phone (615)764-1625, founded 1988, co-editors Errol Hess and Larry Richman, a quarterly. **"We are very open to form, style, length of poems. We see *TSE* as a three-ring circus—with a flair for the visual, which is very much lacking from most poetry journals. The inside ring is the central Appalachian community focused in the area where Tennessee, Kentucky, North Carolina, West Virginia and Virginia come close together. The middle ring is the broader Appalachian region; a culture where we believe a poetry renaissance is beginning. The outer ring is the largest possible community, wherever the English language is spoken and written in poetic form. We encourage submissions from school-age children**

and plan to feature occasionally a previously unpublished poet." They have recently published poetry by Josephine Jacobsen and William Stafford. As a sample the editors selected these lines from "Perfection" by Kerry Shawn Keys:

> When the chips are down
> the axe should be in the air
> feet firmly planted on the ground
> the eyes foursquare and everywhere
> the grain of the wood
> parallel to the spine
> in line with earth and heaven.

TSE is 32 pp. magazine-sized, saddle-stapled, with matte card cover, professionally printed. They accept about 150 of 4,000 poems submitted. Press run: 1,000 for 500 subscribers of which 15 are libraries. Shelf sales: 100-200. Subscription: $10. **Sample postpaid: $3.50. Send SASE for guidelines. Pays 1 copy. Reports in 3-9 months. Simultaneous submissions OK if you tell them promptly when it is accepted elsewhere. Enclose brief bio. "We want to know if the poet has not yet been published or is a youth, as we have features for both." Editor comments on submissions "if poet specifically requests it."** Reviews books of poetry. Richman selects the kids' poems; others chosen by a 3-person board that meets quarterly. They offer an annual contest with fee of $2/poem, $500 prize. For contest, submit 1-5 poems in October-November. Submissions with $10 receive 1 year subscription. 1990 judge: Fred Chappell. Larry Richman says, "We believe you can make an entire line of fantastic invisible accessories out of a mama pig's ear."

SPACE AND TIME (V), #4B, 138 W. 70th St., New York NY 10023-4432, founded 1966, poetry editor Gordon Linzner, is a biannual "publishing **science fiction & fantasy material – particularly hard-to-market mixed genres and work by new writers. They are not accepting MSS at this time.**" They have published poetry by Steve Eng, Denise Dumars and Neal F. Wilgus. The editor selected these sample lines from "In Man's Image" by D.M. Vosk:

> Gull and loon once left their print
> Within the oceans' reach
> Now a robot, stained with mint
> Is dancing on the beach

The 120 pp. digest-sized journal, saddle-stapled, photo reduced from typescript with b/w drawings, has a circulation of 400-500 with 150 subscriptions of which 5 are libraries.

‡**SPARETIME EDITIONS; HMS PRESS; (I)**, Box 340 Station B, London, Ontario N6A 4W1 Canada, phone (519)434-4740, founded 1982, editors Wayne Ray and Joe Blades. They **publish books on a cooperative arrangement. "If any prepayment is asked for it is to cover typesetting cost. I pay for printing."** Pays 10% minimum royalties, 50% maximum, plus "33%" author's copies. They have recently published poetry by Bill Bissett, Milton Acron, Joe Blades and James Deahl. Their books are distributed by The Book Club of the Canadian Poetry Association (see listing under Organizations).

SPARROW PRESS; SPARROW POVERTY PAMPHLETS; VAGROM CHAP BOOKS (V), 103 Waldron St., West Lafayette IN 47906, phone (317)743-1991, publisher Felix Stefanile. This is one of the oldest and most highly respected small press publishers of poetry in the country. "**Sparrow Press announces a change in policy. Henceforth, we shall only publish the work of invited poets. Unsolicited manuscripts will not be considered.**" Subscription for 1992: $10.50 for three consecutive issues of the Sparrow Poverty Pamphlets. These come out erratically, but inevitably. Vagrom Chap Books issued occasionally. Sample copies: $2 for our pamphlets, $3 for chapbooks. "**Correspondence received without self-addressed, stamped return envelope included will not be honored.** We are enthusiastic about our newly declared future." As a sample the publisher selected this excerpt from one of their recent poets, Wally Swist:

> old road through the hills
> fallen leaves
> fill the potholes

"**Modest pay scale planned plus author's copies.** We are working up a contest volume, with good cash prize, as well."

‡**SPECTACLES (II)**, P.O. Box 191534, San Francisco CA 94119-1534, founded 1989, editors Alan Byers and Susan McCarthy McDonald, is a quarterly using "**modern poems in lines or prose poems that take risks. Well-crafted poems of any subject matter by serious writers. Nothing pretentious, amateurish or rhyming.**" They have recently published poetry by Charlotte Muse, Elin Schneeman and William Petersen. As a sample the editor selected these lines (poet unidentified):

> Mysterious, how her center shifts
> with your eyes

> *It is her throat bare and damp, a kind of wrist.*
> *Nothing stops there but you.*

I have not seen an issue, but the editor describes it as 16 pp.,magazine-sized on glossy stock. They accept about 20% of 120 MSS received/year. Press run 500 for 25 subscribers, 50 shelf sales.It is distributed free in coffee shops and cafes. Subscription:$9. **Sample: $3. Pays 1 copy. Submit maximum of 5 poems. Response within 3 months. Comments "if something struck us, or if it's asked for."** They have a special page for "unusual or funny poems — usually short." The editor advises, "Take workshops! Read a lot of poetry — modern and classic. Attend readings. Keep your sense of humor; it's a tough racket!"

SPECTACULAR DISEASES (II), 83B London Rd., Peterborough, Cambridgeshire PE2 9BS UK, founded 1974, Paul Green editor (various invited poetry editors). "The press presents **experimental writing with bias to the current French scene and to current, and past scenes, in the US, and Britain. Most poetry is solicited by the editors.** Long poems will be clearly accepted, if falling in the special categories." They have published poetry by Saúl Yurkievich, Jackson MacLow, and Bernard Noël. *Spectacular Diseases* is an annual digest-sized 40-60 pp." **Sample of *SD* £1.75 postpaid. Query before submitting as most material is invited. Pays in copies.** Under the Spectacular Diseases imprint a number of books and anthologies are printed. For book consideration, **query with about 16 samples; letter helpful but not essential. Pays 10% of run.** Send postage for catalog to buy samples.

SPECTRUM (II), Anna Maria College, Box 72-D, Paxton MA 01612, phone (508)757-4586, founded 1985, poetry editor Joseph Wilson, is a "multidisciplinary national publication with liberal arts emphasis, presenting 6-8 poems in each 66 page issue: **poems of crisp images, precise language, which have something of value to say and say it in an authentic voice. Not the self-conscious, the 'workshop poem,' the cliché, the self-righteous."** They have recently published poetry by William Stafford. *Spectrum* appears twice a year in a 6 × 9" flat-spined format, professionally printed on quality stock with 2-color matte card cover, using b/w photos and art. "We have had to solicit to get the poetry we want, but would rather not." Press run is 1,000 for 650 subscriptions (200 of them to libraries). Per copy: $4. Subscription: $7 for 1 year, $13 for 2 years. **Sample: $3. Pays $20 per poem plus 2 copies. No previously published poems or simultaneous submissions. Reports in 6 weeks.** Editor "occasionally" comments on rejections.

SPINDRIFT (II), Shoreline Community College, 16101 Greenwood Ave., Seattle WA 98133, founded 1962, faculty advisor varies each year, currently Carol Orlock, is **open to all varieties of poetry except greeting-card style.** They have recently published poetry by Judith Barrington, Paula Jones, Sibyl James, Pesha Gertler, Tom Synder, and Richard West. *Spindrift*, an annual, is handsomely printed in an 8" square, flat-spined 125 pp. format, circulation 500. Price per issue: $6.50. **Sample: $5 postpaid. Send SASE for guidelines. Pays 1 copy. "Submit 2 copies of each poem, 6 maximum. Include cover letter with biographical information. We accept submissions until February 1 — report back in March."** The editors advise, "Read what the major contemporary poets are writing. Read what local poets are writing. Be distinctive, love the language, avoid sentiment."

SPINSTERS BOOK COMPANY; (IV-Women), Box 410687, San Francisco CA 94141, phone (415)558-9586, founded 1978, publisher Sherry Thomas, a small-press publisher of paperback books of fiction, non-fiction, limited poetry — **by and for women.** "Publishes 6-8 books a year, but only one poetry title every two years." As a sample, the publisher selected the following lines by Minnie Bruce Pratt:

> *getting to be a grown girl, I iron the cotton sheets*
> *into perfect blankness. No thump shakes Laura, dreaming in the straight-backed chair,*
> *upright, eyes closed, dark brown*
> *face crumpled in an hour's rest from generations of children*

That is from **We Say We Love Each Other**, a handsomely printed and designed flat-spined 6 × 9" paperback, glossy card cover with two-tone photograph, 100 pp. with b/w photo of author on last page. The publisher **accepts freelance submissions but writers should *"query first."*** She reports on queries in 2 weeks, MS in 6 months. Photocopied MSS are OK, dot-matrix OK if double-strike. The cover letter should include credits and bio. Royalties are 7-11%.

THE SPIRIT THAT MOVES US; THE SPIRIT THAT MOVES US PRESS; EDITOR'S CHOICE (IV-Anthology), P.O. Box 820, Jackson Heights NY 11372, phone (718)426-8788, founded 1974, poetry editor Morty Sklar. *"The Spirit That Moves Us* will be continuing its **Editor's Choice** series biennially, and publishing regular issues only occasionally. **Editor's Choice** consists of reprints from other literary magazines and small presses, where our selections are made from nominations made by the editors of those magazines and presses." They have recently published poetry by Thomas McGrath, Michael Hogan, Miriam Halliday-Borkowski and Robert Peters. As a sample the editor selected these lines from "First Snow" by Ellen Biss:

> *Because we have no snow*
> *flames of water flicker*
> *beneath the creek ice*
> *and the sun rests on dark boughs*
> *like first snow.*

The editor's advice: "Write what you would like to write, in a style (or styles) which is/are best for your own expression. Don't worry about acceptance, though you may be concerned about it. Don't just send work which you think editors would like to see, though take that into consideration. Think of the relationship between poem, poet and editor as personal. You may send good poems to editors who simply do not like them, whereas other editors might."

‡SPIT (I, II), 529 2nd St., Brooklyn NY 11215, phone (718)499-7343 or (212)673-3546, founded 1989, edited collectively, appears twice a year using **poetry "judged on artistic merit rather than polemical intent."** They have recently published poetry by Warrick Wynne and Barbara Rosenthal. As a sample the editors selected these lines from "Politics" by Claas Ehlers:

> *On the beach where oceans come in light blue water*
> *At the horizon, more enormous than the tilted moon and gray*
> *—like early morning*
> *Can you see it, Susie, the aircraft carrier, can you see it?*

It is magazine-sized, 50-75 pp., flat-spined, with card cover, desktop published. Press run is 400 for 15 subscriptions of which 1 is a library. Subscription: $12. **Sample postpaid: $2. Send SASE for guidelines. Pays 1 copy. "Poems should be typed and submitted (if possible) in triplicate. Include a cover letter with name, address and a short biographical statement. Do not print name on poems." Previously published poems and simultaneous submissions OK, if so indicated. Reports in 1-6 months. Editors comment on rejections "though not extensive. We are always willing to send more detailed comments if the writer requests."** Joan Dalin advises, "Don't be afraid to be playful, to have *fun* in your poems. Don't work too hard to make a significant statement/metaphor. Imitate your favorite poets. Read a lot. Submit your poems to magazines in which you admire the poetry. Correspond with poets you like. Don't worry too much about publication."

SPITBALL; CASEY AWARD (IV-Sports), 6224 Collegevue Pl., Cincinnati OH 45224, phone (513)541-4296, founded 1981, poetry editor Virgil Smith, is "a unique literary magazine devoted to poetry, fiction and book reviews *exclusively* **about baseball.** Newcomers are very welcome, but remember that you have to know the subject. We do and our readers do. Perhaps a good place to start for beginners is one's personal reactions to the game, *a* game, a player, etc. & take it from there." As a sample I selected the last stanza of "Curt Flood" by Tim Peeler:

> *you are a ghost at barterer's wing,*
> *your smoky gray eyes*
> *are two extra zeroes*
> *on every contract.*

The digest-sized 52 pp. quarterly, saddle-stapled, matte card cover, offset from typescript, has a circulation of 1,000, 750+ subscriptions of which 25 are libraries. Subscription: $12. They receive about 1,000 submissions per year, use 40—very small backlog. "Many times we are able to publish accepted work almost immediately." **Sample: $5 postpaid. "We are not very concerned with the technical details of submitting, but we do prefer a cover letter with some bio info. We also like batches of poems and prefer to use several of same poet in an issue rather than a single poem." Pays 2 copies.** "We encourage anyone interested to submit to *Spitball*. We are always looking for fresh talent. Those who have never written 'baseball poetry' before should read some first probably before submitting. Not necessarily ours. We sponsor the Casey Award (for best baseball book of the year) and the Casey Awards Banquet every January. Any chapbook of baseball poetry should be sent to us for consideration for the 'Casey' plaque that we award to the winner each year."

‡SPLIT PERSONALITY PRESS; HEATHENZINE; TEMM (II), 511 W. Sullivan, Olean NY 14760, founded 1989, editor Ken Wagner. Split Personality Press publishes 6 poetry chapbooks/year. *HEATHENzine* appears every other month. *temm* appears monthly, **"providing an 'overview' forum for all poetic voices. All styles are included, from lyrical/imaginal to naive/primitive, and *everything* in between. Work should be 'accessible' without compromising *truth*. No inauthentic concocted crap."** *temm* has recently published these lines from "making it" by Richard Wilmarth:

> *bills came in the mail*
> *and they opened them with haste*
> *on their way to shop*
> *at the mall in the city*

in a car that was paid for

HEATHEN*zine* wants **poetry that is "really *raw* or *odd*, nothing nicey-nicey/rhymey-rhymey.".** It has recently published poetry by Lyn Lifshin, Todd Moore and John M. Bennett. As a sample the editor selected this poem, "Free Associations," by Stacey Sollfrey:

> *she sucked his beard smiling*
> *as he unhooked all the unchained necklaces*
> *loosely around her neck*
> *giving her a back*
> *with anything it wanted*
> *and everything she chose it to have*

Both magazines are printed in a 4×7" format, photocopied from typescript with matte card cover, saddle-stapled, with press runs of 200-260. Subscription to either is $12/year. **Samples of either: $2 postpaid. Guidelines printed in each issue. Each pays 1 copy. "I prefer to receive cover letter with information concerning latest books, chaps for a contributor's note. Not required. Newcomers and primitives are always welcome providing that the work is of high quality. Previously published poems and simultaneous submissions OK (sometimes). Comments when writer is worth it. I report in 1 week-3 months. Sometimes I don't even send a note that work has been accepted, and just send a contributor's copy with their work in it. This occurs when I receive a strong submission late and choose to bump something else off for it." For chapbook consideration "send bio letter listing credits, along with 3-5 poems. I generally do like to print excerpts from chaps I publish in my magazines." Pays 5-25% royalties plus 25-100 copies. The** editor advises, "create real art straight from your gut or your heart or wherever the hell it comes from, and push it push it push it—someone will publish it. One of my primary talents as an editor seems to be an ability to choose strong work, and then to put it together so that it really works emotionally. Prefer to do chaps by writers who have done at least 3 previously."

SPOON RIVER QUARTERLY (II,IV-Regional, translations), English Dept., Illinois State University, Normal IL 61761, phone (309)438-3667, founded 1976, poetry editor Lucia Getsi, is a "poetry quarterly that features newer and well-known poets from around the country and world;" features **one Illinois poet per issue** at length for the *SRQ* Illinois Poet Series among other national and international poets. (Spoon River Poetry Press, Box 1443, Peoria IL 61655, editor David Pichaske, is still in operation.) "We want interesting and compelling poetry that operates beyond the ho-hum, so-what level, in any form or style about anything; language that is fresh, energetic, committed, filled with some strong voice of authority that grabs the reader in the first line and never lets go. Do not want to see insipid, dull, boring poems, especially those that I cannot ascertain why they're in lines and not paragraphs; poetry which, if you were to put it into paragraphs, would become bad prose." They also use translations of poetry. They have recently published poetry by Frankie Paino, Tim Seibles, Paulette Roeske, Walter McDonald, Elaine Terranova, Jeff Gundy and Kathariné Soniat. As a sample Lucia Getsi selected these lines by Helen Degen Cohen:

> *A darkness, a house*
> *we cannot come out of,*
> *cannot see out of.*
> *Nor even remember*

SRQ has a beautifully produced flat-spined 64 pp., digest-sized, laser set format with glossy card cover using photos, ads. They accept about 2% of 1,000 poems received per month. Press run is 500 for 300 subscriptions (75 of them libraries), and some shelf sales. Subscription: $12. **Sample: $4 postpaid. Pays 3 copies. Reports in 8 weeks. "No simultaneous submissions unless we are notified immediately if a submission is accepted elsewhere. We accept chapbook-length submissions of unpublished poems from poets who have an Illinois connection, by birth or current residence." Editor comments on rejections "many times, if a poet is promising."**

SQUEAKY WHEELS PRESS (IV-Anthology, specialized), 75 DeSoto, San Francisco CA 94127, phone (415)587-2885, founded 1987, editor Cheryl Marie Wade, publishes a semiannual anthology of poetry, prose and art by disabled writers about disability. "We highly encourage submissions by people of color; lesbians and gay men; women and men with cancer, AIDS and other life-threatening disabilities; and people with hearing and/or visual impairments. No more than 6 poems. We welcome all styles and forms. We look for clear and powerful communication." They have published poetry by editor Cheryl Marie Wade, Zara, Neil Marcus and Kenny Fries. As a sample the editor selected these lines from "I Am Not One of The" by herself:

> *I am not one of the physically challenged—*
> *I'm a sock in the eye with gnarled fist*
> *I'm a French kiss with cleft tongue*
> *I'm orthopedic shoes sewn on a last of your fears*

Sample postpaid: $10 for most recent anthology or Close to the Truth (1989). Pays 1 copy, others

at half-price. **Simultaneous submissions and previously published poems OK if noted. Response time: 2 weeks-2 months. No response without SASE. All future books will be published when enough good work is received. Editor comments on submissions when asked.** The 1991 anthology, *Range of Motion*, is 6×9″, flat-spined, professionally printed, 120+ pp. with glossy card cover. "We want work that reflects the rich diversity of our disability community, work that is honest, full-blooded, work that offers insights into the complexity of our lives as disabled women and men. Do not want 'this is what happened to me' stories, or 'poor me' stuff. Think of this as an antidote to telethons."

STAND MAGAZINE; NORTHERN HOUSE (II, IV-Translations), 19 Haldane Terrace, Newcastle on Tyne NE2 3AN, England. US Editor: Prof. Jessie Emerson, P.O. Box 5923, Huntsville AL 35814 (all US contributions to US editor please). *Stand*, founded by editor Jon Silkin in 1952, is a highly esteemed literary quarterly. Jon Silkin seeks more subscriptions from US readers and also hopes "that the magazine **would be seriously treated as an alternative platform to American literary journals.**" He **wants "verse that tries to explore forms. No formulaic verse."** They have recently published poems by such poets as Peter Redgrove, Elizabeth Jennings and Barry Spacks. I selected a sample from "The Meon Hill Picket" by Yann Lovelock:

> Something must be done about this.
> The beech leaves hiss on the hill's verge.
> From the little cars in the field below
> Hang-gliders climb the slope with their women.

Library Journal calls *Stand* "one of England's best, liveliest and truly imaginative little magazines." Among better-known American poets whose work has appeared there are Robert Bly, William Stafford, David Ignatow, Philip Levine and Richard Eberhart. Poet Donald Hall says of it, "among essential magazines, there is Jon Silkin's *Stand*, politically left, with reviews, poems and much translation from continental literature." In its current format it is 6×8″, flat-spined 80 pp., professionally printed in 2 columns, small type, on thin stock with glossy card cover, using ads. Circulation is 4,500 with 2,800 subscriptions of which 600 are libraries. Subscription: $22. **Sample: $6.50 postpaid. Pays £30 per poem (unless under 6 lines) and 1 copy (⅓ off additional copies). Northern House "publishes mostly small collections of poetry by new or established poets. The pamphlets often contain a group of poems written to one theme. Occasionally larger volumes are published,** such as the full-length collection by Sorley Maclean, translated by Iain Crichton Smith." The sample I have seen is a handsomely printed chapbook, digest-sized: **The Constitution of Things** by Michael Blackburn, £1.25 or $2.50.

‡**THE STANDING STONE (I, IV-Horror/Fantasy)**, Ebenrock Enterprises, 120 Perth Ave. #312, Toronto, Ontario M6P 4E1 Canada, founded 1990, editor Gordon R. Menzies, a quarterly (beginning with 2 in 1991), **"publishes short horror and fantasy poetry (high fantasy, traditional, sword & sorcery, speculative), any form or style."** I have not seen an issue, but the editor describes it as 40 pp. digest-sized, photocopied or done on laser printer, saddle-stapled, with light cardstock cover. Press run 150+. Sample: $3 postpaid. **Pays 10/line, minimum $1 plus 1 copy. Send SASE for guidelines. "typed double-spaced with name, address and word count on the top left side of the first page, surname, abbreviation of title and a page number on the top right. No dot matrix. Please include a brief bio with all submissions. Those without SASE will not be returned."** They are planning to start an annual contest with small cash prizes. The editor comments, "If you have regular access to the book you are now holding in your hands, the only excuse you will have for being unpublished is that you're lazy."

STAPLE (I, II), Derbyshire College of Higher Education, Mickleover, Derby, Derbyshire DE3 5GX United Kingdom, phone 0332-47181, founded 1983, editorial contact D. C. Measham, business manager. This literary magazine appears 3 times a year. **"Nothing barred: Evidence of craft, but both traditional and modernist accepted; no totally esoteric or concrete poetry."** They have published poetry by Fleur Adcock, Jon Silkin, Philip Callow, Peter Cash, and David Craig. As a sample D. C. Measham selected these lines from "Two Spring Sonnets" by John Sewell:

> The husks split clean, an early butterfly
> swoons past, a new-lit dung fly plants his feet
> into my dung, his share of my beneficence.

Staple is professionally printed, flat-spined, 80 pp., with card cover. Of up to 2,000 poems received per year they accept about 10%. Their press run is 600 with 300 subscriptions. Subscription: £7 (sterling only). **Sample: £2 postpaid. Guidelines available for SASE. Pays modest fee plus complimentary copy (or free subscription). They consider simultaneous submissions but previously published poems only under special circumstance. Reports in up to 3 months. Editor sometimes comments on rejections.** Send SASE (or SAE with IRC) for rules for their open biennial competitions and for *Staple First Editions* monographs (next competition: 1992).

STAR BOOKS, INC.; STARLIGHT MAGAZINE (I, IV-Spirituality/Inspirational), 408 Pearson St., Wilson NC 27893, phone (919)237-1591, founded 1983, president Irene Burk Harrell, who says they are "very enthusiastically open to beginners. We have published nine volumes of poetry to date, four of which were written by persons who had no previous publication record. All of our poetry is specifically Christian, in line with the teachings of the Bible. We're looking for the fresh and the new. Can't use avant-garde and/or esoteric. For us the impact of the *thought* of a poem is paramount. Need more short poems, with short lines." They have published books of poetry by Rose Ellen Lewis, Norma Woodbridge and Charlotte Carpenter. "Contributors to our *StarLight* magazine are largely previously unpublished." As a sample she selected these lines from Gennet Emery's "Lament for a Child" in her *Wayfarer:*

> Some thought the pain was less
> Because I never saw you
>
> But oh, I did!
> My heart and mind wove textured skin,
> Caressed your cheeks, touched finespun hair
> And smelled sweet breath.

The book is 128 pp., digest-sized, flat-spined, professionally printed, with glossy card cover: $8. *StarLight* is a quarterly, digest-sized, 60 pp., saddle-stapled, professionally printed, with matte card cover. Subscription: $15. Guidelines available for SASE. Sample: $4 postpaid. Submit one poem per page, no cursive type, no erasable bond, no simultaneous submissions or previously published poems. Names and address on each page. Pays 3 copies of magazine; books pay 10% or more royalties. Submit 5-6 samples for book publication with cover letter including bio, publications, "something about yourself, especially about your relationship to God, and why you are writing. We are an exceedingly personal publishing house. Pray about whether to query or send full MS. In some cases one method is best, in some cases another. Either is acceptable." Reports in 1-4 weeks. They also publish approximately four chapbooks each year. Send SASE for guidelines. They hold an annual Star Books Writers' Workshop in October. Irene Burk Harrell says, "Because God seems to be speaking to so many of His children today through poetry, and because established publishing houses are often closed to it on account of the demands of the bottom line, we are looking forward to publishing more and more anointed, God-given poetry of real excellence. Send us your best!"

STAR ROUTE JOURNAL (I, IV-Regional), Box 1451, Redway CA 95560, phone (707)923-3351, founded 1977, publisher/editor Mary Siler Anderson, is a newsprint tabloid publishing 10 issues per year, using poetry, fiction, essays and graphics. "Not overly fond of rhyming. Length unimportant. Partial to Northern California poets. Nature and humanity. Some political poetry. Nothing cute or trite." They have recently published poetry by John Elsberg, Dan Roberts, Edward Mycue, Crawdad Nelson, Nancy L. Clark and Walt Phillips. It is 16-28 tabloid pages. Press run: 1,000 for 250 subscriptions of which 3 are libraries, 300 shelf sales. Subscription: $10. Sample copy: $1. "Back issues not generally available." Send SASE for guidelines. Pays subscription. "Please don't send your only copy; I'm very absent-minded." Include name and address on each poem submitted. Simultaneous submissions and previously published poems OK. Reports in 3 weeks. Editor does not comment on submissions. "I have learned to say 'no'."

STARLIGHT PRESS (II, IV-Anthology, form), P.O. Box 3102, Long Island City NY 11103, founded 1980, editor Ira Rosenstein, is a small press planning to publish an anthology of poetry, its second, within the next two years. This anthology will be dedicated to the sonnet form. To submit for the anthology, send a maximum of 3 sonnets. While strictly metered, 14-line sonnets are welcome, *Starlight* is most open to expansions of the form: 16-line sonnets, sprung-metered sonnets, unmetered, half-rhymed, unrhymed, multi-stanza, use your creativity. What matters is that all poems partake, however tenuous this description may seem, of 'sonnetness', and, beyond that, that they constitute a vivid experience for the reader. As a sample the following lines are offered from "Why Bother?" by Ira Rosenstein:

> Utterly beautiful and penlessly so: she's never written a line.
> Kind and friendly, leggy, imaginative lace, talkative and apt, compelling,
> Caring, illuminating, patient, passionate, interested, interesting;
> Here is a young woman to concede to: great, great fun, and very, very fine.

They will consider simultaneous submissions and previously published poems. Reports in 2 months. Pays 2 copies plus discount on additional Starlight publications.

STARMIST BOOKS (V), Box 12640, Rochester NY 14612, founded 1986, president Beth Boyd, is a small-press publisher of poetry books, "open to all forms except pornography. Responds with encouragement, comments. As of now, submissions by invitation only." StarMist Books has recently published poetry by Virginia JoHe. Beth Boyd has selected as a sample these lines from her book, **Shadows and Rainbows:**

> *We would think of Today as*
> *a Treasure—*
> *all of these things we cannot*
> *measure*
> *The freshness of the*
> *rain—*
> *The sting of the*
> *wind—*
> *The twitter of a*
> *bird—*

Payment is negotiable. Brochures available upon request. Editor sometimes comments on rejections. Advice: "To be aware with each moment of the poetry that surrounds us . . . to ever see it, hear it, taste it, smell it, feel it—write it."

STARSONG (I, IV-Science fiction/fantasy/horror), Rt. 2, Box 260B, St. Matthews SC 29135, founded 1987, editor Larry D. Kirby, III, is a quarterly **"Of sci-fi, fantasy, and horror," using poetry of "any form, any style, very open"** none that is **"pretentious, where meaning is unclear."** He has published poetry by John Grey, Dwight E. Humphries and Steve Sneyd. As a sample he selected these lines from "Burned" by Herb Kauderer:

> *Like a nervous spinster*
> *he clings to an umbilical thread*
> *tied to his ship,*
> *afraid to fly free*
> *afraid even to walk the rings of Saturn.*

Starsong is magazine-sized, 90-100 pp., photocopied with a heavy stock cover. He accepts about 20% of 400 poems received per year. Press run is over 400 for 50 subscriptions of which 5 are libraries. **Sample: $5 postpaid. Send SASE for guidelines. Pays 1 copy. No more than one poem per page, name and address on each page. Reports in 1 month—to be published in the next 2 or 3 issues. Editor usually comments on rejections.** He says, "Say what you mean in your work. Don't try to impress with obscured meanings. I hate that."

STATE STREET PRESS (II), Box 278, Brockport NY 14420, phone (716)637-0023, founded 1981, poetry editor Judith Kitchen, "publishes **chapbooks of poetry (20-24 pp.) usually chosen in an anonymous competition**. State Street Press hopes to publish emerging writers with solid first collections and to offer a format for established writers who have a collection of poems that work together as a chapbook. We have also established a full-length publication—for those of our authors who are beginning to have a national reputation. We want **serious traditional and free verse. We are not usually interested in the language school of poets or what would be termed 'beat.' We are quite frankly middle-of-the-road. We ask only that the poems work as a collection, that the chapbook be more than an aggregate of poems—that they work together."** They have recently published poetry by Stephen Corey, Hannah Stein, Jerah Chadwick, Hilda Raz, and Sally Jo Sorensen. These sample lines are from "Once You Have a Name" by Peter Yovu:

> *There was no one to say a word.*
> *No one to say the sun lay in the sand*
> *like a hub of emptiness, like ambushed love,*
> *or three clouds nearly the same were black*
> *on top, glowing below. There were no tracks*
> *of tumbleweed or wind. There was a mound*
> *of sand in the shape of a turtle,*
> *a shadow coming home.*

The sample chapbook I have seen is beautifully designed and printed, 6 × 9", 30 pp., with textured matte wrapper with art. **Send SASE for guidelines and chapbook contest rules. There is a $5 entry fee, for which you receive one of the chapbooks already published. Simultaneous submissions encouraged. Photocopies OK. Dot-matrix OK "but we don't like it." Pays copies and small honorarium, and authors buy additional ones at cost, sell at readings and keep the profits.** Judith Kitchen comments, "State Street Press believes that the magazines are doing a good job of publishing beginning poets and we hope to present published and unpublished work in a more permanent format, so we do reflect the current market and tastes. We expect our writers to have published individual poems and to be considering a larger body of work that in some way forms a 'book.' We have been cited as a press that prints poetry that is accessible to the general reader."

STEREOPTICON PRESS (V), 534 Wahlmont Dr., Webster NY 14580, founded 1981-2, editor/publisher Etta Ruth Weigl, is a **cooperative publisher (poet shares cost) of "short and well-crafted lyrics showing command of language and more than one level of meaning, but not needlessly obscure. No concrete, performance, 'shock' style, or avant-garde poems."** As a sample she chose these lines from "Winter Walk" by Eleanor A. McQuilkin:

> *The child was "going to a friend's house"*
> *And his voice spoke soft as crayon*
> *Drawing doorways on the land.*

She is temporarily overstocked. Submit query with **4-5 poems, (no more than 1 poem/page) bio, publications. Previously published material OK. Reports on queries in 3 weeks, MSS in 5 months. Pays 30 copies.** "In order to maintain quality production, I reach cooperative agreement with the author, and both of us put money into the project. Arrangements vary, depending on author's needs and wishes. Editor must find MS of merit and marketable before discussion of terms can take place." She **comments on rejections "only if MS comes very close to meeting my standards, but needs a bit more work."**

THE STEVAN COMPANY; SOCIETY OF ETHICAL AND PROFESSIONAL PUBLISHERS OF LITERA-TURE; (II, IV-Translations), 3010 Bee Cave Rd., Austin TX 78746, will be relocating to Micronesia in 1992, address mail % Box 210 CHRB, Saipan, M.P. 96950 (US airmail postal rates), founded 1980, publisher Kathryn Stewart-McDonald. "If you read *The New Yorker, The Atlantic*, and have read textbooks such as Voice Great Within Us, the major Mentor book of poems, e.e. cummings, R.H. Blyth, Li Po, William Blake, you're on track. Well-read poets usually write well. Our readers are very well read and read between 175-210 small press books per year. We prefer to work with experienced writers." They have recently published poetry by Jack Terahata (Japan), Nat Scammacca (Italy), and Dong Jiping (China). In addition to anthologies, they publish collections by individuals. **Query with no more than 5 samples, bio, publication credits.** "No lengthy cover letter, please do not inundate us with all 900 poems you have written. We prefer no previously published poems and usually not simulta-neous submissions. No phone calls. Not necessary to subscribe or join SEPPL." Reading period June-August. They pay in copies. Reports in 6-8 weeks; publication within 1-2 years. Of 75-113 poems received in 30 MSS they accept 60 poems. "We comment on rejections occasionally if requested. We will accept foreign language poems with English translation." Kathryn McDonald says, "We are not a vanity press, sometimes try to solicit grants, will accept money from foundations. The Society of Ethical Publishers agrees to maintain a code of ethics, can make legal referrals, sometimes offers mechanical advice to poets and publishers. This is a private club of like-minded publishers who wish to continue traditions and facilitate rapport between publisher and writer. Board members share mailing lists, copyright attorney and networking information. Members receive free samples, parties and share trade information (i.e., grants available, distributors, printers information, etc.) All members have excellent references, personal and professional. Many can translate and all are committed to their craft."

‡THE WALLACE STEVENS JOURNAL (II, IV-Themes), Liberal Studies, Clarkson University, Potsdam NY 13699, founded 1977, poetry editor Prof. Joseph Duemer, appears biannually using **"poems about or in the spirit of Wallace Stevens or having some relation to his work. No bad parodies of Stevens' anthology pieces."** They have recently published poetry by Elizabeth Spires, Sigman Byrd and editor Joseph Duemer. As a sample the editor selected these lines by William L.M.H. Clask:

> *I. Among twenty silent chairs,*
> *The only moving thing*
> *Was the chalk on the blackboard.*
> *VII. O meager men of Academe,*
> *Why do you imagine silver scholars?*
> *Do you not see how the blackboard*
> *Crumbles about the feet*
> *Of the students around you?*

I have not seen an issue, but the editor describes it as 80-120 pp. 6 × 9″, typeset, flat-spined, with cover art on glossy stock. They accept 10-15 poems of 50-75 received. Press run 900 for 600 subscribers of which 200 are libraries. Subscription: $15. **Sample postpaid: $4. Reports in 2-8 weeks. Pays 2 copies.** "Brief cover letters are fine, even encouraged. Please don't submit to *WSJ* if you have not read Stevens. We like parodies, but they must *add* a new angle of perception. Most of the poems we publish are not parodies, but meditations on themes of interest to Wallace Stevens and those poets he has influenced."

‡STICK (I); LONGHAND PRESS (V), P.O. Box 86, Blackhawk CO 80422, phone (303)582-3465, founded 1988, editors James Taylor III and Eric Paul Shaffer. *Stick* appears in January and July. Longhand Press publishes about 3 books/year, but no unsolicited MSS considered. They have recently published poetry by Steve Sanfield, Art Goodtimes, Gregory Greyhawk, Sarah Backer and Katy McCarville. **"We do not publish lyn lifshin."** As a sample the editor selected these lines (poet unidentified):

> *just to watch it burn*
> *I built a fire*
> *warmest morning of the year*

Stick is digest-sized, 25-40 pp. Press run 200 for 100 subscribers of which 2 are libraries. Shelf sales 5. **Sample postpaid: $4. Send SASE for guidelines. Pays 1 copy. Send no more than 3 poems.**

‡STICKS; STICKS PRESS (II), P.O. Box 399, Maplesville AL 36750-0399, founded 1989, editor/publisher Mary Veazey. *Sticks*, an annual, is **"to publish the best short poems of new and established poets in the tradition of** *Bits* **and** *Eleven.* **All styles, subjects. Maximum length: 25 lines; width: 50 spaces."** As she was just beginning when this listing was written, she offered one of her own poems, "For a Good Ole Boy," as a sample (it was published in **Light Year**):

> *Vodka. Grapefruit juice. In paper cups.*
> *Life discussed among abandoned graves.*
> *Later outside a diner when you threw up,*
> *I finally understood why JESUS SAVES.*
> *Like you'd save me. But Mama knew best—*
> *It's her you'll sleep with is my guess.*
> *But this spring you escape the tomb;*
> *Ride; drink beer; watch dogwoods bloom.*

She planned the magazine to be a 4¼×5½" saddle-stapled booklet with colored card cover, professionally printed, 24+ pp. Press run 250+. **Pays 2 copies. The press publishes 1-2 "mini-chapbooks"/year. Send complete MS to consist of 5 short poems or one longish poem. Reports in "6 weeks or so." Pays 30 copies.** She says, "Almost everything Sticks Press publishes will be small in format. I like tiny poems, tiny books—I'd like to see poems on postage stamps! I wish getting a poem or poems through the mail could be more first-class: speeding rapidly through the countryside with a zip plus four, same size as a greeting card from your favorite person, and with a verse inside decorated with the finest artwork, colorful or even a bit tacky, but with an absolutely essential message."

STILL WATERS PRESS; STILL WATERS WRITING CENTER; WOMEN'S POETRY CHAPBOOK CONTEST; WINTER POETRY CHAPBOOK COMPETITION (II, IV-Women), 112 W. Duerer St., Galloway NJ 08201, phone (609)652-1790, founded 1989, editor Shirley Warren, is a "small-press publisher of poetry chapbooks, short fiction chapbbooks, and poet's handbooks (contemporary craft). Especially interested in **works by, for and about women. We prefer poetry firmly planted in the real world, but equally mindful of poetry as art. The transformation from pain to perseverance, from ordinary to extraordinary, from defeat to triumph, pleases us. But we reject Pollyanna poetry immediately. Nothing sexist, in either direction. We don't want homosexual poetry. Most rhymed poetry doesn't work because it leads to strange manipulations of syntax to achieve rhyme. No patriarchal religious verse. Preferred length: 4 lines—2 pp. per poem. Form: no restrictions—we expect content to dictate the form."** They have recently published poetry by Madeline Tiger and Lynne H. deCourcy. As a sample the editor selected these closing lines from deCourcy's poem "Fire":

> *the leaf arched and flamed and I leapt*
> *to stamp it out, as though I could*
> *stamp out the terror of anything*
> *I started in the world,*
> *as though I could*
> *stamp out the fires of hand and heart*
> *to come, love*
> *leaping from my fingertips and*
> *spreading out of control.*

She publishes 4-8 books a year, including one or two flat-spined paperbacks and chapbooks averaging 28-40 pp. **Query with 3 samples, bio, publications. Simultaneous submissions and previously published poems OK. Pays 10% of the press run. Editor comments on submissions "usually."** Sample chapbooks: $4.95; pamphlets: $3. They hold 4 annual contests, each with $10 reading fee; send SASE for detailed guidelines. The editor says, "read other poets, both contemporary and traditional. Attend some workshops, establish rapport with your local peers, attend readings. Keep your best work in circulation. Someone out there is looking for you." The Still Waters Writing Center offers workshops, writing classes, and some readings.

STONE CIRCLE PRESS (IV-Ethnic), P.O. Box 44, Oakland CA 94604, founded 1987, editor Len Irving, publishes books **"of a Celtic nature. Backgrounded in Scotland, Ireland, Wales, Isle of Man, Cornwall, Brittany." We welcome Stonehenge rather than Acropolis material."** As a sample the editor selected these lines (poet unidentified):

> *Shadows like horses*
> *Down palisades of night*
> *Bunched or racing in death-seeking gallop*
> *See the darkening cloud as their shadows*
> *Break the starting gate*

They publish an average of 2 flat-spined paperbacks per year, averaging 100 pp. **Query with 6 samples. Responds to queries in 1 month. Pays 25 books.** "We are a nonprofit press associated with the Institute of Celtic Studies. We finance and publish the book. The author receives a stated number of books but no royalties." They also subsidy publish, providing "seed money and desk-top publication," seeking donations from all available sources.

STONE PRESS (V), 9727 S.E. Reedway, Portland OR 97266, founded 1968, editor Albert Drake, publishes poetry postcards, posters, broadsides, chapbooks and books. **"Due to other publishing commitments, I'm unable to read poetry submissions during 1992."** He has published books by Earle Birney, Judith Goren, Lee Upton and James Kalmbach. Send for booklist to buy book samples.

STONE SOUP, THE MAGAZINE BY CHILDREN; THE CHILDREN'S ART FOUNDATION (IV-Children), P.O. Box 83, Santa Cruz CA 95063, founded 1973, editor Ms. Gerry Mandel. *Stone Soup* publishes **writing and art by children through age 13; they want to see free verse poetry but no rhyming poetry, haiku or cinquain.** The editor chose as a sample these four lines from "Cancun, A Paradise" by 9-year-old Lisa Osornio:

> *Dangling of the blue*
> *Drops of water splashed from the cool pool,*
> *orange ice drinks cool, going down into the water*
> *and swimming eight different ways.*

Stone Soup, published 5 times a year, is a handsome 6 × 8¾" magazine, professionally printed on heavy stock with 4 full-color art reproductions inside and a full-color illustration on the coated cover, saddle-stapled. A membership in the Children's Art Foundation at $23/year includes a subscription to the magazine, each issue of which contains an Activity Guide. There are 4 pp. of poetry in each issue. Circulation is 12,000, all by subscription; 2,000 go to libraries. **Sample: $4.50 postpaid. Submissions can be any number of pages, any format, but no simultaneous submissions. The editor receives 2,000 poetry submissions/year and uses only 20; she reports in 4 weeks. Guidelines are available for SASE. Pay is $10 and 2 copies plus discounts. Criticism will be given when requested.**

‡STOP LIGHT PRESS; JEANNE DUVAL EDITIONS (I, II), Box 970, Bronxville NY 10708, founded 1989, editors April Lindner and Gerry LeFemina. They publish 4-8 chapbooks/year under their two imprints. **"Stop Light Editions are for poets without a previous collection; Jeanne Duval Editions are for poets with one or two collections of poetry." Sample: $3.50 or $4.50 postpaid. Pays 75 copies. "Open to all styles of poetry. No cliché poetry; no pornography. Do not submit during the summer."** No comments on rejections. They have recently published poetry by Denise Duhamel, editor Gerry LeFemina and Jonathan Wilks. As a sample Gerry Lefemina selected these lines by editor April Lindner:

> *I'd know her home*
> *wherever I found it, even this cinderblock box*
> *she claimed with paint — eggshell blue —*
> *and a rag rug woven from family history.*

The editor advises, "Keep writing! Work in the writer's community, live in the real-world community, that's where the poems are."

STORMLINE PRESS, INC. (V), Box 593, Urbana IL 61801, phone (217)328-2665, founded 1985, publisher Ray Bial, an independent press publishing fiction, poetry and photography, **ordinarily only by invitation. Do not send unsolicited manuscripts. Query with SASE in November and December only.** "We prefer that you first study our publications, such as **A Turning**, by Greg Kuzma, to get an idea of the type of material we like to publish. **We publish both established and new poets, but in the latter case prefer to publish those poets who have been working some years to master their craft. May consider simultaneous submissions. Hard copy MSS are preferred, but photocopied or dot-matrix MSS are OK. Royalties will be negotiated.** The press publishes 1-2 books of poetry each year with an average page count of 48-64. They are 6 × 9", some flat-spined paperbacks and some hardcover.

STORY LINE PRESS; NICHOLAS ROERICH POETRY PRIZE FOR FIRST BOOK OF POETRY (II), Three Oaks Farm, 27006 Gap Road, Brownsville OR 97327-9718, phone (503)466-5352, Story Line Press, founded 1985, poetry editor Robert McDowell. Story Line Press publishes each year the winner of the Nicholas Roerich Poetry Prize for a First Book of Poetry ($1,000 plus publication and a paid reading at the Roerich Museum in New York City; a runner-up receives a full Story Line Press Scholarship to the Wesleyan Writers Conference in Middletown, Connecticut; $15 entry and handling fee). Deadline for submissions: Oct. 15. The press also publishes books about poetry and has in the past published collections of poems by such poets as Colette Inez and Donald Hall. **They consider unsolicited MSS only for the Nicholas Roerich Poetry Prize competition.**

STRAIGHT; STANDARD PUBLISHING CO. (IV-Religious, teens), 8121 Hamilton Ave., Cincinnati OH 45231, editor Carla J. Crane. Standard is a large religious publishing company. *Straight* is a weekly take-home publication (digest-sized, 12 pp., color newsprint) **for teens. Poetry is by teenagers, any style, religious or inspirational in nature. No adult-written poetry.** As a sample the editor selected the first stanza of "Turn to You" by Lonna Aleshire (19):

> *Whenever I'm lonely*
> *or feeling blue*
> *Please teach me to remember*
> *to turn to You.*

Guidelines available for SASE. Pays $5/poem plus 5 copies, reports in 4-6 weeks, publishes acceptances in 9-12 months. Teen author must include birthdate. Photocopy, dot matrix, simultaneous submissions OK. "Many teenagers write poetry in their English classes at school. If you've written a poem on an inspirational topic, and your teacher's given you an 'A' on it, you've got a very good chance of having it published in *Straight*."

THE STRAIN (II), Box 330507, Houston TX 77233-0507, poetry editor Michael Bond, editor Norman C. Stewart, Jr. *The Strain* is a monthly magazine "concentrating on visual, verbal, and performance art to promote interaction between diverse art forms" using **"experimental or traditional poetry of very high quality. Guidelines issue $5 and 8 first-class stamps." Pays "no less than $5" but generally no copies. Simultaneous submissions and previously published poems OK.** "We would **prefer you submit before obtaining the guidelines issue which mostly explains upcoming collections and collaborations."** I have not seen a copy. The editors' advice is to "read Judson Jerome."

‡**STREET PRESS (V),** Box 772, Sound Beach NY 11789-0772, editor Graham Everett. *Street Magazine*, no longer published, was founded in 1973; the press was founded in 1974. Street Press publishes poetry but supplies no information about their criteria, interests, terms, or poets on their list.

STRIDE PUBLICATIONS; TAXUS PRESS: APPARITIONS PRESS (II), 37 Portland St., Newtown Exeter, Devon EX1 2EG England, founded 1980, editor R.M. Loydell. Stride Publications publishes poetry, poetry sequences, prose and novels. **The editor wants to see any poetry that is "new, inventive, nothing self-oriented, emotional, no narrative or fantasy."** He has recently published work by Peter Redgrove, Alexis Lykiard, Sheila E. Murphy and David Miller. Stride Publications publishes paperbacks 40-60 pp. of poetry, plus a few novels and anthologies. **Freelance submissions for book publication are accepted. Authors should query first, sending sample poems. Queries will be answered in 3 weeks and MSS reported on in 3 months or more. Photocopied MSS are OK. Pay is in author's copies, 10% of the press run.**

∫**STRUGGLE: A MAGAZINE OF PROLETARIAN REVOLUTIONARY LITERATURE (I, II, IV-Political, themes, workers' social issues, women, anti-racist),** Box 13261, Harper Station, Detroit MI 48213-0261, founded 1985, editor Tim Hall, is a "literary quarterly, content: the struggle of the working people against the rich. Issues such as: racism, war preparations, worker's struggle against concessions, the over-all struggle for genuine socialism." **The poetry and songs they use are "generally short, any style, subject-matter must highlight the fight against the rule of the billionaires. No material unconnected to the fight to change society, but we welcome experimentation devoted to furthering such content."** They have recently published poetry by L. Ross, Charlie Mehrhoff, Nissa Annakindt, Willie Abraham Howard Jr. and Albert Chui Clark. As a sample the editor selected these lines from "Battlefields" by Rosarius Roy Leonardi:

> *This isn't Bush's war*
> *he's sailing on the coast*
> *of Maine. .*
> *It ain't Teddy's war*
> *he's drinking in a bar*
> *or swimming under bridges.*
> *It's the kids' war.*

1990 style democratic
action
for a sheik,
a prince, a president,
a Nintendo of the damned.

Struggle is digest-sized, 24-36 pp., printed by photo offset using drawings, occasional photos of art work, and short stories, short plays and essays as well as poetry and songs (with their music). Subscription: $6 for 4 issues. **Sample: $1.50 postpaid. Pays 2 copies. Reports in 1-3 months. Accepted work usually appears in the next issue. Editor tries to provide criticism "with every submission."** Tim Hall says, "We want literature and art of discontent with the government and the social and economic system. Specific issues are fine. Show some passion and fire. Formal experiments, traditional forms both welcome. Especially favor works reflecting rebellion by the working people against the rich, against racism, sexism, militarism, imperialism. We support the revolutions and rebellions in Eastern Europe and the Soviet Union, having always considered these regimes state-capitalist and not at all socialist. Especially interested now in protest material against the U.S. war in the Gulf."

STUDENT LEADERSHIP JOURNAL (IV-Students, religious), P.O. Box 7895, Madison WI 53707-7895, phone (608)274-9001, senior editor Robert M. Kachur, is a **"magazine for Christian student leaders on secular campuses. We accept a wide variety of poetry. Do not want to see trite poetry. Also, we accept little rhymed poetry; it must be very, very good."** As a sample the editor selected the middle lines of "Different" by H. Edgar Hix:

You were different, and your scent trail
startled, drew, and tantalized all
the rabbits, timber wolves, and bears.
It was civilized i innocent and strong,
refreshing and stark i new meat.

Student Leadership is as a quarterly, magazine-sized, 28 pp., 2-color inside, 2-color covers, with no advertising, 70% editorial, 30% graphics/art, 10,000 press run going to college students in the United States and Canada. Per issue: $2.95. Subscription: $12. **Sample: $2.95 postpaid. Send SASE for guidelines. Pays $15-50/poem plus 2 copies.** "Would-be contributors should read us to be familiar with what we publish." **Best time to submit MSS is April-August** ("We set our year's editorial plan"). **No simultaneous submissions. Previously published poems OK. Reports in 2-3 months, 1-24 months to publication. Editor "occasionally" comments on rejections.** He says, "Know your market—be familiar with a magazine's target audience and write to that audience."

STUDIO, A JOURNAL OF CHRISTIANS WRITING (II, IV-Religious), 727 Peel St., Albury 2640, New South Wales, Australia, founded 1980, publisher Paul Grover, a small-press literary quarterly "with contents **focusing upon the Christian striving for excellence in poetry**, prose and occasional articles relating Christian views of literary ideas." **In poetry, the editors want "shorter pieces but with no specification as to form or length (necessarily less than 3-4 pages), subject matter, style or purpose. People who send material should be comfortable being published under this banner** *Studio, A Journal of Christians Writing.*" They have recently published poetry by John Foulcher and other Australian poets. As a sample, the editors selected the following lines by Les. A. Murray:

The poor man's anger is a prayer
for equities Time cannot hold
and steel grows from our mother's grace.
Justice is the people's otherworld.

Studio is digest-sized, professionally printed on high-quality colored stock, 32 pp., saddle-stapled, matte card cover, with graphics and line drawings. Circulation is 300, all subscriptions. Subscription $39 (Aud) for overseas members. **Sample available (air mail from U.S.) for $6 (Aud). Pay is 1 copy. Submissions may be "typed copy or dot-matrix or simultaneous." Reporting time is 2 months and time to publication is 9 months.** The magazine conducts a bi-annual poetry and short story contest. The editor says, "Trend in Australia is for imagist poetry and poetry exploring the land and the self. Reading the magazine gives the best indication of style and standard, so send a few dollars for a sample copy before sending your poetry. Keep writing, and we look forward to hearing from you."

SUB-TERRAIN; ANVIL PRESS (II, IV-Social, themes, form/style), Box 1575, Stn. 'A', Vancouver, British Columbia V6C 2P7, Canada, phone (604)876-8710, founded 1988, poetry editor Paul Pitre. Anvil Press is an "alternate small press publishing *Sub-Terrain* as a literary quarterly as well as broadsheets, chapbooks and the occasional monograph. **"Socially conscious literary magazine whose aim is to produce a reading source that will stand in contrast to the trite and pandered." They want "work that has a point-of-view; work that has some passion behind it and is exploring issues that are of**

pressing importance; work that challenges conventional notions of what poetry is or should be; work with a social conscience. In short, what poetry should be: powerful, beautiful, important. No bland, flowery, uninventive poetry that says nothing in style or content." *Sub-Terrain* is 12-20 pp., 7×10" offset with a press run of 500-750. Subscription: $8. Sample: $3 postpaid. Pays money only for solicited work; for other work, 4-issue subscription. They will consider simultaneous submissions, but not previously published poems. Reports in 4-6 weeks. For chapbook or book publication submit 4 sample poems and bio, no simultaneous submissions. "We are willing to consider MSS. But I must stress that we are a co-op, depending on support from an interested audience. New titles will be undertaken with caution. We are not subsidized at this point and do not want to give authors false hopes—but if something is important and should be in print, we will do our best." Editor provides brief comment and more extensive comments for fees. He says, "Poetry, in our opinion, should be a distillation of emotion and experience that is being given back to the world. Pretty words and fancy syntax are just that. Where are the modern day writers who are willing to risk it all, put it all on the line? Young, new writers: show it all, bare your guts, write about what you fear! Believe in the power of the word.The last thing the world needs is soppy, sentimental fluff that gives nothing and says nothing."

SULFUR MAGAZINE (II, IV-Translations), Dept. of English, Eastern Michigan University, Ypsilanti MI 48197, phone (313)483-9787, founded 1981, poetry editor Clayton Eshleman, is a physically gorgeous and hefty (250+ pp. 6×9", flat-spined, glossy card cover, elegant graphics and printing on quality stock) biannual that had earned a distinguished reputation. They have recently published poetry by John Ashbery, Ed Sanders, Gary Snyder, Jackson MacLow, Paul Blackburn and the editor (one of our better-known poets). I selected these sample lines from "Nan's Last Seance" by Peter Redgrove:

> *The gold-searching ants rip up the knotty grains*
> *Of pure gold from the grassy sand, rip grains.*
> *They pile them in flahsing zigguarats.*
> *They are themselves gold-sheened as the summer flies are.*

Publishes by EMU, *Sulfur* has a circulation of 2,000, using approximately 100 pp. of poetry in each issue. Subscription: $13. They use 5-10 of 600-700 submissions received per year. **Sample, postpaid: $6. "We urge would-be contributors to *read* the magazine and send us material only if it seems to be appropriate." Reports in 2-3 weeks. Pays $40 per contributor. Editor comments "sometimes, if the material is interesting."** Reviews 10-20 poetry books per issue. Clayton Eshleman says, "Most unsolicited material is of the "I am sensitive and have practiced my sensitivity' school—with little attention to language as such, or incorporation of materials that lead the poem into more ample contexts than 'personal' experience. I fear too many young writers today spend more time on themselves, without deeply engaging their *selves*, in a serious psychological way—and too little time breaking their heads against the Blakes, Stevens, and Vallejos of the world. That is, writing has replaced reading. I believe that writing is a form of reading and vice versa. Of course, it is the quality and wildness of imagination that finally counts—but this 'quality' is a composit considerably dependent on assimilative reading (and translating, too)."

SUMMER STREAM PRESS (II, IV-Anthologies), Box 6056, Santa Barbara CA 93160-6056, phone (805)962-6540, founded 1978, poetry editor David Duane Frost, publishes a series of books in hardcover and softcover, each presenting 6 poets, averaging 70 text pp. for each poet. "The mix of poets represents many parts of the country and many approaches to poetry. The poets in the initial two volumes have been published, but that is no requirement. We present 1-2 traditional poets in the mix and thus offer them a chance for publication in this world of free-versers. The **6 poets share a 15% royalty. We require rights for our editions worldwide, and share 50-50 with authors for translation rights and for republication of our editions by another publisher. Otherwise all rights remain with the authors.** The first book features Martha Ellis Bosworth and poetry by Ruthann Robson, Clarke Dewey Wells, Robert K. Johnson, Ed Engle, Jr., and David Duane Frost, from whose "Broadsides (Mountain Twilight)" he selected these lines as a sample:

> *There is no song more haunting than this fall*
> *Of noiseless shadows across the sloping snow,*
> *Darkening walls of wilderness valleys, where,*
> *The stillness gathers in listening air.*

To be considered for future volumes in this series, **query with about 12 samples, no cover letter. Replies to query in 30 days, to submission (if invited) in 6 months. Published poetry, simultaneous submissions, photocopy OK. Editor sometimes comments on rejections.**

THE SUN (II), 107 N. Roberson St., Chapel Hill NC 27516, phone (919)942-5282, founded 1974, editor Sy Safransky, is "a monthly magazine of ideas" which uses "all kinds of poetry." They have recently published poems by Wendell Berry, Ellen Carter, Cedar Koons, Louis Jenkins, and Edwin Rommond. *The Sun* is magazine-sized, 40 pp., printed on 50 lb. offset, saddle-stapled, with b/w photos, graphics and ads, circulation 15,000, 10,000 subscriptions of which 50 are libraries. Subscription: $30. They receive 1,000 submissions of freelance poetry per year, use 25, have a 1-3 month backlog. **Sample: $3 postpaid. Submit no more than 6 poems. Reports within 3 months. Pays $25 on publication and in copies and subscription. Send SASE for guidelines.**

SUN DOG: THE SOUTHEAST REVIEW (II), 406 Williams Bldg., English Department, Florida State University, Tallahassee FL 32306, phone (904)644-4230, founded 1979, poetry editors Bland Lawson and Susan Massersmith. "The journal has a small student staff. We publish two flat-spined 100 pp. magazines per year of poetry, short fiction and essays. As a norm, we usually accept about 12 poems per issue. **We accept poetry of the highest caliber, looking for the most 'whole' works. A poet may submit any length, but because of space, poems over 2 pages are impractical. Excellent formal verse highly regarded.**" They have recently published poetry by David Bottoms, David Kirby, Peter Meinke, and Leon Stokesbury. As a sample the editor selected these lines by Tonya Robins:

> The ropes of my hair lengthen
> my fingernails celebrate seasons
> I harvest brittle white crops,
> fields of failed winter wheat,
> tend casks of brilliant seed.

SD is 6×9" with a glossy card cover. Usually including half-tones, line drawings, and color art when budget allows. Press run of 1,250. Subscription: $8 for 2 issues. **Sample: $4 postpaid. Send SASE for guidelines. Pays 2 copies. Poems should be "typed single spaced, between 2-5 submissions at a time. If simultaneous submission say so. No previously published poems. Reports in 3 months. Editor will comment briefly on most poems, especially those which come close to being accepted.**

SUNSHINE MAGAZINE; GOOD READING MAGAZINE; THE SUNSHINE PRESS; HENRICHS PUBLI-CATIONS, INC. (I, IV-Inspirational, humor), P.O. Box 40, Litchfield IL 62056, phone (217)324-3425, founded 1924, poetry editor Peggy Kuethe. *Sunshine Magazine* "is almost entirely a fiction magazine; *Good Reading* is made up of short, current interest factual articles." Both magazines **use some poetry. "We do *not* publish free verse or abstract poetry, no haiku, no negative subjects, no violence, sex, alcohol. We use only uplifting, inspirational poetry that is of regular meter and that rhymes. Inspirational, seasonal, or humorous poetry preferred. Easy to read, pleasantly rhythmic. Maximum 16 lines — no exceptions.**" They have recently published poems by Loise Pinkerton Fritz, Angie Monnens, Eunice Elmore Heizer, Dave Wadley and Marion Schoeberlein. As a sample the editor selected these lines by Edith Summerfield:

> Buds from their bonds unfurl;
> Trees shake out a crown of curls;
> The world becomes a living thing.
> Oh! Glories of eternal Spring.

Both magazines are monthlies. *Sunshine* is 5¼×7¼", saddle-stapled, 36 pp., of which 5 are poetry, circulation to 75,000 subscribers. Subscription: $10. They use about 7% of 2,500 submissions of poetry each year. **Sample: 50¢. Send SASE for guidelines. Absolutely no queries. Submit typewritten MS, 1 poem per page. Reports in 8-10 weeks. Pays 1 copy.** *Good Reading* uses about 4 poems per issue, circulation to 7,200 subscribers. Subscription: $9. **Sample: 50¢. Submission specifications like those for** *Sunshine*. **Pays 1 copy.** The editors comment, "We strongly suggest authors read our guidelines and obtain a sample copy of our magazines. Our format and policies are quite rigid and we make absolutely no exceptions. Many authors submit something entirely different from our format or from anything we've published before — guaranteed rejection."

SUPERINTENDENT'S PROFILE & POCKET EQUIPMENT DIRECTORY (IV-Themes), 220 Central Ave., Box 43, Dunkirk NY 14048, phone (716)366-4774, founded 1978, poetry editor Robert Dyment, is a "monthly magazine, circulation 2,500, for town, village, city, and county highway superintendents and DPW directors throughout New York State," and uses **"only poetry that pertains to highway superintendents and DPW directors and their activities." Submit no more than one page double-spaced.** Subscription: $10. They receive about 50 freelance submissions of poetry per year, use 20, have a 2 month backlog. **Sample: 80¢ postage. Reports within a month. Pays $5/poem.**

SWAMP ROOT (II), Rt. 2, Box 1098, Jacksboro TN 37757, phone (615)562-7082, founded 1987, editor Al Masarik, is a poetry magazine appearing 3 times a year. **"All styles welcome, biased toward clarity, brevity, strong imagery."** They have recently published poetry by Ted Kooser, Naomi Shihab Nye, Linda Hasselstrom, William Kloefkorn and Diane Glancy. As a sample the editor selected these lines by Vivian Shipley:

> Ocean was in early morning fog
> resting heavy on ridges in Harlan County

> *and the frost, ribbed*
> *on the leaf of a blackberry bush.*

It is 6×9″ flat-spined on quality stock with matte card cover or glossy card cover, using b/w photos, drawings and collages interspersed with poetry. They receive about 20 submissions per week, use less than 1%. Press run: 1,000 for 63 subscriptions of which 12 are libraries, few shelf sales. Subscription: $12. **Sample, postpaid: $5. Pays 3 copies plus year's subscription. Simultaneous submissions and previously published poems used "sometimes." Reports in 1-4 weeks. Editor comments on submissions.** Reviews books of poetry.

SWORD OF SHAHRAZAD (I), P.O. Box 10294, Toadsuck Substation, Conway AR 72032, founded 1988, editor Deb'y Gaj, appears 4 times per year, a "small press, workshop-in-a-magazine for fiction writers and poets. **There are no restrictions on form, subject-matter, style, or purpose—but try not to send us epics."** They have recently published poetry by Howard Lakin (head writer for the TV series "Dallas"). As a sample the editor selected (from their Halloween issue) these lines from "Vampire Wine" by Thomas Zimmerman:

> *When your mind and eyes are dull*
> *and slumber's dregs seal your lids,*
> *I'll pierce your neck and madly gulp*
> *the salty wine I find within.*

It is 54 pp. digest-sized, saddle-stapled, typeset, laser printed. They publish "at least 20-25 poems per issue." Subscription: $16. **Sample, postpaid: $3. Send SASE for guidelines. Simultaneous submissions and previously published poems OK. Editor comments on submissions "always."** Reviews books of poetry. We try to give individual criticisms of each poem we get. Our goal is to help writers—to give them feedback instead of just rejection or acceptance. My advice to poets is: read other poets, try all the different forms of poetry, and—most of all—*write!* Like everything else, poetry takes practice."

SYCAMORE REVIEW (II), Department of English, Purdue University, West Lafayette IN 47907, phone (317)494-3783, founded 1988 (first issue May, 1989), editor Michael Kiser. "We accept personal essays (25 pp. max), short fiction (25 pp. max), translations and **quality poetry in any form (6 pp. max). There are no official restrictions as to subject-matter or style."** Recent contributors include Mary Oliver, John Updike, Susan Neville, Marge Piercy, Russell Edson and Maura Stanton. As a sample the editor selected the following lines by Charles Bukowski:

> *look at me in undershirt and shorts,*
> *bare feet bleeding shards of glass.*
>
> *there's some way out that begins with*
> *three bottles*
> *left.*

The magazine is semi-annual in a digest-sized format, 110 pp. flat-spined, professionally printed, with glossy, color cover. Their press run is 1,000 with 300 subscriptions of which 100 are libraries. Subscription: $9. **Sample: $5 postpaid. "We read September through April." Guidelines available for SASE. Pays 2 copies. Reports in 4 months. Cover letters not required but invited. Editor comments on about 20% of rejections.**

‡SYZYGY; THE IMPOSSIBLE UTTERANCE; PLASTER CRAMP PRESS (II, IV-Form), P.O. Box 5975, Chicago IL 60680, founded 1989, publisher Seth Tisue. Plaster Cramp Press publishes the monthly magazine *TIU* and, twice a year, *Syzygy*. Both use **"short-ish language and visual poetry."** They have recently published poetry by Geof Huth, jwcurry and Miekal And. As a sample the editor selected these lines by John M. Bennett:

> *Like a wall of heads drips fat like a small*
> *hand in a lake of gloves like a hill a skull*
> *rolls down . . . what? or, streaking this . . .*

Syzygy is 52 pp., 7×8½″, photocopied and stapled, consisting mostly of prose and graphics. *TIU* is an 8 pp. pamphlet, 4½″, photocopied and stapled, with short poetry and collage. 300 copies of *Syzygy* and 50 copies of *TIU* are printed, distributed to 50 subscribers, publishers, and about 50 shelf sales. For 4 issues, *Syzygy* is $6, *TIU* $1.50. **Reports in one month. Pays 3 copies.** "Please send as wide a selection of work as possible for me to choose from—simultaneous submissions OK."

TAK TAK TAK (II, IV-Translations, themes), P.O. Box 7, Bulwell, Nottingham NG6 OHW England, founded 1986, editors Andrew and Tim Brown, appears twice a year in print and on cassettes, and, in addition, publishes 1-2 collections of poetry per year. **"No restrictions on form or style. However, each**

issue of the magazine is on a theme (i.e. 'Mother Country/Fatherland,' 'Travel'), and *all* contributions must be relevant. If a contribution is long it is going to be more difficult to fit in than something shorter. Write for details of subject(s) etc. of forthcoming issue(s)." They have published poetry by Rudyard Kipling, Michael Horowitz, Karl Blake, Keith Jafrate, Ramona Fotiade and Paul Buck. I have not seen it, but the editor describes it as "100 pp. A5, photolithographed, board cover, line drawings and photographs, plus cassette of poetry, music, collage. Of about 100 poems received in the past year we have used about 25." Press run 500. Subscription: £9, £12.32 postpaid to U.S.A. (includes 2 issues with cassettes). **Sample: £11.16 postpaid to US Pays 1 copy. Submit "a selection of 5 or 6 with a bio of up to 30 words." They consider simultaneous submissions and previously published poems. Reports within 6 months. Editor sometimes comments on rejections.** They also publish 2 or 3 flat-spined paperbacks a year averaging between 40 and 130 pp. For chapbook consideration send as many as possible sample poems, bio, publications. **Reports in 2 months. Pays a negotiated number of copies.** The editors say, "Poetry is just one of the many creative forms our contributions take. We are equally interested in prose and in visual and sound media."

TAKAHE (II, IV-Translations), P.O. Box 13-335, Christchurch 1, New Zealand, phone (03)668659, founded 1989, poetry editors David Howard and Bernadette Hall, is a literary quarterly. **"We have no preconceived specifications as to form, length, subject-matter, style or purpose. We believe that poetry is, among other things, the art of significant silence. It demands an active reader whose trust in language matches that of the writer. No work that batters the reader about the head, that refuses to utilize silence and insists on spelling everything out — as if the reader was incapable of making connections."** They have recently published poetry by Tatyana Shcherbina, Helen Trubek Glenn, Gregory O'Brien, Michael Harlow, Elizabeth Smither and Tony Beyer. As a sample the poetry editors selected these lines by Riemke Ensing:

> *A gesture*
> *of pink in several paper-hats. They alone*
> *are coming to the party.*

I have not seen an issue, but the poetry editors describe it as 56 pp. magazine-sized, desktop publishing with woodcut design on cover and some b/w graphics (including ads). They accept an average of 10% of 1,000 poems received a year. Press run: 200 for 119 subscriptions of which 21 are libraries, 81 shelf sales. Subscription: $24 NZ. **Sample postpaid: $9 NZ. Pays 1 copy plus small emolument at editors' discretion. Submit up to 7 poems. Simultaneous submissions and previously published poems OK (if not published in New Zealand). Reports in 1-2 months. Editors comment on submissions "as a matter of course (particularly if the poem is potentially publishable but needs further work)."** The editors say, "In poetry (as in prayer) the essential thing is the degree to which the silences between words are charged with significance. 'Less is more' — but only if the less is carefully weighed."

TALISMAN: A JOURNAL OF CONTEMPORARY POETRY AND POETICS (II), P.O. Box 1117, Hoboken NJ 07030, phone (201)798-9093, founded 1988, editor Edward Foster, appears twice a year. "Each issue centers on the poetry and poetics of a *major* contemporary poet and includes a selection of new work by other important contemporary writers. **We are particularly interested in poetry in alternative (*not* academic) traditions. We don't want traditional poetry."** They have recently published poetry by William Bronk, Robert Creeley, Ron Padgett, Anne Waldman, Hayden Carruth and Rosmarie Waldrop. As a sample the editor selected a stanza of "The Section Called O" by Rachel Blau DuPlessis (in the Spring, 1990 Susan Howe issue):

> *the wane and wax of*
> *other alphabets, primers*
> *of Adams and of Kings,*
> *their one word*
> *(Xantippe or Xenophon)*
> *for adequate narratives of X.*

Talisman is digest-sized, flat-spined, 152+ pp. photocopied from typescript, with matte card cover. Their press run is 650 with "substantial" subscriptions of which many are libraries. "We are inundated with submissions and lost track of the number long ago." Subscription: $9 individual; $13 institution. **Sample: $5 postpaid. Pays 1 copy. Reports in 1 month.** Reviews books of poetry.

TAMPA BAY REVIEW (II), 5458 N. Rivershore Dr., Tampa FL 33603, founded 1989, managing editor Gianna Russo, is a literary journal appearing twice a year. **"We want poems (and short stories) which are innovative in language, rhythm and subject matter. We tend toward free verse with strong metaphors and vibrant imagery. We are not interested in sentimental rhymed verse or inspirational poetry."** They have recently published poetry by William Stafford, Silvia Curbelo and Richard Mathews. As a sample the editor selected these lines from "Steal this Poem (If You Want To)" by Phyllis McEwen:

> Ride this poem
> like it has a big sleek back
> and a saddle of ice.
> Let it take you
> where you need to be

It is 50-60 pp. digest-sized, saddle-stapled, with matte card cover. Press run: 300 for 50 subscribers. "We accept about 20% of what we receive." Subscription: $8. **Sample postpaid: $4.50, back issue $2** "if available." **Send SASE for guidelines. Enclose up to 3 lines of biographical info with submission. Reports in 8-12 weeks. Payment is in contributor's copies. Editor comments on submissions "often." They "occasionally" use previously published poems. Send no more than 6-8 poems.** "We publish spring and fall. Poems are circulated once or twice to an editorial board, but final decisions are made by our poetry editor. *Tampa Bay Review* is published by Tampa Bay Poets, the area's long-established writers' group. Rights to published works revert to the author. Take risks in your writing. Your goals should be: first, to make your readers understand what you're expressing; and second, to make them sit up and say 'Ah ha!'"

TAMPA REVIEW (III, IV-Translations), P.O. Box 19F, University of Tampa, Tampa FL 33606-1490, phone (813)253-3333, ext. 621, founded 1964 as *UT Poetry Review*, became *Tampa Review* in 1988, editor Richard Mathews, poetry editors Kathryn Van Spanckeren and Donald Morrill, is an elegant annual of fiction, nonfiction, poetry and art (not limited to US authors) wanting **"original and well-crafted poetry written with intelligence and spirit. No greeting card or inspirational verse."** They have recently published poetry by Alberto Rios, Paul Mariani, Mark Halliday, Denise Levertov and Stephen Dunn. As a sample the editors chose these lines by William Stafford:

> Clouds here have dawn before we do,
> but we keep the night and feed it dreams.

It is 96 pp., flat-spined, 7½ × 10½" with a matte card color cover. They accept about 20 of 500 poems received a year. Their press run is 500 with 175 subscriptions of which 20 are libraries. **Sample: $6 postpaid. Pays $10/printed page plus 1 copy and 40% discount on additional copies. Unsolicited MSS are read between October and December. Reports take up to 12 weeks.**

‡**TANGRAM PRESS (III)**, P.O. Box 2249, Granbury TX 76048, phone (817)579-1777, publisher Dayna Fenker. This very small press would like to publish more books such as their handsome coffee-table volume, 12 × 12", hardback, **Where Rainbows Wait for Rain: The Big Bend Country**, combining poems by Sandra Lynn and b/w photographs by Richard Fenker Jr., but "We have a limited staff. **While we do not discourage submissions, we cannot guarantee comments on same. We are not your standard poetry publisher."**

TAPJOE: THE ANAPROCRUSTEAN POETRY JOURNAL OF ENUMCLAW (II, IV-Nature, social issues), P.O. Box 104, Grangeville ID 83530, founded 1987, biannual plus occasional special issues/chapbooks. **"We will consider anything by anyone, however we have a definite preference for free verse poems 10-50 lines with a slant toward nature, social issues, the human environment, which is the environment as a whole. No sexism, racism or unnecessary raw language."** They have recently published poetry by Judith Skillman, Ron Rash, Jess Mills and Sarah Flowers. These sample lines, selected by co-editor Rich Hayden are from "the collected haiku of Albert Einstein" by JB Mulligan:

> The hummingbird motion
> of an opening flower —
> we see a still life.

The magazine is digest-sized, 30-40 pp., saddle-stapled, offset with matte card cover. Accepts 40-60 poems per year with 1,000+ submissions. Print run is 150-300. **Sample: $3 postpaid. Send SASE for guidelines. Pays 1 copy for each accepted poem. "Cover letters appreciated but not necessary. Prefer 4-5 poems per submission." No simultaneous submissions or previously published poems. Reports in 2-8 weeks** "often longer. Each submission is read by several people, which sometimes makes responses slow; however, we feel this is the only way to give each piece fair consideration." **No chapbook submissions at this time.** "We appreciate purchases of sample copies (and subscriptions) but nothing pleases us more than receiving a 'good' poem in the mail—do give us a try." Subscriptions are $10/4 issues. The editors advise, "Read. Read these books: David Wagoner's **Who Shall Be the Sun?**, Mary Oliver's **Dream Work**, Gary Snyder's **Axe Handles**, Robert Sund's **Bunch Grass**. Read Linda Hogan's **Seeing Through the Sun**. Buy books. Buy small press publications."

TAPROOT; BURNING PRESS; KRAPP'S LAST TAPE (II), P.O. Box 18817, Cleveland Heights OH 44118, founded 1980, editor Robert Drake, is a "micropress publisher of avant-garde and experimental literature and art. Also produces a weekly radio show (KLT) of music, noise, language-centered audio art

Share in the discovery of America's best new fiction

Subscribe to STORY, the magazine that made literary history by discovering some of the best-known writing talents of this century. Favorites like Salinger, Cheever, McCullers, Saroyan, Capote, and Mailer are among those writers first published in STORY, and that legacy continues today. After a 22-year interim, STORY was revived in 1989 with its original mission intact: to showcase the country's finest new writing talents.

Each quarterly issue brings you 128 pages of memorable short stories chosen for their strong narratives, engaging styles and challenging subject matter— good fiction that touches the reader long after the final page is turned... fiction that will inspire you as a writer.

Be on hand for the next STORY discovery, and start your subscription to the most widely circulated literary magazine published in America.

☐ I accept! Please enter my 1-year subscription to STORY at the low introductory rate of $17 for 4 quarterly issues.

☐ Payment enclosed ☐ Please bill me

Name_____

Address _____Apt _____

City_____

State_____Zip_____

*Outside U.S. add $7 (Includes GST in Canada) and remit in U.S. funds.
Watch for your first issue in 6-8 weeks!

My 100% Risk-Free Guarantee: If I'm ever dissatisfied with STORY for any reason, I may cancel and receive a full refund for all unmailed issues.   BVPTMKG

The first issues of STORY were cranked out on an old mimeograph machine in 1931 by two American newspaper correspondents in Vienna. Editors Whit Burnett and his wife Martha Foley had no money—just a vision to create a forum for outstanding short stories, regardless of their commercial appeal. The magazine was an instant literary success, and was hailed "The most distinguished short story magazine in the world."

Now STORY returns with the same commitment to publishing the best new fiction written today. It will also provide a workshop for new material from established writers such as Joyce Carol Oates and Madison Smartt Bell. And each issue features a STORY Classic, a story that launched the career of a distinguished writer, reprinted from an early issue of STORY.

Printed on heavy premium paper, each is meant to be read and cherished for years to come. (Those first mimeographed copies of STORY are collector's items today!)

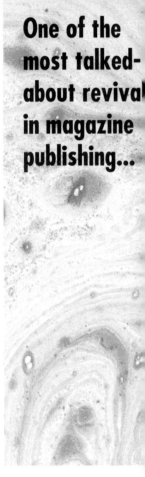

One of the most talked-about revival in magazine publishing...

and a series of audiocassettes." They want **"purposeful experiments with language in which form is the necessary outgrowth of content. No standard academic workshop slop."** I have not seen a copy of their quarterly, *TapRoot*, nor of any of their publications. The editor describes the magazine as "typically 50 pp. photocopied, handmade covers and binding." They accept less than 10% of 1,000-2,000 poems received per year. Press run is 250 typically for 50 subscriptions, 200 shelf sales. **Sample postpaid: $5 when available. Pays 1 copy. "Contributors may buy more at cost." Submit "no more than a dozen at a time unless previously contacted. Simultaneous submissions OK, and previously published poems are sometimes used."** Reviews books of poetry. Burning Press published 8 chapbooks in 1989, averaging 50 pp. **For chapbook publication query with no more than 12 samples. Pays 20% press run. Author may buy more at cost.**

TAPROOT LITERARY REVIEW (I), 302 Park Rd., Ambridge PA 15003, phone (412)266-8476, founded 1986, editor Tikvah Feinstein, is an annual contest publication, very open to beginners. **There is a $5 entry fee for up to 5 poems, "no longer than 30 lines each." Submissions accepted between September 1 and December 31. Nothing previously published or pending publication will be accepted. All entrants receive a copy of** *Taproot*; **enclose $2 for postage and handling.** In addition to contest, each year a guest poet is selected; payment in copies. Writers recently published include Elizabeth R. Curry, Noel M. Valis, Gary Waller and B.Z. Niditch. As a sample the editor selected the following lines of her work:

> *My fingers cascade over the keyboard*
> *falling, flailing, filling a blank screen*
> *with letters woven into images, words*
> *on a magic slate scatter into time*
> *I take from them less than I give*

The review is approximately 80 pages, printed by offset on white stock with one-color glossy cover, art and no ads. Circulation is 500, sold at bookstores, readings and through the mail. Price is $5.50 per issue. **Sample copies for $5 each, includes postage.**

‡TASTE OF LATEX (IV-Erotica), P.O. Box 460122, San Francisco CA 94146, founded 1989, editor Lily Braindrop, is a quarterly using **poetry that is "sex-positive, thoughtful, provocative, nothing misogynist, racist."** The editor describes the magazine as "rebellious, enlightened sleaze for sex-positive peoples of all types. Reviews all sex media!" It is magazine-sized, professionally printed, 40 pp. saddle-stitched, with colored paper cover. Press run 1,000 for 100 subscribers. Subscription: $15/4 issues. **Sample postpaid: $5. Reports in 12-16 weeks. Pays 2 copies. Previously published poems and simultaneous submissions OK if reprint rights are available. "Please stress that** *TOL* **is female edited and published and that** *all* **erotic subject matter will be considered!"**

TEARS IN THE FENCE (II), 38 Hodview, Stourpaine, Nr. Blandford Forum, Dorset DT11 8TN, England, phone 0258-56803, founded 1984, general editor David Caddy, poetry editor Sarah Hopkins, a **"small press magazine of poetry, fiction, interviews, articles, reviews and graphics. We are open to a wide variety of poetic styles. Work of a social, political, ecological and feminist awareness will be close to our purpose. However, we like to publish a balanced variety of work."** The editors do not want to see "didactic rhyming poems." They have recently published Paul Donnelly, Jesse Glass Jr., Astra and Rochelle Lynn Holt. As a sample, they selected the following lines from "Colonial" by Chris Bendon:

> *As I stand in the middle of a sanded*
> *hockey pitch, my spaniel sketches circles,*
> *is rabbit, horse, golden lion. Enormous space*
> *enters my brain but it too shrinks.*

Tears in the Fence appears two times a year. It is magazine-sized, offset from typed copy on lightweight paper with b/w cover art and graphics, 60 pp., one-color matte card cover with black spiral binding. It has a print run of 600 copies, of which 129 go to subscribers and 155 are sold on newsstands. Price per issue is $4, **sample available for same price. Pay is 1 copy. Writers should submit 5 typed poems with IRCs. Reporting time is 3 months and time to publication 8-10 months "but can be much less."** The editor says, "I think it helps to subscribe to several magazines in order to study the market and develop an understanding of what type of poetry is published. Use the review sections and send off to magazines that are new to you."

‡TEMPEST MAGAZINE (II), 231 S. Phillips Ave., #207, Sioux Falls SD 57102, phone (605)334-9772, founded 1989, poetry editor Matthew Mauch, is a monthly tabloid arts, entertainment and opinion magazine **with a special interest in poetry. "Our inhouse requirement is that the poetry we use be 'tempestuous.' Writers have achieved tempestuousness in many different ways. Nothing blatantly pro-religion, no inspirational verse."** They have recently published poetry by Phillip Dacey, Bill Holm and David Stattelman. As a sample the editor selected these lines from "The True Story" by Phil Hey:

> All morning she had wondered whether to leave
> and nothing had told her. The sunlight
> entered the kitchen exactly as the day before,
> making itself at home in the room she had scrubbed
> again and again, hoping to uncover some word
> of what to do after everything was clean.

It is 30 pp., newsprint. They accept about 10% of submissions. Press run 10,000 for 75 subscribers of which 5 are libraries. All issues are distributed free. Subscription: $15. **Sample: $2.50. Pays $5 plus 1 copy. Reports in 1-2 months. Editor comments on rejections "often."** He advises, "Whether or not your work is accepted, continue to write more, for it will all build very slowly and have a monumental impact which will only be measured 100 years from now."

‡TEN LIONS AND THE END OF THE WORLD (II), P.O. Box 4608, New York NY 10185-0039, phone (212)696-8536, founded 1990, editors Alex Vuksic and Jim Allen, appears irregularly, "usually 3-4/ year," using **brave and well-written verse. Any style, form or length. We want works that are truly 'out-there.' No safe, generic verse with a lot of technique and nothing else behind it. *No undue sentimentality.*"** They have recently published poetry by Charles Bukowski, William Packard and Frank Tedesso. As a sample the editor selected these lines from "Lessons of the Sponge" by Rick Hospodar:

> Hole-riddled cell-thing,
> oceanic husk.
> The sponge had an ancestor
> that bathed with African kings.
> I bathe with a corpse;
> it swells and helps me.

It is digest-sized, 20 pp., photocopied from typescript, folded and stapled in the middle with paper cover. Print run 500 for 200 subscribers, distributed free. ("Subscribers only pay p.&h. costs. We survive on contributions." Subscription: $10.) **Sample: $1 postpaid. Send SASE for guidelines. Pays 4 copies (more if requested). Simultaneous submissions OK. Reports in 2 weeks.**

TESSERA (IV-Women, regional, bilingual, translations), 350 Stong, York University, 4700 Keele St., North York, Ontario M3J 1P3 Canada, founded 1984, revived 1988, managing editor Barbara Godard, appears twice a year: "**feminist literary theory and experimental writing by women in French and English, preference to Canadians.**" It is digest-sized, 94 pp., professionally printed, with glossy card cover. Subscription: $18. **Sample postpaid: $10. Submit 4 copies. Deadlines are currently May 15 and Nov. 15. Simultaneous submissions and previously published ("sometimes") poems OK. Pays $5/ page. Editor comments on submissions "sometimes."**

‡TESSERACT PUBLICATIONS; THE BARDIC ROUND TABLE (I), 3001 W. 57th St., Sioux Falls SD 57106-2652, phone (605)361-6942, founded 1981, publisher Janet Leih. "**All my books are subsidized publications. Payment is ⅓ in advance, ⅓ when book goes to printer, balance when book is complete. I help my poets with copyright, bar codes, listings and whatever publicity I can get for them. I have a number of mailing lists and will prepare special mailings for them, work with competent proofreaders, artists and a capable reviewer.**" They held a contest for book publication in 1990 and may hold future contests. I have seen one of their publications: **Quest and other Poems** by Gertrude Johnson. It is digest-sized, saddle-stapled, professionally printed on heavy tinted stock. The Bardic Round Table is a local poetry group meeting monthly that sponsors readings (both for members and others) and engages in other activities primarily to support the poetry of members. Membership: $2.

‡TEXAS TECH UNIVERSITY PRESS (V, IV-Themes), Lubbock TX 79409-1037, phone (806)742-2982, founded 1971, editor Judith Keeling, considers volumes of poetry in four categories only: **Conflict Literature Series:** "Anthologies and single-author works of fiction, nonfiction, and poetry that illuminate unquantifiable aspects of historic tragedy and global conflict"; **First-Book Poetry Series:** "Winning and finalist MSS in the annual competition conducted by Poetry Editor Walter McDonald, who surveys some 20 literary journals throughout the year and invites up to 12 poets to submit MSS for consideration in the competition"; **Invited Poets Series:** "Collections invited from established poets whose work continues to appear in distinguished journals"; and **TTUP Contemporary Poetry Series:** "Winning and finalist works in current national competitions." **Books published on royalty contracts. MS should be submitted with cover letters and attachments to verify eligibility. Editors never comment on rejections.**

TEXTILE BRIDGE PRESS; MOODY STREET IRREGULARS: A JACK KEROUAC NEWSLETTER (IV-Themes), P.O. Box 157, Clarence Center NY 14032, founded 1978, poetry editor Joy Walsh. "**We publish material by and on the work of Jack Kerouac, American author prominent in the fifties. Our chapbooks reflect the spirit of Jack Kerouac. We use poetry in the spirit of Jack Kerouac, poetry of** the working class, poetry about the everyday workaday life. Notice how often the work people spend so much of their life doing is never mentioned in poetry or fiction. Why? **Poetry in any form."** They have recently published poetry by Joseph Semenovich, Marion Perry, Bonnie Johnson, Boria Sax, Michael Basinski, Emanuel Fried, Mildred Crombie, Ted Joans, Michael Hopkins, Tom Clark, Jack Micheline, Carl Solomon and ryki zuckerman. Joy Walsh selected these sample lines from "Indefinite Layoff" by Delores Rossi Script:

> How desperately man
> needs to work.
> Society has shaped it so.
> Without it, it diminishes
> his existence.

Moody Street Irregulars is a 28 pp. magazine-sized newsletter, biannual, circulation 700-1,000 (700 subscriptions of which 30 are libraries), using 3-4 pp. of poetry in each issue. Subscription: $7. They receive about 50 freelance submissions of poetry per year, use half of them. **Sample: $3.50 postpaid. Reports in 1 month. Pays copies.** Textile Bridge Press also publishes collections by individuals. For book publication, query with 5 samples. **"The work speaks to me better than a letter." Replies to query in 1 week, to submission (if invited) in 1 month. Simultaneous submission OK for "some things yes, others no." Photocopy, dot-matrix OK. Pays copies. Send SASE for catalog to buy samples. Editor comments on rejections "if they ask for it."**

THALIA: STUDIES IN LITERARY HUMOR (I, IV-Subscribers, humor), Dept. of English, University of Ottawa, Ottawa, Ontario K1N 6N5 Canada, appears twice a year using **"humor (literary, mostly), preferably literary parodies."** I have not seen an issue, but the editor describes it as 7 × 8½" flat-spined "with illustrated cover." Press run 500 for 475 subscriptions. Subscription: $15. Sample, postpaid: **$7.50. Contributors must subscribe. Simultaneous submissions OK but *Thalia* must have copyright. Will authorize reprints. Editor comments on submissions.**

THEMA (II, IV-Themes), Thema Literary Society, P.O. Box 74109, Metairie LA 70033-4109, founded 1988, editor Virginia Howard, is a literary quarterly **using poetry related to specific themes. "Each issue is based on an unusual premise. Please, please send SASE for guidelines before submitting poetry to find out the upcoming themes. For example: 'these are not the best shoes I own' is the theme for Feb. 1, 1992 (submission deadline); 'unrecognized at the airport' is for May 1, 1992; 'tracks in the snow' is for Aug. 1, 1992. No scatologic language, alternate life-style, explicit love poetry."** They have recently published poetry by Timothy Deshler, Sue Walker and John Brugaletta. As a sample the editor selected these lines by Arlene L. Mandell:

> crisp brittle sliver
> of moon slips
> under her collar,
> digs into the marrow
> of her autumn bones

Thema is digest-sized, 200 pp., professionally printed, with matte card cover. They accept about 25% of 120 poems received per year. Press run 500 for 180 subscriptions of which 22 are libraries. Subscription: $16. **Sample postpaid: $5. Pays $10/poem plus 1 copy. Editor comments on submissions.**

‡**THEMATIC POETRY QUARTERLY (I, IV-Themes)**, 400 Fish Hatchery Rd., Marianna FL 32446, phone (904)482-3890, editor Wilbur I. Throssell, publishes loose-leaf portfolios **of poetry on specific themes, limit 30 lines.** For 1992 the themes and deadlines are: January—Sports & Recreation; March—Landscapes; June—Indians & Pioneers; October—Occupations & Work. Send SASE for list of themes up through 1996. (The tape exchange of poetry, Audio/Visual Poetry Foundation, formerly at this address, has been discontinued.)

‡**THE THIRD HALF LITERARY MAGAZINE; K.T. PUBLICATIONS (I, II)**, 16, Fane Close, Stamford, Lincolnshire PE9 1HG England, founded 1987, editor Mr. Kevin Troop. *TTH* appears 6/year. K.T.P. publishes about 6 chapbooks/year. He wants **"meaningful, human and humane, funny poems up to 40 lines. Nothing obscene."** They have recently published poetry by Lee Bridges, Margaret Munro Gibson

Market conditions are constantly changing! If you're still using this book and it is 1993 or later, buy the newest edition of Poet's Market at your favorite bookstore or order directly from Writer's Digest Books.

and Michael Newman. As a sample I selected this poem, "Pop Goes the Prosperity" by Eddie Flintoff:

> The age borrows
> as always
>   from its tomorrows.
>   The rest
> of time is left
>   to pay interest.

Both the magazine and chapbooks are digest-sized, photocopied from typescript on plain paper with light card colored cover, about 20 pp., saddle-stapled. Press run for the magazine is 250. **Sample postpaid: £1. Reports ASAP. Pays 1 copy. "Procedure for chapbook publication is explained to each author; each case is different."**

THIRD WOMAN PRESS (V, IV-Women, ethnic), Chicano Studies, Dwinelle Hall 3412, University of California, Berkeley CA 94720, phone (415)642-0240, founded 1981, poetry editor Norma Alarcon. **"We do not wish any unsolicited MSS of any kind. Please! Author must query first. Presently we are primarily interested in publishing the literary and artistic work of US Latinas, Hispanic, Native American and other US minority women in general. Our books are in Spanish or English." Query with bio and list of publications, no simultaneous submissions. Editor sometimes comments on rejections.** Occasionally they subsidy publish.

THISTLEDOWN PRESS LTD. (V, IV-Regional), 668 East Place, Saskatoon, Saskatchewan S7J 2Z5 Canada, phone (306)244-1722, founded 1975, Patrick O'Rourke, Editor-in-Chief, is "a literary press that specializes in **quality books of contemporary poetry by Canadian authors. Only the best of contemporary poetry that amply demonstrates an understanding of craft with a distinctive use of voice and language. Only interested in full-length poetry MSS with a 60-80 pp. minimum."** They have recently published books of poetry by Bert Almon, Shelley Leedahl, Charles Noble and Chris Collins. **No unsolicited MSS.** Canadian poets must **query first with letter, bio and publication credits. Poetry MS submission guidelines available upon request. Replies to queries in 2-3 weeks, to submissions (if invited) in 2-3 months. No authors outside Canada. No simultaneous submissions, unsolicited submissions, photocopies or dot-matrix. Contract is for 10% royalty plus 10 copies.** They comment, "Poets submitting MSS to Thistledown Press for possible publication should think in 'book' terms in every facet of the organization and presentation of the MSS: poets presenting MSS that *read* like good books of poetry will have greatly enhanced their possibilities of being published. We strongly suggest that poets familiarize themselves with some of our poetry books before submitting a query letter."

THORNTREE PRESS; GOODMAN AWARD (II), 547 Hawthorn Lane, Winnetka IL 60093, founded 1986, contact Eloise Bradley Fink. This press publishes professionally printed digest-sized, flat-spined paperbacks, 96 pp. selected through competition for the Goodman Award in odd-numbered years. **Sample: $7.95 postpaid.** In **Looking Across,** Marcia Lee Masters' award-winning poems describe her poet-father as "stern as a hatchet … [who] tightened his eyes for silence … treated people like apples, skinning the truth off in strips … [and later she wished for the] "big round table that once clattered with plates, to find some meaning in the fiery thresholds of the past." By spring of 1992, Thorntree Press will have published 13 books or 19 poets. "For the $400, $200 and $100 Goodman Awards we will be selecting three poets for the next **Troika,** Jan. 1-Feb. 14, 1993." Submit a stapled group of 10 pages of original, unpublished poetry, single or double spaced, photocopied, with a $4 reader's fee. MSS will not be returned. (A SASE for winners' names may be included.) "The top fifteen finalists will be invited to submit a 30-page manuscript for possible publication."

THOUGHTS FOR ALL SEASONS: THE MAGAZINE OF EPIGRAMS (IV-Form, humor), % editor Prof. Em. Michel Paul Richard, 11530 SW 99th St., Miami FL 33176, founded 1976, "is an irregular serial: **designed to preserve the epigram as a literary form; satirical.** All issues are commemorative, e.g., 1976, 1984, 1989, 1992." **Rhyming poetry will be considered although most modern epigrams are prose.** Prof. Richard has recently published poetry by David Kelly and offers this sample (poet unidentified):

> God created man in his own image —
> And lo! There stood Pithecanthropus.

TFAS is magazine-sized, offset from typescript on heavy buff stock with full-page cartoon-like drawings, card cover, 84 pp., saddle-stapled. Its press run is 500-1,000. The editor accepts about 20% of material submitted. There are several library subscriptions but most distribution is through direct mail or local bookstores and newsstand sales. Single copy: $4.50 plus $1.50 postpaid. **Send SASE for guidelines. No payment or contributor copies. Simultaneous submissions OK, but not previously published epigrams "unless a thought is appended which alters it." Reports in 30 days. Editor comments on rejections.** The editor says, "This is the only magazine which is devoted to this literary form."

THREE CONTINENTS PRESS INC. (IV-Ethnic, translations), Suite 407, 1901 Pennsylvania Ave. NW, Washington DC 20006, phone (202)223-2554, founded 1973, poetry editor Donald Herdeck. "**Published poets only welcomed and only non-European and non-American poets . . . We publish literature by creative writers from the non-western world (Africa, the Middle East, the Caribbean and Asia/Pacific)—poetry** *only* **by non-western writers or good translations of such poetry if original language is Arabic, French, African vernacular, etc.**" They have recently published poetry by Derek Walcott, Khalil Hawi, Mahmud Dawish and Julia Fields. As a sample the editors selected "The Wind" from **Burden of Waves and Fruit** by the Indian poet Jayanta Mahapatra:

> *My eyes are getting used to the dark.*
> *From time to time*
> *My old father comes at me*
> *with outstretched arms of judgement*
> *and I answer from no clear place I am in.*

This collection is a digest-sized, 98 pp., flat-spined book, professionally printed, glossy card cover with art. They also publish anthologies focused on relevant themes. **Query with 4-5 samples, bio, publication credits. Replies to queries in 5-10 weeks, to submissions (if invited) in 4-5 weeks. 10% royalty contract (5% for translator) with $100-200 advance plus 10 copies. Send SASE for catalog to buy samples.**

THE THREEPENNY REVIEW (II), P.O. Box 9131, Berkeley CA 94709, phone (415)849-4545, founded 1980, poetry editor Wendy Lesser, "is a quarterly review of literature, performing and visual arts, and social articles aimed at the intelligent, well-read, but not necessarily academic reader. Nationwide circulation. **Want: formal, narrative, short poems (and others); do not want: confessional, no punctuation, no capital letters. Prefer under 50 lines but not necessary. No bias** *against* **formal poetry, in fact a slight bias in favor of it.**" They have recently published poetry by Thom Gunn, Frank Bidart, Robert Hass, Czeslaw Milosz, Brenda Hillman, Edgar Bowers and Alan Shapiro. There are about 7-8 poems in each 36 pp. tabloid issue, circulation 7,500 with 6,000 subscriptions of which 300 are libraries. Subscription: $10. They receive about 4,500 submissions of freelance poetry per year, use 12. **Sample: $5 prepaid. Send 5 poems or fewer per submission. Reports in 2-8 weeks. Pays $50/poem. Send SASE for guidelines.**

THUMBPRINTS (I, IV-Themes, regional), 928 Gibbs, Caro MI 48723, phone (517)673-5563, founded 1984, editor Janet Ihle, is the monthly 6 pp. Thumb Area Writers' Club newsletter that uses **poetry about writers and writing, nothing "vulgar."** Maximum 20 lines. As a sample, the editor selected the last stanza of "Simultaneous Submissions" by T. Dunn:

> *So patiently, I mail my verse*
> *With fingers crossed and mumbled prayers,*
> *And should I die before they answer,*
> *Just send the payment to my heirs.*

They sponsor seasonal contests for Michigan amateur writers. Press run: 40 for 26 subscriptions. **Sample postpaid: 75¢. Send SASE for guidelines. Pays 1 copy. Simultaneous submissions and previously published poems OK. Reports in about 2 months.** Editor comments on submissions "sometimes."

‡TIA CHUCHA PRESS (IV-Ethnic, regional, social issues), P.O. Box 476969, Chicago IL 60647, founded 1989, president Luis J. Rodriguez. Tia Chucha **generally discourages unsolicited MS.** They publish 2-4 paperbacks a year, "**multicultural, lyrical, engaging, passionate works informed by social, racial, class experience. Evocative. Poets should be knowledgeable of contemporary and traditional poetry, even if experimenting.**" They have recently published poetry by David Hernandez, Michael Warr and editor Luis J. Rodriguez. As a sample the editor selected these lines from "The Poetry Widow" by Patricia Smith

> *Tonight, I wished I was one of your poems;*
> *strong syllables curled in your throat*
> *awaiting a joyous delivery. I wished I*
> *was that clever, stilted script on the*
> *paper in your hand, words you sweat over.*

That's from her collection **Life According to Motown**, published in a 6×9″ flat-spined professional printed paperback, 74 pp. with glossy card cover, $6.95. "We usually 'select' poets we'd like to publish, those active in a poetry environment (i.e. bar-and cafe scene, magazines, etc.) We believe poetry matters. Although we publish in English, we do not limit our traditions to Western Culture. Poetry should draw on the richness of human cultures, with roots in African, Native American, Asian and Latin sensibilities. We believe in engaging poetry; socially necessary and shaped by political, economic and class realities. Redemptive and relevant. We believe poetry is an art. It needs to be crafted, thought-out and knowledgeable of contemporary and traditional poetics."

‡**TICKLED BY THUNDER: A NEWSLETTER FOR WRITERS (II, IV-Subscribers)**, 7385 129th St., Surrey, British Columbia V3W 7B8 Canada, founded 1990, publisher/editor Larry Lindner, appears 4/year, using poems about **"fantasy, about writing or whatever. Keep them short—not interested in long long poems. Nothing pornographic, childish, unimaginative."** As a sample the editor selected these lines (poet unidentified):

> *So she put a monkee in his tea*
> *marshmallows on the side . . .*

It is 16-20 pp., half magazine-sized, published on Macintosh. Press run 100 for 100 subscribers. Subscription: $12. **Sample: $2.50 postpaid. Pays 1 copy plus cash. Send SASE for guidelines. Include samples of writing with queries. Reply in 1 month. Editor comments on rejections "99% of the time."**

TIDEPOOL (I, IV-Form), 4 E. 23rd St., Hamilton, Ontario L8V 2W6 Canada, phone (416)383-2857, founded 1984, publisher Herb Barrett who says, **"We charge $10 entry fee. Money returned if poetry not used."** Send SASE for guidelines for details. **He wants to see "haiku and contemporary short verse, any style or theme (maximum 34 lines). No scatalogical vulgarity."** He has recently published poetry by Chris Faiers, Dorothy Cameron Smith and Jeff Seffinga. As a sample I selected these lines by Dale Loucareas:

> *holding my heart-beat*
> *the burble of the creek*
> *now polluted*

> *where we played doctor*
> *& later skinny dipped*

Tidepool, published each October, is digest-sized, 80+ pp. saddle-stapled, professionally printed with matte card cover, circulation 400 with 150 subscribers of which 60-70 are libraries. Per issue: $5. **Sample: $5 postpaid. Submit MSS in May and June only. Reports on submissions in 2-3 weeks. No dot-matrix. "Prefer unpublished material." Pays in copies. Sometimes comments on rejections.**

‡**TIGER MOON PRESS; STAR TRIAD 'ZINE; TIGER MOON PRESS CATALOG (I, IV-Fantasy)**, P.O. Box 2371, Vero Beach FL 32961-2371, founded 1988, editor Sara Ryan. The press publishes cards, calendars and other products. They use poetry in their catalog and in *ST*; both appear 3/year. They want **"fantasy, metaphysical, inner growth experiences; I will look at others and have accepted a wide variety."** As a sample, I selected these lines from "Melody" by Stephanie Wong:

> *Follow the magical music,*
> *The melody that sings to you*
> *That whispers your innermost feelings,*
> *That promises to make dreams come true.*

It is magazine-sized, 28-60 pp., desktop published. **Sample postpaid: $4. Send SASE for guidelines. Pays $3-5/poem (depending on length). "I pay one-half in check, one-half in Tiger Moon Press products"; payment also includes a copy of the publication. I prefer a cover letter with a short line or two about the person." Previously published poems and simultaneous submissions OK (if you notify the editor). Reports in 10 days except between October and December, which is more like 1 month.** She buys about 100 poems/year. "Free service to all writers for a listing of any books or credits they want to share on the 'Writer's Preserve' page, which is in all publications."

‡**TIGHT (II)**, P.O. Box 1591, Guerneville CA 95446, founded 1990, editor Ann Erickson, appears every 2 months. *"tight* **uses poetry with concrete vocabulary, everyday or fantastic diction, fragmented form, experiential or surrealist imagery. Avoid academic, didactic or conceptual poetry."** They have recently published poetry by Matt Jasper, Sheila E. Murphy, Keith Abbott, Pat Nolan and John Grey. As a sample the editor selected these lines from "The Room" by Glenn Ingersoll:

> *Both of you are talking and backing*
> *away from each*
> *other. You raise your voices. "Yeah,*
> *oh, yeah."*
> *I remember Joannie's braces. Like my*
>
> *cousin.*

It is 50 pp. photocopied from typescript with matte card cover, digest sized. Press run 150 for 5 subscribers, 50 shelf sales. Subscription $21 (checks payable to Ann Erickson). **Sample postpaid: $2.50 back issue, $3.50 current issue. Submit poetry with seasonal imagery 2 months ahead of season. Pays 1 copy. Previous published poems and simultaneous submissions OK ("If I am warned"). Reports in 1-2 months.**

TIGHTROPE (II); SWAMP PRESS (V), 323 Pelham Rd., Amherst MA 01002, founded 1977, chief editor Ed Rayher. Swamp Press is a small-press publisher of poetry, fiction and graphic art in limited edition, letterpress chapbooks. *Tightrope*, appearing 1-2 times a year, is a literary magazine of varying format, circulation 300, 150 subscriptions of which 25 are libraries. Subscription: $10 for 2 issues. The issue I have seen (January, 1987) is triangular in shape, folded 12" square sheets, elegantly printed on heavy eggshell stock, 44 pp., saddle-sewn, using art (some in colored ink) with colored matte card cover. It contains poems printed in various ways on the pages. As a sample I selected this complete poem (untitled) by Nancy Stewart Smith:

> the sun
> slips down the golden bell's throat
> caught in a dewdrop

Sample of *Tightrope*: $6 postpaid. Send SASE for guidelines. Pays "sometimes" and provides 2 contributor's copies. Reports in 2 months, 6-12 months until publication. No simultaneous submissions. Sometimes comments on rejections. Reviews books of poetry. Swamp Press has recently published books by Edward Kaplan, editor Ed Rayher, Alexis Rotella (a miniature 3×3" containing 6 haiku), Sandra Dutton (a 4 foot long poem), Frannie Lindsay (a 10×13" format containing 3 poems), Andrew Glaze, Tom Hazo, Carole Stone and Steven Ruhl. Send SASE for catalog. **Not presently accepting freelance submissions for chapbook publication but when he publishes chapbooks he pays 5-10% of press run and, if there is grant money available, an honorarium (about $50). Sometimes comments on rejections.** Reviews books of poetry.

TIMBERLINE PRESS (V), Route 1, Box 1434, Fulton MO 65251, phone (314)642-5035, founded 1975, poetry editor Clarence Wolfshohl. "We do limited letterpress editions with the goal of blending strong poetry with well-crafted and designed printing. We lean toward **natural history or strongly imagistic nature poetry but will look at any good work. Also, good humorous poetry. Currently, fully stocked with material."** Recently published poets include Walter Bargen and William Hart. Payment policy: **"50-50 split with author after Timberline Press has recovered its expenses." Reports in under 1 month. Sample copies may be obtained by sending $4 requesting sample copy and noting you saw the listing in Poet's Market.**

‡TIMES CHANGE PRESS (V), P.O. Box 1380, Ojai CA 93024-1380, phone (805)646-8595, founded 1970, publisher Lamar Hoover, publishes nonfiction in areas of antiauthoritarian politics, feminism and gender issues, only rarely poetry. **They accept no unsolicited poetry.**

‡TIN WREATH (I), P.O. Box 13401, Albany NY 12212, founded 1985, "editor/janitor" David Gonsalves, "unindicted co-conspirators" Mark O'Brien and Susan M. Young. *"Tin Wreath* appears 3 times a year with selected late 20th century American visions of the actual and the possible." **The editor wants to see poetry "that transcends the surface elements of experience and makes contact with the deeper forces at work in the world; we're interested in poetry that explores the musical patterns and sculptural qualities inherent in the language; and we'd prefer to read abstract, minimalistic, and/or non-discursive poetry."** He has recently published work by Geof Huth, Deborah Meadows, N. Sean William and Sheila E. Murphy. As a sample, he chose the following poem "Snow/The Spring Afternoon" by Richard Evanoff:

> Blossoms
> caressing concrete/
> > snow
> on a spring afternoon —
> > a girl
> carrying the sun in her
> > > purse
> walks past
> not looking
> > up.

Tin Wreath is digest-sized, no frills, photocopied from handsome, large type on ordinary paper, about 36 pp., folded and saddle-stapled. Circulation is 350. *"Tin Wreath* **is available free upon request and we encourage anyone interested in the magazine to ask for a sample. There are no subscriptions per se or sales, circulation runs between 300-350 per issue."** Contributors receive **3 copies. Writers should send 3-5 poems; photocopy, dot-matrix and simultaneous submissions are all OK. Reporting time is "13 days to 13 weeks"** and time to publication is 3-6 months. The editor comments, "I believe we are in the midst of a transitory phase in American and world poetics (and politics). The movement seems now to be away from the absolute master and masterpiece and toward visionary landscapes both personal and inclusive."

TOAD HIGHWAY (II, IV-Translations), P.O. Box 44, Universal IN 47884, phone (317)832-8918, founded 1988, poetry editors Doug Martin, Brian Beatty, John Colvin, Kevin Anderson and Amanda Marcia. *Toad Highway* is a small magazine appearing irregularly using "all types of artwork, poetry, fiction, essays, reviews and translations. **"We want poetry which proves that the poet is obsessed by each sound, each stress, each image, each line. We'd like to see more scholarly essays and translations of up-and-coming Hispanic poets. No 'happy poems' or work which shows that the poet has not studied contemporary poetry."** They have recently published work by Sandra Russell, Beth Joselow, Connie Deanovich, Jerry Bradley, Barbara Unger and Simon Perchik. As a sample the editors selected these lines from "The Jogger" by Matthew Brennan:

> . . . *While light flows in the road where traffic's stopped;*
> *It blazes on windshields, hubcaps, and chrome;*
> *Farther out, it softens, and in its glow*
> *A woman's jogging West, toward Me — as if*
> *I'm sending forth the light, no matter what she knows.*

TH is a 52 pp. pamphlet, saddle-stapled. Their press run is 250 with 20 subscriptions. "We accept about one in every 100 poems received." Subscription: $12/3 issues. **Sample: $1.50 back issues. Pays 1 copy (discount on others). Submit maximum of 5 poems, single-spaced. No simultaneous submissions, but they will consider previously published poems. Responds to submissions in 3 months maximum. Editor "seldom" comments on rejections.** Reviews books of poetry. *Stone Talk*, a cassette series, is no longer produced. Doug Martin, editor-in-chief, says, "My advice to beginners is to revise their work. Poetry is the quest for wholeness. Approach poetry the same way Nabokov approached fiction. Multiple layers of order is where it's at."

TOLEDO POETS CENTER PRESS; 11 × 30; INMATE ARTS PRESS; GLASS WILL (V), 32 Scott House, University of Toledo, Toledo OH 43606, phone (419)473-0958, founded 1976, poetry editors Joel Lipman and Nick Muska, is a "small press **publisher of area writers, visual literature and of inmate writing (from our writer's workshops at area jails)**" in broadsides, chapbooks and flat-spined paperbacks. **"Submissions are not sought by Toledo Poets Center Press."** *11 × 30* is a "printerly publication of poetry, fiction, articles, literary news and gossip" and appears quarterly. Recent authors include Howard McCord, Michael Kasper, Bern Porter, Christy Sheffield-Sanford, (previously unpublished) Jack Kerouac. *Glass Will* "is a periodic anthology, more book-like (flat-spined) than magazine-like." 6 × 9¼", 266 pp. **It is a regional anthology of poetry appearing "infrequently" and publishing solicited work only. "Please, no unsolicited work. Inquiries welcome." Pays a varied number of author's copies.** All publications are quality offset; samples of 11 × 30 for $1; sample of Glass Will for $5. Joel Lipman notes, **"our focus is on literary life in this region, on strong and provocative writing, and on composition and design that has beauty and permanence."**

‡TOOK: MODERN POETRY IN ENGLISH; NORTON COKER PRESS (V), P.O. Box 640543, San Francisco CA 94164-0543, founded 1988, publisher Edward Mycue. *Took* appears "occasionally." 18 issues have been published. The press publishes 10 chapbooks/year. They have recently published poetry by Laura Kennelly, Jim Gove, Martha King and William Talcott. **Pays copies. No unsolicited MSS.**

TOUCH (IV-Religious, teens, themes), P.O. Box 7259, Grand Rapids MI 49510, phone (616)241-5616, founded 1970, poetry editor Carol Smith: "Our magazine is a 24 pp. edition written **for girls 7-14 to show them how God is at work in their lives and in the world around them.** *Touch* is theme-orientated. We like our poetry to fit the theme of each. We send out a theme update biannually to all our listed freelancers. **We prefer short poems with a Christian emphasis that can show girls how God works in their lives."** They have recently published poetry by Janet Shafer Boyanton and Iris Alderson. The editor selected these sample lines from Jacqueline Schiff's "Love Offering":

> *It isn't easy, my parents say,*
> *To stick to the rules I must obey.*
> *Their rules are a gift of love to me —*
> *That's not always easy for me to see.*

Touch is published 10 times a year, magazine-sized, circulation 15,800 with 15,500 subscriptions. Subscription: $9 US, $10.50 Canada, $15 foreign. They receive 150-200 freelance submissions of poetry per year, use 2 poems in each issue, have a 6 month backlog. **Sample and guidelines free with 8 × 10″ SASE. Poems must not be longer than 20 lines — prefer much shorter. Simultaneous submissions OK. Query with SASE for theme update. Reports in 8 weeks. Pays $5-10 and copies.**

TOUCHSTONE (II), Viterbo College, La Crosse WI 54601, phone (608)784-0268, founded 1950, moderator George Klawitter, is a literary quarterly using mostly poetry, short stories and artwork. **"Any form but no longer than 50 lines/poem. Nothing sentimental."** As a sample the editor selected these lines from "Old Coin In A Cornfield" by Joe Trueblood:

> *Once, in a field on the lake's edge,*
> *you squatted an hour scratching dirt*
> *with a steel claw, and your father did the same*
> *a few yards away.*

The magazine is digest-sized, 48 pp. saddle-stapled, with semi-glossy card cover. Press run 800 for 100 subscriptions of which 25 are libraries. Subscription: $5. **Sample postpaid: $2.50. Send SASE for guidelines. Best poem gets $20. All get 1 copy. Submit 3-5. Reports in 2 months.** The editor says, "Write poetry that is rich in visual imagery. Strive to make your reader *see* what you are talking about. Do not philosophize. Do not moralize. Let the imagery carry the message."

TOUCHSTONE LITERARY JOURNAL; TOUCHSTONE PRESS (II, IV-Translations), P.O. Box 8308, Spring TX 77387-8308, founded 1975, poetry editor William Laufer, is an annual using **"experimental or well-crafted traditional form, translations, no light verse or doggerel. Please include short bio including recent publications for our 'contributors' page.' No mail answered without SASE."** They have recently published poetry by Walter Griffin, Sheila Murphy, Michael L. Johnson, Walter McDonald and Joyce Pounds Hardy. As a sample, I selected these lines from "Women" by Elena Andres:

> *Encircling a motionless water*
> *a hundred arms of women*
> *curve themselves like arches*
> *they move in the wind*
> *like white serpents.*

Touchstone, appearing annually, is digest-sized, flat-spined, 100 pp., professionally printed in small, dark type with glossy card cover. Subscription: $7. **Sample postpaid: $3. "We do not read in December." Pays 1 copy.** Reviews books of poetry.

TOWNSHIPS SUN (IV-Rural, ecological, regional), 7 Conley St., P.O. Box 28, Lennoxville, Quebec J1M 1Z3 Canada, phone (819)566-7424, founded 1972, editor Patricia Ball, is a monthly newspaper in English "concerned with **history of townships, English community, agriculture, ecology, and using poetry on these themes."** As a sample, I selected these opening lines from "A Poem for Bury (Quebec)" by Marjories Stokes Munroe:

> *It's just a little village, where maples line the street,*
> *And graduates of years gone by, come back, their friends to greet.*
> *Three churches in our small town stand,*
> *Three schools, we think, the best ones in the land.*

The tabloid has a press run of 2,500 for 2,000 subscribers of which 20 are libraries, and 500 shelf sales. Subscription: $15/year Canada, $20/year outside Canada. **Sample postpaid: $2. Pays $10-30 plus 1 copy. "Will publish poems specifically about townships, townshippers, or of specific interest to townshippers."** Reviews books of poetry.

TRADESWOMEN MAGAZINE (IV-Women, themes), P.O. Box 40664, San Francisco CA 94140, founded 1982, poetry editor Sue Doro, staff editors Molly Martin and Helen Dozenilek, is a national quarterly "particular to women in non-traditional work" and uses poetry "pertaining to women in trades, tradeswomen as mothers, wives, male co-worker relationships." Subscription: $35. **Sample: $2 postpaid. Guidelines available for SASE. They consider simultaneous submissions and previously published poems. Reports in 4 weeks. No backlog.**

TRAMP (V), P.O. Box 1386, Columbia SC 29202, founded 1987 (first issue March, 1988), poetry editor Alan Howard. **"Publishes short poems in non-traditional forms. Special interest in themes of sensuality and spirituality. Wit is always welcome, from subtle to outrageous. Not interested in rhyming verse, unless it's a bit off-the-wall."** He has published poetry by David Chorlton, Gerald Locklin, Sheila Murphy and Willie Smith. As a sample he selected these lines by Dan Raphael:

> *a tree allergic to its own needles,*
> *a tree standing on its head*
> *a digital tree, statistically significant,*
> *a patented tree, a moon-worshipping tree . . .*

Tramp, appearing 2-3 times a year (plus occasional supplements), is digest-sized, photocopied, saddle-stapled, using some graphics and artwork. Subscription: $10 for 4 issues. **Sample: $3 postpaid. As of March, 1991 *Tramp* is on a temporary hiatus.**

TRANSNATIONAL PERSPECTIVES (III), CP161, 1211 Geneva 16 Switzerland, founded 1975, editor René Wadlow, is a "journal of world politics with some emphasis on culture that crosses frontiers." Uses 4-6 poems per issue, usually illustrated by drawing or photo. They want **"poems stressing harmony of nature, human potential, understanding of other cultures—relatively short. No humor, nationalistic themes, nothing 'overly' subjective."** They have recently published poems by Verona Bratesch and Janet Pehr. As a sample the editor selected these lines by Ondra Lysohorsky:

> Out of all the colours, and shades of colour,
> Out of all shapes, from all perfumes
> A beauty arises I cannot view without pity;
> With all these senses the holiest Silence sings—
> While I know that this beauty so soon fades.

TP appears 3 times a year; it "is oriented toward making policy suggestions in international organizations, especially in the United Nations." It is handsomely produced, magazine-sized, 48 pp., saddle-stapled with coated color paper cover. They receive about 100 poems per year, use 16. Press run is 5,000 for 4,000 subscriptions of which half are libraries. **Sample back issue free on request. Pays 5 copies, more if desired. Simultaneous submissions OK. No previously published poems. Reports in 1 month. Editor comments "rarely, on quality, only why not for *TP*."** René Wadlow says, "Poems in *TP* come from many countries, especially Eastern Europe, Scandinavia and India, often translated into English, usually 'upbeat' since most of articles are on political and economic difficulties of the world."

TRESTLE CREEK REVIEW (II), 1000 West Garden, Coeur d'Alene ID 83814, phone (208)769-3300, ext. 384, founded 1982-83, poetry editor Chad Klinger et al, is a "2 year college creative writing program production. Purposes: (1) expand the range of publishing/editing experience for our small band of writers; (2) expose them to editing experience; (3) create another outlet for serious, beginning writers. **We favor poetry strong on image and sound, the West and country vs. city; spare us the romantic, rhymed clichés. We can't publish much if it's long (more than 2 pp.)"** They have recently published poetry by Benedict Auer, Marcia Hurlow, Edward Lynskey and Martha Vertreace. Chad Klinger selected these lines by Lowell Jaeger:

> Teenage and fond
> of tree limbs glazed like sweets, if she divines
> the odds she is belted snug,
> her knuckles white as the wheel binds,
> as her pulse slides nearer the invisible tug
> of eternal splash toward frozen light
> slipping off maples like chandeliers.

TCR is a digest-sized 57 pp. annual, professionally printed on heavy buff stock, perfect-bound, matte cover with art, circulation 500, 6 subscriptions of which 4 are libraries. They receive freelance poetry submissions from about 100 persons per year, use 30. **Sample: $4. Submit before March 1 (for May publication) no more than 5 pp., no simultaneous submissions. Reports by March 30. Pays 2 copies.** The editor advises, "Be neat; be precise; don't romanticize or cry in your beer; strike the surprising, universal note. Know the names of things."

TRIQUARTERLY MAGAZINE (II), 2020 Ridge Ave., Evanston IL 60208, phone (708)491-7614, founded 1964, editors Reginald Gibbons and Susan Hahn, is one of the most distinguished journals of contemporary literature. Some issues are published as books on specific themes. They have recently published poetry by C. K. Williams, Rita Dove, Alan Shapiro, Li-Young Lee, Lisel Mueller, W.S. DiPiero, Donald Davie, Bruce Weigl, Thomas McGrath and Sandra McPherson. *Triquarterly's* three issues per year are 6×9", 200+ pp., flat-spined, professionally printed with b/w photography, graphics, glossy card cover with b/w photo, circulation 4,500 with 2,000 subscriptions of which 35% are libraries, using about 40 pp. of poetry in each issue. Subscription: $18; per copy: $7.95. They receive about 3,000 freelance submissions of poetry per year, use 20, have about a 12 month backlog. **Sample: $4 postpaid. Submit MSS Oct. 1-April 30. They do not read during the summer months. No dot-matrix or simultaneous submissions. Reports in 10-12 weeks. Payment varies. "We *suggest* prospective contributors examine sample copy before submitting."** Reviews books of poetry "at times."

‡TRONA PRESS; THE RAG OF NO ALLEGIANCE; ARE WE GOING TO A FUNERAL?; THE IDIOT'S FRIGHTFUL LAUGHTER (IV-Form, political), P.O. Box 5342, Athens GA 30604, founded 1989, editor Matthew Beale. *T.R.O.N.A.* publishes **"poetry, prose, interviews, essays, visual pieces, etc. . . . loosely of a, I suppose, philopolitical nature."** *AWGTAF* and *TIFL* are for **"experimental works."** Trona Press publishes chapbooks but is not, at present, open to submissions. They have recently published poetry by Patrick McKinnon, Robert Nagler, Andrew Williams, Ana Pine and Phillip Phuck. As a sample the editor selected these lines (poet unidentified):

> "They can't forget a drug so sweet"

> *uttered Anne in a trance*
> *the stars are dim*
> *they always die*

Sample postpaid: $1 for postage. Pays several copies. Editor always comments on rejections. "Please insure that the submitted work is clearly legible. Beyond that, I am not afflicted with an office paperwork fetish type orientation-and therefore will not burden you with inane demands. In particular, if you wish to include a cover letter, you are thus encouraged to do so. Make it as longwinded as you wish. I am not a metallic slot, I am a human organism—please respond accordingly."

TROUT CREEK PRESS; DOG RIVER REVIEW; DOG RIVER REVIEW POETRY SERIES; BACK POCKET POETS (II), 5976 Billings Rd., Parkdale OR 97041, founded 1981, poetry editor Laurence F. Hawkins, Jr., prefers **"shorter poems (to 30 lines) but will consider longer, book or chapbook consideration. No restrictions on form or content. No pornography or religious verse."** They have recently published poetry by Judson Crews, Gerald Locklin, Arthur Winfield Knight, Connie Fox, Terence Hoagwood and Joseph Semenovich. Laurence Hawkins selected these sample lines from "Measuring Time" by David Chorlton:

> *The eldest son marks a cross*
> *in the crust of a loaf, then cuts*
> *a first piece for his father.*
> *Supper is cheese again,*
> *and the same conversation as the day before . . .*

Dog River Review is a semiannual, digest-sized, 60 pp., saddle-stapled, offset from computer typescript with b/w graphics, circulation 300, 40 subscriptions of which 7 are libraries. Subscription: $6. They receive about 500 freelance submissions of poetry per year, use 40-50. **Sample: $2 postpaid.** Backpocket Poets is a series of $4 \times 5\frac{1}{4}$" chapbooks, professionally printed, 26 pp. saddle-stapled with matte card cover, selling for $2.50 each, a drawing or photo of the author on the back. The Dog River Review Series consists of digest-sized, professionally printed, saddle-stapled chapbooks with matte card covers. **Reports in 1 week-3 months. Payment in copies. Send SASE for guidelines. For book publication by Trout Creek Press, query with 4-6 samples. Replies to queries immediately, to submission (if invited) in 1-2 months. No simultaneous submissions. Photocopy, dot-matrix OK. No payment until** "material costs recovered. We also publish individual authors on cassette tape." Send SASE for catalog to buy samples. **Editor sometimes comments on rejections.** Reviews books of poetry.

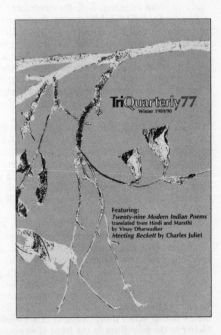

This TriQuarterly *cover is an example of "Xerox art" says editor Reginald Gibbons. The illustration is "real branches that have been photocopied over and over," he says. The cover is light blue, with the branches appearing white. "It wasn't any kind of symbol," says Gibbons. Rather, the cover was designed with the winter season in mind and "it shows the variety of works in our general issues," he says. The artist is Gini Kondziolka, a freelancer who has designed 30 TriQuarterly covers.*

TSUNAMI (II), Earthquake Press, P.O. Box 1442, Venice CA 90294, editor-in-chief Lee Rossi, is a "small press publisher of **poets and poems that aren't afraid to take risks. We have no limitations as to style or subject matter, but we take eight or ten looks at any poem longer than two pages before we accept it.** Our goal is to produce a book full of high-quality poems that tackle a variety of subjects. We enjoy **narrative voice, concrete expressions of modern life, surrealism.**" They have recently published poetry by Clayton Eshleman, Robert Nagler, Fred Voss, Janet Gray and Ellyn Maybe. As a sample they selected these lines from "Next Geraldo" by Roderick Potter:

> *Anjou pears in a meat locker*
> *Man with a mole*
> *Syrian lube jobs*
> *Prewar collapsed lung*
> *Tin: the real story*

Tsunami appears twice a year—digest-sized, 60 pp., perfect-bound, professionally printed, with glossy card cover and full-color art. **Submissions are read twice a year, in March and September.** In their 4th year they received about 2,500 poems, used 100. Press run is 600 for 200 subscriptions, 400 shelf sales. Subscription: $10. **Sample: $6 postpaid. Pays 1 copy. Simultaneous submissions and previously published work not accepted. Reports in "6-10 weeks."** No comments on rejections. The editors say, "We're polyglots—we accept many different voices, styles, tones. We feel that young poets should explore the possibilities of their voice and not stick with one tone or approach. We tap new voices nationwide."

TUCUMCARI LITERARY REVIEW (II), 3108 W. Bellevue Ave., Los Angeles CA 90026, founded 1988, editor Troxey Kemper, assistant editor Neoma Reed, appears every other month. "**Prefer rhyming and established forms, 2-100 lines, but the primary goal is to publish good work. Nothing shaped like a Christmas tree, Easter egg, etc. No talking animals. No haiku.** The quest here is for poetry that will be just as welcome many years later, as it is now. Preference is for readable, understandable writing of literary and lasting quality. Simple, sentimental rhymes and nostalgic recollections, yes, but not stilted, obscure snatches of jumbled words that require a dictionary at hand." They have recently published poetry by Esther M. Leiper, Wilma Elizabeth McDaniel, Gary J. Whitehead, Neill Megaw and Howard G. Baumgartner. As a sample the editor selected these lines from "Flight Path," a villanelle by R.S. Carlson:

> *Soundless lights traverse the turning dark.*
> *Stars, pared moon, outbound jets*
> *Vector for some far, predestined mark.*
>
> *Scattered clouds swing to blur the stark*
> *Rim of moon. Still, the cover lets*
> *Soundless lights traverse the turning dark.*

The magazine is digest-sized, 48 pp., saddle-stapled, photocopied from typescript, with card cover. Their press run is 150-200. Subscription: $12; $20 for overseas. **Sample: $2 plus $2.64 for overseas. Send SASE for guidelines. Pay is 1 copy. Considers simultaneous submissions and previously published poems. Reports within 1 month.** Acquires one-time rights. The editor advises, "Try to write a poem that 'says something,' expresses an idea or mood or *something*—not a jumble of prose words arranged in odd-shaped lines, trying to look like a poem and not saying anything. The established forms still stand as beacons for aspiring poets."

TURKEY PRESS (V), 6746 Sueno Rd., Isla Vista CA 93117, founded 1974, poetry editor Harry Reese along with his wife, Sandra Reese, "is involved with publishing contemporary literature, producing traditional and experimental book art, one-of-a-kind commissioned projects and collaborations with various artists and writers. **We do not encourage solicitations of any kind to the press. We seek out and develop projects on our own.**" They have published poetry by Thomas Merton, James Laughlin, Sam Hamill, Edwin Honig, Glenna Luschei, Tom Clark, Michael Hannon, Keith Waldrop, David Ossman, Peter Whigham, Jack Curtis, Kirk Robertson and Anne E. Edge.

‡TURNSTILE (II, IV-Humor, regional), Suite 2348, 175 5th Ave., New York NY 10010, founded 1988, appears twice a year: "Literary magazine publishing poetry, fiction, articles, art, satire, cartoons, interviews, criticism, reviews, novel excerpts and plays." They want poetry that is "**contemporary, experimental, humor/satire, regional. Nothing badly written. No rhyming poems. None that are well-crafted but lack emotion.**" They have recently published poetry by James Applewhite, Kevin Pilkington, Robert Morgan and Robert Hershon. I have not seen an issue, but the editors describe it as 6×9″, 128 pp., 55 lb. paper, and sent adulatory reviews of the magazine from a number of publications including *Library Journal*. Circulation: 1,500. Subscription: $12. **Sample postpaid $6.50. "Send no more than 4 poems at one time." Reports in 6-8 weeks. Pays 5 copies. Editors often comment on rejections.** "Refer to the guidelines in the front of our magazine."

TURNSTONE PRESS (II, IV-Regional), 607-100 Arthur St., Winnipeg, Manitoba R3B 1H3 Canada, phone (204)947-1555, founded 1975, is a "literary press publishing quality contemporary fiction, poetry, criticism" in flat-spined books (8/year), having **a Canadian emphasis.** They want **"writing based on contemporary poetics, but otherwise wide-ranging. Welcome experimental, graphic, long poems, the unusual. Nothing overly concerned with traditional rhyme and meter."** They have recently published poetry by Di Brandt, Maara Haas and Kristjana Gunnars. As a sample they selected these lines by Robert Kroetsch:

> *This is a prairie road.*
> *This road is the shortest distance*
> *between nowhere and nowhere.*
> *This road is a poem.*

The sample book I have seen, **Waiting for Saskatchewan,** by Fred Wah (a Chinese-Canadian with several previous books of poetry to his credit), is handsomely printed, 98 pp. flat-spined, with glossy two-color card cover, $7.95. It was awarded the Governor General's Award for 1985. **Submit complete MS and bio. Photocopies, good dot-matrix OK, as are poems previously published in magazines. Reports in 2-3 months. Pays $100-200 advance, 10% royalties and 10 copies. Editor comments on rejections "if we believe it has promise." Send 9 × 12″ SASE (or, from the US, SAE with IRCs) for catalog to buy samples.**

TWISTED (IV-Horror, fantasy), 22071 Pineview Dr., Antioch IL 60002, phone (312)395-3085, founded 1985, editor/publisher Christine Hoard, an annual using **poetry of "horror/dark fantasy; humor OK. Form and style open. Not more than 1 page long."** They have recently published poetry by Denise Dumars, Janet Fox, Marge Simon and Wayne Sallee. As a sample the editor selected these lines by poet Steve Sneyd:

> *under dank earth go*
> *white grubs seeking sockets to*
> *see through, souls to save*

I have not seen *Twisted,* but Christine Hoard describes it as "150 pp., magazine-sized, offset, vellum bristol cover, much art, some ads, 60 lb. matte paper. I receive a lot of poetry submissions, use 30-50 per issue." Press run is 300 for single-copy sales. **Sample: $6 postpaid, payable to Christine Hoard. Send SASE for guidelines. Pays 1 copy. "Don't submit more than four poems at a time. You should see a sample copy to get a 'feel' for what we publish." No simultaneous submissions, but previously published poems are sometimes accepted. Reports within 3 months. "We sometimes close when we are preparing next issue or overstocked." Editor often comments on rejections.** She says, "Poets of science fiction, horror, fantasy will be pleased to know there are *lots* of markets in the small press and some organizations are available to offer support and market information."

2 AM MAGAZINE; 2 AM PUBLICATIONS (IV-Science fiction/fantasy, horror), P.O. Box 6754, Rockford IL 61125-1754, phone (815)397-5901, founded 1986, editor Gretta McCombs Anderson, a quarterly, wants **"fantasy, science fiction, heroic fantasy, horror, weird; any form, any style; preferred length is 1-2 pp. We want poetry that leaves an after-image in the mind of the reader."** It has contained poetry by Mark Rich, G. N. Gabbard and Leonard Carpenter, and the editor describes it as 68 pp., magazine-sized, offset on 60 lb. stock, cover printed on glossy stock, illustrations "by leading fantasy artists," uses ads, circulation 1,000 with 250 subscriptions. Single copy: $4.95. Subscription: $19/year. **Sample: $5.95 postpaid. Send SASE for guidelines. Pays 5¢/line or $1 minimum plus 1 copy, 40% discount for more. Reports in 8 weeks, 6-12 months to publication. Submit no more than 5 poems at a time. "Prefer poems no more than 2 pages in length." Photocopies OK. For chapbook consideration (32 pp. 4 × 5″, saddle-stapled) query with 5 sample poems, bio, aesthetic or poetic aims. "Poetry must have concrete images and patterned meter, evoke strong sense of mood and express horror, fantasy or science fiction themes." Payment in royalties and copies. Editor sometimes comments on rejections.** Gretta M. Anderson advises, "Read widely, be aware of what's already been done. Short poems stand a good chance with us. Looking for mood-generating poetry of a cosmic nature. Not interested in self-indulgent poetry."

TYRO MAGAZINE; TYRO WRITERS' GROUP (I, IV-Membership), 194 Carlbert St., Sault Ste. Marie, Ontario P6A 5E1 Canada, phone (705)253-6402, founded 1984, editor Stan Gordon, who says, "This bimonthly is a practice, learning and discussion medium for developing writers, publishing poetry, fiction and nonfiction submitted by members of Tyro Writers' Group. Widely published professionals provide advice, feedback on mail and market opportunities." **Lifetime membership in the group costs $5, and you must be a member to submit.** The magazine publishes "all types" of poetry, but does not want "anything that is morally offensive, legally dangerous or wildly experimental." Poets recently published include Hereward Allix, Bernard Hewitt, Normandie Ann Vigiani, Lucie Adams, R. Erick Ott, Robert James-Huston, Ola C. Gibson, Douglas W. Wardle, Rodene Zimmer, Luther James Maddox and Rita Pozzebon. As a sample here are the last lines of "The Appointed Date" by Jon Davies:

> *In bars*
> *they are discreet,*
> *staring*
> *instead at dancing girls,*
> *hanging ropes*
> *around their necks*
> *before they have to greet.*

The magazine is digest-sized, offset from typeset copy with some b/w graphics, 180-220 pp. flat-spined, one-color coated card cover. Circulation is "about 500 and growing." Price per issue is $10, subscription $27/year. **Sample available for $10, guidelines for SASE. Simultaneous submissions considered. Submissions are reported on in 1 month. Time to publication is 10 weeks. Criticism is "always" provided on rejected MSS.** The editor says, "Writers develop skill through imitation, practice, exposure and feedback. They learn to write by writing, become more published by getting published. We try to provide these experiences to writers with a wide range of skills, from frequently published to never-been-published."

U.C. REVIEW (II), % Office of the Registrar, U.C., University of Toronto, Toronto, Ontario M5S 1A1 Canada, phone (416)978-3170, is a literary magazine appearing twice a year using **"poetry, short prose and criticism, usually experimental in nature. We are open to all forms of literature but prefer challenging and innovative work. No specifications as to style or subject-matter. The work should be engaged to some extent, or at least aware of literary theory. It should be serious about the interaction between form and content, and about its place in the social sphere. No derivative or mainstream commodity poetry."** They have recently published poetry by Patricia Seaman and Yves Troendle. As a sample I selected the first stanza of the 15-line poem "Jocasta's Brooch (The Pasolini Version)" by Chris D'Iorio:

> *To weave backwards from the alleged torment,*
> *to forge sense from strange compulsions,*
> *I wrest vision from that eye, that fragment*

It is digest-sized. Press run 1,200 for 10 subscriptions of which 3 are libraries. Shelf sales in 3 Toronto bookstores. **Sample free. Send SASE for guidelines. Pays 4-6 copies. Reports "1 month after acceptance."** They send copies to small-press publications and some Toronto magazines for criticism. **Editor sometimes comments on rejections.**

ULTRAMARINE PUBLISHING CO., INC. (II), P.O. Box 303, Hastings-on-Hudson NY 10706, founded 1974, editor C. P. Stephens, who says "We mostly distribute books for authors who had a title dropped by a major publisher—the author is usually able to purchase copies very cheaply. We use existing copies purchased by the author from the publisher when the title is being dropped." Ultramarine's recent list includes 250 titles, 90% of them cloth bound, one-third of them science fiction and 10% poetry. **The press pays 10% royalties. "Distributor terms are on a book by book basis, but is a rough split."** Authors should query before making submissions; queries will be answered in 1 week. Simultaneous submissions are OK, as are photocopied or dot-matrix MSS, but no disks.

‡UNCLE (THE MAGAZINE FOR THOSE WHO HAVE GIVEN UP) (IV-Humor, satire); RIVER FRONT READING SERIES; THE KANSAS CITY ARTISTS COALITION, 201 Wyandotte, Kansas City MO 64105, phone (816) 421-5222, appears twice a year using **"high quality humorous and satiric poetry, but not 'epic length.' "** They have recently published poetry by Maxine Chernoff, Malcolm Glass, Miriam Sagan and W.D. Winans. As a sample the editor selected these lines from "The Plague of Disposal" by Eve Merriam:

> *Odors of stale cigars and burning and vomit*
> *shall penetrate thy house*
>
> *and thou shalt spray thy carpets*
> *with daisy-fresh deodorants*
>
> *and the deodorant cans*
> *shall stockpile like armaments*

It is professionally printed, flat-spined, 60-135 pp. with matte card cover. Press run 1,000 for 50 subscribers of which 20 are libraries, 800 shelf sales. **Sample postpaid: $3. Send SASE for guidelines. Pays 2 copies. Reports in 4-8 weeks. 6-12 month delay between acceptance and publication.** The magazine is published as a special project of the River Front Reading Series and is sold during River Front's poetry and fiction readings which take place 3 times a month, sponsored by the Kansas City Artists Coalition.

UNDERPASS; UNDERPASS PRESS (II), #574-21, 10405 Jasper Ave., Edmonton, Alberta T5J 3S2 Canada, founded 1986, editors Barry Hammond and Brian Schulze. *Underpass* is a literary annual. The press publishes chapbooks and flat-spined paperbacks of poetry. They want **"contemporary, urban, avant-garde, concrete, or discursive prose-poems. Any length. No religious or nature poetry."** They have recently published poetry by Brian Burke, Stan Rosal and Alice Major. As a sample, Brian Schulze selected these lines from "Europeanization" by B.Z. Niditch:

> White and blue in the river
> from phantom faces
> every last word escapes
> with the escort of the wind.

Underpass is digest-sized. Their fourth issue was 78 pp., but they hope to increase size and continue the flat-spined format. It is offset printed with a laminated card cover using b/w and color graphics inside. "This year we received about one hundred and fifty submissions and only used twenty-six poets." Press run is 100-300. **Sample: $6.95 postpaid. Send SASE for guidelines. Pays $5/poem plus 2 copies. No simultaneous submissions or previously published poems. Editor sometimes comments on rejections. Deadline for each year is August 31st. Publication in late fall.**

UNDERWHICH EDITIONS (V), Box 262, Adelaide St. Station, Toronto, Ontario M5C 2J4 Canada, and, in western Canada, 920 9th Ave. N., Saskatoon, Saskatchewan S7K 2Z4 Canada, founded 1978, poetry editors Richard Truhlar, Steven Smith, Beverley Daurio, Frank Davey and Paul Dutton are "dedicated to presenting in diverse and appealing physical formats, new works by contemporary creators, **focusing on formal invention and encompassing the expanded frontiers of musical and literary endeavor**" in chapbooks, pamphlets, flat-spined paperbacks, posters, cassettes, records and anthologies. They have recently published poetry by Victor Coleman, Paula Claire and John Riddell. The editors selected these sample lines from "A Knife a Rope a Book" by Mari-Lou Rowley:

> Prefers the body
> raw
> feeling
> his eye
> behind the lens

Currently not accepting poetry submissions. "We have all the MSS we can handle for the foreseeable future."

UNITED METHODIST REPORTER; NATIONAL CHRISTIAN REPORTER; UNITED METHODIST REVIEW (IV-Religious), P.O. Box 660275, Dallas TX 75266-0275, phone (214)630-6495, founded "about 1840." *UMR* is a weekly broadsheet newspaper, circulation 500,000+, "aimed at United Methodist primarily, ecumenical slant secondarily." They use at most one poem a week. The poetry **"must make a religious point — United Methodist or ecumenical theology; short and concise; concrete imagery; unobtrusive rhyme preferred; literary quality in freshness and imagery; not trite but easy to understand; short enough to fill 1-3 inch spaces. Do not want to see poems by 'my 13-year-old niece,' poems dominated by 'I' or rhyme; poems that are too long, too vague or too general; poems without religious slant or point."** As a sample the editor chose the whole poem "The Good Neighbor" by Pollyanna Sedzoil:

> She did her witnessing
> in such ordinary tones
> that only those few
> discerning ones
> who recognize each life
> as a unique poem
> were aware
> of the beautiful psalm
> alive in her daily faithfulness.

Managing Editor John A. Lovelace says they use about 50 of 1,000 poems received per year. Poems may appear in all three publications. **Send SASE for guidelines. Pays $2/poem and 1 copy. Send no more than 3-4 poems at a time. No simultaneous submissions or previously published poems. Time to publication can be up to a year. Editor comments on rejection "if it is promising."**

UNITY; DAILY WORD; WEE WISDOM (IV-Religious, children), Unity School of Christianity, Unity Village MO 64065, founded 1893. "Unity periodicals are devoted to spreading the truth of practical Christianity, the everyday use of Christ's principles. The material used in them is constructive, friendly, unbiased as regards creed or sect, and positive and inspirational in tone. We suggest that prospective contributors study carefully the various publications before submitting material. **Sample copies are sent on request. Complimentary copies are sent to writers on publication. MSS should be typewritten in double space. We accept MSS only with the understanding that they are original and previously unpublished. Unity School pays on acceptance 5¢ a word and up for prose and $1 a line for verse."** *Unity Magazine* is a monthly journal that publishes "articles and **poems that give a clear message of Truth and provide practical, positive help in meeting human needs for healing, supply, and harmony. We pay a $20 minimum."** *Daily Word* is a "monthly manual of daily studies" which "buys a limited number of short devotional articles and poems." *Wee Wisdom* is a monthly magazine for boys and girls. **"Its purpose is character-building. Its goal is to help children develop their full potential. Short, lively nature and science stories and poems, readable by a third-grader. Character-building ideals should be emphasized without preaching."** As a sample I selected the last of three stanzas of "The Prayer of Faith" by Hannah More Kohaus:

> *God is my health, I can't be sick;*
> *God is my strength, unfailing, quick;*
> *God is my all, I know no fear;*
> *Since God and love and Truth are here.*

Many of the poems in the magazine are by children, submitted to the section called "Writers' Guild," edited by Judy Gehrlein. There is no payment for poems in this section except for complimentary copies and an award certificate and letter. Here is a sample, "I Love," by Wendy Strickland (Grade 4):

> *I love the sand,*
> *I love the sea,*
> *I love the waves so high;*
> *But then I saw an airplane*
> *And wished that I could fly.*

Wee Wisdom is 48 pp. saddle-stapled, digest-sized, with colorful art and graphics. **They also buy "rhymed prose for 'read alouds' " for which they pay $15 minimum.**

UNMUZZLED OX (IV-Themes, bilingual/foreign language), 105 Hudson St., New York NY 10013, or Box 550, Kingston, Ontario K7L 4W5 Canada, founded 1971, poetry editor Michael Andre, is a tabloid literary biannual. **Each edition is built around a theme or specific project.** The editor says, "The chances of an unsolicited poem being accepted are slight since I always have specific ideas in mind." He is currently assembling material for issues titled *Poems to the Tune,* "simply pomes to old tunes, a buncha contemporary *Beggar's Opera.* The other is tentatively called *The Unmuzzled OX Book of Erotic Verse.* **Only unpublished work will be considered, but works may be in French as well as English."** Subscription $20.

URBANUS (II), P.O. Box 192561, San Francisco CA 94119, founded 1987, editors Peter Drizhal and Cameron Bamberger, is a twice-yearly journal of poetry. **"Seeks *quality* contemporary and progressive poetry. Does not want to see anything self-indulgent, clichéd, rhymed."** They have recently published poetry by Antler, Martha Vertreace, A.D. Winans, Robert Peters, Cheryl Townsend and Pat McKinnon. As a sample I selected these lines from "harry was talking" by Todd Moore:

> *. . . rain*
> *pounding thru the*
> *rolled down window*
> *stung my face the*
> *skid felt like a*
> *roller coaster ride*
> *thru lightning . . .*

The digest-sized, 48 pp. saddle-stapled magazine uses roughly 5% of the submissions they receive. Their press run is 300. Subscription: $10. **Sample: $5 postpaid. Reports in 4-8 weeks, 9 months-1 year till publication. Pays 1 copy.**

US1 WORKSHEETS; US1 POETS' COOPERATIVE (II), 21 Lake Drive, Roosevelt NJ 08555, founded 1973, is a 20-25 pp. literary tabloid biannual in 11½×17", circulation 500, which uses **high quality poetry and fiction. Sample: $4.** "We use a rotating board of editors; it's wisest to query when we're next reading before submitting." Recently published poets include Alicia Ostreicher, Toi Derricotte, Elizabeth Anne Socolow, Jean Hollander, Pablo Medina and David Keller. **"We read a lot but take very few. Prefer complex, well-written work. Requests for sample copies, queries, and all manuscripts should be addressed to the secretary, % POSTINGS, P.O. Box 1, Ringoes NJ 08551."**

UTAH HOLIDAY MAGAZINE (II, IV-Regional), Suite 200, 807 E. South Temple, Salt Lake City UT 84102, phone (801)532-3737, founded 1971, is a "monthly magazine with a **strong regional focus that publishes a very limited amount of poetry as space permits."** *UHM* says that none of our category designations really applies. **The poetry they use is not necessarily regional, and "We are very open to beginners' submissions.** We don't care if somebody has been published elsewhere or not. We will offer criticism and suggestions to writers, and will also consider accepting something after revision, if we are happy with the revision. But **we do not have much space to run poetry, so writers should be advised there is a high likelihood we will either not accept their poems, or that they will have to wait a considerable amount of time before they see them in print. There are no particular specifications except that the poetry be quality work and that it hasn't been published previously. We are more apt to be able to publish shorter poems just because there is more likely to be space for them. Poems with a strong Utah regional focus would be more acceptable than those which refer to other regions. We like poetry with a unique way of looking at experience or the world."** They have, so far, published only regional writers. As a sample, I selected this haiku by Judith Lundin Lowe:

> *The blue heron . . .*
> *He spreads his wings over her;*
> *The stretched horizon.*

UHM is magazine-sized, 85-130 pages. "We look like any other regional magazine. We have b/w as well as 4-color pages, and regular slick magazine quality paper." Its press run is 14,000 for 10,000 subscriptions, 4,000 shelf sales. Subscriptions: $16.95. Single copy: $1.95. **Sample: $3 postpaid. Pays $25-50 "usually," plus 2-3 copies. They have "an extensive backlog." Simultaneous submissions OK. Reports "within 3 months." Editor sometimes comments on rejections.** She says, "We do not really consider ourselves a very viable market for poetry. We do encourage local people who have poetry, if it is good quality, to submit in hopes that we will have space for it. If people out of region have poems which relate to this region, we would especially encourage them, too."

‡UTAH STATE UNIVERSITY PRESS (V), Logan, UT 84322-7800, phone (801)750-1302, founded 1972, editor Peggy Lee, publishes poetry but is **not open for submissions.**

‡THE VAGABOND (I, II), 6310 Delmar, St. Louis MO 63130, founded 1989, publisher Maria Massey (address "poetry editor" or "literary editor"), is a monthly tabloid newspaper "serving the arts in St. Louis. *The Vagabond* believes that **freedom of speech in all forms is primary in the growth of the arts and that exercising free speech defends and improves existing liberties. Send anything, 300 words or less. Preferably 2-3 poems so we can become acquainted with the poet's work. You may include drawings and photos."** They have recently published poetry by Gerald Malanga, Allen Ginsberg, Francisco Orrego and Tim Leach. As a sample the editor selected these lines from "(K.B.) Between Tickets" by J. Sih:

> *There is an art*
> *to the clean mitering of schedules*
> *to life without maps*
> *Meticulous, polite, laconic*
> *He is living in twenty-four hour measures.*
> *His brow is smooth.*

They accept 60-75% of poetry received. Press run 5,000 for 3 subscribers, distributed free to "poets and artists in St. Louis metro-area. Mailed to various poetry and writers' groups in midwest." Subscription: $6/8 issues. **Sample: 75¢ postpaid. Pays 5 copies. "Please include a short note about yourself. Whatever you want to say. Mainly for my interest. Read within 2-3 weeks."** Editor comments on rejections "often." She advises, "Search out current poets publishing. Read your own poetry aloud, and if you can, perform it or read before an audience (a poetry group or open mike). Be fearless!"

VEGETARIAN JOURNAL; THE VEGETARIAN RESOURCE GROUP; JEWISH VEGETARIANS NEWSLETTER (I, IV-Themes, children/teens), P.O. Box 1463, Baltimore MD 21203, founded 1982, poetry editor Debra Wasserman. *VJ* is bi-monthly, *JV* is quarterly, founded 1983. The Vegetarian Resource Group is a small-press publisher of nonfiction, sometimes incorporating poetry. **They want poetry on themes such as vegetarians, animal rights, and world hunger. "We appreciate humor and/or account of personal feelings about being vegetarian and a factual, scientific approach. Please, no graphic descriptions of animal abuse."** As a sample, the editor selected these lines from a poem by Debbie Israel:

> *I love my nieces, but they add to the problem with their disposable*
> *   diapers*
> *And their bottles of milk, and their meat, and their fish, and their eggs.*
>
> *I love them and I want their lives*
> *To help the world, to be part of the solution, not part of the problem.*

JV is a 16 pp., magazine-sized newsletter, offset from typescript with typeset heads. *VJ* has a circulation of 12,000; *JV* of 800. **Pays copies. Simultaneous submissions and previously published poems OK. Editor makes short comments on rejections.** They offer an annual contest for ages 19 and under, $50 savings bond yearly for the best contribution on any aspect of vegetarianism. "Most entries are essay, but we would accept poetry with enthusiasm." Charles Stahler asks me to "note that *Vegetarian Journal* and *Jewish Vegetarians Newsletter* are published by two separate organizations, but are both edited from the same address." **Sample for *JV* is SASE and two first class stamps. Sample for *Vegetarian Journal* is $3.**

VEHICULE PRESS; SIGNAL EDITIONS (IV-Regional), P.O. Box 125, Station Place du Parc, Montreal, Quebec H2W 2M9 Canada, phone (514)844-6073, poetry editor Michael Harris, publisher Simon Dardick, is a "literary press with poetry series, Signal Editions, **publishing the work of Canadian poets only.**" They publish flat-spined paperbacks and hardbacks. Among the poets published are Louis Dudek, Marie-Claire Blais, Erin Mouré, Don Coles, David Solway, Susan Glickman, and Stephen Scobie. As a sample the publisher selected these lines by poetry editor Michael Harris:

> Soon large in the parish will the thunder bunch
> its fists, the thunder roll its muscle
> and trees fall dead. Nothing rises, Jeffrey,
> as quietly as you. Not the wintering daisy
> at seed in the meadow, the grace of summer fields.

They want Canadian poetry which is **"first-rate, original, content-conscious." Query with 10 poems ("a good proportion of which should already have been published in recognized literary periodicals")** as sample, bio, publication credits, or poetic aims. **Reports in 8 weeks. Photocopy, pays 10% royalities plus 10 author copies.**

VER POETS VOICES; POETRY POST; POETRY WORLD (IV-Members); VER POETS OPEN COMPETI-TION, Haycroft, 61/63 Chiswell Green Lane, St. Albans, County Herts, AL2 3AL England, founded 1965, editor/organizer May Badman, a poetry group **"publishing members' work if it has reached a good standard.** We publish *Ver Poets Voices, Poetry Post,* and *Poetry World,* the last being an information sheet. **We aim at bringing members' work up to professional literary standards if it is not already there.** All members receive our publications free and can buy further copies." Membership costs £10 overseas p.a. They have recently published work by Beth Smith, Ruth Padel, Jane Wight, Dilys Frascella, Lotte Kramer, Daphne Schiller and Alan Dunnett. As a sample, they selected the following lines "Sun to Earth" by May Ivimy:

> You may be running rings round me,
> Blind as you are to my trajectory,
> But you should beware. Your leaps
> May Backfire, sink that puny raft
> Which is all your life; and should
> You penetrate my guard you'd never know
> And I would never notice.

Ver Poets Voices, which appears about twice a year, is digest-sized with a stapled card cover. It goes to the 250 members plus about 50 copies to shops, etc. *Poetry Post,* also a semi-annual, is magazine-sized with a card front cover. It reports on Ver Poets competitions and other matters concerning poetry. *Poetry World,* which appears 4 times/year, is a series of information sheets on national competitions and poetry events. The group organizes the Ver Poets Open Competition (an annual event), which has prizes of £500, £300, and £100 (two equal prizes—total £1,000.). They also organize six competitions per year for members only; winners are published in *Poetry Post.* **Sample copies: *Ver Poets Voices,* £1-50 (£3 includes postage); *Poetry Post,* 80p. (£2 includes postage); *Poetry World,* free for IRC. "All members are encouraged to send work for comment."** Not more than 6 clearly typed or reproduced poems should be submitted at once. **Reporting time is "by return of post" and time to publication is 6 months or less.** Reviews books of poetry if written by members. The editors say, "A lot of work is being done in England by small presses such as ourselves, and we provide continually the first few rungs of the ladder to success as poets. Members are offered free advice on their work and how to present it to editors. Also information on publishing opportunities."

‡VERANDAH (II), c/o TAS, Victoria College, Toorak Campus, 336 Glenterrie Rd., Malvern Victoria, Australia 3144, founded 1986, is a handsome annual. **"We seek poetry of a high quality and literary kind, with no restrictions on length, subject or style."** They have recently published poetry by Vivian Hopkirk, Peter Bakowsski, Adrian D'Ambra and Diane Fahey. As a sample, I selected this haiku by Duncan Richardson:

> Along the cream
> beach they came four pelicans
> playing soft biplanes.

It is flat-spined with full-color glossy card cover, professionally printed on glossy stock, 90+ pp. **Sample postpaid: A$8.50. Pays A$5-10/poem plus 2 copies. Annual deadline May 31. Authors' names are deleted from MS before consideration by editors.**

VERSE (II), English Dept., College of William and Mary, Williamsburg VA 23185, founded 1984, editors Henry Hart, Robert Crawford and David Kinloch, is "a poetry journal which also publishes interviews with poets, articles about poetry and book reviews." They **want "no specific kind; we only look for high quality poetry."** They have recently published poetry by A. R. Ammons, James Merrill, James Dickey, Galway Kinnell, Richard Kenney, John Hollander, Charles Wright, Robert Pinsky, Charles Simic and Wendell Berry. As a sample they selected these lines from "Wolfe Tone" by Seamus Heaney:

> *Light as a skiff, manoeuvreable*
> *yet outmanoeuvred,*
>
> *I affected epaulettes and a cockade,*
> *wrote a style well-bred and impervious*
>
> *to the solidarity I angled for,*
> *and played the ancient Roman with a razor.*

Verse is published 3 times a year in a digest-sized, 90 pp., saddle-stapled format with card cover, using small type, professionally printed. They accept about 100 of 3,000 poems received. Press run: 700, to 600 subscribers of which 150 are libraries, 100 are sold on newsstands or in bookstores. Subscription: $12. **Sample: $4 postpaid. Pays 2 copies. Reports in 1 month, usually 4-5 months to publication. Simultaneous submissions OK.**

VERVE (II, IV-Themes), P.O. Box 3205, Simi Valley CA 93093, founded 1989, editor Ron Reichick, is a quarterly **"open to any style – high literary free verse, traditional – as long as well crafted and fits the theme of issue. No sing-song rhyme, 4-letter words every 4th word."** They have recently published poetry by Diana Chang, Robert Edwards, Maria Gillan and Don McLeod. As a sample the editor selected these lines from "The Mexican Orange Merchant" by S.A. Griffin:

> *... and she will laugh and smile*
> *and throw expensive parties for whales and seals and*
> *starving children*
> *and wars*
> *in places she'll never be or care to be or know of*
> *and she will be as fresh and as beautiful as a*
> *lover's first kiss.*

It is digest-sized, 40 pp., saddle-stitched, using bios of each contributor. Press run 300 for 80 subscriptions of which 3 are libraries. **Sample postpaid: $3.50. Send SASE for guidelines and list of upcoming themes. Pays 1 copy. Submit up to 5 poems, 2 pages maximum per poem; "36 lines or less has best chance."** Simultaneous submissions and previously published poems OK. Reviews books of poetry. They sponsor 2 annual contests, each having prizes of $75, $50 and $25, entry fee $2 each poem. The editor advises, "Keep reading and writing. Listen to criticism, but follow your instinct *and* the poem. *Then* – keep submitting."

VESTAL PRESS, LTD. (IV-Themes, anthologies), 320 N. Jensen Rd., Box 97, Vestal NY 13851-0097, founded 1961, contact Grace L. Houghton, is a "small-press publisher of **books on automatic music, carousels, antique phonographs, antique radios, early film history, postcard histories, many titles geared to hobbyists and collectors"** that has published a book of limericks on the history of the carousel such as this one:

> *The armor you see here is for*
> *those horses that go off to war.*
> *The nice shiny metal*
> *helps the knight prove his mettle*
> *and is intended to minimize gore.*

The verses are by Harvey Roehl, and the charming b/w illustrations by Pat Hyman are suitable for coloring. They have also published an anthology on poetry of the cinema using poems by Vachel Lindsay, Ogden Nash, Gene Lockhart, Howard Moss and about 75 other poets. **If you have a suggested project closely associated with one of the topics listed above, query. Replies to queries in 1-2 weeks. Pays 10% royalties.**

VICTIMOLOGY: AN INTERNATIONAL JOURNAL (IV-Themes), 2333 N. Vernon St., Arlington VA 22207, phone (703)536-1750, is a quarterly **"specifically focusing on the victim, on the dynamics of victimization,** for social scientists, criminal justice professionals and practitioners, social workers and volunteer and professional groups engaged in prevention of victimization and in offering assistance to victims of rape, spouse abuse, child abuse, incest, abuse of the elderly, natural disasters, etc." **Sample: $5 postpaid. Send SASE for guidelines. Uses poetry relevant to the themes of the magazine up to 30 lines. Pays $10-25.**

VIGIL; AMMONITE; VIGIL PUBLICATIONS (II), 12 Priory Mead, Bruton, Somerset BA10 ODZ England, founded 1979, poetry editor John Howard Greaves. *Vigil* was formerly *Period Piece and Paperback*. They want "poetry with a high level of emotional force or intensity of observation. Poems should normally be no longer than 35 lines. Color, imagery and appeal to the senses should be important features. No whining self-indulgent, neurotic soul-baring poetry." They have recently published poetry by John Gonzalez, Roger Elkin, Brian Daldorph and Richard Newman. As a sample the editor selected these lines by Malc Payne:

> he lived with a window
> full of trees
> marking his latest struggle
> to blown end

The digest-sized magazine is 40 pp., saddle-stapled, photoreduced typescript, with colored matte card cover. It appears 3 times a year, press run 200 for 80 subscriptions of which 6 are libraries. They accept about 60 of 200 submissions received. Subscription: £4.50. Sample: £2 postpaid. **Pays 2 copies. Editor sometimes comments on rejections. Submit no more than 6 poems at a time.** *Ammonite* appears twice a year with "myth, image and word towards the secondary millenium . . . a seedbed of mythology for our future, potently embryonic." **Query regarding book publication by Vigil Publications.** The editor offers "appraisal" for £7.50 for a sample of a maximum of 12 poems.

VIKING PENGUIN, 40 W. 23rd St., New York NY 10010. Declined listing.

THE VILLAGE IDIOT; MOTHER OF ASHES PRESS (II), P.O. Box 66, Harrison ID 83833-0066, *The Village Idiot* founded 1970, Mother of Ashes Press founded 1980, editor Joe M. Singer. They want "poetry which breathes." They have recently published poetry by Josephine D. Buffet and Rita Conroy. As a sample the editor selected these lines by Joyce Chandler:

> Are you a nutmeg from brazil finely ground
> a double spice for nose and tongue . . .

The Village Idiot appears triannually in a 6×9″ format, saddle-stapled, 48 pp., with cover, using less than 10% of over 500 poems received a year. Their press run is 300 with 15 subscriptions of which 2 are libraries. Subscription: $15 for 6 issues. **Sample: $3 postpaid. Reports in 1 month. Pays in copies. Editor sometimes comments on rejections.** Reviews books of poetry. Mother of Ashes Press publishes books and chapbooks by invitation only. The editor says, "*The Village Idiot* is good company for an evening; entertaining, informative, provocative, and well enough dressed one does not mind being seen in company with it. Are your poems?"

THE VILLAGER (II), 135 Midland Ave., Bronxville NY 10708, phone (914)337-3252, founded 1928, editor Amy Murphy, poetry editor M. Josephine Colville, a publication of the Bronxville Women's Club for club members and families, professional people and advertisers, circulation 750, appears in 9 monthly issues, October-June. **Sample: $1.25 postpaid. They use one page or more of poetry per issue, prefer poems less than 20 lines, "in good taste only," seasonal (Thanksgiving, Christmas, Easter) 3 months in advance. They copyright material but will release it to author on request. Pays 2 copies. A SASE required.**

THE VINCENT BROTHERS REVIEW (II), 1459 Sanzon Dr., Fairborn OH 45324, founded 1988, editor Kimberly A. Willardson, is a journal appearing three times a year. "We look for well-crafted, thoughtful poems that shoot bolts of electricity into the reader's mind, stimulating a powerful response. We also welcome light verse and are thrilled by unusual, innovative themes/styles. We do not accept previously published poems, simultaneous submissions, or sexist, racist, anti-Semitic poetry. Sloppy MSS containing typos and/or unintentional misspellings are automatically rejected." They have recently published poetry by John Grey, Laura Albrecht and Susan V. Carlos. As a sample the editor selected these lines from "Portrait of a Self" by Richard Stansberger:

> in night's x-ray
> the flesh fades
> bone shows green
> green as the schemes of moss
> bent on taking over

TVBR is digest-sized, 60-80 pp., saddle-stapled, professionally printed, digest-sized with matte card cover. Their press run is 300. We have 100 subscribers, 10 of which are libraries. Subscription: $12. **Sample: $4.50 postpaid. Send SASE for guidelines. Pays 1 copy. Submit no more than**

8 poems at a time, name and address on each page. "We do not read in December." Reports in 6-8 months (after readings by editor and 3 associate editors.) Editor "often" comments on rejections. Reviews books of poetry. She advises, "Don't send your poetry to a magazine you've never seen. Read as much current poetry as you can get your hands on. Read your work aloud to a very tough critic or audience before sending it out."

VIRGIN MEAT (IV-Horror), 2325 West Ave. K-15, Lancaster CA 93536, phone (805)722-1758, founded 1986, editor Steve Blum, appears irregularly with fiction, poetry and art. "Fiction is mildly erotic vampire and spooky happenings. **Poetry: very short, emotionally dark and depressing. No rhyming poetry.**" I have not seen an issue, but the editor describes it as "digest." Press run 300. **Sample: $2 postpaid. Pays "1 copy for each 2 printed. Send no less than 4 at a time. Simultaneous submissions and previously published poems OK. All replies go out in the next day's mail."** Reviews books of poetry "only if it has a cover price."

THE VIRGINIA QUARTERLY REVIEW (III), 1 West Range, Charlottesville VA 22903, founded 1925, is one of the oldest and most distinguished literary journals in the country. It is digest-sized, 220+ pp., flat-spined, circulation 4,000. **They use about 15 pp. of poetry in each issue, pay $1/line, no length or subject restrictions.**

VIRTUE: THE CHRISTIAN MAGAZINE FOR WOMEN (IV-Religious), P.O. Box 850, Sisters OR 97759, founded 1978, editor Marlee Alex, poetry editor Holly Halverson, is a slick magazine, circulation 175,000, appearing 6 times a year, which **"encourages and integrates biblical truth with daily living."** The editor selected these sample lines from "Bending" by Barbara Seaman:

> Down on my knees again, Lord
> and undignified as ever,
> (how to mop mud with grace?)
> attempting to confine the exuberance
> of yesterday's rain to the kitchen only . . .

Virtue is magazine-sized, 80 pp., saddle-stapled, with full-color pages inside as well as on its paper cover. Subscription: $15.95. Price per issue: $2.95. **Sample: $3 postpaid. "We have no specific poetry guidelines. Interested poets should examine poetry in recent issues." Pays $20-40 per poem and 1 copy. Reports in 6-8 weeks, time to publication 3-9 months. Submit "no more than 3 poems, each on separate sheet, typewritten or dot-matrix; notify if simultaneous submission."**

‡VISIBILITIES (IV-Lesbian), P.O. Box 1169, Olney MD 20830-1169, founded 1986, appears every other month using **lesbian poetry.** They have recently published poetry by Leslie Newman. It is 32 pp. **Sample postpaid: $3.50. Send SASE for guidelines. Reports in 2 months. Pays $5 plus 2 copies.**

VISION; TEAM (I, IV-Young Adults), P.O. Box 7259, Grand Rapids MI 49510, phone (616)241-5616, editor Dale Dieleman. *Vision* founded 1977, is "a lifestyles magazine for young adults" appearing every other month. *Team* is a quarterly digest for volunteer youth workers. *Vision* is magazine-sized, 20 pp., professionally printed on good stock, using b/w photos and graphics, with a matte paper cover in 2 colors. As a sample the editor selected this haiku, "On Christmas," by George Ralph:

> still in the pine trees
> sultry Florida night with
> Christmas cicadas

They want **poetry "that reflects feelings and content to which young adults can relate in their personal lives and which will move them to a larger understanding of themselves and the world. We are looking for concise, fresh poetry, packed with images, contemporary in feel." Sample $1 with SAE plus 2 first-class stamps. Guidelines for SASE. No rhymed or erotic poetry. Pays $10-25/poem plus 1 copy. Specify "rights being offered." Simultaneous submissions and previously published poems OK. Reports in 1 month.**

VISION SEEKER & SHARER; RAINBOW PUBLICATIONS (IV-Themes), Trenwyth Higher Penpoll, St. Veep, NR. Lostwithiel, Cornwall PL22 ONG UK, founded 1987, editor David Allen Stringer, is a "libertarian New Age quarterly concerned with **human rights issues, especially Australian aborigines,**

 The double dagger before a listing indicates that the listing is new in this edition. New markets are often the most receptive to submissions.

Native American Indians, Gypsies, 'Hippies,' etc., animal rights and vegetarianism, alternative economics, ecology, visions of a future clean, harmonious and balanced world where humans are 'at one' with the rest of creation, using concerned poetry on social-ecological, etc. issues, 'spiritual' chants/poems/songs of religious or related nature, poems/songs from American Indians, love poems for the earth-mother and natural creation or 'the Great Spirit' in general. No 'purely' personal—like love poems to one person or 'what happened to me in the park yesterday' with no concern for anything beyond." As a sample the editor selected these lines (poet unidentified):

> We build "rainbow bridges" across the world,
> England to the Americas, England to India,
> Everywhere to everywhere from our spirit message centres
> Smoke signals in print or by telepathic powers

It is magazine-sized, typescript, side-stapled with paper cover. Circulation 300 internationally. Subscription: £4.40 UK, £1.10 each; $8 USA, $2 each. **No payment for poems. Editor sometimes comments on rejections.** Reviews books of poetry.

VOICES INTERNATIONAL (II), 1115 Gillette Dr., Little Rock AR 72207, editor Clovita Rice, is a quarterly poetry journal, 32-40 pp., 6×9″ saddle-stapled, professionally printed with b/w matte card cover. **Subscription: $10 per year. Sample: $2 postpaid (always a back issue). Prefers free verse but accepts high quality traditional. Limit submissions to batches of 5, double-spaced, 3-40 lines (will consider longer if good). Publishes an average of 18 months after acceptance. Pays copies.** "We look for poetry with a new focus, memorable detail and phrasing, and significant and haunting statement climax, all of which impel the reader to reread the poem and return to it for future pleasure and reference." The editor selected these sample lines from "Leeward of March" by Evelyn Corry Applebee:

> I leave the rain-warped window
> to descend the basement stairs,
> carrying the ripe-lemon shout
> of a yellow watering can like
> a summer god's wand, to delicacies
> awaiting a warm womb of soil,
> tender transplants from the hothouse
> of my winter.

VOICES ISRAEL (I); MONTHLY POET'S VOICE (IV-Members), P.O. Box 5780, 46157 Herzlia Israel, founded 1972, *Voices Israel* editor Mark Levinson, with an editorial board of 7, is an annual anthology of poetry in English coming from all over the world. **You have to buy a copy to see your work in print. Submit all kinds of poetry (up to 4 poems) each no longer than a sheet of typing paper.** They have recently published poetry by Yehuda Amichai, Eugene Dubnov, Alan Sillitoe and Seymour Mayne. As a sample the editor selected these lines by John Evans:

> The Glen, winnowed by wind and water,
> Is full of white and silence
> And an echo without a beginning.

> There beneath the snow lie all my shadows,
> Overgrown with wild roses, rooted in the rough,
> Attended by thorns, dripping with blood.

The annual *Voices Israel* is 6¼×8″, offset from laser output on ordinary paper, approximately 121 pp. flat-spined with varying cover. Circulation 350, subscription $13.50. **Sample: $10 postpaid. Back copies: $10 postpaid; airmail extra. Contributor's copy: $13.50 airmail. Deadline end of February each year; reports in fall.** *The Monthly Poet's Voice*, a broadside edited by Ezra Ben-Meir, is open only to members of the Voices Group of Poets in English. The editor advises, "Try to forget what you think you should feel, and write what you do feel."

VOL. NO. MAGAZINE (II, IV-Themes), 24721 Newhall Ave., Newhall CA 91321, phone (805)254-0851, founded 1983, poetry editors Richard Weekley, Jerry Danielsen, Tina Landrum and Don McLeod. "*Vol. No.* publishes lively and concise works. Vivid connections. **Each issue has a theme.** "Third World" (Aug. '92) and "The Eros of Eros" (Aug. '93) are pending. Send SASE for descriptions of these. No trivial, clichéd or unthoughtout work. Work that penetrates the ozone within. One-page poems have the best chance." They have recently published poetry by Octavio Paz, Anne Marple, Jane Hirshfield and Julian Pulley. The editors selected these sample lines by William Stafford:

> We stand for hours where sunlight tells us
> it forgives. A golden shaft pours down.
> The air waits. A cardinal sings and sings.
> We stand for hours.

Vol. No. is a digest-sized, saddle-stapled, 32 pp. annual, circulation 300. Subscription: $5. They receive about 600 freelance submissions of poetry per year, use 60, have a 6 month backlog. **Sample: $3 postpaid. Submit limit of 6 poems. Photocopy and simultaneous submissions OK. Reports in 1-5 months. Pays 2 copies.**

W.I.M. PUBLICATIONS (WOMAN IN THE MOON) (IV-Gay, women), 2215-R Market St., Box 137, Dept. PM, San Francisco CA 94114, phone (408)253-3329, founded 1979, poetry editor SDiane Bogus, who says, "We are a small press with trade press ambitions. We publish poetry, business and writing reference books. We generally run 250-1,000 per press run and **give the author half or a percentage of the books. We pay royalties on our established authors. We prefer a query and a modest track record.**" She wants poetry by "gay, black, women, prison poets, enlightened others—contemporary narrative or lyric work, free verse OK, but not too experimental for cognition. We prefer poems to be a page or less if not part of long narrative. No obviously self-indulgent exercises in the psychology of the poet. No sexual abuse themes this year. No gross sexual references; no hate poems." Send 2 first-class stamps for guidelines/catalog. In addition to her own work, she has published poetry by Adele Sebastian. As a sample she selected these lines from "His Life" from **The Book of Lives** by Sherrylynn Posey:

> *I had 4 maybe 5 lovers*
> *in my life*
> *one of them*
> *lied to me*

SDiane Bogus publishes 2-4 chapbooks and flat-spined paperbacks a year each averaging 40-100 pages. **Submit 6 sample poems and a statement of "vision and poetics, vision of the body (or selection) of the work; poetic mentors and $5 reading fee. New poets must take poetry test ($10 plus free critique). Submit between April 1 and June 1 each year. We acknowledge submissions upon receipt. We report at end of reading season June 1-September 7. Simultaneous submissions, previously published poems, photocopies all OK. No dot-matrix.** Authors are asked to assist in promo and sales by providing list of prospective readers and promotional photos. To established authors we pay royalties 5-10% after costs; others half press run in copies. We may take advanced orders; no subsidy. We will accept subscriptions for a book in production at retail price. We produce the book, publish and give author one-half or percentage of books (authorial control). We then fill orders author has provided and others our promo has prompted. *WIM* offers a self-publishing and consultation criticism service for a fee. She says, "W.I.M. promotes readings for its poets and encourages each poet who submits by way of a personal letter which discusses her or his strengths and weaknesses. Often we allow repeat submissions." They sponsor 2 poetry contests year.

WAKE FOREST UNIVERSITY PRESS (IV-Regional, ethnic), P.O. Box 7333, Winston-Salem NC 27109, phone (919)759-5448, founded 1976, director and poetry editor Dillon Johnston. "We publish only poetry from Ireland and bilingual editions of French poetry in translation. I am able to consider only poetry written by Irish poets or translations of contemporary French poetry. I must return, unread, poetry from American poets." They have recently published poetry by John Montague, Derek Mahon, Richard Murphy, Michael Longley, Paul Muldoon, Thomas Kinsella and Eilean N. Chuilleanain. **Query with 4-5 samples. Replies to queries in 1-2 weeks, to submissions (if invited) in 2-3 months. No simultaneous submissions. Photocopy OK. Publishes on 10% royalty contract with $500 advance, 6-8 author's copies.** Dillon Johnston comments, "because our press is so circumscribed, we get few direct submissions from Ireland. I would advise American poets to read your publication carefully so that they not misdirect to presses such as ours work that they, and I, value."

WALKING AND SINNING; ACCELERATOR PRESS (II), 1708 #4 M.L. King, Jr. Way, Berkeley CA 94709, phone (415)549-2815, founded 1988 from *Legumes* (1982-86), poetry editor J.D. Buhl, is an annual "of short poems, 9-10 per issue." Wanting "sparse, mysterious, humorous short pieces, not too much drama or technique, just pictures from the side, words that go together. Nothing long, overly political, self-conscious." They have recently published poetry by Lisa Chang. It is 12 pp., digest-sized, saddle-stapled, with matte card cover. Press run 500. **Sample postpaid: $1. Pays "unlimited" copies. Simultaneous submissions and previously published poems ("if solicited") OK. Editor comments on submissions "even on accepted pieces sometimes."** He says, "*Walking and Sinning* is a small, private publication, but not street level, slap-dash mimeo stuff. It looks simple and attractive, and I try to get it around. For each issue, I want a group of poems that sit well together, create a feel I can be proud of and that the writers can distribute. Send me child-like crazy thoughts and fears. Give it an edge, but don't throw the blade. Let it lie."

WASHINGTON REVIEW; FRIENDS OF THE WASHINGTON REVIEW OF THE ARTS, INC. (II, IV-Regional), P.O. Box 50132, Washington DC 20091, phone (202)638-0515, founded 1974, literary editor Beth Joselow, is a bimonthly journal of arts and literature published by the Friends of the Washington

Review of the Arts, Inc., a non-profit, tax-exempt educational organization. *WR* is tabloid-sized, using 2 of the large pp. per issue for poetry, saddle-stapled on high-quality newsprint, circulation 2,000 with 700 subscriptions of which 10 are libraries. **They publish primarily local Washington metropolitan area poets as well as poets from across the U.S. and abroad. "We have eclectic tastes but lean with more favor toward experimental work."** They have recently published poems by Robert Hershon and Robert Kusch. The editor selected these sample lines by Rod Smith:

> *the climb begun in mist growth sad lush rank*
> abundance—

Sample: $2.50 postpaid. Pays 5 copies. Reviews books of poetry.

WASHINGTON WRITERS' PUBLISHING HOUSE (IV-Regional), P.O. Box 15271, Washington DC 20003, phone (202)543-1905, founded 1975. An editorial board is elected annually from the collective. "We are a poetry publishing collective that publishes outstanding poetry collections in flat-spined paperbacks by **individual authors from the greater Washington, DC area (60 mile radius, excluding Baltimore) on the basis of competitions held once a year.**" They have recently published poetry by Myra Sklarew, Ann Darr, Barbara Lefcowitz, Maxine Clair, Ann Knox, Martin Galvin and Sharon Negri. The editors chose this sample from "A Bracelet of Lies" by Jean Nordhaus:

> *Touch is the last thing*
> *alive in this room.*
> *My hand wrapped in yours*
> *We watch in the gathering dark*
> *for a luminous wave.*

Submit 50-60 pp. MS with SASE only between July 1 and September 30. $5 reading fee. Poets become working members of the collective. "Interested poets may write for a brochure of published poets and sheet of guidelines."

‡WATER MARK PRESS; WATER MARK POETS BOOK AWARDS (V), 138 Duane St., New York NY 10013, founded 1978, editor Coco Gordon, proposes "to publish the best of current writing regardless of form in archival editions with handmade paper and hand done elements in sewn, bound books, broadsides, chapbooks and artworks. I use only avant-garde material." **Currently they accept no unsolicited poetry.** They have recently published poetry by Barbara Roux and Alison Knowles. The editor selected this sample from "After Eden" by Michael Blumenthal:

> *Once again the invasion of purpose*
> *into gesture: the stem towards the vase,*
> *the hands towards the dreaded morning music*
> *of predictability, Indian paintbrush fades*

That's from a collection of his poetry, **Sympathetic Magic**, published by Water Mark in 1980, 96 pp., flat-spined, with art by Theo Fried, printed on archival, matte card cover with colored art, $9. The Water Mark Book Awards are dormant now but Coco Gordon expects to offer the annual Water Mark Book Awards in the future. She advises, "Only well thought out material of significance and original point of view is considered." **Note: Please do not confuse Water Mark Press with the imprint Watermark Press, used by other businesses.**

WATERWAYS: POETRY IN THE MAINSTREAM; TEN PENNY PLAYERS; BARD PRESS (I, IV-Themes, children, anthologies), 393 St. Paul's Ave., Staten Island NY 10304, founded 1977, poetry editors Barbara Fisher and Richard Spiegel, "publishes **poetry by adult and child poets in a magazine that is published 11 times a year. We do theme issues** and are trying to increase an audience for poetry and the printed and performed word. The project produces performance readings in public spaces and is in residence year round at our local library with workshops and readings. We publish the magazine, *Waterways*, anthologies of child poets; child poetry postcard series; chapbooks (adults and child poets). **We are not fond of haiku or rhyming poetry; never use material of an explicit sexual nature.** We are open to reading material from people we have never published, writing in traditional and experimental poetry forms. While we do 'themes' sometimes an idea for a future magazine is inspired by a submission so we try to remain open to poets' inspiration. Poets should be guided however by the fact that we are children's and animal rights advocates and are a NYC press." They have recently published poetry by Albert Huffstickler, Joanne Seltzer, Arthur Knight, and Kit Knight. As a sample, the editors chose these lines by Laurel Speer:

> *For a single individual at any moment in time, to die*
> *is the end. The ghettos live. The survivors remember.*
> *They write books. They ask us not to forget. They make*
> *us look at history. They say, "This is the way it was;*
> *this is the way it is. If you do not read at the very*
> *least, and think, you'll be fleeing, too. Never feel*
> *safe; never assume; keep vigilance; the ghetto lives.*

Waterways is published in a 40 pp. 4¼ × 7″ wide format, saddle-stapled, photocopy and letter-press, from various type styles, using b/w drawings, matte card cover, circulation 150 with 58 subscriptions of which 12 are libraries. Subscription: $20. **Sample: $2.54 postpaid. They use 60% of freelance poems submitted. Submit less than 10 poems for first submission. No dot-matrix. Simultaneous submissions OK. Send SASE for guidelines for approaching themes.** "Since we've taken the time to be very specific in our response, writers should take seriously our comments and not waste their emotional energy and our time sending material that isn't within our area of interest. Sending for our theme sheet and for a sample issue and then objectively thinking about the writers's own work is practical and wise. Without meaning to sound 'precious' or unfriendly, the writer should understand that small press publishers doing limited editions and all production work in house are working from their personal artistic vision and know exactly what notes will harmonize, effectively counterpoint and meld. Many excellent poems are sent back to the writers by *Waterways* because they don't relate to what we are trying to create in a given month or months. Some poets get printed regularly in *Waterways*; others will probably never be published by us, not because the poet doesn't write well (although that too is sometimes the case) but only because we are artists with opinions and we exercise them in building each issue. **Reports in less than a month. Pays 1 copy. Editors sometimes comment on rejections.** They hold contests for children only. Chapbooks published by Ten Penny Players are "by children only — and not by submission; they come through our workshops in the library and schools." Adult poets are published by us through our Bard Press imprint. "Books evolve from the relationship we develop with writers who we publish in *Waterways* and whom we would like to give more exposure." No submissions. The editors advise, "We suggest that poets attend book fairs. It's a fast way to find out what we are all publishing."

WAYNE REVIEW (I, II), Dept. of English, Wayne State University, 51 W. Warren, Detroit MI 48202. Contact Editors. Appears twice a year using **any kind of poetry except that using footnotes.** They have recently published poetry by Ken Mikolowski, Bob Hershon and Adam Cornford. It is magazine-sized and uses 20-30 pp./issue. It is distributed free. **Pays 2 copies and "eternal gratitude." Submit 3-10 poems, nothing handwritten. Simultaneous submissions and previously published poems OK. Reports in 2-3 months.** "We only read from August through January — no summer reading."

‡WE MAGAZINE (III); WE PRESS (V), P.O. Box 1503, Santa Cruz CA 95061, founded 1986, poetry editors Christopher Funkhouser and Stephen Cope. *We* has appeared 13 times in 4 years but is slowing down, becoming a biannual. They want **"experimental poetry with objective base; any length. No urban drivel, personal pronoun, unoriginal."** They have recently published poetry by Francisco X. Alarcôn, Tuli Kupferberg and Ginsberg. As a sample the editor selected these lines from "Really Boomba" by Tory Miller:

> *I saw a blue sky*
> *reflected in the black hair*
> *of a mere man's gut*
> *What magic! No trick I swear*
> *just a single Gift in Sight.*

I have not seen an issue, but the editor describes it as 28-50 pp., offset, using a variety of bindings. Press run 1,000 for 25 subscribers of which 2 are libraries. "Breaks even" on shelf sales. Subscription: $15/3. **Sample postpaid: $3. Reports in 1-5 months. Pays 2 copies, more at discount.** The last 2 issues have been published on cassette. "Our next magazine will be released on compact disk!" We Press publishes paperbacks and chapbooks but does not consider unsolicited or uncontracted books or chapbooks.

WEBSTER REVIEW (II, IV-Translations), Webster University, 470 E. Lockwood, Webster Groves MO 63119, founded 1974, poetry editors Pamela Hadas and Jerred Metz, is a literary annual. They want **"no beginners. We are especially interested in translations of foreign contemporary poetry."** They have recently published poetry by Barbara F. Lefcowitz, Martin Robbins, Will Wells, Margherita Guidacci, and Chang Soo Ko. The editor selected these sample lines from "Wolf Watch," by Jim Barnes:

> *Evil things, the stories go.*
> *I like them, cantankerous*
> *and fussy, murderous*
> *as old maids. Black*
> *as an ace of spades and crooked,*
> *they'll steal you blind*
> *if you get too friendly.*

Webster Review is 128 pp. digest-sized, flat-spined, professionally printed with glossy card cover, circulation 1,000 with 500 subscriptions of which 200 are libraries. Subscription: $5; per copy:

$5. They receive about 1,500 submissions of freelance poetry per year, use 120. **Sample free for SASE. Reports "within a month, usually." Pays $25-50, if funds permit. Contributors receive 2 copies. Editors comment on rejections "if time permits."**

‡THE WESLEYAN ADVOCATE (IV-Religious), P.O. Box 50434, Indianapolis IN 46250-0434, founded 1843, is a monthly magazine using **"short religious poetry only; no long free verse or secular."** I have not seen an issue, but the editor describes it as 36 pp. magazine-sized, offset, saddle-stapled, with 4-color cover. They use 10-15% of 100-200 poems received/year. Press run 20,000 with "some" subscriptions of which 50 are libraries, no shelf sales (so it must be distributed free). Subscription: $12.50. **Sample: $2 plus SASE. Reports in 2 weeks. Pays 15¢/line plus 4-6 copies on request.**

WESLEYAN UNIVERSITY PRESS; WESLEYAN POETRY PRIZE: WESLEYAN POETRY (II), 110 Mt. Vernon, Middletown CT 06459, founded 1957, editor Terry Cochran, is one of the major publishers of poetry in the nation. They have recently published poetry by James Dickey, Joy Harjo, James Tate and Yusef Komunyakaa. I selected as a sample from **White Dress**, by Brenda Hillman, these lines of "Coffee, 3 A.M.":

> You reject the dark but cannot quite
> Without a light from that blue window
> Make it go . . .
> How terror does become you, like a white dress.

Like other books in that series, this is a 6 × 8″, flat-spined cloth and paperback, 64 pp., professionally printed with glossy jacket card cover. **Send query and SASE. Considers simultaneous submissions. Responds to queries in 6-8 weeks, to MSS in 2-4 months. Pays 5-8% royalties plus 10 copies.** They publish 2 paperbacks, 6-8 hardbacks/year. To obtain sample copies, phone 1-800-421-1561. Poetry publications from Wesleyan tend to get widely (and respectfully) reviewed. The Wesley Poetry Prize is for first books. Send SASE for submission policies.

WEST ANGLIA PUBLICATIONS (II), P.O. Box 2683, La Jolla CA 92038, phone (619)453-0706, founded 1982 by editor Helynn Hoffa, is a publishing company that **assumes the cost of putting out a book and pays author in royalties or in books.** Some of the poets they have published are: Gary Morgan, Wilma Lusk, John Theobald and Kenneth Morris. "Other poets we wish we had printed: Sappho, Homer, John Keats, Marianne Moore, Alexander Pope, Elizabeth Barrett Browning and Philip Larkin." And that takes JJ's prize for the most original and effective way of indicating the range of editorial taste that I have encountered. As a sample, the editor chose these lines from "Giancarlo" in Kathleen Iddings' **Selected and New Poems, 1980-1990**:

> Returning to Rome you pulled sheets
> from covered chairs, guided evening
> into the room with Frascati wine
> and mandolins. These weeks in
> Piazza di Spagna were all the same:
> By day earth's core melted the pavement,
> by night the stars cooled and cracked.

To query, send 6 poems, cover letter, bio, and SASE.

WEST BRANCH (II), English Dept., Bucknell Hall, Bucknell University, Lewisburg PA 17837, founded 1977, is a literary biannual. Recently published poems by D. Nurkse, Deborah Burnham, Jim Daniels, Anneliese Wagner, Betsy Sholl, David Citino, Barbara Crooker, and David Brooks. 100-120 pp., digest-sized, circulation 500, using **quality poetry. "We do not consider simultaneous submissions. Each poem is judged on its own merits, regardless of subject or form. We strive to publish the best work being written today."** Reports in 6-8 weeks. Payment in contributors' copies and a subscription to the magazine. One-year's subscription: $7. Two year (4 issues): $11. **Sample: $3.** Reviews books of poetry but only those by writers who have been published in *West Branch*.

WEST COAST LINE; WEST COAST REVIEW BOOKS (II, IV-Regional), English Dept., Simon Fraser University, Burnaby, British Columbia V5A 1S6 Canada, phone (604)291-4287, editor Roy Miki, founded 1965, *West Coast Line* (formerly *West Coast Review*) is published 3 times a year and **"favors work by both new and established Canadian writers, but it observes no borders in encouraging original creativity.** Our focus is on contemporary poetry, short fiction, drama, criticism and reviews of books. The *Line* is *unique* in its continuing programme of publishing West Coast Review Books as part of the regular offering to subscribers." They have published poetry by Roo Borson, Erin Moure, Ron Silliman and Anselm Hollo. The editor chose these sample lines from "A Little Reality" by P.K. Page:

> Gwendolyn,
> your garden of square roots
> grows in this circle:

> *from my pots and pans—*
> *a silver chaparral of leaves and flowers . . .*

The magazine is handsomely printed on glossy paper, 6 × 9″, flat-spined 80 pp. They accept about 20 of the 500-600 poetry MSS received per year. Approximately 26 pages of poetry per issue. Press run 800 for 500 subscriptions of which 350 are libraries, 150 shelf sales. Subscription: $15. Single copies: $8. **Send SASE for guidelines. Pays approximately $10 (Canadian)/printed page plus a one-year subscription. Reports on submissions in 6-8 weeks, 2-8 months till publication. No simultaneous submissions or previously published poetry. MSS returned only if accompanied by sufficient Canadian postage or IRC.**

‡**WEST END PRESS (IV-Political, women, foreign language)**, P.O. Box 27334, Albuquerque NM 87125, founded 1976, publisher John Crawford, publishes 6 paperbacks/year. They want "**political or personal experience, any style. Nothing self-indulgent, 'objective,' or purely descriptive, racist, sexist, elitist, etc. Normally we publish literature of a progressive political orientation. This includes working class literature, literature with political themes and multicultural literature. A majority of our books are written by women. We have published bilingual and intertextual books containing Spanish and Navajo.**" They have recently published poetry by Margaret Randall, Adrian Louis, Ana Castillo and Wendy Rose. As a sample the editor selected these lines from "The Great Pat Smith American Dreampoem" by Pat Smith:

> *One day my customer is Busby Berkeley*
> *He leans on my counter, lights his cigar*
> *likes what he sees*
> *and says in a wise voice*
> *Girlie, can you swim?*

"**Reporting time 3 months, no panel review, at least a year backlog.**" Editor often comments on rejections. **Pays maximum of 6% royalties, but payment is usually in copies, 10% of press run.**

WEST OF BOSTON (II), Box 2, Cochituate Station, Wayland MA 01778, phone (508)653-7241, founded 1983, poetry editor Norman Andrew Kirk, wants to see "**Poetry of power, compassion, originality, and wit—and talent, too.**" As a sample of poetry he likes he selected these lines (poet unidentified):

> *Come to my museum of poetry.*
> *The masterpieces of my mind*
> *are cast about like the misplaced*
> *children of a mad whore.*

For book or chapbook submission query with 5-10 sample poems, credits, and bio. **Simultaneous submissions, photocopies, dot-matrix, previously published poems all OK. Pays 10% of press run.** Editor "sometimes" comments on rejected MSS.

WEST WIND REVIEW (II, IV-Anthology), English Department, Southern Oregon State College, Ashland OR 97520, phone (503)482-6181, founded 1982, poetry editor Geri Couchman, is an annual "**looking for sensitive but strong verse that delights and impresses with its humanistic insights and style. We are seeking rich poetry that celebrates all aspects of men's and women's experiences, both exalted and tragic. We are looking to print material that reflects ethnic and social diversity.**" The *West Wind Review* has grown in size and scope since its beginning in 1982. The editor offers, as a poetry example, these lines by Pete Beckwith:

> *for this fire, this wood.*
> *the moment caught, the fire*
> *inevitable, the joys of solid*
> *returning.*

WWR is handsomely printed, flat-spined, 200 pp., digest-sized, appearing each spring. They receive about 600-700 submissions each year, publish 40-50 poems. Their press run is 500. **Sample: $7 postpaid. Guidelines available for SASE. Do not submit in July or August. Pays 1 copy.** "**Limit of 5 poems not exceeding 50 lines**" per submission. **They will consider simultaneous submissions but not previously published poems. Reports in 8-12 weeks after December 1 deadline.** There is a $50 award for the best poem in an annual contest, $2/poem entry fee.

‡**WESTENRA: THE MISS LUCY WESTENRA SOCIETY OF THE UNDEAD (IV-Horror)**, 125 Taylor St., Jackson TN 38301, phone (901)427-7714, founded 1989, founder and editor Lewis Sanders, appears 3-4/year, using "**vampire poetry, vampire haiku, nothing that does not deal with vampires.**" They have recently published poetry by Carl Brennan, Jane Oz and Cathy Buburuz. I have not seen an issue, but the editor describes it as a magazine-sized newsletter. **Subscription: $10. Sample: cost varies. Pays 1 copy to non-members. Send SASE for guidelines.** Editor comments on rejections "seldom." He advises, "Study, and write, but don't plan on earning a living writing poetry."

WESTERLY; PATRICIA HACKETT PRIZE (II), Centre for Studies in Australian Literature, University of Western Australia, Nedlands 6009, Australia, phone (09) 380-2101, founded 1956, editors Dennis Haskell, Peter Cowan, and Bruce Bennett. *Westerly* is a literary and cultural quarterly publishing quality short fiction, poetry, literary critical, and socio-historical articles, and book reviews. **"No restrictions on creative material. Our only criterion [for poetry] is literary quality. We don't dictate to writers on rhyme, style, experimentation, or anything else. We are willing to publish short or long poems. We do assume a reasonably well read, intelligent audience. Past issues of *Westerly* provide the best guides. Not consciously an academic magazine."** They have recently published work by Les A. Murray, Bruce Dawe, Shirley Lim, Veronica Brady, Peter Porter and Robert Drewe. The quarterly magazine is 7×10", "electronically printed," 96 pp. with some photos and graphics. Circulation is 1,000. Price per copy is $5 (Aus.) plus overseas postage via surface mail, subscription $20 (Aus.)/year. **Sample available for $6 (Aus.) surface mail, $7 (Aus.) airmail. Minimum pay for poetry is $30 plus 1 copy. "Please do not send simultaneous submissions."** Reporting time is 2-3 months and time to publication approximately 12 weeks, sometimes longer. Reviews books of poetry. The Patricia Hackett Prize (value approx. $400) is awarded in March for the best contribution published in *Westerly* during the previous calendar year. The advice of the editors is: "Be sensible. Write what matters for you but think about the reader. Don't be swayed by literary fashion. Read the magazine if possible before sending submissions. Read, Read, Read literature of all kinds and periods."

WESTERN PRODUCER PUBLICATIONS; WESTERN PEOPLE (IV-Regional), P.O. Box 2500, Saskatoon, Saskatchewan S7K 2C4 Canada, phone (306)665-3500, founded 1923, managing editor Michael Gillgannon. *Western People* is a magazine supplement to *The Western Producer*, a weekly newspaper, circulation 135,000, which uses **"poetry about the people, interests, and environment of rural Western Canada."** The editor offers this sample from "Whose Mother" by Ilien Coffey:

> She wheels herself along the gleaming corridors
> Past rooms whose occupants have seen a better day
> her every need is met...Kind strangers see to that;
> she's warm, well fed and yet she yearns for yesterday.

The magazine-sized supplement is 16 pp., newsprint, saddle-stapled, with color and b/w photography and graphics. They receive about 800 submissions of freelance poetry per year, use 40-50. **Sample free for postage (2 oz.) – and ask for guidelines. One poem per page, maximum of 3 poems per submission. Name, address, telephone number upper left corner of each page. Reports within 4 weeks. Pays $15-50 per poem.** The editor comments, "It is difficult for someone from outside Western Canada to catch the flavor of this region; almost all the poems we purchase are written by Western Canadians."

WEYFARERS; GUILDFORD POETS PRESS (II), 9, White Rose Lane, Woking, Surrey, GU22 7JA U.K., founded 1972, administrative editor Margaret Pain, poetry editors Margaret Pain, Susan James, Martin Jones and Jeffery Wheatley. They say, "We publish *Weyfarers* magazine three times a year. All our editors are themselves poets and give their spare time free to help other poets." They describe their needs as **"all types of poetry, serious and humorous, free verse and rhymed/metered, but mostly 'mainstream' modern. Excellence is the main consideration. NO hard porn, graphics, way-out experimental. Any subject publishable, from religious to satire, not more than 40 lines."** They have recently published poetry by David Schaal, Paul Groves, Zbigniew Sas and Jean Hathaway. As an example the editors chose Anne Smith's "Irish Coffee":

> At first,
> silk on the lips
> like early love:
>
> sipped deeper,
> it burns
> as love does
>
> before
> stilling
> the heart again.

The digest-sized saddle-stapled format contains about 28 pp. of poetry (of a total of 32 pp.) The magazine has a circulation of "about 285," including about 180 subscriptions of which 4 are libraries. They use about 125 of 1,200-1,500 submissions received each year. **Sample current issue: $4 in cash USA (or £1-40 UK) postpaid. Submit no more than 6 poems, one poem per sheet. No previously published or simultaneous submissions. Payment 1 copy.** "We are associated with Surrey Poetry Center, who have an annual Open Poetry Competition. The prize-winners are published in *Weyfarers*." They sometimes **comment briefly, if requested,** on rejections. Reviews books of poetry briefly, in newsletter sent to subscribers. And their advice to poets is, "Always read a magazine before submitting. And read plenty of modern poetry."

WHEAT FORDER'S PRESS; PRIMERS FOR THE AGE OF INNER SPACE (IV-Themes), P.O. Box 6317, Washington DC 20015-0317, founded 1974, poetry editor Renée K. Boyle. **This is a 100% subsidy press, asking for camera-ready copy.** "We publish for embassies on topics of interest to Third World countries. We have a series called Primers for the Age of Inner Space. **We seek poetry and book-length essays for this which reflects ideas in sciences, psychology, metahistory reflecting modern thought *at its leading edges.*"** **Considers simultaneous submissions.** As a sample the editor selected these lines from "Graffiti on the Wall of Time":

> *That man himself is dead, who being yet in life*
> *reports that God no longer lives, because in him*
> *the image of that God*
> *no longer rises.*

Query with 5-10 samples and cover letter giving "publication record, precise aim in writing poetry (as fanciful as you wish), express modern thought. Skip modern vulgarities, sex, pot and all that jazz—it's going nowhere." Terms for cooperative publishing, author paying all costs, worked out individually.

WHETSTONE (I, II), Department of English, University of Lethbridge, 4401 University Drive, Lethbridge, Alberta T1K 3M4 Canada, editor Gavian E. Whishaw, appears twice a year with writing by beginners and published authors. **"Open to any kind of poetry, as long as it's of good quality."** They have recently published poems by Susan Musgrave and Rhonda McAdam. As a sample the editor selected lines from "The Technology of Arrogance Which Enters the Mind Unasked and Poisons it with Visions of Paradise" by Kim Maltman:

> *. . . the use of wood becomes like*
> *faith, or love, or sorrows,*
> *that once-removed shadow world in which objects*
> *are inseparable from our desires . . .*

Whetstone is digest-sized, 80+ pp. saddle-stapled, professionally printed in bold face type with two-color matte card cover, circulation 500 with 200 subscriptions of which 25 are libraries, $5 (Can.)/copy, subscription $10. **Sample: $5 postpaid. Guidelines available for SASE. Pays $10 and 1 copy. Any length of poetry. Photocopy, dot-matrix OK. Editor sometimes comments on rejections.** "We have highly specialized poetry and short story competitions. Writers should send $5 for sample copy, plus SASE for rules and regulations."

‡WHETSTONE; WHETSTONE PRIZE (II), P.O. Box 1266, Barrington IL 60011, phone (708)382-5626, editors Sandra Berris, Marsha Portnoy and Jean Tolle, is an annual. **"We emphasize quality more than category. No erotica or haiku."** They have recently published poetry by Paulette Roeske, Jeanne Murray Walker and William Kloefkorn. As a sample the editor selected these lines by Lucia Getsi:

> *The skeleton I found in the thicket wore a collar*
> *tied to a stake, the shape of a dog x-rayed*
> *like my foot at the Buster Brown shoe store. I was nine*
> *and I played on the forbidden bank.*

It is digest-sized, 96 pp., professionally printed, flat-spined with matte card cover. Press run 500 for 100 subscribers of which 5+ are libraries. 350 shelf sales. **Sample postpaid: $3. Reports in 1-4 months. Pays 2 copies.** The Whetstone Prizes are cash awards ($50-$300) for the best work in each issue.

‡WHITE CLOUDS REVUE; WIND VEIN PRESS (IV-Regional), P.O. Box 462, Ketchum ID 83340, founded 1987, editor Scott Preston. *WCR* appears twice a year. They want **"work from divergent Western American traditions, particularly partial to oral performance and/or narrative; no academic reflexes from the William Stafford school of contrived phanopoeia."** They have recently published poetry by Edward Dorn, Bruce Embree, Charles Potts and Rosalie Sorrels. I have not seen an issue, but the editor describes it as 40 pp. 7×8". Press run 250 for 30 subscribers of which 10 are libraries, 10-20 shelf sales. Subscription: $12/4 issues. **Sample postpaid: $3.50. Reports in 2-8 weeks. Pays 2 copies. No submissions until early 1992.** "William Carlos Williams once reputedly wrote to Gilbert Sorrentino, 'A little magazine's only rationale is its editor's belief that the writers he prints must be presented as a group. Anything else is just a collation of pages.' The primary reason I'm not really concerned about encouraging submissions and selling issues is that the primary audience for a small lit mag in this country is and has been the writers associated with it. I'm interested in developing and broadening a certain community of esssentially non-academic Western American writers, and most of the rote submissions I receive simply don't work towards that premise."

WHITE PINE PRESS (V), 76 Center St., Fredonia NY 14063, phone (716)672-5743, founded 1973, poetry editors Dennis Maloney and Elaine LaMattina. White Pine Press publishes poetry, fiction, literature in translation, essays—perfect-bound paperbacks. "At present we are **not accepting unsolicited MSS. Inquire first.**" They have published poetry by William Kloefkorn, Marjorie Agosin, Migel Hernandez, Peter Blue Cloud, Basho, Pablo Neruda, Maurice Kenny and James Wright. As a sample I chose this stanza of "Poems at the Edge of Day" by John Brandi:

> *Poems are acts of death*
> *burning clean*
> *at the edge of day*
> *to renew life.*

Query with 4-5 samples, brief cover letter with bio and publication credits. Reply to queries in 2-4 weeks, to submissions (if invited) in 4 weeks. Simultaneous submissions, photocopy, dot-matrix OK. Pays 5-10% of run. Send $1 for catalog to buy samples.

JAMES WHITE REVIEW: A GAY MEN'S LITERARY QUARTERLY (IV-Gay), P.O. Box 3356, Traffic Station, Minneapolis MN 55403, phone (612)291-2913, founded 1983, poetry editor Greg Baysans **uses all kinds of poetry by gay men.** They have published poetry by Tom Young, James Broughton and Robert Peters. The magazine has a circulation of 3,000 with 1500 subscriptions of which 50 are libraries. They receive about 1,400 submissions per year, use 100, have a 6 week backlog. **Sample: $3 postpaid. Submit a limit of 8 poems or 250 lines. A poem can exceed 250 lines, but it "better be very good." They report in 4 months. Paying $15/poem.** Send SASE for guidelines. Subscriptions $12/year (US). Reviews books of poetry.

‡**WHITE WALL REVIEW; OFF THE WALL AWARDS (I)**, 63 Gould St., Toronto, Ontario M5B 1E9 Canada, phone (416)977-1045, founded 1976, editors Gemma Files and Sarah Wilks, is an annual using **"interesting, preferably spare art. No style is unacceptable. Should poetry serve a purpose beyond being poetry and communicating a poet's idea? Nothing boring, self-satisfied, gratuitously sexual or violent, indulgent."** They have recently published poetry by Lionel Willis and Evelyn Lau. As a sample the editor selected these lines by Harold Rhenisch:

> *and a female grasshopper alone*
> *in a dustry garden*
> *her body extended*
> *bloated*
>
> *pumping her eggs*
> *into the soil*
>
> *her whole body hearing*
>
> *unable to cry out*
> *or sweat*

I have not seen an issue, but the editor describes it as 160 pp., digest-sized. Press run 850 for 3 subscriptions. Subscription: $6. **Sample: $8 postpaid. "Please do not submit between May and July of a given year." Pays 1 copy. Reports "as soon as we can. We comment on all MSS, accepted or not."** they offer Off the Wall Awards, including one for poetry, for Ryerson students and staff.

TAHANA WHITECROW FOUNDATION; CIRCLE OF REFLECTIONS (IV-Ethnic), P.O. Box 18181, Salem OR 97305, phone (503)585-0564, founded 1987, executive director Melanie Smith. The Whitecrow Foundation conducts **one spring/summer poetry contest on Native American themes in poems up to 30 lines in length. Deadline for submissions May 31. No haiku, Seiku, erotic or porno poems. Fees are $2.75 for a single poem, $10 for 4; monetary awards.** Winners, honorable mentions and selected other entries are published in a periodic anthology, **Circle of Reflections.** Winners do not receive free copies but are encouraged to purchase it for $4.95 plus $1 handling in order to "help ensure the continuity of our contests." As a sample Melanie Smith selected these lines by Jack Iyall:

> *Today I'm dirty old man . .*
> *yesterday . . growing old*
> *   was beautiful . .*
> *today I'm a museum piece . .*
> *yesterday . . I could be*
> *   in line for Chief . .*
> *today I'm in the welfare line . .*
> *yesterday . . there was a place for me . .*

Reviews books of poetry for $10 reading fee (average 32 pages). Melanie Smith adds, "We seek unpublished Native writers. Poetic expressions of full-bloods, mixed bloods and empathetic non-Indians need to be heard. Future goals include chapbooks and native theme art. Advice to new writers—keep writing, honing and sharpening your material; don't give up—keep submitting."

WHOLE NOTES; DAEDALUS PRESS (I, II, IV-Children), P.O. Box 1374, Las Cruces NM 88004, phone (505)382-7446, *WN* founded 1984; Daedalus Press founded 1988, editor Nancy Peters Hastings. *WN* appears twice a year. Daedulus Press publishes one chapbook per year by a single poet. **"All forms will be considered."** They have recently published poetry by William Stafford and Harold Witt. As a sample the editor selected these lines from "After a Blizzard" by Don Welch:

> *This morning there's a center to silence,*
> *a snow no one has ever walked upon,*
> *and the wind has folded up like a mastiff*
> *deep in sleep . . .*

WN is 20-24 pp., digest-sized, "nicely printed," staple bound, with a "linen 'fine arts' cover." Press run 400 for 200 subscriptions of which 10 are libraries. They accept about 10% of some 300-400 submissions per year. Subscription: $6. **Sample, postpaid: $3. Pays 2 copies. They prefer submissions of 3-7 poems at a time. Some previously published poems used. Reports in 2-3 weeks. For 20 pp. chapbook consideration, submit 3-15 samples with bio and list of other publications. Pays 50 copies of chapbook. Editor sometimes comments on rejections.** The editor says, "In the fall of each even-numbered year I edit a special issue of *WN* that features writing by young people (under 18)."

WILDERNESS (II, IV-Nature/ecology), 5118 N. Princeton St., Portland OR 97203, (poetry submissions only should be sent to this address), founded 1935, poetry editor John Daniel, is a slick quarterly magazine of "The Wilderness Society, one of the oldest and largest American conservation organizations." Requests for sample and subscriptions should go to *Wilderness*, 900 Seventeenth St. NW, Washington DC 20006. They want **"poetry related to the natural world. Shorter poems stand a better chance than longer, but all will be read. Poetry in any form or style is welcome."** They have recently published poetry by Wendell Berry, Reginald Gibbons, Mary Oliver, Naomi Shihab Nye and William Stafford. The magazine is published on slick stock, full-color, professionally printed, with full-color paper cover, saddle-stapled, 76 pp. Their press run is 340,000 with 300,000 subscriptions. Subscription: $15. **Sample: $3.50 postpaid. Pays $100 plus 2 copies on publication. Responds in 2 months. No simultaneous submissions or previously published material. Editor comments on rejections "occasionally. Don't forget your SASE. Please understand that we have room for only about 15 poems a year."**

WILDFLOWER (II), P.O. Box 4757, Albuquerque NM 87196-4757, founded 1981, editor/publisher Jeanne Shannon, is a leaflet appearing 6-8/year in a 1-page format (either as broadside or folded to digest-size), publishing **short poems on any theme.** They have recently published poetry by Alexis Rotella, Chelsea Adams, Carl Mayfield and Walt Franklin. As a sample the editor selected these lines from "Something About a Letter" by Mary Rising Higgins:

> *Civil divisions wreathe the juniper in shrill*
> *intervals to cool October woodbine. Fused by*
> *deciduous chatter, the present remembers*
> *itself. Merciless growth fleshed into separate*
> *fidelities.*

Subscription: $5. **Sample postpaid: $1. Pays 5 copies. Simultaneous submissions and previously published poems OK. Editor comments on submissions "often."**

WILDWOOD JOURNAL; THE WILDWOOD PRIZE IN POETRY (II, IV-Students), T.H.S. Wallace, Arts 213, 3300 Cameron St. Road, Harrisburg PA 17110-2999, phone (717)780-2487. *Wildwood Journal*, an annual, is **open only to students, alumni and faculty of Harrisburg Area Community College,** but the Wildwood Prize is open to any poet, $500 annually, $5 reading fee. Final selection for the prize is made by a distinguished poet (in 1991 Jeanne Murray Walker) who remains anonymous until the winner is announced. Poems are accepted between September 1 and November 15. Rules available for SASE.

‡WILLAMETTE RIVER PRESS (II), P.O. Box 605, Troutdale OR 97060, founded 1990, editor Douglas Allen Conner, publishes 3-4 paperback and 3-4 chapbooks/year, MSS **selected through competitions (see *Poets & Writers* for rules) with entry fee.** The editor says, "We are open to fresh new voices as well as established ones. We hope to be the publisher for first collections of poets with numerous chapbooks; we hope to publish chapbooks of newer poets who may not yet have published a chapbook but who have a publication history in magazines and small press. All of our books will be of the highest quality in order to adequately showcase the author. **No religious, genre, sloppy, trite, haiku,**

pornography. No unsolicited MSS. Query first with samples, publishing history and awards. Payment for book/chapbook publication arranged with author."

THE WILLIAM AND MARY REVIEW (II), Campus Center, College of William and Mary, Williamsburg VA 23185, phone (804)221-3290, founded 1962, editor William Clark, a 112 pp. annual, "is dedicated to publishing new work by established poets as well as work by new and vital voices." They have published poetry by Dana Gioia, Cornelius Eady, Amy Clampitt, Henri Cole, Julie Agoos, Diane Ackerman and Phyllis Janowitz. They accept 15-20 of about 5,000 poems submitted per year. Press run is 5,500. They have 250 library subscriptions, about 500 shelf sales. Sample: $4.50 postpaid. Pays 4 copies. Submit 1 poem per page, batches of no more than 6 poems. Reports in approximately 2 months.

‡WILLOW REVIEW; COLLEGE OF LAKE COUNTY READING SERIES (II), 19351 West Washington St., Grayslake IL 60030-1198, phone (708)223-6601, founded 1969, edited by Paulette Roeske. The review is a 68 pp., flat-spined annual, 6×9", professionally printed with a glossy cover featuring b/w art. "We are interested in poetry and fiction of high quality with no specifications as to form, length, style or subject." They have recently published poetry by Lisel Mueller, Bruce Guernsey, Larry Starzec and Martha Vertreace. Circulation 1,000, with distribution to most Illinois public, college and university libraries and some in neighboring states. Sample postpaid: $4. Prizes of $100, $50 and $25 are awarded to the best poetry and fiction in each issue. Pays 2 copies. Submit up to 5 poems, no more than 3,000 words, between September and January for April publication. Include name, address, SS#, and information for contributors notes. The reading series, 3-7 readings/academic year, have included Angela Jackson, Ellen Bryant Voigt, Thomas Lux, Charles Simic, Galway Kinnell, Lisel Mueller, Amiri Baraka, Stephen Dobyns, Heather McHugh, Linda Pastan, Katha Pollitt and William Stafford. One of the readings is for contributors to the magazine. These are usually held on Thursday evenings, for audiences of about 100 from students and faculty of College of Lake County and other area colleges and residents of local communities. They are widely publicized in the area, including in the *Chicago Tribune*'s literary arts calendar.

WILLOW SPRINGS (II, IV-Translations), MS-1, Eastern Washington University, Cheney WA 99004, phone (509)458-6429, founded 1977. They have published poetry by Denise Levertov, Carolyn Kizer, Michael Burkard, Russell Edson, Dara Wier, Thomas Lux, Madeline DeFrees, Hayden Carruth, Al Young, Odysseas Elytis, W.S. Merwin, Olga Broumas, Kay Boyle and Lisel Mueller. *Willow Springs* is a semiannual, 6×9", 90 pp., flat-spined, professionally printed, with glossy 2-color card cover with art, circulation 800, 230 subscriptions of which 30% are libraries. They use 1-2% of some 4,000 freelance poems received each year. **Sample: $4 postpaid. Submit September through May. "We do not read in the summer months."** Include name on every page, address on first page of each poem. Brief cover letter saying how many poems on how many pages. No simultaneous submissions. Reports in 1-3 months. Pays 2 copies, others at half price, and pays cash when funds available. Send SASE for guidelines. "We are especially interested in translations from any language or period. We publish quality poetry and fiction that is imaginative, intelligent, and has a concern and care for language." Reviews books of poetry.

WIND MAGAZINE (I, II), Box 809K, RFD #1, Pikeville KY 41501, phone (606)631-1129, founded 1971, poetry editor Quentin R. Howard. "*Wind* since 1971 has published hundreds of poets for the first time and today there are at least 125 who are publishing widely in many magazines and have books to their credit. I have also published about 15 people who had stopped writing and submitting to 'little' magazines because many young editors were not acquainted with much of their work. There's nothing unique about *Wind*; like all 'little' magazines it is friendly (too friendly at times) toward beginning writers who have something to say and do so effectively and interestingly. I have no taboos. I invent my own taboos on reading each MS. But plain old raw vulgarity for shock effect is out. Save your postage! I don't want simple broken prose, neither greeting card-type verse; nor please no love verse and soothing graveyard poetry; none please enamoured of death; believe me it's still being written. I'm not picky about form, style, subject matter nor purpose; but length (pages and pages) makes me frown no matter how much I love it. 'Little' magazines are a squeamish group when it comes to space." They have recently published poetry by Peter Brett, Jacqueline Marcus, Harold Witt, Katharine Privett, Hale Chatfield, Michael Johnson, Real Faucher and Jonathan London. The editor selected these sample lines by Charles Semones:

> Summer is the bad word in our yearly grammar.
> It fits no sensible sentence. No one can write the syntax
> of summer right. Our shared radio clears its throat nightly:
> static the thickness of phlegm drowns out Beethoven and conmen peddling Jesus.

Wind appears irregularly, digest-sized, averaging 86 pp. per issue of which 60 are poetry, saddle-stapled, professionally printed with matte card cover, circulation 455, subscriptions 412 of which

21 are libraries. Subscription: $7 for 3 consecutive issues. They use about 200 of 3,600 freelance submissions of poetry per year, sometimes have as much as a year backlog. **Sample: $2.50 postpaid. Submit at least 3-6 poems. "Photocopies and simultaneous submissions scare me." Shorter poems have a better chance here. Reports in 2-4 weeks. Pays contributor's copies. Editor comments on rejections, "Now and then when time permits. There's many pitfalls about this."** Quentin Howard advises, "Presentation is all-important in deciding on poems."

‡**THE WINDHORSE REVIEW; SAMURAI PRESS (II)**, RR3, Box 3140, Yarmouth, Nova Scotia B5A 4A7, Canada, founded 1982, poetry editor John Castlebury, is an annual magazine that, according to its editor, "**offers a uniquely uplifted and intelligent outlook which commends to it a natural niche among the standard fare of small press publications of poetry in the American marketplace today. All persuasions of poetry are welcome, the only stipulations contrary being solipstic, opinionated and ax-to-grind poems. The only real requirement is that the work express something 'real.' "** They have recently published poetry by Anne Waldman, José Arguelles and Gary Allen. As a sample I selected the first stanza of "Haitian Night" by Nancy Arbuthnot:

> At night French vowels
> soften the breeze blowing
> over the stinking harbor
> or Port-au-Prince: Jean Claude
> singing on the verandah under the mango moon.

Their press run is 500 and *TWR* is sold in bookstores in major cities. It is handsomely printed, uses artistic b/w photos and graphics and has a 2-color paper cover. **Sample: $5 postpaid. Submit 5-10 pp. with brief bio and SASE with IRC or $1 US (US stamps invalid from Canada). Reports in 1 months. Pays copies.** Prisoner copies available free of charge.

THE WINDLESS ORCHARD; THE WINDLESS ORCHARD CHAPBOOKS (II), English Dept., Indiana University, Fort Wayne IN 46805, phone (219)481-6841, founded 1970, poetry editor Robert Novak, a "shoestring labor of love—chapbooks only from frequent contributors to magazine. Sometimes publish calendars." They say they want "**heuristic, excited, valid non-xian religious exercises. Our muse is interested only in the beautiful, the erotic, and the sacred,**" but I could find nothing erotic or sacred in the sample issue sent me, and the kinds of beauty seemed about like those in most literary journals, as these lines by Wayne Kvam, selected by the editors as a sample, indicate:

> Wolfgang, the waiter comes over
> red shirt bulging
> like an apple
> says "crisp oak, birch, and lime"
> into this thin air.

The Windless Orchard appears 3-4 times a year, 50+ pp., digest-sized, offset from typescript, saddle-stapled, with matte card cover with b/w photos. The editors say they have 100 subscriptions of which 25 are libraries, a print run of 300, total circulation: 280. There are about 35 pp. of poetry in each issue. Subscription: $8. They receive about 3,000 freelance submissions of poetry per year, use 200, have a 6 month backlog. **Considers simultaneous submission. Sample: $3 postpaid. Submit 3-7 pp. Reports in 1 day-4 months. Pays 2 copies.** Chapbook submissions by invitation only to contributors to the magazine. Poets pay costs for 300 copies, of which The Windless Orchard Chapbook Series receives 100 for its expenses. **Sample: $3.** Editors sometimes comment on rejections. They advise, "Memorize a poem a day, do translations for the education."

‡**UNIVERSITY OF WINDSOR REVIEW (II)**, University of Windsor, Windsor, Ontario N9B 3P4 Canada, phone (519)253-4232, ext. 2303, founded 1966, poetry editor John Ditsky, appears twice a year. "**Open to all poetry but epic length.**" They have recently published poetry by Ben Bennani, Walter McDonald, Larry Rubin and Lyn Lifshin. As a sample the editor selected these lines (poet unidentified):

> talking to white wolves
> talking to the first
> white wolves ever
> telling of how things are
> in his world.

It is professionally printed, 100 pp., digest-sized. They accept about 15% of 500 poems received/year. Press run 500. Subscription: $12 Canadian, $10 US. **Sample postpaid: $6 Canadian, $5 US. Reports in 6 weeks. Pays $10/poem.**

WINEBERRY PRESS (V, IV-Regional), 3207 Macomb St. NW, Washington DC 20008, phone (202)363-8036, founded 1983, founder and president Elisavietta Ritchie, publishes anthologies and chapbooks of poems by **Washington area poets but accepts no unsolicited MS because of a large backlog.** She has recently published poetry by Judith McComb, Elizabeth Follin-Jones and Beatrice Murphy. As a sample Elisavietta Ritchie selected these lines from "Looking Forward" by Maxine Combs, included in **Swimming Out Of The Collective Unconscious:**

> Nothing is promised
> Like land crabs scuttling
> across a road, unexpected,
> sightings are gifts.

THE WIRE; PROGRESSIVE PRESS (I, IV-Form), 7320 Colonial, Dearborn Heights MI 48127, phone (517)394-3736, founded 1981, editor Sharon Wysocki. *The Wire* is an "alternative arts" publication that appears 2-3 times a year. It publishes **"language and experimental poetry" but no sonnets. "We are also looking for short form erotic poems. Regarding all submissions, the poet has a much better chance for publication in *The Wire* if the poem is in short form."** Poets recently published include Ivan Argüelles, Paul Weinman and Joseph Raffa. As a sample, the editor selected "Kerosene Madonna" by Lyn Lifshin:

> gets you
> hot is
> cheap sucks
> your air

The Wire is photocopied on 8½×11" offset paper, 9 pp., with graphics, stapled at the top left corner. Price per issue is $1 and a subscription is $3.75 (checks should be made out to Progressive Press). **Guidelines are available for SASE. Contributors receive 1 copy. Photocopied and simultaneous submissions are OK, but print must be dark enough for photocopying. Submissions are reported in 6 months and time to publication is the same. Criticism of rejected MSS is provided "sometimes."**

‡WIRE MAGAZINE; EYE OF THE COMET PRESS (II), 2696 Summit Ave., Highland Park IL 60035, founded 1990, editors Michael Barrett and Dean Shavit. *Wire* is a quarterly. Eye of the Comet Press publishes poetry chapbooks. They have recently published poetry by Sterling Plumpp, Barry Silesky, Hilda Morley and David Ignatow. As a sample the editor selected these lines from "Prayerwheel" by Phyllis Janik:

> We can sit on a branch of the family tree
> as a plant or a fish or a piece of human life
> with a goddess: Memory, Lucky, if she's a hawk,
> circling. Or an Elephant, pondering one foot
> after the other. Yes even that.

Wire is magazine-sized, 24-48 pp., professionally printed, saddle-stapled. They accept about 3% of submissions. Press run 5,000 for 100 subscribers, 500 shelf sales. 3,500 are distributed free "to people who attend readings, college writing programs." Subscription: $4/year, $10/3 years. **Sample: $1.25 postpaid. Reports in 1-3 months. Pays 3 copies. Editor comments on rejections "often."** Editor Dean Shavit says, "Truly great poets *always* realize that the problems of human existence are also the same problems of writing a poem."

WISCONSIN ACADEMY REVIEW (IV-Regional), 1922 University Ave., Madison WI 53705, phone (608)263-1692, founded 1954, poetry editor Faith B. Miracle, "distributes information on scientific and cultural life of Wisconsin and provides a forum for **Wisconsin (or Wisconsin background) artists and authors. They want good lyric poetry; traditional meters acceptable if content is fresh. No poem over 65 lines."** They have published poetry by Credo Enriquez, David Martin, Felix Pollak, Ron Wallace and John Bennett. *Wisconsin Academy Review* is a magazine-sized 48 pp. quarterly, professionally printed on glossy stock, glossy card cover with b/w photo, circulation 1,500, with 1,200 subscriptions of which 109 are libraries. They use 4-12 pp. of poetry per issue. Of over 100 freelance submissions of poetry per year they use about 15, have a 6-12 month backlog. **Sample: $3 postpaid. Submit 5 pp. maximum, double-spaced. Photocopy, dot-matrix OK. Must include Wisconsin connection if not Wisconsin return address. Reports in 4-6 weeks. Pays 5 copies. Editor sometimes comments on rejections.** Reviews books of poetry with Wisconsin connection only.

UNIVERSITY OF WISCONSIN PRESS; BRITTINGHAM PRIZE IN POETRY (II), 114 N. Murray St., Madison WI 53715, phone (608)262-4922, Brittingham Prize inaugurated in 1985, poetry editor Ronald Wallace. The University of Wisconsin Press publishes primarily scholarly works, but they offer the annual **Brittingham Prize of $500 plus publication. The contest is the only way in which this press publishes poetry. Send SASE for rules. Submit between September 1 and October 1, unbound MS volume 50-80 pp., name, address, and telephone number on title page. Poems must be previously unpublished in book form. Poems published in journals, chapbooks, and anthologies may be included**

but must be acknowledged. There is a non-refundable $10 reading fee which must accompany the MS. (Checks to University of Wisconsin Press.) MSS will *not* be returned. Enclose self-addressed stamped envelope for contest results. Qualified readers will screen all MSS. Winner will be selected by "a distinguished poet who will remain anonymous until the winner is announced in mid-February." Past judges include C.K. Williams, Maxine Kumin, Mona Van Duyn, Charles Wright, Gerald Stern, Mary Oliver and Donald Finkel. **No translations.** Recent winners are Jim Daniels, Patricia Dobler, David Kirby, Lisa Zeidner, Stefanie Marlis, Judith Vollmer and Renée A. Ashley.

‡WISCONSIN REVIEW; WISCONSIN REVIEW PRESS (II), Box 158, Radford Hall, University of Wisconsin-Oshkosh, Oshkosh WI 54901, (414)424-2267, founded 1966, editor Aaron W. Miller. The elegantly printed *WR* is published 3 times a year, 48-64 pp. **"In poetry we publish mostly free verse with strong images and fresh approaches. We want new turns of phrase."** Some poets recently published are Laurel Mills, Joseph Bruchac, Kenneth Frost, Paul Marion, Dionisio Martinez, Stephen Perry, Margaret Randall, David Steingass, Brian Swann and Peter Wild. As a sample the editors selected these lines from "Early Morning of Another World" by Tom McKeown:

> *After squid and cool white wine there is*
> *no sleep. The long tentacles uncurl*
> *out of the dark with all that was left behind.*
> *Promises expand promises. A frayed mouth*
> *loses its color in the dawn.*

The *Review* is 6×9", quality white stock, glossy card cover with colored art, and black and white art inside. They use 30-40 pp. of poetry in each issue; total circulation is 2,000, with 50 subscriptions, 30 of which go to libraries. Price per issue is $2, subscription $6. **Sample copy: $2 postpaid.** The *Review* receives about 1,500 poetry submissions per year, of which it publishes about 75. **Submit MSS Sept. 15-May 15. Offices checked bi-weekly during summer. Editor requests no more than 4 poems per submission, one poem per page, single spaced with name and address of writer on each page, simultaneous submissions OK; reports to writer within 1-4 months.** Pays 2 contributor's copies; guidelines available for SASE.

THE WISE WOMAN (I, IV-Feminist), 2441 Cordova St., Oakland CA 94602, founded 1980, editor and publisher Ann Forfreedom, is a quarterly journal **"focusing on feminist issues, feminist spirituality, Goddess lore, and feminist witchcraft."** They want **"mostly shorter poetry — by both women and men — dealing with these themes. No Christian-oriented poetry."** They have recently published poetry by Lisa Yount. As a sample the editor selected these lines from"A Universe Beginning," by Kendra Usack:

> *From her blood*
> *comes the first surge,*
> *the hot explosion,*
> *then nebulas unfold . . .*

TWW is magazine-sized, approximately 32 pp., offset. "At least 20 poems received per year; accept about 50% of appropriate poems." Subscription: $15. Sample: $4 postpaid. Pays 1 copy. MS should be typed, double-spaced with writer's name and address on each page. They will consider previously published poems. Ann Forfreedom says, "I prefer poems that are active, come from the writer's deep experiences or feelings, are brief, and are applicable to many kinds of people. A focus on Goddess culture, nature, or feminist issues is helpful. Good spelling is deeply appreciated."

THE WISHING WELL (IV-Membership, women/feminism, lesbian), P.O. Box G, Santee CA 92071-0167, founded 1974, editor/publisher Laddie Hosler, is a "contact magazine for **gay and bi-sexual women** the world over; members' descriptions, photos, some letters, and poetry published with their permission only, resources, etc., listed. I publish writings only for and by members so membership is required." 1-2 pp. in each issue are devoted to **poetry, "which can be 6" to full page — depending upon acceptance by editor, 3" width column."** As a sample I selected this stanza from "Inner Voice" (poet identified only by membership #):

> *The passion I feel for you is warm*
> *Like the color of fall leaves*
> *Hold me; and smell the drifting wood smoke;*
> *as the shadows of the night fall on us.*

It is 7×8½" offset press from typescript, with soft matte card cover. It appears bimonthly and goes to 800 members. **A sample is available for $5. Membership in *Wishing Well* is $55 for 4-7 months. Membership includes the right to publish poetry, a self description (exactly as you write it), and to have responses forwarded to you, and other privileges.** Reviews books of poetry. Personal classifieds section just begun, members and/or nonmembers, $1/word.

WITHOUT HALOS; OCEAN COUNTY POETS COLLECTIVE (II), P.O. Box 1342, Point Pleasant Beach NJ 08742, founded 1983, editor-in-chief Frank Finale, an annual publication of the Ocean County Poets Collective; it prints "good contemporary poetry." The magazine **"accepts all genres, though no obscenity. Prefers poetry no longer than 2 pages. Wants to see strong, lucid images ground in experience."** They do not want **"religious verse, or greeting card lyrics."** Some poets published recently are Marvin Solomon, Thomas Reiter, Jean Hollander, Harold Witt, Shirley Warren and featured Stephen Dunn. As a sample, the editor selected lines from the following poem, "Rilke," by Carol Becker:

> There is no adequate translation.
> You have to come to him in hiking boots.
> High on a mountain in the Swiss Alps,
> outside the town of Sierre, beside its
> little church, he sleeps his impossible
> Sleep, within the sound of cowbells.

Without Halos is digest-sized, handsomely printed with b/w artwork inside and on the cover, 96 pp. flat-spined with glossy card cover. Circulation is 1,000, of which 100 are subscriptions and 100 are sold on newsstands; other distribution is at cultural events, readings, workshops, etc. Price per issue is $5. **Sample available for $5 postpaid, guidelines for SASE. Pay is 1 copy. The editors "prefer letter-quality printing, double-spaced, no more than 5 poems. Name and address should appear in top left-hand corner. Submit between January 1 and June 30 only. No manuscript returned without proper SASE. Sloppiness tossed back."** Reporting time is 2-4 months and all acceptances are printed in the next annual issue, which appears in the winter.

WOLSAK AND WYNN PUBLISHERS LTD. (II), Box 316, Don Mills Post Office, Don Mills, Ontario M3C 2S7 Canada, phone (416)222-4690, founded 1982, poetry editors Heather Cadsby and Maria Jacobs, publishes 5 flat-spined literary paperbacks per year (56-100 pp.). They have recently published collections of poetry by Bill Howell and Lillian Necakov. Here is a sample of "Cultural Differences" from **The Word for Sand** by Heather Spears:

> They have a soft way of touching their genitals
> When they are standing and thinking of something else
> not furtively
> as the men in my culture might
> (even in private furtively)
> but a light touch, simple and unimportant—
> the way a man might touch his pocket for cigarettes,
> or his mouth, as he considers the right word—
> without awkwardness, without arrogance,
> without shame,
> without any emphasis at all.

The books are handsomely printed. **Sample: $8 U.S. or $10 Canadian. Send samples with query, bio, publications. No simultaneous submissions. Reports on queries in 2-4 months. Pays 10% royalties or 10% of press run.** Maria Jacobs says "W&W prefers not to prescribe. We are open to *good* writing of any kind."

WOMAN OF POWER, A MAGAZINE OF FEMINISM, SPIRITUALITY AND POLITICS (IV-Feminist, themes), P.O. Box 827, Cambridge MA 02238-0827, founded 1983. "The purpose of *Woman of Power* is to give women a voice, and we accept submissions from women only. We honor the collective and individual voices of women, and **encourage women from all nations, backgrounds, classes, religions, races, and spiritual paths to submit work.** We read everything that is submitted and try to respond personally to each submission. We are a quarterly publication and **each issue has a theme. Interested poets are encouraged to write (with SASE) for the upcoming themes, for our selection of works greatly depends on how well the poem fits the theme of each issue. We will not print poetry which serves to further separate us from each other, work that could be seen as racist, classist or homophobic.** We encourage work that is sensitive, imaginative, sensual, erotic, clear and that speaks of a woman's experience in the world. It can be all or any one of these, and can be of any length, **120 line maximum. We ask that each poet only submit 5 poems per issue. We have no style specifications. Subject matter should relate to the theme,** but it is in each woman's interpretation that we build the diversity of work. The purpose should be to entertain, enlighten, make the reader laugh or cry, transform or point out something she has discovered that she wishes to share. We are not interested in work that is anti-male, but rather pro-female." They have published poetry by Adrienne Rich, Kalioaka, Yoko Ono, and Veronica Verlyn Culver. As a sample the editors selected these lines by Marge Piercy:

> Nothing living moves in straight lines
> but in arcs, in epicycles, in spirals, in gyres.
> Nothing living grows in cubes or cones or rhomboids

> *but we take a little here and give a little here*
> *and we change*

The quarterly is magazine-sized, 88 pp., saddle-stapled, professionally printed in 2 columns, b/w graphics, photos and ads, glossy cover with photos, circulation 18,000 with 5,000 subscriptions of which 300 are libraries. Subscriptions: $26 (4 issues). They use 10-12 of 300 submissions of freelance poetry per year. **Sample: $7 US, $8 Canada. "Send for deadlines and themes. Thematic quality very important. Photocopy OK. Send only 5 poems, any length. Simultaneous submissions OK, but we must know in the cover letter."** Reports within 1 month of deadline. **Pays 2 copies and 1 year subscription. Send SASE for guidelines. Editor comments on rejections.**

‡**WOMEN'S EDUCATION DES FEMMES (IV-Women/feminism)**, 47 Main St., Toronto, Ontario M6J 2G6 Canada, phone (416)960-4644, founded 1982, editor Christina Starr, is a quarterly using **"feminist poetry, about women."** They have recently published poetry by Linda Wikene Johnson, Chris Wind and Zoë Landale. As a sample the editor selected these lines by Genni Gunn:

> *They are crocuses in February*
> *laughter echoing in hollow valleys*
> *porcelain snowbirds with clipped wings*
> *chamelons in Western clothes*
> *and make-up.*

I have not seen an issue, but the editor describes it as 48 pp., magazine-sized, web offset, saddle-stapled, with one-color cover. Subscription: $17 individual, $30 institution. **Sample postpaid: $2.50. Pays $25/poem plus 2 copies. Reports within about a month.** Occasionally reviews books of poetry.

‡**WOMEN'S PRESS (CANADA) (IV-Women/ethnic)**, 517 College St., #233, Toronto, Ontario M3J 1L6 Canada, founded 1972, co-managing editor Angela Robertson, publishes **"minimum MS 48 pp. Women of colour, feminist, political content, modern or post-modern form, lesbian. No haiku."** As a sample the editor selected these lines by Dionne Brand:

> *this is you girl, this is the poem no woman*
> *ever write for a woman because she 'fraid to touch*

They publish 1 flat-spined paperback/year. **Pays 10% royalties, $150 advance, 6 copies. Reports in 3 months.**

WOMENWISE (IV-Women, feminist), 38 South Main St., Concord NH 03301, phone (603)225-2739, founded 1978, Editorial Committee, "a quarterly newspaper that deals specifically with issues relating to women's health—research, education, and politics." They want **"poetry reflecting status of women in society, relating specifically to women's health issues." They do not want "poetry that doesn't include women or is written by men; poetry that degrades women or is anti-choice."** *WomenWise* is a tabloid newspaper, 12 pp. on quality stock with b/w art and graphics. Its circulation is 3,000+. Price per copy is $2.95, subscription $10/year. **Sample available for $2.95. Pay is a 1-year subscription. Submissions should be typed double-spaced.** Reporting time and time to publication varies. Send for a sample issue.

WOODLEY MEMORIAL PRESS; THE ROBERT GROSS MEMORIAL PRIZE FOR POETRY (IV-Regional), English Department, Washburn University, Topeka KS 66621, phone (913)295-6448, founded 1980, editor Robert Lawson, publishes 1-2 flat-spined paperbacks a year, **collections of poets from Kansas or with Kansas connections, "terms individually arranged with author on acceptance of MS." "We charge $5 reading fee for unsolicited MSS."** Reports on queries in 2 weeks, on MSS in 2 months, published 1 year after acceptance. Samples may be individually ordered from the press for $5. They have recently published poetry by Craig Goad, Michael L. Johnson, Bruce Bond and Harley Elliott. As a sample the editor selected these lines from "In the Old House" by William Stafford:

> *Inside our Victrola a tin voice, faint*
> *but somehow both fragile and powerful, soared*
> *and could be only Caruso, all the way from*
> *Rome: I traced my fingers on the gold letters*
> *and listened my way deeper and deeper*

SASE for Robert Gross Memorial Poetry and Fiction Prize guidelines ($100 and publication).

WORCESTER REVIEW; WORCESTER COUNTY POETRY ASSOCIATION, INC. (II, IV-Regional), 6 Chatham St., Worcester MA 01609, phone (508)797-4770, founded 1973, managing editor Rodger Martin. *WR* appears annually with emphasis on poetry. New England writers are encouraged to submit, though work by other poets is used also. They want **"work that is crafted, intuitively honest, and empathetic, not work that shows the poet little respects his work or his readers."** They have used poetry by Richard Eberhart, William Stafford and Walter McDonald. As a sample I chose the opening of Louise Monfredo's "I Hold Truth":

> that two-faced
> child of mine, over
> sideways in the tub
> to wash its hair
>
> while it screams murder
> soap in the eyes
> you're killing me

WR is 6×9" flat-spined, 64+ pp., professionally printed in dark type on quality stock with glossy card cover, press run of 1,000 for 300 subscriptions (50 of them libraries) and 200 shelf sales. **Subscriptions $10. Sample $4 postpaid. Send SASE for guidelines. Pays $10 per poem, depending upon grants, plus 2 copies. Submit maximum of 5 pages. "I recommend 3 or less for most favorable readings." Simultaneous submissions OK "if indicated." Previously published poems "only on special occasions." Reports in 4-6 months. Editor comments on rejections "if MS warrants a response."** They have an annual contest for poets who live, work, or in some way (past/present) have a Worcester County connection. The editor advises, "Read some. Listen a lot."

THE WORD WORKS; THE WASHINGTON PRIZE (II), P.O. Box 42164, Washington DC 20015, founded 1974, poetry editors Karren Alenier, J. H. Beall, Barbara Goldberg and Robert Sargent, "is a nonprofit literary organization publishing contemporary poetry in single author editions usually in collaboration with a visual artist. We sponsor an ongoing poetry reading series as well as educational programs and the Washington Prize—an award of $1,000 for a book length manuscript by a living American poet." Submission open to any American writer except those connected with Word Works. Send SASE for rules. Entries accepted between February 1 and March 1. Deadline is March 1 postmark. They publish perfect bound paperbacks and occasional anthologies and want **"well-crafted poetry, open to most forms and styles (though not political themes particularly). Experimentation welcomed."** The editors chose "The Inn" from **Farewell to the Body** by Barbara Moore:

> a place like an inn in Chekhov,
> with dirty floors, dirtier icons,
>
> warmed by vodka and salted cucumber
>
> Strange how at home we feel.
> Though our hearts are not good, and
> we're horse stealers, every one of us

"We want more than a collection of poetry. We care about the individual poems—the craft, the emotional content and the risks taken—but we want manuscripts where one poem leads to the next. We strongly recommend you read the books that have already won the Washington Prize. Buy them, if you can, or ask for your libraries to purchase them. (Not a prerequisite.) **Currently we are only reading unsolicited manuscripts for the Washington Prize." Simultaneous submissions OK if so stated. Photocopy OK, no dot-matrix. Payment is 15% of run (usually of 500). Send SASE for catalog to buy samples. Occasionally comments on rejections.** The editors advise, "get community support for your work, know your audience and support contemporary literature by buying and reading small press."

‡WORDS OF WISDOM (I, IV-Humor), 612 Front St. East, Glendora NJ 08029-1133, founded 1981, editor J.M. Freiermuth, appears monthly using **"short, pithy poetry, the stuff that brings a smile to the reader's face on first reading. No religious."** They have recently published poetry by Darcy Cummings and Susan Doro. It is 16-32 pp., phototcopied with plain paper cover. They published about half of 50 submissions received in 1990. Press run 100 for 80 subscribers. **Subscription: $8. Sample postpaid: $1. Reports usually within 60 days. Pays 2 copies. Will publish simultaneous and previously published material only if submitted on floppy disk in ASCII format. No submissions at the end of the year. (Dec. 1-Jan. 31)**

‡WORDSONG; BOYDS MILLS PRESS (IV-Children), 910 Church St., Honesdale PA 18431, phone (717)253-1080, founded 1990, editor-in-chief Dr. Bernice Cullinan, is the imprint under which Boyds Mills Press (in turn, owned by *Highlights for Children*—see that listing) publishes books for children from pre-school to young adult. **"Wordsong encourages poetry which reflects multi-ethnicity, moral standards and fun. We ask poets to think in terms of 30-50 poems. Not interested in poetry for adults or that which includes violence, crass sexuality or promotes hatred. Please send complete book MSS,**

Close-up

Bernice E. Cullinan
Editor-in-chief
Wordsong

Photo by Bachrach

"As far as I know, this is the only imprint totally devoted to poetry for *children*," says Dr. Bernice E. Cullinan, editor-in-chief of Wordsong, an imprint of Boyds Mills Press, which, in turn, was created in 1990 by the publishers of *Highlights for Children*. "Their concern about putting high quality literature in children's hands led to the establishment of the publishing house," Cullinan says, pointing out that Boyds Mills and *Highlights* are totally separate entities.

Besides Wordsong, Boyds Mills Press includes two other imprints devoted to books for children. They are Caroline House, an imprint of hardcover fiction and nonfiction, and Bell Books, an imprint more varied in formats and pricing, and including softcover craft books, how-to-do-it books and books of riddles and jokes.

Cullinan, a professor in Early Childhood and Elementary Education at New York University, seems the natural choice for editor of a poetry-based imprint seeking to publish high quality literature for children. Her primary focus "has always been getting good books into children's hands and getting teachers and librarians to use poetry and literature in classrooms and libraries," and she has written and edited numerous books and articles connecting the teaching of reading and children's literature. Her work includes **Literature and the Child** (Harcourt Brace Jovanovich) and **Children's Literature in the Reading Program** (International Reading Association).

Although she does not write poetry herself, Cullinan has been influential in promoting children's poetry in the United States. She was instrumental in establishing the National Council of Teachers of English Award for Poetry for Children, an award for the entire body of a poet's work given regularly since 1977. Her involvement as a leader in the International Reading Association has also made her a visible leader in the "whole language" movement, promoting a change from a skills-based classroom to a literature-based one—with poetry "at the heart" of the curriculum.

"Our theme at Boyds Mills (and Wordsong) is Walter de la Mare's 'Only the rarest kind of best is good enough for children,' " Cullinan says. Wordsong's first publications, two books of poetry by John Ciardi that were reissued in the fall of 1991, are a testament to that theme. "We intend to keep on bringing back books that we feel should not be out of print," says Cullinan. "Our intent in the beginning was to work with established poets, but now we are issuing works of poets who have never been published before."

However, Wordsong is only interested in book-length manuscripts, not single poems; and all of the imprint's books are theme-oriented. "In some cases, it's a poet's own work all developed around a theme. In other cases, it's a person's collection of other people's poetry for an anthology of work around one particular theme. We have one collection in the works of poems about poetry. We have another one about schools. We even have one about 'my Caribbean childhood,' " Cullinan says. "We will also do individual story poems if it's something that would develop into a picture book, but that's actually under the Caroline House imprint (same address; contact person: Kent Brown)."

At present, Wordsong receives about 100 new poetry submissions a month, says Cullinan, who reads the manuscripts and selects candidates for publication. She also nurtures poets whose work Wordsong would like to publish. "As they're developing their manuscripts, I work with them in reading and reacting and trying to put together a book," she says, noting that Wordsong plans to release six to eight books each spring and fall.

Cullinan specifically looks for poetry that "allows the child to see the world in a different way, that is, words that create an image or help the child understand the essence of an experience." She particularly wants "to hear the poet's voice from *inside* the experience and things that make them cry or things that make them laugh or things that surprise them." Cullinan also points out that "children do not like sophisticated, esoteric poems they do not understand." They want poems that "extend their vision and help them expand their world . . . but they need to be able to go *with* the poet."

Those submitting their work should keep in mind that "children like rhyme, they like rhythm, and they like repetition; but as they become more familiar with poetry, they like more sophisticated poems," Cullinan says. She admits that targeting a particular age group can be difficult because children's "level of maturity in poetry is not necessarily their chronological age. It all depends on how much exposure to poetry they've had." So far, Wordsong's books are aimed at either the primary or intermediate grades, "with only one young adult collection in the hopper."

Even though children like rhythm and repetition, Cullinan does not want to see "the deadly repetition of a rhythm pattern. I want some surprises, some variation." She also does not want anything vulgar or racist. Wordsong wants poetry that is multi-cultural. The imprint is committed to promoting friendship and international understanding, she says, and "we want poetry that makes children laugh."

Cullinan recommends that those who write children's poetry "take their poetry into classrooms and read it directly to children or have someone else read it to children. Better yet, put the poem on a chart and have the children read it themselves." The true test of whether or not a poem is good enough to stand on its own, without the intonations of the poet, is to let the children read the poem aloud, she says. "And children are honest."

—Christine Martin

---

not single poems." They have published poetry by Jane Yolen. As a sample the editor selected these lines from "The Monster Den" by John Ciardi:

> *I met your Mummy long ago.*
> *She said, "How do you do?" I said, "Hello!"*
> *And we talked a little about a lot*
> *And as we talked we sat and thought*
> *A lot or a little. And then, I guess,*
> *I asked her a question, and she said, "Yes."*

"Wordsong prefers original work but will publish anthologies or picture books of poetry previously published by the poet. Wordsong guarantees a response from editors within one month or the poet can call us collect." They offer 4% royalties and advances of $1,000 and more plus 10 author's copies. Dr. Cullinan says, "Poetry lies at the heart of the elementary school literature and reading program. In fact, poetry lies right at the heart of children's language learning. Poetry speaks to the heart of a child. We are anxious to find outstanding poetry—rhyme, free verse and songs—that will appeal to children."

‡WORKING CLASSICS; RED WHEELBARROW PRESS (I, II, IV-Theme), 298 9th Ave., San Francisco CA 94118, founded 1981, editor David Joseph. *Working Classics* is a 30+ pp. "magazine of the creative work of working people. Our poets work at regular jobs like most people do, and/or are parents, homemakers, unemployed; many belong to unions or co-ops. Also our writers are readers. They are vitally interested in a multicultural literature that actively reflects the diversity and strength in American society. They express many points-of-view; encompass many styles and forms. Most of our poetry is by worker poets, who, by the way, bear little resemblance, if at all, to stereotypical thirties' counterparts. No dull, boring, stodgy, humorless, academic alienating, dusty poetry; no poets lulled into thinking everyone has had exactly the same experiences and privileges as themselves; poets not inter-

ested with or listening to their audiences." They have recently published poetry by Sesshu Foster, Julia Stein, Rane Arroyo, Myung-Hee Kim, Steve Rayshich and Mi Sidumo Hlatshwayo. As a sample the editor chose the first lines of "New Hire" by Karen Brodine:

> *just punching in after the clock*
> *jumps to late*
> *staggering from one machine to another*
> *first job I ever got shin splints from*

WC is magazine-sized, offset, usually with a photo of a featured author on the cover. It appears 2-4 times a year. They accept about 10% of poems received. Press run is 1,100. **Sample: $3 postpaid. Pays 3 copies. "We like poets to share with us some of their own background and experiences. Their work doesn't have to be literally about their own job, family, etc., but many write about what they directly know." Simultaneous submissions and previously published poems OK. Reports in 1-3 months. On rejections the editor "frequently comments, often criticizes, tries to be supportive and not off-base, if it can be improved structurally, suggests how."**

WORLDWIDE POETS' CIRCLE; POETRY BY THE SEAS (IV-Membership), P.O. Box 74, Oceanside CA 92049-0074. Commenced publishing in 1985, Jan Renfrow, editor publisher and co-founder. **"We are a membership society. Only members of *WWPC* may submit material to our small monthly magazine, *Poetry By The Seas*. Always include an SASE. We get too many queries and submissions without any return envelopes or postage.** Members are entitled to a variety of benefits and privileges, including participation, either in person or in absentia, in our six-month taping programs, and in any and all scheduled readings. We offer critiquing upon request, and we welcome poets of all ages in all occupations and at all levels of experience and proficiency. You need not be pre-published to join us." Annual membership fee is $15 domestic (including Canada); $20 overseas. Senior citizens and full-time students may join for $13 domestic; $18 abroad. "Please query before sending money—annual membership fee *may* go up within the coming months." Membership includes a year's subscription to *Poetry By The Seas*. Sample copies of *Poetry By The Seas* are available for $2 domestic; $4 overseas. Reviews books of poetry by members. "We strongly believe in the therapeutic healing power of the creative arts."

WORMWOOD REVIEW PRESS; THE WORMWOOD REVIEW; THE WORMWOOD AWARD (II), P.O. P.O. Box 4698, Stockton CA 95204-0698, phone (209)466-8231, founded 1959, poetry editor Marvin Malone. This is one of the oldest and most distinguished literary journals in the country. "The philosophy behind *Wormwood:* (i) avoid publishing oneself and personal friends, (ii) avoid being a 'local' magazine and strive for a national and international audience, (iii) seek unknown talents rather than establishment or fashionable authors, (iv) encourage originality by working with and promoting authors capable of extending the existing patterns of Amerenglish literature, (v) avoid all cults and allegiances and the you-scratch-my-back-and-I-will-scratch-yours approach to publishing, (vi) accept the fact that magazine content is more important than format in the long run, (vii) presume a literate audience and try to make the mag readable from the first page to the last, (viii) restrict the number of pages to no more than 40 per issue since only the insensitive and the masochistic can handle more pages at one sitting, (ix) pay bills on time and don't expect special favors in honor of the muse, and lastly and most importantly (x) don't become too serious and righteous." Marvin Malone wants **"poetry and prose poetry that communicate the temper and range of human experience in contemporary society; don't want religious poetry and work that descends into bathos; don't want imitative sweet verse. Will not consider simultaneous submissions. Must be original; any style or school from traditional to ultra experimental, but *must* communicate; 3-600 lines."** He has recently published poetry by Ron Koertge, Gerald Locklin, Charles Bukowski, Edward Field, and Lyn Lifshin. As a sample he offers these lines by Dieter Weslowski:

> *Why just the other day*
> *I saw a vision of Paradise*
> *above the trees. I think*
> *it was Blake.*
> *No, he wasn't singing,*
> *but his beard was magnificent.*

The digest-sized quarterly, offset from photo reduced typescript, saddle-stapled, has a usual print run of 700 with 500 subscriptions of which about 210 are libraries. Subscription: $8. Yellow pages in the center of each issue feature "one poet or one idea"—in the issue I examined, 8 pp. devoted to Jennifer Stone's "Notes from the Back of Beyond," passages from her diary. **Sample: $4 postpaid. Submit 2-10 poems on as many pages. No dot-matrix. Reports in 2-8 weeks, pays 2-10 copies of the magazine or cash equivalent ($6-30). Send SASE for guidelines.** Reviews books of poetry. For chapbook publication, no query; send 40-60 poems. **"Covering letter not necessary—decisions are made solely on merit of submitted work." Reports in 4-8 weeks. Pays 35 copies or cash equivalent ($105). Send $4 for samples or check libraries.** They offer the

Wormwood Award to the Most Overlooked Book of Worth (poetry or prose) for a calendar year, judged by Marvin Malone. He comments on rejections if the work has merit. He advises, "Have something to say. Read the past and modern 'master' poets. Absorb what they've done, but then write as effectively as you can in your own style. If you can say it in 40 words, do *not* use 400 or 4,000 words."

WRIT (II,IV-Translations), 2 Sussex Ave., Toronto, Ontario M5S 1J5 Canada, phone (416)978-4871, founded 1970, editor Roger Greenwald, associate editor Richard Lush, is a "literary annual publishing new fiction, poetry, and translation of high quality; has room for unestablished writers." **No limitations on kind of poetry sought; new forms welcome. "Must show conscious and disciplined use of language." They do not want to see "haiku, purely formal exercises, and poetry by people who don't bother reading."** They have published poems by Rolf Jacobsen, Paavo Haavikko, Adelia Prado, Pia Tafdrup, Gunnar Harding, Richard Lush, Flavia Cosma, Anne Michaels, Robert Kenter, and Joel Oppenheimer. As a sample the editor selected these lines from "Nineteen Poems" by Charles Douglas:

> But even underground our journey will observe
>
> laws of topography, until an eruption
> becomes like a wart, a small disturbance
> of physiognomy, and each of our acts the weight
>
> of a stone on the hillside, under the freedom system.

The magazine is 6×9″, 96 pp. flat-spined and sewn, professionally printed on heavy stock, matte card cover with color art, circulation 700, for 125 subscriptions of which 75 are libraries, about 125 store and direct sales, $7.50/copy. **Sample: $7.50 postpaid. Pays 2 copies and discount on bulk purchases. Reports in 8-12 weeks. Does not consider submissions between May-July. Acceptances appear in the next issue published. Poems must be typed and easily legible, printouts as close to letter quality as possible with new ribbon. Photocopies OK. No simultaneous submissions. Editor "sometimes comments on rejections."** The editor advises, "Read a copy of the magazine you're submitting to. Let this give you an idea of the quality we're looking for. But in the case of *WRIT*, don't assume we favor only the styles of the pieces we've already published (we can only print what we get and are open to all styles). Enclose phone number and SASE with Canadian stamps or international reply coupons."

WRITE NOW!, (IV-Themes), P.O. Box 1014, Huntington IN 46750, founded 1989, editor Emily Jean Carroll. *Write Now!* **uses a limited amount of poetry up to 36 lines. Payment is 1 copy.** As a sample the editor selected, "Authorship" by Rhoda Rainbow:

> All the happiness
> I seek,
> Is time to write
> A book a week.

Write Now! is bimonthly, digest-sized, 28-32 pages. Subscription $12 ($15 Canada). **Sample $1.50.** "On Assignment" features themed poetry contests each issue with awards of $5 plus copy for first place, $3 plus copy, second place; and $1 plus copy, third place. Poets should send SASE for schedule.

‡THE WRITE WAY; ANN'S ENTERPRISES (I, IV-Themes), P.O. Box 832, Shelburne VT 05482, phone (802)985-8775, founded 1988, editor Ann Larberg. *TWW* is a quarterly using **poems of up to 30 lines on the theme of writing.** It is a 4-page newsletter with articles on writing and ads. Ann's Enterprises publishes a seasonal anthology for Christmas only. **Pays 2 copies. Do not submit in summer. Reports in 6 weeks.** They hold contests quarterly, requiring fees. As a sample the editor selected the concluding lines from her own "Cliché Ultimatum":

> They swim through the
> portholes of his brain
> Emerging again and again
> How to get rid of them?
> Let the clichés rearrange themselves
> until they become sure of what
> they are saying.

Market categories: (I) Beginning; (II) General; (III) Limited; (IV) Specialized; (V) Closed.

THE WRITER; POET TO POET (I, II), 120 Boylston St., Boston MA 02116, founded 1887, "Poet to Poet," quarterly/column by Denise Dumars. This monthly magazine for writers has an instructional column to which poets may submit work for possible publication and comment by Denise Dumars. There is no pay, and MSS are not acknowledged or returned. Submit no more than 3 poems, no longer than 30 lines each, not on onion skin or erasable bond, name and address on each page, one poem to a page. Readers may find suggestions in the column for possible themes or types of poems. As a sample the editor chose "Invitation" by H. Edgar Hix:

> Outside, it's raining.
> It will be dusk all day.
>
> I have hot chocolate
> in red clay cups,
> great quilts, handmade
> by my grandmother,
> and my mother's recipe
> for brownies
> we can make together.

Subscription: $27 (introductory offer: 6 issues for $12). Single copy: $3.

WRITER'S DIGEST (IV-Themes/writing, humor); WRITER'S DIGEST WRITING COMPETITION (II), 1507 Dana Ave, Cincinnati Ohio 45207, phone (513)531-2222, founded 1921. *Writer's Digest,* assistant editor Peter Blocksom, is a monthly magazine for freelance writers—fiction, nonfiction, poetry and drama. "All editorial copy is aimed at helping writers to write better and become more successful. Poetry is part of 'The Writing Life' section of *Writer's Digest* only. These poems should be generally light verse concerning 'the writing life'—the foibles, frenzies, delights and distractions inherent in being a writer. No poetry unrelated to writing. Some 'literary' work is used, but must be related to writing. Preferred length: 4-20 lines." They have recently published poems by Charles Ghigna, Willard R. Espy and Michael Bugeja. As a sample, Peter Blocksom chose this poem, "Epidermal Advice" by Anne Siegrist:

> If you yearn to be a writer,
> why, somehow just begin.
> (But first you'll need a miracle
> to grow a thicker skin!)

They use 2 short poems per issue, about 25 per year of the 1,000 submitted. *Writer's Digest* has a circulation of 225,000. Subscription: $21. **Sample: $3 postpaid. Do not submit to Judson Jerome, poetry columnist for the magazine. Submit to Peter Blocksom, assistant editor, each poem on a separate page, no more than 4 per submission. Dot-matrix is discouraged, photocopy OK. Previously published, simultaneous submissions OK if acknowledged in covering letter. Reports in 3 months. Pays $20-50 per poem. Send SASE for guidelines. Editor comments on rejections** "when we want to encourage or explain decision." Poetry up to 16 lines on any theme is eligible for the annual Writer's Digest Writing Competition. Watch magazine for rules and deadlines, or write for a copy of the contest's rules. (Also see Writer's Digest Books under Publications Useful to Poets.)

THE WRITER'S EXCHANGE; R.S.V.P. PRESS (I, IV-Themes/writing, anthologies), Box 394, Society Hill SC 29593, phone (803)378-4556, founded 1983, editor Gene Boone, is a digest-sized newsletter for writers and poets with a special emphasis on beginners. Gene Boone also publishes an annual poetry anthology. He wants "**upbeat, positive humorous poems, especially short poems to 12 lines, such as haiku,**" especially when they are about writing. He has recently published poetry by Linda Hutton, Dale Loucareas, Vic Chapman, and himself. As a sample he selected these sample lines (poet unidentified):

> A hurried world, spinning too fast
> Modern technology replaces dreams
> With skyscraper nightmares
> God watches as we dance at Satan's feet.

TWE is 6-8 pp., size varies issue-to-issue, saddle-stitched, with a colored paper cover. It is published quarterly. He accepts about half or more of the poetry received. Press run is 75. Subscription: $5 a year. **Sample: $1 postpaid. Send SASE for guidelines. Pays 2 copies. "I prefer typed MSS, one poem per page, readable. Poets should always proofread MSS before sending them out. Errors can cause rejection." No simultaneous submissions. Previously published poetry OK. Responds in 2-4 weeks, usually 4 months until publication.** He offers cash awards for quarterly contests sponsored through the magazine. Send SASE for current rules. He says he comments on rejections, "If I feel it will benefit the poet in the long run, never anything too harsh or overly discouraging."

WRITERS' FORUM (II, IV-Regional), University of Colorado, Colorado Springs CO 80933-7150, *Writers' Forum* founded 1974, Victoria McCabe is poetry editor. *Writers' Forum*, an annual, publishes both beginning and well-known writers, giving "**some emphasis to contemporary Western literature**, that is, to representation of living experience west of the 100th meridian in relation to place and culture. We collaborate with authors in the process of revision, reconsider and frequently publish revised work. We are open to **solidly crafted imaginative work that is verbally interesting and reveals authentic voice. We do not seek MSS slanted for popular appeal, the sentimental, or gentle, pornographic or polemical, and work primarily intended for special audiences such as children, joggers, gays, and so on is not for us. Send 3-5 poems.**" They have recently published poems by William Stafford, David Ray, Kenneth Fields, Harold Witt, and Judson Crews. As a sample the editor chose the closing lines from "Make Believe; Ukraine 1932-33" by Rawdon Tomlinson:

> In the last act the body eats itself;
> Tissue and albumen consumed by breathing,
> The skin colors dust-gray and the hands swell;
> You can't imagine the energy of eating—

The annual is digest-sized, 225+ pp., flat-spined, professionally printed with matte card cover, using 40-50 pp. of poetry in each issue, circulation 800 with 100 subscriptions of which 25 are libraries. **The list price is $8.95 but they offer it at $5.95 to readers of *Writer's Digest*.** They use about 25 of 500 freelance submissions of poetry per year. **Do not submit during June, July or August. Pays 1 copy. Reports in 1-3 months. Simultaneous submissions OK if acknowledged. Photocopy, dot-matrix OK.** Reviews books of poetry.

Poet Laureate of Colorado Thomas Hornsby Ferril
Published by the University of Colorado
at Colorado Springs

"We give some emphasis to Western American literature and Thomas Hornsby Ferril was, at the time of the issue, Poet Laureate of Colorado," editor Alexander Blackburn says of this Writers' Forum cover. Ferril was the subject of the issue's "Western Writers Series." The issue included two articles on Ferril, one by Bill Hornby, reprinted from The Denver Post, and a critical essay by Victoria McCabe, Writers' Forum poetry editor. The logo at the top of the cover "is derived from the Hopi Indians' symbol for emerging consciousness," Blackburn says.

WRITERS FORUM; AND; KROKLOK (IV-Form), 89A Petherton Rd., London N5 2QT England, founded 1963, editor Bob Cobbing, is a "small press publisher of experimental work with occasional issues of magazines dealing with sound and visual poetry in cards, leaflets, chapbooks, occasional paperbacks and magazines. **"Explorations of 'the limits of poetry' including 'graphic' displays, notations for sound and performance, as well as semantic and syntactic developments, not to mention fun. Current interest in computer poetry—visual and verbal.**" They have recently published poetry by Steve McCaffery, Herbert Burke, Bill Griffiths, Peter Finch, Betty Radin and Patricia Farrell. As a sample the editor selected these lines by Robert Sheppard:

> configuration defacing emphasized faces
> dancing word dog said death to words
> alarms trip distortions in a close optic
> mean amputation in surprises

The magazines are published "very irregularly" and use "very little unsolicited poetry; practically none." Press run "varies." **Payment "by arrangement." Many poems should be submitted camera-ready.** Under the imprint Writers Forum they publish 12-18 books a year averaging 24 pp. **Samples and listing: $5. For book publication, query with 6 samples, bio, publications. Pays "by arrangement with author."** The editor says, "We publish only that which surprises and excites us; poets who have a very individual voice and style."

WRITER'S GUIDELINES (I, IV-Themes), (formerly Guidelines Magazine), P.O. Box 608, Pittsburg MO 65724, founded in 1988, Corporation of America, a nonprofit organization, poetry editor Susan Salaki, is a market news magazine, publishing comments by editors and writers on writing and selling MSS and offering the service of distributing guidelines for the editors of various magazine and book publishers to writers. They want **"any form of poetry relating to writing and editing."** They receive about 200 poems a year, 30-40 accepted. **Sample: $4 postpaid. Pays 1 copy. No simultaneous submissions or previously published works. Reports in 2-4 weeks. Submit minimum of 3 samples. Send SASE for guidelines.** "We publish the poems that move us emotionally. Poems that touch the soul of writers and editors are our first choice. Humorous poems also welcome."

WRITERS' JOURNAL (I, II, IV-Teen/young adult), incorporating *Minnesota Ink*, 27 Empire Dr., St. Paul MN 55103, phone (612)225-1306, *Writer's Journal* founded 1980, poetry editor Esther M. Leiper (for the *Minnesota Ink* section, poetry editor Anthoney Stomski). *Writer's Journal* is a bi-monthly magazine "for writers and poets that offers advice and guidance, motivation, inspiration, to the more serious and published writers and poets. Esther Leiper has 2 columns: "Esther Comments," which specifically critiques poems sent in by readers, and "Every Day with Poetry," which discusses a wide range of poetry topics, often—but not always—including readers' work. She says, **"I enjoy a variety of poetry: free verse, strict forms, concrete, Oriental. But we take nothing vulgar, preachy or sloppily written.** Since we appeal to those of different skill levels, some poems are more sophisticated than others, but those accepted must move, intrigue or otherwise positively capture me. 'Esther Comments' is never used as a negative force to put a poem or a poet down. Indeed, I focus on the best part of a given work and seek to suggest means of improvement on weaker aspects. **Short is best: 25 line limit, though** *very* **occasionally we use longer. 3-4 poems at a time is just right."** They have recently published poetry by R. Nikolas Macioci, Kevin Morgan, Miriam Vermilya, Lawrence Schug, Diana Sutliff, Eugene E. Grollmes, and editor Lieper. As a sample the editor selected these lines from "an unidentified author we'd love to hear from":

> I am with Haysie again on God's ranch,
> It is not yet dawn; we ride west
> over the mountains. His face is in shadow
> but I know it is Haysie because
> I have loved his shadow so.

The *Writers' Journal* is magazine-sized, professionally printed, 52 pp. (including paper cover), using 4-8 pp. of poetry in each issue, including columns. Circulation 37,000, They receive about 400 submissions per year of which they use 30-40 (including those used in Esther's column). **Sample copy: $4 postpaid. Photocopy OK, no query. Reports in 4-5 months. Pays 25¢/line. The** section *Minnesota Ink* began as a separate magazine in 1987. Poetry editor Anthoney Stomski, is "open to style, prefer light-hearted pieces and of good taste"; payment varies. *Writers' Journal* has Spring and Fall poetry contests for previously unpublished poetry. Deadlines: April 15 and November 30. *Minnesota Ink* has summer and winter poetry contests. Deadlines: August 15 and February 28. Reading fee for each contest: $2 first poem, $1 each poem thereafter.

WRITERS' OWN MAGAZINE (I, IV-Subscribers), 121 Highbury Grove, Clapham, Bedford, Bedfordshire MK41 6DU U.K., phone 02343-65982, founded 1982, editor Eileen M. Pickering, uses **poetry in "any form up to 32 lines. Definitely** *no* **pornography or blasphemy. Preference given to nature, animals, wholesome deep emotion."** She has recently published poetry by Marjorie G. Harvey and Margaret Munro Gibson. As a sample she selected these lines from "Race Horse" by Marjorie G. Harvey:

> In chestnut thunder
> of thudding hooves,
> turf scuffed speed,
> brushed black tail streaming
> like a young girl's hair,

WOM is digest-sized, 48 pp. including paper cover, offset from typescript, saddle-stapled. **Subscription: $20 per year (or £7-50 sterling money order). You have to subscribe to submit and receive no extra free copies if published. Submit up to 6. May be handwritten (very legibly) or typed. Considers simultaneous submissions. Reports within 1 week, time to publication up to 1 year.** *Writer's Own* also publishes 24 pp. chapbooks on a subsidy basis (unless poet is very well-known.) The magazine holds quarterly poetry competitions with small cash and booklet prizes, open to subscribers only. Eileen M. Pickering advises, "Subscribe to as many poetry mags as you can afford and let your name become well-known within the small mag presses."

‡WRITING (I), P.O. Box 403, Carlton South, Melbourne, Victoria, Australia 3053, founded 1986, supervising editor Sherryl Clark, appears twice a year, **"aims to publish new writers and/or writers in writing groups. Well-published writers should not submit. We think of ourselves as a 'stepping stone' while maintaining the highest possible standard, poetry that is contemporary and fresh, not merely recycling old ideas and images."** As a sample the editor selected these lines from "Granite Day" by Jordie Albiston:

> today
> is a granite day great
> slabs of silence
> cram me in
> thick and impenetrable
> thick with soundlessness

The editor describes it as "48 pp., A5-6×8", stapled, card cover." They accept an average of 25 of 200-300 poems received/year. Press run 350 for 130 subscribers of which 11 are libraries, 50 shelf sales. Subcription: A$14 (in Australia). **Sample postpaid: A$5 in Australia, $7 overseas. Send SASE for guidelines. Pays 1 copy. Editorial committee can take 6 months to respond.**

WRITING (V), Box 69609, Station K, Vancouver, British Columbia V5K 4W7 Canada, phone (604)688-6001, founded 1980, editor Jeff Derksen, is a literary magazine appearing 3 times per year using **"socially committed, innovative writing."** I have not seen a copy, but the editor describes it as 96 pp., 6×9", with "colour cover." They accept about 10% of submissions received. Press run 700 for 300 subscriptions of which 20% are libraries, 200 shelf sales. Subscription: $15 Canada, $18 USA, $20 foreign. **Sample postpaid: $6. Pays subscription. Currently accepts no unsolicited poetry.**

WYOMING, THE HUB OF THE WHEEL . . . A JOURNEY FOR UNIVERSAL SPOKESMEN; THE WILLOW BEE PUBLISHING HOUSE (I, II, IV-Themes, humor), Box 9, Saratoga WY 82331, phone (307)326-5214, founded 1985, managing editor Dawn Senior, who says "We publish a semi-annual literary-art magazine devoted to themes of Peace, The Human Race, Positive Relationships, and the Human Spirit and all its Possibilities. We have a general audience interested in peace, humanism, the environment, society, and universal messages." The editor's instructions are: **"Poetry should be real. We look for a haunting quality in the work which makes the reader want to read each piece again, and again. Usually accept work which is personal and creates emotion in the reader (yet *says* something) rather than works which are purely intellectual, factual. We're especially open to high quality work from minority writers from the U.S. or anywhere in the world."** Her negatives are: **"Don't list emotions. Don't 'sum up' what it is you are saying. Leave some mystery. Strong images, natural rhythms, use of metaphor are necessary; without them, it's merely verse or an editorial."** She has published poetry by Jung-Ja Choi, Gary David, Rochelle Lynn Holt, Graciany Miranda-Archilla and Asher Torren. As a sample, she chose the following lines by Yearn Hong Choi:

> the woods belong to the trees.
> the woods belong to the saint.
> the saint is hiding all the beautiful
> things with the green leaves
> from modern man
> who is passing by
> the woods
> 65 mph.

Wyoming, The Hub of the Wheel is a 6×9" paperback, flat-spined, 100-128 pp., offset with b/w artwork, glossy card cover with b/w illustration. It appears annually. Circulation about 500, of which 40% will be subscriptions. Price per issue is $6.50, subscription $10. **Sample $5 postpaid, guidelines available for SASE. Pay is 1 copy. Writers should submit up to 5 poems, maximum of 80 lines per poem. Photocopies, dot-matrix and simultaneous submissions are OK. "Prefer unpublished poems." Send submissions from September 1 to December 15 only. Submissions are reported on in 4-16 weeks, and time to publication is 6-18 months.** The editor says, "About 10% of our publication is open to new and/or previously unpublished writers. Our editorial biases preclude our accepting material which lauds alcohol or drugs, or which contains sexually explicit passages of a coarse nature. We would reject outright any material which in subject, thought, or language is contrary to our themes. No religious material. Humor is welcome if it is poetry and not verse. If you like our approach, send us something and see what happens."

X-CALIBRE (II, IV-Theme), P.O. Box 780, Bristol, Great Britain B5994 5BB, phone (44)272-715144, founded 1986, editors Ken Taylor and Juli Stevesneyd, have recently published poetry by John Gonzalez, John Light, Falcastron, Juli Stevesneyd and Ann Keith. As a sample they select A Childe's "Lamia":

> *Entranced by the song of the wind*
> *through the wires,*
> *The Lamia raises its arms in*
> *mute wonderment*
> *At the marvels of modern*
> *communication.*

X-Calibre is an **occasional serial devoted either to an author or a theme, usually** with "copious b/w drawings/illustrations," 112 pp., paperback. They accept about 15% of 750 poems received/ year. Press run 500 for 200 shelf sales. **Sample, postpaid: £3. Deadline August 1 annually. Send SAE, IRC for guidelines. Pay is "nominal" with discount on copies. Reports in 1 month.** The editor advises, "Live it!"

‡XENOPHILIA; OMEGA CAT PRESS (II, IV-Themes), 904 Old Town Ct., Cupertino CA 95014, founded 1990, editor Joy Oestreicher. Omega Cat Press publishes 1 chapbook/year. *Xenophilia* appears twice a year using **poetry on "geo-cultural topics; 'xenology'—alien or other cultures, or our society from other's view; exotic rituals, mythic traditions; surreal, beat, punk, fantasy/science fiction, humor and speculative works (to 20 pp.) No greeting-card versification."** They have recently published poetry by Denise Dumars, David Kopaska-Merkel, John Grey, Bruce Boston and Andrew Gettler. As a sample the editor selected these lines from "Distant Mirrors" by Wayne Edwards:

> *here distant mirrors sing at night*
> *mnemotechnic prayers of trust and fear*
> *warnings against civility and progress*
> *the fall of man the slow dissolve*
> *of knowledge and war and love*

The magazine is digest-sized, 30+ pp., saddle-stapled with matte card cover, professionally printed. **Subscription: $5. Sample: $3 postpaid. Pays $5/page plus 1 copy. Send SASE for guidelines. Response in 30 days, longer in December.** Editor comments on rejections "often. I occasionally ask for rewrites." For their annual chapbook competition, submit 30-50 poems "about any national heritage or culture (not necessarily a real culture)—a people's customs, rites, typical social occasions, folkways, etc." **$5 reading fee/submission. Cover letter required. Deadline Dec. 1 for April publication. Write for rules.** All entrants receive a copy of the winning chapbook.

‡X-PRESS PRODUCTIONS (III), 2932 Roundtree Blvd., Ypsilanti MI 48197, founded 1989, editor Eugene Haun, who writes, "Retired, I now have the time and the money to publish poetry; but it *is* my money, and I must put it on serious, talented, disciplined poets. **I do not require a theme, but I do look for integrity and a production which manifests internal consistency. I want poetry, not puzzles. Better known poets do not need my attentions."** The sample chapbook I have seen, **Scenes from Childhood** by Murray Jackson, is professionally printed on inexpensive stock with a glossy card cover with b/w art. The poems titles are all in very different and striking typography. As a sample I chose the first stanza of "To my Brother Larry" from that book:

> *We giggled and watched*
> *The toes of the world*
> *From our basement window.*
> *Archibald, the music teacher,*
> *Petite-ing from his apartment to John R.*

Reports within a month. Pays 50% of earnings after costs. Author owns all but 100 editor's copies. Write for samples.

‡XTRA!; PINK TRIANGLE PRESS; CHURCH-WELLESLEY REVIEW (IV-Gay, lesbian), P.O. Box 7289, Station A, Toronto, Ontario M5W 1X9 Canada, founded 1971. *Xtra!*, appearing every 2 weeks, is **Canada's largest gay and lesbian periodical. They want short, "not epic" poems** for *Church-Wellesley Review*. They have recently published poetry by Daniel David Moses, Sky Gilbert and Antler. Poetry appears only in the annual literary supplement to the tabloid, which has a press run of 21,000 for 500 subscribers—distributed free to the public. **Reports in 3 months. Pays "honorarium."**

YALE UNIVERSITY PRESS; THE YALE SERIES OF YOUNGER POETS (III), 92A Yale Station, New Haven CT 06520, phone (203)432-0900, founded 1908, poetry editor (Yale University Press) Charles Grench. The Yale Series of Younger Poets is one of the most prestigious means available to launch a book publishing career. It is **open to poets under 40 who have not had a book previously published— a book MS of 48-64 pp. Entry fee: $8. Submit February 1-28 each year. Send SASE for rules and**

guidelines. Poets are not disqualified by previous publication of limited editions of no more than 300 copies or previously published poems in newspapers and periodicals, which may be used in the book MS if so identified. Recent winners have been Richard Kenney, Julie Agoos, Pamela Alexander and George Bradley. Publication of the winning volume each year is on a standard royalty contract plus 10 authors' copies, and the reputation of the contest guarantees more than the usual number of reviews.

YANKEE MAGAZINE; YANKEE ANNUAL POETRY CONTEST (II), Main St., Dublin NH 03444, phone (603)563-8222, founded in 1935, poetry editor Jean Burden since 1955, is one of the first places where my own poetry was published—over 30 years ago—and is still going strong, still with the same poetry editor! Though it has a New England emphasis, the poetry is not necessarily about New England or by New Englanders, and it has a national distribution to more than a million subscribers. They want to see **"high quality contemporary poems in either free verse or traditional form. Does not have to be regional in theme. Any subject acceptable, provided it is in good taste. We look for originality in thought, imagery, insight—as well as technical control." They do not want poetry that is "cliché-ridden, banal verse."** They have recently published poetry by William Stafford, Liz Rosenberg, Josephine Jacobsen, Nancy Willard, Linda Pastan, Paul Zimmer and Hayden Carruth. As a sample I selected these lines from "After a Brubeck Concert" by Miller Williams:

> But I will be also, when six hundred years have passed,
> one of seventeen million who made love
> aiming without aiming to at one
> hardly imaginable, who may then be doing
> something no one I know has ever done
> or thought of doing, on some distant world
> we did not know about when we were here.

The monthly is $6 \times 9''$ 170 + pp., saddle-stapled, professionally printed, using full-color and b/w ads and illustrations, with full-color glossy paper cover. They receive over 30,000 submissions a year, accept about 50-60 poems per year. Subscription $19.95. **Submit poems up to 32 lines, free verse or traditional. Uses 4-5 poems/monthly issue. Pays $50/poem, all rights; $35, first magazine rights. Reports in 2-3 weeks. Approximately 18 month backlog. No simultaneous submissions or previously published poems. Submissions without SASE "are tossed." Editor comments on rejections "only if poem has so many good qualities it only needs minor revisions."** Annual poetry contest judged by a prominent New England poet and published in the January issue, with awards of $150, $100 and $50 for the best 3 poems in the preceding year. Jean Burden advises, "Study previous issues of *Yankee* to determine the kind of poetry we want. Get involved in poetry workshops at home."

‡**YARROW, A JOURNAL OF POETRY (II),** English Dept., Lytle Hall, Kutztown State University, Kutztown PA 19530, founded 1981, editor Harry Humes, appears twice a year. They have recently published poetry by Gibbons Ruark, Jared Carter, William Pitt Root and Fleda Brown Jackson. It is 40 pp., $6 \times 9''$ offset. Press run 350. Subscription: $5/2 years. Reports in 1-2 months. Pays 2 copies plus 1 year subscription.

YELLOW SILK: JOURNAL OF EROTIC ARTS, Verygraphics, Box 6374, Albany CA 94706. Declined listing.

‡**YESTERDAY'S MAGAZETTE (I, IV-Senior Citizens),** Independent Publishing Co., Box 15126, Sarasota FL 34277, editor and publisher Ned Burke, founded 1973. This bimonthly magazine says that it is aimed at "plain folks" but it seems to be mainly for the elderly; there is a large "Memories" section. The issue I have contains poems on its "Quills, Quips, & Quotes" page. As a sample I chose the following lines from "The Backyard Pump" by J.E. Coulbourn:

> With two small hands you'd
> grasp the monster's tail
> And try to pump the water in the pail,
> But if his darned esophagus got dry
> No water came no matter how you'd try.

YM is magazine-sized, 22 pp., saddle-stapled, professionally printed on good stock with glossy color cover. A year's subscription is $10 or two years for $16. **Submissions for "Quills, Quips, & Quotes" should be "thoughtful, amusing, or just plain interesting for our 'plain folks' readers. No SASE is required as short items are generally not returned nor acknowledged, unless requested by the contributor. SASE for longer articles. $2 for sample copy and details."**

THE YOUNG CRUSADER (IV-Children, themes), National Woman's Christian Temperance Union, 1730 Chicago Ave., Evanston IL 60201, is a monthly publication for members of the Loyal Temperance Legion and young friends of their age—**about 6-12 years.** The digest-sized leaflet, 12 pp., uses **"short**

WOULD YOU USE THE SAME CALENDAR YEAR AFTER YEAR?

Of course not! If you scheduled your appointments using last year's calendar, you'd risk missing important meetings and deadlines, so you keep update with a new calendar each year. Just like your calendar, *Poet's Market*® changes every year, too. Many of the publishers move, contact names change, and even the publishers' needs change from the previous year. You can't afford to use an out-of-date book to plan your marketing efforts!

So save yourself the frustration of getting your book returned in the mail, stamped MOVED: ADDRESS UNKNOWN. And of NOT submitting your work to new listings because you don't know they exist. **Make sure you have the most current marketing information by ordering *1993 Poet's Market* today.** All you have to do is complete the attached post card and return it with your payment or charge card information. Order now, and there's one thing that won't change from your *1992 Poet's Market* - the price! That's right, we'll send you the 1993 edition for just $19.95. *1993 Poet's Market* will be published and ready for shipment in September 1992.

Let an old acquaintance be forgot, and toast the new edition of *Poet's Market*. Order today!

(See other side for more books for poets)

To order, drop this postpaid card in the mail.

Yes! I want the most current edition of *Poet's Market*.® Please send me the 1993 edition at the 1992 price - $19.95.* (NOTE: *1993 Poet's Market* will be ready for shipment in September 1992.) #10276

Also send me:
___ (#1836) The Poet's Handbook, $10.95* (available NOW)
___ (#10123) On Being A Writer, $19.95* (available NOW)
___ (#10209) Creating Poetry, $18.95* (available NOW)

*Plus postage & handling: $3.00 for one book, $1.00 for each additional book. Ohio residents add 5$1/2$% sales tax.

___ Payment enclosed (Slip this card and your payment into an envelope)
Please charge my: ☐ Visa   ☐ MasterCard

Account # _____ Exp. Date _____

Signature _____ Phone (___) _____

Name _____

Address _____

_____ State _____ Zip _____

*(This offer expires May 31, 1993)

Credit Card Orders Call Toll-Free 1-800-289-0963

1507 Dana Avenue
Cincinnati, OH 45207

6049

MORE BOOKS FOR POETS

The Poet's Handbook
by Judson Jerome
Here's expert instruction on how to use figurative language, symbols, and concrete images; how to tune your ear to sound relationships; the requirements for lyric, narrative, dramatic, didactic, and satirical poetry.
244 pages/$10.95, paperback

Creating Poetry
by John Drury
Designed to encourage budding poets to explore and practice poetry writing skills, Drury's nuts-and-bolts instruction addresses all elements of creating poetry. Each chapter offers an overview of each element discussed, a definition of terms, poetry examples, plus hands-on exercises.
224 pages/$18.95

On Being a Writer
edited by Bill Strickland
Conversational, inspirational, and thought-provoking, this book is a wonderful collection of dialogue, essays and advice from 31 of the greatest writers of our time. Nikki Giovanni and others share tidbits of information and solid technical advice on writing, plus a compelling "inside" look at their writing preferences and passions.
224 pages/32 b&w illus./$19.95

Use coupon on other side to order today!

poems appropriate for the temperance and high moral value and nature themes and their young audience." I selected as a sample the first of 5 stanzas of "Leprechaun's Gold" by Dianne W. Shauer:

> *On the 17th day of March, two*
> *days past the ides, look for wee,*
> *little old men, who, when they see*
> *you, will hide.*

They pay 10¢/line for poetry.

YOUNG VOICES MAGAZINE; YOUNG VOICES MAGAZINE-HIGH SCHOOL EDITION (IV-Children/Teen), P.O. Box 2321, Olympia WA 98507, phone (206)357-4683, founded 1988, publisher/editor Steve Charak, is "a magazine of **creative work of elementary and middle school-age children. The age limit is rigid.**" It appears every other month, press-run 1,000 for 500 subscribers of which 30 are libraries. Subscription: $15 for 1 year, $28 for 2. **Sample: $4 postpaid.** *Young Voices Magazine-High School Edition,* monthly, is for high school students. Subscription: $9 for 1 year. **Sample: $5 postpaid. Send SASE for guidelines. Pays $3/poem plus 1 copy (5 copies if you are a subscriber). Editor comments "definitely, on every piece of writing.**" He says, "Forget the necessity to rhyme. Make each word count with feeling. Feeling determines whether I accept a poem or a story."

‡THE YUKON READER (IV-Regional, form), P.O. Box 4306, Whitehorse, Yukon Y1A 3T3 Canada, phone (403)668-2355, editor Sam Holloway, is a magazine published 6/year using "**rhyming ballads about the North.**" Pays on publication; **$50 plus six magazines.** Subscription: $21. **Sample: free.** It is professionally printed, magazine-sized, 64 pp. with colored paper cover, circulation 25,000. As a sample, I selected the first of 26 stanzas of "Peg Leg McGonagle and the Twin Brother Banker Caper" by Steven C. Levi:

> *Now this tale that I'm telling is quite a peach*
> *of a tavern once known as McGonagle's Reach,*
> *where only the worst of Alaska's bold thieves*
> *could ever meet in the open of old Valdez.*
> *Almost all cut from the same bolt of cloth*
> *they gathered each day blessed with sun, snow or frost.*

Publishes 12 ballads/year. **All manuscripts will receive a personal reply from the editor.**

‡ZEITGEIST (I), P.O. Box 1006, Kalispell MT 59903, founded 1990, publisher/editor John S. Slack, appears 6/year. For poetry, "**best is 1 page or less dealing with personal relationships to world and others. Focused ideas. Disturbing or provocative imagery welcomed. No same old love-death-suicide stuff, graphic sex and/or gratuitous profanity. No blatantly didactic stuff.**" They have recently published poetry by Lowell Jaeger and Ronald Edward Kittell. As a sample the editor selected these lines by Irvin Moon:

> *Noisy as a fistful of coins*
> *you hunch down Pine Street*
> *tempting gaunt stares*
> *from other neon lit warriors.*

It is 35-50 pp. digest-sized, offset, saddle-stapled with matte card cover. They accept about 20% of poems submitted. Press run 200 for 40 subscribers of which 1 is a library, 40 shelf sales. Subscription: $15. **Sample postpaid: $3. Send SASE for guidelines. Reports in 1 day-1 month. Pays $2/page ($1 for very short poems 2-10 lines). Previously published poems and simultaneous submissions OK. "A 3-line bio would help us get a feel of who you are." Editor often comments on rejections.** They offer free space for self-publishers. They feature a poet in each issue with 5 poems. The editor says, "Write often. Sometimes raw is better. Keep your eyes, ears and nose open, alone with your mind. Don't take rejection personally. Sometimes it takes a while to find your audience. We like strong, effective poetry, but you don't necessarily have to strut and flex to reveal literary strength."

ZERO HOUR (IV-Themes), Box 766, Seattle WA 98111, phone (206)323-3648, founded 1987, editor Jim Jones, is "**a thinking person's tabloid. Each issue is devoted to a theme (cults, addiction, pornography, etc.) in which some poetry is printed.**" They have recently published poetry by Jesse Bernstein. I have not seen an issue, but the editor describes it as having 40 pp. It appears 3 times a year. Of 20 pieces of poetry received per year they take about 3. Press run: 3,000 for 2,000 shelf sales. **Sample postpaid: $4. Pays 5 copies. Simultaneous submissions and previously published poems OK.** "We review books of poetry."

ZERO ONE; DANCING PATCH MAGAZINE(V), 39 Minford Gardens, West Kensington, London W14 OAP England, phone 01602-9142, poetry editor and publisher Arthur Moyse. He describes *Dancing Patch Magazine* (which I have not seen) as a "literary quarterly, anarchist oriented, egotistical, clichés.

To avoid disappointments we do not seek submissions for we operate on the 'old pals act' style." He has recently published poems by Cunliffe, Woods and Gould. As a sample he selected these lines by Charles Crute:

> *I rolled Old Laughter on our bed of tears*
> *with tender coppers bought the rose*
> *and found within her vein'd arms*
> *a moments ease, a nights repose*

DPM appears 3-4 times a year. The editor describes it as magazine-sized. He says he receives "too much poetry, takes hardly any." His press run is "secret" as is his number of subscriptions and most other information about it (such as how to buy a sample). He advises, "Just write it and send it off off off. Give up waiting for editorial acceptance or rejection. Just write and post."

ZOLAND BOOKS INC. (III). 384 Huron Ave., Cambridge MA 02138, phone (617)864-6252, founded 1987, publisher Roland Pease, is a "literary press: fiction, poetry, photography, gift books, books of literary interest" using **"high-quality" poetry, not sentimental.** They have recently published poetry by William Corbett, Marguerite Bouvard, and Marge Piercy. They publish 5-8 books a year, flat-spined, averaging 96 pp. **Query with 15 sample poems, bio, publications. No simultaneous submissions. Reports on queries in 6 weeks. Pays 5-10% royalties plus 5 copies. Editor does not comment on submissions.**

ZONE 3; THE RAINMAKER AWARDS (II), Center for the Creative Arts, Box 4565, Austin Peay State University, Clarksville TN 37044, phone (615)648-7031 or 648-7891, founded 1986, editors Malcolm Glass and David Till, *Zone 3* is a poetry journal appearing 3 times a year. "We will 'evolve,' we think, to include stories, essays, reviews, photographs; but emphasis will remain on poetry. **We want poems that match form and function; poems deeply rooted in place, mind, heart, experience, rage, imagination, laughter, and so clearly rooted** *in contemporary language* **that they establish an enduring value. No restrictions on subject-matter, length, etc. No sentimentality, of either the 'left' or 'right.' No poems written primarily because the poet wants to publish poems."** They have published poetry by Greg Kuzma, Dave Etter, Albert Goldbarth, Philip Dacey, Donald Finkel, Laurel Speer, Lynn Luria-Sukenick and Neal Bowers. As a sample David Till selected these lines from Lynn Luria-Sukenick's prose poem "Atlantic Salmon":

> *Maybe the fresher water will seem thick to me,*
> *maybe the river remembering will be heavy with*
> *stories. But they tell me I'm going upriver*
> *to get a story, going to become the alphabet*
> *that will let a million salmon say, "Once upon a time."*

Zone 3 is flat-spined, with a poem on the matte card cover, professionally printed, circulation 500. **Sample: $4 current issue, $4-5 back issues, postpaid. Pays 5 copies and small honoraria when available. Reports in 3-4 months after current deadline. Submit typed MS double-spaced, 2-7 poems. No simultaneous submissions. Subscription: $8 for 3 issues.** The Rainmaker Awards in Poetry, offered by Austin Peay State University, are $500, $300 and $100 and publication in *Zone 3*, spring issue. Fee: 1 year's subscription. Deadline December 31.

Market conditions are constantly changing! If you're still using this book and it is 1993 or later, buy the newest edition of Poet's Market *at your favorite bookstore or order directly from* Writer's Digest Books.

Other Poetry Publishers

Each year we contact all publishers currently listed in **Poet's Market** requesting updated information for our next edition. The following magazine and book publishers were listed in the 1991 edition of **Poet's Market** but are not in the 1992 edition because (a) they did not respond to our request to update their listing (these names appear with no further explanation); (b) their listing was deleted for the reason indicated; (c) their listing information was received after our deadline date.

The reasons some of these publishers are not included in the directory are temporary (e.g., overstocked, temporarily suspending publication, etc.). *If you're interested in any of the following, I suggest you research the publisher and write a brief letter (enclosing SASE) inquiring whether they are now interested in receiving submissions.*

Above the Bridge Magazine
Acta Victoriana
Adara
Aesthetic Rapture (moved, no forwarding address)
Agada
Agassiz Review
Agog Publications (London)
Aireings
Ajax Poetry Letter (moved, no forwarding address)
Albatross
Allegheny Press (no longer publishing poetry)
Alphabox Press
Alternative Fiction & Poetry (ceasing publication)
Amateur Writers Journal (overstocked)
Amazing Stories
Ambergris (no longer accepting poetry)
American Studies Press, Inc. (no longer accepts freelance work)
The American Voice (requested deletion)
And
Anerca
Angel Sun
Anhinga Press
The Archer (ceased publication)
Arete: Forum for Thought (temporarily suspending publication)
Ariel, A Review of International English Literature
Arizona Women's Voice
Arnazella
Ars Poetica Press Newsletter
Artcrimes (overstocked)
Aurora Poetry Letter (ceasing publication)
Axe
Axe Factory Review (defunct)
Axis
Baker Street Publications
William L. Bauhan, Publisher
Beat Scene Magazine
The Belladonna
The Bellevue Press
The Berkeley Review of Books
The Big Mouse

Bitterroot (ceased publication)
BKMK Press
Black Horse (requested deletion)
Blank
Blind Beggar Press (responded too late)
Blue Buildings (ceased publication)
Blue Light Review (responded too late)
Bravo: The Poet's Magazine
Brooklyn Review
Cache Review (stopped publication)
Caesura
The Caitlin Press
California State Poetry Quarterly
Calli's Tales
Capital Magazine
Caring Connection
Carnegie Mellon Magazine
A Carolina Literary Companion
Ceilidh: An Informal Gathering for Story & Song
Celtic Dawn
The University of Chicago Press
Chinese Literature
Christmas, The Annual of Christmas Literature and Art (requested deletion)
Clothespin Fever Press
Columbia University Translation Center
Conditions (moved, no forwarding address)
Corona Publishing Co. (overstocked)
The Coventry Reader
Cover Magazine
Coydog Review (no longer publishing)
Crazyquilt Quarterly (temporarily suspended)
Creativity Unlimited Press (responded too late)
Croton Review
The Cummington Press (no longer accepting MSS)
Daily Meditation
Dark Nerve
Daybreak (ceasing publication)

Decision (no longer accepts unsolicited poetry)
Delhi-London Poetry Quarterly (responded too late)
Detroit Black Writers' Guild
Dialogue: A Journal of Mormon Thought
Dialogue, The Magazine for the Visually Impaired
Door County Almanak
Dragonfly: East/West Haiku Quarterly (out of business)
Dragongate Press
Dramatika, Epistolary Stud Farm
Dream International Quarterly
Earthwise Publications/ Productions (unresolved complaints)
Edge (ceased publication)
El Gato Tuerto
El Tecolote
Eldritch Tales Magazine of Weird Fantasy
Ellipse (responded too late)
Emerald City Comix & Stories
Encounter
Enitharmon Press
Equilibrium
Essence
The Evangelical Beacon
Existere
Exit, A Journal of the Arts
Expecting (no longer publishes poetry)
Fag Rag
Famous Last Words (suspending indefinitely)
Feelings
Fighting Woman News
Firebrand Books
Fireweed: A Feminist Quarterly
First Time
Flights: A Literary Voice for the Miami Valley (going out of print)
Four Zoas Journal of Poetry & Letters (no longer publishing)
Free Venice Beachhead
Galatic Discourse (ceasing publication)
A Galaxy of Verse Literary

Foundation (ceasing publication)
The Galileo Press
Gandhabba (defunct)
Gargoyle (publishing plans uncertain)
Garm Lu: A Canadian Celtic Arts Journal
Gas: The Journal of the Gross Americans Society
Giorno Poetry Systems Records
Global Tapestry Journal
Golf Digest (heavily overstocked)
Green Mountain Review
Green World Press
Grit
Groundswell
Handmade Accents, The Buyers Guide to American Artisans
The Harvard Advocate
Heartland Journal: By Older Writers for Readers of All Ages (ceased publication)
Helikon Press
Herspectives
Hibiscus Magazine (temporarily suspending publication)
Hoosier Challenger
Houghton Mifflin Canada Ltd.
How(ever) (ceasing publication)
Hummingbird
Images (no longer published)
The Independent Review (ceased publication)
Integrity International
Interim
Iris: A Journal About Women
Jam To-Day
Jazziminds Magazine (moved, no forwarding address)
Journal of Poetry Therapy
Just Between Us (out of business)
Kingfisher
Kiosk
Korone (responded too late)
Latest Jokes Newsletter (responded too late)
Latin American Literary Review Press
Latter Day Woman (moved, no forwarding address)
Laughing Dog Press (stopped publishing)
Lip Service
Literary Markets (out of business)
London Review of Books
Lone Star Publications of Humor
Loonfeather
The Madison Review
The Magazine of Speculative Poetry (responded too late)
Magnetic North
Malory Press
Margin (out of business)

Mark
Marriage & Family (undergoing major changes)
The University of Massachusetts Press (may discontinue)
Matilda Publications Productions
Meanjin Quarterly
Memorable Moments
Merlin Books Ltd. (requested deletion)
Metamorphosis
Metamorphous Press
Midwest Villages & Voices
Mina Press (overstocked)
The Mind's Eye, Fiction & Poetry Quarterly
Mirrors
The Moment
Mosaic Press (Cincinnati)
Mots Et Images: Press-Work Project
Moving Parts Press
Mud Creek (defunct)
Muse (out of business)
Music City Song Festival
Music Works
My Restless Soul (moved, no forwarding address)
New Collage Magazine
New Horizons Poetry Club (responded too late)
The New Laurel Review (responded too late)
New Poetry Review (ceased publication)
Night Tree Press
Northern New England Review
Northern Pleasure
Northwest (suspended publication)
The Northwest Gay & Lesbian Reader
Northwest Magazine (no longer accepting poetry)
Notus: New Writing
Oak Square
Off Our Backs
On the Edge
Once Upon a World (responded too late)
Orchises Press
Oregon East
Ouroboros
Overtone Press
Oveta Culp Hobby (ceased publication)
Pacific Review
The Panhandler
Panjandrum Books
Paper Air Magazine
Peacemaking for Children
Peacock Books
Pelican Publishing Company
Pensar Press (moved, no forwarding address)
Permeable Press (moved, no forwarding address)
Phoenix Press
Pirogue Publishing
A Place for Poets (moved, no

forwarding address)
The Plover (Chidori)
The Poem Factory
Poet International
Poet Papers
Poetic Pursuits (responded too late)
Poetry South (temporarily not publishing)
Poetry WLU
Poetry World (ceased publication)
Poets at Work
University of Portland Review
Poultry, A Magazine of Voice
Practical Mystic
Primavera
Prime Times (not publishing poetry)
Prism International (responded too late)
Proem Canada
Proper Tales Press
Prout Journal
The Pterodactyl Press
The Pyramid
Quick Brown Fox
Rackham Journal of the Arts and Humanities (RAJAH)
Read Me (no longer publishing)
Red Bass (overstocked)
The Red Candle Review
Red Cedar Review
Reflections (ceasing publication)
The Renovated Lighthouse Magazine
Repository Press
Rivelin Grapheme Press
Road/House
Rocky Mountain Poetry Magazine
Room Magazine
Rowan Tree Press (discontinued)
The Runaway Spoon Press
St. Andrews Review (reorganizing)
St. Luke's Press (requested deletion)
Salthouse (temporarily discontinued)
Sandscript, Cape Cod Writers Inc.
Sanskrit
Sea Fog Press Inc.
Sea Tails
Ralph W. Secord Press (discontinued publication)
Serpent & Eagle Press
The Shakespeare Newsletter
Shoe Tree: The Literary Magazine By and For Young Writers (out of business)
Shooting Star Review (responded too late)
Singlelife Magazine
Skyline Magazine
Slough Press
Snowy Egret (responded too

late)
The (Something) (ceased
  publication)
The Sounds of Poetry
South End Press
South Head Press
Southern Rose Review
Spider Eyes (ceased
  publication)
Spiritual Quest Publishing
The Stone (suspended
  indefinitely)
Stone Drum (responded too
  late)
Storypoems (no longer
  published)
Straight Ahead (ceasing
  publication)
Tabula Rasa
Tales of the Old West
Talkin' Union (no longer
  publishing)
Tar River Poetry
Tattoo Advocate Journal
Tejas Art Press
Telstar
Tenth Decade (ceasing
  publication)
The Texas Review

Third Lung Review
Third World
13th Moon
Threshold Books
Tidewater
Timbuktu (discontinuing
  publication)
Time of Singing, A Magazine of
  Christian Poetry
Tower Poetry Society
Tradition (responded too late)
Tropos
The Unspeakable Visions of
  the Individual (no longer
  publishing)
University of Utah Press
Valley Women's Voice
The Vanitas Press (responded
  too late)
Vers-Quebec (moved, no
  forwarding address)
Violetta Books
Wainwright (Philadelphia)
Wascana Review
The Washingtonian Magazine
Waterfront Press
Westview: A Journal of
  Western Oklahoma
  (responded too late)

The White Light (no longer in
  business)
The White Rose Literary
  Magazine
The Wicazo Sa Review
  (responded too late)
Windfall (no longer publishing)
Winston-Derek Publishers, Inc.
  (unresolved complaints)
The Wisconsin Restaurateur
Witness (ceased publication)
Witwatersrand University Press
Word & Image: The Illustrated
  Journal (no longer
  publishing)
Writers' Haven Journal
Writer's Lifeline
Writers' Rendezvous
Writer's Rescue
Yellow Moon Press
Young American: America's
  Newspaper for Kids
Young Author's Magazine
The Young Soldier (ceased
  publication)
Z Miscellaneous
Zephyr Press
Zymergy

State and Provincial Grants

Following is a list of arts councils in the United States and Canada that provide assistance to artists (including poets), usually in the form of fellowships or grants. These grants are often substantial and confer some prestige upon recipients; however, only residents of the state or province are eligible. Because deadlines for applications and the amount and nature of available support vary annually, I provide here only the address to which you should send queries in your own state or province:

United States Art Agencies

Alabama State Council on the Arts
Barbara George, Programs Coordinator
1 Dexter Ave.
Montgomery AL 36130
(205)261-4076

Alaska State Council on the Arts
Jean Palmer, Grants Officer
Suite 1-E, 411 W. 4th Ave.
Anchorage AK 99501
(907)279-1558

Arizona Commission on the Arts
Shelley Cohn, Executive Director
417 W. Roosevelt
Phoenix AZ 85003
(602)255-5882

Arkansas Arts Council
Bill Puppione, Executive Director
Heritage Center
Suite 200, 225 E. Markham St.
Little Rock AR 72201
(501)324-9337

California Arts Council
Ann Bourget, Literary Grants
2411 Alhambra Blvd.
Sacramento CA 95817
(916)739-3186

Colorado Council on the Arts and Humanities
Barbara Neal, Executive Director
750 Pennsylvania St.
Denver CO 80203-3699
(303)894-2617

Connecticut Commission on the Arts
John Ostrout, Acting Executive Director
227 Lawrence St.
Hartford CT 06106
(203)566-7076

Delaware State Arts Council
Cecilia Fitzgibbon, Executive Director
State Office Building
820 N. French St.
Wilmington DE 19801
(302)577-3540

Florida Arts Council
Chris Doolin, Director
Division of Cultural Affairs
Florida Department of State
The Capitol
Tallahassee FL 32399-0250
(904)487-2980

Georgia Council for the Arts
Frank Ratka, Executive Director
Suite 100, 2082 E. Exchange Pl.
Tucker GA 30084
(404)493-5780

Hawaii State Foundation on Culture and the Arts
Wendell P.K. Silve, Executive Director
Room 202, 335 Merchant St.
Honolulu HI 96813
(808)548-4145

Idaho Commission on the Arts
Margot Knight, Executive Director
304 W. State St.
Boise ID 83720
(208)334-2119

Illinois Arts Council
Richard Gage, Director of Communication Arts
Suite 10-500, 100 W. Randolph
Chicago IL 60601
(312)814-6750

Indiana Arts Commission
Tom Schorgl, Executive Director
6th Floor, 47 S. Pennsylvania St.
Indianapolis IN 46204
(317)232-1268

Iowa Arts Council
Julie Bailey, Grants Coordinator
State Capitol Complex
Des Moines, IA 50319
(515)281-4451

Kansas Arts Commission
Jay Hawk Tower
Suite 1004, 700 Jackson
Topeka KS 66603
(913)296-3335

Kentucky Arts Council
Charles M. Newell, Executive Director
31 Fountain Pl.

Frankfort KY 40601
(502)564-3757

Louisiana State Arts Council
Gerri Hobdy, Community Development
Coordinator
P.O. Box 44247
Baton Rouge LA 70804
(504)342-8180

Maine State Arts Commission
Martha Dodson, Assistant Director
State House, Station 25
Augusta ME 04330
(207)289-2724

Maryland State Arts Council
Michele Moure, Program Director
15 W. Mulberry St.
Baltimore MD 21201
(301)333-8232

Massachusetts Cultural Council
Eleanor Wachs, Humanities Director
10th Floor, 80 Boylston St.
Boston MA 02116
(617)727-3668

Michigan Council for the Arts
Craig Carvar, Managing Director
Suite 1180, 1200 6th Ave.
Detroit MI 48226
(313)256-3731

COMPAS
Molly LaBerge, Executive Director
305 Landmark Center
75 W. 5th St.
St. Paul MN 55102
(612)292-3249

Mississippi Arts Commission
Kathleen Stept, Arts & Education Program
Director
Suite 207, 239 N. Lamar St.
Jackson MS 39201
(601)359-6030

Missouri Arts Council
Autry Jackson, Program Administrator
Wainwright State Office Complex
Suite 105, 111 N. 7th St.
St. Louis MO 63101
(314)340-6845

Montana Arts Council
Julie Cook, Director of Artist Services
Michael Korn, Director of Folk Life Project
48 N. Last Chance Gulch
New York Block
Helena MT 59620
(406)444-6430

Nebraska Arts Council
Jennifer Clark, Executive Director
1313 Farnam on-the-Mall
Omaha NE 68102-1873
(402)595-2122

Nevada State Council on the Arts
William L. Fox, Director
329 Flint St.
Reno NV 89501
(702)688-1225

New Hampshire State Council on the Arts
Susan Bonaiuto, Director
Phoenix Hall
40 N. Main St.
Concord NH 03301
(603)271-2789

New Jersey State Council on the Arts
Barbara Russo, Acting Executive Director
4 N. Broad St.
Trenton NJ 08608
(609)292-6130

New Mexico Arts Division
Lara Morrow, Director
224 E. Palace Ave.
Santa Fe NM 87501
(505)827-6490

New York State Council on the Arts
Jewelle Gomez, Director, Literature Program
915 Broadway
New York NY 10010
(212)614-2965

North Carolina Arts Council
Deborah McGill, Literature Director
Department of Cultural Resources
221 E. Lane St.
Raleigh NC 27601-2807
(919)733-2111

North Dakota Council on the Arts
Brad Stephenson, Community Services
Coordinator
Suite 606, Black Bldg.
Fargo ND 58102
(701)237-8962

Ohio Arts Council
Joanne Eubanks, Assistant Coordinator
727 E. Main St.
Columbus OH 43205
(614)466-2613

State Arts Council of Oklahoma
Betty Price, Executive Director
Room 640, Jim Thorpe Bldg.
Oklahoma City OK 73105-4987
(405)521-2931

Oregon Arts Commission
Vincent Dunn, Assistant Director
835 Summer St. NE
Salem OR 97301
(503)378-3625

Pennsylvania Council on the Arts
Peter Carnahan, Literature Program Director
Room 216, Finance Bldg.
Harrisburg PA 17120
(717)787-6883

Rhode Island State Council on the Arts
Iona Dobbins, Executive Director
Suite 103, 95 Cedar St.
Providence RI 02903
(401)277-3880

South Carolina Arts Commission
Steve Lewis, Literary Arts Program
1800 Gervais St.
Columbia SC 29201
(803)734-8696

South Dakota Arts Council
Betsi Williamson, A.I.S. Coordinator
108 W. 11th St.
Sioux Falls SD 57102-0788
(605)339-6646

Tennessee Arts Commission
Alice Swanson, Director of Literary Arts
Suite 100, 320 6th Ave. N.
Nashville TN 37243-0780
(615)741-1701

Texas Commission on the Arts
Ricardo Hernandez, Director of Programs
P.O. Box 13406, Capitol Station
Austin TX 78711
(512)463-5535

Utah Arts Council
Sherry Waddingham, Grants Officer
617 E. South Temple St.
Salt Lake City UT 84102
(801)533-5895

Vermont Council on the Arts
Janet Ressler, Grants Coordinator
136 State St.
Montpelier VT 05602
(802)828-3291

Virginia Commission for the Arts
Peggy J. Baggett, Executive Director

James Monroe Bldg.
17th Floor, 101 N. 14th St.
Richmond VA 23219
(804)225-3132

Washington State Arts Commission
Linda Bellon-Fisher, Artists-in-Residence
Program
110 9th and Columbia Bldg.
Mail Stop GH-11
Olympia WA 98504
(206)753-3860

West Virginia Arts and Humanities Division
Allen Withers, Development Coordinator
Department of Education and the Arts
Division of Culture and History
The Cultural Center, Capitol Complex
Charleston WV 23505
(304)348-0220

Wisconsin Arts Board
Dean Amhaus, Deputy Director
Suite 301, 131 W. Wilson
Madison WI 53702
(608)266-0190

Wyoming Council on the Arts
Joy Thompson, Executive Director
2320 Capitol Ave.
Cheyenne WY 82002
(307)777-7742

Canadian Provinces Art Agencies

Alberta Culture and Multiculturalism
Arts Branch - Cultural Industries
Ruth Bertelsen, Manager
11th Floor, CN Tower
10004 - 104 Avenue
Edmonton, Alberta T5J 0K5
(403)427-6315

British Columbia Arts Council
Cultural Services Branch
Kate Wilkinson, Coordinator of Arts Awards
Programs
6th Floor, 800 Johnson St.
Victoria, British Columbia V8V 1X4
(604)356-1728

Manitoba Arts Council
James Hutchison, Literary Arts Consultant
Room 525, 93 Lombard Ave.
Winnipeg, Manitoba R3B 3B1
(204)945-2237

New Brunswick Department of Tourism, Recreation and Heritage
Arts Branch
Bruce Dennis, Program Officer
P.O. Box 12345
Fredericton, New Brunswick E3B 5C3
(506)453-2555

Newfoundland Department of Municipal and Provincial Affairs
Cultural Affairs Division
Elizabeth Batstone, Director of Cultural Affairs
P.O. Box 1854

St. John's, Newfoundland A1C 5P9
(709)576-3650

Nova Scotia Department of Tourism and Culture
Allison Bishop, Director of Cultural Affairs
P.O. Box 456
Halifax, Nova Scotia B3J 2R5
(902)424-5000

Ontario Arts Council
Eleanor Goldhar, Director of Communications
Suite 500, 151 Bloor St.
Toronto, Ontario M5S 1T6
(416)961-1660

Prince Edward Island Council of the Arts
Judy McDonald, Executive Director
P.O. Box 2234
Charlottetown, Prince Edward Island C1A 8B9
(902)368-4410

Organization of Saskatchewan Arts Councils
Barbara Flaten, Executive Director
1102 8th Avenue
Regina, Saskatchewan S4R 1C9
(306)586-1250

Yukon Arts Council
Nina Sutherland, Executive Director
P.O. Box 5120
Whitehorse, Yukon Y1A 4S3
(403)668-6284

Contests and Awards

Included in this section are *only* the contests and awards *not* associated with specific organizations or publishers listed elsewhere. Use the General Index first in order to locate a specific contest or award.

But you will find listed here everything from prestigious honors such as the Pulitzer Prizes and Guggenheim Fellowships to contests with entry fees and small prizes sponsored by local poetry societies and little magazines. Many of the most important are coded **V:** "Don't call us, we'll call you." But there's a place for everyone. Some of the smaller contests seem to be almost family affairs. Subscribers to little magazines apparently enjoy competing with one another and seeing winning poems by names they recognize, if not by themselves, appear in print.

Such recognition may be gratifying, though it means little in regard to establishing a literary reputation. Most of the poets I know rarely, if ever, enter contests, and when they do, they stick to those which confer some prestige among their peers—those sponsored, for instance, by the Poetry Society of America (see listing in Organizations Useful to Poets). But the tastes of judges, even those with a record of publication, are so unpredictable that a contest is very much like a lottery. Winning doesn't mean your poem would be regarded as good by a different judge, and losing doesn't mean another judge might not have given it a prize.

I have tried to weed out those contests that seem to me exploitative of poets, though, for the most part, you have to rely on your own judgment as to whether a contest is a scam. For example, if it costs you $3 a poem to enter and the prizes are $15, $10 and $5, you can figure that it takes only 10 entries to fill the kitty. Sometimes judges are paid fees, and sometimes there are publicity and other costs. But contests with fees are often moneymakers. They may be as innocent as a cake sale as a way to raise money for a small press or organization, but you shouldn't be deluded about your chances of collecting money. Other contests have no fees but are inducements to get you to buy something—for example, an anthology containing your poem. Beware of advertisements in magazines for contests. If you see one saying, in effect, "Poems Wanted," you can be sure that what is wanted is in your wallet.

In general, a beginning poet would be well-advised to put more effort into submitting work for publication than into entering contests unless he enjoys the social aspects of participating in a harmless hobby. But there are many excellent opportunities listed here, especially for poets who have already achieved a substantial publishing record.

In addition to the listings, notice at the end of the section the long list of "Additional Contests and Awards" which cross-refers the many magazines, presses and organizations offering contests and awards in their listings. If a highly reputed literary magazine such as *Negative Capability* or *Poetry* or an organization such as the Academy of American Poets conducts a contest or confers an award, it is likely to be one that is respected in the literary world.

The rules and dates for contests, not to mention their judges or contest chairpeople, change annually. In each case do not enter until you have found out (usually by sending a SASE) the most current rules and deadlines and, where applicable, have obtained appropriate entry forms.

MILTON ACORN POETRY AWARD; PRINCE EDWARD ISLAND LITERARY AWARDS (IV-Regional), The Prince Edward Island Council of the Arts, P.O. Box 2234, Charlottetown, Prince Edward Island C1A 8B9 Canada. Awards are given annually for short stories, poetry, children's literature, novels or historical works, creative writing and playwriting. Writers must have been resident at least 6 of the 12 months before the contest. Submit September 27-February 15. For the Milton Acorn Poetry Award, participants may submit as many entries as they wish, each of no more than 10 pp. Prizes for '90-'91: A trip for 2 via Air Nova to Ottawa, Montreal or Quebec City, first prize; $200 and $100, second and third prizes.

ACTS INSTITUTE, INC. (II), Box 10153, Kansas City MO 64111, this foundation offers money grants to those individuals/teams/groups accepted by artists/writers colonies who need financial assistance to be able to attend. Send SASE for 1992 application materials. Deadlines are June 1 for the following winter and December 1 for the following summer. An anthology of works created by former residents of artists/writers colonies—communities is targeted for publication in 1992.

THE AIR CANADA AWARD (I, IV-Regional), 121 Avenue Rd., Toronto, Ontario M5R 2G3 Canada, is an annual award of two tickets to any Air Canada destination, to a Canadian author, published or unpublished, under 30 who shows the most promise. Nominations are made before April 30 by Canadian Authors Association branches or other writers' organizations, and the award is given at the CAA banquet in June.

ARKANSAS POETRY DAY CONTEST; POETS' ROUNDTABLE OF ARKANSAS (I), over 30 categories, many open to all poets, deadline September 18. Bulletins mailed out in July. For copy send SASE to Verna Lee Hinegardner, 605 Higdon Ferry Rd., Apt. 109, Hot Springs AR 71913.

ARTIST TRUST; ARTIST TRUST GAP GRANTS; ARTIST TRUST FELLOWSHIPS (IV-Regional), 512 Jones Bldg., 1331 Third Ave., Seattle WA 98101, phone (206)467-8734. *Artist Trust* is a nonprofit arts organization that provides grants to artists (including poets) who are residents of the state. It also publishes a 16-page quarterly tabloid of news about arts opportunities and cultural issues.

ARVON INTERNATIONAL POETRY COMPETITION (I, II), Kilnhurst, Kilnhurst Rd., Todmorden, Lancashire OL14 6AX, England, phone 0706 816582, FAX: 0706 816359, jointly sponsored by Duncan Lawrie Limited and *The Observer*. Poems (which may be of any length and previously unpublished) must be in English. First prize is £5,000 ($8,425), and other cash prizes. The competition is biennial. Distinguished poets serve as judges. Though the contest (which raises funds by entry fees) may be better known internationally, the major function of the Arvon Foundation is to offer writing courses at two retreats: At Totleigh Barton, Sheepwash, Beaworthy, Devon EX21 5NS, phone (040923) 338 and at Lumb Bank, Hebden Bridge, West Yorkshire HX7 6DF, phone (0422)843714. These are residential programs at attractive country retreats, offered by established writers in subjects such as poetry, playwriting, short fiction, radio drama, and words and music. The tuition is £175 for, typically, 5 days, which includes tuition, food and accomodations, and there is scholarship available from the foundation for those who cannot otherwise afford to attend.

‡ATLANTIC WRITING COMPETITION; WRITERS' FEDERATION OF NOVA SCOTIA (IV-Regional), Suite 203, 5516 Spring Garden Road, Halifax, Nova Scotia B3J 1G6 Canada, offers prizes of $150, $75 and $50 for 1-15 unpublished poems by residents of the Atlantic Provinces, entry fee $15, deadline January 31. Write for *mandatory* entry form.

BAVARIAN ACADEMY OF FINE ARTS LITERATURE PRIZE (V), Max Josephplatz 3, 8 Munich 22, West Germany, is an award of DM 30,000 awarded annually to an author in the German language to honor a distinguished literary career—by nomination only.

GEORGE BENNETT FELLOWSHIP (II), Phillips Exeter Academy, Exeter NH 03833, provides a $5,000 fellowship plus room and board to a writer with a MS in progress. The Fellow's only official duties are to be in residence while the Academy is in session and to be available to students interested in writing. The committee favors writers who have not yet published a book-length work with a major publisher. Send SASE for application materials. Deadline December 1.

BERLIN ARTISTS' PROGRAM (II), German Academic Exchange Service, (Deutscher Akademischer Austauschdienst), Bureau Berlin Box 12640, Steinplatz 2, 1000 Berlin 12, West Germany, director Dr. Joachim Sartorius, enables 15-20 internationally known and recommended composers, filmmakers and writers to spend a year taking an active part in the cultural life of Berlin. Screening committee meets in March or April.

BOLLINGEN PRIZE (V), Yale University Library, New Haven CT 06520, prize of $10,000 to an American poet for the best poetry collection published during the previous two years, or for a body of poetry written over several years. **By nomination only.** Judges change biennially. Announcements in January of odd-numbered years.

BREAD LOAF WRITERS' CONFERENCE (II), Middlebury College, Middlebury VT 05753, phone (802)388-3711, fellowships and scholarships. Candidates for fellowships must have book published. Candidates for scholarships must have published in major literary periodicals or newspapers. One letter of nomination required by March 15; applications and supporting materials due by April 15. Awards are announced in June for the conference in August.

BUCKNELL SEMINAR FOR YOUNGER POETS; STADLER SEMESTER FOR YOUNGER POETS (IV-Students), Bucknell University, Lewisburg PA 17837, (717)524-1853, director John Wheatcroft. In the spring of 1991, the Stadler Semester for Younger Poets was added to the Seminar for Younger Poets and the Poet-in-Residence Series. The Stadler Semester is distinctive in allowing undergraduate poets almost four months of concentrated work centered in poetry. Guided by practicing poets, the apprentice will write and read poetry and will receive critical response. The two Fellows selected will work with Bucknell's writing faculty. The visiting Poet-in-Residence also will participate in the program. Fellows will earn a semester of academic credit by taking four units of study: a tutorial or individual project with a mentor poet, a poetry-writing workshop, a literature course, and an elective. Undergraduates from four-year colleges with at least one course in poetry writing are eligible to apply; most applicants will be second-semester juniors. Send a 12-15 page portfolio and a letter of self-presentation (a brief autobiography that expresses commitment to writing poetry, cites relevant courses, and lists any publications). Also include a transcript, two recommendations (at least one from a poetry-writing instructor), and a letter from the academic dean granting permission for the student to attend Bucknell for a semester. The Bucknell Seminar For Younger Poets is not a contest for poems but for 10 fellowships to the Bucknell Seminar, held for 4 weeks in June every year. Seniors and juniors from American colleges are eligible to compete for the ten fellowships, which consist of tuition, room, board, and spaces for writing. Application deadline for each year's seminar is March 1 of the previous year. Students chosen for fellowships will be notified on April 1.

THE MARY INGRAHAM BUNTING FELLOWSHIP PROGRAM (IV-Women), Radcliffe College, 34 Concord Ave., Cambridge MA 02138, supports women who want to pursue independent study in the creative arts (among other things). The stipend is $20,500 for a fellowship fulltime July 1-June 30, requiring residence in the Boston area. Applicants in creative arts who do not have doctorates should be at the equivalent stage in their careers as women who have received doctorates two years before applying. Deadline October 2.

BUSH ARTIST FELLOWSHIPS (IV-Regional), E-900 First National Bank Bldg., 332 Minnesota St., St. Paul MN 55101, are for South and North Dakota, Western Wisconsin and Minnesota residents over 25 years of age to help published writers (poetry, fiction, literary nonfiction, playwriting and screen-writing), visual artists, choreographers and composers set aside time for work-in-progress or exploration of new directions. Maximum of 15 awards of a maximum of $26,000 (and up to $7,000 additional for production and traveling expenses) are awarded each year for 6-18 month fellowships. Deadline October 31.

CANADIAN AUTHORS ASSOCIATION LITERARY AWARDS; CANADIAN AUTHORS ASSOCIATION (IV-Regional), 121 Avenue Rd., Toronto, Ontario M5R 2G3 Canada, $5,000 in each of 4 categories (fiction, poetry, non-fiction, drama) to Canadian writers, for a published book in the year of publication (or, in the case of drama, first produced), deadline December 31. Nominations may be made by authors, publishers, agents, or others. (Also see *Canadian Author & Bookman* in Publishers section and The Air Canada Award in this section.)

CAPRICORN POETRY AWARD (II); OPEN VOICE AWARDS (I, II); THE WRITER'S VOICE, Writer's Voice, 5 W. 63rd St., New York NY 10023. Capricorn Poetry Award, publication of a book of poems of 48-68 pp. by an author over 40, a cash prize of $500 and a reading at The Writers Voice. $10 entry fee for nonmembers of The Writer's Voice. January 1 deadline. Write for application guidelines. Open Voice Awards, annual awards, $200 honorarium and a reading in the Fall, open to both published and unpublished poets who have not previously read at The Writer's Voice. January 1 deadline. Write for application form. The Writer's Voice is a literary center sponsoring weekly readings, writing workshops, writing awards, literary film series, a radio program and other activities.

CINTAS FELLOWSHIP PROGRAM (IV-Regional), Arts International, Institute of International Education, 809 United Nations Plaza, New York NY 10017, makes awards of $10,000 to young professional writers and artists of Cuban lineage living outside of Cuba. Deadline for applications March 1.

CLARK COLLEGE POETRY CONTEST (I), % Arlene Paul, 4312 NE 40th St., Vancouver WA 98661, jointly sponsored by Clark College, Oregon State Poetry Association, and Washington Poetry Association, deadline February 15, 1992, $3 per poem entry fee (checks payable to Clark College Foundation), prizes of $50, $75 and $100, for poems up to 25 lines, unpublished, not having won another contest. Entries in triplicate, not identified. Type name, address on a 3×5 card, include title and first line on card. May purchase book of winner's poems for $2.85 postpaid.

INA COOLBRITH CIRCLE ANNUAL POETRY CONTEST (IV-Regional), %Tom Berry, Treasurer, 761 Sequoia Woods Place, Concord CA, 94518, has prizes of $10-50 in each of several categories for California residents only. Poems submitted in 3 copies, no names on copies. Enclose a 3×5" card with name, address, phone number, category, title, first line of poem and status as member or non-member. Members of the Ina Coolbrith Circle pay no fee; others pay $5 for 3 poems (limit 3). Deadline in August. For further information contact Tom Berry.

ABBIE M. COPPS POETRY COMPETITION; GARFIELD LAKE REVIEW (I,II), contest chairperson Linda Jo Scott, Dept. of Humanities, Olivet College, Olivet MI 49076, phone (616)749-7683, annual, $150 prize and publication in the *Garfield Lake Review*, $2/poem entry fee for unpublished poem up to 100 lines. Deadline fixed each year. Submit unsigned, typed poem, entrance fee, and name, address, and phone number in a sealed envelope with the first line of the poem on the outside. Judge to be announced.

COUNCIL FOR WISCONSIN WRITERS, INC.; PAULETTE CHANDLER AWARD (IV-Regional), Box 55322, Madison WI 53705. The Paulette Chandler Award, $1,500, is given annually to a poet (even years) or short story writer (odd years). Wisconsin residents only. Submit letter of application and 5 poems, published or unpublished, by January 16. "Award is based on ability and need." Send SASE for rules. The Council also offers annual awards of $300 or more for a book of poetry by a Wisconsin resident, published within the awards year (preceding the January 16 deadline). Entry form and entry fee ($10 for members of the Council, $15 for others) required.

CREATIVE ARTIST PROGRAM (IV-Regional), Cultural Arts Council of Houston, Suite 224, 1964 West Gray, Houston TX 77019-4808, phone (713)527-9330, offers annual awards of at least $4,000 to individual Houston artists only. Unless funding prohibits, writers are included in the competition. Deadline for entry October 15.

DALY CITY POETRY AND SHORT STORY CONTEST (I), Daly City History, Arts & Science Commission, Serramonte Library, 40 Wembley Dr., Daly City CA 94015, held annually, prizes of $30, $25, $15 and $5 in various categories, entry fee of $1/poem or $1/three haiku, $2/story, poems, published or unpublished, January 4 deadline. Send SASE for rules; attn: Ruth Hoppin, coordinator.

BILLEE MURRAY DENNY POETRY AWARD (II), % Janet Overton, Lincoln College, Lincoln IL 62656, awarded annually, prizes of $1,000, $500 and $250. Open to poets who have not previously published a book of poetry with a commercial or university press (except for chapbooks with a circulation of less than 250). Enter up to 3 poems, 100 lines/poem or less at $2/poem. Poems may be on any subject, using any style, but may not contain "any vulgar, obscene, suggestive or offensive word or phrase." Entry form, and fees, payable to Poetry Contest, Lincoln College, must be postmarked no later than May 31. Winning poems are published in *The Denny Poems*, a biennial anthology, available for $4 from Lincoln College. Send SASE for entry form.

‡MILTON DORFMAN NATIONAL POETRY PRIZE (II), Rome Art & Community Center, c/o Maureen Dunn Murphy, 308 W. Bloomfield St., Rome NY 13440, awarded annually for unpublished poetry, $2 fee/poem, with prizes of $500, $200, $100; poems printed in Center's Newsletter. Contest opens July 1. Deadline Nov. 1. Include name, address and phone on each entry.

ERGO!; BUMBERSHOOT (II), Box 9750-0750, Seattle WA 98109, phone (206)622-5123, founded 1973, producing director, Louise DiLenge, an annual publication *ERGO!* is issued in conjunction with *Bumbershoot* a multi-arts festival at the Seattle Center on Labor Day weekend. "Fifteen hundred will be published for distribution prior to and at the Festival. Included will be selected works by the Writers-in-Performance invitational participants and winners of the Written Works Competitions in addition to the official literary arts program schedule." Six honoraria will be awarded for written works. Considers simultaneous submissions. Deadline for application is mid-February. For application forms and further details write *Bumbershoot* at the address above. *ERGO!* **sample available for $6 postpaid. Competition guidelines available with a SASE.**

FLORIDA STATE WRITING COMPETITION; FLORIDA FREELANCE WRITERS ASSOCIATION (I), P.O. Box 9844, Fort Lauderdale FL 33310, is an annual contest with categories in free verse and traditional, prizes up to $100 in each category, fees $2/poem for members of the FFWA, $2.50 for others. March 15 deadline. Guidelines available each fall through March for #10 SASE.

LEWIS GALANTIERE PRIZE (IV-Translation), American Translators Association, 109 Croton Ave., Ossining NY 10562, $500 awarded in even-numbered years for promising works in literary translation by new translators. Deadline: June 1, 1993.

GEORGIA STATE POETRY SOCIETY, INC.; BYRON HERBERT REECE AND EDWARD DAVIN VICKERS INTERNATIONAL AWARDS; THE REACH OF SONG ANNUAL ANTHOLOGY, ANNUAL CHAPBOOK COMPETITION, GEORGIA STATE POETRY SOCIETY NEWSLETTER (I,IV-Anthologies, form), Box 120, Epworth GA 30541. The society sponsors a number of contests open to all poets, described in their quarterly *Newsletter* (membership $15/year) and sponsors an annual anthology, **The Reach of Song**, and an annual chapbook (for members only) competition. The Byron Herbert Reece and the Edward Davin Vickers International Awards have prizes of $250, $100, $50, $25, $15, and $10. Entry fee: $5, first poem, $1 each additional. Deadline: January 31, Reece Awards; April 30, Vickers Awards. SASE for guidelines. Sample newsletter $2; **Reach of Song**, $10.

‡JOHN GLASSCO TRANSLATION PRIZE (IV-Translation, regional), Literary Translators' Association of Canada, 1030, rue Cherrier, Bureau 510, Montreal, Quebec H2L 1H9 Canada, $500 awarded annually for a translator's first book-length literary translation into French or English, published in Canada during the previous calendar year. The translator must be a Canadian citizen or landed immigrant. Eligible genres include fiction, creative nonfiction, poetry, published plays, children's books. Write for application form. Deadline March 15.

‡GREEN RIVERS WRITERS' CONTESTS (I, IV-Themes, Forms), % Lena Sawyer, Contest Chairman, 4883A Rose Terrace, Ft. Knox KY 40121, offers 8 contests for poetry on various themes and in various forms, entry fee $2/poem for non-members, $1 for members, prizes from $3-$69, July 1 deadline. Send SASE for rules.

GROLIER POETRY PRIZE; ELLEN LA FORGE MEMORIAL POETRY FOUNDATION, INC. (II, IV-Themes), 6 Plympton St., Cambridge MA 02138. The Grolier Poetry Prize is open to all poets who have not published either a vanity, small press, trade, or chapbook of poetry. Two poets receive an honorarium of $150 each. Four poems by each winner and two by each of four runners-up are chosen for publication in the *Grolier Poetry Prize Annual*. Submit 5 poems, not more than 10 double-spaced pages. Opens January 1st of each year; deadline March 15. Submit one MS in duplicate, without name of poet. On a separate sheet give name, address, phone, and titles of poems. $5 entry fee, checks payable to the Ellen La Forge Memorial Poetry Foundation, Inc. Enclose self-address stamped post-card if acknowledgement of receipt is required. For update of rules, send SASE to Grolier Poetry Book Shop, Inc., before submitting MSS. The Ellan La Forge Memorial Poetry Foundation sponsors intercollegiate poetry readings and a reading series, generally five per semester, held on the grounds of Harvard University. These are genereally poets who have a large following or who have new collections of poetry available, for sale at the Grolier Book Shop, which donates money toward costs (such as rental of the auditorium). They pay poets honoraria from $100-400 and occasionally provide overnight accommodations (but not transportation). Such poets as Mark Strand, Stephen Dobyns, Robin Becker, Donald Hall and Brigit Pegeen Kelly have given readings under their auspices. The small foundation depends upon public gifts and support for its activities.

GUGGENHEIM FELLOWSHIPS (II), John Simon Guggenheim Foundation, 90 Park Ave., New York NY 10016. Approximately 170 Guggenheims are awarded each year to persons who have already demonstrated exceptional capacity for productive scholarship or unusual creative ability in the arts. The amounts of the grants vary. The average grant is about $26,500. Application deadline October 1.

HACKNEY LITERARY AWARDS; BIRMINGHAM-SOUTHERN COLLEGE WRITER'S CONFERENCE (II), Birmingham-Southern College, Box A-3, Birmingham AL 35254. This competition, sponsored by the Cecil Hackney family since 1969, offers $4,000 in prizes for novels, poetry and short stories as part of the annual Birmingham-Southern Writer's Conference. Poems must be postmarked by Dec. 31. Send SASE for Hackney guidelines. Winners are announced at the conference, which is held in the spring.

CLARENCE L. HOLTE LITERARY PRIZE (IV-Ethnic), Schomburg Center for Research in Black Culture, The New York Public Library, The Phelps Stoke Fund, 515 Malcolm X Blvd., New York NY 10037, up to $7,500 awarded every other year to a living writer "for an original published work linking the cultural heritage of African peoples with the African diaspora in the new world." The award is made by a jury of scholars of international reputation. The award was given in November 1991. For further information call (212)491-2229.

JOHANN-HEINRICH-VOSS PRIZE FOR TRANSLATION (V), German Academy for Language and Literature, Alexandraweg 23, D-6100 Darmstadt, West Germany, is an annual award of DM 15,000 for outstanding lifetime achievement for translating into German, by nomination only. 1990: Manfred Fuhrmann; 1991: Fritz Vogelgsang.

THE CHESTER H. JONES FOUNDATION NATIONAL POETRY COMPETITION (II), P.O. Box 498, Chardon OH 44024, an annual competition for persons in the USA, Canadian and American citizens living abroad. Prizes: $1,000, $500, $250, and $50 honorable mentions. Winning poems plus others called "commendations" are published in a chapbook available for $3.50 from the foundation. Entry fee $1/poem, no more than 10 entries, no more than 32 lines each. Deadline March 31. Distinguished poets serve as judges.

‡LAMPMAN AWARD (IV-Regional); OTTAWA INDEPENDENT WRITERS/LES ECRIVAINS INDEPENDANTS D'OTTAWA, 134 Caroline Ave., Ottawa, Ontario K1Y 0S9 Canada, phone (613)729-6815, is a $400 award for a published book of English-language poetry by writers in the National Capital region. Submit 3 copies of each title by February 28. Membership in Ottawa Independent Writers is $50/year, and offers their newsletter, programs, a Master Writing Series of workshops, an entry in the OIW Directory, and registration at reduced fees for their annual conference.

D. H. LAWRENCE FELLOWSHIP (II), Dept. of English, University of New Mexico, Albuquerque NM 87131, chair, Scott P. Sanders, offers a creative writer a 3 month summer residence on the Lawrence Ranch near Taos, NM, and a $1,250 stipend. Application fee: $10. Postmark deadline: January 31 annually.

THE STEPHEN LEACOCK MEDAL FOR HUMOUR (IV-Humor, regional), Mrs. Jean Bradley Dickson, Award Chairman, Stephen Leacock Associates, Box 854, Orillia, Ontario L3V 3P4 Canada, phone (705)325-6546, for a book of humour (can be verse) by a Canadian citizen. Submit 10 copies of book, 8×10″ b/w photo, bio and $25 entry fee. Deadline for entry December 31 each year. Prize: Silver Leacock Medal for Humour and J.P. Wiser cash award of $3,500. The also publish *The Newspacket* 3/year.

‡LETRAS DE ORO SPANISH LITERARY PRIZES (IV-Foreign language), North-South Center, University of Miami, Box 248123, Coral Gables FL 33124, include a general prize of $2,500 and the publication of the book length entry, plus an all expenses paid trip to Spain. For creative excellence in poetry written in the Spanish language. Deadline October 12. Contact for guidelines.

‡AMY LOWELL POETRY TRAVELLING SCHOLARSHIP (II), Trust u/w/o Amy Lowell, Exchange Place, 35th Floor, Choate, Hall & Stewart, Boston MA 02109, award directors F. Davis Dassori, Jr., and other Trustees, is an annual award of $27,000 (more-or-less: the amount varies annually), to an "advanced" poet who agrees to live outside of North America for the year of the grant. Deadline for application October 15.

MACARTHUR FELLOWS (V), John D.and Catherine T. MacArthur Foundation, Suite 1100, 140 S. Dearborn St., Chicago IL 60603. An anonymous committee selects individuals to whom the foundation awards large grants.

MAPLECON SF; FANTASY WRITING COMPETITION (I, IV-Themes, science fiction/fantasy), %Madona Skaff, Literary Coordinator, 2105 Thistle Crescent, Ottawa, Ontario K1H 5P4 Canada, no fee. "Total length (1 or more poems) 12-200 lines. Open to anyone regardless of status as a writer. Entry must be based on a science, science fiction or fantasy theme. Please, no resubmissions from previous years." Deadline is in June. Awards (certificates and varying prizes) are made at Maplecon, the Ottawa Regional Science Fiction/Fantasy Convention in October (or mailed to those not present). Please include SASE with all correspondence.

MASSACHUSETTS ARTISTS FELLOWSHIP PROGRAM (IV-Regional), The Artists Foundation, Inc., 8 Park Plaza, Boston MA 02116, fellowships of $10,000 to poets and other artists who are residents of Massachusetts over 18, not students.

MASSACHUSETTS STATE POETRY SOCIETY NATIONAL POETRY DAY CONTEST; GERTRUDE DOLE MEMORIAL CONTEST (I), %Jeanette C. Maes, 64 Harrison Ave., Lynn MA 09105, both contests are open to all poets. The National Poetry Day Contest, with a September 1 deadline, offers prizes of $25, $15 and $10 for each of 12 or more categories; $3 fee for entire contest. The Gertrude Dole Memorial Contest, deadline April 1, offers prizes of $25, $15 and $10; $1 entry fee, one poem per poet. Send SASE for contest flyer.

‡**FREDERIC G. MELCHER BOOK AWARD (IV-Religious)**, 25 Beacon St., Boston MA 02108, is an annual $1,000 prize for a book making a significant contribution to religious liberalism. Books are submitted by publishers only.

MID-SOUTH POETRY FESTIVAL; POETRY SOCIETY OF TENNESSEE (IV-Regional), P.O. Box 11188, Memphis TN 38111, holds an annual poetry festival first weekend in October. Contests deadline in September. There are 24 to 30 categories with cash prizes and other awards totaling approximately $1,500. Eligibility may vary; however, many contests for all poets anywhere; many for Mid-South area poets. Entry fees may vary. Poetry Society of Tennessee is Festival Sponsor with co-sponsorship by other Mid-South poetry societies. Send SASE after June 1 for contest rules and information. Brochure will be sent in June or July. PST publishes a newsletter for members that reviews books of poetry by members or those affiliated with the organization.

MILFORD FINE ARTS COUNCIL POETRY CONTEST (I,II), 5 Broad St., Milford CT 06460. SASE for details.

‡**MISSISSIPPI VALLEY POETRY CONTEST; NORTH AMERICAN LITERARY ESCADRILLE (I, II)**, P.O. Box 3188, Rock Island IL 61204, award director Sue Katz, offers annually prizes of approximately $1,000 for unpublished poems in categories for student (elementary, junior and senior high), adult, Mississippi Valley, senior citizens, jazz, religious, humorous, rhyming, haiku, ethnic, history. Fee: $3 for up to 5 poems. Sept. 15 deadline. Professional readers read winning poems before a reception at an award evening each October.

JENNY MCKEAN MOORE FUND FOR WRITERS, (II), Dept. of English, George Washington University, Washington DC 20052, provides for a Visiting Lecturer in creative writing for about $35,000 for 2 semesters. Apply by November 15 with resume and writing sample of 25 pp. or less.

‡**THE JULIA MOORE POETRY COMPETITION; NEWSLETTER OF HUMOR (IV-Humor)**, International Society for Humor Studies, c/o Don Nilsen, English Dept., ASU, Tempe AZ 85287-0302, is an annual competition for "good bad poetry" in the tradition of Julia Moore, a poet of frontier Michigan, who wrote:

> *My childhood days have passed and gone,*
> *and it fills my heart with pain*
> *To think that youth will nevermore*
> *Return to me again.*
> *And now kind friends, what I have wrote,*
> *I hope you will pass o'er.*
> *And not criticise as some have done Hitherto herebefore.*

The style of Julia Moore is parodied in *Huckleberry Finn*.

NATIONAL ENDOWMENT FOR THE ARTS; FELLOWSHIPS FOR CREATIVE ARTISTS; FELLOWSHIPS FOR TRANSLATORS (II), Literature Program, 1100 Pennsylvania Ave. NW, Washington DC 20506. The Fellowships for Creative Artists comprise the largest program for individual grants available for American poets (and other writers and artists). Dozens of awards of $20,000 are made each year to poets who have published a book or at least 20 poems in magazines in the last 10 years. Decisions are made by a panel of distinguished writers solely on the quality of the submitted material. Guidelines available September of each year. They also offer grants of up to $10,000 to nonprofit organizations to support residencies for published writers of poetry, Fellowships for Translators ($10,000 or $20,000), and other programs to assist publishers and promoters of poetry. Write for complete guidelines.

NATIONAL POETRY SERIES ANNUAL OPEN COMPETITION (II), 26 W. 17th St., New York NY 10011, between January 1 and February 15 considers book-length (approximately 48-64 pp.) MSS, entry fee $15. Manuscripts will not be returned. The five winners are published by participating small press, university press, and trade publishers. Send SASE for complete submissions procedures.

NATIONAL WRITERS CLUB ANNUAL POETRY CONTEST (I), Suite 620, 1450 S. Havana, Aurora CO 80012, award director James L. Young, an annual contest with prizes of $100, $50, $25 and $10 plus honorable mentions. Entry fee $6/poem; additional fee charged if poem is longer than 40 lines. Deadline June 1. All subjects and forms are acceptable.

‡**THE NATIONAL WRITTEN & ILLUSTRATED BY . . . AWARDS CONTEST FOR STUDENTS; LANDMARK EDITIONS (IV-Students)**, P.O. Box 4469, Kansas City MO 64127, award director David Melton, is an annual contest for unpublished work for a book written and illustrated by a student. Three books published, one from each of 3 age categories (6-9; 10-13; 14-19). Each winner receives a $5,000

scholarship provided by the R.D. and Joan Dale Hubbard Foundation, and there are $2,000 and $1,000 scholarship awards for four runners up in each category. Send business-size SASE with 60¢ postage for rules.

NEUSTADT INTERNATIONAL PRIZE FOR LITERATURE; WORLD LITERATURE TODAY (V), University of Oklahoma, Room 110, 630 Parrington Oval, Norman OK 73019, $25,000 given every other year in recognition of life achievement or to a writer whose work is still in progress, nominations from an international jury only.

NEVADA POETRY SOCIETY ANNUAL CONTEST (I), P.O. Box 5741, Reno NV 89513, award director Lorraine Caraway. This contest offers cash awards in several categories. Please send a SASE for exact details. Entries must be postmarked September 1 or before. Winning poems are read at the October meeting of the Nevada Poetry Society.

NEW ENGLAND POETRY CLUB; DANIEL VAROUJAN AWARD; FIRMAN HOUGHTON AWARD; NORMA FARBER AWARD; BARBARA BRADLEY AWARD; ROSALIE BOYLE PRIZE; ERIKA MUMFORD PRIZE (I), 2 Farrar St., Cambridge MA 02138. The contests sponsored by New England Poetry Club have a $2/poem fee for non-members (free to members), all with a June 30th deadline, all judged by well-known poets such as X.J. Kennedy and Peter Viereck. The Varoujan Award of $500 is for a poem "worthy of Daniel Varoujan, an Armenian poet killed by the Turks in 1915." The Firman Houghton Award is $250 (named for a former NEPC president); the Norma Farber Award is $100 for a sonnet or sonnet series; the Rosalie Boyle Prize of $100 is for a poem over 30 lines; the Erika Mumford Prize for a poem of exotic or faraway setting is $250; and the Barbara Bradley Award of $200 for a lyric poem under 21 lines written by a woman. Poems should be sent in duplicate with name of writer on one to Lois Ames, NEPC Contests, 285 Marlboro Road, Sudbury MA 01776, before June 30th annually.

NEW YORK FOUNDATION FOR THE ARTS (IV-Regional), 5 Beekman St., New York NY 10038, annually offers a fellowship of $7,000 for poets who are at least 18 and have resided in New York State for the 2 years prior to application. Submit up to 10 pages of poetry (at least 2 poems), 3 copies of a one-page resume, and support material by September 6. No SASE.

‡NORTHWEST POETS & ARTISTS CALENDAR (IV-Regional), Bainbridge Island Arts Council, 261 Madison S., Bainbridge Island WA 98110, awards $50 each to 25 selected poets and artists each year, work to be used in a 12×12″ full-color wall calendar "featuring outstanding works by Northwest poets and artists (jury-selected)." $6 fee for up to 6 poems, late January deadline. Selected poems and art widely exhibited. Bumbershoot Bookfair 1990 award winner.

OHIOANA BOOK AWARDS; OHIOANA KROUT MEMORIAL AWARD FOR POETRY; OHIOANA QUARTERLY; OHIOANA LIBRARY ASSOCIATION (IV-Regional), Ohioana Library Association, 65 S. Front St., Rm. 1105, Columbus OH 43215. Ohioana Book Awards given yearly to outstanding books published each year. Up to 6 awards may be given for books (including books of poetry) by authors born in Ohio or who have lived in Ohio for at least 5 years, and the Ohioana Poetry Award (with the same residence requirements), made possible by a bequest of Helen Krout, of $1,000 is given yearly "to an individual whose body of work has made, and continues to make, a significant contribution to the poetry of Ohio, and through whose work as a writer, teacher, administrator, or in community service, interest in poetry has been developed." Nominations to be received by December 31. *Ohioana Quarterly* regularly reviews Ohio magazines and books by Ohio authors. It is available through membership in Ohioana Library Association ($20/year).

NATALIE ORNISH POETRY AWARD (IV-Regional); SOEURETTE DIEHL FRASER TRANSLATION AWARD (IV-Translations, regional) TEXAS INSTITUTE OF LETTERS, % James Hoggard, Dept. of English, Midwestern State University, Wichita Falls TX 76308-2099. The Texas Institute of Letters gives annual awards for books by Texas authors in 8 categories, including the Natalie Ornish Poetry Award, a $1,000 award for best volume of poetry. Books must have been first published in the year in question, and entries may be made by authors or by their publishers; deadline January 4 of the following year. One copy of each entry must be mailed to each of three judges, with "information showing an author's Texas association . . . if is not otherwise obvious." Poets must have lived in Texas for at least two consecutive years at some time or their work must reflect a notable concern with matters associated with the state. Soeurette Diehl Fraser Translation Award ($1,000) for best translation of a work into English. Same rules as those for Natalie Ornish poetry award. Write during the fall for complete instructions.

OTTAWA-CARLETON BOOK AWARD (IV-Regional), Carol Sage, Arts Advisory Board, Regional Municipality of Ottawa-Carleton, 111 Lisgar St., Ottawa, Ontario K2P 2L7 Canada, awarded annually to residents of the Ottawa-Carleton Region, deadline January 15.

‡OZARK CREATIVE WRITERS, INC. CONFERENCE AWARDS (IV-Membership), 6817 Gingerbread Lane, Little Rock AR 72204, conference director Peggy Vining. Registrants ($25 prior to Sept. 1) for their annual writers' conference may enter this contest with prizes of $25, 15 and $10 ("a few higher"). Deadline for entry is postmark date Aug. 26. Conference is held in Eureka Springs, Arkansas at the Inn of the Ozarks. Write for brochure.

‡PAUMANOK POETRY AWARD COMPETITION; THE VISITING WRITERS PROGRAM (II), SUNY College of Technology, Farmingdale NY 11735, phone (516)420-2031, director Dr. Charles Fishman. The Paumanok Poetry Award Competition offers a prize of $750 plus expenses for a reading in their 1992-93 series. Submit cover letter, 1 page bio, 7-10 poems and $10 entry fee by Sept. 15. Poets who have read in their series include Hayden Carruth, Allen Ginsberg, Linda Pastan, Marge Piercy, Joyce Carole Oates, Louis Simpson, David Ignatow and many others.

PENNSYLVANIA POETRY SOCIETY ANNUAL CONTEST; WINE AND ROSES POETRY CONTEST; PEGASUS CONTEST FOR STUDENTS; THE ANIMAL KINGDOM CONTEST; SAMUEL FREIBERG MEMORIAL AWARD; LOTTIE KENT RUHL MEMORIAL AWARD (I, IV-Members), 623 N. 4th St., Reading PA 19601, award director Dr. Dorman John Grace. The deadline for the society's annual contest, which has 11 categories open to nonmembers and 4 to members only, is January 15. Grand prize in category 1 (open) will be $100 in 1992; prizes in other categories range from $10-25, plus publication. Entry fees are $1.50/poem for nonmembers except for the grand prize, which requires an entry fee of $2/poem for everybody. For information regarding the Pennsylvania Poetry Society Contest contact Dr. Dorman John Grace (same address as above). The Wine and Roses poetry contest, sponsored by the Wallace Stevens Chapter for unpublished poems in serious and light verse, has prizes of $50, $25, and $15 plus publication and telecast; entry fee $1/poem; deadline June 1; write to Dr. Dorman John Grace. For information about the Pegasus Contest for Students, write to Anne Pierre Spangler, Contest Chairman, 1685 Christian Dr., R.D. #2, Lebanon PA 17042. For information about the Animal Kingdom Contest, the Samuel Freiberg Memorial Award, and the Lottie Kent Ruhl Memorial Award, write to Jessie Ruhl Miller, Contest Chairman, 670 W. Louther St., Carlisle PA 17013. Deadline, December 31. In each category are awards of $20, $15, and $10, fee $1 per poem. The Pennsylvania Poetry Society publishes a quarterly newsletter and an annual **Prize Poems** soft cover book, containing 69 prize and honorable mention award poems. Prize poems in the Wine and Roses and Pegasus contests are published in *PPS Newsletter*.

POETIC PERSPECTIVE, INC. (I), 110 Onieda St., Waxahachie TX 75165, founded in 1989 by Pat Haley, editor. Several poetry contests each year with $3 per poem entry fee, prizes of $50, $25, and $10. Up to 35 lines, maximum of 60 characters and spaces per line. SASE for themes and guidelines. Anthology published yearly in December.

POETRY ARTS PROJECT (IV-Political, social), United Resource Press, 4521 Campus Dr., #388, Irvine CA 92715, holds an annual contest, March 31 deadline, for poems on political and social issues, humorous/series with prizes of "possible publication and definite prizes in U.S. Savings Bonds of various denominations," $3 per poem jury fee. "Absolutely must send SASE to receive entry form. Poetry will not be returned."

‡THE POETRY CENTER BOOK AWARD (II), 1600 Holloway Ave., San Francisco CA 94132. Method for entering contest is to submit a published book and a $5 entry fee; book must be published and copyrighted during the year of the contest and submitted by December 31. "Beginners may enter but in the past winners have published several previous books." Translations are acceptable but "we cannot judge works that are not in English." Books should be by an individual living writer and must be entirely poetry. Prize (only one) is $500 and an invitation to read for the Poetry Center. No entry form is required.

POETRY SOCIETY OF TEXAS (I, IV-Membership), Asst. Corresponding Secretary Faye Carr Adams, 4244 Skillman, Dallas TX 75206, offers approximately 90 contests, prizes $25-350, some open to nonmembers for a fee of $2 per poem, awards at an annual Awards Dinner in November. Send SASE (business size envelope) for rules booklet.

POETS AND PATRONS, INC.; ANNUAL CHICAGOLAND CONTESTS; INTERNATIONAL NARRATIVE CONTEST (II, IV-Regional, form), The Annual Chicagoland Contests, Carol Spelius, Chairman, 373 Ramsay Road, Deerfield IL 60015 are open to all poets residing within 60 miles of Chicago. Send

SASE for rules after March 1. One $3 registration fee for 20 contests in various categories with prizes of $25 and $10 in each, prizes of $75 and $25 for 2 poems judged best of 1st Prize winners and $25 and $15 to 2 judged best of the 2nd Prize winners. Deadline August 1. The International Narrative contest (Chairman Constance Vogel, 1206 Hutchings Avenue, Glenview IL 60025) is open to all. Send SASE after March 1 for rules, deadline Sept. 1 (postmark), no entry fee, prizes of $75 and $25.

POETS CLUB OF CHICAGO INTERNATIONAL SHAKESPEAREAN SONNET CONTEST (II, IV-Form), Chairman June Shipley, 2930 Franklin St., Highland IN 46322. Contest has a deadline of September 1st (postmark). Write for rules, include SASE, not earlier than March. No entry fee. Prizes of $50, $35 and $15.

POETS' DINNER CONTEST (IV-Regional), 2214 Derby St., Berkeley CA 94705. Since 1926 there has been an annual awards banquet sponsored by the ad hoc Poets' Dinner Committee; usually at Spenger's Fish Grotto (a Berkeley Landmark). Three typed copies of poems in not more than three of the eight categories are submitted anonymously without fee (January 15 deadline), and the winning poems (grand prize, 1st, 2nd, 3rd) are read at the banquet and honorable mentions awarded. **Contestant must be present to win.** Prizes awarded cash; honorable mention, books. The event is nonprofit.

POETS OF THE VINEYARD CONTEST (I), %Winnie E. Fitzpatrick, P.O. Box 77, Kenwood CA 95452, an annual contest sponsored by the Sonoma County Chapter (PofV) of the California Federation of Chaparral Poets with entries in 7 categories: A) traditional forms, (38 line maximum); B) free verse, 16 lines or less; C) free verse, 17-28 lines; D) light or humorous (28 line maximum); E) short verse (maximum of 12 lines); F) haiku/senryu and tanka; G) theme poem on grapes, vineyards, wine, viticulture (28 line maximum). Submit 2 copies, 1 with identification; category in upper right-hand corner. Prizes in each category are $20, $15 and $10, with a grand prize chosen from category winners ($50). Deadline February 1, entry fee $2/poem. Prize winning poems will be published in the annual **Winners Anthology.**

POETS RENDEZVOUS CONTEST; INDIANA STATE FEDERATION OF POETRY CLUBS (I), % Paula Fehn, 3302 Bellemeade Ave., Evansville IN 47714, The Poets Rendezvous Contest offers $745 in prizes for poems in 18 categories, $5 fee covers 18 categories in different forms and subjects, September 1 deadline. The Indiana State Federation of Poetry Clubs also has contest with January 15 and July 15 deadlines for poems no longer than 1 page, $1/poem fee, prizes of $25, $15 and $10 with 3 honorable mentions.

THE E.J. PRATT GOLD MEDAL AND PRIZE FOR POETRY (IV-Student), Office of Student Awards, University of Toronto, Toronto, Ontario M5T 2Z9 Canada, to a full- or part-time graduate or undergraduate student for a poem or suite of poems of approximately 100 lines. Entries are submitted under a pseudonym with information on the poet's identity in a separate envelope. Deadline in March.

PRESIDIO LA BAHIA AWARD; SUMMERFIELD G. ROBERTS AWARD (IV-Regional), Sons of the Republic of Texas, Suite 222, 5942 Abrams Rd., Dallas TX 75231. Both may be awarded for poetry. The Presidio La Bahia Award is an annual award or awards (depending upon the number and quality of entries) for writing that promotes research into and preservation of the Spanish Colonial influence on Texas culture. $2,000 is available, with a minimum first prize of $1,200. Entries must be in quadruplicate and will not be returned. Deadline September 30. The Summerfield G. Roberts Award, available to U.S. citizens, is an annual award of $2,500 for a book or manuscript depicting or representing the Republic of Texas (1836-46), written or published during the calendar year for which the award is given. Entries must be submitted in quintuplicate and will not be returned. Deadline January 15.

PULITZER PRIZE IN LETTERS (II), % Secretary of the Pulitzer Prize Board, 702 Journalism, Columbia University, New York NY 10027, offers 5 prizes of $3,000 each year, including one in poetry, for books published in the calendar year preceding the award. Submit 4 copies of published books (or galley proofs if book is being published after November), photo, bio, entry form and $20 entry fee. July 1 deadline for books published between January 1 and June 30; November 1 deadline for books published between July 1 and December 30.

REDWOOD ACRES FAIR POETRY CONTEST (I), P.O. Box 6576, Eureka CA 95502, offers an annual contest with various categories for both juniors and seniors with entry fee of 50¢ per poem for the junior contests and $1 per poem for the senior contests, May 29 deadline.

RHYME INTERNATIONAL COMPETITION FOR RHYMING POETRY (IV-Form), 199 The Long Shoot, Nuneaton, Warwickshire CV11 6JQ England, has 2 categories (open class, up to 50 lines, rhymed poetry; strict form class) with prizes averaging £75-300 in each class each year (at least 60% of fees received); entry fee £2.50 (or $5). Write for entry form. Deadline September 30. Ajudication takes place during a special workshop weekend in England under the supervision of a well-known poet.

MARY ROBERTS RINEHART FOUNDATION AWARD (II), %Roger Lathbury, Mary Roberts Rinehart Fund, English Dept., George Mason University, 4400 University Dr., Fairfax VA 22030-4444. Two grants are made annually to writers who need financial assistance "to complete work definitely projected." The amount of the award depends upon income the fund generates; the 1992 amount will be around $950 in each category. Poets and fiction writes should submit work in odd numbered years, e.g., 1991, 1993. A writer's work must be nominated by an established author or editor; no written recommendations are necessary. Nominations must be accompanied by a sample of the nominee's work, up to 25 pp. of poetry and 30 pp. of fiction. Deadline: November 30.

THE ROBERTS FOUNDATION WRITING AWARDS (II, IV-Anthologies), Box 1868, Pittsburg KS 66762, an annual competition, deadline September 15, for poetry, short fiction and essays. The poetry prizes are $500, $200 and $100, fee $6 for up to 5 poems, $1 for each additional poem. Winners appear in an annual anthology that you may purchase for $4. Send SASE for guidelines and entry form.

ANNA DAVIDSON ROSENBERG AWARD (IV-Ethnic), Judah L. Magnes Museum, 2911 Russell St., Berkeley CA 94705, offers prizes of $100, $50 and $25 (honorable mention) for up to 12 pp. of 1-5 poems on the Jewish Experience in English. There is a Youth Commendation along with the prize if a winner is under 19. Deadline August 31 each year. **Do not send poems without entry form; write between April 15 and July 15 for entry form and guidelines (enclose SASE).**

‡SALMON ARM SONNET CONTEST (IV-Form), Salmon Arm & Dist. Chamber of Commerce, Box 999, Salmon Arm, British Columbia V1E 4P2 Canada, general manager Judi Lowe, is an annual contest, deadline May 1, for unpublished sonnets. Prizes: $100-300 and books. Entry fee $5/poem. Limit 2 entries.

‡SALUTE TO THE ARTS POETRY CONTEST; ARIEL (IV-Themes), Triton College, 2000 Fifth Ave., River Grove IL 60171, open to all poets, any form, published or unpublished, up to 60 lines on specified themes. Poets may submit up to 3 poems. Write for current themes and dates. *Ariel* is a professionally printed magazine-sized annual anthology, 50+ pp. on slick stock with slick card cover publishing only the some four dozen winning entries.

SAN FRANCISCO FOUNDATION; JOSEPH HENRY JACKSON AWARD; JAMES D. PHELAN AWARD (IV-Regional), Suite 910, 685 Market St., San Francisco CA 94105. The Jackson Award ($2,000) will be made to the author of an unpublished work-in-progress in the form of fiction (novel or short stories), non-fictional prose, or poetry. Applicants must be residents of northern California or Nevada for three consecutive years immediately prior to the deadline date of January 15th, and must be between the ages of 20 through 35 as of the deadline. The Phelan Award ($2,000) will be made to the author of an unpublished work-in-progress in the form of fiction (novel or short stories), non-fictional prose, poetry or drama. Applicants must be California-born (although they may now reside outside of the state), and must be between the ages of 20 through 35 as of the January 15th deadline. MSS for both awards must be accompanied by an application form, which may be obtained by sending a SASE to the above address. Entries are accepted between November 15 and January 15.

SAN MATEO COUNTY FAIR FINE ARTS COMPETITION (I), Box 1027, San Mateo CA 94403-0627, phone (415)574-3873, for unpublished poetry. Adult and youth divisions. Write or call for entry form and additional information. Adult Division awards of $100, $50, and $25; fee $6 for 1 poem or $10 for 2. Youth Division awards of $50, $25 and $15; fee $3 for 1 poem or $5 for 2. Limit 2 entries per division. July 5th deadline for poems.

CARL SANDBURG AWARDS (IV-Regional), sponsored by Friends of the Chicago Public Library, 78 E. Washington St., Chicago IL 60602, are given annually to Chicago-area writers for new books in 4 categories, including poetry. Each author receives $1,000. Publisher or authors should submit two copies of books published between June 1 of one year and May 31 of the next. Deadline: Sept. 1.

SASKATCHEWAN WRITERS GUILD ANNUAL LITERARY AWARDS; CITY OF REGINA WRITING AWARD (IV-Regional), SWG Literary Awards Convenor, Box 3986, Regina, Saskatchewan S4P 3R9 Canada, offers 3 prizes of $1,000 for long MS (every fourth year for poetry) and 3 prizes of $150 and $75 honorable mentions for 1 poem up to 100 lines. $15 entry fee for long MSS, $4 for single poems. Deadline February 28. CRWA of $3,300 awarded annually to a writer living in Regina as of January 1 to work for 3 months on a specific project. Deadline March 15.

SCHOLASTIC WRITING AWARDS (IV-Teens), Scholastic Inc., 730 Broadway, New York NY 10003, provide college-bound high school seniors with $100-1,000 grants. Write for rules book between August and December 15.

SCOTTISH INTERNATIONAL OPEN POETRY COMPETITION; THE AYRSHIRE WRITERS' & ARTISTS' SOCIETY, 42 Tollerton Dr., Irvine, Ayrshire Scotland. Open to all poets, Inaugurated in 1972 it is the longest running poetry competition in the U.K. Entries are free, restricted to two per person and should be accompanied by International Reply Coupons and S.A.E. December deadline. Special award ceremony March. First prize, U.K. Section, MacDiarmid Trophy and $100. First prize, International Section, The International Trophy. Scots Section, The Clement Wilson Cup. Diplomas are awarded to runners up. Competition opens September each year.

‡SOCIETY OF MIDLAND AUTHORS AWARD (IV-Regional), c/o Boman, 152 N. Scoville, Oak Park IL 60302, is for authors from Midland states: IL, IN, IA, KS, MI, MN, MO, NE, ND, SD, OH, WI. It is an annual award of $300 minimum and a plaque given at a dinner at the Drake Hotel in Chicago. Books in each calendar year are eligible, not self-published. Deadline 12/15 of year preceding award year. Send SASE for entry form; books must be submitted to each of 3 judges.

SOUTH DAKOTA POETRY SOCIETY CONTESTS (I), Present Chairman of S.D. State Poetry Society Contests Audrae Visser, 710 Elk, Elkton SD 57026, 10 categories, August 31 deadline.

SPARROWGRASS POETRY FORUM (I), Dept. PM, 203 Diamond St., Box 193, Sistersville WV 26175, offers six annual free contests, each of which has $1,000 in prizes, including a $500 grand prize. Entrants are solicited to buy an anthology. I list it because the prizes are substantial. You do not have to buy the anthology to win. Contest deadlines are the last day of every other month. Send 1 original poem, no longer than 20 lines. Name and address at the top of the page. Any style, any subject.

‡SPRINGFEST AND OCTOBERFEST POETRY CONTESTS; MILE HIGH POETRY SOCIETY (I), P.O. Box 21116, Denver CO 80221, phone (303)426-8214, award director Jane C. Schaul. Each spring and fall they offer a contest, $300 1st prize, $100 2nd prize, and two 3rd prizes of $50 each for 36 line poems, $3/poem entry fee, deadlines May 31 and Nov. 30.

WALLACE E. STEGNER FELLOWSHIPS (II), Creative Writing Program, Stanford University, Stanford CA 94305, 4 in poetry, $10,000 plus tuition of $3,500, for promising writers who can benefit from 2 years instruction and criticism at the Writing Center. Previous publication not required, though it can strengthen one's application. Deadline: Postmarked by January 2.

THE TRANSLATORS ASSOCIATION; JOHN FLORIO PRIZE; SCHLEGEL-TIECK PRIZE; SCOTT-MON-CRIEFF PRIZE; BERNARD SHAW PRIZE; PORTUGUESE TRANSLATION PRIZE (IV-Translation), 84 Drayton Gardens, London SW 10 9SB, England. The first three prizes are all for translation of 20th century literature in books published in the U.K. The John Florio Prize of £900 is for the best translation from Italian, awarded every other year. The annual Schlegel-Tieck Prize of £2,000 is for translation from German. The annual Scott-Moncrieff Prize of £1,500 is for translation from French. Publishers only should submit books before December 31. The Association also administers the Bernard Shaw Prize (£1,000 every 3 years) for translations from any period from Swedish into English, and the Portuguese Translation Prize (£3,000 every three years).

LAURA BOWER VAN NUYS CREATIVE WRITING CONTEST (I, II), Black Hills Writers Group, % Larry Budd, 1015 N. 7th, Rapid City SD 57701. "**We will be holding the contest in even-numbered years only.**" Categories: professional and non-professional. $15, $12, and $10 in each category plus a subscription to *The Writer* for the Best of Show award. Fee: $2 per poem. March deadline.

‡THE VICTORIAN FELLOWSHIP OF AUSTRALIAN WRITERS; FAW AWARDS (IV-Regional, Ethnic), 1/317 Barkers Rd., Kew 3101, Australia, all awards for Australian authors. The FAW Barbara Ramsden Award (plaques to author and publisher) is "the major literary award for a book of quality" (book of the year). The FAW Australian Natives Association Literature Award ($1,000) is for "a book of sustained quality and distinction with an Australian theme." The FAW Anne Elder Poetry Award (prizes of $1,000 and $500) is for a first published book of poetry. The FAW Christopher Brennan Award (known in its first years as the Robert Frost Award) is a bronze plaque to honor an Australian poet (entries not required, award by committee). FAW Alan Marshall Award ($500) is a manuscript award for fiction or a long poem with a strong narrative element. The FAW John Shaw Neilson Poetry Award ($550, $30, and $20) is for an unpublished poem of at least 14 lines, December 31 deadline. The FAW Fedora Anderson Young Writers' Poetry Award ($100, $30, $20) is for unpublished poems by Australian writers 15-22 years old, January 31 deadline. The Patricia Weickhardt Award to an

Aboriginal Writer is "to honour the achievement of Aboriginal writers (entries not required, award by committee)."

VOICES OF THE SOUTH CONTEST; SOUTHERN POETRY ASSOCIATION (I), P.O. Box 524, Pass Christian MS 39571. The Southern Poetry Association founded 1986, poetry editor Mildred Klyce. SPA offers networking, publishing, critique service, personal communication and assistance in publication of SPA members chapbooks. $10 annual membership fee includes newsletter. The association sponsors a number of contests, including Yarn Spinner, Poetry in Motion, and Special People. Some are for members only; some, such as the Voices of the South Contest, open to all. Prizes total $200. $2 entry fee/poem (not over 24 lines). June 9 deadline. High scoring poems are published in an anthology (which the poet is not required to purchase). Send SASE for details. Reviews books of poetry in Poet's Voice newsletter.

WESTERN STATES BOOK AWARDS; WESTERN STATES ARTS FEDERATION (IV-Regional), 236 Montezuma Ave., Santa Fe NM 87501, presents biennial book awards to outstanding authors and small publishers of fiction, creative nonfiction and poetry. The awards include cash prizes of $2,500 for winning authors, $5,000 for their respective publishers and other benefits, including the opportunity for the publishers to work with, and learn from, a committee of book industry leaders. MSS must be written by an author living in Alaska, Arizona, California, Colorado, Idaho, Montana, Nevada, New Mexico, Oregon, Utah, Washington or Wyoming. Work must already have been accepted for publication by a publisher in one of these states. Work must be submitted by the publisher, submitted in MS form (not previously published in book form) with a minimum length of 48 pages. Publisher must have published at least 3 books (excluding magazines and chapbooks) since January 1988 and be able to print a first edition of at least 2,000 books. Write for more information.

‡WHITE RABBIT POETRY CONTEST; THE HARBINGER (II), P.O. Box U-1030 USAL, Mobile AL 36688, is an annual, the winners being virtually the only poetry published by *The Harbinger*. Awards are $100, $50 and $25. Deadline 3/31. Send SASE for entry form, which must accompany submisssions (2 copies, author's name on one only).

WHITING WRITERS' AWARDS; MRS. GILES WHITING FOUNDATION (V), Room 3500, 30 Rockefeller Plaza, New York NY 10112, director Gerald Freund. In each of the program's first five years, the Foundation made awards of $30,000 to ten writers of fiction, nonfiction, poetry and plays chosen by a Selection Committee drawn from a list of recognized writers, literary scholars and editors. Recipients of the award were selected from nominations made by writers, educators and editors from communities across the country whose experience and vocations bring them in contact with individuals of unusual talent. The nominators and selectors are appointed by the Foundation and serve anonymously. **Direct applications and informal nominations are not accepted by the Foundation.**

WOODNOTES; SAN FRANCISCO INTERNATIONAL HAIKU COMPETITION; HAIKU POETS OF NORTHERN CALIFORNIA (IV-Form), 478 A Second Ave., San Francisco CA 94118, *Woodnotes* editor and award director Vincent Tripi. Annual haiku competition, prizes of $150, 2 categories, $50 second, $25 third. Fee: $1/haiku, entries on 3×5" cards, on issues pertaining to both sexes and nature, no more than 17 syllables. Deadline October 31. Winning poems published in *HPNC's Woodnotes—Quarterly Journal of Haiku and Senryu*, which also publishes articles, book reviews, news and commentary. Subscription $12, $18 overseas. Single copy $3.

WORLD ORDER OF NARRATIVE AND FORMALIST POETS (II, IV-Subscription, form), P.O. Box 174, Station A, Flushing NY 11358, contest chairman Dr. Alfred Dorn. This organization sponsors contests in at least fifteen categories of traditional and contemporary poetic forms, including the sonnet, blank verse, ballade, villanelle, triolet, limerick, free verse, and new contrapuntal forms created by Alfred Dorn. Prizes total at least $4,000 and range from $20 to $200. Only subscribers to *The Formalist* will be eligible for the competition, as explained in the complete guidelines available from the contest chairman. "We look for originality of thought, phrase and image, combined with masterful craftsmanship. Trite, trivial or technically inept work stands no chance." Postmark deadline for entries: December 10.

WRITERS' FEDERATION OF NOVA SCOTIA ANNUAL ATLANTIC WRITING COMPETITION FOR UN-PUBLISHED MANUSCRIPTS (IV-Regional), Writers' Federation of Nova Scotia, Suite 203, 5516 Spring Garden Road, Halifax, Nova Scotia B3J 1G6 Canada, for up to 15 poems. Deadline January 31. Please write for rules and a mandatory entry form.

WRITERS' GUILD OF ALBERTA BOOK AWARD (IV-Regional), Writer's Guild, 10523 100th Ave., Edmonton, Alberta T5J 0A8 Canada, phone (403)426-5892, awarded in six categories, including poetry. Eligible books will have been published anywhere in the world between January 1 and December

31. Their authors will have been resident in Alberta for at least twelve of the eighteen months prior to December 31. Contact either the WGA head office or the Alberta Playwrights' Network for registry forms. Unpublished manuscripts are not eligible. Except in the drama category, anthologies are not eligible. Four copies of each book to be considered must be mailed to the WGA office no later than December 31. Submissions postmarked after this date will not be accepted. **Exceptions will be made for any books** *published* **between the 15th and 31st of December. These may be submitted by January 15.** Three copies will go to the three judges in that category; one will remain in the WGA library. Works may be submitted by authors, publishers, or any interested parties.

WRITERS UNLIMITED (I), %Voncile Ros, 3020 Frederic St., Pascagoula MS 39567, offers an annual literary competition, deadline September 20. There are up to 20 categories with cash prizes up to $50 and other prizes. Do not use the same poem for more than one category. $5 entry fee covers entries in all categories up to 20. Send SASE for contest rules.

‡ZUZU'S PETALS POETRY CONTESTS (I), P.O. Box 4476, Allentown PA 18105-4476. Quarterly contests have deadlines on the first of each March, June, September and December. Entry fee: $1/ poem, any style, length or subject. 40% of proceeds go to prize winners: 25% to first prize, 10% to second, 5% to third. Free critiques to honorable mentions. The remaining 60% of proceeds goes toward starting a new magazine: *Zuzu's Poetry Forum.*

Additional Contests and Awards

The following listings also contain information on Contests and Awards. Read the listings and/or send SASEs for more details about their offerings. (See the General Index for page numbers.)

Academy of American Poets
Adroit Expression, The
Advocate, The
Alicejamesbooks
Alms House Press
Amaranth Review, The
Amelia
America
American Academy & Institute of Arts & Letters, The
American Collegiate Poets
American Knight
American Poetry Center
American Poetry Review
American Tolkien Society
Americas Review
Analecta
And Review, The
Apropos
Arkansas Press, The University of
Arte Publico Press
Associated Writing Programs
Atlanta Writing Resource Center, Inc.
Bay Area Poets Coalition (BAPC)
Bell's Letters Poet
Black Bear Publications
Black Warrior Review, The
Blue Unicorn, A Triquarterly of Poetry
Breakthrough!
Bristol House Publishers Poetry Review
Brussels Sprout
Cacanadadada
Calapooya Collage
Cape Rock, The
Caravan Press
Chakra
Chaminade Literary Review

Channels
Chelsea
Chicago Review
Chimera Poetry Magazine for Children
Chiron Review
Cincinnati Poetry Review
Cleveland State University Poetry Center
Cochran's Corner
Columbia
Connecticut River Review
Country Woman
Crazyhorse
Creative With Words Publications (C.W.W.)
Cricket
Crucible
Crystal Rainbow
Cutbank
Devil's Millhopper Press, The
Different Drummer, A
Eighth Mountain Press, The
eleventh muse, the
Embers
Envoi
Epoch
Experiment in Words
Explorations
Explorer Magazine
Fairbanks Arts Association
Feelings
Flume Press
Folio: A Literary Journal
Footwork
For Poets Only
Formalist, The
Free Focus
Frogmore Papers
Frogpond: Quarterly Haiku Journal
Golden Isis Magazine

Grain
Greensboro Review, The
Haiku Headlines: A Monthly Newsletter of Haiku and Senryu
Haiku Journal
Haiku Quarterly
Half Tones to Jubilee
Heaven Bone Press
Hippopotamus Press
Hob-Nob
Home Planet News
Housewife-Writer's Forum
Hudson Review, The
Hutton Publications
Icon
Imago Literary Magazine
International Black Writers
International Poets of the Heart
Iowa Press, University of
Iowa Woman
Jeopardy
Kansas Quarterly
Kapok Poetry Press
Keystrokes
League of Canadian Poets, The
Lines n' Rhymes
Literary Focus Poetry Publications
Literature and Belief
Loft, The
Louisiana Literature
Lucidity
Lyric, The
MacGuffin, The
Mainichi Daily News, Haiku in English
Malahat Review, The
Mayberry Gazette, The
Mid-American Review
Midwest Poetry Review

Missouri Press, University of
Mr. Cogito Press
Modern Haiku
Montalvo Center for the Arts
Moving Out: A Feminist
  Literary and Arts Journal
Mss/New Myths
My Legacy
Nation, The
National Federation of State
  Poetry Societies, Inc.
Nebraska Review, The
Negative Capability
New Delta Review
New England Review
New Letters
New Mexico Humanities
  Review
New Press, The
Nimrod International Journal
  of Contemporary Poetry
  and Fiction
North Carolina Haiku Society
  Press, The
North Carolina Writers'
  Network
North, The
Northeastern University Press
Nostalgia: A Sentimental State
  of Mind
Occident Magazine
Ohio State University Press/
  Journal Award in Poetry
Orbis
Owens Publications
Oxalis
Painted Hills Review
Paisley Moon
Palanquin Press
Paris Review, The
Parnassus Literary Journal
Pasque Petals
Pauper's Press/Phaerwind
  Review
Pearl
Pen American Center
Philomel
Piedmont Literary Review
Pikeville Review
Pitt Poetry Series
Plainsongs
Poet
Poetic Page
Poetpourri
Poetry
Poetry & Audience
Poetry Break

Poetry Center of the 92nd
  Street Y, The
Poetry Committee of the
  Greater Washington Area,
  The
Poetry Explosion Newsletter,
  The
Poetry Forum
Poetry Halifax Dartmouth
Poetry Kanto
Poetry Magic Publications
Poetry Miscellany, The
Poetry Nippon Press
Poetry Northwest
Poetry Nottingham
Poetry Only
Poetry Peddler, The
Poetry Review
Poetry Society of America
Poetry: USA Quarterly
Poets House
Poets of Now
Poet's Review
Poets' Roundtable
Portraits Poetry Magazine
Prairie Journal
Prairie Schooner
Press of the Third Mind, The
Princeton University Press
Printed Matter
Prosetry: Newsletter For, By
  and About Writers
Protea Poetry Journal
Psych It: The Sophisticated
  Newsletter for Everyone
Pudding House Publications
Purdue University Press
Pygmy Forest Press
Quarry Magazine
Quarterly Review of Literature
Radcliffe Quarterly
Rainbow City Express
Rhino
Rio Grande Press
River City
Rockford Review, The
San Diego Poets Press
San Jose Studies
Saturday Press, Inc.
Scavenger's Newsletter
Sewanee Review
Shawnee Silhouette
Signpost Press, The
Silver Apples Press
Silver Wings
Silverfish Review
Sing Heavenly Muse!

Sisyphus
Slate & Style
Slipstream
Smith Publisher, Gibbs
Snake River Reflections
Society of American Poets, The
Sonora Review
South Coast Poetry Journal
Southern California Anthology
Southern Humanities Review
Southern Poetry Review
Southwest Review
Sows Ear, The
Sparrow Press
Spitball
Staple
State Street Press
Still Waters Press
Story Line Press
Studio
Taproot Literary Review
Tesseract Publications
Thorntree Press
Thumbprints
Vegetarian Journal
Ver Poets Voices
Verve
W.I.M. Publications (Woman
  in the Moon)
Wesleyan University Press
West Wind Review
Westerly
Weyfarers
Whetstone
White Wall Review
Whitecrow Foundation
Whitman Center for the Arts
  and Humanities, Walt
Wildwood Journal
Willamette River Press
Wisconsin Press, University of
Woodley Memorial Press
Worcester Review
Word Works, The
World-Wide Writers Service,
  Inc.
Wormwood Review Press
Write Now!
Write Way, The
Writer's Digest
Writer's Exchange
Writers' Journal
Writers' Own Magazine
Xenophilia
Yale University Press
Yankee Magazine
Zone 3

Resources

Sponsors of Poetry Readings

Almost always I sell more copies of my books of poetry than do my publishers, and I mostly sell them at readings or at writers' workshops where I am appearing. Few people buy books of poetry on the basis of ads or reviews. They buy when they have had some personal exposure to the poet and want to take something away with them to remind them of the experience. If you are a poet and you want to help sell your books, you'd better tune up your public reading performance. Usually there is a "book table" where patrons may buy copies of poets' work after the reading.

Where do you read? Most poets start at what are called "open readings." Often these occasions feature poets who are traveling through town or are known locally and, after the featured readings, the mike or platform is made available to volunteers—usually with a strict time limit. You put up your hand, go up and read or recite for a couple of minutes in your turn. That's how you meet people—and sometimes can sell books or chapbooks.

Many bookstores sponsor readings. You draw in customers for them and they earn the markup on your books by providing hospitality. Also, many universities sponsor public programs that sometimes include poetry readings. Other organizations that sponsor readings include arts centers, museums, art galleries, literary clubs, libraries, churches, writers' conferences, community and senior citizen centers, state Poets-in-the-Schools programs, YM/YWCAs and YMHAs, coffeehouses, radio and television stations (especially local access channels and PBS stations) and women's centers.

Following is a list of sponsors of readings (aside from those publishers and organizations who mention readings in their market listings). The wide variety of the list suggests that, if you look around in your own community, you may find groups that have sponsored readings or would be willing to do so if asked.

BALCH INSTITUTE FOR ETHNIC STUDIES, *Dr. James Turk, 18 S. 7th St., Philadelphia PA 19106-2314, (215)925-8090.*

BAYLOR UNIVERSITY, *Dr. James E. Barcus, Dept. of English, Waco TX 76798-7404, (817)755-1768.*

BIG HORN BASIN WRITERS, *% Roland Otto, 2097 Lane 10 SR, Powell WY 82435.*

BOCES GENESEO MIGRANT CENTER, *CAMPS Program, % Sylvia Kelly, 211 Holcomb Bldg., Geneseo NY 14454, (716)245-5681.*

THE BOOK SHOP, *Dainis Hazners, 122 N. Main, Sheridan WY 82801, (307)672-6505.*

CABLEARN CHANNEL 27, *Alison S. Beck, 225C Kane Hall, DG-10, University of Washington, Seattle WA 98195, (206)545-TV27.*

CHICAGO HOUSE, *Peg Miller, 607 Trinity, Austin TX 78701, (512)473-2542.*

THE COLLECTED WORKS BOOKSHOP, *Greg Austen, 208-B W. San Francisco St., Santa Fe NM 87501, (505)988-4226.*

THE DISCOVERY CENTER, *Mary Stebbins, 321 S. Clinton St., Syracuse NY 13202, (315)425-9068.*

UNIVERSITY OF FINDLAY WRITERS SERIES, *Diane Kendig, University of Findlay, 1000 N. Main St., Findlay OH 45840-3095, (419)422-8313.*

FIVE TOWNS SENIOR CENTER, *Miriam Bergman, 124 Franklin Pl., Woodmere NY 11598, (516)374-4747.*

FURMAN UNIVERSITY, *Meta Eppler Gilpatrick Series, Gilbert Allen, Box 30881, English Dept., Greenville SC 29613-0001, (803)294-2066.*

GRANITE LINE WRITERS, *Karen Malofy, President, P.O. Box 508, Belleville MI 48112, (313)697-2847.*

THE GUILD COMPLEX, *Michael Warr, 62 E. 13th St., Chicago IL 60605, (312)939-2509.*

ILLINOIS ARTS COUNCIL, *Richard Gage, State of Illinois Center, Suite 10-500, 100 W. Randolph, Chicago IL 60601, (312)814-6750.*

LEHIGH COUNTY COMMUNITY COLLEGE, *Gene Kern, Student Activities Assistant, 2370 Main St., Schnecksville PA 18078-9372, (215)799-2121.*

MALAPROP'S BOOKSTORE/CAFE, *Zoe Rhine, 61 Haywood St., Asheville NC 28802.*

MANHATTAN THEATRE CLUB, *Writers in Performance, Alice Gordon, 453 W. 16th St., New York NY 10011, (212)645-5590.*

MANITOBA WRITERS' GUILD, *206-100 Arthur St., Winnipeg, Manitoba R3B 1H3 Canada.*

MANTEO BOOKSELLERS, *Steve Manteo, 105 Sir Walter Raleigh St., P.O. Box 1520, Manteo NC 27954, (919)473-1221.*

MERCER UNIVERSITY, *Georgia Poetry Circuit, 1400 Coleman Ave., Macon GA 31207.*

MID-HUDSON PSYCHIATRIC CENTER, *Florence Henderson, Box 158, New Hampton NY 10958.*

MIDNIGHT SPECIAL BOOKSTORE, *Margie Ghiz, 1350 3rd St. Promenade, Santa Monica CA 90401.*

MOONSTONE POETRY SERIES, *Moonstone, Inc., 110 S. 13th St., Philadelphia PA 19107, (215)735-9598.*

MULBERRY POETS & WRITERS ASSOCIATION, *P.O. Box 468, Scranton PA 18501.*

MUSICSOURCES, *Rella Lossy, Theatre/Literary Arts Director, 1000 The Alameda, Berkeley CA 94707.*

NEW AGE POETRY SERIES, *Ketan Ben Caesar, North Star Bar, 27th & Poplar St., Philadelphia PA 19130.*

NEW ARTS ALIVE TELEVISION PROGRAM, *Channel 41, Berks Cable, New Arts Program, P.O. Box 82, Kutztown PA 19530, (215)683-6440.*

NORTH CAROLINA WRITERS' NETWORK, *Mark Harrison, Office Mgr., P.O. Box 954, Carrboro NC 27510, (919)967-9540.*

NORTH COUNTRY PUBLIC LIBRARY-WSLU, *Ellen Rocco, St. Lawrence University, Canton NY 13617, (315)379-5356.*

THE NORTHWEST RENAISSANCE, *Marjorie Rommel, 214 N St. NE, Auburn WA 98002, (206)833-4798.*

THE OPEN BOOK, *Marvin Kaye, 525 West End Ave. 12E, New York NY 10024.*

PENN STATE, *Annual Hayfield Poetry Festival, Melissa Norderer, Penn State University/Wilkes-Barre, Box PSU, Lehman PA 18627, (717)675-2171.*

POETRY FORUM AT LARRY'S, *Linda S. Smith, Coordinator, 2040 N. High St., Columbus OH 43201, (614)299-6010.*

POETRY IN THE PARK, *Amy Yore, 549 Franklin Ave., Columbus OH 43215, (614)645-7995.*

PORT WASHINGTON PUBLIC LIBRARY, *Pleasance Coggeshell, 1 Library Dr., Port Washington NY 11050.*

PROVIDENCE COLLEGE, *English Department, Beth Watson Sousa, Public Relations Director, River Ave., Providence RI 02918, (401)455-8090.*

QUEENS COLLEGE EVENING READINGS, *Joe Cuomo, Director, English Department, Queens College, Flushing NY 11367.*

SAN JOSE CENTER FOR POETRY & LITERATURE, *John Mathias, % San Jose Museum of Art, 110 S. Market St., San Jose CA 95113, (408)292-3254.*

SCARSDALE PUBLIC LIBRARY, *Mrs. Timmi Smallens, Post & Olmsted Rds., Scarsdale NY 10583, (914)723-2005.*

SMALL PRESS TRAFFIC LITERARY ARTS CENTER, *Katharine Harer, Director, 3599 24th St., San Francisco CA 94110, (415)285-8394.*

STADLER CENTER FOR POETRY, *John Wheatcroft, Director, Bucknell Hall, Bucknell University, Lewisburg PA 17837-2005, (717)524-1853.*

STATE UNIVERSITY OF NEW YORK-PLATTSBURGH, *Visiting Poets & Writers Series, Alexis Levitin, Department of English, Plattsburgh NY 12901, (518)564-2134.*

SWAN LIBRARY, *Evelyn L. Lyman, 4 N. Main St., Albion NY 14411, (716)589-4246.*

TALKING LEAVES . . . BOOKS, *Jonathan Welch, 3144 Main St., Buffalo NY 14216.*

UTICA COLLEGE LUNCH HOUR SERIES, *Jerome Cartwright, Burrstone Rd., Utica NY 13502, (315)792-3057.*

WAKING OWL BOOKS, *Patrick De Freitas, 1260 S. 13th E., Salt Lake City UT 84102-3247, (802)582-7323.*

WAPPINGERS CENTRAL SCHOOL, *Dennis J. Hannan, Department Head, English 7-12, District English Office, 99 Myers Coners Rd., Wappingers Falls NY 12590-3297.*

WHEATLAND AUTHORS, INC., *% Lois Wright, 1004 13th St., Wheatland WY 82201.*

YM/YWHA OF NORTH NEW JERSEY, *Sheila Hellman, Cultural Arts Director, 1 Pike Dr., Wayne NJ 07470-2443, (201)595-0100.*

Writing Colonies

Are you sitting there trying to concentrate on this book, or on your computer or typewriter, while children are screaming, the phone is ringing off the wall, dinner is boiling over on the stove, or your secretary seems to have a finger stuck on the intercom call button? Maybe you need to get away from it all.

Much fine poetry has been produced at some of the prestigious colonies listed below. Above all, writing colonies are the setting for many new friendships and associations among writers and artists. It is an honor to be accepted by some — and one may go to those as to a temple, awed by the spiritual presence of great poets who have been there over the years.

Writers' colonies are best for those who have a project underway, something definite to work on. Have some alternative plans in mind, in case your project dries up on you. Take with you the reference books and other resources you will need.

I would guess that most of our major poets have spent some time in one or another of these colonies, and it can be an experience that awakens and deepens your sense of what it means to participate in the long fellowship of our art. We may all be grateful that benefactors have provided these "resorts" to foster creativity in the arts — and should learn to use them respectfully and well.

THE EDWARD F. ALBEE FOUNDATION, INC.; THE WILLIAM FLANAGAN MEMORIAL CREATIVE PERSONS CENTER ("THE BARN"), 14 Harrison St., New York NY 10013, phone (212)226-2020, for information and application forms. The Albee Foundation maintains the Center (better known as "The Barn") in Montauk, on Long Island, offering 1-month residencies for writers, painters, sculptors, and composers, open June 1-October 1, accommodating 6 persons at a time. Applications accepted at the Harrison Street address by regular mail only January 1-April 1. Fellowship announcements by May 15. "Located approximately 2 miles from the center of Montauk and the Atlantic Ocean, 'The Barn' rests in a secluded knoll that offers privacy and a peaceful atmosphere. The Foundation expects all those accepted for residence to work seriously and to conduct themselves in such a manner as to aid fellow residents in their endeavors. The environment is simple and communal. Residents are expected to do their share in maintaining the condition of 'The Barn' as well as its peaceful environment."

ATLANTIC CENTER FOR THE ARTS, 1414 Art Center Ave., New Smyrna Beach FL 32168, phone (904)427-6975. The Center was founded in 1979 by a sculptor and painter, Doris Leeper, who secured a seed grant from The Rockefeller Foundation. That same year the Center was chartered by the state of Florida and building began on a 10-acre site. The Center was officially opened in 1982. Since 1982, 40 Master Artists-in-Residence sessions have been held. At each of the 3-week sessions internationally known artists from different disciplines conduct interdisciplinary workshops, lecture, critique work in progress. They also give readings and recitals, exhibit their work, and develop projects with their "associates" — mid-career artists who come from all over the U.S. to work with the Masters. The Center is run by an advisory council which chooses Masters for residencies, helps set policies, and guides the Center in its growth. The process of becoming an associate is different for each master artist. Recent poets in residence at the center include Howard Nemerov (January 1988), James Dickey (June 1987), Fred Chappell (April 1989), Henry Taylor (June 1989) and Ron Padgett (March-April 1990).

‡BANFF CENTRE FOR THE ARTS MAY STUDIOS, Box 1020, 107 Tunnel Mountain Dr., Banff, Alberta T0L 0C0 Canada, offers 4-6 weeks of residence between April 22 and May 31 to writers "who already have a body of work (some of it preferably, but not necesssarily, published) attesting to their commitment and talent. Applicant should have a project in progress . . . . Enrollment is limited to 10 participants." Fee $1,440; room and board $1,591. "Full scholarships for fee and room and board are offered to all successful candidates." Located in an inspirational mountain setting, The Banff Centre for Continuing Education is a unique Canadian institution. Participants are housed in single rooms that also serve as their private work spaces. Three meals per day are provided on campus. Application deadline: Jan. 15.

BELLAGIO STUDY AND CONFERENCE CENTER, The Rockefeller Foundation, 1133 Avenue of the Americas, New York NY 10036, Susan Garfield, Manager, offers five-week residencies in the Italian Alps from January 20-December 20 for artists and scholars. Room available for spouses. Residents must pay their own travel cost.

CENTRUM, % Sarah Muirhead, coordinator, Residency Program, Box 1158, Port Townsend WA 98368, offers 1-month residencies, September through May. Centrum provides individual cottages, a stipend of $75/week, and solitude. Families welcome. Located in Fort Worden State Park on the Strait of Juan de Fuca. Also sponsors the annual Port Townsend Writers' Conference held in July, and other workshops and seminars.

‡CHATEAU DE LESVAULT, c/o Bibbi Lee, Onlay, 58370 Villapourcon, France, phone (33)86-84-32-91, this French country residence is located in the national park "Le Morvan" of western Burgundy, halfway between Nevers and Autun, and is surrounded by green hills and forests. The chateau accommodates five residents at a time in five large rooms with private baths, fully furnished and equipped for working. The facilities of the chateau are at the disposal of residents, including the salon, library and grounds. Requests for residencies from November through April should be made at least two months in advance. The cost is 4,000 FF per month for room, board (five days a week) and utilities.

THE CLEARING, Box 65, Ellison Bay WI 54210, phone (414)854-4088, resident managers Donald and Louise Buchholz, "is first a school, then a place of self-discovery." Made up of cabins and lodges in a rustic setting overlooking Green Bay, it offers a variety of courses, including courses in writing and poetry, May-October. Fees include tuition, room (dormitory or twin-bedded room) and board.

‡COLONYHOUSE: OREGON WRITERS COLONY, c/o Marlene Howard, P.O. Box 15200, Portland OR 97215, phone (503)771-0482, is a seaside cottage owned and operated by Oregon writers. It sleeps 8 and is available for weekly and weekend rentals at (Fall-Winter) $400/week, $200/weekend or (Spring-Summer) $525/week, $325/weekend. 15% discount for Oregon Writers Club members ($20/year).

CUMMINGTON COMMUNITY OF THE ARTS, RR #1, Box 145, Cummington MA 01026, phone (413)634-2172, offers residencies to artists in all disciplines from 1-3 months. Living/studio spaces are in individual cabins or two main houses, on 100 acres in the Berkshires. During July and August, artists with children from age 5-12 are encouraged to apply. Cummington sponsors the Summer Children's Program which offers supervised activity for the children of artists in residence. Application deadlines: Feb. 1 for residences during April, May and June; March 1 for residences during July and August; June 1 for residences during September, October, November.

DOBIE-PAISANO PROJECT, Attn: Audrey N. Slate, Main Building 101, The University of Texas, Austin TX 78712, offers two annual fellowships of $7,200 and 6-month residency at Frank Dobie's ranch, Paisano, for Texans, Texas residents or writers whose work has been substantially identified with the state. Apply by January 22. Write for application and guidelines.

DORLAND MOUNTAIN ARTS COLONY, P.O. Box 6, Temecula CA 92390, established 1979, is a 300 acre Nature Conservancy preserve which offers 1-2 month residences for writers, visual artists and composers in a rustic environment with no elecricity, propane appliances (refrigerator, water heater, cooking stove). Residents provide their own meals. A donation of $150/month is requested. Write for application form. Deadlines the first of September and March.

DORSET COLONY HOUSE RESIDENCIES; AMERICAN THEATRE WORKS, INC.; DORSET THEATRE FESTIVAL, Box 519, Dorset VT 05251, available to writers September-May for periods of 1 week-2 months for intensive work. Requested fee of $75 per week, but ability to pay is not a criterion in awarding residencies. Connected with Dorset Theatre Festival, a production company with an interest in new scripts.

FINE ARTS WORK CENTER IN PROVINCETOWN, Box 565, 24 Pearl St., Provincetown MA 02657, provides monthly stipends of $375 and studio/living quarters for 7 uninterrupted months for 20 young artists and writers (10 of each) who have completed their formal training and are capable of working independently. The Center has a staff of writers and artists who offer manuscript consultations, arrange readings and slide presentations and visits from other distinguished writers and artists. Established writers are invited each year for extended residencies. Each year writing fellows publish *Shankpainter*, a magazine of prose and poetry. Sessions run from October 1 to May 1. Applications, accompanied by a $20 processing fee, must be received by February 1.

‡THE TYRONE GUTHRIE CENTRE, Annaghmakerrig, Newbliss, Co. Monaghan, Ireland, resident director Bernard Loughlin, offers residencies, normally 3 weeks-3 months, for artists, including poets. "Each resident has a private apartment within the house . . . and all the centrally heated comfort an Irish Big House can afford. It is set on a wooded estate of 400 acres and overlooks a large lake. The house is surrounded by gardens and a working dairy farm. Couples or small groups of artists may stay for up to a year in Maggie's Farm, a cottage on the estate, and have use of studios at the Big House. Five newly built, self-contained farmyard cottages are also available for individuals, couples and families for longer stays." To qualify for residence it is necessary to show evidence of a significant level of achievement in the relevant field. Once accepted Irish artists are asked to contribute what they can afford toward the cost of their stay. Overseas artists are expected to pay the whole cost of a residency. "We will give every assistance in obtaining grants from the appropriate cultural insitutions in the artist's home country."

HAMBIDGE CENTER FOR CREATIVE ARTS AND SCIENCES, Box 339, Rabun Gap GA 30568, phone (404)746-5718. The Center is located on six hundred acres of unspoiled wooded slopes, mountain meadows and streams, near Dillard, GA. It is listed on the National Register of Historic Places. Resident Fellowships of 2 weeks-2 months are awarded to individuals engaged in the artistic, scientific, humanistic and educational professions for the purpose of solitude and the pursuit of creative excellence. Those accepted are given a private cottage equipped with a kitchen, sleeping and bathing facilities and a work area. Center is open from May-October. There is also a work-study internship for younger individuals approaching the end of their formal study (requiring 20 hours of work per week). For more information and application forms send SASE (2oz.). Allow approximately 2 months for processing. Applications are reviewed year round.

HAWK, I'M YOUR SISTER, WOMEN'S WILDERNESS CANOE TRIPS, WRITING RETREATS, Beverly Antaeus, P.O. Box 9109, Santa Fe NM 87504. This organization offers wilderness retreats for women, many of them with writing themes including the Voice That is Great Within Us: A Writing Retreat with Linda Trichter Metcalf; Between the Earth & Silence: A Writing Retreat with W.S. Merwin (coed); The River as Metaphor: A Writing Retreat with Sharon Olds; and Friend Sits by Friend: A Writing Retreat with Coleman Barks (coed). The canoe trips are held all over North America and typically last 8-10 days with fees $800-1,250. Write for annual listing of specific trips.

THE MACDOWELL COLONY, 100 High St., Peterborough NH 03458, founded 1907, offers residencies to established writers, composers, visual artists, filmmakers, architects and interdisciplinary artists. Over 3,000 artists have stayed there, many of them producing major works. Apply 8 months before desired residency. Application deadlines: Jun. 15: May-Aug; April 15: Sept.-Dec.; Sept. 15: Jan.-April. Private studio, room and meals provided. Accepted artists are asked to contribute toward residency costs. Current application form is necessary; write address above or call 603-924-3886 or 212-966-4860. Average residency is 6 weeks. Professional work samples required with application.

THE MILLAY COLONY FOR THE ARTS, INC., Steepletop, P.O. Box 3, Austerlitz NY 12017-0003, founded in 1974, assistant director Gail Giles, provides work space, meals and sleeping accommodations at no cost for a period of one month. Apply with samples of your work before February 1 for June-September; before May 1 for October-January; before September 1 for February-May.

MONTALVO CENTER FOR THE ARTS; MONTALVO BIENNIAL POETRY COMPETITION, Box 158, Saratoga CA 95071, presents theatre, musical events and other artistic activities. (I once was on the panel of a poetry workshop there.) They have an Artist-in-Residence program which has 5 apartments available for artists (including poets) for maximum 3-month periods. (No children or pets.) Limited financial assistance available. They offer a biennial poetry competition open to residents of Oregon, Nebraska, Washington and California, with a prominent judge, with a first prize of $1,000 (and artist residency), other prizes of $500, $300 and 8 honorable mentions. Submit 3 poems in duplicate, entry fee $5, October 15 deadline. Send SASE for rules.

THE NORTHWOOD INSTITUTE ALDEN B. DOW CREATIVITY CENTER, Midland, MI 48640-2398, phone (517)837-4478, founded 1979, director Carol Coppage, offers fellowships for 10-week summer residencies at the Northwood Institute Campus. Travel and all expenses are paid. Applicants can be undergraduates, graduates, or those without any academic or institutional affiliation, including citizens of other countries (if they can communicate in English). Projects may be in any field, but must be new and innovative. Write for application. Annual deadline December 31 for following summer.

PALENVILLE INTERARTS COLONY, 2 Bond St., New York NY 10012, offers 1-8 week residencies in Palenville, New York, for seclusion or for interaction among artists of various disciplines in a relaxed and creative atmosphere. Fee (negotiable): $175 per week. Open June 1 to September 30. Application deadline is April 1st.

PUDDING HOUSE PUBLICATIONS, 60 N. Main St., Johnstown OH 43031. See listing in Publishers of Poetry section.

RAGDALE FOUNDATION, 1260 N. Green Bay Rd., Lake Forest IL 60045, founded 1976, director Michael Wilkerson, provides a peaceful place and uninterrupted time for 12 writers, scholars, composers and artists. Meals, linen and laundry facilities are provided. Each resident is assigned private work space and sleeping accommodations. Couples are accepted if each qualifies independently. Residents may come for 2 weeks to 2 months. The fee is $70 per week. Some financial assistance available. The Foundation also sponsors poetry readings, concerts, workshops and seminars in writing. Ragdale is open year-round except for June 15-30 and December 15-January 1. Apply by January 15 for residencies in May-August; April 15 for September-December; September 15 for January-April.

MILDRED I. REID WRITERS COLONY IN NEW HAMPSHIRE, RR5, Box 51, Penacook Road, Contoocook NH 03229, phone (603)746-3625. Winter address Apt. 5, 917 Bucida Road, Delray Beach FL 33483, phone (407)278-3607. The Mildred Reid Writers Colony is run as a private enterprise; there are weekly sessions from July 8 to August 19. The sessions are held at a chalet in the country, 10 miles west of Concord, NH. Cost of a week at the Colony ranges from $130 for a single room and shared bath to $220 double rate for a log cabin in the pines. Fees include room, breakfast, two private conferences and two class sessions weekly. Kitchen facilities are available, and a village with restaurants is within walking distance. Ms. Reid gives private consultations at $5/half hour.

‡THE ROCKY MOUNTAIN WOMEN'S INSTITUTE, 7150 Montview Blvd., Denver CO 80220, phone (303)871-6923, founded 1976, executive director Cheryl Bezio-Gorham, a non-profit organization associated with the University of Denver, offers office or studio space, stipends and support services for one year for artists, writers and scholars chosen from applications. They also offer continuing support for former associates, and they sponsor exhibits, workshops, lectures and performances to highlight and promote the work of current and past Associates. Terms begin each September. Applicants should have a specific project. Applications ($5 processing fee) are received beginning each January. Deadline: closest Friday to March 15. Write for further information.

SPLIT ROCK ARTS PROGRAM, 306 Wesbrook Hall, 77 Pleasant St. SE, University of Minnesota, Minneapolis MN 55455, is a summer series of week-long residential workshops in the visual and literary arts and in the nature and applications of creativity, on the Duluth campus of UM "in the green hills near the city's summit." 1991 writing faculty included Paulette Bates Alden, Christina Baldwin, Michael Dennis Browne, Carolyn Forche, Paul Gruchow, Phebe Hanson, Joy Harjo, Mary LaChapelle, Jane Resh Thomas and Al Young. Tuition ranges from $273-305 for courses taken for credit, $12 less if taken for no credit. Housing is $80 for a double, $115 for a single, in two-bedroom suites. Meals are in UMD's cafeteria, cooked by participants in their apartments or in Duluth restaurants. Other housing options are also available; they range from $114-204 per week.

‡THE SYVENNA FOUNDATION, Rt. 1, Box 193, Linden TX 75563, phone (903)835-8252, associate director Barbara Carroll, has 8 cottages on forested land near the Texas-Louisiana border available to unestablished women writers for 3-month residencies. Pays $300 stipend plus room and utilities. The foundation's name is pronounced Savannah. Women writers of all ages and stages of development as writers are welcome to apply any time of the year.

UCROSS FOUNDATION RESIDENCY PROGRAM, 2836 US Hwy. 14-16, Clearmont WY 82835, phone (307)737-2291, executive director Elizabeth Guheen. There are four concurrent positions open in various disciplines, including poetry, each extending from 2 weeks to 4 months. No charge for room, board or studio space, and they do not expect services or products from guests. Send SASE for information form, which must be accompanied by a work sample and general description of the work you plan to do at Ucross. Residents are selected from a rotating panel of professionals in the arts and humanities in October and March for, respectively, the Spring and Fall residencies. Semiannual application deadlines are March 1 and October 1.

VERMONT STUDIO CENTER; VISUAL ARTISTS AND WRITERS RESIDENCIES, P.O. Box 613, Johnson VT 05656, phone (802)635-2727, founded 1984, offers 4 and 8-week residencies for painters, sculptors and writers, January through April. Applications accepted all year, reviewed monthly. They can accommodate 16 painters, 4 sculptors and 4-6 writers at a time, "who, together with the year-round VSC staff artists, form a dynamic working community" in the Green Mountains. "This environment creates the opportunity for as much solitude and retreat or interchange and support as each fellow wishes. Fellowships available. Writers' work spaces as well as housing for all fellows are provided in individual accommodations in residences in the village of Johnson, all within walking distance of each other as well as the Red Mill complex that contains the dining hall, lounge, offices, gallery. Johnson State College is also within walking distance."

VIRGINIA CENTER FOR THE CREATIVE ARTS, Mt. San Angelo, Sweet Briar VA 24595, director William Smart, provides residencies for 12 writers (and 9 visual artists and 3 composers) for 1-3 months at the 450 acre Mt. San Angelo estate. The normal fee is $20 per day. Financial assistance is available.

THE WRITERS COMMUNITY, West Side YMCA Center for the Arts, New York NY 10023, phone (212)787-6557, offers an advanced 3-month master writing program in poetry, October-December, March-May (application deadline mid-September, mid-February), working with a writer-in-residence. All members are asked to contribute $95 to the program, but there are no other fees. Submit biographical information, a minimum of 10 pp. of poetry, which may be published material. All material should be typed or printed and copies should be retained. MSS cannot be returned. Call for application deadlines.

THE HELENE WURLITZER FOUNDATION OF NEW MEXICO, Box 545, Taos NM 87571, offers residencies to creative, *not* interpretive, artists in all media, rent free and utilities free, for varying periods of time, usually 3 months, from April 1 to September 30, annually. Residents are responsible for their food. No families. No deadlines on application.

YADDO, Box 395, Saratoga Springs NY 12866-0395, founded 1926, c/o President Myra Sklarew, offers residencies to writers, visual artists and composers who have already achieved some recognition in their field and have new work under way. During the summer 35 guests can be accommodated, 14 during the winter, approximately 200 per year. The hours 9-4 are a quiet period reserved for work. There is no fixed charge for a guest stay, but voluntary contributions of up to $20/day to help defray costs of the program are accepted. Write for applications to: Admissions, Yaddo, address above; enclose SASE. Application deadlines are January 15 and August 1. A $20 application fee is required.

Organizations Useful to Poets

An organization of poets may sound like a contradiction in terms, but the truth is, our breed is fairly well organized. You may need support (emotional or financial) and be able to find it if you know how to get in touch with people like yourself nationally or in your local area. For instance, most states have arts councils and many of these offer grants for individual writers (see State and Provincial Grants). Check out, too, the National Federation of State Poetry Societies, Inc. (see their listing in this section) to see whether your state or city has a chapter you might join. Consider joining the Poetry Society of America or the Academy of American Poets (both listed in this section) to receive their publications and to become eligible for their awards. Keep an eye on *Poets & Writers* (see Publications Useful to Poets) for ads and announcements from a wide range of organizations available to you, some of them offering grants and awards for which you may apply.

Though writing is, in general, a lonely occupation, it is sometimes surprising to look up and discover that we are, in fact, surrounded by a vast support system of groups which have been formed to share, encourage and foster our work. There is probably a writers' group or club in your area. If not, it is easy to form one. Just put up notices on public bulletin boards, or take out an ad in your local paper, suggesting that interested writers get together at some specific time and place. Often public libraries have rooms available for such purposes if you don't want to use your home. There are many more closet poets (and other writers) around the country than you might believe.

I have listed here some of the major organizations which offer support of various kinds to poets and some representative samples of smaller groups.

ACADEMY OF AMERICAN POETS; FELLOWSHIP OF THE ACADEMY OF AMERICAN POETS; WALT WHITMAN AWARD; THE LAMONT POETRY SELECTION; HAROLD MORTON LANDON TRANSLATION AWARD; PETER I.B. LAVAN YOUNGER POETS AWARD, 177 E. 87th St., New York NY 10128, founded 1934, by Marie Bullock. I quote Robert Penn Warren, from the *Introduction to Fifty Years of American Poetry*, an anthology published in 1984 containing one poem from each of the 126 Chancellors, Fellows and Award Winners of the Academy: "What does the Academy do? According to its certificate of incorporation, its purpose is 'To encourage, stimulate and foster the production of American poetry. . . .' The responsibility for its activities lies with the Board of Directors and the Board of 12 Chancellors, which has included, over the years, such figures as Louise Bogan, W. H. Auden, Witter Bynner, Randall Jarrell, Robert Lowell, Robinson Jeffers, Marianne Moore, James Merrill, Robert Fitzgerald, F. O. Matthiessen and Archibald MacLeish—certainly not members of the same poetic church." They award fellowships, currently of $20,000 each, to distinguished American poets (no applications taken)—50 to date—and other annual awards. The Walt Whitman Award pays $1,000 plus publication of a poet's first book by a major publisher. MSS of 50-100 pp. must be submitted between September 15 and November 15 with a $10 entry fee. The Lamont Poetry Selection, for a poet's second book, is again a prize of $1,000 and publication. The Academy distributes 2,000 copies to its members. Submissions must be made by a publisher, in MSS form, prior to publication. Poets entering either contest must be American citizens. The Harold Morton Landon Translation Award is for translation of a book-length poem, a collection of poems or a verse-drama translated into English from any language. One award of $1,000 each year to a U.S. citizen. Only publishers may submit the book. Write for guidelines. The Peter I.B. Lavan Younger Poets Awards of $1,000 each are given annually to three younger poets selected by Academy Chancellors (no applications taken). *Poetry Pilot* is an informative periodical sent to those who contribute $20 or more per year or who are members. Membership: $45/year. The Academy sponsors a wide range of poetry readings and symposiums on poetry, including regional symposiums in various areas of the country.

THE AMERICAN ACADEMY & INSTITUTE OF ARTS & LETTERS; THE ARTS AND LETTERS AWARDS; MICHAEL BRAUDE AWARD FOR LIGHT VERSE; THE GOLD MEDAL OF THE ACADEMY; WITTER BYNNER FOUNDATION POETRY PRIZE; FELLOWSHIP TO THE AMERICAN ACADEMY IN ROME; JEAN STEIN AWARD; MORTON DAUWEN ZABEL PRIZE, 633 W. 155th St., New York NY 10032, program assistant John Pratt, offers annual awards in the arts, several of which are given to poets— by nomination only. **No applications for these awards are accepted.** These are: The Arts & Letters Awards of $5,000 each, given to 8 writers annually, some poets; the Michael Braude Award for Light Verse of $5,000, given biennially for light verse in the English language; The Gold Medal of the American Academy and Institute of Arts and Letters, given to a poet every 6 years; Award of Merit of $5,000 for an outstanding artist in one field of the arts, given to a poet once every 6 years; the Witter Bynner Foundation Poetry Prize of $1,500; a fellowship to the American Academy in Rome, including lodging and a stipend to a poet or fiction writer; the Jean Stein Award of $5,000 given every 3rd year to a poet whose work takes risks in expressing its commitment to the author's values and vision; the Morton Dauwen Zabel Prize of $5,000 given every 3rd year to a poet of "progressive, original and experimental tendencies rather than of academic and conservative tendencies." The 7 members of the jury are all Academy-Institute members appointed for a 3-year term. **Candidates (only published writers are considered) must be nominated by a member of the academy-institute.**

AMERICAN POETRY CENTER; ALL MUSE: PENNSYLVANIA'S LITERARY NETWORK NEWSLETTER; YOUNG VOICES OF PENNSYLVANIA POETRY CONTEST; POETS IN RESIDENCE PROGRAM; POETS RESOURCE CENTER; PENNSYLVANIA WRITERS COLLECTION, 1204 Walnut St., Philadelphia PA 19107, phone (215)546-1510, 800-ALL-MUSE (in Pennsylvania), sponsors Poetry Week, Pennsylvania's statewide literary arts festival during the entire month of March, which kicks-off the Center's year-round activities including: Young Voices, a statewide poetry contest for students aged 5-18, the winners of which are published in an anthology and invited to read at libraries during APC's Poetry Week; a Poets-In-Residence Program which brings poets to an inner-city high school in Philadelphia for four weeks; Poets Resource Center which will provide technical resources to Philadelphia writers in the form of comprehensive directories, "how-to" brochures, and a publishing reference library; and *All Muse*, their professionally printed magazine, 20 pp. newsprint publication, which appears in January and September, 20,000 copies distributed free, giving brief reviews of current poetry and fiction works by Pennsylvanians, regional events, publications, workshops, profiles and other news. Their All-Muse hotline provides recorded messages about upcoming literary events statewide; and their Pennsylvania Writers Collection stocks approximately 450 titles, works of poets, fiction writers and presses in Pennsylvania, available for purchase by mail or at the Center in Philadelphia. Though they do not currently sponsor poetry readings, they provide information to the general public regarding when and where readings will be held. They sponsor an annual public symposium on a topic pertinent to poetry, with major poets as speakers, international programs such as Moscow residencies and student poet's tours. They offer technical assistance to writers and literary institutions through periodic workshops and consultations. Center staff members assist schools, corporations and museums in identifying artists for readings and residencies and in organizing literary events. Send SASE for a current list of their activities.

ASSOCIATED WRITING PROGRAMS; AWP CHRONICLE; THE AWP AWARD SERIES, Old Dominion University, Norfolk VA 23529-0079, founded 1967, offers a variety of services to the writing community, including information, job placement assistance, publishing opportunities, literary arts advocacy and forums. Annual individual membership is $45; placement service extra. For $18 you can subscribe to the *AWP Chronicle* (published six times a year), containing information about grants and awards, publishing opportunities, fellowships, and writing programs. They have a catalog of over 250 college and university writing programs. The AWP Award Series selects a volume of poetry each year to be published ($10 entry fee). Deadline: Feb. 28. Send SASE for submission guidelines. Query after September. Their placement service helps writers find jobs in teaching, editing and other related fields.

ATLANTA WRITING RESOURCE CENTER, INC., Room 105, The Arts Exchange, 750 Kalb St., Atlanta GA 30312, phone (404)622-4152, director Malkia M. Moore, "is for everyone with an interest in writing, whether for print or electronic media or simply for personal satisfaction. The Center will provide reference materials, guidelines information samples, standard writing formats and other resources for effective writing and marketing." There is a bimonthly critique group for poets and short story writers, and a monthly open reading and open house called "Writers' Brawl" on the fourth Thursday of each month. The Center has regular open hours (staffed by executive director and volunteers) with personal work space including typewriters, word processors, reference books and other resources. They publish a quarterly newsletter highlighting Center activities and Atlanta's literary events, and they provide news of contests, writers' conferences, etc. They also sponsor an annual contest for previously unpublished original poems. Small cash prizes and honorable mentions. Winners published in *The Chattahoochee Review*. Write for current guidelines. Literary magazines and journals as well as their writers' guidelines are available at the Center. They also hold workshops aimed at improving literary and marketing skills. "People are invited to become mentors for $25/year. Contact us for more information."

‡THE AUTHORS GUILD, INC., 330 W. 42nd St., New York NY 10036, phone (212) 563-5904, executive director Helen A. Stephenson, "is an association of professional writers which focuses its efforts on the legal and business concerns of published authors in the areas of publishing contract terms, copyright, taxation and freedom of expression. We do not work in the area of marketing MSS to publishers nor do we sponsor or participate in awards or prize selections." Send SASE for information on membership.

AUTHORS LEAGUE FUND, 234 W. 44th St., New York NY 10036, makes interest-free loans to published authors in need of temporary help because of illness or an emergency. No grants.

BEYOND BAROQUE LITERARY/ARTS CENTER, P.O. Box 2727, 681 Venice Blvd., Venice CA 90291, phone (213)822-3006, director D.B. Finnegan, a foundation established in 1968 that has been funded by the NEA, state and city arts councils, and corporate donations. Foundation members get a calendar of events, discounts on regularly scheduled programs, and borrowing privileges in the small-press library of 3,000 volumes of poetry, fiction and reference materials, including audio tapes of Beyond Baroque readings. Beyond Baroque contains a bookstore open 5 days a week, including Friday evenings to coincide with regular weekly readings and performances. About 130 writers are invited to read each year; there are also open readings.

BLACK CULTURAL CENTRE FOR NOVA SCOTIA, Box 2128 East Dartmouth, Nova Scotia B2W 3Y2 Canada, phone (902)434-6223, FAX (902)434-2306, founded 1977 "to create among members of the Black communities an awareness of their past, their heritage and their identity; to provide programs and activities for the general public to explore, learn about, understand and appreciate black history, black achievements and black experiences in the broad context of Canadian life. The Centre houses a museum, reference library, archival area, small auditorium and studio workshops."

BURNABY WRITERS' SOCIETY, 6450 Deer Lake Ave., Burnaby, British Columbia V5G 2J3 Canada, contact person Eileen Kernaghan. Corresponding membership in the society, including a newsletter subscription, is open to anyone, anywhere. Yearly dues are $20. Sample newsletter in return for SASE with Canadian stamp. The Society holds monthly meetings at The Burnaby Arts Centre (address above), with a business meeting at 7:30 followed by a writing workshop or speaker. Members of the society stage regular public readings of their own work.

THE WITTER BYNNER FOUNDATION FOR POETRY, INC., P.O. Box 2188, Santa Fe NM 87504, phone (505)988-3251, president Douglas W. Schwartz. The Foundation awards grants exclusively to nonprofit organizations for the support of poetry-related projects in the area of: 1) support of individual poets through existing nonprofit institutions; 2) developing the poetry audience; 3) poetry translation and the process of poetry translation; and 4) uses of poetry. The Foundation "may consider the support of other creative and innovative projects in poetry." Grant applications must be received by February 1 each year; requests for application forms should be submitted to Steven Schwartz, executive director, at the address above.

THE CANADA COUNCIL; GOVERNOR GENERAL'S LITERARY AWARDS; INTERNATIONAL LITERARY PRIZES, 99 Metcalfe St., P.O. Box 1047, Ottawa, Ontario K1P 5V8, Canada, phone (613)598-4365/6, established by Parliament in 1957, "provides a wide range of grants and services to professional Canadian artists and art organizations in dance, media arts music, opera theatre, writing, publishing and the visual arts." The Governor General's Literary Awards, valued at $10,000 (Canadian) each, are given annually for the best English-language and best French-language work in each of seven categories, including poetry. Books must be first-edition trade books which have been written, translated or illustrated by Canadian citizens or permanent residents of Canada and published in Canada or abroad during the previous year (1 Oct-30 Sept). In the case of translation, the original work must also be a Canadian-authored title. Books must be submitted by publishers and be accompanied by a Publisher's Submission Form, which is available from the Writing and Publishing Section. All books must be received at the Canada Council by September 30. The Canada Council administers four International Literary Prizes (Canada-Australia, Canada-French Community of Belgium, Canada-Switzerland and Canada-Japan) of $2,500-3,000 (Canadian) each for the first three prizes and of $10,000 (Canadian) for the Canada-Japan Literary Prize; winners are selected by juries. Except for the Canada-Japan Prize, applications are not accepted.

CANADIAN CONFERENCE ON THE ARTS, 189 Laurier Ave. E., Ottawa, Ontario K1N 6P1 Canada, phone (613)238-3561, was created for "the encouragement of the federal, provincial and municipal governments, as well as the corporate and private sector, to develop policies which will ensure the continued growth of the arts and the cultural industries in Canada." It supplies members with information on political issues affecting the daily lives of artists and writers. Members receive *Arts Bulletin*, a quarterly news magazine of the organization; *Arts News* and other information on cultural issues of the day; counseling, general representation and active support. They sponsor conferences such as taxation and the artist, and offer other services. Membership for individuals is $10 for students and senior citizens, $25 for others, or organizational members on a sliding scale (depending on the organization's budget) of $60-900.

‡CANADIAN POETRY ASSOCIATION; POEMATA, Carrot Common Postal Outlet, P.O. Box 65100, Toronto, Ontario M4K 3Z2 Canada, is a broad based umbrella organization that aims to promote the reading, writing, publishing, purchasing and preservation of poetry in Canada through the individual and combined efforts of its members; to promote and encourage all forms and styles of poetry; to promote communication among poets, publishers and the general public; to promote the establishment and maintenance of poetry libraries and archives in educational institutions across Canada; and to develop an international connection for Canadian poets through *Poemata*, its quarterly newsletter, and events organized by independent, locally-run chapters. Through its ten autonomous local chapters, CPA organizes poetry readings, literary and social events, and runs a book club. Membership is open to anyone with an interest in poetry, including other literary organizations, for $20 per year. Sample newsletter: $3.

CANADIAN SOCIETY OF CHILDREN'S AUTHORS, ILLUSTRATORS & PERFORMERS, Box 280, Station L, Toronto, Ontario M6E 4Z2 Canada, phone (416)654-0903, president Priscilla Galloway, is a "Society of Professionals in the field of children's culture. Puts people into contact with publishers, offers advice to beginners, and generally provides a visible profile for members; 250 professional members and over 800 associates who are termed 'friends.' An annual conference in Toronto the last week of October provides workshops to people interested in writing, illustrating, and performing for children." Membership is $50 per year, which includes a subscription to the quarterly *Canscaip News* and a free copy of the Membership Directory.

‡COMPUSERVE INFORMATION SERVICE, 5000 Arlington Centre Blvd., P.O. Box 20212, Columbus OH 43220, phone (800)848-8199 from outside Ohio or (614)457-0802 from within Ohio or outside the U.S., is an international electronic network available via modem from any computer. On CIS are many forums on specialized topics of interests, including Litforum. This has been described as a 24-hr. nonalcoholic cocktail party: basically a bulletin board where various members post and respond to public messages (though you may communicate with them privately, too, either through the CompuServe mail system or by leaving private messages in Litforum). I usually log onto Litforum about twice a day, so that is the easiest way I know of for you to contact me personally. It costs $39.95 to join CIS (as most of us refer to CompuServe). You can get the stuff at any computer store, or order from them at (800)848-8199. When you join, you get about $25 online credit, so joining is practically free. If you have any telecommunications program on your computer, such as Procomm, you can use that to go online. But CIS can get very expensive ($12.80/hr connect time) by that method. It is better to use one of the many automated programs with which you do whatever you want (write letters, etc.) offline, then go online for a brief time while the program sends whatever you have to send and downloads whatever messages are waiting for you (or any programs you want to download, or material from one of the libraries). The automated program I use, for IBM compatibles, is Tapcis, which has a one-time membership fee of $79, (800)USA-GROUP or (301)387-7322; or you can go online on CIS, type GO TAPCIS at the prompt, and download the program from the Tapcis forum itself (and try it free for 30 days). There are many services available through CIS (in addition to electronic mail), but most of the action is in the forums. In Litforum sometimes the talk is quite funny, often bawdy, and far-ranging, though there is a lot of practical, professional communication, too, and many people make contact via Litforum with agents, editors, other writers, researchers, and so on, that prove quite useful. Sometimes we exchange two or three messages a day, when something is going hot and heavy. You join Litforum (anyone can join; a number of the regulars are not even writers—just people interested in literature, writing, publication, chitchat), read the messages posted in some or all of the 17 sections (on such things as poetry and lyrics, fiction, nonfiction, speculative fiction, and so on), respond to any that you wish to, or just lurk. We've got an unknown audience of lurkers—people who never post a message, just read all the chatter. Each section has a library where you can post material you have written or download material by others, and comment if you wish. There is a workshop for which you can request admission (and you're in automatically) where each writer has a turn to have material criticized by the other workshop members.

COSMEP, THE INTERNATIONAL ASSOCIATION OF INDEPENDENT PUBLISHERS; COSMEP NEWS-LETTER, P.O. Box 703, San Francisco CA 94101. If you are starting a small press or magazine or are embarking on self-publication, you should know about the advantages of membership in COSMEP. Write for information. They are the largest trade association for small press in the U.S. Included among membership benefits is the monthly *COSMEP Newsletter,* which prints news and commentary for small publishers. They also hold publishing conferences.

COUNCIL OF LITERARY MAGAZINES AND PRESSES; DIRECTORY OF LITERARY MAGAZINES; CLMP NEWS, 666 Broadway, New York NY 10012, provides annual grants to various literary magazines and presses and publishes an annual directory useful to writers, The **Directory of Literary Magazines,** which has detailed descriptions of over 500 literary magazines which are supported by CLMP, as well as the tri-quarterly *CLMP News.*

COWBOY POETRY GATHERING; RODEO COWBOY POETRY GATHERING; WESTERN FOLKLIFE CENTER, P.O. Box 888, Elko NV 89801, phone (702)738-7508, FAX (702)738-8771. The Rodeo Cowboy Gathering can be contacted at the same address, though it is held at Cashman Field Theater, Las Vegas. Both of these gatherings are sponsored by Western Folklife Center, Box 81105, Salt Lake City, UT 84158, phone (801)533-5391, FAX (801)533-4233, executive director Hal Cannon. There is an annual 10-day January gathering of cowboy poets in Elko, and a 2-day gathering during the National Finals Rodeo in Las Vegas in December. The Western Folklife Center publishes and distributes books and tapes of cowboy poetry and songs as well as other cowboy memorabilia. The well-established tradition of cowboy poetry is enjoying a renaissance, and thousands of cowboy poets participate in these activities. Membership in the Western Folklife Center is $20/individual, $50/family. Poetry submissions for consideration must be submitted by October 15 with proven ranching experience and no more than three poems performed on a cassette tape. This is not a contest.

FAIRBANKS ARTS ASSOCIATION; FAIRBANKS ARTS MAGAZINE; TANANA VALLEY FAIR CRE-ATIVE WRITING CONTEST, P.O. Box 72786, Fairbanks AK 99707, phone (907)456-6485, editor LeAnn Lowe, Literary Department (Envoy). FAA publishes a bimonthly, *Fairbanks Arts Magazine,* which includes a Literary section ("Envoy") with how-to information, market tips for Alaskan writers, humor and personal experiences pertaining to writing, marketing and lifestyles. They pay $75 on acceptance for articles of 800-1,300 words. **They have a page of poetry in their May-June issue and prefer positive, upbeat poetry for this spring issue. Deadline is January. Pays $20/poem plus 3 copies.** Subscription: $15. **Sample and guidelines: $3.** The FAA conducts the Creative Writing Division for the Tanana Valley Fair and sponsors a Community Reading Series for Alaskan and visiting writers.

FESTIVAL OF POETS AND POETRY AT ST. MARY'S; EBENEZER COOKE POETRY FESTIVAL, St. Mary's College of Maryland, St. Mary's City MD 20686, phone (301)862-0239, is an annual event held during the last two weekends in May of each year. Approximately 18 guest poets and artists participate in and lead workshops, seminars and readings. Concurrent with the Festival, St. Mary's College offers an intensive 14-day poetry writing workshop. The Ebenezer Cooke Poetry Festival is now a bi-annual event in August of even numbered years, held in the name of the first Poet Laureate of Maryland. Poets from Maryland and the surrounding areas are invited to give 5-minute readings, enjoy a crab feast and otherwise celebrate together.

GREAT SWAMP POETRY SERIES; DISTINGUISHED AMERICAN POETS SERIES; THE FIRST AMERI-CAN POETRY DISC, County College of Morris, Randolph NJ 07869, phone (201)328-5471 or 328-5460, DAPS founded 1974, GSPS founded 1986, director Sander Zulauf. Outstanding New Jersey poets and poets who write about New Jersey (such as Maria Gillan, Hal Sirowitz, Jean Hollander, James Richardson, Thomas Reiter, and Laura Boss) are invited to read for GSPS for modest honoraria. "America's best poets" — e.g., they have had readings by James Wright, Elizabeth Bishop, Philip Levine, Howard Nemerov, William Stafford, Lyn Lifshin, Paul Zimmer, and Gwendolyn Brooks — are invited to read in the DAPS for respectable honoraria (at least 2 readings per year). They have produced TFAPD, a laser disk anthology of poetry readings taken from the college archives in 3 volumes: **I. An Introduction to Poetry; II. Contemporary American Poetry; III. James Wright.** All programs are approximately one hour each and are available in laser, Beta and VHS formats.

ILLINOIS WRITERS, INC.; ILLINOIS WRITERS REVIEW; ILLINOIS WRITERS CHAPBOOK COMPET-ITON, P.O. Box 1087, Champaign IL 61820, founded 1975, editor Kevin Stein, associate editor Jim Elledge. The *Review* publishes essays, reviews, and commentary. While reviews and essays often focus on Illinois authors, presses, and journals, the *Review* also publishes work devoted to books and authors of national prominence. Commentary addresses larger issues or movements in contemporary writing. For example, the emergence of language poetry and the present state of the creative writing workshop. "We welcome sample books and chapbooks for review." The *Review* is journal-sized ($8\frac{1}{2} \times 5\frac{1}{2}$) with cover photos or graphic art, appearing semi-annually. Its circulation is about 400. Illinois Writers, Inc., membership, $15/year, includes a subscription to the *Review* as well as six issues of a newsletter which offers manuscript submission information, conference notices, and brief articles of interest to writers, publishers, and libraries. Price per issue is $4. Payment presently in copies but reinstituting payment of $25 per article. Reporting time varies from 6-8 weeks. They also offer a chapbook competition, alternately poetry and fiction and publish the chapbook as a part of expanded efforts. Contest is open to members and to those who pay the $15 membership fee. All entrants and members receive a copy of the winning chapbook. Deadline is October. Watch for announcements of guidelines.

‡INTERNATIONAL BLACK WRITERS CONFERENCE, P.O. Box 1030, Chicago IL 60690, phone (312)995-5195, is "an organization dedicated to the recognition, encouragement and development of writing talent." It has been assisting writers for 20 years. They sponsor "an annual conference, help to create new literary markets, provide an ongoing program of assistance to members and assist communities in the articulation of their needs." Membership: $15/year.

‡JUST BUFFALO LITERARY CENTER, 111 Elmwood Ave., Buffalo NY 14201, phone (716)885-6400, founded 1975 by Debora Ott, has executive director, 3 program directors, an office manager and a director of community relations. They offer readings, workshops, Master Classes, residencies, an annual WNY Writers-in-Residence competition, an annual Labor in Literature competition open to WNY union members, Spoken Arts Radio broadcasts on National Public Radio affiliate WBFO, and Writers-in-Education in the Schools. Just Buffalo acts as a clearing house for literary events in the Greater Buffalo area and offers diverse services to writers and to the WNY region. "Although we are not accepting submissions for publication at this time, we will review works for possible readings."

THE LEAGUE OF CANADIAN POETS; WHEN IS A POEM; WHO'S WHO IN THE LEAGUE OF CANA-DIAN POETS; HERE IS A POEM; POETRY MARKET FOR CANADIANS; NATIONAL POETRY CON-TEST; GERALD LAMPERT MEMORIAL AWARD; PAT LOWTHER MEMORIAL AWARD, 24 Ryerson Ave., Toronto, Ontario M5T 2P3 Canada, phone (416)363-5047, founded 1966, executive director Angela Rebeiro, information Officer Dolores Ricketts. The League's aims are the advancement of poetry in Canada and promotion of the interests of professional, committed Canadian poets. Informa-tion on full and associate membership can be obtained by writing for the brochure, League of Canadian Poets: Services and Membership. The League publishes a biannual **Museletter** (magazine-sized, 30 pp.) plus eight 4-page issues; **When is a Poem**, on teaching poetry to children; a directory volume called **Who's Who in The League of Canadian Poets** that contains one page of information, including a picture, bio, publications and "what critics say" about each of the members; **Here is a Poem**, a companion anthology to **When Is a Poem**, featuring the work of Canadian poets; and **Poetry Markets for Canadians** which covers contracts, markets, agents and more. The League's members go on reading tours, and the League encourages them to speak on any facet of Canadian literature at schools and universities, libraries or organizations. The League has arranged "thousands of readings in every part of Canada"; they are now arranging exchange visits featuring the leading poets of such countries as Great Britain, Germany and the U.S. The League sponsors a National Poetry Contest with prizes of $1,000, $750 and $500; the best 50 poems published in a book. Deadline January 31. Entry fee $5/poem. Poems should be unpublished, under 75 lines and typed. Names and addresses should *not* appear on poems but on a separate covering sheet. Please send SASE for complete rules, info on judges, etc. Open to Canadian citizens or landed immigrants only. The Gerald Lampert Memorial Award of $1,000 is for a first book of poetry written by a Canadian, published professionally. The Pat Lowther Memorial Award of $1,000 is for a book of poetry written by a Canadian woman and published professionally. Write for entry forms. It is also the address of Writers Union of Canada which provides services and information to members, including a writer's guide to Canadian publishers ($3) and a variety of other publications to assist writers.

THE LOFT; LOFT-MCKNIGHT AWARDS, Pratt Community Center, 66 Malcolm Ave. SE, Minneapolis MN 55414, phone (612)379-0754, founded 1974, executive director Susan Broadhead. The Loft was begun by a group of poets looking for a place to give readings and conduct workshops and evolved into a sophisticated hub of activity for creative writing in all genres managed by an 19-member board of directors, and staff of 10. This past year 1,900 members contributed $30/year to the Loft; it was further supported by $46,000 from individuals, plus government, foundation and corporate grants. The Loft offers over 75 eight-week courses each year, in addition to 30 workshops and panels. Its publication readings and emerging voices readings are meant for Minnesota writers whereas the Mentor Series and Creative Non-fiction residency feature nationally known writers. The Loft publishes a monthly newsletter called *A View from the Loft*. The Loft-McKnight Awards are offered annually to Minnesota writers: 8 awards of $7,500 each, 3 in poetry, 5 in creative prose; 2 Awards of Distinction, $10,500 each.

MAINE WRITERS & PUBLISHERS ALLIANCE; MAINE IN PRINT; MAINE WRITERS CENTER, 19 Mason St., Brunswick ME 04011, phone (207)729-6333, founded 1975, according to membership coordinator Paul Doiron, is "a nonprofit organization dedicated to promoting all aspects of writing, publishing, and the book arts. Our membership currently includes over 1,300 writers, publishers, librarians, teachers, booksellers and readers from across Maine and the nation. For an individual contribution of $20 per year members receive a range of benefits including *Maine in Print*, a monthly compilation of calendar events, updated markets, book reviews, grant information, interviews with Maine authors and publishers, articles about writing and more. The Alliance distributes selected books about Maine and by Maine authors and publishers, and it maintains a bookstore, reference library, performance space and word processing station at the Maine Writers Center in Brunswick. MWPA regularly invites writers to read from their works and to conduct Saturday workshops." Reviews books of poetry only by Maine-based presses and poets.

‡**NATIONAL ASSOCIATION FOR POETRY THERAPY,** 225 Williams St., Huron OH 44839, phone (419)433-7767. In many mental and other hospitals, schools, clinics, prisons, nursing homes, half-way houses, recreation and community centers, drug and alcohol addiction centers, hospice programs and other settings professional poetry therapists engage in "the intentional use of poetry and the interactive process to achieve therapeutic goals and personal growth." If you are such a professional you are probably aware of the national organization. If you are not, you may wish to find out about it for many reasons, including the possibility of training and employment. You can become an Associate Member for $55 or a Regular Member with voting rights for $60. Contact NAPT for complete membership information. Members receive the *NAPT Newsletter* and the *Journal of Poetry Therapy*, an interdisciplinary journal of practice, theory, research and education (see their listing under Publishers), and attend NAPT meetings. Subscription to *Journal of Poetry Therapy* for members is $32 annually (4 issues) through Human Sciences Press, 233 Spring St., New York NY 10013-1578.

NATIONAL FEDERATION OF STATE POETRY SOCIETIES, INC., Membership Chairman: Barbara Stevens, 900 E. 34th St., Sioux Falls SD 57105; Contest chairperson: Amy Jo Zook, 3520 State Rt. 56, Mechanicsburg, OH 43044. "NFSPS is a nonprofit organization exclusively educational and literary. Its purpose is to recognize the importance of poetry with respect to national cultural heritage. It is dedicated solely to the furtherance of poetry on the national level and serves to unite poets in the bonds of fellowship and understanding." Any poetry group located in a state not already affiliated but interested in affiliating with NFSPS may contact the membership chairman. Canadian groups may also apply. "In a state where no valid group exists, help may also be obtained by individuals interested in organizing a poetry group for affiliation." Most reputable state poetry societies are members of the National Federation and advertise their various poetry contests through their quarterly bulletin, *Strophes*, available for SASE and $1, editor Kay Kinnaman, Route 3, Box 348, Alexandria, IN 46001. Beware of organizations calling themselves state poetry societies (however named) that are not members of NFSPS, as such labels are sometimes used by vanity schemes trying to sound respectable. Others, such as the Oregon State Poetry Association and the Virginia State Poetry Societies, are quite reputable, but they don't belong to NFSPS. NFSPS holds an annual meeting in a different city each year with a large awards banquet, addressed by an honorary chairman. They sponsor 50 national contests in various categories each year, including the NFSPS Prize of $1,000 for first place; $400, second; $200, third; with entry fees ($3 for the entire contest for members, $5 for NFSPS Award; $1/poem for non-members and $5 for NFSPS award up to 4 poems per entry). All poems winning over $10 are published in an anthology. Rules for all contests are given in a brochure available from Kay Kinnaman at *Strophes* or Amy Jo Zook at the address above; you can also write for the address of your state poetry society.

THE NATIONAL POETRY FOUNDATION; SAGETRIEB; PAIDEUMA, University of Maine, Orono ME 04469, Marie M. Alpert, Publications Coordinator. "The NPF is a non-profit organization concerned with publishing scholarship on the work of 20th century poets, particularly Ezra Pound and those in the Imagist/Objectivist tradition. We publish *Paideuma*, a journal devoted to Ezra Pound scholarship, and *Sagetrieb*, a journal devoted to poets in the imagist/objectivist tradition, as well as one other journal of contemporary poetry and comment—*The New York Quarterly*. [See separate listings for *New York Quarterly*.] NPF conducts a conference each summer and celebrates the centennial of an individual 20th century poet. Marianne Moore's centennial was celebrated in June of 1987, and T. S. Eliot's 100th year was celebrated in August of 1988." Sample copies: $8.95 for *Paideuma* or *Sagetrieb*; $6 for *New York Quarterly*.

NATIONAL WRITERS UNION, 13 Astor Place, Seventh Floor, New York NY 10003, offer members such services as contract bargaining, a grievance committee, contract guidelines, health insurance press credentials, computer discounts, car-rental discounts, and caucuses and trade groups for exchange of information about special markets. Members receive *The American Writer*, the organization's newsletter. Membership is $55 for those earning less than $5,000 per year; $95 for those earning $5,000-$25,000; and $135 for those earning more than $25,000.

NORTH CAROLINA WRITERS' NETWORK: THE NETWORK NEWS; NORTH CAROLINA POETRY CHAPBOOK COMPETITION; THE RANDALL JARRELL POETRY PRIZE, P.O. Box 954, Carrboro NC 27510, established 1985, supports the work of writers, writers' organizations and literary programming statewide. A $25 donation annually brings members the bimonthly *The Network News* newsletter containing organizational news, national market information and other material of interest to writers, and access to the Resource Center, Writers' Exchange, Workshops, Literary Brokerage and Press Service. 1,400 members nationwide. Also sponsors competitions in short fiction, one-act plays and nonfiction essays for North Carolinians and members.

PEN AMERICAN CENTER; PEN WRITERS FUND; PEN TRANSLATION PRIZE: RENATO POGGIOLI AWARD; PEN/REVSON FOUNDATION FELLOWSHIPS; GRANTS AND AWARDS, 568 Broadway, New York NY 10012, phone (212)334-1660, "is the largest of more than 100 centers which comprise International PEN, founded in London in 1921 by John Galsworthy to foster understanding among men and women of letters in all countries. Members of PEN work for freedom of expression wherever it has been endangered, and International PEN is the only worldwide organization of writers and the chief voice of the literary community." Its total membership on all continents is approximately 10,000. "The 2,500 members of the American Center include poets, playwrights, essayists, editors, novelists (for the original letters in the acronym PEN), as well as translators and those editors and agents who have made a substantial contribution to the literary community. Membership in American PEN includes reciprocal privileges in foreign centers for those traveling abroad. Branch offices are located in Cambridge, Houston, Chicago, Portland/Seattle and San Francisco. Among PEN's various activities are public events and symposia, literary awards, assistance to writers in prison and to American writers in need (grants and loans up to $1,000 from PEN Writers Fund). Medical insurance for writers is available to members. The quarterly *PEN Newsletter* is sent to all members and is available to nonmembers by subscription. The PEN Translation prize, sponsored by the Book-of-the-Month Club, 1 each year of $3,000 for works published in the current calendar year. The Renato Poggioli Award, $3,000 annually, to encourage a promising translator from the Italian who has not yet been widely recognized. Candidates with a project in literary translation planning a journey to Italy will be favored. Submit resume, sample translation and description of project before February 1. The PEN/Revson Foundation Fellowships are $12,750 awarded in odd-numbered years to poets (and to writers of fiction in even-numbered years). A fellow writer or editor must nominate candidates age 35 or under by January 15 with three copies of no more than 50 pp. of current work in progress, for someone whose "published work has not yet met with the recognition it merits." They publish **Grants and Awards** biennially, containing guidelines, deadlines, eligibility requirements and other information about hundreds of grants, awards and competitions for poets and other writers: $7.50 postpaid. Send SASE for booklet describing their activities and listing their publications, some of them available free.

PERSONAL POETS UNITED, 860 Armand Ct. NE, Atlanta GA 30324, % Jean Hesse, who started a business in 1980 writing poems for individuals for a fee (for greetings, special occasions, etc.). Others started similar businesses, after she began instructing them in the process, especially through a cassette tape training program and other training materials. She then organized a support group of poets around the country writing poetry-to-order, Personal Poets United. Send SASE for free brochure.

PITTSBURGH POETRY EXCHANGE, 3709 Perrysville Ave., Pittsburgh PA 15214, phone (412)488-8840, founded 1974 as a community-based organization for local poets. It functions as a service organization and information exchange, conducting ongoing workshops, readings, forums and other special events. No dues or fees. "At our open workshop we each drop a dollar into the basket which we turn over to City Books as 'rent' for use of the space. Any other monetary contributions are voluntary, often from outside sources. We've managed not to let our reach exceed our grasp." Their readings programs are primarily committed to local and area poets, with honorariums of $25-50. They sponsor a minimum of three major events per year in addition to their monthly workshop. Some of these have been reading programs in conjunction with community arts festivals, such as the October South Side Poetry Smorgasbord—a series of readings throughout the evening at different shops (galleries, bookstores). Poets from out of town may contact the exchange for assistance in setting up readings at bookstores to help sell their books. Contact Michael Wurster at the above address or phone number.

THE POETRY CENTER OF THE 92ND STREET Y; DISCOVERY/THE NATION POETRY CONTEST, 1395 Lexington Ave., New York NY 10128, phone (212)415-5760, offers annual series of readings by major literary figures (34 readings September-May), writing workshops and lectures. You may join the center to participate in and be informed of these activities. Also co-sponsors the Discovery/The Nation Poetry Contest. Deadline early February. Send SASE for information.

THE POETRY COMMITTEE OF THE GREATER WASHINGTON AREA, The Folger Shakespeare Library, 201 E. Capitol St. SE, Washington DC 20003, phone (202)544-7077, executive director Gigi Bradford. Formed in the mid-70s at the invitation of the poetry coordinator of the Folger Library, meets informally 5 times a year. The membership (by invitation) consists of about 60 people who represent major and minor poetry organizations in the metropolitan area (a few from Baltimore also). Annual sponsors of Celebration of Washington Poetry, a reading and book sale highlighting area poets and presses and the Poetry Committee Book Award for best book of poetry by Washington area poet within the past calendar year.

THE POETRY PROJECT AT ST. MARK'S CHURCH IN THE BOWERY, 10th St. and 2nd Ave., New York NY 10003, phone (212)674-0910, was established in 1966 by the US Dept. of H.E.W. in an effort to help wayward youths in the East Village. It is now funded by a variety of government and private sources. Artistic Director: Ed Friedman. Program Coordinator: Kimberly Lyons. From October through May the project offers workshops, talks, staged readings, performance poetry, lectures and an annual 4-day symposium, and a series of featured writers who bring their books to sell at the readings. If the reading is a publication party, the publisher handles the sales.

POETRY RESOURCE CENTER OF MICHIGAN, 111 E. Kirby, Detroit MI 48202, phone (313)972-5580, "is a nonprofit organization which exists through the generosity of poets, writers, teachers, publishers, printers, librarians and others dedicated to the reading and enjoyment of poetry in Michigan." The *PRC Newsletter* and *Calendar* is available by mail [monthly] for an annual membership donation of $20 or more, and is distributed free of charge at locations throughout the state. To obtain copies for distribution at poetry functions, contact the editor or any member of the PRC Board of Trustees.

POETRY SOCIETY OF AMERICA; POETRY SOCIETY OF AMERICA AWARDS, 15 Gramercy Park, New York NY 10003, phone (212)254-9628, is a nonprofit cultural organization in support of poetry and of poets, member and nonmember, young and established, which sponsors readings, lectures and workshops both in New York City and around the country. Their peer group workshop is open to all members and meets on a weekly basis. They publish a newsletter of their activities. And they sponsor a wide range of contests. The following are open to members only: Gordon Barber Award ($200); Gertrude B. Claytor Award ($250); Gustav Davidson Award ($500); Mary Carolyn Davies Award ($250); Alice Fay Di Castegnola Award ($2,000); Emily Dickinson Award ($100); Consuelo Ford Award ($250); Cecil Hemley Memorial Award ($300); Lucille Medwick Memorial Award ($500). Nonmembers may enter as many of the following contests as they wish, no more than 1 entry for each, for a $5 fee: Ruth Lake Award (II), $100 for a poem of retrospection any length; Elias Lieberman Student Poetry Award, $100 for students in grades 9-12; John Masefield Memorial Award (II) for a narrative poem in English up to 300 lines, $500, translations ineligible; Celia B. Wagner Award (II), $250 any form or length; Robert H. Winner Memorial Award (II), $800 for a poem "characterized by delight in language and the possibilities of discovery in ordinary life," line limit 150. (All have a deadline of December 31; awards are made at a ceremony and banquet in late spring.) The Society also has 3 book contests open to nonmembers, but publishers only may enter books; they must obtain an entry form, and there is a $5 fee for each book entered. Book awards are: Melville Cane Award (II), $500 in even-numbered years awarded to a book of poems, in odd years to prose work on poetry; Norma Farber Award (II), $1,000 for a first book; William Carlos Williams Award (II), $1,250 for a book of poetry published by a small press, nonprofit or university press, by a permanent resident of the U.S.—translations not eligible. The Shelley Memorial Award of $2,000 is by nomination of a jury of 3 poets. For necessary rules and guidelines for their various contests send SASE between September 1 and December 31. Membership: $35.

POETS & WRITERS, INC., See **Poets & Writers** under Publications Useful to Poets.

POETS' CORNER, THE CATHEDRAL CHURCH OF ST. JOHN THE DIVINE, Cathedral Heights, 1047 Amsterdam Ave. at 112 St., New York NY 10025, initiated in 1984 with memorials for Emily Dickinson, Walt Whitman, Washington Irving, Robert Frost, Herman Melville, Nathanial Hawthorne, Edgar Allen Poe, Henry James, Henry David Thoreau, Mark Twain, Ralph Waldo Emerson, William Faulkner, and Wallace Stevens. It is similar in concept to the English Poets' Corner in Westminster Abbey, and was established and dedicated to memorialize this country's greatest writers.

POETS HOUSE; THE REED FOUNDATION LIBRARY; POETRY TEACHER OF THE YEAR AWARD, 72 Spring St., New York NY 10012, phone (212)431-7920, founded 1985, Lee Ellen Briccetti, executive director, "is a library, resource center and meeting place for poets and poetry readers from all parts of the aesthetic spectrum. Programs and events are designed to serve as a platform for discussions and emphasize cross-cultural and interdisciplinary exchange. The Reed Foundation Library is a poetry collection open to the public and is comprised of 20,000 volumes, including books, journals, small press publications and other fugitive poetry materials. Donations to the library are welcomed." Poets House sponsors over 25 public events annually and offers a variety of programs for educators and students. These include a NY/NJ Teachers Conference; a conference for the chairpeople of English Departments; and the Poetry Teacher of the Year Award, which divides a prize of $1,000 between a teacher and her/his school library.

‡**POETS THEATRE**, Rd. 2, Box 155, Conocton NY 14826, sponsors readings and performances with limited funding from Poets and Writers. For a mostly conservative, rural audience.

POETS-IN-THE-SCHOOLS, Most states have PITS programs that send published poets into classrooms to teach students poetry writing. If you have published poetry widely and have a proven commitment to children, contact your state arts council, Arts-in-Education Dept., to see whether you qualify. Three of the biggest are Poets in Public Service (formerly NYSPITS), 1 Union Square, Suite 612, New York, NY 10003, phone (212)206-9000; California Poets-in-the-Schools, 2845 24th St., San Francisco, CA 94110, phone (415)695-7988; and COMPAS, Landmark Center, #308, 75 West 5th St., St. Paul, MN 55102.

‡**THE RED WHEELBARROW; FIDONET,** Austin TX, phone (512)443-5441, is another computer network, or BBS (bulletin board service). This one is "A BBS for poets, dweebs & rascals." If you live outside the Austin area, check your local BBS's to find which might be parts of FidoNet. I quote Joe Barr, sysop of The Red Wheelbarrow, at length because he explains the basic concept: "BBS'ing has become a popular form of electronic communications that will continue to grow as the personal computer revolution marches on and more and more users add a modem to their systems. BBS's are not to be confused with the huge corporations like CompuServe, GEnie, Prodigy, or Bix. Most are run as hobbies by amateur operators (Sysops) and have only a single phone line, unlike the commercial services that can handle hundreds of callers at once. A caller in Oklahoma can read a message entered the day before on a BBS in Hong Kong because they both belong to the same network. The Red Wheelbarrow is part of FidoNet, one of the oldest and most popular of these amateur networks, now linking over 10,000 BBS's around the world and continuing to grow at a rapid pace. Individual sites can pick and choose the topics that interest them and ignore the rest. On FidoNet topics are referred to as Echos (on CompuServe they are Forums), because when a message is keyed in at one site it is 'echoed' throughout the network to whatever other boards carry that topic, or echo. Callers can post their latest work, read poems and comments left by others, check the next meeting of the Austin Writers' League, find out when and where a poetry reading is taking place, or just chat with old friends and make new ones. There is no fee or charge for use and full access is granted on the first call."

‡**SCOTTISH POETRY LIBRARY; SCHOOL OF POETS**, Tweeddale Court, 14 High St., Edinburgh EH1 1TE Scotland, phone (031)557-2876, director Tessa Ransford, librarian Dr. Tom Hubbard, is a central information source and repository for poetic activities in Scotland. Their School of Poets is open to anyone; "at meetings members divide into small groups in which each participant reads a poem which is then analysed and discussed." Meetings normally take place at 7:30 p.m. on the first Tuesday of each month at the library. They publish a calendar containing poems written by members. They also offer a Critical Service in which groups of up to 6 poems, not exceeding 200 lines in all, are given critical comment by members of the School: £15 for each critique (with SASE).

THE SOCIETY OF AUTHORS; THE AUTHOR, 84 Drayton Gardens, London SW10 9SB, England, advises members on business matters, takes up their complaints and institutes legal proceedings, sends them a quarterly journal, *The Author*, publishes guides regarding agents, copyright, income tax, contracts, etc., offers them retirement and medical insurance programs, administers trust funds for their benefit, organizes special interest groups (e.g., broadcasters, children's writers, etc.), and pursues campaigns on behalf of the profession (e.g., for legislative changes).

SONGWRITER'S AND POET'S CRITIQUE, 11599 Coontz Road, Orient OH 43146, phone (614)877-1727, a nonprofit association whose purpose is to serve songwriters, poets and musicians in their area. The president of the organization says, "We provide information on songwriting, how to copyright your work, and contact publishers. We critique songs and poems of our members and guests to improve our craft, and we network songwriters, musicians and lyricists who wish to collaborate. We have a four-track recorder and a library of books and tapes that we circulate among members. We are a talented and diverse group. Some members are published and recorded writers. Dues are $12/year and we invite all songwriters, musicians and poets in the Columbus area to visit and share their creativity. Please call or write for more information."

‡**THE THURBER HOUSE; THE JAMES THURBER WRITER-IN-RESIDENCE**, 77 Jefferson Ave., Columbus OH 43215, phone (614)464-1032, officially opened in 1985, executive director Donn Vickers, who says that it is "one of the most diversely active of all restored writer's homes." The Thurber Center

has a staff of 6 people plus over 30 volunteers and a 21-person Board of Trustees. Half of its budget comes from state, local and national arts councils; 35 percent from foundations; and the rest from sales. The house includes a bookstore which distributes the best small press books the Midwest has to offer. They sponsor a quarter-long writer-in-residence program, The James Thurber Writer-in-Residence, $5,000/quarter plus living accommodations in Thurber's restored house, featuring playwrights, journalists and other writers (poetry and fiction). The house also includes performance spaces and offices. Local writers are invited to use the house as a place to "come together with others who care." They sponsor Evenings with Authors presenting major writers to the public, Literary Picnics on the lawn of Thurber House providing "convivial evenings in the company of both emerging and beloved authors, with delectable menus by some of Columbus's favorite chefs," and other activities.

‡WALT WHITMAN CENTER FOR THE ARTS AND HUMANITIES; CAMDEN POETRY AWARD, 2nd and Cooper St., Camden NJ 08102, program coordinator Joseph Lewis, phone (609)757-7276, a writers' center, founded 1975, offers a variety of programs such as Notable Poets and Writers Series, Walt Whitman Poetry Series, schools programs, adult and children's theater, musical presentations, Fine Art Exhibitions and the Camden Poetry Award. Their regular season runs September through May. During the summer months they provide a four-week Creativity Camp and a children's theater series entitled "10 Fridays of Fun."

‡WITA (WOMEN IN THE ARTS): COLLAGE (IV-Membership), Box 782288, Wichita KS 67278-2288, is a "nonprofit organization that promotes and supports both women and men in the arts." Membership: $8/year, includes quarterly newsletter and admission to a member's show in Wichita exhibiting members' work. Their literary magazine, *Collage,* appears twice a year containing **poetry and short fiction only by members of WITA** (sample copy: $2.50).

WOODLAND PATTERN, Box 92081, 720 E. Locust St., Milwaukee WI 53202, phone (414)263-5001, executive director Anne Kingsbury, who calls it "a semi-glamorous literary and arts center." Ms. Kingsbury regards the Center as a neighborhood organization; it includes a bookstore that concentrates on contemporary literature, much of it small press, much of it poetry and also on multicultural children's literature. It also incorporates a multi purpose gallery/performance/reading space, where exhibitions, readings, a lecture series, musical programs and a reading and study group are held. The *Woodland Pattern Newsletter*, mailed free to 1,900 people, contains an annotated calendar and pieces about visiting writers.

‡WORLD-WIDE WRITERS SERVICE, INC.; WRITERS INK; WRITERS INK PRESS; WRITERS UNLIMITED AGENCY, INC.; WESTHAMPTON WRITERS FESTIVAL; JEANNE VOEGE POETRY AWARDS, 186 N. Coleman Rd., Centereach NY 11720-3072, phone (516)736-6439, founded in 1976, Writers Ink Press founded 1978, poetry editor Dr. David B. Axelrod. "World-wide Writers Service is a literary and speakers' booking agency. With its not-for-profit affiliate, Writers Unlimited Agency, Inc., presents literary workshops and performances, conferences and other literary services, and publishes through Writers Ink Press, chapbooks and small flat-spined books as well as arts editions. **"We publish only by our specific invitation at this time."** *Writers Ink* is "a sometimes newsletter of events on Long Island, now including programs of our conferences." They publish 1-2 books a year, 16-28 pp., **by invitation only.** "We welcome news of other presses and poets' activities. Review books of poetry. We fund raise for non-profit projects and are associates and sponsors of Westhampton Writers Festival and Jeanne Voege Poetry Awards. Arts Editions are profit productions employing hand-made papers, bindings, etc. We have editorial services available at small fees ($50 minimum), but only after inquiry and if appropriate."

THE WRITER'S CENTER; CAROUSEL; POET LORE, 7815 Old Georgetown Rd., Bethesda MD 20814, phone (301)654-8664, founder and chairman of the board Allan Lefcowitz, director Jane Fox. This is an outstanding resource for writers not only in Washington DC but in the wider area ranging from southern Pennsylvania to North Carolina and West Virginia. The Center offers 180 multi-meeting workshops each year in writing, typesetting, word processing, and graphic arts, and provides a research library. It is open 7 days a week, 10 hours a day. Some 2,200 members support the Center with $25 annual donations, which allows for 5 paid staff members. There is a book gallery at which publications of small presses are displayed and sold. The Center's publication, *The Carousel*, is an 12-page tabloid that comes out 6 times a year. They also sponsor 40 annual performance events, which include presentations in poetry, fiction and theater. The Center is now publisher of *Poet Lore* — 100 years old in 1989 (see listing under publishers). Reviews books of poetry.

‡WRITERS' CENTER OF INDIANAPOLIS; WRITERS' CENTER NEWSLETTER, 4040 West 10th St., Indianapolis IN 46222, executive director Jim Powell. The center sponsors readings, workshops and other activities, and publishes a newsletter of markets, contests, awards and other opportunities for Indiana writers. $25/year.

THE WRITERS ROOM, 153 Waverly Pl., 5th Floor, New York NY 10014, phone (212)807-9519, provides a "home away from home" for any writer "with a serious commitment to writing," who needs a place to work. It is open 24 hours a day, 7 days a week, offering desks, storage space and "an alternative to isolation" for up to 150 writers. Space is allotted on a quarterly basis (which may be extended indefinitely) and costs $150 per quarter. "We now offer in-house scholarships for one-quarter year to writers in financial need." The Room is supported by the National Endowment for the Arts, the New York State Council on the Arts, and other public and private sources, and it encourages applications. The Writers Room also offers monthly readings and workshops for its residents, and has occasional exhibits on "writerly" subjects, such as revision.

Additional Organizations Useful to Poets

Also read the following listings for information on other organizations for poets. See the General Index for page numbers.

Publications
Useful to Poets

You are holding in your hands one of the most useful publications for poets that I know of, but there are many more. Even an occupation as haphazard as ours has its quota of professional journals and guides. First you write poetry. Then it occurs to you that you are a *poet*. What does that mean? One thing it is likely to mean is that you have an interest in such publications as are listed in this section where you can read about other writers, about our craft and our business. Below is just a sampling of the many publications responding to that interest. (Also see the Reading List on pages 9-10)

Many take up writing, especially poetry, more for social than artistic reasons. They like to participate in a fellowship, a kind of club-by-mail, in which they can become acquainted with work by a lot of other people like themselves. Some publications cater to that interest; they provide a forum in which beginners can discover and address one another. Often these publications are labors of love by editors/publishers who know firsthand the frustrations of getting started in writing and want to provide a service for beginning writers. Whatever your poetic interests or needs are, you will find useful publications in this section.

Since publications in this list are those that do not, in general, publish poetry, they provide only a sampling of magazines pertinent to our field. Many of our literary magazines are to some degree professional journals and so are useful to us as writers as well as open to us as markets. Those especially focusing on writing are cross-referred at the end of this section, under Additional Publications Useful to Poets.

AD-LIB PUBLICATIONS, 51 N. Fifth St., Fairfield IA 52556-1102, phone (515)472-6617 or (800)669-0773, publisher John Kremer, publishes how-to books about book publishing and self-publishing, such as **1001 Ways to Market Your Books, Independent Publisher's Bookshelf, Directory of Book Printers**, and **Book Publishing Resource Guide** (also available on IBM PC or MacIntosh disk as a database). Send SASE for catalog.

‡AMERICAN POETS IN PROFILE SERIES; FORD-BROWN & CO., (II), Box 2674, Boston MA 02208-2764, founded 1975 (in Birmingham, AL), editor Steven Ford Brown. Ford-Brown will consider prose submissions of critical profiles for its American Poets in Profile Series. Series includes book on Dave Smith, John Logan, Arlien Blaze, Vasson Miller and Carolyn Kizer. Sample: $15.95 postpaid. **Pays advance and copies (amount "depends"). Reports on queries in 2 weeks. No simultaneous submissions.**

‡R.R. BOWKER; LITERARY MARKET PLACE; BOOKS IN PRINT, 121 Chanlon Rd., New Providence NJ 07974, phone (800)521-8110 or (908)464-6800. **LMP** is the major trade directory of publishers and people involved in publishing books and magazines. It is available in most libraries, or individual copies may be purchased (appears in December each year; standing order price $118.70). **BIP** is another standard reference available in most libraries and bookstores. Bowker publishes a wide range of reference books pertaining to publishing. Write for their catalog.

CANADIAN POETRY, English Dept., University of Western Ontario, London, Ontario N6A 3K7 Canada, phone (519)661-3403, founded 1977, editor Prof. D.M.R. Bentley, is a biannual journal of critical articles, reviews, historical documents (such as interviews), and an annual bibliography of the year's work in Canadian poetry studies. It is a professionally printed, scholarly edited, flat-spined 100+ pp. journal which pays contributors in copies. Subscription: $10. Sample: $5. **Note that they publish no poetry except as quotations in articles.**

DUSTBOOKS; INTERNATIONAL DIRECTORY OF LITTLE MAGAZINES AND SMALL PRESSES; SMALL PRESS REVIEW, Box 100, Paradise CA 95967. Dustbooks publishes a number of books useful to writers. Send SASE for catalog. Among their regular publications, **International Directory** is an annual directory of small presses and literary magazines, over 5,000 entries, a third being magazines, half being book publishers, and the rest being both. There is very detailed information about what these presses and magazines report to be their policies in regard to payment, copyright, format and publishing schedules. *Small Press Review* is a monthly magazine, newsprint, carrying current updating of listings in **ID**, small press needs, news, announcements and reviews—a valuable way to stay abreast of the literary marketplace.

LAUGHING BEAR NEWSLETTER; LAUGHING BEAR PRESS (V), Box 36159, Bear Valley Station, Denver CO 80236, phone (303)989-5614, founded 1976, editor Tom Person. *LBN* is a monthly publication of small press information for writers and publishers containing articles, news and reviews. $8/year. Send SASE for sample copy. Laughing Bear Press publishes poetry books and cassette tapes of poetry but accepts no unsolicited MSS.

THE LETTER EXCHANGE, published by The Readers' League, % Stephen Sikora, Box 6218, Albany CA 94706. Published 3 times each year, *The Letter Exchange* is a digest-sized magazine, 36 pp., that publishes four types of listings: regular (which are rather like personal classifieds); ghost letters, which contain lines like "Send news of the Entwives!"; amateur magazines, which publicizes readers' own publishing ventures; and sketch ads, in which readers who would rather draw than write can communicate in their chosen mode. All ads are coded, and readers respond through the code numbers. Subscription to *The Letter Exchange* is $18/year, and sample copies are $8 postpaid for current issue. Poets who are so inclined often exchange poems and criticism with each other through this medium.

LITERARY MAGAZINE REVIEW, %The English Dept., Denison Hall, Kansas State University, Manhattan KS 66506, founded 1981, editor G.W. Clift, a quarterly magazine (digest-sized, perfect-bound, about 80 pp.) that publishes critiques, 2-5 pp. long, of various literary magazines, plus shorter "reviews" (about ½ page), directories of literary magazines (such as British publications) and descriptive listings of new journals during a particular year. Single copies are available for $4 or subscriptions for $12.50 per year.

PARA PUBLISHING, Box 4232-880, Santa Barbara CA 93140-4232, phone (805)968-7277, Orders: 800-PARAPUB, FAX: 805-968-1379. Author-publisher Dan Poynter publishes how-to books on book publishing and self-publishing. **Is There a Book Inside You?** shows you how to get your book out. **The Self-Publishing Manual, How to Write, Print and Sell Your Own Book** is all about book promotion. **Publishing Short-Run Books** shows you how to typeset and lay out your own book. Poynter also publishes **Publishing Contracts on Disk, Book Fairs** and 19 Special Reports on various aspects of book production, promotion, marketing and distribution. *Free* book publishing information kit; send 45¢ SASE.

‡POETRY BOOK SOCIETY, 21 Earls Court Square, London SW5 9DE, England, a book club with an annual subscription rate of £24, which covers 4 books of new British poetry, the *PBS Bulletin*, the annual *Poetry Anthology*, a premium offer (for new members) and free surface postage and packing to anywhere in the world. The selectors also recommend other books of special merit, which are obtainable at discount prices. The Poetry Book Society is subsidized by the Arts Council of Great Britain.

THE POETRY CONNECTION, 301 E. 64th St. #6K (PM), New York NY 10021, phone (212)249-5494, Editor/Publisher: Sylvia Shichman. The Poetry Connection is a poetry contest information grapevine service whereby poetry contest flyers are distributed to poets and writers; provides information on how to sell your poetry/books, chapbook publishing, and mailing of poetry contests for poetry publications and literary organizations and other information about activities pertaining to poetry; also publishes *The Poetry Connection Newsletter* listing poetry contests. Mini-sample: $3.50 plus 2 SASE's. Subscription: $25 (1 year/6 issues), $15 (6 months/3 issues).

‡POETRY EXCHANGE, P.O. Box 85477, Seattle WA 98145-1477, is a monthly newsletter (one I rely on for **Poet's Market** to find new listings), circulation 1,400, $10/year, to which you may subscribe or in which you can buy ads. It has listings of workshops, "manuscripts wanted," and a calendar of regional poetic events, 4 magazine-sized pages in fine print.

POETS & WRITERS, INC.; A DIRECTORY OF AMERICAN POETS AND FICTION WRITERS; WRITER'S GUIDE TO COPYRIGHT; AUTHOR AND AUDIENCE; LITERARY AGENTS; LITERARY BOOKSTORES; POETS & WRITERS MAGAZINE, 72 Spring St., New York NY 10012, phone (212)226-3586 or (800)666-2268 (California only), is our major support organization. Their many helpful publications include *Poets & Writers Magazine* (formerly *Coda*), which appears 6 times a year ($18 or $3.50 for a single copy), magazine-sized, 72 pp., offset, has been called *The Wall Street Journal* of our profession, and it is there that one most readily finds out about resources such as I am listing here, current needs of magazines and presses, contests, awards, jobs and retreats for writers, and discussions of business, legal and other issues affecting writers. *P&W* also publishes a number of valuable directories such as their biennial **A Directory of American Poets and Fiction Writers** ($21.95 paperback), which editors, publishers, agents and sponsors of readings and workshops use to locate over 6,600 active writers in the country. (You may qualify for a listing if you have a number of publications.) They also publish **A Writer's Guide to Copyright; Author And Audience**, a list of over 400 organizations which sponsor readings and workshops involving poets and fiction writers, including a section on how to organize and present a reading or workshop; **Literary Agents: A Writer's Guide; Literary Bookstores: A Cross-Country Guide**, for people who travel; and many reprints of articles from *Coda* and *Poets & Writers Magazine* which are useful to writers, such as "How to Give an Unsolicited Manuscript the Best Chance"; "22 Heavens for Writers (information on writers' colonies)."

POETS' AUDIO CENTER, THE WATERSHED FOUNDATION, Box 50145, Washington DC 20091. This is an international clearinghouse for ordering any poetry recording available, from both commercial and noncommercial producers. Catalog available free ("an introduction to our collection"); they stock over 500 titles. **Not accepting applications at this time.**

BERN PORTER INTERNATIONAL, 22 Salmond Rd., Belfast ME 04915, founded 1911, is a monthly journal that reviews books of poetry. Also provides sleeping bag space for poets and writers May 1 thru November 1 for the cost or free will contribution. No smoking. No drugs. No telephone.

‡PUSHCART PRESS, P.O. Box 380, Wainscott NY 11975, publishes a number of books useful to writers, including the Pushcart Prize Series—annual anthologies representing the best small press publications, according to the judges; The Editors' Book Award Series, "to encourage the writing of distinguished books of uncertain financial value," The Original Publish-It-Yourself Handbook and the Literary Companion Series. Send SASE for catalogue.

REVERSE, 3A, 19 West 73rd St., New York NY 10023, founded 1988, poetry editors Jan McLaughlin and Bruce Weber, appears twice a year with prose on themes relating to poetry planned usually a year in advance. "We are open to unsolicited MSS, and will, on occasion, publish a poem if it concerns a theme, but poems alone are not usually accepted." Prose should be double-spaced, poetry submitted as the poet wishes it to appear in print. Reports in 3-6 months. Submissions should be from 1-10 pp. Reviews books of poetry occasionally.

‡SIPAPU; KONOCTI BOOKS, 23311 County Rd. 88, Winters CA 95694, phone (916)662-3364, founded 1970, Noel Peattie. *Sipapu* consists of reviews of small press publications including poetry, and interviews and conference news, but publishes no poetry. Konocti Books has published poetry but is not currently active.

THE WASHINGTON INTERNATIONAL ARTS LETTER, Box 12010, Des Moines IA 50312, phone (515)255-5577; appears 10 times per year, 6-8 pp. newsletter on grants and other forms of assistance for the arts and humanities—mostly ads for directories to various programs of support in the arts. Reviews books of poetry. Subscription: $124 full rate; $55 for individuals; $82 for institutions.

WORDWRIGHTS CANADA, P.O. Box 456, Station O, Toronto, Ontario M4A 2P1 Canada, director Susan Ioannou, publishes "books on poetics in layman's, not academic, terms," such as **Writing Reader-friendly Poems: Over 50 Rules of Thumb for Clearer Communication** and **Literary Markets that Pay.** They also consider manuscripts of such books for publication, paying $50 advance, 10% royalties, and 5% of press run. They also conduct a "Manuscript Reading Service." Request order form to buy samples.

WRITER'S DIGEST BOOKS; WRITER'S YEARBOOK; WRITER'S DIGEST; WRITER'S MARKET; THE POET'S HANDBOOK, 1507 Dana Ave., Cincinnati OH 45207, phone (800)543-4644 outside Ohio, or (513)531-2222. Writer's Digest Books publishes and distributes a remarkable array of books useful to writers, such as **Writer's Market,** a general guide to about 750 book publishers, of which about 450 publish fiction and/or poetry. *Writer's Digest* is a monthly magazine about writing with frequent articles and much market news about poetry, in addition to my monthly column and Poetry Notes. See entry in Publishers of Poetry section. *Writer's Yearbook* is a newsstand annual for freelance writers, journalists and teachers of creative writing, with articles regarding poetry. WDB publishes my book about writing poetry, **The Poet's Handbook,** and the book you are now using.

‡WRITERS NEWS; WRITERS LIBRARY, P.O. Box 4, NAIRN, 1V12 4HU Scotland, phone 0667-54441. The monthly magazine *Writer's News*, 48 pp., is chock-full of announcements of markets, competitions, opportunities and news of the writing world. A regular feature is their Poetry Workshop, discussing the writing of poetry. Writers Library distributes books on writing, including many published by Writer's Digest Books. Subscription to the magazine: £49-90 or £44-90 if you pay by "direct debit" (charge card). Write for their book catalog.

THE WRITER'S NOOK NEWS, Suite 181, 38114 Third St., Willoughby OH 44094, editor Eugene Ortiz, is a quarterly publishing articles on the craft and business of writing with columns on marketing, contests and awards, conferences, tax legislation, books, prose and poetry, and other topics. It is offset from laser typesetting on 50 lb stock. Sample: $4. Subscription: $14.40 for one year, $33.60 for three, $204 for Lifetime Subscription. "We also publish *The Nook News Conferences & Klatches Bulletin*, a quarterly with the latest information on national and international writers' meetings, *The Nook News Market Bulletin*, a quarterly compiled with the latest market information, and *The Nook News Contests & Awards Bulletin*, which features up-to-date listings of competitions for writers, poets, playwrights, etc. Our latest publication, *The Nook News Review of Writers Publications*, gives detailed reviews of books, magazines, newsletters, etc., written for and about writers and the writing profession. Rates are the same for all four publications."

WRITER'S N.W.; WRITERS NORTHWEST HANDBOOK; MEDIA WEAVERS, Rt. 3, Box 376, Hillsboro OR 97124, phone (503)621-3911, is a professionally published tabloid quarterly giving market news, reviews of books of Northwest authors or presses, software reviews, literary activity, interviews, articles and other pertinent information for writers anywhere. Subscription: $10. **Writers NW Handbook** is like a **Writer's Market** (see listing in this section) for the Northwest (including British Columbia): $16.95 plus $2 p&h ($3 to Alaska, Hawaii and Canada).

‡**WRITING!**, General Learning Corporation, 60 Revere Dr., Northbrook IL 60062-1563, is a monthly magazine (September through May) covering writing skills for junior and senior high school students. **"We accept student-written creative writing for our 'Student Writing' department."**

Additional Publications Useful to Poets

Also read the following listings for other publications useful to poets. See the General Index for page numbers.

Glossary

Bio. Some publishers ask you to send a short biographical paragraph with your submission; it is commonly called a "bio." They may also ask for your important previous publications, or "credits."

Cover letter. Letter accompanying a submission giving brief account of publishing credits and biographical information. See the advice and sample letters in The Business of Poetry article.

Digest-sized. Approximately 5½ × 8½", the size of a folded sheet of conventional typing paper.

Flat-spined. What many publishers call "perfect-bound," glued with a flat edge (usually permitting readable type on the spine).

IRC. International Reply Coupon, postage for return of submissions from another country. One IRC is sufficient for one ounce by *surface mail*. If you want an air mail return, you need one IRC for each half-ounce. Do not send checks or cash for postage to foreign countries: The exchange rates are so high it is not worthwhile for editors to bother with. (Exception: Many Canadian editors do not object to US dollars; use IRCs the first time and inquire.) When I am submitting to foreign countries—or submitting heavy manuscripts within the US—I am likely to instruct the editor to throw the manuscript away if it is rejected, and to notify me by air mail, for which I provide postage. It is cheaper to make another printout or photocopy than to pay postage for such manuscripts.

Magazine-sized. Approximately 8½ × 11", the size of conventional typing paper unfolded.

MS, MSS. Manuscript, manuscripts.

Multiple submission. Submission of more than one poem at a time; most publishers of poetry *prefer* multiple submissions and many specify how many should be in a packet.

P. Abbreviation for pence.

p., pp. Page, pages.

Perfect-bound. See Flat-spined.

Query letter. Letter written to a publisher to elicit interest in a manuscript or to determine if submissions are acceptable. Also see advice and sample cover letter for book or chapbook submission in The Business of Poetry article.

Saddle-stapled. What many publishers call "saddle-stitched," folded and stapled along the fold.

SAE. Self-addressed envelope.

SASE. Self-addressed, stamped envelope. *Every* publisher requires, with any submission, query, request for catalog, or sample, a self-addressed, stamped envelope. This information is so basic I exclude it from the individual listings but repeat it in bold type at the bottom of many pages throughout this book. The return-envelope (usually folded for inclusion) should be large enough to hold the material submitted or requested, and the postage provided—stamps if the submission is within your own country, IRCs if it is to another country—should be sufficient for its return.

Simultaneous submission. Submission of the same manuscript to more than one publisher at a time. Most magazine editors *refuse to accept* simultaneous submissions. Some book and chapbook publishers do not object to simultaneous submissions. In all cases, notify them that the manuscript is being simultaneously submitted elsewhere if that is what you are doing.

Subsidy press. See Vanity press.

Tabloid-sized. 11 × 15" or larger, the size of an ordinary newspaper folded and turned sideways.

Vanity press. A slang term for a publisher that requires the writer to pay publishing costs, especially one that flatters an author in order to generate business. These presses use the term "subsidy" to describe themselves. Some quite respectable presses cannot operate without financial support from their authors and so require subsidies, so it is difficult to tell the difference, but flattery can serve as a warning.

Your Guide to Getting Published

rn to write publishable material and discover the best-paying mar-s for your work. Subscribe to *Writer's Digest*, the magazine that has tructed, informed and inspired writers since 1920. Every month r'll get:

- Fresh markets for your writing, including the names and addresses of editors, what type of writing they're currently buying, how much they pay, and how to get in touch with them.
- Insights, advice, and how-to information from professional writers and editors.
- In-depth profiles of today's foremost authors and the secrets of their success.
- Monthly expert columns about the writing and selling of fiction, nonfiction, poetry and scripts.

s, a $16.00 discount. Subscribe today through this special oductory offer, and receive a full year (12 issues) of Writer's Digest only $17.00—that's a $16.00 savings off the $33 newsstand rate. lose payment with your order, and we will add an extra issue to r subscription, absolutely **free**.

Detach postage-free coupon and mail today!

Subscription Savings Certificate
Save $16.00

Yes, I want professional advice on how to write publishable material and sell it to the best-paying markets. Send me 12 issues of Writer's Digest for just $17...a $16 discount off the newsstand price. Outside U.S. add $7 (includes GST in Canada) and remit in U.S. funds.

☐ Payment enclosed (send me an extra issue *free*— 13 in all).
☐ Please bill me.

Name (please print)

Address   Apt.

City

State   Zip

Basic rate, $24.   VVPM9

Vriter's® DIGEST

arantee: If you are not sfied with your subscrip-s at any time, you may cel it and receive a full nd for all unmailed issues you.

Writer's®
DIGEST

How would you like to get:

- up-to-the-minute reports on new markets for your writing
- professional advice from editors and writers about what to write and how to write it to maximize your opportunities for getting published
- in-depth interviews with leading authors who reveal their secrets of success
- expert opinion about writing and selling fiction, nonfiction, poetry and scripts
- ...all at a $16.00 discount?

Indexes

Chapbook Publishers Index

Chapbook means simply "cheap book." Most chapbooks are pamphlets of 30 pages or less, and an increasing number of publishers are bringing them out—sometimes as awards for the winners of competitions. When a poet has 30-40 poems published in good magazines, he is likely to think in terms of chapbook publication. It is good to have a mini-collection in a relatively inexpensive format—one that is easy (and inexpensive) to mail—to share with friends and family and to sell at readings. Chapbooks are rarely reviewed, rarely sold in bookstores, but they are a common intermediate step between magazine and book publication. And they usually don't disqualify you for first-book competitions.

As is true of most contests sponsored by publishers, chapbook competitions are likely to be thinly disguised money-raisers. But their fees are rarely as high as $10; they rarely get a thousand entrants (I once judged one that had only 13); and a copy of the winning chapbook to all entrants is reasonably generous—and good for the winning poet who is unlikely to have any other way of distributing the book to an interested audience. Moreover, most small press publishers would be unable to afford bringing out chapbooks on any other basis—unless the poet contributed to the cost of publication, a "cooperative" practice that is not uncommon.

But you should not kid yourself about chapbook publication. If you win a competition, you may get a little publicity for it. There may be a cash award, but you may be paid only in copies—for example, a percentage of the press run. Most sales will be those you make yourself and there is unlikely to be much press attention.

Here are the publishers listed in **Poet's Market** that offer chapbook publication. See General Index for page numbers.

Equinox Press
Expedition Press
Feelings
Five Fingers Review
Flume Press
Forest Books
From Here Press
Golden Isis Magazine
Greenhouse Review Press
Green's Magazine
Guyasuta Publisher
Gypsy
Hartland Poetry Quarterly, The
Heaven Bone Press
High Plains Press
High/Coo Press
Hippopotamus Press
Holmgangers Press
Honeybrook Press
Hutton Publications
Imagination Magazine
Inkshed—Poetry and Fiction
Insight Press
International Black Writers
International Poets Academy
Inverted-A, Inc.
Jackson's Arm
Joe Soap's Canoe
Judi-isms
Kapok Poetry Press
Kings Review Magazine
Limberlost Press
Loom Press
Lucidity
Luna Bisonte Prods
M.A.F. Press
Mayapple Press
Mid-American Review
Minotaur Press
Mulberry Press
Nada Press
Negative Capability
New Hope International
New Orleans Poetry Journal
   Press
North, The
Notebook/Cuaderno: A Liter-
   ary Journal
Occident Magazine

Ohio Review, The
Onionhead
Outrider Press
Palanquin Press
Pancake Press
Parting Gifts
Pearl
Peregrine
Perivale Press
Petronium Press
Phase and Cycle
Phoenix Broadsheets
Pikestaff Forum
Poet
Poetical Histories
Poetry Motel
Poetry Peddler, The
Poets of Now
Poets. Painters. Composers.
Poets' Roundtable
Pogment Press
Poked With Sticks
Potato Eyes
Prairie Journal
Press of MacDonald & Rein-
   ecke, The
Proof Rock Press
Prophetic Voices
Prospect Review, The
Pudding House Publications
Quarry Magazine
Rag Mag
Rambunctious Press
Raw Dog Press
Recovering Poet's Registry and
   Exchange
Red Herring Poets
Rhododendron
St. Andrew Press
Samisdat
Score Magazine
Scream Magazine
Scream of the Buddha
Shamal Books
Signpost Press, The
Silver Apples Press
Silver Wings
Silverfish Review
Slipstream

Slow Dancer
Small Press Writers & Artists
   Organization (SPWAO)
Soleil Press
Soundings: Journal of the Liv-
   ing Arts
Sparrow Press
Spitball
Split Personality Press
Spoon River Quarterly
Stand Magazine
Star Books, Inc.
State Street Press
Sticks
Still Waters Press
Stone Circle Press
Stone Press
Stop Light Press
Stormline Press, Inc.
Sub-Terrain
Tak Tak Tak
TapRoot
Textile Bridge Press
Third Half Literary Magazine,
   The
Trout Creek Press
2 AM Magazine
Underpass
Underwhich Editions
Village Idiot, The
W.I.M. Publications (Woman
   in the Moon)
Washington Writers' Publish-
   ing House
Waterways
West Anglia Publications
West of Boston
Whole Notes
Willamette River Press
Windless Orchard, The
Wineberry Press
Wire Magazine
Wormwood Review Press
Writers Forum
Writers' Own Magazine
Xenophilia
X-Press Productions

Subject Index

Use this Subject Index to save time in your search for the best market for your poem(s).

The categories are listed alphabetically and contain the magazines, publishers and contests and awards that buy or accept poetry in these special categories. Most of these markets are coded IV in their listings.

Check through the index first to see what subjects are represented. Then look at the listings in the categories you're interested in. For example, if you're seeking a magazine or contest for your poem on fantasy, look at the listings under *Science Fiction/Fantasy/Horror*. After you've selected a possible market, refer to the General Index for the page number of the listing. Then read the listing *carefully* for details on submission requirements.

In the section *Themes*, there are publishers and magazines which publish poetry on a particular theme or subject or publications directed to a special audience. The *Regional* section lists those outlets which publish poetry about a special geographic area or poetry by poets from a certain region; and the category *Form/Style* contains those magazines and presses that prefer a specific poetic style or form: haiku, sonnets, epic, narrative, etc.

We do not recommend that you use this index exclusively in your search for a market. Most of the magazines, publishers and contests listed in **Poet's Market** are very general in their specifications, and they don't choose to be listed by category. Also, many specialize in one subject area but are open to other subjects as well. Reading *all* the listings is still your best marketing strategy.

Anthology
Anthology of Magazine Verse & Yearbook of American Poetry
Ashland Poetry Press, The
Charnel House
Delaware Valley Poets, Inc.
Envoi
Georgia State Poetry Society, Inc.
Great Lakes Poetry Press
Guild Press
Gypsy
Haiku Journal
Hens Teeth
Insight Press
Judi-isms
Kawabata Press
Kitchen Table: Women of Color Press
Lake Shore Publishing
Lodestar Books
Nada Press
Night Roses
Northwoods Press (C.A.L.)
Papier-Maché Press
Perivale Press
Poetry Magic Publications
Poetry of the People
Poets of Now
Roberts Foundation Writing Awards, The
San Fernando Poetry Journal

Science Fiction Poetry Association
Seven Buffaloes Press
Shamal Books
Spirit That Moves Us, The
Squeaky Wheels Press
Starlight Press
Summer Stream Press
Three Continents Press Inc.
Vestal Press, Ltd.
Voices Israel
Waterways
West Wind Review
Wineberry Press
Word Works, The
Writer's Exchange

Bilingual/Foreign Language
American Collegiate Poets
Atalantik (Bengali)
Bilingual Review Press (Spanish)
Cross-Cultural Communications
Doc(k)s (French)
Ediciones Universal (Spanish)
Five Fingers Review (Spanish)
Footwork (Spanish)
Gairm (Scottish Gaelic)
Gávea-Brown Publications (Portuguese)

Indigo Magazine (French, Spanish)
La Nuez (Spanish)
Language Bridges Quarterly (Polish)
Letras De Oro Spanish Literary Prizes
Maroverlag (German)
Nada Press (Spanish)
New Renaissance, The
Notebook/Cuaderno: A Literary Journal (Spanish)
Osiris (French, Spanish, Polish, Danish, Italian)
Princeton University Press
REAL (Re Arts & Letters)
Sachem Press (Spanish)
Sargasso (Spanish)
Tessera (French)
Unmuzzled Ox (French)
West End Press (Spanish, Navajo)

Children/Teen/Young Adult
Advocacy Press
alive now!
Brilliant Star
Broken Streets
Cat Fancy
Chalk Talk
Chickadee Magazine
Children's Album

Children's Better Health Institute

Chimera Poetry Magazine for Children

Clubhouse

Communications Publishing Group

Coteau Books

Creative With Words Publications (C.W.W.)

Cricket

Dolphin Log

Gospel Publishing House

Hanging Loose Press

Harcourt Brace Jovanovich, Publishers

Hartland Poetry Quarterly, The

Highlights for Children

Holiday House, Inc.

Hopscotch: The Magazine For Girls

Housewife-Writer's Forum

Kau Kau Kitchen Newsletter, The

Kwibidi Publisher

Lighthouse

Lodestar Books

Louisville Review, The

Marks Studio, The Wilton

Mennonite Publishing House

Merlyn's Pen: The National Magazine of Student Writing, Grades 7-10

Nazarene International Headquarters

Night Roses

Oak, The

Owens Publications

Pandora

Pauper's Press/Phaerwind Review

Pennywhistle Press

Pikestaff Forum

Poetry Review

Poetry: USA Quarterly

Primal Voices

Quarry Magazine

Reflections

Scholastic Writing Awards

Seventeen

Shofar

Sow's Ear, The

Stegner Fellowships, Wallace E.

Stone Soup

Straight

Touch

Unity

Vegetarian Journal

Vision

Waterways

Whole Notes

Wordsong

Writers' Journal

Young Crusader, The

Young Voices Magazine

Ethnic/Nationality

Adrift (Irish, Irish-American)

Africa World Press (African, African-American, Caribbean and Latin American)

Afro-Hispanic Review

Aim Magazine

Alchemy Press

Alicejamesbooks (poets of color)

American Dane

Ararat (Armenian)

Arte Publico Press (U.S. Hispanic)

Atalantik (Bengali)

Bear Tribe Publishing (Native American)

Bilingual Review Press (Hispanic)

Black American Literature Forum

Black Books Bulletin

Black Scholar, The

Callaloo (North, South, Central, Latin American; African, Caribbean, European)

Carn (Celtic)

Carolina Wren Press (minorities)

Cencrastus (Scottish)

Chapman (Scottish)

Cintas Fellowship Program (Cubans)

Communications Publishing Group (Asian-American, Black, Hispanic, Native American)

Curley

Eagle Wing Press (American Indian)

Ediciones Universal (Spanish, Cuban)

El Barrio (Latino)

European Judaism

Exit Zero (multicultural)

Gairm (Scottish Gaelic)

Gávea-Brown Publications (Portuguese-American)

Guild Press (minorities)

Hrafnhoh

Holte Literary Prize, Clarence L. (African)

International Black Writers

Israel Horizons

Italian Americana

Japanophile

Journal of Pan African Studies

Judi-isms

Kitchen Table: Women of Color Press (Third World)

Kola (Black)

Kwibidi Publisher (minorities)

La Bella Figura (Italian-American)

Language Bridges Quarterly (Polish)

Lilith Magazine (Jewish)

Middle East Report

Middle Eastern Dancer

Midstream: A Monthly Jewish Review

Minority Literary Expo

Miorita: A Journal of Romanian Studies

New Chicano Writing

New Welsh Review

Notebook/Cuaderno: A Literary Journal (Latino-American, Native American, Black, Asian, Muslim Arab American)

Obsidian II: Black Literature in Review

Oracle Poetry (African)

Path Press, Inc. (African-American, Third World)

Poetry Wales Press (Welsh, Anglo-Welsh)

Rarach Press (Czech)

Rashi (Jewish)

Response (Jewish)

Rosenberg Award, Anna Davidson (Jewish)

Shamal Books (African-American, Caribbean)

Shofar (American Jewish)

Soleil Press (Franco-Americans)

Stone Circle Press (Celtic)

Third Woman Press (US minority women)

Three Continents Press Inc. (non-western; Africa, Middle East, Caribbean, Asia/Pacific)

Tia Chucha Press (African, Asian, Latin, Native American)

Victorian Fellowship of Australian Writers, The

Wake Forest University Press (Irish, French)

Whitecrow Foundation, Tahana (Native American)

Women's Press (women of color)

Form/Style

Alpha Beat Soup (Beat)

Alta Napa Press (epic)

Amelia (all forms)

American Association of Haikuists Newsletter

Ant Farm (four lines or less)

Asylum (prose poems)

Atticus Review/Press (experimental)

Bennett & Kitchel

Brussels Sprout (haiku, senryu)

Charnel House (bad poetry)

DBQP (short language, visual)

Equinox Press (haiku, senryu, tanka)

Figment: Tales from the Imagination

Five Fingers Review

Milim
Miraculous Medal, The
Moore Poetry Competition,
  The Julia
Nazarene International Head-
  quarters
Oblates
Other Side Magazine, The
Our Family
Outreach for Elderly House-
  bound and Disabled
Presbyterian Record, The
Queen of All Hearts
Rolling Coulter
St. Andrew Press
St. Anthony Messenger
St. Joseph Messenger and Ad-
  vocate of the Blind
Sharing the Victory
Shofar
Silver Wings
Sisters Today
Society of American Poets, The
Sojourners
Straight
Student Leadership Journal
Studio
Touch
United Methodist Reporter
Unity
Virtue: The Christian Maga-
  zine for Women
Wesleyan Advocate, The

Science Fiction/Fantasy/
Horror
Aboriginal SF
Acts Institute, Inc.
Alchemy Press
American Association of Hai-
  kuists Newsletter
Argonaut
Auguries
Beyond
Chakra
Companion in Zeor, A
Dagger of the Mind
Dark Side Magazine
Deathrealm
Dreams and Nightmares
Escapist, The
Figment: Tales from the Imagi-
  nation
Gotta Write Network
Grue Magazine
Haunted Sun, The
Haunts
Leading Edge, The
Legend
Lost Magazine
Mage, The
Magic Realism
Maplecon SF
Midnight Zoo
Naughty Naked Dreamgirls
Night Mountains
Nova SF
Pablo Lennis

Pandora
Poetic Knight, The
Poetry Break
Poetry of the People
Rampant Guinea Pig, The
Recursive Angel
Romantist, The
Scavenger's Newsletter
Science Fiction Poetry Associa-
  tion
Scream Magazine
Secret Goldfish
Small Press Writers & Artists
  Organization (SPWAO)
Standing Stone, The
Starsong
Tiger Moon Press
Twisted
2 AM Magazine
Virgin Meat
Westenra

Senior Citizen
Baptist Sunday School Board
Creative With Words Publica-
  tions (C.W.W.)
Mature Years
Outreach for Elderly House-
  bound and Disabled
Passager
Primal Voices
Senior Edition USA/Colorado
  Old Times
Yesterday's Magazette

Social Issues
Aim Magazine
Bad Haircut
Bellflower Press
Black Bear Publications
Christian Century, The
Collages & Bricolages
Communities: Journal of Coop-
  eration
Daughters of Sarah
Deviance
Egorag
Five Fingers Review
Haight Ashbury Literary Jour-
  nal
Implosion Press
Other Side Magazine, The
Peace Newsletter, The
Poetic Space
Poetry Arts Project
Pudding House Publications
San Fernando Poetry Journal
Social Anarchism
Social Justice: A Journal of
  Crime, Conflict, World Or-
  der
Struggle
Sub-Terrain
Tapjoe: The Anaprocrustean
  Poetry Journal of Enum-
  claw
Tia Chucha Press

Specialized
Ag-Pilot International Maga-
  zine (crop dusting)
Anything That Moves: Beyond
  The Myths of Bisexuality
Generation Magazine (SUNY
  at Buffalo affiliation)
New Methods: The Journal of
  Animal Health Technology
  (animals)
Outreach for Elderly House-
  bound and Disabled
Peoplenet (relationships, dis-
  abled)
Poet Gallery Press (American
  poets living outside U.S.)
Poetry Connexion, The (Los
  Angeles radio program)
Radcliffe Quarterly (college-
  related)
Recovering Poet's Registry and
  Exchange (addiction recov-
  ery)
Slate & Style (for blind writers)
Squeaky Wheels Press (by disa-
  bled writers, about disabil-
  ity)

Spirituality/Inspirational
Alchemy Press
Capper's
Chakra
Christian Way, The
Converging Paths
Deviance
Explorer Magazine
Heaven Bone Press
Hrafnhoh
Moksha Journal
New Earth Publications
Oblates
Pocket Inspirations
Poetry Break
Presbyterian Record, The
Rainbow City Express
Recursive Angel
Silver Wings
Star Books, Inc.
Sunshine Magazine

Sports
Aethlon: The Journal of Sport
  Literature
Sharing the Victory
Spitball

Students
Allegheny Review
American Collegiate Poets
Analecta
Ascent, The
Bucknell Seminar for Younger
  Poets
Fiddlehead, The
Hanging Loose Press
Intro
Lyric, The
Merlyn's Pen: The National

Sub-Terrain (social conscience)
Superintendent's Profile & Pocket Equipment Directory
Tak Tak Tak (theme issues)
Texas Tech University Press (historic tragedy, global conflict)
Textile Bridge Press (Jack Kerouac)
Thema (theme issues)
Thematic poetry Quarterly (theme issues)
Thumbprints (writers, writing)
Touch (theme issues)
Tradeswomen Magazine
Unmuzzled Ox (theme issues)
⏸ Vegetarian Journal (vegetarians, animal rights, world hunger)
Verve (theme issues)
Vestal Press, Ltd. (hobbyists, collectors)
Victimology
Vision Seeker & Sharer (social-ecological issues)
Vol. No. Magazine (theme issues)
Waterways (theme issues)
Wheat Forder's Press (science, psychology, metahistory)
Woman of Power (theme issues)
Working Classics (working people)
Write Now! (theme issues)
Write Way, The (writing)
Writer's Digest (writing life)
Writer's Exchange (writing)
Writer's Guidelines (writing, editing)
Wyoming (peace, human race, positive relationships, human spirit)
X-Calibre (theme issues)
Xenophilia (geo-cultural)
Young Crusader, The (temperance, moral values, nature)
Zero Hour (theme issues)

Translations
Abiko Quarterly Litter-ary Rag
Ark, The
Artful Dodge
Ashod
Asylum
Birmingham Poetry Review
Black Apple
Black Buzzard Press
Black River Review
Blue Unicorn, A Triquarterly of Poetry
Chelsea
Classical Outlook, The
Collages & Bricolages
Colorado Review
Coop. Antigruppo Siciliano
Crab Creek Review

Cross-Cultural Communications
Cumberland Poetry Review
Different Drummer, A
Edinburgh Review
Field
Forest Books
Formalist, The
Frank: An International Journal of Contemporary Writing and Art
Frogpond: Quarterly Haiku Journal
G.W. Review
Galatiere Prize, Lewis
Glassco Translation Prize, John
Graham House Review
Guernica Editions Inc.
Hampden-Sydney Poetry Review, The
Hawaii Review
Indigo Magazine
Intertext
Italica Press
Jacaranda Review
Kalliope
Lactuca
Lang Publishing, Inc., Peter
Lines Review
Manhattan Review, The
Mid-American Review
Mr. Cogito Press
(m)öther Tongues
New Directions Publishing Corporation
New Earth Publications
New Renaissance, The
New Rivers Press
New Yorker, The
Ornish Poetry Award, Natalie
Osiris
Partisan Review
Pequod
Perivale Press
Poems for a Livable Planet
Poetry Kanto
Poetry New York: A Journal of Poetry and Translation
Poetry Nippon Press
Polyphonies
Princeton University Press
Puerto Del Sol
Quarterly Review of Literature
REAL (Re Arts & Letters)
Renditions
Rocky Mountain Review of Language and Literature
Rohwedder
Romanticist, The
Sachem Press
Salmon Publishing
Seneca Review
Signal, The
Silverfish Review
Singular Speech Press
Skoob Quarterly Review
Southern Humanities Review
Spoon River Quarterly

Stand Magazine
Stevan Company, The
Sulfur Magazine
Tak Tak Tak
Takahe
Tampa Review
Tessera
Three Continents Press Inc.
Toad Highway
Touchstone Literary Journal
Translators Association, The
Webster Review
Willow Springs
Writ

Women/Feminism
Alicejamesbooks
Anima: The Journal of Human Experience
Atlantis: A Women's Studies Journal
Bellflower Press
Broadsheet Magazine
Bunting Fellowship Program, The Mary Ingraham
Calyx
Carolina Wren Press
Changing Men: Issues In Gender, Sex and Politics
Collages & Bricolages
Cosmopolitan
Country Woman
Creative Woman
Curley
Daughters of Sarah
Deviance
Earth's Daughters: A Feminist Arts Periodical
Eidos Magazine: Erotic Entertainment for Women, Men & Couples
Eighth Mountain Press, The
Encodings
Feminist Studies
Five Fingers Review
Free Focus
Frontiers: A Journal of Women Studies
Good Housekeeping
Heresies
Hurricane Alice
Implosion Press
Iowa Woman
Kalliope
Kitchen Table: Women of Color Press
Lancaster Independent Press
Lilith Magazine
Mayapple Press
Midland Review
Midmarch Arts Press
Miriam Press
Moving Out: A Feminist Literary and Arts Journal
NCASA News
Outrider Press
Perceptions
Plainswoman

Geographical Index

Use this Geographical Index especially to locate small presses and magazines in your region. Much of the poetry being published today reflects regional interests; also publishers often favor poets (and work) from their own regions.

The listings in this index are arranged alphabetically within the geographical sections; refer to the General Index for specific page numbers. Also check your neighboring states for other regional opportunities.

The last three sections, Canada, United Kingdom and Other Countries listings, all require a SAE with IRCs for return of your poetry.

Lullwater Review, The
Old Red Kimono
Parnassus Literary Journal
Poet's Review
Resin
Resurgens
Snake Nation Review
Society of American Poets, The

Hawaii
Aloha, The Magazine of
  Hawaii and the Pacific
Chaminade Literary Review
Hawaii Review
Kaimana: Literary Arts Hawaii
Kau Kau Kitchen Newsletter,
  The
Manoa
Paradise Educational Partner-
  ship
Petronium Press

Idaho
Ahsahta Press
American Cowboy Poet Maga-
  zine, The
Confluence Press
Emshock Letter, The
EOTU
Figment: Tales from the Imagi-
  nation
Honeybrook Press
Hutton Publications
Limberlost Press
Redneck Review of Literature,
  The
Rocky Mountain Review of
  Language and Literature
Signal, The
Snake River Reflections
Tapjoe: The Anaprocrustean
  Poetry Journal of Enum-
  claw
Trestle Creek Review
Village Idiot
White Clouds Revue

Illinois
ACM (Another Chicago Maga-
  zine)
Aim Magazine
Algilmore
Anaconda Press
Ascent
Black Books Bulletin
Brilliant Star
Chicago Review
Christian Century, The
Clockwatch Review
Communities: Journal of Coop-
  eration
Cornerstone: The Voice of This
  Generation
Creative Woman
Cricket
Daughters of Sarah
Farmer's Market
Fox Valley Living

Gotta Write Network
Great Lakes Poetry Press
Hammers
High/Coo Press
Illinois Press, University of
Imagination Magazine
International Black Writers
Journal of the American Medi-
  cal Association (JAMA)
Karamu
Kumquat Meringue
Lake Shore Publishing
Libido: The Journal of Sex and
  Sexuality
Lollipops, The Magazine for
  Early Childhood Educators
Magic Changes
Memory Plus Enterprises Press
Midwest Poetry Review
Mississippi Valley Review
NCASA News
Night Roses
Nomos Press Inc.
Oak, The
Oblates
Outrider Press
Oyez Review
Paper Bag, The
Path Press, Inc.
Pikestaff Forum
Poetry
Poetry East
Poetry Plus Magazine
Press of the Third Mind, The
Rambunctious Press
Red Herring Poets
Rhino
Rockford Review, The
Romancing the Past
Shaw Publishers, Harold
Sou'Wester
Spoon River Quarterly
Stormline Press, Inc.
Student Leadership Journal
Sunshine Magazine
Syzygy
Thorntree Press
Tia Chucha Press
Triquarterly Magazine
Twisted
2 AM Magazine
Whetstone
Willow Review
Wire Magazine
Young Crusader, The

Indiana
Arts Indiana Literary Supple-
  ment
Black American Literature Fo-
  rum
Children's Better Health Insti-
  tute
Evangel
Explorer Magazine
Formalist, The
Indiana Review
Lines n' Rhymes

Living Streams
Night Mountains
Pablo Lennis
Poets' Roundtable
Purdue University Press
Saturday Evening Post
Skylark
Sparrow Press
Sycamore Review
Toad Highway
Wesleyan Advocate, The
Windless Orchard, The
Write Now!

Iowa
Ansuda Publications
Blue Light Press
Coe Review, The
Cramped and Wet
Interstate Religious Writers
  Association Newsletter and
  Workshop
Iowa Press, University of
Iowa Review
Iowa Woman
North American Review
Poet and Critic
Rural Heritage

Kansas
Capper's
Chiron Review
Cottonwood
Kansas Quarterly
Left-Footed Wombat
Midwest Quarterly, The
Mulberry Press
Potpourri
Scavenger's Newsletter
Uncle
Woodley Memorial Press

Kentucky
Appalachian Heritage
Limestone: A Literary Journal
Louisville Review, The
Misnomer
New Madrid
Pikeville Review
Plainsong
River Rat Review
Wind Magazine

Louisiana
Exquisite Corpse
Louisiana Literature
Louisiana State University
  Press
New Delta Review
New Orleans Poetry Journal
  Press
New Orleans Review
Southern Review, The
Thema

Maine
Beloit Poetry Journal, The
Black Fly Review

New Hampshire
Bone and Flesh
Golden Quill Press
Womenwise
Yankee Magazine

New Jersey
Africa World Press
Ararat
Archae A Palaeo-Review of the Arts
Blind Alleys
Chantry Press
Chimera Poetry Magazine for Children
Cokefish
Companion in Zeor, A
Delaware Valley Poets, Inc.
Exit 13
Fellowship in Prayer
First Hand
Footwork
From Here Press
Hardware: The Magazine of Technophilia
Journal of New Jersey Poets
Lilliput Review
Literary Review
Long Shot
Malcontent
Ontario Review
Palanquin Press
Passaic Review
Pegasus Review, The
Princeton University Press
Quarterly Review of Literature
Raritan Quarterly
St. Joseph Messenger and Advocate of the Blind
Saturday Press, Inc.
Scriptor
Sensations
Silver Apples Press
Still Waters Press
Talisman: A Journal of Contemporary Poetry and Poetics
US1 Worksheets
Without Halos
Words of Wisdom

New Mexico
Ant Farm
Dusty Dog
Fish Drum
Frontiers: A Journal of Women Studies
New Mexico Humanities Review
Orphic Lute
Puerto Del Sol
West End Press
Whole Notes
Wildflower

New York
Adrift
Advocate, The

Agog
Alchemy Press
Alms House Press
America
Amicus Journal, The
Antaeus
Art Times: Cultural and Creative Journal
Ascent, The
Ashod
Bad Henry Review, The
Bank Street Press, The
Bantam Doubleday Dell Publishing Group
Beyond
Blue Light Red Light
Blue Ryder
Blueline
Boa Editions, Ltd.
Box 749 Magazine
Braziller, Inc., George
Buffalo Spree Magazine
Camellia
Canal Lines
Central Park
Chakra
Chelsea
Clyde Press, The
Columbia
Commonweal
Confrontation Magazine
Cosmopolitan
Cross-Cultural Communications
CWM
D.C.
DBQP
Different Drummer, A
Earth's Daughters: A Feminist Arts Periodical
Echoes
11th St. Ruse
ELF: Eclectic Literary Forum
Epoch
Faith . . . Works
For Poets Only
Free Focus
Frogpond: Quarterly Haiku Journal
Futurific Magazine
Generation Magazine
Giants Play Well In The Drizzle
Good Housekeeping
Graham House Review
Grand Union
Great Elm Press
Grue Magazine
Hanging Loose Press
Loose
HarperCollins
Heaven Bone Press
Heresies
Holiday House, Inc.
Holt & Company, Henry
Home Planet News
Hudson Review, The
Israel Horizons
Italica Press

Jewish Currents
Judi-isms
Keystrokes
Kitchen Table: Women of Color Press
Knopf, Alfred A.
La Nuez
Lactuca
Ladies' Home Journal
Lake Effect
Lang Publishing, Inc., Peter
Ledge Poetry and Prose Magazine, The
Lilith Magazine
Little Magazine, The
Lodestar Books
Long Island Quarterly
Long Islander
Lookout, The
Lothrop, Lee & Shepard Books
Low-Tech Press
M.A.F. Press
MacFadden Women's Group
McPherson & Company Publishers
Mage, The
Manhattan Poetry Review
Manhattan Review, The
Mellen Press, The Edwin
Midmarch Arts Press
Midstream: A Monthly Jewish Review
Milim
Minnesota Review, The
Miorita
Modern Bride
Moksha Journal
Morrow and Co., William
Mss/New Myths
Mudfish
Nation, The
New Criterion, The
New Directions Publishing Corporation
New Press, The
New York Quarterly
New Yorker, The
1992 Quarterly
Norton & Company, Inc., W. W.
Outerbridge
Overlook Press, The
Oxalis
Oxford Unversity Press
Paragon House Publishers
Paris Review, The
Parnassus
Peace Newsletter, The
Peoplenet
Pequod
Persea Books
Pipe Smoker's Ephemeris, The
Pivot
Poet Gallery Press
Poetpourri
Poetry New York: A Journal of Poetry and Translation
Poetry Peddler, The

My Legacy
Painted Bride Quarterly
Pennsylvania English
Pennsylvania Review
Philomel
Pitt Poetry Series
Pittsburgh Quarterly, The
Poetry Forum
Raw Dog Press
Rolling Coulter
Taproot Literary Review
West Branch
Wildwood Journal
Wordsong

Rhode Island
Aldebaran
Copper Beech Press
Curley
Deviance
Gávea-Brown Publications
Haunts
Italian Americana
Merlyn's Pen: The National
   Magazine of Student Writ-
   ing, Grades 7-10
Northeast Journal

South Carolina
Bench Press, The
Devil's Millhopper Press, The
Emrys Journal
Nostalgia: A Sentimental State
   of Mind
South Carolina Review
Starsong
Tramp
Writer's Exchange

South Dakota
Hens Teeth
Pasque Petals
South Dakota Review
Tempest Magazine
Tesseract Publications

Tennessee
Aethlon: The Journal of Sport
   Literature
alive now!
American Association of Hai-
   kuists Newletter
Baptist Sunday School Board
Co-Laborer
Cumberland Poetry Review
Depot Press
Kapok Poetry Press
Mature Years
Now and Then
Old Hickory Review
Poetry Miscellany, The
RFD
River City
Romantist, The
Sewanee Review
Single Today
Sows Ear, The
Swamp Root

Westenra
Zone 3

Texas
Aileron Press
American Atheist Press
Analecta
Argonaut
Art-Core
Arte Publico Press
Baby Connection News Jour-
   nal, The
Black Tie Press
Channels
Concho River Review
Cross Timbers Review
Dagger of the Mind
Encodings
Experiment in Words
Gopherwood Review, The
Grasslands Review
Great Plains Canal and Avalon
   Dispatch
Gypsy
Inverted-A, Inc.
Julian Associates
Language Bridges Quarterly
Literary Focus Poetry Publica-
   tions
Lucidity
North Texas Press, University
   of
Owens Publications
Prose Poem, The
REAL (Re Arts & Letters)
Red Rampan' Press
Rio Grande Press
Rubber Puppy
Salt Lick
Southwest Review
Stevan Company, The
Strain, The
Tangram Press
Texas Tech University Press
Touchstone Literary Journal
United Methodist Reporter

Utah
Ellipsis Magazine
International Poets of the
   Heart
Leading Edge, The
Literature and Belief
Magic Realism
Manna
Paper Salad Poetry Journal,
   The
Rhododendron
Smith Publisher, Gibbs
Utah Holiday Magazine
Utah State University Press

Vermont
Awede Press
Longhouse
New England Review
Write Way, The

Virginia
Black Buzzard Press
Bogg Publications
Brunswick Publishing Com-
   pany
Chronicle of the Horse, The
Dominion Review, The
Going Gaga
Hampden-Sydney Poetry Re-
   view, The
Hollins Critic, The
Inlet
Intro
Lintel
Lyric, The
Miriam Press
Other Side Magazine, The
Phoebe
Piedmont Literary Review
Pocahontas Press, Inc.
Poetry Explosion Newsletter,
   The
Pogment Press
Proof Rock Press
Reflect
Roanoke Review
St. Andrew Press
Secret Goldfish
Verse
Victimology
Virginia Quarterly Review, The
William and Mary Review, The

Washington
Ag-Pilot International Maga-
   zine
Bad Haircut
Bear Tribe Publishing
Bellowing Ark Press
Box Dog Press
Brussels Sprout
Cacanadadada
Cleaning Business Magazine
Crab Creek Review
Duckabush Journal
Fine Madness
Fredrickson-Kloepfel Publish-
   ing Co.
Happy Lamb
It's A Mad Mad Mad Mad Mad
   World
Jeopardy
L'Epervier Press
Lighthouse
Lithic Review, The
Lynx, A Quarterly Journal of
   Renga
Open Hand Publishing Inc.
Paper Radio
Poetry Northwest
Poets. Painters. Composers.
Portraits Poetry Magazine
Seattle Review
Signpost Press, The
Spindrift
Willow Springs
Young Voices Magazine
Zero Hour

Poetry Voice
Poetry Wales Press
Psychopoetica
Purple Patch
Quartos Magazine
Reality Studios
Rialto, The
Roads
Second Aeon Publications
Smoke
Spectacular Diseases
Stand Magazine
Staple
Stride Publications
Tak Tak Tak
Tears in the Fence
Third Half Literary Magazine, The
Ver Poets Voices
Vigil
Vision Seeker & Sharer
Weyfarers
Writers Forum
Writers' Own Magazine
X-Calibre
Zero One

Other Countries
Abiko Quarterly Litter-ary Rag (Japan)
Blast Magazine (Australia)
Broadsheet Magazine (New Zealand)
Carrefour Press, The (South Africa)
Coop Antigruppo Siciliano (Italy)
Doc(k)s (France)
Frank: An International Journal of Contemporary Writing and Art (France)
Galaxy Press (Australia)
Handshake Editions (France)
Hatbox (Australia)
Imago Literary Magazine (Australia)
International Poets Academy (India)
Landfall (New Zealand)
Lundian, The (Sweden)
Mainichi Daily News, Haiku in English (Japan)
New Cicada (Japan)

Northern Perspective (Australia)
Pinchgut Press (Australia)
Poetry Kanto (Japan)
Poetry Nippon Press (Japan)
Polyphonies (France)
Prakalpana Literature (India)
Rashi (New Zealand)
Renditions (Hong Kong)
Salmon Publishing (Ireland)
Scarp (Australia)
Scripsi (Australia)
Small Times, The (Australia)
Southern Review (Australia)
Studio (Australia)
Takahe (New Zealand)
Transnational Perspectives (Switzerland)
Voices Israel (Israel)
Westerly (Australia)
Writing (Australia)

General Index

Can't find a poetry publisher's listing? Check pages 429-431 at the end of the Publishers of Poetry section for Other Poetry Publishers.

Can't find a poetry publisher's listing? Check pages 429-431 at the end of the Publishers of Poetry section for Other Poetry Publishers.

Can't find a poetry publisher's listing? Check pages 429-431 at the end of the Publishers of Poetry section for Other Poetry Publishers.

Can't find a poetry publisher's listing? Check pages 429-431 at the end of the Publishers of Poetry section for Other Poetry Publishers.

Can't find a poetry publisher's listing? Check pages 429-431 at the end of the Publishers of Poetry section for Other Poetry Publishers.

Can't find a poetry publisher's listing? Check pages 429-431 at the end of the Publishers of Poetry section for Other Poetry Publishers.

Can't find a poetry publisher's listing? Check pages 429-431 at the end of the Publishers of Poetry section for Other Poetry Publishers.

Can't find a poetry publisher's listing? Check pages 429-431 at the end of the Publishers of Poetry section for Other Poetry Publishers.

Ashram (see Moksha Journal 233)

Valley Grapevine (see Seven Buffaloes Press 344)

Van Nuys Creative Writing Contest, Laura Bower 446

Varoujan Award, Daniel (see New England Poetry Club 442)

Vegetarian Journal 395

Vegetarian Resource Group, The (see Vegetarian Journal 395)

Vehicule Press 396

Ver Poets Open Competition (see Ver Poets Voices 396)

Ver Poets Voices 396

Verandah 396

Vergin' Press (see Gypsy 160)

Vermont Council on the Arts 434

Vermont Studio Center 456

Verse 397

Vertical Images (see Fleeting Monolith Enterprises 138)

Verve 397

Vestal Press, Ltd. 397

Victimology: An International Journal 397

Victorian Fellowship of Australian Writers, The 446

Vigil 398

Vigil Publications (see Vigil 398)

Viking Penguin 398

Village Idiot, The 398

Villager, The 398

Vincent Brothers Review, The 398

Virgin Meat 399

Virginia Center for the Creative Arts 457

Virginia Commission for the Arts 434

Virginia Quarterly Review, The 399

Virtue: The Christian Magazine for Women 399

Vishnu-Ala Dav Press (see Left-Footed Wombat 203)

Visibilities 399

Vision 399

Vision Seeker & Sharer 399

Visions, A Success Guide for Native American Students (see Communications Publishing Group 99)

Visions and Revisions (see Primal Voices 307)

Visions-International, The World Journal (see Black Buzzard Press 62)

Visiting Writers Program, The

(see Paumanok Poetry Competition 443)

Visual Artists and Writers Residencies (see Vermont Studio Center 456)

Voege Poetry Awards, Jeanne (see World-Wide Writers Service, Inc. 468)

Voice Without Sides, A (see DBQP 115)

Voices International 400

Voices Israel 400

Voices of the South Contest 447

Vol. No. Magazine 400

Vowel Movement (see Aileron Press 29)

W

W.I.M. Publications (Woman in the Moon) 401

W.W. Publications (see American Tolkien Society 38)

Wake Forest University Press 401

Walking and Sinning 401

Walpurgis Night (see American Association of Haikuists Newsletter 36)

Walt's Corner (see Long Islander 211)

Washington International Arts Letter, The 472

Washington Prize, The (see The Word Works 416)

Washington Review 401

Washington State Arts Commission 434

Washington Writers' Publishing House 402

Water Mark Poets Book Awards (see Water Mark Press 402)

Water Mark Press 402

Watershed Foundation, The (see Poets' Audio Center 472)

Waterways: Poetry in the Mainstream 402

Wayne Review 403

We are Poets and Authors, Too (see Creative with Words Publications 108)

We Magazine 403

We Press (see We Magazines 403)

Weavings (see Alive Now! 31)

Webster Review 403

Wee Wisdom (see Unity 393)

Wesleyan Advocate, The 404

Wesleyan Poetry (see Wesleyan University Press 404)

Wesleyan Poetry Prize (see

Wesleyan University Press 404)

Wesleyan University Press 404

West Anglia Publications 404

West Branch 404

West Coast Line 404

West Coast Review Books (see West Coast Line 404)

West End Press 405

West Florida Literary Federation (see Emerald Coast Review 128)

West of Boston 405

West Virginia Arts And Humanities Division 434

West Wind Review 405

Westenra 405

Westenra Society of the Undead, The Miss Lucy (see Westenra 405)

Westerly 406

Western Folklife Center (see Cowboy Poetry Gathering 462)

Western People (see Western Producer Publications 406)

Western Producer Publications 406

Western States Arts Federation (see Western States Book Awards 447)

Western States Book Awards 447

Westhampton Writers Festival (see World-Wide Writers Service, Inc. 468)

Weyfarers 406

Wheat Forder's Press 407

Wheaton Literary Series (see Harold Shaw Publishers 345)

Wheel of Fire Press (see Crooked Roads 110)

When is a Poem (see The League of Canadian Poets 463)

Whetstone (Canada) 407

Whetstone (Illinois) 407

Whetstone Prize (see Whetstone [Illinois] 407)

White Clouds Revue 407

White Lion Press (see Grand Union 156)

White Pine Press 408

White Rabbit Poetry Contest 447

White Review, James 408

White Wall Review 408

Whitecrow Foundation, Tahana 408

Whiting Foundation, Mrs. Giles (see Whiting Writers' Awards 447)

Can't find a poetry publisher's listing? Check pages 429-431 at the end of the Publishers of Poetry section for Other Poetry Publishers.

Can't find a poetry publisher's listing? Check pages 429-431 at the end of the Publishers of Poetry section for Other Poetry Publishers.

Other Books of Interest

Poetry Books
 Creating Poetry, by John Drury $18.95
 The Poet's Handbook, by Judson Jerome (paper) $10.95
Annual Market Books
 Artist's Market, edited by Lauri Miller $21.95
 Children's Writer's & Illustrator's Market, edited by Lisa Carpenter (paper) $16.95
 Guide to Literary Agents & Art/Photo Reps, edited by Robin Gee $15.95
 Humor & Cartoon Markets, edited by Bob Staake (paper) $16.95
 Novel & Short Story Writer's Market, edited by Robin Gee (paper) $18.95
 Photographer's Market, edited by Sam Marshall $21.95
 Songwriter's Market, edited by Brian Rushing $19.95
 Writer's Market, edited by Mark Kissling $25.95
General Writing Books
 Annable's Treasury of Literary Teasers, by H.D. Annable (paper) $10.95
 Beginning Writer's Answer Book, edited by Kirk Polking (paper) $13.95
 Discovering the Writer Within, by Bruce Ballenger & Barry Lane $16.95
 Getting the Words Right: How to Rewrite, Edit and Revise, by Theodore A. Rees Cheney (paper) $12.95
 How to Write a Book Proposal, by Michael Larsen (paper) $10.95
 Just Open a Vein, edited by William Brohaugh $15.95
 Knowing Where to Look: The Ultimate Guide to Research, by Lois Horowitz (paper) $16.95
 Make Your Words Work, by Gary Provost $17.95
 On Being a Writer, edited by Bill Strickland $19.95
 Pinckert's Practical Grammar, by Robert C. Pinckert (paper) $11.95
 The Story Behind the Word, by Morton S. Freeman (paper) $9.95
 12 Keys to Writing Books That Sell, by Kathleen Krull (paper) $12.95
 The 29 Most Common Writing Mistakes & How to Avoid Them, by Judy Delton (paper) $9.95
 The Wordwatcher's Guide to Good Writing & Grammar, by Morton S. Freeman (paper) $15.95
 Word Processing Secrets for Writers, by Michael A. Banks & Ansen Dibell (paper) $14.95
 The Writer's Book of Checklists, by Scott Edelstein $16.95
 The Writer's Digest Guide to Manuscript Formats, by Buchman & Groves $18.95
 The Writer's Essential Desk Reference, edited by Glenda Neff $19.95
Nonfiction Writing
 The Complete Guide to Writing Biographies, by Ted Schwarz $19.95
 Creative Conversations: The Writer's Guide to Conducting Interviews, by Michael Schumacher $16.95
 How to Do Leaflets, Newsletters, & Newspapers, by Nancy Brigham (paper) $14.95
 How to Sell Every Magazine Article You Write, by Lisa Collier Cool (paper) $11.95
 How to Write Irresistible Query Letters, by Lisa Collier Cool (paper) $10.95
 The Writer's Digest Handbook of Magazine Article Writing, edited by Jean M. Fredette (paper) $11.95
Fiction Writing
 The Art & Craft of Novel Writing, by Oakley Hall $17.95
 Best Stories from New Writers, edited by Linda Sanders $16.95
 Characters & Viewpoint, by Orson Scott Card $13.95
 The Complete Guide to Writing Fiction, by Barnaby Conrad $17.95
 Cosmic Critiques: How & Why 10 Science Fiction Stories Work, edited by Asimov & Greenberg (paper) $12.95
 Creating Characters: How to Build Story People, by Dwight V. Swain $16.95
 Creating Short Fiction, by Damon Knight (paper) $10.95
 Dare to Be a Great Writer: 329 Keys to Powerful Fiction, by Leonard Bishop $16.95
 Dialogue, by Lewis Turco $13.95
 The Fiction Writer's Silent Partner, by Martin Roth $19.95
 Handbook of Short Story Writing: Vol. I, by Dickson and Smythe (paper) $10.95
 Handbook of Short Story Writing: Vol. II, edited by Jean Fredette (paper) $12.95
 How to Write & Sell Your First Novel, by Collier & Leighton (paper) $12.95
 Manuscript Submission, by Scott Edelstein $13.95
 Mastering Fiction Writing, by Kit Reed $18.95

Plot, by Ansen Dibell $13.95
Revision, by Kit Reed $13.95
Spider Spin Me a Web: Lawrence Block on Writing Fiction, by Lawrence Block $16.95
Theme & Strategy, by Ronald B. Tobias $13.95
Writing the Novel: From Plot to Print, by Lawrence Block (paper) $10.95

Special Interest Writing Books

Armed & Dangerous: A Writer's Guide to Weapons, by Michael Newton (paper) $14.95
The Children's Picture Book: How to Write It, How to Sell It, by Ellen E.M. Roberts (paper) $18.95
The Complete Book of Feature Writing, by Leonard Witt $18.95
The Complete Book of Scriptwriting, by J. Michael Straczynski (paper) $11.95
Deadly Doses: A Writer's Guide to Poisons, by Serita Deborah Stevens with Anne Klarner (paper) $16.95
Editing Your Newsletter, by Mark Beach (paper) $18.50
Families Writing, by Peter Stillman $15.95
A Guide to Travel Writing & Photography, by Ann & Carl Purcell (paper) $22.95
Hillary Waugh's Guide to Mysteries & Mystery Writing, by Hillary Waugh $19.95
How to Pitch & Sell Your TV Script, by David Silver $17.95
How to Write a Play, by Raymond Hull (paper) $12.95
How to Write Action/Adventure Novels, by Michael Newton $13.95
How to Write & Sell True Crime, by Gary Provost $17.95
How to Write Horror Fiction, by William F. Nolan $15.95
How to Write Mysteries, by Shannon OCork $13.95
How to Write Romances, by Phyllis Taylor Pianka $13.95
How to Write Science Fiction & Fantasy, by Orson Scott Card $13.95
How to Write Tales of Horror, Fantasy & Science Fiction, edited by J.N. Williamson (paper) $12.95
How to Write the Story of Your Life, by Frank P. Thomas (paper) $11.95
How to Write Western Novels, by Matt Braun $13.95
The Magazine Article: How To Think It, Plan It, Write It, by Peter Jacobi $17.95
Mystery Writer's Handbook, by The Mystery Writers of America (paper) $11.95
Successful Scriptwriting, by Jurgen Wolff & Kerry Cox (paper) $14.95
TV Scriptwriter's Handbook, by Alfred Brenner (paper) $10.95
The Writer's Complete Crime Reference Book, by Martin Roth $19.95
The Writer's Guide to Conquering the Magazine Market, by Connie Emerson $17.95
Writing for Children & Teenagers, 3rd Edition, by Lee Wyndham & Arnold Madison (paper) $12.95
Writing the Modern Mystery, by Barbara Norville $15.95
Writing to Inspire, edited by William Gentz (paper) $14.95

The Writing Business

A Beginner's Guide to Getting Published, edited by Kirk Polking (paper) $11.95
The Complete Guide to Self-Publishing, by Tom & Marilyn Ross (paper) $16.95
How to Write with a Collaborator, by Hal Bennett with Michael Larsen $11.95
How You Can Make $25,000 a Year Writing, by Nancy Edmonds Hanson (paper) $12.95
Is There a Speech Inside You?, by Don Aslett (paper) $9.95
Time Management for Writers, by Ted Schwarz $10.95
The Writer's Friendly Legal Guide, edited by Kirk Polking $16.95
Writer's Guide to Self-Promotion & Publicity, by Elane Feldman $16.95
A Writer's Guide to Contract Negotiations, by Richard Balkin (paper) $11.95
Writing A to Z, edited by Kirk Polking $22.95

To order directly from the publisher, include $3.00 postage and handling for 1 book and $1.00 for each additional book. Allow 30 days for delivery.

Writer's Digest Books
1507 Dana Avenue, Cincinnati, Ohio 45207
Credit card orders call TOLL-FREE
1-800-289-0963
Prices subject to change without notice.

Write to this same address for information on *Writer's Digest* magazine, *Story* magazine, Writer's Digest Book Club, Writer's Digest School, and Writer's Digest Criticism Service.

Notes

Notes

A Poetry Market Plan

Market Categories:

Look for these important codes in the listings to help you decide where to submit your poetry.

I **Beginning:** *Very open to beginners' submissions, often encourage and offer advice to new writers. May require fees, purchase of publication or membership in an organization.*

II **General:** *Usually accept 10% or less of poems received, but in this category a poet developing a list of publication credits will find many names respected in the literary world.*

III **Limited:** *Typically overstocked; do not encourage widespread submissions from poets who have not published elsewhere, although on occasion they publish relatively new and/or little-known poets.*

IV **Specialized:** *Publications which encourage contributors from a specific geographical area or a specific group (by age, ethnic background, etc.), or which accept poems in specific forms (e.g., haiku) or on specific themes.*

V **Closed:** *Listings which do not accept unsolicited manuscripts; you cannot submit without specific permission to do so.*